Mike Meyers' Computer Skills

Survey of Operating Systems

Second Edition

Jane Holcombe and Charles Holcombe

Boston Burr Ridge, IL Dubuque, IA Madison, WI New York San Francisco St. Louis
Bangkok Bogotá Caracas Kuala Lumpur Lisbon London Madrid Mexico City
Milan Montreal New Delhi Santiago Seoul Singapore Sydney Taipei Toronto

MIKE MEYERS' COMPUTER SKILLS: SURVEY OF OPERATING SYSTEMS, SECOND EDITION

Published by McGraw-Hill, a business unit of The McGraw-Hill Companies, Inc., 1221 Avenue of the Americas, New York, NY 10020.

This book is printed on acid-free paper.
Printed in China

3 4 5 6 7 8 9 0 CTP/CTP 0 9 8

ISBN-13: 978-0-07-225773-1
ISBN-10: 0-07-225773-3

Publisher & Sponsoring Editor: *Thomas Casson*
Managing Developmental Editor: *Jonathan Plant*
Marketing Manager: *Lynn Kalb*
Senior Project Manager: *Lori Koetters*
Senior Production Supervisor: *Rose Hepburn*
Lead Media Project Manager: *Audrey Reiter*
Media Technology Producer: *Janna Martin*
Lead designer: *Pam Verros*
Cover Designer: *Brian Perveneckis*
Cover Photos: *LiquidLibrary © Dynamic Graphics, Inc.*
Photo research coordinator: *Lori Kramer*
Photo researcher: *Keri Johnson*
Compositor: *International Typesetting and Composition*
Typeface: *10/13 Palatino*
Printer: *CTPS*

Chapter opener credits: page 1: Keith Brofsky/Getty Images/MGHDIL; page 45: © Doug Wilson/CORBIS; page 93: Jason Reed/RyanMcVay/Getty Images/MGHDIL; page 143: AP Photo/Jeff Christensen; page 199: © Kevin Lee/Getty Images; page 249: © David McNew/Getty Images; page 309: TRBfoto/Getty Images/MGHDIL; page 377: Chad Baker/Getty Images/MGHDIL; page 439: © Randy Faris/CORBIS; page 479: © CORBIS; page 535: © James A. Sugar/CORBIS; page 597: Nick Koudis/Getty Images/MGHDIL; web chapter 13 © Getty Images. Timeline photos in Chapter 1: Page 20: Courtesy of the Computer History Museum. Courtesy Xerox Corporation. Page 21: National Museum of American History, Behring Center. © 2004 Smithsonian Institution. Courtesy Apple Computer. Courtesy Microsoft ® Corp. Page 22: Ralph Morse/Time Life Pictures/Getty Images. Courtesy of the Computer History Museum. Page 23: Courtesy Apple Computer. Courtesy of IBM Corporation. Page 27: Courtesy of palmOne, Inc. Courtesy Apple Computer. Page 28: Courtesy Apple Computer.

Library of Congress Cataloging-in-Publication Data

Holcombe, Jane.
Survey of operating systems/Jane Holcombe and Charles Holcombe.--2nd ed.
p. cm. -- (Mike Meyers' computer skils)
Includes index.
ISBN 0-07-225773-3 (alk. paper)
1. Operating systems (Computers). I. Holcombe, Charles. II. Title. III. Series.
QA76.76.O63H6465 2006
005.4'46--dc22 2005041558

www.mhhe.com

About the Authors

Jane Holcombe (A+, Network+, MCSE, MCT, CTT+, and Novell CNA) was a pioneer in the field of PC support training. In 1983, while working for a financial planning company, she was assigned the task of moving the accounting and client-management operations to IBM PCs. This project included the use of three different operating systems to run the selected software and the installation of a local area network for sharing of the accounting system and client files. While the network was not a complete success, this project revealed the potential of networked PCs in business. Since 1984, she has been an independent trainer, consultant, and course content author, creating and presenting courses on PC operating systems. Through the late 1980s and early 1990s, these courses were taught nationwide. She also co-authored a set of networking courses for the consulting staff of a large network vendor. In the early 1990s, she worked with both Novell and Microsoft server operating systems, finally focusing on Microsoft operating systems and achieving her MCSE certification early, recertifying for new versions of Windows.

Chuck Holcombe has a high-tech background in the use of computers in the nuclear and aerospace fields. In his 15 years at Control Data Corporation, he was successively a programmer, technical sales analyst, salesman, and sales manager in the field marketing force. He ran the Executive Seminar program, was Control Data's liaison to the worldwide university community, and was a market development manager for Plato, Control Data's computer-based education system.

For the past 25 years, he has been an independent trainer and consultant. He has authored and delivered many training courses, is a skilled writer and editor, and is used to creating complex written materials. For a while, he claimed he was semi-retired, but writing books like this one is too much work for him to be able to say that anymore.

The Holcombes have authored the *MCSE Guide to Designing a Microsoft Windows 2000 Network Infrastructure* (Course Technology) and both the *A+ Certification Press Lab Manual* and the *MCSE Certification Press Windows 2000 Professional Lab Manual* (McGraw-Hill/Osborne). They authored *Survey of Operating Systems,* the first book in the Michael Meyers' Computer Skills series, and contributed chapters to The Michael Meyers' *Guide to Managing and Troubleshooting PCs,* The Michael Meyers' *All-in-One A+ Certification Exam Guide, 5th Edition,* and *Windows 2000 Administration* (McGraw-Hill/Osborne). They also wrote several chapters for the Peter Norton *Introduction to Operating Systems, 6th Edition* (McGraw-Hill). The book you are holding is the second edition of *Survey of Operating Systems.*

About the Series Editor

Michael Meyers is the industry's leading authority on A+ and Network+ certification. He is the president and co-founder of Total Seminars, LLC, a provider of PC and network repair seminars, books, videos, and courseware for thousands of organizations throughout the world. Mike has been involved in the computer and network repair industry since 1977 as a technician, instructor, author, consultant, and speaker. Author of several popular PC books and A+ and Network+ courseware, Mike is also the series editor for both the highly successful Mike Meyers' Certification Passport series and the Mike Meyers' Computer Skills series, both published by McGraw-Hill/Osborne. Mike holds multiple industry certifications and considers the moniker "computer nerd" a compliment.

About the Contributors

The depth and breadth of today's operating systems make it almost impossible to be deeply knowledgeable about all of them. We were fortunate to have the help of Fred Shimmin, who provided technical expertise for the chapters on Windows XP, network server operating systems, and Linux, and of Nigel Parry and Ken Harper, who wrote the first edition chapter on Mac OS X and provided guidance for the revisions to this chapter for the second edition. We also owe a great thanks to Timothy Breen, technologist extraordinaire, who provided technical advice and allowed Jane to camp out in his office while she revised the Mac OS X chapter.

About the Peer Reviewers

This book was greatly influenced by the dedicated group of teachers and subject-matter experts who reviewed it and whose suggestions made it so much better. To them we give our heartfelt thanks.

TECHNICAL EDITORS

Gerlinde Brady	Cabrillo College—Aptos, CA
Eric Ecklund	Cambria Rowe College—Johnstown, PA
Wendi Malensek	Seminole Community College—Sanford, FL
Margaret Moore	Coastal Carolina Community College—Jacksonville, NC

PEER REVIEWERS

Gerlinde Brady	Cabrillo College—Aptos, CA
Eric Ecklund	Cambria Rowe College—Johnstown, PA
Christopher J. Gray	Pittsburgh Technical Institute—Oakdale, PA
Farbod Karimi	Heald College—San Francisco, CA
Wendi Malensek	Seminole Community College—Sanford, FL
Margaret Moore	Coastal Carolina Community College—Jacksonville, NC

Acknowledgments

Someone once told us that writing a second edition was easy. We did not find that to be true, as we added a few chapters and quite a bit of content. However, once again, we found all of our efforts supported by the talented team of people at McGraw-Hill. The book's integrity was ensured by this team, which included Chris Johnson, Jonathan Plant, Thomas Casson, Mike Meyers, Laura Stone, and Lori Koetters. The outline for this second edition was based on feedback provided by the many instructors who have used the first edition and responded to surveys. During the writing of this edition, we again turned to technical reviewers and peer reviewers who scrutinized each chapter of the book, giving us invaluable feedback on the relevancy and accuracy of the content. It is hard to imagine a book receiving more attention through its many stages of writing and revision.

As part of the Mike Meyers' Computer Skills series, this book received additional attention from Mike as the series editor.

We greatly appreciate the expertise of the production group. They all worked hard to make the book look wonderful. Creating and laying out the many elements of this complex book design was a huge task, and they handled it with aplomb.

We truly appreciate all who worked hard to make this book what it is. Thank you!

We joyfully dedicate this book to our friend and mentor, Chris Johnson, whose knowledge, market research, editorial acumen, and enthusiasm for our work was a real inspiration to us.

About This Book

Important Technology Skills

Information technology (IT) offers many career paths, leading to occupations in such fields as PC repair, network administration, telecommunications, Web development, graphic design, and desktop support. To become competent in any IT field, however, you need certain basic computer skills. The Mike Meyers' Computer Skills series builds a foundation for success in the IT field by introducing you to fundamental technology concepts and giving you essential computer skills.

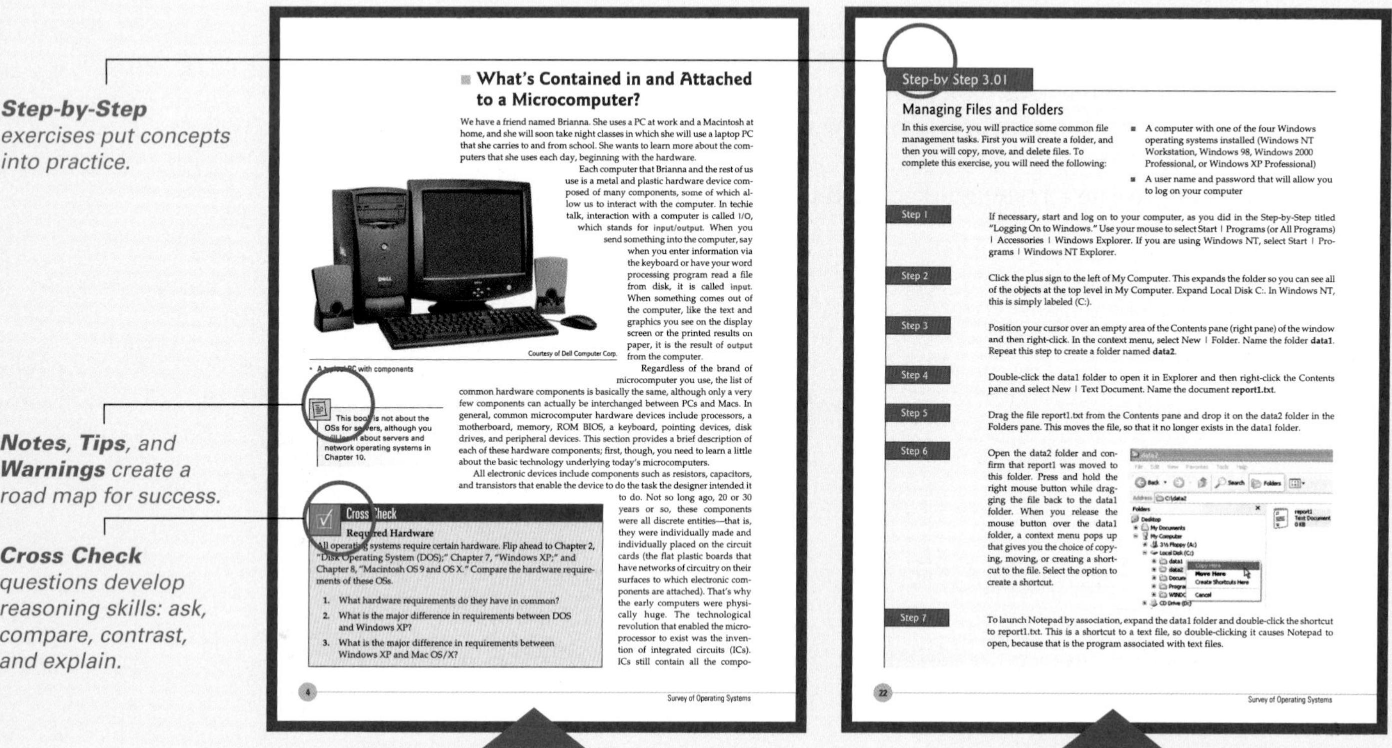

Step-by-Step exercises put concepts into practice.
Notes, **Tips**, and **Warnings** create a road map for success.
Cross Check questions develop reasoning skills: ask, compare, contrast, and explain.
What's Contained in and Attached to a Microcomputer?
Step-by-Step 3.01
Managing Files and Folders

Makes Learning Fun! — *Rich, colorful text and enhanced illustrations bring technical subjects to life.*

Offers Practical Experience — *Step-by-Step tutorials and lab assignments develop essential hands-on skills and put concepts in real-world contexts.*

Proven Learning Method Keeps You on Track

The Mike Meyers' Computer Skills series is structured to give you a practical working knowledge of baseline IT skills and technologies. The series' active learning methodology guides you beyond mere recall and, through thought-provoking activities, labs, and sidebars, helps you develop critical thinking, diagnostic, and communication skills.

Effective Learning Tools

This colorful, pedagogically rich book is designed to make learning easy and enjoyable and to help you develop the skills and critical thinking abilities that will enable you to adapt to different job situations and troubleshoot problems.

Jane Holcombe's and Chuck Holcombe's proven ability to explain concepts in a clear, direct, even humorous way makes these books interesting, motivational, and fun.

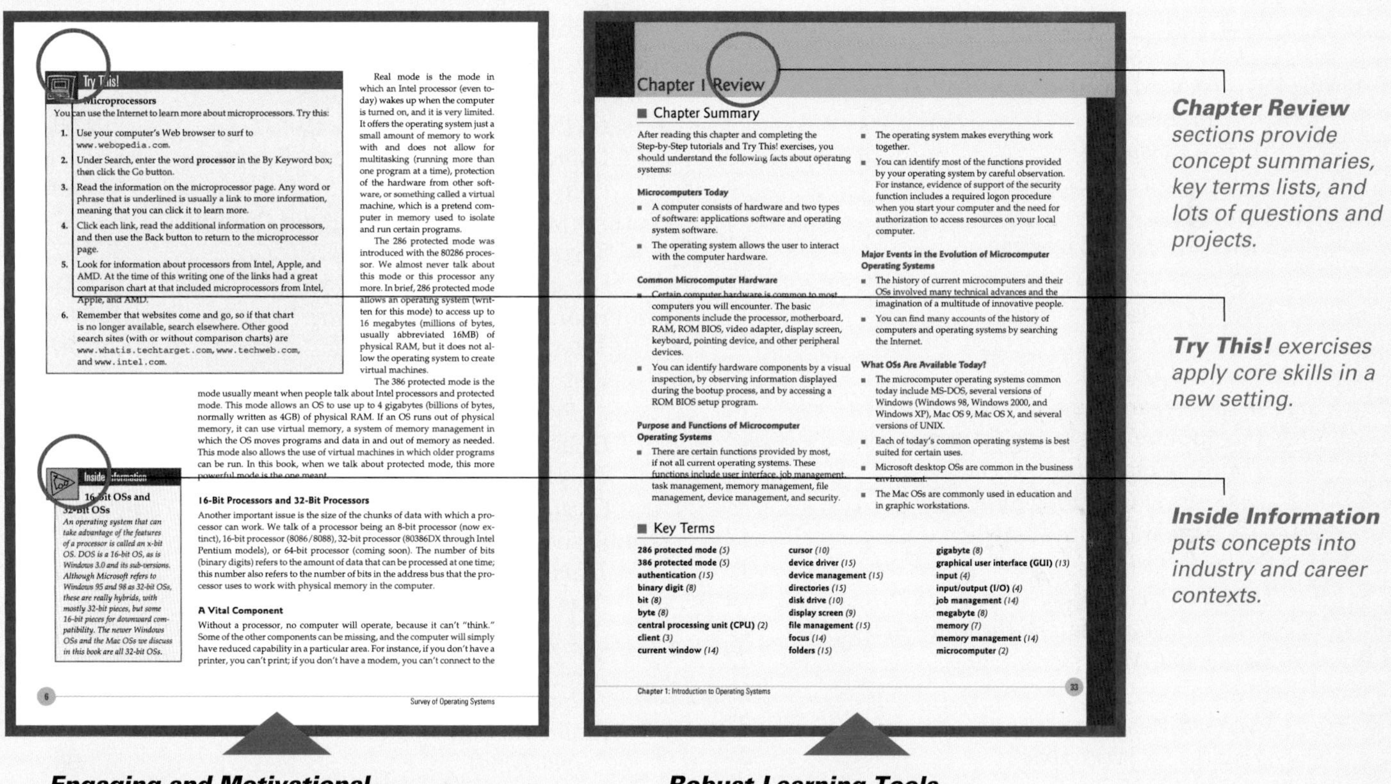

Chapter Review sections provide concept summaries, key terms lists, and lots of questions and projects.
Try This! exercises apply core skills in a new setting.
Inside Information puts concepts into industry and career contexts.

***Engaging and Motivational** — Using a conversational style and proven instructional approach, the authors explain technical concepts in a clear, interesting way using real-world examples.*

***Robust Learning Tools** — Summaries, key term lists, quizzes, essay questions, and lab projects help you practice skills and measure progress.*

Each chapter includes:

- **Learning Objectives** that set measurable goals for chapter-by-chapter progress
- **Four-Color Illustrations** that give you a clear picture of the technologies
- **Step-by-Step Tutorials** that teach you to perform essential tasks and procedures hands-on
- **Try This!** and **Cross Check** sidebars that encourage you to practice and apply concepts in real-world settings
- **Notes**, **Tips**, and **Warnings** that guide you through difficult areas
- **Chapter Summaries** and **Key Terms Lists** that provide you with an easy way to review important concepts and vocabulary
- **Challenging End-of-Chapter Tests** that include vocabulary-building exercises, multiple-choice questions, essay questions, and on-the-job lab projects

CONTENTS

Chapter 7

Managing Local Security in Windows *309*

Chapter 8

A Look under the Hood *377*

FOREWORD

One of the greatest challenges for someone entering the world of computing is trying to get a handle on the many different aspects of this exciting field. There are so many options! Do you want to repair PCs? Perhaps make a web site? Maybe working on networks is the thing you want to do? Perhaps though, you are like so many of us—almost overwhelmed at what all this means and unsure of where you wish to go. If that's you, then you're in for a real treat! *Survey of Operating Systems* is the first of the Mike Meyers' Computer Skills book series. Every book in this series is designed to give you a solid footing in one aspect of the information technologies (IT) industry—to provide you a level of depth to help you understand how all of the many parts of computers work.

So how will this book help you understand what IT is all about? Well, let's start by exploring the text in front of you right now. Like all of the books in this series, it is written in a very relaxed, conversational style that's a pleasure to read. We've tossed the staid, boring technical writing style out the window and instead write as though we're speaking directly to you—because as far as we're concerned, we are. In this and the other books in this series, we aren't afraid of the occasional contraction, nor do we worry about staying in third person. We've pretty much dumped all those other dry, pedantic rules that most technical writing has reduced itself to. I've suffered reading those books, and I swore when it came time to put together this series that we were going to break that mold—and we have! With over a million copies now in print using this series' conversational style, we think a lot of folks agree with what we're doing.

Keep your finger on this page and leaf through this book for a moment. Isn't it beautiful? Sure, there are plenty of exercises and questions for you to use to practice your skills, but let the left side of your brain take a nap, and let the right side appreciate just how attractive a book this is. The four-color printing and all of the colorful elements give the book what I describe very scientifically as a "happy feeling"—akin to walking the aisle at a grocery store.

Last—and this is very important—you'll never find yourself lost in any of these books. You'll never get blindsided by a term that hasn't been defined earlier. You won't find yourself reading one topic and suddenly finding yourself grinding gears as new, totally unrelated topics smack you in the face. Every topic leads from simple to complex, from broad to detailed, and from old to new, building concept upon concept while you read, making the book hard to put down. This is what I call Flow, and it's the most important aspect of these books.

So enjoy your reading. If you have any questions, feel free to contact me @ `michaelm@totalsem.com`.

Mike Meyers

INTRODUCTION

What Will You Learn?

The first edition of this book was well-received by instructors and students. This second edition was designed to update the material, but we did much more than that. Every chapter has been carefully revised as needed, with more illustrations and hands-on opportunities. We have added content to the entire book (over 100 additional pages) so it now covers all of the CompTIA A+ Operating System Technologies Examination Objectives. To include all these objectives, and to respond to feedback we received from instructors, we added three new chapters: Chapter 7, *Managing Local Security in Windows*; Chapter 8, *A Look under the Hood*; and Chapter 10, *The Client Side of Networking*. The former Chapter 5, *Windows 98*, has been removed from the book, but if you still need to learn about this venerable operating system, you can find it as an updated bonus chapter on the book's web site: www.mhhe.com/holcombe2.

In this book, you will learn what OSs are and why they are necessary and so very important to study early in your career. You'll learn about how operating systems work, and perhaps most important for your future peace of mind, you'll learn how to make them behave and do just what you want them to do. You'll learn how different OSs, and different versions of OSs, tackle the same problems. You'll learn where they are similar and where they are different. Best of all, you'll learn to be comfortable with almost any OS. Then when you sit down at a computer in the school library, at the local Internet cafe, or at a friend's house and find that the OS is one you're unfamiliar with, you'll know how to use it, *and you won't be afraid to try it!*

So exactly which OSs will you explore in this book? After a brief overview and some history of microcomputer OSs, you will get hands-on experience with several desktop OSs—from installation through configuration and file management to troubleshooting. These OSs include DOS, several versions of Microsoft Windows, the latest Macintosh OS, and Linux, presented in 12 chapters, plus a bonus Chapter 13 found on our web site (www.mhhe.com/holcombe2).

- Chapter 1, *Introduction to Operating Systems,* will provide an overview of microcomputer hardware and introduce you to the basic functions common to all operating systems, while introducing the operating systems you will study in this book.
- Chapter 2, *Disk Operating System (DOS),* may convince you that this venerable operating system is not yet dead! You will learn how to install MS-DOS, create a startup floppy disk, describe the bootup process, use the command-line interface, enter commands, manage files, and troubleshoot common DOS problems.
- Chapter 3, *Windows NT 4.0 Workstation,* is included because this operating system is still used in many organizations. This chapter will engage you in the installation, configuration, and basic management of Windows NT 4.0, as well as in troubleshooting common problems you may encounter.
- Chapter 4, *Windows 2000 Professional,* will give you hands-on experience with the OS that first combined the consumer-oriented user interface of Windows 98 with the robust nature of Windows NT. In this chapter, you will acquire the skills needed to install, configure, manage, and troubleshoot Windows 2000.
- Chapter 5, *Windows XP Professional,* will give you the opportunity to install, configure, manage, and troubleshoot this popular desktop operating system.
- Chapter 6, *Making the Windows GUI Work for You,* focuses on the Windows GUI and how to navigate, configure, and customize it, manage files, launch applications, and troubleshoot common problems.
- Chapter 7, *Managing Local Security in Windows,* is a new chapter in this edition. This chapter will help you to recognize security threats and vulnerabilities to desktop PCs and users while presenting methods and technologies you can use to protect against these threats to a Windows computer. You will learn to work

with local user accounts; assign permissions to files, folders, and printers; and troubleshoot common security problems in Windows.

- Chapter 8, *A Look under the Hood,* another new chapter in this edition, goes beyond the normal scope of a survey course in order to give even a new Windows user an understanding of some of the inner workings of the Windows operating system. You don't need to be a computer professional to understand the role of the Windows registry and to acquire the simple skills to back up the registry. Even the casual home user needs to install and configure device drivers, and understanding the Windows startup process is key to troubleshooting startup problems. You will also learn very valuable skills to keep your computer up-to-date and to troubleshoot a variety of problems.
- Chapter 9, *Introduction to Network Server Operating Systems,* begins with a brief overview of networking concepts to give you the context in which networks exist, and then provides basic server concepts including the client/server relationship established between client software on your computer and server software on network servers. You will then practice skills to share and protect network resources similar to those required to manage a server.
- Chapter 10, *The Client Side of Networking,* a third new chapter, will give you practice with skills required to configure a computer to work on a network. You will begin with an overview of the TCP/IP protocol suite, and then you will work with the file and print client in your Windows OS to connect to shares, learn about methods for connecting to the Internet, identify and configure Internet clients, and troubleshoot common client connection problems.
- Chapter 11, *Linux on the Desktop,* has been greatly revised and improved since the first edition. In this chapter, you will install Linux, practice skills for working at the Linux command prompt, as well as within a GUI, and troubleshoot common Linux problems.
- Chapter 12, *Macintosh OS X,* will guide you through installing and configuring Mac OS X, and then provide practice using the features of the Mac desktop and workspace. Finally, you will troubleshoot common Mac OS problems.
- Chapter 13, *Windows 98* (available on the McGraw-Hill Higher Education web site: www.mhhe.com/holcombe2), takes you from installing and configuring this OS through the tasks required to customize and manage Windows 98, including updating, creating new users, and managing files and printers. You'll also learn the solutions to common problems encountered in Windows 98.

How Will You Learn?

We don't want to simply give you an encyclopedia of information, because we don't want you to feel like you're standing in front of an information fire hose! We've been there ourselves many times in the past 20-some years, too often with no choice but to use any source available to get the information we needed, even if it was only a technical manual written with no awareness at all of the human audience. Rather, we're going to present just the key points about operating systems and guide you in your own exploration of the specifics of the technology. While there is a ton of good information in this book, one book simply can't give you everything you need to know about operating systems. We do hope to empower you, though, and to increase your ability to use widely available tools and resources to figure out the answers to your questions. Such tools as the Internet and the help program in your OS are aids you should turn to when you need to learn more about a topic and when you want to enhance your skills in working with each of these operating systems—and with computers in general.

Each chapter uses many techniques to help you learn. Each starts with a list of learning objectives followed by lucid explanations of each topic, supported by real-world, on-the-job scenarios and a liberal use of graphics and tables. To give you hands-on experience and to help you "walk the walk," each chapter contains detailed Step-by-Step tutorials and short Try This! exercises to reinforce the concepts. To build vocabulary to help you "talk the talk," each chapter contains definitions of computer terms, summarized in a Key Terms list and compiled into a Glossary at the end of the book. Be ready for a Key Term Quiz at the end of each chapter!

We've also included Inside Information sidebars, which provide insight into some of the subtleties of life with computers. Cross checks help you understand how OSs are similar and how they differ. Notes and Tips are sprinkled throughout the chapters, and Warnings help prevent mishaps (or an emotional meltdown). At the end of each chapter, a Key Term Quiz, Multiple-Choice Quiz, and Essay Quiz help you measure what you've learned and hone your ability to present information on paper. The Lab Projects challenge you to independently complete tasks related to what you've just learned.

Let's Get Down to Work

Okay, enough of this introductory stuff. You've waded through a lot of words to get through the introduction and to this point, but we promise you, it's the last time in this book that you'll see so many words without illustrations. From now on it's downright exciting! Learn a lot and *Have Fun!*

Supplements

For teachers using this book in the classroom, a powerful collection of teaching tools is available on CD-ROM, including:

- An Instructor's Manual that maps to the organization of the textbook
- ExamView® Pro testbank software that generates a wide array of paper or network-based tests, and that features automatic grading
- Hundreds of questions, written by experienced IT instructors
- A wide variety of question types and difficulty levels allows teachers to customize each test to maximize student progress
- Engaging PowerPoint® slides on the lecture topics

Introduction to Operating Systems

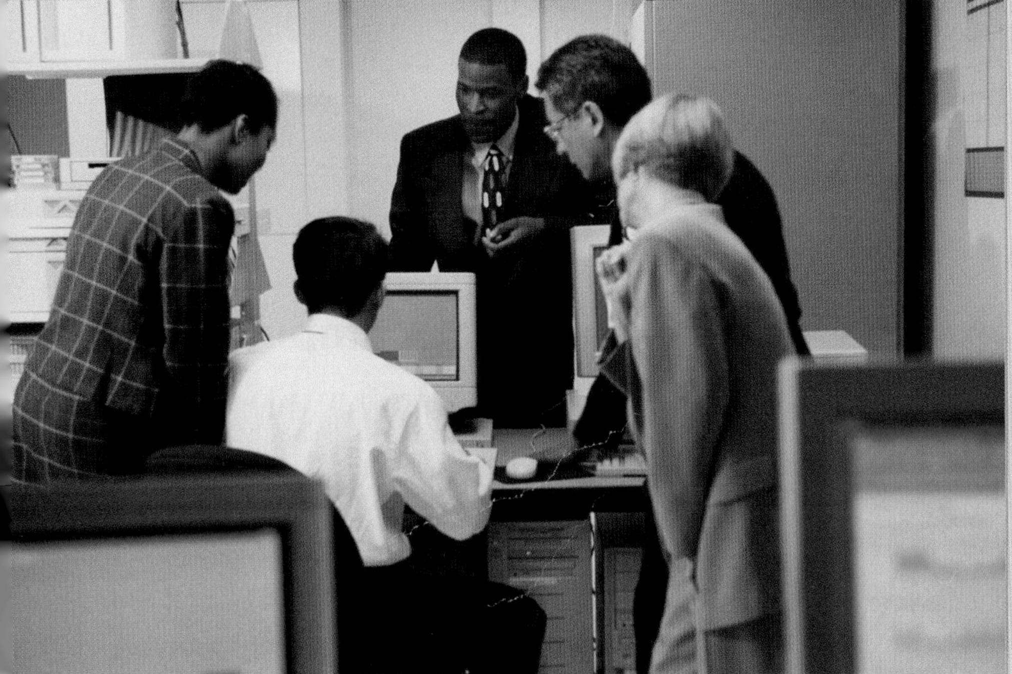

Computers are magnificent tools for the realization of our dreams, but no machine can replace the human spark of spirit, compassion, love, and understanding.

—Louis Gerstner
Former CEO, IBM

You can and must understand computers now!

—Ted Nelson
Computer Lab, 1974

Understanding microcomputer operating systems (OSs) is critical to your future success in life. It is. Just believe us. You don't? You say you drive a car just fine, but you don't understand the engine, transmission, and other systems? So why can't you just use your computer? Why do you have to even know it has an OS? If you can successfully operate a car, you actually know more about its internals than you realize. You turn on the ignition, shift to the correct gear, press the accelerator, and drive down the street without hitting anything. You stop it (in time, usually). Maybe you use your car to drive to work, school, shopping, or the lake or beach, thus making the car your transportation tool. Having only superficial knowledge of the workings of your car is adequate if you never intend to repair your car or to explain to a mechanic the symptoms of a problem. And just as you can use a car without much in-depth knowledge of how it works, you can use your computer to write a letter, send e-mail, create a report, or create a graphic. You only have to know how to turn it on, call up the application program you wish to use, make the application program do what you want it to do, and turn it off.

In this chapter, you will learn how to:

- **Describe the microcomputers in use today**
- **Identify common computer hardware components**
- **Describe the purpose and functions of microcomputer operating systems**
- **Describe major events in the evolution of microcomputer operating systems**
- **List and compare the common microcomputer operating systems**

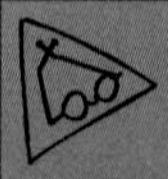

Inside Information

Computers Have Shrunk!

Fifty years ago, most people would have laughed at the thought of dedicating an entire computer to the use of an individual, because computers were far from "micro." They were very large (filling rooms and weighing tons), expensive, high-maintenance machines dedicated to the use of a government agency, university, or company. In 1949, Popular Mechanics *published the following prediction: "Computers in the future may have only 1,000 vacuum tubes and perhaps only weigh 1 1/2 tons." Over the years, computers not only have become physically ever-smaller, but also have become much more powerful than their predecessors.*

But if you ever want to understand how your car actually works, you need to spend time studying it. And if you want to be involved in any aspect of the computer industry, you need to understand how computers work and, in particular, how the most critical software component, the computer's operating system, works.

This chapter provides an overview of microcomputer operating systems. It begins by defining what a microcomputer is, explaining the types of microcomputers you may encounter, and describing the physical components you can expect to find in and connected to a microcomputer. Then, after a brief definition of OSs and their purpose, we present an in-depth discussion of OSs and the functions they perform. You'll take a brief journey back in time to learn the history of microcomputer operating systems, and finally you will be introduced to the microcomputer OSs you will find in homes and offices today.

An Overview of Microcomputers

Before you learn about microcomputer operating systems, you may have a few more general questions: What is a microcomputer? What types of microcomputers are used today? You will find the answers to these questions in this section.

Photo courtesy of Sony Electronics Inc.

• A typical PC with components

What Is a Microcomputer?

A **microcomputer** is a computer built around a special integrated circuit (IC) that performs the calculations, or processing, of the computer. An IC, commonly called a *chip,* is a small electronic component made up of transistors (tiny switches) and other miniaturized parts. Often referred to as the brain of a computer, this chip is the **central processing unit (CPU)**, but is also called a **microprocessor**, or simply a processor. A microcomputer is small enough, and even cheap enough, to be dedicated to the use of a single person. This was a revolutionary idea in the 1970s, when microcomputers first became available, because in the computers of previous decades, bulky vacuum tubes served the purpose that microscopic transistors now serve.

Beware of PC naming confusion! The term *personal computer* (*PC*) actually excludes some microcomputers because it is often interpreted as referring specifically to any computer that complies with the standards that evolved from the IBM PC, which originated in 1981, and that are now manifest in the Microsoft/Intel standards.

What Types of Microcomputers Are Used Today?

In the 1970s, very few computers were small enough to sit on a desk. One computer, the Control Data 160A, actually *was* the desk! But people wanted computers *on* their desks, so what they used was a terminal consisting of a display and a keyboard that was connected to a large mainframe computer. When computers became small enough in the late 1970s to sit on a desk, the word *microcomputer* was coined and widely used to describe the early forms of these computers. We're now more likely to use the term *personal computer (PC)*, which applies to computers that comply with hardware standards set and supported by Microsoft, Intel (the largest computer chip manufacturer), and to a lesser extent, other companies. We call these the Microsoft/Intel standards (also called Wintel). However, many important microcomputers don't comply with these standards—most notably, computers from Apple and the small hand-held computers that are growing in popularity today.

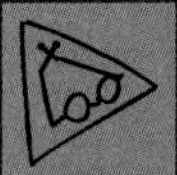

Inside Information

Vacuum Tubes?

In the beginning, digital computers used electronic vacuum tubes as the switches that created the 0's and 1's that a binary computer uses to compute and perform logical operations. Vacuum tubes, although very small compared to the tubes of earlier days, were thousands of times larger than today's microchips that perform the switching function, generated a lot of heat, used a huge amount of electricity, and were fiendishly difficult to keep running reliably. The 1949 Popular Mechanics *quote was referring to electronic digital computers that were room-sized, or larger. One of the authors remembers seeing an air defense computer that was about the size of a city block!*

In the United Kingdom, vacuum tubes were referred to as "valves." If you think about it for a second, you'll realize that a valve in a water pipe can be thought of as a switch—it turns the water on and off. It isn't truly digital, however, because you can adjust a water valve so the water flows somewhere between on and off.

Desktops and Laptops

Today the majority of computers found on desktops in private and public organizations comply with the Microsoft/Intel standard, with Macintosh computers a distant second, at less than 5 percent of the market share. Most of the portable laptop or notebook computers available today are Microsoft/ Intel compatible. Early Macintosh computers came with sophisticated graphics abilities that made them attractive to users in any line of work requiring high-quality graphical and multimedia support. Apple also gave away many computers to schools, so today the Macintosh has ardent supporters in the education area and in graphics businesses. Now the Microsoft/ Intel compatible computers match, or even exceed, the Macintosh graphics and multimedia capabilities. However, when people learn to use a computer, they tend to feel loyalty to the kind of computer they learned on.

Furthermore, microcomputer types can be distinguished by how they are used. A short list includes desktops, laptops, handhelds, and a long list of various devices that don't have "computer" in their name, such as cell phones, games, stoves, refrigerators, TVs, and DVD players. However, this book is dedicated to the operating systems used by individuals on desktop and portable microcomputers, whether they are PCs or Macs.

Servers

A PC or Mac can also be used as a **server**, which is a computer that plays one of several important roles in a network. In all of these roles, it provides services to other computers, which is why they're called servers, and the computers on the receiving end of these services are referred to as **clients**. Although a server may be based on the same hardware components found in microcomputers, those components are beefed up considerably for a server—resulting in the computer equivalent of a professional wrestler versus a jockey. This difference is reflected in the cost, which can run in the tens of thousands of dollars for a server, versus only a few hundred dollars for an average PC.

In this book, we'll use the term *microcomputer* to refer to all small computers as a group, and we'll use the term *PC* when discussing computers that comply with the Microsoft/Intel standards, both desktop and portable. We'll use the term *Mac* to refer to today's Apple computers (which include several models), both desktop and portable.

What kind of services does a server provide? When a server is used to store all of the data files of the users in a department or company, it is called a *file* server. And if a server has one or more printers connected to it that it shares with users on the network, it is called a *print* server. A server doing both tasks is called a *file and print* server. What sounds like two services, is actually combined into one service called a file and print service. Note that one server can offer multiple services at the same time. Servers may offer messaging services (e-mail and fax), web services, and many, many other services.

This book is not about the OSs for servers, although Chapter 9 provides an overview of servers and network operating systems.

Hand-Held Devices

There are also many different hand-held devices, and they are often proprietary devices that comply with no, or very few, standards in their design. Despite their size, they are still called microcomputers because they are built around microprocessors. They include a wide variety of products ranging from simple hand-held computers to multifunction mobile devices. Some hand-held computers are dedicated to a single purpose; examples include the hand-held devices that employees use in grocery stores to track inventory. Others are wireless phones that not only allow voice communications, but also let you connect to the Internet and view your e-mail on their tiny color screens.

What's Contained in and Attached to a Microcomputer?

Our friend Brianna uses a PC at work and a Macintosh at home, and she will soon take night classes in which she will use a laptop PC that she carries to and from school. She wants to learn more about the computers that she uses each day, beginning with the hardware.

Each computer that Brianna and the rest of us use is a metal and plastic hardware contraption composed of many components, some of which allow us to interact with the computer. In techie talk, interaction with a computer is called **input/output (I/O)**. When you send something into the computer, say, when you enter information via the keyboard or have your word processing program read a file from disk, it is called input. When something comes out of the computer, like the text and graphics you see on the display screen or the printed results on paper, it is output from the computer.

Regardless of the brand of microcomputer you use, the list of common hardware components is basically the same. In general, common microcomputer hardware devices include processors, a motherboard, memory, ROM BIOS, a keyboard, pointing devices, disk drives, and peripheral devices. This section provides a brief description of each of these hardware components. First, though, you need to learn a little about the basic technology underlying today's microcomputers.

All electronic devices include components such as resistors, capacitors, and transistors that enable the device to do the task the designer intended it to do. About 20 or 30 years ago, these components were all discrete entities—that is, they were individually made and individually placed on the circuit cards (the flat boards that have networks of circuitry on their

Try This

More About Handhelds

Although this book will mention hand-held devices from time to time, you will not really study these devices in this book. Satisfy your curiosity about this growing area. Try this:

1. Use an Internet search engine, such as `www.google.com`, and search on the term "handheld computer." Browse through the sites you find in the search engine. Results will vary, but some likely sites are `www.Microsoft.com/mobile/handheldpc`, `www.handheldmed.com`, and `www.hhp.com`.
2. What OSs do the hand-held devices you discovered use?
3. What industries are using hand-held devices?

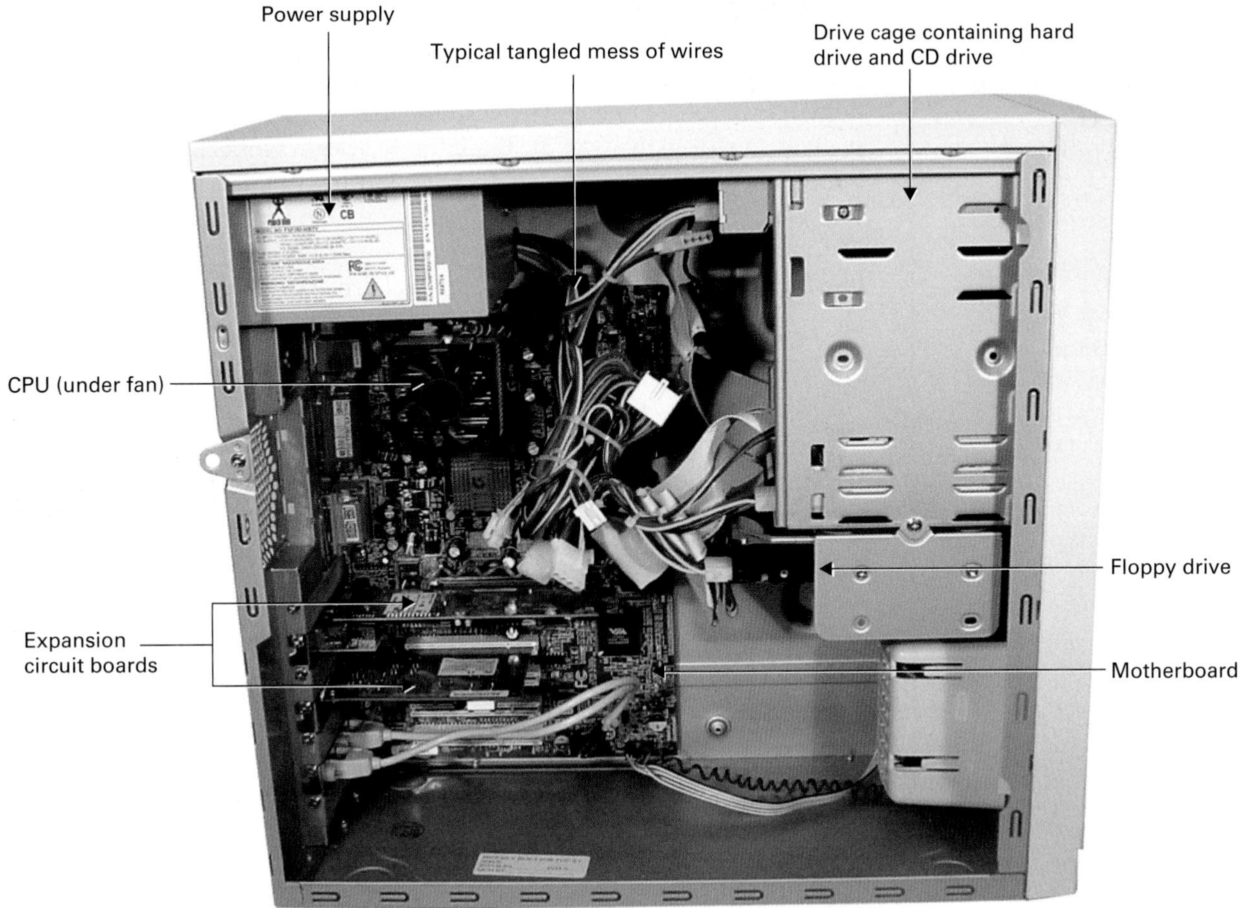

• Open computer showing internal components

surfaces to which electronic components are attached). That's why the early computers were physically huge. The technological revolution that enabled the microprocessor to exist was the invention of integrated circuits (ICs). ICs still contain all the components necessary to make the device work, but they are created by special processes that vastly miniaturize all of the individual pieces and place them on a wafer (or chip) of material. Thus, today a computer chip can contain many millions of devices within it and still be less than an inch or so in size.

Not only the PC, but also just about any modern appliance or machine now uses IC technology, making it one of the most significant inventions—ever. Learn more about the innovative people who made this possible at `inventors.about.com` and search on "inventor integrated circuit."

Microprocessor

A microcomputer always has at least one microprocessor, which is also called a central processing unit (CPU), or simply a processor. Like many of the electronic components in a computer, a processor is an integrated circuit (IC), or chip. The microprocessor is the central component of the computer—its brain. Like your own brain, the processor sends and receives commands to and from the computer's hardware and software. For example, when Brianna wants to print a letter she typed on her computer, she chooses the Print command. This seems like a very simple command, but it actually

Inside Information

Early Intel Processors

For the past decade or so, Intel processors have been variations on the Pentium processor, but in the 1980s there were several major models, such as the CPU in the original IBM PC, the 8088. This was a slightly less capable version of the 8086 (these two models are so similar that they are often considered as one). The next major advance was the 80286 (also called the 286), followed by the 386. Intel often brought out variations on a major model, using letters to distinguish the different CPUs. The 386DX was a specific submodel of the 386, as was the 386SX, which was less capable. For instance, the 386SX could not use as much physical memory as the 386DX. Intel followed this practice with the 486, which also came out in SX and DX versions: one (the SX) lacking and one (the DX) containing a special math coprocessor on the CPU.

causes many commands to be sent to the processor: commands to transfer the file from memory to the printer, commands to communicate with the printer, and many, many others. The processor doesn't just perform calculations; it is involved in nearly everything that happens in your computer. It really is similar to the way the brain/body system works. For example, the brain issues a command to take a step, but the number of processes that command generates is enormous. The autonomic nervous system, which is like an independent computer system, controls the details of the execution of the command, similar to what a peripheral driver does for a PC.

Courtesy Intel.

• Top and bottom views of a microprocessor with many gold pins visible on the bottom

Without a processor, no computer will operate, because it can't "think." Some of the other components can be missing, and the computer will simply have reduced capability in a particular area. For instance, if you don't have a printer, you can't print, or if you don't have a modem, you can't connect to the Internet over a phone line—but the rest of the computer will work fine. However, without a processor, your computer simply will not work.

The capabilities of the processor also define the limits and capabilities of the computer, including the speed of the system. In addition, because operating systems must work closely with the processor and other hardware, an operating system is written to work with a certain range of processors and chipsets. This limits your choice of OSs that you can run on a computer.

Among the distinguishing features of a processor are operation modes and the size of the chunks of data with which the processor can work. Let's look at these features.

Try This

Microprocessors

You can use the Internet to learn more about microprocessors. Try this:

1. Use your computer's web browser to surf to `www.webopedia.com`.
2. Under Search, enter the word **microprocessor** in the Enter A Word For A Definition box; then click the Go button.
3. Read the information on the microprocessor page. Any word or phrase that is underlined is a link to more information, meaning that you can click it to learn more.
4. Click the link titled Microprocessor Comparison Chart and review the information.

Processor Modes

We'll use the Intel processors to briefly look at some basic processor features. The Intel 8086 and 8088 processors used in PCs in the early 1980s had a limited bag of tricks, because they had only one mode of operation: real mode. Later Intel processors beginning with the 386DX had three modes: real mode plus two flavors of protected mode, called 286 protected mode and 386 protected mode.

Real mode is the mode in which an Intel processor (even today) wakes up when the computer is turned on, and it is very limited. It offers the operating system just a small amount of memory to work with and does not allow for multitasking (running more than one program at a time), protection of the hardware from other software, or something called a *virtual machine*, which is a pretend computer in memory, used to isolate and run certain programs.

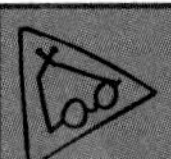

Inside Information

16-, 32-, and 64-Bit OSs

An operating system that can take advantage of the features of a processor is called an x-bit OS. DOS is a 16-bit OS, as is Windows 3.0 and its sub-versions. Windows 95, Windows 98, and Windows Millennium Edition are really hybrids, with mostly 32-bit pieces, but some 16-bit pieces for downward compatibility. The Windows versions, Mac OS X, UNIX, and Linux OSs we discuss in this book are all at least 32-bit OSs, with some being 64-bit. The 64-bit versions include Windows XP 64-bit Edition, MAC OS X Tiger, and various versions of UNIX and Linux.

The 286 protected mode was introduced with the 80286 processor. We almost never talk about this mode or this processor anymore. In brief, 286 protected mode allows an operating system (written for this mode) to access up to 16 megabytes (millions of bytes, usually abbreviated 16MB) of physical RAM, but it does not allow the operating system to create virtual machines. (You'll learn about RAM shortly.)

The 386 protected mode is the mode usually meant when people talk about Intel processors and protected mode. This mode allows an OS to use up to 4 gigabytes (billions of bytes, normally written as 4GB) of physical RAM. If an OS runs out of physical memory, this processor mode supports the use of virtual memory, a system of memory management in which the OS moves programs and data in and out of memory as needed. This mode also allows the use of virtual machines in which older programs can be run. In this book, when we talk about protected mode, this more powerful mode is the one we mean.

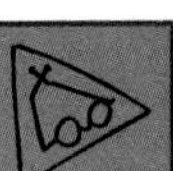

Inside Information

Number Systems

It is probably useful to explain a bit about the various numbering systems digital computers use. During the years of growth and evolution, digital computers have employed many different numbering systems—octal and bi-quinary come immediately to mind (never mind, you won't need to know them). Three number systems, binary, decimal, and hexadecimal, have become common and are being used in most of today's computers. A number system is based on the number of digits available for use. Binary uses only two digits, 0 and 1, hence: binary. Decimal has a ten-digit base and uses the numbers 0 through 9, while hexadecimal has a 16-digit base and uses the numbers 0 through 9 and the letters A through F. Decimal is used to communicate with people; hexadecimal is used to address memory; while binary is used to transfer data. You can add, subtract, multiply, and divide in each of these systems, and fortunately, the calculator found at Start | All Programs | Accessories | Calculator can do that for you. It can also translate numbers from one system to another, since every number in one system has an equivalent number in another system. This is not the place for a detailed tutorial in such translation, so we'll just include a brief table of equivalents so you can get a sense of what numbers in each system look like.

Binary	Decimal	Hexadecimal
1	1	1
10	2	2
11	3	3
100	4	4
101	5	5
110	6	6
111	7	7
1000	8	8
1001	9	9
1010	10	A
1011	11	B
1100	12	C
1101	13	D
1110	14	E
1111	15	F
10000000	128	80
11111111	255	FF

16-, 32-, and 64-Bit Processors

Another important issue is the size of the chunks of data with which a processor can work. We talk of a processor being an 8-bit processor (now extinct), 16-bit processor (8086/8088),

32-bit processor (80386DX through Intel Pentium models), or 64-bit processor (Intel Itanium and Xeon models). The number of *bits* (binary digits) refers to the amount of data that can be processed at one time. A similar number (that does not necessarily match this number) is the number of bits the processor uses in the address bus. The *address bus* is the group of wires leading from the processor that enable the processor to access RAM through assigned addresses.

Motherboard and Chipset

The **motherboard** is the central circuit board of a computer. All other devices are connected to it in one way or another. It contains one or more CPU slots or sockets into which the processor is plugged, the controlling chipset, some memory slots, the voltage regulator module (VRM), the ROM BIOS, and the expansion bus slots. The number of processor sockets, memory slots, and expansion bus slots varies depending on the capabilities of the motherboard. The chipset consists of several chips that control much of the flow of signals to and from the processor and other components. It is another key element in the overall limits and capabilities of the microcomputer. All these new terms are discussed next.

Courtesy Intel.

• A typical motherboard with some components installed

Memory

Memory is a huge topic, but we can condense it to one basic statement: memory *remembers.* Too simple? Let's try again. Computer **memory** involves chips that store programs and data. Got that? That's the short explanation. Here's the low-tech, but long, explanation. Memory, in a computer, refers to one of several different types. In broad terms, there are two types of memory chips in a computer: random-access memory (RAM), and read-only memory (ROM). Programs and data can be stored directly and each memory location can be directly accessed—at random.

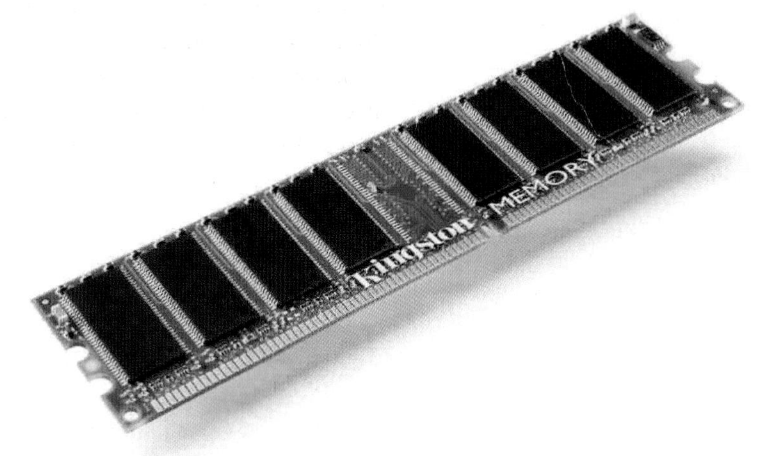

Courtesy of Kingston Technology Company Inc.

• Memory module

To put this into context, a relative of ours just called to boast that he had bought a computer with 1 gigabyte of RAM (roughly a billion bytes of RAM) and a hard drive with 120 gigabytes of disk space. (We know that computer memory and hard drives are growing rapidly, so please don't send us e-mail if that sounds like a ridiculously wimpy computer by the time you read this!)

RAM

The most important memory in your computer is the system memory, also called main or physical memory. It consists of **random-access memory (RAM)** that active programs use when they're running. RAM is volatile, meaning that when you turn off or reboot your computer, whatever is contained in memory disappears. RAM consists of one or more special circuit cards that contain memory chips. It is called random-access memory because the contents of RAM can be created or read by going directly to an address, rather than searching from the beginning to the end every time, as must be done when a computer tape is used.

An address is a pointer to a specific location in memory, used by your OS to organize its use of memory. When an advertisement for a computer states "with 512MB (megabytes) of memory," this is system memory.

Inside Information

A Bit About Bytes

If the words megabyte *and* gigabyte *just sound like jargon, read this. If you learned about megabytes and gigabytes before you ate your first French fries, skip this.*

When we talk about storing things in memory or on disk, we use terms like megabyte and gigabyte to describe amounts of memory or disk space. To understand these terms, first consider the smallest unit of storage (disk or memory), which is a binary digit (abbreviated as bit). You can think of a single bit as being like a light switch: it is either on or off. When it is on, it represents 1; when it is off, it represents 0. Computers (or the folks who make computers) like binary notation because it can be represented by anything that has two states, like on or off. This is exactly how RAM and ROM work: with the equivalent of on and off switches. Floppy and hard disks have a metallic oxide coating that contains particles that can be magnetized (polarized) by a charge, or left unmagnetized, and can thus represent on and off states.

In computers, bits are often used in groups of eight, which we call a byte. A single byte can represent a character, like the letter A *in a word processing document, or a very simple command, like the command to move down one line. When you have 1,024 bytes, you have 1 kilobyte (2 to the 10th power—*kilo *means thousand); 1,048,576 bytes equal 1 megabyte (2 to the 20th power—*mega *means million); 1,073,741,824 bytes equal 1 gigabyte (2 to the 30th power—*giga *means billion); 1,099,511,627,776 bytes equal 1 terabyte (2 to the 40th power—*tera *means trillion). (Notice that the actual number of bytes is not a round number, so when you have a kilobyte of data, you actually have a little more than a thousand bytes—and it really adds up! A gigabyte is actually almost 74 million bytes larger than you would expect.)*

RAM has historically been very expensive, but in recent years, technical advances have vastly increased the amount of RAM available on a single chip while at the same time drastically reducing the cost of each chip. Nowadays, even inexpensive computers have memory capacity only dreamed of a few years ago.

Beyond the system memory, many components in your computer, and the peripherals attached to your computer, also contain memory, but this memory is not included in system memory.

ROM BIOS

Another type of memory is **read-only memory (ROM)**, which is used to store programs more or less permanently. When you turn off your computer, the contents of ROM remain intact. So why did we say "more or less"? Because some ROM can actually be modified, using a special program and sometimes also requiring a temporary change to the hardware, but that is beyond what you need to know right now, so just think of what is contained in ROM as permanent.

The **ROM BIOS** is the chip containing the **read-only memory basic input/output system**. The BIOS is a set of program instructions for starting the computer, as well as for controlling communication between the processor and other components (the input and output). That's why this information is stored in ROM: so that it doesn't vanish when the power is turned off. Also stored in ROM is the system setup program that lets us define the basic configuration information, which is, in turn, stored in another special kind of nonvolatile (its contents do not disappear when power is turned off) RAM, called CMOS RAM.

This basic configuration information includes the following:

- The type and capacity of the installed disk drives (both floppy and hard)
- The disk boot order (the order in which the system searches disks for bootup programs)
- The configuration of system memory
- The configuration of the various connectors
- The configuration of power management
- Other system-level configuration options determined by the makers of the motherboard and the creators of the ROM BIOS

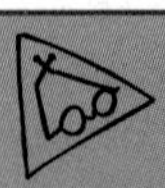

Inside Information

More About ROM

The term ROM BIOS *usually refers to the system BIOS that is central to each computer. However, most components and peripherals have their own ROM that contains program code for operating that component. Because the software that is stored in ROM is nonvolatile, it is often referred to as firmware. If you're quick, you can see information fleetingly displayed on your screen by the system ROM BIOS and the ROM of other devices during bootup, as shown in Figure 1-1.*

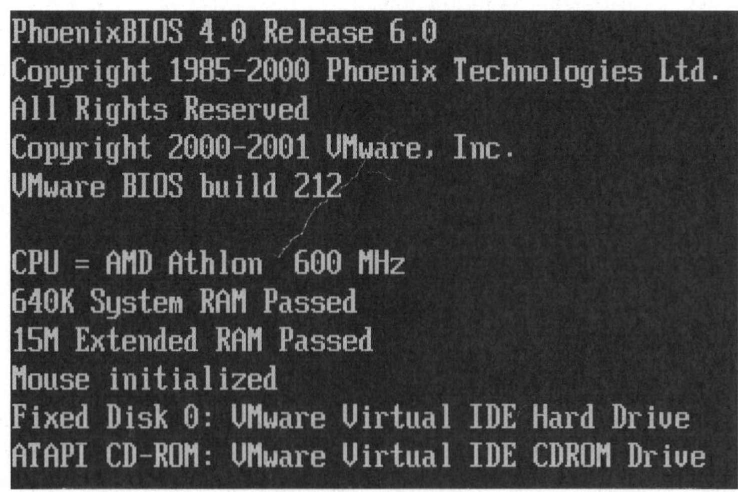

PhoenixBIOS 4.0 Release 6.0
Copyright 1985-2000 Phoenix Technologies Ltd.
All Rights Reserved
Copyright 2000-2001 VMware, Inc.
VMware BIOS build 212
CPU = AMD Athlon 600 MHz
640K System RAM Passed
15M Extended RAM Passed
Mouse initialized
Fixed Disk 0: VMware Virtual IDE Hard Drive
ATAPI CD-ROM: VMware Virtual IDE CDROM Drive

• **Figure 1-1.** BIOS bootup information

Video Adapter and Display

The video adapter is a set of circuitry (either embedded in the motherboard or on a separate circuit board) that receives video control signals from the computer and sends the controlling output signals to the display screen.

A computer will usually have a **display screen**, either a monitor or a flat panel display (FPD), for the visual output from the computer. Traditionally, a display screen was built around a cathode-ray tube (CRT), which is physically bulky and looks like a TV set. However, a FPD has a much smaller footprint on the desktop than a monitor with an equal-sized screen, and this fact, combined with recent improvements in flat-panel displays and rapidly falling prices, make these types of displays increasingly common. There are several types of FPDs with varying characteristics, but they all share the common characteristics of smaller footprints, very thin profile, usually excellent image quality, and a considerably higher price than CRTs.

Copyright ATI Technologies Inc.

• Video adapter

Keyboard

A keyboard is an input device, usually built around a typewriter-style layout of alphanumeric and punctuation keys (commonly known as the *QWERTY* layout after the first six letters in the top letter row) plus additional function, control, arrow, modifying, and editing keys. Most computer keyboards also have a separate numeric keypad, with the exception of portable computer keyboards, which often have the keypad embedded within the alphanumeric keys (doing double duty). Keyboards come in all sizes and shapes including ones you can roll up and ones you can fold up and put in your pocket. One new kind of keyboard actually has no physical keys (`http://www.virtualdevices.net/`). It's a virtual keyboard that projects an image of a keyboard on any flat surface and then senses the movement of your fingers as you type!

Courtesy of Microsoft® Corp.

• Keyboard

Pointing Device

A pointing device is required to move a graphical pointer called a **cursor** around a graphical user interface (GUI). A **mouse**, the most common pointing device, is roughly the size of a bar of soap and connects to the computer by a physical cable or through a wireless connection (using infrared or radio signals). When a mouse is moved around on a flat surface, its device driver (the piece of software that tells the computer what a device is doing) translates its movements into similar movements of the cursor on the display screen. Other pointing devices that provide essentially the same function include track balls, touch pads, and light pens.

Courtesy of Microsoft® Corp.

• Mouse

Disk Drives

Computers today contain one or more **disk drives**, for storing data and programs. A disk drive stores data by putting it onto the surface of small spinning platters using either magnetic or optical technology. Floppy drives and hard disk drives use a magnetic technology in which each disk platter has a metal oxide coating that can be easily magnetized, and data is encoded on this surface magnetically.

Courtesy of Seagate Technology.

• A hard disk drive with the cover removed

Cross Check

Required Hardware

All operating systems require certain hardware. Flip ahead to Chapter 2, Chapter 5, and Chapter 12. Compare the hardware requirements of these OSs.

1. What hardware requirements do they have in common?
2. What is the major difference in requirements between DOS and Windows XP?
3. What is the major difference in requirements between Windows XP and Mac OS X?

A floppy disk has only a single flexible platter, usually made of Mylar, while a hard disk drive will have one or more rigid metal platters. Compact disc (CD) and digital versatile (formerly video) disc (DVD) drives use an optical technology in which a focused light beam generated by a tiny laser is used to read and write information on the disk. CDs and DVDs are plastic with a material embedded that can be altered by the light beam when information is written to the disk, and which reflects variations in the light beam when the disk is read. Floppy and hard disks are always rewriteable, whereas CDs and DVDs come in both read-only and writeable/rewriteable forms.

Storage space is not memory! Don't fall into the trap of confusing memory with storage space. Memory is RAM or ROM. Most of the memory you work with is RAM, used as the temporary workspace for your OS and applications. Storage space is disk space where you save your programs and data as files.

Hard disks are usually found installed inside a computer, but recent developments allow stand-alone hard drives that plug into USB or FireWire ports. They are often used as backup devices. Hard drive capacities have rapidly increased as well, reaching sizes only imagined a few years ago.

Peripheral Devices

Peripheral device is a very broad term that pretty much covers all computer components beyond the motherboard components (processor, basic chipset, and memory). Although this term does include a great deal of "under the hood" stuff (that is, devices that are contained in the computer cabinet along with everything else), we most often use the word *peripheral* to refer to non-essential add-on devices such as digital cameras, printers, scanners, pointing devices, external modems, and disk drives.

Learn more about current hardware technology and future trends at www.hardwarecentral.com, www.aceshardware.com, and www.hwextreme.com.

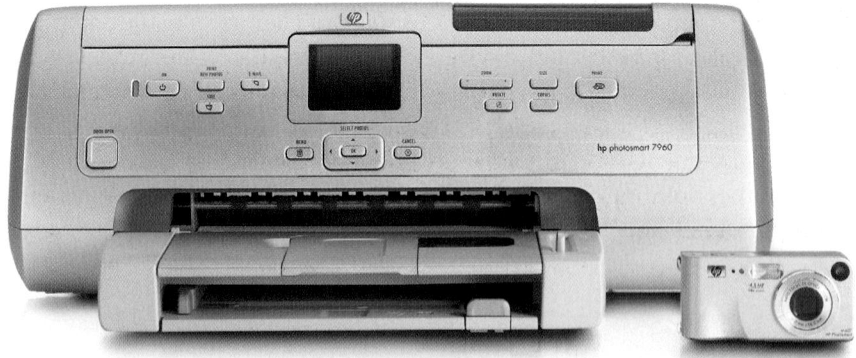

Courtesy of HP.

• An HP Photosmart 7960 photo printer and HP Photosmart digital camera.

Purpose, Types, and Functions of Microcomputer Operating Systems

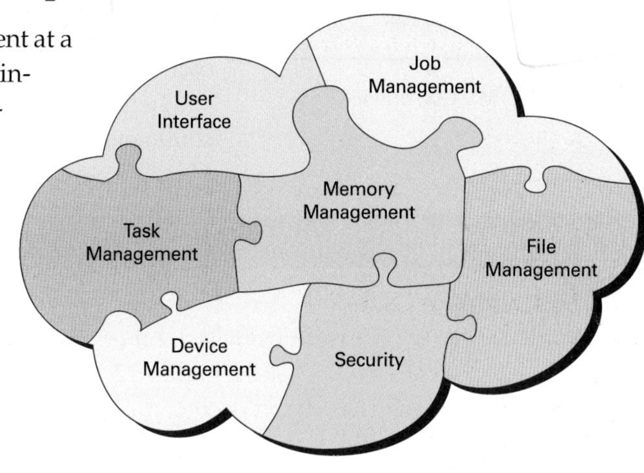

• The functions of an operating system

Bob works part-time in a legal office and is a full-time student at a community college, where he is enrolled in the computer information systems (CIS) track. Recently, he took a Saturday community education class in computer graphics. He finds himself confused by all of the different operating systems that he uses. At work, he has Windows XP Professional on his desktop computer; in the open lab at night school, he uses Windows 2000; and in his recent Saturday afternoon graphics class, he used a Macintosh. His next class at the community college will involve working with Linux. Although Bob's experience might seem extreme, it illustrates a fact: you are likely to encounter different desktop operating systems at work, school, and home. In addition, as computers proliferate, it becomes more important to learn the common characteristics that they share.

Bob spends most of his time on each computer he uses working in one or another specific application, such as a word processor, a graphical drawing program, or an Internet browser. However, he often needs to perform tasks outside of these applications, such as logging onto the computer, launching each application, managing files, and even troubleshooting the occasional problem that may arise with the computer. He has recently gone from not even realizing that such a thing as an operating system existed to wondering how he can learn to perform these common tasks in each of the different operating systems that he encounters. He wants to gain a better understanding of the OSs so that he can both perform better on the job and feel more comfortable while working on the various computers. He has decided to begin by learning what an OS is and what functions it performs, as described in the following sections.

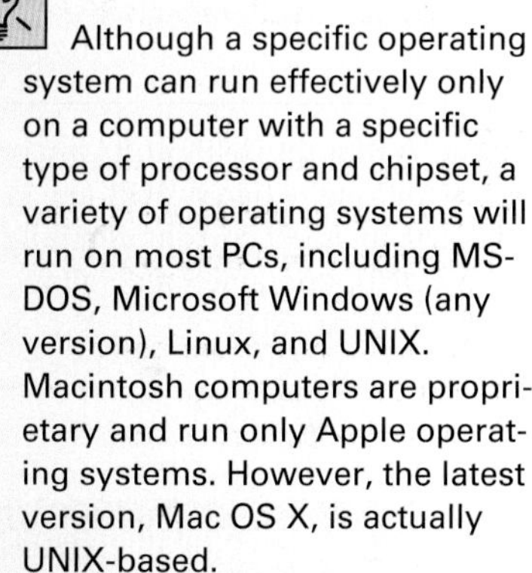

Although a specific operating system can run effectively only on a computer with a specific type of processor and chipset, a variety of operating systems will run on most PCs, including MS-DOS, Microsoft Windows (any version), Linux, and UNIX. Macintosh computers are proprietary and run only Apple operating systems. However, the latest version, Mac OS X, is actually UNIX-based.

What Is an Operating System?

An **operating system (OS)** is the program (or group of programs) that acts as the central control program for the computer. As such, it is loaded (or booted up, a derivation of the adage "lifting yourself by your own bootstraps") when the computer is turned on. Its main component, the **kernel**, always remains in memory while the computer is running. The operating system acts as an intermediary between the applications and the hardware. There are several functions performed by the operating system. We'll study them next.

User Interface

The **user interface** is the software layer, sometimes called the shell, through which the user communicates with the OS. The OS, in turn, communicates with the computer. Thus, the user interface includes the command processor, which loads programs into memory, as well as the many visual components of the operating system (what you see when you look at the monitor).

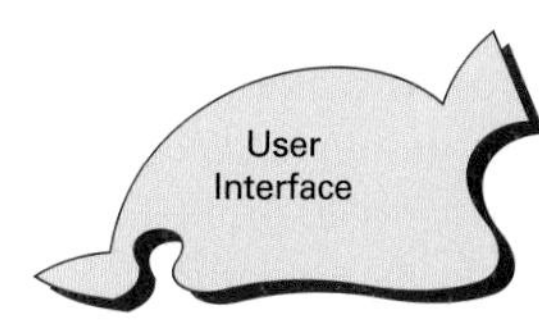

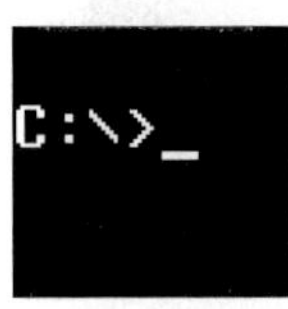

• **Figure 1-2.** MS-DOS prompt

On a computer running DOS, this visual component consists of a character-based command line that provides only sparse amounts of information. Figure 1-2 shows the classic DOS prompt: white characters against a black screen, with a blinking cursor waiting for you to type a command at the keyboard. Only a limited set of characters can appear on the screen, each in its own little equal-sized grid of space.

To become proficient with DOS, you must memorize the somewhat cryptic commands and their modifiers and subcommands. On the other hand, Apple's Mac OSs and Microsoft's Windows operating systems all provide an information-rich **graphical user interface (GUI)** through which you communicate with the OS and the computer. The GUI offers menus and graphical icons (small graphics) that allow you to use the pointing device to select programs to run and to perform many other tasks, such as opening a word-processed file.

Although you do not have to memorize arcane commands, working within a GUI does require you to learn the meaning of the various graphical pieces that make up the GUI and how to navigate among these pieces to find your programs and data. In addition, you must learn how to make a program become active (to start) so that you can get your work or play done. Figure 1-3 shows a GUI screen. Notice the icons and other graphical components, such as the bar at the bottom containing the button labeled "Start."

Cross Check

Compare GUIs

GUIs are not all that different from each other. Flip ahead to Chapter 5, "Windows XP Professional," and Chapter 12, "Mac OS X," and use the illustrations in these two chapters to compare the GUIs of these two OSs. Then answer the following questions:

1. What major differences can you observe between these two GUIs?
2. How are these two interfaces similar?
3. In your opinion, which interface would be more intuitive to use?

Although UNIX and Linux traditionally had a DOS-like interface, most current versions of UNIX and Linux also allow you to use GUIs.

Inside Information

Programmers Make It Work!

When programmers (people who create software programs) write an application, they design the application to interact with the operating system and make all requests for hardware services through the operating system. To do this, they must write the program to use the correct commands to request services from the operating system. The operating system, in turn, interacts with the hardware on behalf of the application and fulfills the requests made by the application.

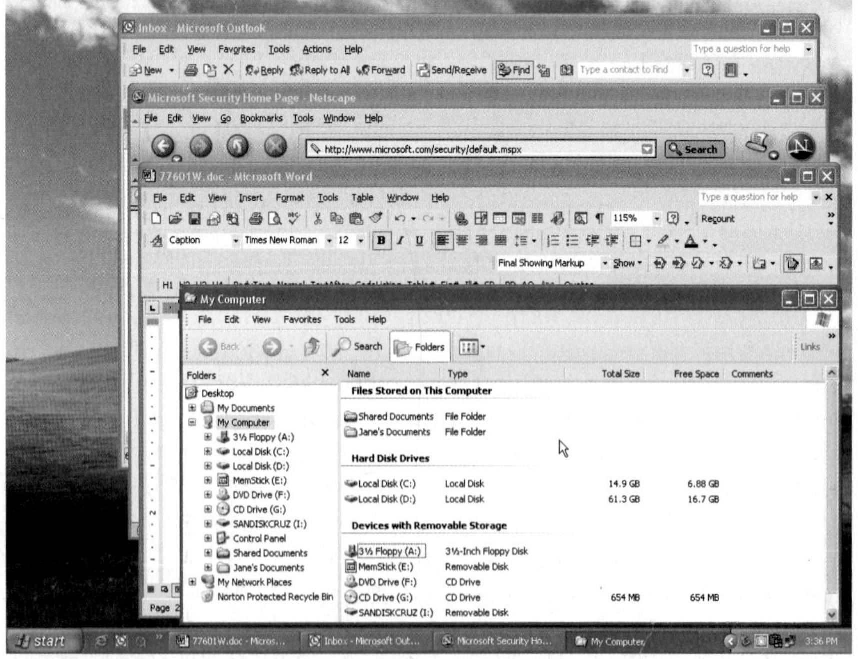

• **Figure 1-3.** A typical GUI screen

Job Management

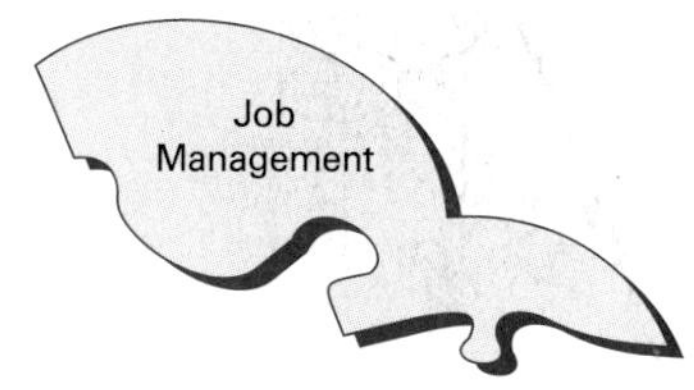

Job management is an operating system function that controls the order and time in which programs are run. Two examples of programs that may perform this function are a scheduling program that schedules other programs or batch files to be run on a certain day and time, and a print program that manages and prioritizes multiple print jobs.

Task Management

Task management is an operating system function found in **multitasking** operating systems. Multitasking implies that a computer is simultaneously running two or more programs (tasks) at the same time. In reality, a computer cannot run more tasks simultaneously than the number of processors that exist within the computer. Because most microcomputers only have a single processor, multitasking is accomplished through a scheme that makes order out of chaos by determining which program responds to the keystrokes and mouse movements.

Task management controls the focus (where the system's attention is at any given moment). It also allows the user to switch between tasks by giving the focus to the application the user brings to the foreground. In Windows, this application runs in the current window. This is the window that is on top of other windows on the screen, and the window that receives input from the keyboard when the user types.

Memory Management

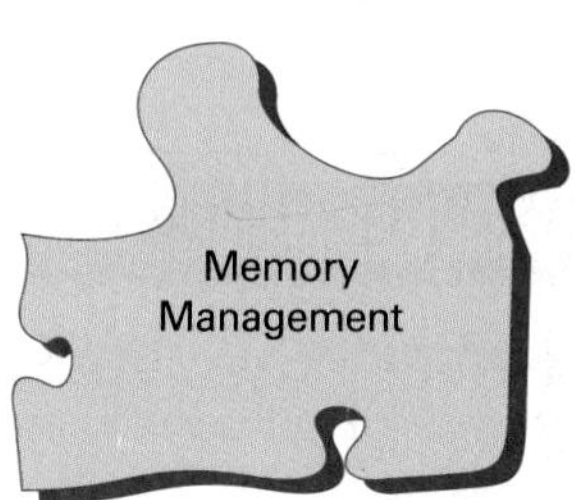

Memory management is an operating system function that manages the placement of programs and data in memory, while keeping track of where it put them. In the case of advanced operating systems, such as Windows NT, Windows 2000, and later similar Windows versions, this involves a scheme for making optimal use of memory. Virtual memory allows more code and data to be in memory than the actual physical system memory can hold. Using a memory management OS component called the virtual memory manager, these operating systems move code and data, as necessary, to a portion of the disk that has been defined as **virtual memory**, meaning that this disk space is used as if it were memory, not just disk storage space. This transfer is performed for code and data that is part of any program that currently does not have the user's attention. Reason? This unneeded-now information does not have to be kept in RAM memory for immediate use, so programs that do need to use the memory now can do so.

> The memory management function may not be included in every definition of an operating system, but it is a very important function, especially in Windows, Macintosh, and UNIX operating systems.

File Management

File management, also referred to as data management, is an operating system function that allows the operating system to read, write, and modify data.

Data is organized into entities called files that are saved to storage devices (usually disks). File management also allows users to organize their files, using other special files that act as containers. These special files are called **folders** or **directories**, and they can contain other folders as well as files.

The user works with a specific logical file organization with which he or she is comfortable, while the operating system file management function relates that logical organization to the actual physical location of the file or folder so that it can store and retrieve the data.

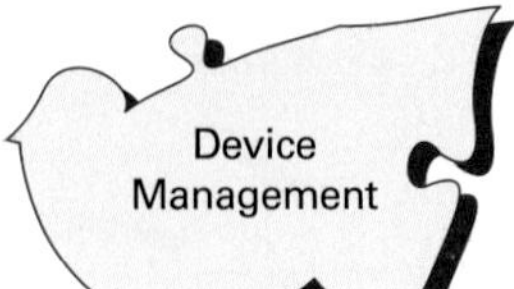

Device Management

The **device management** function controls hardware devices through the use of special software called **device drivers**, which must be installed in the operating system. Device drivers are unique to the device and are created by the manufacturer of the device to work with a specific operating system. For instance, a printer or video adapter will come with drivers for several different operating systems. The device driver contains the commands understood by the device and uses these commands to control the device in response to requests it receives from the operating system. You need a component-specific device driver for each unique hardware component with which the operating system interacts.

Security

The **security** function of an operating system provides password-protected authentication of the user before allowing access to the local computer and may restrict what someone can do on a computer. For example, Rachel is the accounting clerk in a small company. She has confidential information on her computer, and she doesn't want just anyone to be able to walk up to her computer and look at the information stored there. What can be done with the OS to help Rachel secure her computer? You could set up her computer so that anyone getting into it must have a user account. A user account is nothing more than a name and an associated password stored inside the PC.

After you set up Rachel's account, when she logs onto her computer, she must enter her user name and password. Before giving her access to the computer, security components of her operating system will verify that she used a valid user name and password. The validation of the user account and password is called authentication.

A part-time clerk, Kirsten has just been hired to work at night entering accounts payable information into Rachel's computer. To allow Kirsten to also log onto Rachel's computer, you can create a new user account for Kirsten. Although only Rachel and Kirsten can log onto this computer, Rachel does not want Kirsten to be able to access the payroll information, also stored on her computer. Now, this is private information, right? What might be done to help Rachel with this problem? One thing you could do (if her operating system supports it) is to set up Rachel's computer so that she can assign special permissions to the files and folders on her hard disk, giving each user

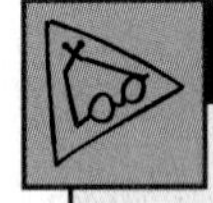

Inside Information

Computer Security and Your Career

Although your operating system may provide a security function, it takes special skills to manage security. If you're pursuing a career that involves managing computers, you will need to learn the skills needed to make computers secure. Here are some types of professionals who need a good understanding of security:

- ***Server administrator*** *A server administrator must understand the security processes of the operating systems on the network servers being administered. A server administrator must know how to use accounts, permissions, and privileges to give users only that required level of access that they need to do their jobs. A server administrator must understand how to implement policies that will protect data, and must have the means to recognize when unauthorized access has succeeded, or even been attempted.*
- ***Network administrator*** *A network administrator is concerned with the larger picture of networkwide security. This type of administrator is involved in implementing a network security plan that complements the security plan implemented on the servers. The network administrator's focus is on the integrity of the network infrastructure of media and connection devices.*
- ***Desktop support analyst*** *A desktop support analyst works on the front line of information technology support. This person works directly with the end user and may be the person who educates the end user on the security policy of the organization. The desktop support analyst must have a good understanding of the security policies of the organization and how users must behave to comply with the policies. Good communication skills are also a real plus!*

account the level of permission needed. For instance, one of Kirsten's tasks is to add accounting information to the accounts payable files, so you could give Kirsten's account the permission that will allow her to write to the files in the accounts payable folder. You will not give Kirsten's account access to any of the other folders, and you will give Rachel's account full control of only the folders that Rachel needs to use.

Categories of Operating Systems

Operating systems are organized into four categories, three of which are based on the number of simultaneous tasks and the number of simultaneous users that can be served, while one category, real-time, is based on an entirely different set of characteristics. Here are the categories:

- Single-user/Single-tasking
- Single-user/Multitasking
- Multi-user/Multitasking
- Real-time

We'll discuss each in turn.

Single-User/Single-Tasking Operating Systems

A single-user/single-tasking operating system is one that allows only a single user to perform a single task at a time. A task is a function such as reading a file from disk, performing a math calculation, printing a document, or sending a request over the Internet to a web server. Small and simple OSs can only manage a single task at a time. (See Figure 1-4.)

• **Figure 1-4.** Single-user/single-tasking

Examples of single-tasking OSs are MS-DOS and the Palm OS, used on the palmOne hand-held computers or other Palm OS-based hand-held computers. Because they take up very little space on disk or in memory when they are running, they do not require a powerful and expensive computer.

Single-User/Multitasking Operating Systems

An operating system that allows a single user to perform two or more functions at once is a single-user/multitasking operating system. Microsoft Windows and the Macintosh operating Systems are examples of this category of OS. Thanks to these OSs and the applications that run on them, people can accomplish more in less time, increasing their productivity. For instance, one person is able to have two or more programs open, can share data between programs, and can instantly switch between them. See Figure 1-5.

• **Figure 1-5.** Single-user/multitasking

A disadvantage of a single-user/multitasking operating system is the increased size and complexity required to support multitasking and other features expected in a modern operating system, such as a GUI interface. People who rely on these features would probably take their large operating system over a small single-tasking one, since they can accomplish in an hour or two tasks that 20 years ago may have taken a couple of days, with or without a computer.

Multi-User/Multitasking Operating Systems

A multi-user/multitasking operating system is an operating system that allows multiple users to run programs simultaneously on a single network server, called a terminal server. This is not at all the same as connecting to a network server for the sake of accessing files and printers. As you will learn in Chapter 9, when a computer is connected to a server to access document files to edit, the client computer performs the processing work locally. Not so with a multi-user OS that gives each user a complete operating environment on the server that is separate from all other users. Software on the user's computer that establishes a connection to the terminal server is called a terminal client. In a multi-user/multitasking operating system environment, all or most of the computing occurs at the server. (See Figure 1-6.)

Examples of multi-user OSs include UNIX, VMS (Virtual Memory System), and mainframe operating systems, such as MVS (Multiple Virtual System), the OS for IBM mainframes. Most of these OSs also support multitasking to each user. The user will usually have a full-fledged PC running the terminal client under Windows, Mac OS, or Linux, but with far lower hardware requirements than it would need if it ran all the processes locally. The terminal server providing a multi-user/multitasking OS to client computers may be UNIX, Linux, NetWare, or a Microsoft Windows server.

Real-Time Operating Systems

A real-time operating system is defined by its speed and ability to work with special real-time application programs. A real-time operating system is a very fast, relatively small OS that is often embedded, meaning it is built into the circuitry of a device and not normally loaded from a disk drive. A real-time operating system is needed to run real-time applications, and it may support multiple simultaneous tasks, or it may only support single-tasking. A real-time application is an application that responds to certain inputs extremely quickly—thousandths or millionths of a second (milliseconds or microseconds, respectively). Real-time applications are needed to run medical

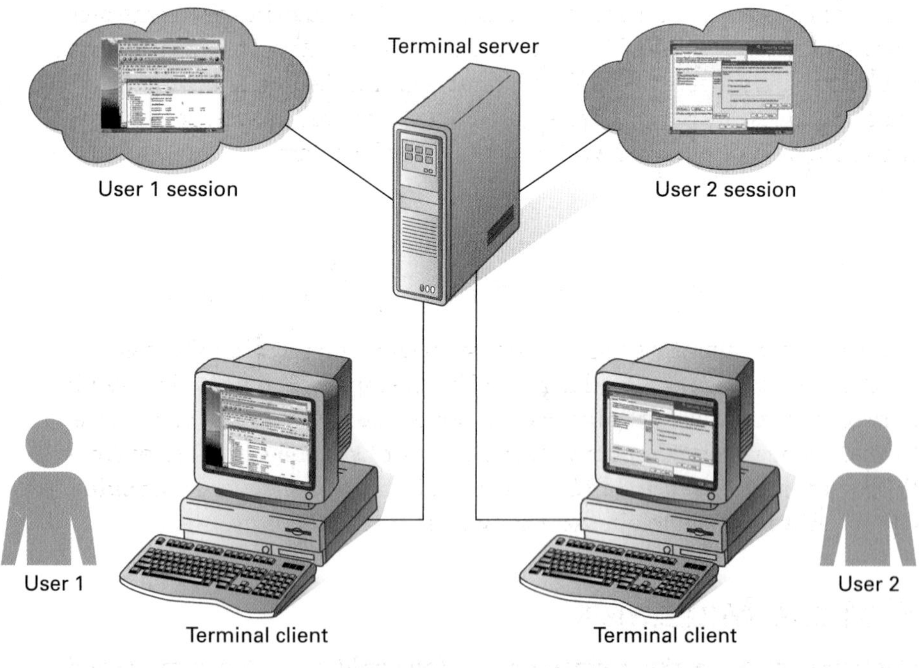

• **Figure 1-6.** Multi-User/multitasking

Photo courtesy of LynuxWorks.

• **Figure 1-7.** Example of a device containing a real-time embedded OS

diagnostics equipment, life-support systems, machinery, scientific instruments, and industrial systems. Examples of real-time operating systems include LynxOS by LynuxWorks, QNX Neutrino by QNX Software Systems, Operating System Embedded (OSE), pSOS, and Windows CE.

Real-time embedded systems are everywhere. Devices with real-time embedded systems control the movement of surveillance cameras suspended by cables over a sports arena. See Figure 1-7. Other devices gather data from race cars and transmit the data and live video images of the race from each car. The latest Hewlett-Packard laser printers contain real-time data controllers. Real-time embedded systems can be found in very large-scale machines, such as the huge sack, parcel, and large parcel sorting machines found in the U.S. Postal Service bulk mail centers.

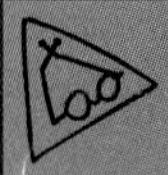

Inside Information

MITS Altair 8800

The MITS Altair 8800 was an important predecessor to the Apple II, TRS-80, and PET computers. It was featured in a cover article of the January 1975 issue of Popular Mechanics, *but it was definitely not for ordinary people. Whether you bought the $395 kit or the fully assembled $495 version, you flipped switches to program it, and the result of these efforts was a pattern of blinking lights. As a portent of the future, the Altair 8800 gave Bill Gates and Paul Allen their very first computer language sale of BASIC.*

Yesterday's Operating Systems

There's an oft-quoted saying: "Those who cannot remember the past are condemned to repeat it." Nothing could be truer in the PC world also—with a small change. Here's the Mike Meyers amendment to that famous phrase: "Those who fail to understand older PC technology will never understand the current stuff." You would be amazed at how much of some of the oldest OSs is still alive and well in the newest ones!

Courtesy Apple Computer.

• Apple II

First the Machines

Computers didn't arrive just yesterday. You could argue that they started with the computers that were designed (but never built) by Charles Babbage

> **Inside Information**
>
> **The Need for OS Functions**
>
> *Until we made the transition from single-purpose machines to multipurpose machines, there was no need for a user interface, because users weren't going to interact with an OS. Anything resembling job management, such as running an analysis of batches of data, was folded into the single-use software. There was no need for task management on a system with only one job to perform. The computers were proprietary (each manufacturer did its own thing, without much regard for program or computer interchangeability), and the software was written to interact with all of the hardware of the system. Therefore, device management was not the big deal that it is today, with the enormous choice of peripheral devices. Memory technologies were also very different from today, because those mammoth computers of the '50s, '60s, and '70s actually had very little memory. Think 16KB, if you can think of such a small amount of memory. Furthermore, memory management was very simple with only a single program running in memory.*

in the 1820s. Or perhaps you would start with the U.S. military's World War II computers. In general, consumers encountered their first microcomputers in 1977 with the introduction of Apple's Apple II, Radio Shack's TRS-80, and Commodore's PET.

Although computers and microcomputers existed before the Apple II, this computer was the first one to combine a number of critical elements to make what today is considered a microcomputer, including a keyboard, monitor, operating system, desirable and useful applications, and a reasonable price tag.

Then the Operating Systems

The idea for an operating system as complex as what you see on your desktop today didn't just pop into someone's head one day. In fact, an operating system as a separate entity didn't exist in the early years of digital computing (defined roughly as from World War II into the 1950s). Each computer was dedicated to a single purpose, such as performing trajectory calculations for weapons or mathematical analysis for a science lab, in addition to the system I/O functions. Operating systems evolved through many small steps, some in the form of technical advances and others in evolutionary changes in how computers were used.

Operating systems evolved because people saw the need to use computers as multipurpose devices. The "user," who at first was a government agency, research institute, or large business, would define the computer's purpose at any given time by the program chosen to run. Some early "operating systems" were developed in the 1950s to manage data storage on tape for mainframe computers, but it was much more common for application programmers to write system I/O routines (the stuff of today's OSs) right into their programs. By the mid-1960s, as disk systems became more common on large computers, operating systems were needed to manage these disks and to perform other common system-level routines.

The computer enthusiasts who bought the earliest microcomputers of the 1970s, such as the MITS Altair, were infatuated with the technology. Slow CPU speeds, very limited memory, clumsy I/O devices, and lack of software did not deter them. They would network with like-minded people, have informal meetings and discussions, and then gather in self-help

1968

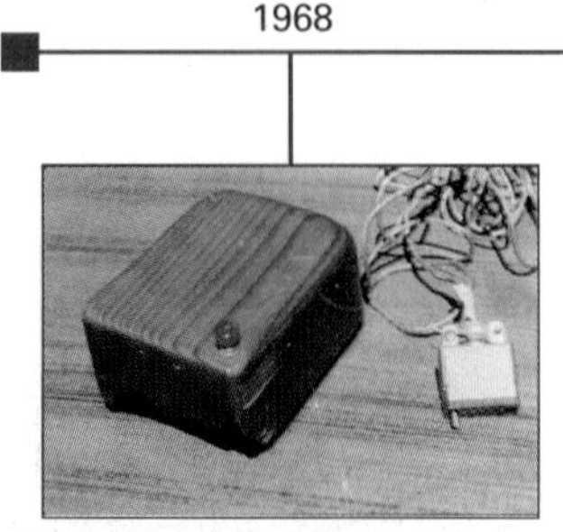

Stanford Research Institute's Douglas Engelbart demonstrates the use of a mouse to move a "bug" around a screen at the Fall Joint Computer Conference in San Francisco.

1969

A small group at Bell Labs works on what eventually becomes UNIX.

ARPANET is created, the first step in the building of the Internet.

1970

Xerox opens Palo Alto Research Center (PARC).

IBM introduces the floppy disk.

Intel creates the 4004 processor, leading the way to the birth of the PC.

1973

PARC creates the Altos, the first "personal computer" with a GUI, laser printer, and a connection to the first Ethernet network.

groups and form clubs like the Home Brew Computer Club in Silicon Valley. They shared their techniques for creating hardware and programming language software for these computers. Almost every one of these early microcomputers exceeded the expectations of their makers and users, but for a variety of reasons, most of the early entrepreneurial companies and their products disappeared before long.

DOS, CP/M, Apple, and the Killer App

For a microcomputer to truly be a successful, widely accepted product—used in businesses as well as by hobbyists—it had to be a tool that performed an important task; it had to have an application that many people needed. That application would be called a *killer app.*

One of these tasks was spreadsheet calculations. Before microcomputers, spreadsheets were created manually, on large sheets of paper. People would enter a column of numbers—say, sales for one product in a drugstore—day-by-day for a month. Then the daily columns would be added up to get the total sales for that product for that month. The next column was for the next product, and so on. The process was tedious and error prone, but very valuable to the manager of the drugstore.

Thus, when VisiCalc, an electronic spreadsheet program that ran on early microcomputers, appeared, it became a very successful application. It automated this thankless job, remembering the formulas for the calculations and allowing people to recalculate a column of numbers after a change was made. VisiCalc did more than this, though: it gave people a reason to want a personal computer. Many people were introduced to VisiCalc on the Apple II computer, and this contributed to the success of the Apple II in the late 1970s. However, as the 1980s arrived, Apple failed to come out with a successor to the Apple II in a timely fashion. This strategic error gave IBM the opportunity to bring out the IBM PC.

Another fateful series of events revolved around the choice of an OS for the IBM PC. IBM representatives came to Microsoft, then a fledgling software company, for the BASIC interpreter, which was being used in other machines at that time, resulting in IBM licensing Microsoft's BASIC interpreter and installing it in the ROM of the IBM PC. The IBM folk also talked to Bill Gates about providing an OS; but he did not have one, and so he sent

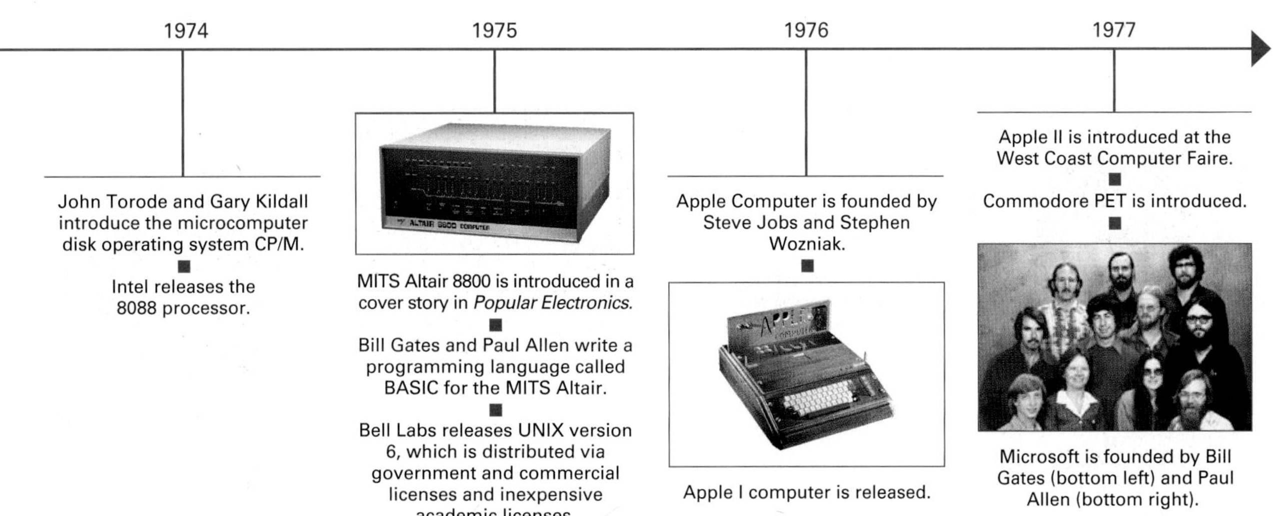

1974
1975
1976
1977
John Torode and Gary Kildall introduce the microcomputer disk operating system CP/M.
Intel releases the 8088 processor.
MITS Altair 8800 is introduced in a cover story in *Popular Electronics.*
Bill Gates and Paul Allen write a programming language called BASIC for the MITS Altair.
Bell Labs releases UNIX version 6, which is distributed via government and commercial licenses and inexpensive academic licenses.
Apple Computer is founded by Steve Jobs and Stephen Wozniak.
Apple I computer is released.
Apple II is introduced at the West Coast Computer Faire.
Commodore PET is introduced.
Microsoft is founded by Bill Gates (bottom left) and Paul Allen (bottom right).

Want to learn more about the history of PCs? Our favorite book on the subject is *Fire in the Valley: The Making of the Personal Computer* (ISBN 0-07-135892-7). You can read excerpts from the book at `www.fireinthevalley.com`.

them to another company, Digital Research, the creators of the then-popular CP/M OS. Digital Research, however, refused to sign a contract with IBM, so they went back to Bill Gates for the OS. To fulfill their contract, Microsoft bought an OS from another company, and this was the basis of the first versions of IBM PC DOS.

The IBM PC came with Microsoft's BASIC interpreter installed in ROM, which allowed programs written in the BASIC programming language to be run on the PC (see the timeline for more details). For those computers that had the optional floppy drive rather than just the tape drive, the IBM PC came with either PC DOS or a version of CP/M as the operating system. IBM, however, priced CP/M far higher than it did PC DOS, which contributed to the demise of CP/M. This computer far exceeded IBM's sales forecast, which was for about a quarter of a million units during the predicted five-year lifetime of the product. According to one account, IBM took orders for half a million computers in the first few days after the IBM PC was introduced. Many who bought it were enthusiasts who bought it, in spite of its roughly $5,000 price tag for a typical configuration, just to see what it could do. However, the "IBM" name behind the product also inspired many business users to buy it because this implied that it was a serious business computer.

The Second Wave

Through the 1980s, PCs with DOS and a variety of DOS applications made great inroads into organizations of all sizes. In the decade after its introduction, thousands of applications were written for DOS, but Lotus 1-2-3, dBase (database management), and WordPerfect (word processing) were the de facto business standards at the end of that decade.

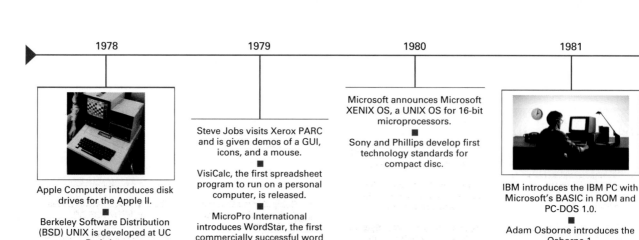

VisiCalc was the killer app that brought attention, and early success, to microcomputers before the IBM PC was released. And although many say that just having the letters *IBM* on the box was what sold that computer, the groundwork laid by VisiCalc was enhanced by a second wave of applications. In 1983, Lotus Corporation starting shipping their new product, Lotus 1-2-3, a DOS spreadsheet application designed to use all of the 640KB of memory available to software (OS plus application) on the IBM PC. Both the 1-2-3 program and the spreadsheet were kept in memory while the user worked. It was very fast compared to VisiCalc, which was written to run under the CP/M OS and designed to use much less memory. And 1-2-3 had additional functionality, such as database functions and a program that would create and print graphs from the spreadsheet data. Lotus 1-2-3 was the killer app, the software that made the IBM PC and PC DOS a must-have combination for

1978

Apple Computer introduces disk drives for the Apple II.

Berkeley Software Distribution (BSD) UNIX is developed at UC Berkeley.

Bell Labs releases UNIX version 7.

1979

Steve Jobs visits Xerox PARC and is given demos of a GUI, icons, and a mouse.

VisiCalc, the first spreadsheet program to run on a personal computer, is released.

MicroPro International introduces WordStar, the first commercially successful word processing program for PCs.

1980

Microsoft announces Microsoft XENIX OS, a UNIX OS for 16-bit microprocessors.

Sony and Phillips develop first technology standards for compact disc.

1981

IBM introduces the IBM PC with Microsoft's BASIC in ROM and PC-DOS 1.0.

Adam Osborne introduces the Osborne 1.

First time *Internet* is used to describe the ARPANET.

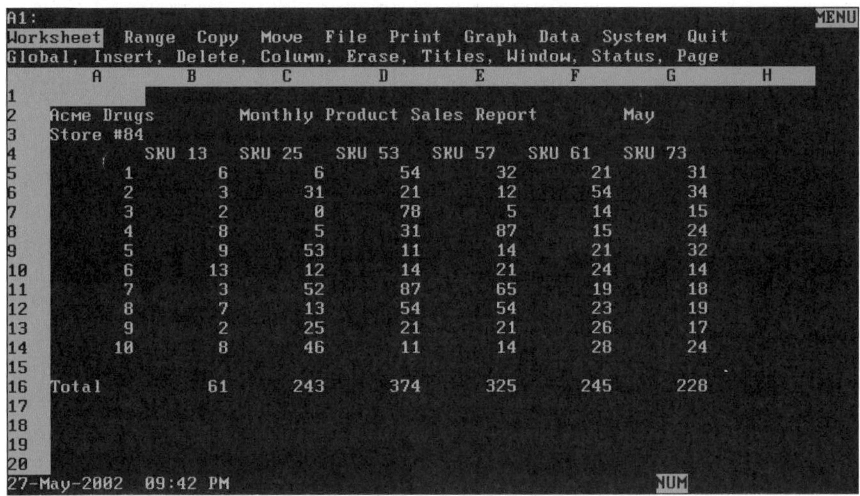

A1: MENU

Worksheet Range Copy Move File Print Graph Data System Quit

Global, Insert, Delete, Column, Erase, Titles, Window, Status, Page

	A	B	C	D	E	F	G	H
1								
2	Acme Drugs		Monthly Product Sales Report				May	
3	Store #84							
4		SKU 13	SKU 25	SKU 53	SKU 57	SKU 61	SKU 73	
5	1	6	6	54	32	21	31	
6	2	3	31	21	12	54	34	
7	3	2	0	78	5	14	15	
8	4	8	5	31	87	15	24	
9	5	9	53	11	14	21	32	
10	6	13	12	14	21	24	14	
11	7	3	52	87	65	19	18	
12	8	7	13	54	54	23	19	
13	9	2	25	21	21	26	17	
14	10	8	46	11	14	28	24	
15								
16	Total	61	243	374	325	245	228	
17								
18								
19								
20								

27-May-2002 09:42 PM NUM

• **Figure 1-8.** Lotus 1-2-3 spreadsheet

people who worked all day crunching numbers and doing what-if calculations. Figure 1-8 shows the Lotus 1-2-3 program with a sample spreadsheet.

OS/2

In 1987, Microsoft and IBM introduced their jointly developed OS/2 (Operating System/2), intended to replace DOS. However, version 1.0 was underpowered in that it was written for the Intel 80286 processor, which had serious memory and mode limits. In spite of the memory limits, it still required much more memory and disk space than DOS (2MB of memory and 8MB of disk space) at a time when 2MB of memory and a 40MB hard drive (considered large in the late 1980s) cost several thousand dollars. Although OS/2 multitasked applications in memory, only one application could be visible on the screen at a time. Also, applications had to be written specifically for OS/2, because it had very limited support for DOS applications.

1982
1983
1984
Mitch Kapor announces Lotus 1-2-3 spreadsheet application for the IBM-PC.
Apple introduces the Lisa, the first commercial computer with a purely graphical operating system and a mouse.
TCP/IP is established as the standard for the Internet.
Lotus 1-2-3 available in retail stores, sells over 200,000 copies the first year.
Microsoft and IBM introduce PC-DOS 2.0 with the IBM PC-XT for its 10MB hard drive.
Microsoft introduces the Microsoft mouse for the IBM PC and compatibles.
Bell Labs releases UNIX System V, release 2 through commercial licenses.
Novell introduces the NetWare network operating system.
Apple Computer releases the Macintosh with the Mac OS System 1.
Apple Computer releases the "Fat Mac" with 512K of memory.
IBM Token Ring networking system is developed.
The IBM PC-AT is introduced with MS-DOS 3.0.
SRI introduces the WordPerfect word processor.

In the 1990s, IBM introduced OS/2 Warp, a greatly improved version of OS/2 with a very nice GUI. After about 18 months, however, IBM pretty much retreated from the battle for the desktop and targeted the high-end

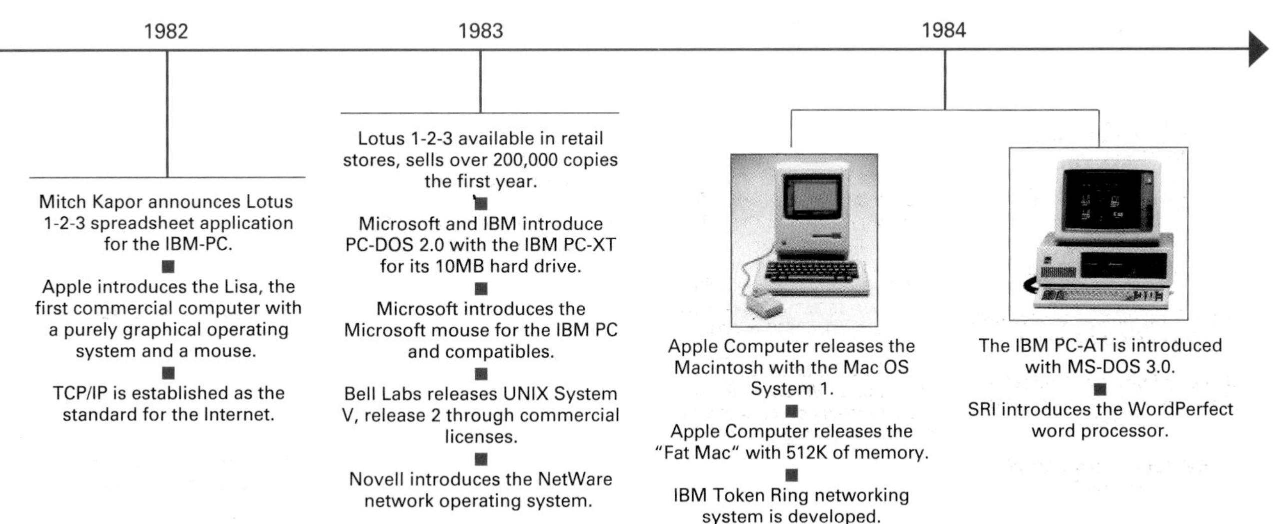

server market. It never rivaled Windows, UNIX, or Linux in terms of sales, and in 2003, IBM announced that it would not develop any future versions of OS/2. They now sell server and desktop computers with a variety of operating systems preinstalled, including Linux, UNIX, Microsoft Windows, and Novell NetWare.

Microsoft Windows

In 1985, when the first version of Windows appeared, it was more smoke than OS. It was a not-very-good GUI balanced precariously on top of DOS. It was slow and had a flat look—you couldn't lay one graphic on top of another. The ability to overlap graphical elements, such as windows and icons, did not show up until a later version. However, the GUI gradually improved with each version.

From 1985 to 1990, Microsoft continued to work on both Windows and DOS, but Windows was not much more than a pretty face until 1990 and Windows 3.0, which supported the three Intel processor modes of operation. Microsoft called the modes Real mode, Standard mode, and 386 Enhanced mode. In Real mode, Windows 3.0 was just a GUI that ran on top of DOS. In the other two modes, it added functionality to DOS to take advantage of the 286 (Standard mode) and 386 (386 Enhanced mode) processor modes.

The most important feature of Windows 3.0 was better support for legacy DOS applications within Windows. This was possible in the 386 processor mode. This meant that DOS apps and Windows apps could both be run simultaneously. This version still had its quirks, but for the first

Inside Information

Versions

When a software publisher, say Microsoft or Apple, creates a new OS, it gives it a version number, usually 1.0. Software publishers receive constant feedback from customers about problems and the need for particular additional features in each OS. In response to this feedback, a publisher often introduces a modified version of the original product, in which case the number to the right of the decimal point will probably change (say, from version 1.0 to version 1.1—"version" is often abbreviated as simply "v"). On the other hand, an important change to an OS, in which significant new features are added or major problems repaired, generally will be reflected in an entirely new version number, with the value to the left of the decimal point being changed. For example, when Microsoft added the ability to work with hard drives to its DOS product, MS-DOS v1.0, the company introduced MS-DOS v2.0. In the last several years, Microsoft has moved away from the old convention and modified the names of four OSs to coincide with the calendar year, as in Windows 95, Windows 98, Windows 2000, and Windows Server 2003. Windows ME and Windows XP were exceptions to this naming convention, and who knows where they'll go from here!

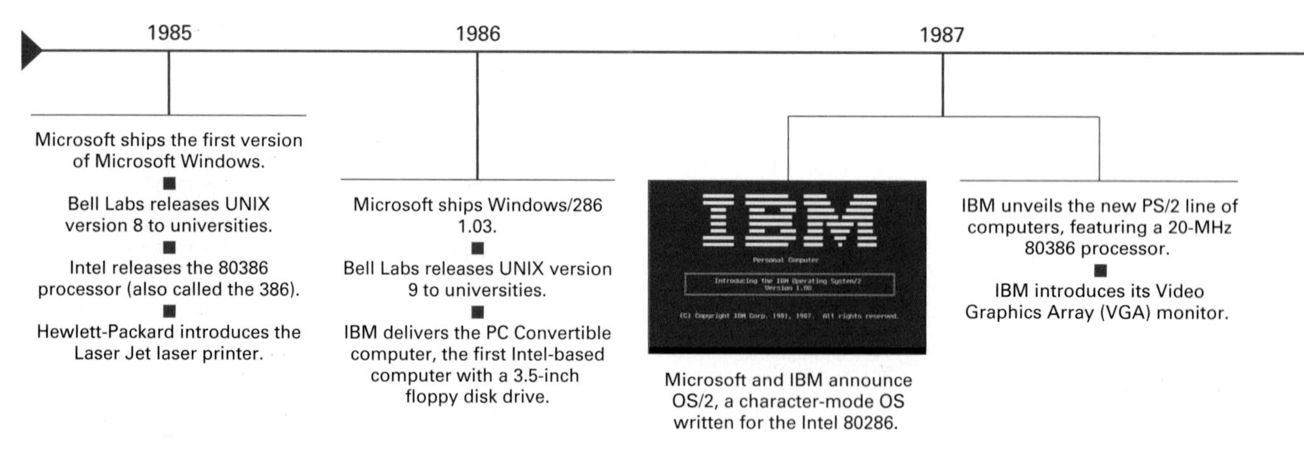

1985
Microsoft ships the first version of Microsoft Windows.
Bell Labs releases UNIX version 8 to universities.
Intel releases the 80386 processor (also called the 386).
Hewlett-Packard introduces the Laser Jet laser printer.
1986
Microsoft ships Windows/286 1.03.
Bell Labs releases UNIX version 9 to universities.
IBM delivers the PC Convertible computer, the first Intel-based computer with a 3.5-inch floppy disk drive.
1987
IBM
Microsoft and IBM announce OS/2, a character-mode OS written for the Intel 80286.
IBM unveils the new PS/2 line of computers, featuring a 20-MHz 80386 processor.
IBM introduces its Video Graphics Array (VGA) monitor.

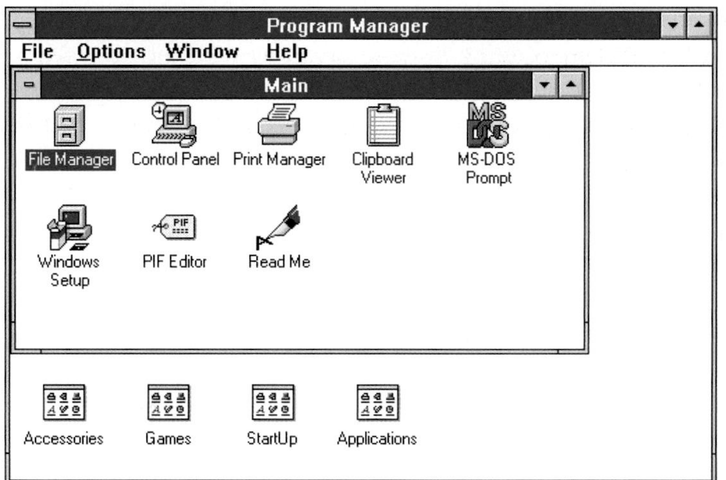

• **Figure 1-9.** MS Windows 3.1 desktop

Inside Information

Protocols

A protocol is a standard, or a set of standards, that everybody agrees to abide by when they build a piece of software or hardware. Products that adhere to a specific protocol will be able to work together, regardless of who made them.

time, IT managers saw a potential GUI replacement for DOS as the desktop OS of choice.

In the spring of 1992, Microsoft brought out a minor upgrade, Windows 3.1, which was adopted as the standard desktop OS by many organizations. The fact that Microsoft's entire suite of applications was also available in versions for Windows 3.*x* helped encourage adoption.

Figure 1-9 shows the Windows 3.1 desktop. Notice that there is no graphical taskbar at the bottom of the screen, just the Program Manager window (the main window) with other windows nested in it.

In this book, when discussing versions that share a major number, such as all of the Windows 3 versions, we'll substitute an *x* for the sub-version number (Windows 3.*x*). When discussing features common to Windows 95, Windows 98, and Windows ME, we'll refer to Windows 9*x*.

Windows for Workgroups

DOS and Windows OSs through Windows 3.*x* included only the operating system functions. If you wanted to connect to a network, you added a **network operating system (NOS)** on top of your installed OS. This separate network operating system might be from 3COM or Novell, or it might be Microsoft's LAN Manager NOS, developed in the late 1980s.

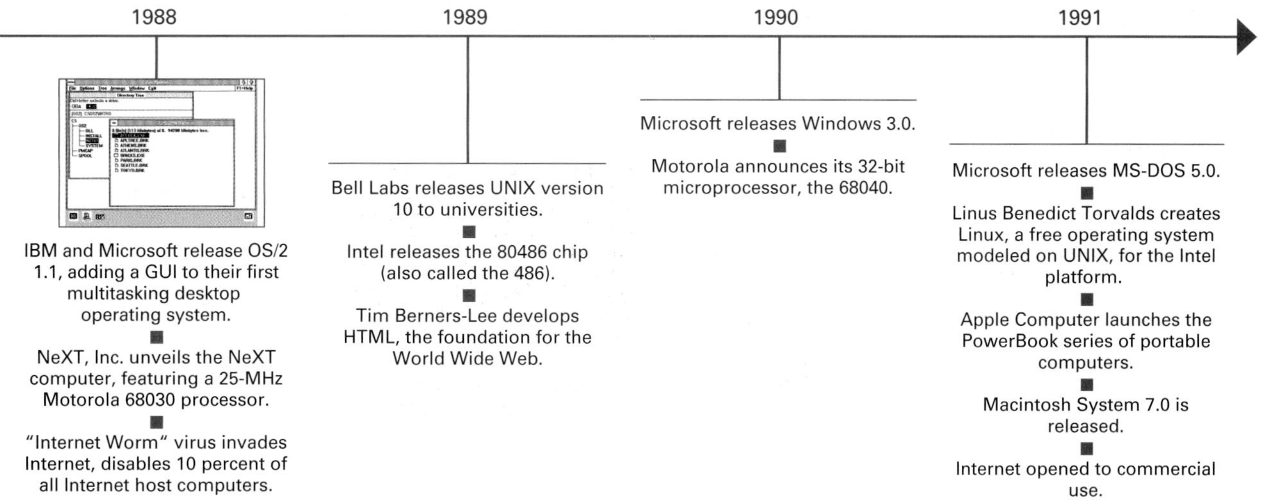

1988
IBM and Microsoft release OS/2 1.1, adding a GUI to their first multitasking desktop operating system.
NeXT, Inc. unveils the NeXT computer, featuring a 25-MHz Motorola 68030 processor.
"Internet Worm" virus invades Internet, disables 10 percent of all Internet host computers.
1989
Bell Labs releases UNIX version 10 to universities.
Intel releases the 80486 chip (also called the 486).
Tim Berners-Lee develops HTML, the foundation for the World Wide Web.
1990
Microsoft releases Windows 3.0.
Motorola announces its 32-bit microprocessor, the 68040.
1991
Microsoft releases MS-DOS 5.0.
Linus Benedict Torvalds creates Linux, a free operating system modeled on UNIX, for the Intel platform.
Apple Computer launches the PowerBook series of portable computers.
Macintosh System 7.0 is released.
Internet opened to commercial use.

Novell and LAN Manager were both server network operating systems that combined the operating system functions with the networking functions, and provided file and print sharing services to other computers. Additionally, to connect to a server, a client computer needs special client software so it can connect and request services from it.

Early client network software, like Novell's client software today, included underlying networking components called drivers and protocols. Among the protocols would be those required to actually "see" a certain server on a network. A Novell client can see and communicate with a Novell NetWare server, while a Microsoft client can do the same with a Microsoft server. The network software Microsoft provided for DOS and for Windows 3.1 on top of DOS included only the client component. However, beginning in October 1992 with Windows for Workgroups 3.1, Microsoft included both the client and server software in all of its Windows OS products. This enabled peer-to-peer networking, meaning desktop computers could act as servers to their peers. This worked well in a small workgroup environment of ten or fewer computers.

Windows for Workgroups 3.1 was followed a year later by Windows for Workgroups 3.11, with the usual obligatory fixes and improvements including faster network and disk I/O operations. However, users were still working with a Windows OS that was running on top of DOS; that is, first DOS was started and then Windows. Windows depended on DOS, which had to be installed on the computer.

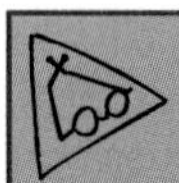

Inside Information

Users Have Evolved Too!

Over the past half-century, a significant change in who interacts with computers has changed the meaning of the term user. *Early computer end users included entire organizations, such as the military, government agencies, and research institutions. The U.S. Army used a very early computer to calculate ballistic tables for firing artillery. Soon scientists discovered the value of using computers to solve complex scientific problems, like those involved in atomic energy research. In each case, the person who touched the computer, or a terminal connected to the computer, had to be a trained computer professional, knowledgeable enough to work with a computer that literally filled a room and cost immense amounts of money. The first business application of computers came in the 1950s when banks started using computers for check processing. This introduced a new class of user, the bank's bookkeepers, which eventually led to other business users directly touching the system, or at least an input device. What was new was that these users were mere mortals, not computer professionals or scientists. At last, ordinary people could access the power of a computer, which paved the way to the development of the personal computer, putting computing power right on the desktop.*

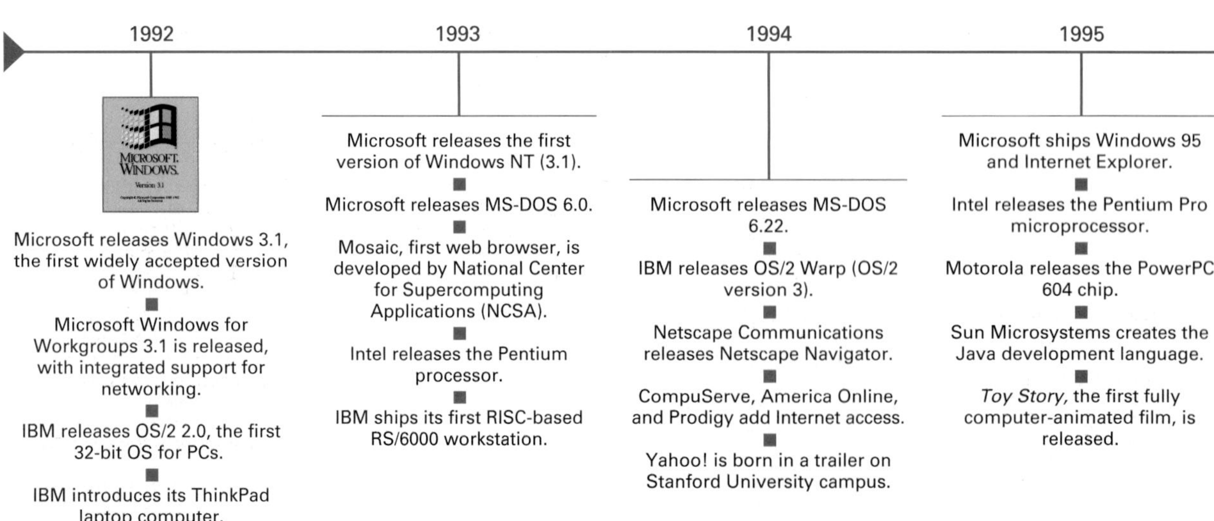

1992
Microsoft Windows Version 3.1
Microsoft releases Windows 3.1, the first widely accepted version of Windows.
Microsoft Windows for Workgroups 3.1 is released, with integrated support for networking.
IBM releases OS/2 2.0, the first 32-bit OS for PCs.
IBM introduces its ThinkPad laptop computer.
1993
Microsoft releases the first version of Windows NT (3.1).
Microsoft releases MS-DOS 6.0.
Mosaic, first web browser, is developed by National Center for Supercomputing Applications (NCSA).
Intel releases the Pentium processor.
IBM ships its first RISC-based RS/6000 workstation.
1994
Microsoft releases MS-DOS 6.22.
IBM releases OS/2 Warp (OS/2 version 3).
Netscape Communications releases Netscape Navigator.
CompuServe, America Online, and Prodigy add Internet access.
Yahoo! is born in a trailer on Stanford University campus.
1995
Microsoft ships Windows 95 and Internet Explorer.
Intel releases the Pentium Pro microprocessor.
Motorola releases the PowerPC 604 chip.
Sun Microsystems creates the Java development language.
Toy Story, the first fully computer-animated film, is released.

Desktop OSs Available Today

The most common desktop microcomputer operating systems in use today include MS-DOS, Windows 98, Windows NT, Windows 2000, Windows XP, the Macintosh OSs, and Linux. DOS is rarely on the desktop, but it survives today in some special devices and is still used by technicians and computer support people. Windows 98 and Windows NT are waning on the desktop as old computers are replaced. This is especially true in corporate settings, where computers are often leased for two or three years and then replaced with new systems with the latest OS under a new lease.

Table 1-1 summarizes the available OSs, listing the publisher, platform, and types of applications that can be run on each OS.

What follows is a brief description of each of these OSs, including a little history here and there to provide perspective. You will also discover where you'll be most likely to encounter each operating system.

We do not include Windows Server 2003 in the list of desktop OSs, because it is not available in a desktop version.

DOS from Microsoft

DOS, which stands for "disk operating system," is an operating system that provides support for interaction, or input and output (I/O), between the memory and disk drives. There have been, and still are, DOS operating

Table 1-1 Summary of Current Desktop/Client OSs

OS Version	Company	Platform	Applications Supported
MS-DOS 6.22	Microsoft	Intel/Microsoft	DOS
Windows NT 4.0 Workstation	Microsoft	Intel/Microsoft	DOS, 16-bit Windows, 32-bit Windows
Windows 98	Microsoft	Intel/Microsoft	DOS, 16-bit Windows, 32-bit Windows
Windows 2000 Professional	Microsoft	Intel/Microsoft	DOS, 16-bit Windows, 32-bit Windows
Windows Millennium Edition	Microsoft	Intel/Microsoft	DOS, 16-bit Windows, 32-bit Windows
Windows XP Professional	Microsoft	Intel/Microsoft	DOS, 16-bit Windows, 32-bit Windows
Mac OS X	Apple	Apple Mac	Macintosh
UNIX	Various	Intel/Microsoft	UNIX/Linux
Linux	Various	Intel/Microsoft	UNIX/Linux

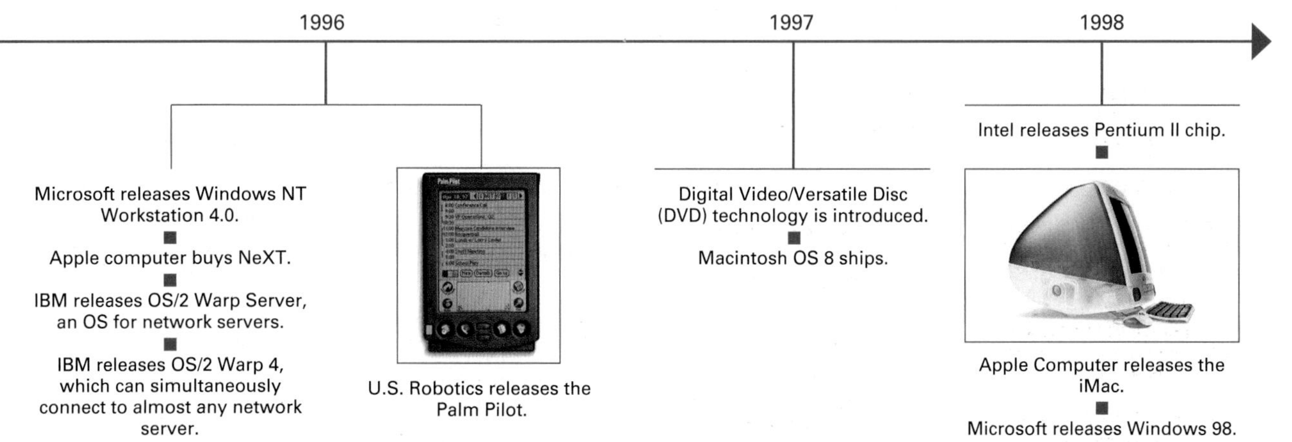
1996
1997
1998
Microsoft releases Windows NT Workstation 4.0.
Apple computer buys NeXT.
IBM releases OS/2 Warp Server, an OS for network servers.
IBM releases OS/2 Warp 4, which can simultaneously connect to almost any network server.
U.S. Robotics releases the Palm Pilot.
Digital Video/Versatile Disc (DVD) technology is introduced.
Macintosh OS 8 ships.
Intel releases Pentium II chip.
Apple Computer releases the iMac.
Microsoft releases Windows 98.

systems for computers other than microcomputers. In addition, all of the popular microcomputer operating systems in use include support for disks.

Each major version of DOS was released to support new disk capacities. PC DOS 1.0 supported single-sided 5¼-inch floppies; PC DOS 1.1 added support for double-sided 5¼-inch floppies; and PC DOS 2.0 was released with the IBM PC-XT and included support for the XT's 10MB hard drives. DOS 3.0 was released with the IBM PC-AT and included support for the larger AT hard drives. Support for 3.5-inch floppies and the larger hard drives of the IBM PS-2 computers was added in DOS 4.0. MS-DOS 6.22 was the last widely used version of MS-DOS.

The DOS Prompt

DOS has a text-mode, command-line interface that requires users to remember cryptic commands and their subcommands in order to perform file management functions and to launch DOS applications. Figure 1-10 shows a good example of how cryptic DOS can be. This assumes knowledge of many, many concepts.

```
A:\>format c: /s /u

WARNING: ALL DATA ON NON-REMOVABLE DISK
DRIVE C: WILL BE LOST!
Proceed with Format (Y/N)?y


Formatting   502M
Format complete.
System transferred

Volume label (11 characters, ENTER for none)?

  526,106,624 bytes total disk space
      212,992 bytes used by system
  525,893,632 bytes available on disk

        8,192 bytes in each allocation unit.
       64,196 allocation units available on disk.

Volume Serial Number is 3A4E-17DA


A:\>_
```

• **Figure 1-10.** MS-DOS prompt with the Format command

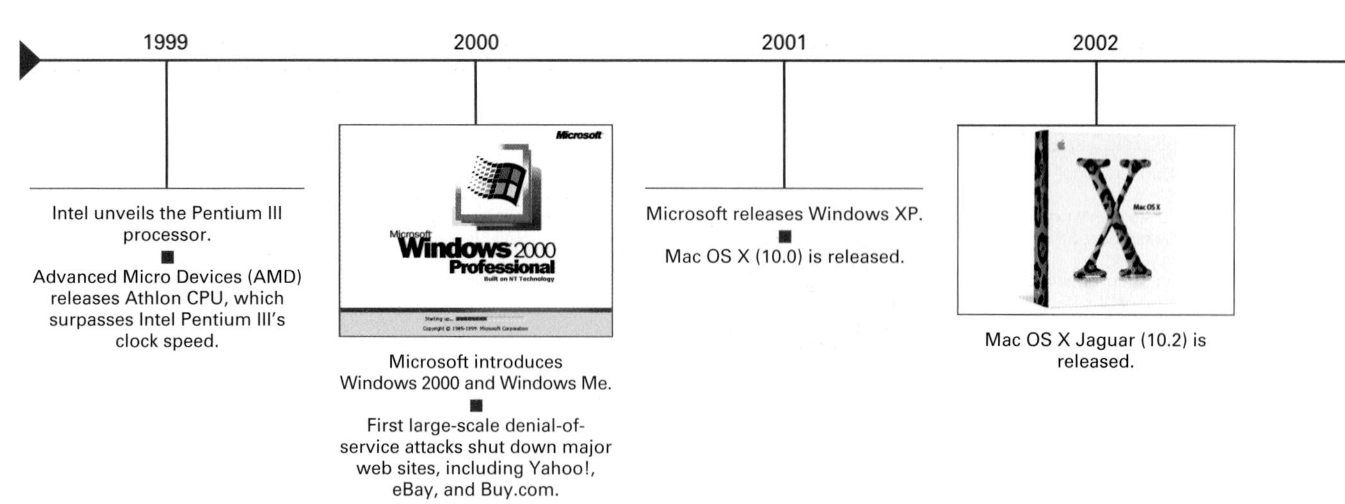

1999
2000
2001
2002
Intel unveils the Pentium III processor.
Advanced Micro Devices (AMD) releases Athlon CPU, which surpasses Intel Pentium III's clock speed.
Microsoft
Microsoft Windows 2000 Professional
Built on NT Technology
Microsoft introduces Windows 2000 and Windows Me.
First large-scale denial-of-service attacks shut down major web sites, including Yahoo!, eBay, and Buy.com.
Microsoft releases Windows XP.
Mac OS X (10.0) is released.
Mac OS X
Mac OS X Jaguar (10.2) is released.

When Would You Use DOS?

Although you would not likely choose it as your main OS on your desktop computer, there are a few exceptions to this rule, as you will see in Chapter 2. Also, you might find DOS as the OS on some hand-held devices that do not require a GUI interface, and computer professionals often find DOS handy as a very small OS that fits on a floppy disk. These will be explored in Chapter 2 as well.

Windows NT

Because it had the same user interface as Windows 3.1, Windows NT was introduced in 1993 as Windows NT 3.1. That was where the similarity ended. To begin with, it was a server operating system, which included server protocols in its integrated network support. Furthermore, unlike Windows 3.*x*, it did not sit on top of DOS, but was an entirely new operating system.

What's Notable in Windows NT?

Windows NT was the first Microsoft OS to take full advantage of the capabilities of the special protected mode that Intel introduced in its processors manufactured after 1986. A major benefit of this was more stability and security in the OS. In fact, NT was so powerful that Microsoft decided to make two versions of NT: one designed mainly for servers, and another geared more toward individual user systems—what some folks call workstations. Thus, the next version of NT (NT 3.5) was also the first Windows OS to have separate products: Windows NT Workstation and Windows NT Server. Both of these used the same kernel (you'll recall that a kernel is the main OS component) and interface, but the Server version had enhancements and components that were needed only on a network server. The Workstation version was configured as a desktop operating system.

In 1996, Microsoft introduced Windows NT 4.0, which had a GUI similar to that of Windows 95 as well as other improvements and enhancements to the OS. Figure 1-11 shows the Windows NT 4.0 desktop.

Another reason Windows NT is included in this book is that there is still a significant installed base of Windows NT servers in organizations. Given enough time, we guarantee that you will run into more than one old workhorse Windows NT Server. Your exposure in this book will guarantee that you won't treat it like an alien being.

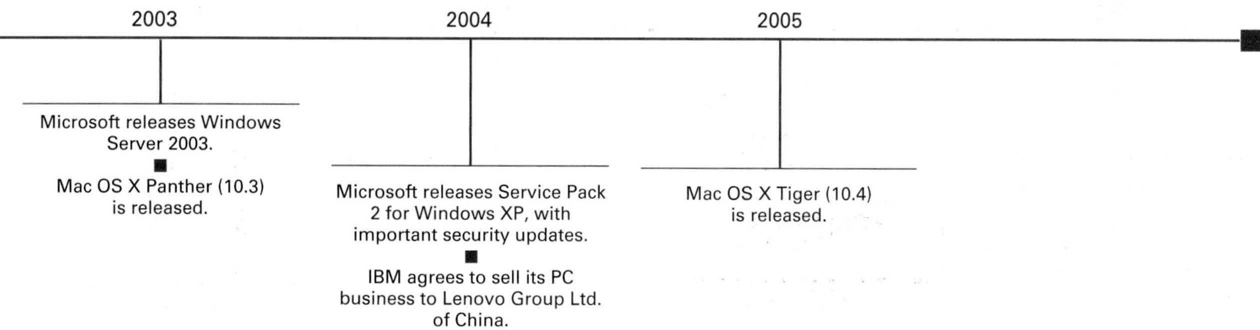

2003
2004
2005
Microsoft releases Windows Server 2003.
Mac OS X Panther (10.3) is released.
Microsoft releases Service Pack 2 for Windows XP, with important security updates.
IBM agrees to sell its PC business to Lenovo Group Ltd. of China.
Mac OS X Tiger (10.4) is released.

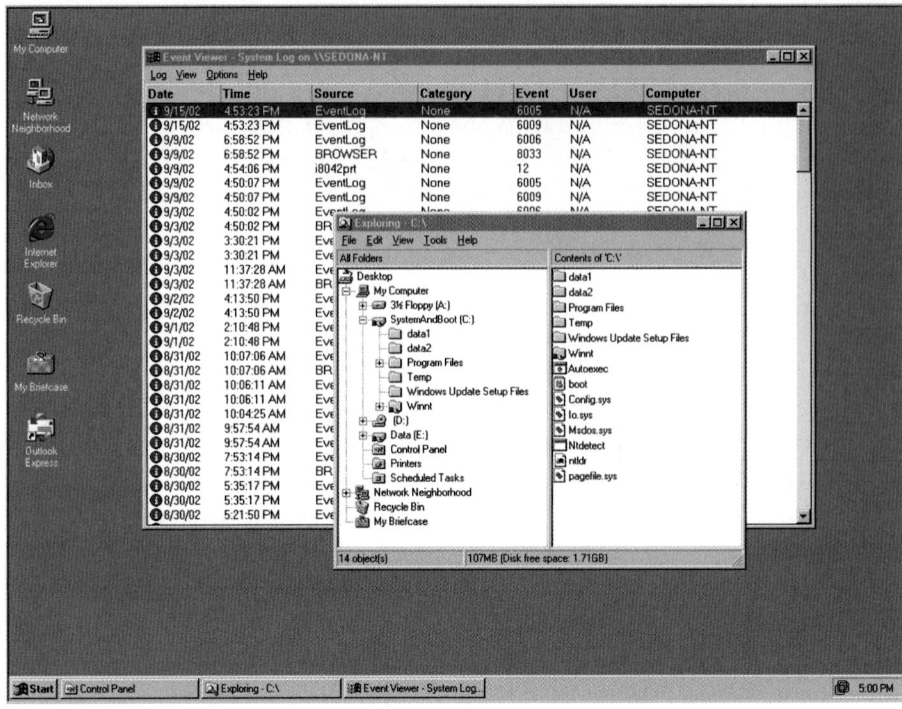

• **Figure 1-11.** MS Windows NT 4.0 desktop with open windows

> Windows 95 predated Windows NT 4 Workstation and has been replaced by Windows 98 and all other subsequent versions of Windows such as Windows 2000 Professional and Windows XP Professional. We will not discuss Windows 95 or Windows 98 in detail in this book but rather the latest of the desktop/client versions. We'll refer to the earlier versions from time to time only to make comparisons with newer OSs or when talking about application support for applications designed for Windows 95 or Windows 98.

When Would You Use Windows NT Workstation?

Even when it was the latest Microsoft OS, you would probably not have used it at home, if only because of the cost, which was more than twice that of the Windows 3.*x* OSs that preceded it and of Windows 95, which was considered the upgrade OS for a Windows 3.*x* OS.

Windows NT 4.0 Workstation is no longer sold or supported by Microsoft. However, you may run into Windows NT Workstation on existing PCs in an organization, and that is the main reason we include it in this book.

Windows 98

Windows 98 was an evolutionary development in the Windows desktop operating system, including improvements in both visible and under-the-hood components. It offered more stability than its immediate predecessor, Windows 95, meaning that it was less likely to stop in its tracks just when you were about to complete that book order on Amazon. Although improved, Windows 98 is not as stable as the newer Windows OSs. Windows 98 is not included in this book, but we did update the first edition's Windows 98 chapter, and you can access it online as Chapter 13 of this second edition. Figure 1-12 shows the Windows 98 desktop.

What's Notable in Windows 98?

Windows 98 offered new options for customizing the GUI, including tighter integration with Microsoft's web browser, Internet Explorer (IE). This feature allows users to configure Windows so that they can, if they wish, always

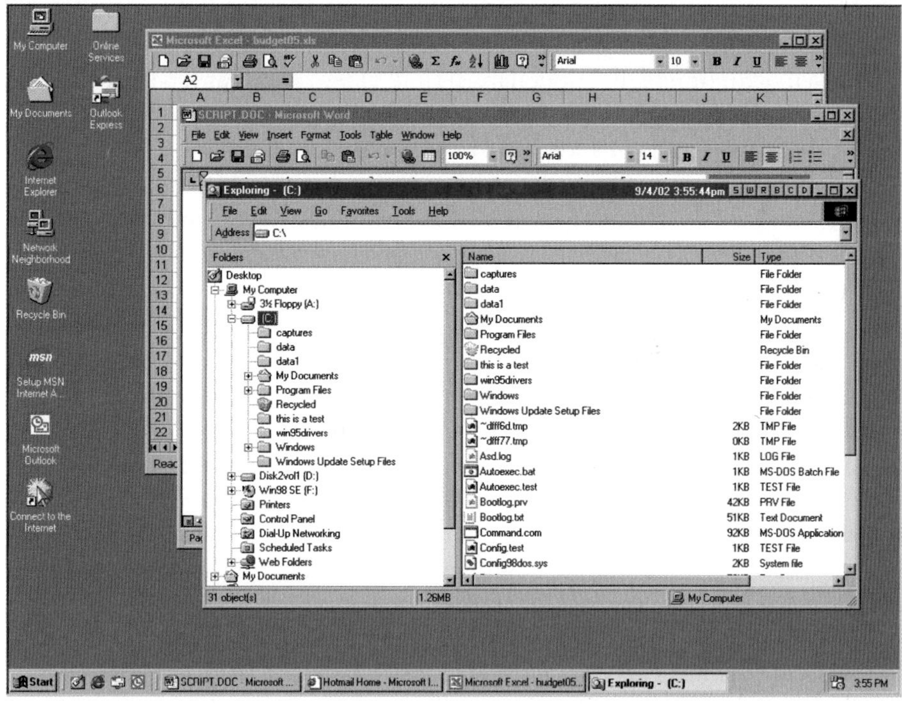

• **Figure 1-12.** MS Windows 98 desktop with open windows

appear to be in an Internet browser, even when they are not browsing the Internet. Windows 98 came with drivers and support for devices, such as DVD drives, that were not included in Windows 95. As usual with an upgrade to an OS, Microsoft cleaned up existing problems and made the OS run faster.

Inside Information

What Is Plug and Play (PnP)?

Plug and play is the capability of a computer to recognize and configure a device when it is installed in or plugged into a computer. Before the introduction of plug-and-play capabilities in computers, peripheral devices, and operating systems, it was necessary to manually configure a device, install the appropriate device driver, and configure the operating system to work with the device. With plug-and-play hardware, the operating system detects that a new device has been installed and automatically searches its own libraries for an appropriate driver. When it finds one, it installs it. Voilà! You're done!

When Would You Use Windows 98?

Windows 98 is now somewhat "long in the tooth," and there are newer choices from Microsoft. At the time it was introduced, however, the two choices of desktop OSs from Microsoft were Windows 95 and Windows NT Workstation. Windows 98 was an upgrade of Windows 95, and Windows NT had only a limited list of supported hardware. NT also did not support an important technology called plug and play (PnP). Therefore, Windows 98 was the choice for PCs with PnP hardware and/or hardware not supported by Windows NT. It's in use today simply because people haven't yet upgraded to Windows 2000 or Windows XP.

Windows Me (Millennium Edition)

Windows Me (Millennium Edition) was targeted at the home market, especially the home gaming user, when introduced in 2000. It is essentially Windows 98 with improved music, video, and home networking support. It included the System Restore utility, which allowed a user to roll back the PC software configuration to a date or time before a bad change was made to the computer. The Windows Movie Maker allowed users to digitally edit, save, and share their home videos, and the Windows Media Player gave users a tool for organizing digital music and video. This was the last Microsoft OS based on the Windows 95 internals (mainly the kernel).

Windows Me is included in this summary only because it was installed on many computers that were sold to individuals, but it is not an OS that was adopted by organizations. You are not likely to encounter it in a work environment.

Windows 2000

In 2000, Microsoft introduced the Windows 2000 family of OS products, which brought together the best of Windows 98 and Windows NT. Microsoft had now united its operating systems in a group of products that all shared the same kernel and covered OS needs from the desktop to the enterprise server. The several versions of Windows 2000 include Windows 2000 Professional (the desktop OS), Windows 2000 Server (for a network server on a small network), Windows 2000 Advanced Server (for a network server in larger networks), and Windows 2000 Enterprise Edition (with lots of features for *really* big servers in *really* big networks).

When Would You Use Windows 2000 Professional?

This is no longer offered as a standard OS when you buy a new desktop computer, but you will find it on existing desktop computers in the workplace for a few more years. Figure 1-13 shows the Windows 2000 desktop. Windows 2000 Professional is included in this book because it is still on many computers; however, today you are most likely to encounter Windows XP Professional on any new PC purchases.

• **Figure 1-13.** MS Windows 2000 desktop

Windows XP

Cross Check

The Many Windows 2000 Products

What's with these different Windows 2000 products? Skip ahead to the beginning of Chapter 4, read more about these variations, and then answer the following questions:

1. Which versions are optimized for the role of network server?
2. Which product cannot be purchased by itself but is sold only in an OEM (original equipment manufacturer) version?
3. Which product is appropriate for a small business that needs only a file and print server?

With its Windows 2000 products, Microsoft brought all of its OSs together, building them on top of the same core internal piece (the kernel). Some of us, especially those whose jobs include support of both desktop and server computers, thought it would simplify our lives. We really liked that idea because we could learn just one OS for both the desktop and server. However, with Windows XP, Microsoft departed from that model. Windows XP is intended only for the desktop or other consumer-type computer, not for the server environment. The new server products introduced after Windows XP begin with Windows Server 2003, which we discuss in Chapter 9.

What's Notable in Windows XP?

There are several Windows XP products: The two most common products are Windows XP Home Edition and Windows XP Professional. Both have the same improved GUI and share many of the same features, but only Windows XP Professional has certain network- and security-related features.

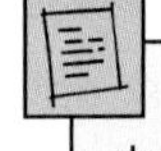

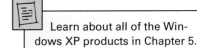

Learn about all of the Windows XP products in Chapter 5.

The Windows XP default desktop is very different from that of previous versions of Windows in that the recycle bin (where deleted files are sent) is the only icon on the desktop. In addition, the Start menu has been redesigned and reorganized, as shown in Figure 1-14.

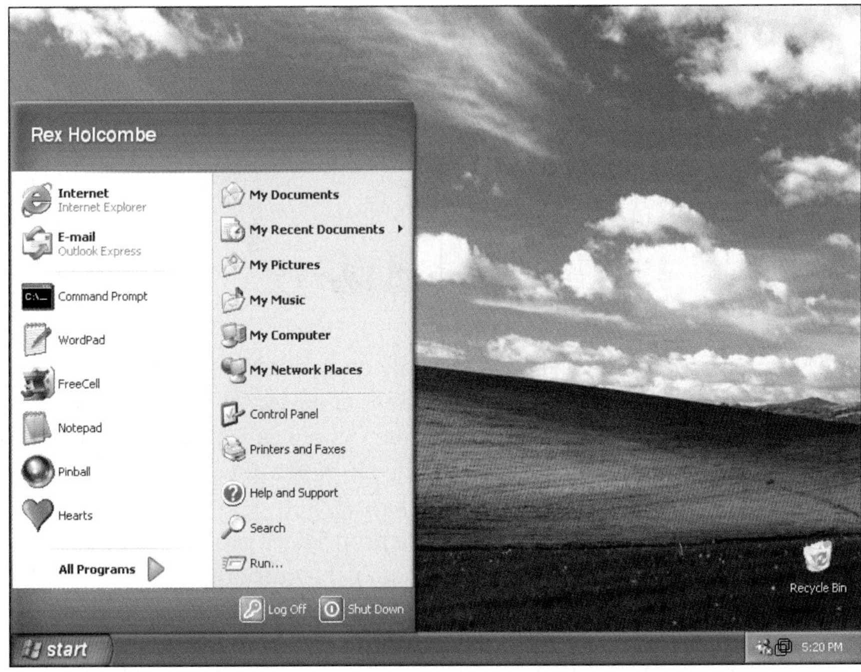

• **Figure 1-14.** MS Windows XP desktop and Start menu

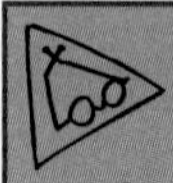

Inside Information

Windows XP Professional vs. Windows XP Home

Here is a short list of features available in Windows XP Professional, but not in Windows XP Home: the ability to join a Windows NT or Active Directory domain (a grouping of users and computers for central administration of security); support for two processors and for multiple (human) languages; a built-in Backup capability; and file encryption on an NTFS volume.

When Would You Use Windows XP?

Introduced in 2001, Windows XP is the successor to Windows 2000, although both are available as of this writing. Windows XP Home Edition is the choice for home users who want a computer based on the Microsoft/Intel standards, who want to run a variety of personal-use software and even many business applications, and who want to connect to the Internet. Windows XP Professional is the choice for corporate or home users who want a Microsoft/Intel standard computer and need to connect as a client computer to Microsoft Windows NT or Windows 2000 servers. The Professional version is also the choice for users who want to be able to run the enormous variety of software written for Windows and to take advantage of the features that are supported only in this version of Windows XP.

Longhorn

The next Windows desktop operating system, code-named Longhorn, is still in development and expected to be released in 2006 or 2007. There was a time when a developing product was given a code name to keep its very existence secret, but Microsoft actually issues announcements about products while they are in development.

What can we expect from Longhorn? It was originally expected to be a minor upgrade to Windows XP (we'll call that "Plan A"), and then it morphed into a major upgrade to both the desktop and server operating systems (our name for this is "Plan B"). As of this writing, announcements have indicated that Longhorn is back to "Plan A" and will just be an upgrade to Windows XP and may include improvements in how Windows handles graphics, files, and communications. Stay tuned…

Try This!

What Is the Latest on Longhorn?

Use a search engine to find out what has happened with Longhorn. You may know without researching!

Try this:

1. Use your favorite search engine to search on "longhorn" and find out what happened to this version of Windows since the writing of this book.
2. Whether this product has been released or not, find the list of features.
3. Do the features still include improvements in how Windows handles graphics, files, and communications? If not, what was omitted? Has anything been added?

Macintosh OSs

The Macintosh operating systems run only on Apple Macintosh computers. The OSs in common use today are Mac OS 9, and Mac OS X (*X* is the Roman numeral for ten). OS 9 reflects evolutionary changes from the first strictly GUI-based Mac operating systems, while OS X is a revolutionary change, based on NextStep, an OS with a UNIX kernel.

Macintosh hardware and software are proprietary products of the Apple Computer Company, which results in better integration of the OS and the hardware, but at a higher price. Apple computers are based on an entirely different architecture than the Microsoft/Intel personal computers. For the past several years, Macintosh computers have used the PowerPC chip with an architecture that is enhanced for graphics and multimedia.

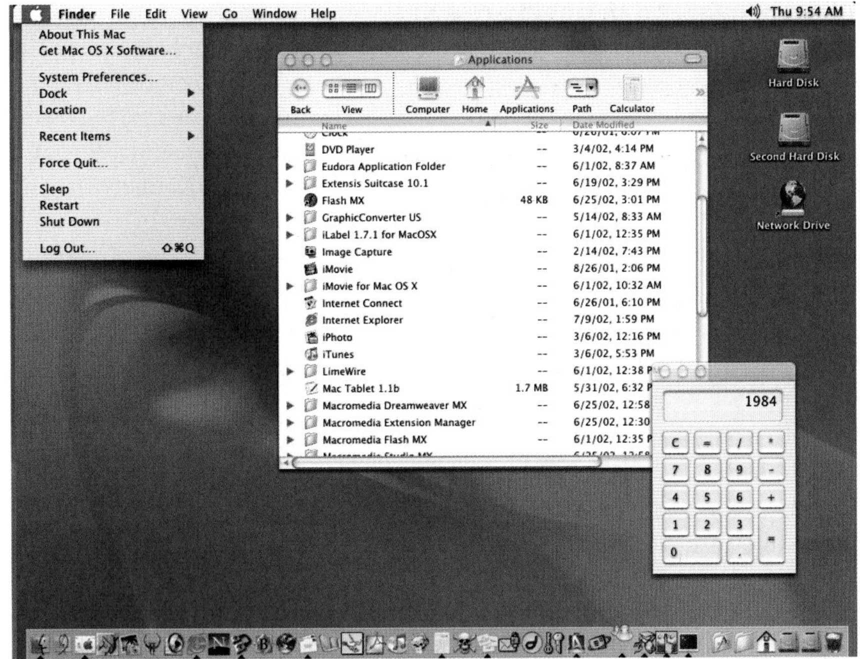

• **Figure 1-15.** Mac OS X GUI

Until Mac OS X, the Macintosh OSs were strictly GUI environments, with no command-line option (see Figure 1-15). Mac OS X, with its UNIX origins, does give you the option of a character-based interface.

The Macintosh has a loyal following among people who first encountered it in school. Early in Apple's history, the company strategically targeted schools and universities as places to sell its products, which, over the years, has resulted in large numbers of people who learned computing on a Mac. However, today the largest market share for the desktop, especially in business and government, belongs to Windows-based computers.

When Would You Use a Macintosh OS?

The Macintosh OS is your only choice if you buy a Macintosh computer. Basically, you can do everything with a Mac that you can do with a PC. Many business applications, including Microsoft Office, come in a version for the Macintosh. One area in which the Macintosh traditionally shines is ease of use, although Windows now provides competition in this area. In addition, the Macintosh is often the OS/computer of choice among graphics professionals and video editing professionals.

UNIX/Linux

UNIX has a longer history than any other popular operating system. It grew out of an operating system developed for an early Digital Equipment Corporation (DEC) computer and went through several generations of changes before it emerged from the Bell Labs Computing Science Research Center (Bell Labs) as UNIX version 6 in 1975. This was a portable operating system for

Try This!

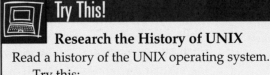

Research the History of UNIX

Read a history of the UNIX operating system.

Try this:

1. Point your web browser to `www.bell-labs.com/history/unix`.
2. Read the article titled "The Creation of the UNIX Operating System."
3. Read about the contributions of Dennis Ritchie and Ken Thompson.

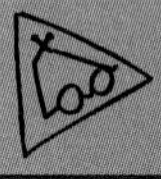

Inside Information

What Is a Portable Operating System?

A portable operating system is one that can be used on a variety of computer systems, with only minor alterations required for the underlying architecture. UNIX can be found today on very large computer systems (still referred to as mainframes) and on Intel desktop systems, as well as on a variety of mid-sized computers.

minicomputers and mainframe computers, and it was distributed via government and commercial licenses and inexpensive academic licenses. The University of California at Berkeley (UCB) licensed UNIX, modified it, and distributed it to other schools as Berkeley Software Distribution (BSD) version 4.2. Later versions have followed. The schools paid licensing fees to Bell Labs. Students and others improved on and added to UNIX, freely sharing their code with each other. This tradition still prevails today.

In addition to portability (the ability to run on different types of computers), UNIX supports timesharing and multiuser systems, and some versions run on personal computers.

The Many Faces of UNIX

The current commercial versions of UNIX include Sun Microsystems' Solaris, Hewlett-Packard's HP-UX, IBM's AIX, and Compaq's Tru64 UNIX. These versions are high-end server OSs and quite expensive, as are the computers they are intended to run on. In addition to the commercial versions, there are also many **open source** versions of UNIX, including FreeBSD and NetBSD. Open source is a certification standard of the Open Source Initiative (OSI) through which a program's source code (the original language in which a program is written) is made available free of charge to the general public. Learn more about open source at `www.opensource.org`. Even with these free versions available, however, it is worthwhile to buy one of the modestly priced packages from companies that charge small fees just for the value they have added to the OS in the form of additional software, installation and configuration instructions, and documentation.

Why Would You Use UNIX?

The Windows family of operating systems presently dominates the desktop, especially in corporate America. Even fierce UNIX advocates do not see UNIX taking over the desktop any time soon. However, it is an excellent server operating system, because it uses resources carefully, allowing you to load only the services currently needed. It is also considered very secure, and versions of UNIX are present on many of the world's Internet servers.

Inside Information

The UNIX Wars

In 1988, a group of UNIX licensees formed the Open Systems Foundation (OSF) to lobby for an "open" UNIX after AT&T formed a partnership with Sun Microsystems to develop a single UNIX with the best of many versions. "Open" means that the code is released to the public so that users can modify the OS to suit themselves. In response, AT&T and other licensees formed UNIX International in order to oppose the OSF. The trade press calls the maneuverings of these two groups the "UNIX wars."

Linux

Linux, an operating system modeled on UNIX and named in honor of its original developer, began as a project in 1991 by Linus Benedict Torvalds while a student at the University of Helsinki in his native Finland. He invited other programmers to work together to create an open-source operating system for modern computers. They created Linux using a powerful programming language called C, along with a free C compiler developed through the GNU project called GNU C Compiler (GCC). Linux has continued to evolve over the years, its code being tested and upgraded by programmers all over the globe. Linus Torvalds could not have predicted in 1991 how well the new operating system would be accepted.

Linux is a 32-bit, multitasking operating system that supports multiple users and multiple processors. It can run on nearly any computer and can support almost any type of application. Although Linux natively uses an awkward command-line interface, windows-like GUI environments, called shells, are available that make it accessible to almost anyone.

The biggest nontechnical difference between Linux and other operating systems is its price and installation. Anyone can get a free copy of Linux on the Internet, and disk-based copies are often inserted in popular computer books and magazines. Commercial versions of Linux, which are very inexpensive when compared with the cost of other powerful operating systems, are also available from a variety of vendors who provide the Linux code free and only charge for the extras, such as utilities, GUI shells, and documentation. At this writing, the most popular Linux vendors are Red Hat and Novell, who both offer special Linux bundles for desktop computers as well as for servers. Novell purchased Ximian in 2003 and now offers Ximian Linux for the desktop. In 2004, they also purchased SuSE Linux AG, so they now have a second desktop Linux product as well as a Linux server product.

For these and other reasons, Linux has become a popular OS in certain circles. Students and teachers have flocked to Linux, not just for its technical advances, but to participate in the global community that has built up around the operating system. This community invites Linux users and developers to contribute modifications and enhancements, and it freely shares information about Linux and Linux-related issues. Although Linux is typically considered to be a server platform, an increasing number of software companies are writing new desktop applications or modifying existing ones for Linux. Figure 1-16 shows an example of a Linux directory.

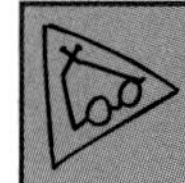

Inside Information

The User Interface

Most versions of UNIX and Linux also offer several different user interfaces. Some use character mode, like the traditional shells, such as the Bourne shell and the C shell. Others use a graphical interface such as GNOME or KDE.

Why Would You Use Linux?

The answer seems to be that you would use Linux for almost any type of computer, because it is fast becoming an accepted OS for all platforms. With several free or inexpensive versions now available for the Microsoft/Intel

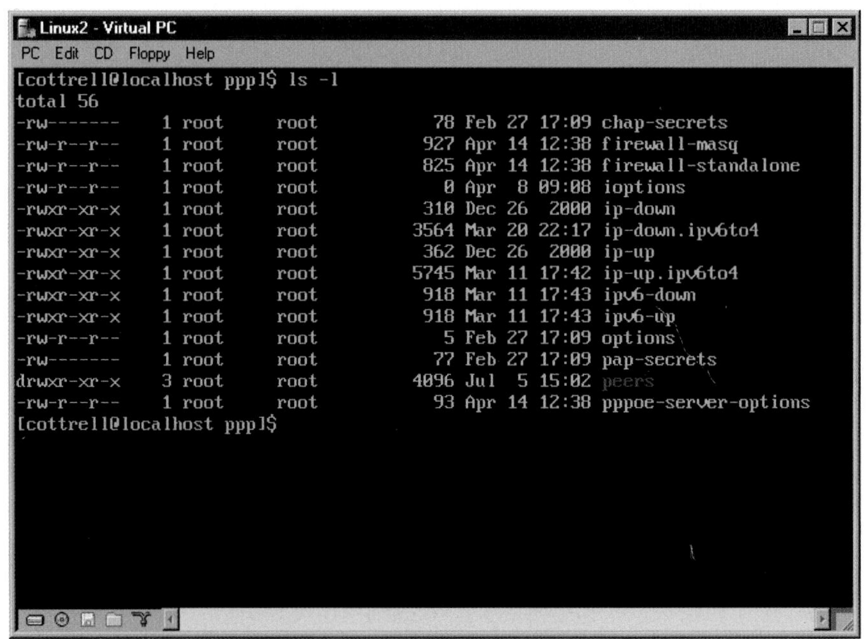

• **Figure 1-16.** Red Hat Linux directory listing (ls command)

platform, this is the OS of choice for present-day hobbyist and computer enthusiasts, who use it to develop new Linux utilities and other software, and to run games. If you're a member of this group, you may be in the market for (or already own) Linux.

Linux is the fastest-growing computer-server software. Until recently, Linux was not considered a contender for the desktop because of the lack of Linux office productivity applications. However, a major bellwether event occurred in the summer of 2004 when the city of Munich, Germany, finalized its decision to make the switch from Windows and Office to Linux and Linux-based office applications on 14,000 desktop PCs. This came after Sun Microsystems, Novell, and Red Hat came out with bundles of Linux and applications, and started marketing all-Linux networks that run open-source software.

Chapter 1 Review

■ Chapter Summary

After reading this chapter and completing the exercises, you should understand the following facts about operating systems:

Microcomputers Today

- A computer consists of hardware and two types of software: applications software and operating system software.
- The operating system allows the user to interact with the computer hardware.

Common Microcomputer Hardware

- Certain computer hardware is common to most computers you will encounter. The basic components include the processor, motherboard, RAM, ROM BIOS, video adapter, display screen, keyboard, pointing device, and other peripheral devices.
- You can identify hardware components by a visual inspection, by observing information displayed during the bootup process, and by accessing a ROM BIOS setup program.

Purpose and Functions of Microcomputer Operating Systems

- Certain functions are provided by most, if not all, current operating systems. These functions include a user interface, job management, task management, memory management, file management, device management, and security.
- The operating system makes everything work together.
- You can identify most of the functions provided by your operating system by careful observation. For instance, evidence of support of the security function includes a required logon procedure when you start your computer and the need for authorization to access resources on your local computer.
- There are four categories of operating systems: Single-user/Single-tasking, Single-user/ Multitasking, Multi-user/Multitasking, and Real-time.
- A single-user/single-tasking operating system is one that allows only a single user to perform a single task at a time.
- An operating system that allows a single user to perform two or more functions at once is a single-user/multitasking operating system.
- A multi-user/multitasking operating system is an operating system that allows multiple users to run programs simultaneously on a single network server, called a terminal server.
- Real-time operating systems are defined by their speed and ability to work with special real-time application programs. A real-time operating system is a very fast, relatively small OS that is often embedded, meaning it is built into the circuitry of a device and not normally loaded from a disk drive.

Major Events in the Evolution of Microcomputer Operating Systems

- The history of current microcomputers and their OSs involved many technical advances and the imagination of a multitude of innovative people.
- You can find many accounts of the history of computers and operating systems by searching the Internet.

What OSs Are Available Today?

- The microcomputer operating systems common today include MS-DOS, several versions of Windows (Windows 98, Windows 2000, and Windows XP), Mac OS 9, Mac OS X, several versions of Linux, and several versions of UNIX.
- Each of today's common operating systems is best suited for certain uses.
- Microsoft desktop OSs are common in the business environment.
- The Mac OSs are commonly used in education and in graphics workstations.

Key Terms List

central processing unit (CPU) *(2)*
client *(3)*
cursor *(11)*
device driver *(16)*
device management *(16)*
directory *(15)*
disk drive *(11)*
display screen *(11)*
file management *(15)*
folder *(15)*
graphical user interface (GUI) *(14)*
input/output (I/O) *(4)*
job management *(15)*
kernel *(13)*
memory *(9)*
memory management *(15)*
microcomputer *(2)*
microprocessor *(2)*
motherboard *(8)*
mouse *(11)*
multitasking *(15)*
network operating system (NOS) *(25)*
open source *(36)*
operating system (OS) *(13)*
peripheral device *(12)*
random-access memory (RAM) *(9)*
read-only memory (ROM) *(10)*
read-only memory basic input/output system (ROM BIOS) *(10)*
security *(16)*
server *(3)*
task management *(15)*
user interface *(13)*
virtual memory *(15)*

Key Terms Quiz

Use the Key Terms List to complete the sentences that follow. Not all terms will be used.

1. The ______ is the hardware component most central to a computer.
2. If you save confidential data on your local hard drive, you should be using an operating system that includes a/an ______ function, which protects local files and folders from unauthorized access.
3. A/an ______ takes care of the interaction between a program and a computer's hardware, freeing application programmers from the task of including such functions in their programs.
4. An operating system that uses ______ will allow you to simultaneously run more programs than the physical memory of the computer will hold.
5. When you run several applications at once and switch between them, you are experiencing the ______ feature of an operating system.
6. Interaction with a computer involving getting data and commands into it and results out of it is called ______
7. A/an ______ is an example of a pointing device.
8. Software that allows the operating system to use a hardware component is called a/an ______.
9. The type of memory used as the workspace for the operating system and applications is ______.
10. Your data and programs are stored on a ______.

Multiple-Choice Quiz

1. Which of the following operating systems will *not* work on a PC?
   - **a.** Mac OS X
   - **b.** Windows 98
   - **c.** Windows NT
   - **d.** Red Hat Linux
   - **e.** Windows XP
2. Which of the following is a small electronic component made up of transistors (tiny switches) and other miniaturized parts?
   - **a.** Peripheral
   - **b.** Integrated circuit (IC)
   - **c.** Handheld
   - **d.** Mouse
   - **e.** Vacuum tube

3. Introduced in 1983, this application program became the "killer app" that made the IBM PC a must-have business tool.
   a. Microsoft Word
   b. VisiCalc
   c. BASIC
   d. PC-DOS
   e. Lotus 1-2-3
4. Which of the following is not available as a desktop operating system?
   a. Windows 98
   b. Macintosh OS X
   c. Windows NT Workstation
   d. Red Hat Linux
   e. Windows Server 2003
5. Which of the following is a computer input device?
   a. Display
   b. Printer
   c. Keyboard
   d. RAM
   e. ROM
6. On a network, the purpose of this computer is to allow end users to save and access files stored on this computer, as well as to print to printers connected to this computer.
   a. Desktop computer
   b. File and print server
   c. Hand-held computer
   d. Laptop
   e. PC
7. Which choice characterizes a real-time operating system?
   a. A GUI and the ability to run great games
   b. Single-tasking
   c. Large and fast
   d. Speed and the ability to support real-time application programs
   e. Runs on a terminal server
8. Which component, if missing, will keep a PC from functioning?
   a. Scanner
   b. Printer
   c. Camera
   d. Microprocessor
   e. Mouse
9. In the early 1950s, a typical computer end user would have been a:
   a. Computer gamer
   b. Medical doctor
   c. Politician
   d. Government agency
   e. Secretary
10. Of the following, which works best in an analogy of the role an operating system plays in a computer?
    a. Salesman
    b. Spreadsheet
    c. Steering wheel
    d. Ignition
    e. Intermediary
11. After reading this chapter, which of the following do you believe accurately describes the overall trend in computing during the last 50-plus years?
    a. Toward physically larger, more powerful computers
    b. Toward physically larger, less powerful computers
    c. Toward physically smaller, less powerful computers
    d. Toward physically smaller, more powerful computers
    e. Toward physically smaller, single-use computers
12. Which of the following is not a peripheral device?
    a. Microprocessor
    b. Printer
    c. Scanner
    d. Mouse
    e. Camera

13. A specialized form of this type of computer would be used by an individual you might see in a grocery store aisle, taking inventory.

 a. Laptop
 b. Handheld
 c. Desktop
 d. Server
 e. Mainframe

14. This chip contains the basic input/output system for a computer.

 a. Microprocessor
 b. CMOS
 c. RAM
 d. ROM BIOS
 e. Floppy disk

15. What is the very first thing each user must do in order to gain access to a secure computer?

 a. Back up all data
 b. Connect to the Internet
 c. Log on with a user name and password
 d. Double-click the Start menu
 e. Reboot

Essay Quiz

1. Write a few sentences describing every interaction you have had with computers in the past 24 hours.
2. If you use more than one operating system on a regular basis, describe some of the similarities and differences you have noticed between two of those operating systems. You are not limited to the operating systems described in this chapter. (If you use a hand-held computer or Internet-enabled cell phone and use a desktop Windows computer, these are two different operating systems.) If you do not work with more than one operating system, find someone who has (classmate or other) and interview that person to answer this question.
3. Explain why Windows 98 is not a good choice of operating system for a laptop computer holding confidential information being used by a person who works from different locations.
4. Describe virtual memory and list an OS that does not use it.
5. In studying the common operating systems, you have considered the availability of software that runs on each OS and the general reasons one may be chosen over the others. Put yourself in the position of an information technology professional in a new company that will open its doors on day one with 50 employees who will need computers on their desks connected to a corporate network and will need to work with standard business applications. What are some other practical considerations that you can think of that must come into play when making this decision? Your answer does not need to specify a particular OS.

Lab Projects

• Lab Project 1.1

Locate as many of the common components (listed next) in your lab computer as possible. If you're doing this in a class lab, you may use any means permitted by the instructor to find this information. You may need to refer to the documentation, use software, or open up the computer. Then write a brief description of the component. For instance, if you discover that your computer has a Pentium 4 processor, record that information, and if you can discover the quantity of memory installed, record that information also. If you're quick, you can discover information about your computer as it is booting up.

1. Processor

   ____

2. Motherboard

   ____

3. Memory

   ____

4. ROM BIOS

   ____

5. Video adapter

   ____

6. Keyboard

   ____

7. Pointing device

   ____

8. Disk drives

   ____

9. Peripheral device

   ____

• Lab Project 1.2

1. To understand the relative cost of each of the operating systems you are studying and the availability of each system, use a paper catalog from a software retailer or a web site such as `www.us.buy.com` or `www.amazon.com` to research the price of each of the operating systems covered in this section. You are not bargain hunting, so you don't need to look for the lowest price; just find the relative cost of the operating systems. You will also find that some are not available as new retail products, although you may find them at other sources. We have listed the full retail versions separately from the upgrade versions. The full versions can be installed on a computer that does not have a previous version of Windows installed. The upgrade versions are cheaper than the full versions, but will not install without a previous version of Windows.

   In Table 1-2, enter the cost of each product. For those that are unavailable, enter **N/A** in the cost column.

2. Once again, using paper catalogs, retail stores, and/or the Internet, research the number of software titles that run in each of these operating systems. This information may be difficult to find. You may have to search other sources. You may find this information at the Microsoft, Apple, and Red Hat web sites or at an Electronics Boutique or Wal-Mart. This will give you a rough idea of the amount of software available for each OS, because it takes into account only software sold at retail through the sites you selected and does not include other free or nearly free software distributed elsewhere. Be careful not to count other versions of the operating system,

Table 1-2 Price and Availability Comparison

Operating System	Cost	Operating System	Cost
MS-DOS (any version)	________	Windows XP Professional full	________
Windows 98 full	________	Windows XP Professional upgrade	________
Windows 98 upgrade	________	Red Hat Linux	________
Windows NT Workstation 4.0 full	________	Red Hat Linux Professional	________
Windows NT Workstation 4.0 upgrade	________	Mac OS 9	________
Windows XP Home Edition full	________	Mac OS X	________
Windows XP Home Edition upgrade	________		

especially when looking for Linux software titles. Only count software that runs on the operating system. At the Buy.com site, we searched on each OS in turn, noticed the total number of titles in the results, and then browsed through them to estimate the total. You're looking only for estimated numbers, because your goal is to gain an understanding of the relative number of software titles available for each OS. While you are at it, notice the type of software available for each OS, which is an indication of the market for that OS. Windows OSs can usually run software written for any of the older versions of Windows, so a low number of titles that name Windows XP in their system requirements does not indicate that there are few applications that will run on XP. Enter your findings on the number of titles in Table 1-3.

Table 1-3 Comparison of the Number of Available Software Titles

Operating System	Estimated Number of Titles	Operating System	Estimated Number of Titles
MS-DOS	N/A	Windows XP	__________
Windows 98	__________	Linux	__________
Windows NT Workstation	__________	Mac OS X	__________

• Lab Project 1.3

Examine the operating system on your class lab computer, and answer questions related to the operating system functions described in this section. If you're not familiar with the operating system on your lab computer, you may need to do some research to answer some of these questions. If so, there are several places you can search. First, look for a Help program in the OS, or read any documentation that is available to you for this OS. If you cannot find the answers in one of these sources, use a search engine on the Internet to find another source of information for your OS.

For this Lab Project, you will need the following:

- A computer with a desktop operating system
- Internet access

1. Start your computer and record the name and version number of your operating system here.

   ____

2. In your own words, describe the user interface.

   ____

   ____

3. Can you see an indication that this operating system provides a job management function? If so, provide a description.

   ____

   ____

4. If your operating system supports task management, explain how you can demonstrate the task management functions to someone else.

   ____

   ____

5. Look for tools used to manage files. Then describe how you can copy a file from a location on your hard drive to a floppy disk.

   ____

   ____

6. Did you see any evidence that this OS provides security? If so, describe why you believe this.

   ____

   ____

Disk Operating System (DOS)

chapter 2

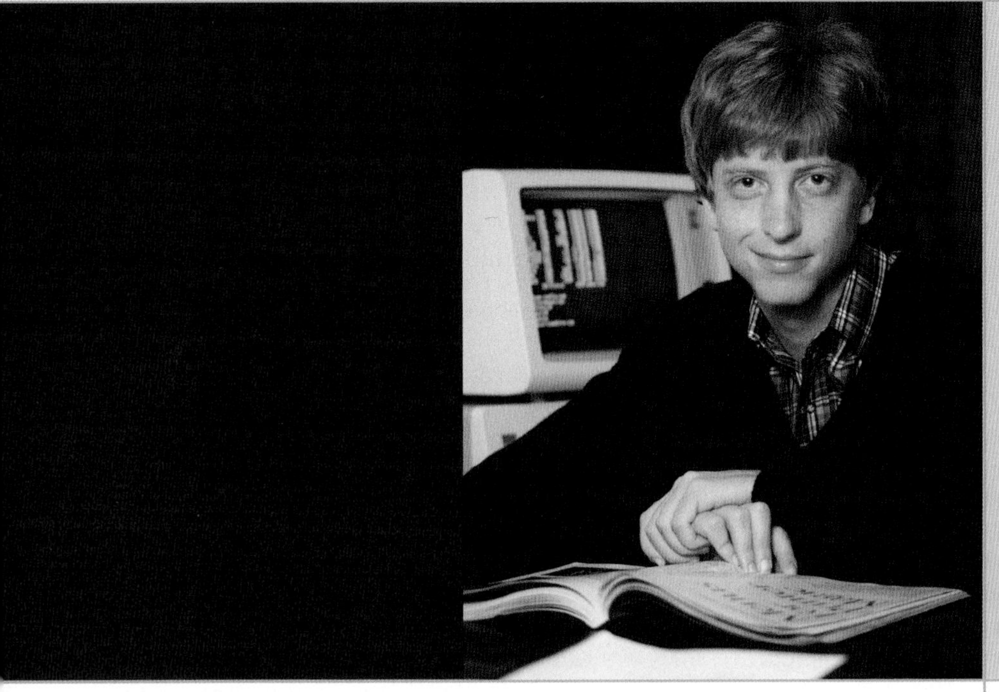

No one needs more than 640K.

—Bill Gates, 1986

In this chapter you will learn how to:

- **Measure the value, strengths, and weaknesses of DOS**
- **Install DOS**
- **Use the FAT file system**
- **Use DOS commands for file management and other tasks**
- **Describe the DOS bootup process and create startup disks**
- **Troubleshoot common DOS problems**

In this chapter you will learn about the following DOS commands:

ATTRIB	ECHO	RD
CD/ CHDIR	EDIT	REN
CHKDSK	FDISK	SCANDISK
CLS	FORMAT	SET
COPY	HELP	SETVER
DEFRAG	LABEL	TYPE
DEL/DELETE	MD	VER
DELTREE	MEM	VOL
DIR	PAUSE	XCOPY

Who cares about DOS? Why should you need to learn about an operating system that was created over 20 years ago and used with the very first PCs? Some organizations still have DOS applications lurking somewhere that they can't or won't replace with newer applications, and some devices (specialized computers) actually still use DOS. In addition, because Windows OSs still have an optimal command-line DOS-like interface, knowing how to use DOS will allow you to accomplish some tasks faster than you can using the standard interface of your OS.

In this chapter you will explore DOS in depth. You'll begin with an overview of the presently available choices for a DOS operating system, explore the two primary reasons DOS is still in use today, and look at the features and limits of DOS OSs. You'll install DOS on your lab computer and practice file management tasks in DOS as you create, copy, move, and delete files and directories. Finally, you will study the DOS bootup process and create a DOS startup disk.

Finding DOS and Understanding Its Strengths and Weaknesses

Your first step in understanding DOS is learning where it still lurks in your world. Then you can begin to understand its strengths and weaknesses. We'll discuss these topics in turn.

Versions of DOS—Past and Present

Many myths are built around the evolution of DOS. We don't wish to add to these myths, but we would like to provide a brief history of DOS, beginning with an important predecessor to DOS, CP/M.

CP/M

In 1975, while on contract to Intel to create a programming language for the Intel 8080 microprocessor, Gary Kildall wrote a simple operating system he named Control Program/Microcomputer (CP/M). Kildall formed a company called Intergalactic Digital Research (later renamed Digital Research) to develop CP/M and other products. CP/M became the OS of choice for the various builders of Intel 8080-based computers. CP/M version 2.2 became a megahit that, by 1978, dominated microcomputing. Eventually more than 500,000 microcomputers would be sold with CP/M as the operating system.

When planning for the 1981 introduction of their IBM PC product, IBM called on Digital Research, hoping to acquire an 8088-compatible version of CP/M for their systems. When they failed to reach an agreement, they turned to Bill Gates. Microsoft was already providing the BASIC interpreter for the new systems, and he agreed to provide a disk operating system.

For more detail on this fascinating history, read the brief article detailing its history at `http://museum.sysun.com/museum/cpmhist.html`. If this URL does not work, use your favorite search engine to find information on CP/M history.

Microsoft DOS

Many versions of DOS have been used in the more than two decades since the introduction of the IBM PCs. The most commonly used versions of DOS came from Microsoft, and there were several variants. First there was PC DOS, which Microsoft licensed to IBM for personal computer (PC) products, beginning with the IBM PC in 1981. To have a product in time for the introduction of the IBM PC, Microsoft purchased a product called QDOS (for

Quick and Dirty Operating System) from Tim Paterson of Seattle Computer Products. They soon realized the shortcomings of this product, and version 1.1 was a heavily revised incarnation of 1.0. Later Microsoft licensed DOS as MS-DOS to many other PC manufacturers. It was often customized to satisfy a manufacturer's particular needs and then sold under that company's name. In such an arrangement, the product is said to be an original equipment manufacturer (OEM) product. IBM sold an OEM version of DOS as PC DOS, Compaq sold an OEM version as Compaq MS-DOS, and many other manufacturers sold versions as well.

Although Microsoft no longer sells MS-DOS 6.22, many organizations still have licenses for it, and you are likely to encounter it. For this reason, we will use MS-DOS 6.22 in the examples in this chapter.

The first version of DOS that Microsoft sold as a retail non-OEM product was MS-DOS 5.0. Microsoft does not presently offer a DOS product, and their last retail version was MS-DOS version 6.22, released in 1994. IBM continued to offer new versions of PC DOS through PC DOS 2000, released in 1998.

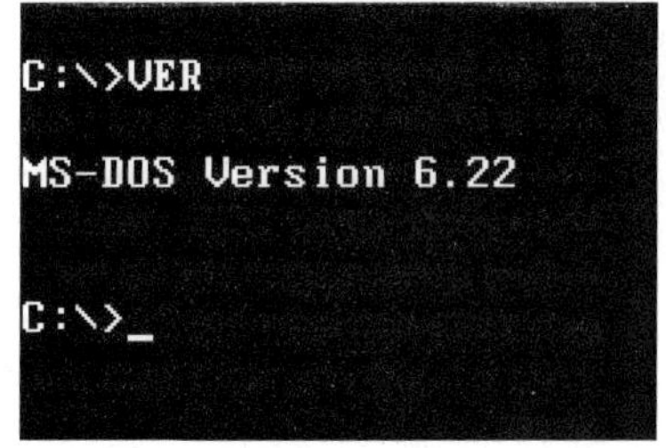

• The VER command

Even though the importance of DOS is greatly diminished in today's computing environment, there is a good chance that you will encounter it in some form on the job. Command-line skills have value with almost any operating system. Even Windows has certain administrative and diagnostic commands that are run from the command prompt. There isn't always a GUI available. For instance, many Internet-related systems have UNIX or Linux installed, requiring skill at the command line. Therefore, you should be familiar with the DOS command line as preparation for working on a variety of OSs.

PC DOS

IBM continues to offer PC DOS, which is no longer designed specifically for IBM PCs, but can be installed on any Microsoft/Intel compatible computer. PC DOS 2000 was released in 1998, but IBM ended defect support for this product on January 31, 2001, meaning that they would no longer provide patches or improvements. Older versions of PC DOS are not available through IBM, but may be found at other retail sources.

For more information about IBM's latest version of PC DOS, point your browser to www.ibm.com and search on "PC DOS."

DR-DOS

Learn more about DR-DOS at www.drdos.com.

In 1987, Digital Research introduced DR-DOS, a DOS product especially for the IBM PC and compatible market. Novell acquired Digital Research in 1991 and briefly offered DR-DOS (then referred to as Novell DOS). Since then, DR-DOS has changed hands several more times—first to Caldera, then to Lineo, and most recently to DeviceLogics in 2002. Lineo updated it to DR-DOS 7.03, adding support for use in ROM or flash memory. DeviceLogics, founded with the goal of offering DOS as a solution for embedded products, continues to offer the 7.03 version and introduced version 8.0 in 2004.

Try This!

Finding the Version Number of DOS

If you have a computer handy with DOS already installed, you can check out the version number by using a command that is common in most DOS versions. You can also try this command from the Windows command prompt (Start | Run | cmd), in which case, it will display the version of Windows. Try this:

1. At the DOS prompt, type **ver** and press ENTER. The version information should appear on the screen.
2. What version are you running? ______________________

DOS for Free

Some versions of DOS are distributed without charge. One of these is FreeDOS, which is distributed under the GNU GPL. GNU (pronounced "guh new") is a project that began many years ago at MIT with the goal of distributing free, open software. People may modify the software, as long as they freely share their modifications with others. This is called the GNU General Public License, or GNU GPL. FreeDOS is designed to be 100 percent compatible with MS-DOS. You can learn more about FreeDOS at `www.freedos.org`.

We have experimented with some of the free DOSs and find that they assume a great deal of knowledge about DOS, which makes them a poor choice for someone just learning DOS, even though you can't beat the price!

DOS' Strengths

DOS has lasted for so many years for two reasons: it works with applications written specifically for DOS, and it takes up only a very small amount of memory. We'll discuss both of these reasons in turn.

DOS for Backward Compatibility

Some people use DOS because they still use one or more special applications that require it. (Applications written for an older operating system are called legacy applications.) Take Christine, for instance. She recently bought a small picture-framing business that included an old PC which uses DOS along with an application program that computes frame prices. The program takes the dimensions of a picture and calculates the amount of matte and frame needed. Whenever prices for her supplies change, she can go into the program and enter the new prices. She likes the program and she feels that it works well.

Because DOS was slow at accessing hardware and programmers wanted to make their applications run faster, many, if not most, DOS applications were written to request services from the hardware in nonstandard ways.

"Working well" should not be the sole reason for using DOS as the operating system for this application, because all versions of Windows can run DOS applications. How well a DOS application runs in Windows depends on how the DOS application was written—and therein lies the problem. If the application program was created to request operating system services in a standard way, then it should run in Windows much as it does under DOS. If the application was written to request services in a nonstandard way (bypassing the operating system), then two outcomes are possible: under Windows it may run much more slowly, or it may not run at all! The best practice is to test your DOS application in Windows before giving up your DOS computer.

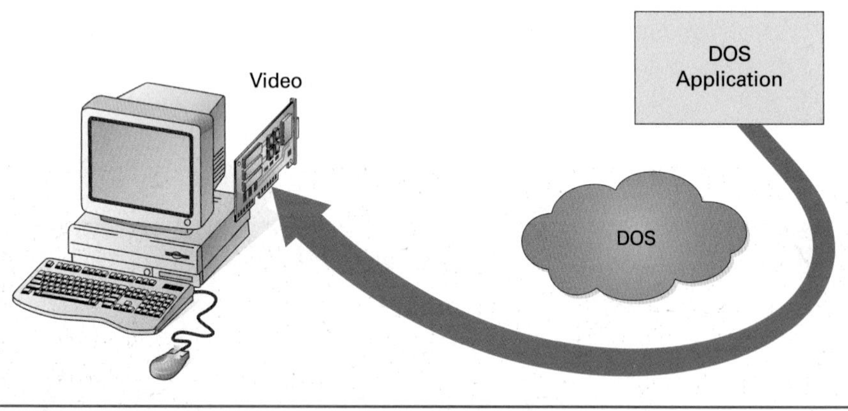

• An application "reaching around" DOS to access hardware directly

DOS When You Need a Small OS

Another reason DOS is still hanging around is that it is more compact than the various Windows OSs and therefore is useful when you need a very small operating system for embedded systems or for portability via a floppy disk.

Embedded systems are ROM-based operating systems running on a computer embedded in a device such as a hand-held computer or a smart kitchen appliance. Although Microsoft does offer scaled-down versions of Windows for those embedded systems that require a sophisticated GUI interface, DOS is a candidate for embedded systems that do not require such an interface.

An interesting use of embedded DOS was shown to us by Lou, who works at a large sporting goods retailer. This company uses hand-held scanning devices to take inventory. Each scanner is a small computer running embedded DOS and, as you can see in Figure 2-1, each scanner has a tiny screen and a keypad to allow users to work in the inventory application and to enter DOS commands. Both DOS and the application are stored on ROM and loaded into only 640KB of RAM. The device scans the Universal Product Codes (UPCs) on in-store inventory and communicates wirelessly with the store's computerized inventory systems.

Photo courtesy of Intermec.

• **Figure 2-1.** A hand-held inventory scanner

Another reason that the small size of DOS makes it attractive to use is that the files required to load DOS into memory (the boot files) easily fit on a 3.5-inch floppy disk. The ability to pack all this onto a single floppy disk makes DOS popular as an OS for the software tools used by computer technicians and other computer professionals. Such a floppy disk, called a **startup disk**, can be used for many tasks, such as booting up a computer that will not boot from its hard drive or running special diagnostic programs to help find a problem. This has been an important use of DOS, but the current trend to omit floppy disk drives from new PCs may eventually make this practice obsolete.

DOS is so small that a startup floppy disk still has plenty of room for additional files, such as drivers and utilities. A **driver** is a special program that works with an OS to allow use of a particular piece of hardware, such as a mouse or CD-ROM drive, or for connecting to a network. A **utility** is a program that allows you to perform handy tasks, usually computer management functions or diagnostics, such as upgrading the program in your computer's ROM-BIOS or looking for errors on your disk. A utility is distinguished from an **application** in that an application is software that allows you to perform useful functions and create results you can use in your personal or business life, such as writing a report or calculating a budget.

If a computer has a brand-new hard drive with nothing yet installed on it, you can boot from a DOS startup floppy disk and prepare the hard drive before installing an OS on it. In coming chapters, you will learn how to use the setup program of each OS to do this preparation without requiring DOS.

You can also use a DOS startup floppy disk to help install a new operating system if the installation files for the new operating system are located on a file server computer on the company network. In that case, you need to use a startup disk with special network drivers to boot up the computer and connect it to the file server. Once it is connected, you can run the installation program for the new operating system over the network and install it on the local hard drive.

```
A:\>dir /w
 Volume in drive A has no label.
 Volume Serial Number is 0000-0000

 Directory of A:\

COMMAND.COM   NOSTACK.COM   ZCOM.EXE      KEYBUS.COM    KEYBUK.COM
KEYBSP.COM    KEYBIT.COM    KEYBFR.COM    KEYBSW.COM    KEYBGR.COM
KEYBDA.COM    KEYBNO.COM    KEYBCHF.COM   KEYBCHG.COM   KEYBGK.COM
CONFIG.SYS    AUTOEXEC.BAT  SETUP.EXE     ASSIGN.COM    CHKDSK.COM
DEBUG.COM     SELECT.COM    EXE2BIN.EXE   FIND.EXE      PRINT.COM
RECOVER.COM   SHARE.EXE     SYS.COM       FORMAT.COM    SORT.EXE
GRAFTABL.COM  LABEL.COM     JOIN.EXE      SUBST.EXE     MORE.COM
REPLACE.EXE   APPEND.COM    XCOPY.EXE     DISKCOPY.COM  DISKCOMP.COM
CONFIGUR.COM  DSKSETUP.COM  MODE.COM      SEARCH.COM    APPLY.COM
TREE.COM      COMP.COM      SHIP.COM      ANSI.SYS      DRIVER.SYS
ATTRIB.EXE    EDLIN.COM     FC.EXE        GRAPHICS.COM  VDISK.SYS
ZCACHE.SYS    EMM.SYS       PART.EXE      PREP.EXE      DETECT.COM
ASGNPART.COM  BOOTF.COM     ZSPOOL.COM    RTCLOCK.COM   BACKUP.COM
RESTORE.COM   LINK.EXE      LIB.EXE
             68 File(s)       623,312 bytes
              0 Dir(s)        766,976 bytes free
```

• A directory listing of an MS-DOS startup floppy disk. Sixty-eight files take up less than half the disk space!

Let's talk for a moment about Nigel, who is an information technology (IT) worker in a large corporation. His tool kit carries an array of hardware tools, but the ones he values most are the software tools. He carries several CDs containing software utilities, driver files, and patches, but he often surprises his clients when he pulls out a DOS startup floppy disk. In fact, he carries several DOS startup floppy disks, each configured for a different purpose. One contains the correct network drivers and software for his client's computers that allow him to boot up a computer and connect to a network server from which he can start the installation of a new OS. Another floppy disk is configured with the drivers and utilities to allow him to update the BIOS on his clients' computers. He certainly never thought the tricks he learned playing on his father's old IBM PC would come in handy so many years later, but customers often are more impressed when he uses these floppy disks than when he troubleshoots a very complicated computer problem requiring much more sophisticated knowledge!

DOS' Weaknesses

DOS has significant processor mode, memory, multitasking, and hard disk usage limitations. We'll discuss each in turn.

DOS Processor Mode Limits

DOS' processor mode limitations are actually the cause of the memory and multitasking limitations. This is because DOS was written for the Intel 8088 processor and the computer architecture (design) of the original IBM PC. The 8088 processor had a limited bag of tricks, because it had only one mode of operation: real mode, in which only 1MB of addresses are available for both RAM and ROM, and only one task at a time can be completed. DOS only understands how to work in real mode.

Newer Intel processors beginning with the 386DX still have real mode. In fact, these processors wake up in real mode; it takes software (the OS) to switch the processor into one of its more powerful protected modes, which were described in Chapter 1. All Windows OSs discussed in this book are capable of using the more advanced protected mode of these processors.

Try This!

Checking Memory Usage

If you already have MS-DOS installed on a computer, you can check out the memory usage with the MEM command. This command also works at the command prompt in Windows. Try this:

1. At the DOS prompt, type **mem** and press ENTER.
2. How much memory is used and how much is available?

   ____

3. If you would like to learn more about the types of memory listed by the MEM command, go to a Windows computer, point your browser to your favorite search engine, and research "DOS memory management."

DOS Memory Limitations

DOS can only access 1MB of address space. Further, the architecture of the PC allows only the first 640KB of this to be RAM used as the workspace for the operating system and the application programs and data. This memory is referred to as **conventional memory**. The remaining 384KB of address space is reserved for the system BIOS and the RAM and ROM used on adapters, such as the video adapter and network cards.

Figure 2-2 shows the result of using the DOS MEM command to look at memory usage on a computer with 16MB of physical memory. It shows that the OS is using 65KB of conventional memory, leaving 573KB of conventional memory for an application to use. The 15,360KB of memory shown as extended memory is the physical memory above 1MB that is not available to DOS. With special drivers added to DOS, certain DOS programs can access this additional memory, but DOS itself is still limited to the first 1MB.

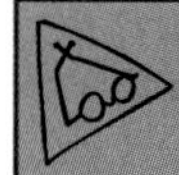

Inside Information

Using Memory More Efficiently

Newer versions of DOS, while still limited to real mode, can use memory more efficiently through special memory management device drivers and through programs that load device drivers and parts of the operating system into the memory areas that DOS cannot use for programs. This leaves more space in the 640KB of main memory for an application program to use.

DOS Multitasking Limits

DOS can't take advantage of the advanced multitasking capabilities of protected mode in the advanced Intel processors. Although DOS can have several drivers and small programs called **terminate and stay resident (TSR)** programs in memory at one time, it can run only one application program at a time. This is called **single-tasking**. The Windows and Mac operating systems you will study in this book allow several programs to run in memory at one time, and users can switch among them. This is called multitasking.

DOS Hard Drive Limitations

Another limitation of DOS is that it does not support hard drives larger than 7.8GB. Further, like most OSs, DOS uses logical drives. A **logical drive** is a portion of a physical hard drive that appears to be a drive with a letter assigned to it. You can have one or more logical drives on a physical drive, but DOS can only use logical drives that are each 2GB or less and within the 7.8GB total space limit.

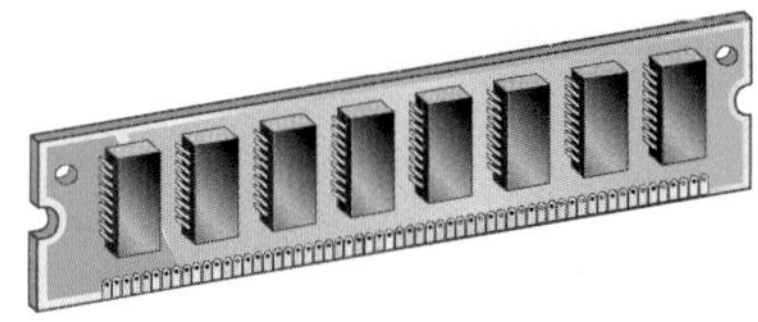

• DOS allows use of only 640KB of memory for programs and data.

Installing DOS

Now that you are familiar with the strengths and weaknesses of DOS, you are ready to install DOS on a PC. In this section you will learn the hardware

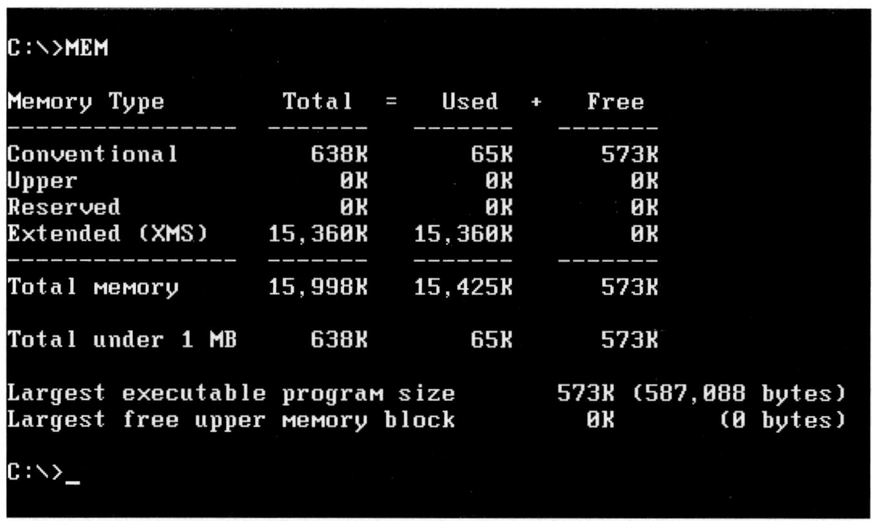

```
C:\>MEM

Memory Type        Total  =   Used  +   Free
----------------  -------   -------   -------
Conventional        638K       65K      573K
Upper                 0K        0K        0K
Reserved              0K        0K        0K
Extended (XMS)   15,360K   15,360K        0K
----------------  -------   -------   -------
Total memory     15,998K   15,425K      573K

Total under 1 MB    638K       65K      573K

Largest executable program size       573K (587,088 bytes)
Largest free upper memory block         0K       (0 bytes)

C:\>_
```

• **Figure 2-2.** The MEM command shows DOS memory usage.

Cross Check

How Does DOS Measure Up as an Operating System?

Consider what you have learned so far about DOS, and look back to the section "Purpose, Types, and Functions of Microcomputer Operating Systems" in Chapter 1. Then answer the following questions:

1. What operating system functions are supported in DOS?
2. What functions are completely unsupported in DOS?
3. Of the functions supported in DOS, which, in your opinion, are only minimally supported?

requirements for DOS and the preparation needed before installing it. Then you'll have an opportunity to install DOS onto a hard drive.

Remember Christine? She is shopping for a new computer because her old computer has failed. She discovered that her picture framing software won't run in any version of Windows, and she's decided that her new computer must have DOS installed so that she can run her picture frame application program—and she's determined to install DOS herself. How will she do this? First, she'll check out the hardware requirements of DOS, then she'll prepare to install DOS, and finally, she will install it.

DOS Hardware Requirements

One of the strong points of DOS is that it can run on the most minimal of PCs—anything from an original 8088-based PC to one of today's lightning-fast Pentium 4 PCs. Therefore, the hardware requirements for DOS are very small. All you need is a personal computer that complies with the old IBM PC standards, or one of its Microsoft/Intel descendents.

Following are general DOS hardware requirements for MS-DOS 6.22 and IBM PC DOS 2000:

- An IBM or compatible personal computer
- 6MB of free hard disk space for the DOS utilities, if installing onto a hard disk
- 512KB of memory

Try This!

How Minimal Are the DOS Requirements?

Computer hardware and prices have come a long way since we bought our first IBM PC for about $5,000. Check out the cheapest computers you can buy for DOS. Try this:

1. Point your Internet browser to the web site of your favorite online computer store (if you don't have a favorite, try `www.dell.com` or `www.gateway.com`).
2. Look for a desktop PC at the cheapest price. Does it meet or exceed the minimum requirements for MS-DOS?

____

Preparing for DOS Installation

To install DOS on a computer hard disk, you must be sure that the computer is physically ready for the installation. That is, make sure the computer is a complete system, with at least the minimal components (see Chapter 1) and that all necessary connections for the components are made. Then, ensure that the computer is plugged into a power outlet.

The computer hard disk does not have to be prepared before the installation, because the MS-DOS 6.22 Setup program can prepare the hard disk. Preparation of a hard disk is a two-step process: the first step is to create a partition, and the second step is to format the partition. A **partition** is an area of a physical hard disk that defines space to be used for file storage. The space within a partition contains one or more logical drives. A logical drive is an area within a partition that is viewed by the OS as a disk drive with a letter assigned to it. (Because this drive is not a physical entity, we use the term *logical* to describe the drive.) These logical drives must, in turn, be formatted by the OS before data can be stored on them. The storage space on a physical hard disk is either a single logical drive, given the letter *C:* when it is the first logical drive on the first hard disk system in a computer, or it can be subdivided into multiple logical drives (for example, C:, D:, E:, and so on).

Partitioning a Hard Disk in MS-DOS

A hard disk comes, fresh from the factory, with its disk space divided into concentric tracks, each of which is divided into equal-sized sectors. This is often referred to as the physical format of the disk. Each sector has a capacity of 512 bytes. The first physical sector on a hard disk is called the master boot record (MBR). Within this sector lies the 64-byte partition table, which a disk partitioning program uses to define the partition boundaries for that hard disk.

The first step in preparing a hard disk for use is to create one or more partitions, the areas of a disk that contain logical drives. Each partition can be formatted with the logical structure required by a file system, often called the logical format. Most operating systems include the partitioning step in a menu-driven process of their installation programs, so that anyone who can answer a few simple questions can at least succeed in creating a partition on which to install the OS. Therefore, most people do not fully understand the basics of partitioning, but this is considered core knowledge for some IT jobs.

Partitioning Programs

While most operating systems include disk partitioning in their setup process, disk partitioning programs come with most operating systems and can be used after the OS is installed to create additional partitions. The one that comes with MS-DOS and with Windows 9*x* is called FDISK. Each of the later versions of Windows has GUI-based partitioning tools. These programs in Windows NT, Windows 2000, Windows XP, and Windows Server 2003 allow for the creation of partitions beyond that on which the OS resides. We'll save discussion of these programs for Chapters 3, 4, and 5. For now, let's look at the basics of hard disk partitioning with MS-DOS' FDISK.

This discussion applies only to standard MS-DOS. Some OEM versions of MS-DOS, as well as third-party DOS operating systems, have partitioning programs that can create more than one primary DOS partition. In addition, they may create larger partitions as well as partition types beyond those discussed here.

Partitioning with FDISK for MS-DOS

> You should use FDISK only after learning how it works. Even then, the safest way to partition a hard disk is from the setup program during the installation of an operating system, because it will include a menu-driven section that will guide you through the disk partitioning process.

Beginning with MS-DOS version 4.0, FDISK can partition hard disks up to 4GB in size, but this partition size is not supported by the FAT16 file system, which is limited to a maximum size of 2GB per partition. Because of this fact, a hard disk larger than 2GB in size must be broken down into multiple partitions, each of which does not exceed 2GB. FDISK can create two types of partitions: primary and extended. A **primary partition** can contain only one logical drive (C:), which uses the entire space of the primary partition, while an **extended partition** can contain one or more logical drives (D:, E:, and so on), each of which can use a portion of the partition. FDISK can create only two partitions on a physical drive; only one can be primary, and one can be extended. MS-DOS will boot from a primary partition, but not from an extended partition. Further, a primary partition must be marked as "active" to be bootable. This is done using the FDISK program. The first hard disk system in a PC being prepared for the installation of MS-DOS must have a primary partition.

The FDISK program is menu-driven. Figure 2-3 shows the FDISK menu for selecting options. If you were preparing a new, unpartitioned hard disk for use, you would first boot from a DOS startup disk that contains the FDISK and FORMAT programs. You would run FDISK, selecting option 1, which would display a menu from which you could choose to create a primary or extended partition, or to create a logical drive on an extended partition (required only for extended partitions). You would select to create a primary partition; then you would follow the instructions, return to this main FDISK options menu, and select option 2, Set Active Partition (or it will not be bootable). Then, after a reboot, run the DOS FORMAT command like so: **format c: /s**. This will format C: and install the system files (discussed later). A partitioned hard drive cannot be used until it is formatted.

Once a hard disk is formatted with the system, reboot and run the FDISK command. Now you can select option 4, Display Partition Information, and see the partition information, as shown in Figure 2-4.

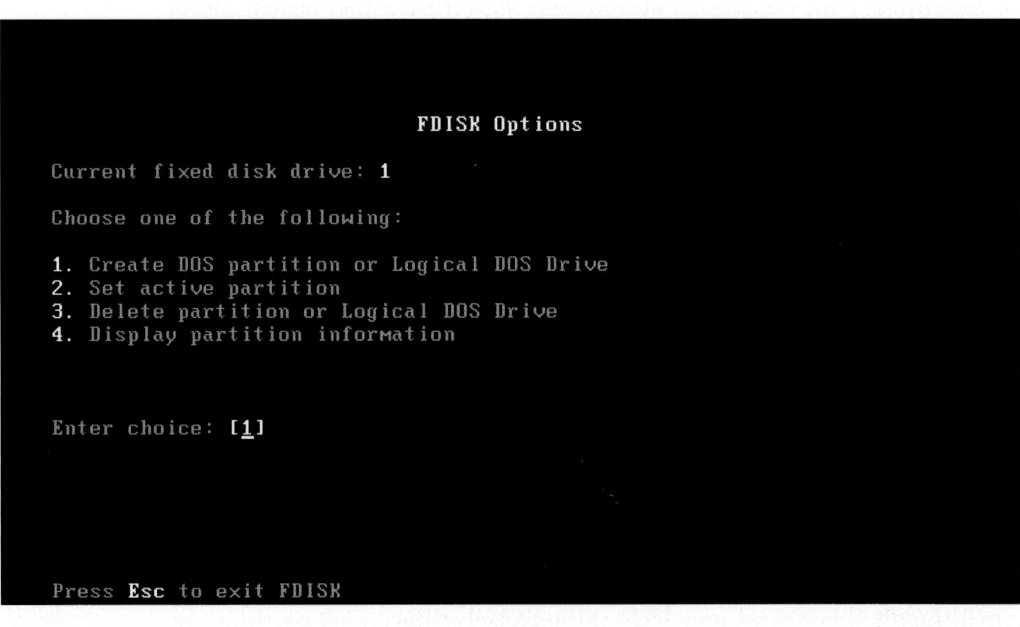

FDISK Options
Current fixed disk drive: 1
Choose one of the following:
1. Create DOS partition or Logical DOS Drive
2. Set active partition
3. Delete partition or Logical DOS Drive
4. Display partition information
Enter choice: [1]
Press Esc to exit FDISK

• **Figure 2-3.** The FDISK Options menu displays the main operations you can perform.

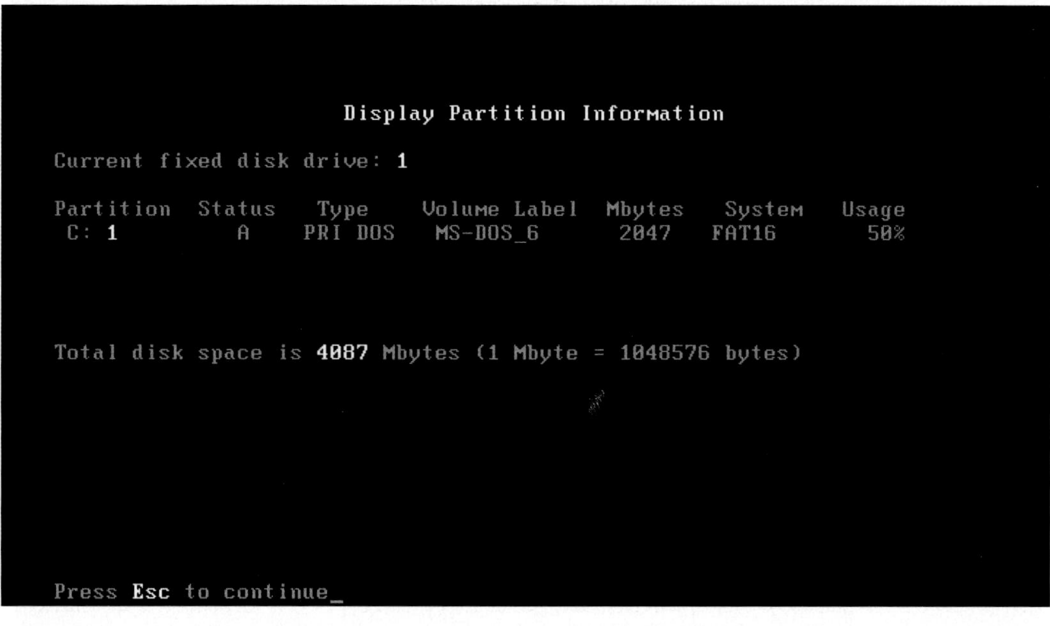

• **Figure 2-4.** The FDISK Display Partition Information page shows the partitioning information for a hard disk.

Cross Check

Using DOS to Prepare a Hard Disk

Consider what you have learned so far about how to use DOS disk utilities. Then answer the following questions:

1. What is the purpose of partitioning a hard disk?

   ____

2. What is the name of the DOS program used for partitioning hard disks?

   ____

3. Once a hard disk contains a partition, what DOS program must you use to further prepare the partitioned space before you can copy files to it?

   ____

Step-by-Step 2.01

Installing DOS on a Hard Disk

In the following steps, you will use the MS-DOS 6.22 setup floppy disks to install DOS on a hard disk. The steps are written assuming that your computer's hard disk is unpartitioned and unformatted. To complete this exercise, you will need the following:

- A Microsoft/Intel standard personal computer (desktop or laptop)
- An unpartitioned hard drive
- The three DOS 6.22 setup disks

Step 1

Insert MS-DOS 6.22 Setup Disk 1 in drive A: and restart the computer. After the computer restarts, you will briefly see a black screen with a message at the top left, "Starting MS-DOS." A blue screen with the "Welcome to Setup" message will follow this. Press ENTER to set up MS-DOS.

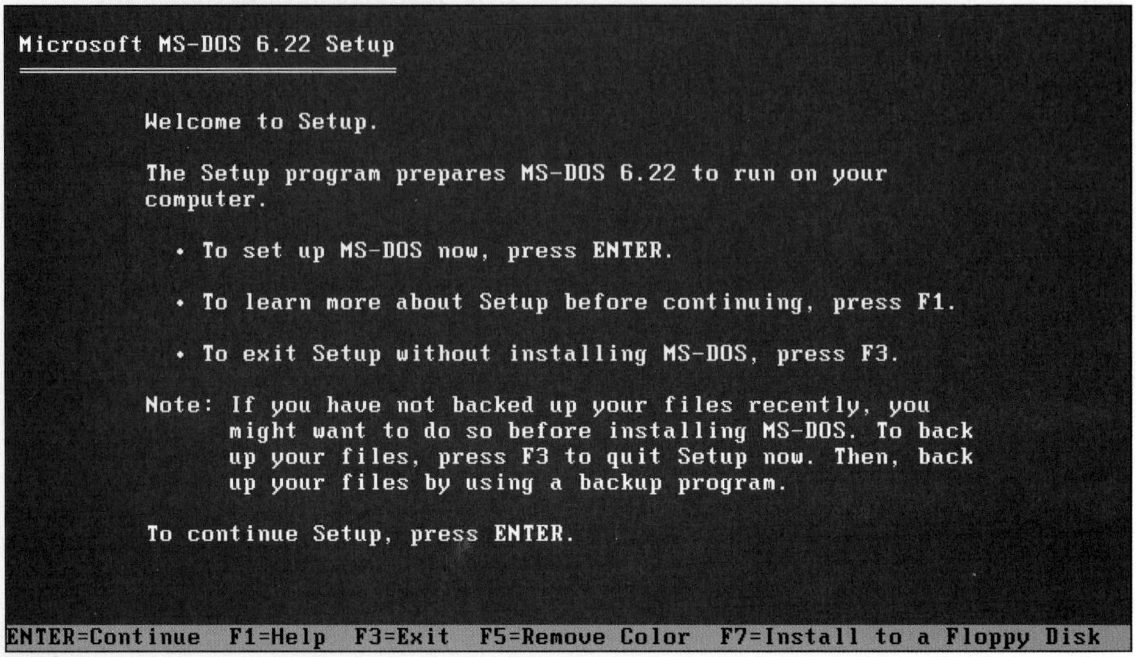

```
Microsoft MS-DOS 6.22 Setup
═══════════════════════════

    Welcome to Setup.

    The Setup program prepares MS-DOS 6.22 to run on your
    computer.

      • To set up MS-DOS now, press ENTER.

      • To learn more about Setup before continuing, press F1.

      • To exit Setup without installing MS-DOS, press F3.

    Note: If you have not backed up your files recently, you
          might want to do so before installing MS-DOS. To back
          up your files, press F3 to quit Setup now. Then, back
          up your files by using a backup program.

    To continue Setup, press ENTER.

ENTER=Continue  F1=Help  F3=Exit  F5=Remove Color  F7=Install to a Floppy Disk
```

Step 2

If your hard disk is unpartitioned, you will see a message saying that Setup needs to configure the unallocated space on your hard disk. With the highlight on Configure Unallocated Disk Space (Recommended), press ENTER.

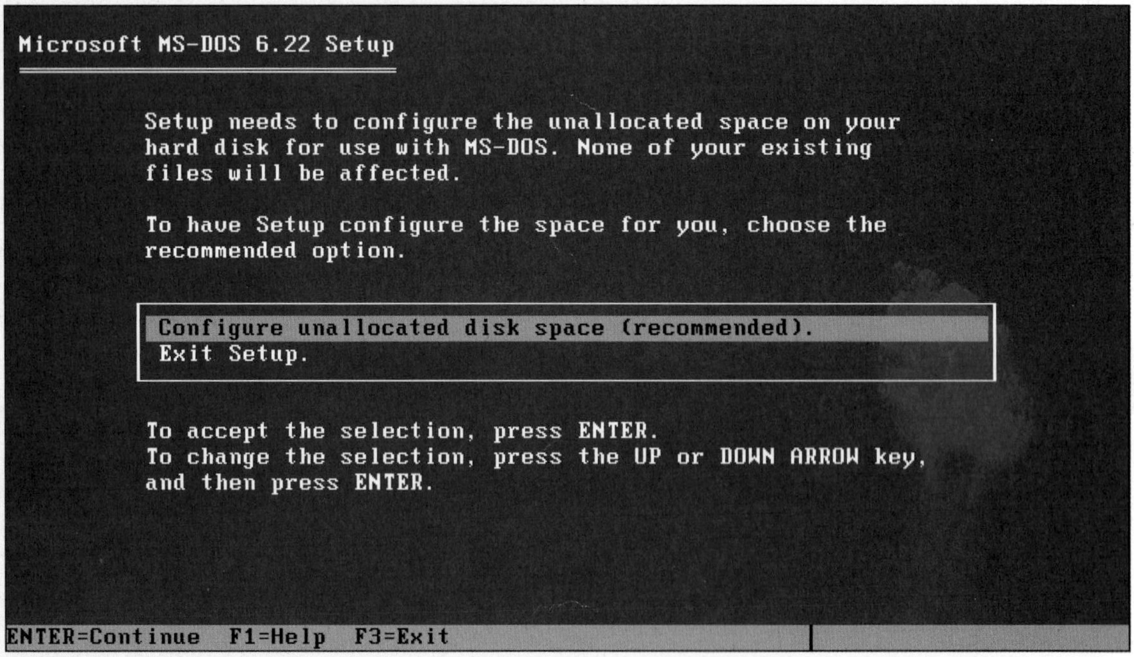

```
Microsoft MS-DOS 6.22 Setup
═══════════════════════════

    Setup needs to configure the unallocated space on your
    hard disk for use with MS-DOS. None of your existing
    files will be affected.

    To have Setup configure the space for you, choose the
    recommended option.

     Configure unallocated disk space (recommended).
     Exit Setup.

    To accept the selection, press ENTER.
    To change the selection, press the UP or DOWN ARROW key,
    and then press ENTER.

ENTER=Continue  F1=Help  F3=Exit
```

Step 3

You will see a message that Setup needs to restart your computer. Be sure Disk 1 is in drive A: and press ENTER to restart. After the restart, you will see the message "Starting MS-DOS" on a black screen, followed by a blue screen and a message saying that Setup is checking your system configuration. Then Setup will format drive C: (which will take a few minutes).

```
Setup will restart your computer now.

Please make sure Setup Disk 1 is in drive A.

• To continue, press ENTER.
```

Step 4

The next screen shows you the system settings Setup will use. This includes the date and time, which Setup found by reading your computer's real-time clock, and the disk and directory where it will install the MS-DOS files. Check the date and time and, if they are correct, continue to Step 5.

If the date or time is not correct, press UP ARROW to move the highlight to the Date/Time line; then press ENTER. Read the instructions on the page that appears, and make the needed correction to the date or time. Then, with the highlight on System Time, press ENTER to return to the previous screen.

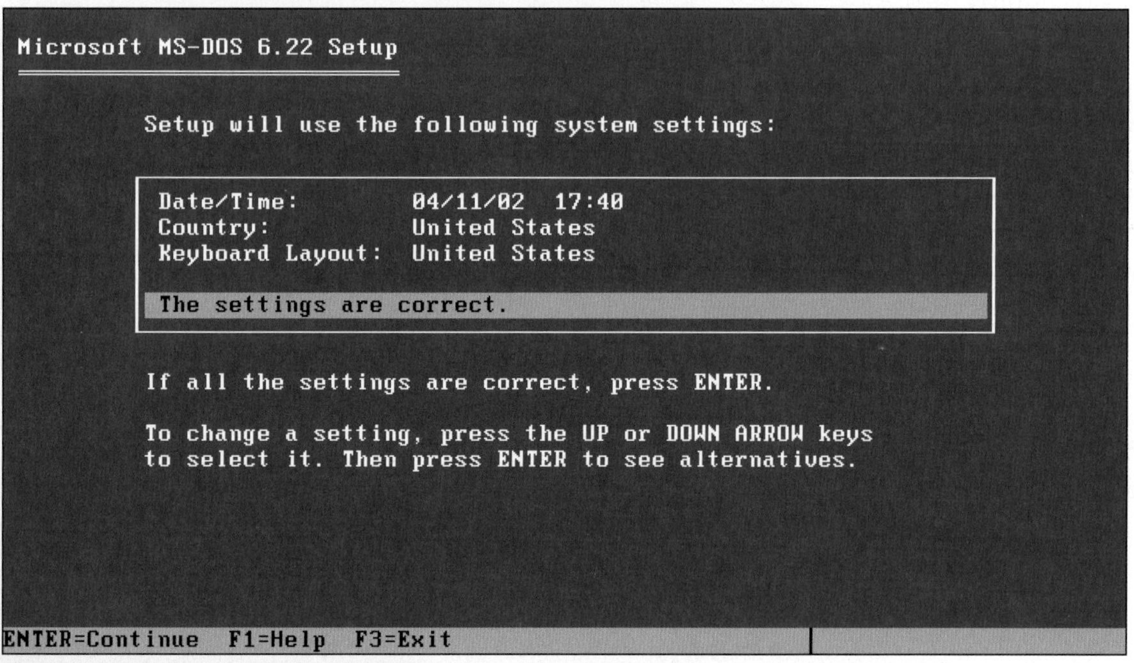

Step 5

Highlight the words *The Settings Are Correct*, and press ENTER to continue the setup process. The next screen shows you the directory to which Setup will copy your MS-DOS files. The default location is C:\DOS. To accept this default, press ENTER.

Step 6

Setup will now copy files onto your hard disk. While it is copying, you can actually see which files are being copied by looking at the bottom right of the screen. A yellow bar shows the progress of the copy operation. Copying from floppy disk is a slow process, but you must still pay attention, because you will be prompted to insert Disk 2 and then Disk 3 at appropriate times as Setup copies files from each of these disks.

```
Microsoft MS-DOS 6.22 Setup

        Now is a great time to fill out your registration card. When
        you send it in, Microsoft will:

           ■ Keep you up to date on the latest product improvements.
           ■ Let you know about related Microsoft products.


          6% complete

                                                    Reading  format.com
```

Step 7

When Setup has copied all the files, you will be prompted to remove all floppy disks. Then press ENTER, and you will see the MS-DOS Setup Complete screen, which prompts you to press ENTER again to restart the computer.

```
MS-DOS Setup Complete

MS-DOS 6.22 is now installed on your computer.

  • To restart your computer with MS-DOS 6.22,
    press ENTER.

  • To learn more about new MS-DOS 6.22 features,
    type HELP WHATSNEW at the command prompt.
```

Step 8

When the computer restarts, you will see a "Starting MS-DOS" message at the top of the screen. This is usually followed by the results of special DOS commands that run during startup, and they will be followed by a **DOS prompt**, which consists of, at minimum, the drive letter followed by a blinking cursor, indicating that the command interpreter is open for business. This is also called the command prompt. Later in this chapter, you will have an opportunity to learn more about working with DOS, and you will run commands at the DOS prompt. When you use the MS-DOS 6.22 Setup program, you may see output resulting from drivers and programs loaded by DOS from commands read from the CONFIG.SYS and AUTOEXEC.BAT files during bootup.

```
Starting MS-DOS...


HIMEM is testing extended memory...done.

C:\>C:\DOS\SMARTDRV.EXE /X
C:\>_
```

How the FAT File System Works

Now that you have installed MS-DOS, you'll learn the FAT file system components that allow an OS to use files and directories, and the file attributes used by an OS to assign certain characteristics to a file or directory.

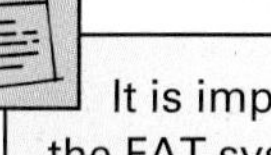

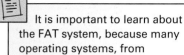

It is important to learn about the FAT system, because many operating systems, from Microsoft and other sources, can work with this file system—even those OSs that can use more advanced file systems.

FAT File System Components

When DOS formats a disk, it places the two primary components of the FAT file system on the disk. These components are the FAT table and the root directory. DOS uses these components to save and retrieve files; you manage your files by creating additional directories under the root directory. The **file allocation table (FAT)** is the component that DOS uses to create a map of where your files reside on disk. A directory is a place where DOS stores information about files, including a reference to the FAT table. Let's consider how these components are organized and how DOS uses them.

FAT Table

The FAT file system gets its name from the acronym for the file allocation table (FAT).

The FAT table is a table in which DOS records how the disk space is used. To do this, DOS divides the entire disk space for one volume (A:, C:, and so on) into equal-sized allocation units called clusters. A **cluster** is the minimum space that can be given to a file, even if the file contains only 14 bytes, and the cluster size is 32,768 bytes. The FAT table has a single entry for each cluster. The entry is a status code, showing that a cluster is empty, occupied, or damaged. If it is occupied, the entry indicates whether the file is continued in another cluster. When saving a file to disk, DOS checks the FAT table to find available space, then updates the FAT table entries for the clusters used for the file. When reading a file from disk, DOS reads the FAT table to determine where all the pieces of the file are located.

FAT12, FAT16, and FAT32

The FAT file system that DOS uses on a hard disk is now called the **FAT16 file system**. It was simply called the FAT file system until an improved version, the **FAT32 file system**, appeared in Windows 95 OEM Service Release version 2 and people had to differentiate between the two. The FAT32 file system can use larger hard disk partitions and allocates disk space more efficiently. Here, in discussing DOS, we will use the term *FAT* to refer to FAT16, unless we want to talk about a feature specific to one of the other versions, in which case, we will use the terms *FAT16* or *FAT32,* as appropriate. And FAT12? That's the file system that DOS and Windows use when they format a floppy disk.

The numbers *12, 16,* and *32* refer to the size of each entry in the FAT table. On a FAT12-formatted floppy disk, each entry is 12 bits long; on a FAT16-formatted drive, each entry is 16 bits long; and on a FAT32-formatted drive, each entry is 32 bits long. The length of the entry limits the number of entries the FAT table can hold, and thus the maximum number of clusters that can be used on a disk. The data space on each disk volume is divided up into the number of clusters the FAT table can handle. There may be one sector per cluster (on a floppy disk), but on hard disk volumes the cluster size may be as large as 64 sectors. Therefore, the FAT32 file system, with its ability to manage more clusters, has the smallest cluster size and wastes the least amount of space.

How Cluster Size Affects Partitions

The FAT file system is limited to 65,525 clusters. The size of a cluster must be a power of 2 and less than 65,536 bytes—this results in a maximum cluster size of 32,768 bytes (32K). Multiplying the maximum number of clusters (65,525) by the maximum cluster size (32,768) equals 2GB, which is therefore the maximum partition size supported by the FAT file system.

```
C:\>dir

 Volume in drive C is MS-DOS_6
 Volume Serial Number is 2C98-8B17
 Directory of C:\

DOS          <DIR>        04-24-02   5:24p
COMMAND  COM        54,645 05-31-94   6:22a
CONFIG   SYS            50 07-25-02  10:18a
AUTOEXEC BAT            68 07-25-02  10:21a
XTREE        <DIR>        07-25-02  12:47p
WORD         <DIR>        07-25-02  12:48p
        6 file(s)         54,763 bytes
                   2,136,473,600 bytes free

C:\>_
```

• Directory listing using the DIR command

Root Directory and Other Directories

A directory is a special file that can contain listings of files and other directories. The **root directory** is the top-level directory, and the only one that the FORMAT command creates. Other programs and users can create additional directories, which will be stored below the root, in a hierarchical structure. A directory that contains other directories is sometimes called a parent directory, and a directory contained within another directory is called a child directory or subdirectory. The information DOS stores in a directory entry for a file includes the file name, extension, date and time of creation or modification, size, attributes, and beginning cluster number. Some of this information is displayed in the directory listing you see when you use the DOS DIR command as shown here.

Using a Directory and the FAT Table to Find a File

How does DOS use a directory and the FAT table to find a file? It uses the directory much like you use a phone directory to find a street address: It searches for the file name in the directory, and when it finds the listing for the file, it learns the starting cluster number (its address) on disk. Then DOS looks up that starting cluster number in the FAT table. The value in the table for that starting cluster tells DOS whether the file spans clusters. If the entire file fits in one cluster, the value in the starting cluster's FAT entry will indicate that the cluster on disk is in use, and that it contains the end of the file. In Figure 2-5, the file AUTOEXEC.BAT shown in the directory begins in cluster 388, and the file allocation table shows that 388 is in use, and that it contains the end of file.

If the file spans two or more clusters, the clusters containing the file's contents are said to be chained together, and the file allocation table will give the address of the next cluster in the chain. The last cluster in the chain contains the end-of-file value. In Figure 2-5 you can see some clusters that are chained to other clusters.

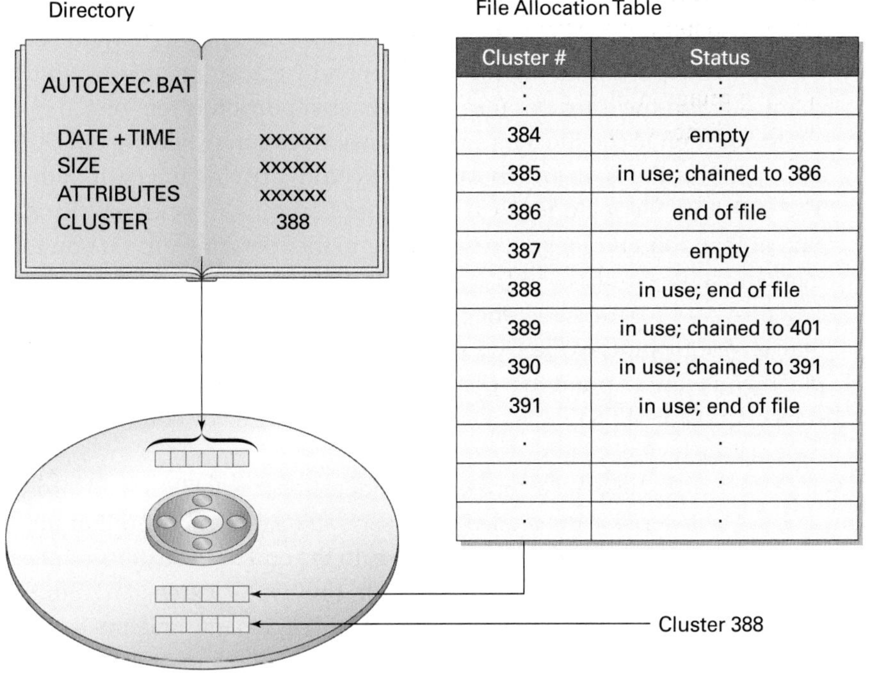

• **Figure 2-5.** DOS uses the directory and the FAT table to find a file.

DOS File-Naming Rules

Try This!

Make DOS Look for a File

The DOS TYPE command displays the contents of a text file on the screen. When you use this command, DOS must find the specified file (AUTOEXEC.BAT in this case) on disk, using the directory information and the FAT information. Try this:

1. Verify that the AUTOEXEC.BAT file is in the root of C: by entering the following: **dir autoexec.bat** and press ENTER.
2. If the AUTOEXEC.BAT file is present, then enter **type c:\autoexec.bat** and press ENTER.

When working with files in DOS, you must understand the rules for naming files, and then you must understand the concept of file type. DOS can only work with files with a file name of up to eight characters, followed by a period, followed by an extension of up to three characters. This basic rule of file naming is called the 8.3 ("eight-dot-three") naming convention. But wait—there is more to it than that. Aside from the dot, which separates the file name from the extension, within the file name and extension you can only use alphanumeric (A to Z and 1 to 0) characters, no spaces, and only a few special characters. These special characters are

$ & # @ ! % ' ^ ( ) - _

Other characters, including math symbols and punctuation characters, are illegal or invalid characters in file names. They are

/ \ [ ] | < > + = ; , * ?

Examples of valid DOS 8.3 file names are README.TXT, FORMAT.COM, FDISK.EXE, AUTOEXEC.BAT, MONOUMB.386, and CONFIG.SYS.

Make life easier for yourself. Don't try to memorize the valid characters—just avoid using anything but alphanumeric characters, or you will make file naming more complicated than it needs to be, and wonder why DOS will not accept your clever file names!

Examples of illegal DOS 8.3 file names are READTHOSE.TXT, FORMAT[.COM, and README.FILE. The first file name is invalid because the file name portion is too long; the second because it contains an illegal character; and the third because the extension portion is too long.

In addition to the file name and extension, you may need to tell DOS exactly where a file is, in which case you need to provide the path to the file. The path to a file includes the drive letter (C:) plus a backslash (\). If you stop at that point (C:\), you are pointing to the root directory. If you follow that with a file name (C:\AUTOEXEC.BAT, for instance), DOS looks in the root directory for the file. If the file is in a subdirectory, you need to include that. C:\DOS points to the DOS subdirectory of the root directory, for example. If you want to point to a file in that directory, you add the name: for instance, C:\DOS\EDIT.COM. Directories within directories are separated by the backslash symbol (\).

In two decades of working with DOS, we have used the asterisk wildcard character about a thousand times more than the question-mark wildcard character. Don't waste too much brainpower on the question-mark character.

You can also use the asterisk (*) and question mark (?) as wildcard characters. The asterisk can be used to replace all characters from that point to the end of the file name, or all characters to the end of the extension. For example, *.DOC refers to all files with the DOC extension. Similarly, README.* refers to all files with the README file name and any extension. The question mark replaces a single character for each instance of the question mark. For instance, DISKCO??.COM refers to all files that match on the provided characters and have any characters in the seventh or eighth place of the file name.

DOS File Types

DOS recognizes several different file types. Some of these file types contain text data, and others contain program code and are referred to as binary files. We don't make DOS guess which is which; we identify the file type of a file with a special extension. Following is a list of common file extensions and the file types each identifies to DOS:

BAK	A file containing backup data
BAS	A BASIC program file
BAT	A batch file (a special text file in which each line is treated like a command at the DOS prompt)
COM	An executable binary file (a program)
DOC	A word processor data file, usually containing text plus the special codes for formatting the text when printed
EXE	An executable binary file using a more complicated structure than a COM file (a program)
SYS	A device driver or operating system file
TXT	A file containing text without special codes for formatting the text

Executable Files

DOS considers three types of files to be executable: COM, EXE, and BAT. COM and EXE files both contain programming code; the difference between these two types of files is not important to us in this chapter. BAT files are batch files, which are not programs, but text files that contain commands that you could type at the command prompt, but which you choose to put in a batch file. When DOS executes a batch file, it uses the command interpreter to interpret each line of the batch file. The batch file acts like a script for the command interpreter. This is called batch processing. Batch processing is a great way to automate tasks you perform frequently. Perhaps you back up the files you are working on every day by copying them to floppy disk; you could create a batch file to automate this process.

Step-by-Step 2.02

Creating a Simple Batch File

You can easily create the batch file for copying files from your hard drive to floppy disk. You would normally do this with data files, but we will do it with some of the files in your DOS directory.

To complete this exercise, you will need

- A computer with MS-DOS 6.22 installed (If you do not have an MS-DOS computer, these steps can be run at the Windows command prompt.)
- A blank formatted floppy disk

Step 1

At the command prompt, type **edit xback.bat** and press ENTER. This opens the EDIT program and names the batch file you are creating. In the Edit program, type the text shown in the illustration, pressing ENTER at the end of each line.

```
 File  Edit  Search  Options                                      Help
                            XBACK.BAT
@ECHO OFF
ECHO Data files will be copied to A:
ECHO Please insert a blank formatted diskette, Then...
PAUSE
XCOPY C:\DOS\*.TXT A:
XCOPY C:\DOS\*.INI A:
ECHO All data files have been copied.
ECHO Remove the diskette and store in a safe place.

F1=Help   Enter=Display Menu   Esc=Cancel   Arrow=Next Item  |  00003:052
```

Step 2

Check your spelling. Case is not significant to DOS. You can enter commands in either uppercase or lowercase. We have used mixed case for the messages that will be displayed, to make this information more readable here. When you are sure that your file is free of typos, save it by pressing ALT plus the F key (they do not have to be simultaneously pressed), which will open the File menu. At the File menu, press S for Save. It will save the file in your current directory, which should be the root directory at present, since we have not yet taught you to change the current directory.

Step 3

Leave the Edit program by selecting the File menu (ALT-F) and pressing X for Exit. Check for the presence of the file at the DOS prompt by typing **dir**. Confirm that XBACK.BAT is listed.

Step 4

Test the batch file by typing **xback** and pressing ENTER. If your batch file is working correctly, you should see the message you typed on the second and third lines of the batch file without the command ECHO at the beginning of the line. We used the ECHO command in two ways here. First, we used ECHO OFF to turn off the echoing of the commands to the screen. We preceded that command with the @ symbol, which turns off echoing of that line to the screen. After that, everything that appears on the screen is the result of the commands, not the commands themselves. The PAUSE command pauses the execution of the commands in the batch file until you press a key. It's the PAUSE command that sends the message "Press any key to continue…".

Step 5

Follow the instructions and press any key. Once more, you do not see the command lines from the batch file, just the results of the commands (the message each command sends to the screen). When the processing is complete, you will see the last two lines of messages. This is a very simple batch file. It could be improved in many ways, but it is a great beginning if you have never created a batch file before.

```
C:\>xback
Data files will be copied to A:
Please insert a blank formatted diskette, Then...
Press any key to continue . . .

Reading source file(s)...
C:\DOS\COUNTRY.TXT
C:\DOS\README.TXT
C:\DOS\NETWORKS.TXT
C:\DOS\DRVSPACE.TXT
        4 File(s) copied
Reading source file(s)...
C:\DOS\DOSSETUP.INI
C:\DOS\SCANDISK.INI
        2 File(s) copied
All data files have been copied.
Remove the diskette and store in a safe place.
C:\>_
```

DOS File Attributes

In addition to file types, DOS uses **file attributes** that are saved in each file or directory entry. These attributes determine how DOS handles the file. For instance, if the file attribute for directory is turned on, or *set*, then the file entry is for a directory, and, rather than pointing to the location of a file, it points to another directory listing. The DOS file attributes are as follows:

- **read-only** An attribute that indicates that a file may not be modified or deleted. DOS automatically puts this attribute on certain files as a small measure of protection. Anyone using a program that ignores this attribute, or using a program that lets them turn off this attribute, can delete the read-only file.
- **archive** An attribute that, when turned on, indicates that a file has been created or modified since the last backup. DOS places this attribute on all new or changed files. Most backup programs can turn off this attribute for each file backed up.
- **system** A special attribute that DOS gives to the system files, IO.SYS and MSDOS.SYS.
- **hidden** An attribute that will cause a file or directory to be hidden from programs that pay attention to this attribute, such as the DIR command.
- **volume label** An attribute used for a special root directory entry, which can be used to give a disk a label or name.
- **directory** An attribute that indicates that the entry is a directory, not a file.

It is worth learning about these attributes, because they are used in the FAT file system in all OSs, and because later, when you work with newer file systems, you will discover that they also have attributes—and some are identical to the FAT file attributes. How are these attributes used? For example, when you format a disk, as shown in Figure 2-6, you may give the disk a name, which is stored as a special file with the volume label attribute.

Try This!

Label Your Disk Electronically!

Format a floppy disk, adding a volume label during the formatting. Then change the label to a different name. You will need a floppy disk that is expendable. Try this:

1. Place the floppy disk in the drive, and at the DOS prompt, type **format a:** and press ENTER.
2. When prompted for a volume label, enter your first name (up to 11 characters) and press ENTER. When asked if you would like to format another, press N and ENTER.
3. Change the volume label. At the DOS prompt, type **label** and press ENTER. When prompted for a volume label, type **datadisk1** and press ENTER.

If a hard disk drive has a volume label and you attempt to format it again, the MS-DOS Format program asks for the volume label name before it will complete the formatting. This is not actually a security measure, since you can use the VOL command or the DIR command to see the volume label, but it does make you stop and maybe think before formatting a disk. That may be just enough to

```
C:\>FORMAT A: /U
Insert new diskette for drive A:
and press ENTER when ready...

Formatting 1.44M
Format complete.

Volume label (11 characters, ENTER for none)? DATADISK1_
```

• **Figure 2-6.** Adding a volume label with the FORMAT command

make you realize that you are trying to format the wrong drive! If you want to add or modify a volume label after formatting a drive, use the LABEL command.

You should never change the directory attribute manually, because it is created by the OS when it creates a directory. This attribute tells the OS that this is not an ordinary file, but a directory. Likewise you shouldn't mess with the system attribute, because it is used by the OS to identify its own special files, such as IO.SYS and MSDOS.SYS. Also it's important for a computer professional to understand the read-only and hidden attributes, because the first one may keep you from editing a file someday, and the second one may keep you from seeing a file on disk. You will soon have opportunities to work with each of these attributes.

One way to display and modify some of these attributes is to use the ATTRIB command, as shown in Figure 2-7. The DOS

Try This!

Make a File Read-Only!

Use the ATTRIB command to make a file read-only. Try this:

1. Use the DIR command to view the list of files in the current directory, and from the files displayed, choose one to use in the next few steps, using its file name and extension when you see *filename.ext*.
2. At the command prompt, type **attrib +r** *filename.ext* and press ENTER.
3. Confirm that the file is now read-only with the Attrib command: type **attrib** and press ENTER.
4. If an *R* is displayed by the file name, it is read-only. Try deleting this file: type **del** *filename.ext*.
5. Remove the read-only attribute: type **attrib -r** *filename.ext*.

Cross Check

The FAT File System

Now that you have learned about the FAT file system, answer the following questions:

1. Consider the components of the FAT file system, and briefly describe the component that gives this file system its name.
2. You have used the DIR command, and in the resulting list of files you see a file with an EXE extension. What type of file should have this extension?
3. Briefly explain the archive attribute.

ATTRIB command lets you view and manipulate all but the directory and volume label attributes. This is an important command if you work with DOS and need to modify a file that has the read-only attribute, or want to make a file read-only to protect it. The ATTRIB command works in all versions of Windows on both the FAT and the newer NTFS file systems. NTFS stands for NT File System, an advanced file system available with the Windows NT, Windows 2000, Windows XP, and Windows 2003 Server OSs.

```
C:\>attrib
     SHR          C:\IO.SYS
     SHR          C:\MSDOS.SYS
       R          C:\COMMAND.COM
  A               C:\WINA20.386
  A               C:\CONFIG.SYS
  A               C:\AUTOEXEC.BAT

C:\>_
```

• **Figure 2-7.** Using the ATTRIB command to view file attributes

Working with the DOS Command Prompt

At a minimum, you need to know the ins and outs of working at the DOS prompt and with the online Help system. You also need to become proficient with the handful of DOS commands that are the most useful for managing directories and files. We'll discuss each in turn.

Success at the DOS Prompt

Up to this point, we have done a few things at the command prompt without much instruction. Were you successful, or did you receive confusing error messages? Success at the DOS prompt is important to you because you will need to use a similar command prompt in almost any OS you encounter as a computer professional—not every day perhaps, but when you want to run small programs that perform a useful administrative or diagnostic task for you. Success at the DOS prompt means correctly entering commands and getting the results you desired. Before you can achieve either of these goals, you need to discover which command will accomplish the task you have in mind, determine the correct syntax for that command, and finally, understand how to correctly enter a command at the command prompt. This requires that you understand how a command is interpreted.

Which Command Will Accomplish the Task?

To discover which command will accomplish the task you have in mind, you must do some detective work. One way to do this is to ask an experienced DOS nerd. Since you probably won't have someone like that handy all the time, a good substitute is the DOS HELP program. Learn to use it! DOS has a fairly simple help program that does not allow you to conduct the more sophisticated searches you will find in other OS help programs. However, many of the command names are actually related to the task the command performs, unlike some of the Linux commands you will study later in this book. At the command prompt, simply type **help**, and you will get a listing of MS-DOS commands with descriptions. Browse through the list to find the command you need.

MS-DOS HELP has onscreen instructions, which are helpful, except that they neglect to tell you that you can use the arrow keys to move the selection highlight and use the ENTER key to select a highlighted item.

Step-by-Step 2.03

Using the Online Help in DOS

In the following steps you will learn how to navigate through the DOS HELP program so that you can turn to HELP whenever you are unsure of what command to use and how to use it. You will also take this opportunity to learn more about the ATTRIB command.

To complete this exercise, you will need:

- A computer with MS-DOS 6.22 installed (If you do not have an MS-DOS computer, these steps can be run at the Windows command prompt.)

Step 1

At the DOS prompt, type **help** and press ENTER. Notice the instructions at the top. If you performed a standard DOS 6.22 installation, you will not have a mouse driver installed and will therefore not be able to use the scroll bars, but you can move around using both the PAGE UP and PAGE DOWN keys and the UP ARROW and DOWN ARROW keys. Press PAGE DOWN to see more of the commands. Press PAGE UP to return to the top of the page.

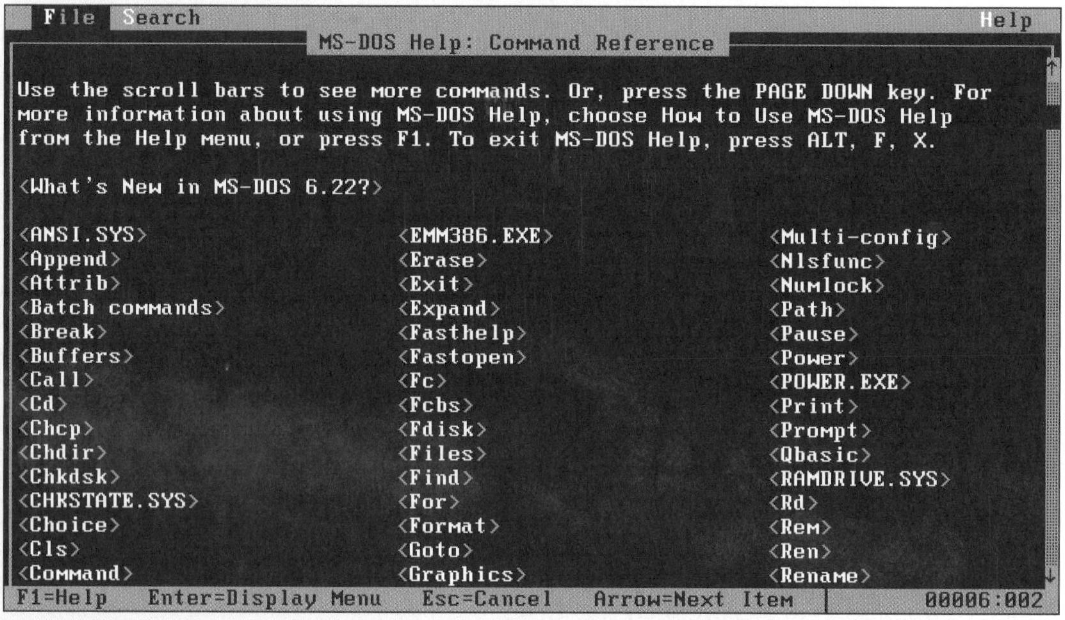

```
 File  Search                                                          Help
                    MS-DOS Help: Command Reference

Use the scroll bars to see more commands. Or, press the PAGE DOWN key. For
more information about using MS-DOS Help, choose How to Use MS-DOS Help
from the Help menu, or press F1. To exit MS-DOS Help, press ALT, F, X.

<What's New in MS-DOS 6.22?>

<ANSI.SYS>                  <EMM386.EXE>                <Multi-config>
<Append>                    <Erase>                     <Nlsfunc>
<Attrib>                    <Exit>                      <Numlock>
<Batch commands>            <Expand>                    <Path>
<Break>                     <Fasthelp>                  <Pause>
<Buffers>                   <Fastopen>                  <Power>
<Call>                      <Fc>                        <POWER.EXE>
<Cd>                        <Fcbs>                      <Print>
<Chcp>                      <Fdisk>                     <Prompt>
<Chdir>                     <Files>                     <Qbasic>
<Chkdsk>                    <Find>                      <RAMDRIVE.SYS>
<CHKSTATE.SYS>              <For>                       <Rd>
<Choice>                    <Format>                    <Rem>
<Cls>                       <Goto>                      <Ren>
<Command>                   <Graphics>                  <Rename>
F1=Help   Enter=Display Menu   Esc=Cancel   Arrow=Next Item     00006:002
```

Step 2

Press ALT and then H followed by ENTER to access the How To Use MS-DOS Help page. It lists seven topics, each enclosed in green brackets. The cursor should be on the first topic, Navigating Through MS-DOS Help. If it isn't, use the TAB key to move there, and then press ENTER to select and read the topic.

Step 3

Read through that topic, and then press and hold ALT while pressing B (ALT-B) to go back to the topic list. Continue through all seven topics, reading the explanations provided. When you are finished, press ESC (twice if necessary) to return to the main MS-DOS Help page.

Step 4

Select the ATTRIB command and press ENTER to view the help information on ATTRIB and to learn how you can see the file attributes of all the files in the current directory.

Step 5 When you are finished, press ALT, then F, and then X to exit MS-DOS HELP and return to the DOS prompt.

Step 6 Now apply what you learned from the MS-DOS HELP program. At the DOS prompt, use the ATTRIB command to see the file attributes of the files in the root of C:.

What Is the Correct Syntax?

You know how to find the command that will accomplish the task, but you also need to know how to tell the command exactly what to do. This requires that you know the syntax of the command. **Syntax** is a set of rules for correctly entering a specific command at the command line. This includes the command name and the parameters that act as instructions to the command. You can use the DOS HELP program to find the syntax for a command, or you can type the command name followed by the "/?" parameter. Figure 2-8 shows the result of typing COPY /? at the command prompt.

Try This!

Check Out the Syntax for DOS Commands

Once you know the name of a DOS command, you can easily discover the correct syntax. Try this:

1. At the DOS command prompt, type **chkdsk /?** and press ENTER. If you are using MS-DOS 6.22, you may be surprised at the suggestion in the last paragraph of the screen output. It recommends that you use SCANDISK rather than CHKDSK.
2. Check out another command: at the DOS command prompt, type **xcopy /?** and press ENTER.

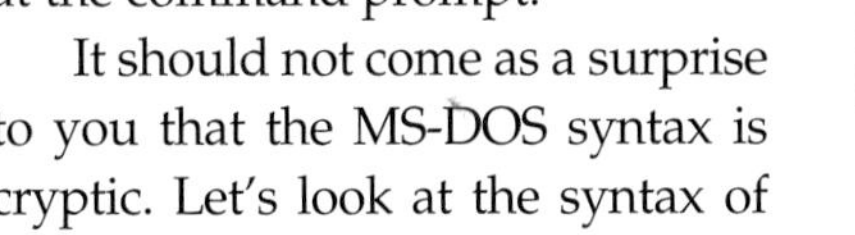

It should not come as a surprise to you that the MS-DOS syntax is cryptic. Let's look at the syntax of the COPY command. To correctly enter the COPY command, you must first type **copy** followed by the optional and required parameters in the order shown. All optional parameters are shown in square brackets with required parameters shown without brackets. The brackets, of course, are not to be used in the actual command line. The source is the only required parameter, and it is the file or files to be copied (you can include the path to a file, as in **c:\dos**). The destination is not required, but if you don't provide it, the directory you're currently in will be assumed.

How Is a Command Interpreted?

At the command prompt, you might enter a command like **dir**, which is only the name of a command. Or, you might enter a command that includes both the command name and instructions to the command, as in **dir a: /a**. In any case, what you enter at the command prompt is interpreted by a special component of your OS called the command interpreter, which in MS-DOS is COMMAND.COM. This component receives commands, finds the actual program code for the command, loads the program code into memory, and passes any additional instructions (such as the **a: /a**) to the command.

Some commands have no additional instructions, such as the VER command, which only displays the MS-DOS version and nothing else, but most DOS commands have many instructions you can use. The list of such commands is quite long, but they include DEL, COPY, REN, and XCOPY, just to name a few. In fact, many commands will not work without additional

Strictly speaking, DOS does not require a space before switches (parameters that begin with a forward slash like /a). But you should get into the habit of always placing a space before each parameter when you type a command, because spaces are required between all parameters when you enter commands from the Start | Run menu in Windows.

```
C:\>copy /?
Copies one or more files to another location.

COPY [/A | /B] source [/A | /B] [+ source [/A | /B] [+ ...]] [destination
  [/A | /B]] [/V] [/Y | /-Y]

  source       Specifies the file or files to be copied.
  /A           Indicates an ASCII text file.
  /B           Indicates a binary file.
  destination  Specifies the directory and/or filename for the new file(s).
  /V           Verifies that new files are written correctly.
  /Y           Suppresses prompting to confirm you want to overwrite an
               existing destination file.
  /-Y          Causes prompting to confirm you want to overwrite an
               existing destination file.

The switch /Y may be preset in the COPYCMD environment variable.
To append files, specify a single file for destination, but multiple files
for source (using wildcards or file1+file2+file3 format).

C:\>_
```

• **Figure 2-8.** The COPY command syntax

instructions. Figure 2-9 shows the output to the screen after we ran all the commands listed in the preceding sentence without any command parameters. Notice that only the VER command works successfully without any further instructions.

Let's look at this process more closely. When you type something into the command line and press ENTER, the DOS command interpreter kicks into action behind the scenes. It takes what you entered at the command line and parses it. In this context, **parse** means to divide the command into its components. DOS' command interpreter parses your entry based on special delimiter characters. The most important delimiter character to remember is the space character (the result of pressing the space bar). When a command line is parsed, the components are called parameters. For instance, **dir /a:/a** has three parameters: dir, a:, and /a. The first parameter must be the command; the other parameters must be valid parameters that the command understands. A parameter that begins with a forward slash (/) is called a switch.

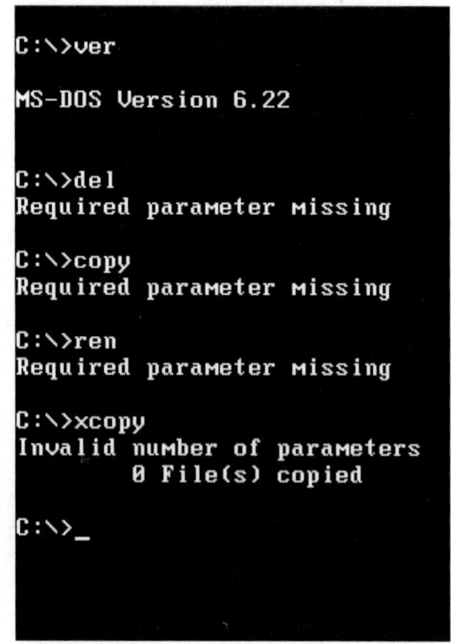

```
C:\>ver

MS-DOS Version 6.22


C:\>del
Required parameter missing

C:\>copy
Required parameter missing

C:\>ren
Required parameter missing

C:\>xcopy
Invalid number of parameters
        0 File(s) copied

C:\>_
```

• **Figure 2-9.** Parameter error messages

How Is a Program Found and Loaded?

The next job for the DOS command interpreter is to load the command named at the beginning of the command line. DOS looks for the command by searching in some special places. Let's say you entered the command CHKDSK. You have not provided a file name extension with the command (which is quite normal), so DOS will first check its own list of **internal commands**. These commands reside within COMMAND.COM and are not stored as separate files on disk. If it finds the command name in that list, DOS doesn't search any further and loads the code into memory, passing on any other parameters that were on the command line. Internal commands are fast because they are small and are already in memory as part of COMMAND.COM.

Our example command, CHKDSK, is not an internal command, which DOS will discover after checking the list of internal commands. Now DOS will look for an external command that matches. An **external command** is a file stored on disk that contains instructions and has one of the following extensions: COM, EXE, or BAT. Typing **chkdsk.exe** on the command line would have told DOS earlier that this was an external command. Because we didn't include the file name extension, DOS is still not sure about the exact file. Now DOS will look for a match, using those extensions. But wait! Where does DOS look for external commands? It first looks in the current directory, and then it consults a list called the search path. The search path is controlled by the PATH command, which should be included in the AUTOEXEC.BAT file. If the PATH command looks like path=c:\dos;c:\word, then to find the CHKDSK command after it has searched the internal list and the current directory, DOS searches in the C:\DOS directory and then in the C:\WORD directory. In each location, DOS first looks for CHKDSK.COM, CHKDSK.EXE, and then CHKDSK.BAT, in that order. If it finds a match, it loads the program into memory and doesn't look any further. In the case of CHKDSK, it would stop after finding CHKDSK.EXE in C:\DOS. Since DOS' external commands can be used only when DOS can find them on disk, they may not be available to use if they haven't been installed.

There are about 30 internal commands, but you will use only about half of them frequently. They include CD, CLS, COPY, DATE, DIR, MD, PATH, PROMPT, ECHO, REM, RD, SET, TIME, TYPE, VER, and VOL. Use the DOS HELP program to learn more about these commands.

Learning to Manage Files and Directories

DOS has a no-frills file management system that is centered on the abilities and limits of the FAT file system. To manage files in DOS, you need to consider strategies for organizing your data in the FAT file system, and you need to know the commands you will use to do this. This is worth learning, because every Microsoft OS and most UNIX OSs can use the FAT file system. Therefore, skills you learn here can be applied in OSs other than DOS.

The DOS directory holds 50 external DOS commands, but you will normally only use a handful, including ATTRIB.EXE, CHKDSK.EXE, DELTREE.EXE, DISKCOPY.COM, EDIT.COM, FORMAT.COM, MEM.EXE, PRINT.EXE, SCANDISK.EXE, SYS.COM, TREE.COM, XCOPY, and UNDELETE.EXE.

Designing a Directory Structure for File Management

Earlier, you studied how the root directory is used by DOS. Now you will take a different view of the root directory as you decide what directories to create within it to hold your data files. You can even create directories within directories, so your directory design can get pretty fancy.

When it comes to organizing data in your computer, think "office supplies," and imagine that your computer is a filing cabinet and that each logical drive (with its root directory) is a drawer in that cabinet. The directories you create at the root would be the large hanging folders, and the directories created at the next level are the smaller folders placed within the hanging folders.

Of course, individual files can be placed in any of these directories, but you should design a directory structure that works for your own need to save and organize your files. Always reserve the root directory for the files needed by the OS during startup and for your top-level subdirectories.

You should never save data files in the root directory because doing so is like dumping things into a filing cabinet drawer without using folders and dividers to organize them. A technical reason for not saving files in the root directory is that, unlike subdirectories, the root directory can't grow. If everything is saved into the root directory, it will eventually reach its limit, and you will get a "Disk Full" error message, even though the disk isn't full!

```
C:\>TREE
Directory PATH listing for Volume MS-DOS_6
Volume Serial Number is 2C98-8B17
C:.
├───DOS
├───DATA
└───APPS
    ├───EXCEL
    └───WORD

C:\>_
```

• **Figure 2-10.** Directories viewed with the TREE command

Figure 2-10 shows the result of using the DOS TREE command to view directories. The DOS setup program created the DOS directory, but a user created the other directories. The DATA directory is where he stores all his data files, while the APPS directory is where he installs all his applications. The directory C:\APPS\EXCEL contains the Microsoft Excel program files, while the directory C:\APPS\WORD contains the Microsoft Word program files. The word processing and spreadsheet files that he creates with these two programs are saved in the DATA directory. The logic behind this design, in which the applications are stored in one directory hierarchy and the data is saved in another directory structure, has to do with backups.

Whether he does his backups with an actual backup program or simply uses the XCOPY command, he can start his backup at the top level (DATA or APPS) and back up the contents of all child directories. His data files change more frequently than the application files, so he will want to back up the DATA directory more often than the APPS directory.

Creating and Removing Directories

Let's say you want to create several new directories to organize your data files. Remember that the directory structure is hierarchical; that is, a directory can contain other directories as well as files. The hierarchy is Drive | Directory | File Name. Remember that a directory that contains other directories is a *parent* directory, and a directory inside a parent directory is a *child* directory, or subdirectory.

The DOS command to create a directory is MD (Make Directory). The syntax is MD [*drive*:]*path*.

The DOS command to move between directories has two possible common names: CD and CHDIR. Both stand for Change Directory and are identical in function. You use the change directory command to change the current directory. After executing either command, you will be in the new directory, and any subsequent commands that you issue that operate on a directory will operate on the directory you are currently in.

Try This!

View Your Directories

If you installed DOS on your lab computer hard disk in Step-by-Step 2.01, you can look at the root directory and a child or subdirectory. Try this:

1. Start your computer. When DOS appears, you will be at the root directory.
2. To see the contents of the root directory, at the command prompt type **dir** and press ENTER. You will see some files and a single directory, DOS.
3. To view the entire directory structure, at the command prompt type **tree** and press ENTER.
4. To look at the contents of the DOS directory, at the command prompt type **dir dos** and press ENTER.
5. To learn more about the DIR command, at the command prompt type **dir /?** and press ENTER.

Use File Management Commands

DOS has several commands you can use for file management tasks. These commands let you copy, move, and delete files, as well as create, move, and delete directories. Remember that some of these commands are internal commands, which are loaded into memory along with DOS, ready to run whenever you need them. These small and fast commands include DIR (Directory), CD (Change Directory), CLS (CLear Screen), COPY, REN (REName), MD (Make Directory), CD (Change Directory), TYPE, and RD (Remove Directory).

Three often-used external commands, XCOPY, DISKCOPY, and DELTREE, are enhancements to internal commands. For instance, XCOPY and DISKCOPY can copy in ways that the internal COPY command can't. XCOPY can copy files and entire directories, while COPY can only copy files—it has no understanding of directories. DISKCOPY can make a floppy disk-to-floppy disk copy, creating an exact duplicate of the original floppy disk. The DELTREE command can delete an entire directory and its contents, while the internal RD (Remove Directory) command can only delete an empty directory.

Another external command is the HELP command (HELP.COM), which you used in Step-by-Step 2.03. In the next Step-by-Step you will use DOS commands to manage files and directories.

One convenient shortcut when moving between directories is to use the double dot (..). When you type **cd ..** (or **chdir ..**), you move to the parent directory of the directory you are in. Thus, you can easily move up a hierarchy without having to enter the name of each parent directory. Similarly, **cd ** moves you directly to the root.

A number of DOS commands have alternate forms. Use whichever form you can remember most easily.

Step-by-Step 2.04

Managing Files and Directories

Let's practice. Say you want to create a new directory named testdata in the root of C:, copy several files into it, examine the files to make sure they are there, and then delete those copied files and the testdata directory.

To complete this exercise, you will need:

- A computer with MS-DOS 6.22 installed (If you do not have an MS-DOS computer, these steps can be run at the Windows command prompt.)

Step 1

At the DOS prompt, type **dir** and press ENTER.

A listing of files and directories in the root (C:\) will be displayed.

Step 2

To move down one level into the DOS directory, type **cd dos** and press ENTER.

Your screen display should look like the one shown here.

```
C:\>dir

 Volume in drive C is MS-DOS_6
 Volume Serial Number is 2C98-8B17
 Directory of C:\

DOS          <DIR>         04-24-02   5:24p
COMMAND  COM        54,645 05-31-94   6:22a
WINA20   386         9,349 05-31-94   6:22a
CONFIG   SYS            71 04-29-02   8:51p
AUTOEXEC BAT            78 04-24-02   6:02p
        5 file(s)       64,143 bytes
                 2,138,013,696 bytes free

C:\>cd dos

C:\DOS>_
```

Step 3

Type **dir** and press ENTER.

You probably only saw a blur as over 5MB of files contained in C:\DOS went streaming past. Clearly you need to do something else to examine the directories contained in C:\DOS.

Step 4

Type **dir /?** and press ENTER to get a listing of the available syntax for the DIR command. Notice that if you use the /p (for Pause) switch, the listing will pause after each screenful of data. Try it now. Type **dir /p** and press ENTER. You can now examine the contents of C:\DOS screenful by screenful. Continue to press ENTER until all screens have been displayed and you are back at the C: prompt.

Step 5

Try a few more switches: type **dir /w** to see a wide listing of directory contents. Then try variations of the sort order switch (dir /o). Try **dir /on** to sort on name.

Step 6

To return to the root of C:, type **cd ..** (that's two periods or dots) and press ENTER—you are now back at the root of C:. Test this by typing **dir**. CD .. actually only takes you up one level, so if you are more than one level below the root and find that you are not back to the root, you may need to issue the command more than once to move up to the root. You can also type CD \, a command that will always take you back to the root of the current drive.

Step 7

To create your testdata directory, type **md testdata** and press ENTER.

Step 8

DOS usually will tell you when a command does not work, but when a command does work, there is often no apparent evidence that it did—so you have to check to see whether it did work. One common way to check is to type **dir** again and read the listing to see if your new directory is shown. You also can simply type **md testdata** again; if you receive the error message that DOS cannot create the directory because it already exists, you know that the command worked. (Checking step-by-step is good.)

Step 9

Notice that the information in the MS-DOS prompt screen simply scrolls up the screen as new lines of text appear and is lost when it rolls off the top—you can't get it back without reentering the command. The screen also becomes cluttered, and it is often useful to clear it.

Type **cls** (for CLear Screen) and press ENTER to clear the screen.

Step 10

It's time to copy some information into your testdata directory. Let's find out what the syntax for the COPY command is. Type **copy /?** and press ENTER. The syntax for the command will be displayed. Complicated, isn't it? This shows how obtuse DOS syntax can be. We'll simplify it for you: the syntax basically is "copy" (space) "from-location" (space) "to-location." Be sure to put the space between each parameter, because that allows the OS to "parse" the command.

Step 11

Type **copy c:\dos*.txt c:\testdata** and press ENTER.

Notice that we used the wildcard character (*) to copy all files with the txt extension—and only those files.

Step 12

Check to see if the command worked. Type **cd testdata** and press ENTER to change focus to the testdata directory. Then type **dir** and press ENTER to display the contents of that directory.

```
C:\>copy c:\dos\*.txt c:\testdata
C:\DOS\COUNTRY.TXT
C:\DOS\README.TXT
C:\DOS\NETWORKS.TXT
C:\DOS\DRVSPACE.TXT
        4 file(s) copied

C:\>cd testdata

C:\TESTDATA>dir

 Volume in drive C is MS-DOS_6
 Volume Serial Number is 2C98-8B17
 Directory of C:\TESTDATA

.            <DIR>           05-01-02   9:52p
..           <DIR>           05-01-02   9:52p
COUNTRY  TXT          15,920 05-31-94   6:22a
README   TXT          60,646 05-31-94   6:22a
NETWORKS TXT          17,465 05-31-94   6:22a
DRVSPACE TXT          41,512 05-31-94   6:22a
        6 file(s)        135,543 bytes
                   2,137,784,320 bytes free

C:\TESTDATA>_
```

You should see a list of files with txt extensions in the testdata directory as shown here.

Step 13

Let's say you have changed your mind, and now you want to get rid of all the files in testdata. You also want to be very sure to delete only the files in testdata.

Type **del c:\testdata*.*** and press ENTER to delete all file names with all extensions.

Type **y** and press ENTER when you see the warning:

```
All files in directory will be deleted!
Are you sure (Y/N)?
```

Notice that we used the wildcard symbol in both the file name and the extension to say that we want to include all files.

Step 14

Again, you need to check on what actually happened.

Type **dir** and press ENTER.

The testdata directory should be empty again, with only the dot (.) and dot-dot (..) files that are part of any subdirectory.

Step 15

We need to get rid of our testdata directory now.

Type **cd ..** and press ENTER to move up to the root of C:.

Step 16

Now use the RD command to remove a directory. Type **rd testdata** and press ENTER. Confirm that the testdata directory was deleted by typing **dir** and pressing ENTER again. There should be no sign of testdata.

The DELTREE command is much more powerful than the DEL command because it can delete a directory that contains files and subdirectories. DELTREE could have been used in Step 13 of the step-by-step to remove the TESTDATA directory without having to delete the files first.

Understanding the DOS Bootup Process and Required Startup Disks

Nigel has found that understanding the boot process has helped him with his job. In this section, you will discover why you should learn the boot process for any OS with which you work. Then you will learn about DOS system files, how the DOS boot process works, and how to create a DOS startup disk.

Why You Should Learn the DOS Bootup Process

Personal computers are multipurpose devices. They become the tools you need them to be only through the installation, first, of hardware components, internal or external to the computer, and then second, through the OS. The OS, in turn, usually has modifications in the form of commands that tell it how to behave and device drivers that add the ability to work with the available hardware. The computer finally becomes the tool you need for the jobs in your personal and business life when application programs are installed. These application programs rely on the OS for services they need.

Nigel has now worked with several different OSs and has found that a significant number of problems with microcomputers occur, or make themselves known, during the bootup (or startup) process. Therefore, understanding the normal startup process for personal computers in general and then for each individual OS helps him to troubleshoot problems that show up during bootup. Careful observation will tell him at what point in the bootup process the failure is occurring. Then he can troubleshoot, using his knowledge of what components must be missing or damaged to cause the problem.

DOS System Files

Three critical DOS files are collectively called the system files. In MS-DOS they are IO.SYS, MSDOS.SYS, and COMMAND.COM. These files must be present in the root of drive C: in order to start DOS from your hard disk, and they must be in the root of a floppy disk in order to start DOS from that floppy. These files make up the bare-bones OS. They are all read-only, and the first two also have both the hidden and system attributes set. IO.SYS handles interaction with hardware and the loading of device drivers during bootup. MSDOS.SYS is the main (or kernel) component of the OS, and COMMAND.COM is the command interpreter that provides you with the famous command prompt and interprets the commands you enter.

Cross Check

Do You Have Command of DOS?

Review what you have learned about working at the DOS command prompt by answering the following:

1. What is the difference between an internal and external DOS command?
2. Describe the difference between the COPY and XCOPY commands.
3. You have copied a group of files to a directory, but received no feedback from DOS. What can you do to confirm that the command was successful?

Figure 2-11 shows the result of running the DIR (Directory) command in the root of drive C: with DOS installed. Notice that we used the /A (All) switch to tell the DIR command to show all files, even those with hidden attributes. You can see the three DOS system files plus the configuration files, CONFIG.SYS and AUTOEXEC.BAT, which you will learn about next.

Try This!

Examine the System Files

If you installed DOS on your hard disk in Step-by-Step 2.01, you can see the system files and their attributes. Try this:

1. At the DOS prompt, type **attrib** and press ENTER.
2. Notice that the list of files displayed includes the three DOS system files and a few others.
3. Notice the file attributes on the files.

DOS Configuration Files

The special DOS configuration files, CONFIG.SYS and AUTOEXEC.BAT, are used by DOS during bootup. These two files are text files (they contain only text), and they have no special formatting codes. What they have in common is that they can be read using any text editor or word processor. Let's see how they differ by looking at when and how these files are used.

CONFIG.SYS The CONFIG.SYS file is used to add device drivers to DOS and to modify DOS settings. To work with a CONFIG.SYS file, you use a text editor to create or modify the file, entering special commands. Then you place the file in the root of the **boot disk**, which is drive C: if DOS is installed on your hard drive, or it can be a bootable floppy. DOS automatically looks for CONFIG.SYS immediately after loading the first two system files and before loading COMMAND.COM. If CONFIG.SYS is present, DOS uses its commands. The most common CONFIG.SYS commands are as follows:

BUFFERS	DOS
DEVICE	FILES
DEVICEHIGH	STACKS

All of these commands are used with an equal sign, as in BUFFERS=30. BUFFERS, DOS, FILES, and STACKS should appear only once in a CONFIG.SYS file, because each modifies a single setting for the OS. The BUFFERS command controls the number of disk read buffers, the area of memory used during file access. The DOS command controls the location in memory of a portion of the operating system. The FILES command controls the number of file handles available to DOS. (File handles are pointers used to keep track of files that are open in memory.) STACKS controls the number of special areas, called stacks, that are used by programs.

The DEVICE and DEVICEHIGH commands are used to load device drivers and will be used in a CONFIG.SYS file as many times as there are device drivers to install. The difference between DEVICE and DEVICEHIGH is that DEVICE loads drivers into the first 640KB of memory, whereas DEVICEHIGH loads drivers into special

```
C:\>dir /a

 Volume in drive C is MS-DOS_6
 Volume Serial Number is 2C98-8B17
 Directory of C:\

IO       SYS        40,774 05-31-94   6:22a
MSDOS    SYS        38,138 05-31-94   6:22a
DOS          <DIR>         04-24-02   5:24p
COMMAND  COM        54,645 05-31-94   6:22a
WINA20   386         9,349 05-31-94   6:22a
CONFIG   SYS            71 04-29-02   8:51p
AUTOEXEC BAT            86 05-03-02   1:51p
        7 file(s)        143,063 bytes
                   2,138,013,696 bytes free

C:\>_
```

• **Figure 2-11.** A directory listing including the system files

Learn more about MEMMAKER in the MS-DOS HELP program.

memory above 640KB, which exists only when DOS is on a computer with a 386 processor or greater, and some special memory management drivers and settings have been loaded. This is a very advanced task, so we suggest that you use the automated method for accomplishing this, using the MEMMAKER program.

A CONFIG.SYS file may be as simple as the following:

```
files=10
buffers=10
dos=high,umb
stacks=9,256
```

The CONFIG.SYS file on a Windows 98 Startup disk is one of the more sophisticated ones you will encounter. The following listing shows this CONFIG.SYS file. There are several lines in which it attempts to load device drivers for a CD-ROM drive. The one that works with your installed CD-ROM drive will be the one that is used. The first of these lines contains the command "device=oakcdrom.sys /D:mscd001." This CONFIG.SYS file also creates a ramdisk, a logical drive that uses RAM memory rather than physical disk space. This file is created automatically for you when you create a Windows 98 Startup disk.

```
 [menu]
menuitem=CD, Start computer with CD-ROM support.
menuitem=NOCD, Start computer without CD-ROM support.
menuitem=HELP, View the Help file.
menudefault=CD,30
menucolor=7,0
[CD]
device=himem.sys /testmem:off
device=oakcdrom.sys /D:mscd001
device=btdosm.sys
device=flashpt.sys
device=btcdrom.sys /D:mscd001
device=aspi2dos.sys
device=aspi8dos.sys
device=aspi4dos.sys
device=aspi8u2.sys
device=aspicd.sys /D:mscd001
[NOCD]
device=himem.sys /testmem:off
[HELP]
device=himem.sys /testmem:off
[COMMON]
files=10
buffers=10
dos=high,umb
stacks=9,256
devicehigh=ramdrive.sys /E 2048
lastdrive=z
```

AUTOEXEC.BAT AUTOEXEC.BAT is, first, a batch file, and second, a special batch file, because DOS looks for it immediately after it loads COMMAND.COM. While we use CONFIG.SYS to tell DOS what to *be,* we can use AUTOEXEC.BAT to tell DOS what to *do* every time it starts up.

For example, you might tell DOS to run a TSR. However, the most common commands found in AUTOEXEC.BAT are commands that place settings in a special area of memory used to store messages to DOS and other programs. This area of memory is called the environment, and commands that add messages to the environment include

PATH	PROMPT	SET

The PATH command allows you to control the search path DOS uses when searching for a command that was entered. The PROMPT command controls the appearance of the DOS prompt. The SET command is used to add other values to the environment. For instance, a DOS application's setup program might add a SET command to the AUTOEXEC.BAT with an entry that contains the directory path to that application's data files. For example, when Norton Utilities for DOS was installed, its setup program put a line in AUTOEXEC.BAT that looked something like this: SET NU=C:\NORTON. This entry would be ignored by other programs, but whenever Norton Utilities runs, it would look in the environment for this setting. You can see the current environment settings by simply typing the SET command at the prompt.

As with the CONFIG.SYS file, you may have a very simple AUTOEXEC.BAT file like the following:

```
path=C:\DOS;
prompt=$p$g
```

You may also have a very complicated AUTOEXEC.BAT file, like the one created by Windows 98 (shown next) when you use the Startup Disk option in Add/Remove programs to create a Windows 98 Startup disk. We won't explain all the commands in this sophisticated batch file. The short explanation is that it expands files that are compressed on the floppy disk in a file named EBD.CAB and copies these files to the RAM drive created by the CONFIG.SYS file. It also tests for the existence of a CD-ROM drive, which it should find if a CD-ROM driver was successfully loaded from the CONFIG.SYS file. If it finds a CD-ROM drive, it loads the Microsoft CD Extensions (MSCDEX.EXE) file system for CD-ROMs.

```
@ECHO OFF
set EXPAND=YES
SET DIRCMD=/O:N
set LglDrv=27 * 26 Z 25 Y 24 X 23 W 22 V 21 U 20 T 19 S 18 R
17 Q 16 P 15
set LglDrv=%LglDrv% O 14 N 13 M 12 L 11 K 10 J 9 I 8 H 7 G 6
F 5 E 4 D 3 C
cls
call setramd.bat %LglDrv%
set temp=c:\
set tmp=c:\
path=%RAMD%:\;a:\;%CDROM%:\
copy command.com %RAMD%:\ > NUL
set comspec=%RAMD%:\command.com
copy extract.exe %RAMD%:\ > NUL
copy readme.txt %RAMD%:\ > NUL
:ERROR
```

Inside Information

Windows Environment Settings

Using environment settings is such a handy practice that it continues today in Windows. One quick way to see the environment settings in Windows is to open a command prompt and simply type the SET command without parameters. You might be surprised at the long list of settings. For instance, the WINDIR value points to the location of the folder in which Windows is installed, and the USERNAME value shows the user name of the currently logged on user.

```
IF EXIST ebd.cab GOTO EXT
echo Please insert Windows 98 Startup Disk 2
echo.
pause
GOTO ERROR
:EXT
%RAMD%:\extract /y /e /l %RAMD%: ebd.cab > NUL
echo The diagnostic tools were successfully loaded to drive
%RAMD%.
echo.
IF "%config%"=="NOCD" GOTO QUIT
IF "%config%"=="HELP" GOTO HELP
LH %ramd%:\MSCDEX.EXE /D:mscd001 /L:%RAMD%
echo.
GOTO QUIT
:HELP
cls
call help.bat
echo Your computer will now restart and the startup menu will
appear.
echo.
echo.
echo.
restart.com
GOTO QUIT
:QUIT
echo To get help, type HELP and press ENTER.
echo.
rem clean up environment variables
set CDROM=
set LglDrv=
```

Some DOS applications would only run in earlier versions of DOS, so Microsoft added a command called SETVER that allowed you to lie to an application. That's right; you would use this command to tell an application that MS-DOS 6.22 was really MS-DOS 4.0. SETVER could be run with the appropriate switches to add MS-DOS 4.0 to a list of versions that was held in memory. Then, when the application requiring MS-DOS 4.0 started, it was "told" that the running OS was MS-DOS 4.0. SETVER could be placed in the AUTOEXEC.BAT file, but more commonly was placed in a batch file used to call up the application.

The DOS Bootup Process

Every time you turn your computer on, your computer "learns" what hardware it has attached to it and looks for an operating system to start. It learns about the essential hardware components by reading information stored in special nonvolatile RAM. It has a standard way of looking for an operating system and loading it into memory. The OS, in turn, learns how it will behave and how it will interact with the hardware. This section offers a somewhat simplified description of the boot process, from turning the computer on through loading the operating system with all its configuration settings and device drivers.

When you boot to DOS, you will be asked to confirm the date and time unless you have an AUTOEXEC.BAT file in the root of the startup disk. That is all you need. The file does not have to have anything in it.

The term "boot up a computer" comes from the old concept of lifting yourself by your own bootstraps—something that is impossible for humans, but necessary for a computer. The computer starts with basically nothing and then executes little programs, each of which performs a necessary task or adds more capability until the entire computer is up and running.

The Intel and similar processors used in our PCs have a unique characteristic tied to the PC architecture: when your PC is powered up, the processor is designed to load a special ROM-based program called the Power-On Self-Test (POST) into memory. POST runs a series of small diagnostic tests on the hardware.

You can boot up (or start) DOS several ways. One way is to turn on the power switch of your PC, which is called performing a **cold boot**. The other two methods are used after a computer is powered up. One is to use a key combination that reboots DOS without a power-down and power-up cycle. This key combination is CTRL-ALT-DELETE (pressed simultaneously), and this method is called a **warm boot**. A third method, also a warm boot, is available on many PCs: press the Reset button, which (depending on the manufacturer) skips the power-down and power-up cycle and runs POST. When POST finishes, it passes control to a small program in the ROM BIOS called the **bootstrap loader**.

CTRL-ALT-DELETE is also fondly referred to as the three-fingered salute.

To understand how the bootstrap loader works, you need to understand a little about how a drive is prepared for use. A disk, whether it is a hard disk or a floppy disk, is divided into individual chunks, called sectors, which are each 512 bytes in size. Further, remember that a hard disk can

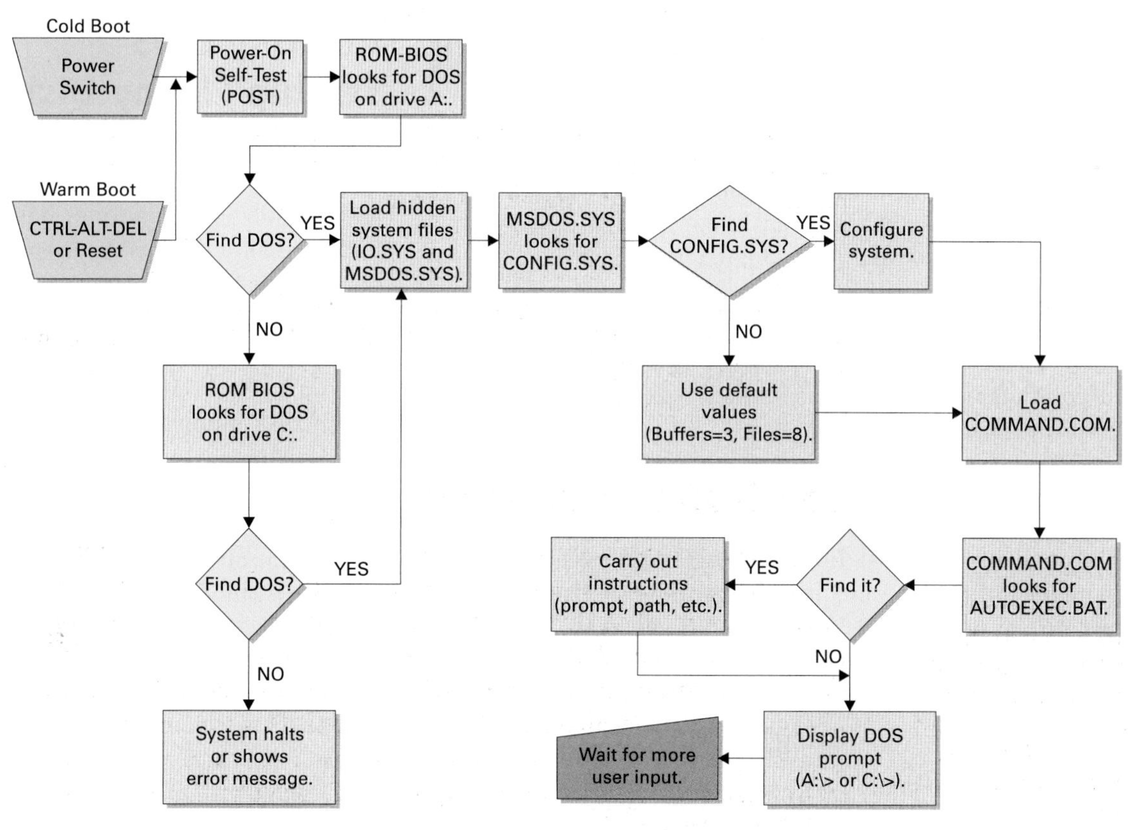

• Flowchart of the DOS bootup process

A floppy disk does not have an MBR, only a boot sector.

This discussion of the bootup process assumes that the boot order in the BIOS is set to first look at the floppy drive, then to the hard drive.

have several areas (partitions) that appear as discrete logical drives (C:, D:, E:, and so on), with many, many sectors in each.

The first sector on each logical drive on a hard disk is the boot sector for that logical drive. When you format a disk (A:, C:, D:, and so on), the OS you are using writes information into the boot sector (not the MBR). This information includes version information about the OS and a small program that calls up the system files for the OS.

The ROM BIOS bootstrap loader looks for a floppy disk in drive A:. If it finds one, it loads the boot sector from that floppy disk into memory, which in turn runs the OS loading program. If the bootstrap loader does not find a floppy disk in drive A:, it looks for an OS on the hard drive. It first looks in the MBR of the first hard drive and reads the partition table, looking for a special type of partition, called a primary partition, that is also identified as "active." This means that it is the specific partition from which to load the OS. The bootstrap loader reads the first sector of the active partition into memory. Remember that this sector is also special. It is the boot sector and contains a special OS loading program.

On a disk formatted by DOS, the OS loading program looks for IO.SYS and MSDOS.SYS. If it finds them, it loads them into memory. MSDOS.SYS looks for CONFIG.SYS in the root directory of the disk from which it is loaded. If it finds this file, it configures the OS based on the commands in CONFIG.SYS. Then COMMAND.COM is loaded into memory. It looks for AUTOEXEC.BAT. If it finds this file, it executes each command in the file. After this, unless an application was loaded by AUTOEXEC.BAT, the DOS prompt is displayed with its little blinking cursor waiting for you to enter a command.

Try This!

Cause a Failure

You can learn what happens when the bootstrap loader fails to find an operating system. If your computer is configured to boot from floppy disk drive first and then from the hard disk, use a blank, formatted floppy disk to "break" your computer and fix it again! Try this:

1. With your computer turned off, insert a blank, formatted floppy disk in drive A:.
2. Turn the computer on. After it fails to find an OS, it should display this message:

```
Non-system disk or disk error
Replace and strike any key when ready
```

3. Simply remove the blank disk from drive A: and press a key. The system should restart and load the operating system from your hard disk.

Creating DOS Startup Floppy Disks

You have seen the term *DOS startup floppy disk,* but what is it and how do you create one? It is a floppy disk that has been prepared with the DOS system files so that it can be used to start DOS on a computer. As simple as DOS is, you cannot create a startup floppy disk simply by copying the three system files onto a formatted floppy disk with the COPY command. You need to use one of the methods you will study next. There are others, but we decided to stop at those that would be most accessible to you.

Using FORMAT to Create a Startup Disk

If you can boot into the DOS OS from either a floppy disk or hard disk, you can then use the FORMAT command to create a DOS startup disk. Using the FORMAT command requires that you use a special switch (/S) with it.

When you use this switch, after the FORMAT command prepares the floppy disk and places a new root directory and FAT on the disk, it will also place the system files (IO.SYS, MSDOS.SYS, and COMMAND.COM) on the floppy disk. You will have no other DOS programs on the floppy disk and will have to manually select and copy the external commands you want on the floppy disk. Use this method when you have an unformatted floppy disk or want to start with a fresh format. You will also have to create the CONFIG.SYS and AUTOEXEC.BAT files appropriate to your computer.

Pay attention to the listing that begins with a value labeled "Bytes Total Disk Space." If FORMAT discovers bad space on your disk, that information will be listed as a number of bytes in bad sectors. Discard the disk. It is a waste of your time to mess with a damaged disk.

Step-by-Step 2.05

Create a Startup Floppy Disk Using FORMAT

You can easily create a simple startup disk using the FORMAT command. To try this, all you need is a computer with a floppy or hard disk that is already started with DOS. You will also need the FORMAT.COM program and a blank floppy disk.

Step 1

At the DOS prompt, enter the following command: **format a: /s**

Step 2

Insert a blank floppy disk in drive A:, and press ENTER when you see the following message:

```
Insert new diskette for drive A:
and press ENTER when ready...
```

Step 3

You can watch the progress as FORMAT checks the floppy disk, saves UNFORMAT information, then continues with the formatting process. Press ENTER when you see the following message:

```
Volume label (11 characters, ENTER for none)?
```

Step 4

Press N and ENTER when you see the following message:

```
Format another (Y/N)?
```

Step 5

Leave the floppy disk in drive A:, and press CTRL-ALT-DELETE to test the startup disk. After a successful test, press ENTER at the date and time prompt (if necessary), remove the disk from drive A:, and label it "Simple Startup Disk." Then reboot the computer.

```
C:\>format a: /s
Insert new diskette for drive A:
and press ENTER when ready...

Checking existing disk format.
Saving UNFORMAT information.
Verifying 1.44M
Format complete.
System transferred

Volume label (11 characters, ENTER for none)?

    1,457,664 bytes total disk space
      200,704 bytes used by system
    1,256,960 bytes available on disk

          512 bytes in each allocation unit.
        2,455 allocation units available on disk.

Volume Serial Number is 0933-1BF4

Format another (Y/N)?n

C:\>_
```

You can also use the MS-DOS Setup program to create a DOS Startup Disk with many of the DOS external commands automatically copied to it.

Using SYS to Create a DOS System Floppy Disk

The SYS command places the DOS system files on a previously formatted floppy disk. The advantage of this command is that it is nondestructive and works as long as there is room on the floppy disk for the system files. To do this, you must boot up a computer to DOS and have the SYS.COM program available on disk in the search path. The actual command you would enter to put the DOS system files on a floppy disk is **sys a:**

The resulting message (if the command is successful) is

```
System transferred.
```

Try This!

Create a Startup Disk with the SYS Command

You can easily create a simple startup disk using the SYS command. All you need is a computer with a floppy or hard disk that is started in DOS, the SYS.COM file in the search path, and a formatted floppy disk (it can even have files on it, as long as there is room for the system files). Try this:

1. Place your floppy disk in drive A:, and enter the following command at the DOS prompt: sys a: and press ENTER.
2. After you see the message "System transferred," remove the disk from drive A: and label it "Startup Disk."

Using Windows to Create a Startup Disk

You can use Windows to create a DOS startup floppy disk:

- If you have Windows 95 or Windows 98 installed on a computer, you can use the Startup Disk option found in Control Panel | Add/Remove Programs | Startup Disk. This creates a Windows 95 or Windows 98 startup disk, which is really just a bootable DOS floppy disk using the Windows version of MS-DOS. The Windows 98 Startup Disk is preferred to that of Windows 95, because it has better CD-ROM drivers.
- If you have Windows XP installed on a computer and you format a floppy disk from within My Computer or Windows Explorer, you will have an option to create an MS-DOS startup disk. This is a nice feature, since we don't always have access to MS-DOS when we need a startup disk. In addition to the system files, this method only copies some basic driver files and creates blank CONFIG.SYS and AUTOEXEC.BAT files. Therefore, you will have to find and copy onto this floppy disk any external commands you wish to use.

Once you create a startup disk, use the DOS DISKCOPY command or the Windows Copy Disk command to duplicate the disk.

Troubleshooting Common DOS Problems

You may encounter some common problems if you work with DOS. Let's examine some of these problems, looking at the symptoms, the possible causes, and solutions.

"Non-System Disk" Error Message

In this scenario, DOS is installed on your hard disk, but fails to boot up, and an error message appears that includes the words "Non-system disk."

This indicates that the OS loader program cannot find IO.SYS or MSDOS.SYS, or both. The most likely cause is that a data floppy disk has been left in drive A:. The OS loader program from the first sector on the disk is loaded into memory and looking for IO.SYS and MSDOS.SYS on drive A:. However, a data floppy disk is one that is formatted to hold data, but is not a bootable disk, so it lacks the system files. To solve this problem, check to see if there is a floppy disk in drive A: and, if so, remove it and press any key. The boot process should continue successfully.

Cross Check

Start Up Your DOS Skills

Review what you learned about MS-DOS startup and answer the following questions:

1. List the three DOS system files.
2. Name the two files used to configure DOS.
3. What command provides locations for the OS to search for executable files?

If you check drive A: and the drive does not contain a floppy disk, then you have a bigger problem, because this means that the OS loader was loaded from the first sector on C: and could not find IO.SYS or MSDOS.SYS during bootup. In this case, you should boot with a bootable disk in drive A: that also has the SYS.COM program. Then type the following command to have the system files placed back on your drive C: **sys c:**.

Next, remove the floppy disk from the floppy drive and reboot your computer. It should now boot to DOS.

"Bad or Missing Command Interpreter" Error Message

In this scenario, DOS is installed on your hard disk, but fails to boot up, and the "Bad or Missing Command Interpreter" error message is displayed. This indicates that the file COMMAND.COM is missing or is a different version than IO.SYS and MSDOS.SYS. To confirm that this is the problem, locate a DOS startup disk of the same version installed on your hard disk, place it in the floppy drive, and boot up again. After the computer boots up, display a directory of the root of C: using the DIR /A command. The /A will display all files, including hidden files. First, verify that COMMAND.COM is missing. If it is missing, then you have confirmed the problem and can solve it. If COMMAND.COM is present, check the file date and time information in IO.SYS, MSDOS.SYS, and COMMAND.COM. If COMMAND.COM has a different date and time, you need to replace it with one with the correct date and time.

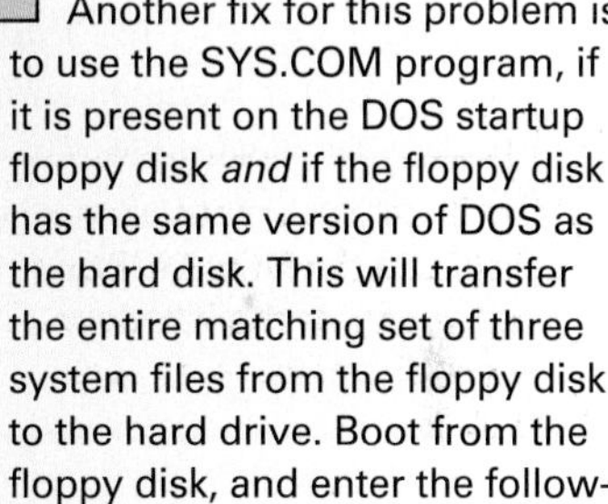

Another fix for this problem is to use the SYS.COM program, if it is present on the DOS startup floppy disk *and* if the floppy disk has the same version of DOS as the hard disk. This will transfer the entire matching set of three system files from the floppy disk to the hard drive. Boot from the floppy disk, and enter the following command: **sys c:**.

To solve this problem, verify that the COMMAND.COM file on the floppy disk is the correct date and time (matching that of IO.SYS and MSDOS.SYS on C:); then copy COMMAND.COM from A: to C:.

"Bad Command or File Name" Error Message

You have just entered a command at the command prompt and receive the "Bad Command or File Name" message. This means that either the command name or a file name (or directory name) in one of the parameters is incorrect. For instance, on a computer with DOS 6.22 installed, we wanted to

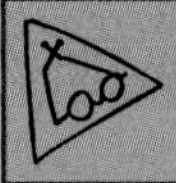

Inside Information

Once Upon a Date and Time

The original IBM PC had a real-time clock that could only keep track of the date and time when the computer was turned on. For this reason, PC DOS and MS-DOS would prompt you for the date and time at every restart. Eventually, battery-supported clocks were added to PCs. Once set, using proprietary programs or the DOS DATE and TIME programs, they continued to keep time—even when the computer was turned off. Each of the earliest battery-supported clocks required a special proprietary program for MS-DOS to read and/or set the clock date and time. This program was usually placed in the AUTOEXEC.BAT file. Therefore, DOS wouldn't prompt for the date and time if an AUTOEXEC.BAT file was present—regardless of whether a clock program was in the AUTOEXEC.BAT file. This behavior changed beginning with MS-DOS for Windows 95. This and newer versions won't prompt for the date and time—with or without the AUTOEXEC.BAT FILE.

delete a directory called DATA1, and we entered the following with a slight typo: **deltree data**.

In this case, there was no DATA directory, only a DATA1 directory, so the result was the "Bad Command or File Name" message.

Whenever you see this error message, whether you are working in DOS or at a command prompt in Windows, look for a typo in the command line you entered, and then reenter the entire line correctly. Typos are the most common cause of this error.

Request to Enter the Current Date and Time

You boot up a computer with DOS, and you are required to enter the current date and time. This means that DOS did not find an AUTOEXEC.BAT file. This was mentioned previously in this chapter, but we include it here to discuss it further. If you previously had an AUTOEXEC.BAT file, you may want to investigate how and why it cannot be found now. Perhaps, rather than booting from drive C:, your computer booted from drive A:, because a bootable startup disk was in the drive. If so, the prompt on the screen should show drive A:. If this is the case, remove the floppy disk and restart the computer.

Chapter 2 Review

■ Chapter Summary

After reading this chapter and completing the Step-by-Step tutorials and Try This! exercises, you should understand the following facts about DOS:

Finding DOS and Understanding Its Strengths and Weaknesses

- One reason DOS is still in limited use today is its small size, which makes it a choice for embedded systems.
- Another reason DOS is still in limited use today is that its system files easily fit on a floppy disk, leaving room for other small programs, which allows technicians to use it to boot up a computer from a floppy disk. They can then run special diagnostic utilities from the floppy disk.
- Windows can run DOS in a virtual DOS machine.
- Another reason for using DOS today is that some DOS applications either run too slowly in a virtual machine or do not work at all in a virtual machine. The applications then must be run on a computer running DOS.
- DOS can access only the real-mode capabilities of the Intel processors.
- DOS is a single-tasking OS.
- DOS provides limited services for DOS applications.
- DOS applications can only use conventional memory.
- Microsoft no longer supports or sells MS-DOS.
- IBM sells PC DOS 2000.
- Digital Research sold its DR-DOS to Novell many years ago. DR-DOS has changed hands several times since then and is now sold through DeviceLogics at `www.drdos.com`.
- Versions of DOS can also be found for free on the Internet.

Installing DOS

- The MS-DOS Setup program will partition and format a hard drive, if needed.
- The hardware requirements for MS-DOS are minimal: an IBM or compatible personal computer, 6MB of free hard disk space for the DOS utilities if you are installing onto a hard disk, and 512KB of memory.

How the FAT File System Works

- DOS uses the FAT file system, which is now referred to as FAT16 to distinguish it from the newer FAT32 file system introduced with Windows 95 OEM edition.
- The FAT file system uses a naming convention for files and directories called the 8.3 (eight-dot-three) naming convention. It allows up to eight characters in the file name, followed by a dot (.), followed by an extension of up to three characters.
- It is best to use only alphanumeric characters for 8.3 file names, even though some non-alphanumeric characters work.
- A file's extension can indicate the type of file (executable, text, and so on).
- File attributes determine how DOS handles a file or directory. The file attributes are read-only, archive, system, hidden, volume label, and directory.

Working with the DOS Command Prompt

- The ATTRIB command allows you to view and manipulate the read-only, archive, system, and hidden attributes.
- Internal commands are commands that are part of COMMAND.COM and are always available to use when you are at a DOS command prompt. They are very fast to access.
- CLS, COPY, REN, DEL, MD, RD, CD, and TYPE are internal DOS commands.
- External commands are in individual files, which must be available where DOS can find them on disk if you wish to use them.
- XCOPY, DELTREE, FORMAT, FDISK, and DISKCOPY are examples of external DOS commands.

Describe the DOS Bootup Process and Create Startup Disks

- It is important to understand the bootup process of an OS in order to troubleshoot failures that occur during bootup.
- A hard boot of a personal computer occurs when you turn on the power switch.
- A soft boot of a personal computer occurs when you press CTRL-ALT-DELETE.
- Many computers have a Reset button, which resets a running computer without a power-down and power-up cycle.
- The order of events during bootup of DOS is cold or warm boot, then POST, and then the bootstrap loader looks on the A: or C: drive and loads the boot record. Then IO.SYS and MSDOS.SYS are loaded, CONFIG.SYS (if it exists) is read and used by MSDOS.SYS, COMMAND.COM is loaded, AUTOEXEC.BAT (if it exists) is read and used by COMMAND.COM, and finally, the DOS prompt is displayed.
- You have many options for creating a DOS startup disk, including use of the DOS Setup program, the SYS or FORMAT command, the Startup Disk option in Windows 9*x*, and the option to create an MS-DOS startup disk when formatting a floppy disk from My Computer or Explorer in Windows XP.

Troubleshoot Common DOS Problems

- A failed startup to DOS that results in the "Non-System Disk" error message means that the OS loader program cannot find IO.SYS and/or MSDOS.SYS. The most likely cause of the problem is that a data floppy disk was left in drive A:. Check for and remove any floppy disks in the drive and reboot the computer.
- A failed startup to DOS that results in a "Bad or Missing Command Interpreter" error message means that the file COMMAND.COM is missing or is a different version than IO.SYS and MSDOS.SYS. Boot from a DOS floppy disk of the correct version, and copy the COMMAND.COM file to the root of C:.
- When you enter a command and see the "Bad Command or File Name" error message, check and recheck your spelling and reenter the command.
- If you are required to enter the date and time when you boot up a computer, this most likely means that there is no AUTOEXEC.BAT on the root of the boot disk. Create an AUTOEXEC.BAT file, even if it is empty, and just about any computer built since 1984 will simply use the internal clock to get this information.

Key Terms List

application *(49)*
boot disk *(77)*
bootstrap loader *(81)*
cluster *(59)*
cold boot *(81)*
conventional memory *(50)*
DOS prompt *(58)*
driver *(49)*
extended partition *(54)*
external command *(71)*
FAT16 file system *(59)*
FAT32 file system *(59)*
file allocation table (FAT) *(59)*
file attribute *(65)*
internal command *(70)*
logical drive *(51)*
parse *(70)*
partition *(53)*
primary partition *(54)*
root directory *(60)*
single-tasking *(51)*
startup disk *(49)*
syntax *(69)*
terminate and stay resident (TSR) *(51)*
utility *(49)*
warm boot *(81)*

■ Key Terms Quiz

Use the Key Terms list to complete the sentences that follow. Not all terms will be used.

1. ______________, the part of the DOS file system from which it gets its name, is used to allocate space to files.
2. The minimum space on disk that a file system can allocate to a file is called a/an ______________.
3. A/an ______________ contains instructions an operating system uses to access and control specific hardware.
4. The 8.3 file naming convention is a feature and a limitation of DOS and the ______________.
5. Computer professionals may carry a DOS ______________ in their tool kit to use in emergencies.
6. The type of memory in which DOS, its drivers, and applications can run is called ______________.
7. A/an ______________ is one of a special set of file directory entries that indicate certain properties, such as read-only, archive, system, and hidden.
8. A DOS command that is part of the COMMAND.COM program and is always available when DOS is running is called a/an ______________.
9. A/an ______________ is the only hard disk partition type from which MS-DOS can be started.
10. A word processor is an example of a/an ______________ program.

■ Multiple-Choice Quiz

1. In the 1980s, IBM sold OEM MS-DOS under this product name.
   - **a.** System X
   - **b.** PC DOS
   - **c.** IBM MS-DOS
   - **d.** Linux
   - **e.** Compaq MS-DOS
2. Why use DOS today?
   - **a.** It uses the FAT32 file system.
   - **b.** It is the OS of choice of gamers.
   - **c.** DOS can take advantage of Intel protected mode.
   - **d.** It does not need much memory or storage space.
   - **e.** It has a great GUI.
3. What DOS operating system product was at one time owned by Novell?
   - **a.** FreeDOS
   - **b.** PC DOS
   - **c.** Compaq MS-DOS
   - **d.** CP/M 86
   - **e.** DR-DOS
4. Which Intel processor mode can MS-DOS use?
   - **a.** Advanced
   - **b.** Protected
   - **c.** Real
   - **d.** Standard
   - **e.** Read-only
5. How much minimum free disk space is required when you install MS-DOS 6.22 or IBM PC DOS 2000 onto the hard drive of a computer?
   - **a.** 512KB
   - **b.** 2GB
   - **c.** 49MB
   - **d.** 6MB
   - **e.** None
6. Which one of the following MS-DOS commands would you use to delete a directory and its contents, including subdirectories, in one pass?
   - **a.** DEL
   - **b.** XCOPY
   - **c.** DELTREE
   - **d.** CHKDSK
   - **e.** ATTRIB

7. Which of the following is true when installing MS-DOS?
   a. You can use the DOS install setup program.
   b. You must have administrator rights to the computer.
   c. You can create a logical drive up to 4GB.
   d. You must install from CD.
   e. You can't use MS-DOS until you have activated it with Microsoft.
8. Which of the following does *not* occur when you format a disk with the MS-DOS FORMAT command?
   a. The FAT table is created.
   b. You will be prompted to give the drive a label.
   c. The boot sector for that logical drive is created.
   d. The DOS subdirectory is created on the disk.
   e. A root directory is created.
9. Where does MS-DOS keep track of disk space allocation?
   a. MBR
   b. Root directory
   c. FAT table
   d. Boot sector
   e. Subdirectory
10. What do you learn from the syntax of a command?
    a. The command's attributes
    b. The rules for entering that command at the command line
    c. The list of possible errors created by the command
    d. The version of the command
    e. How much memory a command uses
11. What BIOS-based program performs diagnostics as a computer is powered up?
    a. IO.SYS
    b. COMMAND.COM
    c. MSDOS.SYS
    d. DEBUG.EXE
    e. POST
12. Which of the following is *not* a method for creating an MS-DOS startup disk?
    a. format a: /S
    b. chkdsk /f
    c. sys a:
    d. The Format command from the context menu of drive A: in My Computer in XP
    e. The Startup Disk option in Windows 98
13. If you are unfamiliar with DOS, have access to computers that are already running DOS, Windows 98, and Windows 2000, and need to create a DOS startup disk with CD-ROM drivers, which should you choose?
    a. format a: /s
    b. chkdsk /f
    c. sys a:
    d. setup a: /S
    e. The Startup Disk option in Windows 98
14. When using FDISK to prepare a primary partition for MS-DOS 6.22, this is the maximum size you can create:
    a. 4GB
    b. 2TB
    c. 512MB
    d. 2GB
    e. 650KB
15. What is the most likely cause of the following error message: "Bad Command or File Name"?
    a. Incorrect switch
    b. Incorrect versions of DOS
    c. Insufficient permissions
    d. You do not have administrator rights
    e. Typos on the command line

Essay Quiz

1. Write a few sentences describing why DOS is in use today, contrasting its strengths with its weaknesses.
2. You're a new employee doing computer support in a small manufacturing company that uses DOS on two computers which run an application written in the late 1980s specifically for this company. They own two legal sets of the software. The company that created the software went out of business ten years ago, and your company has never found an off-the-shelf program to replace this program. For many years the enterprise has maintained the two computers running the program, but now one of them has completely failed. You have been asked to install DOS on a newly purchased computer that has no OS. Your boss left you with the new computer and a copy of the application software. You have found two original sets of MS-DOS 6.22 on 5.25-inch floppy disks, but the new computer only has a 3.5-inch floppy disk drive. The old computer that failed had a 5.25-inch floppy disk drive. The remaining old computer only has a 3.5-inch drive. One of your coworkers believes you must now buy a new copy of DOS. Describe what you believe your options for installing DOS on the new computer are, including the issue of whether you must buy a new copy of DOS.
3. Christine created a DOS startup floppy disk using the SYS command. Now she wants to copy some of the DOS commands from the DOS directory on drive C: of her computer. There are 6MB of files in the DOS directory, so she knows she can't copy all of them. Suggest several useful commands that you would copy to the floppy disk and why you selected each command.
4. In a few sentences, describe the DOS bootup process.
5. Describe the difference between a primary partition and an extended partition.

Lab Projects

• Lab Project 2.1

You have been asked to assist a senior desktop support specialist on a service call to solve a problem with a computer in the distribution warehouse of a large retailer. He installed DOS on a hard drive, as well as a DOS application that the warehouse uses for tracking received orders within the warehouse. He created a CONFIG.SYS file with commands that configure DOS with the settings and drivers needed. Then he created an AUTOEXEC.BAT file that calls the application so that it starts every time the computer is started. Running this one application is to be the only thing that this computer is used for. However, he has had problems with other users deleting the COMMAND.COM, CONFIG.SYS, and AUTOEXEC.BAT files, causing the system to fail to start properly and requiring that someone replace these files on the hard drive. You have been asked to come up with a solution to this problem and to test the solution on the lab computer on which you installed DOS.

You will need a lab computer with MS-DOS installed.

Then do the following:

1. Describe your solution to the problem of users deleting the COMMAND.COM, CONFIG.SYS, and AUTOEXEC.BAT files.
2. Determine the location of the COMMAND.COM, CONFIG.SYS, and AUTOEXEC.BAT files on the hard drive.
3. Implement your solution on your lab computer.
4. Test your solution and explain the results.

• Lab Project 2.2

You are a desktop support analyst in a large corporation. You have computers running several versions of Windows available to you, including Windows 95, Windows 98, Windows 2000, and Windows XP. You do not have DOS available to you. You have been asked to go to a customer site and to take a DOS startup disk with CD drivers installed on it. You need to create this floppy disk before you leave for the customer site.

You will need the following materials:

- A blank floppy disk
- A lab computer with the OS that you need for the task
- A data or distribution CD to use in your test of the startup floppy disk you create

Then do the following:

1. Determine how you will prepare the floppy disk, including the OS you will use and the procedure you will follow in that OS. Your choice of OS depends on which of the available installed operating systems will enable you to create a disk with CD drivers included.
2. Prepare the floppy disk.
3. Test the floppy disk by booting a PC with it and accessing a CD in the CD-ROM drive.

• Lab Project 2.3

To test your proficiency with DOS, your boss has assigned you the task of creating several directories on ten computers. You will create the same directory structure on each computer. In the root of C:, you will create a directory called DATA. Below that you will create two directories: CUSTOMER and SALES. Below CUSTOMER you will create two directories: WHLSALE and RETAIL. Below SALES, you will create three directories: ADS, PROMOS, and PLANS. You realize that manually entering the DOS commands to create those directories at each computer is going to be boring, and when you do a boring job, you tend to make mistakes. Therefore, you have decided to automate this task.

1. To automate the process of creating several directories on ten computers, create a batch file similar to the listing that follows, and name the batch file with a name, such as NEWDIRS.BAT.

```
@ECHO OFF
ECHO Subdirectories will be created on
drive C:.
PAUSE
C:
CD \
MD DATA
MD \DATA\CUSTOMER
MD \DATA\CUSTOMER\WHLSALE
MD \DATA\CUSTOMER\RETAIL
MD \DATA\SALES
MD \DATA\SALES\ADS
MD \DATA\SALES\PROMOS
MD \DATA\SALES\PLANS
ECHO The directories have been created.
```

2. Copy the batch file onto a floppy disk, and take the floppy disk to a computer to test it. Insert the floppy disk, make the drive current by typing **A:**, and then run the batch file by entering the name of the batch file at the command prompt.
3. Report the outcome, including the amount of time you estimate it will take to run the batch file on a total of ten computers. Record how much time you estimate it would have taken to do this task manually at each computer.

Windows NT Workstation 4.0

chapter 3

"Excuse me," growled Moody, "you've got strengths if I say you've got them. Think now. What are you best at?"

—Harry Potter and the Goblet of Fire, by J. K. Rowling

From its introduction as version 3.1, Windows NT has been an entirely different operating system than Microsoft's initial Windows desktop OSs—a better, more secure OS. Windows NT 4.0 Workstation brought an improved user interface and support for more and newer hardware than was previously supported in NT 3.51, and it was offered in parallel with the Windows 9*x* products. Although Windows NT 4.0 Workstation was a more secure and stable alternative, it came at a price: you couldn't use it with the wide range of hardware supported by Windows 9*x*.

In this chapter, you will learn how to install and configure NT 4.0 Workstation and then to manage the desktop. You will learn some maintenance tasks and how to troubleshoot common Windows NT 4.0 Workstation problems.

In this chapter, you will learn how to:

- **Describe Windows NT Workstation 4.0 features and benefits**
- **Install and upgrade Windows NT Workstation 4.0**
- **Configure and manage Windows NT Workstation 4.0**
- **Perform proactive maintenance tasks**
- **Troubleshoot common Windows NT 4.0 problems**

NT Workstation 4.0 Overview

What can NT 4.0 do for you? Are there reasons why you shouldn't have NT 4.0 on your desktop? It's been around a while; how much longer will you be able to buy it? We answer these questions and a few others in the following sections.

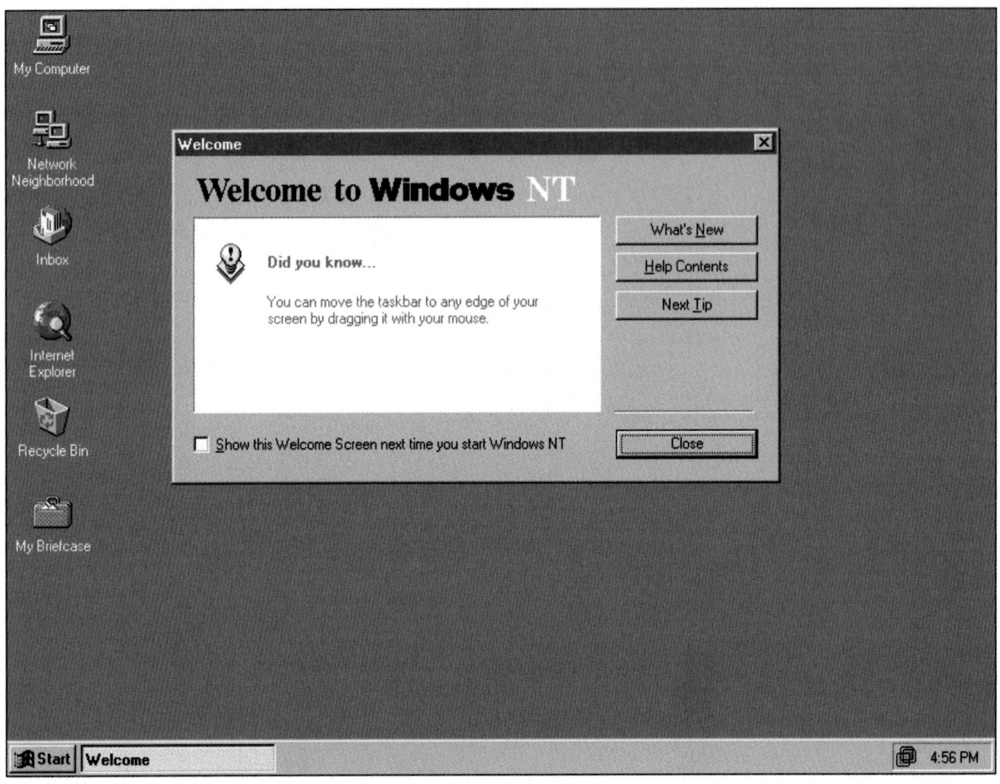

• Welcome to Windows NT

This chapter is about Windows NT Workstation 4.0. In the real world people tend to shorten and/or reorder the wording of a lengthy name like that. We are no exception, so you will see various permutations and abbreviations in this chapter. Don't worry about it! They all refer to the same operating system.

Windows NT 4.0 also personified the Microsoft Internet strategy of including the software needed to be both a client browsing the Internet and an Internet server—even in Windows NT 4.0 Workstation on the desktop.

Features and Benefits

What can Windows NT 4.0 do for you? We'll examine the features and the benefits, but let's first turn the clock back to 1993, the year the first version, Windows NT 3.1, was introduced. Even then, there was more than met the eye. Although it was an entirely different OS than Windows 3.1, Microsoft gave it a Windows 3.1 look and called it Windows NT 3.1. They brought this first version out strictly as a network server OS. This was followed in the next few years by an upgrade, introduced as two products: Windows NT 3.5 Server and a desktop product, Windows NT 3.5 Workstation. This was in recognition of the need for a desktop operating system with more stability and security than Windows 3.1. The last version of NT with the Windows 3.1 desktop was 3.51.

When Windows NT 4.0 was introduced in the fall of 1996, Windows 3.*x* and Windows 95 dominated the PC desktop. Whereas the Windows NT 3.*x* products were stuck in a graphical time warp using the Windows 3.*x* GUI, Windows NT 4.0 adopted the more pleasant and (dare we say?) more intuitive interface of Windows 95. However, behind the scenes, it was an entirely different OS from Windows 95. Let's look at its features in the following categories: desktop, file systems, security, stability, memory, and software compatibility.

Desktop

The Windows NT 4.0 desktop resembles that of the Windows 95 GUI with the familiar objects: taskbar, Start button (with its Start menu), right-click context menus, My Computer, and Windows Explorer (called Windows NT Explorer). Microsoft saw this change to the user interface (or shell) from that of NT 3.1 to be so important that Windows NT 4.0 was called the Shell Update Release.

After all this time, it's hard to remember working with the Windows 3.*x* program groups, which were simple windows containing program icons. They had shortcomings both visually and organizationally. Our biggest complaint was that you couldn't nest program groups to create a hierarchy of programs and other objects. Windows NT 4.0 eliminated this problem because it inherited the new folder and shortcut structure of Windows 95, which allows you to create a hierarchy of folders and shortcuts. Even the menus can be based on this folder structure. The best example of this is the Start menu.

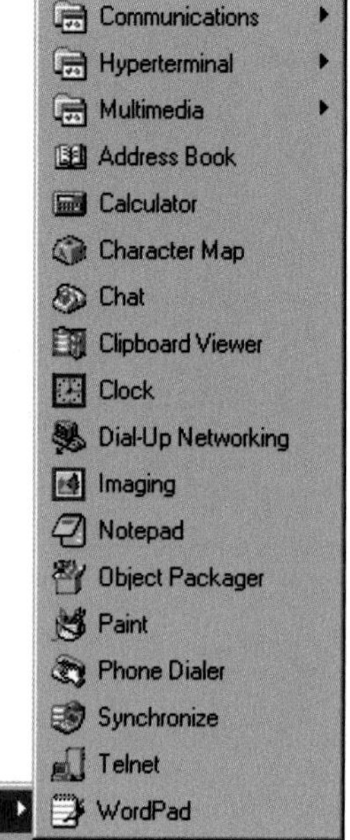

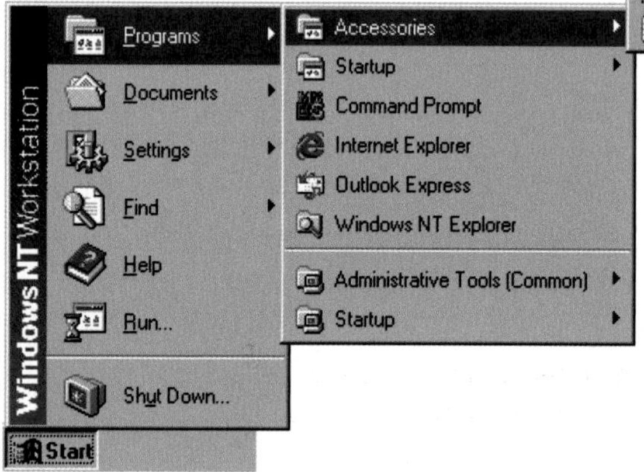

• Windows NT 4.0 Start menu hierarchy

> Quickly open the Start menu by pressing the CTRL-ESC key combination, or simply press the Windows Logo key if it is on your keyboard.

File Systems

Windows NT 4.0 fully supports two files systems: **NT file system version 4 (NTFS4)** and an implementation of FAT16 (introduced in Windows 95) called the **virtual file allocation table (VFAT)**. Both file systems have on-disk components and memory-base (program code) components in the operating system. In other words, the operating system must have some code in memory that can manage the on-disk components of the file system. The on-disk components are placed there when an operating system formats a disk with

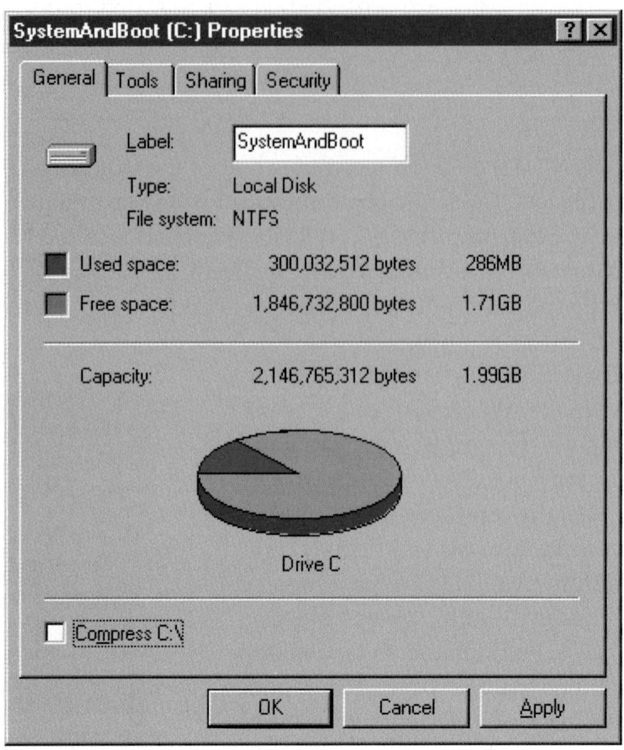

• **Figure 3-1.** The General tab of the Properties of a drive showing NTFS as the file system

one or the other file system. Since a disk partition can only be formatted with a single file system at a time, the General tab of the Properties dialog box of a drive will show which file system is installed on a drive. (See Figure 3-1.)

FAT Although the FAT files system under NT is actually VFAT, it is common to refer to VFAT simply as FAT. It is nearly identical to how FAT16 existed in DOS, except that beginning with Windows 95 and continuing through NT and newer Windows versions, the directory entries are modified to save long file names (with up to 255 characters, including spaces, which were not allowed in 8.3 file names) as well as the legacy 8.3 file names. A **long file name (LFN)** is any file or folder name that breaks the 8.3 file naming convention described in Chapter 2. When you name a file or folder with a file name that does not comply with this convention, Windows saves both the actual name (as a long file name) and an 8.3 version of the name, called an alias, that consists of the first six 8.3-valid characters, followed by a tilde (~) and a number, beginning with zero (0).

NT does not support FAT32, which was introduced in a special release of Windows 95 and is supported in Windows 98, Windows 2000, and Windows XP.

A floppy disk formatted in Windows is automatically formatted with the FAT file system, using a modified version of the FAT12 file system used for floppy disks in DOS. NT supports long file names on floppy disk as well as logical drives on hard disks.

NTFS4 NTFS, however, is a much more advanced file system than any form of the FAT file system. In contrast to the simple FAT table and root directory structure on disk that is the basis for the FAT file system, NTFS4 has a far more sophisticated structure, using a Master File Table (MFT) that allows for additional file attributes. In fact, even a file's actual contents are saved as one or more file attributes. This makes the file system adaptable to future changes. In addition, NTFS4 works like a transaction-based database, in that it sees all file access as transactions, and if a transaction is not complete, it will roll back to the last successful transaction. NTFS4 will also avoid saving files to damaged portions of a disk, called bad sectors. Windows NT will not allow you to format a floppy disk with NTFS4, because it requires much more space on disk for its structure than FAT. This is referred to as the file system's overhead. You may format a fairly small hard disk partition, but because of the space required for overhead, the smallest recommended size is 10MB.

NT supports long file names (LFNs) in NTFS similar to the way in which it supports LFNs in the FAT file system. NT creates 8.3 aliases for long file names on both FAT and NTFS partitions.

Finally, NTFS provides folder and file security, which allows permissions to be applied to any file or folder on an NTFS partition. This is one of the most important differences between the NTFS and FAT file systems. This leads us to the next feature, security.

At the time Windows NT 4.0 was introduced, NTFS4 was referred to simply as **NTFS**. After Windows 2000 came out with version 5 of NTFS, called NTFS5, it became important to use the version-specific name (NTFS4 or NTFS5).

Security

Windows NT 4.0 can be made secure on the desktop, meaning that even a stand-alone Windows NT 4.0 computer has significant security components. This is a claim that can't be made for Windows 95, Windows 98, or Windows ME. Windows NT 4.0 requires a logon, by means of a user account (either on the local computer or in a network domain). If the user account is local, it is an actual user account in a local security accounts database, which the Windows 9*x* products do not have. Moreover, Windows NT 4.0 has file- and folder-level security if you use Windows NT 4.0's advanced file system, NT File System version 4 (NTFS4), on your local hard drive. The Properties dialog box of each folder and file on a drive formatted with NTFS will have a Security tab (see Figure 3-2) with a Permissions button that brings up a dialog box in which you can assign permissions (Read Only, Full Control, No Access, and so on) controlling user access to the file and folder. Learn more about file and folder security in Chapter 7.

While Windows NT uses folders graphically, many of the dialog boxes and messages continued to use the old term of *directory* for what we now know as a disk folder. These two terms are frequently used interchangeably even to this day.

Stability

Windows NT 4.0 is more stable than Windows 3.*x* or 9*x*. What does stability in an OS mean? Mainly, it means that you can work all day in many different applications without risking loss of your data because the system has *hung up*—a term that means that your computer has stopped responding to input from the keyboard and the mouse. Back when Windows NT 4.0 was the newest Windows OS, the best reason for installing it on a desktop computer was its stability. This appealed to a significant number of users and to IT people who had to support desktop computers. In Chapter 8 you will learn more about the "under-the-hood" components that contribute to this stability.

The proof is in the performance. Hermione is a believer in the stability of NT 4.0 compared to earlier versions of Windows. During the five years that she used Windows NT 4.0 on her desktop computer, her coworker Neville

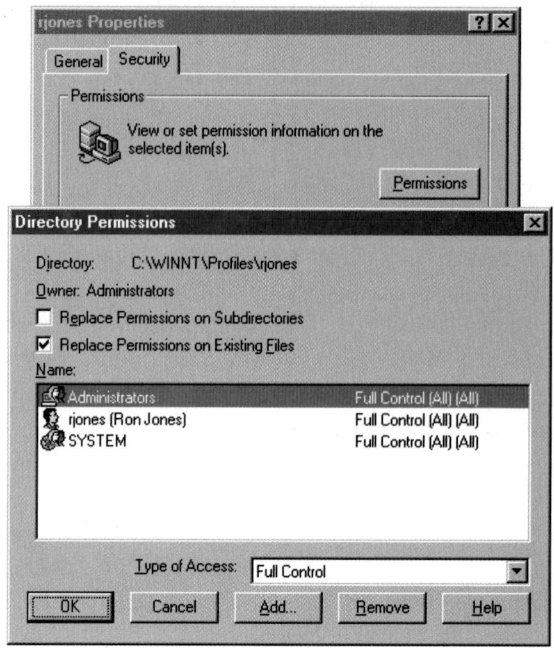

• **Figure 3-2.** The Directory Permissions dialog box

Inside Information

The Memory Race

When NT 4.0 came out several years ago, 4GB sounded like a truckload of RAM, but in the context of today's desktop PCs with ever increasing amounts of RAM, 4GB seems generous, but not outlandish. The programs being created today are increasing in size, too. Therefore, the way Windows NT 4.0 handles memory begins to make sense.

was using Windows 95 and then Windows 98. As the two worked in adjacent cubicles, Hermione would occasionally hear an anguished cry from Neville: his computer had hung up, had to be restarted, and he frequently lost his current work. Hermione might go for months without problems.

Memory

Windows NT 4.0 can use up to 4GB of RAM. On top of that, it uses virtual memory, which simply means that it can use some of your hard disk storage space as RAM. You can have more programs and data in memory than your physical memory can hold, thanks to the Virtual Memory Manager, which decides what can be safely moved out of RAM and onto a special disk area that the OS uses as memory. The file the operating system creates for this purpose is called the **swap file**.

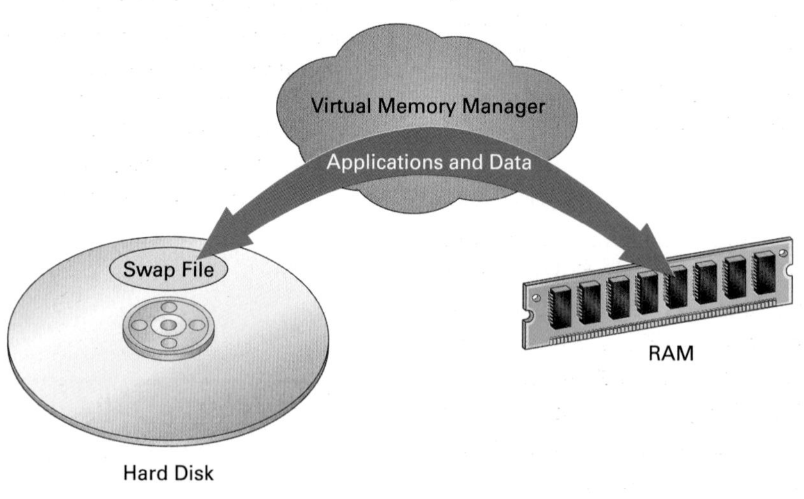

• The Virtual Memory Manager maximizes memory by swapping programs and data between RAM and the hard disk.

Software Compatibility with Legacy Applications

Just because you're running Windows NT 4.0 doesn't mean that all of your software must be written just for Windows NT 4.0. You may not even be able to find updated replacements for your important business applications; Microsoft thought about that problem. Windows NT Workstation 4.0 can run the following types of software:

- MS-DOS applications
- 16-bit Windows-based applications (written for Windows 3.*x*)
- 32-bit Windows-based applications (written for Windows 9*x* and NT 4.0)
- OS/2 version 1.*x* character-based applications
- OS/2 16-bit Presentation Manager applications (with separate add-in product)
- POSIX1-based applications (POSIX is short for portable operating system interface for computing environments)

Windows Applications and DOS Applications Windows NT 4.0 runs applications in environments called *subsystems.* The "native" applications of Windows NT are 32-bit Windows applications. These applications are written to a specific set of rules, and they run in the Win32 subsystem. DOS applications can run in the Win32 subsystem, with a little help. A DOS application runs, within a virtual DOS machine (VDM), as does any 16-bit Windows applications (written for Windows 3.*x*).

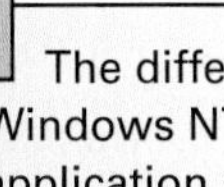

The difference between how Windows NT 4.0 handles a DOS application and how it handles a 16-bit Windows application is that NT adds a copy of Windows 3.*x* to the VDM before loading the 16-bit Windows application.

OS/2 and POSIX Applications Using subsystems, Windows NT 4.0 provides support for the other types of applications by creating simulated environments that look and feel like the OS for which the application was written. Recall OS/2 from Chapter 1? When an OS/2 application is started, Windows NT 4.0 starts an OS/2 subsystem, but it simulates a very old version of OS/2. Finally, the POSIX1 subsystem emulates POSIX1, a special UNIX environment. When one of these programs is launched, Windows NT 4.0 loads the correct subsystem for it.

To learn more about POSIX, point your browser to `en.wikipedia.org` and search on "POSIX."

The Limitations of Windows NT

How can an operating system with a name that stands for "new technology" be obsolete? Easy—in the computer world, nothing is new after six months, and a decade is like a geological era. The Windows NT 4.0 user interface began to show its age when Windows 98 came out two years later with some subtle changes to the GUI. It has really shown its age since Windows 2000 was introduced in 2000, and then Windows XP was introduced in 2001.

Hard Drive Limits

When you install Windows NT 4.0, the Setup program is able to create a hard disk partition with a maximum size of only 4GB—the partition limit of a FAT partition in Windows NT. Even when you tell the Setup program that you want the new partition to be formatted with NTFS, which has a far larger size limit, the Setup program still can create only a 4GB maximum partition. This is because the Windows NT 4.0 Setup program does not have the ability to format a drive as NTFS. Therefore, it formats using FAT and creates a script telling the newly installed OS to perform the NTFS conversion the first time it starts. Once you have Windows NT 4.0 installed and

Inside Information

Partition Limits Are Beyond NT

A partition is a portion of a hard disk that can be formatted to hold one or more logical drives. When you partition a drive, the maximum partition size is the lesser of two values: the maximum partition size supported by the hardware or the maximum partition size supported by the file system. The FAT16 file system has a 4GB partition size limit in Windows NT 4.0 (a 2GB partition size limit in Windows 9x); the NTFS file system has a partition size limit of 16 exabytes (an exabyte is one billion billion bytes). Now, this is obviously theoretical, because the hardware limit (mostly a BIOS thing) is more like 137GB, although this is changing.

running, you can create additional, larger partitions in unpartitioned free space on the same hard disk or other hard disks in the computer.

Windows NT and the Latest Hardware

As for Neville? He eventually outgrew his old computer and now uses a multi-GHz screamer with Windows XP. He now has stability as well as the latest gadgets.

Remember Hermione and Neville? She used Windows NT 4.0 for several years, whereas Neville used first Windows 95 and then Windows 98. Have you wondered why Neville put up with the instability of those OSs? He never considered putting Windows NT 4.0 on his computer because he needs and uses the latest and greatest hardware on his desktop computer, and Windows NT 4.0 doesn't support a great variety of hardware. Its biggest shortcoming in that area is that it doesn't support plug and play. There are many people like Neville, and for them, stodgy old Windows NT is, well, too stodgy. And realistically, this hardware limit has only become worse as more and newer peripherals continue to become available.

Windows NT and Legacy Software

Although Windows NT 4.0 has built-in support for applications written for several other OSs, some applications, most notoriously some DOS applications and 16-bit Windows applications, won't work in NT's simulated environment. Actually, Windows NT 4.0 can work with some applications, but you need to test each one to see if it will run at all, or if it runs too slowly under Windows NT 4.0 to be useful to you.

Why Is Windows NT 4.0 Still in Use?

Technology does not stand still, and today you're simply not going to select Windows NT 4.0 for your next new desktop PC. However, for the next few years of your career, you are sure to encounter it on the job from time to time. Here are some reasons why.

Windows NT 4.0 for Backward Compatibility

Installing Windows NT 4.0 on new machines to use existing licenses is a pretty weak reason for continuing to use it. Because of its limited hardware support, you are likely to run into hardware that Windows NT 4.0 simply can't use.

We have heard clients and students say that they're still using Windows NT 4.0 on the desktop because of a vertical market application (one specific to their industry) that was designed to run in Windows NT. Or perhaps it would actually run in newer Windows versions, but the vendor will support it only in Windows NT 4.0. Until that application is revised to run on a newer version of Windows, the user will stay with Windows NT. If you work in such an organization, you may have to install Windows NT 4.0 on replacement machines that will run the same application.

Windows NT—When That's All You Have!

Many organizations lease their computer systems and therefore use an OS for the length of the lease. A few years ago, a typical computer lease was for three years, but budget cuts have forced many companies to extend current leases, often to five years. This extends the life of old OSs and application suites, and also extends the length of time you need to stay knowledgeable about older technologies. Similarly, an organization that owns licenses for Windows NT 4.0 may continue to use those licenses when it replaces old computers with new.

Where Can I Find Windows NT 4.0 Today?

Microsoft publishes their Windows product life-cycle guidelines at www.microsoft.com/windows/lifecycle (see Figure 3-3). On this page they describe their policy and provide links to all the Windows products.

Use the link at the bottom of the Windows Life-Cycle Policy to view the Windows Service Pack Roadmap.

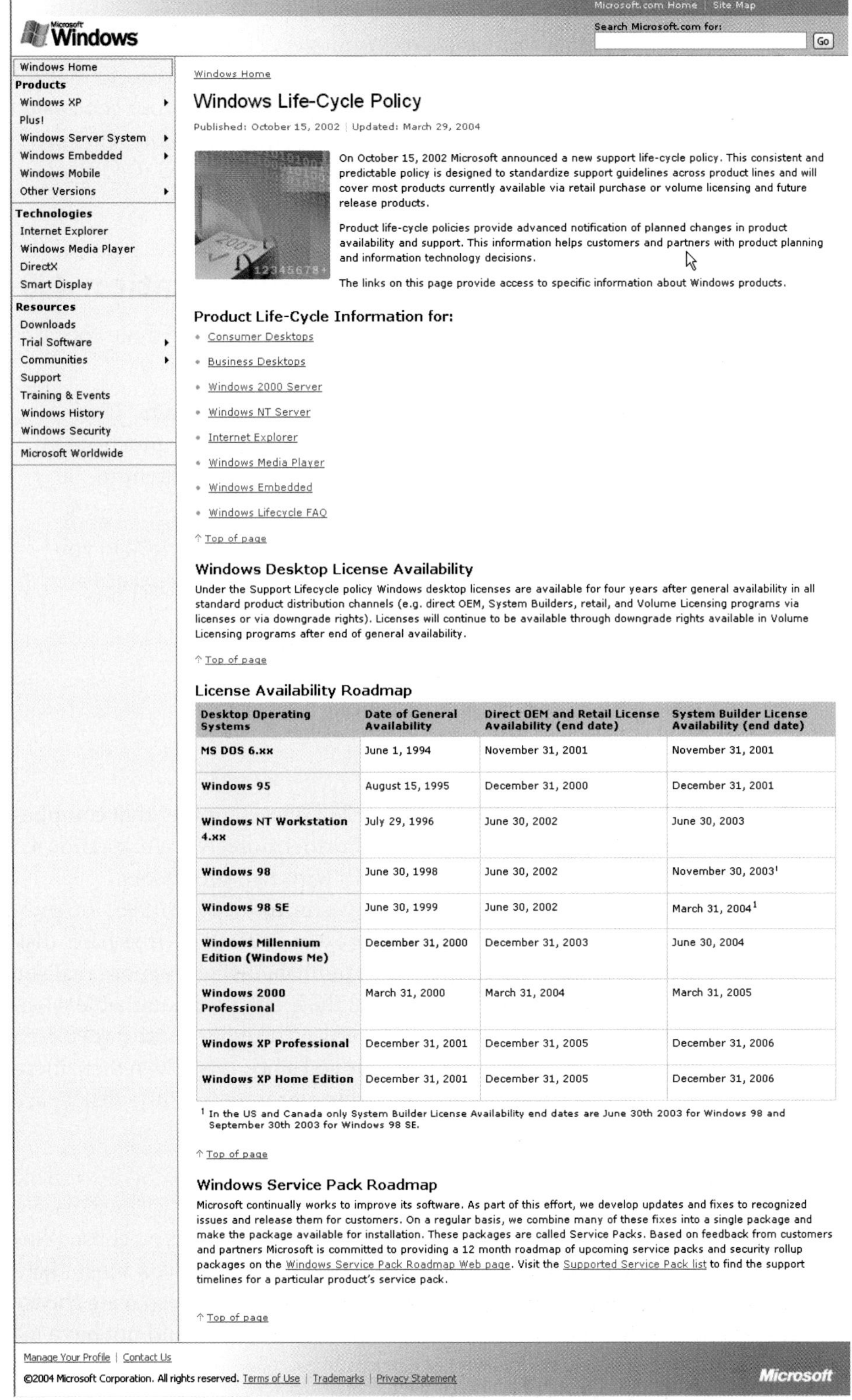

Microsoft.com Home | Site Map

Search Microsoft.com for: Go

Microsoft Windows

Windows Home

Products

- Windows XP
- Plus!
- Windows Server System
- Windows Embedded
- Windows Mobile
- Other Versions

Technologies

- Internet Explorer
- Windows Media Player
- DirectX
- Smart Display

Resources

- Downloads
- Trial Software
- Communities
- Support
- Training & Events
- Windows History
- Windows Security

Microsoft Worldwide

Windows Home

Windows Life-Cycle Policy

Published: October 15, 2002 | Updated: March 29, 2004

On October 15, 2002 Microsoft announced a new support life-cycle policy. This consistent and predictable policy is designed to standardize support guidelines across product lines and will cover most products currently available via retail purchase or volume licensing and future release products.

Product life-cycle policies provide advanced notification of planned changes in product availability and support. This information helps customers and partners with product planning and information technology decisions.

The links on this page provide access to specific information about Windows products.

Product Life-Cycle Information for:

- Consumer Desktops
- Business Desktops
- Windows 2000 Server
- Windows NT Server
- Internet Explorer
- Windows Media Player
- Windows Embedded
- Windows Lifecycle FAQ

Top of page

Windows Desktop License Availability

Under the Support Lifecycle policy Windows desktop licenses are available for four years after general availability in all standard product distribution channels (e.g. direct OEM, System Builders, retail, and Volume Licensing programs via licenses or via downgrade rights). Licenses will continue to be available through downgrade rights available in Volume Licensing programs after end of general availability.

Top of page

License Availability Roadmap

Desktop Operating Systems	Date of General Availability	Direct OEM and Retail License Availability (end date)	System Builder License Availability (end date)
MS DOS 6.xx	June 1, 1994	November 31, 2001	November 31, 2001
Windows 95	August 15, 1995	December 31, 2000	December 31, 2001
Windows NT Workstation 4.xx	July 29, 1996	June 30, 2002	June 30, 2003
Windows 98	June 30, 1998	June 30, 2002	November 30, 2003[1]
Windows 98 SE	June 30, 1999	June 30, 2002	March 31, 2004[1]
Windows Millennium Edition (Windows Me)	December 31, 2000	December 31, 2003	June 30, 2004
Windows 2000 Professional	March 31, 2000	March 31, 2004	March 31, 2005
Windows XP Professional	December 31, 2001	December 31, 2005	December 31, 2006
Windows XP Home Edition	December 31, 2001	December 31, 2005	December 31, 2006

[1] In the US and Canada only System Builder License Availability end dates are June 30th 2003 for Windows 98 and September 30th 2003 for Windows 98 SE.

Top of page

Windows Service Pack Roadmap

Microsoft continually works to improve its software. As part of this effort, we develop updates and fixes to recognized issues and release them for customers. On a regular basis, we combine many of these fixes into a single package and make the package available for installation. These packages are called Service Packs. Based on feedback from customers and partners Microsoft is committed to providing a 12 month roadmap of upcoming service packs and security rollup packages on the Windows Service Pack Roadmap Web page. Visit the Supported Service Pack list to find the support timelines for a particular product's service pack.

Top of page

Manage Your Profile | Contact Us

©2004 Microsoft Corporation. All rights reserved. Terms of Use | Trademarks | Privacy Statement

Microsoft

• **Figure 3-3.** Microsoft has a published policy for availability and support for their products.

Another reason to learn about Windows NT 4.0 Workstation is that Windows 2000 and Windows XP are simply new versions of Windows NT. What you learn here is worthwhile because, although those OSs improved on Windows NT 4.0, they still have many of the same features and characteristics.

Information on this page shows that Direct OEM licenses and System Builder licenses have not been available for Windows NT 4.0 since June 30, 2002, and June 30, 2003, respectively. These types of licenses are for companies that preinstall and bundle the OS with new computers. At this writing, the retail version of NT 4.0 Workstation is still available through online retailers.

According to the Business Desktops link on the Life-Cycle page, support for Windows NT 4.0 Workstation ended June 30, 2004. Microsoft will leave the technical support information for Windows NT 4.0 Workstation at its web site, but can discontinue this with 12 months' notice. Add to that the newer replacements for Windows NT 4.0 Workstation, and your conclusion must be that Windows NT 4.0 Workstation is no longer a viable retail product. However, we urge you to learn about it because it is still used in many organizations.

Hardware and Windows NT Workstation 4.0

When you prepare to install an operating system, you have three concerns regarding the computer hardware:

- What are the minimum requirements for running the OS? How much "horsepower" is required in the processor, how much RAM and hard disk space, what video capabilities, and what input devices?
- What will support the job you want this computer to do? Do you need a more powerful processor? More RAM or disk space? Fancy video?
- What hardware is compatible with this OS?

Let's take a closer look at these concerns.

Inside Information

Symmetric Multiprocessing Support in Windows NT

Most desktop computers are built around a single processor. Symmetric multiprocessing (SMP) computers are built around multiple identical processors. In these systems, the processors have equal access to physical memory, and an OS must be specifically designed to take advantage of the horsepower of these multiple processors. Whereas Windows NT Workstation, Windows 2000, and Windows XP support SMP with two processors, the Windows Server operating systems from Windows NT Server through Windows Server 2003 support more than two processors—up to 32 with the most advanced versions of Windows Server 2003. Hmmm...it's a pretty safe bet that your desktop computer has only a single processor.

Requirements

Windows NT 4.0 Workstation can be installed on a computer that complies with the Intel/Microsoft set of standards. Furthermore, NT Workstation 4.0 supports symmetric multiprocessing (SMP) with two processors.

When Windows NT Workstation 4.0 was introduced in 1996, the published minimums included a 486/33 processor, 110MB of free hard disk space, and 12MB of RAM. Microsoft later published slightly more realistic minimum requirements on its web site, but these still seem laughable when you think of the computers you see advertised in your local paper each week. This shows how far the world has moved since 1996. Even then, these minimums would have left you with a computer with too little disk space and RAM to install an office suite of software.

Ideal Hardware Configuration

In the first two years that Windows NT 4.0 was available, if you chose Windows NT Workstation for your desktop over Windows 95, you most likely had a very good reason, such as security and stability. You also were choosing a much more expensive OS than Windows 95. You would not have installed this OS on an underpowered computer.

The ideal hardware configuration varies based on the needs of the applications to be run on the computer, but, for us, the ideal configuration for Windows NT on a desktop computer with a standard set of office applications (word processor, spreadsheet, mail, and so on) installed looks like the following:

- Intel Pentium processor
- 128MB RAM
- 2 to 4GB available hard disk space
- CD-ROM drive
- SVGA or higher-resolution video adapter
- Microsoft mouse

Cross Check

How Does Windows NT 4.0 Measure Up as an Operating System?

Consider what you have learned so far about Windows NT 4.0, and look back to the section "Purpose, Types, and Functions of Microcomputer Operating Systems" in Chapter 1. Then answer the following questions:

1. What operating system functions are supported in Windows NT 4.0?
2. Are any functions completely unsupported in Windows NT 4.0?
3. Of the functions supported in Windows NT 4.0, which, in your opinion, need to be improved on? Please elaborate.

Compatible Products

Although official support has ended for Windows NT, Microsoft maintains a site called the Windows Quality Online Services, where you can download a text file of the last Hardware Compatibility List (HCL) they created for NT. See Figure 3-4. The HCL is a list of hardware that has passed Microsoft's compatibility tests for Windows NT 4.0. You can also check out any driver disk that comes with your hardware to see if it lists an NT driver. Finally, check out the web site of the hardware manufacturer.

A very outdated HCL is on the Windows NT 4.0 CD. Don't use it! The best information is on the Microsoft web site.

If you aren't sure how you would search for compatible hardware products, consider Keisha, who is getting ready to install Windows NT 4.0 on a replacement computer because the previous computer had an application that requires it. Keisha wants to add a device that requires an Institute of Electrical and Electronic Engineers (IEEE) 1394 (FireWire) controller, and her department is converting from a wired Ethernet network to a wireless network. She has heard that Windows NT doesn't support IEEE 1394 controllers or wireless network adapters and so has decided to learn whether NT does, indeed, support these hardware devices. She will start by downloading the HCL.

Try This!

Check Out the HCL for Windows NT 4.0

To complete this task, you will need a computer with an Internet connection and a web browser. Try this:

1. Point your web browser at `https://winqual.microsoft.com/download/default.asp`.
2. In the download column, click on NT40xHCL.txt. This will open the Hardware Compatibility List for Windows NT 4.0.
3. Search through the list for "1394 Controller." You will see just one controller listed under this category. Now you would have to research the availability of this controller.
4. Further search of manufacturers' web sites might turn up more controllers that have device drivers for Windows NT 4.0.

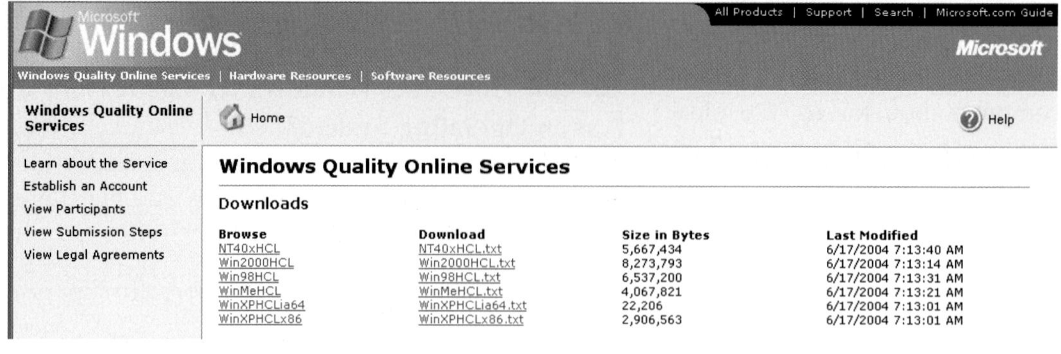

• **Figure 3-4.** Download the Windows NT 4.0 HCL from the Windows Quality Online Services page.

Installing Windows NT Workstation 4.0

You've completed an overview of the features and limits of Windows NT, considered the hardware requirements and recommendations for installing NT, and know where to go to find out if your hardware and software is compatible with Windows NT. Now you need to install Windows NT so you can learn how to work with it.

Before you install Windows NT, or any OS, you need to perform the following tasks: choose between an upgrade or clean installation, select and prepare the hardware, determine what service packs and updates are needed, determine the method of installation, and gather the materials (disks, drivers, applications, and so on) you'll need to complete the installation.

Upgrade vs. Clean Installation

An upgrade installation of an operating system involves installing a new operating system on top of an existing operating system. A **clean installation** is an installation onto a completely empty hard disk.

The Reality of Upgrading

The goal of an upgrade is to save work by having the new OS assume all the settings of the previous OS, and to avoid having to reinstall the applications into the new installation. With any version of Windows, you perform an upgrade by installing into the existing Windows installation directory.

But it may not be as simple as you would hope. Some previously installed applications may be incompatible with the new operating system, or need to be uninstalled or disabled before beginning the upgrade. This is especially true of antivirus software. There is also the possibility that an installed device may not be supported in the new operating system. We had this happen with a "name brand" external CD-ROM drive when we upgraded a laptop from Windows 95 to Windows 2000. So, an upgrade is not as simple as it sounds, requiring research into all the installed applications, utilities, and drivers before you begin the upgrade.

The Reality of Performing a Clean Installation

The goal of a clean installation is to avoid inheriting problems from a previous installation. For this reason, when performing a clean installation, if the hard disk was previously used, you would have the Windows Setup program repartition and format the disk. A partition defines the boundaries of a logical drive, and repartitioning rewrites the partition information in the master boot record (MBR), making the previous logical drive and its contents unavailable. Once you repartition, you must format each logical drive within the partition (one for each primary partition, and one or more for each extended partition).

There are subtle differences in how different OSs partition disks, and some installed utilities (or viruses) may have altered the MBR and boot record on the disk. A repartition and format will truly give you a clean disk.

Now for the bad news: a clean installation is a lot of work when done manually. For this reason, many organizations now use other more advanced methods, such as a hands-free, scripted install, or use of an **image**, which is an exact duplicate of the entire hard drive contents, including the OS and all installed software. But these methods are, for the most part, only employed in large organizations. Even then, it's important to know how to build a desktop, meaning to install an operating system and all appropriate software, as well as to configure it for daily use.

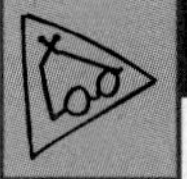

Inside Information

Images

The use of images is very popular in medium to large organizations that have dozens, hundreds, or thousands of desktop computers. You create a custom image for a large number of users by installing the OS on a reference computer identical to those on which the images will eventually be placed. Then you install all the necessary applications, and finally, you customize the desktop, complete with shortcuts, and add the corporate wallpaper. Next, you use special imaging software, such as Symantec's Ghost (`www.ghost.com`) to copy the image of the hard drive. It can be copied onto a CD, but it is usually copied to a network server and then distributed from there. Other similar products include Paragon's Hard Disk Manager (`http://www.paragon-gmbh.com/`) and Drive Image by PowerQuest. (At the time of this writing, you could access their web site at `www.powerquest.com`, but PowerQuest was purchased by Symantec in December 2003, so this URL may change.)

Select and Prepare the Hardware

To install Windows NT on a computer hard disk, you must be sure that the computer is physically ready for the installation. That is, ensure that the computer is a complete system, with at least the minimal hardware recommendations, and that all of the hardware is compatible with Windows NT 4.0. You also need to ensure that all necessary connections are in place for the installed components and that the computer is plugged into a power outlet. The computer hard disk does not have to be specially prepared for Windows NT installation, because the Windows NT Setup program can prepare the hard disk.

Determine the Service Pack and Updates to Use

After any software company releases complex software such as Windows NT, the programming staff continues to work on the software. Programmers receive feedback about problems from customers, and they re-create the problems and come up with software fixes called **patches** or updates. Those that solve security problems and/or problems that can potentially cause major failures are now called critical updates.

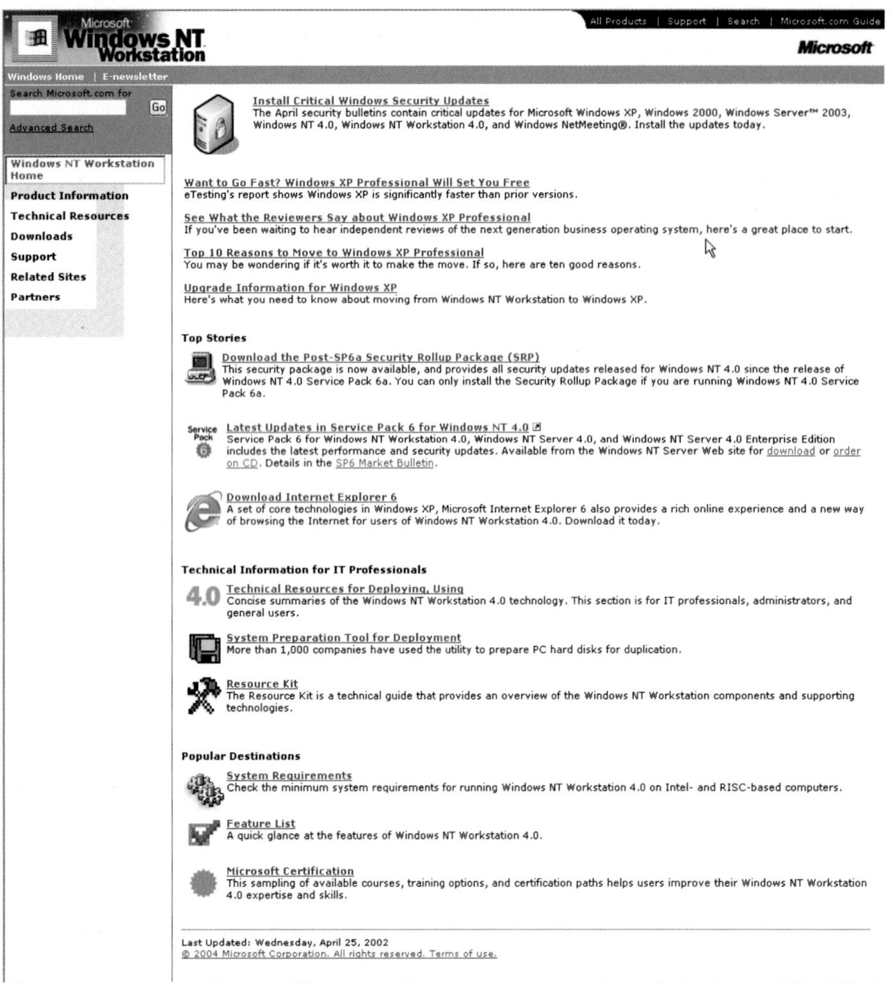

Microsoft Windows NT Workstation
All Products | Support | Search | Microsoft.com Guide
Microsoft
Windows Home | E-newsletter
Search Microsoft.com for
Go
Advanced Search
Windows NT Workstation Home
Product Information
Technical Resources
Downloads
Support
Related Sites
Partners
Install Critical Windows Security Updates
The April security bulletins contain critical updates for Microsoft Windows XP, Windows 2000, Windows Server™ 2003, Windows NT 4.0, Windows NT Workstation 4.0, and Windows NetMeeting®. Install the updates today.
Want to Go Fast? Windows XP Professional Will Set You Free
eTesting's report shows Windows XP is significantly faster than prior versions.
See What the Reviewers Say about Windows XP Professional
If you've been waiting to hear independent reviews of the next generation business operating system, here's a great place to start.
Top 10 Reasons to Move to Windows XP Professional
You may be wondering if it's worth it to make the move. If so, here are ten good reasons.
Upgrade Information for Windows XP
Here's what you need to know about moving from Windows NT Workstation to Windows XP.
Top Stories
Download the Post-SP6a Security Rollup Package (SRP)
This security package is now available, and provides all security updates released for Windows NT 4.0 since the release of Windows NT 4.0 Service Pack 6a. You can only install the Security Rollup Package if you are running Windows NT 4.0 Service Pack 6a.
Service Pack 6
Latest Updates in Service Pack 6 for Windows NT 4.0
Service Pack 6 for Windows NT Workstation 4.0, Windows NT Server 4.0, and Windows NT Server 4.0 Enterprise Edition includes the latest performance and security updates. Available from the Windows NT Server Web site for download or order on CD. Details in the SP6 Market Bulletin.
Download Internet Explorer 6
A set of core technologies in Windows XP, Microsoft Internet Explorer 6 also provides a rich online experience and a new way of browsing the Internet for users of Windows NT Workstation 4.0. Download it today.
Technical Information for IT Professionals
4.0
Technical Resources for Deploying, Using
Concise summaries of the Windows NT Workstation 4.0 technology. This section is for IT professionals, administrators, and general users.
System Preparation Tool for Deployment
More than 1,000 companies have used the utility to prepare PC hard disks for duplication.
Resource Kit
The Resource Kit is a technical guide that provides an overview of the Windows NT Workstation components and supporting technologies.
Popular Destinations
System Requirements
Check the minimum system requirements for running Windows NT Workstation 4.0 on Intel- and RISC-based computers.
Feature List
A quick glance at the features of Windows NT Workstation 4.0.
Microsoft Certification
This sampling of available courses, training options, and certification paths helps users improve their Windows NT Workstation 4.0 expertise and skills.
Last Updated: Wednesday, April 25, 2002
© 2004 Microsoft Corporation. All rights reserved. Terms of use.

• Windows NT Workstation home page

What Do I Need and Where Do I Look?

Microsoft releases updates individually, as they are completed, and the company also periodically bundles together a series of accumulated updates into a larger package called a **service pack**. These, in turn, are made available in versions, or levels, such as Service Pack 1 and Service Pack 2. NT 4.0's service packs were numbered through 6a (a post–Service Pack 6 release), which was followed by the post–SP6a Security Rollup Package (SRP). You can find out more about the updates and service packs for Windows NT 4.0 at `www.microsoft.com/ntworkstation`.

The service pack level in NT 4.0 is critical; you should never install and use Windows NT 4.0 without planning to add a service pack immediately after the installation.

Although service packs that fix problems are a fact of life with today's very complex OSs, Windows NT 4.0 service packs were also renowned not just for fixing problems with the OS, but for adding new features. However, sometimes the fixes and/or new features actually cause new problems. Therefore, most organizations that exercise standards and control over their desktop computers mandate that a new service pack can't be installed until it has been thoroughly tested on nonproduction PCs in a test lab.

> If you have reason to install NT 4.0 on a PC at school or at work, be sure to check with an administrator to learn the approved service pack level.

Determine the Method of Installation

To install Windows NT (without using a third-party product), you can choose a manual installation or an automated installation, both of which have variations.

Manual Installation

A manual installation is high maintenance, requiring your attention throughout the entire process to provide information and to respond to messages. You will perform a manual installation in Step-by-Step 3.02. This is the method you would choose for a unique installation, or if the number of computers is too few to warrant the time, effort, and expense that an automated installation requires.

After deciding on a manual installation, you still have choices to make:

- Will the distribution files (those in the i386 directory on the Windows NT 4.0 CD-ROM) be located on the local computer or on the network server? If you don't have a CD-ROM drive in the computer, but it is connected to a network, then you'll have to boot the computer with an operating system that has the network components installed so you can connect to the server where the source files are stored.
- If the computer does have a CD-ROM drive, will it work for the installation—that is, will the Windows NT 4.0 Setup program recognize it, and will the computer boot from the CD-ROM drive? If you can boot from the CD-ROM drive, then your manual installation can be completed as shown in Step-by-Step 3.02.
- If a CD-ROM drive is present and is recognized by Windows NT Setup (which you may be able to determine only by trying), but you can't boot from it, you will need the three Windows NT 4.0 Workstation setup disks, as well as the CD-ROM disk. Place the first disk in the drive, restart, and follow the onscreen instructions.

The OS you use to boot the computer and connect to the network can be DOS or another version of Windows. Once you connect to the source location, you run the NT Setup program using WINNT.EXE (for DOS) or WINNT32.EXE (for Windows).

If your computer won't boot from the CD-ROM drive, a change to the computer's system settings may be required. Don't try to change the settings without expert help, because the wrong changes to the system settings can disable your computer.

Step-by-Step 3.01

Creating the Windows NT 4.0 Setup Disks from Windows or DOS

To create the Windows NT 4.0 setup disks, you can use any version of Windows or MS-DOS, as long as it recognizes the installed CD-ROM drive. The preferred method is to do this from Windows. If you do not have a spare computer with Windows on which to create the Setup Disks, you can use the Windows 98 Startup Disk. Boot up and select CD-ROM support. This startup disk also loads drivers that speed up the copying process. Once you are at an A: prompt, remove the Windows 98 Startup Disk. You will not see the GUI dialog boxes shown next, but will see equivalent pages in character mode with a blue background.

You will need the following:

- A computer running MS-DOS or Windows 3.*x* or greater
- The Windows NT CD-ROM
- Three formatted, blank, high-density 3.5-inch floppy disks

Step 1

Place the Windows NT CD in the drive. If your computer supports AutoPlay for CDs, the Windows NT CD window will appear. Close the window.

In Windows 95 or greater, select Start | Run. In the Open box, type the following:

```
d:\i386\winnt32 /ox
```

Replace *d* with the drive letter of your CD-ROM drive; i386 is the directory where the installation program is located, winnt32 is the 32-bit NT installation program used by Windows 95 or greater, and /ox is a switch used to create a set of installation floppy disks.

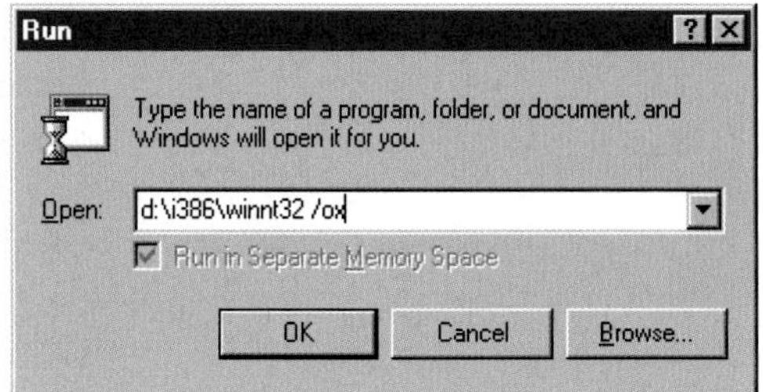

In MS-DOS or Windows 3.*x*, enter the following from a command prompt and click OK:

```
d:\i386\winnt /ox
```

Replace *d* with the drive letter of your CD-ROM drive; i386 is the directory where the installation program is located, winnt is the 16-bit NT installation program used by DOS and Windows 3.*x*, and /ox is a switch used to create a set of installation floppy disks.

Step 2

On the Windows NT 4.00 Upgrade/Installation page, verify that the location of the Windows NT 4.0 files includes the drive letter for your CD-ROM drive and also the i386 directory; then click Continue.

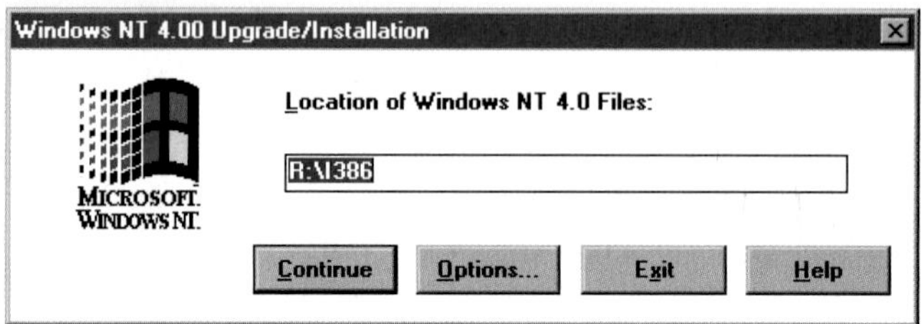

Step 3

Follow the instructions in the Installation/Upgrade Information box, and label three formatted, blank, high-density 3.5-inch floppy disks. Insert the one labeled "Windows NT Workstation Setup Disk #3" in the floppy drive and click OK or press ENTER.

Step 4

Follow the instructions on the screen; when Disk #3 has been prepared, you will be prompted to replace it with Disk #2. When Disk #2 has been prepared, you will be prompted to replace it with the disk labeled "Windows NT Workstation Setup Boot Disk." When this disk has been prepared, you have your entire set.

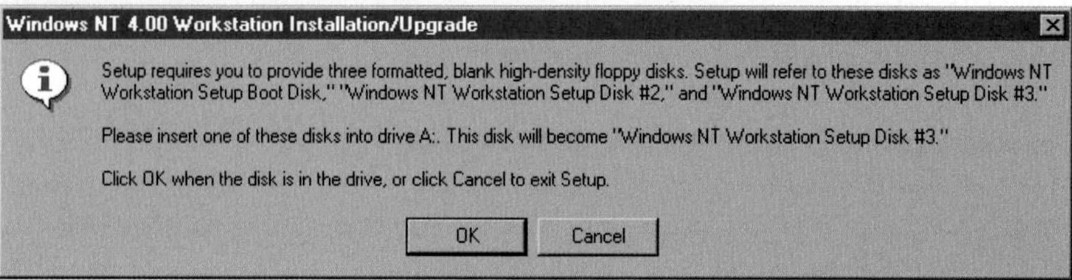

Step 5

If you are installing NT on the same computer, leave the floppy disk in the drive and restart the computer. However, if you want to install NT on a different computer, remove the floppy disk and keep all three floppy disks together until you are ready to use them in Step-by-Step 3.02.

Automated Installation You perform an automated installation of Windows NT 4.0 using scripts that someone (often a team of people) has prepared ahead of time. This method is used by organizations with large numbers of desktop computers that need identical applications and desktop configurations. This method requires training and planning by one or more people.

The WINNT and WINNT32 Setup Programs Automated installations and some manual installations may require the use of the WINNT.EXE or WINNT32.EXE program.

- An automated installation using the scripting method for Windows NT 4.0 provided by Microsoft uses either of these programs with appropriate command-line switches to select the scripts.
- A manual installation in which you don't boot from the CD or the setup boot disks requires the use of one of these programs; which one depends on the operating system in control at the time. Did you boot from a DOS disk to install from source files over the network? Then you need to use WINNT.EXE, the version for DOS or Windows 3.*x*. Are you upgrading from Windows 95 to Windows NT? Then you need to boot into Windows 95 and run WINNT32.EXE.

To learn about the syntax of either the winnt or winnt32 command, open a command prompt and run the command followed by the /? parameter.

A Windows NT Installation Strategy

Regardless of the method you choose to use for your installation, we strongly suggest a strategy commonly used with Windows NT 4.0: install Windows NT 4.0 using the generic drivers provided with the OS, especially for your video adapter. You will not be able to access all of the capabilities of the adapter right away, but hang in there—we have a reason for this strategy. After you have the OS installed and running with basic drivers, then you should apply service packs. It turns out that some newer drivers do install, but they do not work until you apply service packs. This is because support for such newer technology as the AGP video adapters wasn't included in Windows NT 4.0, but was added in service packs. After applying the appropriate service pack, install the new drivers.

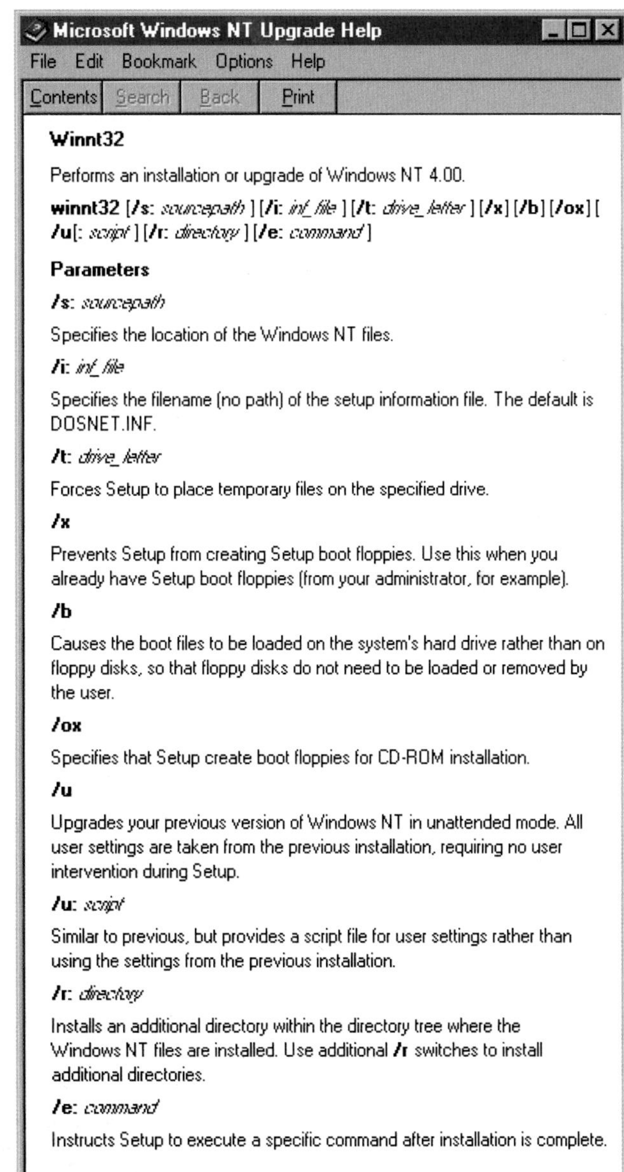

Winnt32

Performs an installation or upgrade of Windows NT 4.00.

winnt32 [**/s:** *sourcepath*] [**/i:** *inf_file*] [**/t:** *drive_letter*] [**/x**] [**/b**] [**/ox**] [**/u**[: *script*] [**/r:** *directory*] [**/e:** *command*]

Parameters

/s: *sourcepath*

Specifies the location of the Windows NT files.

/i: *inf_file*

Specifies the filename (no path) of the setup information file. The default is DOSNET.INF.

/t: *drive_letter*

Forces Setup to place temporary files on the specified drive.

/x

Prevents Setup from creating Setup boot floppies. Use this when you already have Setup boot floppies (from your administrator, for example).

/b

Causes the boot files to be loaded on the system's hard drive rather than on floppy disks, so that floppy disks do not need to be loaded or removed by the user.

/ox

Specifies that Setup create boot floppies for CD-ROM installation.

/u

Upgrades your previous version of Windows NT in unattended mode. All user settings are taken from the previous installation, requiring no user intervention during Setup.

/u: *script*

Similar to previous, but provides a script file for user settings rather than using the settings from the previous installation.

/r: *directory*

Installs an additional directory within the directory tree where the Windows NT files are installed. Use additional **/r** switches to install additional directories.

/e: *command*

Instructs Setup to execute a specific command after installation is complete.

• WINNT32.EXE syntax

Gather the Materials Needed for Installation

If your computer and its components are newer than 1996 (and we hope they are!), Windows NT 4.0 will not have all of the correct drivers for your system. A driver is a special file containing program code that allows an OS to interact with and control a hardware device. You will need the device drivers for your installed hardware. Driver files are supplied by the manufacturer of the device, so if you can't locate the driver disk that came with the device, contact the manufacturer. Today that's as easy as connecting to the manufacturer's web site and downloading the driver.

If you'll be installing Windows NT 4.0 from source files on a network server, you won't need the CD, but you will need to be able to start your computer with an

OS configured with the correct drivers and network client software to access the network and the server.

If your computer will boot from a CD-ROM, you need only the Windows NT 4.0 Workstation CD; if your computer has a CD-ROM drive but can't boot from it, you'll also need the three Windows NT Workstation setup disks. If that's the case, and if you don't have the floppy disks, you can create a new set. Step-by-Step 3.01 has instructions to do this.

You should also have a 3.5-inch floppy disk ready so that you can create an **emergency repair disk (ERD)**. An ERD is important to create and keep up-to-date, because it is needed to recover from damage to the operating system files through the emergency repair process, described in the troubleshooting section of this chapter.

Begin Installation

If you have selected and prepared the hardware, determined your strategy for installation, and checked out the service pack level approved for use at your school or at work, then you are nearly ready to install.

Whenever possible, do a clean installation of a new operating system. We even prefer to start with an unpartitioned hard disk. Unless it is a brand-new hard disk, we remove the old partition and allow the setup program to create a new partition and format it during the installation process.

Step-by-Step 3.02

Installing Windows NT Workstation 4.0

The steps in this exercise assume a clean installation on an unpartitioned hard drive. To complete this exercise, you'll need the following:

- A Microsoft/Intel standard personal computer (desktop or laptop) configured to boot from CD-ROM
- An unpartitioned hard disk (disk 0, the first hard disk)
- The Windows NT Workstation 4.0 CD
- Three Windows NT setup disks, if your computer doesn't boot from CD-ROM
- One 3.5-inch floppy disk to use as an emergency repair disk
- The CD key code from the envelope of your NT CD
- A 15-character (or less) name for your computer, unique on your network
- The name of the workgroup to be used in the class lab
- A 14-character (or less) password for the Administrator account on your computer
- The TCP/IP configuration information for your computer, or confirmation from your instructor that you should configure Windows NT to get an IP address automatically

Step 1

Insert the Windows NT Workstation 4.0 CD and restart the computer. After the computer restarts, you'll briefly see a black screen with a message at the top left: "Setup is inspecting your computer's hardware configuration…" Then a nearly empty blue screen appears, labeled simply "Windows NT Workstation Setup." This is the preparation for text mode of the setup program. When all of the NT Setup files are loaded into memory, the setup program's version of the NT kernel will be loaded and initialized (made active).

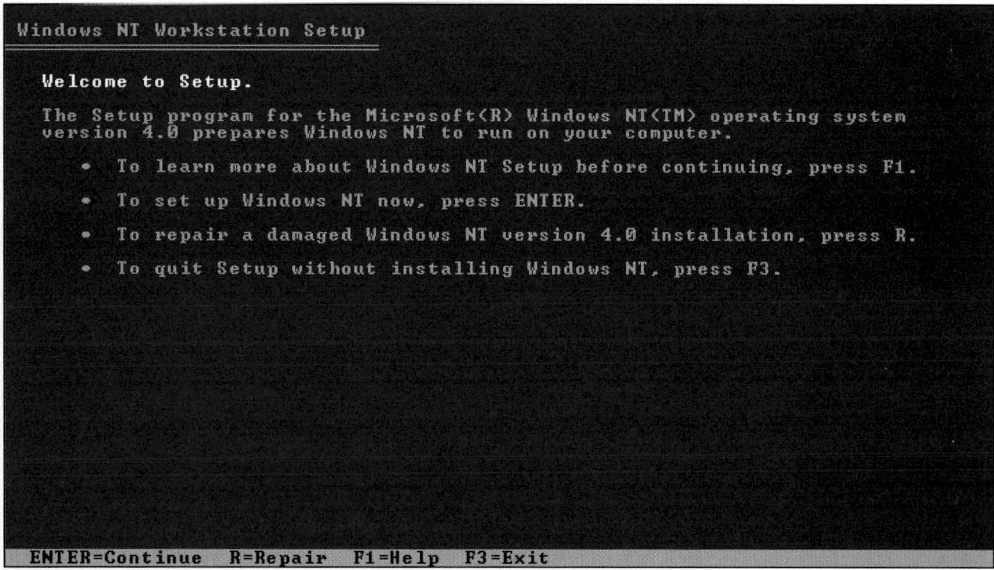

Step 2

For the next several screens, follow the instructions, responding based on the list at the beginning of this step-by-step. In addition, if your hard disk is unpartitioned, have NT Setup create a partition that is greater than 500MB and that leaves unpartitioned space available for use later. Select NTFS as the file system for the new partition. Accept the default location for the setup program to install the OS. At the conclusion of the text-mode setup, you will be prompted to remove the CD and floppy disk (if present) and your computer will reboot.

Step 3

After the reboot, NT Setup starts in GUI mode, and the words "Windows NT Setup" appear over blue and black wallpaper. This will be the background for NT Setup until the next reboot. The first message box on this background shows the progress of files being copied. Reinsert your Windows NT 4.0 CD now.

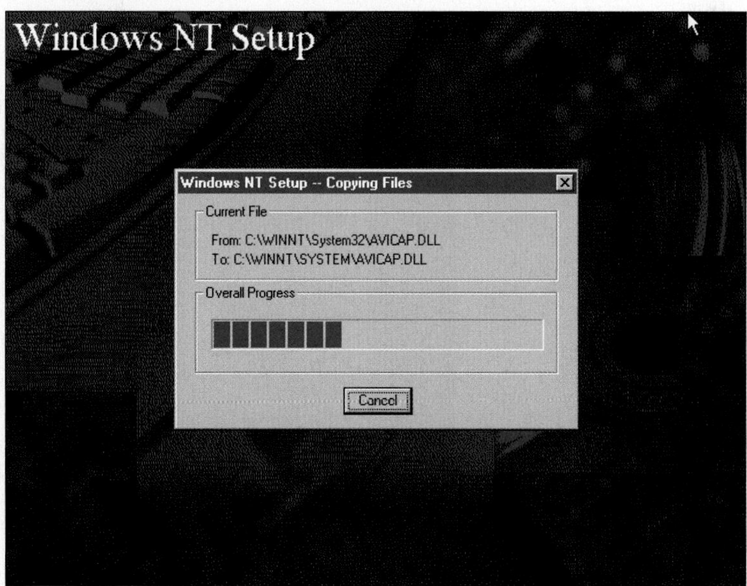

Step 4

The "Welcome to the Windows NT Setup Wizard" message appears, informing you that it will perform three parts: gathering information about the computer, installing Windows NT networking, and finishing setup. Notice that the first step is highlighted. This message will reappear at the beginning of the next two parts of the setup. To continue, press ENTER or click the Next button.

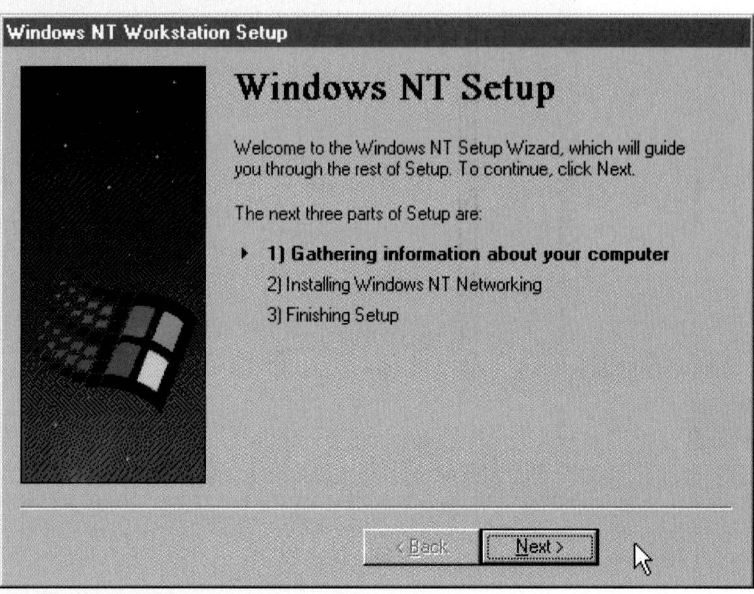

Step 5

The wizard will guide you through the information gathering steps. You will have to make choices and provide more information. Select Typical on the Setup Options page, fill in the Name and Organization page, and have NT Setup install the most common components. Provide the setup program with the information from the list at the beginning of this step-by-step.

Step 6

During the steps for installing Windows NT networking, use the information about your network settings that you prepared at the beginning of this step-by-step.

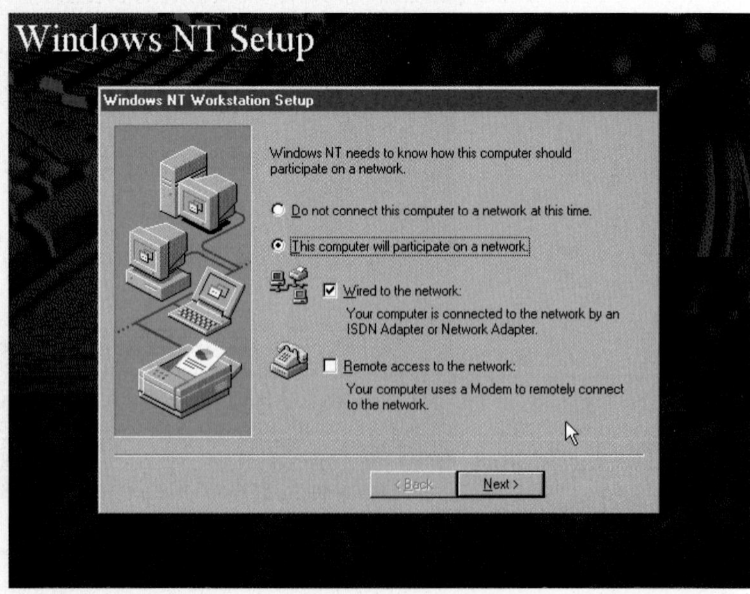

Step 7

During the steps for finishing setup, select your time zone and test your display settings; then NT Setup will copy the files necessary to complete the installation and configure the components. When it is finished, you will be prompted to restart the computer. A test of a successful installation is a successful reboot, so remove any floppy disks and CDs, and then click the Restart Computer button. Log on with the Administrator account, using the password you provided during setup.

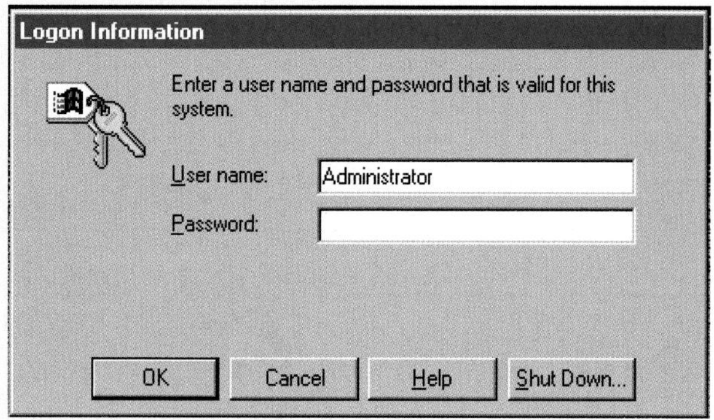

Performing Post-Installation Tasks

After Windows NT 4.0 is installed, you have a few necessary post-installation tasks. They include verifying network access (assuming you are connected to a network) and installing the necessary service pack. These tasks should be completed before moving on to customizing the desktop for yourself or another user and performing other desktop management tasks.

Copy Distribution Files Once the operating system is installed, if you have sufficient free hard disk space, it is a good practice to copy the i386 directory from the distribution CD-ROM to the local hard drive. Then, when you add device drivers and other components, you won't have to locate the CD so that the component can be installed; you simply browse to the new location.

Verify Network Access You have successfully installed Windows NT Workstation on a user's desktop. If the user requires access to a LAN and the computer was connected to the LAN during installation, it should have all the right stuff to work on the LAN, but you must verify that the computer can connect to the other computers on the network. We're saving the details of networking for Chapter 10, but right now we'll have you do a simple test of network connectivity, because this is a task normally done immediately after installing an OS.

The simplest test, although it is not entirely reliable, is to use Network Neighborhood to see other computers on your network. In the example here, the list includes an NT Server named HTC1, a Windows XP computer named LAGUNA, and the computer on which we installed Windows NT 4.0 Workstation, SEDONA-NT. If you encounter problems with your network connection in the class lab, ask your instructor to help you solve the problem.

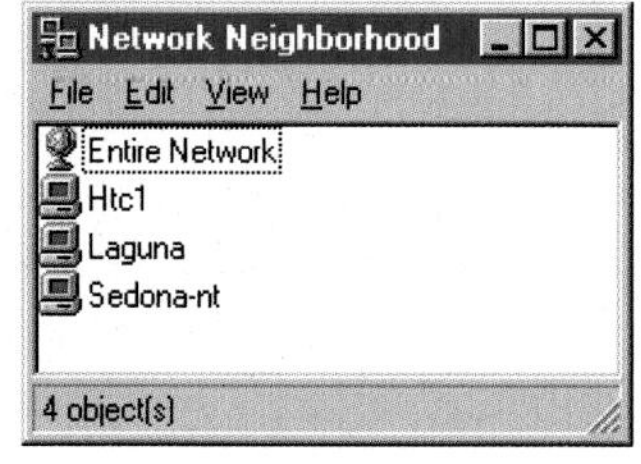

• Network Neighborhood

Inside Information

What Computers Are Visible in Network Neighborhood?

Computers are visible in Network Neighborhood only if they have a special service called the Server service turned on, meaning that the computer is capable of sharing its file folders and printers with others on the network. Windows NT Workstation has this service turned on by default. It makes sense that such a service would exist on server operating systems because that is, after all, their reason for being, and those OSs are tuned to support even a high volume of user access. It is available in desktop operating systems so users can share file folders and printers with a small number of other users. This is called peer-to-peer networking. You will learn more about networking in Chapters 9 and 10.

Try This!

Verify Network Access Using Network Neighborhood

Your instructor will tell you what computers should be visible on your network. Try this:

1. On the desktop, locate and double-click the Network Neighborhood icon.
2. When the Network Neighborhood window opens, you will see a listing of the computers visible on your network. If other computers are visible to you, then you are connected to the network, even if you cannot see your own computer listed.

Windows NT 4.0 Service Packs

When you install any software, it is important always to check for the latest updates to the software.

There are several ways to find the version information in Windows NT, but using **WINVER** from Start | Run is our favorite because it's fast. This option displays the About Windows NT message box that contains version and licensing information, as well as the amount of memory available. It also shows the service pack level, right after the version information, if a service pack has been installed. This is the same message box you see if you select Help | About from the menu in Windows NT Explorer or My Computer.

The Windows NT 4.0 service packs include new support for hardware, such as the AGP video standard, which was added in Service Pack 3 but seemed to work even better with Service Pack 6.

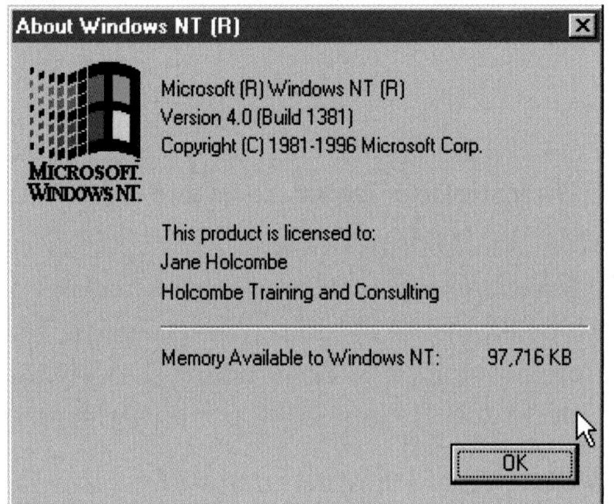

• About Windows NT

Because Windows NT is not a current product, we recently ran into a problem that we solved in two different ways. You decide which way you want to try.

Updating Windows NT—Method I After installing the OS, we used Internet Explorer to connect to the Microsoft site and downloaded the latest service pack (6a). Because we were using the version of Internet Explorer that comes with Windows NT, version 2.0, we experienced difficulty viewing web pages. In spite of that, we made it to the Service Pack 6a download page. Our mistake was selecting the button labeled "Start SP6a Express Download." This downloaded what turned out to be a small program that reconnected to the site to complete the actual download and installation, but when we ran the program and it tried to do just that, an error message popped up stating that Internet Explorer version 3 or greater was required to complete the operation! So, we found the Internet Explorer page (`www.microsoft.com/windows/ie`) on the Microsoft site and found the download page for Internet Explorer version 6. On a hunch, we read the system requirements and discovered that it required Windows NT to have Service Pack 6a installed first.

Next, we went searching for a download source for Internet Explorer 3 to install so that we could install Service Pack 6a, and then install Internet Explorer 6. Using another computer with a newer version of Internet Explorer, we found a link to Internet Explorer 3.02 at `www.oldversion.com`. We downloaded and copied it to a CD.

Cross Check

Comparing Installations

Now that you have installed Windows NT 4.0 Workstation, compare the installation process with that of MS-DOS 6.22, which you studied in Chapter 2. Then answer the following questions:

1. Overall, how are the setup programs for the two OSs similar?
2. Overall, how are the setup programs for the two OSs different?
3. Compare tasks required after installation of DOS with those required after the installation of Windows NT 4.0.

Armed with the CD containing Internet Explorer 3.02, we returned to our NT Workstation computer and installed IE 3.02. Using this, we connected to the Microsoft site and successfully downloaded and installed SP6a. Finally, we connected to the Internet Explorer page and downloaded and installed IE 6.

Updating Windows NT—Method 2 Once we recovered from Method 1, we went back to the SP6a web page and discovered we had an option for downloading SP6a. Download it by clicking the button labeled "Start SP6a Network Download." While the first method downloads a small program that is then used to download and install the required components of SP6a for your computer, this button downloads the full service pack (34.5MB). Once it is downloaded, start the service pack installation by running the program file. The benefit of this is that it does not require a newer version of IE to install first. Once the service pack is installed, you can upgrade your Internet Explorer.

Step-by-Step 3.03

Installing Service Packs

In this step-by-step, you will use the second method to update Windows NT 4.0 to Service Pack 6a (SP6a).

To complete this exercise, you will need the following:

- The computer on which you successfully installed Windows NT in Step-by-Step 3.02, connected to a LAN, with the correct drivers and protocols for your network
- A user name and password for an account that is a member of the Administrators group
- High-speed Internet access from your lab computer, or a location on the local network or on your hard drive where the instructor has placed the service pack for you to download

Step 1

Log on as an administrator. If your instructor has placed the service pack program on your hard disk or in a network location, skip this step. Otherwise, point your Internet browser to `www.Microsoft.com/ntworkstation`. On the Windows NT Workstation page, select the link for the latest updates, and on the Windows NT 4.0 Service Pack 6a page choose and click a download version. On the resulting page, locate and click the link

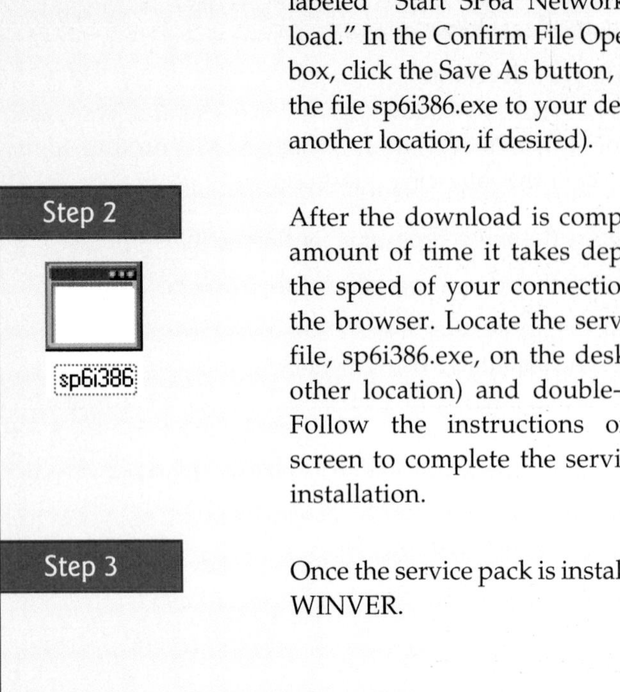

labeled "Start SP6a Network Download." In the Confirm File Open dialog box, click the Save As button, and save the file sp6i386.exe to your desktop (or another location, if desired).

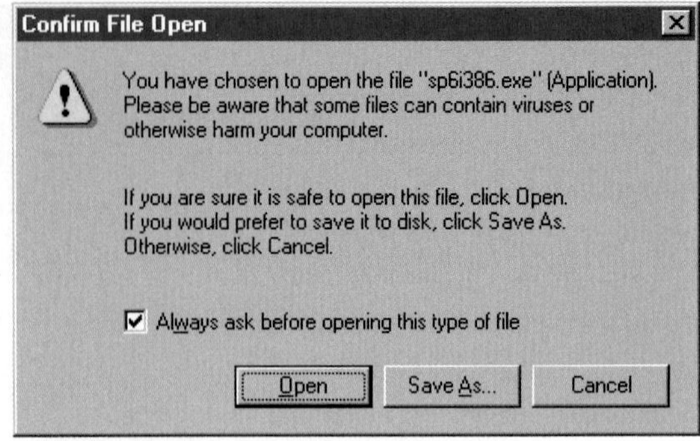

Confirm File Open
You have chosen to open the file "sp6i386.exe" (Application).
Please be aware that some files can contain viruses or otherwise harm your computer.
If you are sure it is safe to open this file, click Open.
If you would prefer to save it to disk, click Save As.
Otherwise, click Cancel.
Always ask before opening this type of file
Open
Save As...
Cancel

Step 2

sp6i386

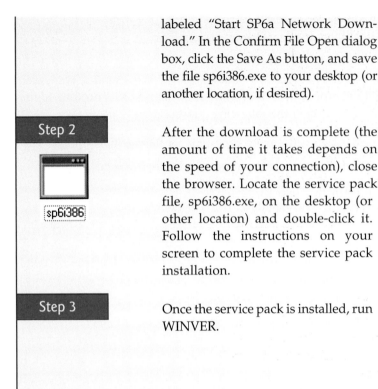

After the download is complete (the amount of time it takes depends on the speed of your connection), close the browser. Locate the service pack file, sp6i386.exe, on the desktop (or other location) and double-click it. Follow the instructions on your screen to complete the service pack installation.

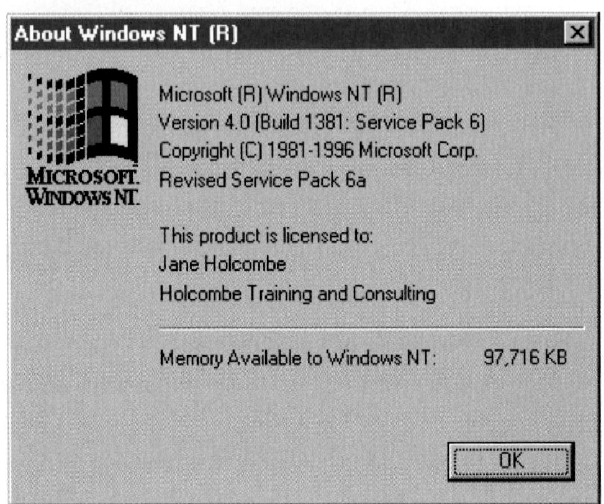

Step 3

Once the service pack is installed, run WINVER.

Customizing and Managing Windows NT Workstation 4.0

Once you've installed an OS, you need to configure and manage it for the person who will use it. This can involve a variety of tasks, including creating a new hard disk partition, installing or removing programs, and customizing the desktop. Take some time now to learn about these tasks.

Creating a New Hard Disk Partition

Creation of a disk partition may seem like an advanced task for a survey class, but if you install Windows NT 4.0 Workstation on a new computer, the probability that you will have unpartitioned disk space after the installation is very high because of the small size of the partition that Windows NT Setup creates relative to the very large hard disk systems common today. Therefore, creating a new hard disk partition once in a lab situation is a valuable experience for you.

Windows NT Partitioning Basics

As you learned in Chapter 2, a partition defines the boundaries on a hard disk that can be used as if it were a separate physical disk. The two standard partition types are primary and extended. A primary partition can have a single drive letter assigned to the entire partition. An extended partition can have multiple logical drive letters. Each area that is defined as a drive letter is a **volume**, so a primary partition has a single volume, and an extended partition can contain one or more volumes. A PC will start an OS from a primary partition that is also marked as active. An extended partition cannot be marked as active and therefore cannot be used to start an OS.

Under Windows NT, a hard disk can have a total of four partitions, but never more than one extended partition. Extended partitions came about to get around the limits of the DOS, Windows 3.*x*, and Windows 9*x* OSs. You don't need or want an extended partition if you are not using one of these OSs. When you create a new extended partition, you must define the size and number of logical drives. When you create a new primary partition under Windows NT, it is automatically assigned a logical drive letter, but you will have to format it before it can be used to store files and folders.

Windows NT Disk Administrator

The tool you use to manage disks in Windows NT is **Disk Administrator**, which you will use in the following step-by-step. When you use Disk Administrator, you will see that the Partition menu has an option called Create and another called Create Extended. Be sure to select Create. Selecting Create in Disk Administrator will create a new primary partition, and selecting Create Extended will create a new extended partition (you can have no more than one per physical disk). Without going into the boring details of what is wrong with extended partitions, simply remember that an extended partition is not a good thing unless you are dual-booting between Windows NT 4.0 and an OS that cannot use more than one primary partition per physical disk and needs to use the new partition.

If you are dual-booting between NT and a less capable OS, such as DOS, Windows 3.*x*, or Windows 9*x*, any drive that the second OS needs must use the FAT file system. Also, the drive can be on only the first primary partition or in a logical drive in an extended partition. All other drives and partitions will be unavailable when one of these other OSs is active.

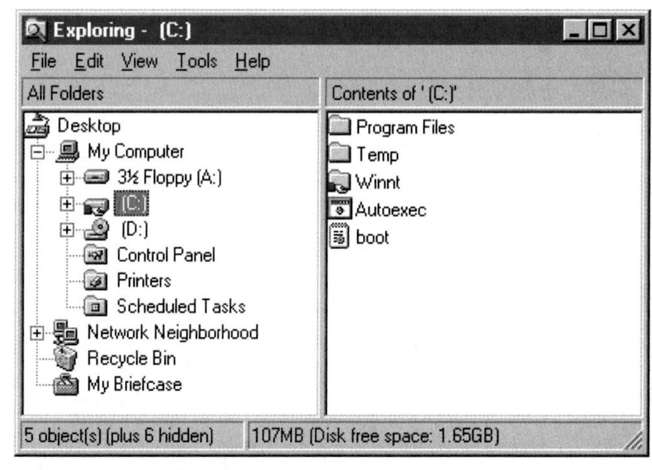

• Drive letters

Step-by-Step 3.04

Creating a New Partition

In this exercise, you will create a new partition on your hard disk.

To complete this exercise, you will need the following:

- The computer on which you successfully installed Windows NT in Step-by-Step 3.02
- Unpartitioned hard disk space
- A user name and password for an account that is a member of the Administrators group
- A blank floppy disk

Step 1

Log on as an administrator and launch Disk Administrator by selecting Start | Programs | Administrative Tools | Disk Administrator. The first time you run Disk Administrator, you will see a message box stating that it will update system configuration information.

Step 2

Click OK to close the message box, and Disk Administrator will start. On the first startup screen, you'll also see a message stating that Disk Administrator needs to write information (the signature) on the disk. Click OK to allow it to do this, and then click Yes in the Confirm box. You don't have any choice, but you won't see this message again.

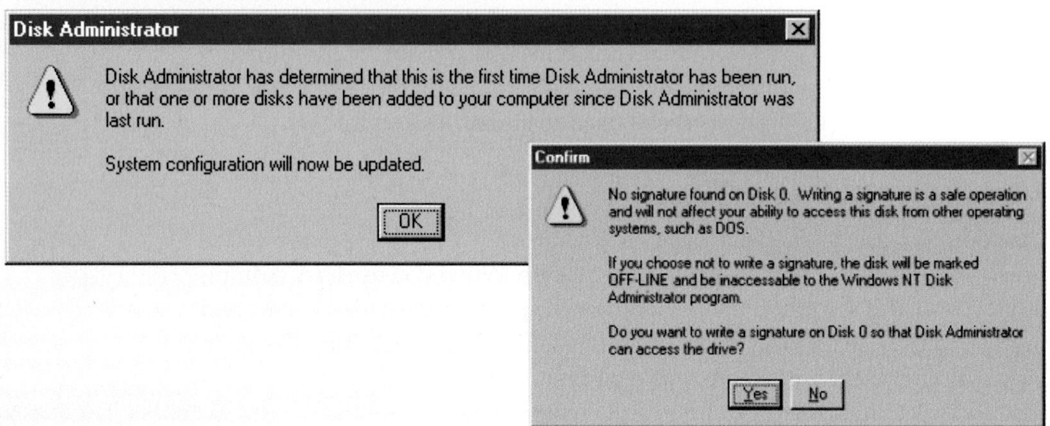

Step 3

In Disk Administrator, each physical disk is numbered, beginning with zero. The partitions are defined and labeled in boxes with color-coded bars at the top. The key is in the bottom of the window. If you installed NT according to the instructions in Step-by-Step 3.02, drive C: is a primary partition with the NTFS file system. Drive letters are assigned to hard disk volumes first and then to optical disk drives.

Step 4

To create a new partition in the unpartitioned space, click the area labeled "Free Space," and then go to the menu bar and select Partition | Create. Read the resulting message in the Confirm box, and click Yes to confirm and continue.

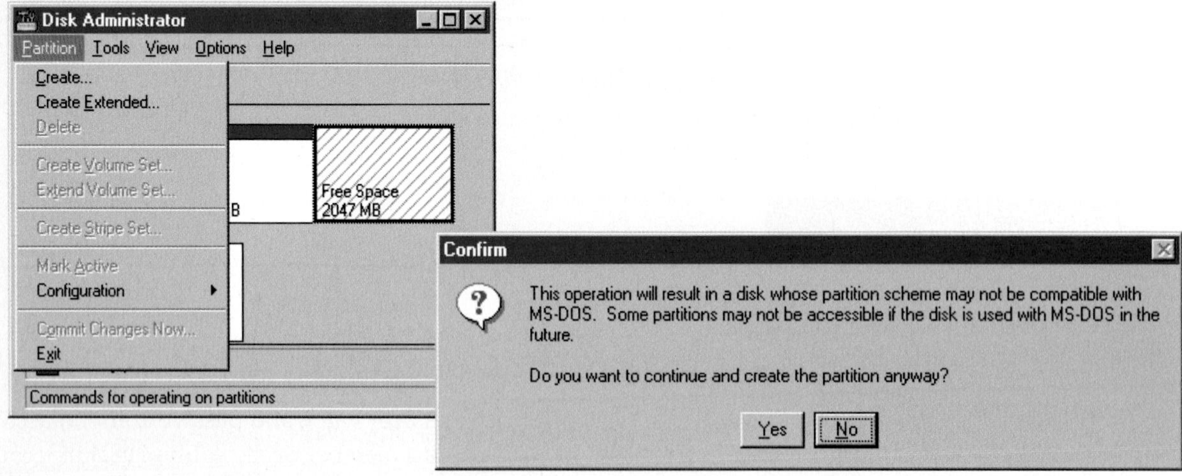

Step 5

In the Create Primary Partition dialog box, enter a size for the new partition in the entry box or accept the maximum size; then click OK. Ask your instructor for guidance if you are not sure what size to create.

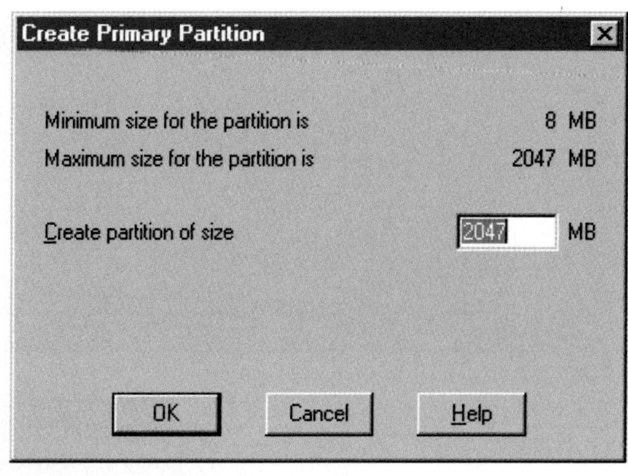

Step 6

The new drive will show a drive letter (if you created a new primary partition). Before you can format the new drive, you must commit the changes, which saves the changes in the registry—a huge listing of all of the settings for the OS. To commit the changes, right-click the new partition, select Commit Changes Now, and then click Yes in the Confirm box. An information box labeled "Disk Administrator" reminding you to update the emergency repair configuration will follow this. Click OK.

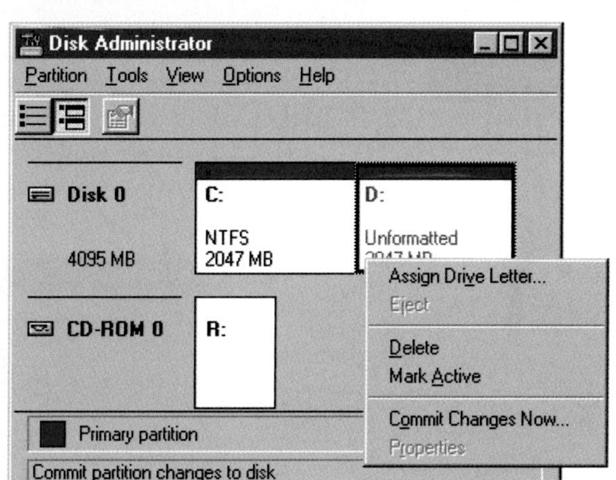

Step 7

To format the drive, right-click the drive letter and select Format. In the Format box, select the NTFS file system, leave the allocation unit size at the default value, and type **DATA** in the Volume Label box. Do not select either format option; then click Start. In the warning box, click OK. A progress bar will appear in the Formatting box. Click OK when the box pops up with the "Format Complete" message; then click Close in the Format dialog box.

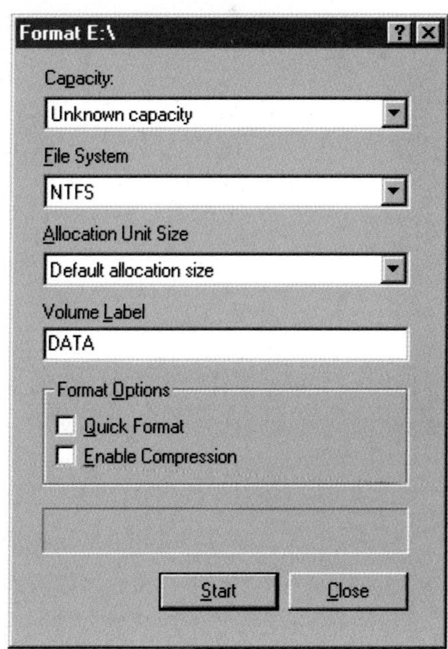

Step 8

Confirm that you now have two drives, C: and the new drive, each of which is a primary partition on your hard disk, and then close Disk Administrator.

Step 9

Update the emergency repair configuration information in the registry, and create a new emergency repair disk. Select Start | Run. In the Run box, type **RDISK** and press ENTER. Click Update Repair Info. This updates the Repair folder (C:\WINNT\REPAIR if NT is installed in WINNT) with a copy of portions of the registry which now contains information about the new drive.

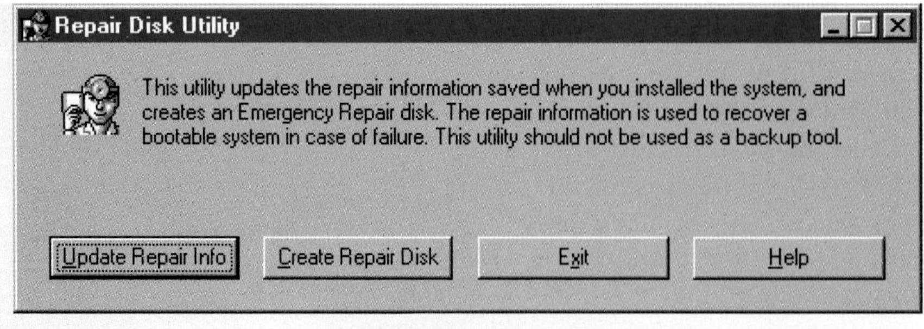

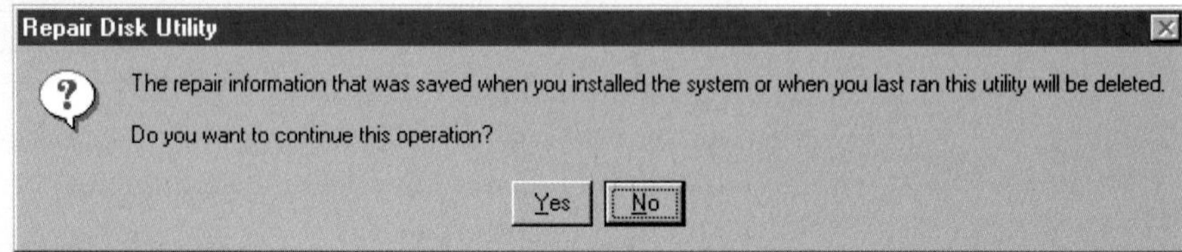

Step 10

When the repair information has been updated, you will be prompted to create an emergency repair disk. Click Yes and follow the instructions. Disk Administrator will format the disk and then copy the contents of the Repair folder to the disk. When this process is complete, remove the disk and place it in a safe location.

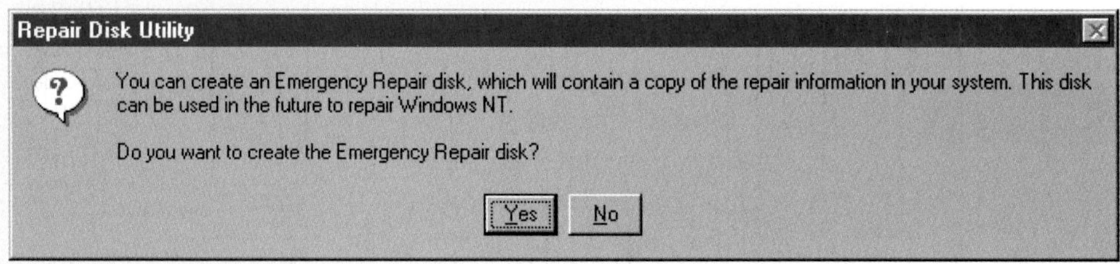

Installing and Removing Applications and Windows Components

After you have installed the OS, you need to install the applications required by the user. Many applications have their own installation programs. In addition, Windows NT has a special Control Panel applet, Add/Remove Programs, which you can use to install and uninstall applications and Windows components.

Step-by-Step 3.05

Using Add/Remove Programs to Install Applications

In this exercise, you will use Add/Remove Programs to verify which programs and Windows components have been installed and to uninstall one of those components. To complete this exercise, you will need the following:

- The computer on which you successfully installed Windows
- A user name and password for an account that is a member of the Administrators group

Step 1

Log on as an administrator and select Start | Settings | Control Panel | Add/Remove Programs. Note the programs listed on the Install/Uninstall page.

Step 2

Click the Windows NT Setup tab, and note the Windows components listed on that page. Be very careful not to click a check box unless you really want to check or uncheck that component. Click each name (not its check box) and note the Details button. This button becomes active when the listed item includes more than one component. Select Accessories; then click the Details button to see all of the Accessories.

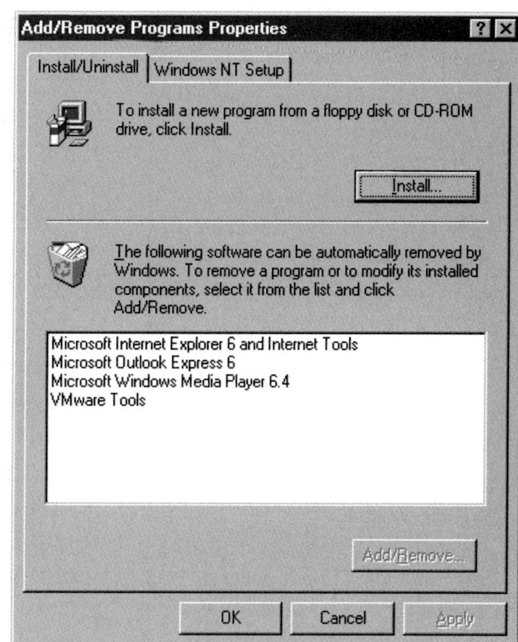

Step 3

Click Cancel to close the Accessories details box. Back on the Windows NT Setup page, notice that no Games components have been installed. Install a game now. Click Games and then click Details. Click the check box by FreeCell, and then click OK to close the Games box; click OK to close Add/Remove Programs.

Step 4

Verify that the FreeCell game was installed by locating it on the Start menu and starting it. You will find it at Start | Programs | Accessories | Games | FreeCell. Exit FreeCell when you are done.

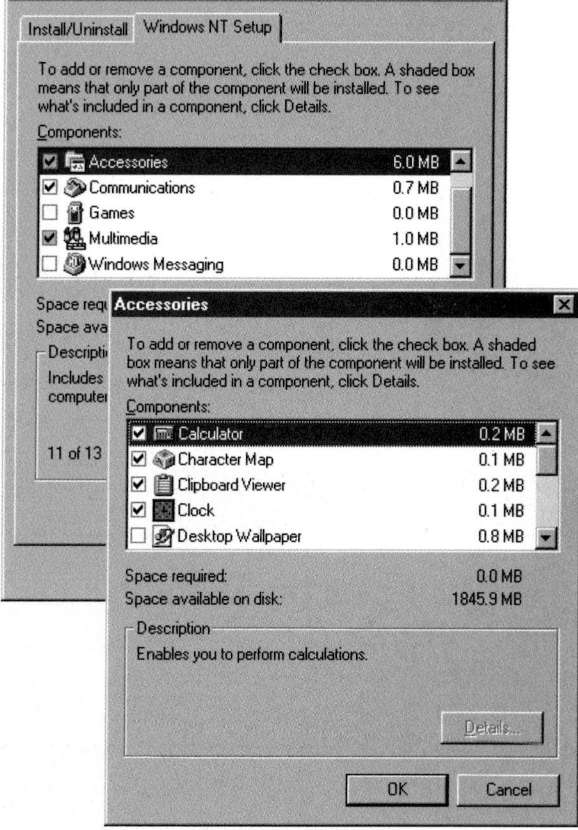

Inside Information

When to Click Apply

Countless times, when Jane (one of the authors) has demonstrated Windows to a class, students have pointed out that she closes dialog boxes without clicking Apply and, therefore, that the changes won't take effect. This isn't true. The Apply button appears in dialog boxes that have multiple tabbed sheets. If you make changes on one tabbed sheet and want to move to another within the same dialog box, click Apply. This applies the changes from that tabbed sheet without closing the dialog box. When you are done working in a dialog box, you don't have to click both Apply and OK to have changes take effect—OK applies all changes and closes the dialog box.

EXPLORER.EXE works behind the scenes as the program that provides your desktop and opens folders.

Preparing the Desktop for Users

After you have installed Windows and tested any required network connectivity, added required service packs, created new partitions, and installed applications, you are ready to customize the desktop. Your goal should be to make the desktop visually pleasant for the user and to make any necessary changes that make using the OS easier.

Users Will Customize the Desktop

One observation many professionals have related to us is that they continue to encounter client users who are new to working with computers and need to be guided through the procedures for turning on the computer, logging on, and performing new tasks. Revisiting the same novice user within a week, they find a customized desktop with a picture of their children or pet poodle as wallpaper. This tells us that they were given a good introduction. Some organizations don't allow such personalization for a variety of reasons, such as corporate image, propriety, and security when computers are in a public area. However, when it is allowed, this type of customization can make the user feel more comfortable with the computer.

Respect the Chair/Keyboard Interface

In two decades of working with users and teaching desktop and server support skills, Jane heard thousands of professed true-life stories about human-computer interactions—many of them hilarious, but that's another book. Many of these stories reflect human nature when confronted with a new situation. It's important always to remember what it is like to be introduced to something very new and strange to you and to be told that you have to master its use for school or work. (You may be going through this right now!) A good desktop support person helps the new user feel comfortable with the computer and the required programs. Beyond the training and one-on-one tutoring of the user you may perform, you need to set up the desktop so that it works for the individual. The chair/keyboard interface is a human being!

Step-by-Step 3.06

Customizing the Desktop

Experience will teach you the best methods for customizing the desktop. In this exercise, you will customize the settings for My Computer and Windows NT Explorer and use the Display applet to modify the desktop. Although the particular changes you make in this exercise may not be appropriate for most users, you will have an opportunity to view many of the settings available to you.

To complete this exercise, you will need the following:

- The computer on which you successfully installed Windows
- A user name and password for an account that is a member of the Administrators group

Step 1

Log on as an administrator and right-click My Computer. This brings up the context menu. Notice that one of the options, Open, is in bold. The bold item in a context menu is the default action that occurs when you double-click an object. You are going to change this default behavior. But first, click an empty portion of the desktop to close the context menu without making a choice (the ESC key also closes open menus and dialog boxes).

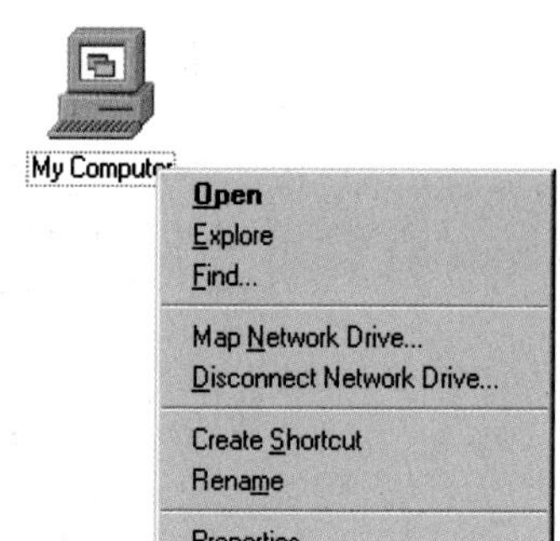

Step 2

Double-click My Computer. This brings up Folder view. This is what Open means for this object. Leave this window open and go back to the desktop. Right-click My Computer and select Explore to start My Computer in Explorer view. Compare the two views and see which you prefer. Do you like the one-dimensional, single-pane window of Folder view or the double-pane window of Explorer view, with a hierarchy of objects in the left Folder pane and the contents on the right?

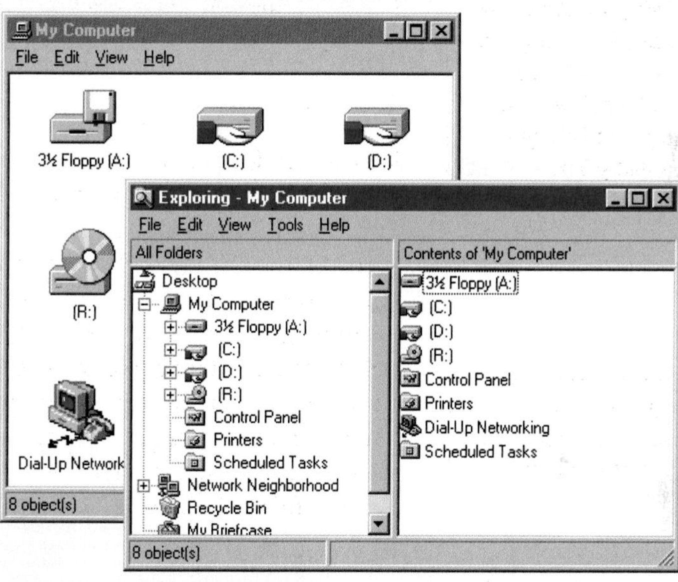

Step 3

We prefer Explorer view. Therefore, one of the first things we do for our own desktops is to make Explorer view the default, as you will do next. (Let's pretend that this is your preference, too!) Click one of the open My Computer windows and select View | Options. In the Options dialog box, click the File Types tab. In the list of registered file types, scroll down and select Folder (*not* File Folder).

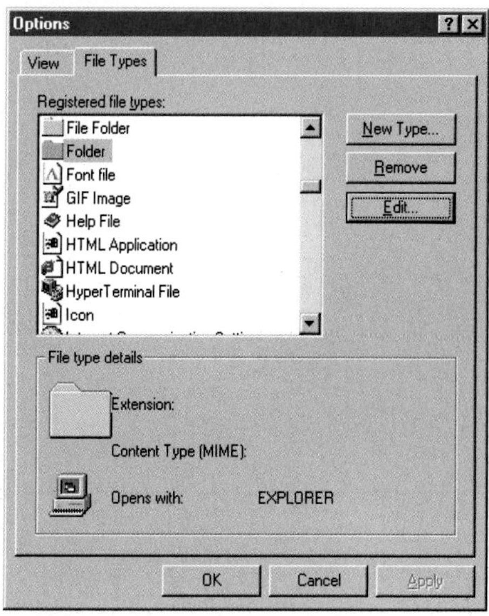

Step 4

Notice under File Type Details that Folder opens with Explorer, which opens a folder, whether it is opened in Folder view or Explorer view. With Folder selected, click the Edit button. In the Edit File Type dialog box, the word *Open* in the list of Actions is bold. That indicates that it is the default action. To change the default, click Explore and then click the Set Default button.

Step 5

Click Close to close the Edit File Type dialog box. Click the OK button to close the Options dialog box and to make the change take effect. Test the change by right-clicking on My Computer. Explore should now be in bold. Test it further by double-clicking the My Computer icon. It should now open in Explorer view.

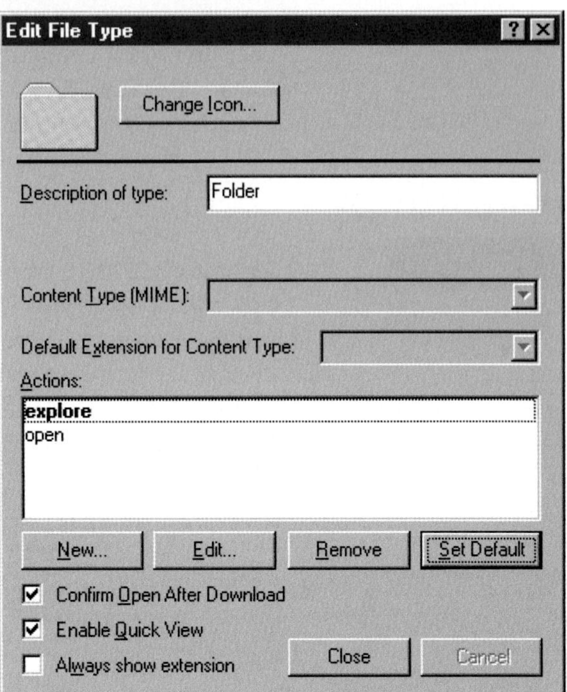

Step 6

Make a change to your desktop. Right-click the desktop to open the Display Properties dialog box and click the Appearance tab. Select each of the schemes in the drop-down list box, and use the preview box at the top to choose a new scheme. When you find one that suits you, select it; then click OK to close the Display Properties dialog box and to apply the change you made.

Creating and Managing a Local Printer

Before anyone can use a local printer (one connected directly to the PC), an administrator must install the printer driver. After it is installed, users on that computer can print to the printer. Members of the Users, Administrators, and Power Users groups have different rights to the printer for management tasks.

Only the Administrator user or another member of the Administrators group can install a printer driver. NT comes with many printer drivers, but these drivers are of a 1996 vintage. That presents the administrator with two main scenarios: installing a printer driver from the Windows NT CD (only for old printer models), and installing a printer driver that comes with the printer. In Step-by-Step 3.07, you will install a printer driver from the Windows NT CD.

If you need to install a new printer in a Windows NT 4.0 system, you can use the Have Disk button on the Manufacturers page of the Add Printer wizard to point to the location of the drivers for the new printer. Then you continue on through the Add Printer wizard. However, it has been our experience that you almost never need to use the Add Printer wizard if your printer driver is not on the Add Printer wizard list. Every recently manufactured printer that we have installed has come with its own setup program. Recently, we installed a Samsung laser printer in a Windows NT 4.0 system. Following the instructions, we installed the printer driver in five mouse clicks and did not have to enter any information.

Be sure to read the documentation that comes with the printer. Most manufacturers use the Install Shield installation program, which works very well with Windows.

Step-by-Step 3.07

Installing a Printer Driver from the Windows NT CD

In this exercise, you will install a printer driver for a local printer. This is an older printer, and the drivers for it are on the Windows NT CD.

To complete this exercise, you will need the following:

- The computer on which you successfully installed Windows NT
- The Windows NT 4.0 Workstation CD
- A user name and password for an account that is a member of the Administrators group

You do not need a printer connected to your computer.

Step 1

Log on as an administrator and select Start | Settings | Printers. Double-click Add Printer to start the Add Printer wizard.

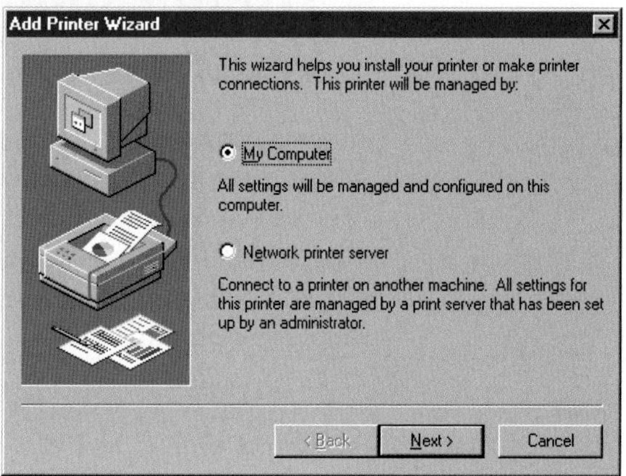

Step 2

Select My Computer and click Next. In the Available Ports list, select LPT1; then click Next. In the Manufacturers list, scroll down and select HP. In the Printers list, select HP LaserJet 5; then click Next. The Printer Name box will default to the model name of the printer, but you can give the printer a friendly name, such as Accounting Printer; then click Next. Leave the printer as unshared. You will learn about sharing printers in Chapter 10. Click Next.

Step 3

Select No on the Printer Test page, unless this specific printer is actually attached. Click Finish. The Add Printer wizard will attempt to find the files it needs. If it doesn't find them, it will prompt you to provide the location. It is looking for the Windows NT CD. Change the drive letter in the Files Needed box if it does not point to your CD drive. Insert the CD and then click OK. A Copying Files box will appear very briefly, and the desktop will be displayed.

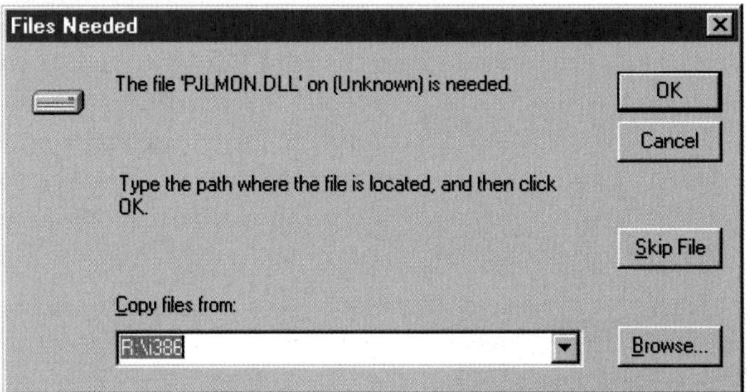

Step 4

Verify the installation of the printer by selecting Start | Settings | Printers. The new printer should appear in the Printers folder.

Troubleshooting Common Windows NT 4.0 Problems

Anyone using a computer eventually runs into a situation where something fails or the computer just sort of behaves differently. For those occasions when no one is handy to solve the problem for you, we have some suggestions. In this section, you'll learn where you can find help and how to perform some simple maintenance tasks, as well as learn some Windows NT 4.0 troubleshooting tips.

Proactive Tasks

There are tasks you can perform on your computer that will either help prevent certain problems, or help you more quickly recover from a problem. Creating backups, having an NT repair disk handy, and becoming familiar with sources of help will make your life easier.

Creating Backups

It is better to be prepared for loss of data than to find a "cure" for it after the data is gone. Prevention is at least a twofold process. First you need a plan for organizing your data so that it can be easily backed up, and then you must perform backups at regular intervals.

Any plan for organizing data should make sense to the user so he or she will actually follow it, it should keep data files separate from the application program files, and it should set up a hierarchical structure to make backup easier. A simple hierarchical structure has a folder at the top level and several subfolders stored within that folder, with the subfolders containing files organized by type of data file or by the names of the projects the user works on or by whatever scheme makes sense to the user. With just one folder at the top of the entire hierarchy, you can point a backup or copy program to the top folder and back up all data files at one time.

Back up all valuable files! Windows NT 4.0 Workstation has a backup program, available through Start | Programs | Administrative Tools | Backup. However, this program works only if you have a tape backup system installed, and it must be a tape backup system that is on the list of tested hardware at the Microsoft site. This makes the NT Backup program almost useless for a desktop computer. If your data files are stored on your local computer and you don't have a tape backup system, find another backup method. This is very important! Use a network server, writeable CD-ROM, or other removable media. Third-party backup programs also are available for Windows NT 4.0. Later versions of Windows include greatly improved backup programs.

If you need an alternative to the Windows NT backup program, you might go to `www.dantz.com` or `www.novastor.com` to see what they offer.

The NT Repair Disk and the Repair Process

Repair information saved when you run the emergency repair disk program, RDISK, includes the hardware and software configuration information critical to running your operating system and hardware components. This configuration information is affected by changes made, such as creating new partitions and formatting a drive, and during the installation and configuration of device drivers and other components. Make a habit of updating the repair information and the emergency repair disk (ERD) every time you add a new driver or make other changes, such as when you create or remove a disk partition. Step-by-Step 3.04 includes the steps for running the RDISK program to create an up-to-date ERD.

Finding Sources of Help

Our two favorite places to find help for problems with Windows are the Microsoft web site and the Windows NT Help program. The NT Workstation home page is at `www.Microsoft.com/ntworkstation`. From there, you can select Technical Resources and look for a topic. The Windows NT

Help program is available on the Start menu. Browse through key topics using the Index tab, or search for a word or phrase using the Find tab, a technique you will use in the following Step-by-Step.

Step-by-Step 3.08

Finding Help in Windows NT

In this step-by-step, you use the Find tab, which is more powerful because you can search for words and terms within topics.

To complete this exercise, you will need the computer on which you successfully installed Windows.

Step 1

Select Start | Help. In the help program, click the Find tab. If this is the first time you have clicked Find, the Find Setup wizard needs to create a search list. Select Maximize Search Capabilities; then click Next twice, and the Find tabbed sheet will appear, and the Help Topics window will open. Click the Options button, and under Search For Topics Containing, select The Words You Typed In Exact Order; then click OK.

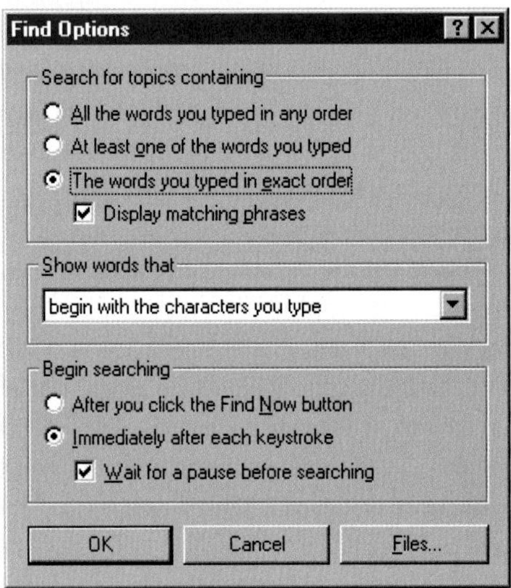

Step 2

Let's see what Windows NT Help has to say about disk space. Type the words **disk space** in the top box. The second box shows some matching words, and the bottom box shows the topics related to those words.

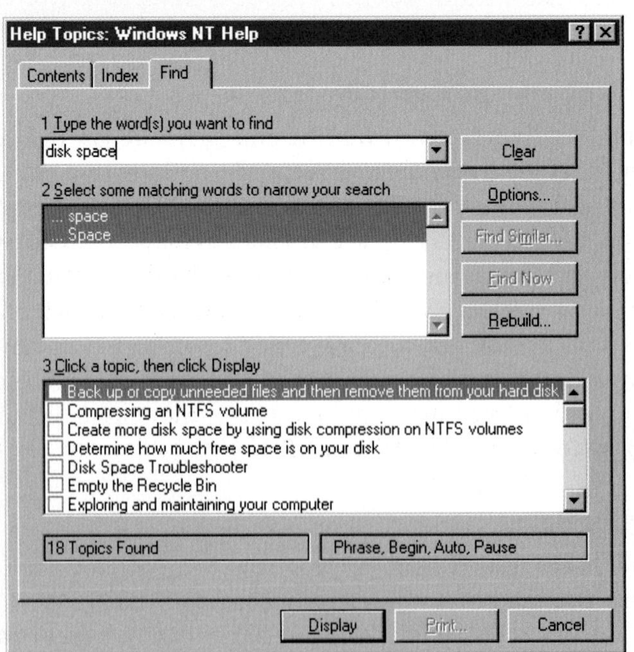

In the bottom box, locate Disk Space Troubleshooter and click the check box to select it; then click Display.

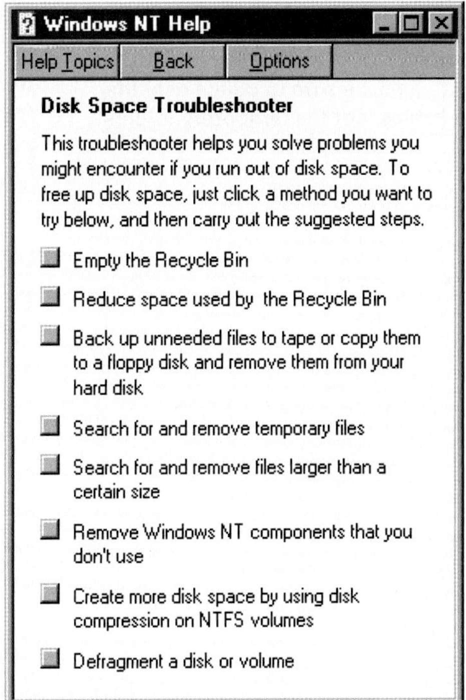

Step 3

In the Disk Space Troubleshooter, click Empty The Recycle Bin. You will see instructions on emptying the Recycle Bin, which holds files that have been deleted from your local hard disk. Follow these instructions; then click the Back button to return to the last box. Back in the Disk Space Troubleshooter, repeat the last two steps for each of the suggested steps shown in the troubleshooter.

In this exercise, you used Windows NT Help to research disk space problems. The suggestion you saw for removing temporary files is a little vague, but the next step-by-step will guide you through this process.

When Problems Sneak Up on You

Have you ever heard of the term "bit-creep"? A friend once said, "Over time, my OS seems to deteriorate through a mysterious process I call bit-creep. Therefore, once a year I back up my data, reformat the hard drive, and reinstall the OS or install a new OS."

We have heard similar stories countless times from computer professionals and savvy users. Our theory was that this bit-creep phenomenon had something to do with unstable OSs. So in 1996, when we installed NT 4.0 on a desktop computer in our office, we decided to use it as a test of that concept. As advertised, it was a more stable OS than its contemporary, Windows 95, and it stayed fairly stable through daily use for over four years, although that could be because we were conservative about adding new software to the computer, except the occasional service pack. After that, however, it did get weird, and each time it suffered a hardware failure, we were on the verge of removing the OS and replacing it because of the increased frequency of software hang ups (no response to the mouse or keyboard). By the time we were ready to replace it, we did not choose to install a newer OS, but instead replaced the computer with a brand-new faster one on which we installed Windows 2000 Professional, which has since been upgraded to Windows XP Professional.

Possible Cause

Let's look at some of the possible causes of "bit creep." If your computer seems to have become slower over time, the cause may be a hard drive issue, but not truly a hardware issue. Data is stored on hard drives in a

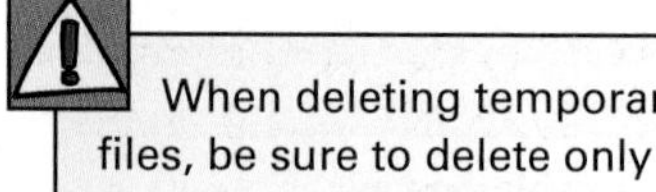

When deleting temporary files, be sure to delete only the files, not the temporary folders!

way that can lead to pieces of individual files being stored in widely separated areas of the disk. Then, when reading the files into memory, the system takes longer to gather up all the pieces. This is called disk fragmentation, and at the very least will cause slower file access and program startups. In the extreme, it may cause your computer to hang or produce other errors.

Solution

The solution is to run a program on your hard disk that reorganizes, or defragments, the data on your hard disk. This process is called **defragmentation**, or defragging. Windows NT doesn't come with a defragmentation program, but programs are available from other sources, such as Executive Software, which publishes Diskeeper. Use a disk defragmentation program on FAT and NTFS volumes. At one time, Microsoft stated that NTFS volumes did not require defragmentation. We used Diskeeper to analyze an NTFS drive on an NT 4.0 computer that had been used for just a few days. It found 203 fragmented files, with a total of 1,642 excess fragments.

Before you defragment your hard drive, you should clean up your hard disk. That includes removing unnecessary or obsolete programs and deleting unnecessary files. The biggest offenders in this second category are temporary files. Many applications save temporary files on your hard disk. When such an application is closed, it should remove the temporary files. Some may not get removed, though, if the application isn't closed properly or if it fails to complete the removal process, but other applications purposely don't clean up their temporary files. Your Internet browser may be in this second category.

Temporary files are often stored in a folder named TEMP, and temporary Internet files are stored in a folder named Temporary Internet Files (depending on the version of Internet Explorer). On a regular basis, clean out these locations. You can also check your software to see if it has a setting to manage the temporary files.

Step-by-Step 3.09

Removing Temporary Files

In this exercise, you will look for and delete temporary files and change the settings for temporary Internet files.

To complete this exercise, you will need the following:

- The computer on which you successfully installed Windows NT Workstation 4.0
- Internet Explorer version 6

Step 1

Log on as Administrator. Close any open applications.

Step 2

Search for the temporary folders. Select Start | Find | Files Or Folders. In the Find: All Files dialog box, type **temp** in the Named text box, and select Local Hard Drives in the Look In text box. Be sure that Include Subfolders is checked and then click Find Now.

Step 3

You should find a single TEMP folder on drive C:, and perhaps a Temporary Internet Files folder for each user. These folders may have few or no temporary files, depending on what applications you have used since installing NT.

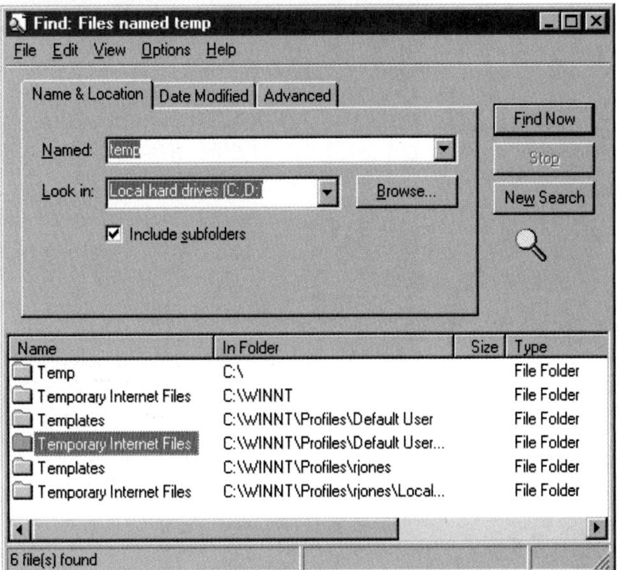

Step 4

Double-click the TEMP folder to open it; select the TEMP folder contents and press DELETE. You can do the same with the Temporary Internet Files folder.

Using the Emergency Repair Disk

If your Windows NT computer will not boot check out the use of Windows startup disks in Chapter 8. If that method does not solve your problem, you may need to perform an emergency repair. This requires having up-to-date information in the Repair folder (C:\WINNT\ REPAIR). You should also have a backup of this information, in the form of a special floppy disk called an emergency repair disk (ERD). In this chapter, you had two opportunities to create an ERD: once during the installation (Step-by-Step 3.02) and once after creating a new partition (Step-by-Step 3.04).

To perform an emergency repair, you need the Windows NT CD, the ERD, and if your computer will not start from CD-ROM, you will need the three setup disks. See Step-by-Step 3.01, "Creating the Windows NT 4.0 Setup Disks from Windows or DOS." The procedure is as follows:

1. Using the CD-ROM or the setup disks, boot to the Windows NT 4.0 setup program.
2. At the Welcome To Setup screen, press R to repair a damaged Windows NT version 4.0 installation.
3. On the following screen, select or deselect the desired actions in the box; then press ENTER to continue.

Windows NT, Windows 2000, and Windows XP all have the same startup process. You will learn more about this common Windows startup process in Chapter 7, where you will also learn how to solve problems at startup. Can't wait? Then, connect to `www.microsoft.com/technet` and search for the article titled "What Happens When You Start Your Computer." This is Chapter 19 of the *Windows NT Workstation Resource Kit.*

```
Windows NT Workstation Setup

  As part of the repair process, Setup will perform each optional task
  shown below with an 'X' in its check box.

  To perform the selected tasks, press ENTER to indicate "Continue."
  If you want to select or deselect any item in the list, press the
  UP or DOWN ARROW key to move the highlight to the item you want
  to change. Then press ENTER.

      [X] Inspect registry files
      [X] Inspect startup environment
      [X] Verify Windows NT system files
      [X] Inspect boot sector
          Continue (perform selected tasks)

 F1=Help  F3=Exit  ESC=Cancel  ENTER=Select/Deselect
```

• Emergency repair menu

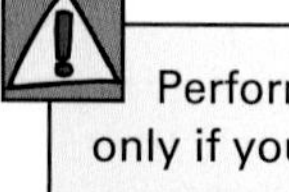

Perform an emergency repair only if you are unable to boot up, cannot repair with the startup disk, and have kept the repair information up-to-date. You should also first browse the emergency repair topics at the Microsoft Technet site: www.microsoft.com/technet.

4. On the following screen, press ENTER to continue with detection of mass-storage devices or S to continue after skipping mass-storage device detection. Unless you have tried this and failed previously on this computer, choose the first option.
5. Continue, following the instructions on the screen. When the procedure is complete, remove all disks and restart the computer.

The Blue Screen of Death (BSOD)

The **Blue Screen of Death (BSOD)** strikes horror in the hearts of IT professionals new and old. We actually have yet to hear of someone dying from a blue screen, but it would be fair to say that more than a few important data files have met an untimely demise when a Windows NT computer has crashed and displayed a Stop message on a blue screen. First, we'll answer the question, "What is the BSOD?" and then we'll show you an approach to troubleshooting BSOD problems—and this is well worth learning because both Windows 2000 and Windows XP have similar Stop screens, and the action you take for those OSs is much like what you will learn here.

What Is the BSOD?

The BSOD is actually a feature (rather than a bug) of Windows NT. It's a blue character-mode screen that displays a message that includes the word *Stop* near the top left of the screen, and seemingly nothing else that makes sense. Stop error screens exist by design. The OS stops everything when it detects that something very bad (also known as a Fatal Error) has happened to make it unstable.

Windows NT 4.0 is not the only OS that is designed to behave like this, although others may not produce the infamous BSOD. When something occurs to make an OS unstable, it is assumed that more damage could be done by allowing things to continue out of control, so the OS stops and displays a blue screen with an error message. Although in-depth study of the handling of stop errors is a more advanced topic for another day, another course, there are several common blue-screen errors that you can learn to decipher just from reading the first few lines of information on the Stop screen.

Inside Information

Stop Error

First, let's have some kind words about this stop error business. The screen appears by design and may keep even worse things from happening. You wouldn't really want to continue driving your car if the oil pan were ruptured and the car were leaking oil by the quart. The oil light shows up on your dash, nice and bright so you can't ignore it. Now if it weren't for the risk of bodily harm to drivers and passengers, we're sure manufacturers would have the car stop itself at the first sign of a major oil leak, so that you wouldn't ruin your engine. A desktop OS is not usually involved in propelling humans at freeway speeds, so stopping is considered a good choice if something has happened to make the OS question its own sanity.

What Can Cause a BSOD?

Some programs can go bad without causing a BSOD. These are programs, like your application programs, that are isolated from the kernel of the operating system and cannot usually cause harm. With these programs, Windows NT can usually maintain enough control to let you remove an offending program through the Task Manager. Other programs, notoriously drivers, are given the same privileges as the OS kernel and can cause a BSOD. A bad driver can cause the BSOD during installation and during startup.

Solving the Problem by Observation and Research

A BSOD is intimidating because most of the screen is filled with geeky-looking hexadecimal numbers, as shown in Figure 3-5. Ignore them and just

```
*** STOP: 0x69696969 (0x00000000,0x00000000,0x00000000,0x00000000)

CPUID:GenuineIntel 7.1.2 irql:1f  SYSVER 0xf0000565

Dll Base DateStmp - Name                  Dll Base DateStmp - Name
80100000 3255a915 - ntoskrnl.exe          80010000 31ee6c52 - hal.dll
80001000 31ed06b4 - atapi.sys             80006000 31ec6c74 - SCSIPORT.SYS
8000e000 31ed06b4 - buslogic.sys          80223000 31ed237c - Disk.sys
80227000 31ec6c7a - CLASS2.SYS            8022b000 31eed0a7 - Ntfs.sys
f5a90000 31ec6c8d - Floppy.SYS            f5aa0000 31ec6ca1 - Cdrom.SYS
f5ab8000 31ec6c7d - Cdaudio.SYS           f5d0a000 31ec6df7 - Fs_Rec.SYS
f5dc9000 31ec6c99 - Null.SYS              f5c64000 31ed868b - KSecDD.SYS
f5dca000 31ec6c78 - Beep.SYS              f5ad0000 31ec6c90 - i8042prt.sys
f5c6c000 31ec6c97 - mouclass.sys          f5c74000 31ec6c94 - kbdclass.sys
f5ae8000 31f50722 - VIDEOPRT.SYS          f5c84000 31ec6c6d - vga.sys
f5b00000 31ec6ccb - Msfs.SYS              f5800000 31ec6cc7 - Npfs.SYS
f5792000 31eed262 - NDIS.SYS              a0000000 31f954f7 - win32k.sys
f577c000 31ee8583 - vga.dll               f5830000 31ec6e8f - Cdfs.SYS
f5cd8000 31ec6e6c - TDI.SYS               f56c3000 31f130a7 - tcpip.sys
f56a7000 31f50a65 - netbt.sys             f5ac8000 31ec6e04 - amdpcn.sys
f58d0000 31f8f864 - afd.sys               f5b08000 31ec6e7a - netbios.sys
f5920000 31ec6cb1 - Serial.SYS            f5646000 325c3856 - srv.sys
f55df000 31f5003b - rdr.sys               f55ce000 31f7a1ba - mup.sys
f5d8c000 2f2131c8 - crashdrv.sys

Address  dword dump   Build [1381]                            - Name
f58bfdd0 f5d8c756 f5d8c756 69696969 f5d8c410 04515f10 808ccd30 - crashdrv.sys
f58bfdd8 f5d8c410 f5d8c410 04515f10 808ccd30 f58bfe14 8011139b - crashdrv.sys
f58bfde8 8011139b 8011139b 808ccd30 809bf2c8 808cab4c 809bf2c8 - ntoskrnl.exe
f58bfdfc 8016af42 8016af42 04515f10 00000000 80165a01 f58bfdec - ntoskrnl.exe
f58bfe08 80165a01 80165a01 f58bfdec f58bfdf4 f58bfea0 8016b6d3 - ntoskrnl.exe
f58bfe18 8016b6d3 8016b6d3 808ccd30 809bf2c8 808d03a8 809bf200 - ntoskrnl.exe
f58bfe2c 80165a01 80165a01 8bfe3801 00000002 f58bff04 0012fc88 - ntoskrnl.exe
f58bfe40 80165a54 80165a54 00000000 0012019f 038ed025 f58bfe98 - ntoskrnl.exe
f58bfe94 801382d4 801382d4 80141ab0 ffffffff f58bfed4 80165a7c - ntoskrnl.exe
f58bfe98 80141ab0 80141ab0 ffffffff f58bfed4 80165a7c 00000044 - ntoskrnl.exe
f58bfea4 80165a7c 80165a7c 00000044 00000000 00000000 00000000 - ntoskrnl.exe
f58bfed8 8013b519 8013b519 00000044 00000000 00000000 00000000 - ntoskrnl.exe
f58bff04 f5658c12 f5658c12 00000000 00000001 00000001 f5651718 - srv.sys
f58bff14 f5651718 f5651718 f5659032 00000000 00000000 00000000 - srv.sys
f58bff18 f5659032 f5659032 00000000 00000000 00000000 00000000 - srv.sys
f58bff80 8013f9ea 8013f9ea f5659055 f56514f8 00000000 0000027f - ntoskrnl.exe
f58bff84 f5659055 f5659055 f56514f8 00000000 0000027f          - srv.sys

Restart and set the recovery options in the system control panel
or the /CRASHDEBUG system start option. If this message reappears,
contact your system administrator or technical support group.
```

• **Figure 3-5.** A BSOD displays a Stop error code near the top of the screen.

concentrate on the first few lines on your screen. Observe and record what you see on the screen in preparation for either reporting it to a computer support person or researching the cause yourself. Look for the stop code (the first string of characters after the word *Stop*) and write it down (*yes,* the entire string), and then look for a description at the left of the line immediately below the line containing the Stop code and above the line that begins "CPUID." As Figure 3-5 shows, sometimes there is no description. An example of a description is "IRQL_NOT_LESS_OR_EQUAL." If a description is present, write it down, also. After displaying a Stop screen, the computer may restart on its own. If not, once you have recorded this information, you should restart it. It is possible that the computer will restart and function normally, but you should still report the problem or research the cause of the Stop screen.

Using just the stop code, search the Microsoft Technet site (`www.microsoft.com/technet`) for possible causes and solutions (using another computer if this one won't work). When you find information on this stop code, it may have different solutions based on the description found on the screen.

Preparing for the BSOD

To be prepared for a BSOD, you should decide how you want your computer to behave after a stop error. You do this by modifying the Recovery settings on the Startup/Shutdown tab of the System applet of Control Panel.

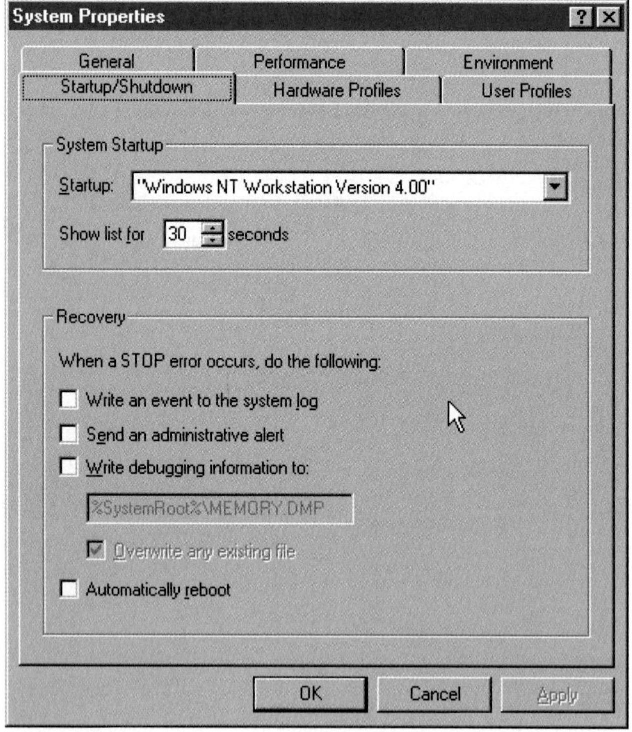

• The Recovery settings on the Startup/Shutdown tab

- **Write An Event To The System Log** will cause NT to write an event to the system log, which is one of several log files that can be viewed using Event Viewer (Start | Programs | Administrative Tools |

Event Viewer). This means that even if the computer reboots after a Stop screen, you can read the stop error information that was on the screen in the system log. We recommend you select this setting, if it is not already selected.

- **Send An Administrative Alert** is a setting that we recommend you select. This sends an alert message to the administrator that will appear on the administrator's screen the next time the administrator logs on.
- **Writing Debugging Information To** is a setting we don't recommend for a desktop computer, because it creates a file containing an image of the contents of memory at the time of the fatal error. This file can be sent to Microsoft for evaluation of a problem, but this amount of effort and cost (Microsoft charges for these services) is normally only expended on a critical computer, such as a network server.
- **Automatically Reboot** is a setting we recommend, as long as you have also selected the first option, which preserves the stop error information.

Stalled Print Job

You have sent a print job to your printer, but it either does not print at all, or only partially prints before stalling. To troubleshoot this, you double-click on the printer icon that appears on the right side of the taskbar while a document is printing. This opens the print queue. The status of the document is "printing" although it is not actually doing so. Now you turn to the printer and check that it has paper, is connected, turned on, and online. Return to your computer and the print queue, select the document, and attempt to cancel it from the queue. The status may change, but the print job never leaves the queue. In fact, if you try to send other print jobs, they will also fail to print. This is a sure sign of a stalled print spooler, and the only solution is to restart the Spooler service. You may do this by restarting your computer, or by stopping and starting just the Spooler service. You can do the latter from the Services applet in Control Panel. From the list of services, select Spooler and click the Stop button. When the status column shows that this service is stopped, restart it by selecting the Start button. Open the print queue from Start | Printers. The problem document is usually

Try This!

Setting Recovery Options

You can set the recovery options on your computer now. To do this, you must be logged on as an administrator. Try this:

1. Right-click My Computer and select Properties. In the Properties dialog box, select the Startup/Shutdown tab.
2. Select Write An Event To The System Log (if it is not already selected), Send An Administrative Alert, and Automatically Reboot. Click OK to close the System Properties dialog box.
3. If the System Control Panel applet message that the Alerter service is not running appears, click OK. Click No when prompted to restart the computer, and perform the next step. Otherwise, skip to step 5.
4. To start the Alerter service, open a command prompt and type **net start alerter** and press ENTER. Then restart your computer and skip step 5.
5. If you did not receive the Alerter message in step 3, click Yes to restart your computer.

deleted when the spooler restarts. If it has not been deleted, you will find that you are able to manually delete it now. Finally, resend the print job.

Internet Explorer Displays Junk

> Learn about the protocols of the Web in Chapter 10.

Windows NT 4.0 comes with Internet Explorer version 2.0, which does not understand the newer versions of the code used on web sites today. Since much of the code is really text-based instructions to your Internet browser, anything it does not understand is considered to be text and is displayed. The result may look like Figure 3-6.

The solution to a problem like this is to update to a newer version of the browser. This sometimes places you in a Catch-22 situation, because the current version of Internet Explorer will not install without the latest service pack—and you can't use the Express Install for the latest service pack without the latest version of Internet Explorer.

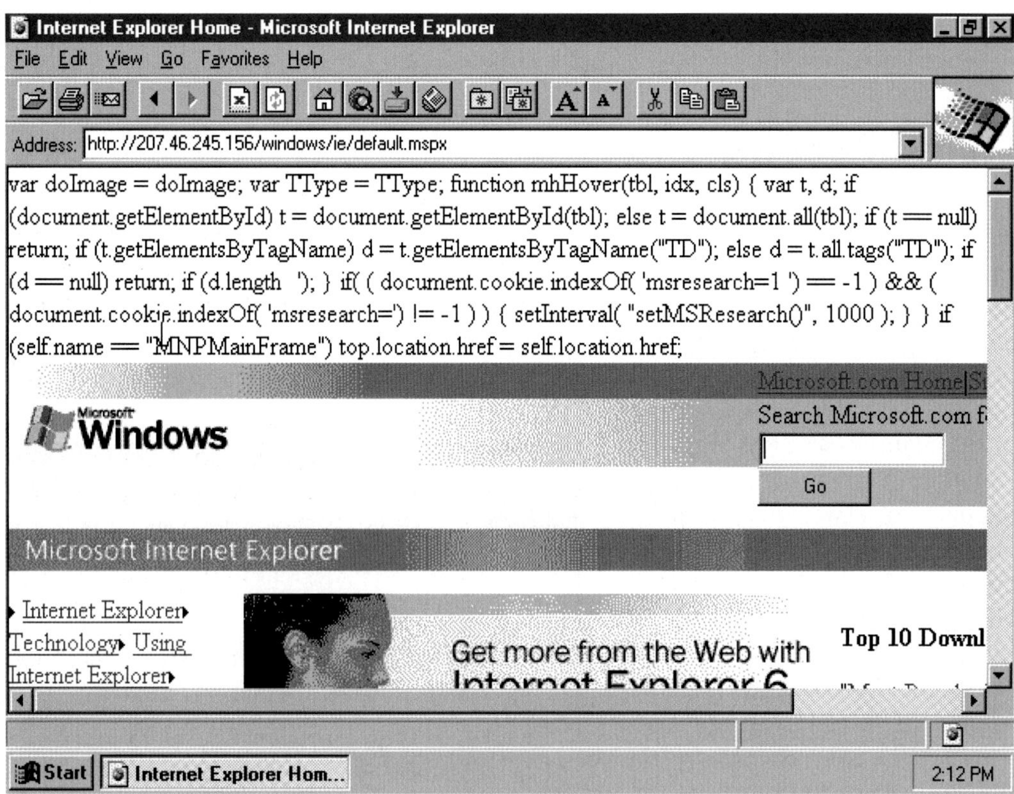

• **Figure 3-6.** An old version of Internet Explorer displays the code it cannot interpret.

■ Chapter Summary

After reading this chapter and completing the Step-by-Step tutorials and Try This! exercises, you should understand the following facts about Windows NT:

Windows NT 4.0 Workstation Overview

- Windows NT Workstation is a more stable OS than Windows 3.*x* and Windows 9*x*.
- Windows NT Workstation provides local security.
- The Windows NT 4.0 Workstation desktop resembles Windows 95.
- Windows NT 4.0 supports the NTFS4 and FAT16 file systems.
- Windows NT 4.0 can run applications written for MS-DOS, Windows 3.*x*, Windows 9*x*, and Windows NT.
- Some DOS and Windows 3.*x* applications will not work in Windows NT 4.0.

Install and Configure Windows NT 4.0 Workstation

- The Windows NT 4.0 Setup program can create a partition with a maximum size of 4GB. If more partitions are desired, create them after installing NT.
- NT requires special software drivers for all hardware.
- You can download the latest Windows NT 4.0 Hardware Compatibility List (HCL) found at `winqual.microsoft.com/download/`.
- The minimum hardware requirements for NT 4.0 Workstation are a Pentium processor, 16MB of RAM, 120MB of available disk space, CD-ROM drive (or other access to the source files), VGA or higher-resolution video adapter, and Microsoft mouse (or compatible pointing device).
- Don't stop at the minimum hardware requirements when you install NT 4.0; you will need more memory, hard disk space, and perhaps more processing power, depending on the applications you install.
- Microsoft's published recommended minimum hardware included an Intel Pentium processor, 32 to 48MB of RAM, 2GB available hard disk space, CD-ROM drive, SVGA or higher-resolution video adapter, and Microsoft mouse.
- Before installing NT, prepare your hardware, determine the installation method, and gather the materials needed to complete the installation.
- The Windows NT setup disks are required when you want to install NT from CD-ROM, but the computer cannot boot from the CD drive.
- You can create a set of NT setup disks by running *d*:\i386\WINNT32 /OX. (from Windows) or *d*:\i386\WINNT /OX (from Windows 3.*x* or DOS).
- You cannot install Windows NT 4.0 without the CD key, a code that appears on the envelope containing your NT CD.
- Service packs are very important for Windows NT 4.0.
- Service packs for Windows NT 4.0 Workstation can be found on the Microsoft NT Workstation page at `www.microsoft.com/ntworkstation`.
- You can view other computers on the network through Network Neighborhood.
- When uncertain about the service packs installed in Windows NT, run the WINVER program, which will tell you what (if any) service packs are installed.
- By default, Windows Explorer view options hide hidden files and hide most file extensions.
- If you have an NTFS volume, you can assign permissions to folders and files to protect data from unauthorized users.

Customize and Manage Windows NT 4.0 Workstation

- A Windows NT 4.0 Workstation installation must be configured and managed for the person who will use it. This may include creating a new hard disk partition, installing or removing programs, and customizing the desktop.
- Disk Administrator is the program an administrator uses to create and format partitions and to manage drive letters.
- If there is only one hard drive partition and a CD-ROM drive, the NT Setup program will assign

the hard drive partition drive letter C:, and the CD-ROM drive letter D:. If you create more hard drive partitions, they will get drive letters beginning with letter E:. Disk Administrator will allow you to assign a different drive letter to the CD-ROM drive.

- Unless you are dual-booting between NT and a less capable OS, such as DOS, Windows 3.*x*, or Windows 9*x*, you should not create extended partitions.
- If you are dual-booting between NT and a less capable OS, such as DOS, Windows 3.*x*, or Windows 9*x*, any drive that the second OS needs must use the FAT file system. Also, the drive can be on only the first primary partition or in a logical drive in an extended partition.
- You can remove programs with the Add/Remove Programs Control Panel applet.
- Making the desktop visually pleasant to the user will enhance the user's work experience.
- Simple maintenance tasks include removing temporary files, uninstalling unneeded software, and running a disk-defragmenting program.
- The infamous Blue Screen of Death (BSOD) is actually caused by the operating system responding to a serious error, called a stop error, which threatens to make the system so unstable that the operating system shuts down rather than continue.
- Observe and record information from a BSOD so that either a support person or you may research the cause.
- A computer may restart on its own, or need to be restarted manually after a BSOD.
- A computer may restart normally after a BSOD, but the cause should still be researched in case there are steps you can take to prevent it from happening again.
- Be prepared for possible Windows NT stop errors by setting recovery options.

Troubleshooting Common Windows NT 4.0 Problems

- If you do not know how to perform a task in Windows NT, you can search the help program. It has many tutorials with step-by-step instructions.
- Restart the Spooler service to remove a stalled print job.
- If Internet Explorer displays junk, upgrade to a newer version.

Key Terms List

Blue Screen of Death (BSOD) *(132)*
clean installation *(104)*
defragmentation *(130)*
Disk Administrator *(117)*
emergency repair disk (ERD) *(110)*
image *(105)*
long file name (LFN) *(96)*
NTFS *(97)*
NT file system version 4 (NTFS4) *(95)*
patches *(105)*
service pack *(106)*
swap file *(98)*
virtual file allocation table (VFAT) *(95)*
volume *(117)*
WINVER *(114)*

Key Terms Quiz

Use the Key Terms list to complete the sentences that follow. Not all the terms will be used.

1. It is important that the most current _______________ be installed to fix bugs and add new features.
2. An exact duplicate of the entire hard drive contents, including the OS and all installed software, is called a/an _______________.
3. Although the screen seems to be covered with what looks like computer code, careful observation may help you discover the cause of a/an _______________.
4. A quick way to show the About Windows NT message box that contains version and licensing information, the amount of memory available, and the service pack level is to run the program _______________.

5. Each area in a partition that is assigned a drive letter is a/an ___________________.

6. The ___________________ file system has a theoretical partition size limit of 16 exabytes (one billion billion bytes).

7. Programmers at Microsoft create ___________________, which are software fixes to individual problems discovered in a software product.

8. To perform a/an ___________________, you begin with a computer with an empty hard disk, or repartition the hard disk during the installation of the OS.

9. Although we don't usually use this term, ___________________ is the updated version of FAT16 found in Windows NT.

10. ___________________ of a disk will reorganize a drive so that the pieces of each file are stored contiguously on disk.

Multiple-Choice Quiz

1. What security feature sets NTFS apart from the FAT file systems?
   - **a.** File and folder permissions
   - **b.** User authentication
   - **c.** Password policy
   - **d.** Personal firewall
   - **e.** Spam filter

2. Which of the following was *not* a graphic element first introduced in Windows 95 and included in Windows NT 4.0?
   - **a.** Taskbar
   - **b.** Menus
   - **c.** My Computer
   - **d.** Network Neighborhood
   - **e.** Start button

3. Of the following, which would have been a likely reason for someone to have chosen Windows NT 4.0 Workstation as a desktop OS in 1996 over the popular Windows 95?
   - **a.** Great screen savers
   - **b.** Less expensive than Windows 95
   - **c.** Stability and security
   - **d.** Hardware support
   - **e.** Easy to install

4. Which word or phrase that follows describes something that Windows NT 4.0 and Windows 95 have in common?
   - **a.** NTFS
   - **b.** Common kernel
   - **c.** Local user accounts
   - **d.** GUI features
   - **e.** Administrator

5. Which of the following will not run in Windows NT 4.0?
   - **a.** 64-bit UNIX applications
   - **b.** 16-bit Windows-based applications
   - **c.** MS-DOS applications
   - **d.** OS/2 version 1.*x* applications
   - **e.** 32-bit Windows-based applications

6. The special environments in which NT runs applications are called:
   - **a.** Addresses
   - **b.** Accounts
   - **c.** Shells
   - **d.** Subsystems
   - **e.** Windows

7. The largest partition size you can create with the Windows NT 4.0 setup program is:
   - **a.** 7.8GB
   - **b.** 16TB
   - **c.** 2GB
   - **d.** 500MB
   - **e.** 4GB

8. As a new OS in 1996, a major drawback NT 4.0 Workstation had was:
   - **a.** The GUI
   - **b.** Security
   - **c.** Hardware support
   - **d.** Memory
   - **e.** Hard disk limits

9. The Windows NT GUI tool for creating and managing hard disk partitions is:
   a. Windows Explorer
   b. FDISK
   c. Disk Defragmenter
   d. Disk Administrator
   e. Windows NT Diagnostics
10. Which of the following statements is true of service packs for Windows NT 4.0?
   a. Remove applications
   b. Fix file corruption
   c. Install MS Office
   d. Upgrade to a new OS
   e. Fix bugs and sometimes add new features
11. To remove an installed Windows component or application, you would use the following:
   a. Add/Remove Programs
   b. My Documents
   c. My Computer
   d. Start | Run
   e. Recycle Bin
12. An operating system that supports this can take full advantage of a computer built around multiple identical processors.
   a. Protected mode
   b. Multitasking
   c. Symmetric multiprocessing (SMP)
   d. Single-tasking
   e. Co-processing
13. When preparing to install Windows NT 4.0 on a computer that will not boot from the CD drive, you will need to create a set of Windows NT 4.0 setup disks. How many floppy disks will this require?
   a. One
   b. Five
   c. Four
   d. Three
   e. Two
14. The RDisk utility allows you to create one of these:
   a. Emergency repair disk (ERD)
   b. NT Boot disk
   c. MS-DOS boot disk
   d. Configuration disk
   e. Data disk
15. When an NT computer fails with the dreaded Blue Screen of Death (BSOD), it displays this piece of information that can be used to find the solution to the problem causing the failure.
   a. Serial number
   b. Product ID
   c. Version number
   d. Stop error code
   e. Service pack version

Essay Quiz

1. Write a few sentences describing why Windows NT 4.0 Workstation is in use today. Select the one reason you believe to be the most significant and support your viewpoint.
2. Describe the weaknesses of Windows NT 4.0 Workstation. Select the one weakness you believe to be the most compelling reason not to use it. Support your viewpoint.
3. You work for a small accounting firm that has just purchased a new PC from a local company that builds PCs from standard components. That computer will be running a special application that requires Windows NT 4.0 with Service Pack 5 or greater. Without describing the actual installation, describe the steps you'll take before and after you install Windows NT 4.0 and before the installation of the new application.
4. You're a new employee doing computer support in a small manufacturing company that uses Windows NT in a workgroup on a small network. One of the printers is a sophisticated graphics printer that is expensive to run. It is shared on the network, and your boss has asked you to set it up so that only two people can send print jobs to the printer. Describe what you will do.

5. A friend calls you with a problem. He installed Windows NT 4.0 Workstation on a computer that is not connected to the Internet, but he has access to another computer with Internet access and a writeable CD drive. He wants to upgrade NT on the first computer to Service Pack 6a. Write a few sentences describing what steps he should take.

Lab Projects

• Lab Project 3.1

A virus hit your computer, and many critical files were destroyed. The only data you kept on that computer consisted of some files that luckily were copied to a writeable CD (CD-RW) the day before the virus hit. You have decided it is easier to reinstall Windows NT 4.0 than to try to repair the damaged files, and you have decided to repartition and format the hard disk to ensure that all traces of the virus and its damage are gone.

You will need the following:

- The lab computer on which you previously installed Windows NT
- The Windows NT 4.0 Workstation CD
- The CD key code from the envelope of your NT CD
- The list of configuration information you used for the first installation

Then do the following:

1. Perform the installation.
2. Complete any necessary tasks after the installation.
3. Record your observations on performing an installation of NT for the second time.

• Lab Project 3.2

You and your boss are the entire IT department for a small company with a very limited budget. He has identified ten computers that should be replaced as slow and obsolete equipment. He has found a nonprofit organization that has agreed to accept the old equipment, with all software removed from the hard drives. The computers presently run Windows NT Workstation 4.0. He plans to build the new computers, with your assistance, out of purchased components. Because of budget constraints, he would like to install NT 4.0 on the new computers and has verified that the components he is purchasing for the new computers are compatible with NT 4.0. He plans to use NT 4.0 on the new machines for three years. He would like you to investigate the status of Microsoft's support for NT 4.0 Workstation and how this might affect the company's use of this OS. Do the following:

1. Determine where you will find the information.
2. Do the research your boss requested, and write a report including whether or not Microsoft will discontinue support and what impact this will have on his plans.

• Lab Project 3.3

Your spouse's company is upgrading to all-new computers with new operating systems and has offered to give their existing computers to employees for their personal/family use. The computers will have Windows NT 4.0 Workstation and a full suite of Office products installed on them. They also will include licenses for the OS and application software, but no peripherals will be included. By sheer coincidence, you have also been offered a functioning laser printer for free by the father of a friend. It's an oldie but a goodie—an HP LaserJet IIID. This big, old, business workhorse is a duplex printer (which means that it can print on both sides of the paper), and it is ideal for a project you have that requires that capability.

You have decided to accept both offers. To ensure that Windows NT 4.0 Workstation will be reliable and stable, you need to research its current status. You also need to verify that the computer and the printer will function together. There are several steps you should take to accomplish these tasks.

Perform the following tasks:

1. Explain how you are going to discover the present status of the OS.
2. Describe how you will eliminate any known problems with the OS.
3. Explain the steps you will take to learn whether the computer and printer can work together. Then perform those steps and describe the results.

Windows 2000 Professional

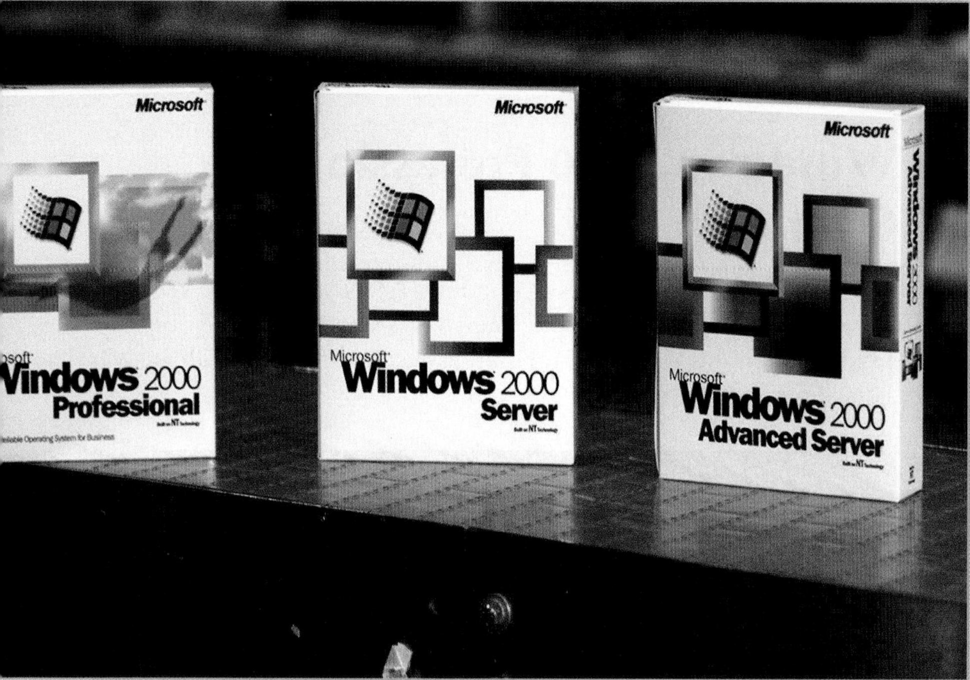

It seems very pretty, but it's RATHER hard to understand!

—THROUGH THE LOOKING GLASS,
BY LEWIS CARROLL

Windows 2000 Professional was the first Windows version that combined the friendly nature of the consumer-oriented versions of Windows (Windows 9*x*) with the robustness introduced in Windows NT. Its user interface was familiar enough to legions of Windows 95 and Windows 98 users for them to feel quickly at home when using a Windows 2000 Professional–based PC. This was important because it meant that businesses didn't have to give up the advanced features of a Windows NT–based OS to keep their employees happy with the way their desktop PCs functioned. By combining the best of both worlds, Windows 2000 Professional provides a powerful core and a very usable interface for maximum productivity. It's not an upgrade to Windows 98, however. Switching to Windows 2000 is more like replacing the engine in our old Honda Prelude with that of a Mustang V8.

In this chapter, you will learn how to:

- **Describe Windows 2000 Professional benefits, features, and weaknesses**
- **Install and configure Windows 2000 Professional**
- **Customize and manage Windows 2000 Professional**
- **Perform proactive maintenance tasks**
- **Troubleshoot common Windows 2000 Professional problems**

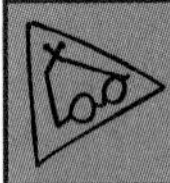

Inside Information

Different Versions

Windows 2000 is actually available in several different versions. The version designed for use in the typical desktop PC is Windows 2000 Professional. For server systems, Microsoft offers Windows 2000 Server, Windows 2000 Advanced Server, and Windows 2000 Datacenter Server—all of which are optimized for the role of network server. The first two are available through retail: Windows 2000 Server is targeted as a departmental file, print, and communication server; and Windows 2000 Advanced Server is targeted as a web server and as the tool for running line-of-business applications. Windows 2000 Datacenter Server is available only through server manufacturers, preinstalled on very high-end servers. All of the Windows 2000 versions have substantially identical appearances, and the differences become apparent only when you are given the task of managing a large network installation. Windows 2000 Professional can be used as a file, print, and communications server for a small number of client computers. It has limits—both legal licensing limits and capacity limits—that prevent it from being an effective server OS.

While it is not the latest desktop version of Windows, you'll still encounter Windows 2000 Professional in the business world. This chapter will help you prepare so that you will feel comfortable with the essentials of Windows 2000 Professional. You will learn the hardware required to use Windows 2000 Professional, as well as how to configure Windows 2000 Professional for efficient operation, how to install application programs, and how to install and configure a printer in Windows 2000 Professional. Finally, you'll learn what to do to resolve some of the problems you are likely to encounter.

Windows 2000 Professional Overview

What are the benefits and features of Windows 2000 Professional? What are its weaknesses? Why would anyone want Windows 2000 Professional on the desktop when there are other operating system choices? We'll answer these questions in this section.

• Windows 2000 Professional desktop with several open applications

Benefits and Features

To be successful, an OS must offer benefits for the user. In the case of Windows 2000 Professional, the benefits are in the areas of stability, software compatibility, security, and support for several file systems to suit the performance and security needs of the user. In the following sections, we explore these benefits by exploring the features of Windows 2000 Professional that make them possible.

Desktop

Windows 2000 has a familiar desktop that shows only subtle changes from previous Windows OSs. The taskbar offers the customizable Quick Launch toolbar with the Show Desktop button, a feature introduced in Windows 98. There are familiar desktop icons (My Documents, My Computer, Recycle Bin, and Internet Explorer) and slightly modified icons, like the Network Places desktop icon, which is now My Network Places (see Figure 4-1).

Security

Since Windows 2000 Professional is a member of the Windows NT family, it is also far more secure than Windows 95 or Windows 98. Not only is a logon to Windows 2000 Professional mandatory, but this logon must be performed from an account that is a member of a security database—either the local security accounts database built into Windows 2000 Professional on the local computer, or a network-based security database, such as in a Windows NT or Active Directory domain. A **Windows NT domain** is one in which all servers maintaining the domain database are running a Windows NT Server OS. An **Active Directory domain** is one in which at least one of the servers maintaining the domain database is running a Windows 2000 Server OS or greater.

In addition, it's possible to restrict access to local resources such as files, folders, and printers to specific user accounts or group accounts, which contain user accounts. This is done through the use of permissions. A **permission** is a level of access to an object (in this case a file or folder) that is granted to a user account or group account. An example of a permission is read-only, a permission that allows a user to view the contents of a file or folder, but not alter the file or folder.

Up to this point, these features reflect security as it existed in Windows NT 4.0. However, Windows 2000 Professional offers several improvements to security. A short list of these improvements includes the following:

- New tools are provided for administering security in Windows 2000 Professional, including group policies and new console tools available through the Control Panel.

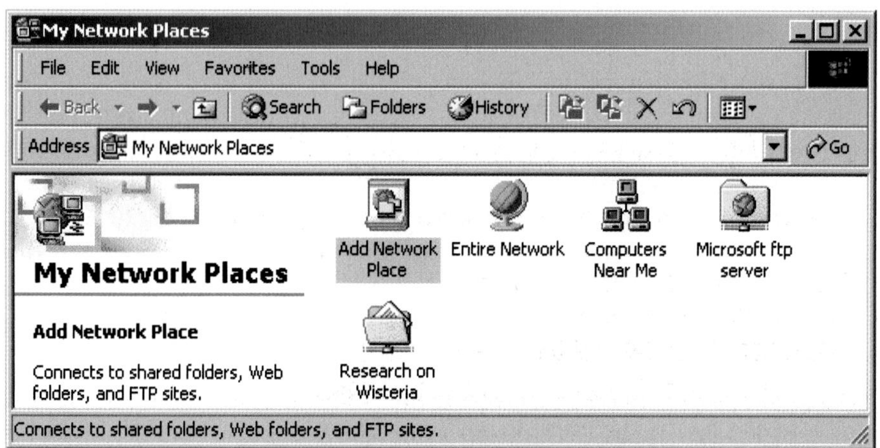

• **Figure 4-1.** My Network Places with links, as well as added links (shown as folder icons)

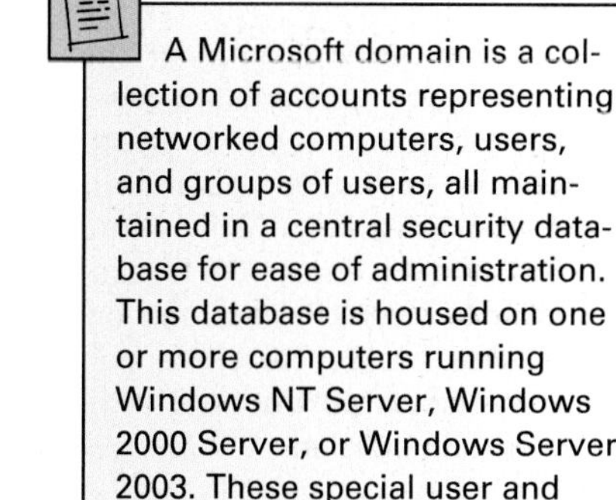

A Microsoft domain is a collection of accounts representing networked computers, users, and groups of users, all maintained in a central security database for ease of administration. This database is housed on one or more computers running Windows NT Server, Windows 2000 Server, or Windows Server 2003. These special user and group accounts are often simply referred to as "users" and "groups," even though we are talking about accounts that are stored on disk, not the actual people involved.

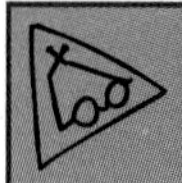

Inside Information

Meet the Families!

As with European royalty, there are separate houses, or genealogical lines, of Windows. First, there is what we'll call the "House of DOS" Windows family, which evolved from the first version of Windows (in 1985) that simply put a graphical interface on top of DOS (16-bit program code). Each new version was an improvement over the last, but still depended on DOS as a core component. The last two versions in this line are Windows 98 and Windows Me, which use primarily 32-bit code, but they still have some 16-bit components and depend on DOS to start.

The other major Windows line could be called the "House of NT," because this line evolved from the first version of Windows NT (3.1). This is an entirely separate line from the House of DOS Windows family, based on a different kernel (the main core programming code) and on other internal components than the House of DOS versions of Windows. This line includes all versions of Windows NT, Windows 2000, Windows XP, and Windows Server 2003.

For a desktop computer, the important ingredients for centralized management of group policies for that computer are membership in an Active Directory domain and an OS level of Windows 2000 Professional or greater; a lesser (older) version of Windows will not be affected by group policies!

Group policy is an extremely advanced topic, but it is key to successfully managing Windows 2000 Professional. If you want to learn more, connect to `http://support.microsoft.com` and search the Knowledge Base for the topic Group Policy.

- The Internet Protocol Security (IPSec) protocols can be used to make network communications more secure.
- Logon authentication from a Windows 2000 Professional computer to a Windows Active Directory domain is more secure with the use of the Kerberos security protocol. When a user logs onto an Active Directory domain, a unique value is assigned to that user and used to identify all traffic from that user to any Active Directory server.
- Files on an NTFS5 volume can be encrypted to further secure them.

Group Policies Our nomination for the best improvement in security in Windows 2000 Professional is the use of group policies to centrally manage security when a Windows 2000 Professional computer is part of an active directory domain. Group policy is a very advanced topic, so we'll just give you the abridged version here. **Group policy** is a grouping of policies for controlling not only the many security settings, but also configuration settings for the OS. This is done to give administrators the ability to centrally manage many hundreds of settings using a single administrative tool.

If a Windows 2000 Professional computer is a stand-alone computer or a member of a workgroup, the administration of these settings must be done at that computer; in which case you are merely setting policies for that one computer (local policy), rather than group policy, as applied in a domain. The real power of group policies comes into play when your Windows 2000 Professional computer is a member of an Active Directory domain. An Active Directory domain is one that has one or more Windows 2000 Server or newer Microsoft server operating systems in the role of domain controller (the computer that maintains the Active Directory database). Only then can group policies be centrally administered for all member computers (both servers and clients) that have Windows 2000 or newer Microsoft operating systems.

The primary tool used for managing group policies is the Group Policy Editor. Using this one tool, an administrator can create a set of group policies to modify settings on a single computer or on hundreds of computers (in an Active Directory domain). Figure 4-2 shows the Group Policy Editor with a view of the Local Computer Policy. When administering a workgroup, a clever administrator can learn the advanced technique of creating templates that can be copied to each individual computer.

More Secure Authentication When you log on, your user name and password are compared with those in the security accounts database through a process called authentication. A Windows 2000 Professional computer that is not a member of a Windows domain can only authenticate users who have accounts in the local accounts database. When a Windows 2000 Professional computer is a member of a Windows NT domain or an Active Directory domain, a user logs on using a user name and password of a domain account, and Windows 2000 Professional passes the user's authentication information (user name and password) to a domain controller for authentication. This is called **pass-through authentication**. If the authentication is successful, the user is logged on to both the network and to the local computer. Kerberos is the authentication protocol that Windows 2000 Professional uses when you log onto an Active Directory domain. This is a more secure protocol than the previous Windows authentication protocols, but it is not

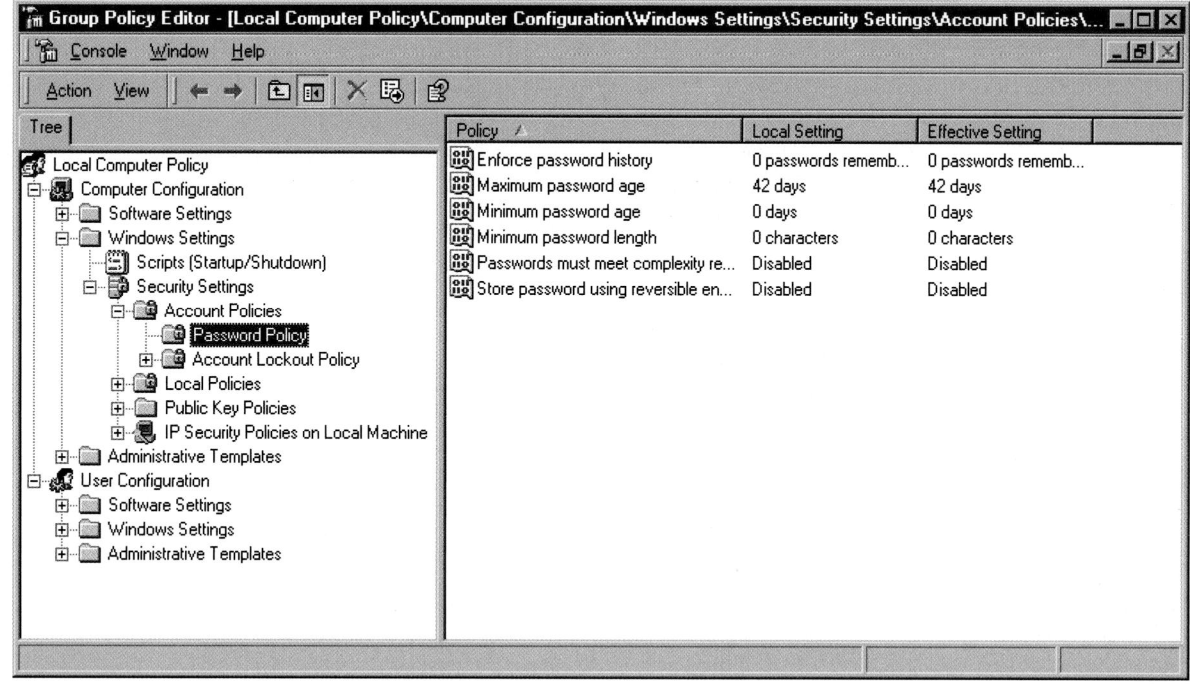

• **Figure 4-2.** Group Policy Editor showing Local Computer Policy

the only authentication protocol that Windows 2000 Professional can use. Several others are used either together with Kerberos or separately, depending on your method of authentication.

File Encryption File encryption, as implemented in Windows 2000, is the process of transforming the contents of a file so that the file is unintelligible to anyone other than the person who encrypted it. This is a new feature of NTFS introduced in Windows 2000 Professional. In short, a user can encrypt a folder or individual files. The process is as simple as opening the Properties of a file or folder, clicking the Advanced button, and placing a check in the box by Encrypt Contents To Secure Data, as shown in Figure 4-3. When you turn on encryption for a folder, the folder itself isn't really encrypted; rather, any files already in or added to the folder are encrypted. If an encrypted file is moved or copied to an NTFS volume, it will retain its encryption, even if it is moved to a folder that does not have encryption turned on. Be sure to only use cutting and pasting (or saving from within an application) to move files into an encrypted folder, because moving files with a drag-and-drop operation will not result in the file automatically being encrypted. Further, if an encrypted file is moved or copied to a non-NTFS volume, it will be decrypted.

File encryption sounds simple, right? Well, there are drawbacks to it, and you should not use file and folder encryption until you learn more about it in Chapter 7.

You cannot use both the Compress and Encrypt attributes on the same file or folder. You may use only one or the other. Clicking the Encrypt box will clear the Compress box, and vice versa.

Walk Before You Run! Here we go again—introducing a really advanced topic and then sort of patting you on the head and saying you don't need to know it right now. Though going any further with the security topic at this point would be overwhelming, it's important for your future career that you be aware of computer security. In the United States, recent laws mandate that the health care industry and others implement high-security standards to protect individual privacy. This applies to the handling of computer-based records as

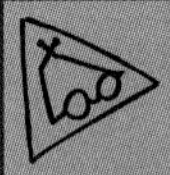

Inside Information

Don't Blink!

The most common method of authentication is the simple logon in which you enter your user name and password using the keyboard and mouse. Other methods may include special devices to authenticate you. One such mechanism is a credit-card-size device called a smart card, which provides a token, or password. Other devices allow you to prove who you are through biometrics (measuring a biological characteristic). For example, you might log onto your computer by entering your user name at a keyboard and then placing your thumb on a device that scans your fingerprint. A similar approach is retinal scanning, which confirms your identity by examining the retina of your eye. These are all options if you're logging onto an Active Directory domain from a Windows 2000 Professional computer, but they require special equipment and configuration of all the computers involved.

A handy place to begin learning more about computer security is the Help program in Windows 2000 Professional. Select Help from the Start menu and then search on Security. To begin, *skip* the topics Cluster Control, Network Load Balancing, Message Queuing, and Security Hosts. Come back to these other topics only if you plan to work in network or server administration. Enjoy!

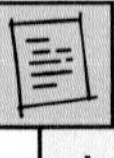

Learn more about driver signing and working with signed and unsigned drivers in Chapter 8.

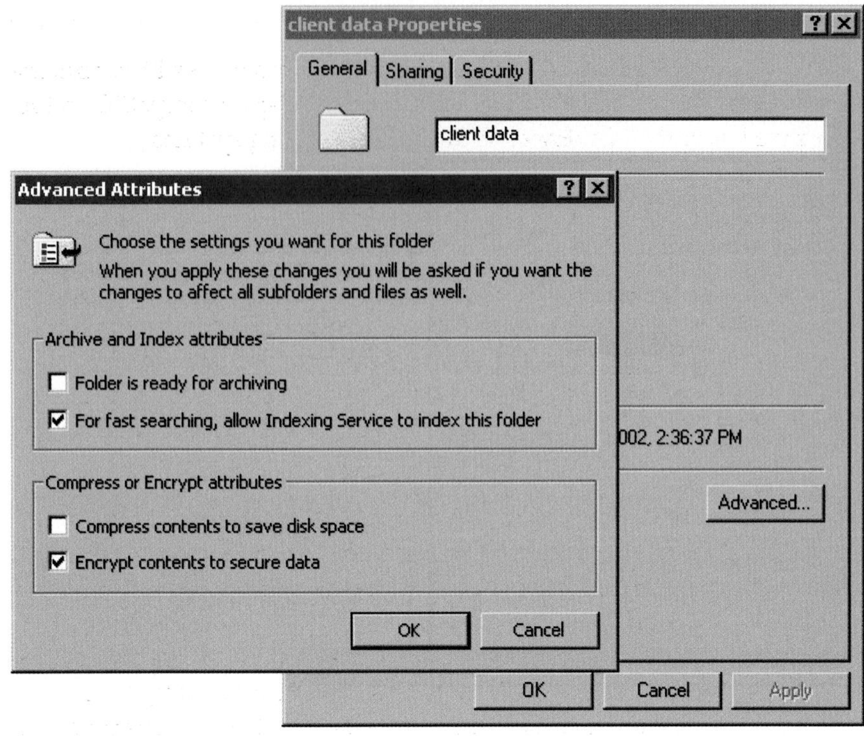

• **Figure 4-3.** Turn on encryption in the Advanced Attributes dialog box of a file or folder's properties

well as paper records. In addition, anyone who uses the Internet should learn about security threats and how to protect themselves from them. So it's important that you eventually learn more about security options for networked desktop computers. You will learn more about security in Chapter 7.

Stability

Windows 2000 Professional is really just an upgrade version of Windows NT 4.0. It was in development for about four years, and for much of that time Microsoft planned to name it Windows NT 5.0. In the fall of 1998, over a year before the new version was released, Microsoft announced that the new OS would be named Windows 2000 Professional. It still has the same 32-bit architecture of Windows NT, which offers an important advantage over Windows 9*x*: stability. Like its predecessor, Windows 2000 Professional runs each application program in its own **protected memory space**. Essentially, this means that a poorly written application program can crash without affecting any other running applications or Windows 2000 Professional itself. This "clean room" approach to applications means that a PC running Windows 2000 Professional can often run for months without ever having to be restarted. In addition, Microsoft introduced **code signing** in Windows 2000, which means that all of the operating system code is digitally signed to show that it has not been tampered with. Code signing of device drivers is called **driver signing**. Driver signing indicates two things: the integrity of the file or files, and that the device driver has passed Microsoft's tests for compatibility.

Hardware Compatibility

Windows 2000 has a long list of hardware that is compatible with it, and, unlike Windows NT, Windows 2000 is fully plug-and-play compatible, a first for a member of the Windows NT family of operating systems.

When Windows 2000 was introduced, the latest version of the Universal Serial Bus (USB) standard that it supported was version 1.1. If your computer includes USB 2.0 support, you will want to be sure to install Service Pack 4 to add support for this newer and faster USB standard.

Software Compatibility

Another important benefit of Windows 2000 Professional is the ability to choose from a large selection of application software written to run on Windows computers. Although many application programs are available for Macintosh, Linux, and other OSs, software developers do tend to develop more applications intended for Windows-based PCs than for PCs running any other OS, simply because the vast majority of all PCs run some version of Windows.

16-Bit and 32-Bit Windows Applications and DOS Applications As a member of the Windows family of operating systems, Windows 2000 Professional quite naturally was designed to run a specific group of programs. Although it maintains a limited ability to run many DOS applications, as well as older 16-bit Windows programs, Windows 2000 Professional was specifically designed to perform at its best when running 32-bit Windows programs.

Windows 2000 Professional, like Windows NT 4.0, runs applications in environments called subsystems, and as with Windows NT, 32-bit Windows applications are the "native" applications of Windows 2000. These applications are written to a specific set of rules, and they run in the Win32 subsystem. Many programs designed for Windows 95 (or later) or Windows NT 3.51 (or later) are 32-bit Windows programs. This compatibility across both lines of the Windows OS family is one reason why Windows 2000 Professional has been considered by many people to be an excellent solution to the need for an operating system that both runs popular application programs and provides the security required to protect the user's data.

Applications that depend on Windows 9*x* **virtual device drivers (VXDs)** cannot run under Windows 2000 Professional. A program that uses a VXD in Windows 9*x* may be able to work if it is modified to use a service that provides the same functionality in Windows 2000 Professional.

Applications Written for Non-Microsoft OSs In addition to 16-bit and 32-bit Windows applications, Windows 2000 Professional can run the same types of applications as NT 4.0. For details, review "Software Compatibility with Legacy Applications" in Chapter 3.

Cross Check

Windows 2000 Professional vs. Windows NT 4.0 Workstation

Compare Windows 2000 Professional to Windows NT 4.0, discussed in Chapter 3, and then answer the following questions:

1. Considering what you have learned about the features and benefits, briefly compare the security features of Windows 2000 Professional and Windows NT 4.0 Workstation.

   ____

2. Downward compatibility with older applications (DOS, 16-bit Windows, and 32-bit Windows) is important to the success of any version of Windows. Compare the application support in Windows 2000 to that in Windows NT.

   ____

Windows 2000 File Systems

Recall that a file system is the means an operating system uses to organize information on disks. For CD-ROMs, Windows 2000 uses the compact disc file system (CDFS), and it uses the universal disk format (UDF) for digital versatile discs (DVDs). A benefit of Windows 2000 Professional is that it supports more file systems than the previous Microsoft OSs. Like all the previous versions of Windows, it supports the FAT file systems, including FAT12 for diskettes and FAT16 for hard disks. Like Windows 98, it also supports the improved FAT32 file system. In fact, during Windows 2000 installation, if you choose to format a partition larger than 2GB with the FAT file system, the Setup program will automatically format it as FAT32. After Windows 2000 installation, if you select FAT as the file system when you format a hard disk larger than 512MB, Windows 2000 will automatically format it as FAT32.

Like Windows NT, Windows 2000 supports NTFS, but introduces new features in NTFS version 5 (NTFS5). NTFS has always been a more efficient file system than FAT, and it is more secure than the FAT file systems, because you can set permissions on each file and folder on an NTFS volume. NTFS also uses a superior method of storing files that guards against file damage or loss, but it now has more features, such as file encryption (mentioned earlier) for better security and a feature that supports indexing to make searches of files and folders faster. This is called the **Indexing Service** and must be turned on through the Properties of a drive if this feature is desired. All of these features make NTFS5 the preferred file system for Windows 2000.

Disk Storage Improvements in Windows 2000

Windows 2000 introduces the concept of disk types—basic and dynamic. While the basic disk type is the default disk type of Windows 2000, and the one you are most likely to use in Windows 2000 Professional, take a few minutes for an overview of these disk types:

Basic Disks Basic disks are disks prepared and managed in the manner of Windows NT 4.0. A **basic disk** can have up to four partitions and is compatible with older operating systems. The partition types are primary and extended, of which there can be a maximum of four primary partitions or three primaries and one extended partition. Each primary partition may have only one drive letter assigned to it, while an extended partition must have one or more logical drives (each with a drive letter). See Figure 4-4.

Dynamic Disks The dynamic disk type is a new way to allocate disk space and manage hard disks. **Dynamic disk** types have space allocated in volumes, not partitions, and do not have the limits that are imposed on basic disks.

Leave your options open! To convert a disk from basic to dynamic, there must be at least 1MB of unallocated space on the physical disk to hold the disk configuration information. Therefore, when creating partitions on a basic disk, be sure to leave at least 1MB of unallocated space free.

- There is no limit to the number of volumes on a dynamic disk.
- A volume can be extended to include available space on any hard disk in the computer.
- The configuration information for a dynamic disk is saved on the disk, rather than in the registry.

However, the default disk type in Windows 2000 is the basic disk type. Once the operating system is up and running, you may choose to convert a basic disk to dynamic, but the benefits of dynamic disks are really aimed at disks on network servers. In fact, the best features of dynamic disks (volume types that support fault tolerance) are not available in Windows 2000 Professional, but only in the Windows 2000 Server products. Table 4-1 shows the volume types that can be created with dynamic disks and the versions of

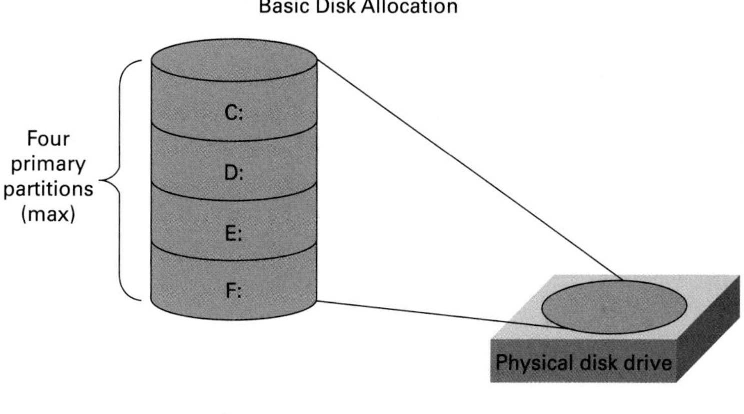

Or

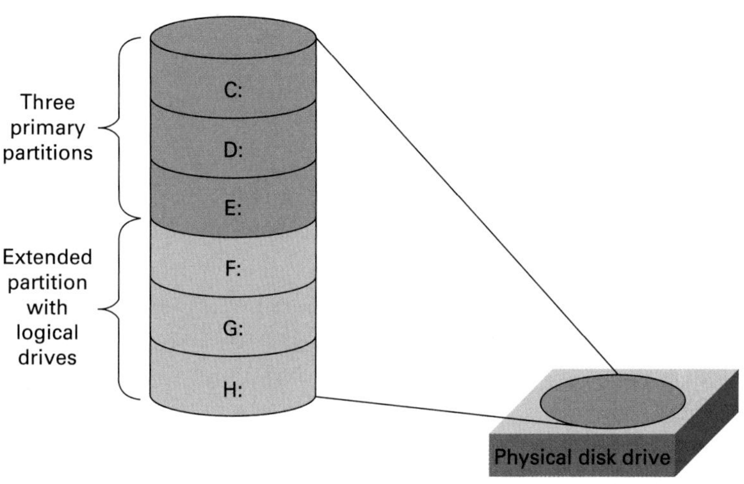

Figure 4-4. Basic Disk Allocation allows for a maximum of four partitions.

Windows 2000 that support each volume type (denoted by an *X*). Following are definitions of each dynamic disk volume type.

- **Simple Volume** This dynamic disk volume type includes disk space on a single hard disk. When you convert a basic disk to a dynamic disk, each existing volume becomes a **simple volume**. A simple volume can be created in Windows 2000 Professional or Windows 2000 Server. See Figure 4-5.

Table 4-1 Dynamic Disk Volume Types

	Windows 2000 Professional	Windows 2000 Server (all versions)
Simple Volume	X	X
Striped Volume	X	X
Spanned Volume	X	X
Mirrored Volume	N/A	X
Raid-5 Volume	N/A	X

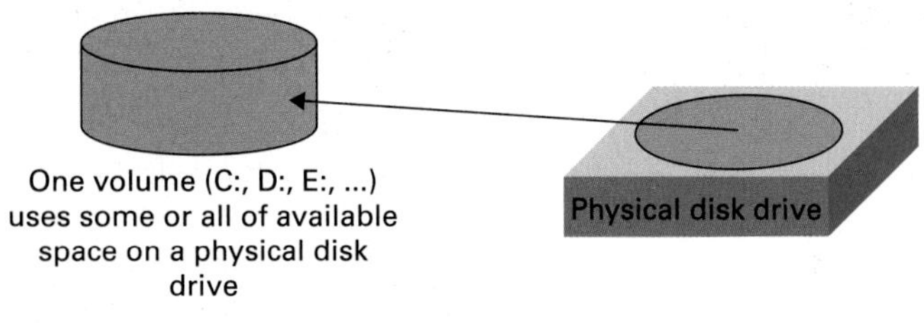

• **Figure 4-5.** A simple volume can be created on a dynamic disk in Windows 2000 Professional or Windows 2000 Server.

- **Striped Volume** This dynamic disk volume type combines space on two or more disks into a single volume. Data on a **striped volume** is written in 64KB blocks across all the physical disks in the volume in turn, using up to 32 disks, and must use an equal amount of disk space on each disk. This provides better performance if the hardware supports simultaneous reads and writes across the disks in the volume, but does not provide fault tolerance, which in this case is the ability to survive the failure of one of the disk drives in the volume. See Figure 4-6.
- **Spanned Volume** This dynamic disk volume type combines space on two or more physical disks. The operating system writes data into the first disk; and when the first disk runs out of space in the portion allocated to the spanned volume, the operating system moves on to the second disk in the spanned volume, writing to it until it is full, and then moving on to the next disk with space allocated to the **spanned volume**. A spanned volume has no fault tolerance; if one disk in a spanned volume fails, the entire volume fails. There is also no increase in performance. All you get from a spanned volume is the ability to store data on more than one physical disk but have it treated as a single volume. See Figure 4-7.
- **Mirrored Volume** Now we're talking fault tolerance! However, this is available only in the Windows 2000 Server products (and newer Windows Server products), not in Windows 2000 Professional. A **mirrored volume** includes two identical copies of a simple volume, on separate physical disks, created nearly simultaneously. Therefore, if one disk in a mirrored volume fails, Windows 2000 will "fail-over" to the still-working member of the mirrored volume. This means it will drop the failed member and only use the surviving member.
- **RAID-5 Volume** Another example of fault tolerance that is also unavailable in Windows 2000 Professional is a **RAID-5 volume**. This is a striped volume with added information that enables it to recover from a failure of one of the physical disks in the volume. It requires at least three physical disks in a computer running a Windows 2000 Server OS or greater.

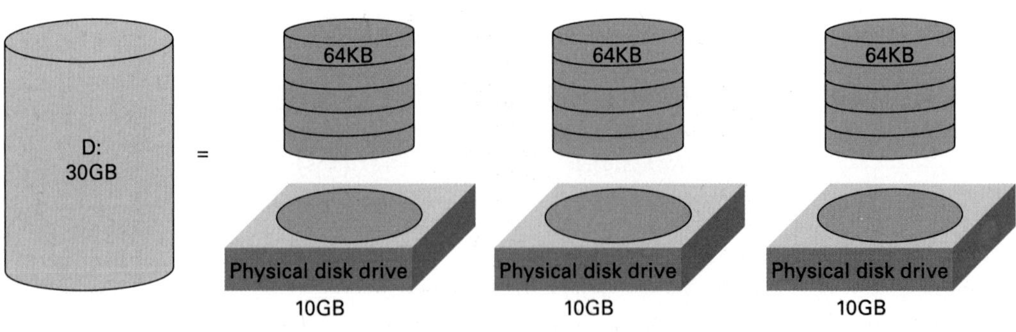

• **Figure 4-6.** A striped volume has data written across all disks included in the striped volume. It can be created on dynamic disks in a Windows 2000 Professional or Windows 2000 Server system.

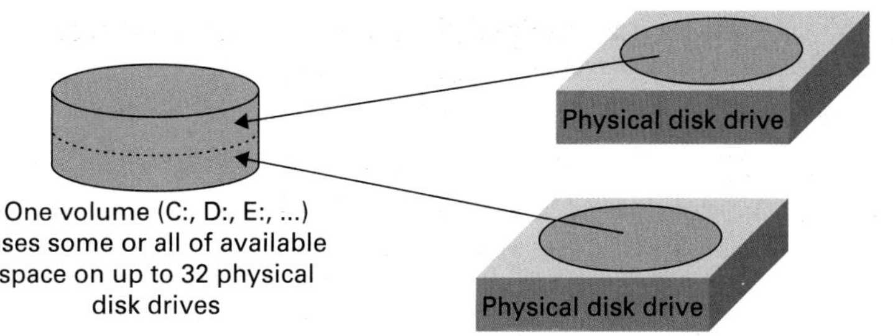

• **Figure 4-7.** A spanned volume can be created on dynamic disks in Windows 2000 Professional and all Windows 2000 Server systems.

Drive Paths and Mounted Volumes When it comes to assigning drive letters to primary partitions or logical drives on a basic disk or to volumes on dynamic disks, we are limited by the 26 letters of the alphabet. In fact, the first two letters, *A* and *B*, are reserved for floppy disk drives, and you are left with 24 letters for other drives. This limit is extended in two ways in Windows 2000. First, if you do not have floppy disk drives, you can assign letters *A* and *B* to other drives. Second, a feature using drive paths and mounted volumes allows you to avoid using drive letters altogether. This new feature is available on both basic and dynamic disks. Now, a partition (basic disk) or volume (dynamic disk) need not have a drive letter assigned at all, but can be "connected" to an empty folder on another drive. This connection of a partition or volume to a folder is called a **mount point**; the path to the partition or volume is called a **drive path**. This requires NTFS on the partition or volume hosting the drive path. A partition or volume can have both a drive letter and one or more drive paths. In My Computer or Windows Explorer, the mount point is listed with local folders, but with a drive icon. Figure 4-8 shows a mount point labeled "Q1-2006"; the contents of the mounted volume are shown in the right-hand pane.

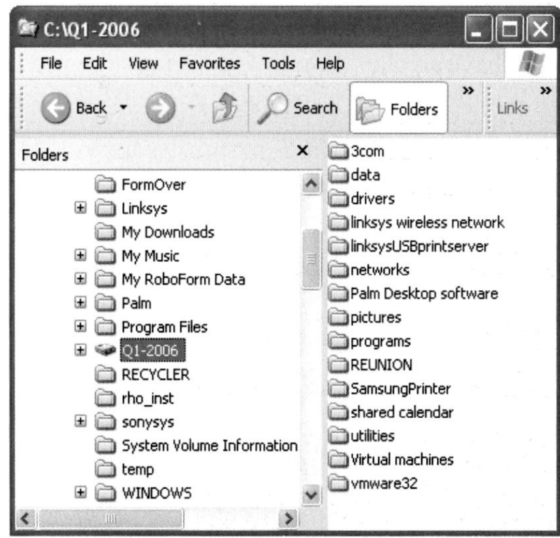

• **Figure 4-8.** A mount point and drive path can be created in Windows 2000 Professional or greater OS.

Inside Information

RAID Basics

Striped volumes, mirrored volumes, and RAID-5 volumes are implementations of redundant array of independent disks, most often referred to as RAID, followed by a version number. RAID involves the use of two or more disks for the purpose of better performance or (most often) to provide redundancy of data. A striped volume is an example of RAID-0; a mirrored volume is RAID-1. When RAID provides redundancy, as it does in mirrored volumes and RAID-5 striped volumes, if one disk fails, the data is not lost. Check out the information on RAID at `www.acnc.com/raid.html`*, and/or use your favorite Internet search engine to research "RAID levels."*

Don't confuse disk type with file system. All the file systems supported by Windows 2000 (FAT16, FAT32, and NTFS5) can be used on either disk type—basic or dynamic. Once you partition a basic disk, you may format it with any of these file systems. This is also true of dynamic disk volumes. We prefer to use the NTFS5 file system.

Cross Check

Compare File Systems

If it seems that you have heard about FAT16, FAT32, and NTFS before in this book, it is because we mentioned them in Chapters 2 and 3. Flip back to those chapters, and review the information on these file systems; then answer the following questions:

1. Which versions of Windows support any version of the NTFS file system?

   ____

2. Which version of Windows first offered the FAT32 file system?

   ____

Weaknesses of Windows 2000 Professional

Windows 2000 Professional is not a perfect OS—as if there were such a thing anywhere! You may be surprised to learn that some of its benefits appear to also be weaknesses. "What?" you say, "We can't have it both ways?" Just watch! We believe that the enhanced security and support for DOS and 16-bit Windows applications can be seen as weaknesses. We also believe that the more capable an OS is, the more complex it is to work with, especially when you encounter problems. We see this complexity not exactly as a weakness, but as an obstacle to adoption.

Support for Old DOS and Windows Applications

Windows 2000 does not provide optimal support for all old DOS and Windows applications. The weaknesses in this area are twofold. First, some old applications will not run in Windows 2000 Professional. Second, some applications that do run, do so more slowly than in Windows 9*x*.

Some Applications Just Won't Run Backward compatibility issues are not new. There have long been some DOS and 16-bit Windows applications that won't run in newer versions of Windows, but some applications written for Windows 9*x* also won't run in Windows 2000 Professional. An application written for Windows 9*x* should be a 32-bit application written to comply with certain rules. Problems occur when an application is not carefully created and, while it runs well in Windows 9*x*, simply breaks too many rules to run in Windows 2000 Professional. Even though this incompatibility may not be the fault of Microsoft, if you have an older Windows program that you enjoy or rely on that won't run in Windows 2000 Professional, you will see this as a severe limitation of Windows 2000 Professional.

Some Applications Will Run More Slowly DOS and Windows 3.*x* applications may run more slowly in Windows 2000 Professional than in Windows 9*x*. This slowness has to do with the virtual environment that must be created, and the fact an application may be behaving in a nonstandard way, even for DOS or Windows 3.*x*. Therefore, this problem also depends on the program and how it was written. Because time has diminished the chance that you'll ever need to run DOS or Windows 3.*x* applications, this is a very minor weakness of the OS.

The Need to Reboot After Modifying the OS

When Windows 2000 Professional was in development, we heard that Microsoft was working to make the OS behave so that the computer would not need to be restarted every time an OS component is added or removed. Microsoft only partially succeeded, and you will find that although there are fewer event types that require a reboot, plenty still exist. You don't have to reboot when you reconfigure TCP/IP for your network or after installing some OS components and applications, but you still have to reboot after adding some components and applications and after you apply a service pack.

When Is Windows 2000 Professional Needed?

Although Windows 2000 Professional is far more stable and secure than Windows 9.*x*, the latter has lingered on the desktop in many organizations. Quite honestly, this is because when Windows 2000 Professional was introduced, Windows 9.*x* was far less expensive for PC manufacturers to install on most systems (less than half the cost of Windows 2000 Professional). Individual consumers were far more interested in saving a few dollars than in having a more stable and secure OS on their PCs. It is reasonable, therefore, to ask "When is Windows 2000 Professional actually necessary?"

Consider Carlos, who runs a business that auctions off historical memorabilia from the days of the California Gold Rush and the Comstock Lode. He has several employees who each work on an individual PC connected to a small network. A substantial part of Carlos' business derives from the extensive research his employees do on the various items contained within each auction. Carlos' company requires security, and when he purchased new computers in 2000, he bought Windows 2000 Professional for its security and integrity to protect his company's research data from loss and to control access to that data so that only authorized people could view or modify information. A year later, when Windows XP was introduced, he chose not to upgrade, but to stay with Windows 2000 for the usable life of the computers.

Alanna owns a small computer programming company. When she is working on developing an application program, she can't afford to have computer problems that might wipe out days of work. She, too, appreciates the stability that Windows 2000 Professional provides so she can spend her time making sure that her programs run properly and not spend time worrying about losing her work.

These are just two examples of why Windows 2000 Professional is so popular. Compared to an OS like Windows 98, Windows 2000 Professional is a far better choice if you simply want to get work done without constantly worrying about crashes and downtime. Windows 2000 Professional is also a much better choice than operating systems such as Linux or the Macintosh OS for people who want compatibility with the broadest range of fully supported applications at a reasonable price.

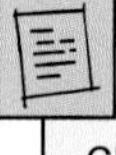

The world is changing, and in Chapter 11, you will learn more about the inroads the Linux OS has made on desktops worldwide.

Here are some examples of when Windows 2000 Professional would be preferred over Windows 9.*x* as a desktop operating system:

- Although most Windows programs will run under Windows 9.*x*, a few very demanding business-oriented programs (such as certain CAD programs) will run only under a member of the Windows NT family. In this case, Windows 2000 Professional would be an excellent choice.

- If it is vitally important that a PC be reliable (such as in a medical monitoring application), the far greater stability of Windows 2000 Professional may be required.
- A publicly accessible PC (such as one providing Internet access in a business' lobby) likely could benefit from the advanced security features of Windows 2000 Professional to prevent users from performing unauthorized actions.
- In a business environment, it is often very important to maintain precise control over access to resources such as sensitive files. The security features of Windows 2000 Professional make this far easier to accomplish than on a system running Windows 9.*x*.
- A desktop computer that is a member of a Windows Active Directory domain can be managed and administered better if it is a Windows 2000 Professional or Windows XP Professional computer, because these OSs can be centrally managed and secured through the use of group policies.

Installing and Configuring Windows 2000 Professional

Now that you understand the benefits and weaknesses of Windows 2000 Professional and when you might consider using this OS, you are ready to install this OS on your lab computer. But first, you have tasks to complete, such as checking out the hardware requirements for Windows 2000 Professional and the compatibility of your hardware and software, choosing the method of installation, gathering the materials and information needed for installation, and preparing the Windows 2000 Professional setup disks (if necessary).

Hardware and Software for Windows 2000 Professional

Before you install or upgrade a computer to Windows 2000 Professional, you have four concerns regarding the computer hardware and software: the minimum hardware required by the OS, the ideal hardware for the job you hope to do with the computer, the compatibility of your hardware, and the compatibility of the software you want to use. Let's take a closer look at these concerns.

> Although you can install Windows 2000 Professional on a computer that just meets the minimum hardware requirements, you'll get far better performance with a more generous system configuration. You will get the biggest performance boosts from a faster CPU and increased RAM and disk space.

Hardware Requirements

Windows 2000 Professional has more demanding hardware requirements than previous versions of Windows, but these requirements are still very modest considering the way most PCs have been configured for quite a few years. At minimum, Windows 2000 Professional requires a 133-MHz Pentium or higher microprocessor (or equivalent), 64MB of RAM, a 2GB hard disk with 650MB of free space, a VGA or higher-resolution video adapter with a compatible monitor, a keyboard, and a Microsoft mouse or compatible pointing device. Additionally, a CD-ROM drive is required if you want to install from the Windows 2000 Professional CD.

The Ideal Hardware Configuration

If you ask us what the ideal hardware configuration is, we would simply answer, "It all depends." You might recognize that as the consultant's answer to every question. It is, however, the correct answer. The ideal hardware configuration depends on what you hope to do with your Windows 2000 Professional computer. Therefore, here we will suggest a middle-of-the-road configuration that would be overkill for most ordinary tasks, but may not be quite adequate if you are using your computer to play very sophisticated Internet games or to run some other type of sophisticated program with high demands on processor, memory, and disk—or that requires some exotic piece of hardware. If you are not a computer gamer or other super-high-tech computer user, the following should be ideal:

- Intel Pentium 4 processor
- 256MB RAM
- 30GB of available hard disk space
- Fast CD-ROM drive
- DVD drive
- SVGA or higher-resolution video adapter
- Microsoft mouse

Configuring a computer to boot from CD-ROM is done through the computer's system setup utility, independent of the operating system installed. Don't try this on a computer at school or work without explicit permission. For your home computer, check out the manufacturer's documentation to see how to start the system setup utility and how to change the boot order (which drives are bootable, and in what order the system will search them for an operating system).

In addition, if this is a clean installation, with no previous OS on the computer, your computer should boot from the CD-ROM drive. This has been a standard feature in PCs for many years, configurable in the system setup program. If your computer will not boot from CD and has no previous OS installed, then a 3.5-inch disk drive is also required, and the computer must be configured to boot from the floppy drive. A Windows 2000 Professional–compatible network adapter is also required if your computer is to be on a network.

Checking Hardware and Software Compatibility

When you search the Microsoft compatibility site, double-check spelling. For instance, when we searched for the Hewlett-Packard 7400C scanner, we left out the hyphen and failed to find the scanner. Repeating the search with the hyphen included worked!

Before you install Windows 2000 Professional or add new hardware or software to an existing installation, spend a few minutes to determine whether Windows 2000 Professional will work with the hardware or software you have. If you don't have Internet access, you should check the **hardware compatibility list (HCL)** contained in the HCL.txt file in the Support folder on the Windows 2000 Professional CD. This text file lists all of the system components and peripherals that were tested and shown to be compatible with Windows 2000 Professional at the time Windows 2000 Professional was prepared for release. Note that the HCL.txt file has a date of December 1999, so any products introduced after that time won't be shown.

If you have Internet access, see the online compatibility list for Windows 2000 by connecting to `www.microsoft.com/whdc/hcl/search.mspx`. The posting dates shown on these pages are much more recent than the Windows 2000 CD release date of December 1999.

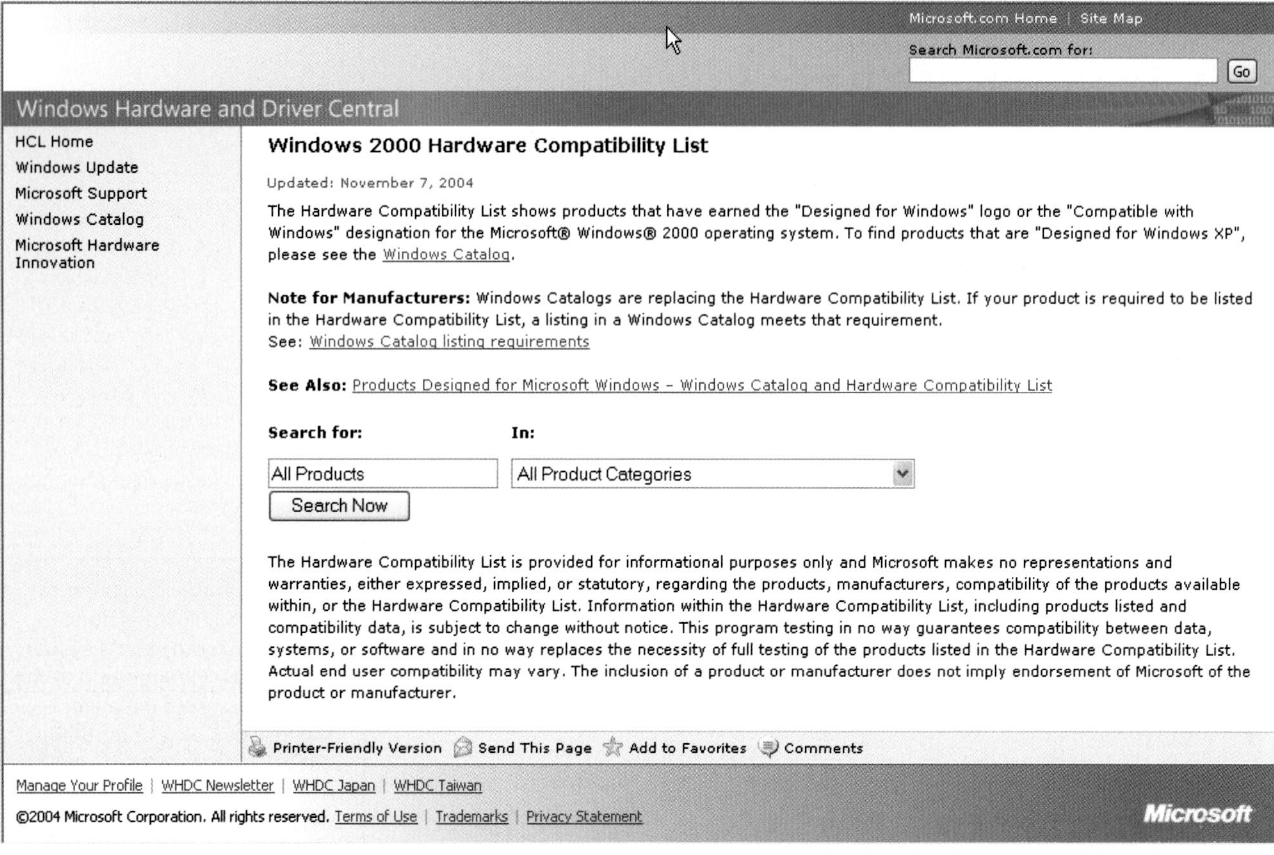

• Windows 2000 Professional hardware compatibility

It's important to check out compatibility before installing Windows 2000 Professional and any time you want to add new hardware or software to the computer. Consider Veronica, who has a computer with Windows 2000 Professional installed. She's been very happy with this computer and would now like to add an HP Scanjet 7400C scanner. Since she hasn't yet bought the scanner, she is going to check Microsoft's site first.

This is especially important for a device released after Windows 2000 Professional was released, since that means that its device driver is not included on the Windows 2000 Professional CD. If Veronica checks the Microsoft site and finds that the drivers for this scanner are not on the CD, and that there is no link at the Microsoft site

Try This!

Check Out the Compatible Products

Look for the HP Scanjet 7400C device driver that Veronica needs. To complete this task, you will need a computer with an Internet connection and a web browser. Try this:

1. Point your web browser to `www.microsoft.com/whdc/hcl/search.mspx`.
2. In the Search For box, type **Hewlett-Packard** (replacing the previous text in the box). Then tab to the box labeled "In," and select Imaging/scanner from the drop-down list. Click the Search Now button.
3. Use the Legend link to decipher the meaning of the icons shown to the right of each product.
4. You may have to scroll the screen to see the results. If you find that the device driver is not available for download, you can connect to the manufacturer's site (`www.hp.com`) and search for a device driver there.

to download the driver, then she can check out the manufacturer's web site to see if the manufacturer has posted a new driver.

Keep in mind, however, that older devices (such as printers) that were available long before the release of Windows 2000 Professional (and which do not appear in the HCL) will probably not have new drivers written for Windows 2000 Professional. In some cases, you can use Windows 2000 Professional drivers for a similar model, but full device functionality may not be available.

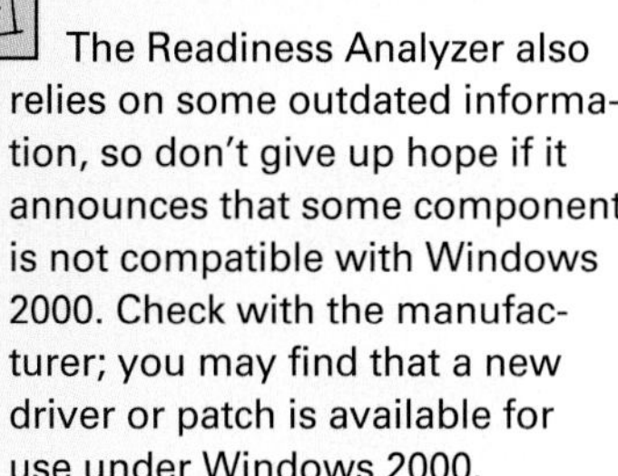

The Readiness Analyzer also relies on some outdated information, so don't give up hope if it announces that some component is not compatible with Windows 2000. Check with the manufacturer; you may find that a new driver or patch is available for use under Windows 2000.

Use the Readiness Analyzer to Check Out Compatibility The Windows 2000 Professional installation program also performs a hardware compatibility test before beginning the installation. Although you could rely on this test to ensure that your system meets the minimum requirements for Windows 2000 Professional compatibility, we don't advise doing so. If incompatible hardware is found, you'll have to abort the installation and resolve the compatibility issues before proceeding. Generally, this means removing any incompatible hardware and replacing it with compatible hardware.

As an alternative, you may want to use the Readiness Analyzer, a stand-alone compatibility test for both hardware and software that you can launch by running the WINNT32 program with the `checkupgradeonly` switch (WINNT32/checkupgradeonly). WINNT32 is the program that starts an upgrade installation from Windows 9*x*. When you run it with the `checkupgradeonly` switch on, it runs the compatibility test without starting the upgrade installation. The result is an upgrade report on the compatibility of all detected hardware and software. This report can be viewed on the screen or printed, and it is saved in a file called upgrade.txt, although you can choose a different name from within the Readiness Analyzer. Figure 4-9 shows the upgrade report information after we ran the Readiness Analyzer on a computer with a video adapter unknown to Windows 2000 Professional. In a case like this, try to obtain a Windows 2000 Professional device driver from the vendor.

Use the Windows Catalog (`http://www.microsoft.com/windows/catalog/`) to find compatible software for Windows 2000. While this site appears to be for Windows XP only, Microsoft recommends it for checking out software for Windows 2000.

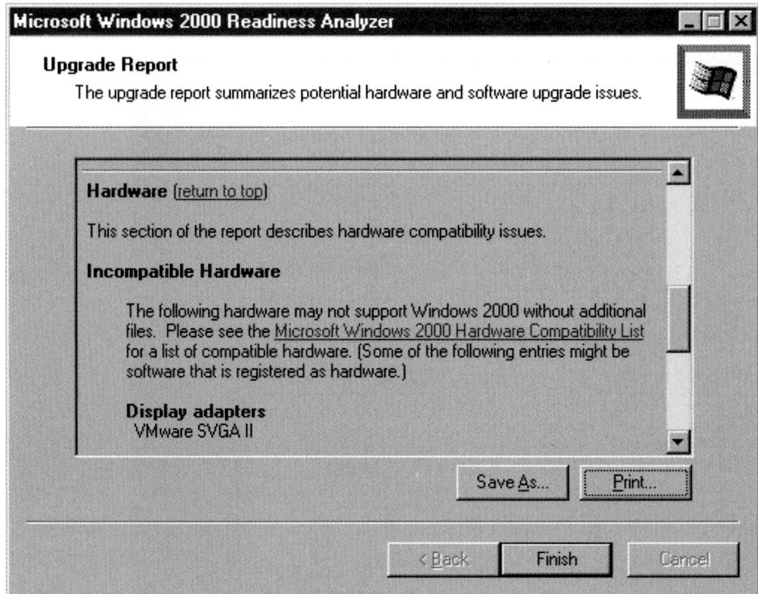

• **Figure 4-9.** Readiness Analyzer upgrade report

Step-by-Step 4.01

Run the Hardware and Software Compatibility Test

You can test the compatibility of the hardware and software on your lab computer. To complete this task, you will need the Windows 2000 Professional CD and a computer running any 32-bit version of Windows.

Step 1

Insert the Windows 2000 Professional CD. If your computer uses autorun (if it automatically runs a program when a CD is inserted), close any messages or windows that open.

Step 2

Open a command prompt and enter the following commands (where *d* is your CD-ROM drive letter; be sure to press ENTER at the end of each line):

```
d:
cd \i386
winnt32 /checkupgradeonly
```

Readiness Analyzer will take a few minutes to detect your hardware and software and prepare the upgrade report.

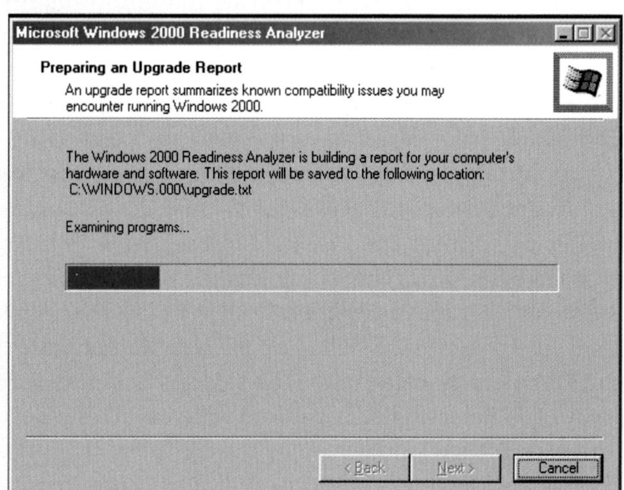

Step 3

When the upgrade report appears, scroll through the summary information and look for any information about incompatible hardware or software.

Step 4

When you have finished, click Save As and save the report as **Upgrade.txt** on the root folder of your local hard drive. Then click Finish to close the Readiness Analyzer.

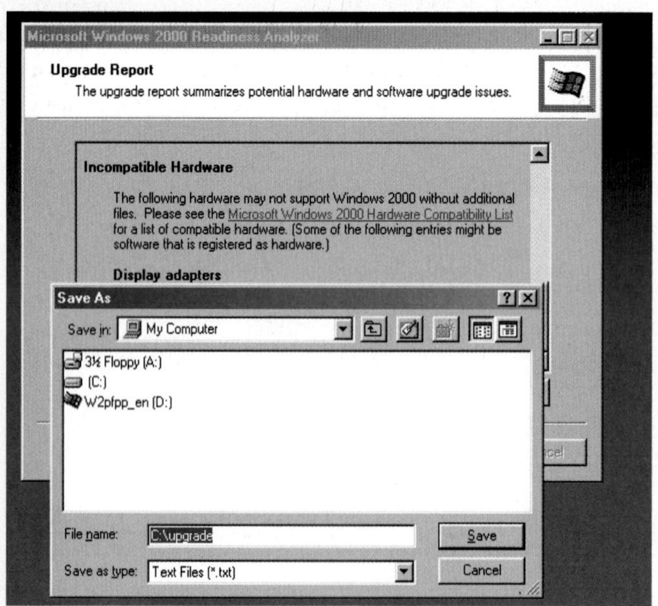

Pick a File System

If you plan to dual-boot between Windows 2000 and any previous Microsoft OS, the boot drive must be formatted with a file system compatible with both operating systems. Any drive that Windows 9*x* needs must use the FAT file system. Also, the drive can only be on the first primary partition or in a logical drive in an extended partition. All other drives and partitions will be unavailable when one of the other OSs is active. Table 4-2 shows the file systems each dual-boot combination can use.

Determine the Service Packs and Updates to Use

Service packs and updates have become critical for any operating system. They often are needed to correct a vulnerability discovered by the growing number of hackers, people who find ways to break into networked computers and wreak havoc. You will most certainly want to apply any necessary service packs or updates immediately after installation. For most of us, that means that we connect to Microsoft's Update site at `windowsupdate.microsoft.com` immediately after installation and install the recommended updates and service packs.

However, if you are using a computer at home or work, keep in mind that some organizations do not allow service packs or updates to be installed unless they have first been tested by their own IT staff. In this case, you should check out what has been approved and where the appropriate service packs and updates are. They will probably be somewhere on the local network or on a CD.

Determine the Method of Installation

You can install Windows 2000 Professional manually, or you can use an automated method. There are variations of each of these approaches.

The following operating systems can be upgraded to Windows 2000 Professional: Windows 95, Windows 98, Windows NT 3.51 Workstation, and Windows NT 4.0 Workstation.

Manual Installation A manual installation requires that someone be present during the entire installation, providing responses to questions asked by the installation program. You may perform a manual installation for an empty hard disk (also called a clean installation) or for an upgrade to a computer with an existing Windows OS installed. An upgrade is an installation that directly replaces an existing Windows operating system, preserving all the configuration information from the previous OS and applications and applying them to the new OS.

You would usually choose a manual installation for a single computer or if the number of installations is too few to justify spending the time, effort,

Table 4-2 File Systems for Dual Booting

Older Version	Windows 2000
Windows 95	FAT16
Window 95 SR2, Windows 98, Windows Me	FAT16, FAT32

There are two versions of Makeboot: the 16-bit version for DOS, Windows 3.1, and Windows 9*x* called MAKEBOOT.EXE, and the 32-bit version for 32-bit Windows called MAKEBT32.EXE. The second version is much faster than the first, and therefore should be used whenever the OS will support it.

and expense of an automated installation. Once you decide on a manual installation, you need to make more decisions.

- Where are the source files? Will you install from the Windows 2000 Professional CD, from the local hard drive, or from a share on a network server? If this will be a clean installation, you must either boot directly from the CD or from the Windows 2000 Professional setup disks, which start the Setup program but require the presence of the CD. If you are upgrading, you will start your old OS, insert the CD, and, if autorun is enabled, you will select Install Windows 2000 from the Microsoft Windows 2000 Professional CD window, as shown in Figure 4-10. Otherwise, run WINNT32 (the upgrade program) from the i386 folder on the CD or on a file server.
- If you are planning to perform a clean installation from the CD, test whether the computer will boot from the CD. If your computer will not boot from CD, you will have to create a set of Windows 2000 Professional setup boot disks. This can be done using the Makeboot program, which is located in the Bootdisk folder on the Windows 2000 Professional CD. Most likely, you will need to run the Makeboot program on another

Try This!

Create Setup Boot Disks for Windows 2000

If you have access to a computer running any version of DOS or Windows, you can create a set of setup boot disks for Windows 2000. You will also need four blank, high-density diskettes. Try this:

1. Place the Windows 2000 Professional CD in the drive. Then enter the following (pressing ENTER at the end of each line):

   d*:** (where ***d is the drive letter of the CD-ROM drive)

   cd bootdisk

   makeboot (for DOS, Windows 3.1, or Windows 9*x* only)

   makebt32 (for Windows NT, Windows 2000, Windows XP, or greater)
2. Respond to the requests on the screen, and then label and insert the diskettes.
3. On completion, store the four diskettes until needed.

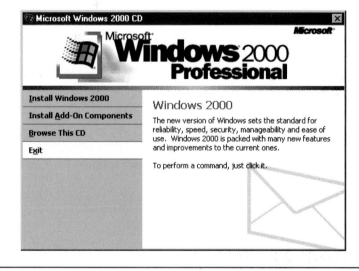

Any existing content on the four disks you use with the MAKEBOOT.EXE program will be destroyed. It is very important that you use disks that do not contain any files that you may need in the future since those files will be overwritten.

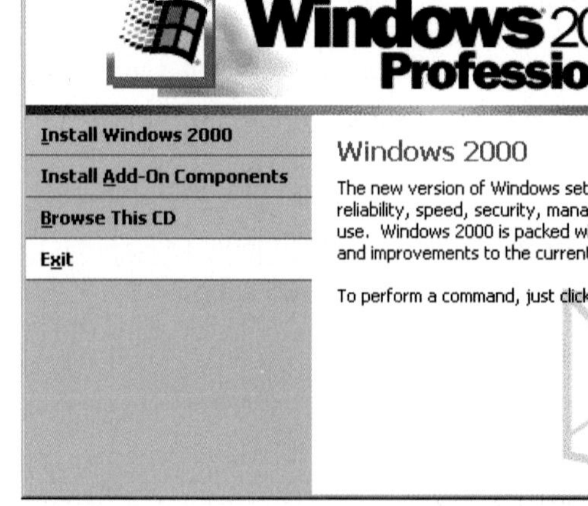

• **Figure 4-10.** Autorun menu on a Windows 2000 Professional CD

computer (other than the one on which you want to install Windows 2000 Professional) since you probably will not be able to access the CD drive if no OS is installed. MAKEBOOT.EXE is a character-mode program, not one with a graphical user interface.

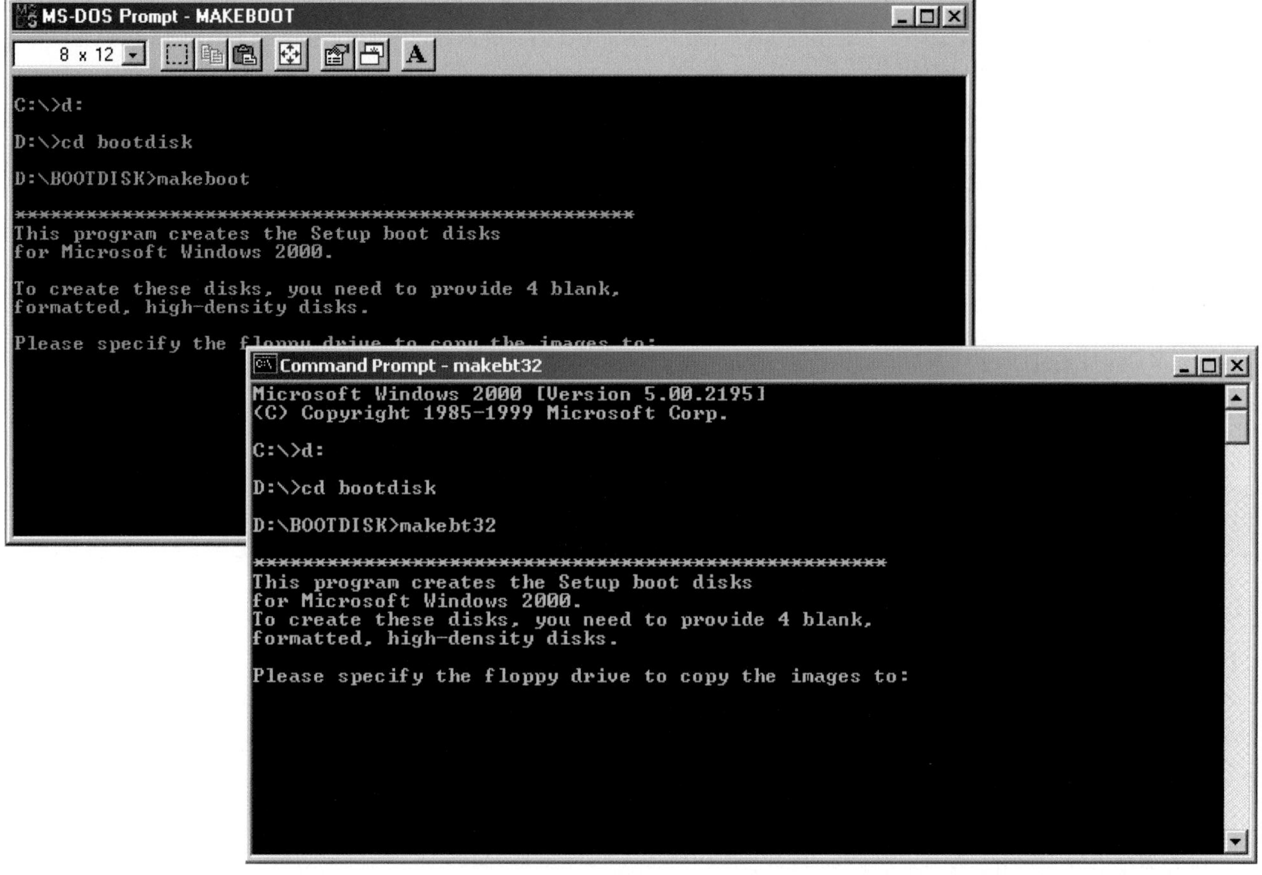

• MAKEBOOT is used to create setup boot disks for installing Windows 2000 Professional.

Automated Installation You can perform an automated installation of Windows 2000 Professional using one of several methods. One method is to use special scripts that are called up using special switches in the WINNT or WINNT32 programs that are in the i386 folder of the Windows 2000 Professional CD. The creation of these special scripts and how you prepare the source files for the installation process are advanced topics.

Many organizations use images as their method of automated installation. An image is a copy of an entire hard disk containing an OS and all applications. This image is copied using special software, and it can then be copied to one or many computers, also using special software. Most medium-size to large organizations have used this method for many years. The most popular imaging software is Ghost, from Symantec (`www.symantec.com/ghost`).

> If you are determined to learn more about setup scripts, check out the Windows 2000 Professional web site at `www.microsoft.com/windows2000/professional`. Search on Deployment. Most of these documents will cure insomnia!

Symantec offers two Ghost products: Symantec Ghost Corporate for corporations, which may use it for thousands of desktop installations, and Norton Ghost for a single computer. They also offer Ghost bundled with other Symantec products.

Whenever possible, perform a clean installation by installing Windows on an empty hard disk. We even prefer to start with an unpartitioned hard disk and have the setup program create a new partition and format it.

Gather the Materials Needed for Installation

The materials you will need for an installation depend on the decisions you have made about the installation and what you have learned about the compatibility of your hardware. You should, at minimum, have the Windows 2000 Professional CD or know a location on the network from which you can run the Windows upgrade program. If you plan to install from the CD but you either do not have an OS installed to access the CD or cannot boot from the CD, then you will need the four Windows 2000 Professional setup boot disks.

If you did your homework and checked out the compatibility of your hardware, you have gathered any drivers that won't be on the Windows 2000 Professional CD. You can install these drivers when prompted during the installation, or in the case of noncritical devices such as printers, you can wait until after the installation is complete to install them.

Everything else you will need is listed at the start of Step-by-Step 4.02. Make sure you have all of the items before you begin.

Step-by-Step 4.02

Installing Windows 2000 Professional

The steps in this exercise describe a clean installation on an unpartitioned hard drive. To complete this exercise, you will need the following:

- A Microsoft/Intel standard personal computer (desktop or laptop) compatible with Windows 2000 Professional, with at least the minimum hardware and configured to boot from CD
- An unpartitioned hard disk (disk 0, the first hard disk)
- The Windows 2000 Professional CD
- The four Windows 2000 Professional setup disks, if your computer doesn't boot from a CD-ROM drive
- One 3.5-inch diskette to use as an emergency repair disk
- The CD key code from the envelope of your Windows 2000 Professional CD
- A 15-character (or fewer) name, unique on your network, for your computer
- The name of the workgroup to be used in the class lab
- A password for the Administrator account on your computer
- The IP address, subnet mask, and other necessary TCP/IP configuration information, or confirmation from your instructor that you should configure Windows 2000 Professional to get an IP address automatically

Step 1

Insert the Windows 2000 Professional CD and restart the computer. After the restart, a blue character-mode screen will appear while the setup files are loaded into memory. This will take several minutes, during which the gray status bar at the bottom of the screen will name the files as they are loaded. Once all of the setup files are loaded, you'll see the message on the status bar that Setup is starting Windows 2000 Professional. Then the Welcome To Setup screen will appear. Press ENTER to continue.

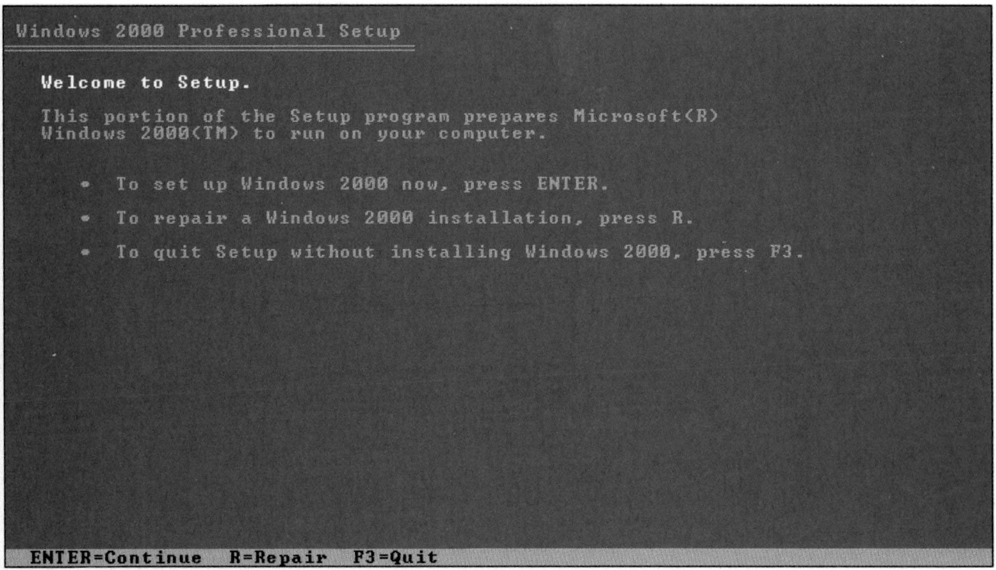

Windows 2000 Professional Setup
Welcome to Setup.
This portion of the Setup program prepares Microsoft(R)
Windows 2000(TM) to run on your computer.
• To set up Windows 2000 now, press ENTER.
• To repair a Windows 2000 installation, press R.
• To quit Setup without installing Windows 2000, press F3.
ENTER=Continue R=Repair F3=Quit

Step 2

The next screen shows that Setup has detected that the computer startup hard disk is new or has been erased. Press C to continue. Read the license agreement, and then press F8 to accept it. On the next several screens, follow the instructions to create a partition of at least 2GB (2,048MB), select the new partition as the location for Windows 2000 Professional, and format it with NTFS. Setup will then take several minutes to copy files to the new partition (C:), and your computer will reboot.

Windows 2000 Professional Setup

Please wait while Setup copies files to the Windows 2000
installation folders.
This may take several minutes to complete.

Setup is copying files...
41%

Copying: mdmspq28.inf

Step 3

After the reboot, Setup starts in GUI mode, with the message, "Please wait...." Then GUI mode setup begins, and the first screen may flash past before you can read it. Setup will then detect basic hardware, such as the keyboard and mouse, and install device drivers. This will take several minutes, during which time your screen may flicker and flash several times.

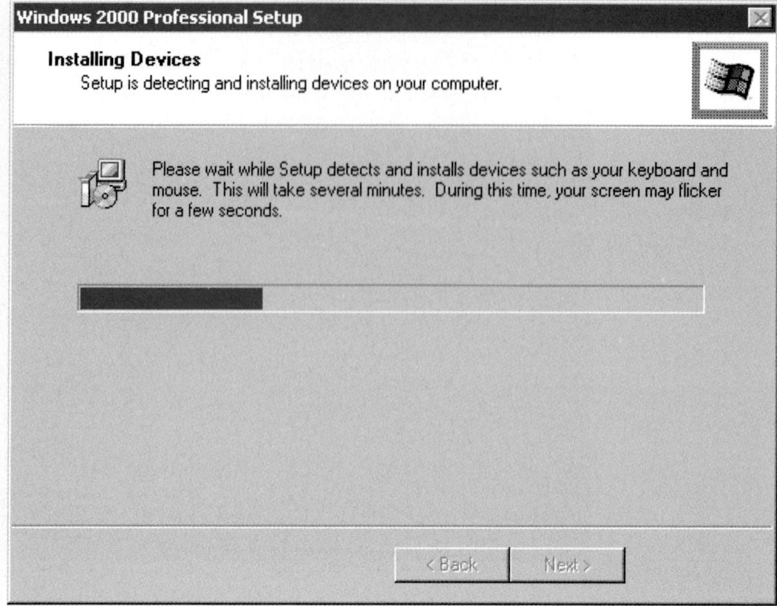

Step 4

On the Regional Setting page, leave the default, unless you need to customize Windows for a different locale. Follow the instructions to continue through the next several pages, providing the necessary responses from the information you gathered before beginning this step-by-step exercise. On the Network Settings page, select Typical Settings unless your instructor has told you otherwise, in which case you should select Custom Settings. That's where you enter TCP/IP configuration information (IP address, subnet mask, and so on). Enter your workgroup name on the Workgroup Or Computer Domain page.

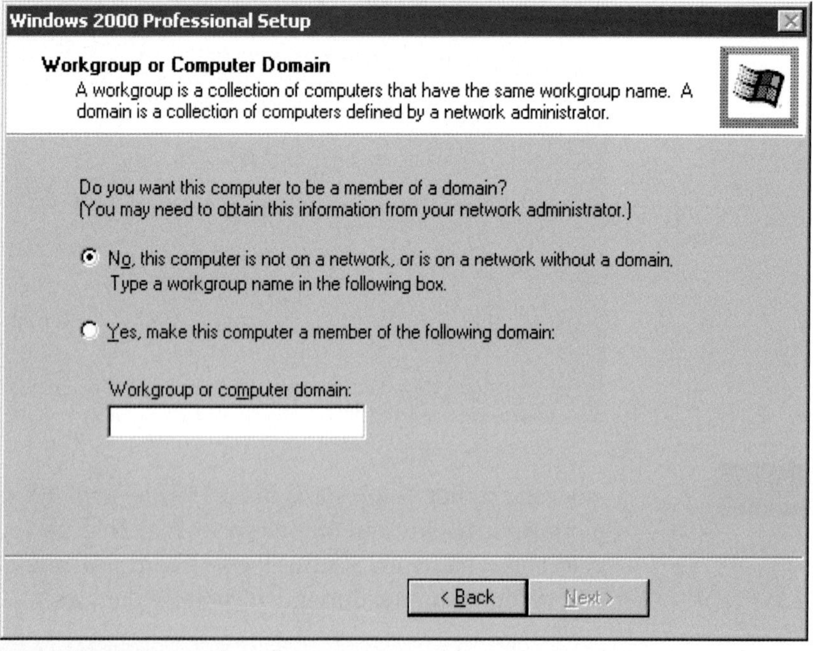

Step 5

Setup will take several minutes to copy the files necessary to complete the installation; then the Performing Final Tasks page will appear while Setup installs Start menu items, registers components (with the OS), saves settings, and removes temporary files created during the installation. At the conclusion, the Completing The Windows 2000 Professional Setup Wizard page will appear. Follow the instructions and then click Finish. After the reboot, the Network Identification wizard appears.

Step 6

Follow the onscreen instructions to complete the wizard. The default setting on the Users Of This Computer page—Windows Always Assumes The Following User Has Logged On To This Computer—is the least secure. It uses the name you entered on the Name And Organization page. If you choose this option and provide a password, Windows 2000 Professional will create a user account in its security accounts database (the SAM), but Windows will automatically perform the logon for you. Therefore, anyone who can turn on your computer is logged onto the computer using your local account.

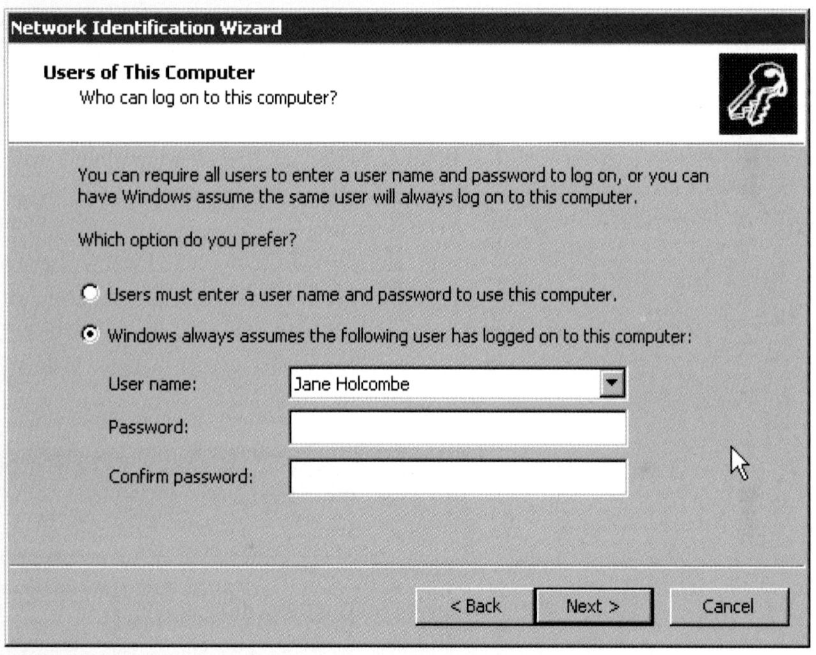

Step 7

Select the setting Users Must Enter A User Name And Password To Use This Computer. This is a more secure setting. The previous setting is okay for a computer in a low-risk, low-security environment and, preferably, not on a network, but this setting is for computers in most businesses. However, it requires a little more work to create the individual accounts. When you have completed this wizard, the Log On To Windows dialog box will appear, unless you selected the less-secure option.

Step 8

Log onto Windows as Administrator, supplying the password that you gave during the installation. After you log on, you should see the desktop with the Getting Started dialog box. You can use this to learn more about Windows, by clicking Discover Windows (you will need to insert the Windows 2000 Professional CD).

Try This!

Verify Network Access Using My Network Places

Your instructor will tell you what computers should be visible on your network. Try this:

1. On the desktop, locate and open My Network Places.
2. In the My Network Places folder, open Computer Near Me.
3. Confirm that you can see your own computer and any others specified by your instructor.

Remember that the only computers visible in My Network Places are those with the Server service running. A Windows 2000 Professional computer has this service installed and enabled by default, so your computer should be visible in My Network Places.

Verify Network Access

If this computer is on a network, you should verify that it can communicate with other computers on the network. A less-than-perfect, but easy, low-tech test is to open My Network Places and see if you can see any computers on the network besides your own.

Figure 4-11 shows My Network Places opened in Explorer view (right-click My Network Places and select Explore). With all the icons under Entire Network expanded, you have a pretty good view of the network. There are three domains or workgroups, named Htc, Research, and Workgroup. In fact, Htc is a Windows NT domain, and Research and Workgroup are both workgroups. Then you can see the computers in each of these groups. Finally, Computers Near Me contains all the computers in the workgroup or domain to which the local computer belongs.

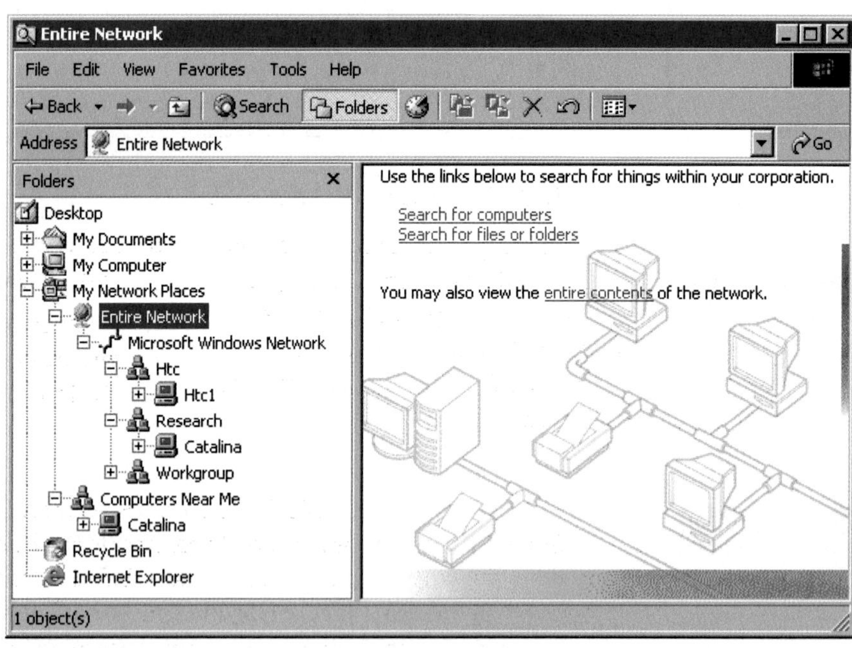

• **Figure 4-11.** My Network Places expanded to show workgroups, domains, and computers.

Verify Windows 2000 Professional Updates and Service Packs

One reason it's important to verify your network access after installing Windows 2000 Professional is that you may need network access to complete the next important task: installing any necessary updates or service packs. Since updates and service packs often fix security problems, it is important to install the latest ones as soon as possible. These are available on the Microsoft web site for free download.

If you're permitted to get the very latest from the Microsoft Update site and you have Internet access to your computer, you can use the Windows Update program on the Start menu to connect.

Do not browse to any web site other than the Windows Update site until you have obtained the necessary security updates from Microsoft and taken additional steps to secure your computer against computer viruses, spam, spyware, and other threats you will learn about in Chapter 7.

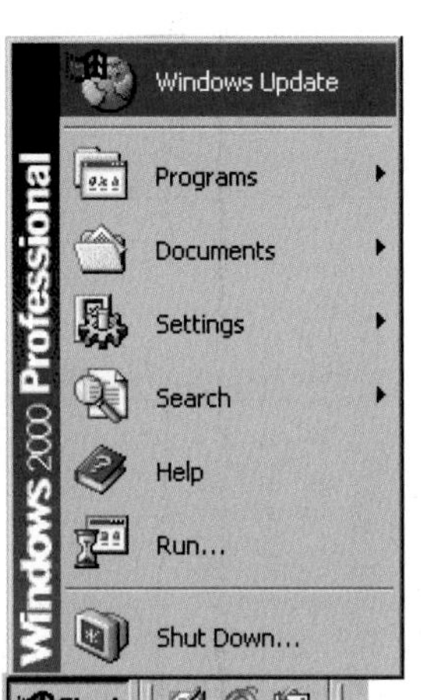

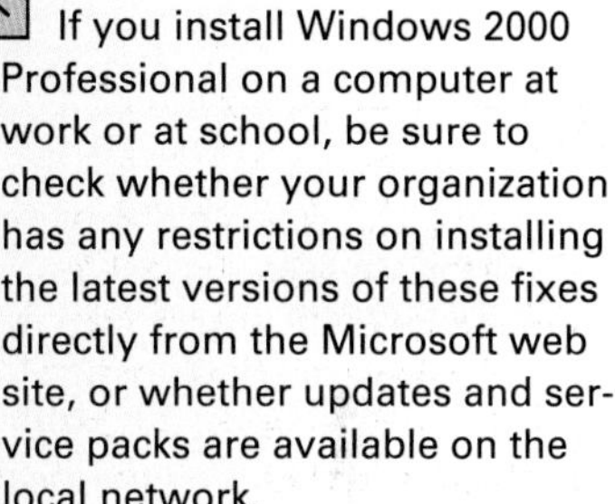

If you install Windows 2000 Professional on a computer at work or at school, be sure to check whether your organization has any restrictions on installing the latest versions of these fixes directly from the Microsoft web site, or whether updates and service packs are available on the local network.

• Windows Update is on the Start menu.

Step-by-Step 4.03

Installing Updates and Service Packs

In this step-by-step exercise, you will use Windows Update to connect to the Microsoft Update site; test your computer for installed components, updates, and service packs; and install the recommended updates and service packs. To complete this exercise, you will need the following:

- A PC with Windows 2000 Professional installed as described in Step-by-Step 4.02
- Internet access (before beginning, confirm that you can access the Internet using Internet Explorer)

Step 1

From the Windows 2000 Professional Start menu, select Windows Update. If this is the first time you have attempted to connect to the Internet from this computer, you may see a Windows Update page with a link labeled "Connect me to the Internet." Selecting this link will open the Internet Connection wizard, which will take you through configuring an Internet connection (with the guidance of your instructor). Once this is accomplished, move on to the next step.

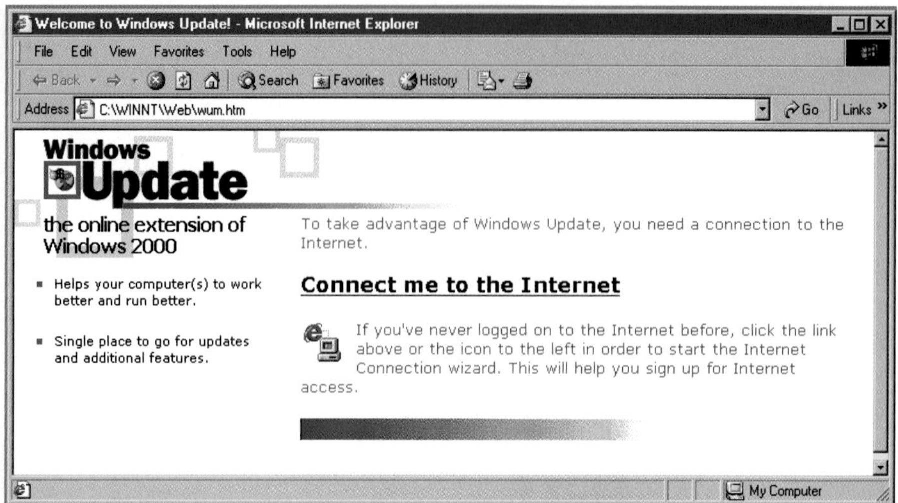

Step 2

Once connected to the Windows Update page, a detection program will check the locally installed version of Windows Update and install a newer version the first time you connect and any time after that when a new version is available. Before the new version of Windows Update can be installed, you must click Yes in the Security Warning dialog box.

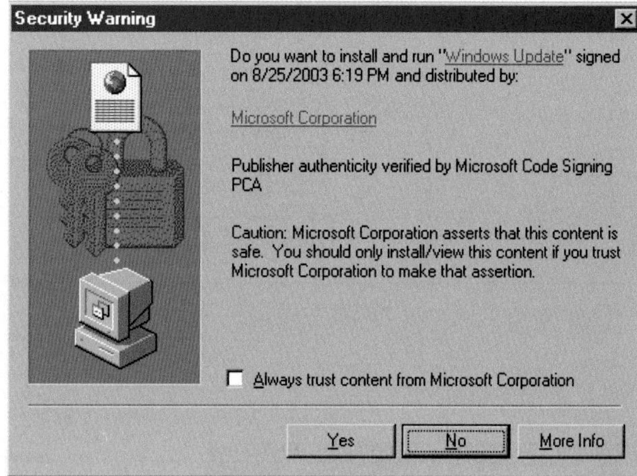

Step 3

After the new version of Windows Update is installed, the Welcome to Windows Update page displays. Click Scan for Updates. In the Pick updates to install page, click Review and install updates.

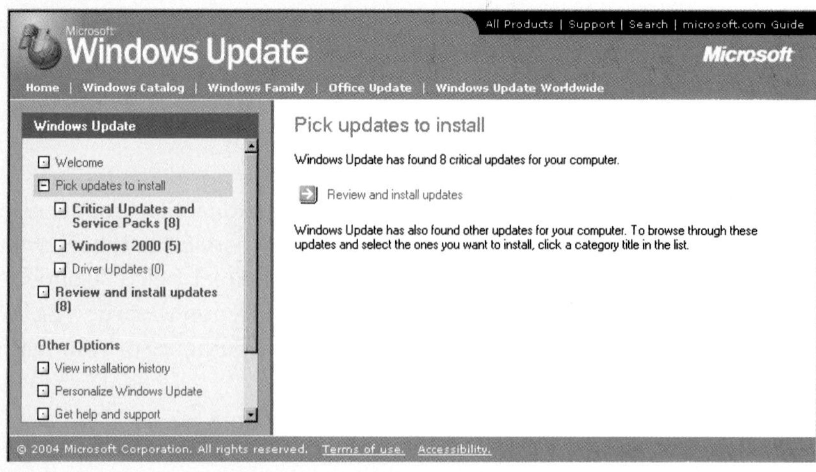

Step 4

You may have to use the scroll bar to view all of the updates. Some can be installed together. Some are described as exclusive and must be installed separately from others. Follow the instructions on the screen and install the updates now.

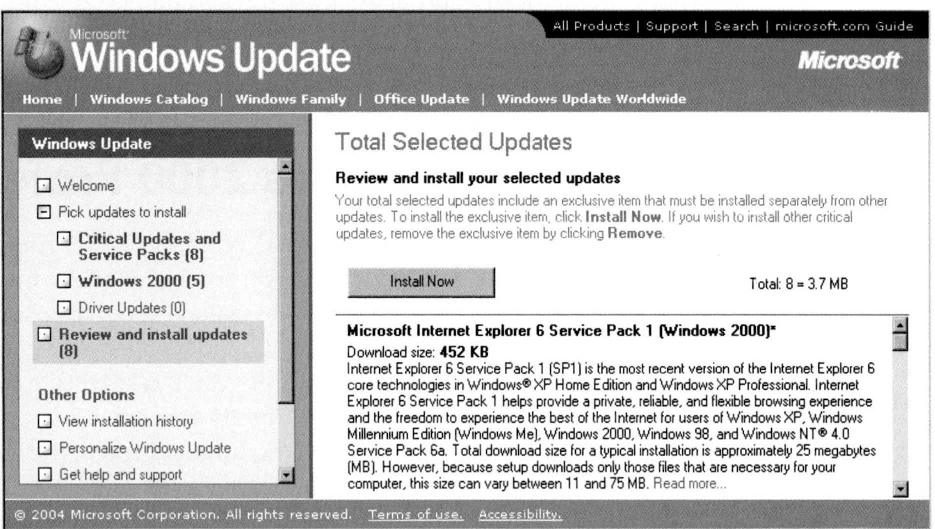

Step 5

The Windows Update wizard will download and install each update. You may be prompted to restart your computer after an update is installed. After the restart, if you have not installed all of the recommended updates, restart Windows Update, rescan your computer, and review the remaining updates. Install the other updates. The smaller updates can often be installed together. Repeat until all of the recommended updates have been installed.

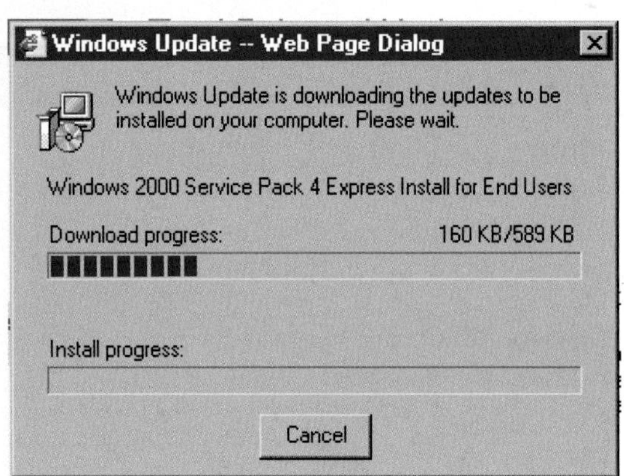

Step 6

After you have installed all of the Windows Updates to correct any potential problems with the OS, look for any updates for your applications programs. For instance, if you are using Microsoft Office, you can select Office Update from the Windows Update site and go through a process similar to that for installing the Windows updates. If you have applications from other companies, wait to check out their web sites for updates until after you have taken steps to protect your computer from viruses and other threats you may encounter on the Internet.

Further Securing Windows 2000 Professional

Once you have installed the updates, including critical security updates, install an antivirus program and other software to protect your computer against threats from spyware and the annoyances of advertising pop-ups. You will learn more about these threats and the remedies for them in Chapter 7.

Customizing and Managing Windows 2000 Professional

Once you have installed Windows 2000 Professional, configured the OS to work with your network, and installed recommended updates and service packs, you can get down to the real fun of customizing the OS for the person who will use it. In addition to being a very stable and robust operating system, Windows 2000 Professional is also quite easy to customize and manage for one user or for hundreds of users.

In this section, we examine several of the tools you can use to customize and manage Windows 2000 Professional. You'll look at the options for making a computer more accessible and the options for customizing display settings. You will practice adding and sharing a printer and customizing the Start menu. Then you'll explore the options for managing files and folders and practice searching the hard drive for a file. You will practice other customization tasks, including installing and removing applications.

Creating a New Hard Disk Partition

If after installing Windows 2000 you have unpartitioned hard disk space, you will need to partition that space and create one or more logical drives. We prefer to plan on this, purposely creating a partition of about 4GB (or more, depending on the total disk size) during installation for the operating system and applications, and to partition the remaining disk space after installation. Then we use the additional logical drive(s) for storing data files. This makes backup of data much simpler and minimizes the fragmentation of the system partition that results from working with data files.

Cross Check

Review Windows NT 4.0 Disk Partitioning

To understand basic disk types in Windows 2000, you can simply review what you learned about Windows NT 4.0 and disk partitioning in Chapter 3. Then answer the following questions:

1. You want to have more than four logical drives on a disk. What are your options?

   ____

2. You would like to divide the space of a single physical disk into four logical drives. Describe the partitions you would create.

   ____

3. You plan to dual-boot between Windows 2000 and Windows 98 on a 120GB disk. You want Windows 98 to have access to all the hard disk space. Describe the partitions you would create.

   ____

Windows 2000 Partitioning Basics

Windows 2000 introduces the concept of disk types—basic and dynamic. Before Windows 2000, we did not use "basic" to describe disks, but now we do, because

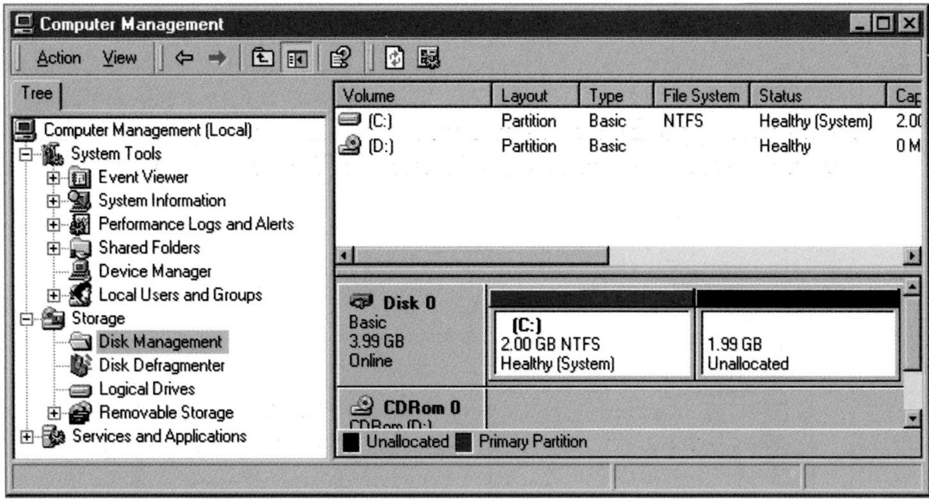

• **Figure 4-12.** Disk Management is one of several tools found in the Computer Management console.

there is a new way. This is similar to the issue of versions of the NTFS file system, where we only needed to talk about NTFS5 versus NTFS4 after version 5 was introduced in Windows 2000. Windows 2000 can use either disk type, and by default, begins with the basic disk type.

Windows 2000 Disk Management

The tool you use to manage disks in Windows 2000 is **Disk Management**, which can be found in the Computer Management console (see Figure 4-12), launched from the context menu of My Computer or from the Administrative Tools folder. Disk Management appears in the right pane of the Computer Management window, where you will see that each physical hard disk is numbered, beginning with zero, and each optical disk is numbered, beginning with zero. Each partition or unallocated space is labeled in boxes with color-coded bars at the top. The key is at the bottom of the pane. You will use Disk Management in the following step-by-step in which you will create a new partition, format the partition, and then change the drive letters of the partition and the CD-ROM drive.

If you change the drive letter of a CD-ROM drive after you have used that drive to install software, you may need to manually enter the new drive letter whenever you make a change or uninstall a program that was installed previous to the drive letter change.

Step-by-Step 4.04

Creating a New Partition

In this exercise, you will create a new partition on your hard disk. It is assumed that the disk type has not been changed from basic since the installation.

To complete this exercise, you will need the following:

- The computer on which you successfully installed Windows 2000 in Step-by-Step 4.02
- Unpartitioned hard disk space
- A user name and password for an account that is a member of the Administrators group
- A blank diskette

Step 1

Log on as an administrator, right-click My Computer, and select Manage from the context menu. This will open the Computer Management console. This console can also be opened from Start | Programs | Administrative Tools or from within Control Panel.

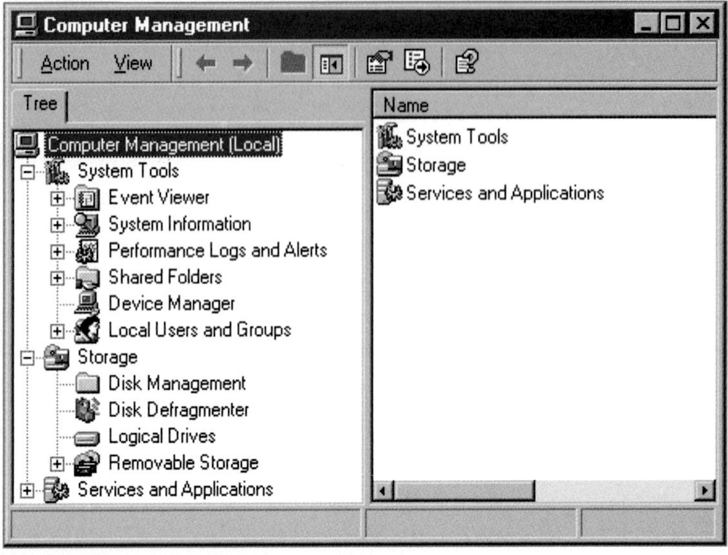

Step 2

In Computer Management, click the Disk Management folder under the Storage node. After a brief delay, the Disk Management snap-in will appear in the right window pane of the console. If you installed Windows 2000 according to the instructions in Step-by-Step 4.02, drive C: is a primary partition with the NTFS file system. Drive letters are assigned to hard disk drives first and then to laser disk drives. Right-click in the box labeled "Unallocated," and click Create Partition to launch the Create Partition wizard.

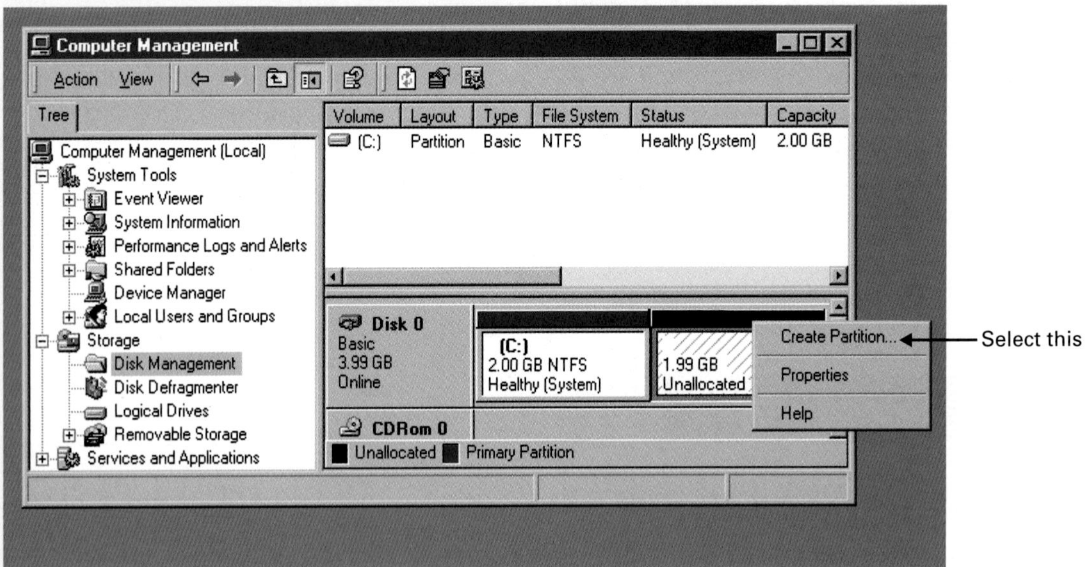

Step 3

In the Welcome page of the Create Partition wizard, select the Next button. In the Select Partition Type page, select Primary Partition. In the Specify Partition Size page, select a partition size that is at least 1MB smaller than the maximum space. Then click Next.

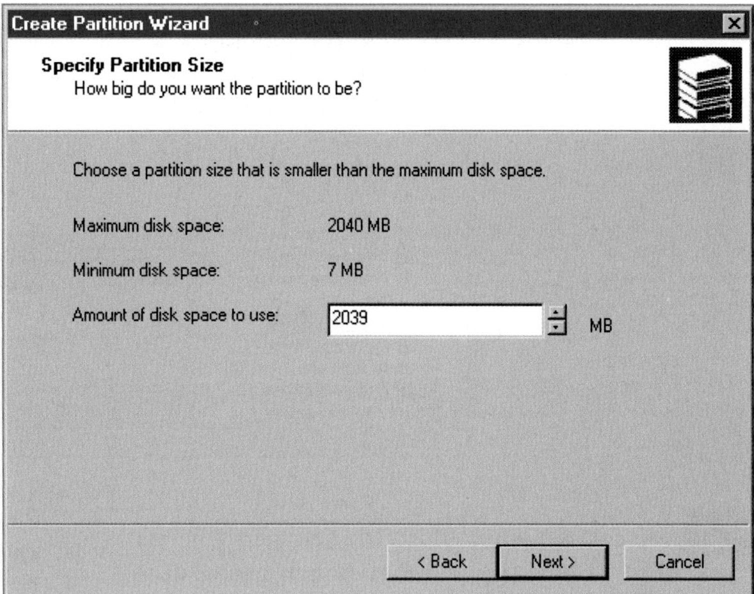

Step 4

In the Assign Drive Letter page, keep the default drive letter setting and click Next. In the Format Partition page, keep the default selection, which will format the drive with NTFS (actually NTFS5) and click Next.

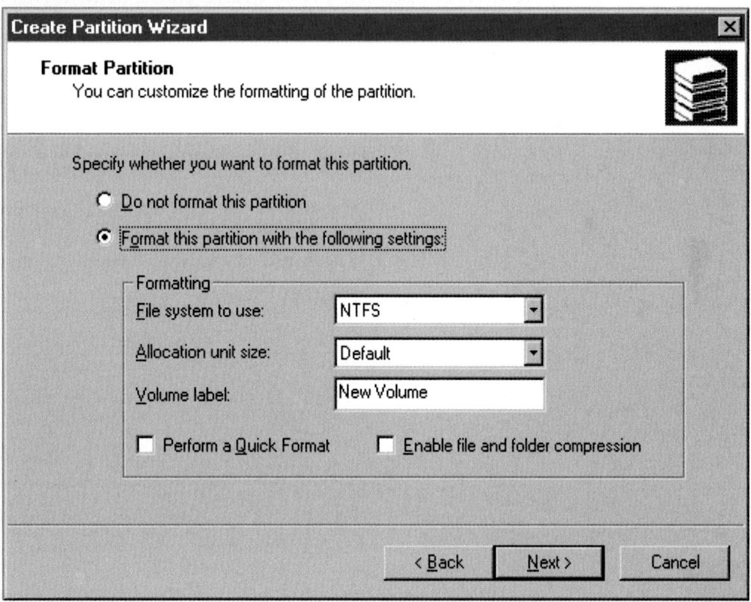

Step 5

The Completing The Create Partition Wizard page displays a summary of the settings you have selected. Review these settings. If you wish to change any of the settings, use the Back button to find the page for the setting. Otherwise, click Finish to complete the partitioning. If you watch Disk Management carefully, you will see the Unallocated space change to a partition, then to a formatted New Volume.

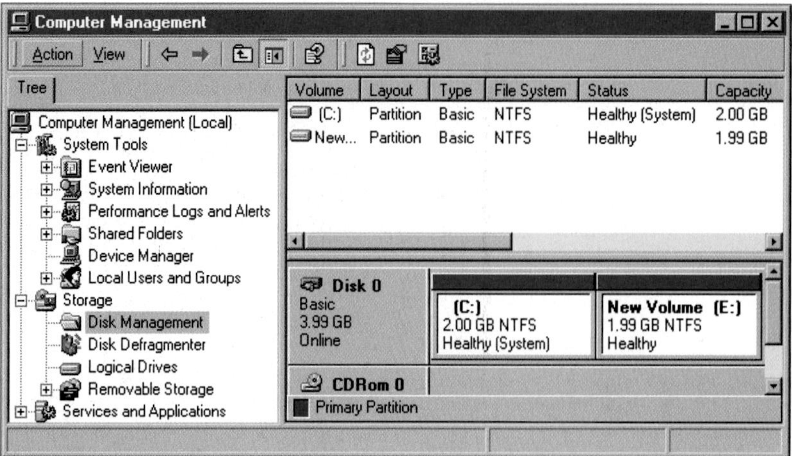

Step 6

But what's this? The new partition has letter *E:*, while the partition created during installation has letter *C:*. This is because during Windows Installation, the CD-ROM drive received the letter *D:*, but this is not set in stone. So change the CD-ROM drive to a letter beyond that which you expect to need for hard disks and removable disk drives. Do this now by right-clicking the box representing the CD-ROM drive and selecting Change Drive Letter And Path. In the dialog box, click Edit and in the Edit Drive Letter Or Path dialog box, use the spin box to select drive letter *M:* and then click OK. Click Yes in the Confirm box.

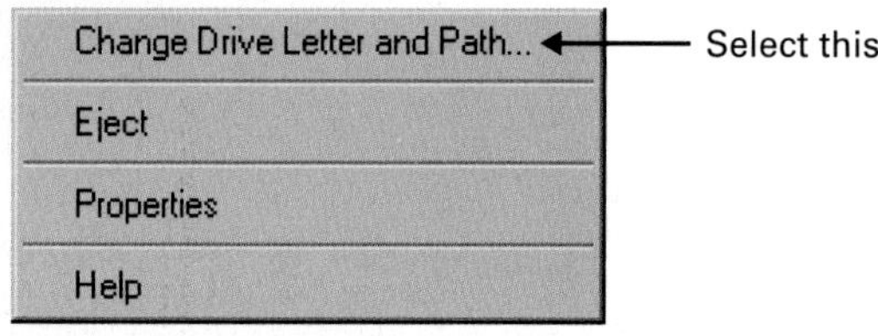

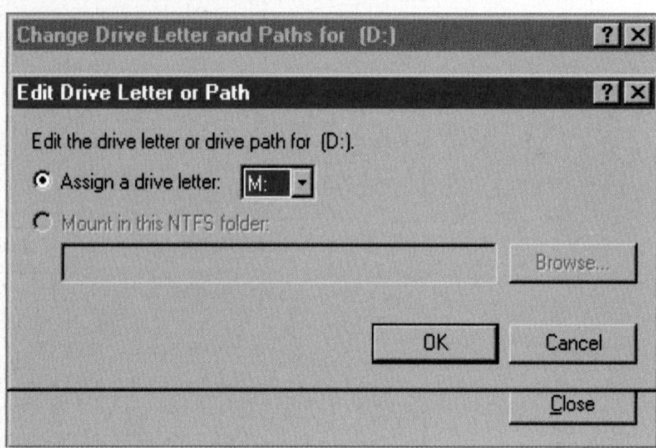

Step 7

Use what you learned in the previous step to change the drive letter of the newly created partition to drive *D:*.

Step 8

Learn more about your new volume, and give it a new label (name). In Disk Management, right-click on the new volume and select Properties. On the General tab, notice the amount of disk space shown as used. This is the amount used by the NTFS file system—space that is referred to as overhead. This space varies somewhat by drive size, but the large amount used explains why Windows cannot format a diskette with NTFS (any version). On the General tab, you will see that the new volume was given the label "New Volume," which is not very descriptive. Rename it now by clicking in the Label box and typing **data** as the new name. Finally, click OK. Close Computer Management.

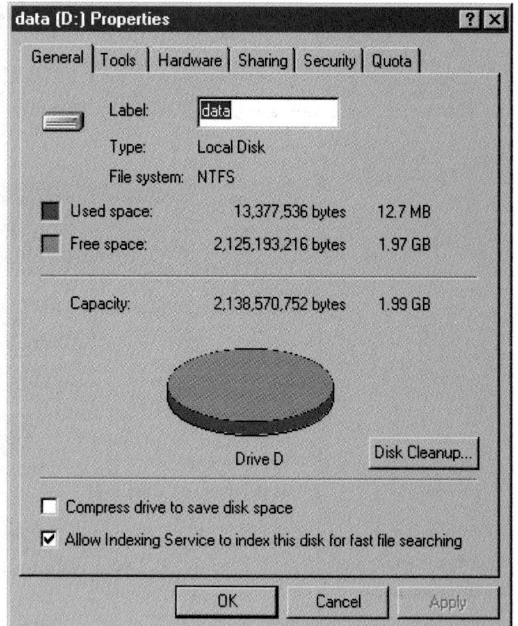

Step 9

Update the emergency repair configuration information and create a new emergency repair disk. Select Start | Run. In the Run box, type **NTBACKUP** and press ENTER. Click the button labeled "Emergency Repair Disk." Click to place a check in the check box to also back up the registry to the Repair folder (the default location for this is C:\WINNT\REPAIR). Then click OK and follow the instructions on the screen for the labeling and handling of the diskette. When done, click OK to close the Emergency Repair Diskette dialog box, and then close the Backup program.

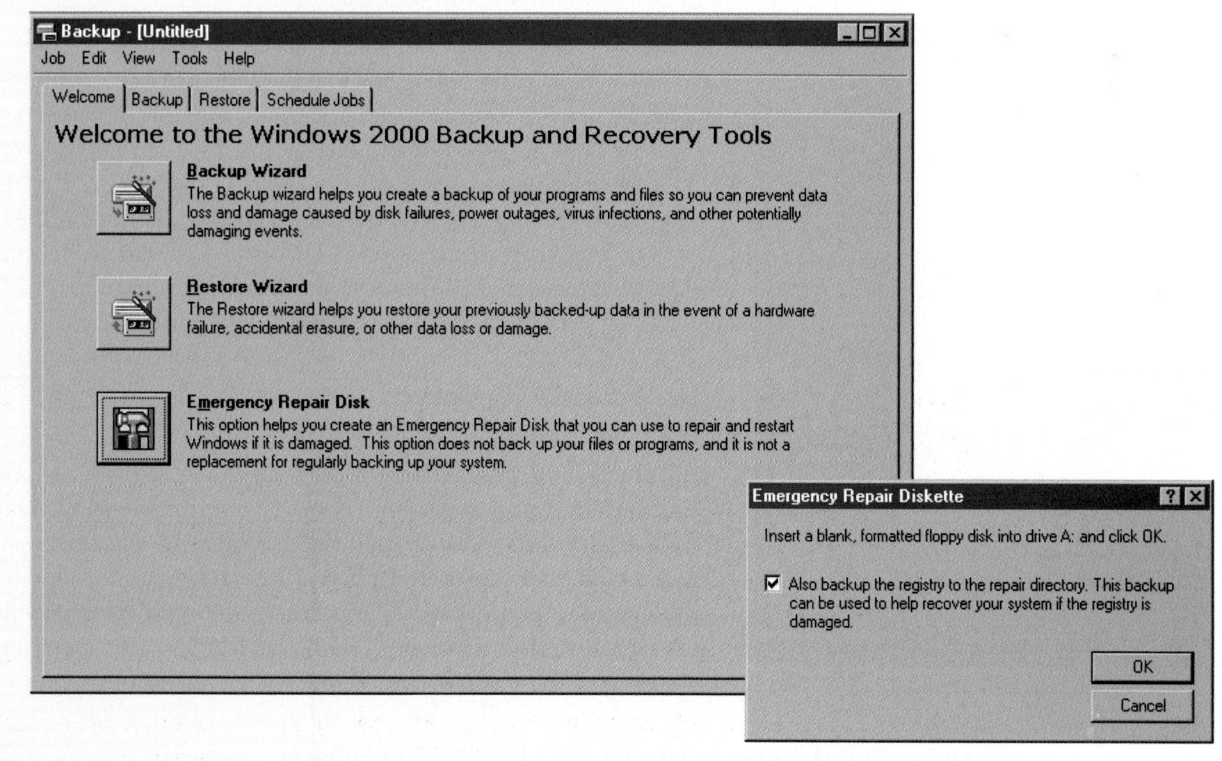

Using the Control Panel Applets

The Windows 2000 Professional **Control Panel** contains numerous applets that you can use to adjust the configuration of many different aspects of the OS.

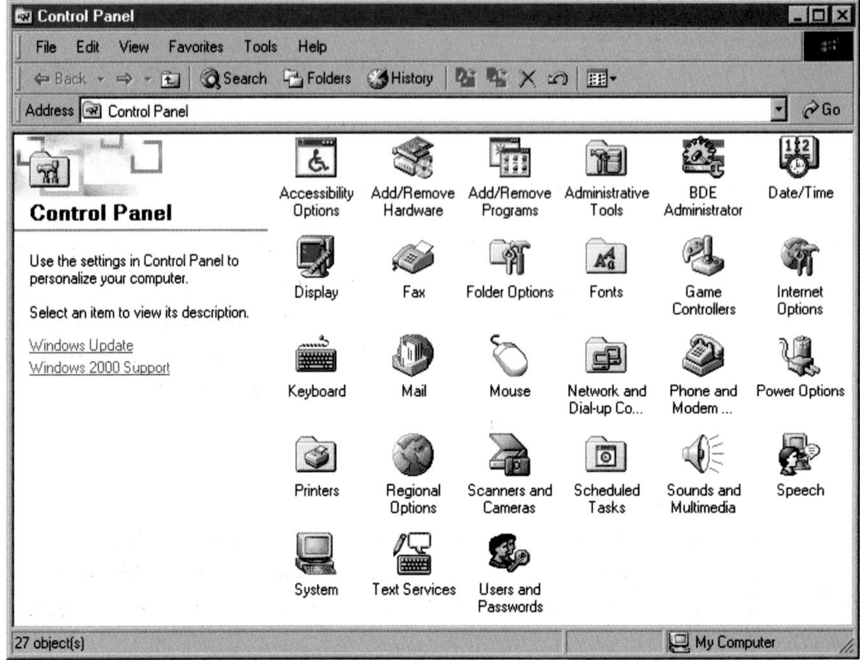

• The Windows 2000 Professional Control Panel

Your Control Panel may not look exactly like the Control Panel shown here. Depending on the configuration of your system, your Control Panel may have more or fewer icons.

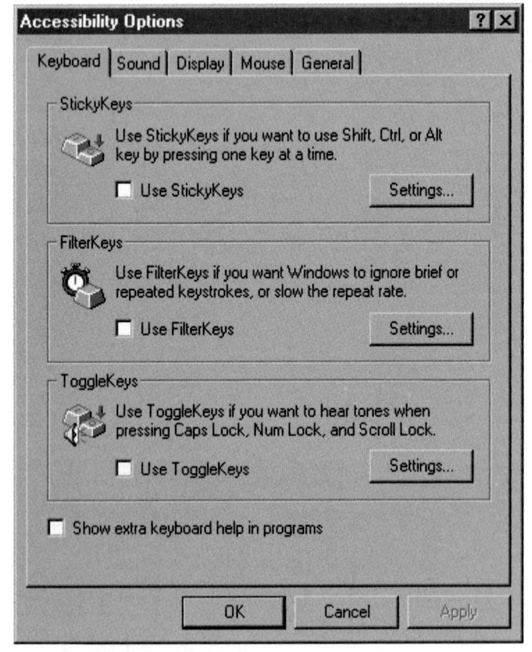

• Accessibility Options

As you learned in Chapter 3, each of these applets typically opens a window or a dialog box in which you can make a number of important adjustments. Remember that the Control Panel provides just one of several methods for opening a particular tool.

Although we do not have the room to discuss each of the new Control Panel applets, we'll look closely at a few of them. As will quickly become apparent, you use similar techniques with all of these tools, so you should have no trouble using additional Control Panel tools in the future on your own.

The Accessibility Options

Windows 2000 Professional has a number of built-in features that are designed to make computers more accessible for people with certain common disabilities such as restricted vision, hearing loss, or difficulty with mobility. Some of these features can be enabled and configured through the Accessibility Options applet on the Control Panel, and others are in the form of utilities (small, useful programs) that you turn on and configure from Start | Programs | Accessories | Accessibility.

The Accessibility Options dialog box has several tabs that you can use to configure various aspects of the accessibility options. For example, on the Keyboard tab, you can set the StickyKeys option, which is helpful for someone who must use a pointer stick for typing. The CTRL, ALT, and SHIFT keys are often used along with a second key to issue various commands, but holding down multiple keys simultaneously is not possible with a pointer stick. When StickyKeys is enabled, pressing any of those keys and then following that with another keypress is considered the equivalent of pressing the two keys simultaneously.

Inside Information

Accessibility for Special Needs

Several federal and state laws bar discrimination against people based on disabilities. It is important to understand how to use the various accessibility options in Windows 2000 Professional so that a disabled user can be correctly accommodated and to comply with these regulations. We strongly urge you to view the Accessibility for Special Needs topic in the Windows 2000 Professional help system to learn more about these tools. You can access the Windows 2000 Professional help system by clicking the Start button and choosing Help from the Start menu.

Customizing Display Settings

The Display applet in Windows 2000 is not too different from that in past versions of Windows, and by now you should be able to find your way around this applet to change the background, add a screen saver, and otherwise customize the desktop to your own needs and taste. However, there is one, easy-to-overlook button on the Settings tab that you should take at look at.

The Advanced Button

The Advanced button in the Display Properties dialog box includes an extremely important button that many Windows users seem to miss. The Advanced button displays an additional dialog box that combines the video adapter card and monitor properties so that you can choose settings that are appropriate for the pair.

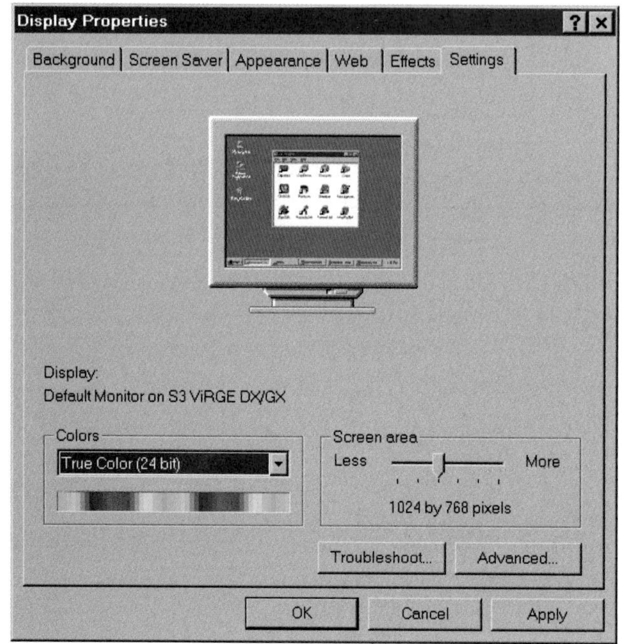

• Select the Advanced button on the Settings tab

• Select a refresh rate above 60 Hertz

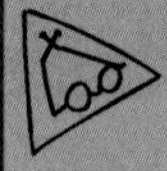

Inside Information

Headaches and Nausea!

In the early days of motion pictures, people sometimes became nauseated or suffered from headaches when watching a movie. Research showed that the human eye has persistence—that is, the brain retains an image for a fraction of a second after the image is turned off. When about 20 images per second are shown, the human eye can still detect the flickering on and off of the images. Movies are shown in theaters at a rate of at least 32 frames per second so that motion on a screen appears to be continuous. On a CRT monitor, other problems, like the alternating current from an electric wall socket outlet, can cause the flicker to be noticeable if the rate is below about 60 Hz.

Remember that a printer that is directly connected to your computer (local) is still local even if you intend to share it on the network.

Probably the most important tab in this dialog box is the Monitor tab, where you can choose the **refresh rate** for the display. The refresh rate defines how often the display is refreshed to keep the image flicker-free. In every case, this setting must be above 60 Hertz (hertz—Hz—a rate of repetition in cycles per second) to reduce eyestrain. The reason for this is that at 60 Hertz or below, the monitor flickers—often causing users to develop headaches or other vision-related problems. Depending on the quality of the monitor, you may need to select a lower screen resolution to permit a refresh rate above 60 Hertz.

Creating and Managing a Local Printer

In spite of optimistic predictions heard many times over the years, the "paperless office" is still pretty much a pipe dream and is likely to remain so. Most computer users still need printers, so we now look at the process of installing a printer in Windows 2000 Professional (which you can do only if you are a member of the Administrators group). Adding a printer in Windows is really adding a printer driver, which you need to do whether the printer is directly connected to your computer or connected elsewhere on the network. When you install a local printer and then share it so that others on your network can use it, your computer plays the role of a print server.

When you send a print job to a network print server, that computer actually does the real work of putting the job in a print queue (if the printer is busy) and sending it to the printer when its turn comes. That means that the print server clearly needs a driver for the printer, so it knows how to communicate with the printer. However, your computer also needs a print driver to prepare the print job with all the correct commands to tell the printer how you want your printed document to appear.

Step-by-Step 4.05

Adding a Printer in Windows 2000

Take a few minutes to add a local printer. To complete this step-by-step exercise, you will need the following:

- The computer on which you successfully installed Windows 2000 Professional in Step-by-Step 4.02

Note: A physical printer is *not* required.

Step 1

Open the Printers folder by choosing Start | Settings | Printers. Click the Add Printer icon, and the Add Printer wizard will start. At the first screen, click Next to continue. On the Local Or Network Printer page, choose Local Printer and clear the check box next to Automatically Detect And Install My Plug And Play Printer, because you don't really have this printer connected. Then click Next.

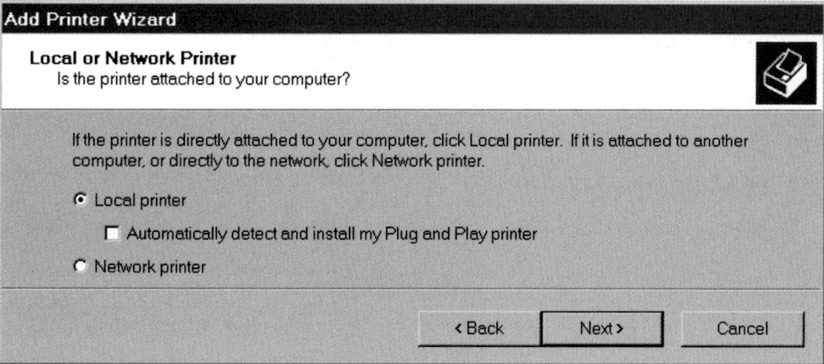

Step 2

On the Select The Printer Port page, ensure that Use The Following Port is selected and then click Next. On the next page, select HP from the list of manufacturers and HP Color LaserJet 4500 from the list of printers and then click Next. On the Name Your Printer page (no, it's not a new game), you may enter a name that is friendlier than the model name. This is not mandatory—the illustration shows the model name—but you may want to do this to identify how the printer is being used: for example, Brochure Printer or Accounting Printer.

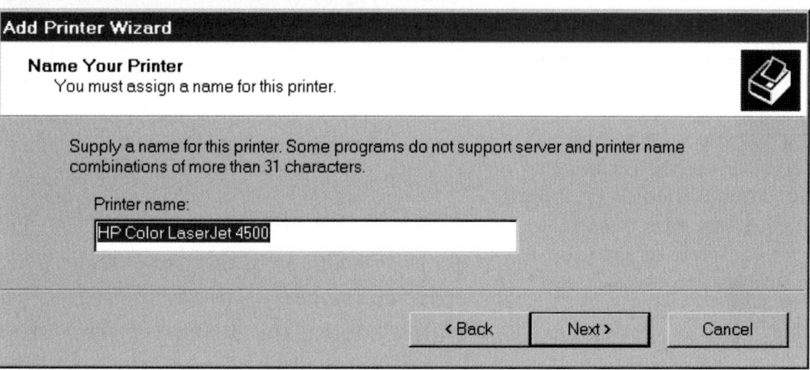

Step 3

On the Printer Sharing page, ensure that the Share As option is selected, and give the printer yet another name—this time a share name by which it will be known on the network. Leave the default, or enter a short, friendly name; then click Next.

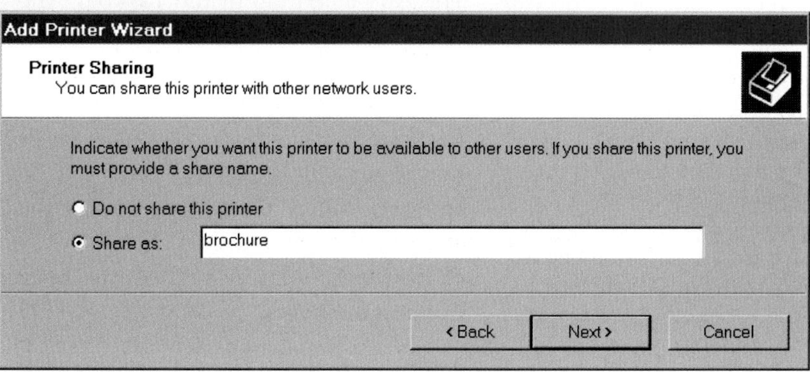

Step 4 On the Location And Comment page, you can give a location for the printer and add a description in the Comment box. Then click Next.

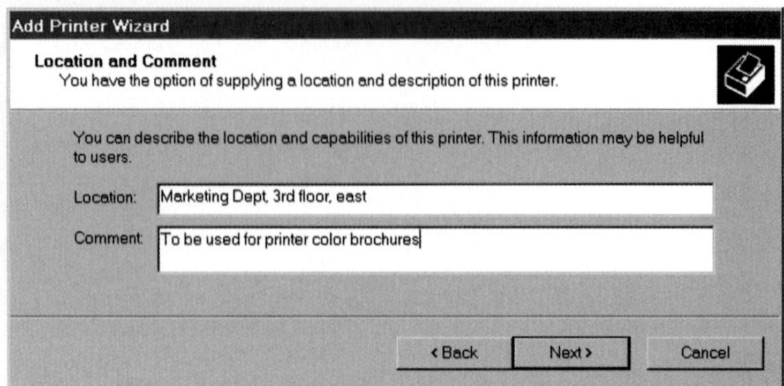

Step 5 When the Add Printer wizard offers to print a test page, you will normally accept the offer, but in this case, you don't have the printer. To close the wizard, click Finish.

Configuring the Start Menu

For the final example of Windows 2000 Professional customization, we'll look at the Taskbar And Start Menu Properties dialog box. You display this dialog box by right-clicking a blank space on the taskbar and choosing Properties from the pop-up menu.

> The Use Personalized Menus option is confusing. When this option is first turned on, nothing changes. Then, after the OS watches for a few days to see what options you use and don't use, each menu shows only recently used items—which can be very confusing for users who don't understand where the missing items have gone. To see hidden menu items in a truncated menu, click the chevrons at the bottom of the menu.

The General Tab

As in Windows 98, the General tab of the Taskbar And Start Menu Properties dialog box, shown in Figure 4-13, includes several options. These primarily control the display of the taskbar; however, some affect the Start menu. You can use the taskbar and Start menu options to ensure that the taskbar is always visible, or to hide it when you want the maximum amount of desktop space for your applications.

The Advanced Tab

The Advanced tab of the Taskbar And Start Menu Properties dialog box, shown in Figure 4-14, enables you to further customize the Start menu by adding or removing Start menu items and configuring settings.

Some of the more interesting items on the Advanced tab are located in the Start Menu Settings area near the bottom of this tab. For example, items that begin with the word *Expand* will create a menu from the items in the respective folder. Thus, if you select the Expand Control Panel option and click Apply, you can then choose the Control Panel objects from a submenu of the Start menu instead of first opening the Control Panel and double-clicking the items.

> You don't have to open the Taskbar And Start Menu Properties dialog box to re-sort the Start menu. Just right-click the Start menu, and choose Sort By Name from the pop-up menu to sort the menu in alphabetical order.

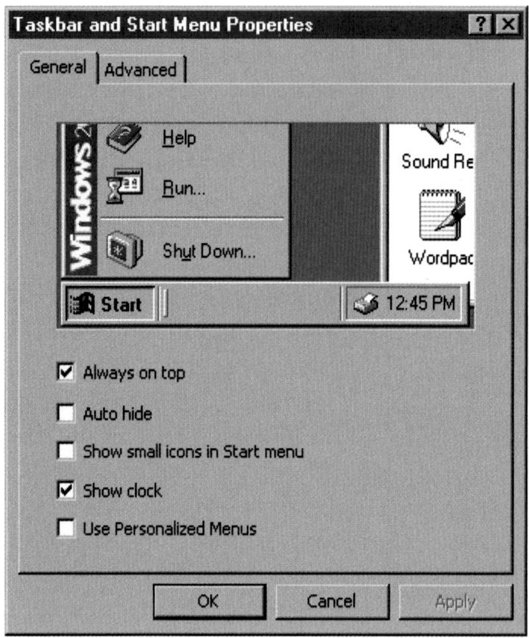

• **Figure 4-13.** Set the taskbar and Start menu options.

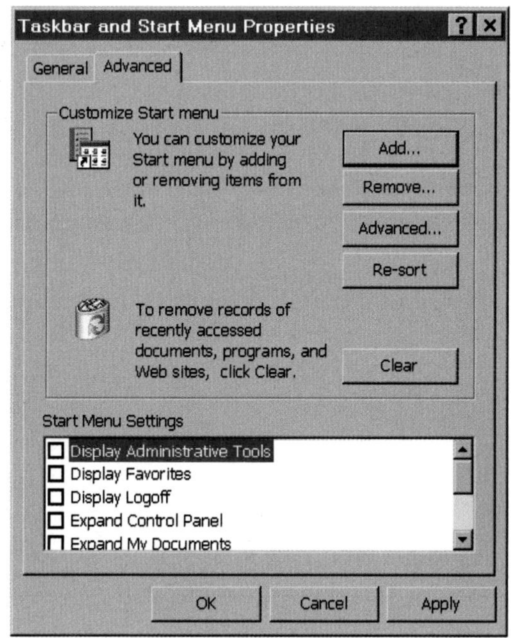

• **Figure 4-14.** Advanced taskbar and Start menu properties

Try This!

Customize the Start Menu

Today you're a desktop support person who's been asked to customize the Start menu for one of your client users. He doesn't like personalized menus, would like a shortcut to the Favorites folder on the Start menu, and would also like the contents of the My Documents folder to appear as a menu when he selects My Documents from the Start menu. Try this:

1. Open Taskbar And Start Menu Properties, and clear the check box next to Use Personalized Menus.
2. Select the Advanced tab of Taskbar And Start Menu Properties, and place a check in the box next to Display Favorites.
3. Scroll through the list of Start menu settings, and place a check in the box next to Expand My Documents.
4. Click OK to close the dialog box, and then test for the results of these changes. If you only very recently installed Windows 2000, it may not have truncated (personalized) your menus yet, so you may not yet see a difference. The results of the other two settings are easy to observe.

Installing and Removing Applications and Windows 2000 Components

Any OS is simply a vehicle for running applications. Therefore, installing the applications a user needs is a necessary task when customizing Windows 2000. In this section, we look briefly at how you install and remove application programs in Windows 2000 Professional.

Before attempting to install an application, check to make certain that the program is actually compatible with Windows 2000 Professional. If the program's requirements do not state that the program is compatible with Windows 2000 Professional, you may have to determine its compatibility through the Microsoft Windows Catalog site at `www.microsoft.com/windows/catalog/`.

Try This!

Install an Application

To begin the installation process manually, try this:

1. Open the Add/Remove Programs item in the Control Panel by clicking the Start button and choosing Settings | Control Panel. Then double-click the Add/Remove Programs icon.
2. Click the Add New Programs button along the left side of the Add/Remove Programs dialog box. Be sure you have placed the installation CD in the drive and that you have any registration numbers available.
3. Click the CD Or Floppy button to display the Install Program from Floppy Disk Or CD-ROM dialog box. When you are ready, click Next and then follow the onscreen directions to complete the installation.

You should shut down all other open applications before beginning a software installation. You also may be required to restart Windows 2000 Professional to complete the installation process.

Installing Applications

Most application programs are distributed on CDs (although some very small programs are still distributed on floppy disks). Luckily, Windows 2000 supports autorun, a feature that enables it to look for and read a special file called **autorun** immediately after a CD is inserted and to run whatever program is listed in autorun.inf. Most application programs distributed on CD have an autorun file that calls up the installation program.

Sometimes, however, it is simply necessary to institute the installation sequence yourself. Perhaps the install CD lacks an autorun installation program, or perhaps your PC is configured so that autorun programs must be started manually. In some cases, a CD may contain more than one program, and you must choose which of them to install. Regardless of the reason, beginning the installation process manually is a simple and straightforward process using the Add/Remove Programs applet in the Control Panel, which will search the CD drive for an installation program.

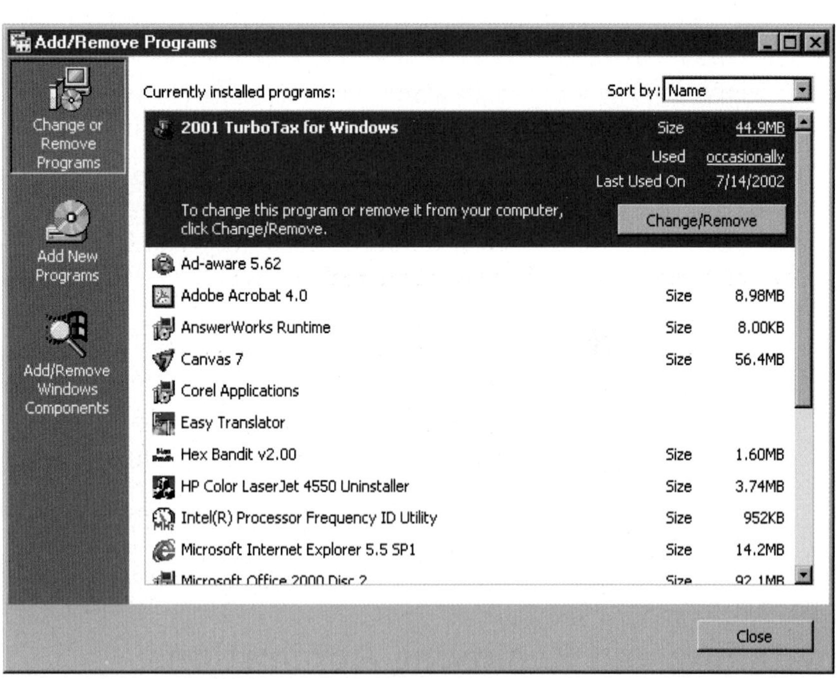

• The Change or Remove Programs page in Add/Remove Programs.

Typically, you will have to accept the terms of the software license before you are allowed to install the application. These steps are not optional since the installation simply won't proceed until you accept any terms the software manufacturer provides and enter the correct code. You may also be asked to make several decisions during the installation process. For example, you may be asked where you would like to install the program and if you would like certain optional components installed. Generally speaking, it is best to simply accept the suggested settings.

Removing Applications

Each application program you have installed takes up space on your computer's hard disk. Programs that you no longer need or use simply waste space that could be used for other purposes, so removing those can be an important piece of housekeeping.

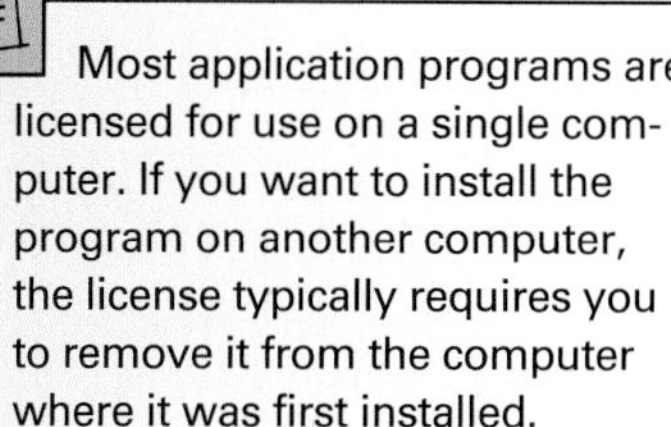

Most application programs are licensed for use on a single computer. If you want to install the program on another computer, the license typically requires you to remove it from the computer where it was first installed.

You remove a program from a Windows 2000 Professional PC in much the same manner as you installed it. That is, you begin by opening the Add/Remove Programs dialog box. Next, with the Change Or Remove Programs button clicked, you select the program you want to remove and click the Change/Remove button.

You may next see a message similar to the one shown here warning you that the program will be permanently removed from your PC. If you are certain you want to continue, click Yes.

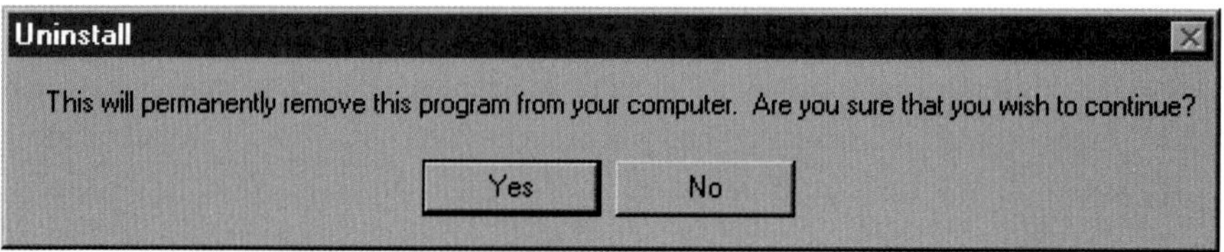

• Confirm that you want to remove the program

Often you will also see a message telling you that a shared file that appears to no longer be in use is about to be deleted. Generally speaking, it is safe to delete such files. If you don't delete them, they will likely be orphaned and remain unused on your hard disk forever.

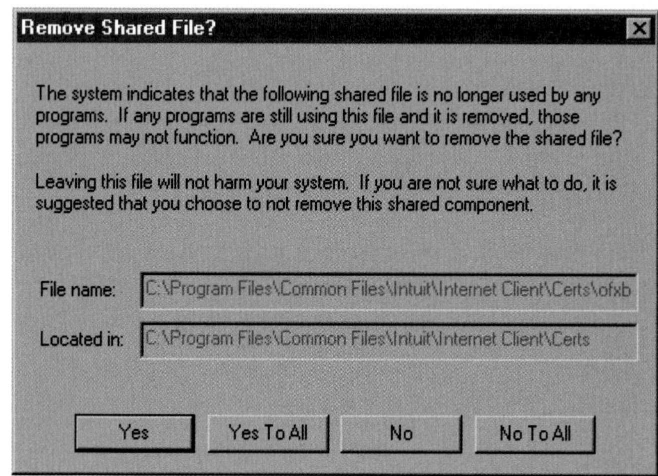

• Shared files that are no longer in use waste disk space.

An application may even be a component of Windows 2000, such as a game, WordPad, or Calculator. In that case, the application can be installed or removed using Add/Remove Programs | Add/Remove Windows Components.

Try This!

Remove an Application

Removing an application is quite simple. Try this:

1. Log onto your PC using an account with Administrator rights.
2. Open the Control Panel.
3. Select the Add/Remove Programs icon.
4. Examine the list of installed programs, and remove one you no longer use.

In some cases, clicking the Change/Remove button will start the application's install program so that you can modify the features that are installed. This is completely a function of the program you are attempting to remove, however.

Troubleshooting Common Windows 2000 Professional Problems

Let's face it—any computer can experience problems no matter how stable and secure its operating system. Windows 2000 Professional is certainly one of the most stable and trouble-free operating systems you will find, but you still may encounter difficulties from time to time. In this section, we'll first look at some of the tools used in troubleshooting: Registry Editor, Event Viewer, and Device Manager. Then we will take the proactive approach with best practices to keep the wolves at bay. Finally, we'll look at some common problems and their possible causes and resolutions.

An Approach to Troubleshooting

Our hope is that, with the correct preventative practices (discussed later), you will never suffer a failure or major problem with Windows 2000. However, experience tells us that even smart, savvy people often fail to take even the most basic preventative steps, and even those who do will occasionally be confronted with an OS problem.

When trouble comes calling, your response, depending on your experience, should be to:

1. Carefully observe and record the error messages or other symptoms of a problem.
2. Use the information you gathered to find the cause.
3. Research the solution.
4. Apply the solution.
5. Test the results.

Where to Find Help

Where can you find help in discovering a problem's cause and solution? A great place to begin is the Windows 2000 Professional Help program (assuming that you have access to a working computer). Search on key words related to the symptoms, and look through the troubleshooters.

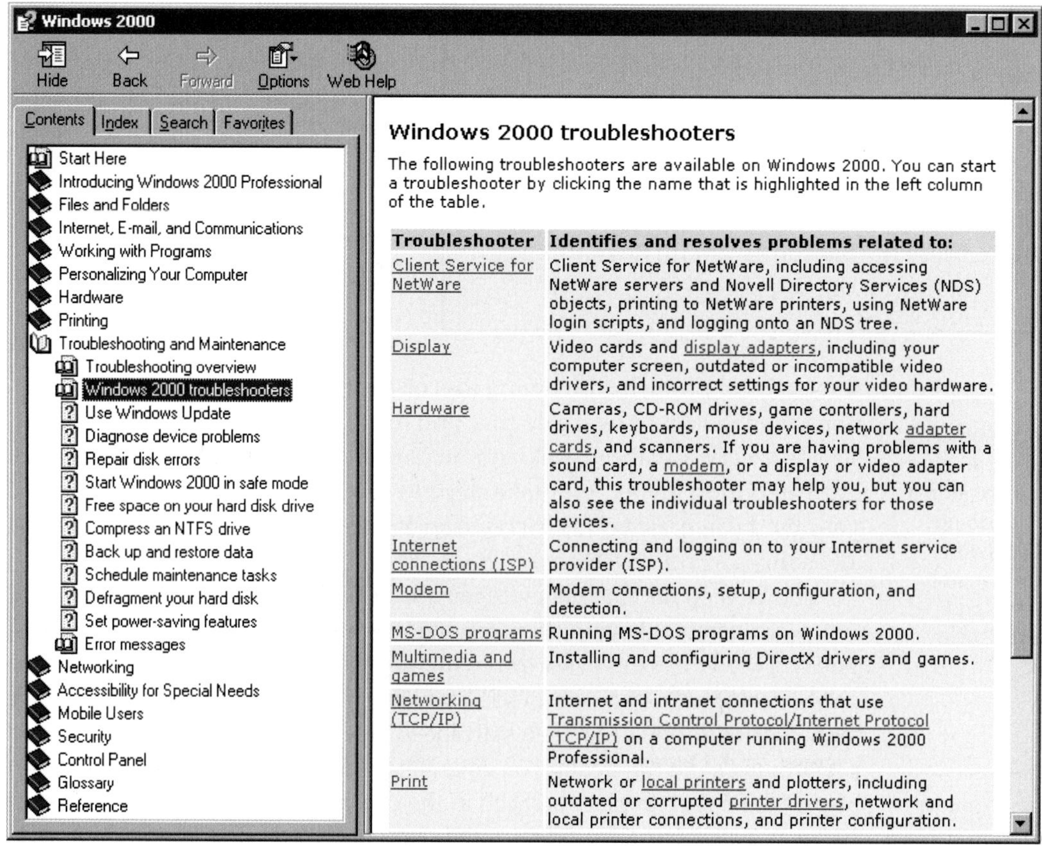

• The Windows 2000 Help troubleshooters

We have had a great deal of good luck searching Microsoft's Technet site, at `www.microsoft.com/technet`. Sometimes a broader search of the Microsoft site, not confined to just the Technet area, yields better results. If you need to cast an even larger net, point your web browser to an Internet search engine, such as `www.google.com`, and enter a few key words from an error message. This has worked for us several times!

Proactive Maintenance Tasks

Someone once said that the best offense is a good defense. Don't wait for problems to occur before you take action. Have a defensive strategy in which you take steps to avoid problems. Your strategy should include backing up data, disk defragmenting, and periodic housekeeping of the files and folders. In addition, you should install and configure an antivirus program, which will be discussed in Chapter 7.

Try This!

Create an Emergency Repair Disk

If you did not create an emergency repair disk in Step-by-Step 4.04, create one now. First, locate a blank formatted diskette. Try this:

1. Open the Backup program from Start | Programs | Accessories | System Tools.
2. In the Welcome page, click the button labeled "Emergency Repair Disk."
3. In the Emergency Repair Diskette dialog box, click the check box to insert a check mark. Then click OK. When the disk has been created, the dialog box will inform you, and you can click OK to close the dialog box. Close the Backup program. Remove the diskette and put it in a safe place.

Creating Backups

Yes, we know you've heard it over and over. But you still need to actually back up your data files on removable media or to another computer. It is not possible to overemphasize how important it is to do this! Do it often and do it right. Windows 2000 Professional has a backup program, available through Start | Programs | Accessories | System Tools.

Preparing for an Emergency Repair

In Windows 2000, as in Windows NT 4.0, you can recover from some critical problems involving loss or damage of configuration information saved in Windows. To do this, you must perform an emergency repair. This is a very advanced task and an extreme solution. However, it is not even an option if you don't take steps to save configuration information to your hard drive, as well as to create an emergency repair disk after any and all changes to your system.

You created an emergency repair disk (ERD) during the Windows 2000 Setup program, and again after creating a new partition in Step-by-Step 4.04. You will need to do this every time you make a change to hardware or software on your computer. To create an ERD, you first need a formatted, blank, 3.5-inch high-density floppy disk. Then start the Windows 2000 Backup Program, and perform the steps for creating an emergency repair disk at the end of Step-by-Step 4.04. Be sure to place a check in the check box in the Emergency Repair Diskette dialog box. This will save the updated configuration information in the Repair folder on the hard drive, as well as create the repair diskette.

On your personal computer, keep your emergency repair disk up-to-date, even if you are intimidated by the thought of doing an emergency repair on your own. If you experience a major failure of your computer, and take it to a service center, take the ERD with you also.

You will learn more about advanced recovery options, including the emergency repair and the recovery console, in Chapter 8.

Periodic Housekeeping

Keep your computer "lean and mean." If you simply can't resist acquiring new programs that look just a little interesting because they are free or inexpensive, you may find trouble in the form of undesirable changes to your system and outright hard drive bloat. Periodically, you should do some serious housecleaning, which should include removing any applications you no longer need, deleting any data files you no longer need, and deleting temporary files. After you have done this, defragment your hard drive, because file fragmentation (even on an NTFS volume) can slow down a computer. In Chapter 6 you'll learn more about the Windows 2000 utilities for accomplishing these tasks: Disk Cleanup and Disk Defragmenter.

Common Problems and Solutions

There are several common problems that you might encounter with almost any OS. You'll look now at five common problems and the actions you might take when you encounter them.

Unable to Access Another Computer on Your Network

If you are unable to access another computer on your network, check the following possibilities:

- Make certain the other PC is turned on, is physically connected to the network, and has shared the folder or printer you want to access.
- Try restarting the other PC. Sometimes computers seem to disappear from the network when a power-saving mode kicks in; restarting the PC makes the computer reappear.
- If this is the first time you have attempted to access the other computer, make certain that you have access rights to that computer. You may also need to check the network settings using the Network icon on the Control Panel to ensure that both systems are using the same networking protocols.

Unable to Print

If you are unable to print, try these solutions:

- Make certain that the printer is on, is connected, has paper, and is not in offline mode. In offline mode, a printer does not "listen" to the computer. This mode may be set by the printer after experiencing an error. Many printers will simply resume after the error is resolved, but some printers require that a button or switch be pressed to put the computer back into the online "listening" mode.
- Try opening the Properties dialog box for the printer and sending a test page to the printer. If this fails, open the Help program and look in the Index for "Troubleshooters, Print." Use the Print Troubleshooter to debug the problem.
- If you are attempting to print to a network printer, make certain that you have the proper permissions and that the printer is currently available.
- Try printing from another application such as Notepad. If this works, make certain the application that cannot print is set to use the correct printer.
- Sometimes simply turning the power off and then on again to a printer and to any attached print server device can help when a printer stops responding.

Unable to Locate a File

Even experienced computer users who are very comfortable working with files and folders find themselves searching for a file they remember storing in the perfect folder location. In some offices, several people share one computer and create files for common access. That sounds like Janelle, an office manager for a small antique furniture appraisal company. She has several appraisers who produce their own files on antique items and save them on a computer they all share. When a customer asks for detailed information on a particular item, Janelle must be able to locate the specific file that describes it. To do so, she often turns to the Windows 2000 Professional Search facility.

This allows her to search not only her local hard drive, but also any shared folders on the network.

To open the Windows 2000 Professional search tool, click the Start button and choose Search | For Files Or Folders from the Start menu. Once the Search Results window is open, you use the various options in the window to define your search. The Search Results window contains text boxes and other controls you use to customize the search. These include the following:

Turn on the Indexing Service only if you do very frequent searches, because you may find the frequent disk activity of index updating annoying, and this service can actually make other programs run more slowly.

Each search condition that you add must be satisfied in addition to all existing search conditions. That is, if you specify that the file must be at least 128KB and that it must contain the text "proposal," both of those conditions must be met. A file of less than 128KB that contains the text will not be included in the results.

- **Search For Files Or Folders Named** This text box enables you to enter the name (or partial name) of the file or folder you want to find. You can use the question mark (?) as a wildcard to replace a single character, or the asterisk (*) as a wildcard to replace any number of characters. To search for a name that includes spaces, enclose the search phrase in quotation marks.
- **Containing Text** This text box allows you to specify text contained in the file you want to find. For example, Janelle is searching for a file containing research she did on an 18th-century candlestick table, but she has forgotten the file name she used for it. She remembers that she used the phrase "mahogany candlestick table." Therefore, she enters *.* in the Files Or Folders Named box, and the phrase "mahogany candlestick table" in the Containing Text box.
- **Look In** Use this drop-down list to select the locations you want to search. You might want to limit the search to likely locations to speed the search process.
- **Date** Select this check box to display additional date-related search options so that you can find files based on the date they were modified, created, or last accessed. For instance, if Janelle recalls that she modified the mahogany candlestick table file in the past week, she can narrow her search by date to the past seven days.
- **Type** Use this option when you want to locate specific types of files such as Word documents, applications, or image files.
- **Size** This option enables you to specify that the file must be of a certain size.
- **Advanced Options** Select this option to specify that the search should include subfolders or be case sensitive, or that you want to search files that will take a long time to search.
- **Indexing Service** Select this option to enable or disable the Indexing Service, which will maintain indexes of the files (both properties and contents) on your hard drive. This service watches for changes on the drive and updates the indexes every time changes occur. These indexes speed up searches by any program (such as the Search program) that knows to use them.

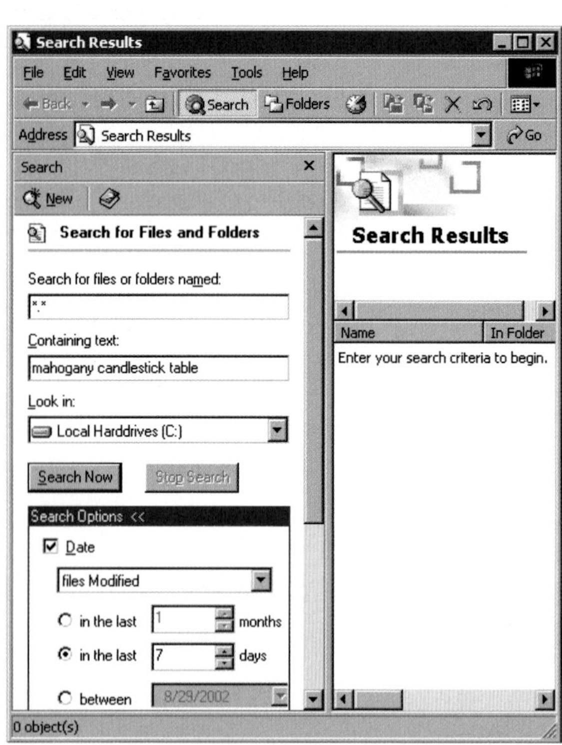

• The Search window

Try This!

Practice Doing a Search

Although the concept of searching for a particular item or group of items is easy to understand, the more options available to help you search, the more complicated the actual search becomes. Searching is a skill that requires practice! Try this:

1. Open the search window from Start | Search | For Files And Folders.
2. Specify that you want to search your hard disk for all application files by using the wildcard ***.exe** as the name of the file. Search, and note the number of results you get.
3. Narrow the search by specifying that you want to see only files created within the past three months. Search, and again note the number of results.
4. Finally, see what happens when you narrow the search so that only those files that are under 25KB are located. Take note of how adding conditions reduces the number of results returned.

Cannot Connect to the Internet

If you are unable to connect to the Internet, here are some things to watch for:

- Make certain that your modem (or other connection device) is on, is properly connected, and that you have established the Internet connection correctly.
- If you are connecting through your network, make certain that the computer or router through which your network connects to the Internet is functioning properly.
- Check your user name and password (if your Internet connection requires these). Remember that these are often case sensitive and that they are usually not the same as your Windows 2000 Professional logon.
- If you are on cable or DSL service, resetting the modem can correct outages or Internet access slowdowns.

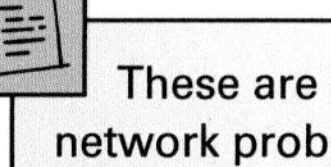

These are simple solutions to network problems. In Chapter 10 you will learn more about troubleshooting network problems.

These are simple solutions for device driver problems. In Chapter 8 you will learn more about troubleshooting device driver problems.

Cannot Install a Hardware Device Driver

If you attempt to install a new hardware device and cannot successfully do so, try these options:

- Make certain that the device is on the hardware compatibility list found either on the Windows 2000 Professional CD or at the Microsoft web site.
- If Windows 2000 Professional does not offer a native driver for the device, check the disks that came with the device or Microsoft's or the manufacturer's web site to locate Windows 2000 Professional–compatible drivers.

Cannot Play Audio, Video, or Other Multimedia Files

If you are unable to play multimedia content on a Windows 2000 Professional PC, consider these possibilities:

- Make certain that the speakers are properly connected and powered on.
- Make certain that the Windows 2000 Professional volume control is not muted. Check this by clicking the speaker icon in the system tray and then clicking the slider. When you do, the speakers should produce a sound.
- If the system was upgraded from Windows 9*x*, it's possible that Windows 2000 Professional drivers have not been installed for the multimedia devices. Open the Sounds and Multimedia applet in the Control Panel, and then click the Hardware tab of the Sounds And Multimedia Properties dialog box to verify that each device is working properly. If a device is not working properly, click the Properties button, and check out the installed driver. You may need to find and search the manufacturer's web site for a new device driver, or to replace the device.

Chapter 4 Review

Chapter Summary

After reading this chapter and completing the Step-by-Step tutorials and Try This! exercises, you should understand the following facts about Windows 2000 Professional:

Windows 2000 Professional Overview

- Windows 2000 Professional provides benefits through enhanced features in the areas of the desktop, security, stability, compatibility, and file systems.
- Windows 2000 Professional weaknesses are in support for old DOS and Windows applications and in the fact that reboots are still required after some changes to the OS, although reboots are required for fewer reasons than in previous OSs.
- The file systems Windows 2000 supports are FAT12, FAT16, FAT32, and NTFS5, although we usually refer to any of the FAT file systems as FAT, and the versions of NTFS as simply NTFS, unless making explicit statements or comparisons.
- Windows 2000 Professional is preferred over Windows 9*x* when stability, reliability, and security are required, when a software publisher lists this OS as a requirement for installing an application, and when remote administration of a computer is required.

Installing and Configuring Windows 2000 Professional

- Before installing Windows 2000, be sure that the hardware you plan to use will be adequate for the work you hope to accomplish on that computer.
- Determine whether Windows 2000 is compatible with the hardware and software you plan to use. You can find out by reading the documentation for the hardware and software items, looking at the compatibility information at `www.microsoft.com/whdc/hcl/search.mspx`, or contacting the manufacturer. You can also run a compatibility test that comes with Windows 2000, called the Readiness Analyzer.
- You can install Windows as an upgrade on a computer with an earlier version of Windows, or you can install a clean installation, beginning with an empty hard drive.
- Whether you are performing an upgrade or a clean installation, you can choose to do it manually, which requires your attention and interaction, or automatically, which requires the least amount of hand-holding. The automatic methods involve more work, technical understanding, and even financial investment.
- The four Windows 2000 setup boot disks are required if you are installing from the local CD-ROM drive and the computer will not boot from the CD. The Makeboot program will generate these disks. This program comes in two forms: MAKEBOOT.EXE (for DOS and 16-bit Windows) and MAKEBT32.EXE (for 32-bit Windows OSs).
- Install service packs and updates immediately after installing an OS, and after that, periodically check for updates. A shortcut installed on the Start menu, called Windows Update, makes this process easy, provided you have an Internet connection.
- You should check network connectivity after you install Windows 2000 on a computer connected to a network.

Customizing and Managing Windows 2000 Professional

- After installing Windows 2000, you will need to customize and manage Windows 2000. The Control Panel applets are your main tools for doing this.
- Make a Windows 2000 computer easier to use for someone with restricted vision, hearing loss, or mobility difficulties. Some built-in accessibility components can be enabled and configured using the Accessibility Options applet, and some accessibility utilities can be enabled from Start | Programs | Accessories | Accessibility.

- The Display applet lets you modify the desktop background, enable or disable a screen saver, and further customize the desktop. In addition, the Settings tab allows you to configure certain video adapter and monitor settings.
- Add a printer using the Add Printer wizard. You can further manage a printer in the properties for an installed printer. This includes assigning permissions to control access to the printer.
- Use the Taskbar And Start Menu Properties dialog box to control the display of the taskbar and Start menu, much as in Windows 98. The new Personalized Menus option is enabled by default, but it may confuse users. If it does, disable it from the Advanced tab.
- Windows 2000 Professional has several default folders that organize files. Some of these folders store files used by the OS, and some, such as My Documents and My Pictures, are created for each user and intended as default locations for data files created by the user. Avoid deleting or modifying system files.
- The Windows 2000 Search option has been expanded with more search options. To enhance the speed of file searches on an NTFS volume, enable the new Indexing Service in the Search Options area of the Search Results window.

Troubleshooting Windows 2000 Professional

- When a problem occurs, observe and record all symptoms and error messages; then research the cause and solution using Windows 2000 Help, the Internet, or other sources. Once you have found a solution, apply it and test the results.
- Normally, you should not modify the Windows 2000 registry, but if a recommended solution includes editing the registry, use one of the registry editors that comes with Windows 2000, back up the registry, and only then make the recommended change.
- When you see an error message in Windows 2000, use the Event Viewer to see if the error was logged in one of the log files it maintains. The information in the error message may lead you directly to the solution, or you may be able to use the information to search for a solution at Microsoft or elsewhere.
- Use Device Manager when you suspect that a problem is related to a device or device driver. With Device Manager, you can disable or enable a device, update a device driver, or configure a device.
- Take preventative measures to avoid problems. This includes running an antivirus program on your computer, not opening suspicious e-mail messages or attachments from unknown sources, performing periodic housekeeping to remove unneeded files and programs, and defragmenting the disk periodically.
- Be aware of several common problems and their solutions, including the inability to access another computer on the network or the Internet, to print, to install a hardware device driver, and to use multimedia content.

Key Terms

Active Directory domain *(145)*
autorun *(184)*
basic disk *(150)*
code signing *(148)*
Control Panel *(178)*
Disk Management *(173)*
drive path *(153)*
driver signing *(148)*
dynamic disk *(150)*
group policy *(146)*
hardware compatibility list (HCL) *(157)*
Indexing Service *(150)*
mirrored volume *(152)*
mount point *(153)*
pass-through authentication *(146)*
permission *(145)*
protected memory space *(148)*
RAID-5 volume *(152)*
refresh rate *(180)*
simple volume *(151)*
spanned volume *(152)*
striped volume *(152)*
virtual device driver (VXD) *(149)*
Windows NT domain *(145)*

■ Key Terms Quiz

Use the Key Terms List to complete the sentences that follow. Not all terms will be used.

1. To make searches faster on an NTFS volume, enable the ____________________.
2. To determine whether the devices on a PC are compatible with Windows 2000 Professional, examine the ____________________.
3. ____________________ is a new disk type introduced in Windows 2000.
4. Tools for configuring Windows 2000 Professional are on the ____________________.
5. ____________________ is the practice of digitally signing the contents of a device driver file to show that it has not been tampered with.
6. Programs that rely on Windows 9*x*–style ____________________ cannot run under Windows 2000 Professional.
7. A/an ____________________ is one in which at least one of the servers maintaining the domain database is running a Windows 2000 Server OS or greater.
8. Because Windows 2000 places each running application program in its own ______________, a program can fail without affecting other programs or the OS.
9. The screen ____________________ should be above 60 Hertz to avoid eyestrain.
10. ____________________ is a grouping of policies for controlling not only the many security settings, but also configuration settings for Windows 2000.

■ Multiple-Choice Quiz

1. Which of the following is *not* a reason to choose Windows 2000 Professional?
   - **a.** Stability
   - **b.** Compatibility with Windows applications
   - **c.** New, improved version of NTFS
   - **d.** Compatibility with Macintosh programs
   - **e.** Security
2. The minimum amount of memory needed for Windows 2000 Professional is:
   - **a.** 16MB
   - **b.** 24MB
   - **c.** 64MB
   - **d.** 128MB
   - **e.** 4GB
3. When you install Windows 2000, be prepared to provide a password for this user account.
   - **a.** Power user
   - **b.** Administrator
   - **c.** Visitor
   - **d.** Guest
   - **e.** Operator
4. When adding a printer driver for a physical printer that is directly connected to your computer and that you plan to share on the network, which option should you select in the Add Printer wizard?
   - **a.** Network Printer
   - **b.** FILE
   - **c.** Generic
   - **d.** Remote Printer
   - **e.** Local Printer
5. If you want to enable the StickyKeys feature, which Control Panel applet do you use?
   - **a.** Keyboard
   - **b.** Mouse
   - **c.** System

d. Administrative Tools

e. Accessibility

6. Which is the preferred file system for Windows 2000 Professional?

a. FAT32

b. NTFS5

c. HPFS

d. Linux32

e. FAT

7. Which of the following terms is *not* a part of Windows 2000 Professional security?

a. Families

b. Users

c. Groups

d. Rights

e. Permissions

8. To what family of Microsoft OSs does Windows 2000 Professional belong?

a. Windows UNIX family

b. Microsoft LAN Manager family

c. House of DOS Windows family

d. Windows NT family

e. Consumer Windows family

9. The default disk type of Windows 2000.

a. NTFS5

b. Dynamic

c. Basic

d. NTFS4

e. FAT32

10. Which of the following should *not* be part of a standard approach to troubleshooting?

a. Carefully observe and record the error messages or other symptoms of a problem.

b. Use the information you gathered to find the cause.

c. Repartition and format the hard drive.

d. Research the solution.

e. Test the results.

11. Which of the following is out of place in a defensive strategy to prevent problems in Windows 2000?

a. Antivirus program

b. Freeware games

c. Data backup

d. Disk defragmenter

e. Deletion of temporary files

12. The greatest benefit from group policy can be achieved when a computer is a member of a/an:

a. Active Directory domain

b. Windows NT 4.0 domain

c. Workgroup

d. Group

e. File system

13. The setting Use Personalized Menus affects which GUI component?

a. Taskbar

b. Desktop

c. Start menu

d. Notification area

e. Context menus

14. Windows 2000 Professional uses this authentication protocol for pass-through authentication when you log onto a Windows Active Directory domain.

a. IPSec

b. TCP/IP

c. NTFS

d. Kerberos

e. Autorun

15. Why should you defragment your hard drive on a regular basis?

a. Defragmenting alphabetizes your files, making them easier to find.

b. Defragmenting may improve the performance of your computer.

c. Defragmenting makes your files more secure.

d. Defragmenting cleans out all temporary files.

e. None of the above.

Essay Quiz

1. You are given the task of installing Windows 2000 Professional on 50 identical computers built especially for your company by a local computer company. The computers will arrive with no operating system on the hard disk. You have purchased the necessary licenses and software to install Windows 2000 Professional and an office suite on all systems before delivering them to the users' desktops. The computers will be delivered to your office in two weeks, and then you will have another three weeks to complete the installation. You have arranged for sufficient space to store the boxed computers, and you have network connections to the workspace in the computer assembly area. Describe briefly your overall strategy for preparing for and implementing this task.
2. You presently have a single hard disk system and a CD-ROM drive in your Windows 2000 Professional desktop computer. The hard disk is a basic disk, configured with two primary partitions, drives C: and D:, and the CD-ROM drive has letter E:. You have purchased a new hard disk to add to the computer. Once it is physically installed, you will partition it so that it has two primary partitions. You would like to have the drive letters *E* and *D* assigned to these new partitions. Describe how you will achieve this.
3. Describe the periodic housekeeping that was recommended in the Troubleshooting section of this chapter.
4. You have just installed Windows 2000 Professional on a computer at home that is connected to the Internet via broadband. Describe how you will update the operating system.
5. Your boss wants you to install Windows 2000 Professional on his PC. You go to his office, and you discover that he has an old printer and an old scanner that look like they've been sitting around pretty much unused for a long time. How can you be sure that these items will be compatible with Windows 2000 Professional before you begin the installation process?

Lab Projects

• Lab Project 4.1

You have just been given a PC in which the hard disk has failed and been replaced by a new one with no operating system. The system has a CD-ROM drive, but when you try to install Windows 2000 Professional by booting directly from the CD, nothing happens.

You will need the following:

- A lab computer with no operating system installed

Then do the following:

1. Describe what you must do to install Windows 2000 Professional on this PC.
2. Determine how you can create boot disks.
3. Implement your solution on your lab computer.
4. Test your solution and explain the results.

• Lab Project 4.2

After completing this chapter, you realize the value of proactive maintenance and have decided to implement it on your computer.

You will need the following:

- A lab computer with Windows 2000 Professional installed

Then do the following:

1. Develop a proactive maintenance plan for your home or lab computer. Consider how it is configured as far as removable, writeable media such as floppy disk drives and CDR drives. Write a description of the proactive maintenance tasks you will be able to do on this system and how often you will do each task.
2. Test the individual tasks in your plan. Revise your plan if you discover a limit in one of these programs.
3. Present your plan to the class or to a fellow student.

Windows XP Professional

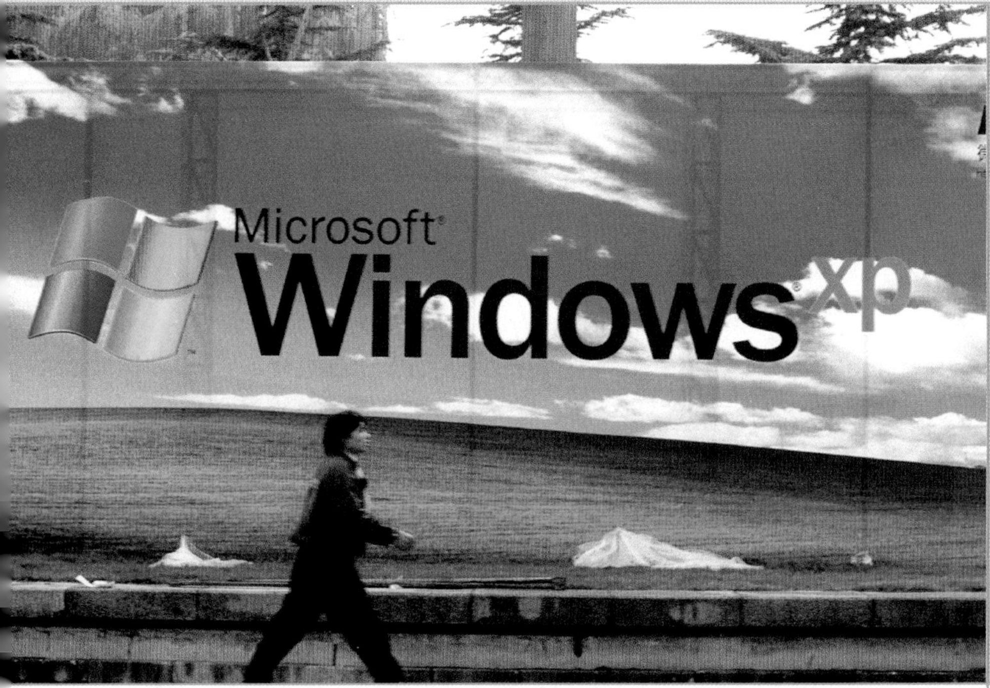

Windows XP... is worthwhile for one reason: under-the-hood, deep-into-geekdom stability.

—David LaGesse,
U.S. News and World Report

Windows XP Professional, the subject of this chapter, was introduced in October 2001 as a business desktop product. A separate product, Windows XP Home Edition, was introduced at the same time, and since then, they have brought out additional Windows XP products.

In this chapter, you will work with Windows XP Professional because this (or its successor) is the desktop OS you will encounter in most organizations. You will learn its benefits, features, and weaknesses, and you will install it, configure it, and customize it. In addition, you will learn some basic proactive measures you should take to prevent problems. Finally, you will learn to troubleshoot common Windows XP Professional problems.

In this chapter, you will learn to:

- **Describe Windows XP Professional benefits, features, and limits**
- **Install and configure Windows XP Professional**
- **Customize and manage Windows XP Professional**
- **Perform proactive maintenance tasks**
- **Troubleshoot common Windows XP Professional problems**

Windows XP Professional Overview

Windows XP is an upgrade to Windows 2000. In Chapter 4 we used the analogy of replacing the engine in our old Honda Prelude with that of a Mustang V8 to illustrate the move from Windows 98 to Windows 2000 Professional. If you now make the transition from Windows 2000 Professional to Windows XP Professional, it'll be like replacing that old Honda car body with a sleek, new one, and adding some features that will give you the benefit of more security and ease-of-maintenance. This overview includes a description of the various Windows XP versions, the enhanced features and benefits of Windows XP, and the limitations of Windows XP.

Windows XP Versions

As with Windows 2000, there are several versions of Windows XP—some that were introduced many months after the initial release. All are designed for consumers at home or in business. The Windows XP lineup and target customers include

- Windows XP Professional, for the business and power users
- Windows XP Home Edition, for the home or very small business
- Windows XP Media Center Edition, which allows users to use a TV remote control to view TV listings and to catalog songs, videos, and pictures
- Windows XP Tablet PC Edition, for tablet devices and notebooks
- Windows XP Embedded, for other devices (usually small, hand-held devices)
- Windows XP 64-bit Edition, for more advanced PCs with one 64-bit or two symmetric 64-bit processors, and up to 16GB of RAM

What you won't find in this list is a server version of Windows XP. With the Windows XP products, Microsoft officially separates their small system OSs from their server system OSs.

Although Windows XP Home Edition can work well in a small office that has simple security needs, it is not appropriate for a larger business environment, because it doesn't include many of the security and remote management features of Windows XP Professional. The most significant shortfall of Windows XP Home Edition is the inability to join a Microsoft domain. This is a real problem for a small business that decides to bring in a Small Business Server edition of either Windows 2000 Server or Windows Server 2003, which includes a Microsoft Active Directory domain. The business would have to upgrade every Windows XP Home Edition computer to Windows XP Professional before users could enjoy the benefits of logging onto a domain.

Windows XP's Enhanced Features and Benefits

Edgar owns a computer consulting business that specializes in small businesses. Because he knows so much about what small business users need, we'll let him guide us through Windows XP's features and why they are so useful. Edgar's company is a Microsoft Solution Provider, which means it participates in a special Microsoft program to provide appropriate Microsoft solutions to its customers. In their own office, they use Windows 2000 servers and Windows XP Professional on their desktop and laptop computers. They've put together a list of features for their customers who are considering purchasing new desktop or laptop computers, or upgrading existing computers. We'll discuss the features they feel are most important.

Windows XP Professional has benefits in the areas of desktop usage, speed, security, stability, and compatibility. It also supports several file systems to suit the performance and security needs of the user. In the following sections, we explore these features and benefits.

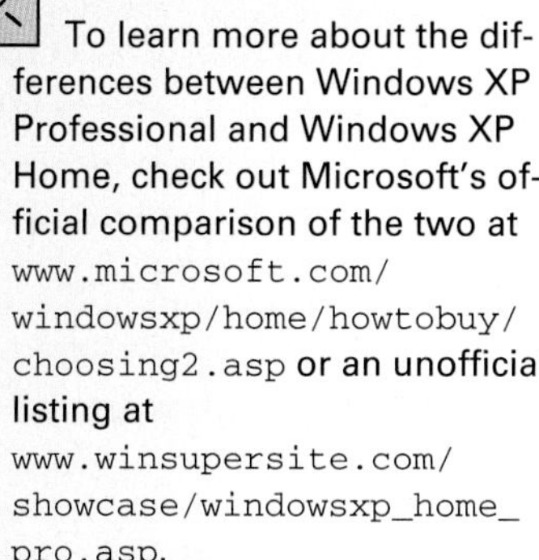

To learn more about the differences between Windows XP Professional and Windows XP Home, check out Microsoft's official comparison of the two at `www.microsoft.com/windowsxp/home/howtobuy/choosing2.asp` or an unofficial listing at `www.winsupersite.com/showcase/windowsxp_home_pro.asp`.

Desktop Beauty and Usability

People will buy a product that is visually appealing, and the designers at Microsoft have made Windows XP downright beautiful. This reflects the efforts Microsoft has put into making it more usable.

Visual Appeal If you are a veteran Windows user, you'll see the changes Microsoft implemented in Windows XP immediately upon booting it up. Gone is the boring, subdued color scheme. In its place is a larger, brighter, blue-and-green default scheme. The desktop pictures are all quite appealing. Even the text on the icons has been improved.

Usability It is an understatement to say that the default desktop is uncluttered, since it contains only the Recycle Bin icon. The desktop icons formerly visible have been moved to a reorganized, two-column Start menu that can be customized (through the Start menu properties) to suit the needs and experience of the user (see Figure 5-1). The improvements, however, are more than just visual and go far beyond the changes you can make to the Start menu. The desktop actually seems to learn from you, and you'll notice that the Start menu constantly adjusts itself. The most frequently used programs are listed on the left side of the Start menu, with all other programs available on the All Programs submenu. The more you use a program, the higher it rises on the list of frequently used programs. Figure 5-1 shows that Microsoft Word is the most frequently used program on this system.

The Display applet has been logically reorganized with a new Themes tab replacing the former Background tab. Now you can choose a Theme, which is a predefined set of desktop choices such as color scheme, screen saver, sounds, and more. The desktop reorganizes itself as well. If you have used earlier versions of Windows, you are probably familiar with cluttered desktops. Every program you installed seemed to place its own icon on the desktop. Windows XP solves this problem by periodically moving unused

• The Windows XP desktop (with the Bliss wallpaper)

desktop icons into a folder named Unused Desktop Shortcuts (with your approval, of course). So even if every new program places a shortcut on the desktop, only the shortcuts you actually use stay there.

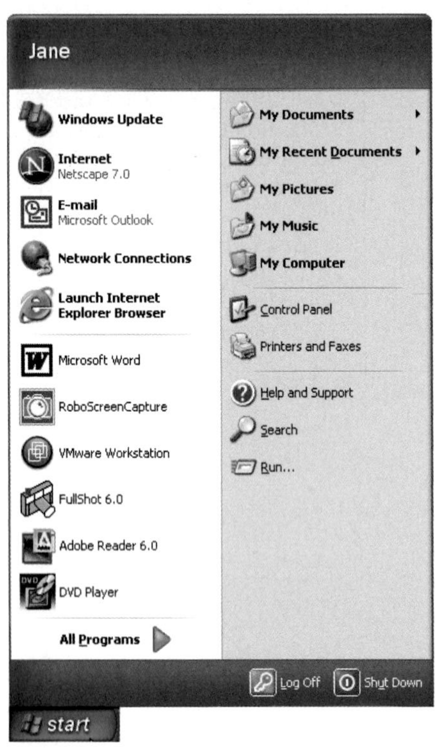

• **Figure 5-1.** The Windows XP Start menu

Speed

Windows XP is much faster than previous editions of Windows. It boots faster and runs programs better than either Windows 2000 or Windows 98. Faster computers allow you to get more done—and can help lower your stress level. Figures released by Microsoft suggest a boot time 34 percent faster than for Windows 2000. In other words, if your computer used to boot in 1 minute, it may now boot in under 40 seconds.

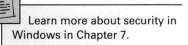

Around the time Windows XP was introduced, TechTV (now G4TechTV) ran several tests comparing Windows XP to Windows 2000 and determined that Windows XP ran 20 percent faster than Windows 2000.

Faster Bootup How did Microsoft decrease the boot time? By improving the drivers for hardware and by a special scheme in which Windows XP learns what is needed at bootup and creates a list of code or data that it can bring into memory before it is needed. This is called **prefetching**.

Programs Run Faster Programs run faster in Windows XP thanks, in part, to prefetching for applications, which works much like prefetching for bootup. Windows XP keeps track of the files an application uses and creates a prefetch list. The next time that application is run, Windows XP uses the appropriate prefetch list, bringing code the program has used in the past into memory before it's requested. Windows XP also rearranges the placement of programs on disk so that they will launch faster.

Microsoft examined the applications that users work with most often and discovered that CD burning, digital photo manipulation, and Internet messaging (implemented as Windows Messenger in Windows XP) were the three fastest-growing applications. Microsoft thus made each easier and faster in Windows XP. CD creation in particular has become much simpler.

Security

Learn more about security in Windows in Chapter 7.

As with Windows NT and Windows 2000, XP's grandparent and parent, Windows XP Professional contains security components, including required logon authentication and the ability to set file and folder permissions on an NTFS volume. These security features, and others, have been enhanced, while new security features have been added, especially in the area of the network.

Required Logon A logon to Windows XP Professional is mandatory, and this logon must be performed from an account that is a member of a security database—either the local security accounts database built into Windows XP Professional on the local computer, or a network-based security database, such as in a Windows NT or Active Directory domain. When you install Windows XP, you are given an opportunity to automate this logon, so that you will not have to manually enter your user name and password. In a casual environment in which security is not an issue, this is a good thing, but in any situation in which you need computer security, do not automate the logon. It defeats the purpose of the required logon, which is to prevent unauthorized access to your computer.

NTFS5 Introduced in Windows 2000, NTFS version 5 (NTFS5) continues to be supported in Windows XP. NTFS5 inherited both the file compression feature from NTFS4 and security for files and folders, which has been part of NTFS since it first appeared in Windows NT. It has improved on file and folder security by adding flexibility and power through new permissions and an improvement in the interface for setting permissions. As in Windows 2000, NTFS5 in Windows XP allows you to encrypt files for extra security and to create mount points for drive paths, as explained in Chapter 4.

In Chapter 7 you will learn more about the security features of NTFS5 including file encryption and the new file and folder permissions.

Stability and Compatibility

Edgar has been using Windows XP Professional on his office desktop for several months. During this time, he has experienced precisely one unrecoverable crash, which occurred after he installed a bad memory module into the motherboard and booted the computer. Nothing else has caused his computer to crash or to stop responding. He routinely runs at least six applications at any given time, each a memory hog. In the rare event that a program has stopped responding, he has been able to stop it without affecting any other applications. This is awesome. In contrast, his home computer running Windows 98 crashes frequently (on bad days, hourly!).

Microsoft attacked the stability problem from three angles. They strengthened driver signing, originally introduced in Windows 2000; they added the Program Compatibility options for older-program support; and they made Windows updates an (optionally) automatic process.

Code Signing/Driver Signing Like Windows 2000, the Windows XP program code is digitally signed by Microsoft before it is released, and Windows XP checks for this signature to ensure that the code has not been damaged or tampered with. A subset of this is driver signing; Microsoft certifies Windows XP drivers before the vendor ships the product. A certified driver is called a signed driver. Microsoft provides the vendor with a digital signature that is incorporated into the driver file. Signed drivers are supposed to eliminate hardware conflicts and unnecessary delays. Figure 5-2 shows a network card driver with a digital signature.

Learn more about code signing and driver signing and the related features in Windows 2000 and Windows XP in Chapter 8.

• **Figure 5-2.** Signed network card driver

Program Compatibility Settings Hardware issues are just part of the stability issue. Older programs, often called legacy applications, exist in computers around the globe. In the past these programs did not run well on newer versions of operating systems. For example, perhaps your favorite game program was written to take advantage of the way that Windows 98 interacted with the video card. After buying a new computer with Windows XP, you install the program and it does not work at all, or does not display properly on the screen. You can use the Compatibility settings in the properties dialog box of the executable program file to tell Windows XP to emulate, or pretend, that it is Windows 98. Simply pick Windows 98/Windows Me from the Compatibility Mode list, as shown in Figure 5-3, and Windows XP will run the program in a modified environment that will not affect other running programs. A display problem may or may not be resolved by a

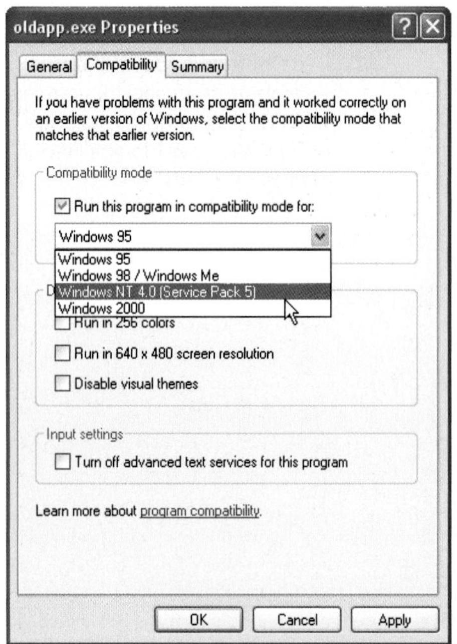

• **Figure 5-3.** The Compatibility page allows you to select settings that enable an older program to run.

compatibility mode. You may also force Windows XP to use a different screen resolution and/or color depth in the Display Settings on the Compatibility page. Alternatively, you can run the Program Compatibility wizard, as described later in this chapter under "Troubleshooting Common Windows XP Problems."

Automated Windows Update Windows updates have been an important, but often neglected, task for computer users. Typically, Microsoft finds and corrects problems with its software in a timely fashion. Earlier versions of Windows let the users decide when, if ever, to update their computers. The net result could be disastrous, as seen a few years ago when the worm Code Red and the worm-virus Nimda caused thousands of computers across the country to go down. Both viruses exploited flaws in Internet Information Server (IIS) installed on Windows 2000 Server. The flaws had been corrected in a security update released by Microsoft several months earlier. If administrators had updated their computers, the virus-caused damage would not have been so widespread.

Microsoft received a lot of bad press from these incidents. While it's true that Microsoft programming caused the flaw, the company provided the solution well before the incidents. The real fault lies squarely on the shoulders of the administrators who failed to implement the updates. To help avoid this problem in the future, Microsoft has improved their Windows Update web page (`http://windowsupdate.microsoft.com`), provided a **Windows Update** program that allows you to interactively connect to this web page, and provided a second program, **Automatic Update**, which can be configured to automatically connect to the Microsoft site and download updates.

> For a complete list of features and benefits, check out `www.microsoft.com/windowsxp/pro/evaluation/features.asp`.

Windows XP actually nags you to enable Automatic Update. Soon after installing Windows XP (a day or two in our experience), a message balloon, as shown in Figure 5-4, will pop up from the taskbar suggesting that you automate updates. If you click on this message, the Automatic Updates Setup wizard will run, allowing you to configure the update program.

> Both the Windows Update and Automatic Update programs require Internet Explorer. Updates to these programs may also require updates to Internet Explorer.

You say you've never seen this message balloon, and would certainly like to automate the update process? No problem—simply right-click on My Computer (on the Start menu), select Properties, and then click the Automatic Updates tab and select the settings you desire. Then, whenever your computer connects to the Web, it checks the Windows Update page. What happens next depends on the setting you chose. See Figure 5-5, which shows the Automatic Updates page from the version of Automatic Updates released in the summer of 2004 in advance of Service Pack 2. Service Pack 2 was released in August of 2004 and included many security updates.

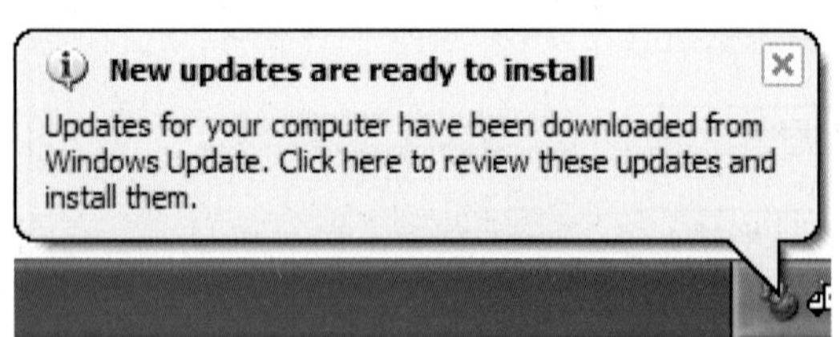

• **Figure 5-4.** Windows Update balloon message

If you have a slow Internet connection (dial-up), you may want to disable Automatic Updates and opt to use Windows Update to manually connect and download the updates at times that will not interfere with your work. If you have a faster connection, you may elect to have the updates downloaded automatically, and review and select the updates you wish to install. Whichever option you choose, keeping Windows XP up-to-date should reduce the number of viruses that exploit system flaws.

File System Support

As stated earlier, Windows XP supports NTFS version 5. It actually has the same file support you learned about in Windows 2000—that is, support for FAT12 for diskettes, and NTFS5, FAT16, and FAT32 for hard disks. Of these choices, only NTFS5 offers file and folder security. While FAT32 does use disk space more efficiently and can be used on very large hard disk partitions, the only reason to choose FAT32 under Windows XP is when you wish to dual-boot between Windows XP and a version of Windows 9*x* that supports FAT32. In both cases, the system partition and any partitions you wish to have available to the older OS should be formatted as FAT32. Similarly, FAT16 would be your choice when dual-booting between Windows XP and OSs such as Windows 95 (previous to Service Release 2) or MS-DOS. FAT16 should be your file system of last resort, as it offers neither security nor efficient disk usage.

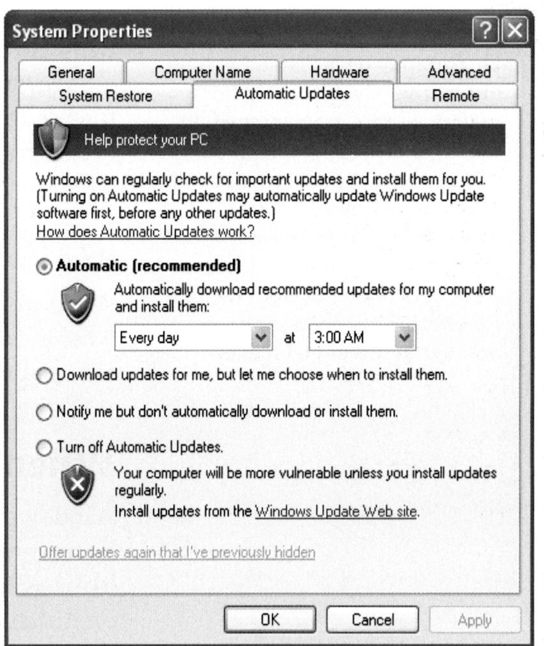

• **Figure 5-5.** Choosing to enable automatic updates

New and Improved Recovery Tools

In the area of disaster recovery tools, Windows XP has inherited the best of its predecessors in both Windows families, and it has discarded and replaced an old tool. That is, it has such vintage Windows NT tools as the Last Known Good Configuration startup option for startup failures due to a configuration change, and the Task Manager for removing errant programs. It has the Recovery Console that was introduced in Windows 2000. From the Windows 9*x* family, it inherited Safe Mode startup options and the Device Manager, improving on both. A new, and excellent, recovery tool is called **System Restore**, which was actually introduced in Windows ME and upgraded in Windows XP. System Restore creates **restore points**, which are snapshots of Windows, its configuration, and all installed programs. If your computer has nonfatal problems after you have made a change, you can roll it back to the last restore point. We have used it and it works! And finally, to recover from damage that prevents the operating system from being started up in any way, **Automated System Recovery (ASR)** is available from the Backup program (NTBACKUP.EXE). ASR replaces the Emergency Repair process of Windows NT and Windows 2000. Learn more about System Restore and ASR later in this chapter under "Troubleshooting Common Windows XP Problems," and learn about the other recovery features, Safe Mode, Recovery Console, and Device Manager, in Chapter 8.

Automated System Recovery and the Backup Utility are not included in Windows XP Home Edition. Since Home Edition is often preinstalled on computers, many manufacturers attempt to make up for this with a custom system recovery tool, but may not include a backup utility.

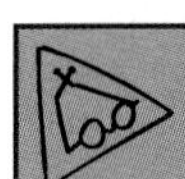

Inside Information

Problems with Last Known Good

Last Known Good (LKG) only lets you restore the system to a single restore point (not called that), and it seems to work only on alternate Thursdays. That's because you only have a narrow window of opportunity to use LKG—on the first reboot after making a configuration change, and before *logging on. Once you log on, the former LKG settings are deleted, and the new settings with the changes included become the LKG.*

The Limitations of Windows XP

In our view, Windows XP is a very good desktop/laptop OS—it offers the stability of the NT family of OSs, while giving us an improved, attractive GUI. We feel the weaknesses of Windows XP are minor and are just in the areas of hardware support and increased hardware requirements.

Hardware Support

If you have an older device that does not have a signed driver, you may be in trouble. Microsoft frowns on the use of a nonsigned driver, so there is no guarantee that the product will work properly. In addition, using the product

You may be surprised at how often drivers you receive from manufacturers are unsigned. In our experience, the unsigned drivers usually perform just fine. The one exception to this rule was a driver for a device from a small manufacturer, and we were able to use System Restore to roll back the changes made during the driver installation.

may actually slow down boot times. However, in all likelihood the product will work just fine. Experiment on a noncritical system.

We know several network administrators who are choosing to be safe by forcing their Windows XP systems to use only signed drivers. The Automatic Updates page of the System applet in Windows XP's Control Panel allows an administrator to choose the desired level of protection.

Hardware Requirements

While the hardware requirements of Windows XP are certainly less than what is commonly provided by the typical new PC, if you are upgrading an old computer, you may find these requirements to be a bit high. See Table 5-1.

When to Use Windows XP

Windows XP is an improvement over previous versions of Windows, but its features may not be for everybody. If you are purchasing a new PC, it most likely will come with Windows XP Home or Windows XP Professional preinstalled. However, if you are upgrading an older computer, you need to answer several questions.

- First, consider the adage, "If it ain't broke, don't fix it." If your computer is doing everything you need it to do, there is no reason to upgrade. If you are happy with your current OS, leave it alone. You are used to it and know how to work with it—new is not always better.
- Second, ask yourself if you are ready to deal with the work of upgrading. Even though Windows XP is compatible with most equipment, several commonly used pieces of software and hardware do not work with Windows XP. Edgar's upgrade to XP required the purchase of a new video card. The Voodoo 2000 card he had been running for several years did not support DirectX 8.1, the minimum version supported by Windows XP. He also had to uninstall Symantec's Norton Utilities before upgrading to Windows XP and then reinstall it after the upgrade. This process was made more tedious by that program's need to reacquire all the latest virus definitions.

What Version to Use?

When Edgar's customers consider upgrading or replacing their Windows PCs, how does he decide which of the many versions of Windows XP to install for them? Of all the versions, the two that are most appropriate for most desktops or laptops are Windows XP Home and Windows XP Professional. The Home edition is suited to the average home user, and the Professional edition is designed to work in an office. However, the distinction is not really all that clear. For some very small businesses, Windows XP Home may be adequate, and because of the price differential, they may choose it. But for most business users, Windows XP Professional is the most appropriate of the Windows XP versions, both for their new PC purchases and their upgrades.

To help choose between the Home and Professional products for his customers, Edgar asks them the following questions:

- Will the user need to connect to the computer remotely?

- Will the computer be connecting to a Microsoft NT or Active Directory domain-based network? (Users cannot log onto either type of domain from a Windows XP Home computer.)
- Is it important to easily rebuild your machine in the event of a catastrophe?
- Is it important to make individual files secure?

If the customer answers yes to any of these questions, Edgar will recommend Windows XP Professional, but in the case of an upgrade, they need to first compare the existing computer configuration with the hardware requirements for Windows XP.

> **Cross Check**
>
> **Differences Count!**
>
> Now that you have had an overview of Windows XP, answer the following questions in the space provided:
>
> 1. In general terms, how is Windows XP Home Edition different from Windows XP Professional?
>
>   ______________________________
>
> 2. Describe the difference between the Windows Update program and Automatic Update.
>
>   ______________________________

Installing and Upgrading Windows XP Professional

The average person may buy a computer with an OS preinstalled, and use that same OS until the computer fails or becomes obsolete to the user. But you aren't the average person. You are either preparing for a technical career, or you may simply wish to be a very knowledgeable computer user. In either case, the best way to begin learning a new OS is to successfully install it from scratch. To that end, we will focus on a clean installation.

As with previous versions of Windows, you must first learn the tasks required to prepare for Windows XP installation, perform the installation, and then complete post-installation tasks.

Please keep in mind that IT professionals may use scripted installations or some type of imaged installations, as discussed in previous Windows chapters. These methods are best when you must install an OS onto many computers, using identical configurations.

Preparing for Windows XP Installation

Prepare to install Windows XP Professional by ensuring hardware requirements are met, verifying hardware and software compatibility, determining how to boot into Windows XP setup, and finally, taking time to understand the difference between activation and registration and how to handle both tasks when it comes time to do them during installation.

Cross Check

Planning for an Upgrade or Clean Installation

This is the third time in this book that you are confronting the issue of upgrading versus doing a clean installation. Flip back to the section titled "Upgrade vs. Clean Installation" in Chapter 3 and "Installing and Configuring Windows 2000 Professional" in Chapter 4 and answer the following questions:

1. Briefly outline your strategy for doing a clean installation on a computer with an existing partition.

___

2. Describe the tasks to be completed before doing an upgrade to Windows XP Professional.

___

Ensure Windows XP Hardware Requirements

Windows XP is not a small operating system—in terms of both disk space needed for storage, and the CPU and RAM needed to run it and supported programs. The published minimum requirements are not about compatibility, but about quantity and power; it takes a modern CPU to run this operating system well. In addition, the programs we choose to run on desktop computers have grown in their processor, storage, and memory requirements. Table 5-1 shows the minimum requirements, as well as our recommended minimums for installing Windows XP on a typical desktop computer in preparation for daily use by an office professional, using a productivity suite such as Microsoft Office 2003.

Verify Hardware and Software Compatibility

The Installation wizard for Windows XP includes a Compatibility wizard, which checks your system. The results this wizard returns are both displayed on the screen and saved in a file. Since you can run the compatibility checker as the **Upgrade Advisor** separately from installation, why wait until you are ready to install? Before installing, be sure that you resolve any compatibility problems. You will need to check hardware and software compatibility before installing Windows XP Professional—either as an upgrade or as a new installation. Of course, if you purchase a computer with Windows XP preinstalled, you are spared checking out hardware compatibility, but you will still need to verify that the application software you plan to add to the computer will be compatible.

Table 5-1 Windows XP Minimums vs. Our Recommended Minimums

Minimums for Windows XP Professional	Recommended Minimums for Windows XP Professional
Any Intel or AMD 300-MHz or higher processor	Any Intel or AMD 600-MHz or higher processor
128MB of RAM	256MB of RAM
1.5GB of hard drive space	4GB of hard drive space
Super VGA video card that supports 800×600 resolution or greater	Super VGA video card that supports 1024×768 resolution or greater
CD-ROM or DVD drive	CD-R, CD-RW, or DVD-R drive

Luckily, you have two tools for determining whether your hardware is compatible: the Windows Catalog on the Microsoft web site and the Upgrade Advisor on the Windows XP CD.

Windows Catalog The Windows Catalog is a searchable list of hardware and software that is known to work with Windows. The Windows Catalog can be found at `www.microsoft.com/windows/catalog`. Once at the Windows Catalog page, you can search on specific hardware or software products, or browse through the catalog of hardware and software products that will work with Windows XP. If you are checking on the compatibility of software, select the Software tab, and for hardware, select the Hardware tab.

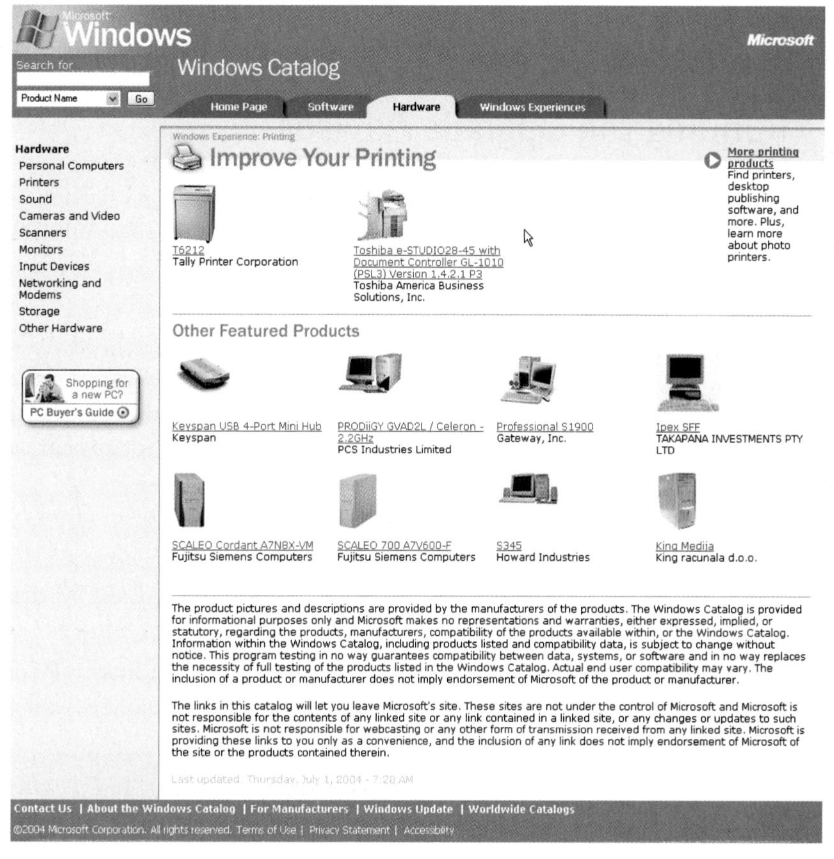

• The Hardware page of the Windows Catalog

Upgrade Advisor In our experience, Windows XP supports a wide range of hardware and software, even some rather old "no name" computers, but we like to be proactive when planning an installation, especially an upgrade. You may not have the luxury of time in upgrading a computer—you may be asked by your boss or client to perform an upgrade *now*. Fortunately, the upgrade advisor is the first process that runs on the Windows XP installation CD. It examines your hardware and installed software (in the case of an upgrade) and provides a list of devices and software that are known to have issues with Windows XP. Be sure to follow the suggestions on this list!

The Upgrade Advisor can also be run separately from the installation. You can run it from the Windows XP Professional CD, or, if you want to find out about compatibility for an upgrade before purchasing Windows XP, connect to the Windows XP Compatibility web page at `www.microsoft.com/windowsxp/pro/upgrading/advisor.mspx`. Scroll to the bottom of the page, and follow the instructions under "How Do I Use Upgrade Advisor?"

When he was first learning about Windows XP, Edgar ran the advisor on a test computer at the office that was running Windows 98. It produced a report that found only one incompatibility—an antivirus program. The details stated that the program was compatible only if installed after Windows XP was installed. Therefore, it suggested removing the program before installing the OS, then reinstalling it after the OS is installed. Don't ignore the instructions provided by the Upgrade Advisor! On a test computer, like that on which Edgar ran the Upgrade Advisor, you can afford to see what the consequences are of ignoring advice, but you don't always have that luxury or time. Edgar always likes to find out what the consequences are of ignoring advice. He says that helps to troubleshoot problems that his clients run into.

Inside Information

What Did Edgar Learn?

Edgar ignored the advice to remove the antivirus program before upgrading his test computer. After the upgrade, Windows XP did not run, and he could not even boot up into Windows XP's Safe Mode. After several hours of trying to fix the installation, he had to wipe the hard drive clean and start from scratch. He has a few customers who like to try things first and then call him for help. After this experience, he sent a friendly e-mail to his customers, offering his company's services for installing or upgrading computers, and warning them that if they do it themselves, they should follow the Upgrade Advisor instructions very carefully!

Step-by-Step 5.01

Running the Upgrade Advisor

In this step-by-step, you will run the Upgrade Advisor for your system. To complete this task, you will need the following:

- A PC with Windows XP or older version of Windows
- The Windows XP CD
- Internet access (optional)

Step 1

Insert the Windows XP CD. If autorun is enabled, the Welcome To Microsoft Windows XP screen will appear. If this does not appear, select Start | Run, enter the following, and click OK:

```
d:\setup.exe
```

where *d* is the drive letter for the CD-ROM drive.

Step 2

At the Welcome To Microsoft Windows XP screen, select Check System Compatibility. On the following page, select Check My System Automatically.

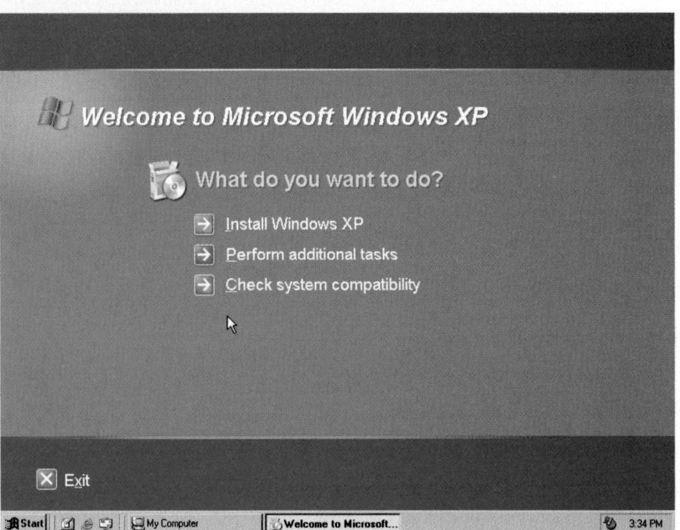

Step 3

The Upgrade Advisor dialog box opens and gives you two choices. If you have an Internet connection, select the first choice, which will download the updated Setup files. If you don't have an Internet connection, select No, Skip This Step And Continue Installing Windows. (Don't worry, you aren't really going to install, yet). Click Next. The Upgrade Advisor will show the tasks that Upgrade Advisor is performing, and then it may restart Setup.

Step 4

If Setup does not restart, The Report System Compatibility page will display the results of the test. If Setup restarts and you find yourself back at the page in the Upgrade Advisor in which you chose to download the updated Setup files, select No, Skip This Step And Continue Installing Windows and click Next. The Report System Compatibility page appears next. Read the findings that the Upgrade Advisor presents. If a problem was found, click the Details button for instructions. Remember Edgar's experience and follow the instructions. You can save the information in a file by clicking Save As and selecting a location. If incompatible items are found, report this to your instructor; then click Finish.

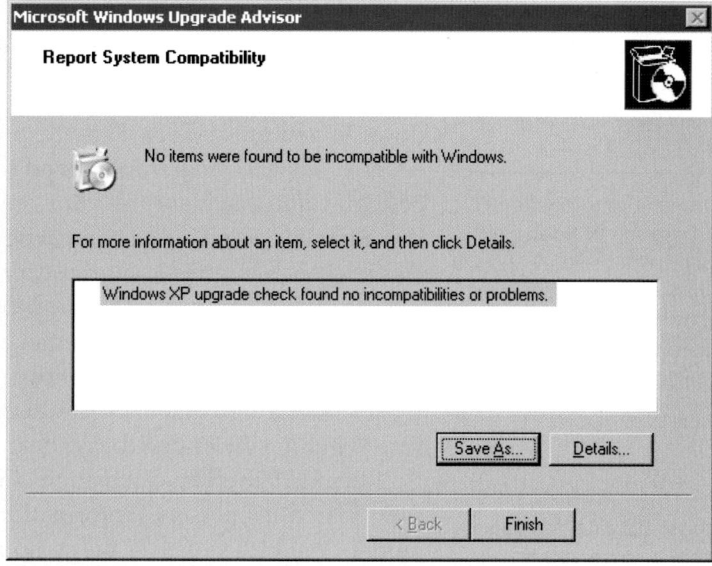

Booting into Windows XP Setup

The Windows XP CDs are bootable, and Microsoft no longer includes a program to create a set of setup boot disks. This should not be an issue, because PCs manufactured in the last several years have the ability to boot from CD-ROM. This is a system BIOS setting, usually described as "boot order," controlled through a PC's BIOS-based setup program. While we don't recommend that you modify the system settings on your lab computer, if you find that you cannot boot from the Windows XP CD, ask your instructor to help you configure the PC to boot from a CD.

In the unlikely event that your lab computer can't be made to boot from CD, you can create a set of six (yes, six!) Windows XP setup boot disks using a program downloaded from Microsoft's web site.

> If you need to create the setup boot disks, connect to `www.support.microsoft.com/winxp` and search on "310994." This is the number of an article that explains how to create the disks and provides links for several versions of the program to create them.

Registration vs. Activation

In one of the final steps during setup, you will be prompted to register your product and to activate it. Many people confuse activation with registration. These are two separate operations. Registration is informing Microsoft who the official owner or user of the product is and providing contact information such as name, address, company, phone number, e-mail address, and so on, about them. Registration is still entirely optional. **Activation** is a new method designed to combat software piracy, meaning that Microsoft wishes to ensure that each license for Windows XP is used solely on a single computer. It's also more formally called **Microsoft Product Activation (MPA)**. Learn more about activation so that you won't be misinformed.

Mandatory Activation Within 30 Days of Installation Activation is mandatory, but you may skip this step during installation. You will have 30 days in

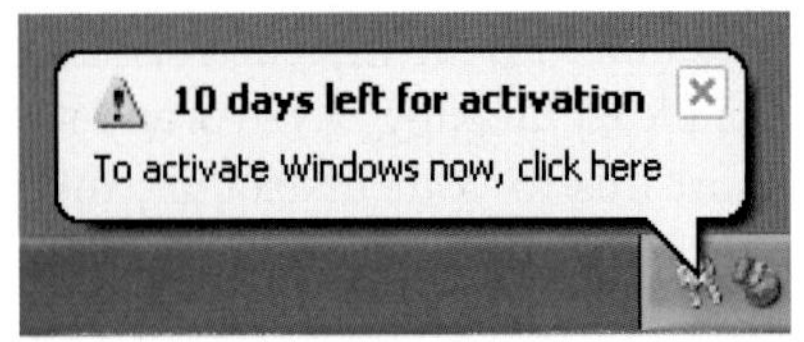

• The reminder balloon message to activate Windows XP

which to activate the product, during which time it will work normally. If you don't activate it within that time frame, it will automatically be disabled at the end of the 30 days. Don't worry about forgetting, because once it's installed, Windows XP frequently reminds you to activate it with a balloon message over the tray area of the taskbar. The messages even tell you how many days you have left.

It is important to understand activation, because Windows XP Professional is not the only Microsoft product requiring activation, and Microsoft is not the only software vendor using an activation process.

Activation Mechanics Here is how product activation of Windows XP works. When you choose to activate, either during setup or later when Windows XP reminds you to do it, the product ID, which is generated from the product key code that you entered during installation, is combined with a 50-digit value that identifies your key hardware components to create an installation ID code. This code must be sent to Microsoft, either automatically if you have an Internet connection, or verbally via a phone call to Microsoft. Microsoft then returns a 42-digit product activation code. If you are doing this online, you do not have to enter any codes; it is automatic and very fast. If you are activating over the phone, you must read the installation ID to a representative and enter the resulting 42-digit activation code into the Activate Windows By Phone dialog box.

If you must activate Windows XP by phone, be sure you are sitting at your computer. Our experience is that you have to do all this in real time, entering the code while it is being dictated by the representative; you cannot write the number down and use it later. Your experience may be different than ours.

Microsoft Product Activation does not scan the contents of the hard disk, search for personal information, or gather information on the make, model, or manufacturer of the computer or its components. No personal information about you is sent as part of the activation process. Figure 5-6 shows the dialog box that will open when you start activation by clicking on the reminder message balloon.

Reactivation The hardware identifier that is used during activation is referred to as the "hardware hash" because it is generated by applying a special mathematical algorithm to values assigned to the following hardware:

- Display adapter
- SCSI adapter
- IDE adapter
- Network adapter media access control address
- RAM amount range (for example, 0–64MB or 64–128MB)
- Processor type
- Processor serial number
- Hard disk device
- Hard disk volume serial number
- CD-ROM/CD-RW/DVD-ROM drive

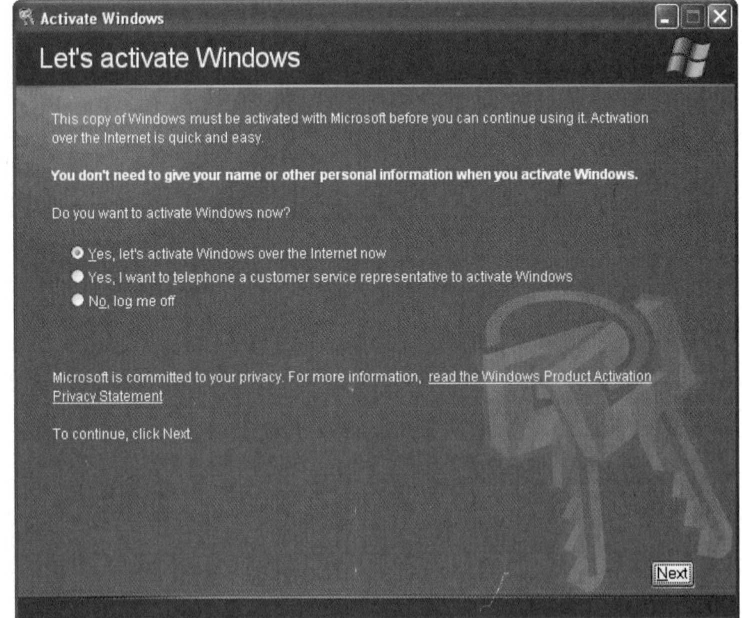

• **Figure 5-6.** Activation will take just seconds with an Internet connection.

MPA will occasionally recalculate the hardware hash, and compare it to the one created during activation. When it detects a significant difference in the hardware hash, you will be required to reactivate, and may be asked to call and confirm the reason for the reactivation. Adding new hardware, such as disk drives, will not require reactivation, but replacing components in the preceding list, or repartitioning and reformatting a drive, will affect the hardware hash. We have had to reactivate after making a great many changes to a computer, and again when we decommissioned a computer and installed Windows XP on a different computer.

Learn more about Microsoft Product Activation (MPA) by connecting to `www.support.microsoft.com` and searching on "activation." You will find articles on activation for Windows XP and other Microsoft products. Notice that software purchased with a volume license agreement does not require product activation.

Getting Down to the Business of Installing Windows XP Professional

So you've convinced yourself that it's time to install Windows XP. Any apprehension you may have about the process should be thrown out the window. Installing Windows XP is simple. The Windows Setup wizard will guide you through every step of the process. The onscreen directions are correct and clear, and you will need to make very few decisions. If you are in doubt about a setting, pressing ENTER will likely perform the correct action by selecting a default setting.

Overall, the installation process takes about an hour. Most of that time will be spent watching the screen. Feel free to walk away as the installation is taking place. If input is needed, the installation program will stop and wait until you click the correct buttons.

If you are not available to respond to a prompt on the screen during installation, it will only delay completion. Microsoft has greatly improved the installation process over that of Windows NT and Windows 2000. Those installations required input from you fairly frequently across the entire process. The installation process for Windows XP only requires input from you at the very beginning and at the very end.

Step-by-Step 5.02

Installing Windows XP Professional

In this step-by-step, you will do a clean installation of Windows XP Professional. To complete this exercise, you will need the following:

- A Microsoft/Intel standard personal computer (desktop or laptop) compatible with Windows XP Professional, with at least the minimum hardware and configured to boot from CD
- An unpartitioned hard disk (disk 0, the first hard disk)
- The Windows XP Professional CD
- The Product ID code from the envelope or jewel case of your Windows XP Professional CD (The Product ID code used to be called the CD key.)
- A 15-character (or less) name, unique on your network, for your computer
- The name of the workgroup to be used in the class lab
- A password for the Administrator account on your computer
- The IP address, subnet mask, and other necessary TCP/IP configuration information, or confirmation from your instructor that you should configure Windows XP Professional to get an IP address automatically

Step 1

Insert the Windows XP CD and boot the computer. After inspecting your hardware configuration, Windows XP Professional Setup will show the blue screen of character mode setup and copy files to your computer. After the files are copied, you will be prompted to remove the CD and reboot the system. Windows Setup will start, load system devices, and display the Welcome To Setup screen. Press ENTER to start the installation.

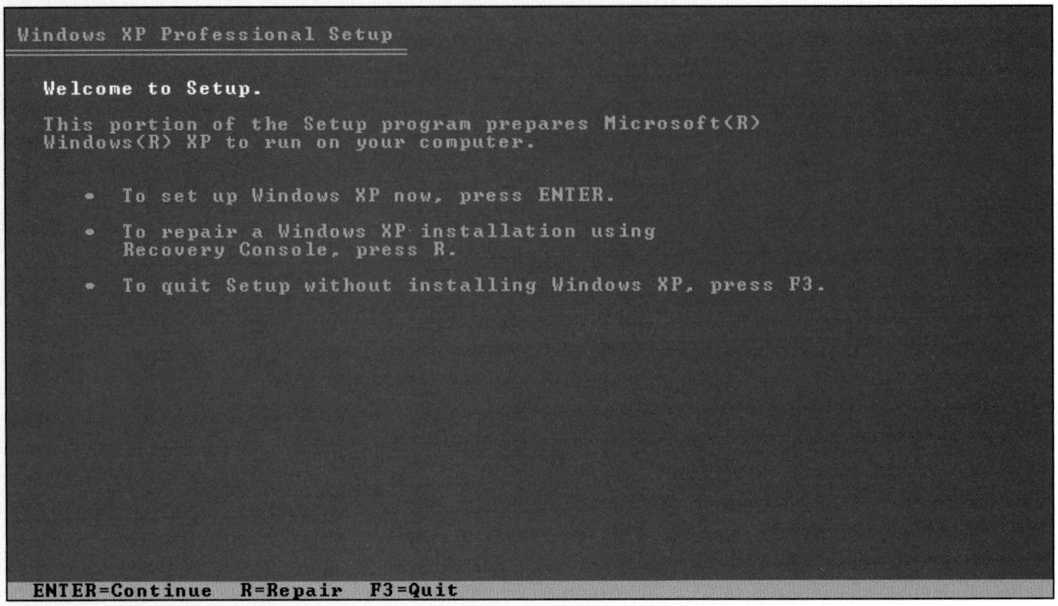

```
Windows XP Professional Setup

  Welcome to Setup.

  This portion of the Setup program prepares Microsoft(R)
  Windows(R) XP to run on your computer.

     •  To set up Windows XP now, press ENTER.

     •  To repair a Windows XP installation using
        Recovery Console, press R.

     •  To quit Setup without installing Windows XP, press F3.

 ENTER=Continue   R=Repair   F3=Quit
```

Step 2

The End User License Agreement (EULA) appears. This is your agreement to comply with your license to use Windows XP Professional. Basically, you are allowed to install Windows XP Professional on one computer for each license that you own. Read the EULA; press F8 to acknowledge acceptance of the agreement and to continue.

Step 3

If your hard disk is unpartitioned, you will need to create a new partition by ensuring that the highlight is on "Unpartitioned space," and then pressing C to create a partition in the unpartitioned space. On the following screen, you can either accept the default size for the partition, or enter a smaller value in the highlighted box. In our example, we wanted a 2,048MB partition and had to first use the BACKSPACE key to overwrite the default value and enter 2048.

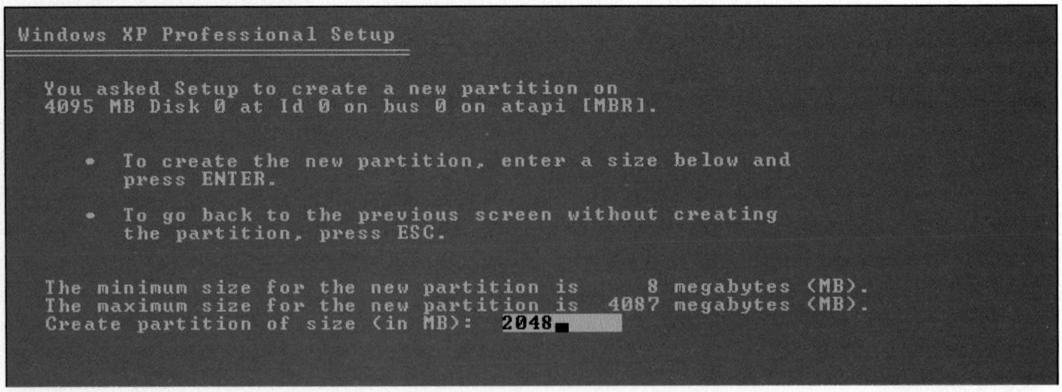

```
Windows XP Professional Setup

  You asked Setup to create a new partition on
  4095 MB Disk 0 at Id 0 on bus 0 on atapi [MBR].

     •  To create the new partition, enter a size below and
        press ENTER.

     •  To go back to the previous screen without creating
        the partition, press ESC.

  The minimum size for the new partition is     8 megabytes (MB).
  The maximum size for the new partition is  4087 megabytes (MB).
  Create partition of size (in MB):  2048
```

Step 4

The next screen is similar to the one in which you first chose to partition the hard disks, only now you'll select the new partition and press ENTER to install Windows XP on that partition. Then, you need to decide on the file system format for the new partition. Select

Format The Partition Using The NTFS File System and then press ENTER. The screen will show a progress bar while the partition is being formatted.

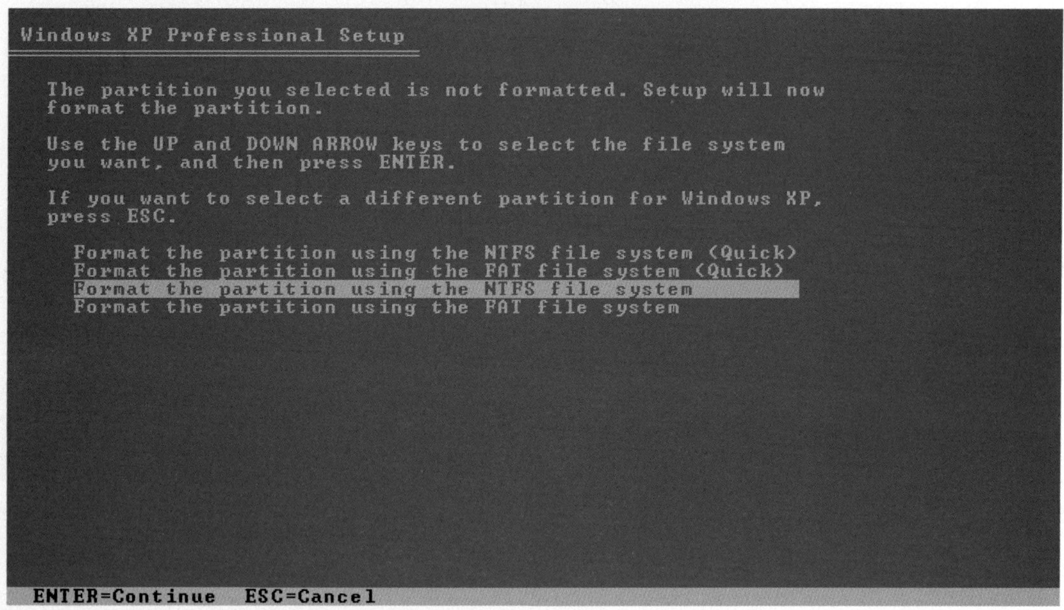

Step 5

Next, setup copies files to the newly formatted partition, displaying another progress bar. On a clean installation, setup creates a folder named Windows in C:\ into which it installs the OS, creating appropriate subfolders below this folder. After it completes copying the base set of files to this location, your computer reboots, and the graphical mode of Windows XP setup begins. On the left of the screen, uncompleted tasks have a white button, completed tasks have a green button, and the current task has a red button.

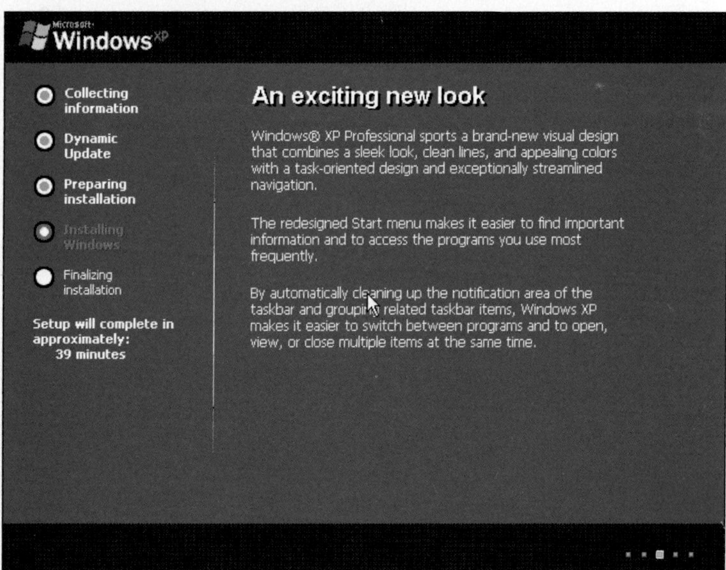

Step 6

On the Regional And Language Options screen, leave the defaults and click Next, unless told otherwise by your instructor. On the Personalize Your Software page, enter your name and the name of your school or employer. Next, you must enter a valid product key for Windows XP. This can be found on the CD case containing your copy of Windows XP. Be sure to enter it exactly, or you will be unable to continue.

Step 7

Next, you need to name your computer, which identifies your computer on a network. Check with your instructor or network administrator for an appropriate name. In addition to a valid name for your computer, you need to create a password for the Administrator user account. This will be the password that allows you to modify and fix the computer. Next, set the date, time, and time zone.

Step 8

If a network card was detected, the network components will be installed, and you'll have an opportunity to configure the network settings. On the Network Settings page, select Typical Settings, unless told otherwise by your instructor. Once the networking elements are installed, you need to configure the network. Relax, Windows Setup will do most of the work for you. Unless you have specific instructions from your instructor or network administrator, the default settings are the preferred choices.

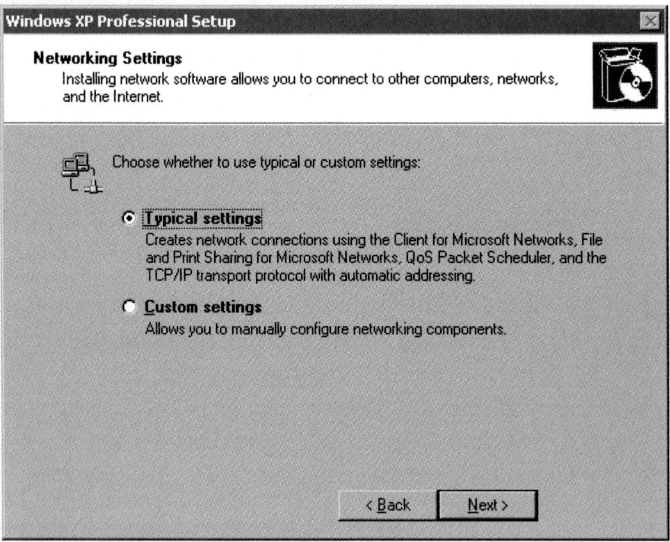

Step 9

If your computer participates in a domain-based network, you need to set the domain options. The computer shown here is on a network without a domain, and we have supplied a workgroup name. Enter the workgroup name provided by your instructor, and click Next. Be prepared to wait for several minutes while Windows Setup copies files.

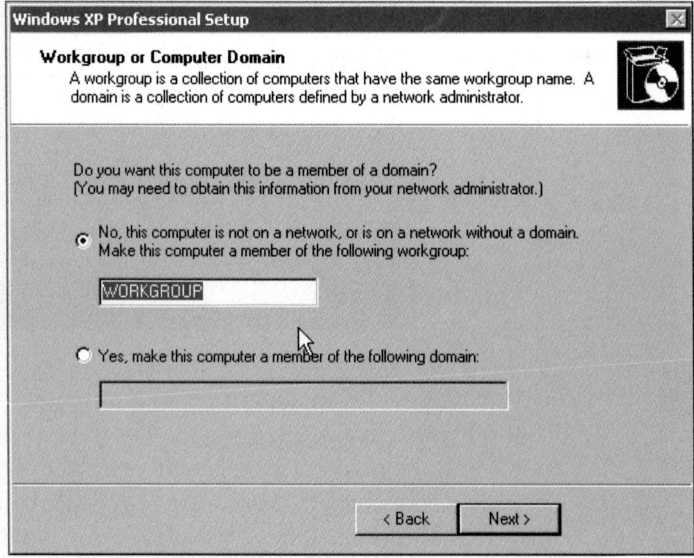

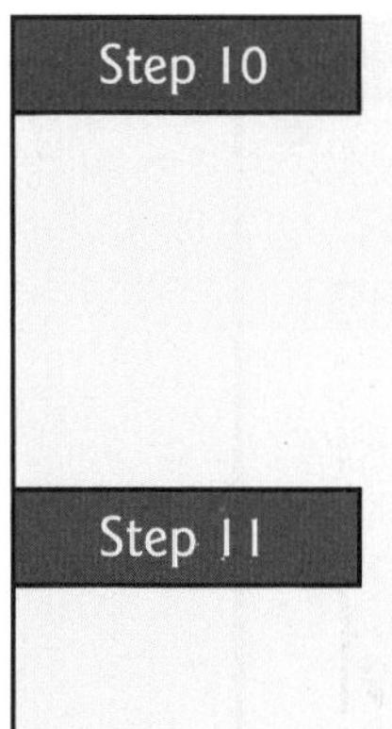

After the files required for the final configuration are copied, Windows XP will reboot. During this reboot, Windows XP determines your screen size and applies the appropriate resolution. This reboot can take several minutes to complete, so be patient. Once the reboot is complete, you must log on as the Administrator. There may be balloon messages over the tray area of the taskbar. A common message concerns the display resolution. Click the balloon and allow Windows XP to automatically adjust the display settings.

Another message reminds you that you have 30 days left for activation. We suggest that when you do a single install, you test it for a few days before activating it, in case you need to make any significant changes in the hardware. It might appear to the activation program that you have installed on a different computer or made sufficient changes to a computer after product activation to require reactivation. Delaying activation also allows time to work out any problems with network connectivity. If you are not choosing to activate at this time, click on the close button of the message balloon. Congratulations! You have completed the Windows XP installation and should have a desktop with the default Bliss background.

Performing Post-Installation Tasks

After Windows XP is installed, you have a few necessary post-installation tasks. They include verifying network access (assuming you are connected to a network) and installing updates. These tasks should be completed before moving on to customizing the desktop for yourself or another user and performing other desktop management tasks.

Verify Network Access

Once you have completed the installation, if the computer is connected to a network, verify that it can communicate with other computers on the network. Use My Network Places as you did in Chapter 4, and see if you can see any computers on the network besides your own. The only catch is that My Network Places is not where it used to be! You'll find it in My Computer, which is on the Start menu. Once you open My Network Places, click on View Workgroup Computers, a link in the task pane on the left. This will show all the computers in the workgroup or domain in which your computer resides (recall the workgroup or domain setting from the installation). In Figure 5-7 you can see just one computer, Webster01, in the workgroup. If you also used a workgroup name that was different from that chosen by your fellow students, your computer may also be alone like Webster01 is.

• **Figure 5-7.** Osborne workgroup with one computer showing

This is the computer on which we installed Windows XP during Step-by-Step 5.02. To see other workgroups and domains, find and click the link labeled "Microsoft Windows Network" in the task pane under Other Places. (This link is not visible in Figure 5-7; it can be found using the scroll bar). Figure 5-8 shows three workgroups or computers:

My Network Places refers to all groupings of computers as workgroups, even though in Figure 5-8, Htc is a domain, and the others are workgroups.

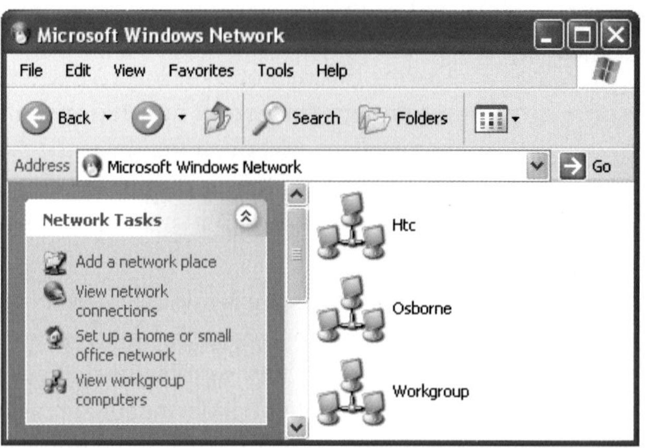

• **Figure 5-8.** Microsoft Windows Network with three workgroups or domains showing

> **Try This!**
>
> **Check Out Your Neighborhood**
>
> If your Windows XP computer is connected to a network, verify that you can see other computers on the network. Remember that only computers with the Server service turned on are visible. This is turned on by default during Windows XP installation, so you should see your computer and others on the network. Try this:
>
> 1. Select Start | My Computer. In My Computer, under Other Places, select My Network Places. If any folders have been shared on your network, you may see them in this view. If you see folders, you have verified network connectivity.
> 2. Under Network Tasks (in the task pane), select View Workgroup Computers. You should, at minimum, see your computer in the workgroup you specified during installation (see title bar).
> 3. Under Other Places, select Microsoft Network to see other workgroups on your network. When you have finished, close all open windows.

Htc, Osborne, and Workgroup. Just seeing other workgroups and domains on the network is confirmation that a network connection is working, because you must be connected and communicating on a network to be aware of the other workgroups, domains, and computers. However, if you are eager to see other computers, open one of these workgroups or domains.

Install Updates

Now that you have verified network access, your next task should be to install updates. This is important, especially if you are on a network and/or the Internet, because many of the updates are to close security holes that are most likely to be exploited over a network. How you actually obtain updates will depend on the organization (school or business) where you install Windows XP. In some organizations, the IT department may distribute updates intended for new installations on CD so that they can be installed before a computer is even connected to a network. Other organizations may make them available on a shared folder on the network. If you have an Internet connection, you can connect to the Microsoft web site and download them for free.

Updates can bring their own problems. Therefore, at school or at work, do not install updates unless directed to do so by your instructor or an administrator. Before applying an update to a PC at home, be sure to read all the information provided by Microsoft, and do some additional research to determine if there are any incompatibilities between your computer or applications and the new update.

If you're permitted to get the very latest from the Windows Update site and you have Internet access from your computer, you can use the Windows Update program from the Control Panel, which is accessed from the Start menu.

Step-by-Step 5.03

Installing Updates

In this step-by-step exercise, you will use Windows Update to connect to the Microsoft Update site; test your computer for installed components, updates, and service packs; and install the recommended updates and service packs. To complete this exercise, you will need the following:

- A PC with Windows XP Professional installed as described in Step-by-Step 5.02
- Internet access (confirm that you can access the Internet using Internet Explorer)
- A user name and password for an account that is a member of the Administrators group

Step 1

Log on as Administrator and then select Start | Control Panel. Then click Windows Update. Internet Explorer will connect to the Windows Update web page, and you will see a message asking if you want to install the latest version of Windows Update. Click Yes, and follow instructions to install any further updates to the Windows Update program.

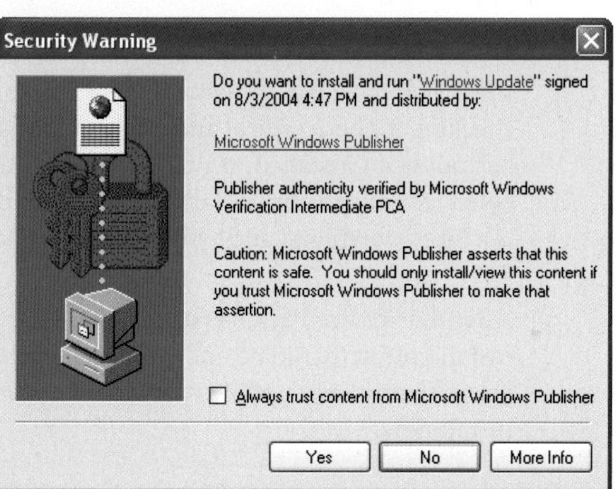

Step 2

After installing the latest updates to Windows Update, the Welcome page will be displayed. Click Express Install to start a quick scan of your computer that will determine what high priority updates should be installed. There will be a delay while it scans and looks for available updates. Then the Express Updates page will display the list of high priority updates Microsoft recommends for your computer. Click Install to proceed.

Step 3

Read and accept any End User License Agreements (EULAs). The updates will be downloaded and installed. After the critical updates have been installed, allow the computer to be restarted.

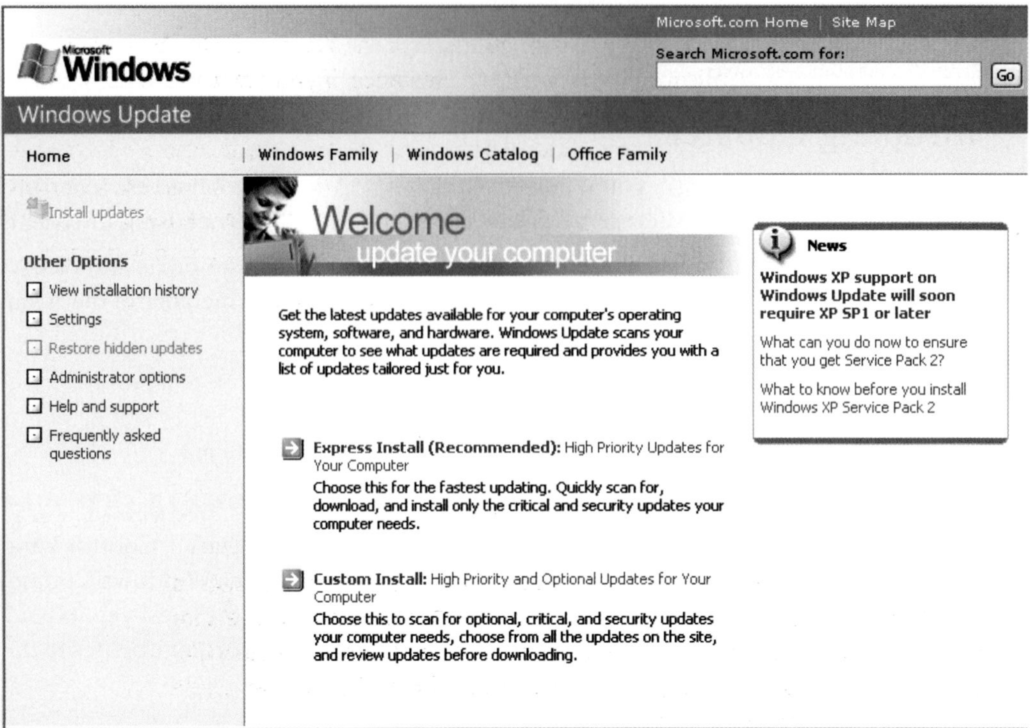

Step 4

Once Windows has restarted, use the Windows Update program to reconnect to the web site. Click the Custom Install button and another scan will be made of your computer, checking for both critical and optional updates. If Windows XP Service Pack 2 (or newer) has not been installed, it will be listed in the results, in which case, click the button labeled Download and Install Now. Accept the EULA, and it will proceed. A service pack is a large download and will require a restart.

Step 5

After the Service Pack has been installed, run Windows Update again, click the Custom Install button to initiate another scan. At the conclusion of this scan, review the updates listed, remove any updates you don't wish to install at this time, and click Download and Install now.

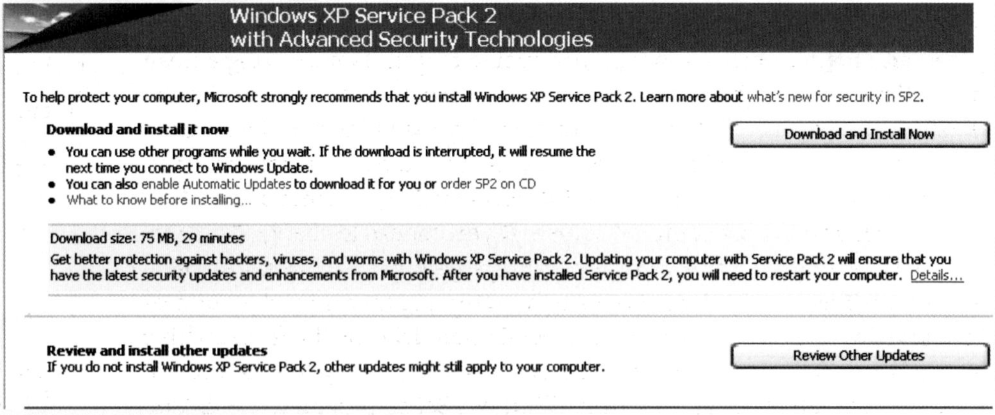

Step 6

After you have installed all of the Windows Updates, look for any updates for your applications programs. For instance, if you are using Microsoft Office, you can select Office Family from the Windows Update site and go through a process similar to that for installing the Windows Updates. If you have applications from other companies, check out their web sites for updates. We realize that you probably have not installed any other software yet, but include this step for future reference, because you will need to do this on any computer on which you have installed applications.

Customize and Manage Windows XP Professional

Once you have installed Windows XP Professional, configured the OS to work with your network, and installed recommended updates and service packs, it's time to customize Windows for the user. In the case of a new OS, the first few times you do this, you will need to find familiar tools and perhaps learn how to use new ones.

In this section, you will practice some of the common procedures for customizing and managing Windows XP, creating a new partition, installing and removing applications and Windows components, and preparing the desktop for users, including modifications to display settings and adding a printer.

Creating New Partitions in Windows XP

With the very large hard disks, often over 100GB, that come standard in desktop computers, we prefer a strategy of dividing the hard disk space into two (or more) partitions. This allows the operating system and applications installed into the operating system to "own" the system partition, the partition on which the OS is installed. This also provides a distinct drive or drives that can be devoted purely to data. They are therefore easier to back up. To that end, we plan for our disk space needs ahead of time, deciding on the portion of the hard disk that should be devoted to the OS and other programs, and the portion that should be devoted to data. Next, during a clean installation of an OS, we create a system partition of the size planned. Immediately after the installation, we perform the essential post-installation tasks. Then, before installing new applications, we create the new partition or partitions. This order is important if you install applications from CD-ROM, which is the most common source. If you choose to change the drive letter of the CD-ROM drive, as shown in Step-by-Step 5.04, this is best done before installing applications, because the setup programs for the applications usually remember the program installation drive as the former drive letter of the CD-ROM drive. Anytime you want to modify the application using its installation program, or the Windows Setup program, it will look for application components at the original location. If you change the drive letter of the CD-ROM drive after installing applications from CD, you will

The partition sizes shown in the step-by-steps are not indicative of the sizes we would choose on a very large hard disk, but reflect the smaller hard disk sizes students often encounter in classroom or lab computers. On a 100GB hard disk, we might create a 20GB system partition and an 80GB data partition. The point is that for most of us, our data storage needs are going to far exceed our program storage needs.

have to manually change the drive path whenever you run an installation program that requires that remembered location. The following step-by-step will walk you through the procedure for changing drive letters, creating a new partition, renaming the new partition, and creating a restore point for these changes.

Step-by-Step 5.04

Creating a New Partition After Installation

In this exercise, you will create a new partition on your hard disk. It is assumed that the disk type has not been changed from basic since installing Windows XP Professional in Step-by-Step 5.02.

To complete this exercise, you will need the following:

- The computer on which you successfully installed Windows in Step-by-Step 5.02
- Unpartitioned hard disk space
- A user name and password for an account that is a member of the Administrators group

Step 1

Log on as an Administrator, open the Start menu, right-click My Computer, and select Manage from the context menu. This will open the Computer Management console. This console can also be opened from Start | Control Panel | Administrative Tools.

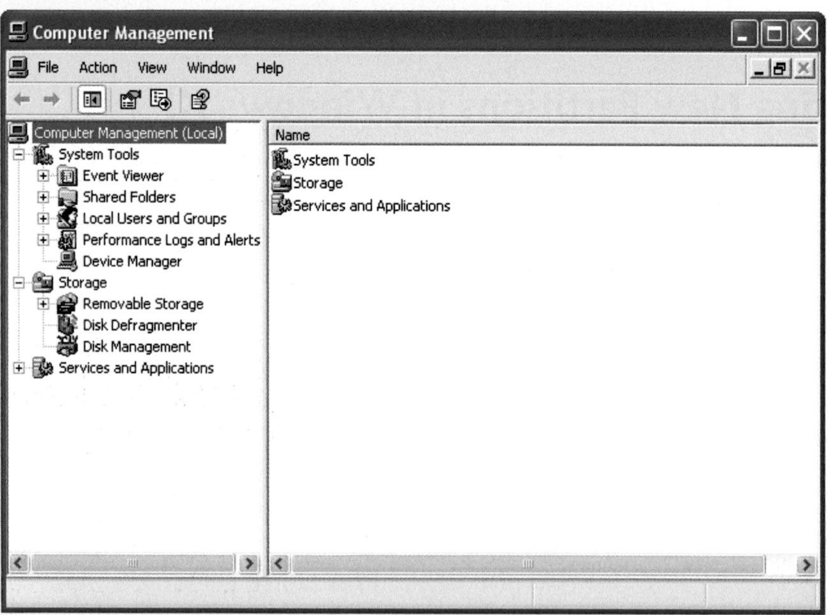

Step 2

In Computer Management, click the Disk Management folder under the Storage node. After a brief delay, the Disk Management snap-in will appear in the right pane of the console. If you installed Windows XP according to the instructions in Step-by-Step 5.02, drive C: is a primary partition with the NTFS file system. Drive letters are assigned to hard disk drives first and then to laser disc drives. If there is unallocated space remaining on the hard disk, you will see an area labeled "Unallocated" with the amount of space.

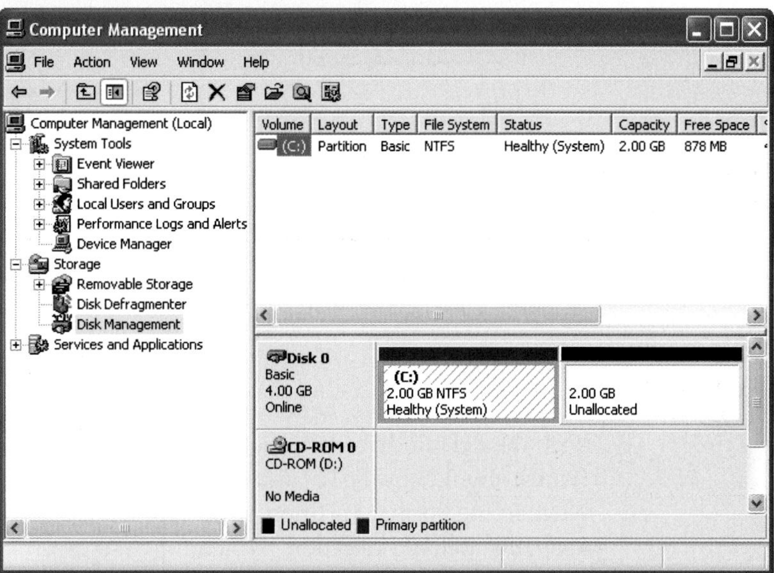

Step 3

Before creating the new partition on the hard disk, change the drive letter of the CD-ROM drive: Right-click on the area labeled "CD-ROM 0," and select Change Drive Letter And Paths from the menu. In the Change Drive Letter And Paths dialog box, select the Change button and then choose a new drive letter for the CD-ROM drive. Click OK, then click Yes in the Confirm box, and keep the Computer Management console open to Disk Management.

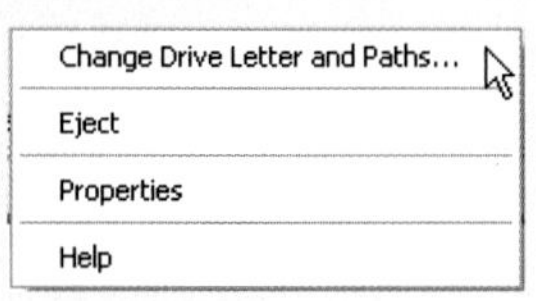

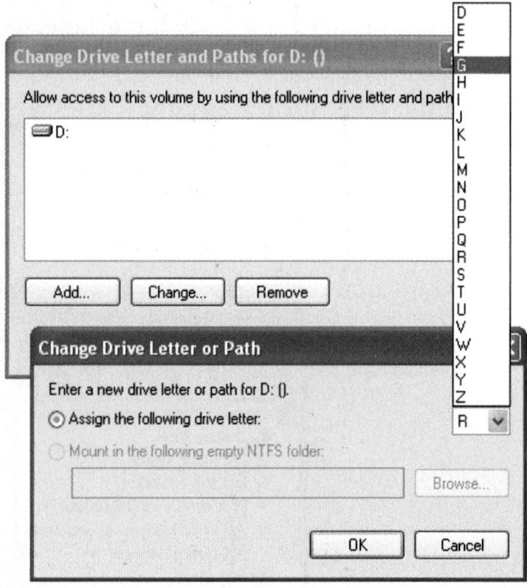

Step 4

Right-click in the box labeled "Unallocated," and click New Partition to launch the New Partition wizard. In the Welcome page of the New Partition wizard, select the Next button. In the Select Partition Type page, select Primary Partition and click Next. In the Specify Partition Size page, select a partition size that is at least 1MB smaller than the maximum space. Then click Next.

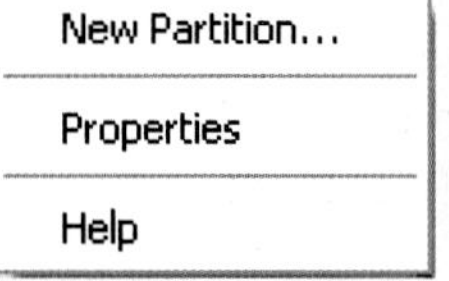

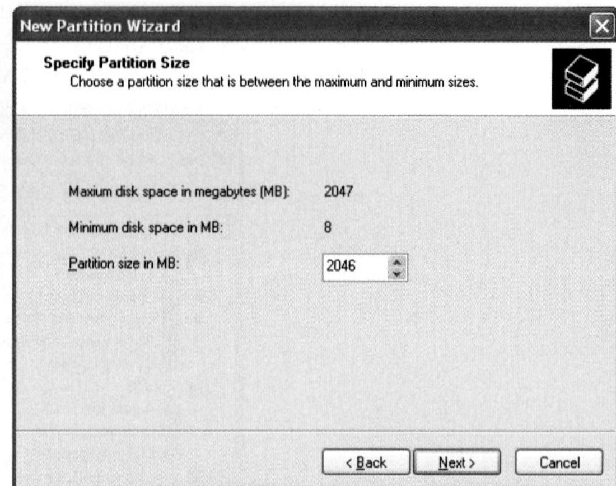

Step 5

In the Assign Drive Letter page, keep the default drive letter setting (which should now be D:) and click Next. In the Format Partition page, keep the default selection, which will format the drive with NTFS (actually NTFS5), using the Default allocation size (Don't mess with this!), and will name (label) the volume New Volume. Click Next.

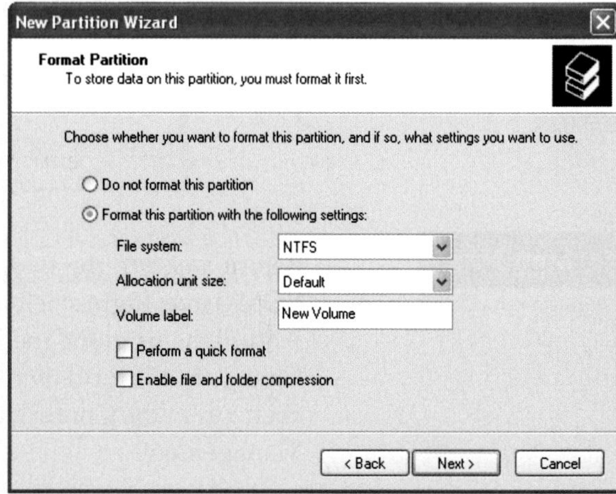

Step 6

The Completing The New Partition Wizard page displays a summary of the settings you have selected. Review these settings. If you wish to change any of the settings, use the Back button to find the page for the setting. Otherwise, click Finish to complete the partitioning. If you watch Disk Management carefully, you will see the Unallocated space change to a partition, then the formatting progress will be displayed, and finally it will be shown as a Healthy volume. Leave the Computer Management console open to Disk Management.

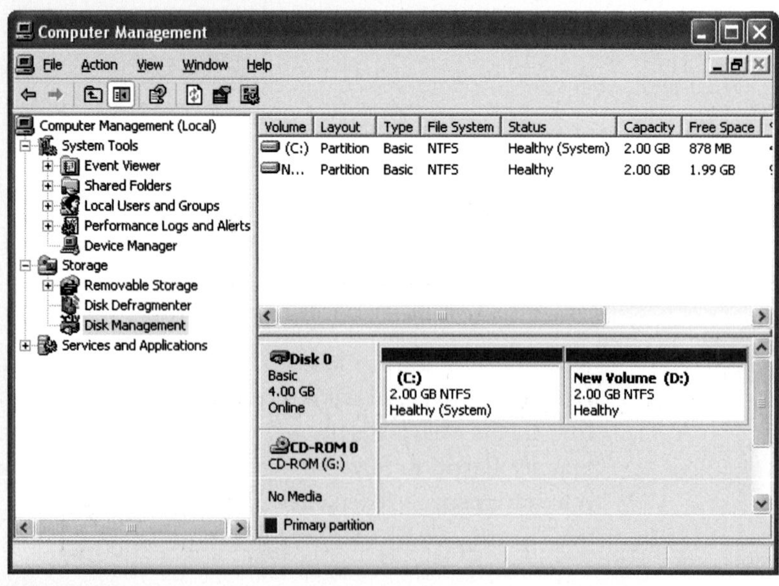

Step 7

Learn more about your new volume, and give it a new label (name). In Disk Management, right-click on the new volume, and select Properties from the context menu. On the General page, notice the amount of disk space shown as used. This is the amount used by the NTFS file system before any files or folders are created—space that is referred to as overhead. This space varies somewhat by drive size, but the large amount used explains why Windows cannot format a diskette with NTFS (any version). On the General page, you will see that the new volume was given the label "New Volume," which is not very descriptive. Rename it now by clicking in the label box and typing **Data** as the new name. Finally, click OK. Close Computer Management.

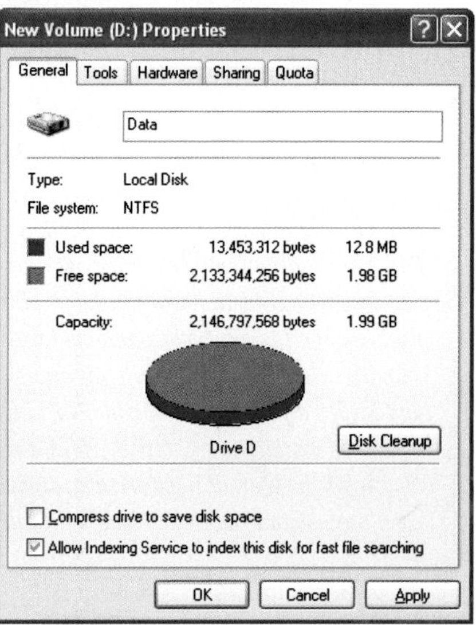

Step 8

Now create a system restore point that will include the new drive letters and the new volume label. Select Start | All Programs | Accessories | System Tools | System Restore. On the Welcome To System Restore page, select Create A Restore Point, and click Next. On the Create A Restore Point page, enter a descriptive name for this restore point, such as **Name for partition and new drive letters**. Click Create and then click Close on the Restore Point Created page to close the System Restore program.

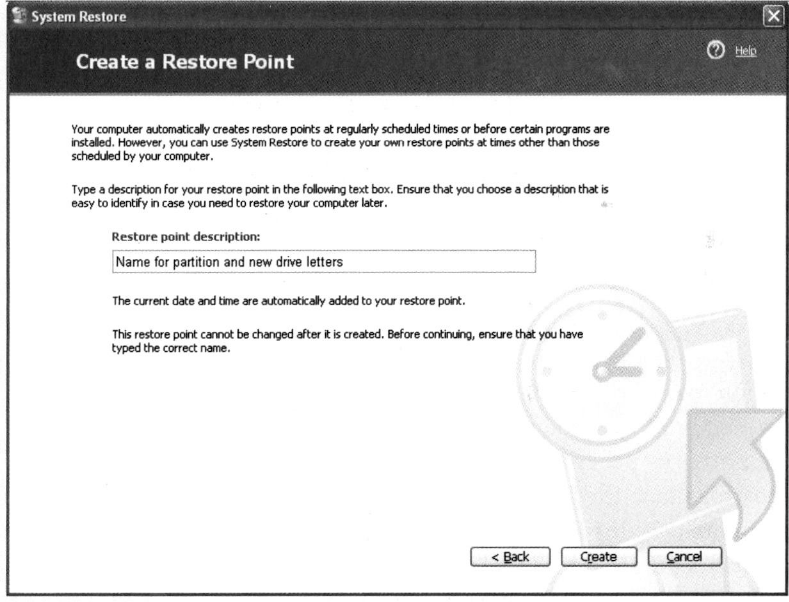

Installing and Removing Applications in Windows XP

For most people, a computer in itself is not important; it's the work (or play) that we can accomplish with the computer that is important. Therefore,

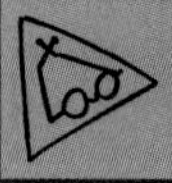

Inside Information

InstallShield

No matter what type of application program you install, if it needs to make changes to Windows, it probably uses a special installation program that runs as a wizard. That program is very often ***InstallShield****, from InstallShield Software Corporation, which was recently purchased by Macrovision Corporation. While the InstallShield Software Corporation may cease to exist after the recent purchase by Macrovision, we expect the InstallShield name for the products to be retained. Software companies purchase the InstallShield products for creating installations for Windows because InstallShield enables their programmers to create installation programs that work in a standardized fashion. The InstallShield Company specializes in the intricacies of Windows installations, so that programmers in thousands of companies don't have to. Watch for the InstallShield wizard, and/or go to* `www.installshield.com` *to learn more about the InstallShield products.*

Inside Information

Not Just for Windows!

InstallShield claims to be the complete installation-authoring solution for any platform, and they currently run a ticker-tape-like banner on their web site (`www.installshield.com`*) that lists Linux, Windows, Mac OS X, AIX, Solaris, HP-UZ, OS/400, and other operating systems.*

Windows XP is no more than a pretty face until you install the applications that will enable the user to do the desired tasks. Installing an application in Windows XP is very much like installing one in Windows 2000 or Windows 98, but you should always practice common tasks in a new OS. In this section, we look briefly at how you install and remove application programs in Windows XP.

Windows XP, like its immediate predecessors, allows you to add programs through a Control Panel applet, now revamped and slightly renamed as Add Or Remove Programs. As with its predecessors, you will rarely need to use this option, as setup programs often start as soon as you insert the CD (if Autorun is enabled, which it is by default). But if this is not the case, use the Add New Program button in Add Or Remove Programs, and it will search for the setup program.

Step-by-Step 5.05

Installing an Application in Windows XP

In this step-by-step, you will practice installing an application into Windows XP. The application we have chosen is a free 30-day evaluation copy of a popular antivirus program, PC-cillin by Trend Micro, available on the Internet. Since web pages change frequently, the following steps may not exactly match the steps you will need to take when you access the Trend Micro web site. You may also choose to install a different application, in which case, the steps will only generally apply.

To complete this step-by-step, you will need the following:

- The computer on which you successfully installed Windows XP Professional in Step-by-Step 5.02
- Fast Internet access (A 56K modem connection will take hours to download the file)
- A user name and password for an account that is a member of the Administrators group

Step 1

Log on as an Administrator. Use Internet Explorer to connect to `www.trendmicro.com`. Click on Personal to find the antivirus software appropriate for a single user. Click Try Now under the latest version of PC-cillin (PC-cillin Internet Security 2004 at this time). This will take you to the Update Center page. Select the link for the Trial Download only (at this time the link has the name of the file).

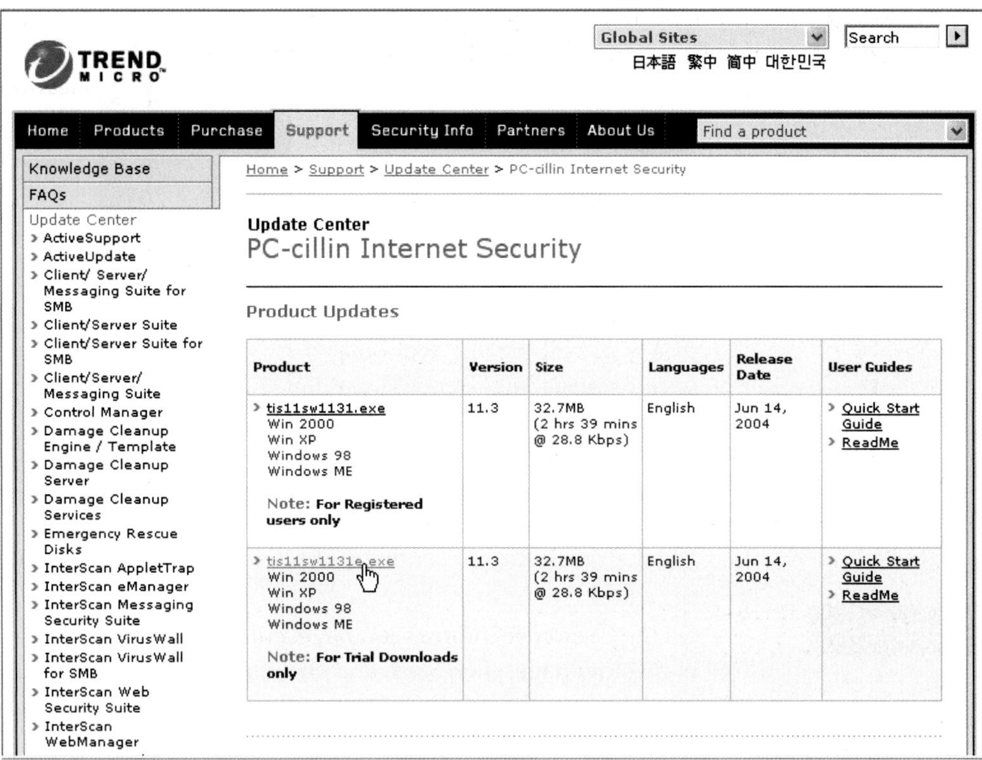

Step 2

In the File Download box, select Save. This will open the Save As dialog box. Use the drop-down text box labeled "Save in" to select the My Documents folder, and then click Save.

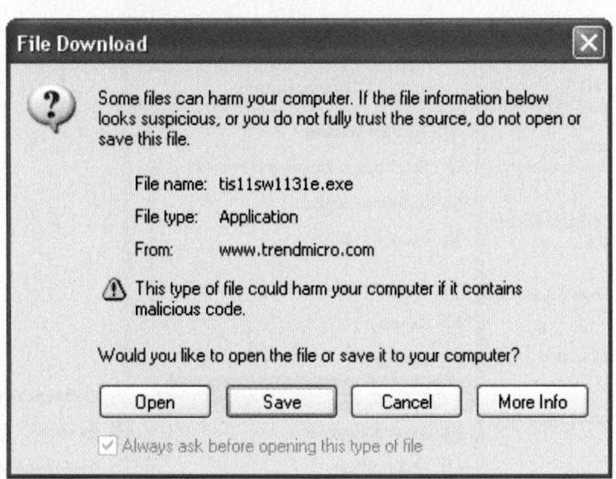

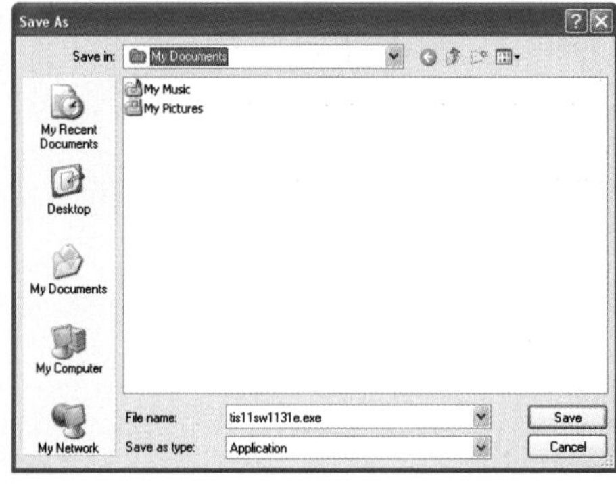

Step 3

When the download is complete, select the Open Folder button in the Download Complete dialog box. This will open the My Documents folder, the location where the file was downloaded. Double-click on the file to start the installation. The InstallShield program will run. On the Location To Save Files page, click Next to save in the default location (shown in the text box).

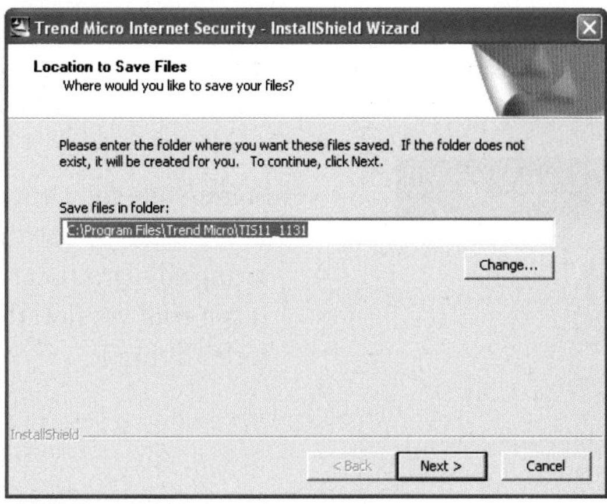

Step 4

Next, you will see the Extracting Files page, as the InstallShield wizard extracts all the individual files from the same executable file that contained the wizard. This is why the download was so huge! Once the files are extracted, the Preparing To Install page is shown briefly, and then you will see the welcome page for installing Trend Micro Internet Security. Click next and read the License Agreement page, click the radio button to accept the license agreement, and then click Next to continue. This will begin a virus scan of your computer.

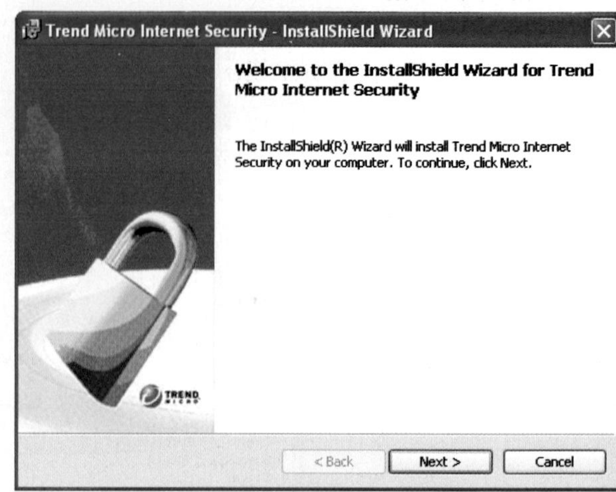

Step 5

On the Customer Information page, enter a User Name and click Next. On the Destination Folder page, click Next, and click Install on the Ready To Install The Program page. The Installing Trend Micro Internet Security page will be shown for a few minutes, and when the installation is done, close the wizard by clicking the Finish button on the InstallShield Wizard Completed page. You will find shortcuts for the program on the Start menu.

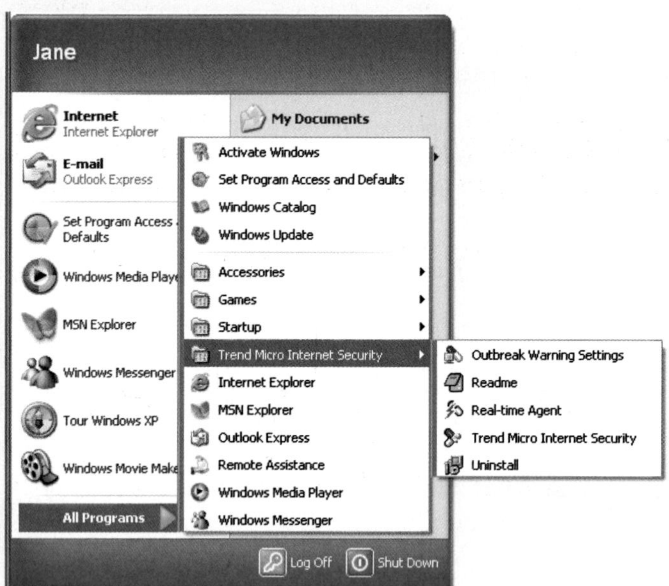

Step 6

A message may appear as a pop-up over the notification area of the taskbar. Use the close button on the message box. Registering this product requires payment, but until it is registered, it is a trial version that allows you to examine its features before buying it.

Removing Programs

The longer you have an OS installed on a user's computer, the more housekeeping it requires. One cleanup task is to remove programs that are no longer needed (or never really were). Because Windows XP requires that most software be installed by an administrator, the problem of user-installed harmful or unnecessary programs has almost disappeared, as long as users are not given access to the Administrator account or to any other that is a member of the computer's Administrators group. (Learn more about users and groups in Chapter 7.)

Even when only trained IT staff install programs, it's eventually necessary to remove some programs for a variety of reasons. Maybe an application didn't meet expectations, or it outgrew its usefulness. Computers purchased with Windows XP preinstalled often have many additional programs installed that you'll never use. These programs are taking up disk space that can be used for needed programs and data files. In Windows XP, removing programs is much like in previous versions of Windows. You can look for the application's uninstall program or use the Add Or Remove Programs applet in Control Panel (which often uses the same uninstall method as the application). Figure 5-9 shows Add Or Remove Programs on a

Try This!

Use Add or Remove Programs

Although you may not need to remove any programs just yet, familiarize yourself with the new look of the Add Or Remove Programs applet, and look at the list of currently installed programs. In addition to applications, any updates will be listed here. Try this:

1. Open the Control Panel. Select Add Or Remove Programs.
2. Browse through the list of Currently Installed Programs, expanding each one. This list may be empty if you have not updated Windows or installed any programs.
3. If you find a program that should be removed, click the Change/Remove button to begin the uninstall process. Sometimes you must provide the installation CD before the program can be removed!
4. When you have finished exploring, exit from Add Or Remove Programs. If you uninstalled an application, you may need to allow the uninstall program to restart the computer.

Never remove a program by simply deleting it from disk. Even if you succeed in removing all its files, Windows and other programs may still try to start the program, and you will be left with error messages and no easy solution to stop this from occurring.

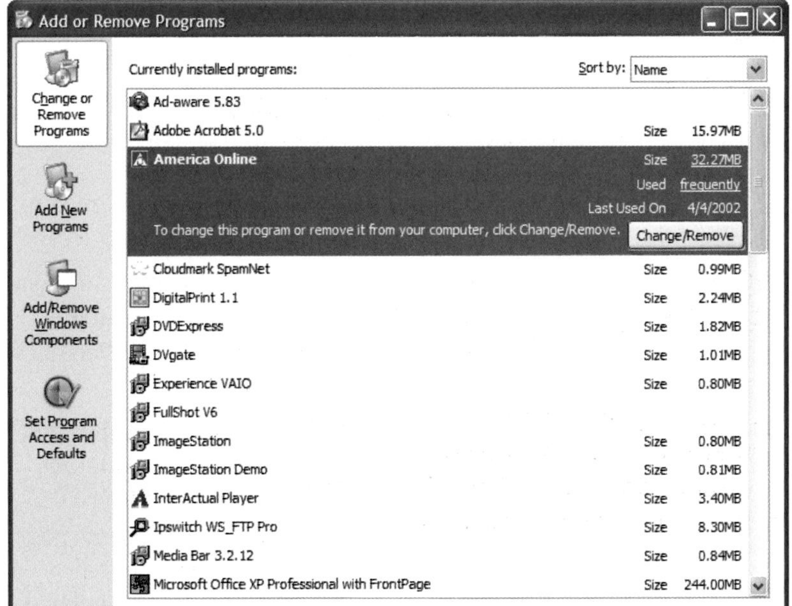

• **Figure 5-9.** Add or Remove Programs

computer with a combination of preinstalled applications and user-installed applications. When you click on a program name, the information expands and often shows you when it was last used and how frequently it's used. In this example, it shows that AOL was frequently used, when in reality we never used it!

Add or Remove Windows XP Components

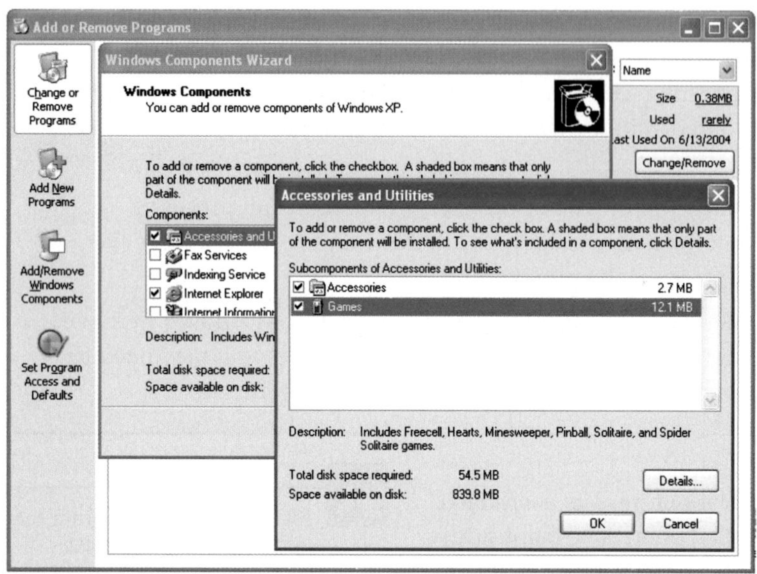

- Add or Remove Components wizard showing the details of accessories and utilities

The Windows XP Professional CD contains many Windows components beyond the basic operating system files. When you installed Windows XP Professional, the Setup program tried to guess which of these components you would need and installed Notepad, modem support, and games on your computer. These Windows components can be removed from your system if you like. Other components from the CD can be added as well. If you are adding components, you will need a copy of your Windows XP Professional CD or need another location where the Windows XP Professional source files are stored. This is a task that really hasn't changed from previous versions of Windows. The CD is not needed if you are removing components.

Try This!

Modifying Windows Components

The default installation of Windows XP Professional installs the Internet games, and many organizations don't approve of computer games at all and find that Internet games add to network traffic. Therefore, you will now remove this component from your lab computer. Try this:

1. Log on as Administrator and open the Control Panel, and run the Add Or Remove Programs applet.
2. Click the Add/Remove Windows Components button, and wait while the screen is updated. Being careful *not* to click on the check box, select the Accessories And Utilities entry. Then click the Details button.
3. Being careful *not* to click on the check box, select the Games entry and click the Details button. Click in the check box by Internet Games to remove the check mark. Click OK twice to accept the change you made and return to the Windows Components page, where you must click Next to have the changes made. The Configuring Components page will display; then click Finish in the Completing The Windows Components Wizard page.

Preparing the Desktop for Users

It can be argued that installing Windows and performing all the tasks detailed in this chapter so far come under the heading of preparing the desktop for users. Therefore, the tasks outlined here may be just the final steps before the computer is truly ready for use. In this section, you'll learn about working with the display applet to customize the desktop and about adding a local printer.

Customizing Display Settings

Microsoft and most users believe that users should control how their computer looks. The argument is that if a user has to stare at the screen for eight or more hours a day, then he or she should be able to make the desktop appealing. Therefore, a PC support person may only change a few things about the desktop before turning it over to the owner/user for customization. As in previous versions, Windows XP includes the Display applet for changing the display resolution, background picture, color themes, and the screen saver. During installation, Windows Setup usually leaves the display adapter at the lowest resolution (800×600), which most users dislike. You can use the Display applet to select a higher resolution. In a nod to the ordinary users' desire to control their desktop, you do not have to be logged on as an Administrator to make preference changes to your desktop—you only need administrator privileges to install, upgrade, or remove the driver itself, or to do just a few other advanced tasks. Therefore, the following step-by-step can be completed while logged on with an ordinary user account.

Many organizations don't like users to change their desktops, especially if they can be seen by customers. A standard look on the desktop looks more professional. It also reduces the chance that an employee may offend a customer or coworker with a poorly chosen desktop.

Step-by-Step 5.06

Using the Display Applet

In this step-by-step, you will familiarize yourself with the reorganized Display applet and make a few changes to the desktop. To complete this task, you will need the following:

- A PC with Windows XP

Step 1

A quick way to open the Display applet is to right-click on the desktop and select Properties from the context menu. In the Display applet, notice the tabs labeled "Themes," "Desktop," "Screen Saver," "Appearance," and "Settings." Explore each page, being careful not to make changes (just yet).

Step 2

Make the first change. On the Appearance page, click the Effects button. In the second drop-down list, select ClearType. This setting is especially important for displaying text on laptops and desktop computers with flat panel displays (FPDs). Then click OK just once to close the Effects box, and leave the Display Properties box open for the next step. Click the Apply button in the Appearance page. This button simply saves the changes without closing the dialog box. It ensures that if you accidentally click Cancel, the changes you have made will not be lost.

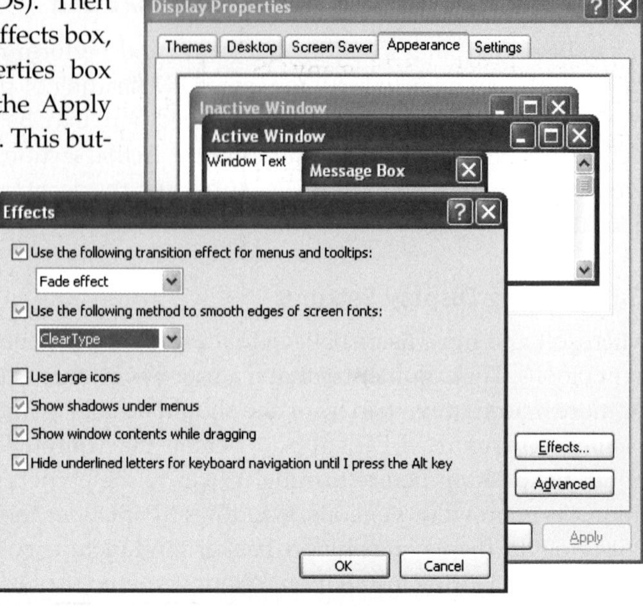

Step 3

Now move to the Settings page, where the screen resolution may be as low as 800 by 600. Move the slide toward "More" to the desired resolution (there may only be one or two places where the slide will work). Click Apply, click Yes in the Monitoring Settings dialog box (if the display looks OK), and leave the Display applet open.

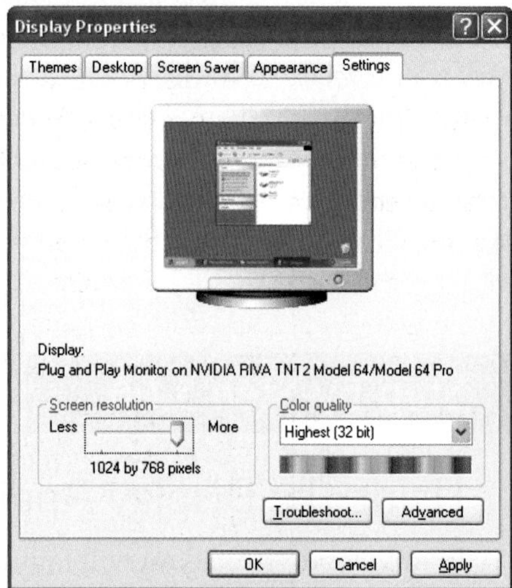

Step 4

On the Settings page, select the Advanced button. In the resulting dialog box, select the Monitor page and ensure that the screen refresh rate is in excess of 60 Hertz. If it is not, you will want to change it, or inform your instructor. When done, click OK to exit completely out of the Display Properties dialog box and to save the last changes (if any).

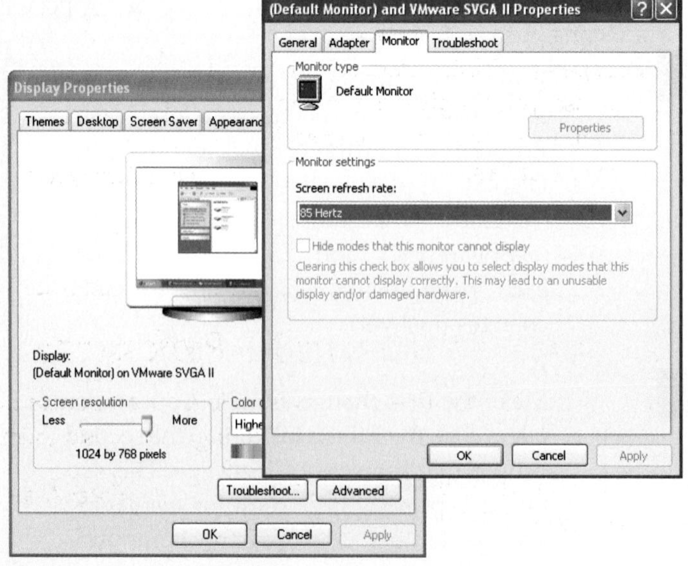

Adding a Local Printer

Another customizing task that you will do soon after installing any OS is to add a printer. This involves two parts: attaching the physical printer, and installing the correct driver into the OS—referred to by Microsoft as "creating a printer." Microsoft has made this task nearly transparent, so that in the best of circumstances you are hardly aware that much of anything happened, except that you can print to a new printer.

Because Windows XP is a plug-and-play OS, most new printers seem to install themselves, especially if the printer uses an IEEE 1394 (FireWire) or infrared port. Because they are completely plug and play, you simply connect the printer to your computer, and Windows will install the driver and configure the device for you. You should hang around, though, because you may have to insert the Windows XP CD or a disk from the printer manufacturer, if requested. You'll usually have similar success installing a plug-and-play printer connected to a parallel port. Our experience has also shown that you have the best success when installing a plug-and-play printer on a USB connection if you first run the manufacturer's installation program from the CD-ROM before connecting the printer (after reading the instructions, of course). This will prevent problems that can occur when Windows has an older driver for the printer and installs that instead of the newer one.

If you are installing a non-plug-and-play printer, you will have to use the **Add Printer wizard**, which you can start by selecting Add A Printer from the Printer Tasks list after opening Printers And Faxes on the Start menu. In this case, you simply follow the instructions on the screen. Even without a plug-and-play printer this is pretty painless.

Cross Check

Windows XP Tasks

Think back to the tasks you performed to customize and manage Windows XP, and then answer the following questions:

1. Of the following tasks, which ones will not require logging on as an Administrator: partitioning a disk, installing an application, or modifying desktop preferences?

   ____

2. You notice that you are getting low on hard disk space on a computer that came with Windows and with many applications preinstalled. Which task, practiced in this chapter, might help you free up more disk space beyond simply deleting files?

   ____

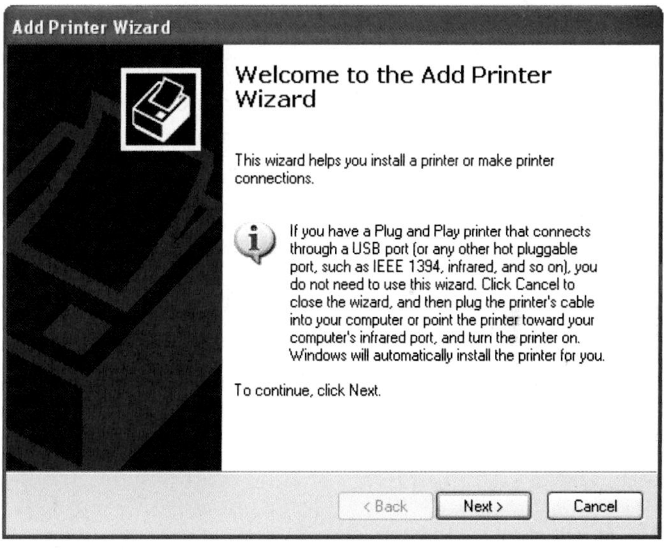

• Add Printer wizard

Step-by-Step 5.07

Adding a Printer in Windows XP Professional

Take a few minutes to add a local printer. To complete this step-by-step exercise, you will need the following:

- The computer on which you successfully installed Windows XP Professional in Step-by-Step 5.02
- A user name and password for an account that is a member of the Administrators group

Note: A physical printer is *not* required.

Step 1

Log on as an Administrator. Open the Printers folder by choosing Start | Printers And Faxes. Under Printer Tasks, select Add A Printer to open the Add Printer wizard. Click Next on the Welcome page.

Step 2

On the Local Or Network Printer page, choose Local Printer Attached To This Computer, but clear the check box by Automatically Detect And Install My Plug And Play Printer, and click Next. (You don't really have this printer connected.)

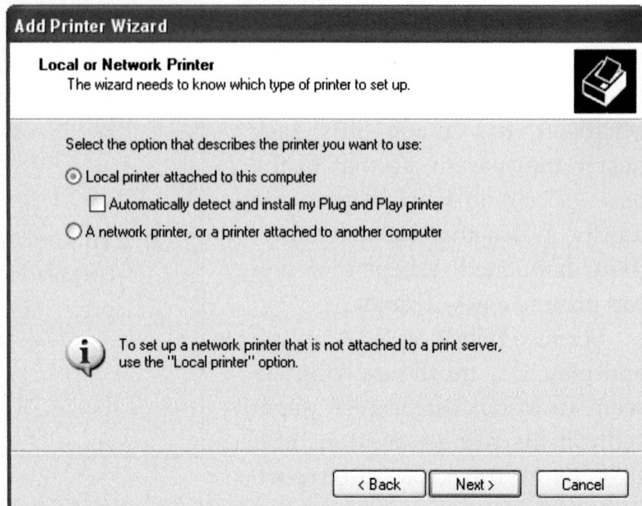

Step 3

On the Select A Printer Port page, select Use The Following Port, keep the port that is shown in the text box, and then click Next. On the next page, select HP from the list of manufacturers and HP Color LaserJet 4500 from the list of printers and then click Next. On the Name Your Printer page (no, it's not a new game), you may enter a name that is friendlier than the model name. This is not mandatory—the illustration shows the model name—but you may want to do this to identify how the printer is being used: for example, Brochure Printer or Accounting Printer.

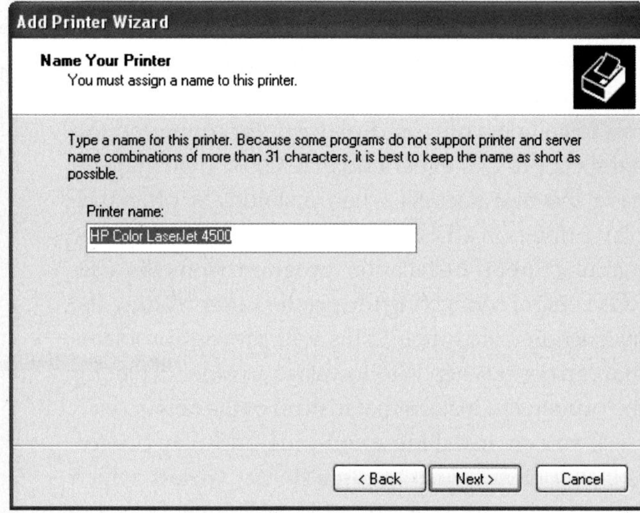

Step 4

On the Printer Sharing page, ensure that Do Not Share This Printer is selected and click Next. On the Printer Test page, select No, because you do not actually have this printer attached. Click Next, and then click Finish to complete the task and close the wizard. Verify that there is an icon for the new printer in the Printers And Faxes folder.

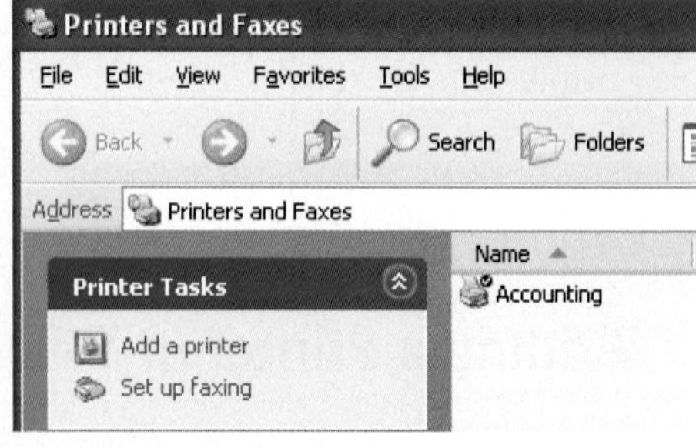

Troubleshooting Common Windows XP Problems

If life were perfect, then your computer would work all the time, with no problems. However, no matter how hard you work, your computer will find new ways to annoy you. In this section, we will review some of the new features for being prepared for problems and troubleshooting. We will introduce you to the new Windows XP Help and Support Center and to proactive tasks that can be performed with the Backup Utility and System Restore.

Where to Find Help

The Help program in Windows XP has been expanded into the **Help and Support Center**, an improvement over all the previous versions. Launch it from Start | Help And Support, and see a large menu of options for troubleshooting. From here you can invite someone to connect to your computer and remotely access your desktop to help you correct a problem (see Chapter 8). You can connect to Microsoft's support site or to a newsgroup to research a problem or to seek help and advice. We won't detail all the choices, but don't overlook this program when you need to troubleshoot, or when you simply wish to learn more about Windows.

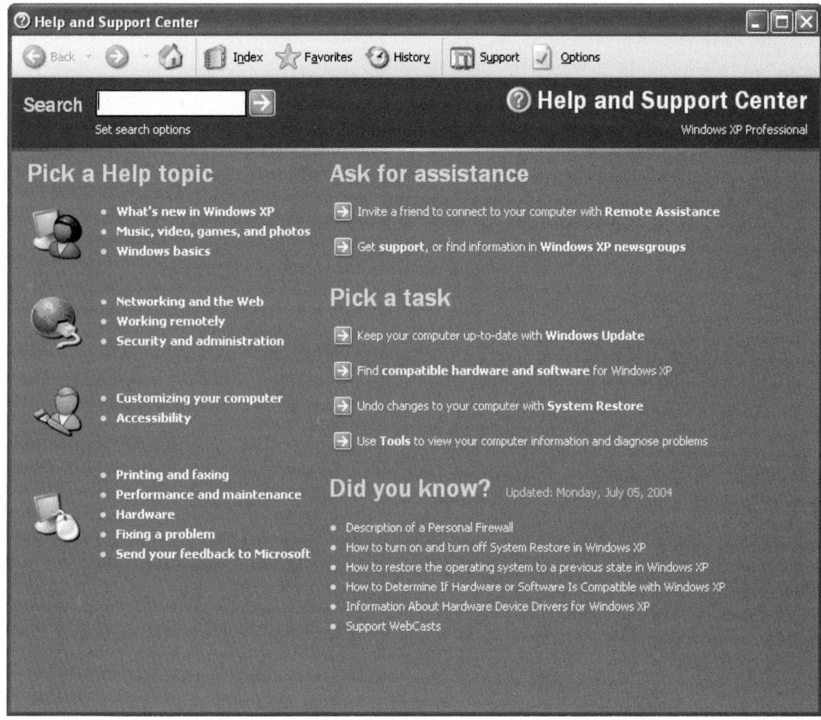

• The new Help and Support Center should be the first place you look for answers.

Perform Proactive Maintenance Tasks

Someone once said that the best offense is a good defense. Don't wait for problems to occur before you take action. Have a defensive strategy in which you take steps to avoid problems. Your strategy should include backing up data, disk defragmenting, and periodic housekeeping of the files and folders. Be prepared to use the System Restore and Automatic System Recovery features. You should install and configure an antivirus program, which will be discussed in Chapter 7.

Creating Backups and Creating Automated System Recovery Disks

Yes, we know you've heard it over and over. But you still need to actually back up your data files onto removable media or to another computer. It is not possible to overemphasize how important it is to do this! Do it often and do it right. Windows XP Professional, like previous versions, has the Backup Utility, available through Start | All Programs | Accessories | System Tools.

Windows XP Professional has a new recovery feature, Automated System Recovery (ASR), that replaces the Windows NT/Windows 2000 Emergency

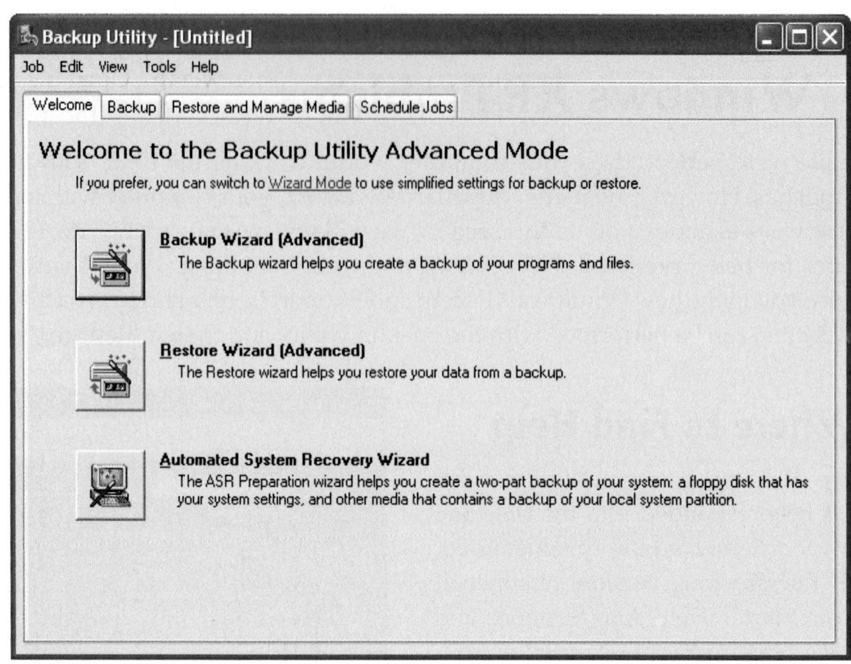

• **Figure 5-10.** The Automated System Recovery wizard will walk you through the creation of an ASR disk set.

Repair process, which depended on restoring a special backup of system settings. ASR, in contrast, uses a backup of the entire system partition (where the OS is installed) and therefore provides a more holistic repair, restoring your operating system to a certain point in time. ASR requires some planning. You must use the Advanced Mode of the **Backup Utility** (NTBACKUP.EXE) to create an ASR backup set, which includes an ASR diskette to initiate a bootup into the ASR state, and a system partition backup to media, such as tape, another local hard disk, or a network location that is accessed via a drive letter (a "mapped" drive). Figure 5-10 shows the Advanced Mode of the Backup Utility with the option for running the Automated System Recovery wizard to create an ASR set. An ASR backup set does not include a backup of other partitions, nor does it allow you to select data folders. Therefore, your Windows XP Professional backup strategy should include the occasional creation of an ASR set, and frequent backups to save data and changes to the OS since the last ASR set.

Step-by-Step 5.08

Explore the Backup Program (NTBACKUP)

The backup program NTBACKUP is the tool provided with Windows XP Professional for creating backups, ASR backups, and ASR diskettes. You should familiarize yourself with this program. To complete this step-by-step exercise, you will need the following:

- The computer on which you successfully installed Windows XP Professional in Step-by-Step 5.02
- A user name and password for an account that is a member of the Administrators group

Step 1

Log on as an Administrator. First, run the Backup Utility and examine the Automated System Recovery Preparation wizard. Open the Backup program quickly by entering the command **NTBACKUP** in the Run box (from Start | Run). In the Welcome page of the Backup Or Restore wizard, click Advanced Mode.

Step 2

In the Welcome page of Advanced Mode, click on the button labeled "Automated System Recovery Wizard." This will open the Automated System Recovery Preparation wizard. Click Next.

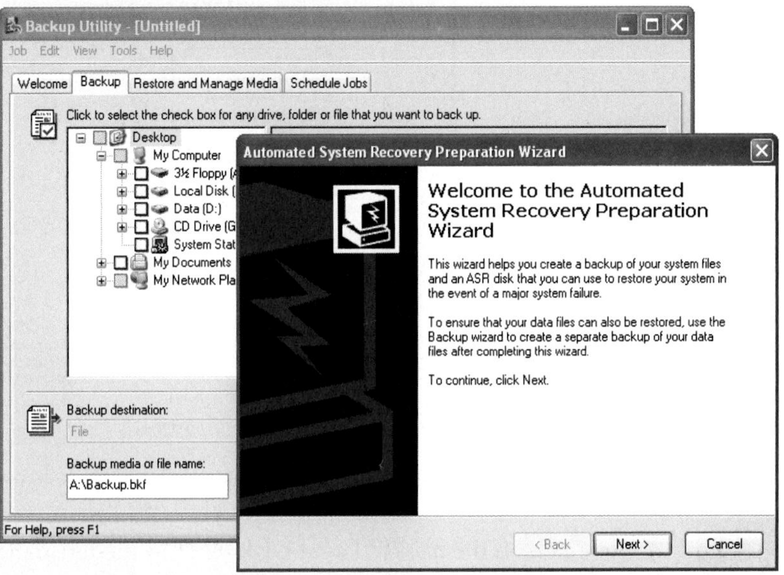

Step 3

On the Backup Destination page, notice the Backup Media Type box. If your system includes a tape backup system (very unlikely), it will give you a choice between tape and file. If the Backup Media Type box is grayed out (like the illustration), you can only back up to a file (rather than to tape), and you must provide a destination for this file on any local hard drive or network location available to you.

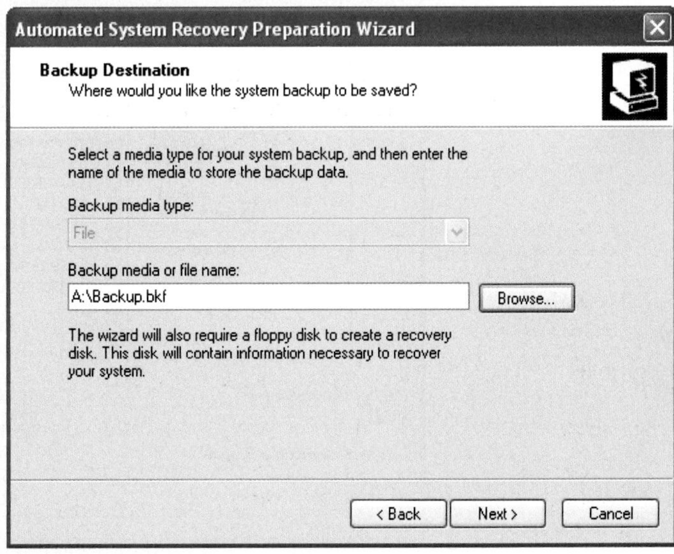

Step 4

Cancel the Automated System Recovery wizard and explore the Backup page. In the left pane, notice the check boxes that allow you to select drives and folders to back up. Click on the *words* "System State," and the contents of System State will display in the right pane. Placing a check in the box to the left of System State will back up all these items. The grayed-out boxes show you that you can back up all the components of System State, or none of them, but you cannot select individual System State components.

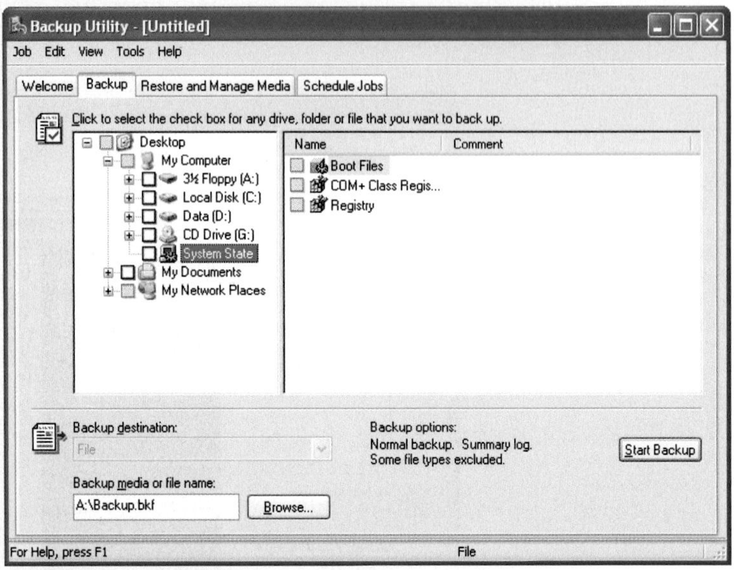

Step 5

Click on the *words* "Local Disk (C:)" in the left pane, and the right pane will reveal the contents. Now click on the check box to the left of "Local Disk (C:)," and notice that all the check boxes in the right pane are selected *except* pagefile.sys. This is a special file used by the system for virtual memory and should *not* be backed up; it cannot be selected for backup in the Backup Utility. You will learn more about pagefile.sys and virtual memory in Chapter 8.

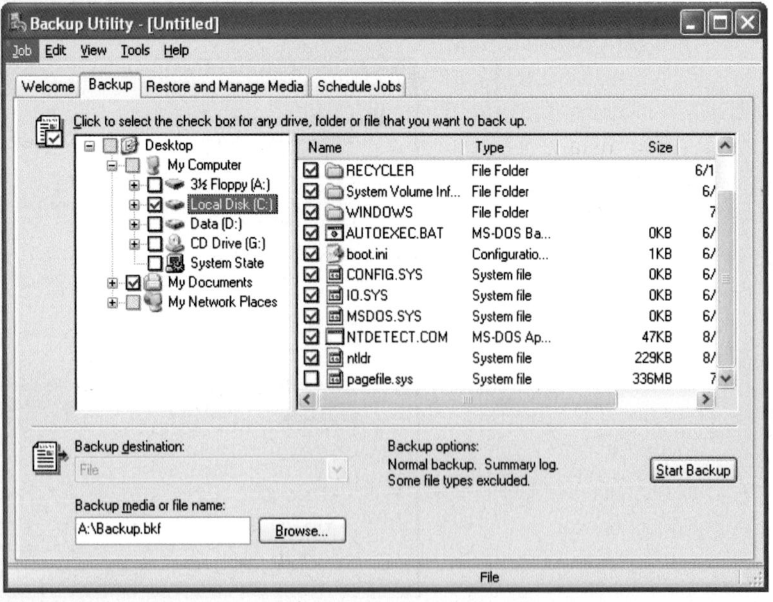

Step 6 Click some of the folders on drive C:, and notice that you can move around in them, much as you can in My Computer, selecting and deselecting folders to include in a backup. When you have explored the folders, close the Backup Utility.

Periodic Housekeeping

Keep your computer "lean and mean." If you simply can't resist buying programs that look just a little interesting because they are only $30 or so, you may find trouble in the form of undesirable changes to your system and outright hard drive bloat. Periodically, you should do some serious housecleaning, which should include removing any applications you no longer need, deleting any data files you no longer need, and deleting temporary files. After you have done this, defragment your hard drive, because file fragmentation (even on an NTFS volume) can slow down a computer. In Chapter 6 you'll learn more about the Windows XP utilities for accomplishing these tasks: Disk Cleanup and Disk Defragmenter.

Safe Mode is a special startup option that was introduced in Windows 95. Startup options have been improved upon in each version since then, and you will learn more about Windows startup options in Chapter 8.

Create Restore Points for System Restore

Windows XP has a great new tool, System Restore, which was actually introduced in Windows ME but has been improved in Windows XP. Several years ago, Edgar had a bad experience after making some changes to a client's Windows 95 computer. The client was a small engineering company. The chief engineer had made several software and hardware changes, and now every time they turned the computer on, it entered a self-reboot loop when loading Windows 95. They weren't even able to go into Safe Mode, and the chief engineer couldn't quite remember all the changes he had made. Edgar finally had to reformat the disk to clean it and reinstall all of the software and data. If only Edgar had Windows XP and System Restore!

The System Restore tools allow you to restore your computer to its configuration at a previous point in time, called a restore point. Some of these points in time are set automatically. For instance, by default, every time you install new software, Windows XP creates a restore point. Thus, if installation of a program causes your computer to malfunction, simply restore the system to a time point before that installation, and the computer should work.

During the restore process, only settings and programs are changed. No data is lost. Your computer will include all programs and settings as of the restore date and time. This feature is invaluable for overworked administrators and consultants like Edgar. A simple restore will fix many user-generated problems.

To restore to a previous time point, start the System Restore wizard by choosing Start | All Programs | Accessories | System Tools | System Restore. Select the first radio button, Restore My Computer To An Earlier Time, and then click Next.

Learn more about the registry, how to edit it, and how to back up the registry in Chapter 8.

The second screen shows a calendar with restore points. Any day with a boldface date has a restore point. These points are created after you add or remove software, or install Windows updates, and during the normal shutdown of your computer. Figure 5-11 shows a restore point when a program was installed. Select a date to restore to and click Next.

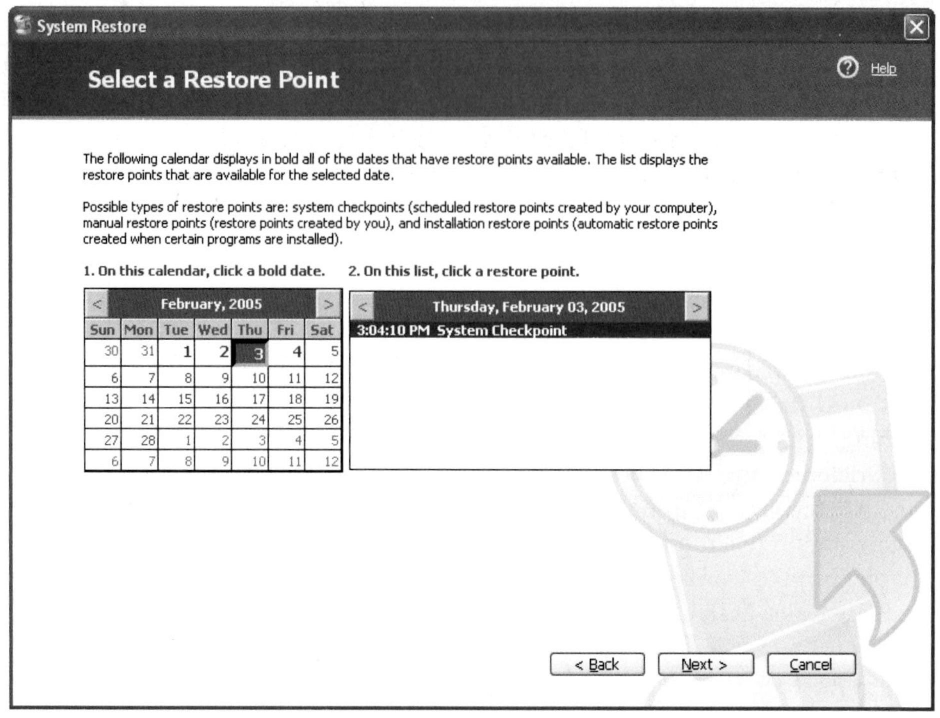

• **Figure 5-11.** Selecting a restore point

The last screen before the system is restored is a warning. It advises you to close all open programs and reminds you that Windows will shut down during the restore process. It also states that the restore operation is completely reversible. Thus, if you go too far back in time, you can restore to a more recent date.

You don't have to count on the automatic creation of restore points. You can open System Restore at any time and simply select Create A Restore Point, similar to what you did in Step 8 of Step-by-Step 5.04. This is something to consider doing before making changes that might not trigger an automatic restore point, such as directly editing the registry.

System Restore is turned on by default and uses some of your disk space to save information on restore points. To turn System Restore off or change the disk space usage, open the System Properties applet in Control Panel, and select the System Restore tab, where you will find these settings. Disabling System Restore is now a common part of cleaning off many virus infections to make sure that a virus isn't hiding in the restore files, but be aware that turning System Restore off, even for a moment, deletes all old restore points.

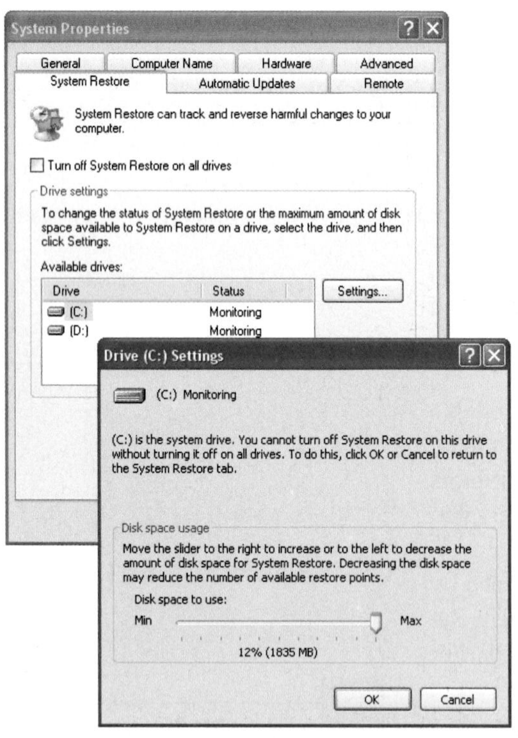

• System Restore settings

The Blue Screen of Death (BSOD) Revisited

The Stop screen, often referred to as the Blue Screen of Death (BSOD), which you learned about in Chapter 3, may still show up in Windows XP. Recall that a Stop screen will appear if the OS detects that a fatal error has occurred. A fatal error is one that could cause too much instability to guarantee the integrity of the system and prevent loss of data in open files. Such an event is called a stop error.

Turning System Restore off, even for a moment, deletes all old restore points!

Preparing for Stop Errors in Windows XP

As in Windows NT and Windows 2000, to be prepared for a BSOD, you should decide how you want your computer to behave after a stop error. You do this by modifying the System Failure settings on the Startup And Recovery page. These settings can be found by opening the System applet in Control Panel, selecting the Advanced tab, and clicking the Settings button under Startup And Recovery.

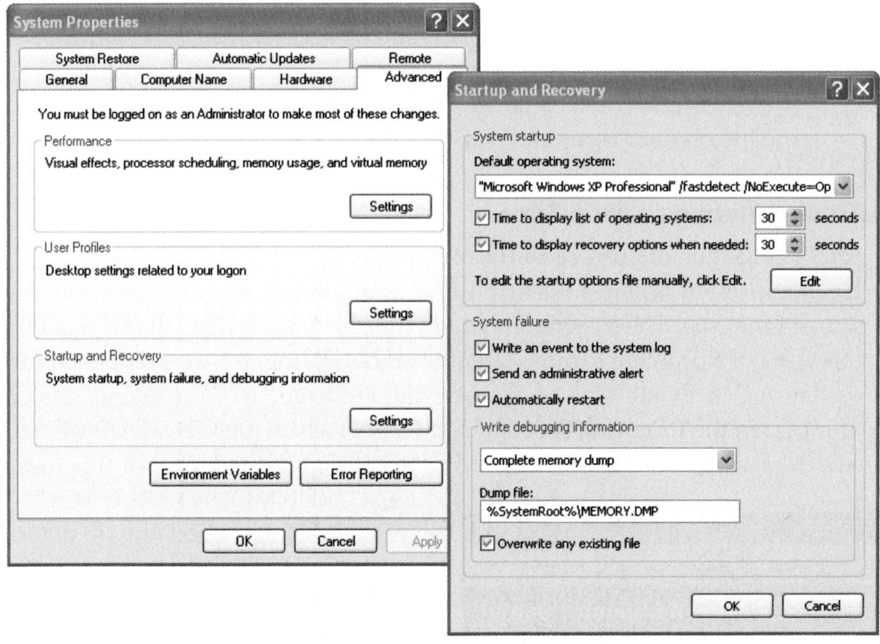

• The default System Failure settings on the Startup and Recovery page

- **Write An Event To The System Log** causes Windows to write an event to the system log, which is one of several log files that can be viewed using Event Viewer (found under Administrative Tools). We highly recommend this setting, because it means that even if the computer reboots after a Stop screen, you can read the stop error information that was on the screen in the system log. You'll learn to use the Event Viewer in Chapter 8.
- **Send An Administrative Alert** is a setting that sends an alert message to the administrator that will appear on the administrator's screen the next time the administrator logs on. This is a useful setting if your computer is part of a domain, so that a domain administrator will be alerted.

- **Automatically Restart** is a setting we recommend, as long as you have also selected the first option, which preserves the stop error information in the system log file.
- **Writing Debugging Information** contains a drop-down list, a text box, and a check box. The drop-down list allows you to control the existence and the size of the file containing debugging information. This file is called a **dump file**, and the settings include None, Small Memory Dump (64KB), Kernel Memory Dump, and Complete Memory Dump. A complete memory dump contains an image of the contents of memory at the time of the fatal error. This file can be sent to Microsoft for evaluation of a problem, but this amount of effort and cost (Microsoft charges for these services) is normally only expended on a critical computer, such as a network server. For a desktop computer, a small memory dump should be adequate, unless you are advised otherwise by a support person. The text box allows you to specify the location of the dump file. The default is %SystemRoot%, which is a variable way of pointing to the folder in which Windows is installed. In a clean install, the default location will be C:\Windows. The final setting is the check box labeled "Overwrite any existing file." We recommend selecting this option so that dump files do not accumulate on your computer's hard drive.

Troubleshooting a Stop Error

Eric, a colleague of ours, recently experienced a stop error in Windows XP. He was present when it occurred and scanned the first few lines on the screen for a clue. The system rebooted while he was viewing the screen, but this was not a problem to him. After the reboot, he logged on and opened the system log in Event Viewer. He saw the message "STOP [several sets of numbers in the form 0x00000000] UNMOUNTABLE_BOOT_VOLUME." A search of `support.microsoft.com` using just the last part of this message (UNMOUNTABLE_BOOT_VOLUME) described how to determine the cause and action to take by examining the values that preceded it. Eric discovered that the solution to his problem was to restart Windows using the recovery console and to run a command from the command line. You'll learn more about the recovery console in Chapter 8.

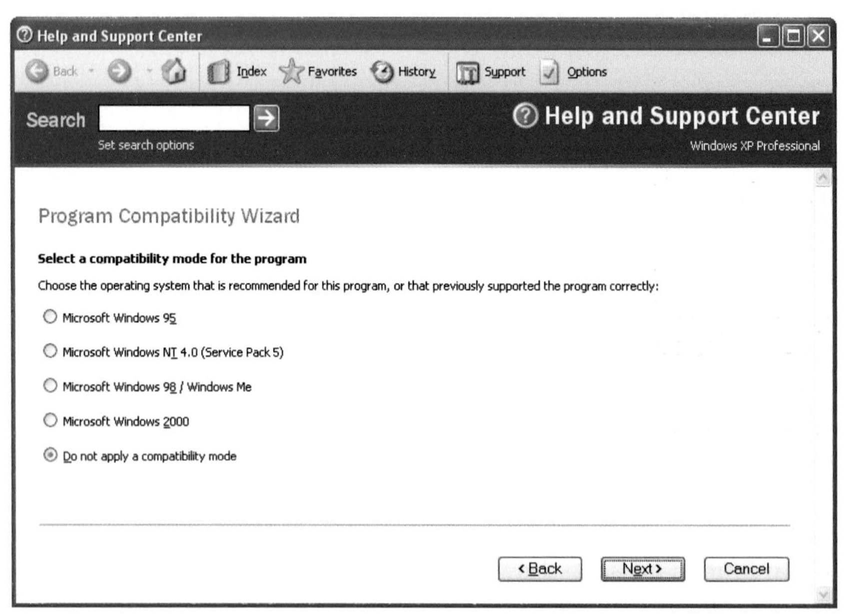

• The Program Compatibility wizard walks you through assigning settings to allow an older program to run under Windows XP.

An Old Application Will Not Run

You have a brand-new Windows XP computer. You need to run a program that worked nicely on your now-defunct Windows 95 computer. However, when you start the program in Windows XP, it doesn't perform correctly. Maybe the screen doesn't look quite right, or perhaps the program frequently hangs. To solve this problem, Windows XP allows you to trick the program into thinking that the OS is actually Windows 95 by using compatibility options. You can set these options by running the **Program Compatibility wizard** from the Help and Support Center or by setting the options manually from the properties of the shortcut or program file.

To run the Program Compatibility wizard, select Start | All Programs | Accessories | Program Compatibility Wizard. Following the instructions, you may choose to have the wizard display a list of all installed programs from which you can select your problem program. Then you can move through the wizard, selecting settings for emulating earlier versions of Windows and/or modifying the display settings for the program. Then test the program to see if there is an improvement.

Alternatively, you can set compatibility settings manually. On the Start menu, locate the shortcut for the offending program. Right-click and select Properties. Select the Compatibility tab. On this page, place a check in the box under Compatibility Mode, and then select Windows 95 in the drop-down list below it (see Figure 5-12). Click OK and test the program. If it still has problems, go back to the Compatibility page, and tweak the Display Settings and/or turn off advanced text services. If you need help, click the Program Compatibility link at the bottom of the page.

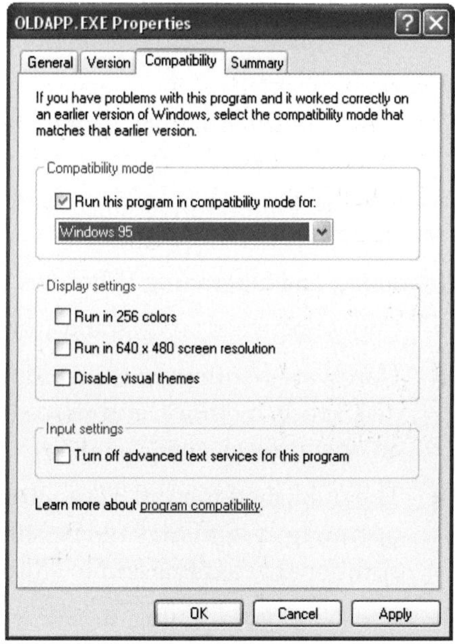

• **Figure 5-12.** Use the Compatibility page to make manual settings.

Chapter 5 Review

■ Chapter Summary

After reading this chapter and completing the Step-by-Step tutorials and Try This! exercises, you should understand the following facts about Windows XP:

Windows XP Professional Benefits, Features, and Weaknesses

- There are several Windows XP products, but none of them is designed to be a true network server operating system.
- The Windows XP products include
  - Windows XP Professional
  - Windows XP Home Edition
  - Windows XP Media Center Edition
  - Windows XP Tablet PC Edition
  - Windows XP Embedded
  - Windows XP 64-bit Edition
- Windows XP Professional is the focus of this chapter.
- Windows XP Professional features and benefits include
  - Desktop beauty and usability
  - Speed (faster at bootup and running programs than previous versions of Windows)
  - Security, including the required logon, and security features in the NTFS5 file system
  - Stability and compatibility
  - File system support of NTFS5, FAT32, and FAT16 on hard drives
  - New and improved recovery tools, including Last Known Good Configuration startup option; Task Manager, Recovery Console, Safe Mode startup options; Device Manager; System Restore; and Automated System Recovery
- Windows XP Professional has just a few limitations including
  - Hardware support is limited—older device drivers may have a problem during installation because they do not have signed drivers. Older device drivers may actually slow down boot time.
  - The hardware requirements are pretty high if you are planning to install on an older machine. (Newer machines are likely to come standard with disk, processor, and memory that far exceed the requirements.)
- While Windows XP (Home or Professional) comes standard on most PCs today, choosing it for an upgrade of an older computer requires research to ensure that it will be compatible with the computer and all other hardware, as well as the installed software.
- When choosing between Windows XP Professional and Windows XP Home, a "Yes" to any of the following questions indicates that Windows XP Professional is needed:
  - Will the user need to connect to the computer remotely?
  - Will the computer be connecting to a Microsoft NT or Active Directory domain-based network?
  - Is it important to easily rebuild your machine in the event of a catastrophe?
  - Is it important to make individual files secure?

Installing and Upgrading Windows XP Professional

- Choose between an upgrade and a clean installation.
- Hardware requirements include the amount of disk space, memory, and processor required to run an operating system.
- The published minimum requirements for an operating system may not be sufficient to run additional programs and to store data.
- The Windows Catalog at `www.microsoft.com/windows/catalog` is a searchable list of hardware and software known to work with Windows XP.
- You should run the Upgrade Advisor and perform any tasks suggested by it before upgrading a computer to Windows XP.
- No Setup startup disks are included with Windows XP. If you need to make them, you must connect to their web site and create them from a program available there.

- To combat software piracy, Microsoft requires that you activate Windows XP within 30 days of installation.
- Registration is still optional.
- Soon after installing Windows XP, you should verify network access and install new updates.

Customize and Manage Windows XP Professional

- To create and manage disk partitions, use Disk Management in the Computer Management console.
- When you install new programs in Windows, you will often use an installation program that comes with the new application.
- To uninstall a program, use the Add Or Remove Programs applet in Control Panel.
- Programs should be removed correctly using an uninstall program.
- To add or remove a Windows component, use the Windows Components wizard from the Add Or Remove Programs applet in Control Panel.
- Use the Display applet in Control Panel to ensure that the screen resolution is set properly.
- A new setting to select a display method called ClearType for smoothing screen fonts is accessed by the Effects button on the Appearance page. Enabling ClearType is especially important for displaying text on laptops and desktop computers with flat panel displays (FPDs).
- Windows XP supports both plug-and-play and non-plug-and-play printers.

Troubleshooting Common Windows XP Problems

- Help and Support Center is the new and improved help program containing a large menu of options.
- Proactive tasks include
  - Creating backups and creating automated system recovery disks
  - Periodic housekeeping
  - Creating restore points for System Restore
- If an old application will not run, or causes problems with the display, locate the executable file for the application, and select options in the Compatibility page of the file's properties dialog box.

Key Terms

Activation *(211)*
Add Printer wizard *(233)*
Automated System Recovery (ASR) *(205)*
Automatic Update *(204)*
Backup Utility *(236)*
dump file *(242)*
Help and Support Center *(235)*
InstallShield *(226)*
Microsoft Product Activation (MPA) *(211)*
prefetching *(202)*
Program Compatibility wizard *(243)*
restore point *(205)*
System Restore *(205)*
Upgrade Advisor *(208)*
Windows Update *(204)*

Key Terms Quiz

Use the Key Terms list to complete the sentences that follow.

1. When unsure about hardware and software compatibility before upgrading, use the Windows XP CD to run the Windows XP ______________ on the computer.
2. ______________ allows you to return your computer to a previous working state.
3. ______________ is a new feature of Windows XP that enables it to start up faster and to run programs faster.
4. One of the most common programs used to install applications into Windows is called ______________
5. A great place to look for solutions to problems, troubleshooting tips, and other information about Windows XP is the new ______________

6. A new recovery tool that backs up the system partition can be found in the Advanced Mode of the Windows XP ______________

7. If a program written for an older version of Windows does not run under Windows XP, use the ______________

8. For ______________ to work, you must have a set of disks that includes a system backup to back up media, and a special diskette that can boot up the computer and start the new recovery.

9. A ______________ is like a snapshot of Windows XP settings at a certain point in time.

10. Registration is optional, but ______________ is mandatory.

■ Multiple-Choice Quiz

1. Which file system has security features?
   - a. FAT32
   - b. FAT16
   - c. NTFS5
   - d. FAT12
   - e. NTFS32

2. Why does Windows XP use a process called prefetching?
   - a. To restore system state
   - b. To speed up OS bootup and to make programs run faster
   - c. To create a restore point and restore the system
   - d. To activate Windows XP
   - e. To authenticate users

3. Which version of Windows XP is intended for general business users?
   - a. Windows XP Home Edition
   - b. Windows XP Media Center Edition
   - c. Windows XP Tablet PC Edition
   - d. Windows XP Professional
   - e. Windows XP 64-bit Edition

4. Why does the Windows XP desktop reorganize itself?
   - a. To keep your disk defragmented
   - b. To update your mailing list
   - c. To remind you of to-do tasks
   - d. To run programs more efficiently
   - e. To eliminate desktop clutter

5. Which term best describes the logon to Windows XP Professional?
   - a. Insecure
   - b. Optional
   - c. Mandatory
   - d. Customary
   - e. Character-mode

6. What is the latest version (as of Windows XP) of Windows' most advanced file system?
   - a. NTFS32
   - b. FAT32
   - c. FAT16
   - d. FAT12
   - e. NTFS5

7. Why must you activate Windows XP after installation?
   - a. This is how you register your product.
   - b. It won't start up after installation unless it is activated.
   - c. To detect computer viruses.
   - d. Microsoft requires it to protect itself against software piracy.
   - e. To create limited users.

8. Why should you install updates for Windows XP?
   - a. To install new applications
   - b. To create a new computer administrator account
   - c. To correct general problems and security problems with the program code
   - d. To install new games
   - e. To be kept up-to-date on the latest Windows products

9. Why would you use the ClearType option in Display Properties | Appearance | Effects?
   a. To make the text on the screen translucent
   b. To smooth the edges of screen fonts
   c. To personalize your desktop
   d. To make printed documents more readable
   e. To select the Bliss wallpaper
10. Why do software publishers use products like InstallShield?
   a. It acts as an antivirus program
   b. To create standardized installation programs
   c. To upgrade from Windows Me
   d. To repartition hard disks
   e. To activate Windows XP
11. Windows XP checks for this in a file's program code to ensure that the code has not been damaged or tampered with.
   a. Restore point
   b. Digital signature
   c. Virus
   d. Worm
   e. Developer's signature
12. What mode, selectable from the properties of a shortcut or program file, allows you to run an old program in an environment that emulates an older version of Windows?
   a. Compatibility mode
   b. Safe mode
   c. Real mode
   d. Protected mode
   e. Standard mode
13. Last Known Good (LKG) only works within a narrow window of time that ends when the following occurs:
   a. An administrative alert is sent
   b. Any user logs on
   c. The computer reboots
   d. The disk is defragmented
   e. A new partition is created
14. You have just installed Windows XP Professional and did not choose to activate it when prompted to do so during the installation process. How long do you have to activate it before Windows XP stops working?
   a. 10 days
   b. 120 days
   c. 6 months
   d. 30 days
   e. Indefinitely
15. You installed Windows XP Professional on a 15GB partition created during installation. You are now creating a second partition in the remaining 65GB of available space on the hard disk. The computer is not configured for dual-boot. What type of partition and which file system should you choose (is preferred) for this new partition?
   a. Extended partition with FAT32
   b. Primary partition with FAT16
   c. Extended partition with NTFS5
   d. Primary partition with NTFS5
   e. Primary partition with FAT32

Essay Quiz

1. What methods are available for booting into the Windows Setup program on a stand-alone PC?
2. In your own words, describe the difference between activation and registration. Be sure to explain which one is mandatory, and why each is used by Microsoft.
3. Briefly describe why you might partition a very large hard disk into two or more partitions.
4. Why does Windows XP Professional have the two recovery tools System Restore and Automatic System Recovery? Isn't one of these enough?
5. In your opinion, what is the most important feature of XP? Why?

Lab Projects

• Lab Project 5.1

Currently your Windows XP Professional computer is working just fine, but you would like to prepare for a disaster—such as an unrecoverable hard disk failure in which the hard disk needs to be replaced—and get yourself up and running as quickly as possible with your computer restored to its previous state before the failure.

You will need the lab computer on which you installed Windows XP Professional in Step-by-Step 5.02. If the computer has a writeable CD or DVD drive, have some media on hand to use for backup. You will also need a blank diskette.

Then do the following:

1. Given the available drives and media, determine what recovery options, from those featured in this chapter, are available to you. The recovery options featured in this chapter include Last Known Good, System Restore, and Automatic System Recovery.
2. Write a plan for using the recovery option or options that would be appropriate for the scenario described. Explain why each of the featured recovery options will or will not work.
3. Do any proactive work that is possible to do on your computer to prepare for the chosen recovery option.
4. Present your plan to your fellow students, and describe the proactive steps you have taken on your lab computer.

• Lab Project 5.2

Windows XP Professional is running on an older computer. You want to increase its speed by turning off extraneous animation and features in Windows XP.

You will need the following:

- A computer running Windows XP
- The administrator password for this computer

Then do the following:

1. Go to the Performance tab of the My Computer icon.
2. Turn off all video enhancements.
3. Set a dedicated virtual RAM size. A good formula is 1.5 times the size of your RAM.

Making the Windows GUI Work for You

So, Daddy, if 50 years ago a computer was as big as our garage, how big was the mouse?

—A CHILD TO HIS FATHER (PARAPHRASE)
MINNEAPOLIS STAR TRIBUNE

The interaction of humans with computers has changed in scale and method since computing's early days. In scale, it has changed from an interaction engaged in by a handful of highly trained experts to one involving millions of people using computers for everyday business and personal tasks. In method, human interaction has also moved from the tedious flipping of switches or feeding of punch cards to the common use of a pointing device to navigate a graphical user interface (GUI) based on the desktop metaphor. The little boy who asked the preceding question can't imagine a computer without a mouse, and two generations from now, his grandson may have trouble imagining using something as crude as a mouse!

In this chapter, you will consider this whole idea of how humans interact with computers and how the desktop metaphor describes the graphical user interfaces of Windows, UNIX, Linux, and Mac OSs. You will learn concepts and skills common to the GUIs of five versions of Windows (NT, 9*x*, 2000, XP, and Windows Server 2003) while you acquaint yourself with the capabilities of today's Windows desktops. In the process, you will learn skills that will help you in all of your future interactions with computers.

In this chapter, you will learn how to:

- **Explain the nature and history of the Windows GUI**
- **Navigate the Windows GUI**
- **Configure and customize the Windows desktop**
- **Manage files in Windows**
- **Launch applications in Windows**
- **Select a method for leaving the desktop**
- **Troubleshoot common Windows desktop problems**

Who Invented the Desktop?

Remember Douglas Engelbart? He was listed in the timeline in Chapter 1 because in 1968, at the Fall Joint Computer Conference in San Francisco, he and his team members gave a demonstration that included the use of a mouse to move a "tracking spot" around a screen containing both text and graphical elements. Even back when the user was most likely to be a highly trained computer or scientific professional, visionaries like Engelbart and his team could see the need to make computers more user-friendly.

Douglas Engelbart's vision of human interaction with computers extended far beyond the mouse and user interface. One biographical article we found on the Internet stated that he could "envision people sitting in front of displays, 'flying around' in an information space where they could formulate and organize their ideas with incredible speed and flexibility." This was decades before the World Wide Web made the Internet just this type of environment for many millions of people worldwide.

Years later, in the lab of Xerox's now-famous Palo Alto Research Center (PARC), others continued to work on giving computers a more intuitive (or immediately understandable) user interface. The physical components of the Xerox Alto computer they developed consisted of a display, keyboard, and mouse on the desktop plus a dishwasher-sized cabinet containing the processor and disk storage. It also carried a hefty $35,000 price tag. In the late 1970s, some of the pioneers in personal computing visited this lab and were inspired by the technology demonstrated there as Xerox engineers worked on what was to become the Xerox Star, with its more refined graphical user interface. You might even say these

Try This!

Learn More About Douglas Engelbart

There is a wealth of information on Douglas Engelbart on the Internet. Among the treasures we have found is a 90-minute video of the 1968 public demonstration presented by Engelbart and the group of researchers who worked with him at the Augmentation Research Center at Stanford Research Institute in Menlo Park, California. Previously, portions of the presentation, edited into 35 video clips formatted for RealVideo streaming video were available at `sloan.stanford.edu`. As of this writing, the video is not available, but you may be lucky and find it posted there again. Try this:

1. Use your favorite Internet search engine to search on Douglas Engelbart.
2. Look for references to the 1968 demo. There are many written accounts and a few instances of audio and video clips.
3. Find other innovative ideas credited to Douglas Engelbart.

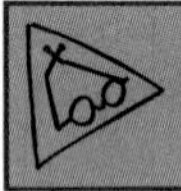

Inside Information

What Does *Intuitive* Really Mean?

Harry has been an IT professional for over 20 years, beginning in 1983 on the front lines as PCs were first brought into his company. He now manages the corporate desktop support department, responsible for all end user computing in the corporation. He believes that the Windows GUI is "intuitive"; he can't imagine anyone not understanding how to perform basic tasks in Windows.

Carl, in contrast, has had a long career with a major passenger airline as an airplane maintenance manager. For many years, his primary use of his office desktop computer was to access a mainframe-based corporate e-mail system. Several years ago, the airline switched to a Windows environment. Today, Carl spends nearly half his workday on his computer reading and sending e-mail, reviewing updates to airplane maintenance bulletins accessed using his web browser (Internet Explorer), and using software that allows him to schedule his team of mechanics. He still finds learning new tasks in Windows to be difficult. In spite of the "intuitive" interface, every time he needs to perform a new task, someone must show him the steps, and he has to practice them before he feels competent to repeat the task.

As you can see, the definition of intuitive *depends on the person and that person's experience with computers. If you pursue a career as an information services or information technology professional, you will encounter people whose experiences fall everywhere within the range between Harry and Carl.*

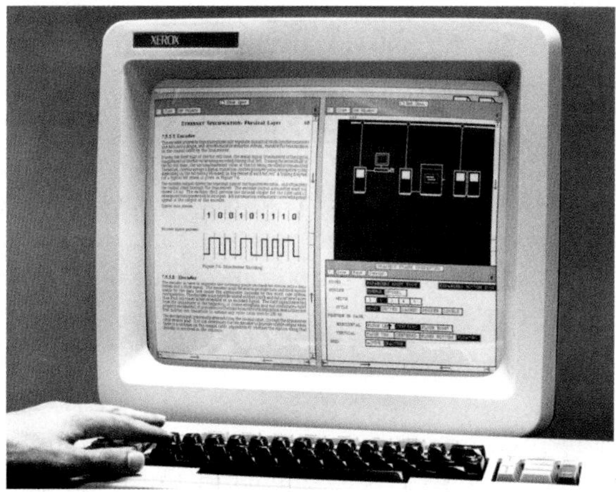

Courtesy Xerox Corporation.

• **Figure 6-1.** A very early computer developed at Palo Alto Research Center (PARC)

visitors "borrowed" a few ideas. Figure 6-1 shows one of the computers developed at PARC.

Apple's Macintosh computer, introduced in 1984, was the first successful consumer product influenced by the user interface innovations at PARC. Microsoft soon followed suit with its first Windows product.

So what's the big deal about the GUI desktop? It is simply an imaginary workspace where you store objects such as programs and data in **windows**, each of which is a bordered area of the desktop used by a single program. If you were lucky enough to have a Windows-based PC or Macintosh at home as a child, you probably take the desktop metaphor for granted.

Today's Windows and Mac OSs, as well as GUI shells for UNIX and Linux, continue to use the metaphor of a desktop for the GUI. This metaphor has endured over decades with the same basic principle—the mouse and keyboard are the primary input devices used to select from objects and menus on the "desktop" display. The graphic display is the primary output device for real-time interaction.

You can learn more about the history of Windows. Point your Internet browser to your favorite search engine (ours is `www.google.com`), and search on "History of Windows." You will find some interesting, and sometimes quite biased, accounts of the history of Microsoft Windows.

Navigating the Windows GUI

Early microcomputer OSs, such as DOS and CP/M, used a **command prompt** in a simple character-mode interface. Then **menu**-based interfaces (nongraphical, character-based interfaces offering lists of choices) were added to individual applications and to each operating system. Today, Windows and Macintosh each offer an integrated GUI that makes accomplishing tasks easy and fast (most of the time), and menus are such a good idea that Windows and Mac OSs also have plenty of menus in their GUIs. In this section, we'll go for a spin around the Windows desktop.

The menu-based interface used with DOS was referred to as a shell.

We assume knowledge of Windows GUI and mouse elements. If you need to review GUI and mouse skills, your instructor will help you.

Getting to the Desktop via Logon

You can't navigate in Windows until you get to the Windows user interface. Is that a problem? Not really. You may just have to turn on your computer

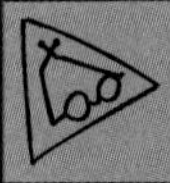

Inside Information

Don't Blink!

The most common method of authentication is the simple logon in which you enter your user name and password using the keyboard and mouse. Other methods may include special devices, such as a credit-card-size device called a smart card, which provides a token, or password. Some devices allow you to prove who you are through biometrics (measuring a biological characteristic). For example, you might log onto your computer by entering your user name at a keyboard and then placing your thumb on a device that scans your fingerprint. A similar approach is retinal scanning, which confirms your identity by examining the retina of your eye. These are all options that require special equipment and configuration of all the computers involved.

and wait about a minute for the Windows interface (the desktop) to appear. However, depending on the version of Windows you're using and how it is configured, you may not be able to see the desktop and start working until you log on. That is, you must provide a user name and a password that are verified against a security database, either local or on a server on the network. Let's look at how each of four Windows desktop versions behaves at startup. If you work with only one of these versions, you may want to skim the information about the other versions and focus on the version of Windows you have on your desktop.

User Accounts

When you log onto a Windows computer, you are prompted to enter a user name and password. In most cases, the correct user name and password identify you as a valid user because they are compared to a user name and password in a **user account**. A user account is a record in an accounts database. This database may reside on a local computer or on one or more network computers (servers), in which case it can be multi-mastered, meaning that the same database is replicated on many servers, and users can be authenticated by any server containing a copy of the accounts database.

On a stand-alone Windows 9*x* computer, the user name is not terribly significant, since there is no notion of a local user account in Windows 9*x*. People often mistake the ability of Windows 9*x* to remember user names and passwords (saved in a file for each user who logs on locally) with the ability to maintain an accounts database, which does not exist in Windows 9*x*. The purpose of logging on with a user name is twofold: if your Windows 9*x* computer is configured to allow you (the user) to log onto a Microsoft Windows domain (either Windows NT or Active Directory), the logon information is passed on to a domain controller for authentication to any domain resources on the network. If you do not log onto a domain, the user name and password are simply used to identify a file that is kept locally and used to save your user name and password information to resources on the private network or the Internet. In addition, if individual user profiles are enabled on the Windows 9*x* computer, the user name is used to identify which profile to use for each person.

There is no option in the identification pages for a Windows 9*x* computer to join a domain, because it cannot!

Workgroups and Domains

Windows computers participate in a network through membership in one of two types of logical groups: a workgroup or a domain. In a Microsoft network a **workgroup** is a grouping of computers on a network for the sake of sharing printers and folders with other users in the group. Generically, this is called a peer-to-peer network. A Microsoft workgroup must have a unique name on the network, but the only user accounts available in a workgroup exist independently on member computers that are capable of maintaining a local accounts database (Windows NT, Windows 2000, Windows XP, and Windows 2003 have this capability). These user accounts can only be used to authenticate users to the local computer and to give them rights and permissions to the resources on the local computer such as files and printers. All it takes to be a member of a workgroup is to specify the workgroup name, either in the identification page of the Windows 9*x* setup program, or in the identification page of the Windows 9*x* Network properties dialog box.

A Microsoft Windows **domain** has a centralized security accounts database maintained on one or more special servers called domain controllers. This centralized database contains accounts for users, groups, and computers participating in the domain and can be used to authenticate a user for access to any resource of the domain. You will revisit workgroups and domains in Chapter 10.

> A **dialog box** is a computerized form that you fill in much like a paper form, using the keyboard and mouse rather than a pen or pencil. You encounter many dialog boxes in Windows. Some are as simple as a logon box, while others may have many pages. With all dialog boxes, once you enter the information required, you either press ENTER or click a special object resembling a button (labeled "Close," "Enter," or "Exit") to have the computer close the box and process the information you provided.

The use of CTRL-ALT-DELETE Before Logon

With the exception of the Windows 9*x* versions, all the Windows OSs discussed either default to, or can be configured to, prompt for the CTRL-ALT-DELETE key combination before showing the logon dialog box in which you enter your user name and password. This is done for security purposes, clearing memory of certain types of viruses that may be lurking. If not disabled by this action, they would do mischief or damage. For instance, some of these viruses wait to capture the keystrokes you enter for your user name and password. In some instances, you may be able to disable this requirement to press CTRL-ALT-DELETE, but you'll lose the security it offers. A standard installation of Windows XP will not require CTRL-ALT-DELETE, but it should be added by an administrator who desires a higher level of security.

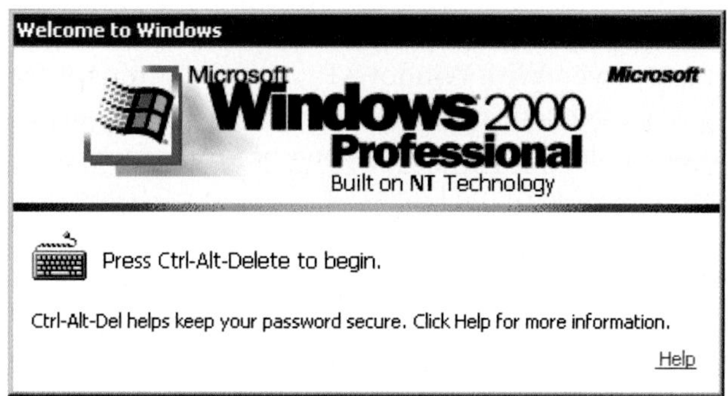

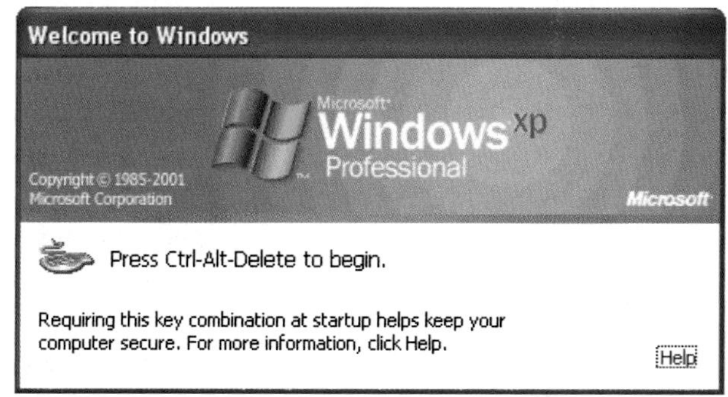

• Windows 2000 and Windows XP messages requiring CTRL-ALT-DELETE to log on

Working with Logon Dialog Boxes

Logon dialog boxes vary from version to version of Windows and can even vary by the computer's role on a network. They vary in both complexity and in the title shown in the title bar. For instance, all the logon dialog boxes for Windows NT are simply titled "Logon Information," while the Windows 98 logon dialog box may be titled "Welcome to Windows" or "Enter Network Password," and the Windows 2000 and Windows XP dialog boxes are titled "Log On to Windows." If a Windows computer is not connected to a network, or is on a network but is not participating in a domain, you will see a very simple dialog box that only allows logging onto the local computer with a select button entitled "Options" to configure domain entry information. If a Windows computer is on a network and participating in a Windows domain, you will see a dialog box that allows you to log onto a Windows domain using your user name and password.

Inside Information

Why Is It Possible to Cancel from a Windows 98 Logon, But Still Access the Computer?

Security is not the strong point of Windows 98, but ease-of-use is. If you cancel the logon, you can still get to the local computer in Windows 98. But if you try to access a network resource that requires authentication, you will have to log on to get network access.

Logging Onto a Stand-Alone or a Workgroup Computer The simple dialog boxes for stand-alone or workgroup computers may look like the simple Welcome To Windows screen of Windows XP, or they may include text boxes for user name and password that appear only if your computer is not a member of a Microsoft Windows domain—that is, if your computer is a stand-alone computer (meaning that it is not on a network), or if it is on a peer-to-peer network as a member of a workgroup.

The Windows NT 4.0 logon dialog box is titled "Logon Information" and its simple version is shown in Figure 6-2.

Windows 98 can be used without having to log on, but generally this is done only if you have a stand-alone computer that is not on a network. Even without network access, your Windows 98 computer may be configured to request a logon, in which case you will see the Welcome To Windows dialog box, shown in Figure 6-3. If the computer is on a network, the dialog box is titled Enter Network Password, as shown in Figure 6-4. The user name and password may then be compared to the user name and password in a local password file, unless the computer is configured to send authentication information to a network server (either a Microsoft Windows server or a Novell server). This logon does not make the local computer secure, because you can cancel the dialog box and still have access to your Windows 98 computer. But you won't have access to network resources that require a user name and password unless you provide them at the time you connect to a network resource, such as a server. With Windows 9*x*, security begins at the network servers. More secure versions of Windows provide local security.

When logging onto a Windows 2000 stand-alone or workgroup computer, you will see a simple version of the Log On To Windows dialog box, as shown in Figure 6-5.

In Windows XP, Microsoft made significant changes to the look of the user interface. These changes are apparent before you even reach the desktop, as you can see in Figure 6-6, which shows the logon screen you will see the first time you log onto a stand-alone or workgroup member computer.

Logging Onto a Microsoft Windows Domain If you have a user account in a Microsoft Windows domain, you may log onto the domain and access those domain resources to which you are given permission. A computer can also be a member of a domain, allowing domain administrators to manage the

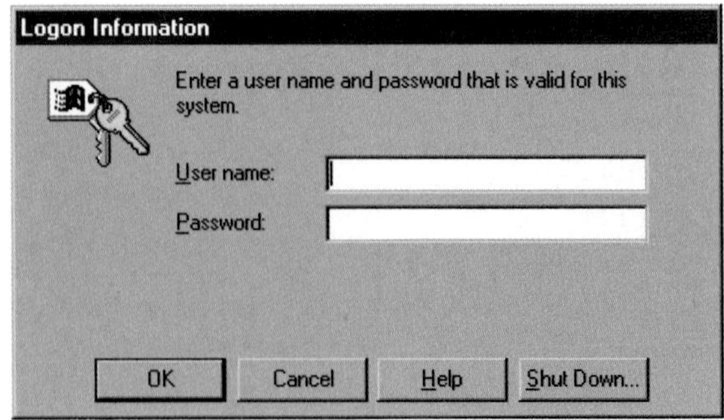

• **Figure 6-2.** Windows NT Logon Information screen for a stand-alone or workgroup computer

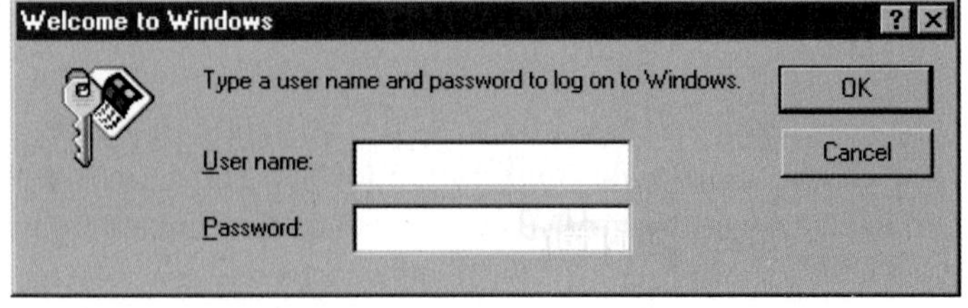

• **Figure 6-3.** Windows 98 Welcome to Windows logon screen for a stand-alone computer

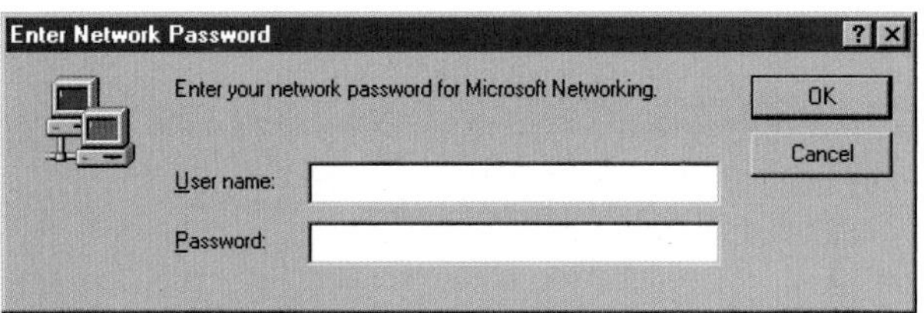

• **Figure 6-4.** Windows 98 Enter Network Password dialog box for logging onto a workgroup

• **Figure 6-5.** Windows 2000 Log On to Windows dialog box for a stand-alone or workgroup computer

resources of the computer. Computers running Windows NT, Windows 2000, Windows XP, and Windows Server 2003 can be members of a domain.

When you log onto a domain from a Windows computer, it must also be a member of the domain to which you are logging on or a member of a domain with a special relationship with the domain to which you belong. The exception is Windows 9*x* computers. A Windows 9*x* computer cannot be a member of a domain, but a user who is a member of a domain can log onto the domain from a Windows 9*x* computer if it has been configured to send the user's logon requests to the domain, in which case it will have a third text box, labeled "Domain."

What does domain membership mean to a computer? There are several very important administrative and technical differences, but the simple answer

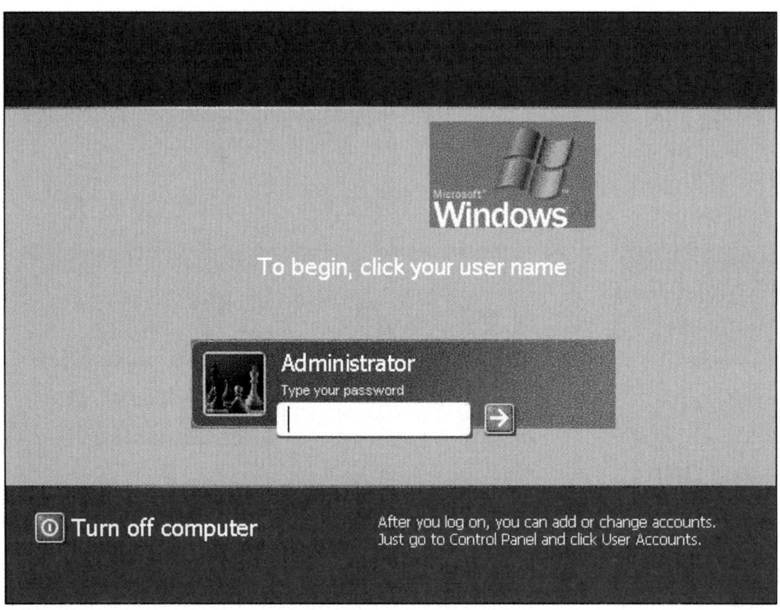

• **Figure 6-6.** Windows XP default logon screen for a stand-alone or workgroup computer

is that because a Windows 9*x* or Windows XP Home Edition computer cannot be a member of a domain, it does not have all the benefits of membership that a Windows NT, Windows 2000, Windows XP Professional, or Windows Server 2003 computer enjoys. To an administrator of many desktop computers, the difference is in not being able to centrally manage the Windows 9*x* or Windows XP Home Edition computers on the network in the same manner that she can manage computers that have the more advanced Windows OSs.

> **Inside Information**
>
> **Domain Users Can Access Shares on a Windows 9x Computer**
>
> *If you want to share files (or printers) on your Windows 9x computer with other members of your domain, you can give access to a shared folder on your computer to users in the domain. This is an advanced task, and if your computer is part of a network at school or work, you should talk to your network administrator before doing this.*

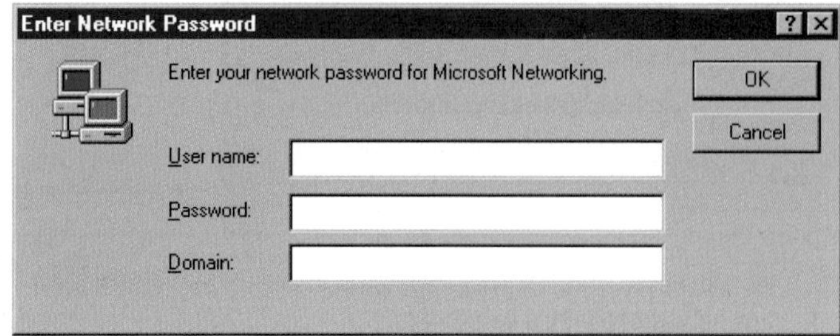

• Windows 98 Enter Network Password dialog box for logging to a domain

If a Windows NT, Windows 2000, or Windows XP Professional computer is a member of a Microsoft Windows domain, as is most likely the case in a corporate environment, the logon dialog box will have a drop-down list box. Figure 6-7 shows the Windows NT Logon Information dialog box. Notice the drop-down list box labeled "Domain." This allows you to select between a domain or the local computer. In this case, SEDONA-NT is the name of the local computer. Selecting this will allow you to log on using a local user account.

Figure 6-8 shows the same dialog box with a domain name, HTC, selected. Logging on with a domain name selected allows you to log on using a domain user account. If you have a choice between a local computer or a domain logon, you will normally log onto the domain. How can you tell the difference between logging onto the computer-based user account and the domain-based user account in Windows NT? You can't tell the difference just by looking at the Logon Information dialog box. Either of these names would be a valid computer or domain name in a Microsoft network. If you are using NT, you simply have to learn the difference between your computer

• **Figure 6-7.** Windows NT logon screen with the local computer SEDONA-NT selected

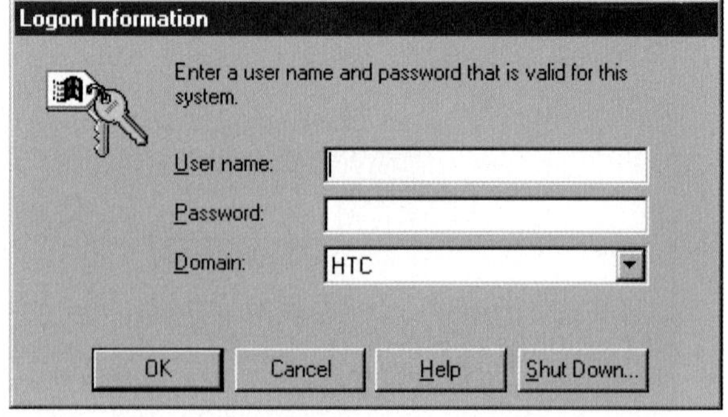

• **Figure 6-8.** Windows NT logon screen with the domain HTC selected name and the domain name. If you work in an organization that has a Microsoft Windows domain, IT professionals will have configured your computer to log onto the domain and will normally tell users which name to select to do so. Fortunately, the logon dialog box will default to displaying what you last logged onto.

Beginning with Windows 2000, this dialog box has been renamed Log On To Windows and it is greatly improved—the troublesome Domain drop-down list box is now labeled "Log on to," and they have added the description "this computer" when displaying the computer name.

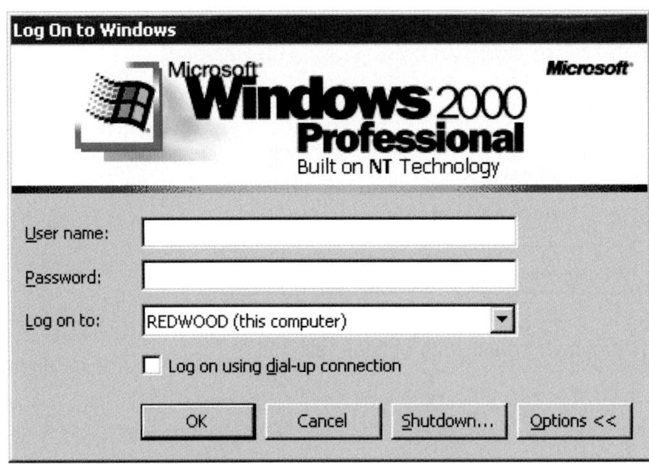

• Windows 2000 Log On to Windows dialog box with a local computer selected, as indicated by the label "(this computer)"

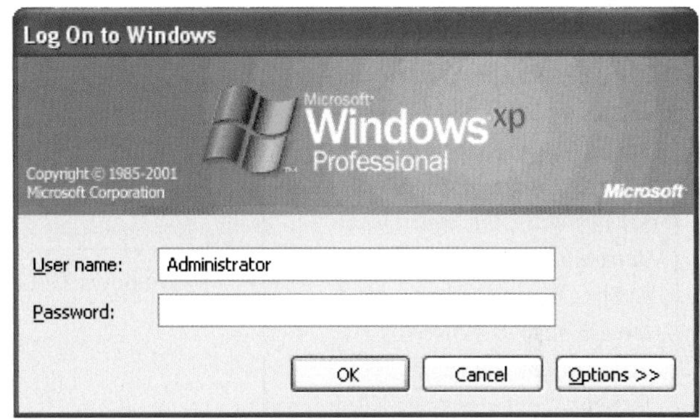

• Windows XP Log On to Windows screen

Buttons in the Logon Dialog Boxes Windows dialog boxes vary somewhat in the buttons they display. Following is a list of the buttons and when you might see them:

- Expect to find the OK button in all versions. After you have entered the necessary information into the dialog box, press ENTER or click the OK button to have your logon processed.
- The Cancel button is normally visible, but (with the exception of Windows 9*x*) it is disabled on a computer that is a workgroup member. It is enabled on a domain member computer. It allows canceling a local or domain logon, presumably because you have changed your mind about which type of logon you wish to make.
- The Help button appeared in the Windows NT logon dialog box, but it really wasn't much help. More recent versions will display a pop-up help message if you fail when attempting to log on.
- With the exception of Windows 9*x*, the logon dialog box has a Shut Down button, which allows someone who has not yet logged on to shut down the computer. By default, this button is enabled in desktop versions of Windows (Windows NT 4.0 Workstation, Windows 2000 Professional, and Windows XP Professional) but disabled in server versions of Windows like Windows 2000 Server and Windows Server 2003.

Inside Information

Only Administrators Can Shut Down Servers

While this book is about desktop operating systems, we just can't help telling you a little about other computers you may encounter. Network servers normally play very important roles in an organization, with many users depending on being able to connect to them over the network to access files and printers. For that reason, servers should not be shut down by anyone but people who have the right to shut down the server and the knowledge to know when it is appropriate to do so. Therefore, the Shut Down button is normally disabled on a server OS and enabled on a desktop OS such as Windows NT Workstation, Windows 2000 Professional, and Windows XP; it is assumed that the desktop computer is not playing the role of a server. If the desktop computer is playing the role of a server, then an administrator can disable this button (an advanced task).

- The Options button did not exist for Windows 9*x* or Windows NT, but is seen beginning with Windows 2000. It controls the display of two items in the Log On To Windows dialog box—the Log On To drop-down list box and the Log On Using Dial-Up Connection check box. Clicking the Options button will hide or display these items. This type of button is called a "toggle" because it turns a setting on or off.

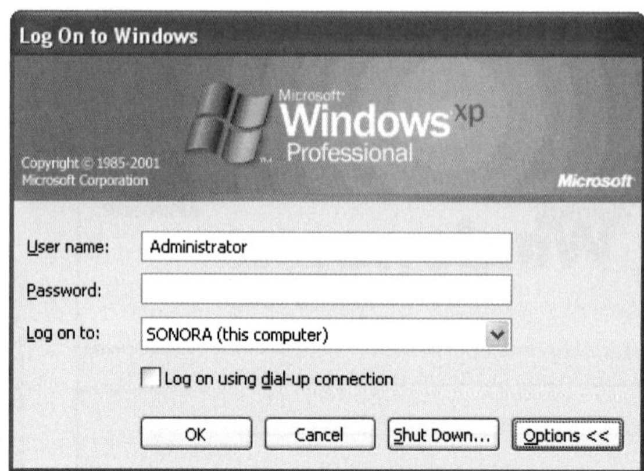

• Windows XP Log On to Windows screen with Options selected

Try This!

Use the Options Button

If you have access to a computer running Windows 2000 or a newer version, check out the Options button. Try this:

1. If necessary, start or restart your computer.
2. If prompted, press CTRL-ALT-DELETE.
3. If the Options button is available, click it once and notice the change. Click it again to return the dialog box to its previous state.

Step-by-Step 6.01

Logging Onto Windows

In this exercise, you will log onto your computer. To complete this exercise, you need the following:

- A computer with one of the four Windows operating systems installed (Windows 98, Windows NT Workstation, Windows 2000 Professional, or Windows XP Professional)
- A user name and password that will allow you to log onto your computer

Step 1

If necessary, turn on your computer.

Step 2

If you are prompted, press CTRL-ALT-DELETE.

Step 3

Enter your user name, press TAB or use the mouse to move to the Password box, enter your password, and then press ENTER.

Step 4

If instructed to do so, select the computer or domain from the Log On To drop-down list box.

Step 5

Leave the desktop open while you read the next section in the book.

A Tour of the Desktop

After you have logged onto your computer, you see your desktop—the entire screen area where all of the graphical objects appear. If at all possible, read the following while sitting at a computer running Windows, and locate each object described on your desktop.

All descriptions of Windows graphical elements are based on a standard installation of the retail product. You may see an almost infinite number of variations in Windows if it has been pre-installed on a new computer or customized since installation.

Getting Started

The first time you log onto Windows, it offers you a little extra help getting started. This may come in the form of a special dialog box, as you see in NT, Windows 98, and Windows 2000. Or it may be a simple cartoon-style message balloon, as you will see in Windows XP. They have similar objectives: to help you begin your use of Windows.

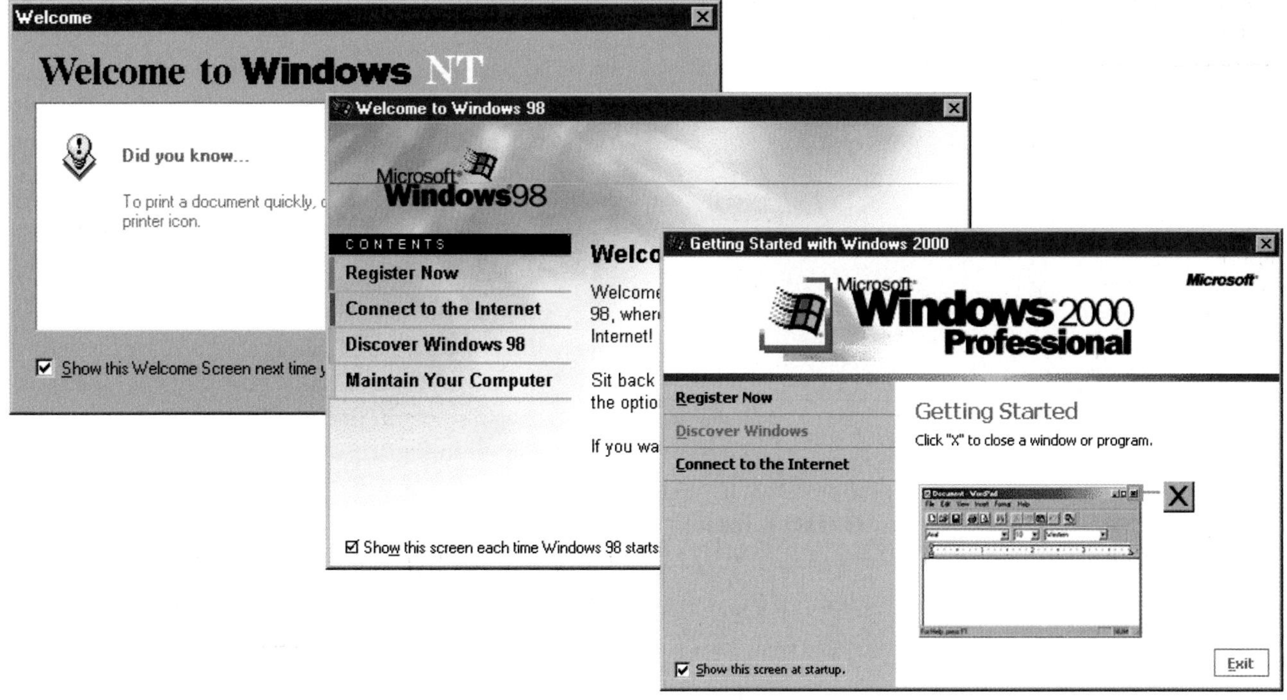

• Getting Started screens for Windows NT, Windows 98, and Windows 2000 Professional

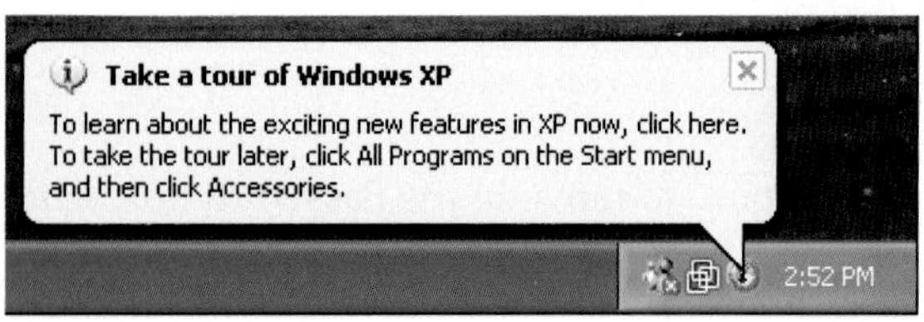

• At startup, Windows XP may display a balloon message.

All versions of Windows discussed here offer getting-started information when you first log on. In Windows NT, the Welcome window gives a different tip every time it appears and has buttons that give you access to What's New in Windows NT and Help Contents. The Welcome To Windows 98 screen in Windows 98 has links to Register Now, Connect to the Internet, Discover Windows 98 (a tutorial), and Maintain Your Computer. The Windows 2000 Getting Started window has links to Register Now, Discover Windows, and Connect to the Internet. In all of these, you can remove a check from the Show This Screen At Startup check box so that you will not see the welcome information every time you log on. In Windows XP you will see a balloon message over the system tray area offering a tour of Windows XP. You can reopen these Windows and tutorials anytime you wish from the Accessories menu.

After you get past the welcoming efforts of your OS, you can explore the desktop. Let's look at the common elements you may see on the desktop, including the taskbar, icons, and other objects.

First Look

Windows has a variety of graphical objects, including the mouse pointer, icons, shortcuts, dialog boxes, windows, folders, buttons, toolbars, menus, and the taskbar. If your desktop hasn't been modified since Windows was installed, you will see a mouse pointer, taskbar, Start menu, and one or more icons. An **icon** is a tiny graphic representing an object such as a file, folder, disk, menu item, or program. A **shortcut** is an icon that represents a link to any object that can be represented by an icon. Activating a shortcut (by clicking on it) is a quick way to access an object or to start up a program from any location without having to find the actual location of the object on your computer. A single object, like a program file, can be represented by more than one shortcut, and a shortcut can be placed on the desktop, taskbar, and other places within the Windows GUI. Shortcut icons are often (but not always) distinguished by a small bent arrow, as seen in the shortcut to Microsoft Word shown in Figure 6-9.

• The Windows XP desktop

Desktop Icons

The biggest variation on the desktop is in the displayed icons. The default desktop icons are as follows:

- Windows NT 4.0, Windows 98, and Windows 2000 all have My Computer, Internet Explorer, and the Recycle Bin as default icons. In addition, if any one of these versions of Windows is on a network, Network Neighborhood (My Network Places in Windows 2000) will also appear.

• **Figure 6-9.** MS Word shortcut icon

- Inbox appears only on the Windows NT 4.0 desktop. Similarly, Windows 98 has a desktop icon for Outlook Express.
- My Briefcase is on the NT desktop, and My Documents is on the Windows 98 and Windows 2000 desktops.
- Windows 98 also contains several additional icons, including MSN Internet Account, Online Services, and Connect To The Internet.
- The default Windows XP desktop is very, very clean, with just the Recycle Bin icon showing.

- Windows NT

- Windows 98

- Windows 2000

- Windows XP

Try This!

Lock and Unlock the Taskbar

If you have a Windows computer handy, experiment with the taskbar. Try this:

1. Use your mouse to drag the taskbar to a different position on the desktop. If it did not move, then it may be locked.
2. Right-click on an empty portion of the taskbar. See if there is a setting, Lock The Taskbar.
3. If the Lock The Taskbar setting is available, experiment with turning it on and off, testing your ability to move the taskbar.

Taskbar

Beginning with Windows 95, all Windows versions for PCs display the **taskbar** across the bottom of the screen, with some variations in the default buttons on the bar. The Windows XP taskbar shown in Figure 6-10 includes a Start button, the notification area, the Quick Launch toolbar, and buttons for programs that are running. Most of the taskbar area is used to display buttons for running programs.

The notification area (also called the system tray or systray), located on the far right of the taskbar, is used by programs and some hardware devices to display status icons. These icons may represent devices such as network adapters and software such as a battery meter, antivirus program, and so on. Pausing the mouse pointer over one of these icons will cause a rectangular status box to pop up. Another type of pop-up box, a message balloon, will pop up near the notification area for events relating to one of the icons.

• Status messages display when the mouse pointer is paused on an icon.

• When an event occurs related to a notification area icon, a message displays in a balloon over the icon.

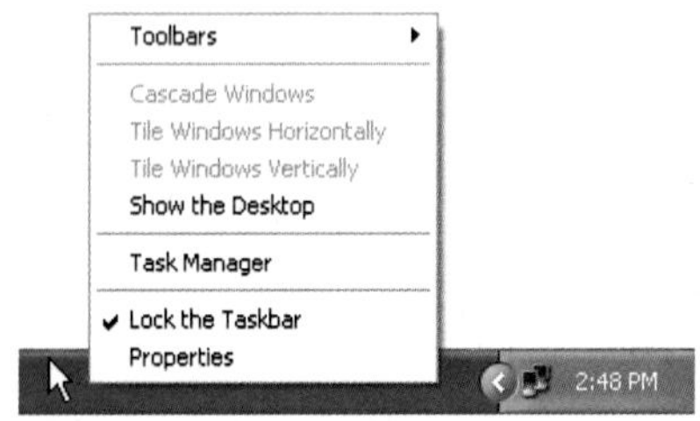

• Lock the taskbar position from the taskbar's context menu.

You can reposition the entire taskbar by simply moving the pointer to an "empty" area and dragging it to a new position. You can also resize the taskbar by dragging just an edge of it until it is the desired size. The Windows XP taskbar option, Lock The Taskbar, locks the taskbar in place so that it can't be moved until the option is turned off. This is turned on by default, and you can turn it on or off by right-clicking on the taskbar and selecting or deselecting Lock The Taskbar.

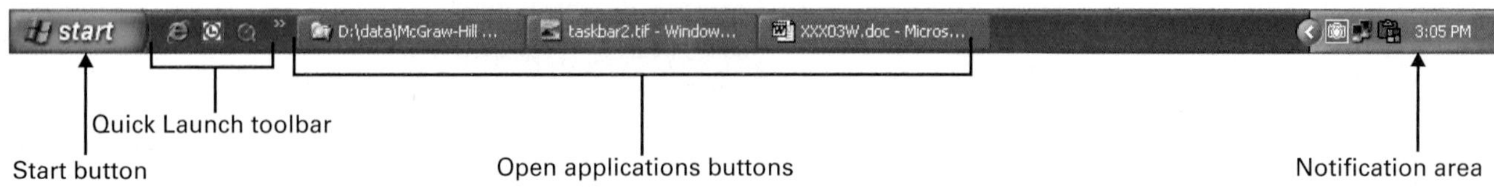

• **Figure 6-10.** Windows XP taskbar with components identified

Start Menu

The Start button on the taskbar opens a very important menu, called the Start menu. This menu is divided into areas containing shortcuts and submenus. It is the central tool for finding and starting a variety of programs in Windows. Microsoft increased the importance of the Start menu in Windows XP, moving all but one of the default desktop icons off the desktop and onto the Start menu, which required more space for the Start menu—two columns as opposed to the previous default of one column. (See Figure 6-11.) On the top left of the Start menu is an area called the pinned items list, your choice of programs for browsing the Internet and using e-mail. The shortcuts in the pinned items list remain there unless you choose to remove or change them. In Windows XP, a separator line marks the end of this list and the beginning of the recently used programs list. In all four versions, the Start menu contains shortcuts for programs and folders which in turn may contain more folders, shortcuts, and files. An arrow on a folder icon indicates that the folder item can be expanded to display the contents, or submenu. In the following sections, you'll look at the areas of the Start menu and the menu shortcuts that are common to all or most of these OSs. Some of the shortcut names have been altered slightly between Windows versions, in which case we present the alternative names.

Programs/All Programs Before Windows XP, the Programs menu item had an icon of a folder with an overlapping program icon. This indicates that it is a folder containing links to programs and other folders containing programs. In Windows XP it serves the same function, but does not have an

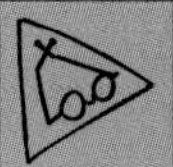

Inside Information

Special Folders

Windows treats certain disk folders called ***special folders*** *differently than others. These folders include Start Menu, My Documents, Favorites, Desktop, and many others. A set of special folders is saved on disk for each user who logs on. These are called* ***personal folders****. In addition, a generic set is saved with shortcuts and folders that appear on the desktops of all users who log onto the local computer.*

You can add additional shortcuts to the pinned items list on your Windows XP computer. The setting for doing this is in the Customize Start Menu page of the Properties dialog box for the Start menu (right-click on the Start button and select Properties). Or you can right-click any shortcut and choose Pin To Start Menu.

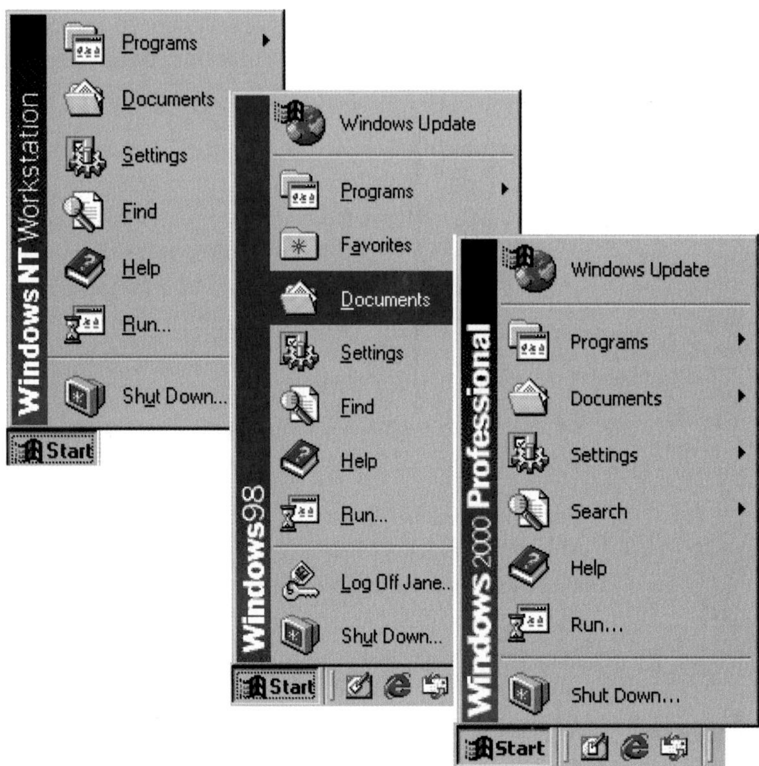

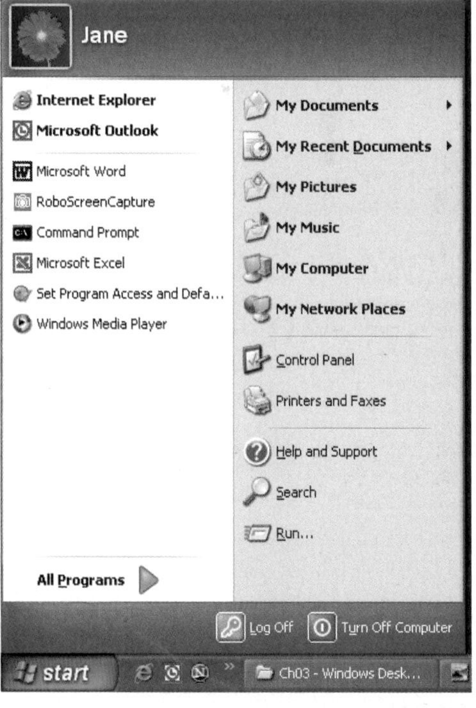

• **Figure 6-11.** Compare the Start menus in four versions of Windows.

• Windows 2000 Program menu

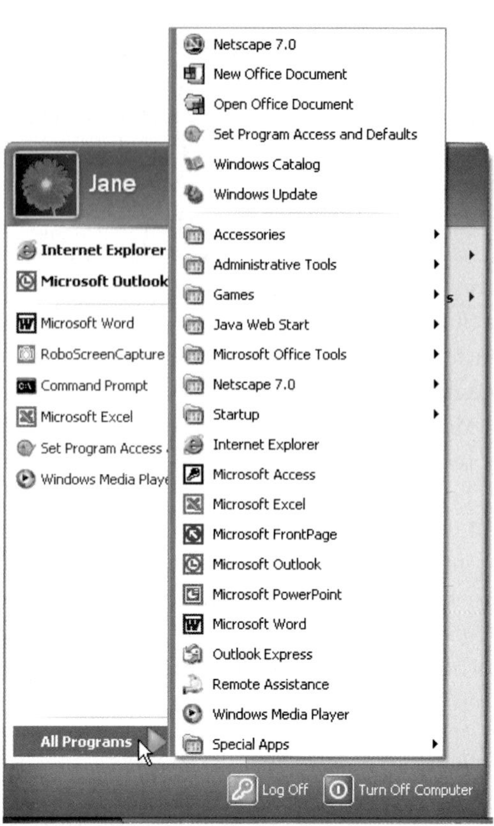

• Windows XP All Programs menu

icon and is renamed All Programs. Click this Start menu shortcut to open a menu with a list of programs and program categories. When you install a new application in Windows, it will usually add a folder or program icon to this menu.

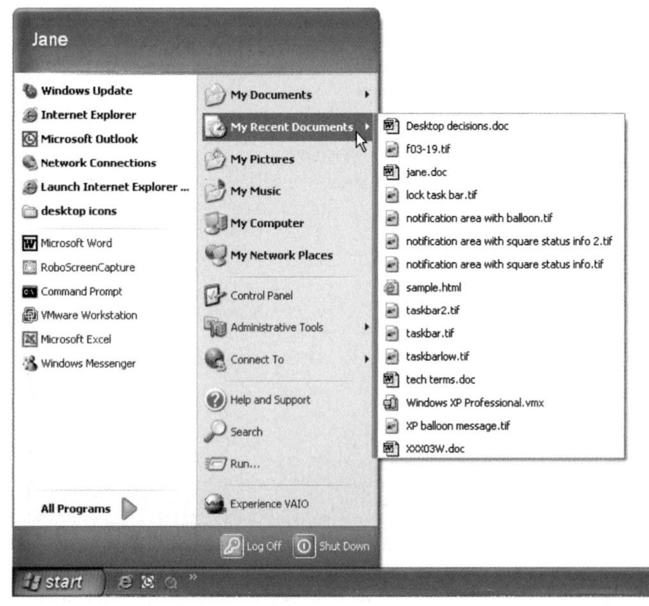

• Windows XP My Recent Documents

Documents/My Recent Documents The Documents shortcut icon (Windows NT, Windows 98, and Windows 2000) appears to be an open folder with papers in it. This folder contains shortcuts to recently opened data files. In Windows XP, this folder is named My Recent Documents and only appears on the Start menu if the "List my most recently opened documents" check box is selected in the Advanced options accessed through the Customize button in the Start Menu Properties dialog box. See Figure 6-12.

Personal Folders Personal folders are a significant subset of special folders that Windows creates on disk to hold files and folders for each user. Included are files containing desktop configuration and preference information, as well as each user's own data files. Shortcuts to some of these personal folders are on the Start menu. In Windows 98 and Windows 2000, the Documents shortcut menu contains a shortcut to the personal folder, My

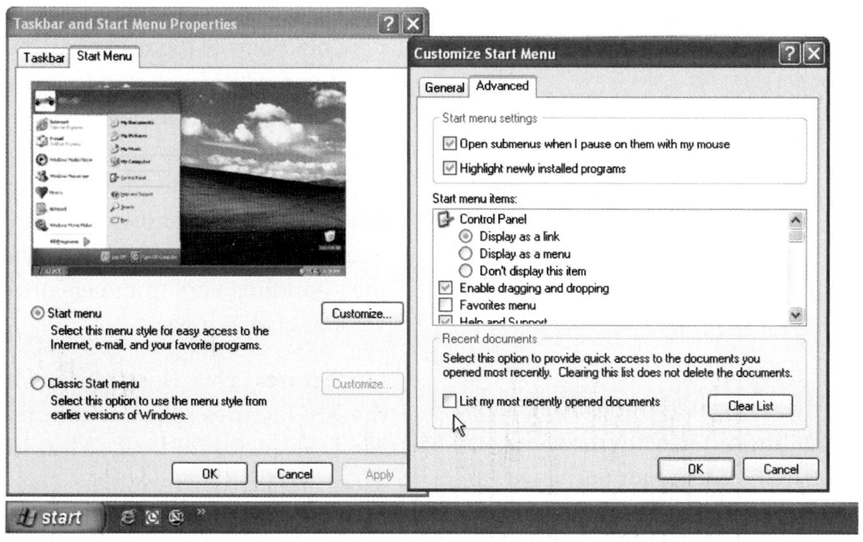

• **Figure 6-12.** Select "List my most recently opened documents" on the Advanced page of the Customize Start Menu dialog box.

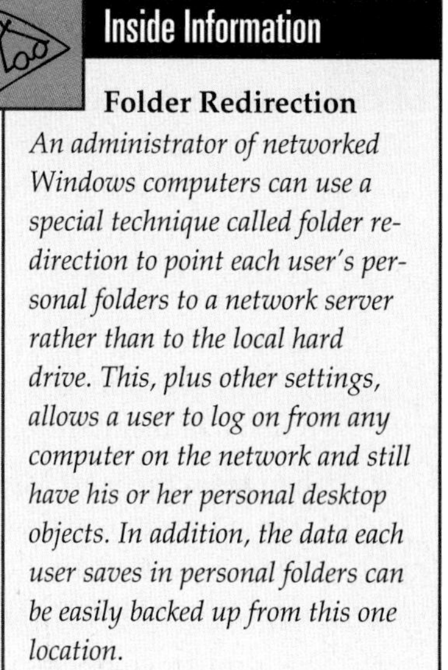

Inside Information

Folder Redirection

An administrator of networked Windows computers can use a special technique called folder redirection to point each user's personal folders to a network server rather than to the local hard drive. This, plus other settings, allows a user to log on from any computer on the network and still have his or her personal desktop objects. In addition, the data each user saves in personal folders can be easily backed up from this one location.

Documents, in which you can save your data files. In Windows XP, My Documents on the Start menu is a shortcut to the personal My Documents folder where you can save data files. Each user has personal folders, separate from those of all other users. Each user's personal folders are saved under a special folder named with the user's logon name. (See Figure 6-13.) Many Windows applications are aware of this folder and will default to My Documents for saving and opening files.

Additional personal folders may be added by Windows and other applications. They can be quite numerous, depending on the installed

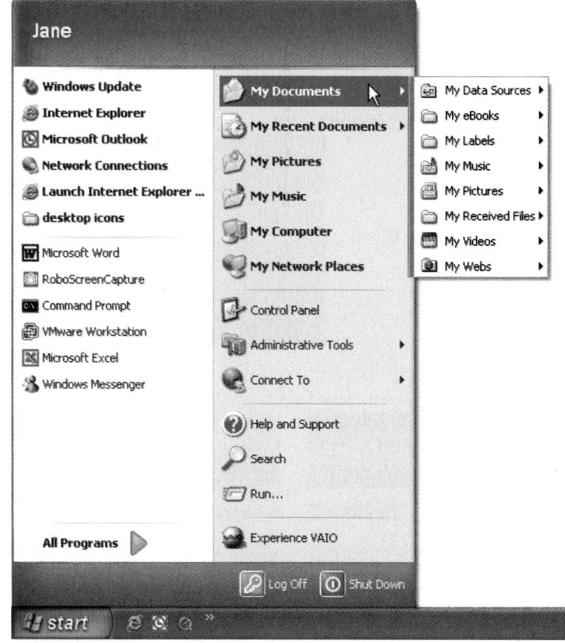

• Windows XP My Documents

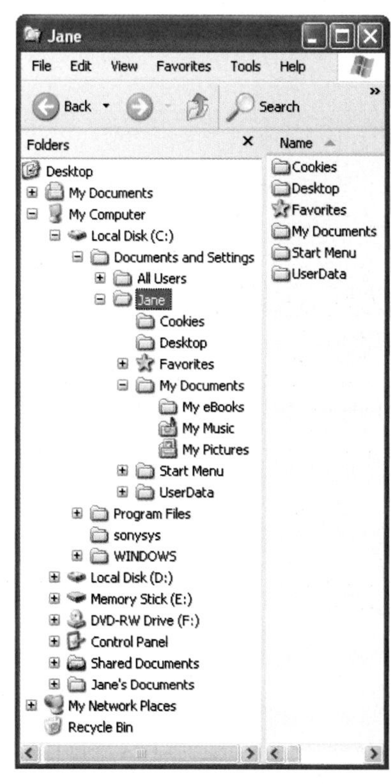

• **Figure 6-13.** Each user has a set of personal folders within a folder named with the user's logon name.

Try This!

Explore the Personal Folders

The shortcuts that appear on your Start menu are contained in two locations on disk: the Start Menu folder in your profile folders and the Start Menu folder in the All Users folder. Browse through these folders now. Try this:

1. Right-click on the Start button and select Explore. This will open the Start Menu folder within your profile folders. Note the contents of the Start Menu folder.
2. Then open the Start Menu folder that is located under All Users. Look at the contents that appear in this folder. The combined folders and shortcut files are those that appear on your Start menu, plus others that appear there through other means.
3. Do a similar comparison of the Programs folder located under the Start Menu folder in each location. The Programs folders should contain the folders and shortcuts that appear on your All Programs menu.

applications and Windows components. Some of them, like My Pictures and My Music, reside in the My Documents folder, while others may reside elsewhere. These additional personal folders may or may not have separate shortcuts on the Start menu. Special folders and their handling vary from version to version of Windows.

My Pictures This is a shortcut to the My Pictures folder within the My Documents folder. Use this location to save picture files. There are benefits to doing this, because this is a special folder designed just for picture files. The task list for this folder includes tasks for working with your pictures: View As A Slide Show, Order Prints Online, Print This Picture, Set As Desktop Background, and Copy To A CD. Similarly, the context menu for each file will contain tasks appropriate for this type of file. This last feature is true for a picture file in any disk folder. The Filmstrip option on the View menu allows you to view the files in the folder as you would a filmstrip. This view is shown in Figure 6-14.

My Music This is a shortcut to another special folder, the My Music folder within the My Documents folder. Here also, you will find tasks appropriate

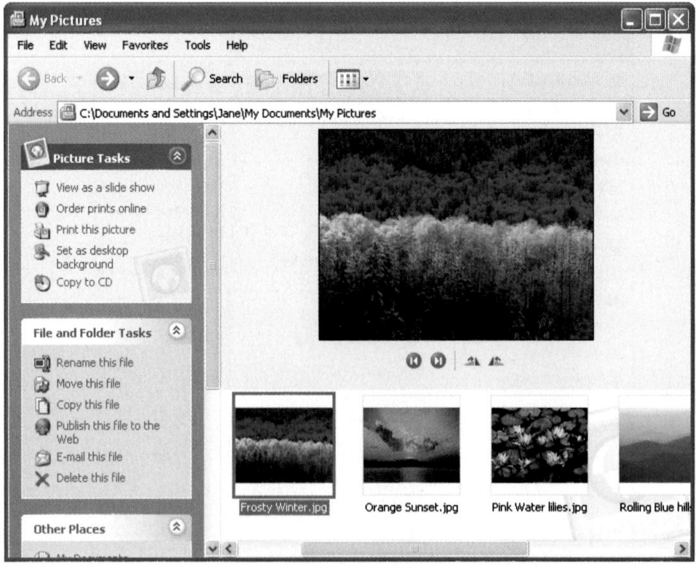

• **Figure 6-14.** The My Pictures folder has a task list with appropriate tasks for picture files.

for music files in the task list and the context menus, such as Play and Copy To Music CD. Use this location to save music files.

My Computer This shortcut is on the desktop or the Start menu, depending on your version of Windows. It opens the My Computer folder in Windows Explorer, displaying file folders, hard disk drives, and removable storage on the local computer. The actual objects vary from version to version and also depend on how the computer is configured. Clicking on the Folders button on the toolbar will change the view from the default, single-pane view to a two-pane view showing a folder hierarchy in the left pane and the contents of the currently selected folder on the right. (See Figures 6-15 and 6-16.) Use this folder when you need to work with disk folders beyond your personal folders, for instance to access folders on a removable drive.

Most keyboards today include the Windows key, a key with the Microsoft Windows logo usually located to the left of the space bar. This key pressed in combination with other keys acts as a shortcut to open menus and folders in Windows. Pressing WINDOWS KEY-E will open Windows Explorer focused on the My Computer folder.

Network Neighborhood/My Network Places This shortcut opens a special folder containing shortcuts to network locations—on the LAN or the Internet. Once again, the task list includes tasks appropriate for working with network locations, such as Add A Network Place, View Network Connections, View Workgroup Computers, and Set Up A Home Or Small Office Network.

Settings Windows NT, Windows 98, and Windows 2000 have a Settings shortcut on the Start menu. This shortcut opens a menu of choices that differs depending on the version of Windows. Control Panel, Printers, and Taskbar icons are common to all three OSs that have the Settings menu. Other items you will find, depending on the version of Windows, are Network and Dial-up Connections, Folder Options, Active Desktop, and Windows Update.

While Windows XP does not have the Settings menu, it does have Control Panel and Printers

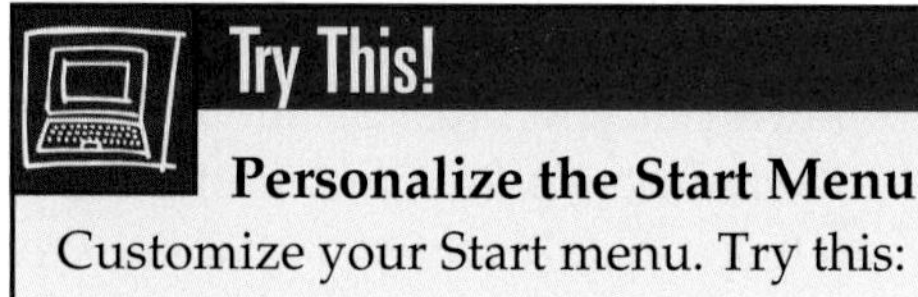

Try This!

Personalize the Start Menu

Customize your Start menu. Try this:

1. Right-click on the Start button and select Properties.
2. On the Start Menu page, ensure that the Start Menu radio button is selected, and click the Customize button to its right.
3. Make changes to some of the settings on the General page, such as the icon size or the Show On Start Menu items. Close the Taskbar And Start Menu Properties dialog box and test your changes.

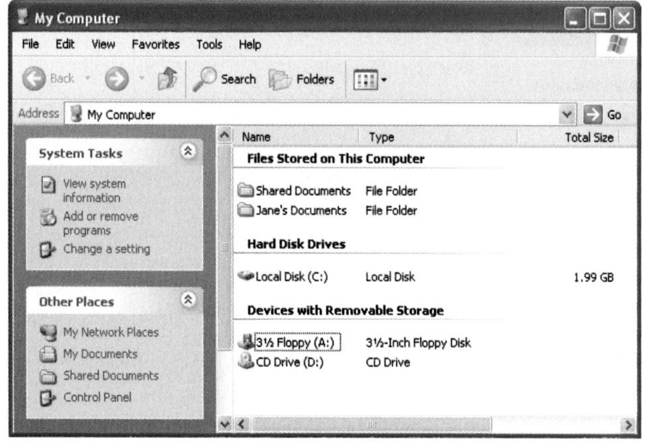

• **Figure 6-15.** Windows XP My Computer—Default view

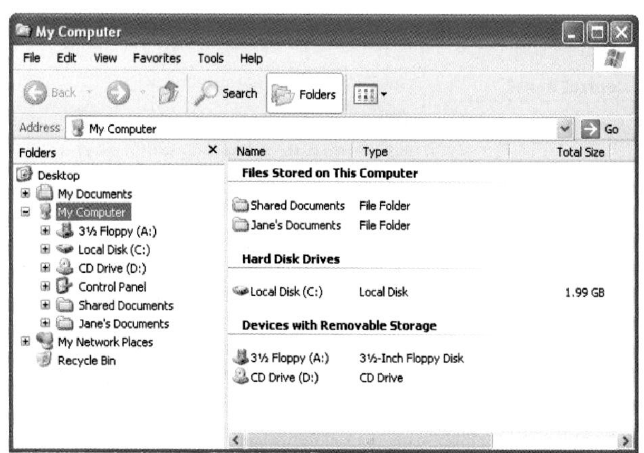

• **Figure 6-16.** Windows XP My Computer—Dual-pane view with folder hierarchy

And Faxes as shortcuts on the Start menu. All of the items you usually find on the older Settings menus (with the exception of Control Panel itself) are really links to options within Control Panel.

Control Panel The Control Panel item on the Settings menu is a link to the Control Panel special folder, which contains a variety of **applets** (mini-application programs) that exist to allow you (or an administrator) to configure your software and hardware. Many of these applets can be accessed elsewhere. For instance, activating the Display applet in Control Panel opens the Properties dialog box for the display, which you can also open by right-clicking an empty area of the desktop and selecting Properties from the context menu.

The Control Panel changed very little through the various versions of Windows, until Windows XP, when it underwent a major reorganization. Compare the classic Control Panel from Windows 2000, shown in Figure 6-17, with the Control Panel from Windows XP, shown in Figure 6-18. In the classic version, you see icons for the individual applets themselves. To use that version, you think about the task you need to do, and then you search for the right tool to do that task. (Let's see. I want to switch the primary and secondary buttons on the mouse for a left-handed user. Because it's a mouse, I'll begin by opening the Mouse applet, and then I'll make the appropriate choice.)

The Windows XP Control Panel, however, is organized by functional category. So, as before, you think of the task you want to perform. Next, however, you must decide which category fits your task. Modifying how the mouse works comes under the category Printers And Other Hardware. It helps that this category happens to have a graphic of a mouse (obviously a huge mouse, since in the graphic it is bigger than the printer). So you click the printers and hardware category, and then you have another choice, as you can see in Figure 6-19. You can select a task, but those listed have nothing to do with the mouse, or you can pick a Control Panel icon. Finally… there's

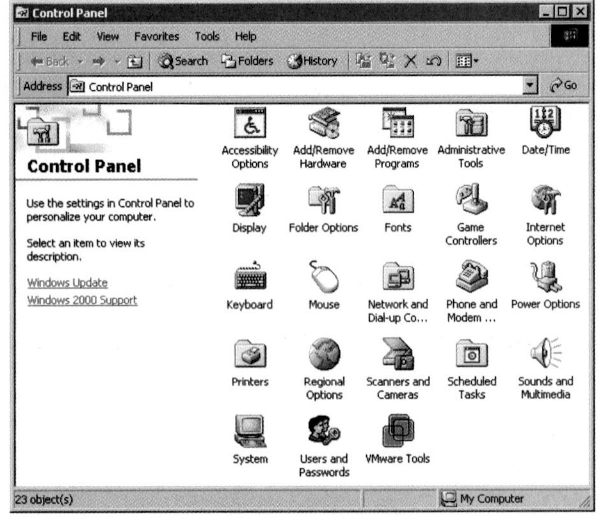

• **Figure 6-17.** Windows 2000 Control Panel

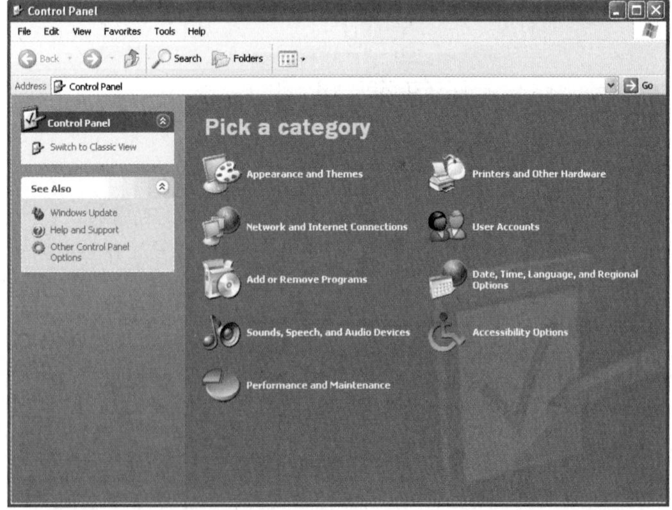

• **Figure 6-18.** Windows XP Control Panel

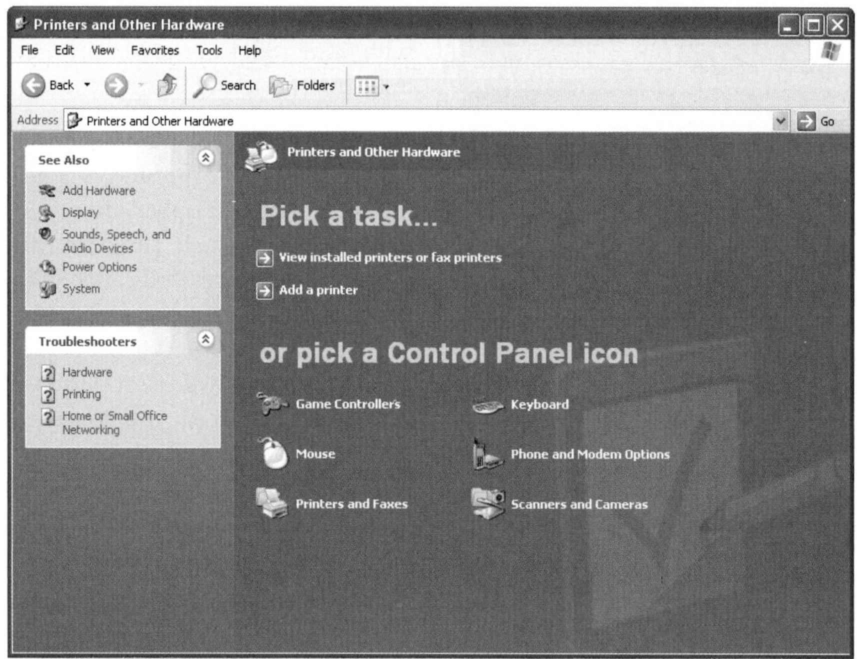

• **Figure 6-19.** Pick a task...or pick a Control Panel icon.

the Mouse icon! A single mouse-click will now bring up the Mouse Properties dialog box, and you can work from there.

It can be argued that Control Panel is easier to use in XP, especially if you are new to Windows or, like our friend Carl, have not found previous versions easy to use. However, experienced Windows users and computer professionals, like Harry, will discover that the more advanced options are somewhat more difficult to find. More experienced users, therefore, may choose to use the Windows XP option for viewing Control Panel in the Classic view.

Printers and Faxes Printers And Faxes on the Start menu is a shortcut to the Printers And Faxes folder in Control Panel. From this folder, you can install and manage printers and install and manage the Fax client that comes with Windows. This client is not installed by default.

• Manage printing and faxing from the Printers and Faxes folder.

Help All four versions of Windows include a Help option on the Start menu. The Help program itself has improved with each version, and with Windows XP, the Help And Support option opens up the Help And Support Center window, which gives you links to your local Help program, Internet sources, Remote Assistance, Microsoft's Windows XP newsgroups, and various programs to help you update your software, restore the system, and diagnose problems. Whatever version of Windows you have, take time to check out Help. You will find answers to most of your questions about Windows in Help. All versions have troubleshooting scripts that walk you through a problem. Don't forget this great

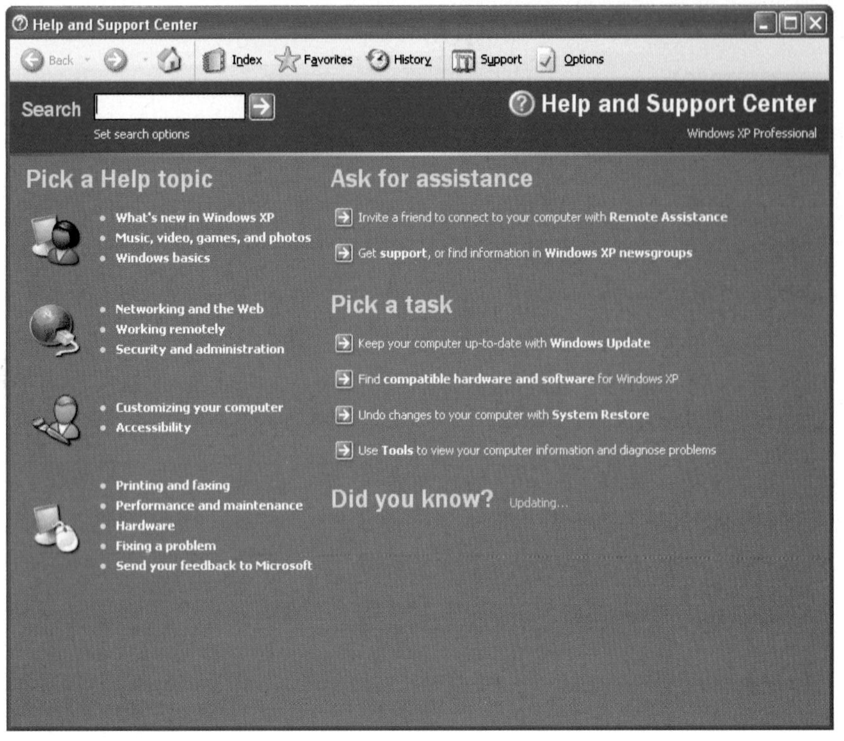

• Windows XP Help menu

resource when you have problems with your computer or simply want to learn more about using Windows.

Find/Search All of the versions of Windows that you are studying here have a Start menu option that opens a Find or a Search program (the name change occurred after Windows 98). These programs have increased in capability with each version of Windows, from Windows NT, which allowed you to search only for files, folders, and computers, to Windows XP, which offers a comprehensive search program that allows you to search for almost anything you want on a small or large network—or even on the Internet. The list of items has been expanded to include people, files in online tape backup storage, various types of files, help topics, and more.

Run The Run option allows you to launch any program that can run under Windows. When you select Start | Run, a dialog box appears. You can enter the name of the program to be launched, or click the Browse button to search for the program on disk (local or network). Some programs, such as the registry editor (regedit or regedt32), cannot normally be started by an icon or menu entry, but are routinely started from Start | Run. Other

> Use the size option on a regular basis to find space-hogging files on your drives. For instance, search for files of at least 10,000KB and then browse through them. Are there large zipped files that you no longer need? Media files you no longer care to see or hear? Delete all the unwanted files. This is a handy "tidying up" technique. This will find files that can be missed by the Disk Cleanup utility you will learn about later in this chapter.

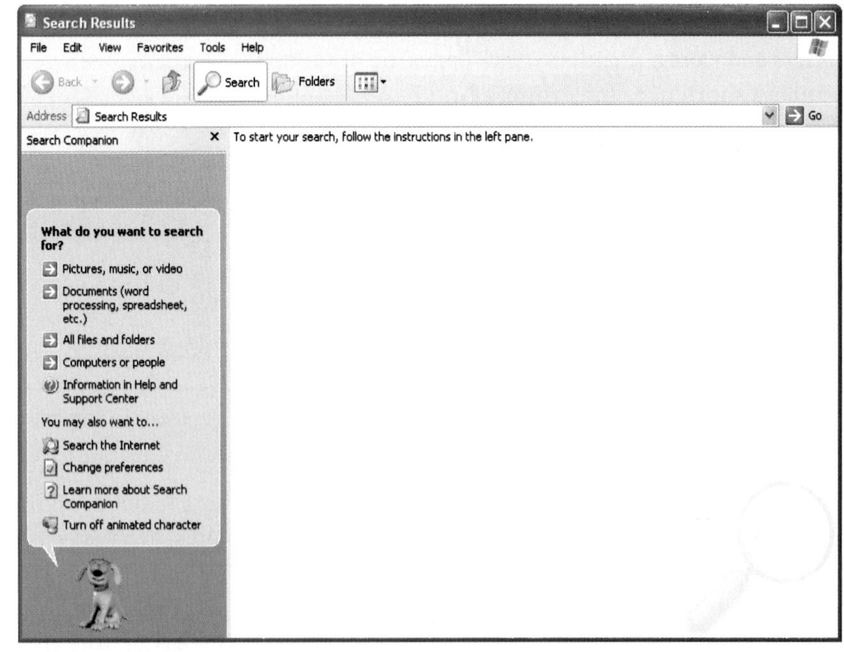

• Windows XP Search menu

commands seem to be buried in the Start menu, and intermediate to advanced users will often discover the executable name for their favorite programs and start them from the Run box. One good example is the System Information utility, launched from a shortcut located at Start | All Programs | Accessories | System Tools. It is clearly easier to remember its executable file name, msinfo32.exe, and start it from the Run box. This important GUI utility allows you to view hardware and software configuration information, and to start several diagnostics and repair utilities from its Tools menu.

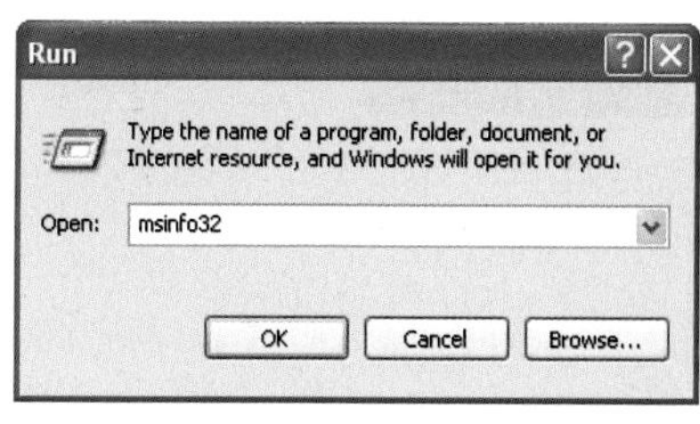

• Launch a program from Start | Run.

Shut Down For years we have heard users say, "Why can't there be a 'Turn off' switch for a PC?" They really are asking for a single hardware switch that will gracefully shut down their programs and OS as well as power off the hardware. This has finally come to the PC world, at least for Windows XP, but it requires a special setting found on the Advanced tab of the Power Options applet. This setting defines the action that should occur when you press the power button on your computer. In all other cases, pressing the power button will not gracefully shut down the OS, and you should not use the hardware switch before properly shutting down the OS, or you will risk losing data and/or damaging program files. Windows NT, Windows 98, and Windows 2000 all have a Shut Down option on the Start menu, which leads to other options, including Log Off and (finally) Shut Down. Shut Down in Windows 98, Windows 2000, and Windows XP will also power off your hardware if this feature is supported by your computer's motherboard and chipset. On older machines, after you select Shut Down, the OS is shut down and then a message such as the following will appear: "You may safely turn off your computer." In Windows XP, Start | Shut Down has been replaced by two buttons, Log Off and Turn Off Computer, at the bottom of the Start menu. You will work with your OS' shut down or turn off option in the section "Logging Off and Shutting Down."

Although any program that can run under Windows can be launched from Start | Run, it isn't practical for running most command-line utilities, because the command prompt will not remain open long enough for you to see the result of running the command! For these programs, first launch the command prompt; then run the program.

Step-by-Step 6.02

Using the Start Menu

In this exercise, you will use the shortcuts and submenus of the Start menu. To complete this exercise, you will need the following:

- A computer with one of the four Windows operating systems installed (Windows 98, Windows NT Workstation, Windows 2000 Professional, or Windows XP Professional)
- A user name and password that will allow you to log onto your computer

Step 1

If necessary, start and log onto your computer, as you did in Step-by-Step 6.01.

Step 2

Start a program from the Run box: Select Start | Run. Type **notepad** in the Run box and then click OK or press ENTER. Notepad is a text editor that comes with Windows. It can only create and edit text files, which are files that do not have hidden formatting codes like those that a word processor embeds in a file to control the way data is displayed and printed. Text files usually have a TXT extension. Create a text file in Notepad just for fun.

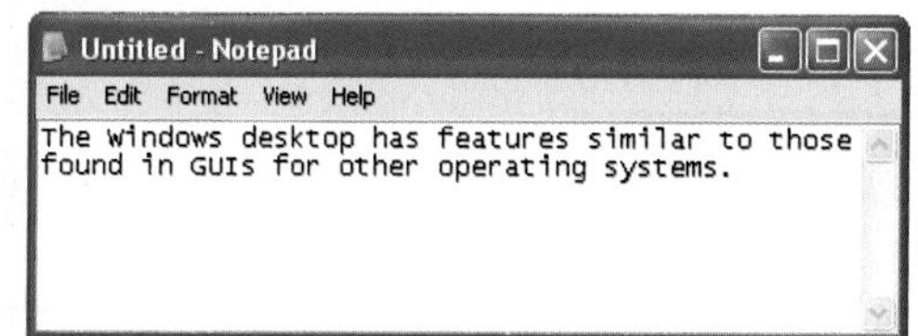

Step 3

Close Notepad. When prompted to save the file, save it in My Documents as **mysample.txt**.

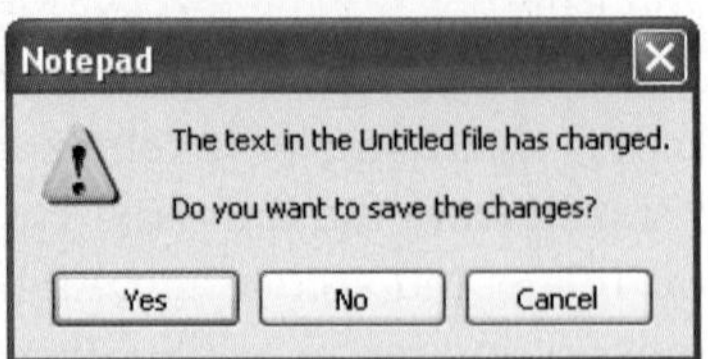

Step 4

Start a program from a menu. Select Start | All Programs (or Programs) | Accessories (in some versions of Windows) | Games | Solitaire (or the game of your choice). Play exactly one game to enhance your mouse skills. If you do not know how to play, click the Help button (you may even find Strategies and Tips). After you are done, close the game.

Step 5

Open a command prompt. If you are using Windows 2000 or Windows XP, select Start | All Programs (or Programs) | Accessories | Command Prompt.

If you are using Windows NT or Windows 98, select Start | Programs | Command Prompt (or MS-DOS Prompt).

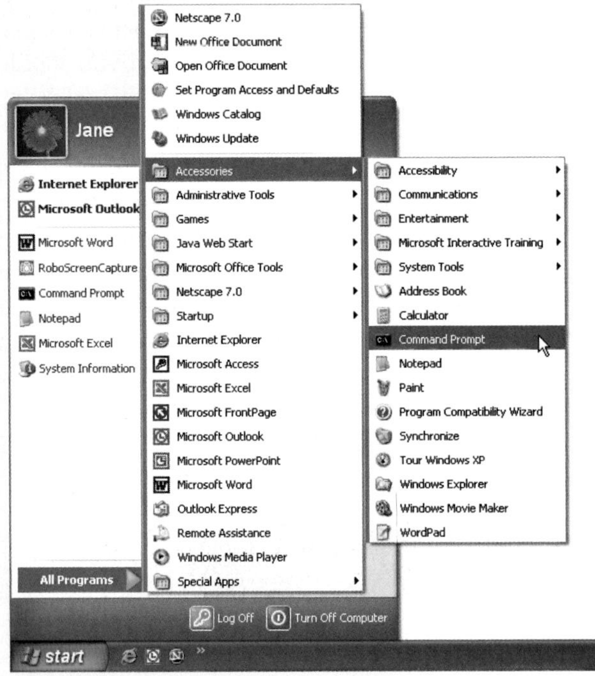

Step 6

At the command prompt, type **ipconfig**. Press ENTER. This is a very advanced command, but one that you should learn even if you are new to computers, especially if you are responsible for your own computer. This command gives you information about your network or Internet connection. If you have a network problem, a network administrator or your ISP may ask you to run this command and give them the resulting information.

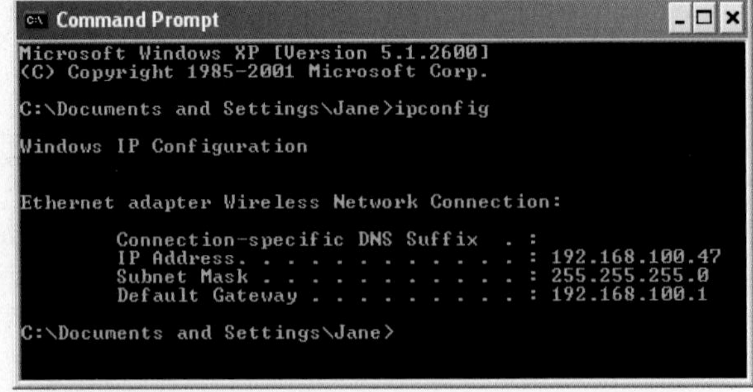

Step 7

At the command prompt, type **exit** and press ENTER to close the command prompt window.

Configuring and Customizing the Windows Desktop

Windows allows each user to create the desktop environment that suits his or her particular personality and way of working. Some people like icons all over the desktop on a simple background, others like elaborate graphic backgrounds with icons, while yet others like simple, peaceful scenes with few icons. Customizing is easy. In this section, we'll explore some of your options for customizing the Windows desktop: choosing the Classic Desktop or the Active Desktop, changing the background wallpaper or pattern, selecting color schemes, and making video settings.

Classic Desktop vs. Active Desktop

Microsoft introduced the concept of the Active Desktop with Internet Explorer (IE) 4.01 and the versions of Windows that came after it. **Active Desktop** is a feature that lets you put web content directly on your Windows desktop. If Active Desktop is installed, you can choose between the classic Windows desktop and Web view. In classic Windows desktop, you double-click to open an object on the desktop or in My Computer, while in Web view, objects on the desktop behave like links in a web page so you can open them with a single click. You can have a combination of the old and the new, with your standard desktop icons requiring a double-click to open, and other objects shown as links with an underline that indicates that they are links and so require only a single-click. Furthermore, you can display web content directly on your desktop, even content that changes, like stock quotes. Figure 6-20 shows web content (from two web sites) displayed on the Windows XP desktop. Moving the mouse pointer over one of the web windows brings up a bar with buttons for a context menu and for expanding or closing the window. These windows stay on your desktop, even when you are offline, displaying the content from the last update.

You use the Display properties applet to enable, customize, or disable Active Desktop. In all but Windows XP, look for the Web tab in the Display properties dialog box. In Windows XP, you must first select the Desktop tab in Display Properties, click the Customize Desktop button, and then click the Web tab. However, to enable single-click in XP, you must go to the Tools Folder of Windows Explorer and select Folder Options. On the General page, you will see the single-click versus double-click options under Click Items As Follows. This setting affects Windows Explorer and the entire Windows desktop.

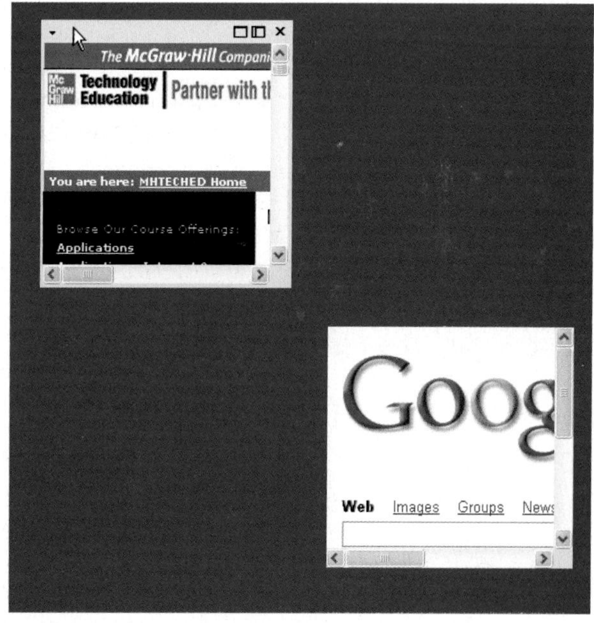

• **Figure 6-20.** Windows XP with two Active Desktop web-content windows

Decorating the Desktop: Background, Color Schemes, and Settings

You have many choices when it comes to how your desktop is decorated. You can have wallpaper on the background, or no wallpaper—there are many designs available, and you can also buy designs or get them free from many sources. You may even make your own from a photo or any graphics file. You can also change the colors of the desktop items, select a screen saver, or select a theme, each of which is a combination of individual settings. All of this can be done by right-clicking the desktop, selecting Properties, and using the various individual tabs in the Display Properties dialog box. The names change on some of these tabs from version to version of Windows.

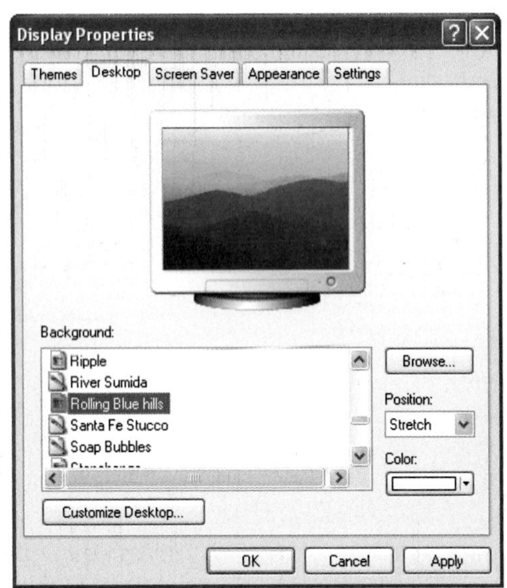

• The Windows XP Desktop page (formerly Background) allows you to select the background color and wallpaper.

Customizing the Taskbar

One clever thing you can do is to make use of the Quick Launch toolbar. The icons on this toolbar are smaller, thereby saving valuable desktop real estate, and can be activated with a single click. We arrange our icons in the order of frequency of use, putting the ones we use the most on the Quick Launch toolbar, and placing those we use less frequently on the desktop.

One of our purposes in writing this book is to help you become comfortable enough with Windows that you are able to figure out how to do things on your own, without needing a step-by-step explanation. Modern computers in general, and Windows OSs in particular, usually have a number of ways to do a task or to activate a specific function. The procedure you choose to do the task is often the first one you find. People tend not to look for other, perhaps easier, ways to do a task after they have found one that works for them.

Step-by-Step 6.03

Customizing the Desktop

In this exercise, you will customize the desktop by adding or changing the screen saver and by adding an icon to your Quick Start menu. To complete this exercise, you will need the following:

- A computer with one of the four Windows operating systems installed (Windows NT Workstation, Windows 98, Windows 2000 Professional, or Windows XP Professional)
- A user name and password that will allow you to log onto your computer

Step 1

If necessary, start and log onto your computer, right-click an empty area of the desktop, and then select Properties. In the Display Properties dialog box, click the Screen Saver tab.

Step 2

On the Screen Saver page, select a screen saver from the Screen Saver drop-down list. This will cause other buttons and boxes on that page to become active. Keep in mind that although some screen savers, such as those identified as OpenGL in Windows NT and Windows 2000, are really cool, they may slow down your computer and interfere with other programs. In Windows XP these screen savers are not clearly defined, but a rule of thumb is that the more a screen saver draws on your screen, as opposed to simply moving a small graphic around, the more processing it may require. So, if you have more important tasks for your computer than displaying a fantastic screen saver, don't choose one of these elaborate screen savers.

Step 3

Click the Preview button to preview the screen saver on the full screen. Moving the mouse or pressing a key will stop the preview. The value in the Wait box controls how long the computer will have to go without mouse or keyboard activity before the screen saver comes on. Adjust this number to the setting you desire.

Step 4

If you have confidential information on your computer that you do not want others to access when you step away from your computer, one option is to put a password on your screen saver. If you select the On Resume, Password Protect check box, a password will be required to access your computer once the screen saver has become active. Password protection on screen savers is available in all four versions of Windows used in this book. In all but Windows 9*x*, this password is the password you used to log onto the computer. In Windows 9*x*, this password is one you create just for the screen saver using the Change button. Select Password Protected. Then click OK to close the Display Properties dialog box.

Step 5

A better alternative to password-protected screen savers in Windows NT, Windows 2000, and Windows XP is the ability to lock your computer. This is more secure than using a screen saver (among other advantages, you can do it immediately). This option is only available if CTRL-ALT-DELETE is required for a logon, in which case, the Lock Computer option is available on the Security menu, accessed from the desktop by pressing CTRL-ALT-DELETE. Press CTRL-ALT-DELETE and select Lock Computer. The "Computer Locked" message will appear on your screen. To use the computer, enter your password in the Unlock Computer box.

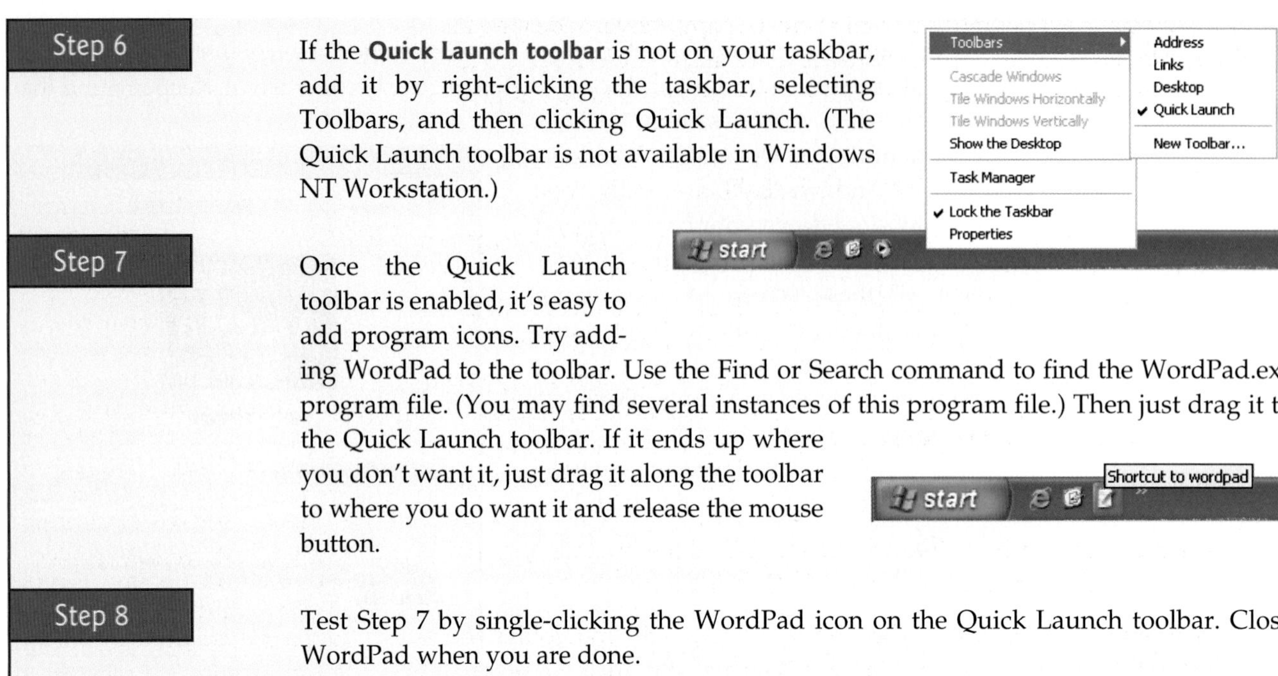

Step 6

If the **Quick Launch toolbar** is not on your taskbar, add it by right-clicking the taskbar, selecting Toolbars, and then clicking Quick Launch. (The Quick Launch toolbar is not available in Windows NT Workstation.)

Step 7

Once the Quick Launch toolbar is enabled, it's easy to add program icons. Try adding WordPad to the toolbar. Use the Find or Search command to find the WordPad.exe program file. (You may find several instances of this program file.) Then just drag it to the Quick Launch toolbar. If it ends up where you don't want it, just drag it along the toolbar to where you do want it and release the mouse button.

Step 8

Test Step 7 by single-clicking the WordPad icon on the Quick Launch toolbar. Close WordPad when you are done.

Managing Files in Windows

While any GUI operating system you use may have its own methods for allowing you to manage your files, the Windows OSs have many things in common. In this section, check out file and folder basics, organizing files using folders, creating files, GUI and non-GUI techniques for managing files, and maintenance of files and disks.

File and Folder Basics

A file is information organized as a unit. The author of a file determines just how much information to save in a single file. For instance, the chapter you are reading right now is saved as a single file. We could have chosen to save all of the chapters of this book in a single file, but chose instead to save them in individual files, because it breaks the information up into more workable "chunks" for us. That's the key to working with information in general—using chunks that you can manage well. In addition, a file is saved into a special file on disk called a folder (named "directory" in MS-DOS). When you are working in an application, such as a word processor, it will usually have a default folder into which it saves your files, but you can choose to save any file in other folders—you can even create additional folders. You have choices like these when you are working with data files.

As part of managing your files, you'll perform different actions—such as opening, closing, copying, and moving files and folders. Compared to file management in DOS, file management in Windows is infinitely easier and safer. File management is easier because you don't have to memorize commands that use cryptic syntax. Moreover, you don't have to feel like you are taking a typing test every time you want to create, copy, move, or delete a file or folder. File management is somewhat safer because you can see exactly what files and folders you have selected for a file management operation.

What Files Should You Manage?

Windows computers use several file types including, in broad terms, program files and data files. Program files (also called binary files) contain programming code (instructions read by the OS or special interpreters). Program files include those that you can directly run, such as files with the COM or EXE extension, and those that are called up by other programs, such as files with the DLL extension. When it comes to file management, it is necessary to manage data files. Management of program files is best left to the experts. Leave program files where their installation programs place them. Before studying file management of data files, take a brief look at the folder structure created by Windows for the use of the operating system files, add-on components, and applications. They include

- **Documents and Settings** This folder, located in the root folder of the boot partition, is where Windows 2000 and Windows XP place the personal folders for all users who log on.
- **Windows** This folder, located in the root folder of the boot partition, is where the Windows operating system is stored. Note that before the operating system is installed, the setup program will allow you to give this folder a different name, but we strongly suggest you resist any urge to do this!
- **Program Files** This folder is the location of subfolders where your application programs are typically installed.
- **Fonts** Here you will find the various fonts installed on the PC. This folder is always a subfolder of the Windows folder and is considered a special folder.
- **System and System32** These are subfolders of the Windows folder and are used to store many very important files necessary for the proper operation of Windows. Stay out of these folders unless you are confident that you know what you are doing.
- **Temp** This is a folder used to temporarily store files, such as those used during the installation of new application programs, and those temporary files created by a program while it is working. This folder often contains out-of-date files left over from an installation operation.

The rule for the Temp folder is that any program writing files to it should delete those files when the program is given the command to close. If a program ends abnormally (you trip over the power cord or the OS hangs up), the program can't do this important chore. Therefore, it is generally considered safe to delete files from the Temp folder that have not been used in over a week. In practice, we delete all temporary files dated before the last restart.

Hands Off System Files!

Quite a few files, called system files, are part of the OS and are very important to the proper operation of Windows. Some are located in the root of drive C:, while others are located in the folder in which Windows is installed. The default name for this folder is WINNT or WINDOWS, depending on the version of Windows. This folder in turn contains many additional folders containing important operating system files. In Windows 2000 and Windows XP, the default settings for My Computer or Explorer will hide the contents of a folder in which system files and other important files are stored. When this occurs, you have to take an additional action to view the contents.

Hiding the folders in the GUI does not depend on the hidden file attributes. My Computer or Explorer will hide the contents of a folder without regard to the file attributes.

In Windows 2000, you click on a link titled "Show Files"; in XP, you click on the words "Show the contents of this folder." By default, Windows XP hides both the root folder and the Windows installation folder, while Windows 2000 only hides the latter. If you decide to make them visible, do not make manual changes to these folders. Other changes you make to Windows through Control Panel applets and setup programs will alter the contents of these folders.

In addition, some files in these folders have the hidden attribute turned on so that Windows hides them, even when you view the folder contents. But when you are studying or troubleshooting an OS, you may want to change this default so that you can see the hidden files. You can change these defaults in My Computer or Windows Explorer if you choose Tools | Folder Options and modify the settings on the View tab. Figure 6-21 shows the settings we use when we want to be able to see all files, including file extensions.

Inside Information

Text File Editors

A type of application called a text editor allows you to create and edit text files using only the simplest of formatting codes (like carriage return, line feed, and end of document codes). A text editor uses only one set of characters and does not use or understand codes for special character fonts or special paragraph formatting. Windows comes with two text editors—one, Notepad, is a Windows application. Another, Edit, is a DOS application. When you call up Edit in Windows, it is loaded into a DOS virtual machine, which looks and feels to the DOS application like a real computer running MS-DOS. You will learn more about virtual machines later in this chapter. Notepad is a typical Windows GUI application and uses the standard Windows commands and mouse actions. Other applications (WordPad and Microsoft Word) can create and edit text files, but they are primarily word processors, which can create documents with fancy formatting instructions included. To create a text file with a word processor, you must choose to save the file as a text file. Notepad and Edit create only simple text files without the extra formatting.

These files are hidden.

This folder contains files that keep your system working properly. You should not modify its contents.

Show the contents of this folder

• A message about hidden files

Remember DOS file attributes from Chapter 2? Windows uses file attributes on all of its file systems; its hidden, archive, and system attributes are employed in the same way as described in Chapter 2. But in Windows 2000 and Windows XP using the NTFS file system, if you open the properties for a file and select the Advanced button, you'll see the advanced attributes: index, compress, and encrypt.

Although the default View setting that hides the important operating system files is pretty effective, it does not provide absolute protection for those files. When logged on as an Administrator, you can delete a folder containing those files. You would receive a warning message, but you could choose to ignore the warning.

Managing Data Files

The techniques discussed next are mainly for data files. Data files are the files you create with application programs, and there are a large number of data file types. A short list of data file types includes

- **Text files**, which most often have the TXT extension
- **Word processing document** files (Word uses the DOC extension)
- **Graphic files** (with a variety of extensions, such as BMP, DIB, GIF, JPG, and TIF)
- **Database files** (Access uses the MDB extension)
- **Spreadsheet files** (Excel uses the XLS extension)

Organizing Files Using Folders

All information on a computer is stored in files, and those files are typically organized by separating them into folders containing related files. It's important for you to understand how to organize files and folders properly so that you can easily access important files, and so that you know which files should not be touched. And because even the best file organization won't guarantee that you'll always remember the name of that very important file or even where you saved it, you should practice searching for files.

Any filing system needs a level of organization if it is to be useful. If you use a filing cabinet to hold a number of important documents, most likely

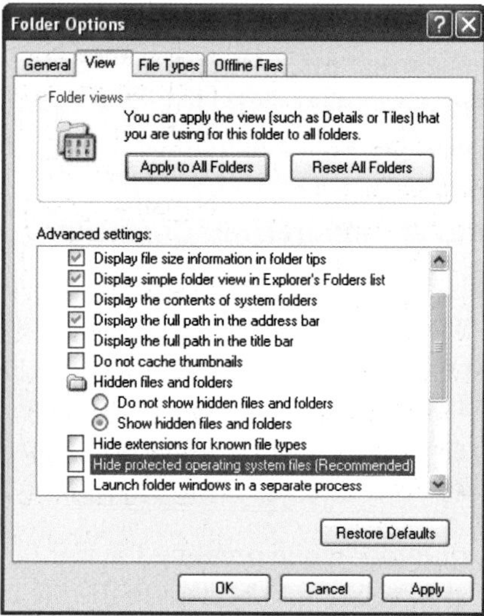

• **Figure 6-21.** Modified View settings

you organize those documents into separate file folders and use some sort of alphabetical arrangement of the folders so that you can locate the documents quickly when you need them. Imagine what a difficult time you would have finding your tax-related documents if all year you simply threw everything into a large box and then had to sort through each piece of paper to find the few important ones out of thousands.

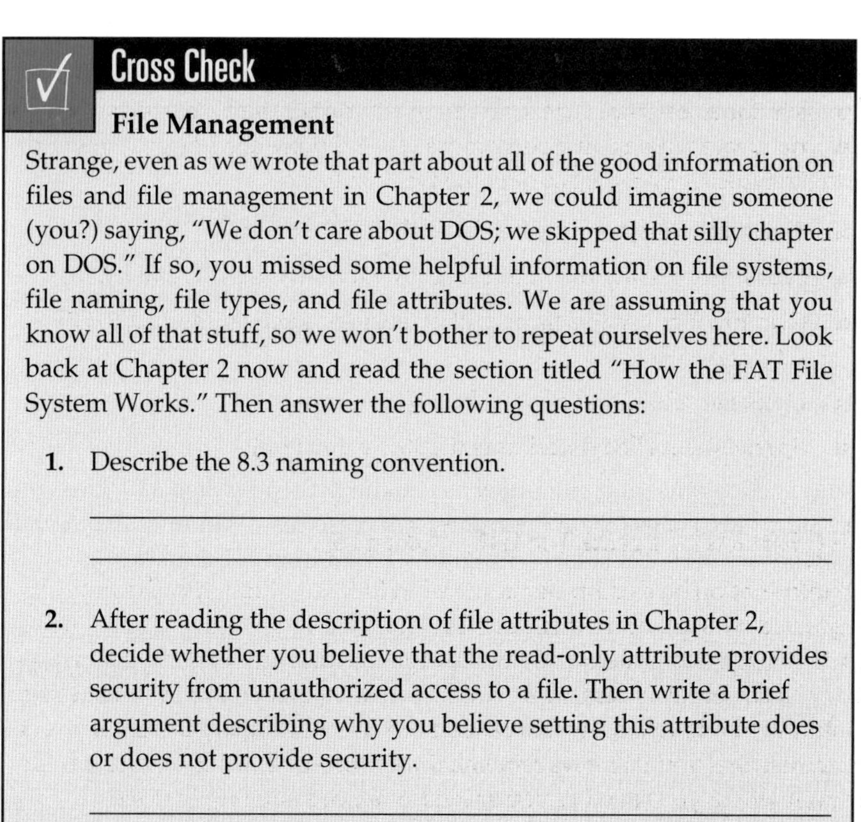

Cross Check

File Management

Strange, even as we wrote that part about all of the good information on files and file management in Chapter 2, we could imagine someone (you?) saying, "We don't care about DOS; we skipped that silly chapter on DOS." If so, you missed some helpful information on file systems, file naming, file types, and file attributes. We are assuming that you know all of that stuff, so we won't bother to repeat ourselves here. Look back at Chapter 2 now and read the section titled "How the FAT File System Works." Then answer the following questions:

1. Describe the 8.3 naming convention.

   ____

   ____

2. After reading the description of file attributes in Chapter 2, decide whether you believe that the read-only attribute provides security from unauthorized access to a file. Then write a brief argument describing why you believe setting this attribute does or does not provide security.

   ____

   ____

• Windows installation automatically creates dozens of folders!

GUI Techniques

Building on what you learned in Chapter 2, we'll now look at the GUI tools you will use for file management, primarily My Computer and Windows Explorer; then we'll practice basic file management tasks.

Drag-and-Drop Rules in Explorer/My Computer

Dragging is a basic GUI action in Windows that is accomplished by selecting a screen object and then, while pressing and holding down a mouse button, moving the mouse to where you want the object to be placed. When you release the mouse button, the object is "dropped" or positioned at the new location. This complete operation is called drag-and-drop. When you perform drag-and-drop on folders and files in Windows Explorer, certain rules apply:

1. Dragging a file or folder while pressing the right mouse button allows you to move, copy, or create a shortcut to the file in the new folder.
2. Pressing CTRL while dragging results in a move.
3. Dragging an item to another drive results in a copy, as opposed to a move.
4. Pressing and holding down SHIFT while pressing the left mouse button and dragging a file or folder to another drive results in a move.
5. Program files are treated differently than data files: when you drag a program file to a new folder, the program file is not moved or copied. Instead, a shortcut to the program is created. To actually move a program, you must be logged on as an Administrator.

Step-by-Step 6.04

Managing Files and Folders

In this exercise, you will practice some common file management tasks. First you will create a folder, and then you will copy, move, and delete files. To complete this exercise, you will need the following:

- A computer with one of the four Windows operating systems installed (Windows NT Workstation, Windows 98, Windows 2000 Professional, or Windows XP Professional)
- A user name and password that will allow you to log onto your computer

Step 1

If necessary, start and log onto your computer, as you did in Step-by-Step 6.01. Use your mouse to select Start | Programs (or All Programs) | Accessories | Windows Explorer. If you are using Windows NT, select Start | Programs | Windows NT Explorer.

Step 2

Click the plus sign to the left of My Computer. This expands the folder so you can see all of the objects at the top level in My Computer. Expand Local Disk C:. In Windows NT, this is simply labeled "(C:)."

Step 3

Position your cursor over an empty area of the Contents pane (right pane) of the window and then right-click. In the context menu, select New | Folder. Name the folder **data1**. Repeat this step to create a folder named **data2**.

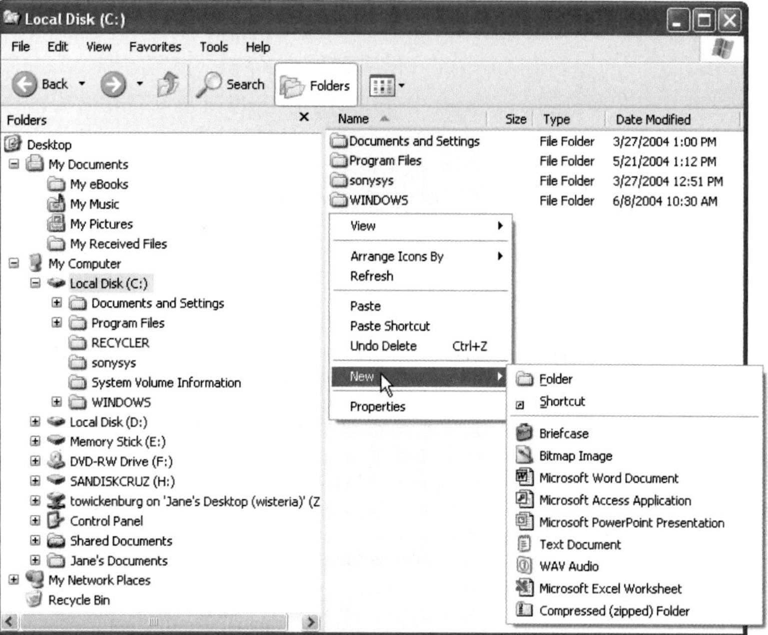

Step 4

Double-click the data1 folder to open it in Explorer, then right-click the Contents pane, and select New | Text Document. Name the document **report1.txt**.

Step 5

Drag the file report1.txt from the Contents pane, and drop it on the data2 folder in the Folders pane. This moves the file, so that it no longer exists in the data1 folder. A drag-and-drop operation between folders on the same drive is a **move** operation, and a drag-and-drop operation between folders on different drives is a **copy** operation.

Step 6

Open the data2 folder and confirm that report1 was moved to this folder. Press and hold the right mouse button while dragging the file back to the data1 folder. When you release the mouse button over the data1 folder, a context menu pops up that gives you the choice of copying, moving, or creating a shortcut to the file. Select the option to create a shortcut.

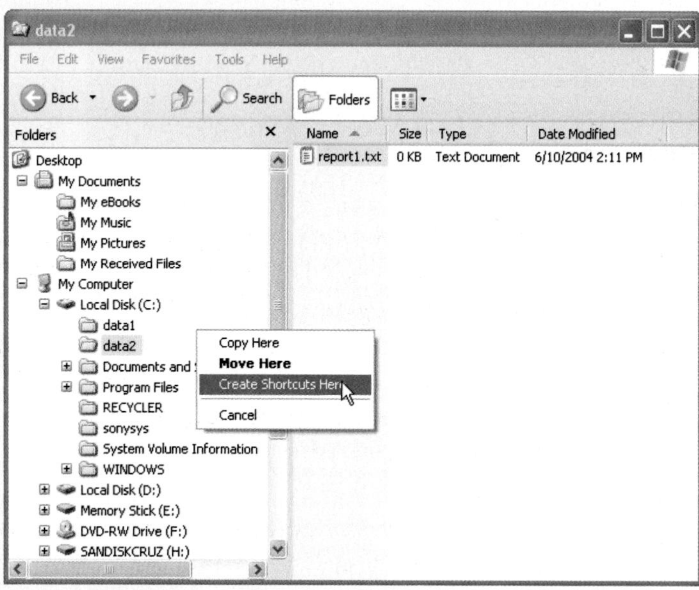

Step 7

To launch Notepad by association, expand the data1 folder and double-click the shortcut to report1.txt. This is a shortcut to a text file, so double-clicking it causes Notepad to open, because that is the program associated with text files.

Step 8

To ensure that the text you enter displays within the Notepad windows, select the Format menu and place a check in front of Word Wrap. Now type a few sentences describing what happens when you drag a file from one folder to another folder on the same drive. Then save the file by selecting File | Save. Exit from Notepad by using the ALT-F4 shortcut key combination.

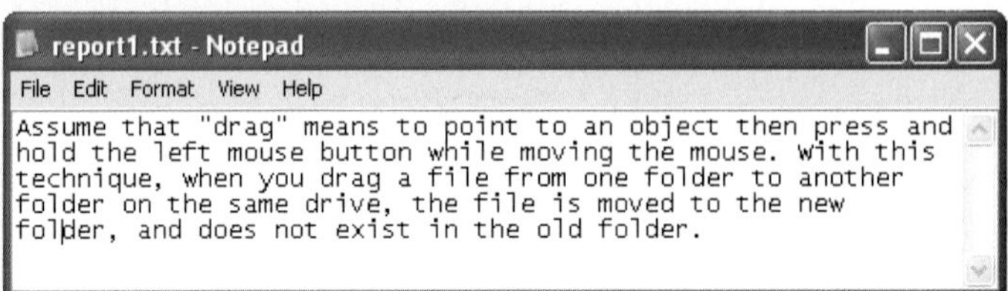

Step 9

Open the data2 folder and double-click the report1 file. The sentence you typed should be in the file. Exit from Notepad.

In this exercise, you practiced a few file management tasks, including creating directories and files, copying a file, and creating a shortcut to a file. You also edited and saved a file.

Non-GUI Techniques—The Command Prompt

In Windows you may open a command prompt, and run commands. Some may be traditional DOS commands such as FORMAT, XCOPY, ATTRIB, and DISKCOPY, updated and modified to run from a Windows command prompt. These programs are examples of command-line utilities that quickly perform a task, and then are gone from memory. Other commands may start programs that we call applications, which stay in memory, have a user interface, and allow us to do work, such as creating and modifying text or word processing documents, or creating, modifying, and manipulating data with a database. Windows NT, Windows 2000, and Windows XP all allow any program that will run in Windows to be launched from a command prompt.

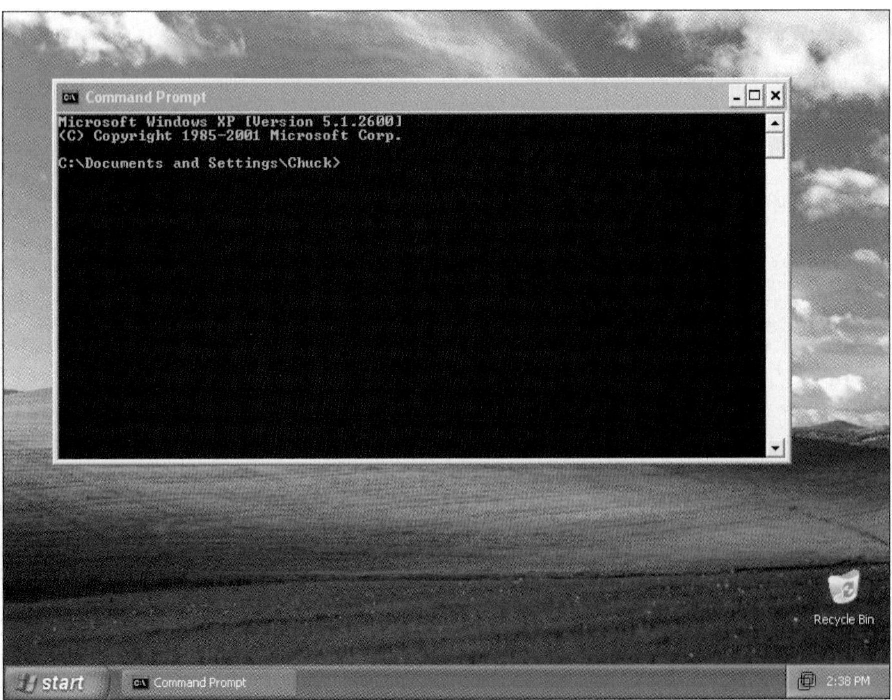

All versions of Windows allow you to work at a command prompt while the OS is running. Although people frequently refer to the command prompt as being DOS, that statement is not always true—it may not actually be DOS. Because Windows 95 and 98 have only one way of presenting the command prompt to you while running Windows, you would be correct in calling this DOS. The more advanced Windows OSs give you two options for working at a command prompt within Windows, but only one of these methods is DOS. The other is simply non-GUI Windows.

In addition to these methods of working at the command prompt from within Windows, Windows 9*x*, Windows 2000, and Windows XP have startup options that allow you to start at a command prompt. Accessing the command prompt in this way is valuable for troubleshooting startup problems. You will have a chance to look at the startup options in a later chapter. In this chapter, learn about working at the command prompt after Windows has been started normally.

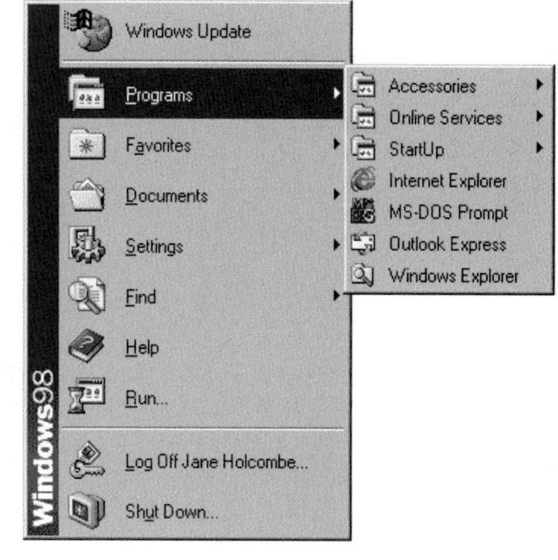

• **Figure 6-22.** MS Windows 98—Start | Programs | MS-DOS Prompt

The Command Prompt in Windows 9x

In Windows 95 and 98, the command prompt that you can select from Start | Programs runs in a DOS **virtual machine**. In fact, to start it without going through the menus, you can use Start | Run, and then type **command** in the Run box. This has the same effect as the Start | Programs method, because both call up the DOS command shell (COMMAND.COM), which in turn causes Windows to launch a DOS virtual machine.

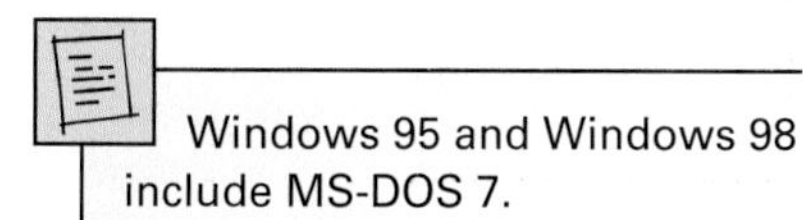

Windows 95 and Windows 98 include MS-DOS 7.

Notice in Figure 6-22 that the choice from the Programs menu in Windows 98 is MS-DOS Prompt. This is a subtle hint that the program you launch is MS-DOS running in a virtual machine in Windows 98.

The Command Prompt in Windows NT, Windows 2000, and Windows XP

In Windows NT, Windows 2000, and Windows XP, the choice you will see when you browse through the Start menu hierarchy is Command Prompt, which reflects a significant difference between these OSs and the Windows 9*x* OSs. The program that is launched when you select the Command Prompt option from the Start menu hierarchy is CMD.EXE. This offers you a full 32-bit, character-mode command prompt that is not a virtual machine with the limits of DOS, and it doesn't take up nearly as much space in memory when it is opened. Now, if you are using Windows and really miss DOS, you can use the Start | Run | Command method to launch a virtual machine!

Figure 6-23 shows the differences between the two methods for opening a command prompt. The command prompt at the top

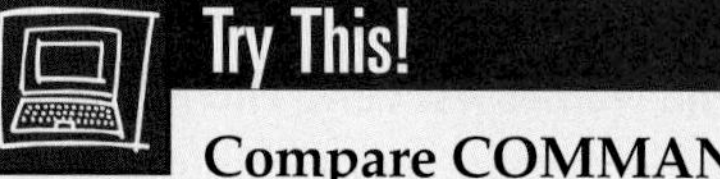

Try This!

Compare COMMAND to CMD

If you have a computer handy with Windows NT, Windows 2000, or Windows XP installed, compare the two methods for opening a command prompt. Try this:

1. Open an MS-DOS command prompt with Start | Run | Command.
2. Leave the first command prompt window open, and open a 32-bit text mode command prompt with Start | Run | CMD.
3. Notice the differences between the two, including the version information at the top and the inability of the MS-DOS command prompt to display long file names.

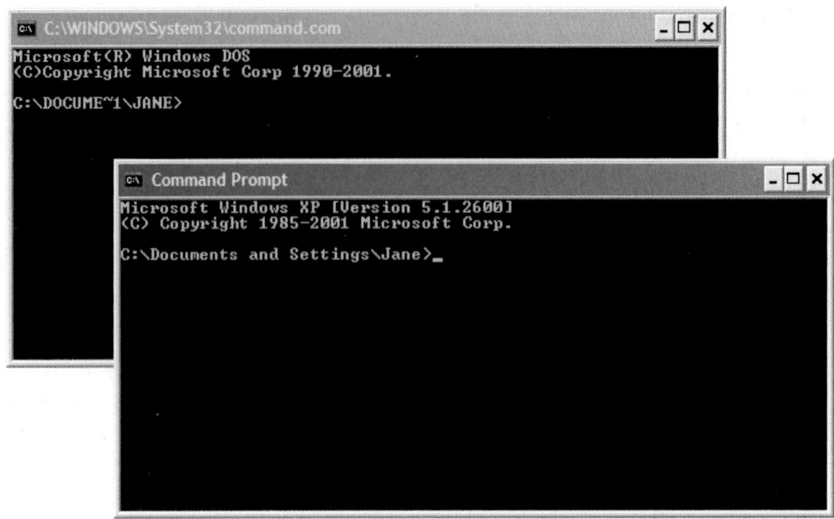

• **Figure 6-23.** Compare the two methods for opening a command prompt.

left was opened with Start | Run | COMMAND, which creates a DOS virtual machine, while the bottom command prompt was opened with the Command Prompt option found in the Accessories menu in Windows XP. Notice the lack of long file name support in the DOS virtual machine and the differences in version information seen at the top of each window. In addition, in the CMD version, you can use the up arrow key to browse through a list of commands you have entered during that session. This capability is not turned on by default in the MS-DOS Command Prompt.

Do No Harm! When working at the command prompt in Windows, the first rule is "Do no harm!" The best way to follow this rule is to never perform file management at the command prompt and to never run third-party disk utilities at the command prompt. The no-file-management rule is important mainly because without a GUI, you are in danger of deleting or moving the wrong files. The no-third-party-disk-utility rule is important if you are using Windows 95 or Windows 98, which cannot protect against such programs. The more advanced Windows versions will not allow these programs to run.

8.3 File Names vs. Long File Names Another important reason not to perform file management at the command prompt relates to the issue of 8.3 file names. Beginning with Windows 95, Windows allows you to create long file names that go beyond the limits of the 8.3 naming convention, allowing up to 255 characters in a file name. If you create a file with a long file name, Windows maintains both that long file name and a downward-compatible 8.3 file name for each file. If you create a file with a valid 8.3 file name, that is the only file name associated with the file. You can cause problems with this dual file name system if you copy and modify files from the command prompt using the 8.3 file name. This will cause the file to lose its association with the long file name. Then someone working in Windows may not be able to find their long file name files. Be sure to do all your file management in Windows using the GUI rather than the command prompt.

Any program that will run in Windows can be launched from a command prompt. If the program is written for DOS, a virtual machine will launch to hold the program, but you will still remain in the Command Prompt window. If the program is a 32-bit GUI program, it will launch in a separate window. If it is a character mode program, it will run within the command-line interface.

The Dangers of FDISK and Other DOS Utilities Some DOS utilities are included in Windows 9*x* but not included in other versions of Windows, either because they don't run in these versions or because they are considered too harmful to be included. An example of such a program is the FDISK utility. It cannot be run in Windows NT, Windows 2000, Windows XP, or Windows Server 2003, but it is the only disk management tool included with Windows 95 and Windows 98. Fortunately, if you run it at the MS-DOS Prompt in Windows 98, it will not allow you to do any damage, but if you run it after booting up with a Startup disk that contains the FDISK program, there is no such safeguard. Therefore, you should use FDISK only after learning how it works. Unless you understand how it works, the best time to partition a hard disk for Windows 9*x* is when you run the setup program for Windows 9*x*. It will then run FDISK for you, gathering information from you and guiding you through the process.

Step-by-Step 6.05

Working at the Command Prompt in Windows

In this exercise, you will run some simple file management and disk maintenance commands from the command prompt. To complete this exercise, you will need the following:

- A computer with one of the four Windows operating systems installed (Windows NT Workstation, Windows 98, Windows 2000 Professional, or Windows XP Professional)
- The data1 folder created in Step-by-Step 6.04

The steps in this exercise are written for Windows XP, but will work in other versions of Windows with only slight variations.

Step 1

If necessary, start and log onto your computer, as you did in Step-by-Step 6.01. Use your mouse to open the command prompt: Start | All Programs | Accessories | Command Prompt. The command prompt will display the version information and the current folder. In XP the current folder is normally your personal folder under the Documents and Settings directory. At the Command Prompt, type **dir** and press ENTER. A listing of files and folders within the current folder will be displayed. If they scrolled off the screen, type the command again with the pause switch: **dir /p**.

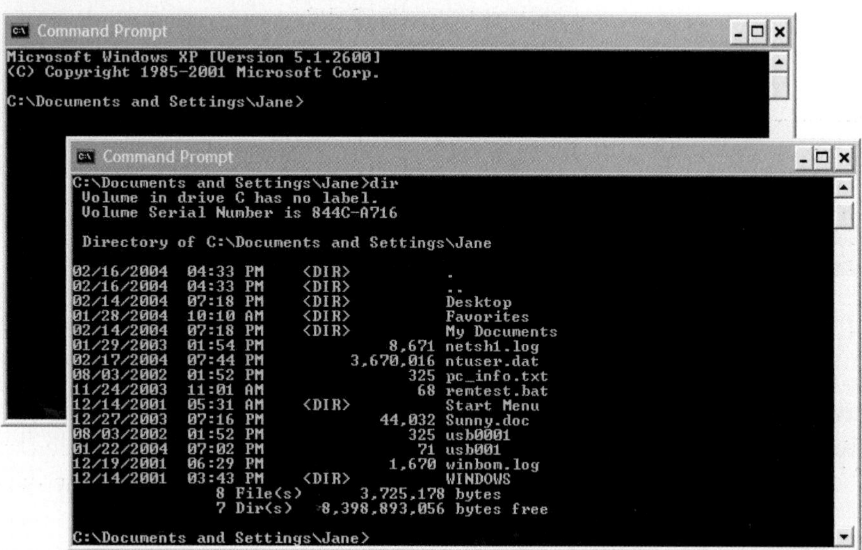

Command Prompt
Microsoft Windows XP [Version 5.1.2600]
(C) Copyright 1985-2001 Microsoft Corp.
C:\Documents and Settings\Jane>
Command Prompt
C:\Documents and Settings\Jane>dir
Volume in drive C has no label.
Volume Serial Number is 844C-A716
Directory of C:\Documents and Settings\Jane
02/16/2004 04:33 PM <DIR> .
02/16/2004 04:33 PM <DIR> ..
02/14/2004 07:18 PM <DIR> Desktop
01/28/2004 10:10 AM <DIR> Favorites
02/14/2004 07:18 PM <DIR> My Documents
01/29/2003 01:54 PM 8,671 netsh1.log
02/17/2004 07:44 PM 3,670,016 ntuser.dat
08/03/2002 01:52 PM 325 pc_info.txt
11/24/2003 11:01 AM 68 remtest.bat
12/14/2001 05:31 AM <DIR> Start Menu
12/27/2003 07:16 PM 44,032 Sunny.doc
08/03/2002 01:52 PM 325 usb0001
01/22/2004 07:02 PM 71 usb001
12/19/2001 06:29 PM 1,670 winbom.log
12/14/2001 03:43 PM <DIR> WINDOWS
8 File(s) 3,725,178 bytes
7 Dir(s) 8,398,893,056 bytes free
C:\Documents and Settings\Jane>

Step 2

Type the clear screen command, CLS, to clear the screen and press ENTER. Check out the syntax for the DEFRAG command. Type **defrag /?** and press ENTER. Now enter the command to run an analysis only of drive (volume) C:. To do this type **defrag C: -A** and press ENTER.

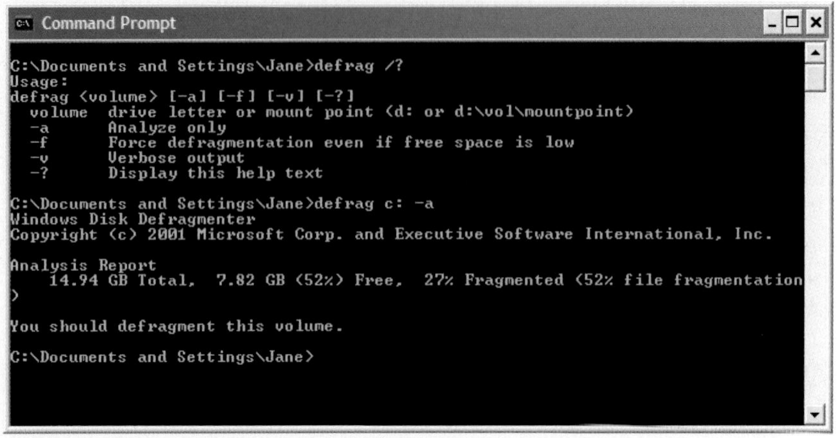

```
Command Prompt

C:\Documents and Settings\Jane>defrag /?
Usage:
defrag <volume> [-a] [-f] [-v] [-?]
  volume  drive letter or mount point (d: or d:\vol\mountpoint)
  -a      Analyze only
  -f      Force defragmentation even if free space is low
  -v      Verbose output
  -?      Display this help text

C:\Documents and Settings\Jane>defrag c: -a
Windows Disk Defragmenter
Copyright (c) 2001 Microsoft Corp. and Executive Software International, Inc.

Analysis Report
    14.94 GB Total,  7.82 GB (52%) Free,  27% Fragmented (52% file fragmentation
)

You should defragment this volume.

C:\Documents and Settings\Jane>
```

Step 3

Notice how quickly this command returned the results, which, in our example, included a recommendation to defragment the volume. If you have ever run the Windows defragmentation tool found on the Tools menu of the Properties of a volume, you will be surprised at the speed of this command-line version of the same utility. You could use this method to make a quick check and then, if it recommends defragmentation, you can either run it from the command line or from the GUI utility. The latter method is explained later in this chapter.

Step 4

Now check the disk for errors: type **chkdsk** and press ENTER. Running CHKDSK without the /F parameter is like running DEFRAG with the -A parameter—it only analyzes the disk. If errors were found, rerun the command and include the /F parameter. If the volume is in use (as is always the case with drive C:), you will see a message asking if you would like to schedule the volume to be checked during the next system restart. Press **y** and ENTER to schedule this.

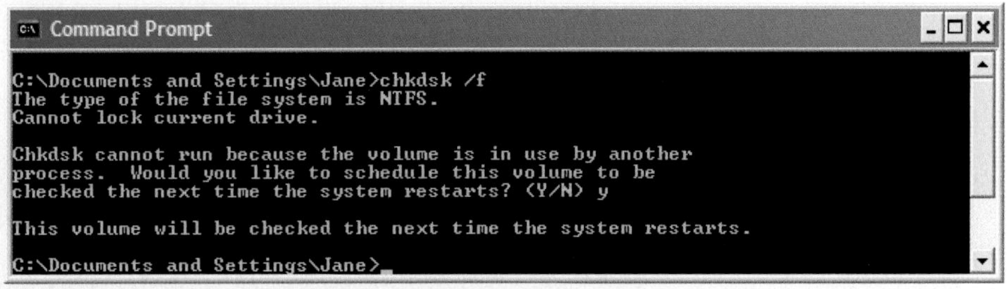

```
Command Prompt

C:\Documents and Settings\Jane>chkdsk /f
The type of the file system is NTFS.
Cannot lock current drive.

Chkdsk cannot run because the volume is in use by another
process.  Would you like to schedule this volume to be
checked the next time the system restarts? (Y/N) y

This volume will be checked the next time the system restarts.

C:\Documents and Settings\Jane>_
```

Step 5

At the command prompt, change to the My Documents directory by typing **cd mydocuments** and pressing ENTER. Create a new directory in the MY DOCUMENTS directory: At the command prompt type **md testdata** and press ENTER. Type **dir** and confirm that the new folder was created within the current folder.

Step 6

Copy the Data1 folder and its contents (including subdirectories) to the TESTDATA directory. Type **xcopy data1 testdata**.

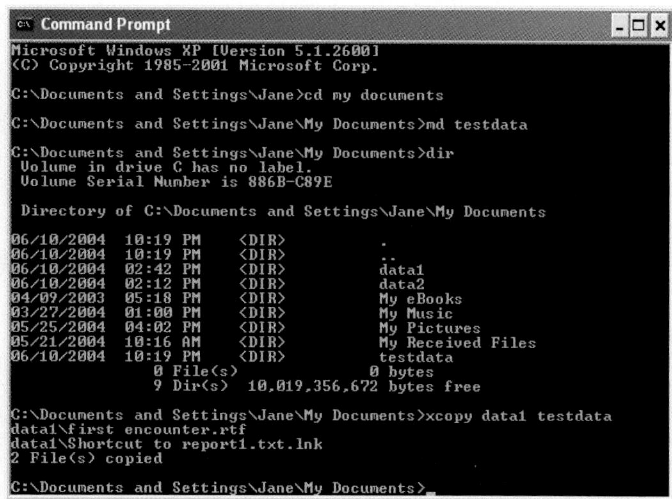

Command Prompt
Microsoft Windows XP [Version 5.1.2600]
(C) Copyright 1985-2001 Microsoft Corp.
C:\Documents and Settings\Jane>cd my documents
C:\Documents and Settings\Jane\My Documents>md testdata
C:\Documents and Settings\Jane\My Documents>dir
Volume in drive C has no label.
Volume Serial Number is 886B-C89E
Directory of C:\Documents and Settings\Jane\My Documents
06/10/2004 10:19 PM <DIR> .
06/10/2004 10:19 PM <DIR> ..
06/10/2004 02:42 PM <DIR> data1
06/10/2004 02:12 PM <DIR> data2
04/09/2003 05:18 PM <DIR> My eBooks
03/27/2004 01:00 PM <DIR> My Music
05/25/2004 04:02 PM <DIR> My Pictures
05/21/2004 10:16 AM <DIR> My Received Files
06/10/2004 10:19 PM <DIR> testdata
0 File(s) 0 bytes
9 Dir(s) 10,019,356,672 bytes free
C:\Documents and Settings\Jane\My Documents>xcopy data1 testdata
data1\first encounter.rtf
data1\Shortcut to report1.txt.lnk
2 File(s) copied
C:\Documents and Settings\Jane\My Documents>_

Step 7

Unfortunately, the command prompt in Windows does not give you the handy DELTREE command of MS-DOS that would allow you to delete a folder full of files in one step. To delete the folder you just created, delete each of the files within that folder, and then use the RD command to remove the directory. Type cd testdata. Delete all the files in this folder by typing DEL *.*. Then move up one level to the My Documents folder: type **cd** ..—that is, CD followed by two periods (..). Then type **rd testdata**. The folder you created is now removed.

Maintenance of Disks and Files

You can do certain basic maintenance tasks on a regular basis to achieve three different results:

1. Remove excess files that accumulate over time.
2. Reorganize how files are saved on disk.
3. Back up valuable data and system files so that you can restore them if your computer has a major failure.

You can perform these tasks with tools that come with Windows, or you can choose to use third-party tools, which may offer more options or related functions. You can also schedule some of these tasks to run on a regular basis, using either the built-in scheduling function found in Windows, or a third-party scheduler.

Following are overviews of the built-in Windows software tools for performing these tasks:

Remove Excess Files with Disk Cleanup

Disk Cleanup is available in Windows 98, Windows 2000, and Windows XP. Figure 6-24 shows a shortcut to this GUI utility that can be found in Start | All Programs | Accessories | System Tools. You can also start it from Start | Run by entering the following: **cleanmgr**. Use it to remove the following types of files:

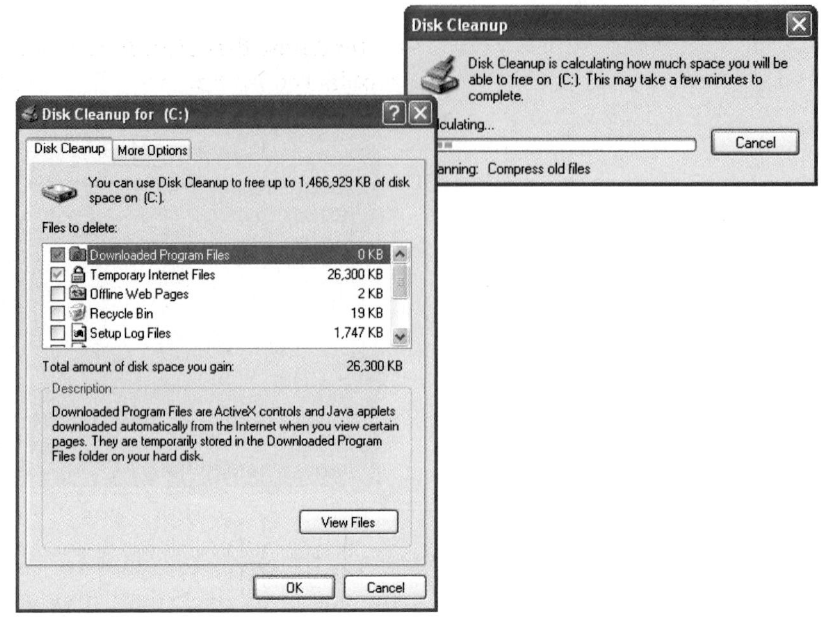

• **Figure 6-24.** The Disk Cleanup utility

Downloaded Program Files These are small program files, called applets, which are automatically saved on your local hard drive when you browse various web pages. The most common applets used at web sites are Java applets, ActiveX controls, and Flash components, but you may find other types, too. The files are typically saved in the C:\Windows\Downloaded Program Files folder.

Temporary Internet Files When you view a web page, a number of files are downloaded to your computer and used by your web browser to compose and display the page on your screen. To save time when you view the same page again, your browser stores these locally in a folder created in the Temporary Internet Files folder located within your personal folders. Then, when you revisit that same web site, Internet Explorer can load the page more quickly by comparing the files downloaded to your Temporary Internet Files folder with those at the web site. It will only download those files that are new or have changed, and combine them with the locally stored unchanged file. In this way it can display the page faster than the first time you visited the site.

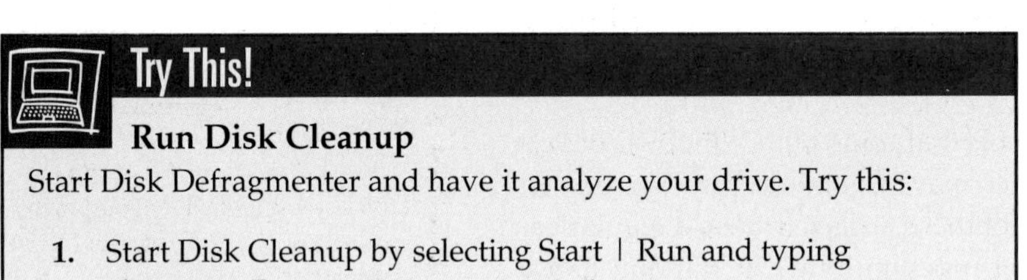

Try This!

Run Disk Cleanup

Start Disk Defragmenter and have it analyze your drive. Try this:

1. Start Disk Cleanup by selecting Start | Run and typing **cleanmgr**. Press ENTER.
2. Select a drive volume; then Disk Cleanup will calculate how much space can be freed up.
3. After the calculation, the Disk Cleanup dialog box will open. Select or deselect file categories.
4. Click OK to have Disk Cleanup proceed; click Yes in the warning box asking "Are you sure …?" A message box with a progress bar will display while files are deleted and compressed. This box will close automatically when the cleanup is completed.

Defragmenting a Disk

Operating systems have become smarter about how they store files on disk, but over time Windows still develops a problem called fragmented files that can cause it to take longer to retrieve files from disk. As files are created, deleted, and revised, empty spaces open up, and new files, folders, or pieces of files and folders are saved in the spaces. As a result, the disk read/write heads must be repositioned to pick up all the pieces when one of these fragmented files or folders must be read into memory. The solution to this is to use a program that reorganizes the files and folders so that each one is stored in contiguous disk space. Use a third-party program or the Disk Defragmenting utility. This program can be run from a shortcut found in Windows XP at Start | All Programs | Accessories | System Tools | Disk Defragmenter. You can also start it from Start | Run by entering **dfrg.msc**.

Before running a disk defragmenter, be sure to delete unnecessary files and folders. The Disk Cleanup utility will help with that task.

Try This!

Run the Windows Disk Defragmenter

Start Disk Defragmenter and have it analyze your drive. Try this:

1. Start Disk Defragmenter by selecting Start | Run and typing **dfrg.msc**. Press ENTER.
2. Select a drive volume; then click the Analyze button.
3. After the analysis is complete, a small message box will open informing you that your volume either does or does not require defragmenting.
4. Unless instructed otherwise by your instructor, close the message box and then close Disk Defragmenter.

Backing Up Data

The data created and stored on computers is far more valuable than the computer hardware and software used to create and store the data. This is true for individuals as well as organizations. For this reason, your backup strategies, the hardware and software used for backup, and the actual habit of backing up are critical to maintaining both data and computers. In case of the accidental destruction of data and/or the disks containing the data, having a recent backup on removable media can be the difference between personal or professional disaster and the minor inconvenience of taking the time to restore the data. Therefore, most versions of Windows include backup programs. Also, excellent third-party backup programs offer additional features and capabilities. The executable name of the backup program that comes with Windows NT, Windows 2000, and Windows XP Professional is NTBACKUP.EXE, which opens the Backup wizard. It can be accessed through a shortcut in the System Tools folder, or from Start | Run using the executable name. The Windows NT version only worked with tape backup systems and had a rather short list of compatible tape backup systems. Since Windows NT, the backup program has been improved in each version of Windows—both in capabilities and in the backup media it will use. It will now back up to a tape drive, local hard disk, or to a network location that is available as a drive letter (a "mapped" drive). Figure 6-25 shows the Windows XP Backup or Restore wizard.

MSBACKUP.EXE is the backup program provided with Windows 98.

If you find yourself working with Windows XP Home Edition, you may still install Windows Backup (NTBACKUP). If you have the distribution CD for XP Home, NTBACKUP and its installation program are located under VALUEADD\MSFT\NTBACKUP. Simply launch the installation program located in this directory (it has an MSI extension), and NTBACKUP will be installed. If your computer came preinstalled with XP Home and you do not have the distribution CD, search for this folder on your hard drive, because it may have been placed there, along with the other distribution files.

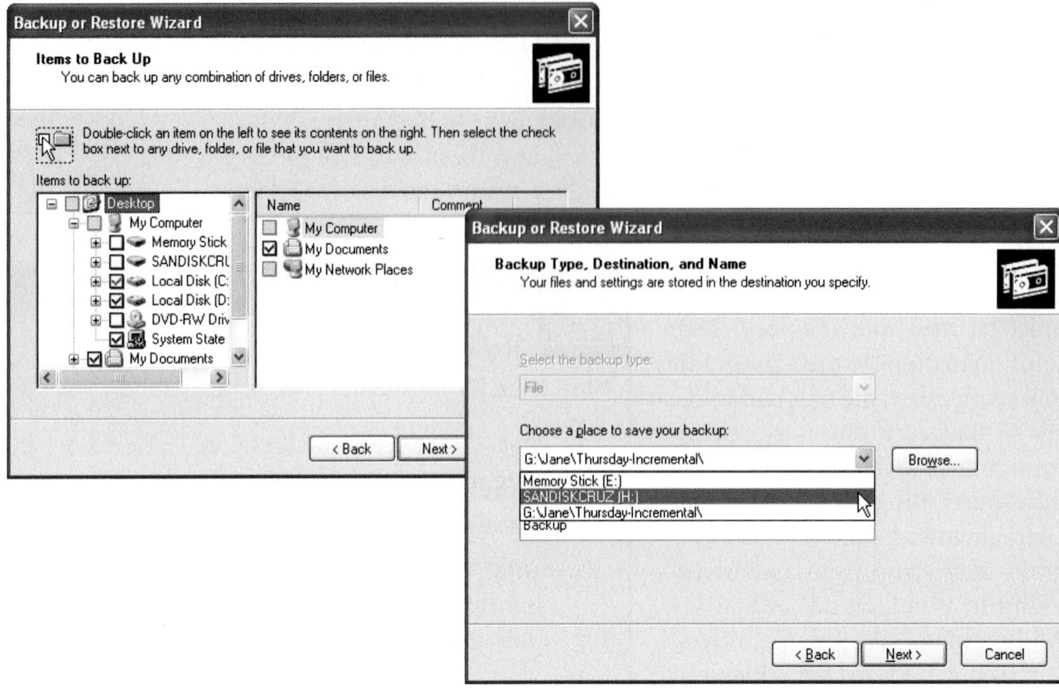

• **Figure 6-25.** The Windows XP backup wizard showing its support for any location on a logical drive

Launching Programs in Windows

Someday you may only have to think about a task, and your computer will load the correct program and lead you through the task—or complete it for you. Until that day, you generally must know what program you need for your task. Then you have to take some action to start the program. The discussion in this section of the chapter will help you become a "champion launcher."

Start Menu

Programs can be launched when they are selected from the Start menu or one of its submenus. For instance, to launch the Calculator program, we simply use the mouse to select Start | All Programs | Accessories | Calculator.

Program Shortcut

Double-clicking a shortcut to a program will launch the program. Shortcuts can be on the Start menu, as mentioned earlier, on the desktop, on the taskbar, or in a folder.

Start | Run

A program can be launched from Start | Run, which is a handy way to run a program you don't use very frequently. An administrator working on a client's computer might use Start | Run to launch an administrative or diagnostics tool that is available on the user's computer but is not something she wants the user to easily run. An example of this is a program called Regedit, which is very dangerous in the wrong hands, but at times is very necessary for an administrator to use. (Now, don't go running Regedit until you learn more about it!) We also like to use Start | Run to launch applications that are several menu levels down in the Start menu, but for which we don't want to add a shortcut to the taskbar or desktop, when we are familiar with the file name. For instance, **winmsd** is a command that opens System Information. We don't need to run this every day, but when we sit down at someone's computer and want to get a quick summary of their hardware and software, we simply select Start | Run and type **winmsd** in the Run box.

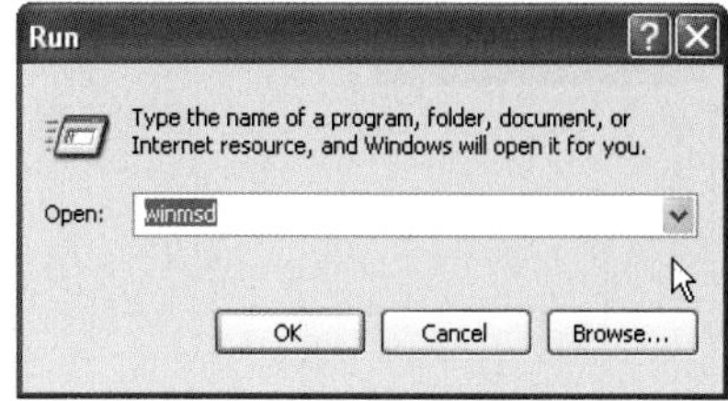

Launch by Association

When you install an application program, the installation program informs Windows of the file types that it understands and provides Windows with the file name extension of the file type, such as DOC, RTF, TIF, and so on. The program and the file type are then registered with Windows, and the file type is associated with the program. Then, when you double-click a data file, Windows checks its list of associations, loads the program that can use that type of data file into memory, and hands the file to the program. If you have several programs that can work with the same data file format, Windows will give one of them first priority when it comes to **launch by association**. Changing this priority is an advanced task that is not included in this book.

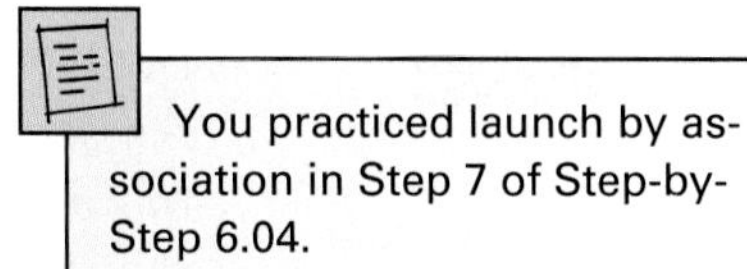

You practiced launch by association in Step 7 of Step-by-Step 6.04.

Step-by-Step 6.06

Launch Programs in Windows

Practice launching a program using different methods. While you are performing these steps, consider which methods you would use.

To complete this exercise, you will need the following:

- A computer with one of the four Windows operating systems installed (Windows NT Workstation, Windows 98, Windows 2000 Professional, or Windows XP Professional)
- A user name and password that will allow you to log onto your computer
- Completion of Step-by-Step 6.04

Step 1

If necessary, start and log onto your computer, as you did in Step-by-Step 6.01. Use your mouse to select Start | Programs (or All Programs) | Accessories | WordPad. Then, in WordPad, type a paragraph or two describing your first encounter with a computer.

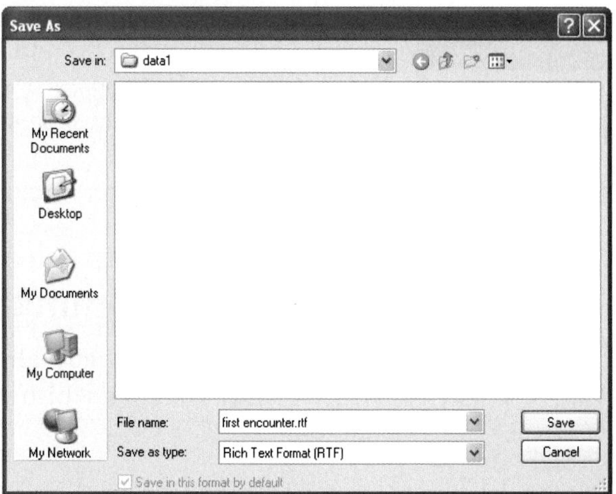

Step 2

Save the file. Use your mouse to select File | Save As. Next to the Save In box, click the down arrow, click Local Disk C:, and double-click data1 in the Contents pane. In the File Name box, type **first encounter**; then select Rich Text Format in the Save As Type box and click Save. Select File | Exit to close WordPad.

Step 3

Now open My Computer and locate the data1 folder, which now contains two objects: First Encounter and a shortcut to report1.

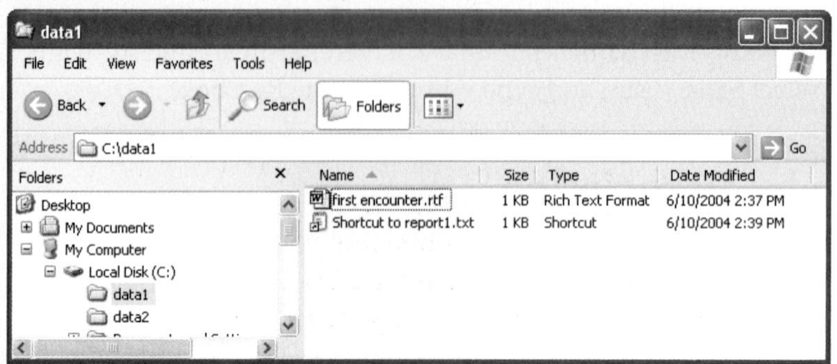

Step 4

Double-click First Encounter. It should open in WordPad because this type of file (RTF) is associated with WordPad by default. If it opens in another word processing program, this indicates that your Windows settings have been modified to associate a different program with RTF. In either case, you have successfully launched a program associated with your data file. Exit from the program.

Step 5

Another way to launch a program is by using its executable name. Do this now for WordPad: select Start | Run and type **wordpad** in the Run box. After WordPad appears, you can click File or the Open icon to find your document and read it. When you are finished, exit from WordPad.

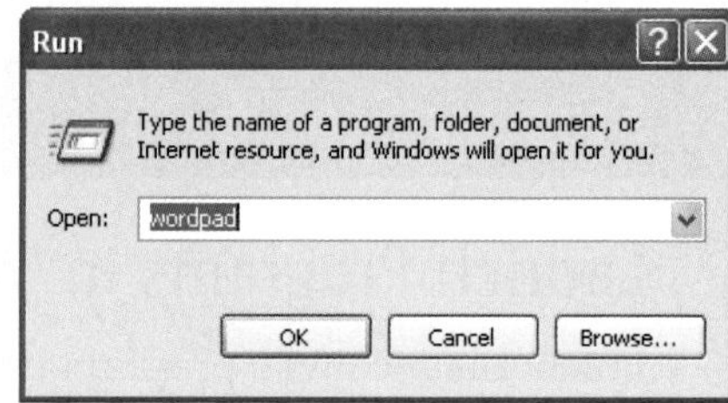

Step 6

Now you will test the launching of programs from the command prompt. If you have Windows NT, Windows 2000, or Windows XP, select Start | Run and type **cmd** in the Run box; then press ENTER. If you have Windows 98, type **command** in the Run box.

Step 7

At the command prompt, type **notepad** and press ENTER. This should launch the Notepad program. This approach works only for a program that is in a location where Windows will search for programs. This is called the *search path,* and it is a special setting in Windows.

Command Prompt

As we've already discussed, Windows has a text-based command prompt from which you can launch any program that can be run in Windows.

Launching Windows Programs from the Command Prompt

If the program is a Windows program, it will open in a window and run exactly as it would if launched by any other method.

Running DOS Applications in Windows

When a DOS application runs in Windows, it runs in a virtual machine. Using DOS applications in Windows has at least three disadvantages:

- The virtual machine for a DOS application takes up quite a bit of memory and also requires a lot of processor cycles. To illustrate this, we ran two DOS apps in Windows XP. You can see the memory usage of these two apps in Figure 6-26, which shows the Windows Task Manager, a program that allows you to look at memory usage and other properties of programs that are currently in memory. The highlighted process, NTVDM.EXE, is the primary software component for creating a virtual DOS machine. It appears here twice because there are two DOS apps running, and each one is in its own virtual machine. As you can see in the memory usage column, each instance of NTVDM.EXE is using approximately 2MB of memory. This will vary based on the individual application and its memory needs.
- Some DOS applications cannot run in the artificial environment of a virtual machine because their programmers wrote them to bypass DOS and to access the hardware using older programming methods. While Windows 95 and 98 allow this to some extent, Windows NT, Windows 2000, and Windows XP do not. Therefore, these DOS applications will not run in these OSs.

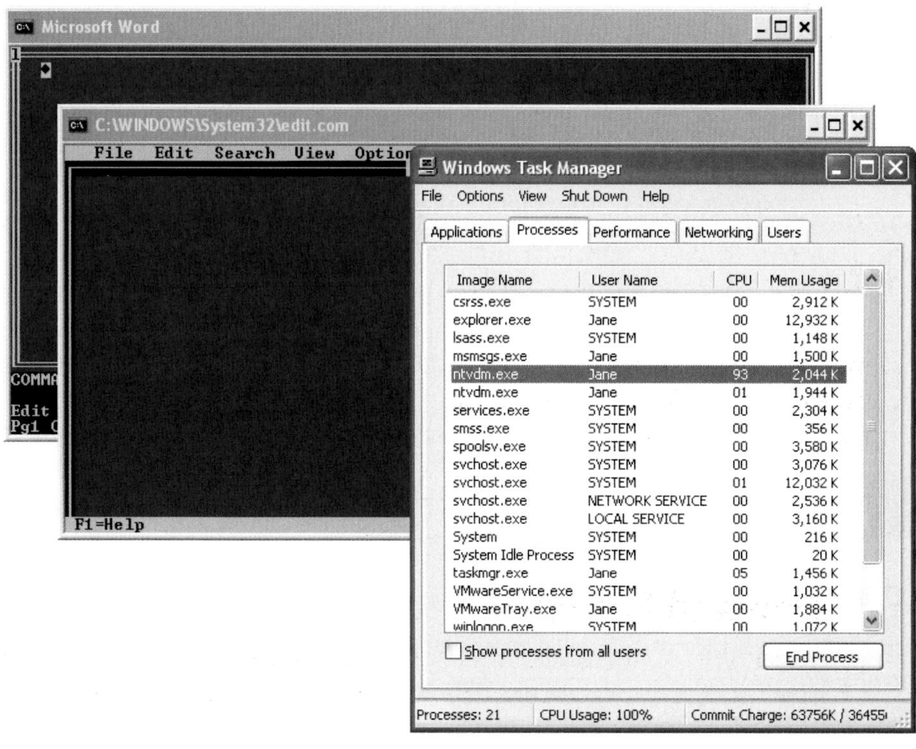

• **Figure 6-26.** The virtual machines for these two DOS applications require a great deal of memory.

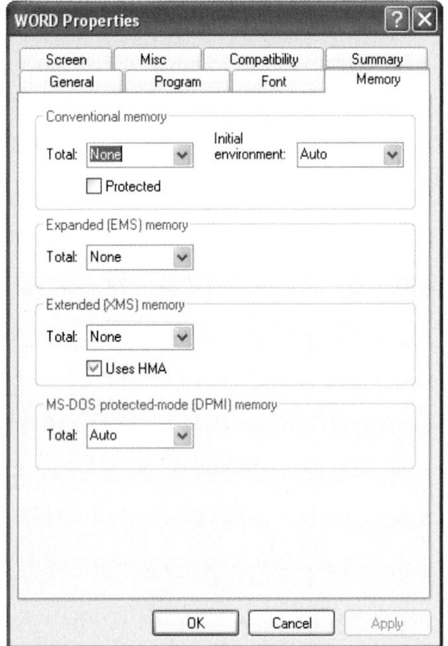

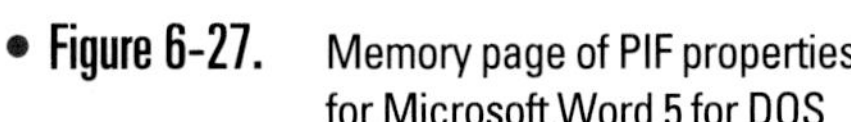

• **Figure 6-27.** Memory page of PIF properties for Microsoft Word 5 for DOS

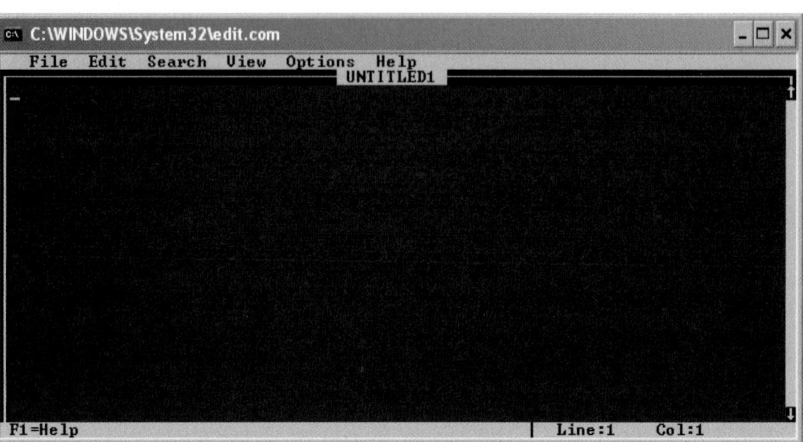

• **Figure 6-28.** The MS-DOS Editor—Edit

- DOS applications running in Windows rely on a special file called a program information file (PIF) that tells the OS how to furnish the virtual machine with the memory and other options for the application. If you have a DOS application that will not run in Windows, you can try modifying the PIF file setting for that application. It may be that the application behaves well enough to run in a virtual machine but has special memory or screen needs. However, you must be familiar with very old DOS technologies and understand how to modify the PIF for the application. Figure 6-27 shows just one page, the memory page, of the PIF properties for Microsoft Word 5. There are memory terms here that even many experienced IT professionals do not understand, because knowledge of these is not required if you don't support DOS applications.

The DOS editor, Edit, shown in Figure 6-28, has its own simple nongraphical user interface, with a menu bar and menu commands that you can access using the alt key plus a letter key from the commands on the menu bar.

Step-by-Step 6.07

Running MS-DOS Editor in Windows

In this step-by-step, you will run MS-DOS Editor in Windows. The instructions are written specifically for Windows XP, but you may use any of the Windows OSs listed here. There may be slight variations in the steps due to differences in the GUI.

To complete this step-by-step, you will need a PC running Windows NT, Windows 2000, or Windows XP.

Step 1

If necessary, start and log onto your computer, as you did in Step-by-Step 6.01. Press CTRL-SHIFT-ESC to start the Windows Task Manager. By default, this application runs on top of all other open windows. To change this behavior, choose the Options menu and remove the check mark from Always On Top.

Step 2

Click the Processes tab and notice that NTVDM.EXE is not listed in the image name column. Click the Minimize button for Windows Task Manager. This is the button labeled "-" at the top right of the window.

Step 3

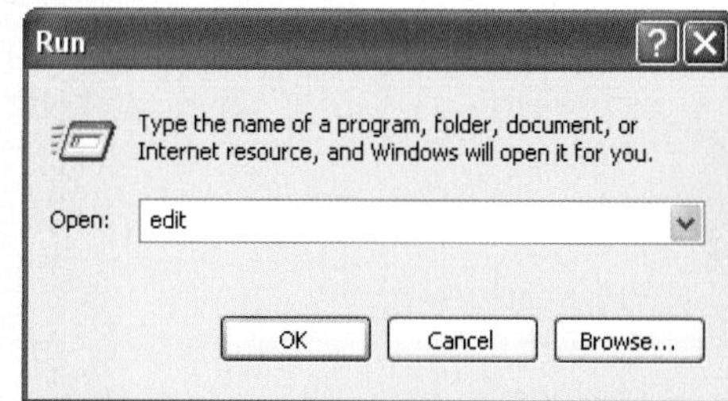

From the taskbar, select Start | Run. In the Run box, type **edit** and press ENTER. The DOS edit application should open in a Window on your desktop.

Step 4

Press and hold ALT while pressing and releasing TAB. Do not release ALT until Task Manager is selected. In Task Manager, click on the Processes tab, and locate the file NTVDM.EXE in the Image Name Column. After you have confirmed that NTVDM.EXE is running, close Task Manager by clicking on the button with an *X* in the top right of the Task Manager window.

Step 5

Switch to the Edit program by clicking inside the Edit window. Type a sentence into the MS-DOS Editor window.

Step 6

Save the file by pressing the ALT-F key combination, and then pressing S. The Save As dialog box will appear as shown here.

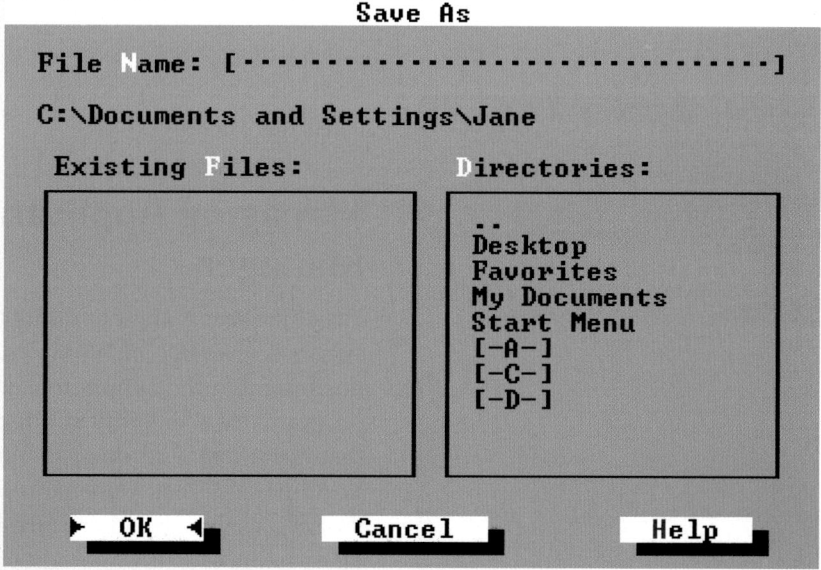

Step 7

The blinking cursor should be in the space next to File Name. Press TAB twice so that the cursor is in the Directories box. Use the down arrow until My Documents is selected and appears on the File Name line above. Press TAB four times until the blinking cursor is after My Documents on the File Name line. Press the right arrow key so that the highlight is removed from My Documents, but the cursor remains in place. Type the name **test1.txt**. Your Save As dialog should look similar to the one shown here.

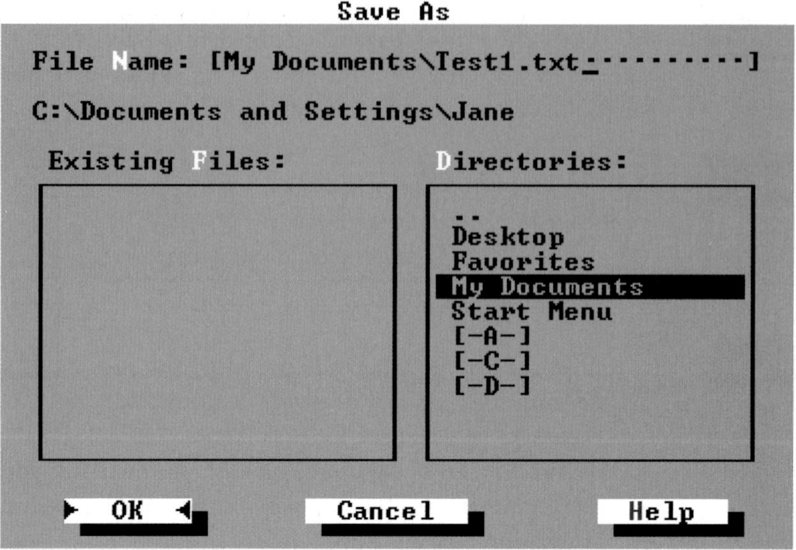

Step 8

To exit from the MS-DOS Editor, press ALT-F to bring up the File menu; then press X to select Exit. The Editor will close, as will the entire window.

If you have never worked in a DOS application but are experienced in working in Windows or with Macintosh computers, the step-by-step you just finished should help you to understand why most organizations have moved on to applications that run in a GUI, like Windows and the Mac OSs.

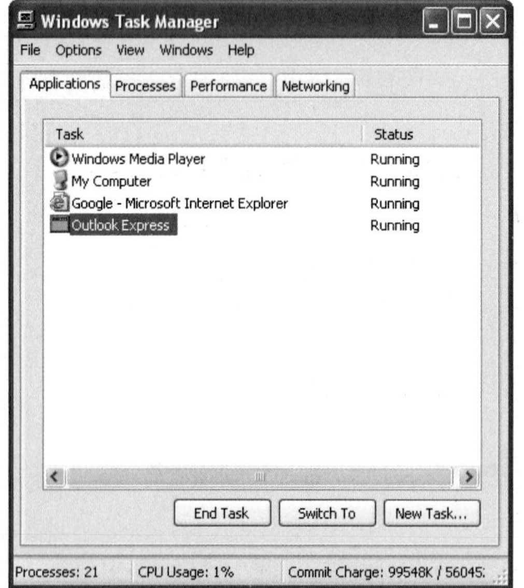

- Use Task Manager to view the status of applications and to stop any that are not responding.

Managing Applications with Task Manager

Task Manager is another utility that has been improved with each successive version of Windows. The current Task Manager does not resemble the simple tool we used to remove unresponsive programs from memory in Windows 9*x*, but you can still use it for that same task and more in Windows NT, Windows 2000, and Windows XP. Task Manager is now a very sophisticated program that allows you to end an unresponsive program and to do other tasks. For now, it is important to know how to start it, and how to stop an unresponsive program. Earlier, you learned the special shortcut to open this program (CTRL-SHIFT-ESC). Another way to start Task Manager is to press CTRL-ALT-DELETE. If your computer is not configured to use the Security dialog box, Task Manager will open at this point. If your computer is configured to use the

Security dialog box, that will open, and from there you can click the Task Manager button. Task Manager has several tabbed sheets; the Applications tab is the one from which you view and manage GUI applications.

Selecting a Strategy for Leaving the Desktop

At the end of the day, or whenever you leave your computer, you should select a proper method for leaving the desktop. In Step-by-Step 6.03 you worked with two options: Screen Saver and Lock Computer. In addition, depending on the version of Windows, you may choose from simply logging off and leaving the computer running, logging off and shutting down, or two special modes: Standby and Hibernate. Let's take a look at these options.

Logging Off and Shutting Down

Which you choose to do—log off, shut down, or both—depends on whose computer it really is and who makes the rules for its use. If it is your home computer, you will probably log off (if necessary) and shut down each day. If you use a computer at school or work, you will obey the rules of the organization. For instance, some organizations require that all users log off at the end of the day but leave their computers on. In fact, some organizations even configure Windows so that there is no Shut Down choice (an advanced administrative task). This may be so that a centralized backup of all of the computers, or some other maintenance, can occur. In this case, you will simply log off at the end of the day.

At work or in your school lab, you are more likely to be required to power down your computer. This actually means that, in most cases, you will simply select Shut Down, which will perform both functions for you. If you are certain that your computer can safely be shut down from the power button, you may use that, which will have the same effect as the Shut Down choice.

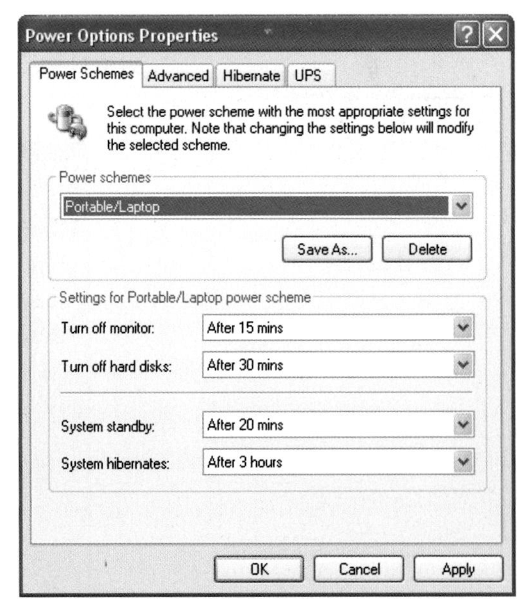

• System Standby setting in the Power Options applet

System Standby

System Standby puts your computer into a "sleep" state in which it consumes minimal power, and when you resume use of your computer, all the same programs are open on your desktop as before the standby state. If your Windows 2000 or Windows XP computer includes support for power management, you will have the option to put the computer in Standby. System Standby settings are found in the Power Options applet in Control Panel. It can be configured to occur automatically after a specified period of mouse and keyboard inactivity, or you can simply select Standby from the Shutdown menu. If you use this, remember

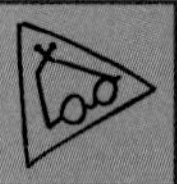

Inside Information

Wake-on-LAN

Newer technologies in computer motherboards and network adapter cards, such as Wake-on-LAN, have reduced the necessity for leaving computers on around the clock. Wake-on-LAN technology allows a program on the network to access a computer through the network adapter even when it's not powered up. Thus, a centralized task like backup or software installation can be performed while the computer is not being used.

that the computer is not really turned off, and if it is running on battery, it may eventually run out of power and turn off completely—in which case, any data in memory and not saved to disk before standby will be lost.

Hibernate

Another option for stopping work on your computer and being able to quickly pick up where you left off is Hibernate. When a Windows computer hibernates, it first saves everything in memory to disk, thus creating a snapshot of the current state, including open applications and data. Only then does it power down the computer. When bringing the computer out of hibernation, you can resume work in the same applications working with the same data. Hibernate is available in Windows 2000 and Windows XP, and configurable from the Hibernate tab of the Power Options applet. You can choose to have your computer hibernate automatically after a period of inactivity, or you can select it from the Shutdown menu.

Start Menu

Selecting Shut Down from the Start menu in Windows NT and Windows 2000 opens the Shut Down Windows dialog box. Selecting Turn Off Computer at the bottom of the Windows XP Start menu leads to a Turn Off Computer dialog box with choices to Stand By, Turn Off, or Restart.

Ctrl-Alt-Delete

Pressing CTRL-ALT-DELETE leads to the Security menu in Windows NT, Windows 2000, and Windows XP. You can select Log Off and Shut Down from this menu. Selecting Log Off will log off only the current user, but will not shut down the computer. Selecting Shut Down will do both tasks.

Cross Check

Windows GUI Comparison

Now that you have studied and practiced working with the Windows desktop, and practiced skills to navigate, manage files, configure the desktop, and launch programs, answer the following questions:

1. List three visual differences between the Windows 98 desktop and the Windows XP desktop.
2. Describe the use of the Documents folder, available in Windows 98, Windows 2000, and Windows XP, and provide the name of the equivalent folder in Windows XP and how to make it available.
3. Discuss methods you can use to make it more convenient for a user to launch programs from the desktop.

Troubleshooting Common Windows Desktop Problems

Some common Windows desktop problems include disappearing dialog boxes, an inability to find something, failure of Windows to start, and failure of Windows when you are working at the desktop or in My Computer or Windows Explorer. Let's look at these problems and how you might solve them yourself.

> You can even move backward through the fields in a dialog box by holding down the SHIFT key while you press TAB.

Disappearing Dialog Box

You have just entered something in a dialog box, but you're not finished and want to move to another field in that same dialog box, but suddenly the dialog box disappears. This most often happens because you have pressed ENTER at the wrong time. Within a dialog box, you can move from field to field by pressing TAB or clicking the field you want. For each field, you type something or click a button or check box. Only when you are done should you press ENTER. At that point, your entries are accepted, and the box closes. The solution to the disappearing dialog box problem is to be careful not to press ENTER until you have finished working in a dialog box.

Inability to Find Something

Maybe the other day you wrote a rough draft of a paper on the life cycle of amoebas that is due next week. Today you want to continue to work on it, but you can't remember where you saved it. You're not even sure of the exact name of the file, except that you used *amoeba* in the name. If you are using any of the versions of Windows you are studying in this book, there is one quick way to find a file or folder: use the Find or Search function from the Start menu. For instance, to find a file with the word *amoeba* in its name, use Start | Find (or Start | Search). Then enter **amoeba** in the Named box. Selecting C: in the Look In box will then start a search of your entire drive C: for any file (or folder) with *amoeba* in its name. The results will look something like Figure 6-29, depending on your version of Windows.

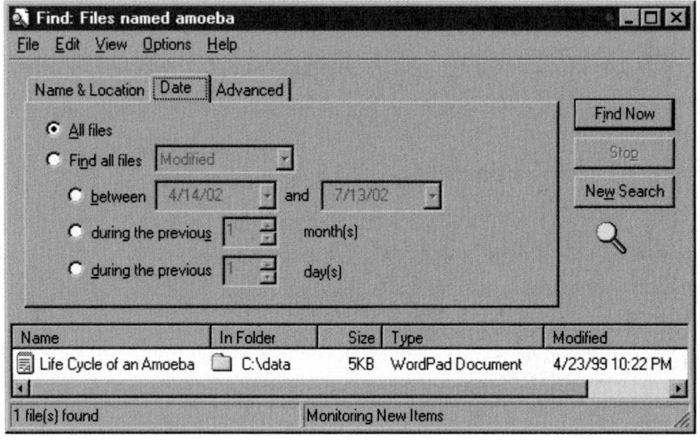

• **Figure 6-29.** Results of a search for "amoeba"

Windows Fails to Start

Strictly speaking, if Windows fails to start, this is not a failure of the desktop but an inability to get to the desktop. There can be many causes of a failure of Windows to start. A common one that is easy to fix is leaving a data disk in your floppy drive; when you start your computer, it tries to boot from the data disk. Unless the floppy disk has been configured in a special way, your computer will not boot to your Windows OS. You may see a message referring to a nonsystem disk or saying that the system could not find NTLDR. In either case, check the floppy drive. If a floppy disk is in the drive, remove it and restart your computer.

Another reason for a failure to start may be a problem with the configuration. Perhaps this is the first restart after installing a new device driver, or after making a significant change to the system, such as modifying the settings for a device. In this case, you can try one of the solutions detailed here.

Last Known Good

Windows NT 4.0, Windows 2000, and Windows XP allow you to go back to the last working configuration. This option has its limits and is not available in Windows 9*x*. In Windows NT 4.0, you select your OS from the OS Loader screen on startup, and then, before the GUI loads, press the space bar. The Hardware Profile/Configuration Recovery menu appears, as shown in Figure 6-30. From here, press L to load the Last Known Good Configuration. In the new OSs, press F8 before the GUI loads during startup. This will bring up the Advanced Options menu from which you select Last Known Good.

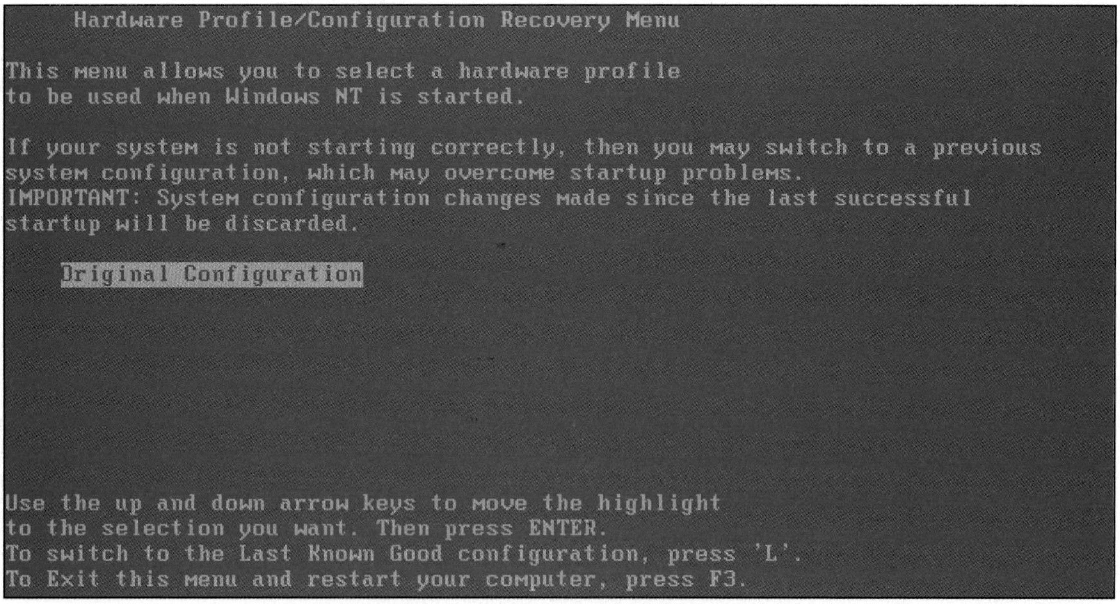

```
    Hardware Profile/Configuration Recovery Menu

This menu allows you to select a hardware profile
to be used when Windows NT is started.

If your system is not starting correctly, then you may switch to a previous
system configuration, which may overcome startup problems.
IMPORTANT: System configuration changes made since the last successful
startup will be discarded.

    Original Configuration

Use the up and down arrow keys to move the highlight
to the selection you want. Then press ENTER.
To switch to the Last Known Good configuration, press 'L'.
To Exit this menu and restart your computer, press F3.
```

• **Figure 6-30.** Switch to the Windows NT 4.0 Last Known Good Configuration from this screen.

Advanced Options Menu

When Windows 9*x*, Windows 2000, and Windows XP fail on startup, try working with the choices on the Advanced Options menu. Figure 6-31 shows the Windows XP version of this menu. There are many options here, including Safe Mode, which allows you to start Windows without some of the components that may be causing the startup failure. Then you can remove, replace, or reconfigure the failed driver or other component.

Windows Stalls

Have you ever been working in Windows when it suddenly stops responding? It won't let you close your applications. Maybe the cursor seems to be stuck in busy mode (usually you see the hourglass). If you are using Windows 98, you can press CTRL-ALT-DELETE; you'll then see a message about Explorer not responding. If you are using one of the other three OSs, you can press CTRL-SHIFT-ESC to open the Task Manager; you'll then see the message saying that Explorer is not responding. The best solution is to shut down Windows and restart. Normally, this takes care of the problem, at least for a day, a week, or a month.

If the system is really locked, you may not be able to shut it down from the GUI. In that case, you'll have to actually turn off the system with the power switch. When you turn it back on, it will probably automatically run CHKDSK or SCANDISK to make sure the hard drive was not damaged during the shutdown.

An Application Fails to Start

Harry is working late one night because he is preparing a presentation for a planning meeting in the morning. He is working in Windows 2000 Professional, and he has several applications open. He created a great, complex spreadsheet in Excel, a report in Word, and a slide presentation in PowerPoint. He needs to read a file he found on the Internet during his research on reducing cost of ownership for desktop computers. The file is in

```
Windows Advanced Options Menu
Please select an option:

    Safe Mode
    Safe Mode with Networking
    Safe Mode with Command Prompt

    Enable Boot Logging
    Enable VGA Mode
    Last Known Good Configuration (your most recent settings that worked)
    Directory Services Restore Mode (Windows domain controllers only)
    Debugging Mode

    Start Windows Normally
    Reboot
    Return to OS Choices Menu

Use the up and down arrow keys to move the highlight to your choice.
```

• **Figure 6-31.** Use the Windows XP Advanced Options menu to troubleshoot startup problems.

PDF format. He double-clicks the file, expecting it to load into the Acrobat Reader program. The hourglass icon appears briefly, and Acrobat does not start. No error message appears. He opens the Task Manager, which shows current tasks. He expects to see Acrobat listed with a status of "not responding," but it isn't listed. One possible problem is that there is not enough memory to run the additional program. The solution is to close one or more applications, then attempt to open Acrobat.

Chapter 6 Review

■ Chapter Summary

After reading this chapter and completing the Step-by-Step tutorials and Try This! exercises, you should understand the following facts about the Windows desktop:

Who Invented the Desktop?

- The origins of the desktop metaphor go back several decades.
- Many innovative people contributed to the desktop metaphor; the earliest we found was Douglas Engelbart, who demonstrated the use of a mouse with a computer in 1968.
- The mouse and keyboard are your primary input devices.
- The Palo Alto Research Center (PARC) was a major contributor to the desktop metaphor.
- The Apple Macintosh was the first successful consumer product using a graphical desktop and a mouse.
- The desktop metaphor endures today in many different operating systems including Windows, Macintosh OS, and various GUI interfaces for UNIX and Linux.

Navigating the Windows GUI

- In most organizations, you will have to log on and be authenticated before you can get to your Windows desktop.
- A user account is a record in an accounts database that may exist locally (except for Windows 9*x*) or on a network server.
- Logging onto a computer requires a user name and password that match those in a user account.
- A workgroup is a grouping of computers on a network for the sake of sharing printers and folders with other users in the group.
- A Microsoft Windows domain has a centralized security accounts database, maintained on one or more special servers called domain controllers. This centralized database contains accounts for users, groups, and computers participating in the domain and can be used to authenticate a user for access to any resource of the domain.
- For a more secure logon, CTRL-ALT-DELETE is required to bring up the logon dialog box in all but Windows 9*x*.
- By default, Windows XP, Windows 2000 Professional, and Windows NT Workstation allow users to select Shutdown even though no one is logged on. This is not allowed on Windows server computers.
- Windows Help has improved with each version of Windows. Use it!
- Windows now has a variety of graphical objects, including the cursor, icons, shortcuts, dialog boxes, windows, folders, buttons, toolbars, menus, and the taskbar.
- The Start button gives you access to menus from which you can launch programs.
- The Documents shortcut icon (Windows NT, Windows 98, and Windows 2000) contains shortcuts to recently opened data files. In Windows XP this folder is named My Recent Documents, but is not enabled by default.
- Personal folders are a significant subset of special folders that Windows creates on disk to hold files and folders for each user. Included are files containing desktop configuration and preference information, as well as each user's own data files. Shortcuts to some of these personal folders are on the Start menu.
- Personal Folders include Start Menu, My Documents, Favorites, Desktop, and many others.

Configuring and Customizing the Windows Desktop

- If Active Desktop is enabled, you can choose between the classic Windows desktop and Web view. In classic Windows desktop, you double-click to open an object; in Web view, objects on the desktop behave like links in a web page, so you can open them with a single click.
- Shortcuts added to the Quick Launch area of the taskbar can be launched with a single click.
- Control Panel contains many applets that allow you to configure your hardware and software.

- Right-clicking on the desktop and choosing Properties opens the Display Properties box, a Control Panel applet that allows you to customize many aspects of the desktop.

Manage Files in Windows

- A file is information organized as a unit, and the author of a file determines how much information is stored in a file.
- Files allow you to put information into manageable chunks.
- A special type of file called a folder in Windows, but previously called a directory in MS-DOS, acts as a container for files. You can create folders in a hierarchy, enhancing the organization of your files.
- File management in the Windows GUI is easier and safer than in DOS because you don't have to memorize commands that use cryptic syntax; you don't have to feel like you are taking a typing test every time you want to create, copy, move, or delete a file or folder; and because you can see exactly what files and folders you have selected for a file management operation.
- Two important file types are program files and data files. Program files (also called binary files) contain programming code, and data files contain the data you create and work with in your application programs.
- It is best not to attempt to manage program files, especially those the operating system requires, called system files. Leave them in the folders in which the operating system or installation programs place them.
- Manage data files.
- A short list of data file types includes
    - **Text files**, which most often have the TXT extension
    - **Word processing document** files (with the DOC extension)
    - **Graphic files** (with a variety of extensions, such as BMP, DIB, GIF, JPG, and TIF)
    - **Database files** (Access uses the MDB extension)
    - **Spreadsheet files** (Excel uses the XLS extension)
- The Find/Search option has been improved with each version of Windows. In Windows NT, you can search for files, folders, and computers, but in Windows XP, this search function has been greatly expanded. If you have an Internet connection, you can search for almost anything in the world that is searchable over the Internet.
- Users can manage files and folders in My Computer and Windows Explorer and from the command prompt. The last is not recommended.

Launching Programs in Windows

- Users can launch programs by using the Start menu.
- Another method for launching programs is with the use of shortcuts on the desktop or other locations.
- Using the file extensions of data files, Windows associates the files with applications that can create and read that file type. When you click on a file that has an extension for which Windows has an association, Windows will start the associated program and load the file as data for the program.
- Another method for launching a program is to use the Run command from the Start menu. Then you enter a command name in the box to launch a program.
- You can also launch a program from the command prompt. If the program is a GUI program, it will be launched in a window.

Leave the Desktop by Logging Off and Shutting Down

- Your end-of-day procedure depends on the rules for using the computer.
- In some organizations, users are required to log off but to leave the computer running.
- In other organizations, users are required to log off and shut down the computer.
- You should never just switch off your desktop computer with the on/off switch. You should always do so from within Windows.

Troubleshoot Common Windows Desktop Problems

- Pressing ENTER when you intended to select a new field may cause a dialog box to disappear.
- Use the Find or Search function to find lost files.
- Leaving a floppy disk in the drive is a frequent cause of startup failure.
- If Windows stops responding, you may have no other choice but to restart your computer.

Key Terms List

Active Desktop *(273)*
applet *(268)*
command prompt *(251)*
copy *(281)*
dialog box *(253)*
domain *(253)*
icon *(260)*
launch by association *(291)*
menu *(251)*
move *(281)*
personal folder *(263)*
Quick Launch toolbar *(276)*
shortcut *(260)*
special folder *(263)*
taskbar *(262)*
user account *(252)*
virtual machine *(283)*
windows *(251)*
workgroup *(252)*

Key Terms Quiz

Use terms from the Key Terms List to complete the sentences that follow. Not all terms will be used.

1. The ____________________ is a portion of the taskbar that can contain buttons that let you launch programs with a single click.
2. A/an ____________________ is a way to display a list of options and programs from which a user can make a choice.
3. The Display icon in the classic Control Panel represents a/an ____________________ that allows you to change configuration settings for your Display.
4. The ____________________ contains the Start menu, buttons for currently open applications, and the system tray, and it may also contain the Quick Launch bar.
5. A/an ____________________ is a bordered area of the desktop used by a single program.
6. The ____________________ feature lets you put web content directly on your Windows desktop.
7. The only security accounts available in a/an ____________________ exist on individual member computers that are capable of maintaining a separate local accounts database.
8. A Microsoft ____________________ has a centralized security accounts database, maintained on special servers called domain controllers.
9. Starting an application by double-clicking on a document file is an example of ____________________.
10. My Documents is a/an ____________________ and as such is treated differently by Windows than an ordinary folder.

Multiple-Choice Quiz

1. Who demonstrated the use of a mouse with a user interface at a conference in 1968?
   - **a.** Bill Gates
   - **b.** Steve Wozniak
   - **c.** Bob Metcalfe
   - **d.** Steve Jobs
   - **e.** Douglas Engelbart
2. Which of the following is not an element of a Windows desktop GUI?
   - **a.** Windows
   - **b.** Menus
   - **c.** Command prompt
   - **d.** Shortcuts
   - **e.** Taskbar
3. What key combination may be required before you can enter your user name and password in Windows?
   - **a.** CTRL-SHIFT-DELETE
   - **b.** CTRL-ALT-DELETE
   - **c.** CTRL-ESC
   - **d.** CTRL-SPACE BAR
   - **e.** CTRL-ENTER
4. Which of the following will launch a program?
   - **a.** Selecting a program icon from the Start menu
   - **b.** Pressing ALT-F4
   - **c.** Pressing CTRL while clicking the mouse
   - **d.** Selecting a program from the Recycle Bin
   - **e.** Clicking the minimize button

5. If you have a problem with Windows that you do not know how to solve, you can begin by:
    a. Pressing ALT-F1
    b. Using the mouse
    c. Using the Windows Help program
    d. Calling the Microsoft toll-free number
    e. Opening the Tools menu
6. A user's judgment that an OS is or is not intuitive may depend largely on the person's:
    a. Experience with computers
    b. Age
    c. Income level
    d. Job title
    e. Education
7. You can change the appearance of your Windows desktop using:
    a. Microsoft Word
    b. Outlook Express
    c. The Display applet in Control Panel
    d. The System applet in Control Panel
    e. WordPad
8. Which of the following can be used for managing files and folders?
    a. Windows Explorer and My Computer
    b. The Display applet in Control Panel
    c. Notepad
    d. MSN Explorer
    e. Disk Management
9. What could cause a dialog box to close before you have completed all the desired changes?
    a. Activation of the screen saver
    b. Pressing ENTER
    c. Entering invalid information
    d. Automatic Update
    e. Not having administrator rights
10. What should you do if you are confused about where you saved a file?
    a. Use Windows Help
    b. Record file locations on paper
    c. Use the Search or Find program
    d. Learn memory association tricks
    e. Save all files in the root of C:
11. What is the first task of the day for most Windows users—something they must do before they even see their Windows desktop?
    a. Open My Computer
    b. Run Windows Explorer
    c. Log on
    d. Select Run
    e. Click Start
12. What disk maintenance task should be performed on a regular basis to keep files well organized for quick access?
    a. Run Disk Defragmenter
    b. Reformat the disk
    c. Search and replace
    d. Delete temporary files
    e. Enable Active Desktop
13. What word describes the type of files you should not move, delete, edit, or try to manage directly?
    a. Text
    b. Spreadsheet
    c. Data
    d. Program
    e. Database
14. Notepad is an example of this category of application.
    a. Spreadsheet
    b. Text editor
    c. Word processor
    d. Database
    e. Accounting
15. What standard desktop object can be modified to allow you to launch your programs quickly and to see status information of certain running programs?
    a. Recycle Bin
    b. Cursor
    c. Start menu
    d. Taskbar
    e. Control Panel folder

■ Essay Quiz

1. In your own words, describe why the desktop metaphor, as implemented in Windows, is intuitive (or not) for you. Maybe you like parts of it, but not others. Elaborate.
2. Rosemary is an order processor and office assistant in the small manufacturing company that recently hired you. She has been working in Windows 98, but her present computer will be replaced with a new Windows XP Professional computer and Microsoft Office 2003. Previously, she kept all of her files in a folder named Data on her local hard drive. You have suggested that she now keep her data files in her My Documents folder, and you have arranged to have these files transferred from her present computer to the new computer. She has asked for an explanation of why she should work with the My Computer folder. Write an explanation that you might give Rosemary for this recommendation.
3. Your department is writing a computer-use policy manual. Your boss has asked you to write a paragraph for the manual selling the benefits of taking advantage of the desktop customization capabilities of Windows. The versions currently used in your company are Windows 2000 and Windows XP. Write a paragraph selling the benefits and inviting the users to schedule appointments to have you help them customize their systems to their preferences.
4. You have double-clicked a graphics file that you want to edit. Rather than launch your favorite graphics editor program, Windows started a different program and loaded your data file. You do not know how to use this program, but you want to edit the graphic. You know that the other program is on your computer, because you used it earlier today. Explain what is happening and describe what you can do so that you can edit this file with the program you like.

Lab Projects

• Lab Project 6.1

As a desktop support consultant for a real estate brokerage firm, you often help agents with their home office computers. You have been asked to help an agent organize his data files on a new computer with Windows XP. On his previous computer, he saved his data files in a variety of folders in several of the four hard drive volumes, which was awkward when it came time to back up his files. To help him organize his files, you created a table of the applications he uses and the business functions of the data he creates with each application.

Application	Business Function(s)
Microsoft Access	Client list database Contractor list database
Microsoft Word	Introductory letters Proposal presentations Offer presentations
PowerPoint	Listing brochures Self-marketing brochures

1. Using this table, design a file management strategy for the agent that will be logical to use and that will make the backup process easier for him. Write a description and justification of this design to present to the agent.
2. Using your lab computer, create the folders that will be required to fulfill your design.
3. Present this plan to a fellow student or to the class in general. You may want to create drawings of your design or to use the folders you created in step 3 to demonstrate it.

• Lab Project 6.2

A small manufacturing company has hired you to be a desktop support person. As such, you must know how to install and configure operating systems on the company's computers and, eventually, learn all the software applications used in the company so that you can train and support the employees in the use of their computers. Your boss has just asked you to help a new user personalize her Windows desktop. You have learned that she will frequently use two applications and less frequently use another three applications. You have noticed that she is a "clean desk" sort of person, and you believe that she may want her Windows desktop to reflect her physical work habits. Since some of the data she will be working with is confidential, she is required to log off whenever she leaves her computer.

You will need a lab computer with any of the four versions of Windows installed.

Then do the following:

1. Describe the strategy you will suggest to her for giving her appropriate access to her applications, addressing her clean-desk work behavior, and the security issues. All solutions should involve desktop customization.
2. Assume that she agreed with your suggestions. Now implement your suggested changes on your lab computer. Remember that two applications should be very quickly available to her, and that three others should be convenient, but don't need to be as quickly available. Use any applications available to you for the five applications in the scenario.
3. Test your solution.
4. Demonstrate your solution for one or more of your fellow students.

• Lab Project 6.3

Loretta is an IT employee at a large company, presently assigned to a group that researches and tests future and alternative computing technology. Her present assignment is to research possible alternatives to the desktop metaphor—both in new OSs and in add-ons to Windows. Give Loretta some help with this project.

1. Use an Internet search engine to search on "desktop metaphor." Browse through the results to find two potential metaphors that may replace the present desktop metaphor.
2. For each alternative you select, write a paragraph or two that describes the new metaphor, gives the author's reason for its superiority to the desktop metaphor, and gives your personal opinion of that metaphor.
3. Present your findings to one or more of your classmates.

Managing Local Security in Windows

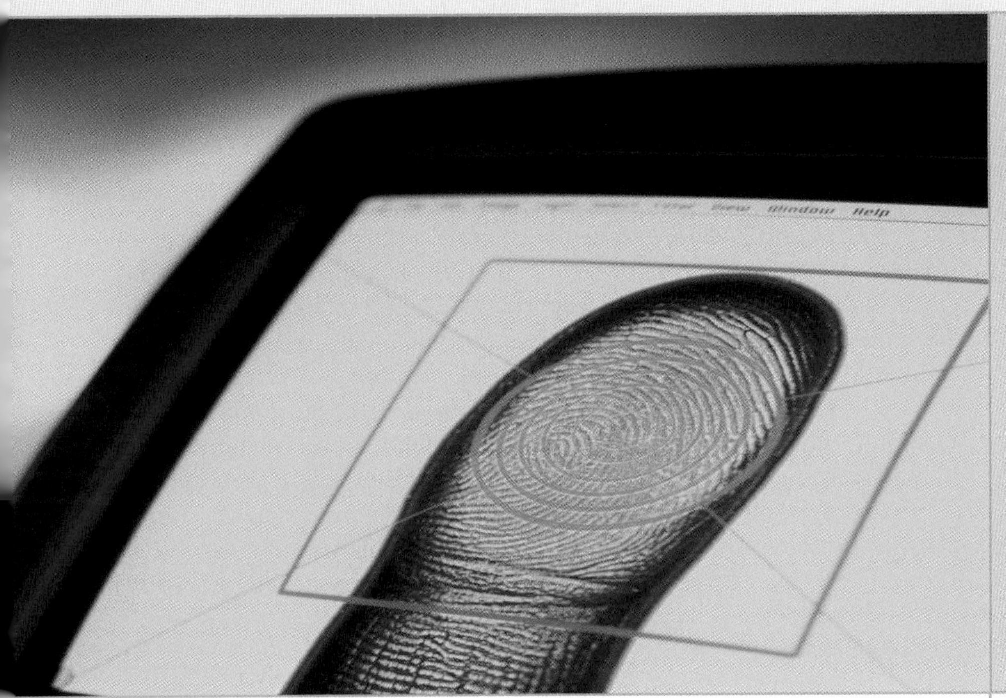

The only truly secure system is one that is powered off, cast in a block of concrete and sealed in a lead-lined room with armed guards.

—Eugene H. Spafford, Professor and Executive Director of the Purdue CERIAS (Center for Education and Research in Information Assurance and Security)

Why do our latest operating systems have a long list of security features? Why do we need to frequently apply security patches to Windows operating systems? Why has computer security become a multi-billion-dollar business worldwide? It's because it's dangerous out there. And, as you will learn in this chapter, "out there" seems to be everywhere, because no place or technology seems safe from some sort of threat. That includes the Internet, corporate networks, and even your cell phone or PDA! Learn what the threats are, who the perpetrators are, and the methods, practices, and technologies for protecting your computer system.

Once we have instilled a healthy dose of paranoia in your mind, you will learn how to work with the security features of the latest versions of Windows. This will include creating local accounts, viewing user rights, defining security policy, and assigning permissions to files, folders, and printers.

In this chapter, you will learn how to:

- **Recognize security threats and vulnerabilities to desktop PCs and users**
- **Implement methods and technologies that protect against threats**
- **Create local user accounts in Windows**
- **Assign permissions to files, folders, and printers in Windows**
- **Troubleshoot common security problems in Windows**

Threats to Computers and Users

What are you risking if your computer is not secure? Let's look at some ways you can be affected. You can experience computer hardware theft, loss of valuable data, your financial security, and even your personal identity. For instance, just about everyone who uses a computer uses e-mail, and just about everyone who uses e-mail receives unwanted e-mail. In this section, you will learn that this type of e-mail is not just a threat to your personal productivity, but is also a favorite doorway for threats to computers and networks worldwide.

Computer Hardware Theft

Of course, security includes something as simple as locking doors, keeping hardware locked away from prying eyes and sticky fingers. That's obvious. What may not be obvious to you, especially if you use a laptop as your principal computer, is what happens if your computer is stolen. You would be astonished at how many computers, especially laptops, are stolen each year, and unless your computer has been properly secured, there goes your business information, your data files, your financial information, your address book, everything! Although a large percentage of computer theft occurs just so the thief can sell the hardware quickly and get some quick cash, an increasing number of thieves are technically sophisticated and will go through your hard drive looking for bank account, credit card, and other financial data so they can steal your identity.

> To learn more about identity theft in general, how to protect yourself, and how to report suspected identity theft, point your browser to `http://www.consumer.gov/idtheft/`, the Federal Trade Commission's ID Theft web site.

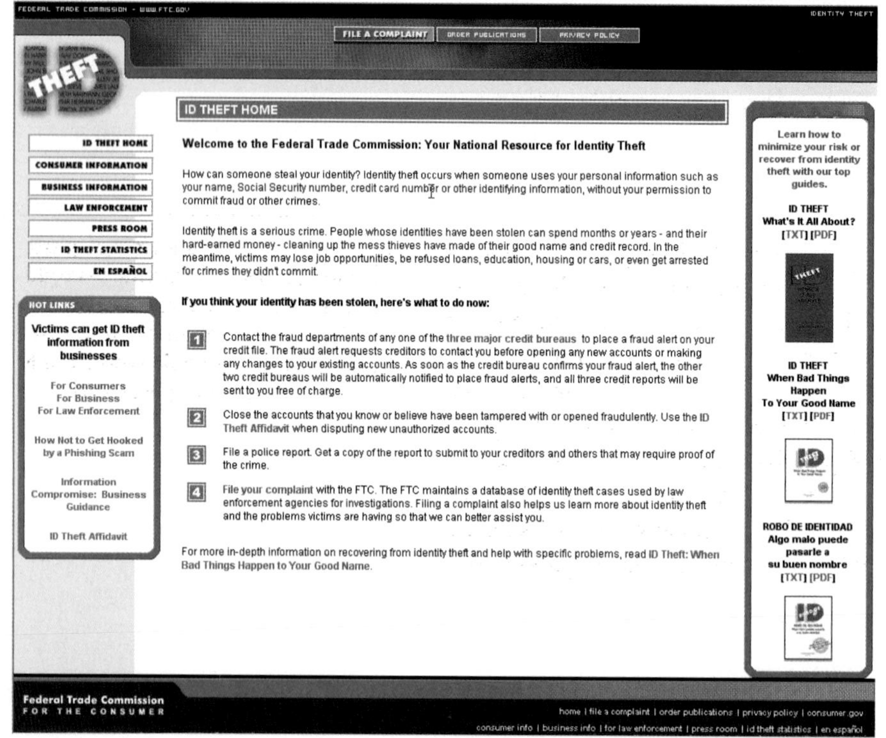

• The Federal Trade Commission's ID Theft web page

Identity Theft

Identify theft occurs when someone collects personal information belonging to another person and uses that information to fraudulently make purchases, open new credit accounts, and even obtain new driver's licenses and other forms of identification in the victim's name. They may not even be interested in actual financial information; simply obtaining your social security number and other key personal information may be enough to steal your identity. Thieves can steal your identity in many ways that aren't directly involved with computers. Several web sites maintained by the U.S. government offer all kinds of valuable information for consumers who wish to protect themselves from identify theft.

Fraud

Fraud is the use of deceit and trickery to persuade someone to hand over money or other valuables. Fraud is often associated with identify theft, because the perpetrator will falsely pose as the victim when using the victim's credit cards and other personal and financial information.

Accidents, Mistakes, and Natural and Unnatural Disasters

Accidents and mistakes happen. We don't know of anyone who hasn't accidentally erased an important file, pressed the wrong button at the wrong instant, or created a file name they can't remember. Disasters also happen in many forms. Just a few are fires, earthquakes, and weather-induced disasters such as tornadoes, lightning strikes, and floods. Predicting such events is imperfect at best. The principal way to protect against accidents, mistakes, and disasters is to make frequent, comprehensive backups. You can make backups of an entire hard drive using programs that make an image of the drive, or use programs that back up your critical data files on a periodic basis. Organizations that have a lot of valuable data even make multiple backups and keep copies off-site. Then, in case of fire, flood, earthquake, or other natural disasters that destroy not only the on-site backups but also the computer, they can still recover.

Deliberate Attacks

You probably have heard of threats against computers like viruses, worms, Trojan horses, or spam. But have you ever heard of pop-up downloads, drive-by downloads, war driving, Bluesnarfing, adware, spyware, back doors, spim, phishing, or hoaxes? Read on—it'll make the hair on your head stand straight up!

Password Crackers

A huge number of programs and techniques are available to people who want to discover passwords. One commonly used technique is to invade an unsecured web site to access information unwitting users provide to the site, such as user names and passwords. Another technique is to use a password cracker, a program used to discover a password. Some password crackers fall into the category of "brute-force" password crackers, which simply means the program tries a huge number of permutations of possible passwords. Often, because people tend to use simple passwords such as their initials, birthdates, addresses, and so on, the brute-force method works. Other password crackers use more sophisticated statistical or mathematical methods to discover passwords.

> If you enter the words "password cracker" into your favorite search engine, you will be horrified at the number of programs available for people who want to try to guess your password.

Virus

A **virus** is a program that is installed and activated on a computer without the knowledge or permission of the user. At the least the intent is mischief, but most often it is intended to be genuinely damaging in one way or another. Like a living virus that infects humans and animals, a computer virus can result in a wide range of symptoms and outcomes. Loss of data, damage

"In the wild" is a term frequently used to describe the overall computing environment—most notably including the Internet.

to or complete failure of an operating system, or theft of personal and financial information are just a few of the potential results of viruses infecting an individual computer. If you extend the range of a virus to a corporate or government network, the results can be far reaching, and even tragic. There are thousands of viruses "in the wild" today.

Worm

Like a virus, a **worm** is a program that is installed and activated on a computer without the knowledge or permission of the user. But a worm replicates itself on the computer, or throughout a network. In other words, a worm is a replicating computer virus, and it can have a similar range of outcomes. Worms travel between machines in many different ways. Several worms in recent years have moved from one computer to another as zipped (compressed) attachments to e-mail, often with an innocent-sounding or enticing subject line. When the user opens the zipped attachment, the program executes, scanning the local address book and replicating itself to the addresses it finds. Typical of this type of worm, variants of the Netsky and MyDoom worms caused chaos and loss of productivity just in the amount of network traffic they generated.

Trojan Horse

The modern day **Trojan horse** program is used to gain access to computers much like the ancient Greek warriors who, in Homer's famous tale the *Iliad,* gained access to the city of Troy by hiding in a large wooden horse, presented as a gift to the city (thus, a Trojan horse). A Trojan horse program is installed and activated on a computer by appearing to be something harmless, which the user innocently installs. This is a common way that a virus or a worm can infect your system.

Pop-Up Download

A **pop-up download** is a program that is downloaded to a user's computer through the use of a pop-up page that appears on your computer while surfing the Web. It requires an action on the part of a user, such as clicking on a button that implies acceptance of something like free information, although what that something may actually be is not made really clear. The program that is downloaded may be a virus or a worm.

Try This!

Research the Latest Virus Threat

Many organizations, including antivirus vendors and security services, post information on the Internet about the latest virus threats. Learn about the latest virus threats on the Internet. Try this:

1. Open your browser, connect to the web site of an antivirus vendor, and look for a link for the latest virus threats. You may use a search engine to find such a web site. The following URL will connect to the web page maintained by Symantec: `http://securityresponse.symantec.com/`.
2. Make a list of the top five virus threats listed on the page. Then use the links for each virus threat to learn more about each one.
3. Check out information on other security issues on the page, such as recently discovered vulnerabilities in operating systems.

Drive-By Download

A **drive-by download** is a program downloaded to a user's computer without consent. Often the simple act of browsing to a web site or opening an HTML e-mail message may result in such a surreptitious download. A drive-by download may also occur when installing another application. This has been found to be particularly true of certain file-sharing programs, installed to allow the sharing of music, data, or photo files over the Internet. Some drive-by downloads may alter your Internet Explorer home page and/or redirect all your browser searches to one site. Any drive-by download may also install a virus, a worm, or even more likely, adware or spyware (which are described later in this chapter).

War Driving

War driving is the name given to the act of moving through a neighborhood in a vehicle or on foot, using either a laptop equipped with Wi-Fi wireless network capability, or a simple Wi-Fi sensor available for a few dollars from many sources. War drivers are searching for open hotspots, areas where a Wi-Fi network is connected to the Internet without the use of security to keep out intruders. They will often make a mark on a building where a hotspot exists that people "in the know" can understand so they can later use that hotspot to access the Internet, a practice called war chalking. Not only are they gaining Internet access illegally by riding on the subscription of the hotspot owner, but they can capture keystrokes, passwords, and user names. And if the individual computers on the wireless network, or other networks connected to it, are not protected, unauthorized people may access those computers. Some hotspots are created intentionally, and more and more hotspots are being made available for free or for a small charge by various businesses, such as coffee shops, bookstores, restaurants, hotels, and even campgrounds.

Bluesnarfing

Similar to war driving, Bluesnarfing is the act of covertly obtaining information broadcast from wireless devices using the Bluetooth standard, a short-range wireless standard used for data exchange between desktop computers and mobile devices such as personal digital assistants (PDAs) or cellular phones. Bluetooth devices have a range of 10 centimeters to 100 meters, depending on the power class of the device. Using a cell phone, a Bluesnarfer can "eavesdrop" to acquire information, or even use the synchronizing feature of the device to pick up all the user's information—all without being detected by the victim.

Keystroke Logger

A keystroke logger is either a hardware device or a program that monitors and records a user's every keystroke, usually without the user's knowledge. In the case of a hardware logger, the person desiring the keystroke log must physically install it before recording and then remove it afterward in order to collect the stored log of keystrokes. A software keystroke logger program may not require physical access to the target computer, but simply need a method for downloading and installing it on the computer. This could occur through the use of spyware, a pop-up downloader, or a drive-by downloader. Once installed, such a program may be configured to send the logged information over the Internet via e-mail, or using other methods, to the person desiring the log.

Some parents install keystroke loggers to monitor children's Internet activity, but such programs have the potential for abuse by people with less benign motivations, including stalking, identify theft, and more.

Spyware

Spyware is a category of software that runs surreptitiously on a user's computer, gathers information without permission from the user, and then sends that information to the people or organizations that requested it. Internet-based spyware is sometimes called tracking software or a spybot, and it may be installed on a computer through a virus, or by many other means of secretly installing software. Spyware can be used by companies to trace users' surfing patterns to improve the company's marketing efforts; it can be used for industrial espionage; it can be used by law enforcement to find sexual predators or criminals (with appropriate legal permissions); and it can be used by governments to investigate terrorism.

Adware

Adware is a form of spyware software that is downloaded to a computer without permission. It collects information about the user so as to display targeted advertisements to the user, either in the form of inline banners or pop-ups. Inline banners are advertisements that run within the context of the current page, just taking up screen real estate. **Pop-ups** are a greater annoyance, because they are ads that run in separate browser windows that you must close before you can continue with your present task. Clicking to accept an offer presented on an inline banner or a pop-up may trigger a pop-up download that can install a virus or worm.

Web Browser Hijacking

We received a call the other day from Dave, a finance officer at a large farm implement company. Every time he opened Internet Explorer, the home page pointed to a site advertising adware removal software. This is an example of web browser hijacking, a practice that has been growing. The motivation for people to do this varies, but some unscrupulous people do this so that their web site will register more visitors, and then they can raise their rates to advertisers.

Dave was able to reverse this by changing the default page in Internet Options, but it was very annoying. He was lucky, because sometimes hijackers make it very difficult to defeat the hijack, by modifying the registry so that every time you restart Windows or Internet Explorer, the hijack is reinstated. Or you may even find that Internet Options are not available because of a registry change.

Back Door

In computing, a **back door** is a way in which someone can gain access to a computer, bypassing security. Sometimes a back door is installed into a single program by its author so that it can be easily accessed later for administering the program and/or for troubleshooting the program. Or a back door may be created by an attacker taking advantage of a discovered weakness in the system's security. In one well-known situation, the Code Red worm took advantage of a vulnerability in Microsoft's Internet Information Server to install a back door. Then, the Nimda worm took advantage of the back door left by the Code Red worm.

Try This!

Research Spam Statistics

Find out the latest bad news on the amount of Internet e-mail identified as spam. Try this:

1. Open your browser and connect to your favorite search engine, such as Google or AltaVista.
2. Search on "spam statistics."
3. In the results list, many of the links will be for anti-spam programs that provide individual statistics. Review the results and select a link that appears to give actual statistics on spam occurrences for Internet e-mail users. Discuss the results with your classmates.

Spam

Spam is unsolicited e-mail. This includes e-mail from a legitimate source selling a real service or product, but if you did not give them permission to send such information to you, it is considered spam. Too often spam involves some form of scam—a bogus offer to sell a service or product that does not exist or tries to include you in a complicated money-making deal. If it sounds too good to be true, it is! The perpetrators of spam are called spammers, and laws have been passed making spam illegal. Some corporate network administrators report that as much as 60 percent of the incoming e-mail traffic is spam. Spam accounts for a huge amount of traffic on the Internet and private networks, and a great loss in productivity as administrators work to protect their users from spam and as individuals sort through and eliminate spam.

Spim

Spim is an acronym for **Sp**am over **I**nstant **M**essaging, and the perpetrators are called spimmers. Instant messaging screen names are often collected by small programs, called **bots** (short for robot, a program that runs automatically), that are sent out over the Internet to collect information. The spimbot then sends unsolicited instant messages to the screen names. A typical spim message may contain a link to a web site, where, like spam, the recipient will find products or services for sale, legitimate or otherwise.

Phishing

Phishing is a fraudulent method of obtaining personal financial information through the use of pop-ups or e-mail that purports to be from a legitimate organization, such as a bank, credit card company, retailer, and so on. They often (falsely) appear to be from well-known organization's web sites, such as eBay, PayPal, MSN, Yahoo, BestBuy, and America Online. In a typical phishing scenario, the e-mail may contain authentic-looking logos, and even links to the actual site, but the link

Try This!

Take a Phishing IQ Test!

It is often not easy to discern which e-mails are legitimate and which are "phish." Try this:

1. Use your web browser to connect to the phishing IQ test at `http://survey.mailfrontier.com/survey/quiztest.html`.
2. You will be presented with ten e-mails, and you must decide whether each is legitimate or phish.
3. When you finish, you will be presented with the correct answers. Each e-mail also has a detailed explanation as to why it is either legitimate or phish. Read these explanations carefully.

specified for supplying personal financial information will take recipients to a "spoofed" web page where they are asked to enter their personal data. The web page may look exactly like the company's real web page, but it's not at their site. A common practice is for a phisher to use the credit information to make purchases over the Internet, choosing items that are easy to resell and having them delivered to a destination address to which the phisher has access, such as a vacant house.

Be very suspicious of e-mail requesting personal financial information. Legitimate businesses will never contact you by e-mail and ask you for your access code, social security number, or password. Phishing is just an old-fashioned scam in high-tech dress.

Exposure to Inappropriate or Distasteful Content

The Internet, and especially the World Wide Web, is a treasure trove of information. It is hard to imagine a subject that cannot be found somewhere on the Internet. However, some of this content may be inappropriate or distasteful. What is inappropriate or distasteful content? To some extent, this can only be judged by an individual. However, there are circumstances in which content should be filtered to avoid exposing a certain group or individual to content that is inappropriate or distasteful. A company may choose to enable content filtering to avoid having employees or customers offended by certain content visible on a company computer being used by an employee. Parents often use content filters to protect children from exposure to content the parents believe would be harmful.

Invasion of Privacy

Many of the threats discussed so far can also be viewed as invasions of privacy. Protecting against privacy invasion includes protecting your personal information at your bank, a credit union, both online and bricks-and-mortar retail stores, athletic clubs, or almost any organization in which you are a customer, member, or employee. All steps you take to make your computer more secure also contribute to the protection of your privacy.

A more subtle form of privacy invasion involves the misuse of something called cookies. **Cookies** are very small files an Internet browser saves on the local hard drive at the request of a web site. The next time you connect to that same web site, it will request the cookies saved on previous visits. Cookies are text files, so they cannot contain viruses, which are executable code, but what they may contain includes the following:

- User preferences when visiting a specific site
- Information you may have entered into a form at the web site, including personal information
- Browsing activity
- Shopping selections on a web site

> From now on, when you browse the Web, look for links to, and read, the privacy statement or site policy at each web site you visit.

The use of cookies is a convenience to a user who does not have to reenter preferences and pertinent information on every visit to a favorite web site. In fact, users are not overtly aware of the saving and retrieving of cookies from their local hard disk, although most good web sites clearly detail whether they use cookies and what they are used for. This information can be found in the privacy statement or policy of the site. Cookies can only be accessed by the web site that created them, or through some subterfuge of the web site creator. A problem that is connected with the use of cookies is that various banner ad creators use cookies to track your web surfing habits.

Hoaxes use weaknesses in human behavior to ensure they are replicated and distributed. In other words, hoaxes prey on the Human Operating System.
—Stewart Kirkpatrick

Hoaxes

A hoax may take many forms. One is an e-mail message claiming to be from Microsoft notifying the receiver of the availability of an update, and providing a link to a web site for downloading the fix. (Microsoft never sends out updates through e-mail.) When recipients click on the link, rather than receive the latest security update, they may be downloading a virus or other invasive program.

In Addition...

We cannot begin to cover all the methods currently being used to victimize computer users.

However, various organizations work to keep track of these threats, counter them, and inform the public. The Federal Trade Commission (FTC) is one such organization. They maintain a web site with a list of documents about various consumer issues and threats. The URL for that site is `http://www.ftc.gov/bcp/menu-internet.htm`. These documents are worth reviewing from time to time.

Check Fraud Alerts

Browse through the list of alerts at the FTC web site. Try this:

1. Point your browser to `http://www.ftc.gov/bcp/menu-internet.htm`.
2. Select an alert to read by clicking on one of the links.

Defense Against Threats

There are no simple solutions to all the damaging and mischievous threats that lurk on the Internet, as well as on private networks, but doing nothing is not an option! We need to make our best efforts to thwart these threats, even if a determined and skilled invader can still defeat our efforts. The point is that most people do not have the necessary skills, motivation, or access to sophisticated tools, and implementing basic security will keep the majority out. Below are some basic defensive practices that you can apply in Windows to avoid being a victim. Sometimes you will need to install a third-party program (free or commercial) to add a type of protection not provided in Windows.

Use Windows Help to Learn More about Security

The Windows Help program is a great aid to learning and to on-the-job troubleshooting. You can use Help to learn about the security features listed here. Try this:

1. From the Start menu, select Help (Help And Support in Windows XP).
2. In Windows 2000, search on the word "security." In Windows XP, click the link labeled "Security and privacy."
3. Select one or more topics in the results to learn more about security in Windows. When you are done, close the Help program.

Authentication and Authorization

One of the first defenses against threats is authentication and authorization by a security system built into the operating systems on your local computer and on network servers. **Authentication** is the verification of who you are. **Authorization** determines your level of access to a computer or a resource (files, folders, printers, and so on). Both of these are available in most Windows desktop OSs.

Authentication

Authentication may be one-factor, two-factor, or even three-factor. One-factor authentication is based on your use of a user name and password as you log onto your computer. In this case, you are authenticated based on something you know—your user name and password. Two-factor authentication involves the use of something you know plus something you have, referred to as a **token**. If you use a cash card at an ATM, you are familiar with two-factor authentication, because the something you know is your PIN (Personal Identification Number) code, while the token is your cash card. For even more security, consider three-factor authentication—adding biometric data such as a retinal scan, voice print, or fingerprint scan to the token and password.

Authorization

Authorization includes authentication, plus verification of your level of access to a computer or resource, including permissions and/or rights. When you connect to a shared folder on your LAN, the security system of the computer hosting the share will perform authorization, authenticating you and verifying that your account has some level of access to the folder. This level of access is called a permission. A permission describes an action that may be performed on an object. An example of a permission found on NTFS volumes is the read permission that allows reading of the contents of a file or folder.

Blank passwords or those that are easily visible on a sticky note provide no security. Always insist on nonblank passwords that are not sitting out in the open.

Passwords

A **password** is a string of characters that you enter, along with an identifier such as a user name, in order to be authenticated. A password is an important piece of the security puzzle. Don't take your password for granted. In fact, that should be "passwords," because you should not use the same password everywhere, and you should put a great deal of thought into creating passwords that truly help you protect yourself. This is important because, unless you deal strictly in cash and do all your transactions in person at the bank, secure authentication is your basic defense against an invasion of your privacy, and your password is central to having secure authentication. Passwords are a very important part of any security system. Most experts recommend using passwords that are at least eight characters long and contain a mixture of numbers, letters (both uppercase and lowercase), and non-alphanumeric characters. Passwords that use common words—such as the name of a pet—are easily guessed, and therefore offer little in the way of real security.

Best Practices with User Names and Passwords

You may actually have habits that make you vulnerable to identity theft or to another type of attack on your computer, data, or personal information. Consider the following questions:

- Do you have too many passwords to remember?
- When you have an opportunity to create a new password, do you use your favorite password—the one that you use everywhere?
- At school or work, do you have your password written on sticky notes or your desk calendar?
- Have you used the same password for more than a few months?

If you've done any of these things, you are at risk! And, hey, the risk is not only with your password. Since many web sites allow you to provide a user name to be used when you log in, you may also be reusing the same user name and password combination. Wow! Now a hacker doesn't even have to guess your account name!

Don't Give Away Your User Name and Password

If you use the same user name and password at your bank as you do at a web site where you took what seemed like a harmless personality test, you may have put your bank account and your other financial assets at risk. The web site might have been created to surreptitiously gather just such personal information, or it may have an innocent mission but simply employs weak security practices. Either way, the outcome may be the same—someone now has information that could enable them to access your bank account. "But," you say, "I didn't provide them with my bank account information." Are you sure? If you provided any personal information to the web site, they may be able to use it to search online databases (some containing information illegally gathered), and to discover, or guess, which bank you use. Then, even though the bank has much better security practices than the web site you went to, you have just given someone the key (so to speak) to your assets.

Create Strong Passwords

A strong password is one that meets certain criteria, and these criteria change over time as hackers create more techniques and tools for discovering passwords. Microsoft defines a strong password as one that contains at least eight characters, includes a combination of letters, numbers, and other symbols (+, -, $, and so on), and is easy for you to remember but difficult for others to guess.

Learn more about protecting your computer with passwords. Use an Internet search engine to search on "strong passwords." You will find great tips on how to create complex passwords that are easy to recall but hard for others to crack.

Never Reuse Passwords

Every account should have a unique name (if possible) and a unique password (always). Many web sites require your e-mail address as the user name, so these will not be unique.

Avoid Creating Unnecessary Online Accounts

Many web sites ask that you create an account and "join," but what are the benefits of joining? Why do they need information about you?

Don't Provide More Information than Necessary

Avoid creating accounts with web sites that request your social security number and other personal and financial information. Avoid having your credit card numbers and bank account information stored on a web site. Although it's not easy to do online, you can do the following with a merchant in person. If they ask for your social security number, ask these four questions:

1. Why do you need it?
2. How will you protect it?
3. How will you use it?
4. What happens if I don't give it to you?

You may have to make a decision as to whether to do business with that merchant if they don't give you satisfactory answers.

Always Use Strong Passwords for Certain Types of Accounts

Use a strong password for the following account types:

- Banks, investments, credit cards, and online payment providers
- E-mail
- Work-related
- Online auction sites and retailers
- Sites where you have provided personal information

Security Accounts

A **security account** is an account that can be assigned permission to take action on an object (such as a file, folder, or printer) or the right to take some action on an entire system, such as install device drivers into an operating system on a computer. A security account may identify a single entity (individual or computer) or a group of entities. Security accounts exist in security databases, such as those maintained by Novell servers, UNIX or Linux systems, and Windows server and desktop operating systems (excluding the Windows 9*x* family).

User Accounts

The most common type of security account is an individual account, called a user account and assigned to a single person. In the security database, a user account contains, at minimum, a user name and password used to authenticate a user. Depending on the structure of the security accounts database, a user account may contain additional identifying information. Typically, a user account will include the user's full name, a description, and a variety of other fields including e-mail address, department, phone numbers, and so on. User accounts exist in all Windows security accounts databases.

Group Accounts

A **group account** is a security account that may contain one or more individual accounts, and, in some security accounts databases, it may contain other groups. Group accounts exist in all Windows security accounts databases.

Computer Accounts

Computers (and sometimes devices) may also have security accounts within a security accounts database maintained by a network server, such as in a Microsoft Windows domain.

Encryption

Encryption is the transformation of data into a code that can only be decrypted through the use of a secret key or password. A **secret key** is a special code that can be used to decrypt encrypted data. Encryption can be used on data files that are stored on a local computer or network server. In addition, data that is being sent over a network can be encrypted. Encryption is used to protect sensitive or valuable data, and only someone who knows the password or holds the secret key can decrypt the data back to its original state. The secret key may be held in a **digital certificate**, which is a special file stored on a computer. Encryption is very useful for data stored on a laptop or in professional settings, where data theft is a real concern. The NTFS5 file system includes the ability to encrypt files and folders.

Firewalls

Firewalls are designed to protect you against the dangers presented by having an unprotected connection to the Internet. A firewall sits between a private network and the Internet (or other network) and examines all traffic in and out of the network it is protecting. It will block any traffic it recognizes as a potential threat, using a variety of techniques. Table 7-1 lists some of the most common technologies associated with firewalls. Your ISP and most corporations employ hardware firewalls, expensive and specialized computers manufactured by companies such as Cisco, 3COM (now owned by Cisco), NetGear, and others, and these sophisticated firewalls require highly trained people to manage them. At work or at school the network is probably protected by such a firewall.

Working Behind a Firewall in a Large Organization

A firewall makes decisions about allowing traffic into the private network, based on how it (the firewall) is configured, and that is determined by the types of computers residing within the private network, and how they will interact with the Internet. If all the computers on a private network are simple desktop computers, connecting to the Internet to browse web pages and access FTP sites, the firewall protecting the network has a simple job. It simply blocks all in-bound traffic that is not the result of a request from a computer on the internal network. In other words, it matches incoming traffic with previous outgoing traffic that made requests that would result in incoming traffic. For instance, when you connect to a web site, there is outgoing traffic from your computer to the web site requesting to see a page.

Table 7-1 Firewall Technologies

Technology	Description
IP packet filter	Often used on routers, an IP packet filter inspects (or filters) each packet that enters or leaves the network, applying a set of security rules defined by a network administrator. Packets that fail inspection are not allowed to pass between the connected networks.
Proxy service	Sometimes referred to as an application-layer gateway, a proxy service is designed to watch for application-specific traffic. For example, a web proxy only examines web browser traffic. Acting as a stand-in (proxy) for internal computers, it intercepts outbound connection requests to external servers and directs incoming traffic to the correct internal computer. A proxy service can be configured to block traffic from specific domains or addresses.
Encrypted authentication	Some firewalls require external users to provide a user name and password before they can open a connection through a firewall. Since the authentication information (user name and password) must pass over the Internet, it is important to encrypt it. This is called encrypted authentication and involves the use of one of several encryption protocols to encrypt the authentication information. Encrypted authentication is a security service that is not limited to firewalls and is not always implemented on a firewall.
Virtual private network (VPN)	Also not a true firewall technology, a virtual private network is a virtual tunnel created between two endpoints over a public network. This is done by encapsulating the packets. Other security methods are also usually applied, such as encryption of the data and encrypted authentication. When set up in combination with properly configured firewalls, a VPN is the safest way to connect two private networks over the Internet.

That page comes to you in the form of incoming traffic. A firewall will allow it through based on your initial request.

If, however, the private network includes servers that offer services on the Internet, then initiating traffic must be allowed to come through the firewall, but it does not allow all incoming traffic through. In this case, a firewall is configured to allow incoming traffic of the type that can communicate with the internally based servers. The various types of traffic include e-mail, web, FTP, and others. Each type of traffic has a certain characteristic recognizable by the firewall. Figure 7-1 shows a firewall protecting a network containing both servers and desktop computers (shown as clients).

> **Inside Information**
>
> **DMZs**
>
> *A network professional would look at the simplified example of a firewall shown in Figure 7-1 and immediately talk about setting up a DMZ, a network between the internal network and the Internet with a firewall on both sides. The DMZ, named for a wartime demilitarized zone, would contain any servers an organization wishes to use to offer services to the Internet.*

Working Behind a Firewall at Home or on a Small LAN

Many products for home and small business use, described as "broadband routers," are actually true multifunction network devices that serve as bridges, routers, and firewalls. You may also choose to install a "personal" software firewall utility on any desktop computer that's directly connected to the Internet. Windows XP comes with a simple firewall, and there are many third-party firewall programs. The pre–Service Pack 2 version is called Internet Connection Firewall, which you can optionally turn on through the properties of the network connection you wish to protect. Figure 7-2 shows this dialog box.

Windows XP Service Pack 2 (SP2) installed a new firewall called Windows Firewall, which is turned on by default. This firewall can be turned off or on and configured through an entirely new dialog box accessible via a

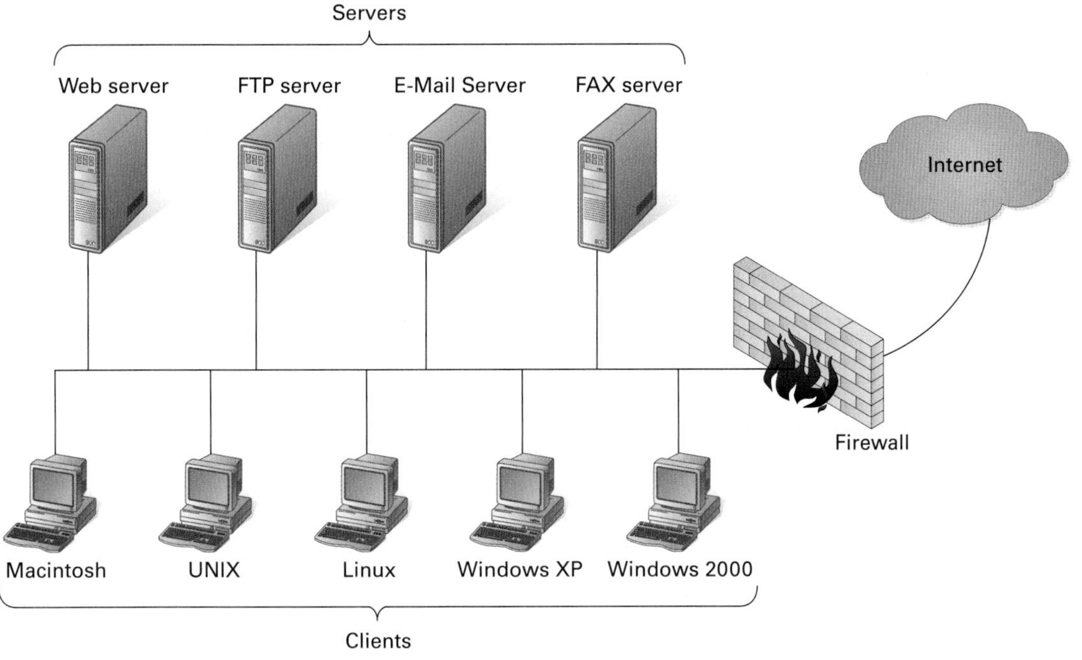

• **Figure 7-1.** A private network protected by a firewall

new applet in the Control Panel or through a Settings button on the Advanced page of the properties dialog box of a network connection.

The Windows Firewall is much more configurable than its predecessor, but because it is a *personal* firewall, and not an expensive network firewall, it allows you to modify the firewall settings without needing to understand advanced concepts, such as how the firewall identifies the types of traffic

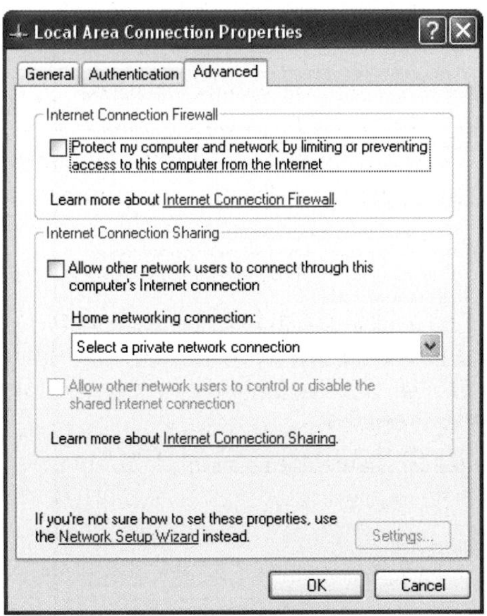

• **Figure 7-2.** The Advanced tab, pre-SP2, shows the Internet Connection Firewall settings. The Internet Connection Sharing portion of this dialog box will only exist on a computer with two network connections.

Zone Labs (`www.zonelabs.com`) offers many excellent security products, including Zone Alarm, a personal firewall.

coming to your computer. Step-by-Step 7.01 will lead you through configuring the post-SP2 Windows Firewall. Windows Firewall is an improvement over Internet Connection Firewall in protecting your computer from attacks from outside, but it also has its limits. It does not intercept messages sent from your computer by spyware. You will need to manually turn off Windows Firewall if you have installed a third-party firewall or wish to rely on an external firewall located on your network.

Step-by-Step 7.01

Configure the Windows Firewall

The Windows Firewall, installed as part of Windows XP SP2, is easy to configure through a Control Panel applet. In this exercise, you will view the configuration options. To complete this exercise, you will need the following:

- The computer on which you successfully installed Windows XP Professional in Step-by-Step 5.02
- Windows XP Updated to SP2
- A user name and password for an account that is a member of the Administrators group

Step 1

Log onto your lab computer as Administrator. Select Start | Control Panel | Windows Firewall. It is turned on by default. If you find that yours is not turned on, select the radio button to turn it on. The Don't Allow Exceptions check box is checked only if you have no need for others to connect to your computer.

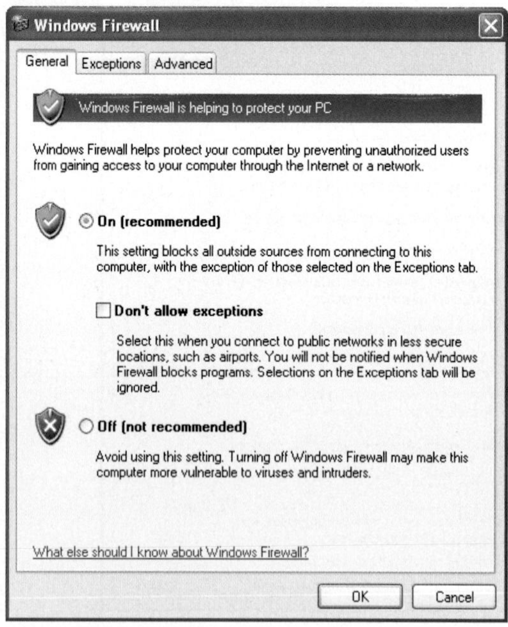

Step 2

Click on the Exceptions tab to see a list of the type of traffic that can be allowed through your firewall as exceptions. Only the items checked will be allowed through; all other incoming traffic that was not requested by your computer will be blocked.

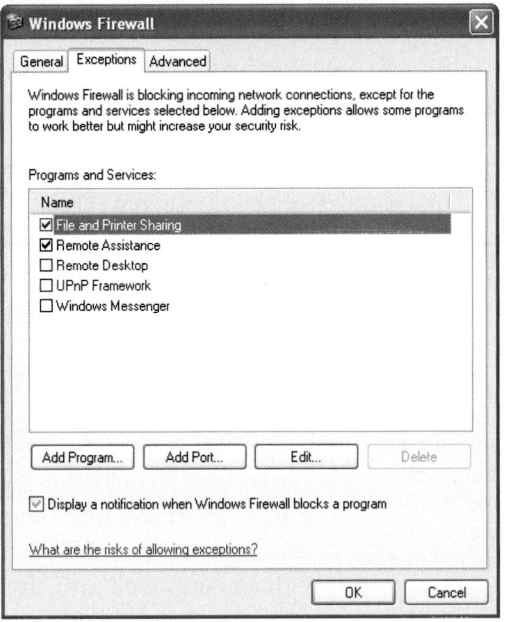

Step 3

Only place a check in boxes next to services you need to use. For instance, turn on File And Printer Sharing only if you have enabled this on your computer and have created one or more shared folders for others on your network to access. You will learn more about using these services on a desktop computer in Chapter 10.

Step 4

Double-click on "File and Printer Sharing" to open the Edit A Service dialog box for this service. The information in the column labeled "Name" reveals the information (called port IDs) the firewall uses to identify the type of traffic used for the file and printer sharing service. Click the Change Scope button if you wish to modify the scope. The Scope column limits incoming traffic for this service to your subnet (local portion of a network), any computer, or computers with specific addresses.

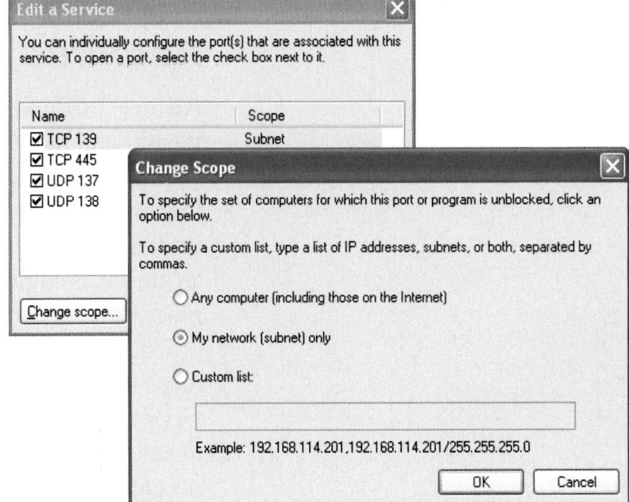

Step 5

Click the Cancel button to return to the Exceptions page. The Add Program button will allow you to add a program or service to the list of programs and services in the exceptions list. We do not recommend that you do this, because the selection list includes many programs that would be inappropriate or impossible to allow others to access over a network. If you have clicked on this button, click Cancel now.

Step 6

Similarly, the Add Port button should only be used if you have expert advice on adding a port, or port ID, the identifying information you viewed in the Edit A Service dialog box in Step 4. Cancel out of the Windows Firewall now, unless your instructor advises you to make and save changes to the settings.

Anti-Spam

> If your e-mail program does not include a spam filter, you will want to install one or upgrade to e-mail software that will include this feature (if that is an option for you). Research your options by using your favorite web search engine. Search on "spam filter."

There are many software products—often called spam filters—designed to combat spam. In a larger organization with centralized network and computer management, special filter software installed on central mail servers can remove spam before it gets to a user's desktop. Other network administrators are using Internet-based spam filtering services that filter out incoming spam even before it reaches the corporate network. However, individuals connected to the Internet at home or in small businesses are often on their own when it comes to eliminating spam. Luckily, many e-mail clients now offer spam filtering. Without some sort of spam filter, you must sort through your own e-mail to find and delete the spam. Spam filters are not perfect—they often filter out legitimate messages while allowing some spam messages through. For this reason, most spam filters require some configuration on the part of the user, through the use of rules that will automate the process of removing spam from known sources. And the user will still often need to review a list of suspected spam messages.

Antivirus

An antivirus program can examine the contents of a disk or RAM for hidden viruses and files that may act as hosts for virus code. Effective antivirus products not only detect and remove viruses, but they also help you recover data that has been lost because of a virus. To remain current, they require frequent updating as to the virus threats to watch for. An antivirus program includes an antivirus engine (the main program) and a set of patterns of recognized viruses, usually contained in files called definition files. It has become common practice among retailers of antivirus software to charge an annual fee for updates to the antivirus engine and the definitions. There are excellent free services for home users. One example is AVG Anti-Virus from Grisoft. Once installed, most antivirus programs can be configured to automatically connect to the manufacturer's web site and check for these updates.

Anti-Pop-Up

Many free and commercial programs are available that effectively block various forms of adware, especially pop-ups. These are the easiest to block and the most annoying, because a pop-up advertisement appears in its own window and must be closed or moved before you can see the content you were seeking. Such a blocking program is called a pop-up blocker, and it is usually configured so that it will block pop-ups quietly, but you can also configure it to make a sound and/or display a message allowing you to make a decision on each pop-up. We have found a few web sites where blocking all pop-ups has blocked much of the content we were seeking. In that case, we may disable our pop-up blocker altogether for that session, or configure it to display a message allowing for a decision to be made for each pop-up. Windows XP SP2 installs a pop-up blocker for Internet Explorer. You can enable this new feature on the Privacy page of the Internet Options dialog box. Once enabled, click the Settings button to open the Pop-Up Blocker Settings page, as shown in Figure 7-3. You can also get third-party programs, such as Stopzilla, available at `www.stopzilla.com`.

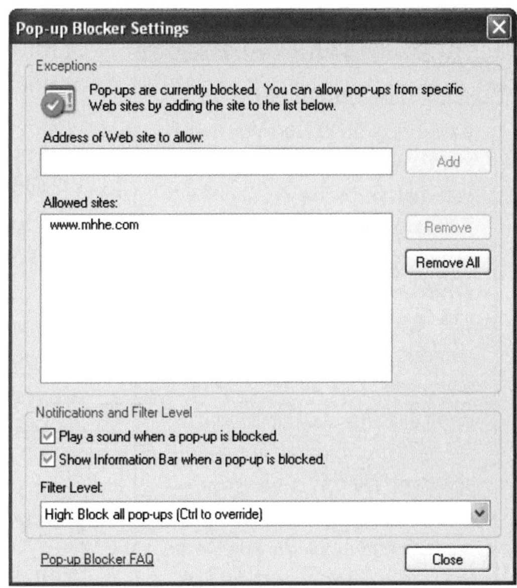

• **Figure 7-3.** The Internet Explorer Pop-up Blocker Settings page available with Windows XP SP2

More Help from Windows XP Service Pack 2

In addition to Windows Firewall and the pop-up blocker for Internet Explorer, both just discussed, Windows XP Service Pack 2 came with a new Control Panel applet called the Windows Security Center. It monitors the security status for three functions: Firewall, Automatic Updates, and Virus Protection. While antivirus software is not part of SP2, it will recognize the existence of some third-party antivirus programs and whether or not the program is enabled.

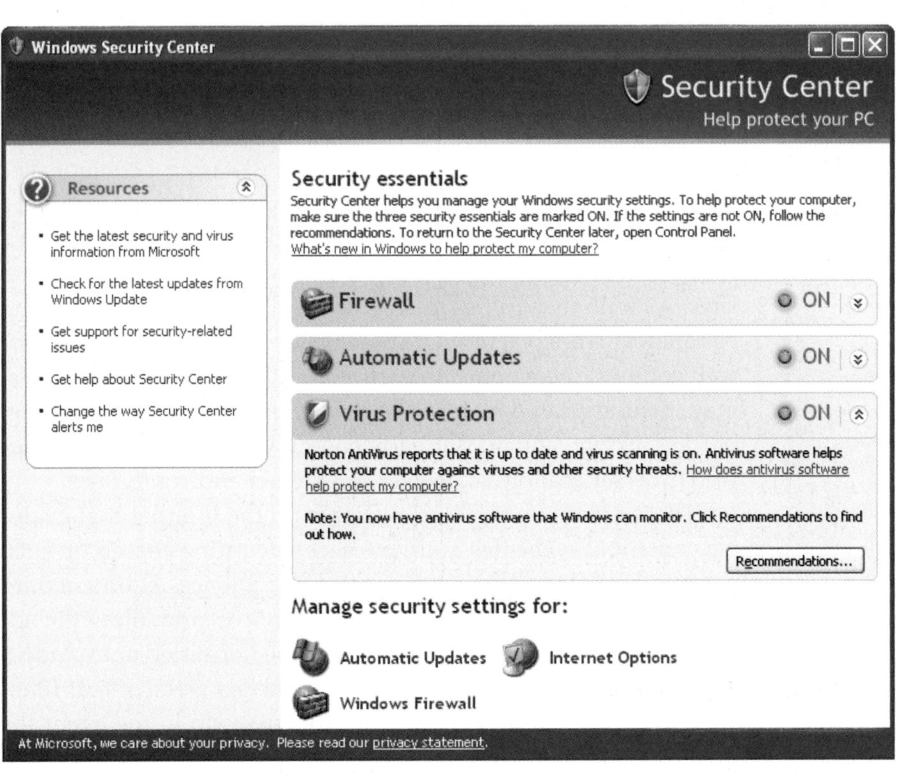

• Windows Security Center

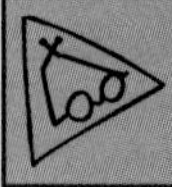

Inside Information

The Quick Cure

Creators of the threats discussed in this chapter, especially viruses, pop-ups, and drive-by downloads, will target the most commonly used software in order to have the greatest effect for their efforts. The most common software used on desktop PCs is currently from Microsoft. This includes the operating systems, desktop productivity software, and web browser software. Therefore, the quick (but not always easy) cure is to use different software. For the average user it is not a trivial task to switch from Microsoft Windows to a Linux OS, but to avoid the threats that target Internet Explorer, you can switch to an alternative web browser, such as Netscape Navigator, Opera, or Firefox. These web browsers will be discussed in more detail in Chapter 10.

Service Pack 2 also adds a Manage Add-ons button to the Programs page of Internet Options. This opens a dialog box that allows you to view, disable, or enable the many add-ons that are installed in Internet Explorer. In addition, add-ons will no longer silently install as drive-by downloads. When an add-on attempts to install, a pop-up dialog box will request your permission.

Outlook Express, Internet Explorer, and Windows Messenger all now provide warnings before you can open files that could contain viruses, and you will find that the file has been quarantined. You will need to locate the file on disk, right-click it, and select Unblock from the context menu. Not terribly intuitive!

Other security enhancements in SP2 involve under-the-hood changes to prevent a variety of attacks that for years have targeted Windows operating systems.

Privacy Protection

Web browsers and third-party programs—both free and commercial products—offer privacy protection options. In Microsoft Internet Explorer, privacy settings can be configured through the Internet Options dialog box, accessible from either the Control Panel or the Tools menu in Internet Explorer. These privacy settings determine how Internet Explorer handles cookies. The settings range from block all cookies to allow all cookies, with a variety of settings in between. Experiment with the settings by selecting one and then spending some time browsing the Internet. The balance here is between the convenience of cookies for frequently accessed sites, and the risk of an invasion of privacy.

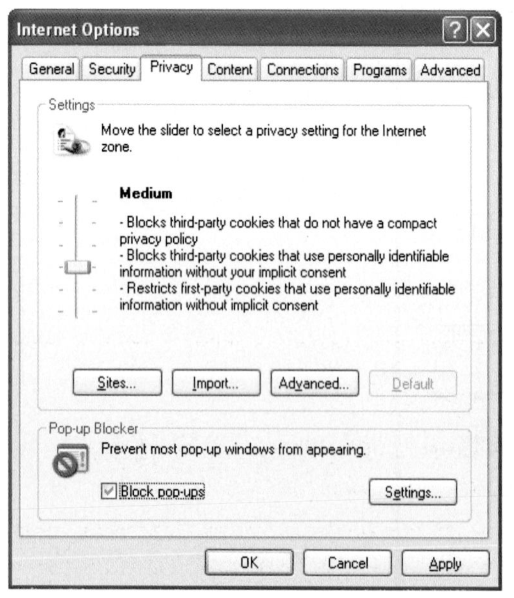

• Use the privacy page to control the use of cookies.

Protection from Inappropriate or Distasteful Content

You can use software that blocks content, called a **content filter**, to enable protection from inappropriate or distasteful content. The most common type of content filter used on the Internet is called a web content filter, a software program designed to work with a web browser to either block certain sites or to only allow certain sites. As with most types of software, you can find both free and commercial versions of web content filters on the Internet. Some web content filters come as part of a multifunction package that may include related features, such as a privacy filter and pop-up blocker. In fact, you may already have a web content filter in your web browser that only needs to be enabled and configured.

There are many services available on the Internet that evaluate content of web sites and give each site ratings based on such parameters as language, nudity, sex, and violence. A content filter may use one or more of these rating services, and allow the administrator to choose the rating level to be permitted or excluded. Not all web sites are rated, so if you enable a web content filter, you will also have to decide what it should do in the event the user connects to an unrated site.

Microsoft Internet Explorer comes with a content filter called Content Advisor. It can be enabled and configured through the Internet Options dialog box, which is accessible from either the Control Panel or the Tools menu in Internet Explorer. Clicking the Enable button will turn on this service as well as open a new dialog box for configuring the Content Advisor. From here you have a variety of choices to make. The Ratings page will allow you to configure the level of ratings for language, nudity, sex, and violence. At this writing, the current version of Internet Explorer uses the Recreational Software Advisory Council (RSACi) ratings service, an organization that has been replaced by the Internet Content Rating Association (ICRA). You may also choose a different rating bureau. Before you can use such a bureau, you will need to contact one separately and arrange for this service, which will usually involve a fee. Learn how to configure the Content Advisor options in Step-by-Step 7.02.

Using your favorite web search engine, search on "web content filter" to learn more about this topic and to find third-party web content filters.

Microsoft warns that using a different ratings bureau than the default will add a delay to web browsing, as the new ratings bureau is contacted for each new web page visited.

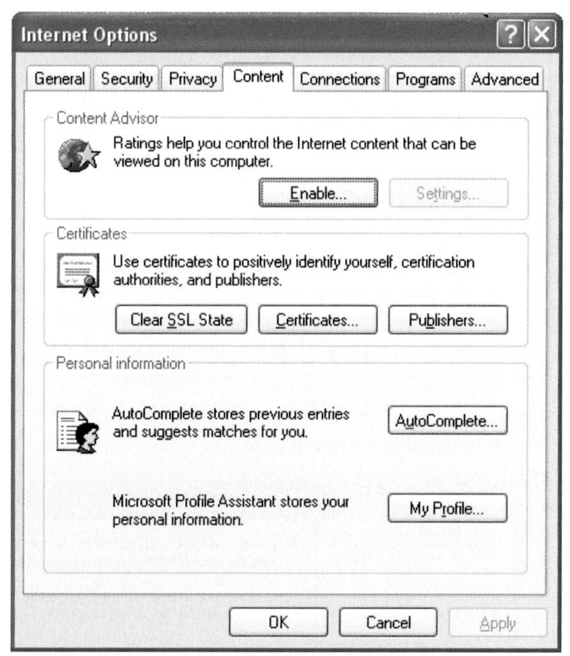

• Enable the Content Advisor in the Content page of Internet Options.

Step-by-Step 7.02

Check Out the Content Advisor in Internet Explorer

The Internet Explorer Content Advisor is easy to enable, but not so easy to configure once enabled. In this exercise, you will enable the Content Advisor, create a supervisor password, and view the configuration options. To complete this exercise, you will need the following:

- A computer running Windows and Internet Explorer version 6 (or greater)
- A user name and password for an account that is a member of the Administrators group

Step 1

Log onto your computer with the Administrator account and open Internet Explorer. Select the Tools menu and then select Internet Options. In the Internet Options dialog box, select the Content page. Click the Enable button located in the Content Advisor area of the page. This will open the Content Advisor dialog box.

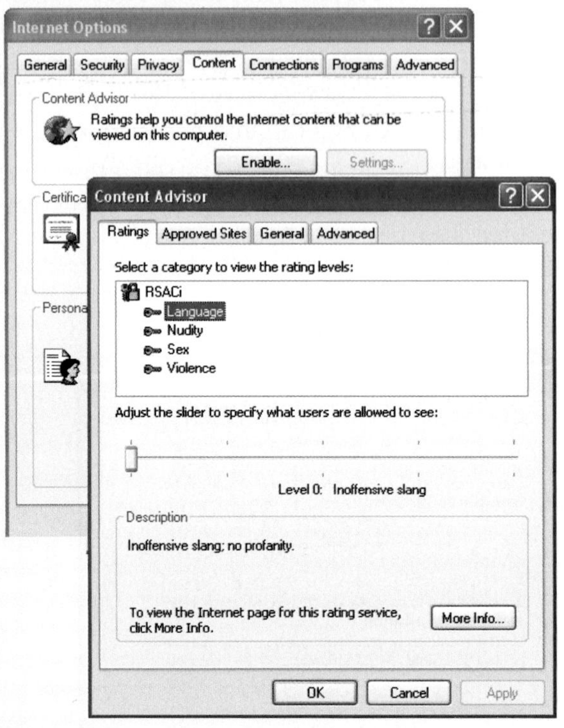

Step 2

Now create a supervisor password, because Content Advisor does not work without one. Select the General tab and under Supervisor Password, click the Create Password button. Create a password, entering it twice, and then type a Hint to help you remember this password. Click OK to close the message box confirming the creation of the supervisor password.

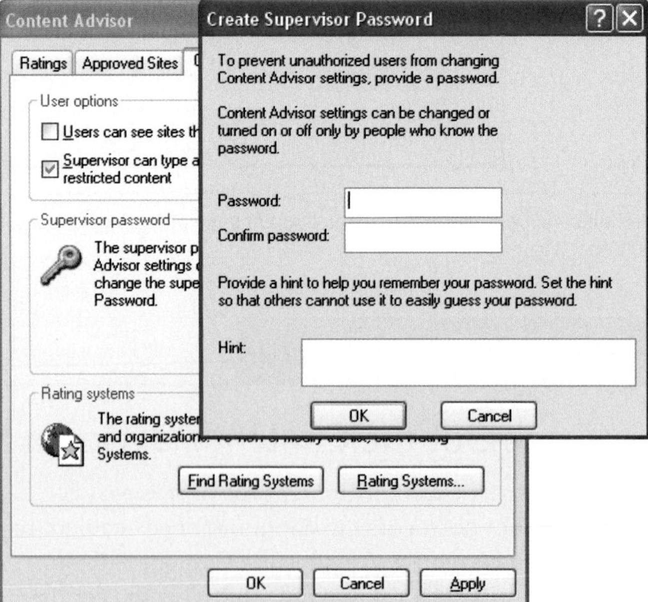

Step 3

On the General page, you'll notice that the first setting under User Options is deselected. This means that, by default, once Content Advisor is turned on, users may not view pages that have not been rated by the ratings service selected in Content Advisor. The second option is turned on by default; with this selected, the user will be prompted to enter the supervisor password to view restricted sites.

Step 4

Return to the ratings page. Next to the lock-and-key icon is the name of the rating service that will be used to rate sites. Below that are the categories this service has rated. When you select one of the categories, a slider will be displayed in the middle of the box. This slider can be used to select what rating level the user will be allowed to view in each category. Examine each of the categories, and move the slider to see the descriptions of each of the rating levels.

Step 5

Click on the Approved Sites tab. This is where you can create a list of web sites that are either always viewable or never viewable. This is configurable per web site. Enter a web site and click the Always button. Enter another web site and click the Never button. To remove a site from the list, select it and click the Remove button.

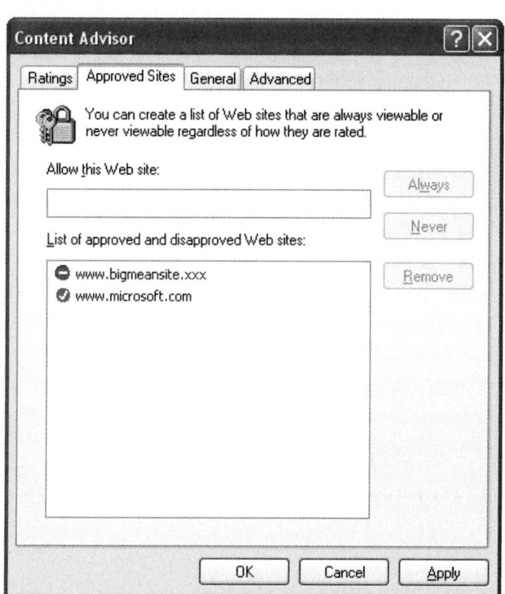

Step 6

Return to the General page; the Ratings Systems portion at the bottom of the page allows you to configure the ratings system(s) available to this computer. To see the current list of ratings systems, click the button labeled "Rating Systems," which will display the default rating system as RSACi. Click the Add button to see if other rating systems files are available on your computer. You should see the file for the default rating system (rsaci.rat). Click Cancel twice to return to the Content Advisor dialog box.

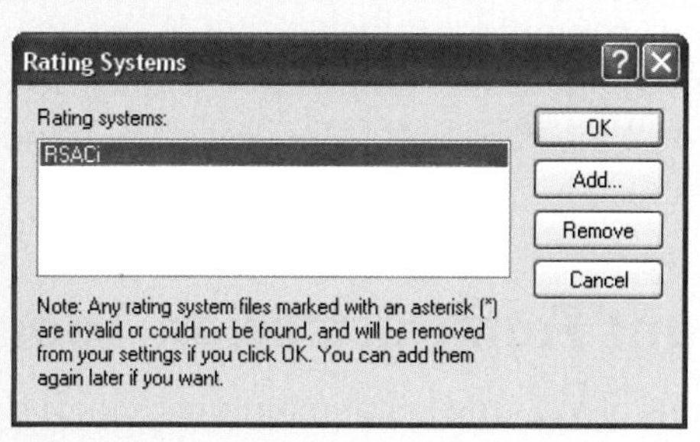

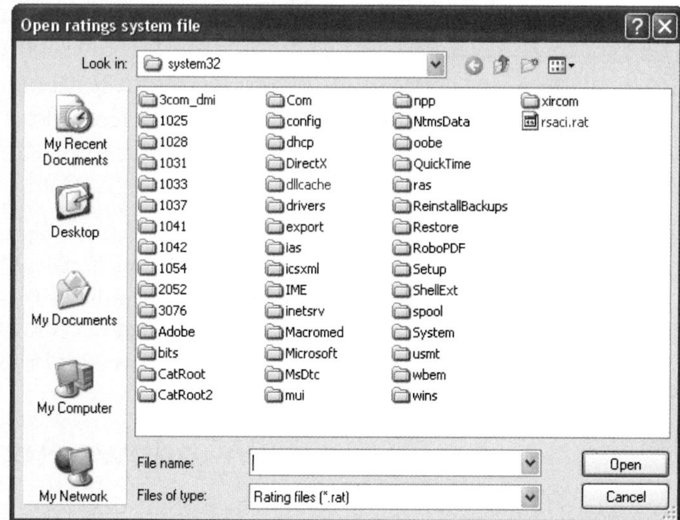

Step 7

Click the Advanced tab and view the options available here. The section labeled "Ratings Bureau" will allow you to enter the name of the new ratings bureau (do not do that now). Once a ratings bureau name is entered, you would click the Import button under PICRules and enter the name of the rules file supplied by your new ratings bureau. After viewing the Advanced page, click OK to close the Content Advisor. Click OK again to close the message box advising you that Content Advisor has been enabled, and then click OK to close the Internet Options dialog box.

Step 8

Before the Content Advisor settings will take effect, you need to close and restart Internet Explorer. Do that now. Depending on your settings, you may be surprised at what you are not permitted to view!

Windows Local Security Accounts

Now that you have learned the threats to computer security and common defenses against these threats, including the use of security accounts, explore the use of Windows local security accounts in securing a Windows desktop operating system.

All versions of the Windows 9*x* family are excluded from this discussion of local security accounts, because these operating systems do not maintain local security accounts.

Windows NT 4.0 Workstation, Windows 2000 Professional, and Windows XP Professional all contain local security account databases for user and group accounts. A skillful administrator can use these accounts to protect sensitive information on a computer. Permissions to use printers and to access files and folders on an NTFS volume can be assigned to users and groups. In a Microsoft workgroup, the only security accounts are on the individual Windows desktop computers (when using Windows NT, Windows 2000, and Windows XP). In this section, you will study local security accounts in the Windows desktop versions of Windows NT, Windows 2000, and Windows XP Professional.

Windows Account Administration Tools

Each of the desktop versions of Windows that maintains a local security accounts database has a tool (or several) for administering security accounts. While advanced administrators managing security accounts for a medium-to-large organization will use scripting tools—from Microsoft or from other vendors—to create or modify many accounts at once, our discussion here is confined to the GUI tools that come with Windows. Here is an overview of the account administration tools for Windows desktop operating systems that you will use later in this chapter.

Windows NT 4.0 Workstation

The one GUI administration tool for local accounts in Windows NT 4.0 Workstation is User Manager, which you open by selecting Start | Programs | Administrative Tools | User Manager.

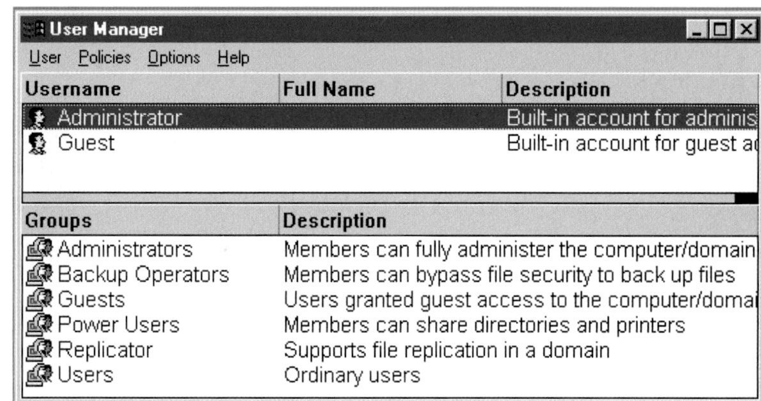

• User Manager in Windows NT 4.0

Simple Account Management in Windows 2000 and Windows XP Professional

Windows 2000 Professional and Windows XP Professional each have two user management tools—a simpler tool intended for home and small business use, and an advanced tool for professional administrators.

Windows 2000 Professional Users and Passwords In Windows 2000 Professional, a simple user management tool, the Users and Passwords applet is found in Control Panel. This is a simple tool for managing user accounts, with some limitations, as you will see later in this chapter. This may be sufficient for managing accounts on a desktop or laptop computer at home or in a very small business.

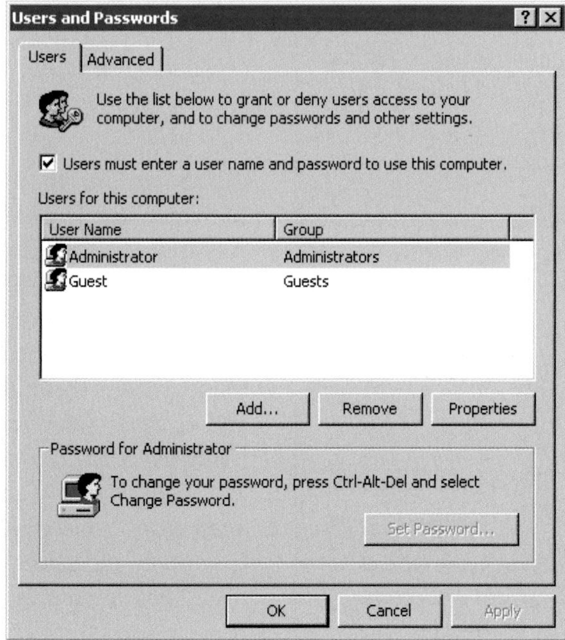

• Users and Passwords in Windows 2000 Professional

Control Panel in Windows XP has two views: the default category view, with just a few categories listed, and Classic view, with all choices listed. If you worked with Windows before Windows XP, you may want to switch to Classic view.

Windows XP Professional User Accounts In Windows XP, a simple user management tool, the User Accounts Control Panel applet, replaces the former Users and Passwords applet and further simplifies the user management tasks. This may be sufficient for managing accounts on a desktop or laptop computer at home or in a very small business.

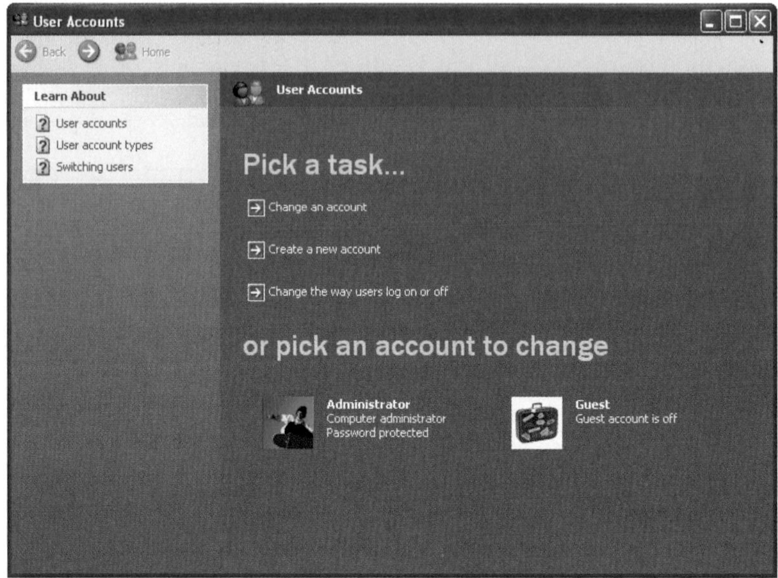

• Windows XP Professional User Accounts

Try This!

Add Administrative Tools to the Windows XP Professional Start Menu

Administrative Tools is a special folder containing helpful tools for administration. Make it handy by adding it to your All Programs folder now. You will need the computer on which you successfully installed Windows XP Professional in Step-by-Step 5.02. Try this:

1. Right-click the Start button, select Properties, select the Start Menu tab, and then click the Customize button next to the words "Start Menu."
2. In the Customize Start Menu dialog box, select the Advanced tab, and scroll the list under Start Menu Items to the bottom, to System Administration Tools. Then select the radio button next to Display on the All Programs Menu.
3. Click OK twice to close the Customize Start Menu dialog box as well as the Taskbar and Start Menu Properties dialog box.
4. Confirm that Administrative Tools is now displayed on the All Programs list. You will use Administrative Tools in upcoming step-by-step exercises in this chapter and later in this book.

Advanced Account Management in Windows 2000 and Windows XP Professional

Local Users and Groups, an advanced tool for managing local security accounts in Windows 2000 and Windows XP Professional, can be found in the Computer Management console (Figure 7-4). A knowledgeable administrator of either Windows 2000 Professional or Windows XP Professional computers will choose to create and manage users through Local Users and Groups, which reveals all existing users and groups.

To open the Computer Management console, right-click on My Computer and select Manage from the context menu. In addition, this console and others can be found in the Administrative Tools folder located in Control Panel in both operating systems. In Windows 2000,

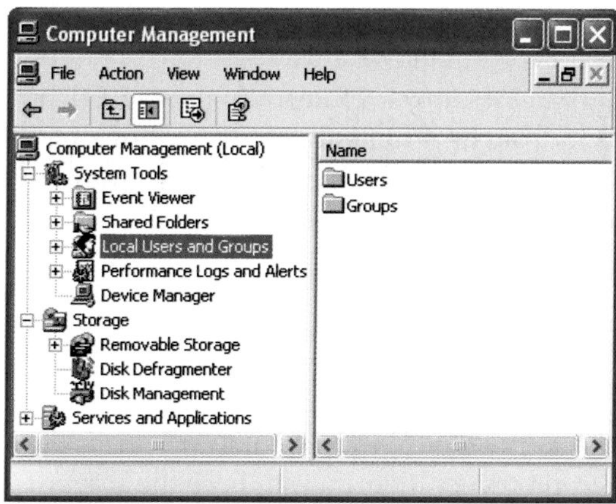

• **Figure 7-4.** The Windows XP Computer Management console

you will also find Administrative tools by selecting Start | Programs | Administrative Tools. In Windows XP, you can customize the Start menu to add the Administrative Tools folder to the All Programs menu.

Windows Local User Accounts

Windows NT, Windows 2000, and Windows XP each require an authenticated logon with a valid user name and password. For these operating systems, the most basic element of security is the user account. A user account is a record in a security database, and each user must present a valid user name and password of a local or domain user account to log onto a Windows computer.

Built-In Local User Accounts

There are two built-in user accounts in Windows: Administrator and Guest. These two accounts are at opposite ends of the power spectrum. The Administrator account is all-powerful and active by default, while the Guest account has no special powers and is disabled by default.

We strongly urge you to create a user account that is only a member of the local Users group. Use this account when you are doing ordinary work on your computer. Log on as an Administrator only when you need to do things that require a privileged account!

Administrator When you installed Windows on your lab computer, you had to provide the password for the Administrator. The local Administrator account is an all-powerful account able to do anything to the local computer. If a malicious person gets access to it, that person has full control of your computer. This account cannot be deleted, but it can be renamed, which is a good practice, as long as you remember the new name when you need to log on as a powerful user. Using the Administrator account is just fine when you're doing administrative tasks, such as installing updates, adding printers, adding and removing programs and Windows components, and creating users and groups. However, even on your own computer, if you are on a network or connected to the Internet, you should never log on with such a powerful account when you are doing ordinary tasks, such as writing and printing reports, browsing the Internet, and playing games (certainly not!).

Only an Administrator can modify update settings, connect to the Microsoft Windows Update web page, or install updates.

In a Microsoft domain, security accounts are contained in a centralized accounts database on special servers called domain controllers. A special relationship then exists between the domain security accounts database and the security accounts database on individual desktops.

Guest During installation, another user account, **Guest,** is created. When enabled, the Guest account allows a user without an account to log on. It is disabled by default in Windows NT and Windows 2000, but it is enabled by default in both Windows XP Professional (when the computer is not a member of a domain) and Windows XP Home. Even though it is enabled, it is turned off, which simply means it cannot be used for a local logon. In these versions of Windows, this account has functions relating to security and network shares.

User-Created Accounts

In the lab, when you installed Windows, you supplied the password for the Administrator account. Since then, this has been the account you have used to log on, unless you created a new local account or unless you joined the computer to a domain. It is the administrator's job to create additional accounts.

Windows Local Group Accounts

Each local user account is also a member of one or more local groups. A local group is a security account that contains one or more local user accounts and, when a computer is a member of a Windows domain, may also contain domain user or group accounts. Groups are used by the system administrator to easily assign the same rights and permissions to all members of the group without the need to set those rights and permissions individually.

Built-In Local Group Accounts

In addition to the built-in user accounts, there are several built-in group accounts. They include Administrators, Backup Operators, Guests, Power Users, Replicator, and Users. Windows XP Professional also includes the new Network Configuration Operators group that has a set of privileges needed to change the network configuration without having full administrator privileges. To view these groups in Windows 2000 Professional and Windows XP Professional, right-click My Computer and select Manage to open the Computer Management console. Then expand Local Users And Groups and then Groups.

By default, Administrator is the only member of the Administrators group, and Guest is the only member of the Guests group. The other groups are empty until an administrator creates additional local user accounts, at which point all local user accounts are automatically members of the Users group. The administrator may make users members of any group, including groups the administrator creates.

The Power Users group, while more privileged than the Users group, is more limited than the Administrators group, and some administrators assign the primary user of a computer to this group.

Automatically Created Groups

In addition to the default set of built-in groups, you will see groups created automatically when certain services were installed, and groups created by an Administrator. See Figure 7-5.

Special Groups/Built-In Security Principals

In addition to the built-in groups and those that an administrator can create and administer, there are special built-in groups that cannot be created or

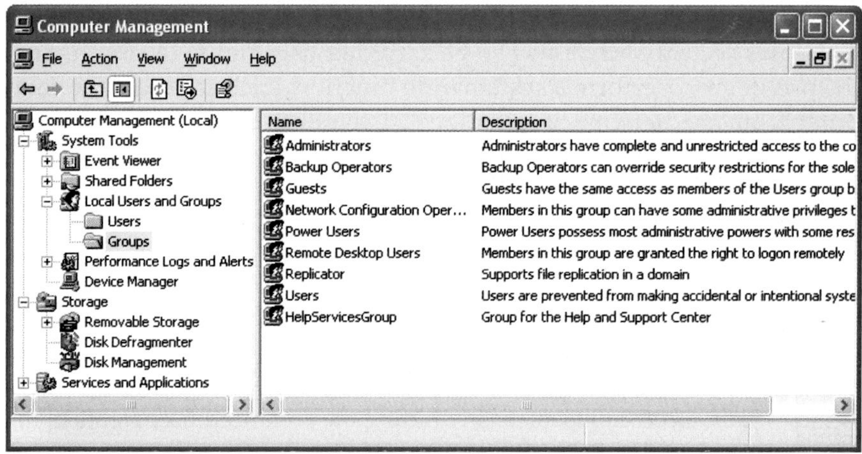

• **Figure 7-5.** The list of groups in Windows XP

modified. Their membership is predefined, and some of them are available to you only when you assign permissions or rights. In Windows NT and Windows 2000, these groups are called special groups; in Windows XP, these are referred to as built-in security principals. Figure 7-6 shows a list of these groups on the computer named Klamath. A few important special groups are Creator Owner (the user who created the file or folder), System (the operating system), and the Everyone group, which includes all users on a network, even those who haven't been authenticated.

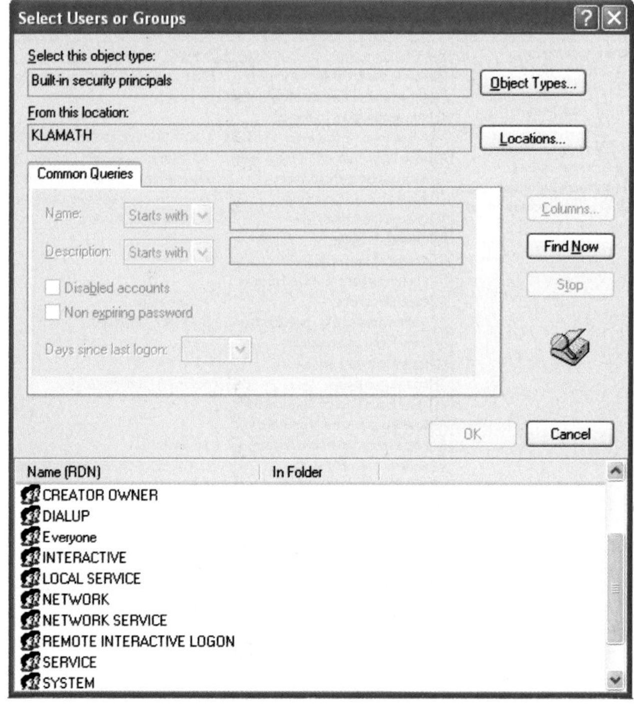

• **Figure 7-6.** In Windows XP, the Select Users or Groups dialog box can be used to view built-in security principals (special groups).

Later in this chapter, we will show you how to access the Select Users or Groups dialog box.

User Rights

Windows security accounts can be assigned user rights. A **user right** is the privilege to perform a systemwide function, such as access the computer from the network, log on locally, log onto a computer from the network, back up files, change the system time, or load and unload device drivers. The method you use to view user rights depends on your version of Windows.

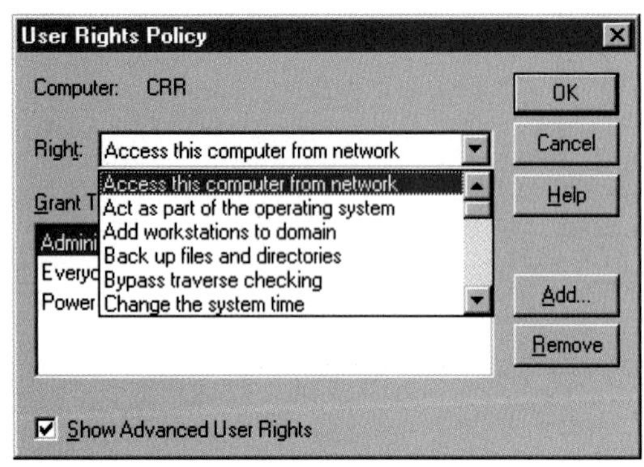

• The user rights list for Windows NT 4.0 Workstation

Windows NT 4.0 Workstation You can view the user rights of a Windows NT 4.0 Workstation computer by opening User Manager and selecting User Rights from the Policies menu. Windows NT 4.0 Workstation also distinguishes between basic rights and advanced rights, normally hiding the advanced user rights in the User Rights Policy dialog box.

Windows 2000 Professional and Windows XP Professional To view user rights in Windows 2000 Professional and Windows XP Professional, open the Local Security Policy console and select User Rights Assignment. In both OSs Administrative Tools is located in the Control Panel. You may optionally Add Administrative Tools to the Start Menu in Windows XP Professional by following the steps in the Try This exercise on page 334. Add it to the Windows 2000 Start Menu in a similar fashion; accessing the Properties dialog box for the Start Menu by right-clicking an empty area of the taskbar.

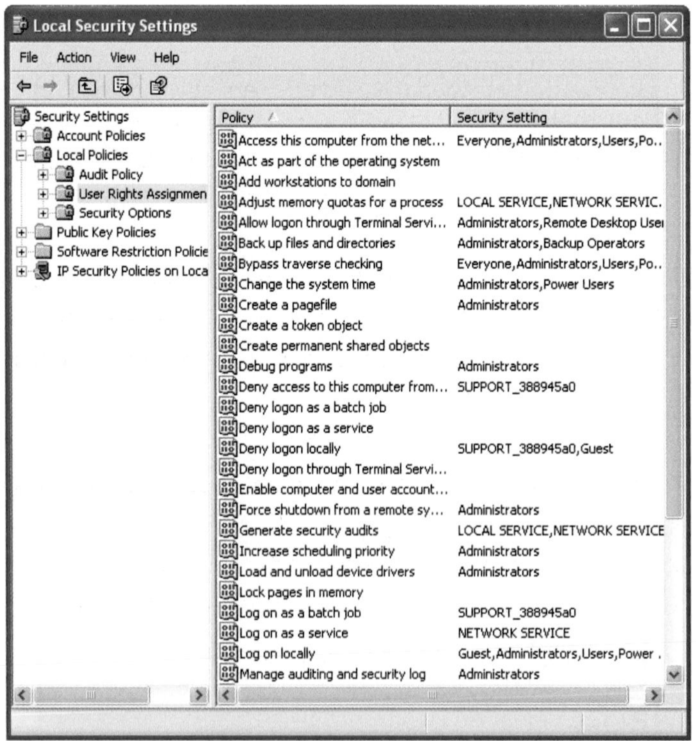

• The list of user rights in Windows XP Professional

Table 7-2 shows the built-in groups with their default rights. The user rights shown in red were added in Windows 2000, while the items shown in green were added in Windows XP.

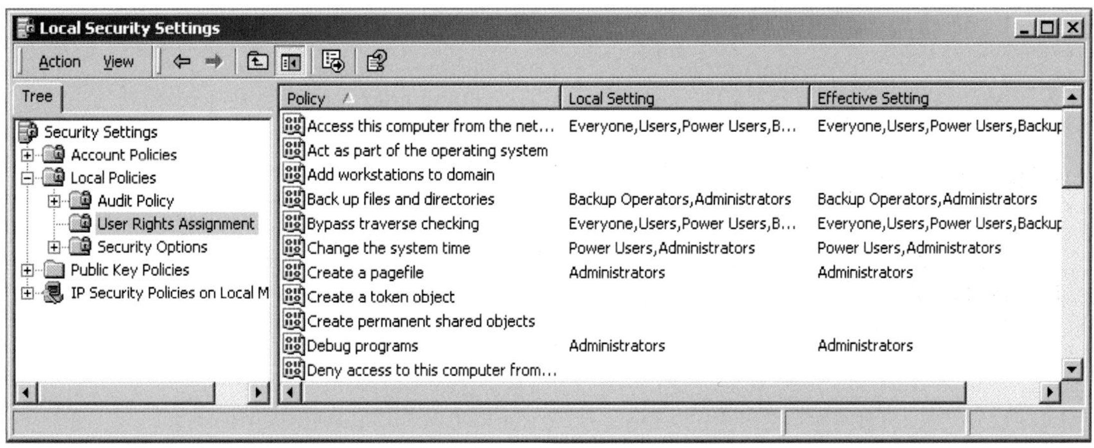

• The list of user rights in Windows 2000 Professional.

Granularity of Control with Groups

With Windows 2000, and even more so in Windows XP Professional, Microsoft has added granularity of control using groups. What does this mean? It used to be that you had just a few built-in groups to which you could assign rights to perform certain tasks or permissions to certain objects. The default groups ranged from the all-powerful Administrators to groups with no default rights and permissions (Guests), or groups with a little more than nothing (Users), and then the Power Users group with a few elevated rights. The new Network Configuration Operators group is an example of granularity of control. While you cannot view any rights assigned to this new group in Local User Settings, it has default permissions to perform the following:

- Modify the Transmission Control Protocol/Internet Protocol (TCP/IP) properties for a local area network (LAN) connection
- Rename the LAN connections or remote access connections that are available to all of the users
- Enable or disable a LAN connection
- Modify the properties of all of the remote access connections of the user
- Delete all of the remote access connections of the user
- Rename all of the remote access connections of the user
- Issue ipconfig, release, or renew commands

Planning for Users and Groups

If a Windows computer is used only by a single user, then you need to create only one additional user account beyond Administrator. Windows XP Professional requires that you create one additional account that is a

Table 7-2 Default User Rights for Windows NT 4.0 Workstation, Windows 2000 Workstation, and Windows XP Professional

Group Name	User Rights
Administrators	Access this computer from network **Adjust memory quotas for a process** Back up files and directories **Bypass traverse checking** Change the system time Create a page file Debug programs Force shutdown from a remote system Increase scheduling priority Load and unload device drivers Log on locally Manage auditing and security log Modify firmware environment values **Perform volume maintenance tasks** Profile single process Profile system performance **Remove computer from docking station** Restore files and directories Shut down the system Take ownership of files or other objects
Backup Operators	**Access this computer from network** Back up files and directories **Bypass traverse checking** Log on locally Restore files and directories Shut down the system
Everyone	Access this computer from network Bypass traverse checking Log on locally Shut down the system
Guests	Log on locally
Power Users	Access this computer from network **Bypass traverse checking** Change the system time Force shutdown from a remote system Increase Scheduling Priorities (NT only) Log on locally Profile single process **Remove computer from docking station** Shut down the system
Remote Desktop Users (W2K, WXP)	**Allow logon through terminal services**
Users	**Access this computer from network** **Bypass traverse checking** Log on locally **Remove computer from docking station** Shut down the system

member of the Administrators group before creating any ordinary accounts. If the computer is used by more than one local user, you should create an additional local account for each person. If the computer is a member of a Windows NT or Active Directory domain, you can give access to files, folders, and printers on that computer to the users and groups in the domain. If the computer is a member of a workgroup, and you wish to share local files, folders, and/or printers, then it must have local accounts for granting access to network users.

Passwords are case sensitive; therefore take that into consideration during planning, and pay attention to case when creating new passwords and when entering a password for authentication.

You must be logged on as a member of the Administrators group to create users or groups, and you must provide certain information for each user you create. To be prepared to create a new user, have this information at hand. We like using planning forms as we prepare to create accounts. A completed planning form for new users might look like Table 7-3. Although all users are automatically members of the Users group, we included it in the planning form. Full Name and Description are optional, but it is good practice to complete these fields. If User Must Change Password At Next Logon is turned on, users log on with the password assigned in the New User dialog box, but will be prompted to immediately change the password. The default groups are normally sufficient for a local user account; therefore no new groups are included.

Administering Local Windows Accounts

If a Windows computer is a member of a Windows NT or Active Directory domain, management of users and groups is mainly done at the domain level, and each user who logs onto the local computer will use a domain user account. But if a computer is a stand-alone computer or a member of a workgroup (as you will often see in very small organizations), users and groups will have to be managed on each computer. For that reason, it is good practice to create users on a desktop computer. You are also working with the same concepts on a small scale that an administrator must work with in a domain. Now let's create some local security accounts.

Creating a New User

Creating a new user account enables that user to log in with a user name and password. This allows an administrator to set the rights and permissions for the user. Unless otherwise specified, as in Table 7-3, you should create one account that is only a member of the local Users group, and an account that is a member of the local Administrators group (in addition to the Administrator account created during installation).

To create and manage users, you must be logged on as the Administrator or a member of the local Administrators group. Be sure to assign a password to the Administrator account so that only authorized users can access this all-powerful account.

Table 7-3 User and Group Planning Form

User Name	Full Name	Description	Password	Groups
Ssmith	Sue Smith	Manager	Ssmith	Users Power Users
Rjones	Ron Jones	Clerk	Rjones	Users

User Administration in Windows NT 4.0 Workstation

In the following step-by-step, you will create new users in Windows NT 4.0 Workstation using User Manager. Using this tool requires some knowledge of Windows security accounts, reflecting the positioning of Windows NT Workstation in the mid-1990s as an OS for an advanced user or for a user in an organization with knowledgeable desktop support staff.

Step-by-Step 7.03

Creating New Users in Windows NT 4.0 Workstation

Now you will create the users listed in Table 7-3, the User and Group Planning Form. To complete this exercise, you will need the following:

- The computer on which you successfully installed Windows NT in Step-by-Step 3.02
- A user name and password for an account that is a member of the Administrators group

Step 1

Log onto your lab computer as Administrator. Select Start | Programs | Administrative Tools | User Manager. On the menu bar, select New User.

Step 2

Complete the New User form for Sue Smith, filling in the correct fields from Table 7-3. You must enter the password two times, first in the Password field and again in the Confirm Password field. Leave the check by User Must Change Password At Next Logon; then click Groups.

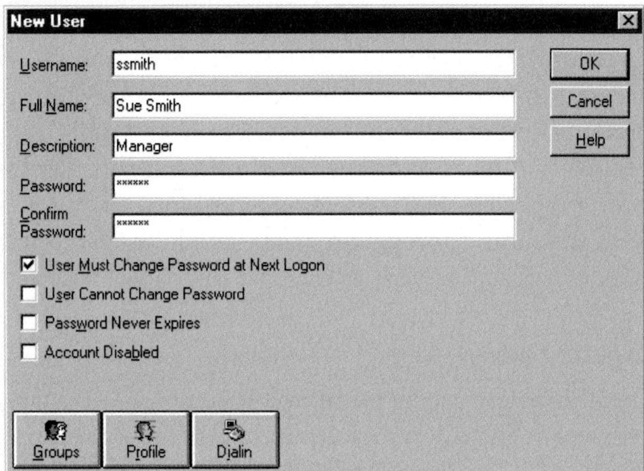

Step 3

In the Group Memberships dialog box, notice that Sue Smith is automatically a member of the Users group. To add her to the Power Users group, click Power Users in the Not Member Of list; then click the Add button. Click OK to add Sue to the Power Users group. Confirm that the information is correct in the New User dialog box; then click OK in the New User dialog box to create the new account.

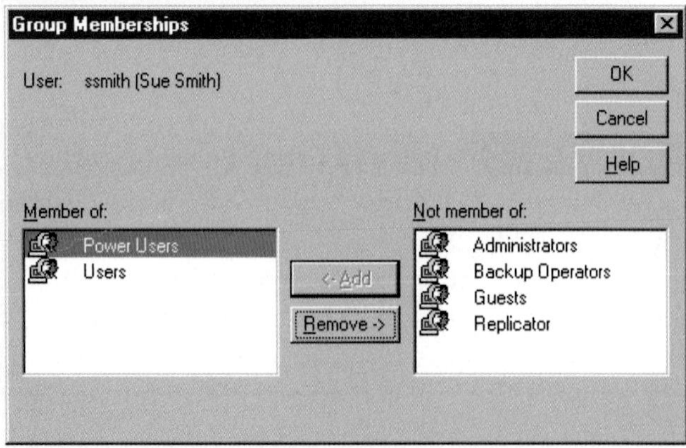

Step 4

Repeat Steps 2 and 3 to create a user account for Ron Jones. Do not add him to the Power Users group.

Step 5

Test the new accounts by logging off as Administrator and logging on as each new account. When you log on as each user, you will have to change the password.

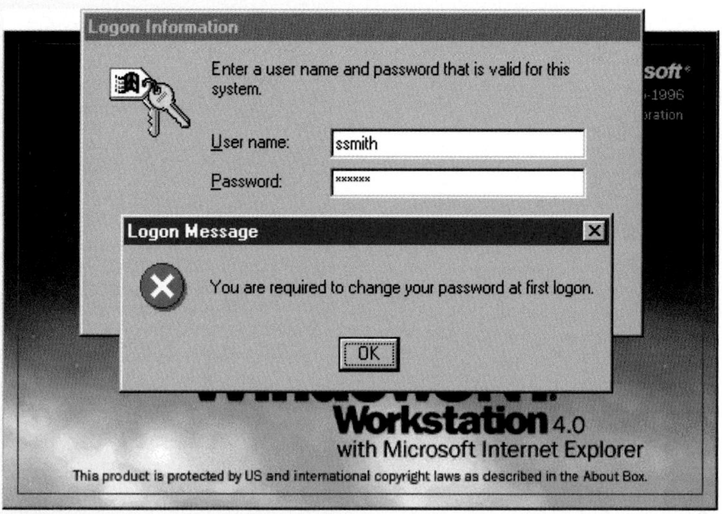

User Administration in Windows 2000 Professional

Before creating new accounts in Windows 2000 Professional, you will first view some default settings that can compromise the security of your computer. When you install Windows 2000 Professional, if your computer is not made a member of a domain, you can choose to let the OS assume that you are the only user of the computer and that you don't want to see the logon dialog box. This does not mean that there is no user account and no authentication, only that the authentication is automatic, and void of any security benefit. You can check this setting after installation (and refresh your memory) by opening the Users and Passwords applet in the Control Panel to see the setting for Users Must Enter A User Name And Password To Use This Computer. In Windows 2000, security begins with turning on User Must Enter A User Name And Password, because if this setting is turned off, anyone with physical access to your computer can use it without entering a user name and password.

There's a second setting in Users and Passwords that's important to enable for the sake of security—the setting on the Advanced tab under Secure Boot Settings. If checked, as shown in Figure 7-7, it requires users to press CTRL-ALT-DELETE before logging on. This setting is a defense against certain viruses that try to capture your user name and password, sometimes by presenting a fake logon prompt. Pressing CTRL-ALT-DELETE will remove a program like that from memory and allow the actual logon dialog box to appear. If you installed Windows 2000 Professional per the instructions in Step-by-Step 4.02, you should choose the more secure options.

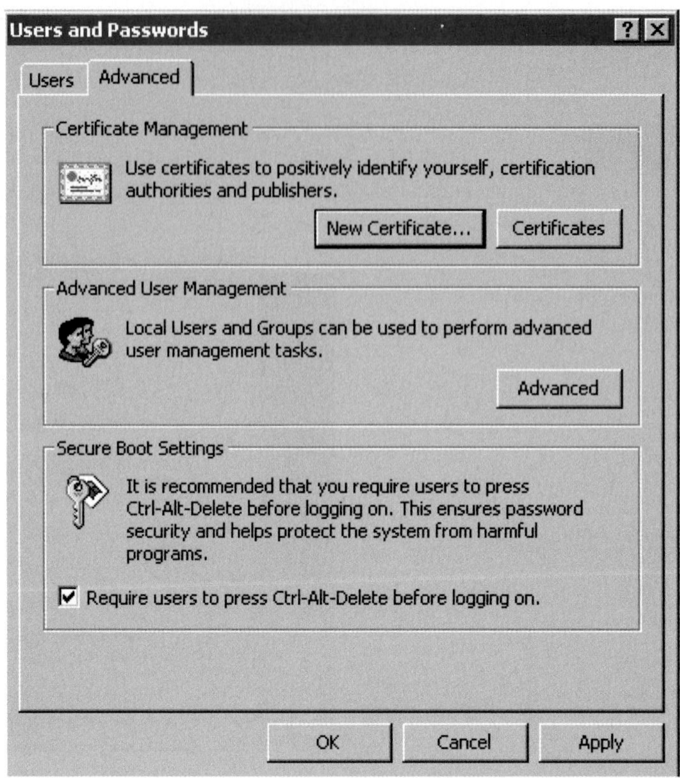
Users and Passwords
Users
Advanced
Certificate Management
Use certificates to positively identify yourself, certification authorities and publishers.
New Certificate...
Certificates
Advanced User Management
Local Users and Groups can be used to perform advanced user management tasks.
Advanced
Secure Boot Settings
It is recommended that you require users to press Ctrl-Alt-Delete before logging on. This ensures password security and helps protect the system from harmful programs.
Require users to press Ctrl-Alt-Delete before logging on.
OK
Cancel
Apply

• **Figure 7-7.** Make your computer more secure by enabling Secure Boot Settings.

Step-by-Step 7.04

Creating and Configuring a New User Account in Windows 2000 Professional

Now you will create the users listed in Table 7-3, the User and Group Planning Form. To complete this exercise, you will need the following:

- The computer on which you successfully installed Windows 2000 Professional in Step-by-Step 4.02
- A user name and password for an account that is a member of the Administrators group

Step 1

Log onto your lab computer as Administrator or as a member of the Administrators group. Open the Users and Passwords applet in the Control Panel, and click the Add button.

Step 2

In the first page of the Add New User wizard, fill in the correct information for Sue Smith, using Table 7-3. After you have entered the User Name, the Full Name, and the Description, click Next.

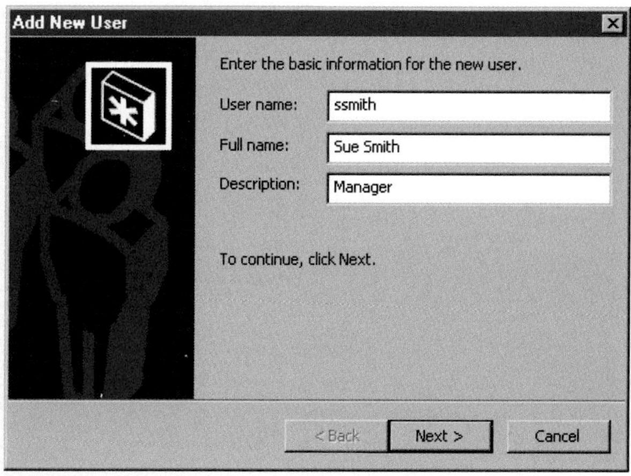

Step 3 Enter and confirm the initial password for this new user, using the password in Table 7-3, the User and Group Planning Form. Then click Next to continue.

Step 4 Now assign the new user to one or more groups. There are two suggested options—Standard User and Restricted User—or you can select the Other option button, and choose a group from the drop-down list. For Sue Smith, select Standard User, which on a Windows 2000 Professional desktop makes her a member of the local Power Users group, as well as the local Users group. Click the Finish button to close the dialog box.

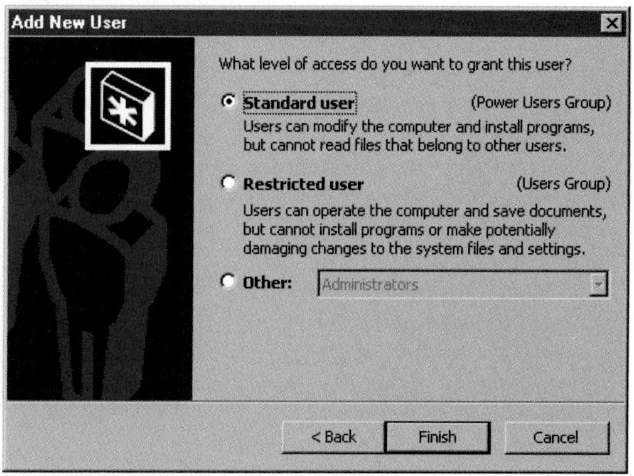

Step 5 You should see your new user listed in the Users And Passwords dialog box. Now suppose you have changed your mind about the password you created and want to change it. Select the new user in the Users For This Computer list on the Users page. Then click the Set Password button on the Users page. Enter and confirm the new password, and then click OK to apply the changes.

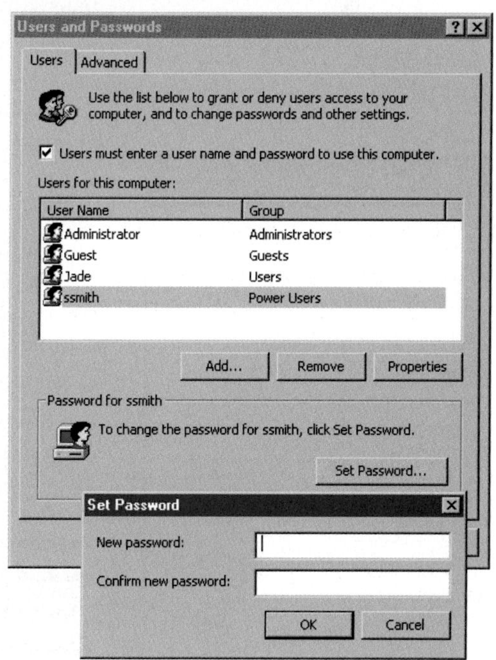

Step 6 Repeat Steps 2, 3, and 4 to create a user account for Ron Jones using the User and Group Planning Form, but do not add him to the Power Users group.

Step 7 Test each new account by logging off as Administrator and logging on as the new account. When you have tested both accounts, log off.

When creating new user accounts on your own computer, create both a Computer Administrator account and a Limited account for yourself. Use the administrator account whenever you need to install new software or to make changes to the computer. Use the Limited account for your day-to-day work. This protects your computer from viruses that might use the elevated privileges of your Administrator account to cause damage.

User Administration in Windows XP Professional

In Windows XP, the User Accounts applet hides the complete list of users, using a simplistic reference to account types that is actually a reference to its group membership. An account that is a member of the local Administrators group is said to be a Computer Administrator, while an account that only belongs to the Local Users group is said to be a **Limited account**. Which users it shows depends on the currently logged-on user. When an Administrator is logged on, he or she will see both types of accounts and the Guest account. When a user with a Limited account is logged on, only that user's account will be visible in User Accounts.

More About Windows XP Accounts Creating users in User Accounts is a straightforward process. You need to provide a user name and an initial password. The user can change the password later. You also need to know the type of account to create: Computer Administrator or Limited.

Unless otherwise specified, as in Table 7-3, you should create one Limited account (member of the Users group) per user of the computer and an account that is a member of the local Administrators group (in addition to the one created during installation). The reason Windows XP Professional requires two administrator accounts is so that if one administrator is not available, or is not able to log onto the computer, another one can. It's simple redundancy. Windows XP actually reminds you to do this; the first time you try to create a local account after installing Windows XP, it will only allow you to create a Computer Administrator account. After that, it will allow you to create Limited accounts.

If you upgrade from Windows NT or Windows 2000 or from a Windows 9*x* installation in which user profiles were enabled, Setup will migrate the existing accounts to Windows XP Professional.

Inside Information

The Password Reset Disk as Both a Convenience and a Threat

The password reset disk only has to be created once; regardless of how many times the user may later change the password. This is both a convenience and a threat. It is a convenience in that you only have to make it one time and it will always work. It is a threat in that it will always work on your machine, no matter who has it and uses it!

Password Reset Disk Windows XP Professional allows the currently logged-on user to create a password reset disk that can be used in the case of a forgotten password. This is very important to have, because if you forget your password, and an administrator resets the password using User Accounts or Local Users and Groups, then when you log on using the new password, you will find that you will lose access to some items, including files that you encrypted when logged on with the forgotten password. When you reset a password with a password reset disk, you can log on using the new password, and still have access to previously encrypted files.

Best of all, with the password reset disk, users have the power to fix their own passwords. You only have this power if you think to create a password reset disk before you forget the password!

If you need to create a password reset disk for a computer on a network (domain), search the help system for "password reset disk," and follow the instructions for password reset disks for a computer on a domain.

Encryption is a very advanced feature that should only be used after studying it carefully. It would take more than a chapter just to talk about encryption in depth!

Step-By-Step 7.05

Creating User Accounts and a Password Reset Disk in Windows XP

In this step-by-step, you will create new user accounts. First, you will create an account that is a member of the Administrators group, because in Windows XP Professional, the first new account you create after installation must be a Computer Administrator account (in addition to the user, Administrator), giving you two accounts that are members of the Administrators group. Only then will you be allowed to create Limited accounts, which you will create using the User and Group Planning Form found in Table 7-3. You will also create a password reset disk for one of the new accounts.

To complete this step-by-step, you will need the following:

- The computer on which you successfully installed Windows XP Professional in Step-by-Step 5.02
- The password for the Administrator
- A blank formatted floppy disk

Step 1

Log on as Administrator and open Control Panel. Select the User Accounts applet. Click Create A New Account. On the Name The New Account page, enter the first letter of your first name, followed by your last name, and click Next.

Step 2

On the Pick An Account Type page, the option for Limited is grayed out (unavailable) because this is the first account you have created since installation. This first new account can only be a Computer Administrator account. Notice the tasks a computer administrator can do, and then click Create Account.

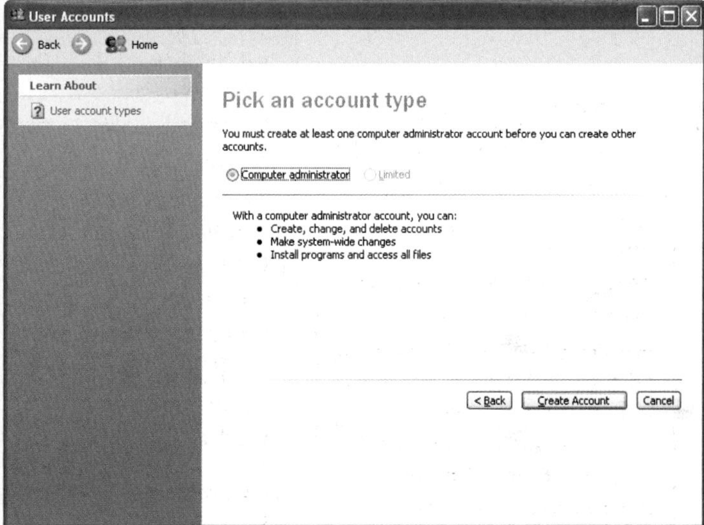

Step 3

The account is created, and you're returned to the main page of User Accounts, where you should see your new account.

Step 4

Now you can create Limited accounts. In this case, you'll create two, using the User and Group Planning Form in Table 7-3. Follow the steps you used to create the previous account to create the accounts for Sue Smith and Ron Jones, but make both of them limited users. *Be sure to read the description of the Limited account type on the Pick An Account Type page.*

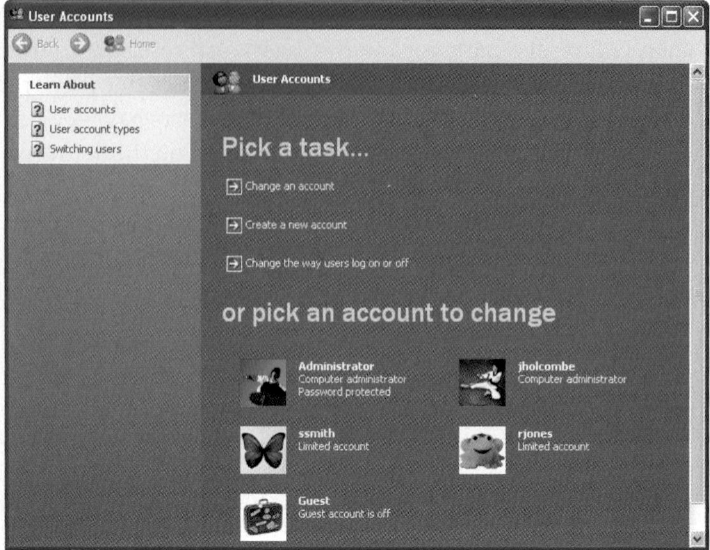

Step 5

Back in the main page, ssmith and rjones will appear as Limited accounts. Your two new accounts have blank passwords, which is only tolerable in a very low-security environment.

Step 6

Create new passwords, beginning with the Computer Administrator account you just created for yourself. In User Accounts, select Change An Account. On the Pick An Account To Change page, select the new Computer Administrator you just created.

Step 7

On the following page, select Create A Password. Before creating a password, click on each of the items in the Learn About list to learn how to create a secure password as well as a good password hint, and a message about what to do when you forget your password. Then, use what you learn to fill in the text boxes for the new password and a password hint, and then click Create Password.

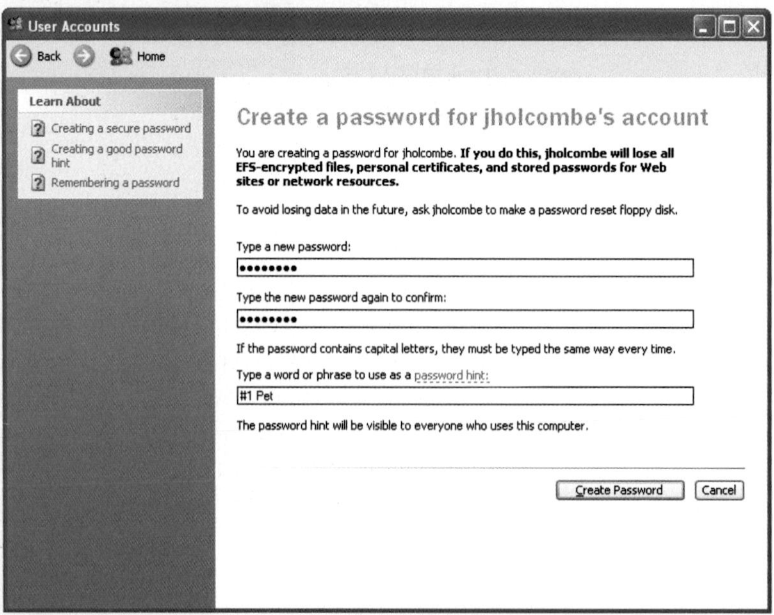

Step 8

Use the Back button to go back to the Pick An Account To Change page, select ssmith, and create a password and password hint for that account. Do the same for the rjones account. When you have created passwords for all your accounts, close the User Accounts Pick A Task page.

Step 9

While you were able to create accounts and to create passwords, you were unable to place users in any group accounts other than Administrators or Users, and not able to add any additional information. If you want to go beyond the capabilities of the User Accounts tool, you need to open the Computer Management console. Do that now. Right-click on My Computer and select Manage.

Step 10

In the Computer Management console, select Local Users And Groups and click on Users. The users you created in the previous steps will be displayed, as well as users that are not shown in User Accounts.

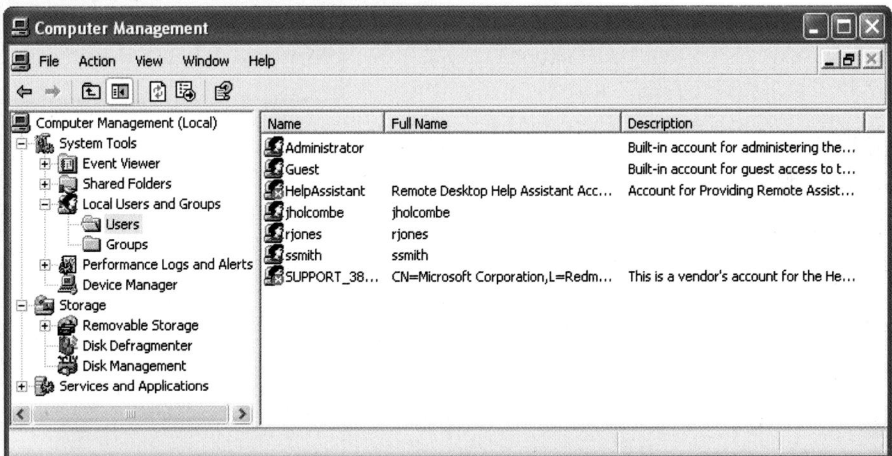

Step 11

Double-click ssmith to open the Properties for this user account. The User Accounts tool used "ssmith" as both the user name and full name. Change the Full Name to **Sue Smith**, and add the description from the User and Group Planning Form in Table 7-3.

Step 12

Select the Member Of tab and click the Add button. In the Select Groups dialog box, click the Advanced button to bring up another Select Groups dialog box that will allow you to view all the local groups in a list from which you can make a selection.

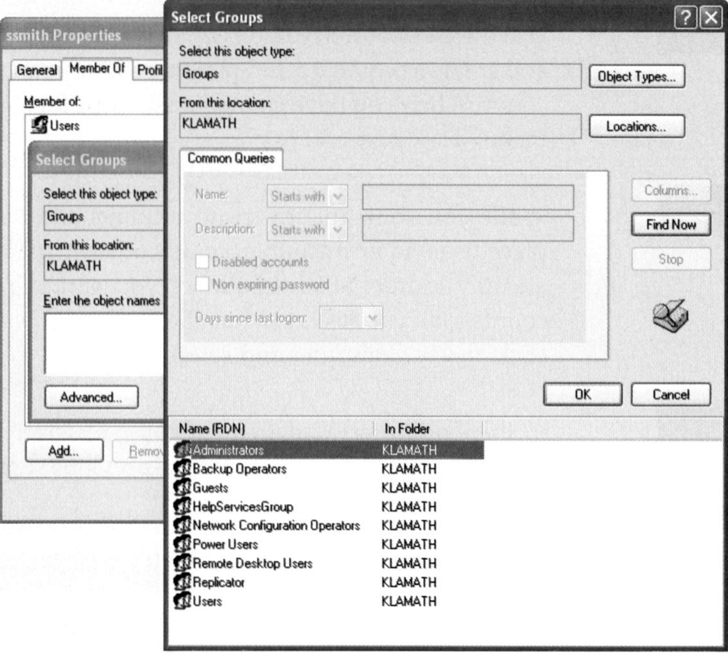

Step 13

Select Power Users from the list. Then click OK three times to close the three open dialog boxes. When you return to the Computer Management console, you may have to refresh the Users node by selecting the Users folder and pressing F5. The full name and description should now be shown for the ssmith account. Close Computer Management.

Step 14

Now create the password reset disk. Open User Accounts and on the Pick A Task page, select the account that you are currently logged in on as (Administrator). On the next page, select Prevent A Forgotten Password from the list of Related Tasks (on the left). Read the Welcome page of the Forgotten Password wizard, and then click Next.

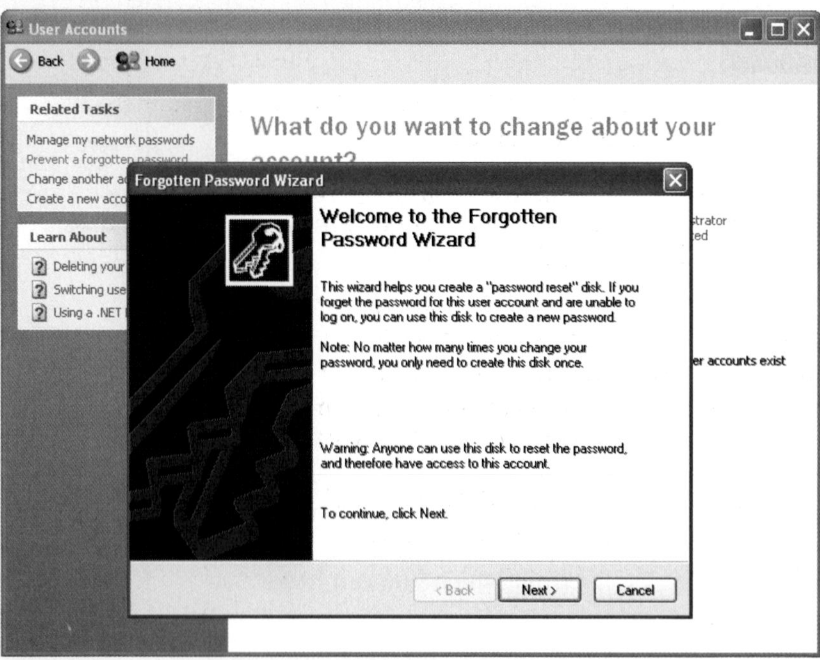

Step 15

Insert a blank, formatted floppy disk in drive A: and click Next. On the Create User Account Password page, enter the current user account password and click Next. The Creating Password Reset Disk page will show a progress bar while creating the disk. When it is completed, click Next, and then click Finish to close the wizard. Make sure the disk is properly labeled, including the account name and computer; then store in a safe and secure place.

Account Policies

Account policies for a local computer are settings stored on the computer that control how user accounts can interact with the computer. Account policies exist in Windows NT 4.0 Workstation, Windows 2000 Professional, and Windows XP Professional. There are also account policies that control user interaction with a domain, but domain-level account policies are beyond the scope of this book. Account policies that affect a Windows computer that is not part of a domain include two subsets:

- **Password policy** is a group of settings for passwords, such as the requirement for password length, and the length of time before a password must be changed.
- **Account lockout policy** includes three important settings: one involves the number of tries a user has when entering a password before being locked out, and the second one sets the length of time that an account will be locked out of the system. The third one controls when the counter for the number of attempts is reset to zero.

Windows NT 4.0 Workstation Account Policies In Windows NT 4.0 Workstation, account policies are set from the Policies menu in User Manager. In the Account Policy dialog box, the two subsets of policies are labeled "Password Restrictions" and "Account lockout."

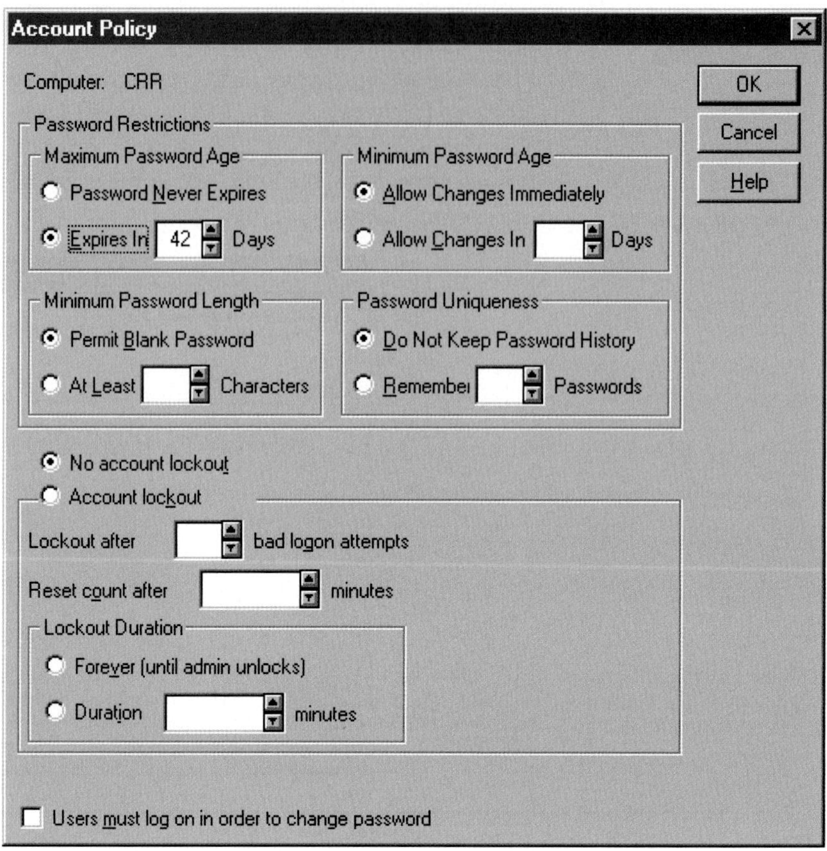

• The Windows NT 4.0 Workstation account policies

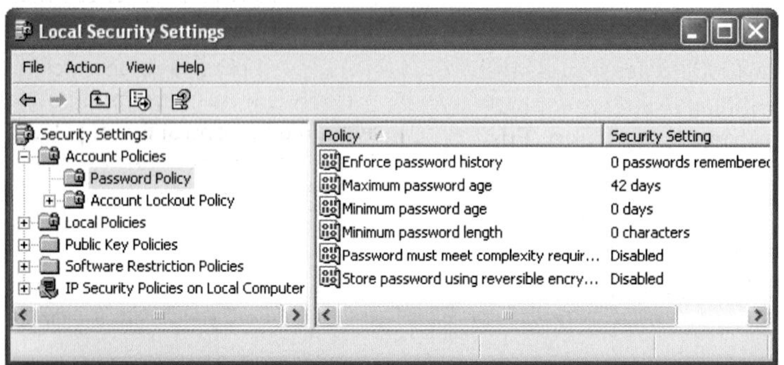

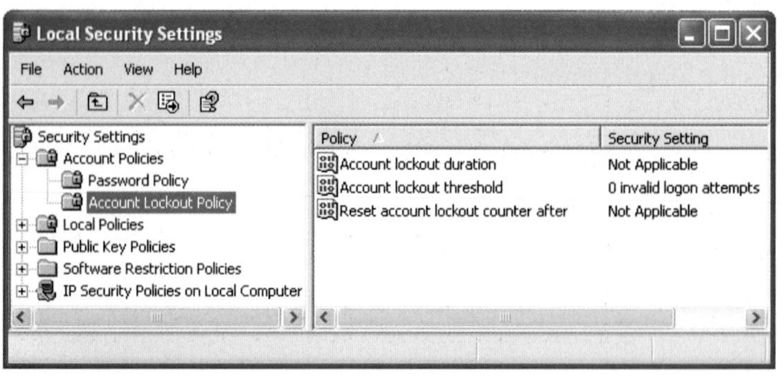

• The Windows XP Professional account policies

Windows 2000 Professional and Windows XP Professional Account Policies In Windows 2000 and Windows XP Professional, account policies are set from the Local Security Policy console. Open this console from Administrative tool, and then select the Account Policies node. Although the GUI is very different from that used in Windows NT, many of the settings are the same.

Configuring Windows Protection When an Intruder Has Physical Access

Many threats to computers come from within—from someone who has physical access to a computer. An infinite number of scenarios involve such access. What follows is a true story that points out a significant vulnerability that you can avoid. After that we offer suggestions for protecting your system from attacks from within.

Consider the case of two students we'll call Jeff and Sam, who did not get along with each other; in fact, every encounter involved an exchange of insults. One day, Jeff left the school computer lab without logging out of the network. Sam, seeing this, sat down at Jeff's computer, connected to Jeff's personal folders, and proceeded to modify the files for one of Jeff's courses with incorrect information and disparaging remarks about the instructor. Luckily for Jeff, the instructor in the course knew what Sam had done because several other students witnessed Sam's actions and reported him. Without the other students, Jeff might have failed the course.

This story provides a simple moral: do not leave your computer vulnerable to attack when you walk away from your desk at work or at school. On a corporate network, your account may have access to files containing sensitive data crucial to the continued success of the company. A disgruntled employee could destroy (or steal) these files and hurt the company, and if the damage was done through your account, the blame will fall on your shoulders. The best way to avoid this risk is to do one of the following before leaving your computer:

- Log out (powering off is optional)
- Lock computer (see Step-by-Step 6.03 in Chapter 6)
- Use a password-protected screen saver (see Step-by-Step 6.03 in Chapter 6)
- Select Standby or Hibernate options from the Shut Down Windows menu (see Chapter 6)
- Enable Switch User

All but the last solution have already been discussed in Chapter 6, so we'll just provide an overview with an emphasis on security and an explanation of the final choice, enabling Switch User.

The Downside of Logging Out and the Search for a Better Solution The trouble with the log out solution is that many of us work under distracting conditions and constantly changing priorities. In fact, the more focused you are in your work, the less likely you are to consciously log out every time you leave your desk, and it would be better to have an automatic solution. Further, logging off closes all your open programs, requiring when you return that you log back on and figure out where you left off in your work.

Lock Computer will not work if you have chosen to use the Welcome Screen, an option available in Control Panel | User Accounts | Change the way users log on or log off.

Microsoft has kept these objections in mind while working on this problem with Windows NT, Windows 2000, and Windows XP, gradually achieving better results with each one. These included computer locking capabilities in Windows NT, as well as password-protected screen savers. The solutions at this point (in addition to simply logging off) are pretty good.

Lock Computer Lock Computer is an option in Windows NT, Windows 2000, and Windows XP Professional. This is preferred to logging off, when you want to leave all your programs running exactly where you left off. It is very simple to do. Before leaving your computer unattended, simply press CTRL-ALT-DELETE to open the Windows Security dialog box and click Lock Computer. That's it. Your desktop will disappear, and the Computer Locked dialog box will appear on the screen. Then when you return, simply press

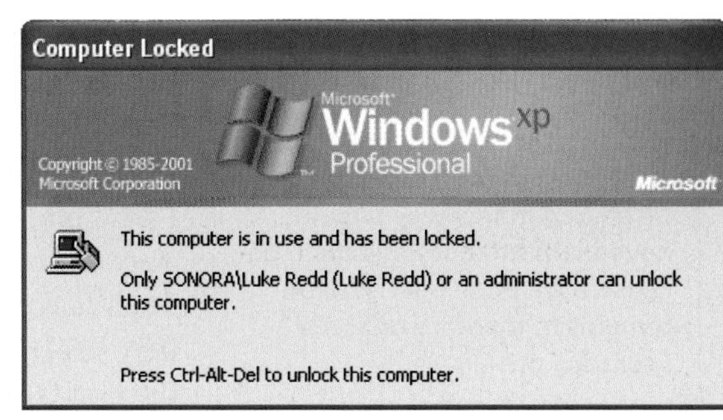

• The Windows XP Professional Computer Locked dialog box

CTRL-ALT-DELETE, enter the password for your account, and you will be back to the desktop exactly as you left it.

Password-protected screen saver is only available when you are logged on with a password-protected account.

Password-Protected Screen Saver Another option that can be used to restrict access to your Windows computer when you walk away is a screen saver with password protection turned on. There are two caveats to using a screen saver for security:

- A screen saver is not secure unless you configure it to be password protected, and then it is only as secure as your password.
- Even with password protection, the computer is vulnerable during the wait period. A screen saver doesn't turn on until a sustained period of no keyboard or mouse activity. If someone walks up to an unattended computer and uses the mouse or keyboard before the wait period ends, he has as much control of the computer as the logged-on account will allow (another reason to not use an Administrator account while doing ordinary tasks).

You enable and configure a screen saver by using the Screen Saver tab on the Display Properties dialog box, as you did in Step-by-Step 6.03 in Chapter 6.

Switch User can't be used on a computer that is a member of a domain, and it will disable Serial Keys, an accessibility feature.

Switch User If you have Windows XP Professional, the last walk-away-from-your-computer-with-no-worries option is Fast User Switching, which adds the Switch User option to the Log Off menu. We like Fast User Switching. It's a great feature for a stand-alone computer or one that is on a network as a member of a workgroup. This is a step up from Lock Computer in that more than one user can have his or her current desktop session remain in memory. This feature allows multiple users to share a computer when their use of the computer overlaps.

• The Log Off Windows box with the Switch User button

Two users, Aretha and Roscoe, work in a small home improvement store's customer service area and share a computer during the same eight-hour shift, using it to schedule flooring product deliveries and installations. No problem—an administrator set up the computer to allow for fast user switching so that neither user has to lose the work she or he is doing, and yet each has an open user session. When Aretha is working on the computer but must walk away or allow Roscoe access, she simply selects Start | Log Off | Switch User. Then she can walk away knowing that she can return with her desktop in the exact state she left it. Roscoe can also now log on. When he needs to leave the computer, he also selects Switch User.

Only a computer administrator can turn on Switch User. To do this, open User Accounts in Control Panel, and select Change The Way Users Log On Or Off. Select Fast User Switching, and click Apply Options. You may see a message that Fast User Switching cannot be turned on because Offline Files is currently enabled. If so, click OK to open the Offline Files Settings page of Folder Options, clear the check in the box labeled "Enable Offline Files," and click OK. After that detour, you'll be back in the first page of User Accounts. Here you will have to first select (to place a check mark by) Use The Welcome Screen, and then you may select Use Fast User Switching. Test it by selecting Start | Log Off. Confirm that the Switch User button is now in the Log Off Windows box.

A computer that is going to be shared in this way should have extra memory installed, because each open user session remains in memory until the user logs off.

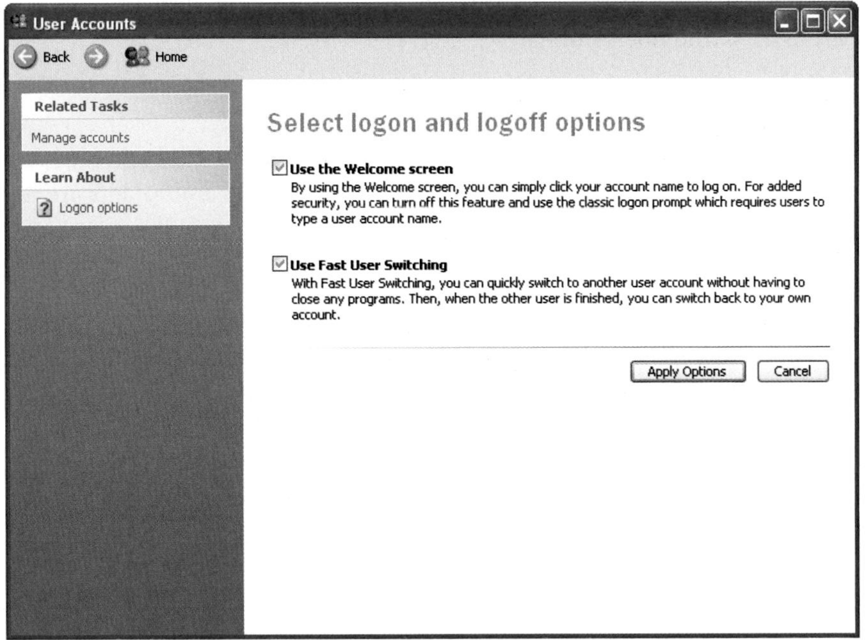

- Fast User Switching can be turned on only if the Enable Offline Files feature is disabled, and if Use The Welcome Screen is enabled.

Applying Security to Files, Folders, and Printers in Windows

Windows NT 4.0 Workstation, Windows 2000, and Windows XP Professional all fully support the use of permissions to protect files folders and printers. Permissions for files and folders depend on the use of the NTFS file system, as does a new security feature, file encryption, which is available beginning with Windows 2000. Printer permissions are supported in all three OSs regardless of the file system in use. In this section, you will explore NTFS permissions for files and folders, encryption on NTFS volumes, and printer permissions.

Securing Files and Folders on an NTFS Drive

Windows NT 4.0 Workstation, Windows 2000, and Windows XP all support the NTFS file system. Windows NT 4.0 supports what is now called NTFS version 4 (NTFS4), and the other two support the more capable NTFS version 5 (NTFS5). Both versions of NTFS allow you to control who has access to specified files and folders by assigning permissions. These permissions restrict access to local users and groups as well as to those who connect to these resources over the network. Although, in the case of those connecting over a network, the share permissions (not related to NTFS permissions) take effect first and may totally block access to the underlying files and folders. Only NTFS volumes allow you to assign permissions to files and folders. The differences between NTFS4 and NTFS5 are mainly in granularity. That is, there are more permissions now, and the permissions in the newer file system are a superset of those in the older file system, giving more precise control over how each user or group accesses data. In this section, we will focus on the security features of NTFS5, including file and folder permissions and encryption.

File and Folder Permissions

On a volume formatted with the NTFS file system, each folder and file has a set of security permissions associated with it. While files and folders are not the only objects to which you may assign permissions, we will limit our discussion of permissions to these objects for now.

ACLs and ACEs Each file and folder on an NTFS volume has an associated access control list (ACL), which is a table of users and/or groups and their permissions to the file or folder. Each ACL has at least one access control entry (ACE), which is like a record in this tiny ACL database that contains just one user or group account name and the permissions assigned to this account. The ACEs are created by an administrator or someone with the permissions to create ACEs for the file or folder. To view the ACEs in an ACL for a file or folder, open the properties dialog box and select the Security tab. Figure 7-8 shows the Security page for a folder named Spreadsheets. Notice the list of permissions for the user jholcombe. This is an ACE.

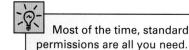

The permissions you can set on folders differ slightly from those that you can set on files. In both cases, there are standard permissions, each of which is composed of several special permissions. For example, the standard file permission called Read permission consists of the following special permissions: Read Data, Read Attributes, Read Extended Attributes, Read Permissions (the permissions on the file), and Synchronize.

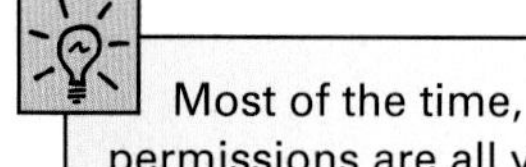

Most of the time, standard permissions are all you need.

The standard file permissions are as follows:

- Full Control
- Modify
- Read and Execute
- Read
- Write

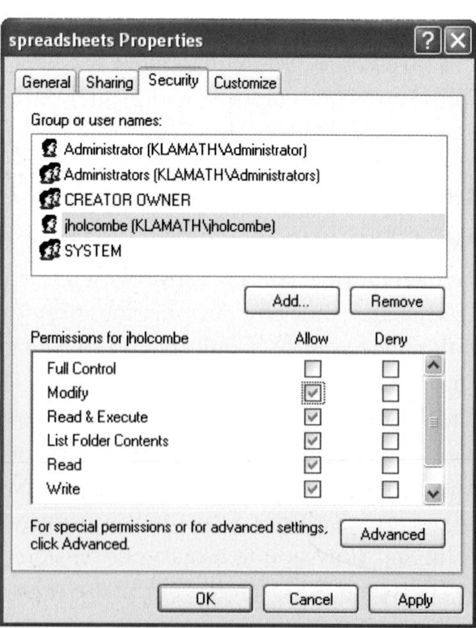

• **Figure 7-8.** The list of permissions for a folder

The standard folder permissions are the same as the standard file permissions with the added permission of List Folder Contents.

Do you have a folder that contains sensitive information such as payroll files? Such folders should be protected from unauthorized access. To do this, you can assign permissions to certain users and groups, and you can keep others out, implicitly or explicitly. This is possible because each of the standard permissions and each of the special permissions has three states: Allow, Deny, or implicit denial. Only one box can be checked at a time for any permission. If both the Allow and Deny boxes are clear, that permission is not applied at all—it's implicitly denied. If the Allow box is checked, that permission is allowed, and if the Deny box is checked, that permission is denied—it's explicitly denied. Why have these three-state permissions? If a user account is only implicitly denied access to a file or folder by being left off the permissions list, that user can be given access to the file and folder through membership in a group that has access. On the other hand, an administrator can explicitly grant access to a group, and also explicitly restrict access to a member of the group using the Deny state of a permission. This will override the users Allow permission to the file or folder that was granted to the group.

NTFS4 permissions are only two-state—each permission is on or off. Therefore, when applying file and folder permissions in Windows NT 4.0, keep users out implicitly by not including them in a file or folders list of permissions. Keep users out explicitly by including them in the list and granting them the No Access permission—which is as clear as you can get.

Try This!

Research Special Permissions

It is important to understand permissions so that you can protect resources from unauthorized access or damage. Don't try to memorize them—remember that help is just a few mouse clicks away. Use the Windows 2000 Help program or the Windows XP Help and Support Center now to see the list of special permissions that make up each of the standard permissions listed here. Try this:

1. Start the Help program (Help and Support in Windows XP) from the Start menu.
2. In Windows 2000, search the Index for "file permissions" and examine the list of file permissions, including the special permissions. Repeat the search for "folder permissions".
3. In the Windows XP Help and Support Center, use the search box to find articles on "special permissions." In the Search Results list, open the article "How to set, view, change, or remove special permissions for files and folders in Windows XP," and read the descriptions of each of the special folder permissions.
4. When you have completed your research, close Help.

Permissions Assigned to Personal Folders

In earlier step-by-steps, you created new user accounts and tested those accounts by logging on as each new user. When a new user logs onto Windows, the operating system will create personal folders just for that user. In addition, if the local drive is an NTFS partition, it will assign a default set of permissions to those folders designed to keep other users out of those folders. In Chapter 6 you learned about these folders and their default location on the hard drive. Now you will explore the default permissions set on these folders.

To be safe, change NTFS permissions only for data files and folders that you create to actually hold data, not on any files and folders created for and used by the operating system, located in a folder named "windows" or "winnt." During installation, the Windows setup program sets default permissions within this folder that allow the OS to function, but that keep ordinary users from harming the OS. You can cause harm to the OS if you change these default settings.

NTFS Permission Inheritance

The folders and files on a disk volume are arranged in a hierarchy, with the drive itself at the top, followed by the root folder and subfolders. When a new folder or file is created, it inherits the permission settings of the parent folder, unless you choose to block this inheritance, which is an option in the Security dialog box of the file or folder. When you view permissions on a file or folder, the permissions that have been inherited from the parent will be grayed out, and you will not be able to modify those permissions at that level.

New permissions can be assigned, but inherited permissions cannot be altered. They can be modified in the folder in which they originated. You can choose to block inheritance on a folder or file to which you wish to assign different (usually more restrictive) permissions. If you block inheritance, you will be prompted with the option to copy the previous inherited permissions.

Step-by-Step 7.06

Viewing Permissions on Personal Folders

In this step-by-step exercise, you will explore the NTFS permissions that are assigned automatically to personal folders. To complete this exercise, you will need the following:

- The computer on which you successfully installed Windows 2000 Professional or Windows XP Professional in earlier step-by-steps in this book
- The user accounts created in Step-by-Step 7.04 or 7.05, listed in Table 7-3, the User and Group Planning Form
- Drive C: set up as an NTFS partition (per the instructions in the installation step-by-steps)

Step 1

Log on as Sue Smith (ssmith). Open My Computer, browse to C:\Documents and Settings, and notice the folders. There should be one for each user who has logged on, plus one titled All Users.

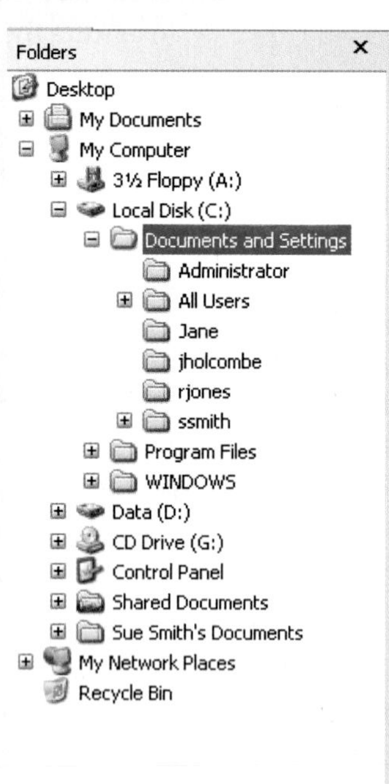

Step 2

Open the folder named ssmith and view the contents. These folders make up the user profile for user Sue Smith. They were created the first time that user logged on, and they contain the files that hold that user's desktop files, favorites, the Start menu, and several other important folders and files. These folders are created on any file system that Windows supports, even FAT16 or FAT32.

Folders
Desktop
My Documents
My Computer
3½ Floppy (A:)
Local Disk (C:)
Documents and Settings
Administrator
All Users
Jane
jholcombe
rjones
ssmith
Cookies
Desktop
Favorites
My Documents
Start Menu
Program Files
WINDOWS
Data (D:)
CD Drive (G:)
Control Panel
Shared Documents
Sue Smith's Documents
My Network Places
Recycle Bin

Step 3

When a user first logs onto a computer that has NTFS on the boot drive (the drive in which the system files are installed), Windows sets permissions on the personal folders it creates for the user. To view these permissions, right-click the folder named ssmith, select Properties, and then click the Security tab. Click the Permissions button, and you will see the list of users and groups that have permissions to the folder. Notice that the Everyone group is not on the list.

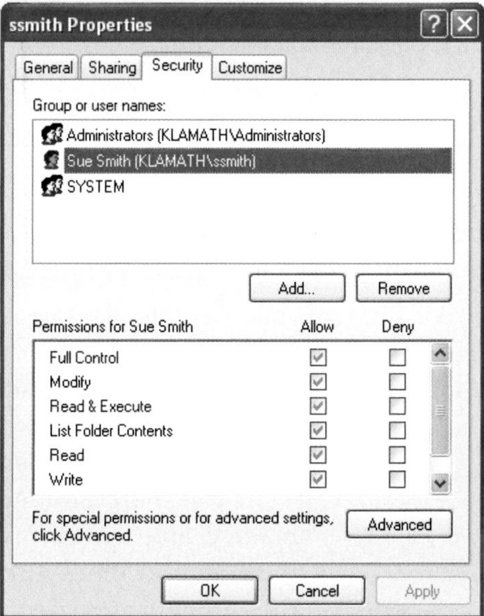

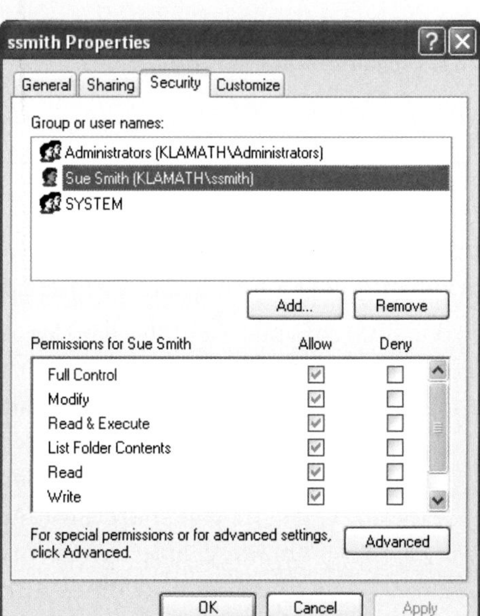

Step 4

By default, the Security page shows only the standard permissions and lets you assign only the standard permissions. Notice the check boxes for Allow and Deny for each standard permission. To see the special permissions, click the Advanced button, and then click the View/Edit button to see the special permissions assigned to the selected user. You will rarely need these special permissions. Click Cancel three times to close the Properties dialog box.

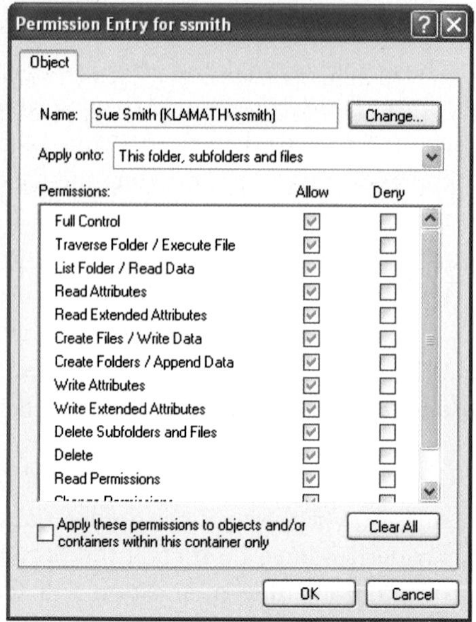

Step 5

Try to open the folder named rjones. You will not be able to do this, because the user account you are using (Sue Smith) does not have permissions to access the personal folder of Ron Jones. Log off.

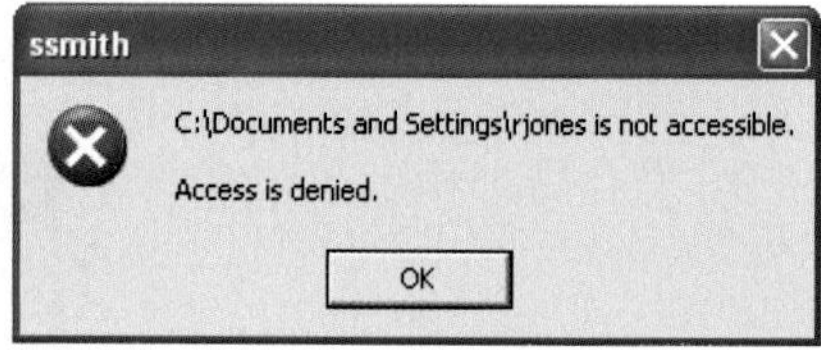

> In Chapter 10 you will create shares and set permissions.

Combining NTFS and Share Permissions

Anyone sitting at your computer who logs on can access files and folders on an NTFS volume if the permissions allow. You might say that person has to go through two security "doors": the authentication door (during logon) and the authorization door in which the security system checks the ACL on each file or folder for NTFS permissions for that user.

If you share a folder on that same NTFS volume, it is made visible to network users, and anyone coming over the network comes through three doors. Only this time, the authentication door is between the computer and the network (yes, even though it is not apparent, an incoming user authenticates). Then there are two authorization doors: one at the share point (the shared folder) at which point permissions on the share are checked to see if the incoming user is authorized to have access, and another at the NTFS file and folder level where the NTFS permissions are checked.

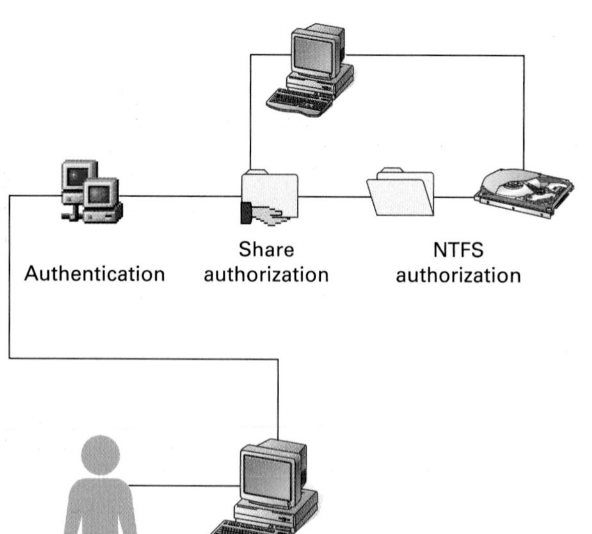

• Accessing an NTFS file or folder through a network share

NTFS File and Folder Encryption

If you use Windows 2000 or Windows XP Professional, you can make individual files or folders even more secure. NTFS5, introduced in Windows 2000, supports a new security feature: the ability to encrypt files and folders. Actually, NTFS5 doesn't do this all by itself. It partners with the **Encrypting File System (EFS),** a new component of the operating system, to encrypt files and folders that are saved on an NTFS5 volume. This new encryption feature, combined with other secure practices, is a welcome feature for those who keep confidential or valuable data on portable computers. See how this is applied in the following scenario:

Jaime is a financial planner who carries his laptop to meetings with his clients. On his hard drive he has files containing confidential data on each of his clients. He needs to be sure to keep this information secure from prying eyes, and he worries that if his laptop were stolen, this information would fall into the wrong hands. To guard against this, Jaime has four good practices:

> Encryption and compression are mutually exclusive; you can do one or the other, but not both.

1. He encrypts all confidential data files on his laptop, which is running Windows XP Professional.
2. He makes sure that he always uses a complex password that would be difficult to guess.
3. He changes his password frequently and never reuses old passwords.
4. He always uses the Lock Computer option in the Windows Security dialog box whenever he leaves his computer unattended, even briefly.

Encrypting a File or Folder Jaime has encrypted a folder on his laptop that is called Data. While the folder itself is not actually encrypted, all files in this folder are now encrypted, and any new files he saves into that folder are automatically encrypted. This may sound rather high-tech and inconvenient, but it was quite simple to do, and once Jamie turned on encryption for this folder, he never had to think about it again. As long as he is logged on with the same account that he used when he turned on encryption, he simply opens the encrypted files using his normal applications. The security components of the OS verify that he is authorized to access these files *and* that he is the person who encrypted them. Someone logged onto his computer with a different account will not be able to open these files, even if the person uses an account with Full Control permission to the files. To encrypt a file or

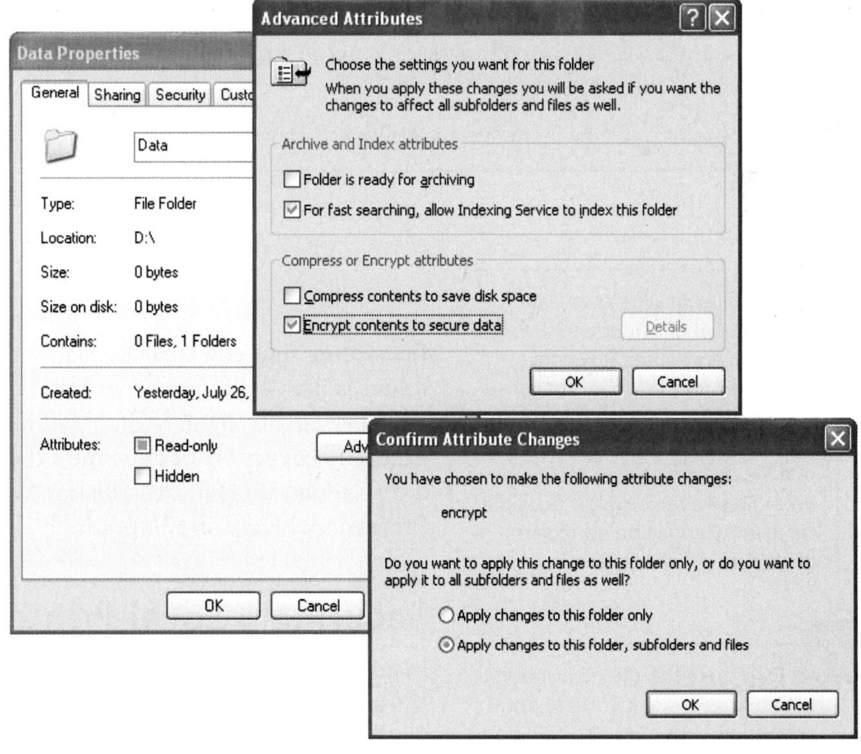

• Accepting the default will encrypt the current and future contents of a folder.

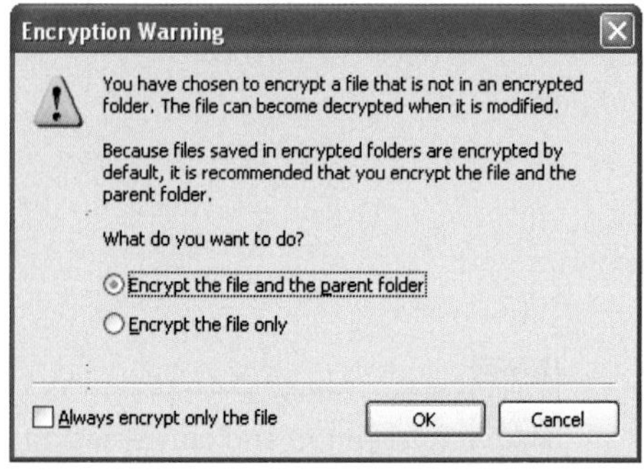

• The warning message when encrypting a file

folder, simply open the properties dialog box, click the Advanced button, and place a check mark in the box labeled "Encrypt contents to secure data." When you click OK to close the Properties dialog box, you must make a decision. In the case of a folder, you must decide whether to encrypt the current contents of the folder and all new contents, or to only encrypt the new contents. In the case of a file located in an unencrypted folder, a warning message asks you to select between encrypting the file and the parent folder, or only encrypting the file. If an encrypted file is moved or copied to an NTFS volume, it will retain its encryption, even if it is moved to a folder that does not have encryption turned on. Conversely, moving an unencrypted file into an encrypted folder by using drag-and-drop will not result in the file being encrypted. Be sure to only use cutting and pasting (or saving from within an application) to move files into an encrypted folder. Further, if an encrypted file is moved or copied to a non-NTFS volume, it will be decrypted.

Cross Check

NTFS Folder and File Permissions

Review the NTFS folder and file permissions, and then answer the following questions:

1. List the standard NTFS file permissions in Windows XP.

   ____

2. How do the standard NTFS folder permissions differ from the standard NTFS file permissions?

   ____

3. You need to assign the modify folder permissions to an account. When you do this in Windows XP, what other standard permissions are also selected?

   ____

EFS in Windows XP Professional

EFS in Windows XP Professional has the following features not available in Windows 2000:

- A user can share encrypted files with other users.
- A user may encrypt offline files, which are files that are stored on a network server but cached in local memory when the local computer is disconnected from the server.

If you use a Windows 2000 Professional or Windows XP Professional computer at school or work, you may discover that encryption isn't available when you look at the Advanced Properties of a file or folder on an NTFS volume. This is because it is possible for a knowledgeable administrator to turn off encryption.

Decrypting Files and Folders The only person who can decrypt a file or folder is the person who encrypted it or a member of a special group called recovery agents. By default, only the local administrator is a member of this group. Recovery is not the same as being able to directly access the data; it is a very advanced task, described in Windows 2000 Help and in Windows XP Professional Help and Support.

Don't use the file encryption capabilities unless you are an advanced user who has researched it first, or unless you have the support of skilled professionals who can take steps to ensure that your encrypted data can be successfully recovered.

Securing a Local Printer

In addition to setting permissions on files and folders, you may set permissions on your local printer. A printer has a single set of permissions that affect both the locally logged-on user and users accessing the printer as a share on the network. Printer permissions are simple compared to NTFS permissions. Printer permissions consist of:

- **Print** Permission to send documents to the printer.
- **Manage Printer** This permission includes the print permission plus permission to pause and restart the printer, change spooler settings, share the printer, assign printer permissions, and change printer properties.
- **Manage Documents** Permission to pause, resume, restart, cancel, and rearrange the order of documents submitted by all users. This permission does not include the print or manage printer permission.

When you add a printer driver, the default permissions allow any user to print; a special group called Creator Owner has Manage Documents permission, but only members of the Power Users and Administrators groups are assigned all of the permissions. Creator Owner, in this case, refers to anyone printing a document, giving each user the right to manage just their own documents. Figure 7-9 shows the default permissions for the printer named Accounting.

While all users are assigned the print permissions through the Everyone group, an administrator can assign more restrictive permissions if needed. One way to do that is to remove the Everyone group and explicitly assign permissions to users and groups. Another method is to leave the Everyone group as is, but to explicitly deny Print permission to a single user or group.

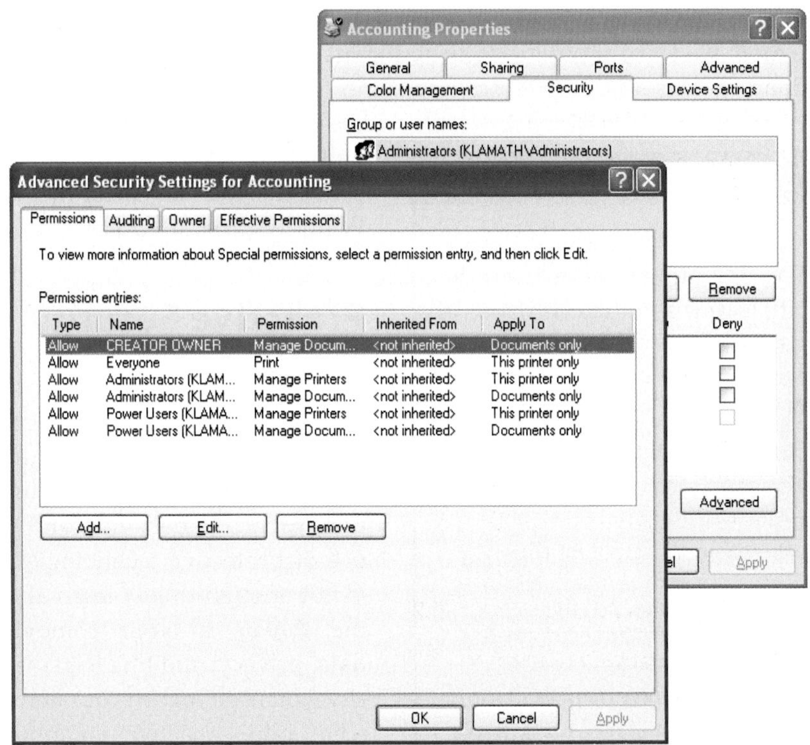

• **Figure 7-9.** The Advanced button on the printer properties page shows printer permission details.

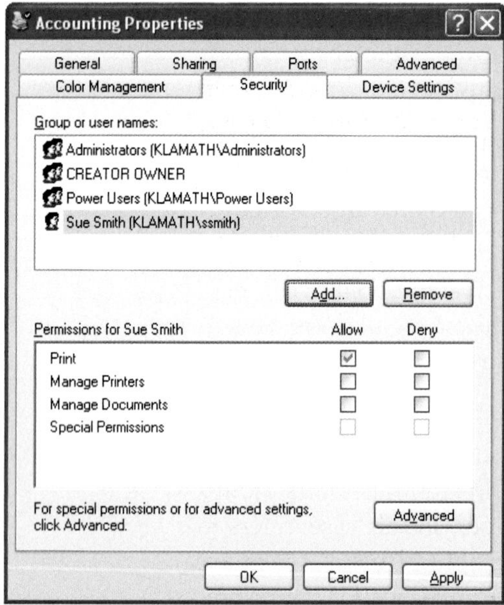

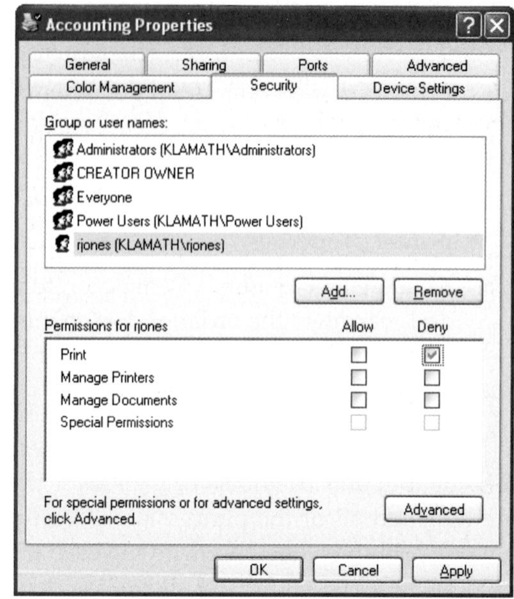

• Restrict permissions by removing the Everyone group or by explicitly denying the Print permission.

Troubleshooting Common Windows Security Problems

The more we learn about the security threats, the more we learn about prevention. In this section, we provide some proactive security tasks that a desktop user can perform, and we will also look at a few common problems you may encounter as a Windows desktop user.

Proactive Security Tasks

The most powerful protection against computer-based security threats is a combination of education, proactive behavior, and the use of protective technologies. It is not enough to just learn about the threats to your computer, data, privacy, and financial integrity; you need to turn your knowledge into proactive computing behavior.

> **Cross Check**
>
> **Compare Security Features**
>
> Security features are very important in an operating system. Consider what you have learned about the security features in three versions of Windows and answer the following questions:
>
> 1. Of these operating systems, which offers the most robust security features?
>
> ______________________________
>
> ______________________________
>
> 2. Which operating system makes it the easiest to protect files using encryption?
>
> ______________________________
>
> ______________________________
>
> 3. Which operating systems enable you to create one or more groups of users to which you can apply permissions to access resources and grant rights to perform certain systemwide actions?
>
> ______________________________
>
> ______________________________

Education

This chapter may be just a beginning of your education about how threats, such as viruses, get access to computers and networks—and how our own behavior can make us vulnerable to threats such as identity theft. Beyond understanding how these things can happen, also be alert to signs of a virus or symptoms that someone is using your credit.

Any unusual computer event may indicate that your computer has been infected by a virus, some sort of browser hijack, or other form of spyware, adware, and so on. Some signs to look for include

- Strange screen messages
- Sudden computer slowdown
- Missing data
- Inability to access the hard drive

Similarly, unusual activity in any of your credit or savings accounts can indicate that you are a victim of identity theft including

- Charges on credit accounts that you are sure you or your family did not make
- Calls from creditors about overdue payments on accounts you never opened
- A turndown when applying for a new credit, for reasons you know are not true
- A credit bureau report of existing credit accounts you never opened

Prevention

If you use a computer at home, work, or school, and are on a network and/or the Internet, a touch of paranoia is healthy; just don't let it distract you from your day-to-day tasks. Take proactive, responsible steps, as outlined in this chapter and summed up next.

Authentication, Authorization, and Passwords These are your friends! Rather than work at ways to avoid the task of logging on or using strong passwords, respect this first line defense. Apply the recommendations listed in the section titled "Best Practices with User Names and Passwords" earlier in this chapter.

Some programs will help you create your passwords. To find such programs, use your favorite Internet search engine to search on "random password generator." You may also find programs that will help you manage many passwords, such as Symantec's Norton Password Manager.

At work or school, if you are logging into a Microsoft domain or a NetWare network, they may enforce a password policy that only accepts strong passwords. How a strong password is defined depends on the settings they select, such as minimum password length or complexity. Complexity requirements may say that the characters must include a combination of lowercase alphabetical characters, uppercase alphabetical characters, numerals, punctuation characters, and math symbols. In addition, they may require that you create a new password every month, and that you cannot repeat any of the last ten passwords.

Here is a suggestion to help you create passwords that comply with such a password policy. Begin by thinking of a phrase that is easy to remember, such as: "I love the Boston Red Sox." Then take the first letter of each word in that phrase and string the letters together. In our example, the result is:

"iltbrs." Now turn it into a more complex password by capitalizing some of the alpha characters and inserting numbers and other symbols between the letters: "i-l,T.b+r-s." Now, if this meets the minimum password requirements, you have a password. The trick is to remember this password without the use of sticky notes!

Security for Mobile Computing

In addition to the practices just outlined for authentication, authorization, and use of passwords, important practices are required when traveling with laptops or other mobile computing devices.

Be Extra Wary of the Danger of Theft Portable computer devices of all types are obviously more susceptible to physical theft, so you should be alert to that threat.

Encrypt Sensitive and Confidential Data In addition to applying permissions, any sensitive data on the laptop should be further protected with encryption, as described in the section "NTFS File and Folder Encryption" earlier in this chapter.

Common Problems

Security is a huge topic, and troubleshooting security problems is also a huge topic. Therefore, this chapter has tried to limit security to the desktop operating system, and here we have selected what we have found to be some common security problems encountered on desktop computers.

Troubleshooting Logon Problems

Everyone does it! You're in a hurry and when you type in your user name and password, you don't notice the placement of your hands, and one or both of them are incorrect. You receive the message shown in Figure 7-10. No problem, you type it in again, but don't notice that you have the Caps Lock on. Windows XP will warn you of this, but other versions of Windows will not; be careful about the placement of your hands, and ensure that Caps Lock is off before entering your user name and password.

You may modify the account lockout policy in Windows NT 4.0 Workstation by opening User Manager, opening the Policies menu, and selecting Account Lockout.

On a really bad day, like your first day back at work after a vacation, you may try several times before you enter the password correctly. If you're logging onto a corporate network, all these tries are being counted and may exceed a limit on the number of logon attempts. This limit is part of account policies, which you learned about earlier in this chapter. Exceeding the number of invalid logon attempts (account lockout threshold) may result in your user account being locked out of the computer and the network for a period of time (account lockout duration), and you will see a message similar to that in Figure 7-11. There is usually a third parameter that is used for account policy: the period of time after which the counter for the number of logon attempts is reset to zero.

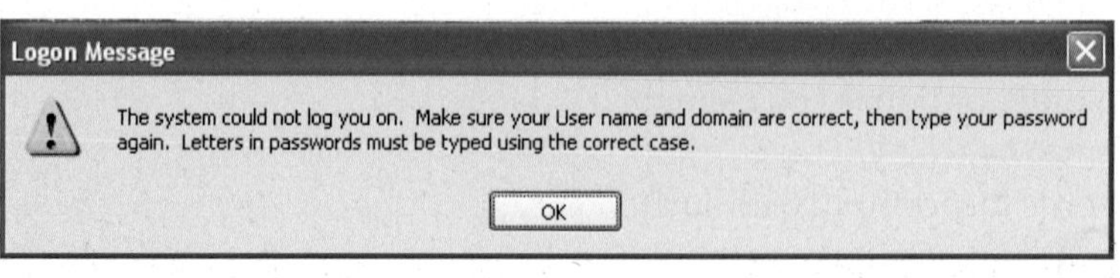
Logon Message
The system could not log you on. Make sure your User name and domain are correct, then type your password again. Letters in passwords must be typed using the correct case.
OK

• **Figure 7-10.** Logon error message

If a message like this appears when you are trying to log onto a network at school or work, you will have to call an administrator

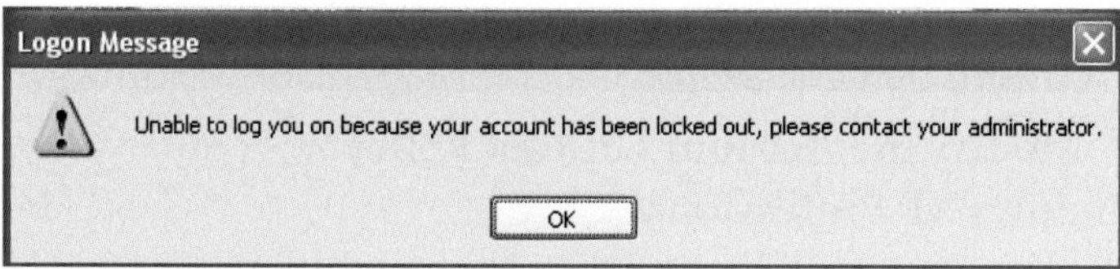

• **Figure 7-11.** Logon lockout message

for help. An administrator may be able to override the lockout so that you may try again. Type carefully this time!

If no administrator is available, you will have to wait for the account lockout time to expire. These settings are configured by an administrator, usually to comply with a company's security standard. So, it could be a matter of minutes, or it could even be days! Although at the time it can be a huge inconvenience, this is your protection against password crackers, who may need to make many tries before they guess the correct password.

In the unlikely event that you receive a lockout message when attempting to log onto a stand-alone or workgroup Windows computer, someone will have to log on with an account that is a member of the Administrators group and unlock your account, or you will have to wait out the lockout period.

Inside Information

Administrators and the Account Lockout Policy

On a local computer, the Administrator is the only account that is not affected by the Account Lockout Policy. All other users, including other members of the Administrators group, are affected by the restrictions of the Lockout Policy and will be locked out if they exceed the number of logon attempts.

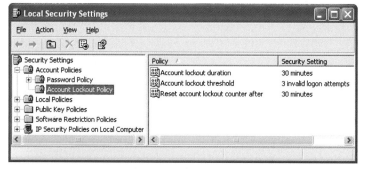

• The Account Lockout Policy with values set for lockout duration, threshold, and a period of time after which the counter is reset

Unknown Account Type in the User Accounts Applet in Windows XP Professional

You are logged on as an Administrator and open the User Accounts applet in Control Panel. You are confused to see that one or more of the local accounts is labeled as an "Unknown account type." Why has this occurred? What should you do?

User Accounts is a very simple account administration program, and as such it is not too smart. It only recognizes two account types: Computer Administrator and Limited account. Recall that computer administrator is a member of the local Administrator group, and limited user is a member of the local Users group. An account that is a member of any other group confuses the User Accounts applet. What should you do? Nothing, unless you wish to find out more about the unknown account type or make changes to an account that User Accounts will not allow, in which case you should open the Computer Management console (right-click on My Computer and select Manage), and then open the Local Users and Groups.

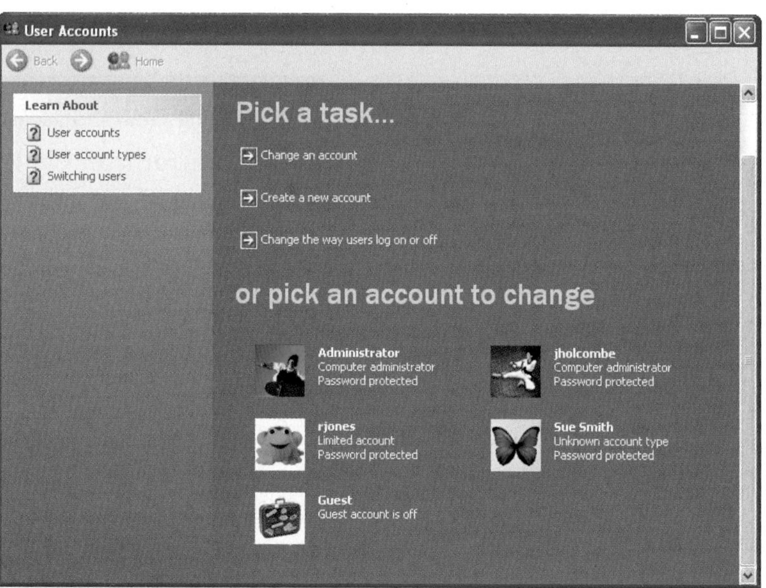

• Unknown account type listed in User Accounts

Try This!

Modify the Account Lockout Policy in Windows XP Professional

Modify the Account Lockout Policy. Although these instructions are written for Windows XP Professional, the steps are nearly identical to those required in Windows 2000. Therefore, all you need is a Windows 2000 or Windows XP Professional computer and the use of an account that is a member of the Administrators group. Try this:

1. Select Start | All Programs | Local Security Policy. In the Local Security Policy console, select the Account Policies node, and then select Account Lockout Policy.
2. Double-click on Account Lockout Threshold, and use the spinner box to change the value. Any nonzero value will turn on the Account Lockout Policy and open a box with recommended values for the other two settings.
3. Log off as Administrator and use incorrect information in the Log On To Windows dialog box enough times to exceed the account lockout threshold.
4. Log back on as an Administrator, and set the Account Lockout Threshold to zero to turn it off.

Reacting to a Suspected Virus Attack

If you suspect a computer has been infected by a virus and have an antivirus program installed, run a scan of all drives and memory to see if you can discover and remove the virus. If this does not discover a virus, but you are still suspicious, or if you do not have an up-to-date antivirus program installed, you can connect to one of many web sites that offer free online scans. Just one example of such a scanner is Housecall, found at `housecall.trendmicro.com`. This scanner is by Trend Micro, who also offers a commercial antivirus suite at `www.trendmicro.com`.

Web sites change frequently. If a free virus scanner is no longer available at `www.trendmicro.com`, simply find another one. Use your browser to connect to a search engine, such as Google, and search on "free virus scan."

Try This!

Perform an Online Virus Scan

Try out one of the online virus scanners. All you need is a Windows computer with a web browser and a connection to the Internet. Use the online scanner at Trend Micro, or search the Internet for another one to use. Try this:

1. Open your browser and connect to `housecall.trendmicro.com`.
2. On the Housecall page, select the option to scan now. You will need to answer a question or two, including responding to a Security Warning before the engine and pattern file are downloaded, installed, and you can finally choose the drive or drives to scan. Follow the onscreen instructions to run the scan.
3. When finished, close out of all open windows.

Chapter 7 Review

■ Chapter Summary

After reading this chapter and completing the exercises, you should understand the following facts about the Windows desktop:

Threats to Computers and Users

- Computer security includes keeping the hardware itself safe from theft. Laptops, in particular, are frequently stolen.
- Identify theft occurs when someone collects personal information belonging to another person and uses that information fraudulently to make purchases, open new credit accounts, and even obtain new driver's licenses and other forms of identification in the victim's name.
- Fraud is the use of deceit and trickery to persuade someone to hand over money or other valuables; identity theft is a form of fraud.
- Losses due to accidents, mistakes, and natural and unnatural disasters will happen. Prepare for such losses by creating frequent backups, and, if necessary, store backups off-site.
- Deliberate attacks against computers, networks, and data come in many forms. Just a few of these threats include spam, viruses, and spyware.
- To keep up-to-date on computer security threats, contact the Federal Trade Commission (FTC) at `http://www.ftc.gov/bcp/menu-internet.html`.

Defense Against Threats

- Authentication and authorization are performed by a security system built into the operating systems on your local computer or on network servers.
- A password is a string of characters that you enter, along with an identifier such as a user name, in order to be authenticated.
- Adopt best practices with user names and passwords.
- A security account is an account that exists in a security accounts database on a server or desktop computer.
- Security accounts can be assigned a level of access (permission) to an object (such as a file, folder, or printer) or the right to take some action on an entire system.
- An individual security account, called a user account, is assigned to a single person. In a network, individual security accounts may also be assigned to computers.
- A group account is a security account that may contain one or more individual accounts, and, in some cases, it may contain other groups.
- Encryption is the transformation of data into a code that can only be decrypted through the use of a secret key or password.
- A firewall sits between a private network and the Internet (or other network) and examines all traffic in and out of the network it is protecting, blocking any traffic it recognizes as a potential threat.
- Many products for home and small business use, described as "broadband routers," are actually true multifunction network devices that serve as bridges, routers, and firewalls.
- There are also personal firewall utilities for use on any desktop computer that's directly connected to the Internet.
- An antivirus program can examine the contents of a disk or RAM for hidden viruses and files that may act as hosts for virus code.
- Anti-pop-up programs block the pop-up advertising seen at many web sites.
- Web browsers usually have privacy settings that allow you to control how and when cookies are saved on your local computer by web sites.
- A content filter is software that can be used to block inappropriate or offensive content while browsing the Web. One can be obtained separately, or you can use the content filtering capabilities of your web browser.

Local Security Accounts in Windows Desktop Operating Systems

- Windows NT 4.0 Workstation, Windows 2000 Professional, and Windows XP Professional all contain local security account databases for user and group accounts.
- Each person who uses one of these versions of Windows must be logged on using a user name and password of a local or domain security account.
- The one GUI administration tool for local accounts in Windows NT 4.0 Workstation is User Manager.
- Windows 2000 Professional and Windows XP Professional each have two user management tools—a simple tool for home and small business use, and an advanced tool for professional administrators.
- In Windows 2000 Professional, the Users and Passwords applet is the simple tool.
- In Windows XP, the *User Accounts* Control Panel applet, replaces the former *Users and Passwords* applet and further simplifies the user management tasks.
- A standard GUI, called the Microsoft Management Console (MMC), is used for many system management tasks in Windows 2000 and Windows XP.
- There are two built-in user accounts in Windows: Administrator and Guest.
- Each local user account is also a member of one or more local groups.
- There are several built-in group accounts, including Administrators, Backup Operators, Guests, Power Users, Replicator, and Users. Windows XP Professional also includes the new Network Configuration Operators group created to give group members permissions to change the network configuration without having full Administrator privileges.
- Other groups are created automatically when certain services are installed and groups are created by an administrator.
- There are also special built-in groups that cannot be created or modified, whose membership is predefined, and some of whom are available to you only when you assign permissions or rights. In Windows NT and Windows 2000, these groups are called special groups; in Windows XP Professional, they are called built-in security principals.
- Windows security accounts can be assigned user rights, which are privileges to perform system-wide functions, such as access the computer from the network, log on locally, log onto a computer from the network, back up files, or change the system time.
- If a computer is used by only one person, create an ordinary user account for that person. If the computer is used by more than one local user, you should create an additional local account for each person.
- If the computer is a member of a Windows NT or Active Directory domain, you can give access to files, folders, and printers on that computer to the users and groups in the domain.
- If the computer is a member of a workgroup, and you wish to share local files, folders, and/or printers, then it must have local accounts for granting access to network users.
- You must be logged on as a member of the Administrators group to create users or groups.
- If a Windows computer is a member of a Windows NT or Active Directory domain, management of users and groups is mainly done at the domain level, and each user who logs onto the local computer will use a domain user account.
- If a computer is a stand-alone computer or a member of a workgroup, users and groups will have to be managed on each computer.
- In Windows 2000, security begins with turning on User Must Enter A User Name And Password, because if this setting is turned off, anyone with physical access to your computer can use it without entering a user name and password.
- There's a second security setting in Users and Passwords that's important to enable—the setting on the Advanced tab under Secure Boot Settings. If checked, it requires users to press CTRL-ALT-DELETE before logging on.

- In Windows XP, the User Accounts applet hides the complete list of users, using a simplistic reference to account types that is actually a reference to its group membership.
- Windows XP Professional allows the currently logged-on user to create a password reset disk that can be used in case of a forgotten password.
- Account policies for a local computer are settings stored on the computer that control how user accounts can interact with the computer.
- When at work or school, you should secure your computer when you walk away from your desk.

Applying Security with the NTFS File System

- Windows NT 4.0 supports NTFS version 4 (NTFS4), while Windows 2000 and Windows XP support NTFS version 5 (NTFS5). Both versions allow you to apply permissions to files and folders.
- Each file and folder on an NTFS volume has an Access Control List for storing permissions. Each record in an ACL is an Access Control Entry (ACE).
- Standard file and folder permissions are each comprised of one or more special permissions, but standard permissions are often all you need to use.
- Standard file permissions include Full Control, Modify, Read and Execute, Read, and Write.
- Standard folder permissions include Full Control, Modify, Read and Execute, Read, Write, and List Folder Contents.
- A set of personal folders is created for each user who logs on locally, and if the boot volume is NTFS, Windows creates permissions on the folders that only allow the Administrator, the System, and that user to access the folders.
- When accessing files and folders on an NTFS volume, an interactive user (sitting at the computer) must pass through two security "doors"—one for authentication, and another for authorization.
- A user connecting over the network to a shared folder pointing to a folder on an NTFS volume must come through three doors: authentication to the computer, authorization to the share, and authorization to the NTFS file or folder.
- An additional security feature, file and folder encryption, is available in Windows 2000 and Windows XP Professional through combining NTFS5 and a new component of these operating systems, the Encrypting File System (EFS).
- The only person who can decrypt a file or folder is the person who encrypted it, or a member of a special group called recovery agents.
- A local printer has a simple set of permissions: Print, Manage Printer, and Manage Documents.

Troubleshooting Common Windows Security Problems

- The most powerful protection against computer-based security threats is a combination of education, proactive behavior, and the use of protective technologies.
- Any unusual computer event may indicate that your computer has been infected by a virus.
- Unusual activity in any of your credit or savings accounts can indicate that you are a victim of identity theft.
- If you suspect a computer has become infected by a virus but do not have an up-to-date virus scanner, you may connect to one of many web sites offering free online antivirus scans.
- Logon failure may simply be the result of a typo when entering the user name or password, or it may result from exceeding the number of failed logon attempts configured in the Account Lockout Policy for a network or an individual computer. An administrator may need to modify the policy.
- If the User Accounts applet shows "Unknown account type," for a user it simply indicates that the user account belongs to a group that User Accounts does not recognize. Use the Users and Password node in Computer Management to view the account.

■ Key Terms List

authentication *(318)*
authorization *(318)*
back door *(314)*
bot *(315)*
content filter *(328)*
cookies *(316)*
digital certificate *(321)*
drive-by download *(312)*
Encrypting File System (EFS) *(361)*
encryption *(321)*
group account *(321)*
guest *(336)*
identity theft *(310)*
limited account *(346)*
password *(318)*
pop-up *(314)*
pop-up download *(312)*
secret key *(321)*
security account *(320)*
spam *(315)*
spim *(315)*
spyware *(314)*
token *(318)*
Trojan horse *(312)*
user right *(338)*
virus *(311)*
war driving *(313)*
worm *(312)*

■ Key Terms Quiz

Use terms from the Key Terms List to complete the sentences that follow. Not all terms will be used.

1. ________________ is a category of software that runs surreptitiously on a user's computer, gathers information without permission from the user, and then sends that information to the people or organizations that requested the information.
2. Programs on a web site may send very small text files called ________________ to a web browser along with a request that the web browser save the file to disk.
3. Unsolicited e-mail, usually sent to market a service or product (legitimate or otherwise), is called ________________.
4. ________________ occurs when someone collects personal information belonging to another person and uses that information fraudulently to make purchases, open new credit accounts, and even obtain new driver's licenses and other forms of identification in the victim's name.
5. In Windows, a/an ________________ defines what systemwide action users and groups may perform, such as logging onto a computer or installing device drivers.
6. ________________ includes authentication, plus the determination of a person's level of access to a computer or a resource.
7. NTFS combined with the ________________ adds another level of security to files beyond the use of permissions.
8. ________________ is verification of who you are.
9. A parent wanting to protect a child from inappropriate web content may use a ________________.
10. A secret key may be held in a ________________, which is a special file stored on a computer.

■ Multiple-Choice Quiz

1. Which printer permissions are normally assigned to the Everyone group?
   - a. Maintain Printer
   - b. Manage Printer
   - c. Manage Documents
   - d. Restore Printer
   - e. Print
2. If two people working different hours use the same Windows computer (excluding Windows 9*x*), what can you do to protect files in folders on a FAT volume on that computer?
   - a. Create local user accounts
   - b. You can't protect files on a FAT volume from local users
   - c. Copy files to My Briefcase

d. Save files in the Inbox

e. Set folder permissions

3. Since Windows XP Professional creates the local Administrator account automatically, why would you need a local limited user account?

   a. To log onto a domain
   b. To install updates
   c. To use when you are not doing administrative tasks
   d. To install software
   e. To manage printers

4. When you use the Windows XP User Accounts Control Panel applet to manage local accounts, it shows an account type called Limited account. What is the only built-in local user group to which Limited accounts belong?

   a. Administrators
   b. Users
   c. Guests
   d. Backup Operators
   e. Managers

5. You are the only user of your Windows XP Professional computer. You want to be able to leave your desk and keep your data secure, but you do not want to have to shut it down and restart it. Which of the following options is the best choice?

   a. Fast User Switching
   b. Automatic System Recovery
   c. System Restore
   d. CTRL-ALT-DELETE
   e. Lock Computer

6. A program installed and activated on a computer without the knowledge or permission of the user, and which replicates itself on the computer or throughout a network, is called this.

   a. Virus
   b. Utility
   c. Worm
   d. Scam
   e. Spim

7. A virus hidden inside a seemingly harmless program is called this.

   a. Worm
   b. Trojan horse
   c. Antivirus
   d. Optimizer
   e. Cookie

8. The man driving around downtown with his laptop would occasionally get out of his car and make cryptic marks on the walls of buildings. What was he doing?

   a. War painting
   b. Drive-by downloading
   c. Password cracking
   d. War driving
   e. Bluesnarfing

9. Strange screen messages, sudden computer slowdown, missing data, and inability to access the hard drive may be symptoms of what?

   a. War riding
   b. Spam
   c. Encryption
   d. Virus infection
   e. Fraud

10. This device sits between a private network and the Internet (or other network) and examines all traffic in and out of the network it is protecting, blocking any traffic it recognizes as a potential threat.

   a. Router
   b. Firewall
   c. Bridge
   d. Worm
   e. Keystroke logger

11. After several failed logon attempts, a message appears stating that your account has been locked out. This is the result of exceeding this setting in Account Lockout Policy.

   a. Password length
   b. Account lockout threshold
   c. Account lockout duration
   d. Maximum password age
   e. Password complexity requirements

12. While NTFS5 in both Windows 2000 and Windows XP Professional supports file and folder encryption, there have been some improvements in encryption in Windows XP Professional. What is one of those improvements?
    - **a.** Encapsulation
    - **b.** Decryption
    - **c.** Recovery agents
    - **d.** Sharing of encrypted files
    - **e.** Folder encryption
13. Combined with NTFS5, this component in Windows 2000 and Windows XP Professional makes file and folder encryption possible.
    - **a.** Encrypting Data System (EDS)
    - **b.** Private key
    - **c.** Encrypting File System (EFS)
    - **d.** Secret password
    - **e.** File compression
14. When a network user connects to a shared folder on an NTFS volume, what occurs between the time the user is authenticated to the computer security system and the time he is authorized to access a file or folder on the NTFS volume?
    - **a.** Authentication to the network
    - **b.** Authorization to access the network
    - **c.** A token is passed to the network
    - **d.** Biometric testing occurs
    - **e.** Authorization to the share
15. The first time a user logs onto a Windows 2000 or Windows XP Professional computer, this set of folders is created. If they exist on an NTFS volume, Windows will set permissions on the folders to protect the users' data from other users. What folders are created?
    - **a.** System folders
    - **b.** Personal folders for the new user
    - **c.** Personal folders for the default user
    - **d.** Shared folders for the new user
    - **e.** Shared folders for the default user

■ Essay Quiz

1. Describe the process for adding a user in Windows XP.
2. Why should you have multiple Computer Administrator accounts?
3. Why should the Guest account be disabled?
4. In your own words, describe why the use of Internet cookies can be an invasion of privacy.
5. Differentiate between permission and user right.

Lab Projects

• Lab Project 7.1

Research identity theft in order to answer the following questions:

1. What is the estimated annual cost of identity theft in the United States? What is the cost of identity theft in another first world country?
2. Find a recent article on an identity theft ring that used the Internet and describe how they operated.
3. Share your findings with others in your class, and compare the information you found.

• Lab Project 7.2

You have been hired by a small company with ten Windows XP Professional computers networked in a workgroup. They have access to the Internet through a broadband router that also acts as a firewall. Each computer contains sensitive data, each user is the only user of that computer, each user connects to several web sites as part of his or her work, and each is required to maintain unique user names and password for each of these accounts, as well as his or her local user name and password.

1. Using pen and paper or a word processing program, create two tables for security settings that you recommend be configured in the account policies of the Local Security Policies of each computer (use the same set for all computers). One table should contain your recommended settings for Account Lockout Policy, and the other should contain your recommended settings for Password Policy. When you are finished, discuss your reasons for recommending these settings.
2. With many online accounts, these users could really use a password generator and manager. Your boss would like you to research the available software in this category and to find and recommend one that would cost less than $500US for ten users.

• Lab Project 7.3

Planning is a very important step that an administrator must learn to take before implementing security changes to a computer. Part of that process involves gathering information about the security needs, such as user group accounts required and the permissions needed for each account. Once you gather this information, it is very helpful to organize it by creating a form to contain it. In this lab, you will create a permissions planning form for setting permissions on a single computer. In this scenario, a small import company has just seven employees, each using a desktop computer with Windows XP Professional. An eighth computer is located in a conference room and is configured so that any of the seven employees may log onto that computer. Table 7-4 is the planning form used to create the accounts on this computer.

The following folders have been created on the conference room computer:

C:\Sales\Database	C:\Sales\Promos
C:\Sales\ExcelDocs	C:\Sales\WordDocs

Use the following information to create a folder permissions planning form to be used to create the appropriate permissions on the folder of the conference room computer.

- Your plan includes giving the built-in Administrators group Full Control permissions for all folders and files in the Sales folder and blocking inheritance to the Sales folder from the parent folder.

Table 7-4 User and Group Accounts Planning Form

User Name	Full Name	Group(s)
Lpederson	Laura D. Pederson	Managers, Sales, Staff, Users
Mfrost	Marvin B. Frost	Sales, Users
Nrjones	Nancy R. Jones	Sales, Users
Sfisher	Sandra H. Fisher	Users
Njones	Norman A. Jones	Sales, Users
Jsmith	John I. Smith	Sales, Staff, Users
Jfrank	Jill K. Frank	Administrators, Sales, Staff, Users

- You will also remove all permissions for the Everyone group from the Sales folder, and all folders and files below the Sales Folder.
- Members of the Users group should only have permission to list folder contents on the Sales folder hierarchy, and read and execute on the WordDocs folder.
- All members of the Sales group must have read and write access to the WordDocs folder.
- All members of the Sales group should be able to read documents in the ExcelDocs folders, but only members of the Staff group can create and modify these documents.
- All members of the Sales groups should be able to read documents in the database folder, but only members of the Managers group may modify the contents of this folder.
- The Database folder contains a product database that is updated once a month from a master file by the manager, who makes final decisions about pricing data in this file before making it available to the rest of the Sales department.
- All members of the Sales group should be permitted to modify the contents of the Promos folder.

Using pen and paper, or a word processor, create a planning form to organize this information.

A Look under the Hood

chapter 8

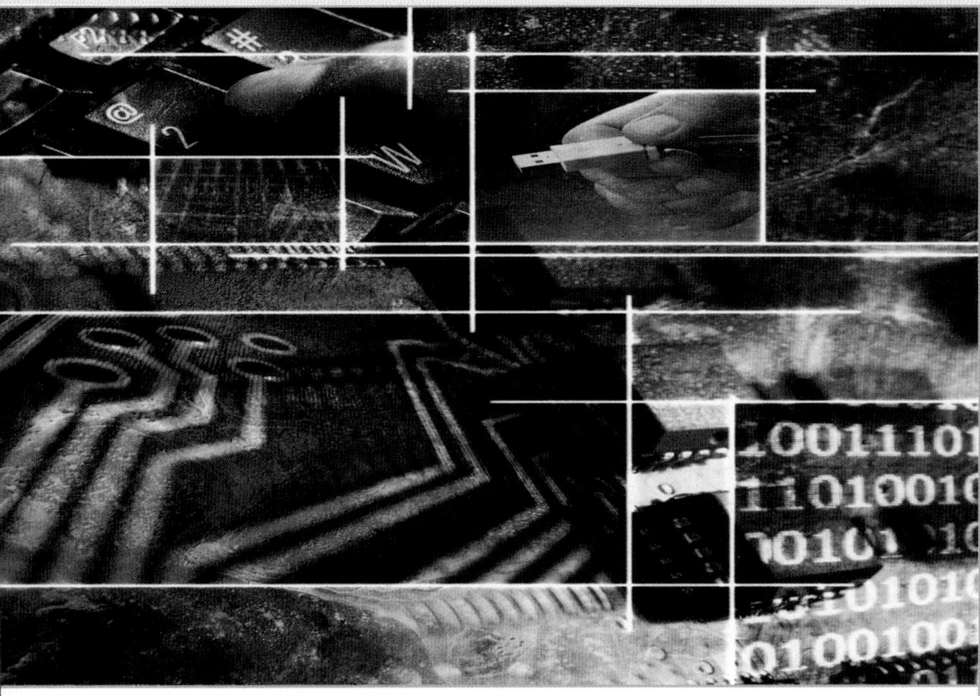

An operating system is something like a duck … it's calm on the surface but paddling like crazy underneath.

—Chuck Holcombe

When the IBM-PC was introduced in 1981, it was a computer with a mostly open architecture. Because of this open architecture, computer users came to expect that they could make a personal computer into the tool they needed by adding the right mix of software and hardware. Today, we have even greater expectations. To many, a PC is an office automation tool with office productivity software, a printer, and maybe a scanner and Internet connection. Others may make it their video workstation with the addition of elaborate video editing and movie production components. A PC might be the unifying component in a music studio. It may run manufacturing equipment or automotive test equipment.

For the PC to be such a versatile machine, it must first have a hardware architecture that allows you to add your choice from a huge variety of hardware components. You also must have an operating system that can be configured to control all the devices you choose to plug in. And you probably want a visually pleasing, easy-to-use GUI operating system, along with GUI applications that are compatible with the OS and that complement your master plan for the PC.

In this chapter, you will learn how to:

- **Define the role of the registry in Windows and back up and modify the registry when needed**
- **Install, configure, and manage device drivers**
- **Monitor and optimize performance in Windows**
- **Compare the file systems supported by Windows**
- **Describe the Windows startup process**
- **Troubleshoot common Windows problems**

Windows is just such a configurable operating system—but the price to pay for having so much variable potential in an operating system is complexity. In this chapter, you'll look under the hood at some of that complexity, including the registry, device drivers, file systems, and the critical files used in the startup procedure. You'll look at performance tuning and monitoring features, and related troubleshooting topics.

Understanding the Registry

The registry, introduced in Windows 95, is one of several technical features of Windows that has made it easier to configure and support than the earlier Microsoft operating systems. Ironically, it is also one of the most complicated and least understood features of Windows. In this section, you'll learn about the registry—its role in Windows and how to modify the registry when needed.

The Registry Defined

The Windows **registry** is a database of all configuration settings in Windows. It includes settings for:

- Device drivers
- Services
- Installed application programs
- Operating system components
- User preferences

Remember that the registry only contains settings, not the actual device drivers, services, or applications to which the settings apply!

The registry is created when Windows is installed, and it continues to be modified as you configure Windows and add applications and components. During startup, Windows depends on the registry to tell it what services, drivers, and components to load into memory, and how to configure each component.

• Adding a new device creates changes in the registry.

Automatic Registry Changes

Any change to the operating system or an installed application will result in a change in the registry. The registry will automatically be changed when:

- Windows starts up or shuts down
- During Windows Setup (which is run more often than you may think)
- Changes are made through a Control Panel applet
- A new device is installed
- Any changes are made to the Windows configuration
- Any changes are made to a user's desktop preferences
- An application is installed or modified
- Changes are made to preferences in any application

Registry Files

The registry is loaded into memory during startup and remains in memory while Windows is active. Although it is considered a single entity, the registry is actually stored in a number of binary files on disk. A **binary file** contains program code, as opposed to a file containing simple text. The Windows registry files include the following:

- SYSTEM
- SOFTWARE
- SECURITY
- SAM
- DEFAULT
- NTUSER.DAT

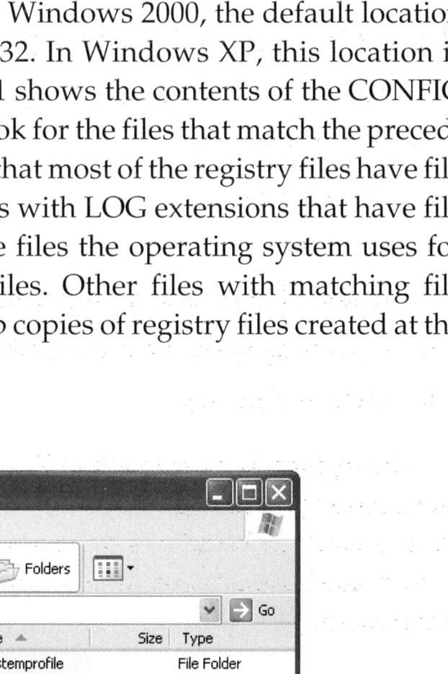

The portion of the registry represented in one of these registry files is called a **hive**—so named because someone decided that the registry structure resembled a beehive. These are the permanent portions of the registry, with all the changes saved from use to use. With the exception of the NTUSER.DAT file, these registry files are saved in a disk folder named CONFIG. In Windows NT and Windows 2000, the default location of this folder is C:\WINNT\SYSTEM32. In Windows XP, this location is C:\WINDOWS\SYSTEM32. Figure 8-1 shows the contents of the CONFIG folder in Windows XP Professional. Look for the files that match the preceding list (except NTUSER.DAT). Notice that most of the registry files have file names without file extensions. The files with LOG extensions that have file names that match the registry files are files the operating system uses for logging transactions to the registry files. Other files with matching file names, and SAV extensions, are backup copies of registry files created at the end of the text mode stage of setup.

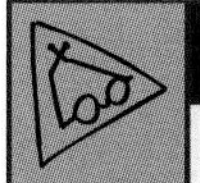

Inside Information

Windows 9*x* Registry Files

The Windows 9x registry files have different file names (SYSTEM.DAT and USER.DAT) from the registry files in Windows NT, Windows 2000, and Windows XP. All Windows hardware and software configuration settings are contained in SYSTEM.DAT, while user preference settings for the desktop and applications are saved in USER.DAT.

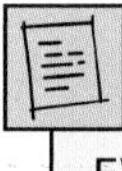

The files that end with the EVT extension are log files from Event Viewer. You'll learn more about Event Viewer later in this chapter.

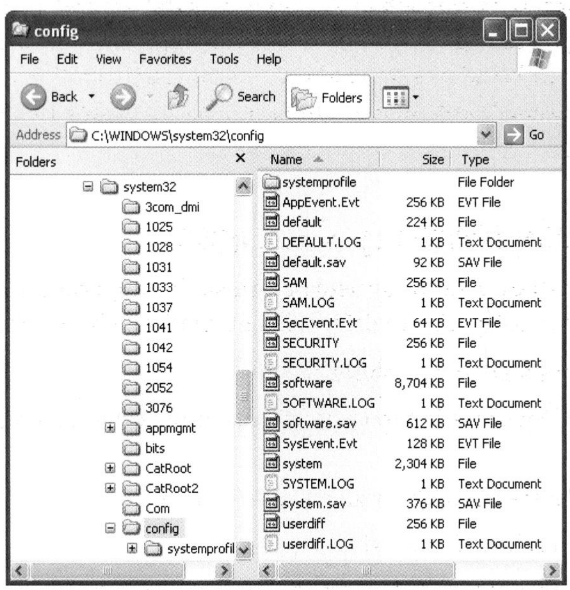

• **Figure 8-1.** The CONFIG folder contains most of the registry files as well as Event Viewer log files.

SYSTEM

The SYSTEM hive contains information used at startup, including device drivers to be loaded, as well as the order of their loading and configuration settings, the starting and configuring of services, and various operating system settings.

SOFTWARE

The SOFTWARE hive contains configuration settings for software installed on the local computer, along with various items of miscellaneous configuration data.

SECURITY

The SECURITY hive contains the local security policy settings for the computer, including those that you studied in Chapter 7.

SAM

The SAM hive contains the local security accounts database; SAM is an acronym for Security Accounts Manager.

DEFAULT

The DEFAULT hive contains user desktop settings, called a user profile, used when no user is logged on. This may sound counterintuitive, but you do need desktop settings for the GUI even before you log on. Evidence of this profile is seen in the desktop settings used for the Log On To Windows dialog box and the desktop background.

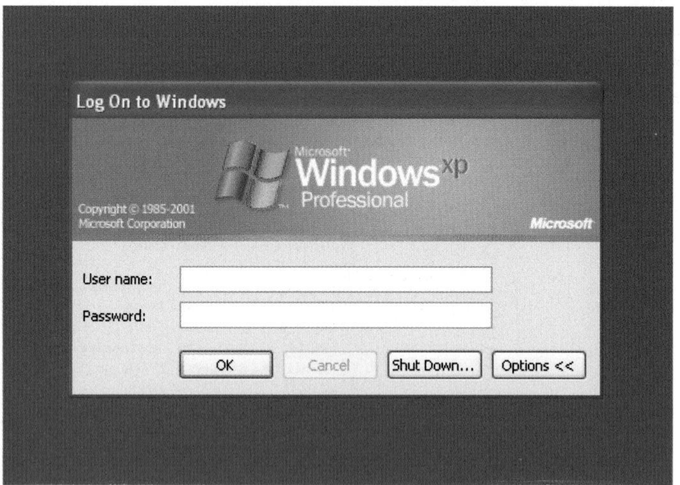

• The default user profile is used until a user logs on.

Inside Information

USERDIFF

The USERDIFF file shown in the CONFIG folder is not a registry hive. This file has a role when a computer has been upgraded from an earlier version of Windows. As each user who previously had a profile on that computer logs on, the USERDIFF file is used to create the new NTUSER.DAT file that will be compatible with the new version of the registry.

NTUSER.DAT

The NTUSER.DAT hive file contains the user profile for a single user. These settings include application preferences, screen colors, network connections, and other personal choices. There is a separate NTUSER.DAT file for each user who logs onto the computer, as well as one located in the

DEFAULT USER folder. During startup, the other registry hives (located in the CONFIG folder) are used to load and configure the operating system. One of the last tasks of the operating system at startup is to request a user logon. When a user logs on, the settings from that user's NTUSER.DAT file are applied and become part of the current registry. The first time a user logs onto a computer, the NTUSER.DAT file from the DEFAULT USER folder is used to create the initial profile for the user. The NTUSER.DAT file is saved in the top-level personal folder for that user. Figure 8-2 shows the files and folders that make up a user profile. Notice the NTUSER.DAT registry file, the NTUSER.DAT.LOG log file, and the NTUSER.INI initialization file.

Personal folders were defined in Chapter 6.

Do not directly edit the registry with a tool like Regedit unless it is absolutely necessary—there are many safer ways to make a change to the registry.

Viewing the Registry Structure

You can view and edit the registry as a hierarchical structure using registry editing tools, such as REGEDIT.EXE or REGEDT32.EXE, both of which come with Windows (except Windows 9*x*, which only has REGEDIT.EXE). Until Windows XP, these were two separate programs, with some differences in capabilities and the user interface, but in Windows XP, either command name brings up the same registry editor.

Start Regedit

It is simple to open Regedit from any of the versions of Windows you have installed in the previous chapters. Try this:

1. Open the Run box by selecting Start | Run.
2. Type **regedit** in the Run box and select OK.

Viewing the Registry with Registry Editor

The registry editor executable file, REGEDIT.EXE, is located in the folder in which the operating system is installed (C:\WINDOWS or C:\WINNT), but it does not have a shortcut on

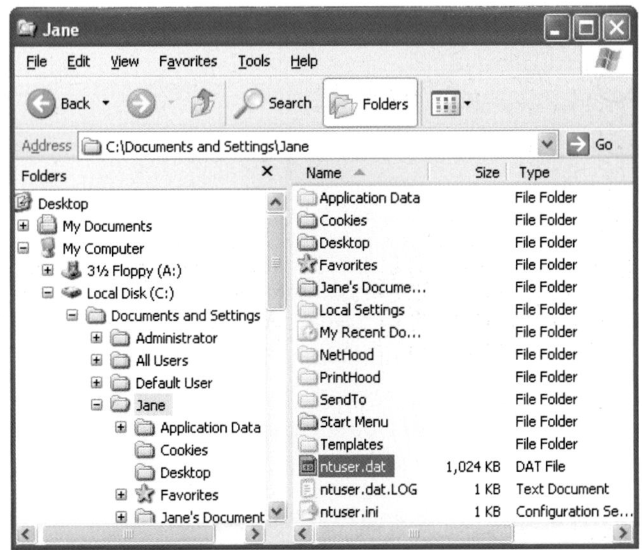

• **Figure 8-2.** The NTUSER.DAT registry file in the personal folders for the user Jane

Inside Information

Regedit.exe vs. Regedt32.exe

In Windows NT and Windows 2000, the most obvious difference between the two registry editors is in the user interface. Regedt32 looks more like a Windows 3.x application, with a separate window for each registry root tree, while Regedit shows the entire registry structure in a single window. Of the two, Regedit has a better registry search function, but whenever direct editing was required, we preferred to work with Regedt32 because it displayed the actual data types more accurately. Windows XP has only one registry editing program, no matter which name you use to start it. This registry editor displays all data types.

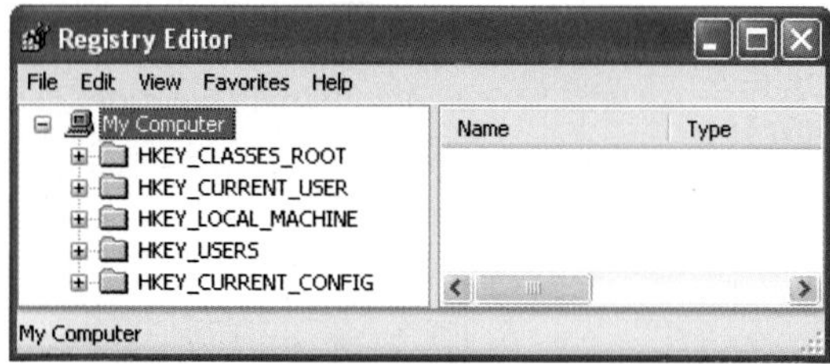

• **Figure 8-3.** The registry subtrees

the Start menu. This is for a very good reason; it should not be too handy. Because Microsoft doesn't want to make it too easy for us to casually run Regedit, we must start it from the Run box. It will aid your understanding of the registry if you open the Regedit program now and refer to it as you read the following descriptions of the registry components.

You can navigate the registry with your mouse in the same way you navigate any disk folder, by opening and closing folders. The first time Regedit is run on a computer, it looks like Figure 8-3. Each folder represents a **key**, an object that may contain one or more sets of settings as well as other keys. The top five folders are **root keys**, often called **subtrees** in Microsoft documentation. Each of these subtrees is the top of a hierarchical structure. A key that exists within another key is called a **subkey**. The settings within a key are called **value entries**. When you click on the folder for a key, it becomes the active key in Regedit, its folder icon "opens," and the contents of the key are shown in the right pane. Table 8-1 gives an overview of the information stored within each subtree of the registry.

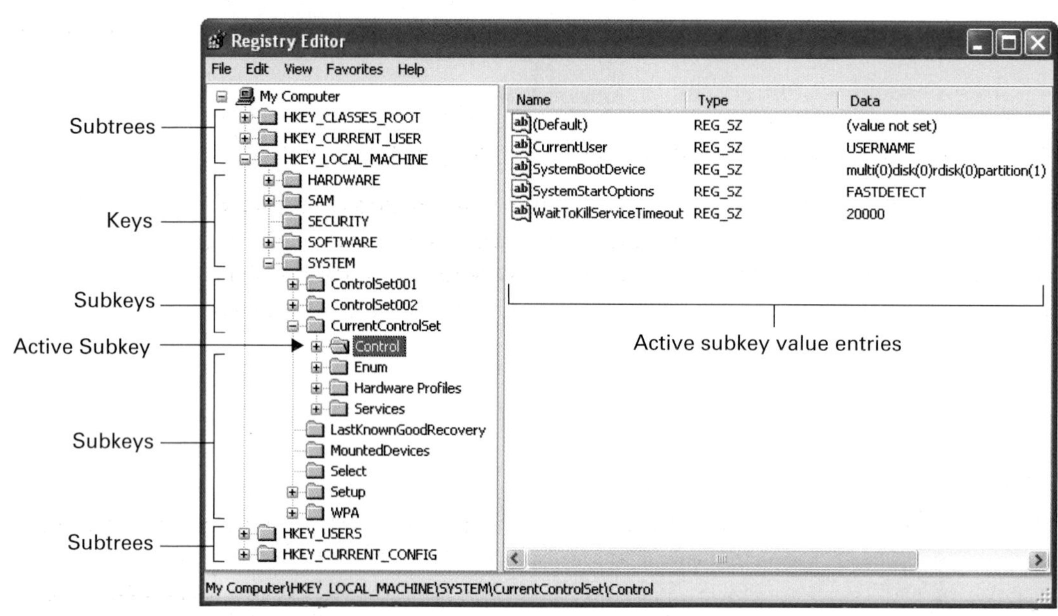

• Registry components

To describe a registry location, use a notation that shows the path from a subtree down through the keys and subkeys, similar to that used to describe file and folder locations on disk: HKEY_LOCAL_MACHINE\SYSTEM\CURRENTCONTROLSET\CONTROL.

Data Types in Value Entries In Regedit each value entry is shown in three columns labeled "Name," "Type," and "Data." The Type column shows a label that describes the format of the data in that key, also called **data type**. There are many data types in the registry; take a few minutes to study Table 8-2, which shows just a few registry data types to give you an idea of how diverse the data in the registry can be.

The Permanent Portions of the Registry: Registry Hives Earlier you learned about the files used to store portions of the registry. Table 8-3 shows the

Table 8-1 Contents of Registry Subtrees

Subtree	Description
HKEY_LOCAL_MACHINE	Detected hardware, software and hardware configuration information, security settings, and the local security accounts database.
HKEY_CLASSES_ROOT	Relationships (called associations) between applications and file types defined by file extension. Information used for object linking and embedding (OLE) and special objects called COM objects. This subtree is actually all the information located in HKEY_LOCAL_MACHINE\Software\Classes.
HKEY_CURRENT_CONFIG	Configuration information for the current hardware profile, which is a set of changes (*only* changes) to the standard configuration in the Software and Systems subkeys under HKEY_LOCAL_MACHINE.
HKEY_CURRENT_USER	The user profile for the currently logged-on user, which consists of the NTUSER.DAT file for the user along with any changes since logon.
HKEY_USERS	All user profiles that are loaded in memory, including the profile of the currently logged on user (also shown under HKEY_CURRENT_USER), the default profile, and profiles for special user accounts that are used to run various services. Except for the default profile, each is labeled with a **security ID (SID)**, a unique string of numbers preceded by *S-1-5* that identifies a security principal in a Windows security accounts database.

registry hive files and their location in the registry. Use this table to browse to the locations in the registry for each of these hives, using Regedit.

The Temporary Portion of the Registry The information stored in HKEY_LOCAL_MACHINE\Hardware is temporary information, gathered during the hardware detection process of the detect and configure hardware phase of Windows startup. It is not saved to disk in a file, as are other portions of the registry.

Table 8-2 Windows Registry Data Types (The Short List)

Data Type	Description
REG_BINARY	Raw binary data. Some hardware data is shown in binary. Ironically, binary data is shown in hexadecimal and might look like this: ff 00 ff ff 02 05
REG_DWORD	A number 4 bytes long in binary, hexadecimal, or decimal format. It may look something like this in hexadecimal: 0x00000002
REG_EXPAND_SZ	A single string of text including a variable. A variable is a value to be replaced when called by an application. An example of a common variable is *%systemroot%*, which, when used by Windows, is replaced by the path of the folder containing the Windows system files. Example: a registry entry containing *%systemroot%*\regedit.exe becomes c:\windows\regedit.exe
REG_MULTI_SZ	Multiple strings of human-readable text, separated by a special NULL character that is not displayed. Example: System\CurrentControlSet\Control\ProductOptions System\CurrentControlSet\Control\Print\Printers System\CurrentControlSet\Control\Server Applications
REG_SZ	A sequence of characters representing human-readable text. This data type may be used when the data is quite simple, such as a numeric value—for example, 16—or to represent an entire list: comm.drv commdlg.dll ctl3dv2.dll ddeml.dll.

Table 8-3 Locations of the Hives Within the Registry

Hive File	Registry Location
SYSTEM	HKEY_LOCAL_MACHINE\SYSTEM
SOFTWARE	HKEY_LOCAL_MACHINE\SOFTWARE
SECURITY	HKEY_LOCAL_MACHINE\SECURITY
SAM	HKEY_LOCAL_MACHINE\SAM
DEFAULT	HKEY_USERS\.DEFAULT
NTUSER.DAT of the currently logged-on user	HKEY_CURRENT_USER and HKEY_USERS

Working with Device Drivers

A device driver is program code that allows an operating system to control the use of a physical device. A manufacturer of a device will create device drivers for common operating systems and make the drivers available with the device. The range of physical devices that work in Windows is quite broad. Just a short list includes printers, network interface cards, video adapters, video capture and editing cards, scanners, cameras, sound cards, and joysticks.

Try This!

Locate a Device Driver on the Web

Assume that you are looking for a Windows XP device driver for a Logitech trackball device called the TrackMan Wheel. Try this:

1. Point your web browser to `www.logitech.com`. Select a location and language. On the main page, select Downloads.
2. On the Software Updates And Downloads page, look for the TrackMan Wheel. If it is listed, select the link. If it is not listed, select another product.
3. View the page for the device you selected, and notice the list of operating systems for which Logitech provides device drivers. Unless you actually need this device driver, do not download.

Finding Device Drivers

A new device normally comes with a floppy disk or CD containing an installation program and device drivers for one or more operating systems. But these disks have a way of disappearing after they are purchased. Or, you wish to install the device into a newer operating system, and cannot find the driver files on disk for the new OS. In that case, connect to the web site of the manufacturer of the device, and look for a link titled "Downloads" or "Device Drivers." Then search for the model name or number of your device and the OS version you need.

• **Figure 8-4.** Insufficient security privileges to install or uninstall a device

Permissions Required for Installing and Configuring Device Drivers

You must be logged on as Administrator or a member of the Administrators group in order to install any device driver in Windows. If you attempt to install a new device while logged on with a non-administrator account, you will see a message similar to that shown in Figure 8-4.

However, once a device has been installed, any member of the local Users group may disconnect and reconnect the device without restriction. So, if an administrator installed a USB-connected network card on your computer and you unplug the device, when you plug it back in, it will operate, because the driver is not uninstalled from your computer when you unplug a device, it is just given a status of not present.

Try This!

Test the Permissions Required to Install a Device Driver

The versions of Windows you have studied that include security components will not allow just any user to install, configure, or remove device drivers. Try this:

1. If necessary, log off as Administrator, and log on as a user who is not a member of the Administrators group.
2. Open Control Panel and attempt to start the Add Hardware wizard.
3. An error message should appear.

Working with Signed vs. Unsigned Device Drivers

Because a device driver becomes a part of an operating system, a poorly written device driver can cause problems, or even system crashes. For this reason, bad device drivers have long been the number one cause of operating system instability. To help users avoid badly written program code, Microsoft has developed several features in Windows 2000 and Windows XP.

The central feature is code signing, the use of a digital signature provided by Microsoft as its seal of approval on program code. A Microsoft **digital signature** is encrypted data placed in the file that can be unencrypted by Windows in a process called **file signature verification**. The digital signature includes information about the file so that the operating system can detect whether the file has been altered in any way. If you attempt to install a program that contains unsigned code, you may see the warning shown in Figure 8-5.

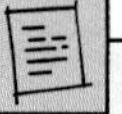

Only someone with Administrator rights can modify the Driver Signing settings.

Driver signing is simply code signing of device drivers. This does not mean that all device drivers that aren't digitally signed are bad. What it does mean is that Microsoft has provided a process that a manufacturer can choose to use in order to have their device drivers tested and signed by Microsoft. This is part of the process of having a device added to Microsoft's compatibility list.

Try This!

Check Out the Driver Signing Settings

Check out the driver signing settings on your lab computer. Try this:

1. Open the System applet in Control Panel.
2. Select the Hardware tab and click the Driver Signing button.
3. Notice the action currently selected, and then click Cancel to close the Driver Signing Options and System Properties dialog boxes.

An administrator can control how Windows reacts when you attempt to install a program or device driver that is not digitally signed. This is done through the Driver Signing button located on the Hardware page of the System applet. The three settings are

- **Ignore** Windows will install drivers and not inform you when code is found not to contain a digital signature.
- **Warn** When Windows detects unsigned code, it will display a warning (see Figure 8-6) and not proceed until you make a decision about using the device or canceling the installation.
- **Block** Windows will block the installation of unsigned code.

Installing and Configuring a Plug-and-Play Device

The plug-and-play standard is an industry standard that relieves the computer user of the onerous task of manually installing and configuring a device driver for a new device. Support for plug and play (PnP) was introduced in Windows 95 and improved in each later version of Windows beginning with Windows 2000, but it was not fully supported in any version of Windows NT.

A plug-and-play device must still have a device driver, but because the device, the computer, and the operating system support the plug-and-play standard, when you install or attach the device, Windows XP Professional will detect the device, install the device driver, and configure the device so that it does not conflict with other devices. You may still have to provide the device driver

Try This!

Install a Plug-and-Play Device

Locate a plug-and-play USB device that has not previously been installed on your computer. Try this:

1. Power up the computer and log on as an Administrator. After the desktop appears, install the device driver, if required.
2. Then plug the USB device into a USB port. You may see a balloon by the notification area as the device is automatically recognized.

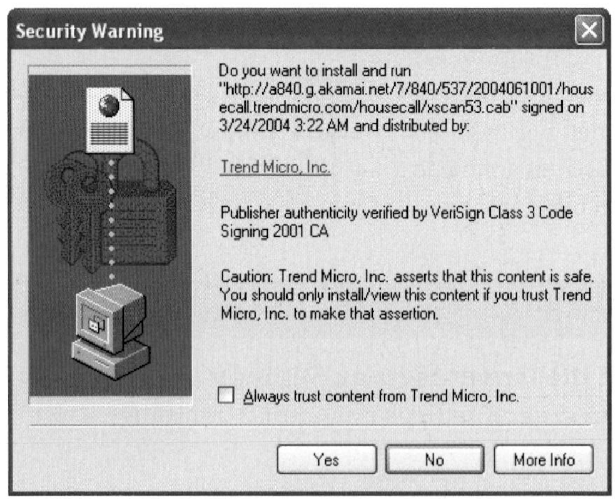

• **Figure 8-5.** Security warning asking if you want to install unsigned code

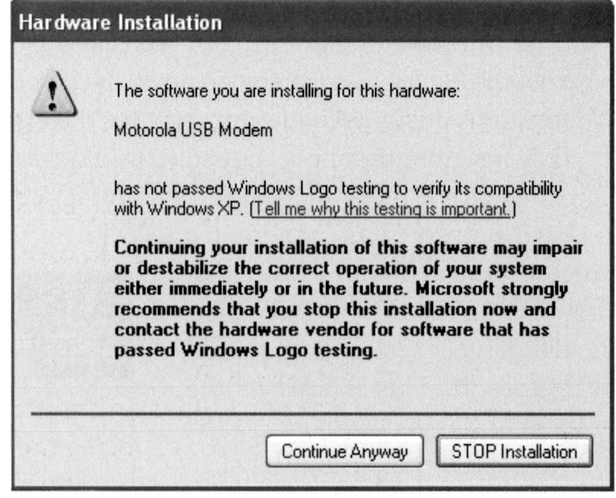

• **Figure 8-6.** When you see this warning, you may stop the installation or continue, even though the driver is not digitally signed.

if Windows does not already have the driver file. In that case, you will be prompted to insert a disk or provide the location of the device driver. Sometimes, the plug-and-play device installation requires a reboot.

While you will need to power down your computer before installing a plug-and-play bus card, external plug-and-play devices that connect through certain interfaces can be connected to the computer while it is up and running. They will be automatically detected. Those interfaces include

- Universal Serial Bus (USB)
- IEEE 1394 (FireWire)
- SCSI

After a new device has been installed or connected, the Found New Hardware wizard will open. Follow the instructions to install the device driver for the new device.

Always read the documentation before installing any device. In some cases, the device driver must be installed *before* installing or connecting the plug-and-play device. We have found this to be true of several USB devices, as well as those that use the IEEE 1394 interface.

• Found New Hardware wizard requesting directions

Disconnecting a Plug-and-Play Device

Windows plug-and-play support also allows you to disconnect USB and IEEE 1394 external plug-and-play devices without first powering down the computer, but Windows would like to be warned about the change! In Windows terminology you are *removing* the device, and you notify Windows of your intention by double-clicking the Safely Remove Hardware icon located in the notification area of the taskbar. Figure 8-7 shows the Safely Remove Hardware dialog box, listing the devices that may be removed, and the Stop A Hardware Device box, which opened when the Stop button was clicked.

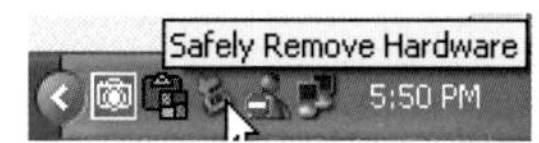

• Safely Remove Hardware icon

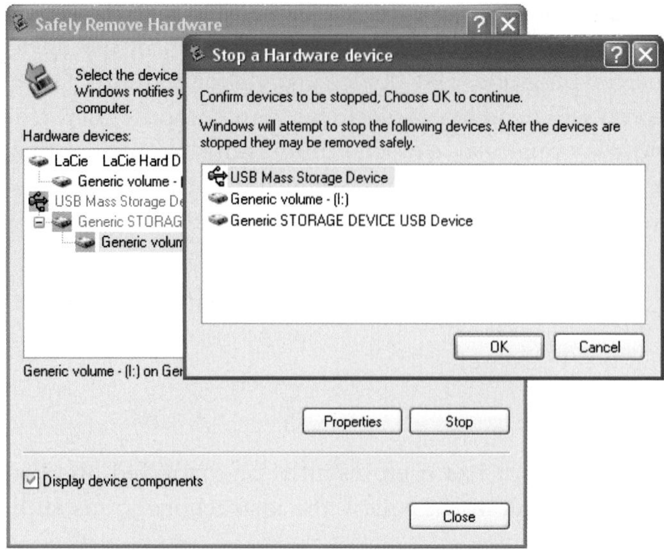

• **Figure 8-7.** Safely Remove Hardware dialog box

Installing and Configuring a Non-Plug-and-Play Device

Happily, most new devices for PCs are now plug and play. If you should encounter a non-plug-and-play device, read the documentation either that comes with the device or which may be found at the manufacturer's web site. Then follow the instructions. An installation program available from the manufacturer is the preferred method. If you have an appropriate device driver, but no installation program is available, then use the Add Hardware applet, and provide the location of the device driver when prompted by the Add Hardware wizard.

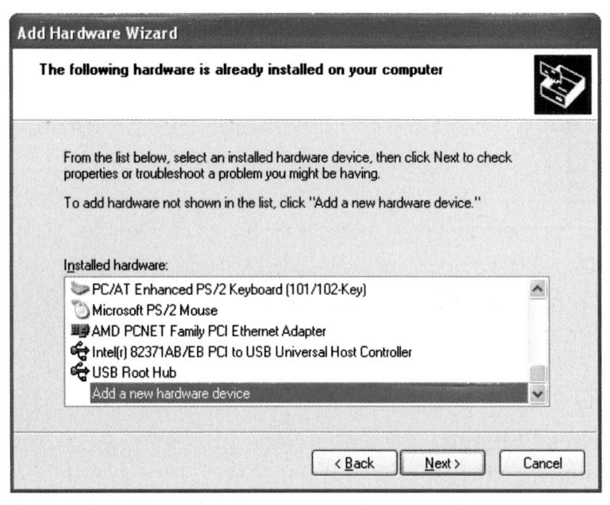

• The Add Hardware wizard

Using Device Manager to Manage Device Drivers

Device Manager is a tool that allows an administrator to view and change device properties, update device drivers, configure device settings, and uninstall devices. Windows XP Device Manager will even allow an administrator to roll back a driver update. Device Manager did not exist in Windows NT, but has been in every other version of Windows since Windows 95. Microsoft has worked to improve this utility in each successive version.

In Windows 2000 and Windows XP, Device Manager can be found through the System applet by selecting the Hardware tab, and then clicking the Device Manager button. It is an MMC snap-in and opens up into a separate console window. Only administrators can make modifications in Device Manager in Windows 2000 and Windows XP. Device Manager in Windows XP

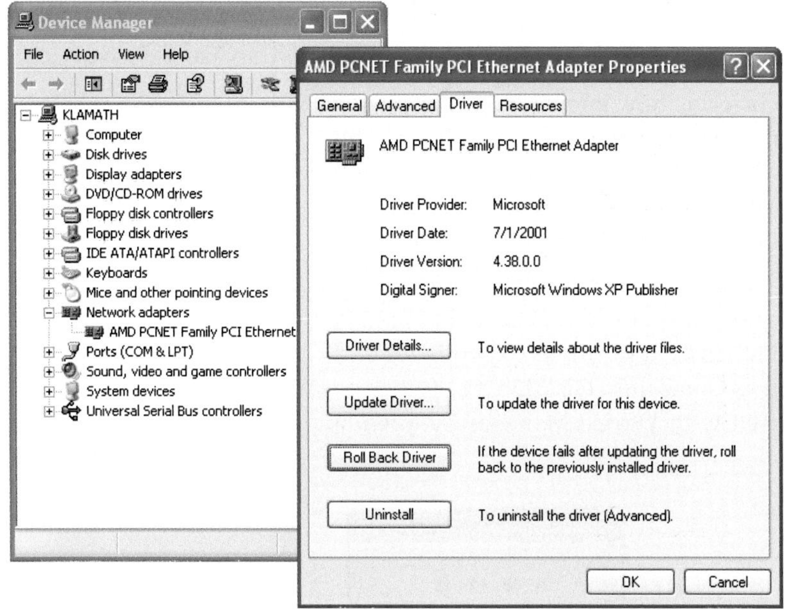

• Device Manager

works almost exactly as in Windows 2000, with some small changes in how information is viewed, and with the addition of the new Roll Back Driver button on the Driver tab of the Properties dialog box. This feature works on device drivers that have been updated with new drivers. It is quite handy for those times when you find the new device driver causes new problems.

Step-by-Step 8.01

Getting to Know Device Manager

In this step-by-step, you will first open Device Manager in a conventional manner, and then you will create a shortcut to Device Manager on the desktop to make it more convenient to open. You'll then examine the information shown in Device Manager. For this step-by-step, you will need a computer running Windows 2000 or Windows XP Professional.

Step 1

Log on as a local administrator, and open the System applet in Control Panel. In the System Properties dialog box, select the Hardware tab, and then click the Device Manager button. The window that opens gives you access to all the devices on the machine. Close the Device Manager and System Properties windows.

Step 2

In this step, you will create a custom shortcut on the desktop so that you can open Device Manager more quickly. Right-click on an empty area of the desktop and select New | Shortcut. In the Create Shortcut wizard, a text box prompts you to enter the location of the item. Simply enter the file name and extension for the Device Manager console: **devmgmt.msc**. Click the Next button. In the text box labeled "Type a name for this shortcut," type **device mgr**, and click the Finish button.

Step 3

Test your new shortcut by double-clicking on it to open Device Manager. Use the View menu to experiment with various ways of changing how information is displayed. You have two options for viewing devices and two options for viewing resources, which you can choose from the View menu. You will normally view devices by type, because this approach is simpler and more understandable.

Step 4

When viewing devices by type, there is a node for each device type, such as Computer, Disk Drives, and so on. Familiarize yourself with Device Manager by opening the nodes.

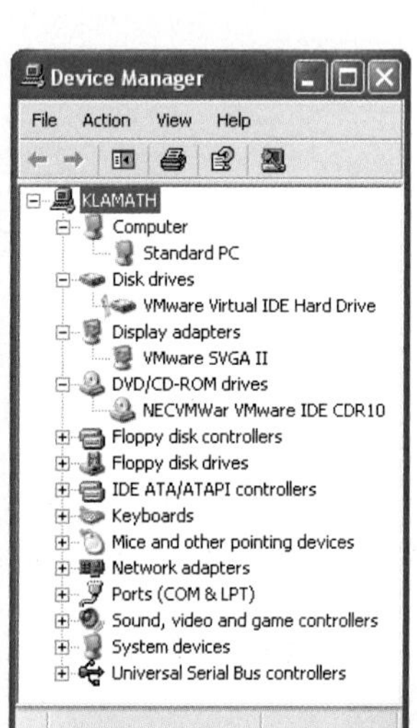

Step 5

Click the yellow question mark in the toolbar to open Device Manager Help; browse through the topics to learn more. Find out how you can print information about a device—a handy trick if you need to give information about a problem device to someone helping you. When you are finished, close all open windows. You will use other features of Device Manager in the troubleshooting section of this chapter.

Hardware Profiles

On a Windows computer, a **hardware profile** includes registry keys that contain the following: settings defining the devices that must be started during Windows startup, the list of files associated with each device, and configuration settings for each device. During Windows installation, the hardware profile created on a desktop computer is titled "Profile 1" (see Figure 8-8). This first profile defines all the existing hardware at the time of installation, and by default every device is enabled. On a desktop computer, you will probably always have a single hardware profile, and you may never be aware of it or need to configure a second profile. You can view, create, copy, rename, and modify hardware profiles by clicking the Hardware Profiles button on the Hardware page in System Properties (the System applet in Control Panel).

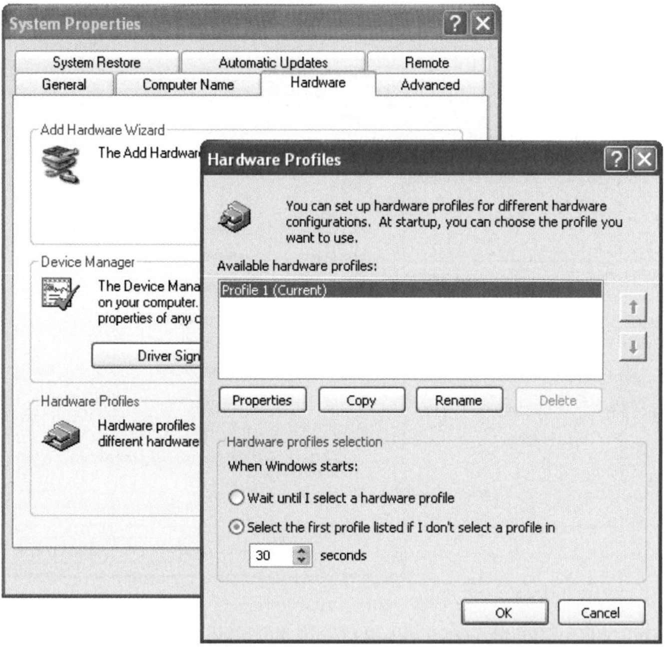

• **Figure 8-8.** The Hardware Profiles dialog box showing a single hardware profile and the default settings

When there are two or more hardware profiles, Windows startup pauses and displays the Hardware Profile/Configuration Recovery menu from which you may select a profile. On a multiboot computer, this menu will be displayed after the OS Selection menu. The default setting will display the menu for 30 seconds to give the user time to choose a profile. If a selection is not made within that time, the first profile listed will be selected.

Hardware profiles are nice to have on a laptop computer that has two or more different hardware configurations available to it. Let's say you use a laptop at school or work that connects to a docking station. If Windows 2000 or Windows XP was installed on this laptop while it was docked (and the docking station was successfully detected), the profile is named Docked Profile. The docking station has a network interface card, diskette drive, and a nice sound card connected to great speakers. When you use this same laptop at home or when traveling, it is "undocked" from all that great hardware left behind on your desktop, and you use the laptop's modem to connect to the Internet. A hardware profile for this set of hardware could be created and named "Undocked." To do so, first use the Copy button to copy the first profile, and

```
        Hardware Profile/Configuration Recovery Menu

This menu allows you to select a hardware profile
to be used when Windows is started.

If your system is not starting correctly, then you may switch to a
previous system configuration, which may overcome startup problems.
IMPORTANT: System configuration changes made since the last successful
startup will be discarded.

     Docked
     Undocked

Use the up and down arrow keys to move the highlight
to the selection you want. Then press ENTER.
To switch to the Last Known Good configuration, press 'L'.
To Exit this menu and restart your computer, press F3.
```

• The Hardware Profile/Configuration Recovery menu

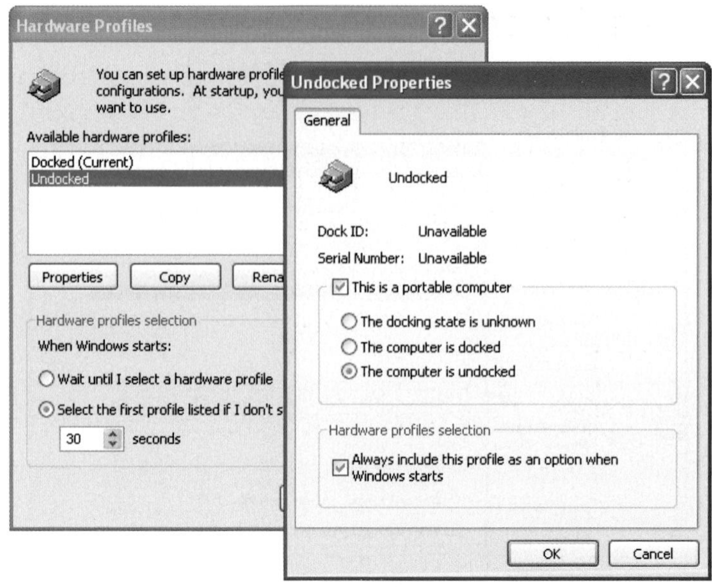

• Use the Hardware Profiles dialog box to create and modify new profiles.

• A disabled device in Device Manager

name it "Undocked." The last step is to use the Properties button and ensure that the check box labeled "This is a portable computer" is selected and that the check box under Hardware Profiles Selection is selected.

You can further fine-tune your new hardware profile by disabling the devices that are not available when the computer is undocked. To do so, start Windows and select the hardware profile in question. Then open Device Manager, locate the device, right-click on it, and select Disable from the context menu. Disabling a device will not uninstall the device driver from your computer; Windows simply won't load the device driver into memory during startup, and a disabled device will have a red X on its icon in Device Manager.

Managing Performance in Windows

The average desktop user may not care about the details of managing computer performance. In fact, to most of us, the performance of a desktop is subjective, as we each believe a computer performs well if we are not inconvenienced by any noticeable delays and as long as it doesn't fail. Microsoft has attempted to give us tools to measure performance so that we can make objective judgments and even compare different computer systems running Windows. Frankly, these tools are most often used on network servers rather than on desktop and laptop computers. Therefore, learning about them gives you a small insight into the work of network server administrators, but you will not usually change the performance settings or attempt to monitor the performance of your desktop computer.

Windows Performance Settings

The Windows Performance settings, found on the Advanced tab of the System Properties dialog box, allow you to adjust settings that control visual effects, processor scheduling, memory usage, and virtual memory. They are included here so that you understand these settings and how they may affect your Windows installation, but we strongly advise you not to manually change them. Windows fine-tunes some of these settings on-the-fly to adjust to variations in how the memory and processor are used. Making manual adjustments can interfere with Windows' ability to adjust to changes. Now that we've done our duty by warning you, we'll tell you about these settings.

Windows NT 4.0 and Windows 2000 Performance Settings

Windows NT 4.0 and Windows 2000 have limited Performance settings compared to Windows XP. Figure 8-9 shows the Windows NT 4.0 Performance settings, while Figure 8-10 shows the Windows 2000 Performance settings. The discussion that follows describes the Windows XP Professional settings, a superset of these earlier settings.

Windows XP Visual Effects

The **Visual Effects** page of the Windows XP Performance Options is a group of settings that includes treatments of the GUI that make Windows more visually interesting and even fun to use. But many, if not all, of these treatments come at a price—the increased use of processor and memory. Therefore, choosing visual effects settings represents a trade-off between performance and interesting visual effects. The four choices are as follows:

Let Windows Choose What's Best for My Computer This user "hands-off" setting gives Windows complete control over the selection of visual effects.

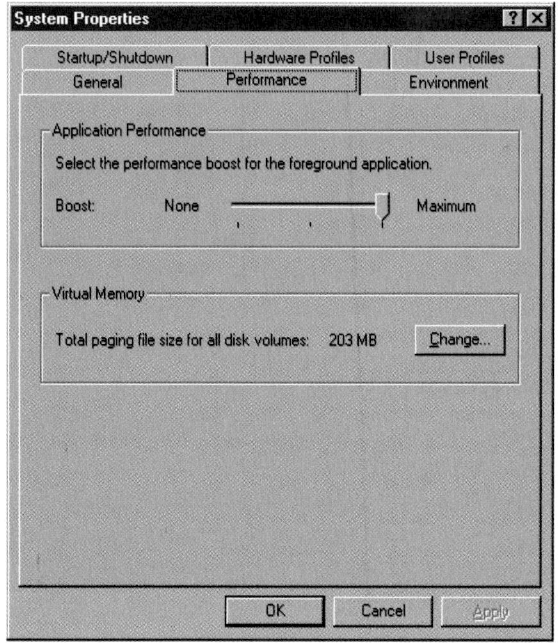

• **Figure 8-9.** Windows NT 4.0 Performance options

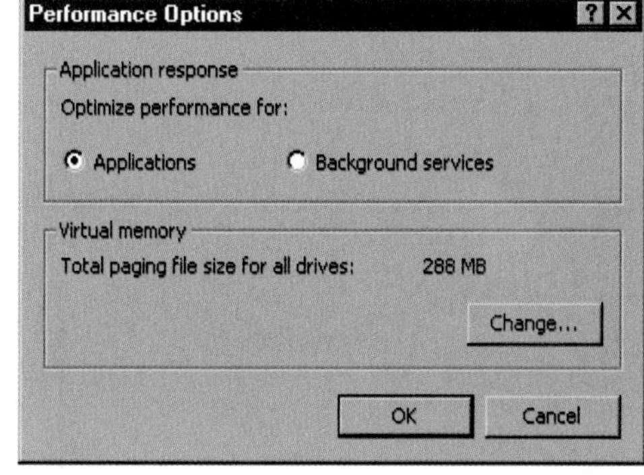

• **Figure 8-10.** Windows 2000 Performance Options

And Windows might just decide to turn on every visual effect if the computer has sufficient memory, processor, and video resources, as shown in Figure 8-11. Because new computers often come equipped with advanced video adapters and 512MB or more of physical memory, don't be surprised to see Windows turn on all visual elements.

Adjust for Best Appearance Selecting this setting is equivalent to telling Windows that nice visual effects are more important to you than processing speed. You are still allowing Windows to make the decisions, but you are tipping the scales in favor of visual effects. On a computer with plenty of video and memory resources, this may not hurt performance. On a minimally configured computer, you may see a performance difference if you run applications that require a lot of processing power.

Adjust for Best Performance This setting tells Windows that the best performance must be achieved at the expense of all visual effects, so choosing this option automatically deselects *every* visual effect. After this is selected, and the OK button is pressed, there will be a pause while the new setting is applied. In Windows XP the effect of this setting is an interface that looks just like Windows 2000!

Custom Custom allows an administrator to select any desired combination of settings. In fact, if an administrator selects or deselects any of the check boxes under Custom when one of the other radio buttons is selected, the Custom radio button is automatically selected.

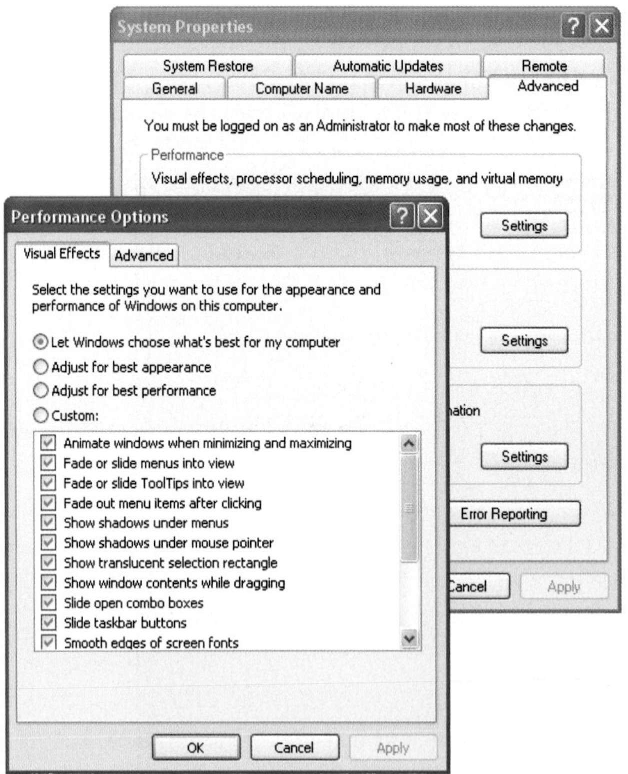

• **Figure 8-11.** The Visual Effects default settings

Step-by-Step 8.02

Experiment with Visual Effects

On a Windows XP computer, selecting Adjust For Best Performance produces a dramatic change to the user interface. In this step-by-step, you will experiment with visual effects settings.

Step 1

Log on as an Administrator. Open the System applet in Control Panel and select the Advanced tab. On the Advanced page, locate the Performance area and select the Settings button for that area. This will open the Performance Options dialog box.

Step 2

On the Visual Effects page, select Adjust For Best Performance. Notice that the entire list of visual settings is deselected, and then click the OK button to close the page and to accept the changes. There will be a pause during which a "Please Wait" message will be displayed while the changes are applied to the desktop.

Step 3

The changes to the desktop are apparent immediately in the System Properties dialog box. If you wish to change back to the previous settings, return to System Properties | Advanced | Performance Options, and select Let Windows Choose What's Best For My Computer.

Advanced Performance Options

The Advanced Performance Options page has even more settings, including Processor Scheduling, Memory Usage, and Virtual Memory.

Processor Scheduling By default, the Processor Scheduling setting has Programs selected, which gives a higher priority to the active window, rather than to the other user programs running in background. You will normally leave this setting at the default. Changing it to Background Services may cause the current application to run noticeably slower, but will give a higher priority to such background tasks as backup or very large spreadsheet calculations.

Memory Usage The memory usage settings control how Windows allocates memory between user programs and the operating system. The default setting of Programs will allocate the most memory to the applications a user runs, while the System Cache setting will allocate a greater portion of memory to the operating system. Your applications

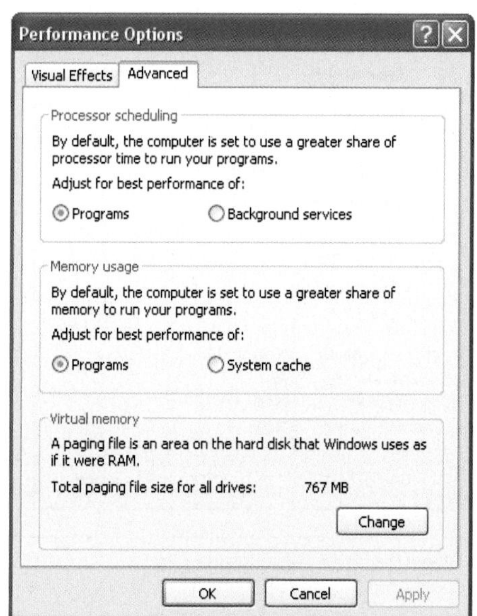

• The Advanced page of Performance Options

will perform better if you keep the default setting, but you may not experience any change if your computer has plenty of memory—as is true of many computers sold today that have memory of 512MB or greater.

Virtual Memory

> The swap file in Windows 9*x* is named win386.swp and is located in the directory in which Windows is installed (usually C:\Windows).

When a Windows computer is running low on memory available for the operating system and any loaded application programs, it will use and manage a portion of disk space as if it were RAM. This is called **virtual memory**, and Windows uses a special paging file, pagefile.sys, to allocate disk space for virtual memory. By default, Windows creates this file in the root of C: and sets the size to one and a half times the installed physical RAM.

Your life will be much simpler, and Windows' overall performance will be better and more stable, if you do not modify the default settings on your computer. The Virtual Memory settings on the Advanced page of Performance Options is the place to go if you can't resist taking control of such settings. Simply click the Change button to see the options for modifying Virtual Memory settings. These settings include the size and location of the page file, and the number of page files used. On Windows servers, administrators may relocate the page file to another volume, preferably on a separate hard disk that does not contain the operating system files, but this is not usually necessary on the desktop versions of Windows, because the performance demands are not anywhere near those required of network servers. Also, moving the page file may disable a feature in Windows—when Windows experiences a stop error, it can write debugging information to the paging file, but only if the paging file is on the boot partition. Therefore, although an optimum virtual memory configuration would have the paging file on a separate physical hard disk, one should also be created on the boot partition in case of a stop error.

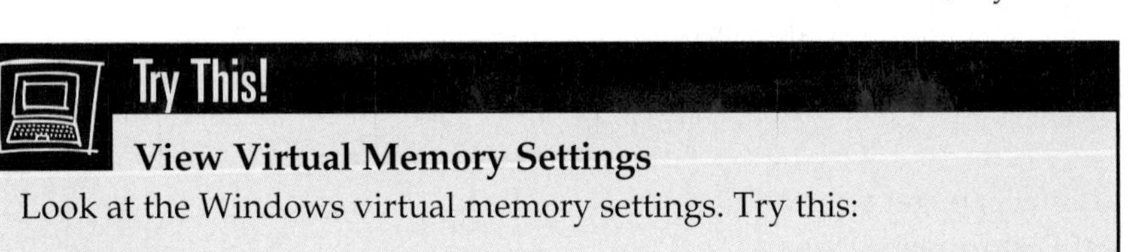

Try This!

View Virtual Memory Settings

Look at the Windows virtual memory settings. Try this:

1. Log on as an Administrator. Open the System applet in Control Panel and select the Advanced tab.
2. On the Advanced page, locate the Performance area and select the Settings button for that area. This will open the Performance Options dialog box. Select the Advanced page.
3. On the Advanced page, locate the Virtual Memory section and select the Change button.
4. View, but do not change, the settings; then click Cancel to close each of the open dialog boxes.

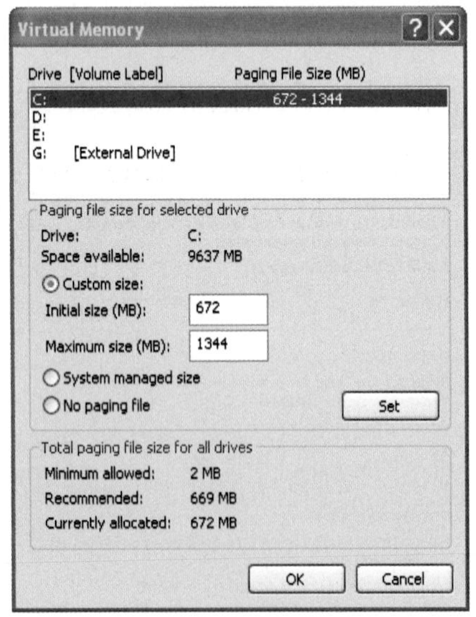

• The Virtual Memory dialog box

Performance Monitoring

Performance monitoring is something that is usually done on network servers, not on Windows desktop computers. Server administrators use performance monitoring to ensure that the quality of service is maintained, and as an early warning of potential problems that show up first as performance problems. All Windows server products have performance monitoring tools, and several of these tools are also available in the desktop versions of Windows (Windows NT 4.0 Workstation, Windows 2000, and Windows XP). One such tool, Performance Monitor, is found in Windows NT 4.0 in Start | Administrative Tools | Performance

Monitor. Beginning with Windows 2000, Performance Monitor is replaced by a console called Performance containing two nodes: System Monitor and Performance Logs and Alerts.

System Monitor is even prepared for the occasion when a computer has more than one of an object, like two physical hard drives or two processors. Each of these can be monitored as a different instance.

System Monitor

System Monitor, available in both Windows 2000 and Windows XP Professional, is much like Windows NT 4.0's Performance Monitor in that it allows an administrator to gather and view performance data involving memory, disks, processor, network, and other objects. Each object has one or more counters that you may select for monitoring. System Monitor displays the data in real time in a report, graph, or histogram (bar chart). Open System Monitor in Windows XP Professional by selecting Start | All Programs | Administrative Tools | Performance. When you first open System Monitor, it displays three commonly used counters, each from a separate object:

- A counter for pages per second of the memory object
- A counter for average disk queue length of the physical disk object
- A counter for the percent of processor time used by the processor object

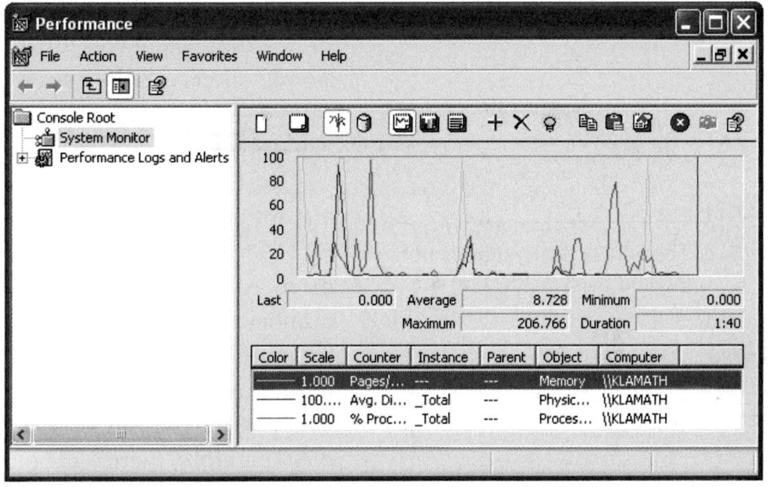

• System Monitor displaying data in a graph

To learn more about System Monitor, first select the System Monitor node in the Performance console, and then click the Help button (yellow question mark).

Performance Logs and Alerts

The Performance Logs and Alert node in the Performance console actually allows three types of activities. You can create alerts, which are discussed in the troubleshooting section of this chapter, and you can create two types of logs files, described here:

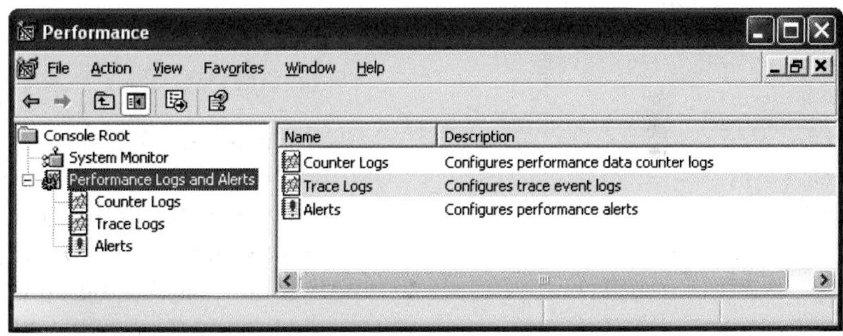

• Performance Logs and Alerts options

- **Counter Logs** track the same performance counters that you can track in real time with System Monitor, but save the information in a log file to be reviewed after the fact.
- **Trace Logs** track events rather than performance counters.

Windows File Systems

As you learned in earlier chapters, a file system is the on-disk logical organization of a disk volume for storing files, as well as code, within an operating system that allows the OS to store and manage files on disk. The on-disk logical structure is placed there when an operating system formats a disk. Depending on the version of Windows you use, you can select from two or three supported file systems when you format a disk. File systems have been discussed in previous chapters, so we will just provide some summary information here.

FAT File Systems in Windows

The FAT file systems have a logical structure that includes a file allocation table (FAT—hence the name of the file system) and a directory structure. The FAT enables the OS to allocate space on disk to files, while a directory gives the OS a place for identifying information about each file. The FAT file system used by DOS on a hard disk is now called the FAT16 file system. The FAT32 file system was introduced in Windows 95 OEM Service Release version 2. The FAT32 file system can use larger hard disk partitions and allocates disk space more efficiently. The FAT12 file system is used by DOS and Windows OSs when formatting floppy disks.

The FAT32 file system is not supported by Windows NT 4.0.

The numbers *12, 16,* and *32* refer to the size of each entry in the FAT table. On a FAT12-formatted floppy disk, each entry is 12 bits long; on a FAT16-formatted drive, each entry is 16 bits long, and on a FAT32-formatted drive, each entry is 32 bits long. These entries hold binary values used to number the allocation units on the volume. Therefore, the length of the entry limits the number of entries the FAT table can hold, and thus the maximum number of clusters that can be used on a disk. The data space on each disk volume is divided up into the number of clusters the FAT table can handle. Therefore, there will be 1 sector per cluster on a floppy disk, but on hard disk volumes the cluster size may be as large as 64 sectors. Of all the FAT file systems, FAT 32, with its ability to manage more clusters, has the smallest cluster size and wastes the least amount of space.

Windows NTFS File Systems

The NTFS file systems are available in all versions of Windows beginning with Windows NT, but excluding the Windows 9*x* versions. The main NTFS logical structure is a Master File Table. Windows uses a transaction processing system to track changes in NTFS, adding a measure of transaction-level recoverability to the file system. It is similar to what your bank uses to track transactions, and it will roll back incomplete transactions. NTFS allocates disk space more efficiently than FAT, and NTFS5 theoretically supports a volume size of 256TB (terabytes), but the current actual limit within Windows 2000 and Windows XP is 2TB.

From the beginning, the NTFS file system provided file and folder security not available on FAT volumes. Since the introduction of NTFS5 in Windows 2000, the version of NTFS in Windows NT 4.0 is now referred to as NTFS4. In addition to file and folder security, NTFS4 supports file compression, while NTFS5 has added file encryption and an indexing service.

File Systems for CDs and DVDs

Optical disks require special Windows file system drivers. The CD-ROM File System (CDFS) allows Windows OSs to read CD-ROMs and to read and write to writeable CDs (CD-R) and rewriteable CDs (CD-RW). Windows NT 4.0 does not natively support any writeable or rewriteable CDs. The universal disk format (UDF) is a file system driver required for Windows to read DVD ROMs and to read and write DVD-R and DVD-RW. Windows XP has a DVD-RAM driver that supports the 4.7GB DVD-RAM disk standard.

The Windows Startup Process

Now you'll learn more about the Windows startup process common to Windows NT 4.0, Windows 2000, and Windows XP Professional. You will learn the roles of the critical files for Windows startup and the locations of these files. This information is important to know so that if a failure occurs due to a missing file during startup, you can identify the missing file. You will also learn how to create a Windows startup disk, an important tool for solving Windows startup problems. In this discussion, the term "Windows" applies to any of these three operating systems, and we will only refer to the specific Windows version name when necessary to address a difference among these three versions.

Windows 9*x* OSs are excluded from the following discussion. They have a different startup process using the following files: IO.SYS, MSDOS.SYS, CONFIG.SYS (if present), IFSHLP .SYS, COMMAND.COM (for non-GUI startup), AUTOEXEC.BAT (if present), HIMEM.SYS, WIN .COM, WIN.INI, SYSTEM.INI, SYSTEM.DAT, USER.DAT, and VMM32.VXD.

Windows Boot and System Files

Windows is a very large and complicated OS, and for it to start, many files have to be brought into memory while the OS is starting up. These include **boot files**, which reside in the root of drive C:, and **system files** that reside in folders below the folder in which you installed Windows. In Microsoft terminology, the partition that contains the boot files is called the **system partition**, and the partition containing the system files is called the **boot partition**. Counterintuitive? Definitely, but in most cases, the system partition and the boot partition are one and the same—the partition given the volume letter C:. However, it is possible to install Windows with C: as the system partition, and another volume, D: or E:, as the boot partition. Table 8-4 lists the Windows boot files, all located in the root of the system partition.

Try This!

Use My Computer to View the Boot Files

By default, many of the files listed in Table 8-4 are hidden from view in My Computer/Windows Explorer. You can view the boot files in My Computer, but first, look at your current view settings and modify them, as necessary, to display the boot files on the root of C:. Try this:

1. Open My Computer and look at the contents of the root of C:. Are NTLDR and NTDETECT.COM visible? Can you see the file name extensions on the files that are visible? If you can answer yes to both questions, do not make changes to your view settings and skip to step 3. If the answer is no, go to step 2.
2. Select Tools | Folder Options. On the View page, select Show Hidden Files And Folders and deselect two boxes: Hide Extensions For Known File Types and Hide Protected Operating System Files. Then click OK to close the Folder Options dialog box.
3. Confirm that you can see NTLDR and NTDETECT.COM, and that file extensions are visible. Many other files will also be visible.

Now consider the location of the system files. The full path to this location, including the drive letter and subdirectories, will vary based on the folder location in which Windows is installed. In the following table and elsewhere in this chapter, we use the variable *systemroot* to represent this

Table 8-4	Windows Boot Files	
File Name	**Location**	**Description**
BOOT.INI	C:\	Contains the OS Selection menu
BOOTSECT.DOS	C:\	Only present when a computer is configured to dual-boot between Windows NT/2000/XP and Windows 9*x* or DOS
NTBOOTDD.SYS	C:\	SCSI device driver (rarely needed)
NTDETECT.COM	C:\	Hardware detection program
NTLDR	C:\	Windows operating system loader started by the OS loader program in the boot sector of C:

location, since it may be different from system to system. Most often the *systemroot* is C:\WINNT in Windows NT and Windows 2000, or C:\WINDOWS in Windows XP. Table 8-5 lists the system files used during Windows startup, a brief description, and the location of each file.

Most of the registry hives are loaded during Windows startup. The DEFAULT hive is used as a user profile until a user logs on locally. Table 8-6 lists the registry hives loaded during startup.

Phases of the Startup Process

The Power-On Self-Test and initial startup phase are common to all PCs and were described in Chapter 2.

The Windows startup process has several phases on a typical desktop computer: the Power-On Self-Test phase, initial startup phase, boot loader phase, detect and configure hardware phase, logon phase, and plug-and-play device detection phase. Through these phases, the operating system is built, much like a building, from the ground up, with more levels and complexity added at each phase. Learn about these phases in the order in which they occur:

BIOS and CMOS were described in Chapter 1.

Power-On Self-Test

This phase, common to all PCs, starts when a computer is turned on or restarted. The CPU loads the BIOS programs from a special read-only memory (ROM) chip, beginning with the Power-On Self-Test (POST). POST tests system

Table 8-5	Windows System Files	
File Name	**Location**	**Description**
CSRSS.EXE	*systemroot*\SYSTEM32\	User-mode portion of the Windows subsystem
Device driver files	*systemroot*\SYSTEM32\DRIVERS	For example: acpi.sys, disk.sys, ftdisk, and hundreds of others
HAL.DLL	*systemroot*/SYSTEM32	Hardware abstraction layer software provided by a computer manufacturer as a software layer between the hardware and the OS, hiding (abstracting) the details and making all systems appear the same to the OS
PAGEFILE.SYS	C:\	The file used by the virtual memory manager
SERVICES.EXE	*systemroot*\SYSTEM32	Service controller contains code for several services
SMSS.EXE	*systemroot*\SYSTEM32	Session manager initializes drivers and services
Win32k.sys	*systemroot*\SYSTEM32	Kernel-mode portion of the Windows subsystem

Table 8-6	Windows Registry Files Loaded During System Startup (NTUSER.DAT is not listed here because it is not loaded until a user logs on.)	
File Name	**Location**	**Description**
DEFAULT	*systemroot*\SYSTEM32\CONFIG	The default user profile used until a user logs on
SECURITY	*systemroot*\SYSTEM32\CONFIG	The security hive of the registry
SOFTWARE	*systemroot*\SYSTEM32\CONFIG	The software hive of the registry
SYSTEM	*systemroot*\SYSTEM32\CONFIG	The system hive of the registry

hardware, determines the amount of memory present, verifies that devices required for OS startup are working, and loads configuration settings from CMOS memory into main system memory. During the POST, the BIOS briefly displays information on the screen as it tests memory and devices.

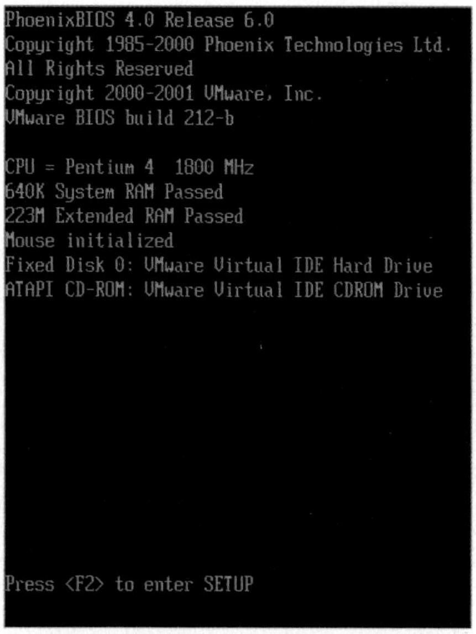

```
PhoenixBIOS 4.0 Release 6.0
Copyright 1985-2000 Phoenix Technologies Ltd.
All Rights Reserved
Copyright 2000-2001 VMware, Inc.
VMware BIOS build 212-b

CPU = Pentium 4  1800 MHz
640K System RAM Passed
223M Extended RAM Passed
Mouse initialized
Fixed Disk 0: VMware Virtual IDE Hard Drive
ATAPI CD-ROM: VMware Virtual IDE CDROM Drive

Press <F2> to enter SETUP
```

• Power-On Self-Test information is displayed briefly.

Initial Startup Phase

In this phase, the BIOS code uses CMOS settings to determine what drives can be used to start an OS, and the order in which the system will search these drives in attempting to begin the OS startup process. One common order is A:, then a CD drive, then C:, in which case, the system will look for a bootable floppy disk in drive A:. If one is not there, it will try to boot from a CD-ROM (if present). If there is no bootable CD-ROM present, then it will try to boot from the hard disk, loading the master boot record (MBR), the first sector on a hard disk, into memory. The BIOS passes control of the system to this code, which then uses information in the partition table (also located in the MBR) to find the first sector of the active partition (the boot sector), which is then loaded into memory as the boot code. The job of the boot code is to identify the file system on the active partition, and to find the NTLDR file and load it into memory.

Boot Loader Phase

Once NTLDR is loaded into memory, it takes control, switches the processor to protected mode, starts the file system (the in-memory code that can read and write to an NTFS or FAT volume), reads the BOOT.INI file, and in some cases, displays the OS Selection menu. Windows NT 4.0 displays this menu by default, but Windows 2000 and Windows XP only display this menu if it lists more than one operating system, as in the case of a dual-boot configuration. Then, if you select Windows *9x* or DOS from the OS selection menu, NTLDR loads the

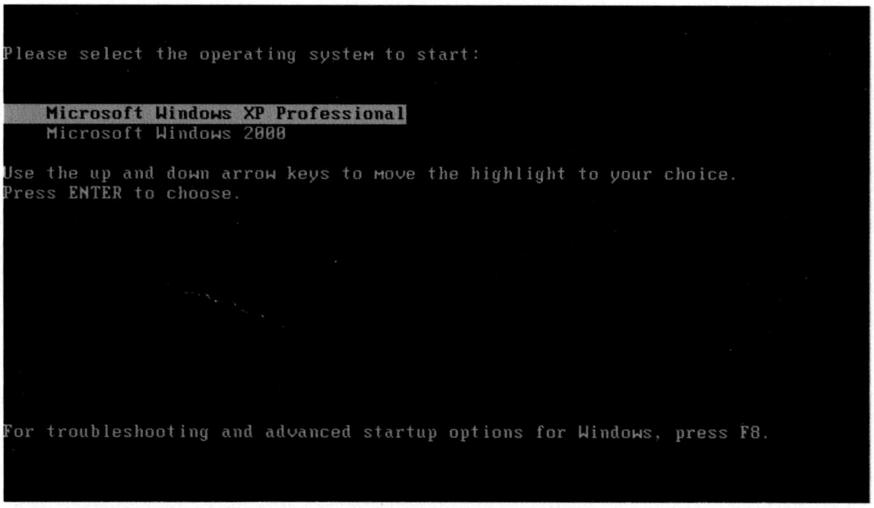

```
Please select the operating system to start:

    Microsoft Windows XP Professional
    Microsoft Windows 2000

Use the up and down arrow keys to move the highlight to your choice.
Press ENTER to choose.

For troubleshooting and advanced startup options for Windows, press F8.
```

• The Windows XP OS Selection menu showing two OS choices

Inside Information

Windows Environment Settings

Windows, like DOS, has a special location where it stores messages, in the form of environment variables. In Windows these variables are stored in the registry and can be placed there through the Environment Variable button on the Advanced page of the System Properties dialog box. These variables are used by the OS and other programs.

file called BOOTSECT.DOS, and NTLDR is out of the picture while BOOTSECT.DOS loads one of the earlier OSs. Normally, one of the three Windows OSs studied here is selected from the OS selection menu (either automatically as the default, or manually), and NTLDR moves to the next phase.

Detect and Configure Hardware Phase

NTLDR starts NTDETECT.COM, which in turn scans the hardware in the computer and reports the list to NTLDR for later inclusion in the registry.

Kernel Loading Phase

NTLDR loads NTOSKRNL.EXE (the kernel) after locating it through the BOOT.INI file. Or if no BOOT.INI file is present, NTLDR loads the kernel from the default location for this version of Windows. NTLDR then passes the hardware information to the kernel. The hardware abstraction layer file for the system, HAL.DLL, is also loaded into memory. NTLDR loads the SYSTEM portion of the registry and the drivers that are configured (through registry settings) to load at startup. All of this code is loaded into memory but not immediately initialized (made active). Once all startup components are loaded, the kernel is initialized and takes over the startup process. The kernel initializes the components (services and drivers) required for startup. Once that is accomplished, the kernel scans the registry for other components that were not required during startup but are part of the configuration, and then loads and initializes them. The kernel also starts the session manager (SMSS.EXE), which creates the system environment variables and loads the kernel-mode Windows subsystem code that switches Windows from text mode to graphics mode. Then session manager starts the user-mode Windows subsystem code (CSRSS.EXE). Just a few of session manager's other tasks include creating the virtual memory paging file (pagefile.sys) and starting the Windows logon service (WINLOGON.EXE), which leads us to the next phase.

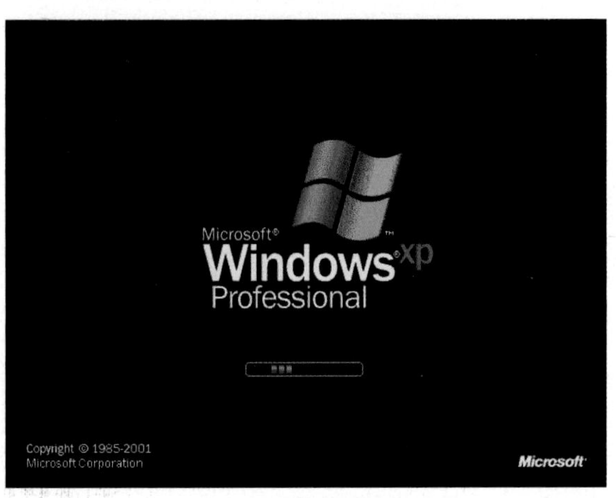

• This screen is displayed during the kernel loading phase.

All Windows-based applications run in the Windows subsystem, which has two parts: a kernel-mode portion, which handles requests for access to system resources from the user-mode portion (the second part), which is restricted in its access and must therefore make requests through the kernel-mode portion.

Logon Phase

The key player in this phase is the Windows logon service that supports logging on and logging off and also starts the service control manager (SERVICES.EXE) and the local security authority (LSASS.EXE). At this point, the Begin logon prompt appears. When a user presses CTRL-ALT-DELETE, the Windows logon service responds by displaying the Logon To Windows dialog box. A user enters a user name and password, which the local security authority uses to authenticate the user in the local security accounts database.

But a lot of other things happen during this phase. Logon scripts are run (if they exist), startup programs for various applications are run, and noncritical services are started. Windows finds instructions to run these programs and services in the following registry locations:

- HKEY_LOCAL_MACHINE\SOFTWARE\Microsoft\Windows\CurrentVersion\RunOnce

- HKEY_LOCAL_MACHINE\SOFTWARE\Microsoft\Windows\CurrentVersion\Policies\Explorer\Run
- HKEY_LOCAL_MACHINE\SOFTWARE\Microsoft\Windows\CurrentVersion\Run
- HKEY_CURRENT_USER\Software\Microsoft\Windows NT\CurrentVersion\Windows\Run
- HKEY_CURRENT_USER\Software\Microsoft\Windows\CurrentVersion\Run
- HKEY_CURRENT_USER\Software\Microsoft\Windows\CurrentVersion\RunOnce

Windows also starts programs located in the following folders:

- *systemdrive*\Documents and Settings\All Users\Start Menu\Programs\Startup
- *systemdrive*\Documents and Settings*username*\Start Menu\Programs\Startup

Inside Information

Plug-and-Play Detection

During the Logon phase, Windows 2000 and Windows XP perform plug-and-play detection, using BIOS, hardware, device drivers, and other methods to detect new plug-and-play devices. If a new device is detected, Windows allocates system resources and installs device drivers.

Modifying System Startup with the BOOT.INI File

The BOOT.INI file holds important information used by NTLDR to locate the operating system, and in the case of a dual-boot configuration, to display an OS selection menu. In Windows NT, this menu is displayed by default, even if the system is not dual-boot. This file can be edited directly, but it is an advanced task performed by system administrators. However, you can edit this file indirectly through the GUI. In Windows NT, you could do this through System Properties | Startup/Shutdown. In Windows 2000 and Windows XP, you can do this though System Properties | Advanced | Startup And Recovery. In all versions, the information that modifies the BOOT.INI file is in the top of this dialog box, in the System startup section. You learned about the System Failure settings shown on the bottom of this page in Chapter 5.

In all three versions, a drop-down list lets you choose the default OS in a dual-boot system, and another setting allows you to set

Cross Check

DOS Startup

Go back to Chapter 2, review the section "The DOS Bootup Process," and then answer these questions:

1. What is the difference between a cold boot and a warm boot?

   ____

   ____

2. Where is the bootstrap loader found, and what role does it play?

   ____

   ____

3. What is located in the first physical sector of a hard disk?

   ____

   ____

4. What is located in the first sector of each logical drive?

   ____

   ____

Still curious? Learn more about the BOOT.INI file and an alternative way to edit it. Point your browser to `www.microsoft.com`, and search for the article "HOW TO: Edit the Boot.ini File in Windows XP." Learn more about BOOT.INI switches in another article on the Microsoft site: "Available switch options for the Windows XP and the Windows Server 2003 Boot.ini files."

the length of time the OS selection menu is displayed. In Windows XP you also have a setting that controls the length of time recovery options are displayed, when needed. Plus, you have an Edit button that opens Notepad with the BOOT.INI file loaded in it for editing. We strongly recommend that you do not directly edit the BOOT.INI file without a great deal of preparation and/or expert advice.

Here is an example of a BOOT.INI file for a dual-boot installation in which Windows 2000 is booted from the first partition on the hard disk (C:) and Windows XP is booted from the second partition on the hard disk (D:):

```
[boot loader]
timeout=30
default=multi(0)disk(0)rdisk(0)partition(1)\WINDOWS
[operating systems]
multi(0)disk(0)rdisk(0)partition(1)\WINDOWS="Windows XP
Professional" /fastdetect
multi(0)disk(0)rdisk(0)partition(2)\WINNT="Windows 2000
Professional" /fastdetect
```

The lines beginning with "multi" provide the location information to NTLDR in a format called an ARC path: `multi (0) disk (0) rdisk (0) partition (1)\WINDOWS`. In brief, this identifies the disk controller, the hard disk on that controller, the partition on that hard disk, and finally, the folder in that partition in which the OS is located. The words that appear in quotes on these lines will be displayed on the OS Selection menu; anything after the quotes is a switch that affects how Windows starts up. For instance, the /fastdetect switch is the default switch used with Windows 2000 and Windows XP. It causes NTDETECT to skip parallel and serial device enumeration. While there are many other BOOT.INI switches, you should not normally need to manually add any to your desktop installation of Windows.

Troubleshooting Windows Problems

When troubleshooting Windows problems, you should first apply a strategy for gathering helpful information about the problem. For those times when you are troubleshooting another person's computer problems, we have some suggestions in a topic we call "Cooperative Troubleshooting." Then, before you roll up your sleeves and dive into troubleshooting, see our suggested proactive tasks. Learn how to use Event Viewer for troubleshooting, how to modify the registry, how to use the Last Known Good Configuration, when to troubleshoot startup problems by first using a startup disk, and then how to use Safe Mode.

Cooperative Troubleshooting

In Chapter 4 we introduced a simple five-step approach to troubleshooting. Now we'll add some tips for working with a person who is experiencing problems with a Windows computer. That requires knowledge, powers of observation, and people skills. Keep in mind that although a computer may be of great interest to you, most people just want it to behave and be a reliable tool. Patience pays off!

You may be called upon to help another user because computer support is in your job description, or just because you seem more knowledgeable to the other person and you are handy, working in the next cubicle at the office or sitting at another computer in the school lab. Whatever the situation, remain respectful of the user. In fact, for this discussion, we will call the person requesting help the "customer" so that we remember to be respectful to them. Whatever the circumstances, or your troubleshooting experience, it may be enhanced by the following three suggestions:

Elicit Problem Symptoms from Customers

Ask the customer to carefully describe the symptoms relating to the problem, including anything unusual that happened immediately before the problem occurred, such as unusual disk activity (noise), the hourglass icon indicating that the system was busy, or any error messages (exactly as they were displayed, if possible). Many people want to tell you their interpretation of what's wrong, rather than the actual symptoms they observed. So try to get them to focus on actual events.

Can't reproduce the problem? Many, but not all, error messages can be viewed "after the fact" in Event Viewer. Learn more about Event Viewer later in this chapter.

Have Customers Reproduce Errors as Part of the Diagnostics Process

If possible, have the customer demonstrate the problem to you and perhaps even reproduce the error messages so that you may document the exact language of the message. This may allow you to use a search engine on the Web to find a solution to the problem. Or, from what the error message shows, you may draw on your own experience to immediately correct the problem.

Windows XP may provide your answer to "What has changed?" in Windows Event Viewer, as well as in System Restore. A change to the system configuration will trigger a restore point.

Identify Recent Changes to the Computer by the User

Whenever you are troubleshooting a problem on a computer that previously functioned normally, you need an answer to the question "What has changed?" This is an important part of the information gathering process. The answer to this question may lead you directly to the cause of the present troubles, and then you can move on to researching the solution, applying it, and testing the results.

Only it's not that easy! The customer may not consider something he or she did to be a change to the computer system. Or, he or she may be afraid of the consequences of accepting responsibility for the current problem. Or, they may simply not know that someone made a change to their system overnight. So tread lightly, and find creative ways to ask this same question. In fact, asking this question directly and too aggressively can result in the response "Nothing! I didn't do anything!"—and things can go downhill from there, because the customer now needs to defend this position of innocent victim. To avoid this pitfall, you might ask when the computer last behaved normally, and then try to work chronologically from there, slowly learning what event may be linked to the problem. Ask if the computer has been moved or any components disconnected recently. Has a new light or other electrical device been added to the vicinity near the computer?

• Trying to get a customer to describe the problem

Proactive Tasks

Several proactive tasks will make troubleshooting easier, or even prevent problems. These include keeping Windows updated, knowing how to use administrative tools like the Runas command, preparing startup disks for each computer, maintaining backups, backing up the registry, and configuring alerts.

Keeping Windows Updated

In Chapters 3, 4, and 5 we explained why Microsoft publishes service packs and updates to Windows and emphasized that you should keep your computer up-to-date. At work or at school the distribution of new service packs and updates may be managed centrally, and you may not be personally involved at all. At home or in a small organization, you may be the administrator of your own computer, and therefore, should know how to configure Automatic Update and how to use Windows Update.

Windows XP Service Pack 2 Windows XP Service Pack 2 (SP2), originally planned for release in fall of 2003, was actually released in August 2004. The reason for the delay was that Microsoft added many new security features, not just patches. They added a central security management console called Security Center, replaced Internet Connection Firewall with an all-new Windows Firewall, and improved the wireless network support so it is both easier and more secure. They also made security improvements in Internet Explorer, Outlook Express, and Instant Messaging—not to mention many changes to the internal code to make the OS more stable and more secure.

Configuring Automatic Update If you are the administrator of your computer and you have Internet access to your computer, you can configure Automatic Update to automatically download critical updates and to optionally automatically install them. This feature is provided with Windows XP, Windows 2000 SP3 (or later), and Windows Server 2003. To configure it, open the Automatic Updates applet in Control Panel, or click on the Automatic Updates tab on the System applet. Figure 8-12 shows the options available for having critical Windows updates downloaded and installed. We prefer the options selected in the figure, which will automatically download the updates, notify the user, and then the user can review the information provided on the update and decide when or if to install it. Automatic Update only looks for critical updates; it is not designed to download the optional updates from the Microsoft web site. To learn how to download optional updates, read on.

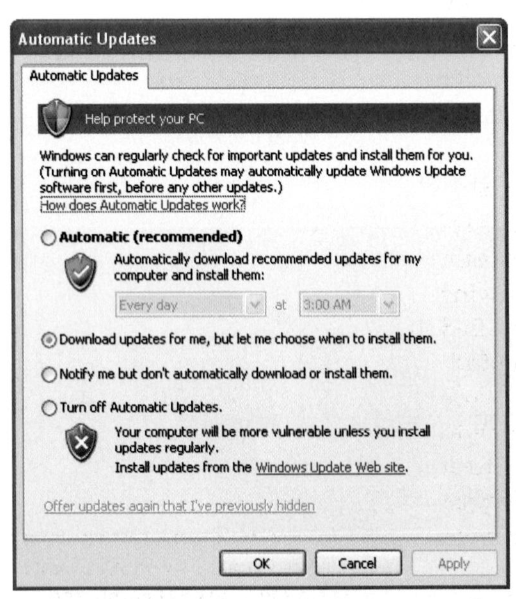

• **Figure 8-12.** Configure Automatic Updates

Working with Windows Update Windows Update is an application with a shortcut on the Start menu of both Windows 2000 and Windows XP. When you open Windows Update, it will connect to the Microsoft Windows Update web site, where you can choose to have it check the status of your computer and then provide a list of updates that you may choose to download and install. It differs from Automatic Update in that you must initiate this connection and that Windows Update allows you to download and install more than just critical updates. In preparation for SP2, Microsoft modified the Windows Update web site to make it easier to use. The Express Install option will scan your computer and then download all the appropriate critical updates combined together in one package.

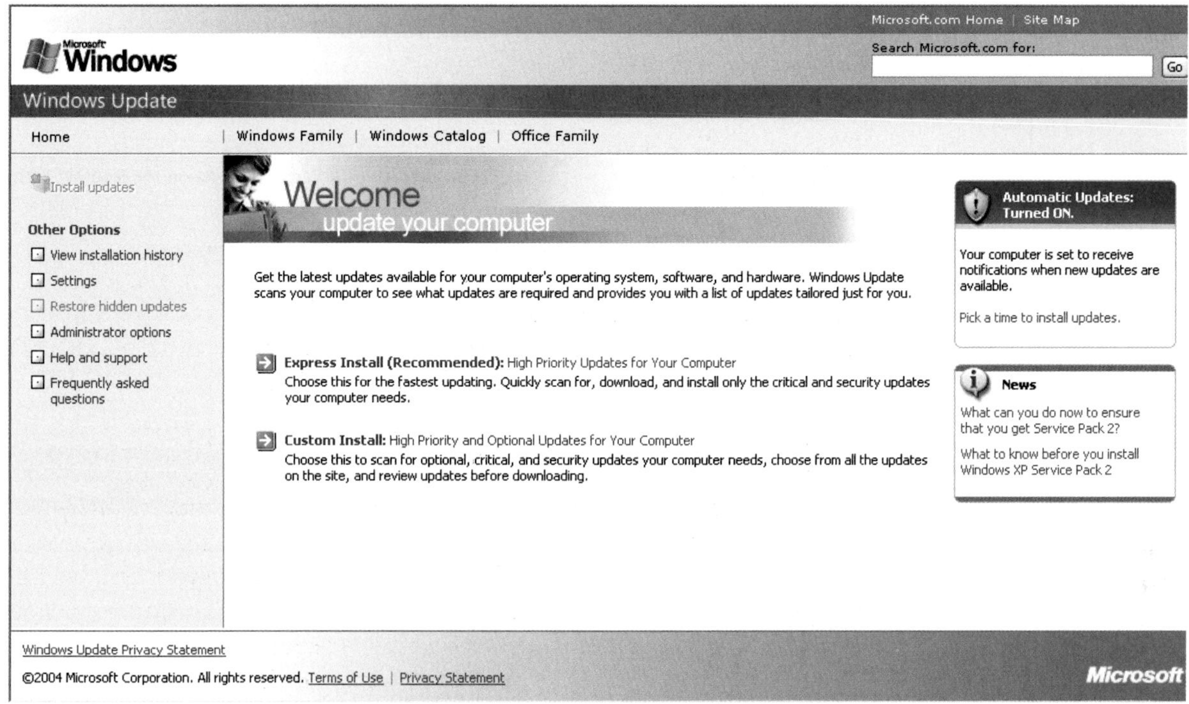

• The improved Windows Update web site

The new Custom Install option also scans your computer and then provides a list of critical updates, noncritical system updates, and updates to your installed drivers (see Figure 8-13). You may then browse through the results and examine the details of each update, select the ones you wish to install, and initiate the download and installation of those that you have selected.

Using Runas

Runas is a command-line command that allows you to run a single command using a user account other than the one with which you logged on. The use of Runas is not, in itself, a proactive task. However, it is being proactive to learn what this command is, and to learn a way to use it for managing and solving problems on computers before you need it. Support professionals often find themselves working on a customer computer, logged on as a user without administrative rights, but needing to install software, update or roll back device drivers, or to perform another function that requires administrative rights to the user's computer. Remember, an ordinary user account can look but not touch, which you can test by trying to open Device Manager when logged on as an account other than an Administrator. Device Manager will open after first displaying the message shown in Figure 8-14.

You could log off and then log back on as a local administrator, but beginning with Windows 2000, there is a command, Runas, that will let you stay logged on with the user's account, but run a command as an administrator.

> The Runas command is similar to the Linux SU command, which you'll learn about in Chapter 11.

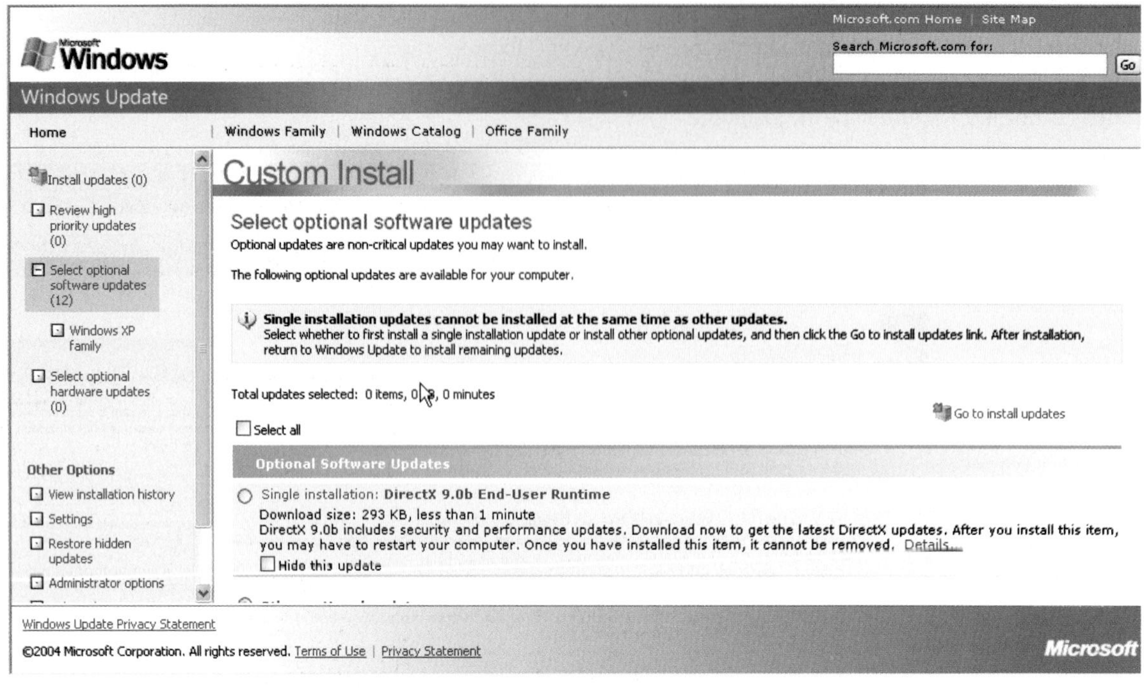

• **Figure 8-13.** Use Custom Install to download and install critical and noncritical updates.

If you use the Windows Help program to research the Runas command or to open a command prompt and enter **runas /?**, you will see all the options for using this command, and you will probably decide that it is simply too complicated! Don't give up, because although the Runas command has many options, the syntax for using it to run a command using a local administrator account is quite simple:

```
runas /user:<username> <program>
```

where <username> is the user account for this Runas command, and <program> is the name of the program to be run in the context of the user account.

You may enter the Runas command from Start | Run, but if not entered correctly, it will fail (often without displaying an error message), so we prefer a strategy of creating a shortcut in which you have entered the Runas command correctly to call up the command prompt. The exact syntax for the command you will enter in the shortcut is

```
runas /user:administrator cmd
```

If you log on as an ordinary user and use the Runas command with an Administrator account to run a software installation, the software will be installed into the profile of the logged-on user.

Once the shortcut is tested, copy it to a floppy disk that you can carry to any Windows 2000 Professional or Windows XP Professional computer that has a floppy drive. This will work as long as you know the password of the local Administrator account. A password is required every time you use the Runas command, so other users cannot use this shortcut unless they know the Administrator's password. The next step-by-step will show you how to create the Runas shortcut just described.

• **Figure 8-14.** After closing this dialog box, Device Manager will be displayed in "Don't Touch" mode.

Step-by-Step 8.03

Create and Test a Runas Shortcut

In this step-by-step, you will create a shortcut that you will use to execute the Runas command to allow you to open a command prompt under the context of the Administrator. To complete this exercise, you will need a computer running Windows 2000 or Windows XP Professional. You will need the user name and password for both a local administrator account and a local non-administrator user account.

Step 1

Log onto Windows 2000 or Windows XP Professional as any user account that is not a member of the local Administrators group. Right-click the desktop and select New | Shortcut.

In the text box labeled "Type the location of the item," enter **runas.exe /user:administrator cmd**. (Be sure to include the spaces within the text you must type!) Click Next.

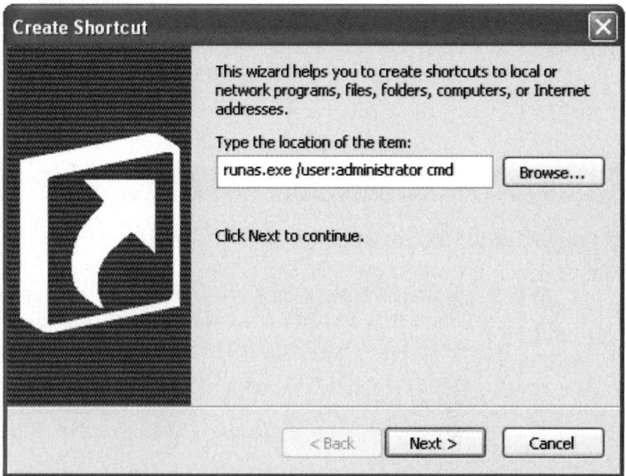

Step 2

In the text box labeled "Type a name for this shortcut," type **Admin CMD Prompt**. Click Finish.

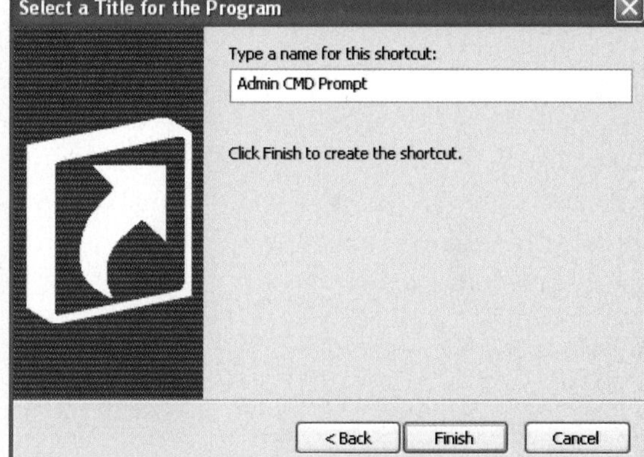

Step 3

Locate the new shortcut on your desktop and open it. At the prompt, type the password for the administrator and press ENTER.

Step 4

You now have a command prompt open in an account that you can use to administer the computer, even when logged on as a user without administrative permissions. You can start any command from this prompt, and it will run in the context of the Administrator.

Step 5

To test this, start Device Manager from the Admin CMD Prompt by entering the name of the management console for Device Manager: **devmgmt.msc**. Device Manager will open without first displaying the message that you don't have sufficient rights, which would happen if you ran it using a non-administrative user account.

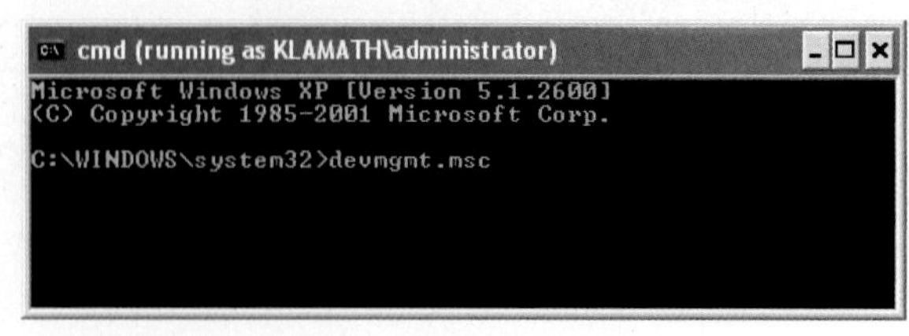

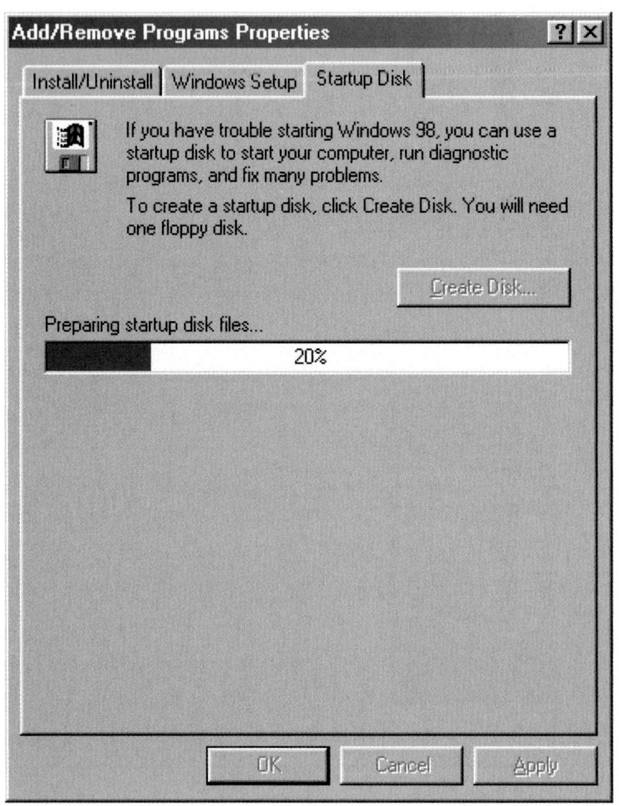

• Create a Windows 98 startup disk from Add/Remove Programs.

Create Startup Disks

Ask anyone with long experience supporting Windows desktop computers if they use startup disks (actually, floppy disks), and you will probably hear about more than one type of startup disk. They will talk about MS-DOS, Windows 98, and Windows NT/2000/XP startup disks. The disks allow you to start an operating system either completely, in the case of MS-DOS and Windows 98 startup disks, or less completely, as in the case of Windows NT/2000/XP startup disks. In either case, these are handy to have when troubleshooting startup problems, and even when preparing a new hard disk for use. Learn how to create these three types of startup disks.

Windows NT/2000/XP Startup Disks One basic fact you can't have missed while learning about the Windows startup process: it is a very complicated OS! A large number of files are critical to getting Windows up and running. Have you wondered what can be done if one of those files is damaged? Not knowing how to solve a problem like this could affect your computing career, or at least ruin your day. The Windows NT 4.0, Windows 2000, and Windows XP startup disks are similar and can only be used through the detect and configure hardware phases. After that, there must be Windows system files on the hard disk to complete the Windows startup. A startup disk should be created for each Windows computer that is configured to boot from a floppy disk drive and it should be kept in a safe place where you can quickly access it in the event of a startup failure.

Windows is far too big to fit onto a floppy disk the way DOS does, but you can easily fit the Windows boot files from the system partition (the root of drive C:) onto a floppy disk. Although you cannot reliably use a startup disk for one version of Windows on a computer running another version of Windows, a startup disk should work on most computers running the same version, as long as both installations of Windows were installed using default locations. The exception will be if one of the computers has a SCSI controller that requires the use of an NTBOOTDD.SYS file. To keep life simple, create a Windows startup disk on each computer, and keep it handy to that computer.

To create a Windows startup disk for Windows NT 4.0, Windows 2000, or Windows XP, first format a floppy disk in Windows. Then copy NTLDR, NTDETECT.COM, BOOT.INI, and (if present) NTBOOTDD.SYS to the floppy disk.

You can use the floppy disk to bypass the Windows boot files in the root of C:. You will find this capability very handy if, when you try to boot normally from the hard disk, an error message indicates that one of those files was not found.

Step-by-Step 8.04

Creating and Testing a Windows Startup Disk

In this step-by-step, you will create a Windows startup disk. You can complete this exercise on any computer running one of the three versions of Windows discussed earlier. To complete this exercise, you will need the following:

- The computer on which you successfully installed Windows NT 4.0 Workstation, Windows 2000, or Windows XP Professional
- A floppy drive A: that is bootable (not all computers today include floppy drives, and not all floppy drives are bootable)
- A single blank floppy disk
- A user name and password for an account that is a member of the Administrators group

Step 1

Log on as an Administrator, insert the floppy disk into the drive, open My Computer, and right-click the icon for drive A: in My Computer (be careful not to click it before you right-click, or it will not allow you to format). Select Format and click Start in the Format dialog box. Click OK in the Warning box. The formatting may take a few minutes (floppy disk drives are slow).

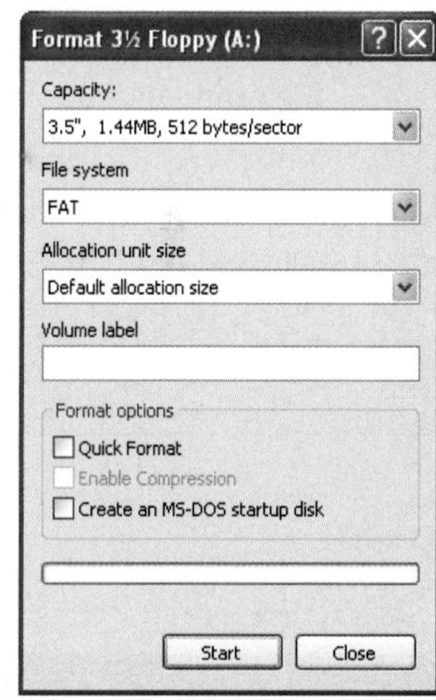

Step 2

When formatting is complete, close the dialog box and return to My Computer. Expand drive C: and locate the following files: NTLDR, NTDETECT.COM, BOOT.INI, and NTBOOTDD.SYS. Don't be concerned if the last file is not present; it is present only if needed for certain hard disk controllers. CTRL-click to select each of the boot files; then use the CTRL-C and CTRL-V method to copy (*not* move!) them to drive A:.

Step 3

When the files have been copied, leave the floppy disk in the drive and restart your computer. The restart should work exactly like a normal restart, except it will be slower, and you will hear drive A: work as the boot files are read from there. After a successful restart, remove the floppy disk, label it "Windows *X* Startup Disk" (where *X* is the version of Windows used), and set it aside for later.

MS-DOS and Windows 98 Startup Disk In addition to a Windows startup disk like the one described earlier in this chapter, you may also need to create MS-DOS startup disks (as described in Chapter 2) and Windows 98 startup disks. Even people who no longer support MS-DOS or Windows 98 desktops still use Windows 98 startup disks. These startup disks actually run MS-DOS. The need for a Windows 98 startup disk depends on the file systems used on Windows computers. This is because these floppy disks will give you access to the hard disk of almost any operating system, provided the system partition has been formatted with FAT16. The FAT16 file system is not normally recommended when the operating system supports FAT32, NTFS4, or NTFS5, but you may encounter systems with advanced OSs that still use the FAT16 file system.

The Windows 98 Startup disk that came packaged with the Windows 98 CD-ROM can be used as an MS-DOS startup disk. You will recognize this floppy disk because it has a printed Microsoft label, which calls the disk a "Boot Disk," and provides setup instructions. When a computer is started with this floppy disk and the menu appears, select choice 2 or 3, which will simply start up MS-DOS (see Figure 8-15). Choice 2 will load a CD-ROM device driver, while choice 3 will not. Both choices will allow access to any local hard disk partitions under 2GB in size formatted with FAT16 or FAT32.

The problem with this floppy disk is that it does not give you many useful MS-DOS utilities. To create a more useful MS-DOS startup disk, one that will include CD-ROM drivers as well as many MS-DOS utilities, create it from within Windows 98. To do this, you will need a computer with the Windows 98 operating system—then use the Startup Disk option of the Add/Remove Programs applet in Control Panel. When you boot from the resulting floppy disk, you will see a menu similar to the one produced by the original Windows 98 Boot Disk, but it will not include the option for starting Windows 98 Setup.

Try This!

Use Regedit to Back Up the Registry

It is quite simple to back up the registry using Regedit. Try this:

1. Launch Regedit by selecting Start | Run, and type **regedit** in the Run box.
2. If you only wish to export a portion of the registry, first select the range in the folder window, and then select File | Export.
3. Notice the Export range at the bottom of the Export Registry File dialog box. It should show the portion of the registry that you selected. You may keep this choice, manually enter another range, or select All if you wish to back up the entire registry.
4. Select a location, enter a file name, and click Save.

• **Figure 8-15.** The Startup Menu from the Windows 98 "Boot Disk" packaged with the Windows 98 CD-ROM

Maintaining Backups and Backing Up the Registry

When troubleshooting, you may need to make changes to Windows that may change the files on disk and may also change the registry—directly or indirectly. Therefore, before attempting any possible solution that involves installing, uninstalling, or reconfiguring *anything,* it is a very good idea to back up the files on the hard disk before you start. If regular backups of the entire computer are maintained, then they will include the entire registry, as well as the operating system files and data files. Before you make any changes, at least do an incremental backup that will include all changes since the last full backup.

If you need to make a change to the registry, you may only need to back up that portion of the registry you will alter.

One of the easiest ways to save your registry settings is to use the Export Registry File option in the Regedit program. You will find this option on the File menu in Regedit for Windows XP, and on the Registry menu in Regedit for Windows NT 4.0 and Windows 2000. If you damage the registry, you can reload the old registry using the Import option from the same menu and selecting the REG file you created.

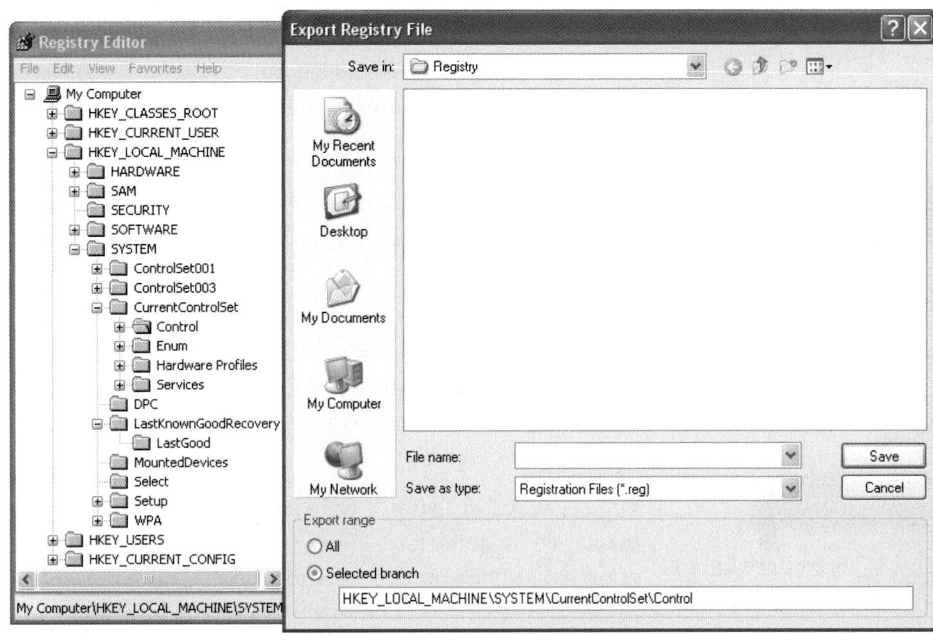

• Use Export Registry File in Regedit to back up all or part of the registry.

Another option for backing up the registry is to use a backup program that is capable of backing up the registry. You can choose among many third-party backup programs, and the Windows Backup program (NTBACKUP .EXE) that comes with Windows NT 4.0, Windows 2000, and Windows XP Professional.

The NT version of Backup only works with a locally attached tape backup system, while the newer versions support local hard disks and can back up to network locations. To back up the registry in Backup for Windows NT 4.0, you must select the folder containing the operating system, normally located at C:\WINNT for Windows NT 4.0. In Windows 2000 and Windows XP Professional, choose Advanced mode and select the System State option. This backs up the registry, boot files, and some related files, but does not back up all of the operating system files or any user data.

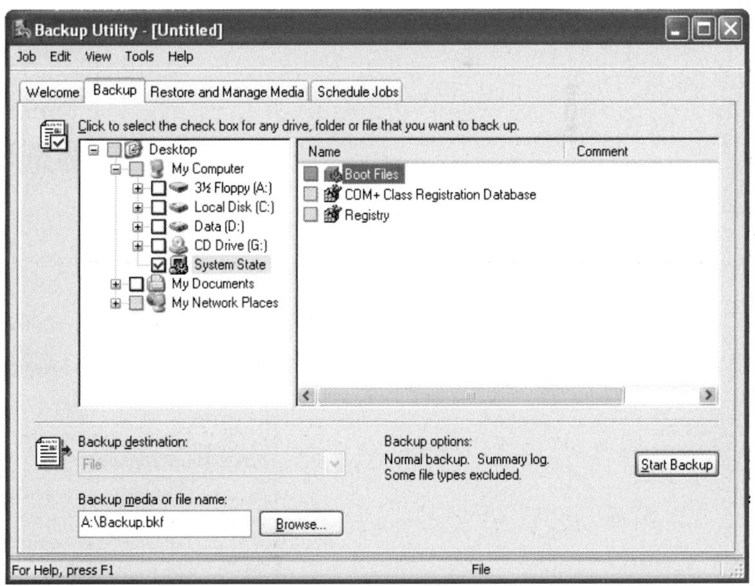

• Select System State to back up the registry.

Alerts

An alert is a notification triggered by some system event. Windows NT 4.0 has a GUI tool, found in the Server applet of Control Panel, that allows an administrator to configure where alert messages are sent, but it does not allow an administrator to configure what events will trigger an alert. Windows 2000 and Windows XP Professional have a GUI tool that gives an administrator a great deal of

A quick way to open the Performance console is Start | Run | **perfmon.msc**.

flexibility in selecting triggering events to configure alerts. For instance, if a hard disk becomes too full, you may have a variety of problems, ranging from extreme slowness to the inability to install an update, but most of us are too busy to notice that our graphic or music files are gobbling up disk space. Configuring an alert would warn you in plenty of time to prevent a major inconvenience. If you would like to be notified when the amount of free disk space reaches 80 percent of its capacity, configure an alert for this threshold. This is done from the Performance Logs and Alerts console found in Windows 2000 and Windows XP in the Performance node of Administrative tools or launched by entering "perfmon.msc" in the Run dialog box.

Step-by-Step 8.05

Configuring an Alert

In this step-by-step, you will use the Performance console in either Windows 2000 or Windows XP Professional to configure an alert.

Step 1

Log on as Administrator (or a member of the Administrators group), and open the Performance console: Start | Run | **perfmon.msc**. Expand the Performance Logs and Alerts node, right-click on Alerts, and select New Alert Settings. In the Name box, type **Disk Space** and select OK. Leave the Comment field blank, and click on the Add button below the Counters box.

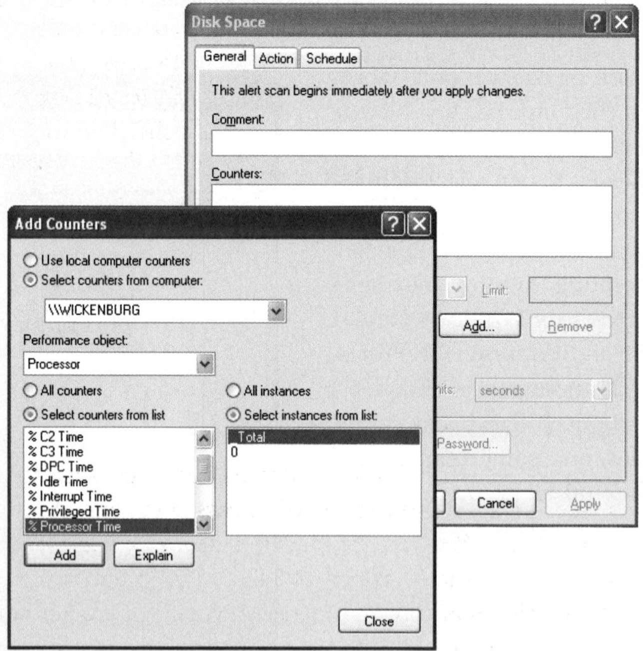

Step 2

In the Add Counters dialog box, open the Performance Object list box, and select Logical Disk. Ensure that Select Counters From List is selected, and then choose % Free Space from the list. Then ensure that Select Instances From List is selected and choose C:. Click Close to return to the Disk Space dialog box.

Step 3

In the Disk Space dialog box open the drop-down list labeled "Alert when the value is" and select Under. In the Limit box, enter **20**, and under "Sample data every," change the Interval to one (1) and change the Units to hours. *Do not* close the Disk Space dialog box.

Step 4

Select the Action tab, which allows you to select the action or actions to be taken when disk space is below the threshold. Leave the default setting, and it will log an entry in the application log. Select the Schedule tab and notice that the scan will begin immediately. Click OK to accept the settings and to close the Disk Space dialog box. The Performance console should now have a new alert named Disk Space. The icon will be red at first, but then will change to green as the alert is started.

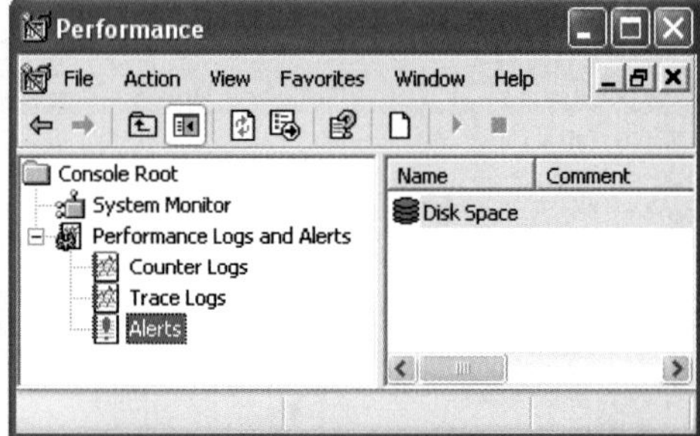

Troubleshooting with Event Viewer

When troubleshooting Windows NT 4.0, administrators often wish for Device Manager, which exists in Windows 9*x*, Windows 2000, and Windows XP. However, we also have often wished that Windows 9*x* had the event logging capabilities of these other versions of Windows. In the versions of Windows that include this great tool, error messages are no longer something fleeting that users must write down in order to troubleshoot—most error messages are saved in event logs. Become familiar with Event Viewer before a problem occurs, so that you will be comfortable using it to research a problem. Use Event Viewer to view logs of system, security, and application events, paying attention to the warning and error logs for messages that can be used to solve problems.

> Open Event Viewer quickly from Start | Run in Windows 2000 or Windows XP by using its file name: **eventvwr.msc**. Or create a shortcut and copy it to a diskette for portability.

Event Logs

Event Viewer has three categories of events: system, application, and security. You can open Event Viewer in Windows NT by selecting Start | Programs | Administrative Tools | Event Viewer. You will find it in Windows 2000 and Windows XP Professional in the Computer Management console found at Start | Control Panel | Administrative Tools | Event Viewer.

System Events The system log shows events involving the OS system components (drivers, services, and so on). The types of events range from normal events, such as startup and shutdown, to warning of a situation that may lead to an error, to actual error events. Even the dreaded "Blue Screen of Death" error messages show up in the system log as stop errors. The system log is the first place to look when a message indicates failure of a component, such as a driver or service. Double-click an event to see the details, including the actual message that appeared on the desktop in a warning. The message itself may lead you to the solution. Each event also has an ID number. We have had varied success in searching the Microsoft Technet web site for a solution using either a portion of the error message or the event ID.

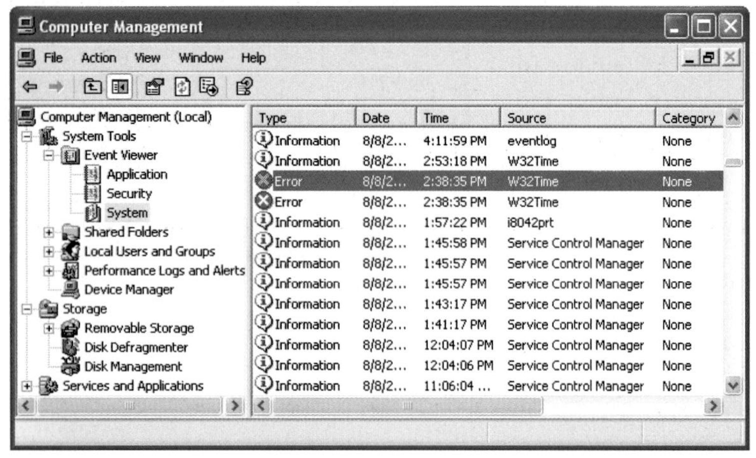

• System event log showing information, and error events

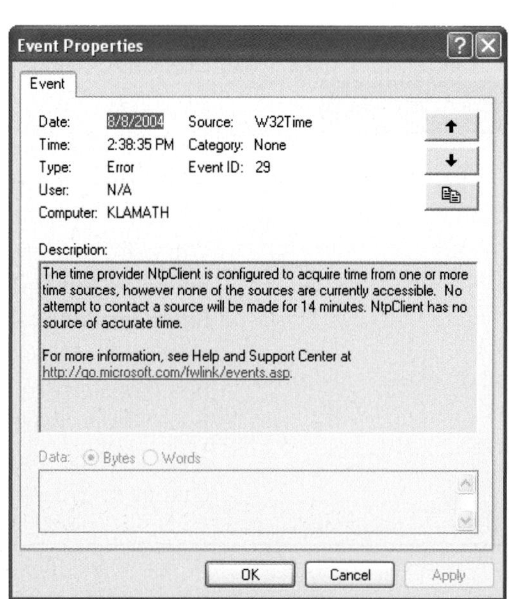

• The details of a system error

Application Events The application log shows events involving applications. These applications may be your office suite of applications or Windows components that run in the GUI, such as Windows Explorer. Some application events are recorded in the application log by a special program called Dr. Watson. If you see a Dr. Watson error on your screen, you will find the error in the application log.

Security Events Security events are not recorded by default; therefore, don't be surprised to find an empty security log in Event Viewer. Security events will only be logged after an administrator turns on auditing. Several types of events can be logged. Auditing is turned on in Windows NT 4.0 by opening User Manager, choosing Policies | Audit, and selecting Audit These Events.

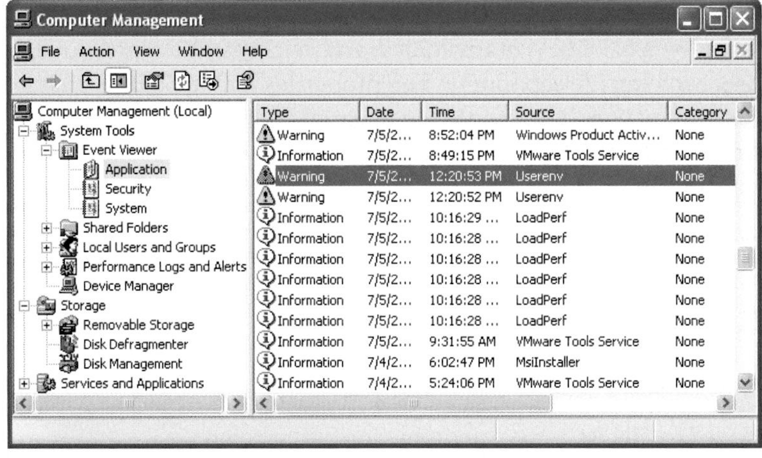

• The application log showing information, warning, and error events

To learn more about Event Viewer, use the help program from within Event Viewer.

Even then, nothing will appear in the security log until events are selected. If the event selected is File and Object Access, the administrator must then select a file or folder and modify its properties so that it is audited.

In Windows 2000 and Windows XP, auditing can be turned on through the Local Security Policy shortcut on the Administrative Tools menu. Auditing is controlled through two sets of settings: Security Settings | Local Policies | Audit Policy, and Security Settings | Local Policies | Security Options. For instance, if Audit Account Logon Events is enabled, the security log will log each successful and/or failed logon attempt. Logging security events comes under the heading of managing security, rather than troubleshooting.

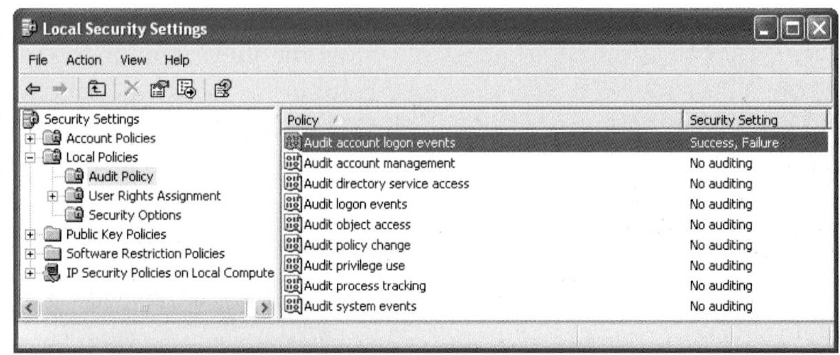

• Turn on auditing in the Local Security Settings.

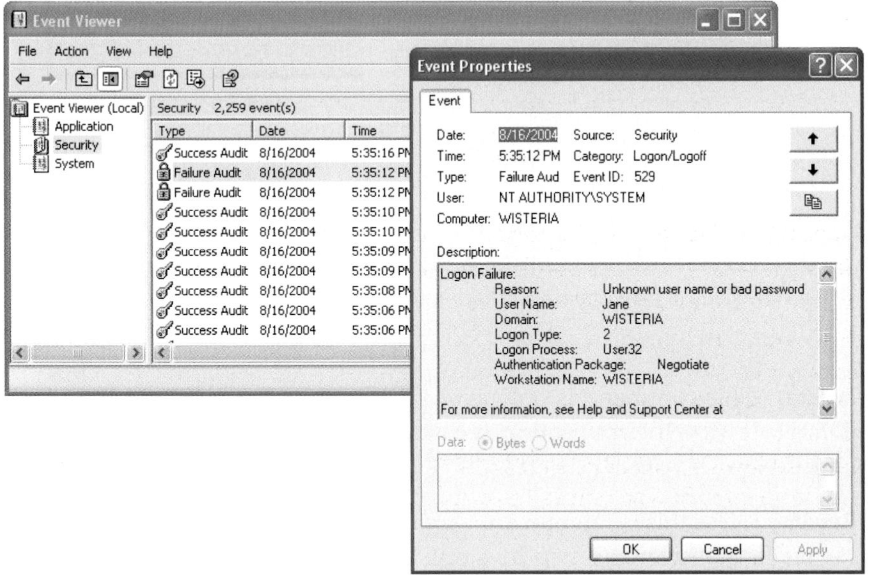

• Events in the security log

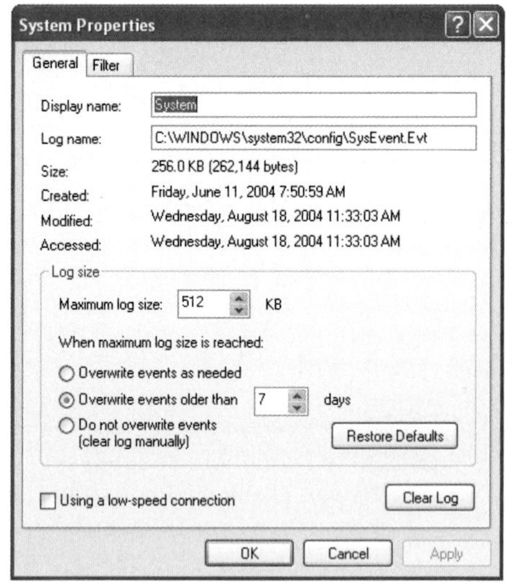

• The properties dialog box for the System log file

Configuring and Saving Event Logs

Windows NT 4.0, Windows 2000, and Windows XP allow you to manage each log file separately. The properties dialog box for each log file will allow you to configure the maximum size to which each event log may grow and the action to take when the event log is full (reaches the maximum size).

In addition, you may clear each log file, save the log file to view later, open a previously saved log file, and create multiple views of the log files. In Windows XP, simply right-click on a log file to choose one of the following actions from the context menu:

Open Log File Use this command to open a previously saved log file.

Save Log File As Save a log file for future reference.

New Log View Create a new node in the Event Viewer console, and then use the View settings to filter the events viewed.

Clear All Events Use this to clear out the event log; this option prompts you to save the log file before clearing, but you may also choose to "lose" all the events.

View This choice brings up the View menu (identical to the list of options from the View item on the menu bar), which allows you to add or remove columns in the detail pane, view all the records, filter the records that are viewed, display events from newest to oldest or oldest to newest, find a record based on search criteria, and customize the view.

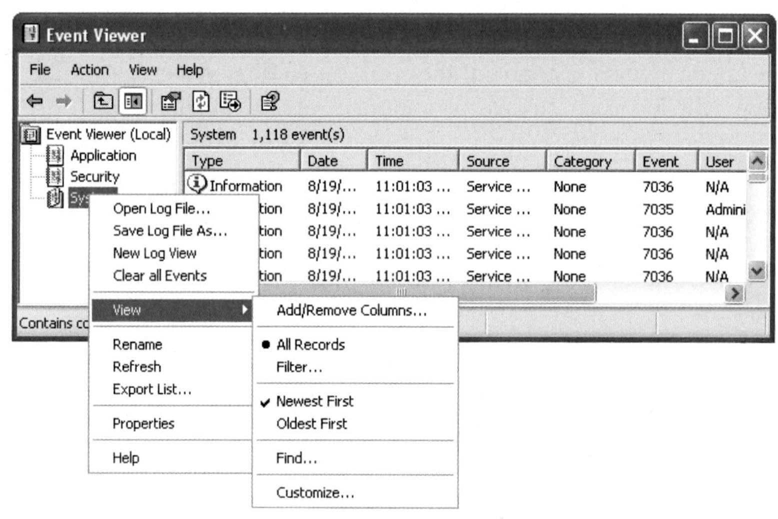

• The View menu of the System event log

Delete This command is only available for any views added beyond the default views of the application, security, and system logs. When used on an added view, it *instantly* deletes it!

Rename Use this command after creating a new view of an Event Viewer log (as in the following step-by-step). Otherwise, the new view has a less-than-meaningful name like "System (2)"!

Refresh Logging is occurring even while you are using Event Viewer. This command will update Event Viewer to show any new events recorded in the log files.

Export List Use this command to export the event list to a file for import into a word processor, spreadsheet, or database program. There are four file format choices to choose from, depending on the type of file your application can import.

Properties Use this command to open the properties dialog box of the selected log. Figure 8-16 shows the Properties dialog box of the System event log.

Solving Problems by Modifying the Registry

The registry is modified frequently: anytime you run the Windows Setup program, anytime you install and/or configure a new device, anytime you make a change through a Control Panel applet, and anytime you change an application preference. In short, the registry is altered whenever you make a change in the operating system or in an application. These are all indirect methods of modifying the registry.

Normally, the only methods you should use to modify the registry are indirect. However, sometimes when you have a problem, the solution you find (after some research) is to modify the registry. The tool you use to do this is the Registry Editor.

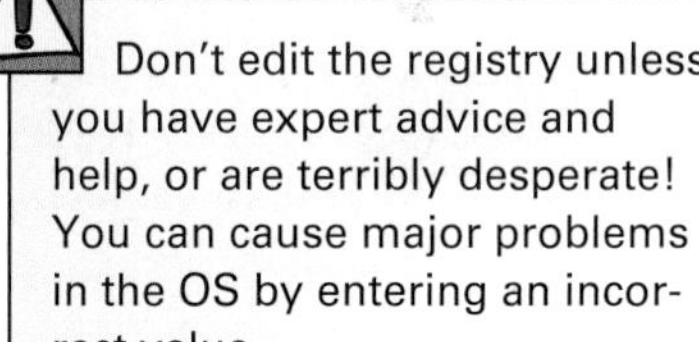

Don't edit the registry unless you have expert advice and help, or are terribly desperate! You can cause major problems in the OS by entering an incorrect value.

When you are troubleshooting, you will run into situations in which it is suggested that you edit the Windows registry. Modifying the registry directly with a registry editor should only be done when there is no other choice. The following step-by-step will allow you to experiment with modifying the registry both indirectly and directly.

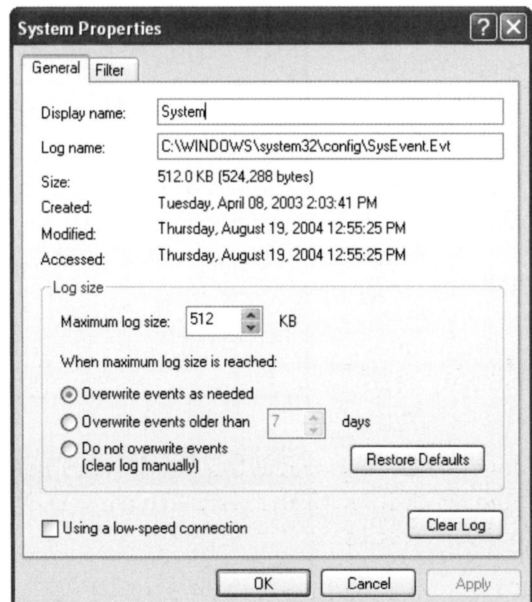

• **Figure 8-16.** The Properties dialog box of the System event log

Step-by-Step 8.06

Modifying the Registry

Step 1

View the registry before making a change. Start Regedit from the Start | Run box. In Regedit, navigate to HKEY_CURRENT_USER\Environment. Make note of the existing value entries for the Environment key, shown in the right pane. The variable %USERPROFILE% represents the location of the user profile, which is most often C:\Documents and Settings*username*.

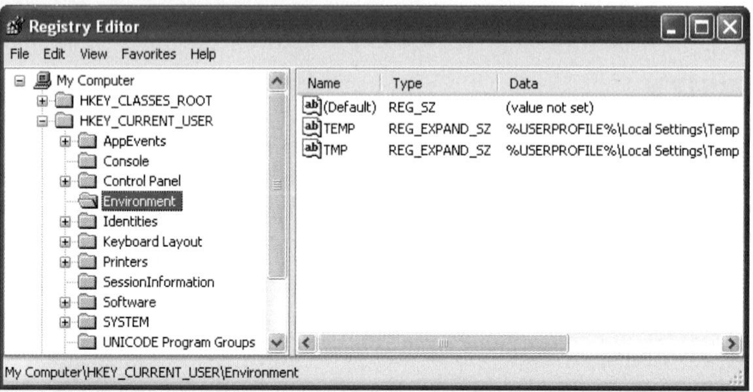

Step 2

Back up this key before modifying it. Right-click the Environment key and select Export. In the File Name text box of the Export Registry File dialog box, enter **environ** (the REG extension will automatically be added when you save the file), click Save, and then close Regedit.

Step 3

From Control Panel, open the System applet and select the Advanced tab. On the Advanced page, select the Environment Variables button. The values shown in the top box show the environment variable for the currently logged-on user, and are the same as the value entries you viewed in the registry, with one exception—they now show the actual path to the user profile.

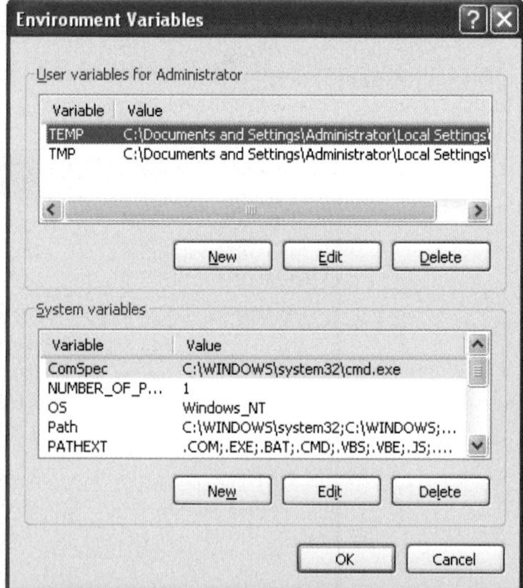

Step 4

Now add a new environment variable for the current user. Click the New button below the User Variables For Administrator box. In the Variable Name box, type **Myname**. In the Variable Value box, type ***yourname*** (your first name). Then click OK to close the New User Variable box, and twice more to close both the Environment Variables box and System Properties.

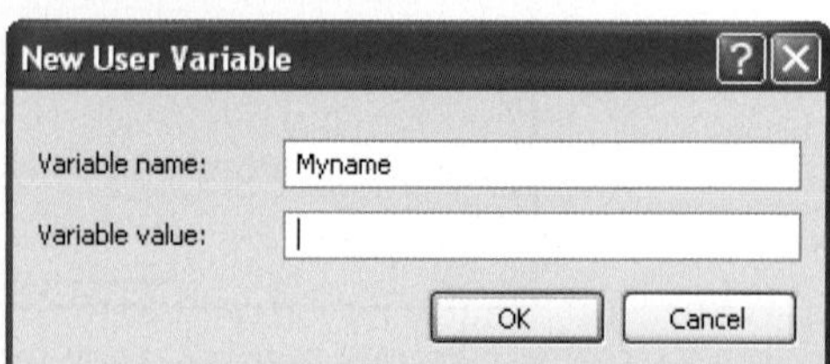

Step 5

Open Regedit and view the changes to the Environment key under HKEY_CURRENT_USER.

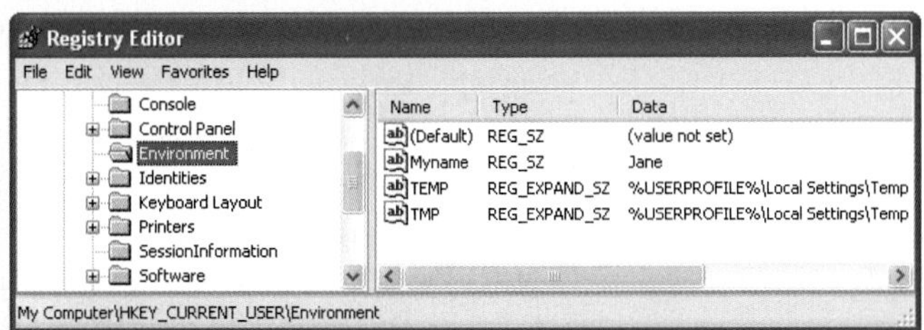

Step 6

Now edit the registry to remove the new value entry. Right-click *Myname* and select Delete. Click Yes in the Confirm box. Confirm that the correct value is removed and close Regedit.

Last Known Good Configuration Recovery

Windows NT 4.0, Windows 2000, and Windows XP all have a startup option called Last Known Good Configuration. Choosing this will select the last set of configuration changes since the last successful user logon and allow you to recover after making a configuration change that causes problems. In all of these operating systems, if you make a change to the configuration, such as adding a new device or modifying the configuration of a device or program, you may recover as long as you have not logged back on since the change. Until a new logon, Windows maintains a copy of the configuration at the last logon—the last known good. A successful logon signals that the new configuration is good, and the old configuration is no longer saved. The modified configuration is now considered to be the last known good.

```
Windows Advanced Options Menu
Please select an option:

    Safe Mode
    Safe Mode with Networking
    Safe Mode with Command Prompt

    Enable Boot Logging
    Enable VGA Mode
    Last Known Good Configuration (your most recent settings that worked)
    Directory Services Restore Mode (Windows domain controllers only)
    Debugging Mode

    Start Windows Normally
    Reboot
    Return to OS Choices Menu

Use the up and down arrow keys to move the highlight to your choice.
```

• The Windows XP Advanced Options Menu

If, after making a configuration change, you experience problems you believe are related to the change, do not log on again, but instead restart Windows. The actual steps after that depend on the version of Windows.

- In Windows NT 4.0, when the OS selection menu appears during the restart, make a selection, and then watch for the prompt to press the space bar to bring up the Hardware Profile/Last Known Good Menu. Then press L to switch to the last known good configuration.
- In Windows 2000 and Windows XP, carefully watch the screen during the restart. You must press the F8 key after the POST and before the Microsoft Windows "splash" screen appears—a graphical screen with the version information. This will bring up the Advanced Options menu from which you can select the Last Known Good Configuration.

Troubleshooting Startup Problems with the Windows Startup Disk

Earlier you created a Windows startup disk for the version of Windows on your lab computer. Now that you're armed with this handy disk, learn how to use it to troubleshoot and solve problems with startup that involve damaged or missing boot files. If your computer fails to start and you see any of the following messages, use the startup disk you created for your computer to start Windows. Once Windows is successfully started from the startup disk, copy the missing file to the root of C:. For startup failures with different messages, check out the use of the Startup options.

The message "NTLDR is missing" may appear when a formatted disk that is not configured to start Windows is left in a floppy drive during startup. Therefore, when you see this message, be sure to first check that there is no disk in the floppy drive.

NTLDR or NTDECTECT.COM Is Missing

This error message indicates that files in the root of C: may be missing or corrupt. If startup fails and you see a message that NTLDR or NTDETECT.COM is missing when you boot from your hard disk, simply boot with your Windows startup disk, and copy the missing file from A:\ to C:\.

NTOSKRNL Is Invalid or Missing

The error message "NTOSKRNL is invalid or missing" does not occur too often, but when it does, this message is usually incorrect and misleading—it is highly unlikely that this file is either invalid or missing. What is more likely is that NTOSKRNL is not where the NTLDR expects it to be. NTLDR finds this location by reading the BOOT.INI file. If a BOOT.INI file is not present, NTLDR attempts to locate this file in the default location for the version of Windows being used. In Windows NT 4.0 and Windows 2000, that location is C:\WINNT32\SYSTEM32, while in Windows XP, the default location is C:\WINDOWS\SYSTEM32. If Windows was not installed in the default location, and the BOOT.INI file is damaged or missing, Windows will fail to start and will display the "NTOSKRNL invalid or missing" error. Similarly, if the BOOT.INI is present but contains incorrect information, NTLDR will look in the wrong location and once again display the error message. If the computer previously started without failure, and if you have a Windows Startup disk for the computer, use the disk to start Windows. If Windows starts when using the Startup disk, correct the problem by copying the BOOT.INI file to the root of C:. If Windows does not start properly with the disk, then you have a more advanced problem. It still may be related to the BOOT.INI file, but may involve a change to the partitioning of the disk, and is a very advanced problem. If this is the case, research the Microsoft site for articles on the BOOT.INI file and how it describes the path to NTOSKRNL.EXE using an ARC path.

Inside Information

Why Is Windows Busy When I Log On?

Have you ever wondered why Windows seems busy after you see the logon screen and even after you log on? This busy status is indicated by disk activity, and sometimes the mouse pointer displays the busy icon (usually the hourglass). This is because the Begin Logon dialog box appears before the service controller is done loading services. This also means that after you log on, you might see an error message indicating that a service didn't load properly.

Troubleshooting Startup Problems with Startup Modes

As you work with Windows computers, you may run into computers that fail to start up normally. When this occurs immediately after a configuration change, but before you have logged on again, you may want to try the Last Known Good option you learned earlier. Beyond this, your startup options depend on the version of Windows you're using.

Windows NT 4.0 Startup Options

The Windows NT 4.0 default installation provides two OS Loader menu choices. The first one is the normal Windows startup, while the second one starts Windows with a standard VGA driver rather than the manufacturer's driver. This option applies to problems with video that occur after installing the manufacturer's video driver. You can use VGA mode as a very simple test. If Windows NT 4.0 will not start normally, but starts up just fine when you select the VGA mode, then the problem is the video adapter. While Windows is running in the Standard VGA mode, uninstall the problem video driver.

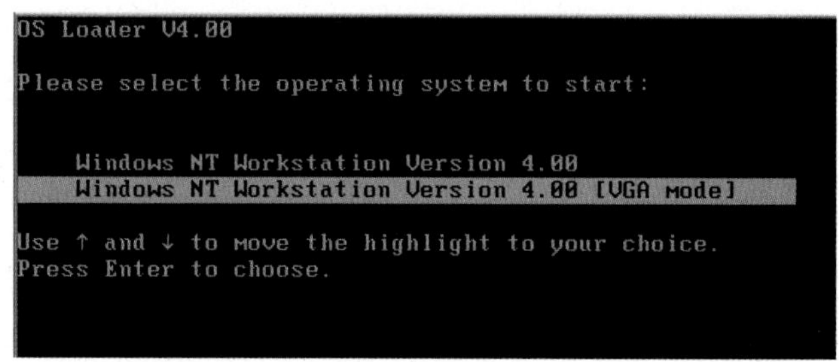

• The Windows NT 4.0 OS Loader menu

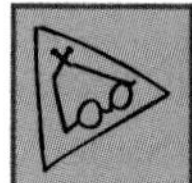

If your computer is configured to dual-boot, you will press F8 when you see the text-mode operating system selection screen. That screen is not displayed on a Windows 2000 or Windows XP computer that is not configured to dual-boot.

Windows 2000 and Windows XP Professional

Windows 2000 and Windows XP have several startup options available from the Advanced Options menu, accessed by pressing F8 before the graphical Windows splash screen appears.

Safe Mode If Windows will not start normally, but starts just fine in Safe Mode, use Safe Mode while locating the problem using Device Manager, and then correct the source of the problem. Safe Mode does not disable Windows security. You are required to log on in all three variants of Safe Mode, and you can only access those resources to which you have permissions.

Three Safe Mode variants are available from the Advanced Options menu:

- **Safe Mode** starts up without using several drivers and components that would normally be started, including the network components. It loads only very basic, non-vendor-specific drivers for mouse, video (loading Windows' very basic VGA.sys driver), keyboard, mass storage, and system services.
- **Safe Mode With Networking** is identical to plain Safe Mode, except that networking components are also started. Use the following debug sequence with Safe Mode With Networking:
    - If Windows will not start up normally, but it starts OK in plain Safe Mode, restart and select Safe Mode With Networking.
    - If it fails to start in Safe Mode With Networking, the problem area is network drivers or components. Use Device Manager to disable the network adapter driver (the likely culprit), and then boot up normally. If Windows now works, replace your network driver.
    - If this problem occurs in Windows XP immediately after upgrading a network driver, use Device Manager to roll back the updated driver. In Windows 2000, remove the device driver. When a better updated driver is available, install it.
- **Safe Mode With Command Prompt** is Safe Mode with only a command prompt as a user interface. Windows would normally load your GUI desktop, but this depends on the program EXPLORER.EXE, the GUI shell to Windows. In place of this GUI

Inside Information

Where Is EXPLORER.EXE?

Are you wondering where you would find an uncorrupted version of EXPLORER.EXE? You will find a compressed version of it in the I386 directory of the Windows 2000 or Windows XP Professional CD. Open a command prompt and use the Expand command (it is installed with Windows) to expand it. The syntax is

```
EXPAND d:\I386\
EXPLORER.EX_ PATH\
EXPLORER.EXE
```

In this command, the d *represents the drive letter of the CD-ROM drive, and* PATH *represents the full* path *to the directory in which you want the file expanded. The actual command line you type may look like this: EXPAND E:\i386\EXPLORER.EX_ C:\WINDOWS\EXPLORER.EXE (you do not need to capitalize).*

shell, Safe Mode With Command Prompt loads a very limited GUI with a command prompt (CMD.EXE) window. This is a handy option to remember if the desktop does not display at all. Once you have eliminated video drivers as the cause, corruption of the EXPLORER.EXE program may be the problem. From within the command prompt, you can delete the corrupted version of EXPLORER.EXE and copy an undamaged version. This requires knowledge of the command-line commands for navigating the directory structure, as well as knowledge of the location of the file that you are replacing. You can launch programs, such as the Event Viewer (eventvwr.msc), the Computer Management console (compmgmt.msc), or Device Manager (devmgmt.msc) from the command prompt.

Step-by-Step 8.07

Using Safe Mode

In the following steps, you will explore the three Safe Mode variants available from the Advanced Options menu. For this step-by-step, you will need a computer running Windows 2000 or Windows XP Professional. The illustrations shown are from Windows XP.

Step 1

Restart your computer. Press F8 after the POST messages, when you see the black text-mode screen with the "Starting Windows" message. From the Advanced Options menu, select Safe Mode, and then press ENTER. A small "Welcome to Windows" message box is displayed against a black background with the build version number at the top of the screen and "Safe Mode" in each corner of the background.

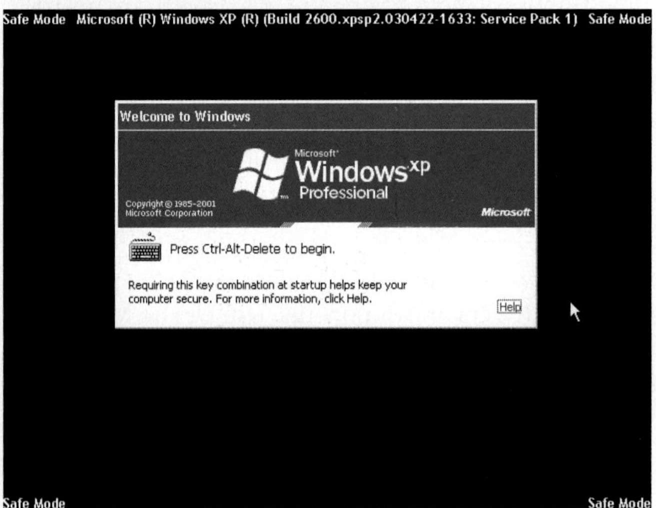

Step 2

Press CTRL-ALT-DELETE. Log on as Administrator (or a member of the Administrators group). A Desktop dialog box will be displayed to inform you that Windows is running in Safe Mode. Select the Yes button to proceed with Safe Mode. Recall that only the standard video drivers are installed, and some components are not loaded, so the desktop will not look normal, although it will still have all the GUI components displayed.

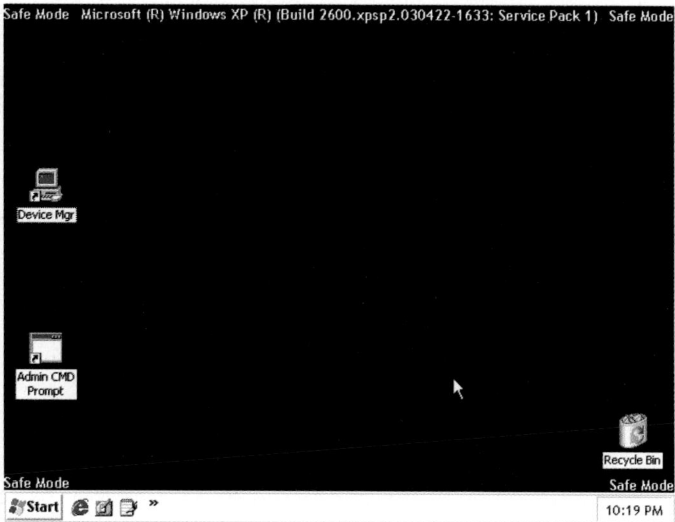

Step 3

Open Device Manager and browse through the list of devices. Double-click on a device to access its properties; then select the Driver tab, where you can disable any suspect device or perform other tasks, such as removing, updating, or rolling back drivers. (Rollback is not available in Windows 2000.) Close Device Manager.

Step 4

Restart your computer, press F8 after the POST, and select Safe Mode With Networking. This mode looks just like standard Safe Mode. Log on as an Administrator (or a member of the Administrators group), and attempt to connect to a network share. If you were troubleshooting a startup problem, successfully starting in Safe Mode With Networking would rule out networking components. Conversely, if you are able to start in Safe Mode, but cannot start in Safe Mode With Networking, the problem *is* with a networking component.

Step 5

Restart your computer, press F8 after the POST, and select Safe Mode With Command Prompt. A text-mode background will display, and then a small GUI box with the message "Starting Windows," followed by the Log On To Windows dialog box. Log on as you have previously. The command prompt will display within a window, but the GUI desktop will not exist, because Explorer and other GUI components are not started in this mode.

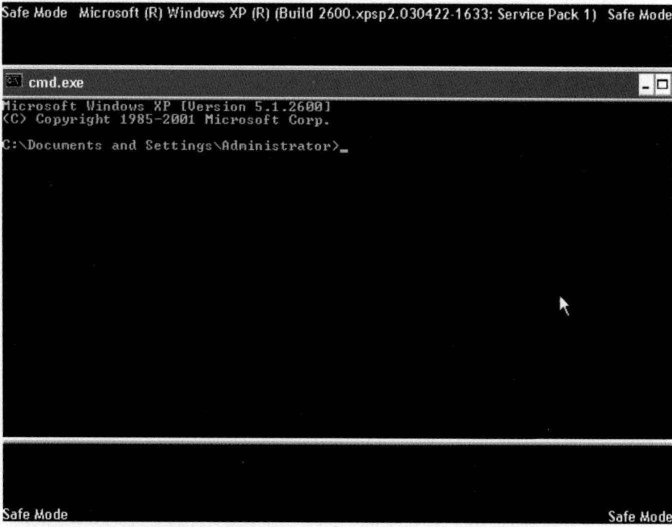

Step 6	After logging on, take a few minutes to try some of the command-line commands like **DIR** and **CD**. Typing **Help** at the command line will give you a list of the commands, and typing a command name followed by **/?** will give you the syntax for that command. Have fun!
Step 7	Now start Device Manager from the command prompt by typing **devmgmt.msc** and pressing ENTER. Check out the Device Manager GUI in Safe Mode, opening some of the device nodes. When you are done, exit by pressing CTRL-ALT-DELETE, which will bring up the security menu. Then select Shut Down.

Enable Boot Logging When boot logging is turned on, a log of the Windows startup is created in a file named NTBTLOG.TXT and saved in the *systemroot* folder. This log file creates an entry for each component as it is loaded into memory. It also lists drivers that were not loaded. An administrator viewing this file can discover what drivers were loaded into memory. Boot logging occurs automatically with each of the three Safe Modes. Selecting this option from the Advanced Options menu will turn on boot logging and proceed with a normal startup.

Enable VGA Mode This option starts Windows normally, except that the video mode is changed to the lowest resolution (640×480), using the currently installed video driver. It does not switch to the basic Windows video driver. Select this option after making a video configuration change that is not supported by the video adapter and that prevents Windows from displaying properly.

Directory Services Restore Mode This mode is available in Windows Servers acting as domain controllers.

Debugging Mode This is an advanced option used to send debugging information about the Windows startup over a serial cable to another computer that is running a special program called a debugger.

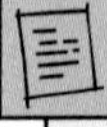

In place of the two options Start Windows Normally and Reboot, Windows 2000 has only one option, Reboot Normally, which behaves like the Windows XP Reboot option.

Start Windows Normally Use this option to start Windows normally from this menu. You would use this after using F8 to view the Advanced Options menu and deciding to continue with a normal startup. It does not restart the computer.

Reboot This option restarts the computer, acting like a warm reboot (CTRL-ALT-DELETE) from MS-DOS or like Restart Windows from the Windows Shut Down menu. You may then choose to allow Windows to start normally or to open the Advanced Options menu with the F8 key.

If you are logged on as a non-administrative user and start Device Manager, you will receive a warning that you do not have sufficient privileges to install or modify device drivers. However, if you click the OK button on this warning box, Device Manager will open, allowing a non-administrative user to look but not touch!

Return to OS Choices Menu Selecting this option on a multiboot computer will return to the OS Choices menu (OS Loader menu).

Troubleshooting Device Problems

If Windows detects a problem with a device, you will quickly learn this when you open Device Manager. The device type will be expanded, and the problem device will have a yellow exclamation mark next to it. The problem may be with the device itself, its device driver, or the ability of the operating system to automatically configure it. If you see this symbol on a device, double-click the device to open its Properties dialog box, which will give you more information. In the example in Figure 8-17, the yellow icons on the communications ports indicate that Windows discovered problems. The Properties dialog box for one of these devices reports that there are not enough free resources for the device.

You may be surprised that we didn't attempt to fix this problem, but we simply have no need to use these devices. If we did need one of these devices, we could follow the instructions in the Device Status box and click the Troubleshoot button to get help on resolving the problems. Familiarize yourself with the contents of Device Manager by opening the nodes, such as Computer and Disk Drives.

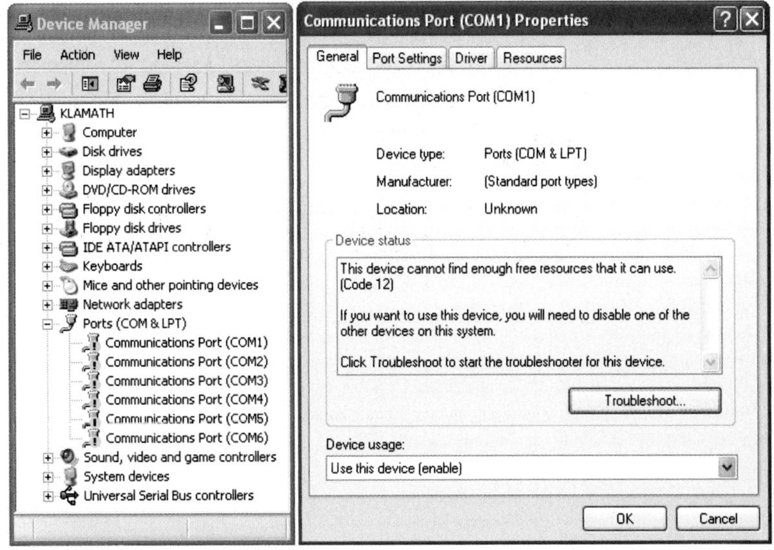

• **Figure 8-17.** The exclamation marks in the yellow circles indicate problems. The Properties dialog box provides an explanation.

Step-by-Step 8.08

Working with Device Manager

In this step-by-step, you will use Device Manager to verify that your devices are recognized by Windows and are functioning normally. Then you will explore the options for removing or rolling back a faulty device driver. This step-by-step was written for Windows XP Professional, but can be completed in either Windows 2000 or Windows XP Home. Windows 2000 will not have the Rollback option.

Step 1

Log onto Windows as an Administrator and open Device Manager. Expand a device category node, such as Network Adapters or Display Adapters, and select a device.

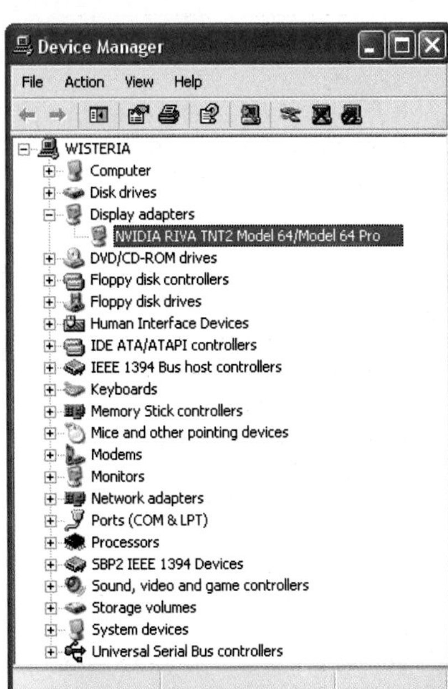

Step 2

Double-click the device to open the Properties dialog box. Select the Driver tab and click the Driver Details button to view information about the device driver, including the name and location of the driver file or files, the provider, file version, copyright information, and the digital signature. This information is valuable when a manufacturer has issued more than one version of a device driver and you need to identify the version installed to decide if it should be replaced with a newer version.

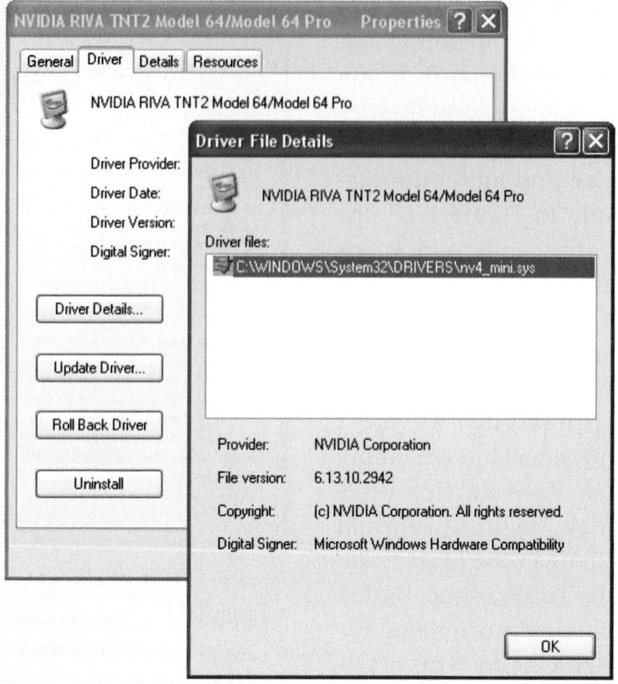

Step 3

Click OK to close the Driver Details page, and select Update Driver to open the Hardware Update wizard. This is similar to the Add Hardware wizard found in Control Panel. Close the Hardware Update wizard after noting its characteristics. When an installed device driver is updated, Windows creates a backup of the old driver files for use by Driver Rollback.

Step 4

If you are using Windows XP, select the Driver Rollback button. If the driver was previously updated, you will see a message asking if you are sure you would like to roll back to the previous driver. Select No. Do not actually roll back the driver! If the driver was never updated, you will see a message stating that no device driver was backed up. Click No to close this box if it appears.

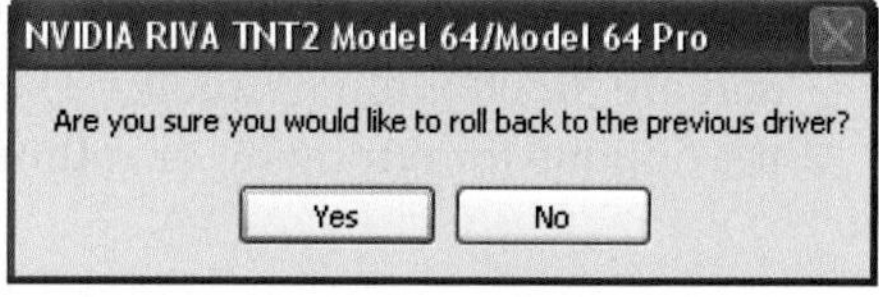

Step 5

Now select Uninstall. The Confirm Device Removal box warns that you are about to uninstall the device. Cancel out of this box. Then close Device Manager.

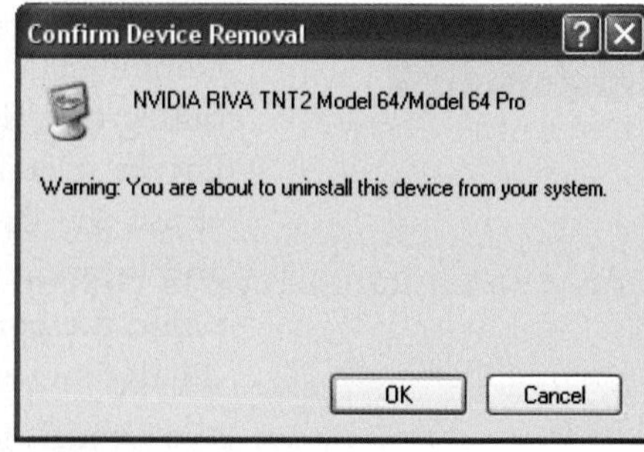

Recovery Options

If your computer will not start in any form of Safe Mode, use one of the more advanced recovery options available in Windows. Your options include the Emergency Repair Process (using the emergency repair disk (ERD)) in Windows NT 4.0 or Windows 2000; the Recovery Console in Windows 2000 or Windows XP Professional; System Restore, beginning with Windows Me; and Automatic System Recovery, available beginning with Windows XP Professional. All of these options require some proactive steps for these solutions to work.

Emergency Repair Process

The Emergency Repair Process in Windows NT 4.0 and Windows 2000 requires an up-to-date ERD, or recent emergency repair information stored on the local hard disk. In Windows NT 4.0, using the RDISK command with the /S switch will both save configuration information to hard disk and create an ERD with some of the basic emergency repair information. In Windows 2000, the RDISK command was replaced by a button on the Welcome page of the Windows Backup program. After you click this, an Emergency Repair Diskette dialog box guides you through the process, including providing an option to also back up the registry to the Repair directory located in the *systemroot*.

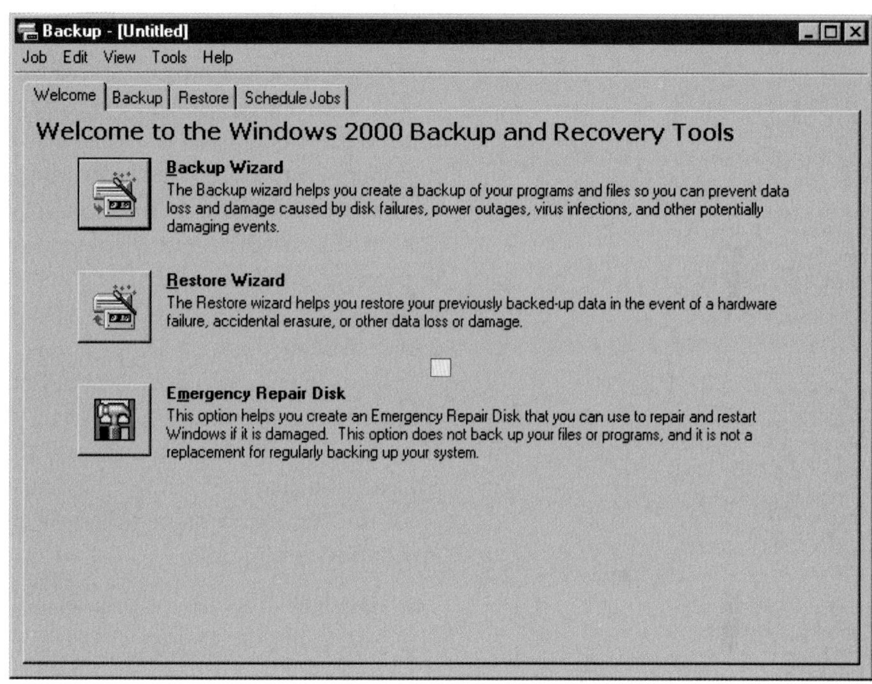

• The Emergency Repair Disk option in the Windows 2000 Backup program

Recovery Console

The Recovery Console was introduced in Windows 2000 and is an advanced option for recovering from a failure of the OS when all else has failed. The Recovery Console is a totally non-GUI command-line interface. If you have the Windows 2000 or Windows XP Professional CD, you can start the Recovery Console by booting from the CD, running Setup and selecting Repair, and then selecting Recovery Console. However, if you like to be proactive, you can install the Recovery Console on your hard drive so that it is one of your startup options and does not require the Windows CD to run. The steps to do this in Windows 2000 and Windows XP are identical.

Log on as an Administrator, and insert the Windows 2000 or Windows XP Professional CD-ROM. If Autorun starts the Setup program, click the No button. Then open a Windows command prompt by selecting Start | Run and typing **CMD** into the dialog box. In the command prompt, enter the following command:

```
d:\i386\winnt32 /cmdcons
```

where *d* is your CD drive letter.

> As with most command-line interfaces, the previous information stays on the screen until the screen is full.

Just follow the instructions on the screen. If you are connected to the Internet, allow the Setup program to download updated files. After the Recovery Console is installed, at each restart, the OS selection menu will show your Windows OS (Windows 2000 Professional or Windows XP) and the Microsoft Windows Recovery Console. It may also show other choices if yours is a multiboot computer. When you select the Recovery Console, it will start, and then you will see the Recovery Console command prompt.

The cursor is a small white rectangle sitting to the right of the question mark on the last line. If there is only one installation of Windows on your computer, type **1** at the prompt, and press ENTER. If you press ENTER before typing in a valid selection, the Recovery Console will cancel and the computer will reboot. Once you have made your selection, a new line appears on the screen prompting for the Administrator password.

Enter the Administrator password for that computer and press ENTER. The password will not be displayed on the screen; only asterisks will show in place of the password. The screen still shows everything that has happened so far, unless something has happened to cause an error message. It now looks like Figure 8-18.

Now what do you do? Use the Recovery Console commands, of course. Recovery Console uses many of the commands that worked in DOS as well as some uniquely its own. To see a list of Recovery Console commands, simply enter **help** at the prompt. To learn more about an individual command, enter the command name followed by **/?**. Below is a brief description of a few handy commands:

- **DISKPART** The Windows equivalent to FDISK
- **EXIT** Exits the Recovery Console and restarts your computer
- **FIXBOOT** Writes a new partition table from the backup MST
- **FIXMBR** The equivalent to FDISK /MBR
- **HELP** Displays a Help screen
- **LOGON** Logs onto a Windows installation
- **SYSTEMROOT** Sets the current directory to the root of the system partition—usually C:\

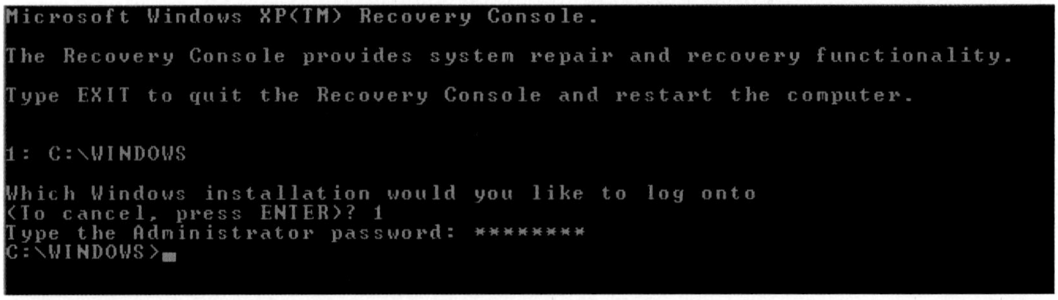

```
Microsoft Windows XP(TM) Recovery Console.

The Recovery Console provides system repair and recovery functionality.

Type EXIT to quit the Recovery Console and restart the computer.

1: C:\WINDOWS

Which Windows installation would you like to log onto
<To cancel, press ENTER>? 1
Type the Administrator password: ********
C:\WINDOWS>
```

• **Figure 8-18.** Microsoft Windows XP Recovery Console

The files that make up the Recovery Console reside on drive C:, making the Recovery Console unavailable if this partition is badly damaged. The Recovery Console shines in the business of allowing an administrator to manually restore registries, stopping problem services, rebuilding partitions (other than the system partition), or using the EXPAND program to extract copies of corrupted files from a CD-ROM or floppy disk.

You can reconfigure a service so that it starts with different settings, format drives on the hard disk, read and write on local FAT or NTFS volumes, and copy replacement files from a floppy or CD. The Recovery Console allows you to access the file system and is still constrained by the file and folder security of NTFS. Recovery Console is a very advanced tool—definitely not for amateurs!

System Restore

For those of us who like to add the latest software or device to our Windows computers, only to find that nothing seems to work right after the change, Microsoft has System Restore. You learned about System Restore in Chapter 5, and it is only available in Windows Me, Windows XP, and later versions of Windows.

Automated System Recovery (ASR)

For times when a hard disk has failed completely, or Windows appears to be so corrupted that you have found no means of recovering, Windows XP Professional has the Automatic System Recovery (ASR) option that you learned about in Chapter 5. This option replaces the Emergency Repair process found in Windows NT 4.0 and Windows 2000. A set of ASR disks created with the Automated System Recovery Preparation wizard can be used to totally restore the Windows operating system. The ASR disk set consists of a special bootable floppy disk and a backup of the local system partition to tape, another local hard disk, or a network location. A more conventional set of backups can then be used to restore data files as well as any system files that were backed up after the ASR set was created.

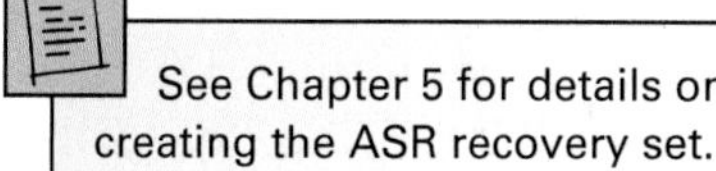

See Chapter 5 for details on creating the ASR recovery set.

Chapter 8 Review

Chapter Summary

After reading this chapter and completing the Step-by-Step tutorials and Try This! exercises, you should understand the following facts about the Windows desktop:

Understanding the Registry

- The registry is a database of all configuration settings in Windows. Avoid directly editing the registry, because you can cause severe damage. The Control Panel applets provide a safe way to edit the registry.
- The registry is created during Windows setup, anytime a setup or installation program is run after that, and during startup and shutdown. It is also modified anytime a device driver is installed, and whenever any application, Windows component, or device is configured.
- Most of the registry is saved in several files, called hives. They include SYSTEM, SOFTWARE, SECURITY, SAM, DEFAULT, and NTUSER.DAT.
- Two registry editors are found in Windows—Regedit.exe and Regedt32.exe. Until Windows XP, these were two separate editors with different features. Beginning with Windows XP, either command name brings up the same, new and improved version of the registry editor.
- The registry is viewed in a hierarchical folder structure in Registry Editor.
- A key is a folder object that can contain one or more sets of settings as well as other keys.
- The five top-level keys, or root keys, in the registry are called subtrees.
- A key that exists within another key is called a subkey.
- Settings within a key are called value entries. Each value entry has a name, type, and data.
- The permanent portions of the registry are contained in the registry hives, saved in the files described earlier.
- HKEY_LOCAL_MACHINE\Hardware contains the temporary portion of the registry, the information gathered during hardware detection during each Windows startup.

Working with Device Drivers

- A device driver is program code, created by the device manufacturer, which allows an OS to control the use of a physical device.
- Look for device drivers on the floppy disk or CD that comes with a device, or at the web site of the manufacturer.
- You must be logged on as Administrator or a member of the Administrators group to install any device driver in Windows.
- Once a device has been installed, a user may disconnect and reconnect the device without restriction—the driver will not be uninstalled.
- Code signing is designed to avoid problems caused by badly written code. It involves a digital signature, provided by Microsoft as a seal of approval of program code.
- Windows uses a process called file signature verification to check for code signing, and an administrator can configure what action Windows takes when it detects code that does not contain a digital signature. Configure with the Driver Signing button located on the Hardware page of the System applet.
- Always read the manufacturer's documentation, and follow the instructions before attempting to install a device driver, whether it is plug-and-play or not.
- When an administrator installs or connects a plug-and-play device to a Windows computer, the device will be automatically detected, and the driver will be installed and configured with little or no interaction from the user, except to provide the device driver disk if requested.
- Plug-and-play devices connected to USB or IEEE 1394 (FireWire) can be disconnected without restarting Windows.
- Install non-plug-and-play devices by using the manufacturer's instructions and installation program, if available. If the device does not come with an installation program, and you have the correct device drivers, use the Add New Hardware applet in Control Panel.

- Device Manager is the tool in Windows 2000 and Windows XP for managing and troubleshooting device problems.
- A hardware profile includes the registry keys that contain the settings defining the devices that must be started during Windows startup, the files associated with each device, and configuration settings for each device.
- Most Windows computers, especially desktops, only have a single hardware profile.
- Hardware profiles are very handy for a laptop computer that has two or more configurations, usually including one when it is connected to a docking station and another when it is undocked.

Managing Performance in Windows

- Windows performance settings are available on the Advanced tab of the System Properties dialog box, but you should not have to make any changes to these settings, because Windows automatically adjusts to system changes to provide good performance.
- Visual effects include treatments of the GUI that make Windows more visually interesting and even fun to use, but which may come at a price—the use of processor and memory.
- The Advanced page of Performance Options has even more settings, including Processor Scheduling, Memory Usage, and Virtual Memory.
- When a Windows computer is running low on memory for the operating system and any loaded application programs, it will use and manage a portion of disk space as RAM. This is called virtual memory.
- Windows virtual memory uses a paging file called pagefile.sys, which is usually located on the root of C:.
- Normally, Windows manages virtual memory, adjusting for changing memory needs, but an administrator can control the size, location, and even the number of paging files.
- Performance monitoring is something that is usually done on network servers, not on Windows desktop computers. Server administrators use performance monitoring to ensure that the quality of service is maintained, and as an early warning of potential problems that can show up first as performance problems.
- Beginning with Windows 2000, Performance Monitor is replaced by a console called Performance containing two nodes: System Monitor and Performance Logs and Alerts.
- System Monitor, available in both Windows 2000 and Windows XP Professional, allows an administrator to gather and view performance data involving memory, disk, processor, network, and other objects.
- The Performance Logs and Alert node in the Performance console actually allows three types of activities—creating alerts and creating two types of log files, counter and trace.

Windows File Systems

- The FAT file system supported in Windows 2000 and Windows XP includes FAT12, FAT16, and FAT32.
- Windows NT 4.0 supports FAT12, FAT16, FAT32, and NTFS4.
- The NTFS5 file system is supported in both Windows 2000 and Windows XP.
- The CD-ROM File System (CDFS) allows Windows OSs to read CD-ROMs and to read and write to writeable CDs (CD-R) and rewriteable CDs (CD-RW). Windows NT 4.0 does not natively support any writeable or rewriteable CDs.
- The universal disk format (UDF) is a file system driver required for Windows to read DVD ROMs and to read and write DVD-R and DVD-RW. Windows XP has a DVD-RAM driver that supports the 4.7GB DVD-RAM disk standard.

Windows Startup Process

- The Windows boot files, used during the boot sequence of startup, are NTLDR, NTDETECT .COM, BOOT.INI, and NTBOOTDD.SYS.
- The Windows system files, used during the load sequence of Windows startup, are NTOSKRNL .EXE, SYSTEM, and many components and driver files.
- A Windows startup disk is created by formatting a diskette and copying the boot files from the root of C: to the root of A:.
- A Windows startup disk can be used in case of damage to the boot files on an NT computer.

- There are several phases to the Windows startup process: Power-On Self-Test (POST), initial startup, boot loader, detect and configure hardware, logon, and plug-and-play device detection.
- You can view System, Application, and Security logs in Event Viewer.

Troubleshooting Windows Problems

- Cooperative troubleshooting is a method to use when troubleshooting problems on another person's computer. It involves
  - Eliciting problem symptoms from customers
  - Having customers reproduce errors as part of the diagnostics process
  - Identifying recent changes to the computer by the user
- Several proactive tasks make troubleshooting easier, or even preventable. These include keeping Windows updated, knowing how to use administrative tools like the Runas command, preparing startup disks for each computer, maintaining backups, backing up the registry, and configuring alerts.
- Automatic Update is provided with Windows XP, Windows 2000 (SP3 or later), and Windows Server 2003. It can be configured to automatically download critical updates and, optionally, to automatically install them.
- Windows Update is an application that connects to Microsoft's Windows Update web site, checks the status of your computer, and then provides a list of critical and recommended updates that you may choose to download and install.
- Runas is a command-line command that allows you to run a single command using a user account other than the one with which you logged on.
- A startup disk allows you to start up a computer from the floppy disk drive, a handy thing to do when you troubleshoot startup problems.
- The Windows NT 4.0, Windows 2000, and Windows XP startup disks are similar and can only be used through the detect and configure hardware phases; after that, there must be Windows system files on the hard disk to complete the Windows startup.
- A Windows 98 or MS-DOS startup disk will boot up a computer to the command prompt from which you can run a variety of MS-DOS programs, including FDISK to partition a hard disk or FORMAT to format a hard drive.
- Maintain current backups of the entire system and the registry so that you can restore a system to its previous state after troubleshooting.
- The Windows Backup program in Windows NT 4.0 will back up the registry when the system partition is selected for backup. In Windows 2000 and Windows XP Professional, the Windows Backup program will back up the registry when System State is selected.
- An administrator can configure alerts to warn of events that could lead to problems if not dealt with.
- Use Event Viewer to view logs of system, security, and application events, paying attention to the warning and error logs for messages that can be used to solve problems.
- While directly editing the registry should be avoided, learn how to edit it in case a registry edit is the only way to solve a problem.
- Last Known Good Configuration is a startup option that will select the last set of configuration changes since the last successful user logon.
- Use a Windows startup disk to troubleshoot and solve problems with startup that involve damaged or missing boot files.
- Windows NT 4.0, Windows 2000, and Windows XP all have a startup option called VGA mode that can be used successfully when there is a problem with a manufacturer's video driver.
- Windows 2000 and Windows XP have Safe Mode startup options, inherited from Windows 98. They include Safe Mode, Safe Mode With Networking, and Safe Mode With Command Prompt.
- Device Manager is the primary tool for troubleshooting device problems. A yellow exclamation mark on a device in Device Manager indicates a problem. Open the properties dialog box to see an explanation.
- Use Device Manager to uninstall, update, and remove device drivers. You can also use it to disable a device without removing the driver.
- Windows Recovery options include the Emergency Repair Process (Windows NT 4.0 and Windows 2000), the Recovery Console (beginning with Windows 2000), System Restore (beginning with Windows Me), and Automated System Recovery (beginning with Windows XP Professional).

Key Terms List

binary file *(379)*
boot files *(399)*
boot partition *(399)*
data type *(382)*
digital signature *(385)*
file signature verification *(385)*
hardware profile *(390)*
hive *(379)*
key *(382)*
registry *(378)*
root key *(382)*
security ID (SID) *(383)*
subkey *(382)*
subtree *(382)*
system file *(399)*
system partition *(399)*
value entries *(382)*
virtual memory *(396)*
Visual Effects *(393)*

Key Terms Quiz

Use terms from the Key Terms List to complete the sentences that follow. Not all terms will be used.

1. NTLDR, NTDETECT.COM, and BOOT.INI are Windows ________________.
2. Windows system files must reside in the ________________.
3. When viewed with a registry editor, a/an ________________, or root key, is a registry key located at the top level.
4. Many of the settings available on the ________________ page of Windows XP Performance Options settings come at a price—the increased use of processor and memory.
5. The Windows ________________ is a database of all configuration settings in Windows.
6. When a Windows computer has more than one set of hardware available to it, create a/an ________________ and disable the unavailable components in one of the profiles.
7. A/an ________________ contains program code.
8. When Windows runs out of sufficient RAM memory for the program code and data in memory, it uses ________________.
9. REG_DWORD is an example of a registry ________________.
10. A/an ________________ is a unique string of numbers preceded by *S-1-5* that identifies a security principal in a Windows security accounts database.

Multiple-Choice Quiz

1. Which of the following is not found in the registry?
   a. Device driver settings
   b. Services settings
   c. User data files
   d. User preferences
   e. Application program settings
2. Any change to Windows or an installed application results in a change to this special database.
   a. Microsoft SQL Server
   b. Microsoft Excel
   c. NTUSER.DAT
   d. Registry
   e. DEFAULT
3. Most of the Windows registry files are saved in this location.
   a. *systemroot*\SYSTEM32\CONFIG
   b. D:\WINDOWS
   c. *systemroot*\SYSTEM32\REGISTRY

- **d.** *systemroot*\WINDOWS
- **e.** *systemroot*\WINNT

4. The source of the user profile settings used until after a user logs onto Windows.

- **a.** NTUSER.DAT
- **b.** USER.DAT
- **c.** SYSTEM.DAT
- **d.** DEFAULT
- **e.** SYSTEM

5. HKEY_LOCAL_MACHINE\hardware contains data collected during the detect and configure hardware phase of startup; this information is said to be:

- **a.** Permanent
- **b.** Temporary
- **c.** Binary
- **d.** Hexadecimal
- **e.** Digital

6. Which statement is true?

- **a.** Only an Administrator may disconnect or reconnect a device after it has been installed.
- **b.** Only members of the Administrators group may disconnect or reconnect a device after it has been installed.
- **c.** Only members of the Guests group may disconnect or reconnect a device after it has been installed.
- **d.** Any member of the local Users group may disconnect or reconnect a device after it has been installed.
- **e.** No one may disconnect or reconnect a device after it has been installed.

7. Which statement is true?

- **a.** An unsigned device driver can be installed if the Driver Signing settings allow it.
- **b.** An unsigned device driver cannot be installed.
- **c.** Only a manufacturer can install an unsigned device driver.
- **d.** Unsigned device drivers should never be installed.
- **e.** Unsigned device drivers are always dangerous.

8. A Device Manager feature introduced in Windows XP.

- **a.** Uninstall driver
- **b.** Rollback driver
- **c.** Disable driver
- **d.** Update driver
- **e.** Remove driver

9. The Windows XP Visual Effects settings involve a trade-off between interesting visual effects and ________.

- **a.** Security
- **b.** Stability
- **c.** Performance
- **d.** Wallpaper
- **e.** Sound effects

10. By default, the Processor Scheduling setting is set to this option.

- **a.** Programs
- **b.** Background
- **c.** Once a week
- **d.** Daily
- **e.** Never

11. Monitor performance in Windows 2000 and Windows XP using ______.

- **a.** Event Viewer
- **b.** System applet
- **c.** Device Manager
- **d.** Recovery Console
- **e.** Performance Console

12. Which statement is true?

- **a.** The system partition contains the system files.
- **b.** The boot partition contains the boot files.
- **c.** The extended partition contains the boot files.
- **d.** The Windows partition contains the system files.
- **e.** The system partition contains the boot files.

13. The first file to be loaded into memory during bootup is:

- **a.** NTBOOTDD.SYS
- **b.** NTLDR

c. BOOT.INI

d. NTDETECT.COM

e. NTBIO.SYS

14. A program used to download and install both critical and noncritical Windows updates.

a. Automatic Updates

b. Device Manager

c. Automatic System Recovery

d. Recovery Console

e. Windows Update

15. A Windows command-line command that allows you to run another command using a user account other than the one with which you logged on.

a. SU

b. Runas

c. RDISK

d. FDISK

e. CMD

■ Essay Quiz

1. As you were leaving your office for the day yesterday, a desktop-support person came in and announced that he had to make some changes to your computer. When you powered up your computer this morning, Windows would not start. Instead, you saw the message "NTLDR is missing. Press any key to restart." When you press a key, the computer restarts, but you get the same message. You call the help desk, but no one can talk to you or come to your desk for at least an hour. Describe what you would do in this case.

2. Your Windows XP computer is having display problems when starting up. You suspect that the cause is a video driver update that you installed. You managed to log on at the first restart after the update, in spite of being barely able to see the distorted logon dialog box. Then you found that, even though you were logged on, it was hopeless to try to work with the GUI. Describe how you would confirm that the problem is the video adapter and how you will correct the problem.

3. Your brother-in-law has informed you that he read on the Internet that the optimum configuration for a Windows paging file is 250MB on drive C:, and that you should configure your Windows XP computer accordingly. Will you follow his advice? Why or why not? In your own words, describe your response to this suggestion.

4. In your own words, describe what you believe is the most important proactive task to take to avoid problems with Windows, and give a reason why you believe this is true.

5. Briefly explain the effects on attempting to install an unsigned device driver if Driver Signing is set to Warn.

Lab Projects

• Lab Project 8.1

Your Windows XP computer will not start up, and you believe the cause is a network card you recently installed.

1. Describe the steps you will take to isolate the problem.
2. Demonstrate how you will do this.

• Lab Project 8.2

You have a laptop computer in a docking station at work. Windows XP was installed on this computer while it was docked, and it has a single hardware profile named "Docked Profile." You need to configure this laptop computer with a second hardware profile that will not use a network card or a floppy disk drive, because these devices are not available when the computer is undocked.

1. Describe the steps you will take to create this second hardware profile.
2. Use your lab computer to create a second profile.
3. Test your solution and demonstrate the loading of each of the two profiles.
4. Demonstrate your solution for one or more of your fellow students.

• Lab Project 8.3

You are having a problem with your Windows computer that is isolated to a single graphics editing program that you use every day in your work. When you described the problem to the customer service support person for this product, you were told that the one and only fix for it is to edit a key under HKEY-LOCAL_MACHINE\SOFTWARE. He or she has assured you that this fix will work without causing any problems, but you are wary of doing this.

1. Describe the steps you will take before making the suggested registry changes.
2. Demonstrate these steps on your lab computer.

Introduction to Network Server Operating Systems

chapter 9

In all large corporations, there is a pervasive fear that someone somewhere is having fun with a computer on company time. Networks help alleviate that fear.

—John C. Dvorak

A stand-alone PC—one with no connection whatsoever to a network—is a rare thing today. Most of us can find some reason or need to connect to a network, whether it is a small home network, a corporate intranet, or the Internet. Without a network connection, a PC is like a remote island where the inhabitants have resolved to be isolated from civilization. And it does take resolve today to be so isolated, because there are means by which a computer in even the most remote location can be connected to the Internet or other network. The heart and soul of all networks are servers, the computers that provide the services we, as clients, seek on a network. These services are those that give us access to files and printers, web pages, applications, and much more. Each of these services is considered to have an important role on a network.

In this chapter, we will explore the basics of networking, starting with an overview of the hardware and software components and the purposes of network server operating systems. We will examine a simple classification of networks based on geography, along with some network administration considerations. We will consider the various roles computers play on a network, and we will see that there are many ways to be "served" on a network. Finally, we will explore the common roles of network servers, both on private networks and on the Internet, and the server operating systems that support these roles.

In this chapter, you will learn how to:

- **Explain the basic concepts of networking**
- **Describe basic server concepts**
- **Describe the common roles of network servers**
- **Share and protect network resources**

Networking Basics

If you connect two or more PCs using communications media, you have a computer network. But why would you want to connect computers? We will look at the main reasons for creating networks and then examine networks classified by geography and by administrative model. We will wrap up with a discussion of the components of a network.

Why Network PCs?

Why network PCs? If you think of a stand-alone PC as being like an island without any connection to the rest of the world, you can immediately see how limited it is. You cannot reach out through the computer and over the network to access data on other computers, you cannot browse the Internet to research your school project, and you cannot buy things from faraway places. For these and many other reasons, the vast majority of the world's PCs now have the ability to join and become part of a computer network. The fundamental reasons for connecting computers are to share resources, to communicate, and to manage network resources. These functions are usually provided by specialized computers, called servers, which provide a variety of roles. We will describe these reasons for networking now, and later in the chapter, we'll discuss some server roles.

Resource Sharing

We asked our friend Avtar if he knew what it is that computers actually share over a network, and he gave a very common answer: data. To an extent, that is true, but the broader answer, and what makes modern computer networks so powerful, is that networks allow individual computers to share **network resources**—anything that can be shared over a network.

It is the ability for a user at one computer to access a resource on another computer that makes today's computing so powerful. A resource is not simply, or only, data. Resources include objects such as data files and folders, of course, but resources also include physical entities, such as modems, printers, CD and DVD player/recorders, and backup devices. Resources also include services such as e-mail and fax. You can even sit in front of one PC and take over and control the function of another PC on the network.

Communicating

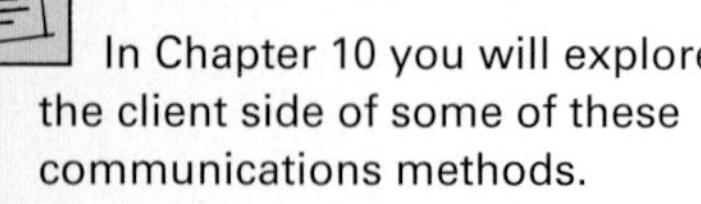

In Chapter 10 you will explore the client side of some of these communications methods.

People can communicate over a network using a variety of methods on both privately owned networks and the Internet. These include electronic mail (e-mail), list servers, newsgroups, and chat rooms. All of these methods allow electronic messages to pass between people. Some allow you the immediacy of a real-time conversation (similar to a phone conversation), and others send messages to you or post them in a place where you can read them. You can even communicate in real time and face-to-face using videoconferencing.

Network Resource Management

Placing resources on networks has led to the need for centralized management of those resources. Network resource management can involve many different tasks, for example, making a resource such as a file folder or printer available on the network. On a Microsoft Windows network, this is called creating a **share**. Additional tasks include centralizing data backup and performing myriad other tasks for managing data and physical resources on a network. Possibly the most important tasks on a network are applying and managing the necessary security to network resources and to the network in general.

Data Backup We cannot overstress the importance of data backup as being part of network resource management. Networks were not always an easy sell to managers in the 1980s. Many just did not see the need to spend the money to connect PCs for the sake of sharing data. However, even these holdouts approved LAN installations once they understood the benefits of centralized backups. With a network, all users can save their data to a server. Then, at the end of the day, the data files on the server can be backed up to tape. Centralized backup is much superior to the many haphazard methods used before networks.

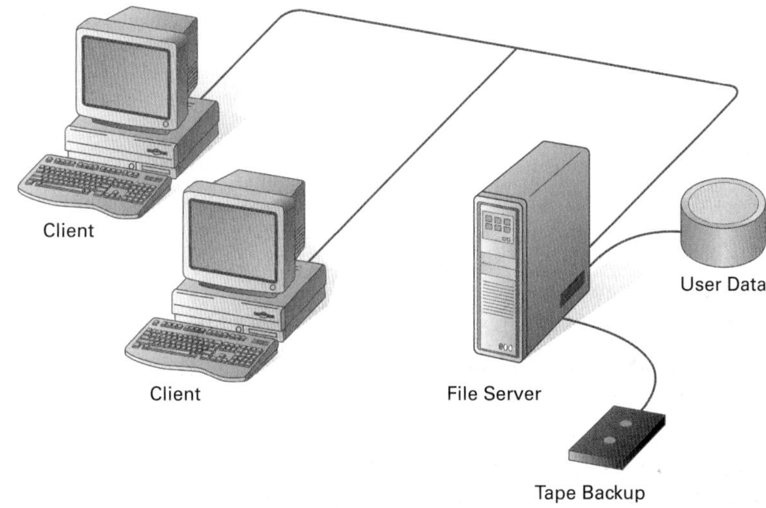

• Centralized backup is superior to the methods used before networks.

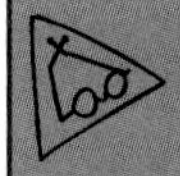

Inside Information

Sneaker Net Backup

If you were not there, you cannot imagine how bad it really was! In 1987, we visited a company with 40 computer users and no LAN. The daily "centralized backup" was a great example of what was called "sneaker net," the transportation of data via floppy disks carried from computer to computer by a human being. At the end of every day, each user copied the day's new or modified files onto carefully labeled floppy disks and placed them on the far left corner of his or her desk. At 5 P.M., an employee walked from desk to desk and collected the disks. They were then stored in a filing cabinet as the backup archive. It is so much better to have users save all of their data to a network server that can be backed up every day!

Single-Server Security In early PC networks, network security existed only on the individual server computers on the LAN and closely resembled the local security for modern desktop operating systems described in Chapter 7.

Even today, local security on a single server follows this model. Each server has a database of security accounts used by its security components to grant access to users wanting to connect to the server. In a server-based security database, an account was (and still is) a listing of information about a user or group of users. To access a server in the single-server model, you must go through an authentication process using a valid user name and password of an account that exists on that server. Further, once authenticated, you must go through an authorization process to gain access to each resource on the server. This process will confirm what, if any, permissions you have to each resource. Authentication and authorization are central to any computer security system. The differences occur in the location of the security accounts database.

Cross Check

NTFS Folder and File Permissions

Authorization is based on permissions assigned to a resource, such as NTFS and share permissions. Review the information on combining NTFS and share permissions in Chapter 7. Then answer the following questions:

1. What permissions are available to protect files from users accessing a share from over a network when a share exists on a FAT32 volume?

   ____

2. How do the share permissions and NTFS folder permissions work together?

   ____

This security model is still used in small business and isolated offices or departments. Figure 9-1 shows the permissions for a network resource, a shared folder named Sales, on a server running Windows Server 2003. The server is named 2K3SRVR. The users, Elaine Long and Sarah Brown, have accounts in the server's security accounts database, and they have been granted permissions for this share. As Figure 9-1 shows, Sarah has only the Read permission.

Multi-Server Security The biggest problem with the single or autonomous server model is that it does not scale well for a large multiple-server scenario. What works in a network with a single server does not work well in a network with hundreds of servers, because you (the user) have to have an account on each server you want to access. Even if you use the same user name and password in each account, the administration of the accounts has to be done on each server. Imagine changing a user's password when the user has an account on each separate server! This, and other administrative problems with the single-server model, was addressed in the 1990s, when server security grew beyond the single-server security model to a more centralized model that allows users a single logon to access all network resources. In addition, an account database could be multi-mastered, meaning that it is duplicated across two or more servers. This provided fault tolerance for the list of accounts, because if a single server failed, the accounts were saved on other servers. It also provided better availability, because the servers could be placed in different locations so that users could be authenticated by a server on their local LAN. The servers themselves still needed to communicate with each other in order to keep the accounts database synchronized across all the copies. But this could be done with less traffic by server-to-server communication over LANs or WANs, while the logons of many users at one location can be handled by one or more servers placed physically close to those users.

The real advancement came with the development of various forms of the **directory service**, a network service that can manage all types of network resources, based on certain international standards. Any single server participating in a directory service uses a procedure called pass-through authentication in which the server passes the authentication information provided by a user through to the central accounts database, stored on a directory services server, for

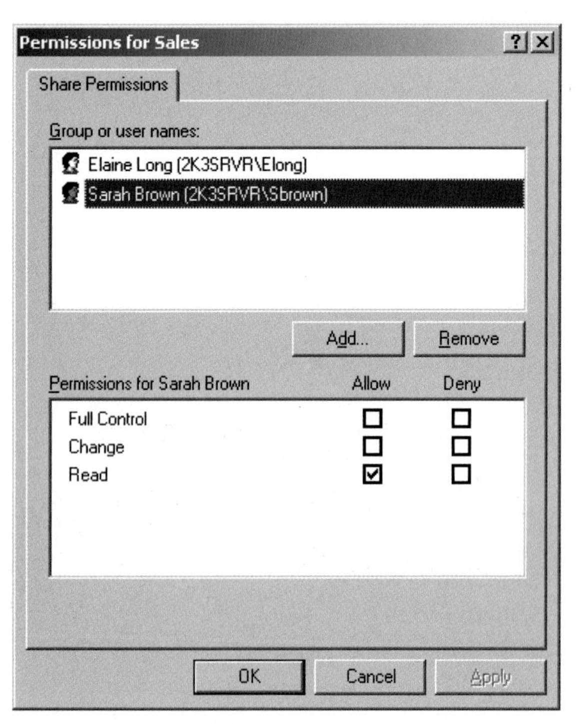

• **Figure 9-1.** Windows folder sharing

authentication. It also uses these central accounts for authorization purposes to assign permissions for the local resources to users and groups. Current directory services can manage larger numbers of objects and more types of objects.

Theoretically, all of an organization's data (e-mail, customer lists, inventory, and so on) can be stored in a directory service database. All that is needed is software that knows how to store, manage, and retrieve data from the directory service. This is one reason why each vendor, such as Microsoft or Novell, wants its particular directory service solution to become the central network service for organizations.

Networks, Small to Large

Today, network boundaries seem blurred, especially to the casual user. However, networks can still be classified by size and geography. These traditional classifications include local area networks (LANs), metropolitan area networks (MANs), and wide area networks (WANs).

LANs

A LAN is geographically the smallest type of computer network. It is two or more computers connected by communications media in a small geographical area. That could be a room, a floor of a building, an entire building, or a business or academic campus all connected with a common network technology, and usually at the fastest speeds. We talk about LAN speeds in terms of millions of bits per second or even billions of bits per second, as in 10 Mbps, 100 Mbps, 1 Gbps, and 10 Gbps. These translate to 10 megabits, 100 megabits, and 1 or 10 gigabits (billions of bits) per second.

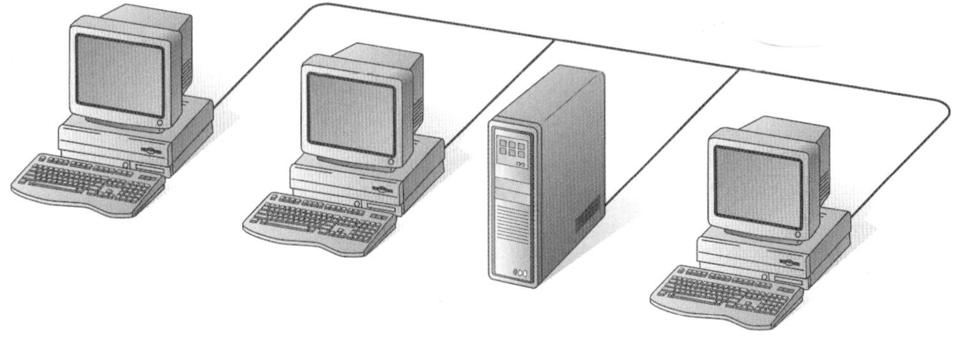

• Local area network (LAN)

MANs

A MAN is a network that covers a metropolitan area, usually using high-speed fiber-optic cable (operating in the gigabits-per-second range). Although people tend to be less aware of MANs, they exist nonetheless. In fact, a MAN may well be somewhere between you and the Internet. A MAN allows a community of LANs to connect to each other and to the Internet.

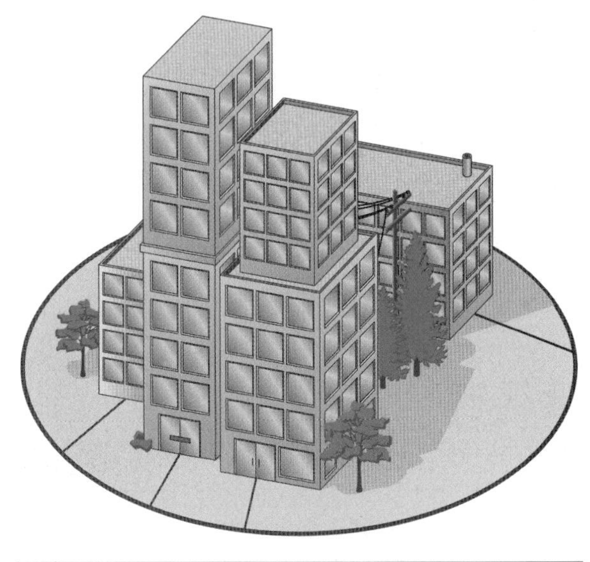

• Metropolitan area network (MAN)

WANs

A WAN may cover the largest geographic area. It is defined as two or more networks connected over long distances using phone lines, cable networks, or satellite communications. The connection between the networks is called a WAN

The speed of your communications on any network is a function of the speed of the slowest pathway between you and the servers you are accessing. The weakest link determines your speed.

connection. The generic term for such connected networks is **internetwork**. The most famous and largest of these is the Internet. Your Internet connection from home is a WAN connection, even when the network at home consists of a single computer connected to a phone line.

WAN speeds range from thousands of bits per second up into the millions of bits per second. At the low end today are 56-Kbps modems (56,000 bits per second). At the high end of WAN speeds are parts of the Internet backbone, the connecting infrastructure of the Internet, which runs at hundreds of millions of bits per second and faster.

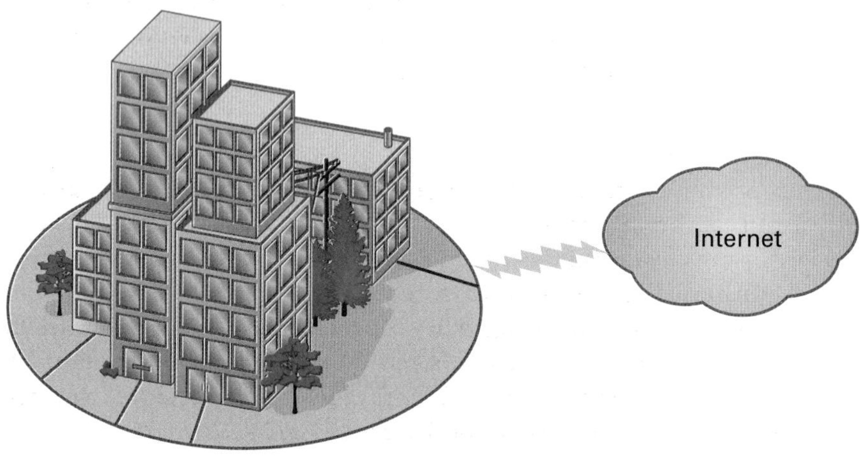

• Wide area network (WAN)

Logical Network Organization

How the computers on a network are organized for administration, where data is stored, and where the programs you are using actually run are functions of the logical organization of a network. There are two ways to organize a network: using peer-to-peer and server-based arrangements.

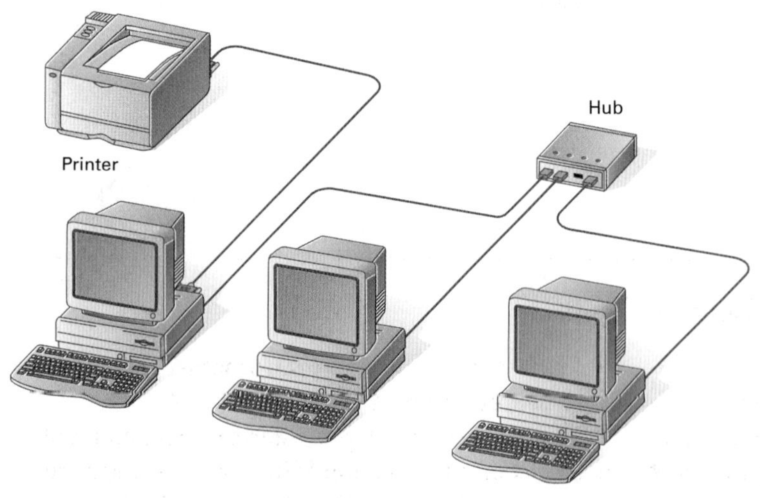

• Peer-to-peer network

Peer-to-Peer Networks

In a peer-to-peer logical network organization, data and other resources are distributed around the network among the desktop PCs that are connected to the network—the same computers that the users use for their work. More important, there is no built-in central management of security. Our accountant, Tom, has a peer-to-peer network in his office. There are a total of three PCs sitting on the desktops of the two accountants and the staff person. The most important files are in a share on Tom's computer. Another set of files is in a share on Tom's assistant's computer, which also controls a shared printer.

At each PC hosting a resource, an administrator must make that individual resource available as a share, and that computer is considered an equal, or peer, of all others. In addition to taking steps to allow a folder or printer to be shared on the network, the administrator has to consider security needs and take whatever steps are necessary and possible to give file or printer access only to those who should have access. Peer-to-peer is not the status quo in medium to large organizations. In Microsoft networks, a solely peer-to-peer network is called a workgroup. Microsoft does not recommend a workgroup of more than ten computers because of the administrative headaches involved in managing the accounts, shares, and permissions on more than ten systems. Even in such small networks, a workgroup is not recommended if there are high security needs.

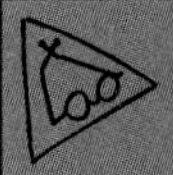

Inside Information

Microsoft Domain Names

Windows NT domain names were simple one-word names, while those used in Microsoft domains since Windows 2000 look like the domain names you see on the Internet, such as "Microsoft.com," and may have more names to the left separated by the decimal point symbol in the format of "third.second.first."

Server-Based Networks

The most common administrative organization for PC networks is a server-based arrangement, where each client computer on a network interacts with one or more servers. And since a server is nothing without clients to serve, this is often called a client/server network. The servers provide a central place for keeping and controlling the resources. The servers are dedicated to providing network services and are not used as desktop computers. A Microsoft server-based network with central administration is called a domain. Each domain must have a special label, called a **domain name**.

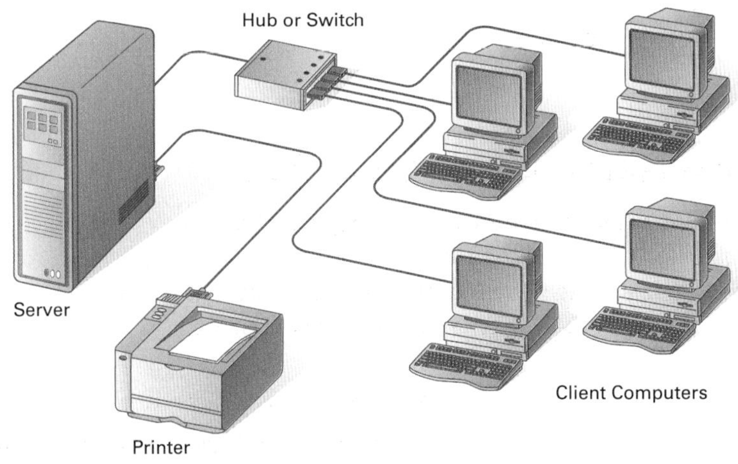

• Server-based network

Step-by-Step 9.01

Peer-to-Peer or Server-Based Network?

In this step-by-step exercise, you will use the OS to determine whether your class lab is on a network. Yes, we realize that you could just walk around and look at the back of each computer for physical proof that it is or is not on a network, but see if you can determine that status through your OS. Then you will look for clues that tell you whether it is peer-to-peer, server-based, or both.

To complete this step-by-step exercise, you will need a computer running Windows. The steps are written for Windows XP, but are very similar to those you will take in other versions of Windows.

Step 1

As you log onto your computer, take a close look at the Log On To Windows dialog box. If the Log On To pull-down menu gives you a domain to which to log on, then you have access to a Microsoft server-based network. If the only choice is to log onto your computer, rather than to a domain, your computer may be part of a peer-to-peer network.

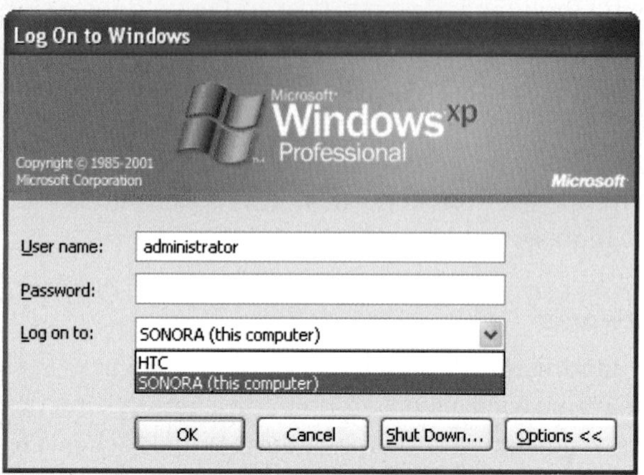

Step 2

If you could not determine whether your computer was on a network in the previous step, open My Network Places. Any computers you are able to see are file and print servers on your network. The fact that you can see them means that you are successfully connected to a network. Remember that this service is often turned on by default, even in desktop versions of Windows.

Step 3

Now view the properties of the computers that are acting as servers on your network. In My Network Places, right-click on a server and select properties. If it is a Windows Server computer running Windows 2000 or Windows Server 2003, you may not be allowed to view its properties. The computer Sonora is running Windows XP Professional, shown as "Windows Professional."

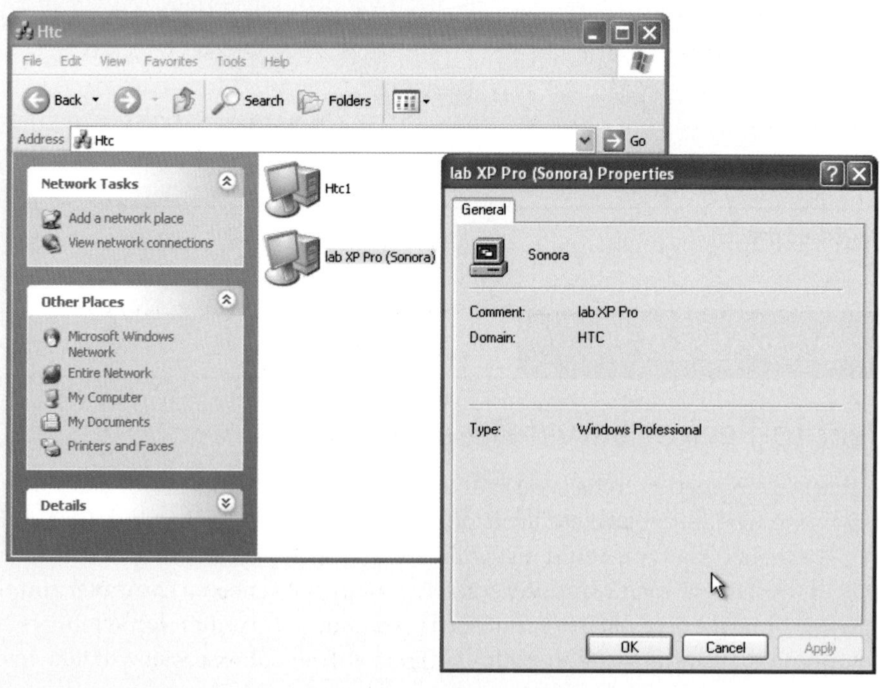

Network Pieces and Parts

So what are the pieces and parts that make up a network? Obviously, there are PCs, but there are many other components as well. Some components are physical, like the hardware used to connect to the network, the media (wires, or broadcast and receiving antennas in the case of wireless) that make the connections work, and the connection points the communications media connects to—the nodes. Yet other components include the software that makes everything work together—the drivers, network operating systems (NOSs), and services—and the protocols. Build your understanding of basic network theory by examining these pieces.

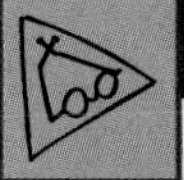

Inside Information

Skipping a Step

It is interesting that in the United States and most of Europe, a significant majority of network transmission is over existing, or upgraded, telephone media. But in Africa, South America, parts of Asia, and other areas of the world where an elaborate wired communication system is largely nonexistent, computer networks are rapidly being established using radio and satellite communications media. They are bypassing the ground-based wiring stage.

Physical Components

Several types of hardware components connect your computer to the network and connect networks to other networks.

Network Interface and Media Start with the computer in front of you, which is called a **node** when it is connected to a network. To connect to a network, your computer must have a network interface—a device that sends and receives signals over the network media. The network interface to connect to a LAN is an integrated circuit card installed in or connected to your computer called a network interface card (NIC) or a network adapter. The network interface device for a dial-up connection to a network is a modem (*mo*dulator/*dem*odulator). Whatever the device, it must be able to work with the specific media of your network. A wireless device must have a NIC with antennas for sending and receiving radio frequency (RF) signals.

The **media** carrics the signals between devices on the network. In the beginning, of course, network media was metal wire (think telephone cable), and the vast majority of it in developed countries still is. But other types of media work well for specific needs and are gaining ground rapidly. Optical signals are fed through fiber-optic cables, which, though still cables, are made of glass instead of metal. Fiber-optic media can transmit data much faster than wire-based media. The media that is getting a lot of attention lately is wireless—in which the radio or infrared signals are transmitted to receivers through the air around us. This wireless media makes physical connection unnecessary. These different media all do essentially the same thing: they carry data bits from one place to another.

Other Network Connection Devices So what else is needed to make a network work, in addition to the network connection devices in each computer plus the media? Various other network devices are required to move data between computers and between connected networks. They include the following:

- Network **hubs** and **switches** that the media from each node connects to.
- Network connection devices called **bridges** and **routers** that carry traffic from network to network.
- Network security devices, especially firewalls. A firewall is a hardware component with specialized software that is usually placed at the point where a private network (or group of networks) connects to a public, untrusted network, the Internet. A firewall works to prevent malicions traffic from entering a network.

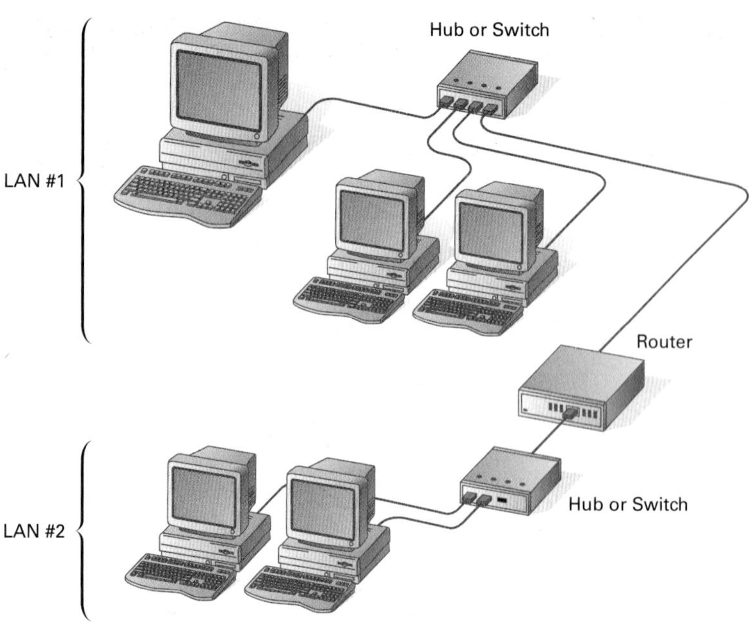

• Network components

Software Components

The software components that make it possible to use a computer network include drivers, network operating systems, and services.

Drivers You need a driver to allow your OS to control the network interface device (NIC or modem). Most NICs or modems come with drivers for several different OSs. If your interface device does not have a driver for your OS, you should check the manufacturer's web site or the Microsoft web site.

Network Operating Systems (NOSs) A network operating system (NOS) contains the basic program code that allows your computer to communicate on a network. Other software components are installed in the NOS to provide network access. The term *NOS* had more meaning when the OS and NOS were separate programs, or were even from different vendors. In the 1980s, a desktop computer usually ran DOS, and you added a NOS to connect to a network. In all Microsoft OSs since Windows for Workgroups, the OS and the NOS are combined. This is also true of the Mac OSs and the many flavors of UNIX and Linux. Today the term *NOS* is often used to refer to OSs designed primarily to function as network servers.

Services Services are individual programs that provide a certain function or set of functions and are usually active behind the scenes. Each Windows OS has many services that provide both network and non-network functions. Figure 9-2 shows part of the list of services on a Windows XP computer. The workstation service enables your computer to access network shares as a client, and the server service allows a computer to provide basic server services such as file and print sharing. Another service, Net Logon, sends your authentication request from your PC to a server, when you log onto a Windows domain.

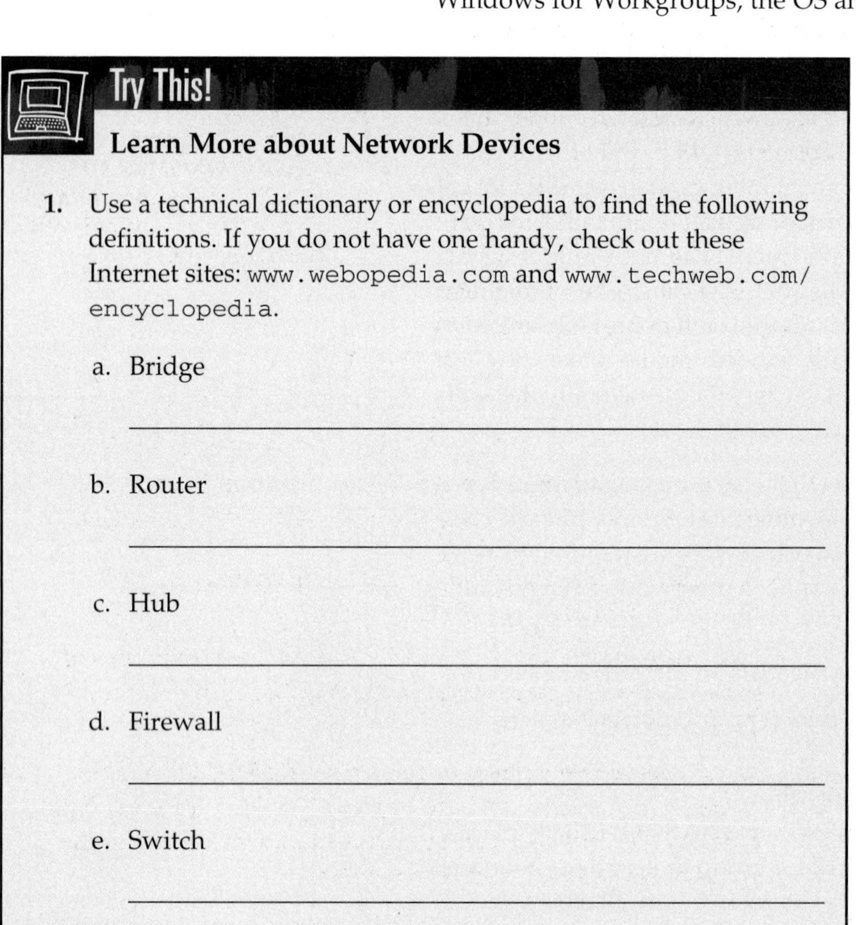

Try This!

Learn More about Network Devices

1. Use a technical dictionary or encyclopedia to find the following definitions. If you do not have one handy, check out these Internet sites: `www.webopedia.com` and `www.techweb.com/encyclopedia`.

   a. Bridge

   ____

   b. Router

   ____

   c. Hub

   ____

   d. Firewall

   ____

   e. Switch

   ____

Protocols

Because there are so many kinds of media, network devices, and ways of arranging nodes in a network, some agreed-upon rules are needed that each component has to follow for the network to function correctly. These rules are called **protocols**. There are numerous different protocols and various kinds, or levels, of protocols. Some apply directly to the way that data is placed on the hardware; these are often called transport protocols. Other protocols, called network communication protocols, work at a level above the hardware. Network communication protocols depend on the hardware, but are not concerned with how the hardware works.

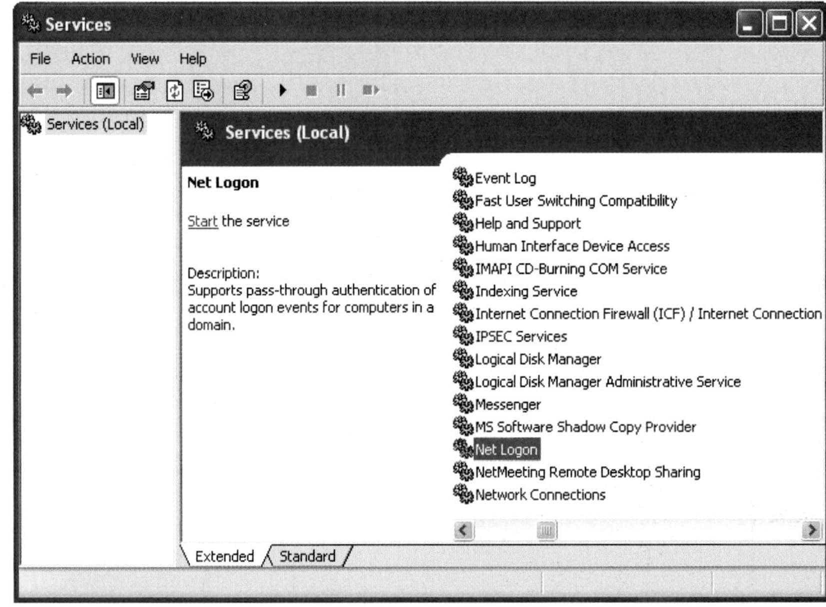

• **Figure 9-2.** Windows XP services

Of course, someone has to pay attention to the hardware protocols, at least to ensure that your network hardware devices can connect your computer to the network and can communicate with the other devices on the network. For instance, certain wireless network devices comply with incompatible standards and so cannot communicate with each other.

Network Communication Protocol Suites Network communication protocols are usually combined into suites that work together. The most common protocol suite on networks today (and the standard protocol suite of the Internet) is TCP/IP, but other network protocol suites are still in use in small- to medium-sized departmental LANs. These include Microsoft's NetBEUI (very rarely used today), Apple's AppleTalk (replaced in newer versions of the Mac OS by TCP/IP), and Novell's IPX/SPX, which still has a greater presence than the other two, but is also being replaced with TCP/IP. Windows 2000, Windows XP, and Windows Server 2003 install TCP/IP by default, but there are other protocols that you can optionally install, as shown in Figure 9-3. To see this dialog box in Windows XP, click Install on the General page of the Local Area Connection Properties dialog box, select Protocol, and then click Add.

NWLink IPX/SPX/NetBIOS Compatible Transport Protocol is Microsoft's version of Novell's IPX/SPX protocol.

Try This!

See the List of Services on Your Lab Computer

You will need a computer running Windows XP or Windows 2000.

1. Select Start | Run and enter the following command: **services.msc**. Then press ENTER.
2. Scroll through the list of services, and read the descriptions of some of the network services. Notice the Status and Startup Type columns.
3. Try an alternative method to quickly see what services are started. Open a command prompt and type **NET START**. Then press ENTER. This command displays the services that had the status of Started in the Services window.

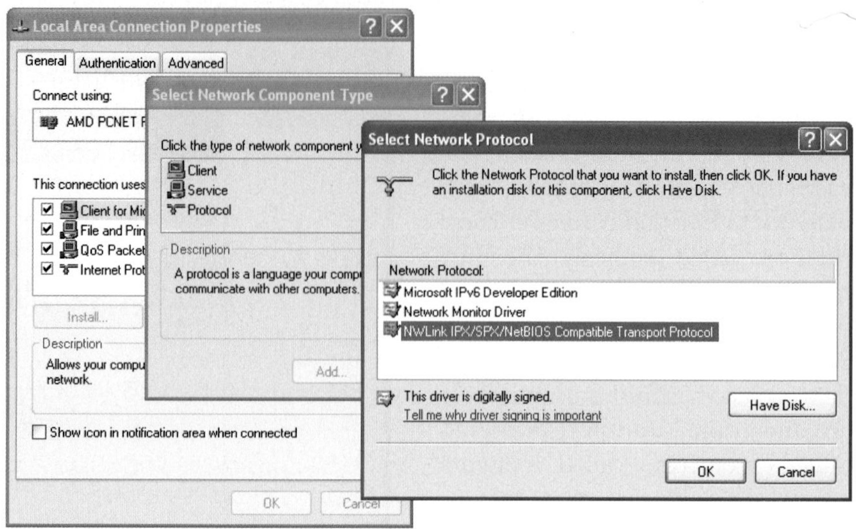

• **Figure 9-3.** Select Network Protocol dialog box

Basic Server Concepts

A server is a computer on a network that provides one or more services to other computers. Servers are the heart and soul of a network of any size. A client is a computer, or rather a software component on that computer, that accesses a service of a server. In this section, you will learn more about this client/server relationship. The first service provided in early LANs, and still in use even today, is the service that allows a server to provide access to its local files to users over the network.

The Two Sides of the Equation

One problem with understanding networking is the somewhat ambiguous nature of the terminology. Now go back to the concept of resource sharing. When we discuss sharing, we have to ask who does the sharing, and who just accesses the resource. To make the answer a little less ambiguous, we use the terms *server* and *client,* the two sides of the networking equation.

Any system that wants to share its resources must run a program or service that does the sharing. At that instant, the system is a server. Any system that wants to access resources must run a program that does the accessing. At that instant, the system is a client. In a peer-to-peer network, each system must have both client and server software available. All current versions of Windows desktop OSs are capable of playing both

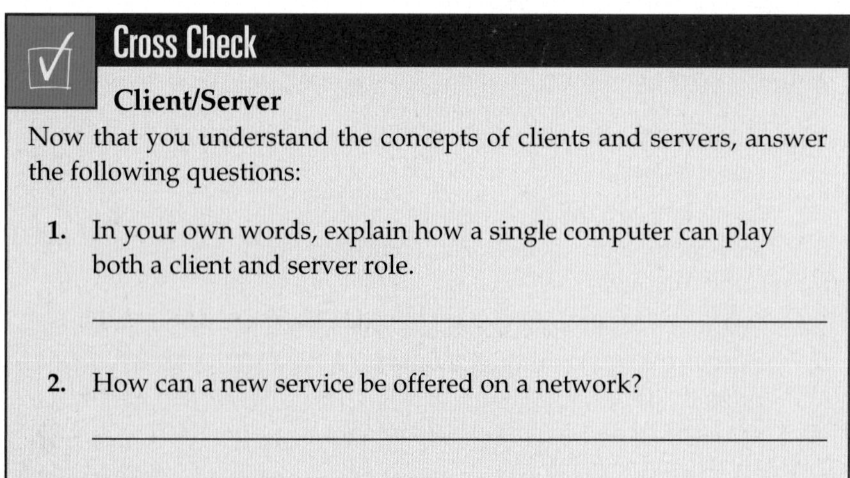

Cross Check

Client/Server

Now that you understand the concepts of clients and servers, answer the following questions:

1. In your own words, explain how a single computer can play both a client and server role.

   ____

2. How can a new service be offered on a network?

   ____

roles simultaneously. Thus, the role of server is not limited to powerful computer systems with vast resources, although that is the common perception. In fact, any computer connected to a network may play many roles at once.

There is specific client software for each type of resource a client accesses. Each client performs all tasks necessary to request the specific resources and to work with them locally. The server side performs all of the necessary processing on the server to provide the requested services. In this way, processing is distributed. This relationship is referred to as **client/server networking**.

The OSs Supporting the Services

This leads us to the topic of the complexity of network servers. Network servers offer many services, but most of these services run on top of one of a handful of network operating systems from Microsoft, Novell, or any of several UNIX or Linux vendors. To complicate matters, Novell offers separate Linux products, for servers and desktops, as well as its flagship NetWare product.

Most network servers in use today—on both private and public networks—have modular software components. The server administrators select the services needed and install them in the NOS. The services may or may not be from the same vendor as the NOS. The underlying NOS will be a server product from Microsoft or Novell or will be a variant of UNIX or Linux. In the following sections, we explore the NOSs available today.

Windows Server Operating Systems

In addition to their desktop products, Microsoft has several server operating system products under each of their major Windows versions. The server versions in use today include Windows NT Server 4.0, Windows 2000 Server, and Windows Server 2003. Each of these is actually a product family, with individual products targeted to a certain range of server hardware and even to specific purposes. Any one of these server OSs may offer one or more network roles, depending on the services installed and configured. One role that can be played by any of these is that of a **domain controller**, a server that maintains the directory service accounts database in a Microsoft network. When a Windows 2000 Server or Windows Server 2003 is configured as a domain controller, it runs Active Directory, Microsoft's directory service for maintaining accounts for users, client computers, servers, printers, networks, and other objects that can participate in a network. This replaces the SAM used by Windows NT domain controllers, but the SAM has not gone away entirely. SAM is still the accounts database for local accounts on Windows desktop computers and non-domain controller servers. The server products are as follows:

Windows NT Server 4.0 Although not truly a current product, since it was introduced in 1996, Windows NT Server 4.0 is still running on many network servers. Its server products include the following:

- **Windows NT Server 4.0** is a general-purpose server used for file and print services and as a domain controller in small- to medium-sized organizations.

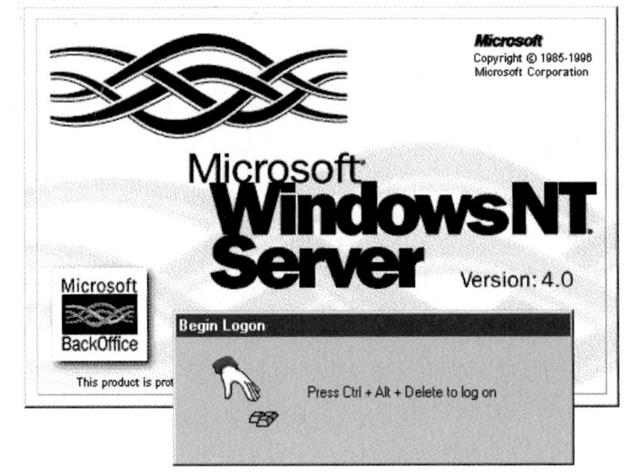

• The Windows NT Server 4.0 Splash screen and logon prompt

- **Windows NT Server 4.0 Enterprise Edition** is designed for larger network servers and came only as an OEM product preinstalled on servers.

Windows NT 4.0 Server products have not been offered for sale by Microsoft through any channel since July 1, 2003, and they discontinued all support for Windows NT 4.0 Server as of January 1, 2005.

Windows 2000 Server The Windows 2000 Server product line was introduced early in 2000 as three products:

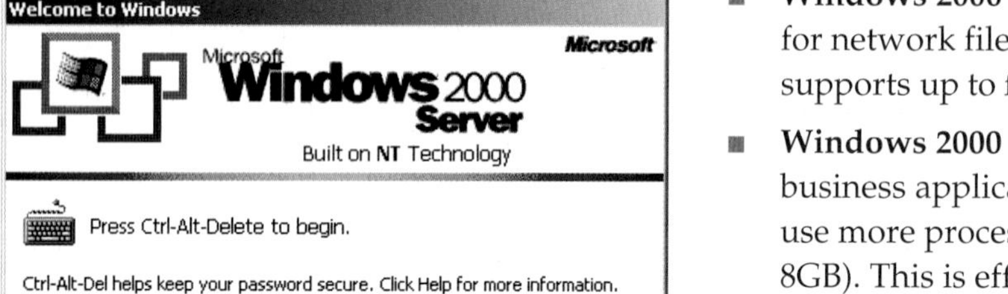

• The Windows 2000 Server logon prompt

- **Windows 2000 Server** is the base server operating system for network file, print, intranet, and application servers. It supports up to four processors and 8GB of physical RAM.
- **Windows 2000 Advanced Server** is targeted at line-of-business applications, e-commerce, and web servers. It can use more processors (up to eight) and more memory (up to 8GB). This is effectively an upgrade to the Windows NT 4.0 Enterprise Edition.
- **Windows 2000 Datacenter Server** is available only in OEM versions on very high-end servers with up to 32 processors and up to 64GB of memory. This version is targeted at very large data warehousing, econometric analysis, science and engineering applications, and very large web sites.

Microsoft's Small Business Server (SBS) products are special bundles of their server products targeted to small businesses and offered at bargain prices. These products have been offered for several years and include the latest Microsoft Windows Server plus valuable add-on services. For instance, Windows Small Business Server 2003 is targeted to small businesses with up to 75 client computers. See the list of features offered with this product at `http://www.microsoft.com/windowsserver2003/sbs/`.

Windows Server 2003 Windows Server 2003 was introduced in April 2003. At this writing the Windows Server 2003 operating system product line includes the following:

- **Windows Server 2003 Standard Edition** is designed for small- to medium-sized networks, offering a full suite of services needed by these networks. It is ideal for small business or department-level business units. It supports up to four processors, 4GB of physical RAM.
- **Windows Server 2003 Enterprise Edition** is designed for large networks, or those small-to-medium networks for which network growth is predicted during the organization's planned useful life of the server. This NOS is highly **scalable**, meaning that it is capable of easily adapting to increased demands. It has features required by large, highly reliable networks that are not supported in the Standard Edition. It is offered in a 32-bit version for the Intel Pentium and Xeon processors, as well as a 64-bit version for the Intel Itanium processor. The Itanium processor was designed for the extremely processor-intensive tasks required on some large networks. Further, the Enterprise Edition supports up to eight processors and 64GB of RAM.
- **Windows Server 2003 Web Edition** is designed for the role of a dedicated web server. Because web services do not require the same RAM and processor levels as some of the other Windows Server 2003 products, it only supports up to 2GB of RAM, up to two processors, and is offered only in a 32-bit version for the Intel Pentium and Xeon processors. All services deemed unnecessary for a web server are removed from this edition in order to optimize it to focus on the

tasks of hosting web sites and serving up web pages. It is an inexpensive (relative to its siblings), single-purpose tool. It costs about 60 percent less than the Standard Edition.

- **Windows Server 2003 Datacenter Edition** is Microsoft's answer to the organization that cannot tolerate any loss of service on their networks and/or must handle immense amounts of data. It is available only in OEM versions, preinstalled on very high-end server computers. To support high availability and mission-critical service, this product comes with Microsoft's comprehensive support system called the Windows Datacenter High Availability Program, administered by Microsoft or by the vendor. Like Enterprise Edition, it comes in a 32- and 64-bit version. The 32-bit version supports up to 32 processors and 64GB of RAM, while the 64-bit version supports up to 64 processors and up to 512GB of RAM.

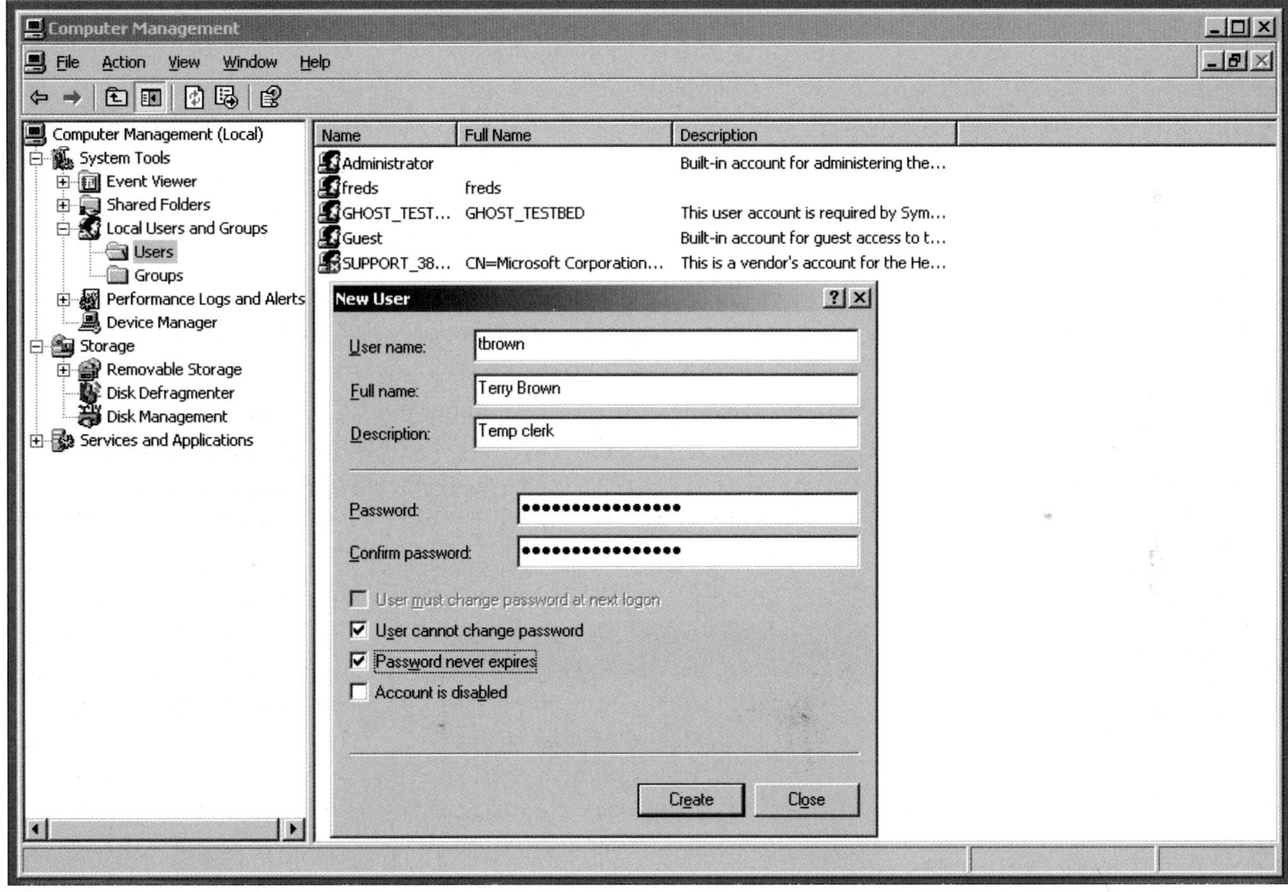

• Windows Server 2003 Enterprise Edition Computer Management Console

UNIX Server Operating Systems

There are many versions of UNIX, and they run on a variety of hardware platforms. Add to this UNIX's power and stability (it rarely crashes), and it is no wonder UNIX has long been the server OS of choice for hosting various

Try This!

Learn More about the Open Source Initiative

The Open Source Initiative is part of a worldwide movement toward making more software available under the open source terms. Use your favorite search engine to research the Open Source Initiative, and then answer the following questions:

1. Why is it significant that the Open Source Initiative supports software licensing over software patents?
2. Why has the use of open source software become acceptable in places where it was not previously used?

network infrastructure services. DNS and DHCP services on the Internet and within many organizations are commonly run on UNIX servers. Feeling the competitive pressure from Linux, the latest UNIX products from IBM, Compaq, Caldera, Hewlett-Packard, and Sun are even more scalable, secure, and manageable than their previous versions. They also offer both 32- and 64-bit versions that support multiple processors. In large organizations, UNIX remains a popular network operating system, especially on servers that host large databases shared by thousands of users. Many types of specialized database-specific software programs have been developed for the UNIX platform, and they are deeply entrenched in industries such as insurance, medicine, banking, and manufacturing. UNIX is also widely used on web servers, especially those that support online transactions and that make heavy use of databases.

Linux Server Operating Systems

The many versions of Linux are growing in popularity within various sizes of organizations. It is also becoming more accepted in the small business and home markets as the server OS for computers providing Internet and networking services. Linux is an open operating system, available by itself for free, or available from certain vendors who bundle it and charge a fee for add-on software, installation programs, documentation, and user support. It is a cost-effective alternative to other operating system for sharing files, applications, printers, modems, and Internet services. A large number of Linux servers host web sites and perform other roles on the Internet. Linux is competing with all other server operating systems in many arenas. Among the Linux vendors are Red Hat, Novell, Hewlett-Packard, the Gentoo Foundation, and MandrakeSoft SA. Linux is considered open source software, meaning that the source code (program code in its original and changeable form) is freely available to anyone. That is the generic definition. The manner in which most Linux vendors distribute Linux complies with the Open Source standard, as defined by the Open Source Initiative (`www.opensource.org`).

Cross Check

UNIX vs. Linux

Flip back to Chapter 1, and review the information about the history of UNIX and Linux. Then answer the following questions:

1. Who played key roles in the development of UNIX? Who is considered to be the father of Linux?

   ____

2. Do you regard these two OSs as variations of the same OS? Why?

   ____

Novell Server Operating Systems

In the 1980s, Novell, Inc. produced some of the earliest hardware and software for corporate networks. They continued to update their flagship product, the NetWare network operating system, to meet the growing need for more services and larger networks. By the early 1990s, Novell's NetWare operating system, using the IPX/SPX protocol suite, led this market with a nearly 70 percent share. Their fortunes declined in the mid-1990s, however, as they lost market share to Microsoft server products. Still innovative, Novell introduced their directory service, Novell Directory Services (NDS), in their NetWare 4.0 product in 1994, years ahead of Microsoft's introduction of a competing directory service in Windows 2000. And in 1998, NetWare 5 shipped with native support for TCP/IP, the protocol suite standard of the Internet and corporate networks.

Novell still is an important server OS vendor, bringing out new versions of NetWare and developing and improving the services that run on its server OSs. At this writing, Novell's latest version of NetWare is Open Enterprise Server (OES). While in development, this version was referred to as NetWare 7, but by release was given a name that more accurately reflects the evolution of the NetWare server products from platforms for proprietary products to a platform for open systems services and applications—a "marriage" of NetWare and Linux. OES is just one server product line offered by Novell, and it appears to be a departure from the NetWare brand. They also offer SUSE Linux Enterprise Server, for a broad range of computers up to mainframes, and will be adding more server products for target markets, such as retailers. This strategy has brought them increasing market share.

Try This!

Find the Latest NOSs and Related Products

Microsoft and Novell both have basic NOS server products and many add-on services. Connect to their web sites and browse through the list of products. Try this:

1. Connect to `www.microsoft.com` and look for products. Browse through the Windows desktop and server operating systems and the Office products. Then find the products that can be added to the Windows servers, such as the e-mail server, Exchange Server.
2. Connect to `www.novell.com` and click the link to Products. The list is long and growing, including the server operating systems, desktop (Linux) operating system, and services that can be added to Novell's basic server OSs.

Server Roles—Past and Present

Think of all of the reasons for using a network, and you will find that there is a server role for each reason. Learn how server roles evolved over the last few decades as networking itself grew to touch the lives of people throughout the world. Then learn about some of the key roles servers play on networks—both private and public.

Server Roles in the Past

Early LANs in the 1980s focused on file and printer sharing, because hard drives and printers were expensive, and it was worth connecting computers just to share them. At that time, the mission-critical network services in large organizations were provided by very large mainframe computers running proprietary operating systems and applications, and the users worked at dedicated terminals connected to the mainframe over a proprietary network. Therefore, a typical early LAN was separate from the corporate network, located within a department, and provided file and print services to PC users of MS-DOS-based office applications. These systems were sometimes brought in and installed under the direction of a middle manager, without the help or approval of the department that ran and supported the mainframe services. One or two servers would meet the needs of an entire department.

Over the years, PC-based servers have improved at both the hardware and OS levels so that the servers now have capabilities that rival the mainframe systems and therefore, the number of roles played by these servers has increased. The mantra of IT professionals has become "interoperability," meaning that all systems must have the capability to interact. Network services have moved off the proprietary networks, and hardware and software from nearly all vendors will communicate and work together. All the connected networks of a single organization and all the resources on that network are now referred to as an **enterprise network**. An organization's data may be anywhere on the enterprise network. Applications—even mission-critical applications—may reside on a mainframe system or on a server.

Server Roles Today

Today there are many additional server roles on both private intranets and on the Internet. One physical server computer may be dedicated to a single role, or it may play a combination of roles. These roles sometimes come in the form of elaborate services such as e-mail that can be added to a network operating system, in which case, the service is an extra-cost option not built into the server OS. The source of an added service may be the same vendor as the OS, or a third-party vendor. In the following sections, we look at just a few of the many roles that servers play in today's networks.

Directory Service Server

A generic term for a server that maintains the directory service database for an organization is a directory service server. In a Windows Active Directory (AD) domain, the servers running the AD directory service must be running one of the Windows 2000 Server or Windows Server 2003 products. These servers are called domain controllers. An administrator of a directory services network uses special administrative tools to manage the directory service accounts. In an Active Directory domain, the administrator may use any Windows 2000 or Windows XP Professional computer on the network to remotely manage the accounts, or she may sit at the keyboard of one of the AD domain controllers. In both cases, the administrator uses the same tool: the Active Directory Users and Group console.

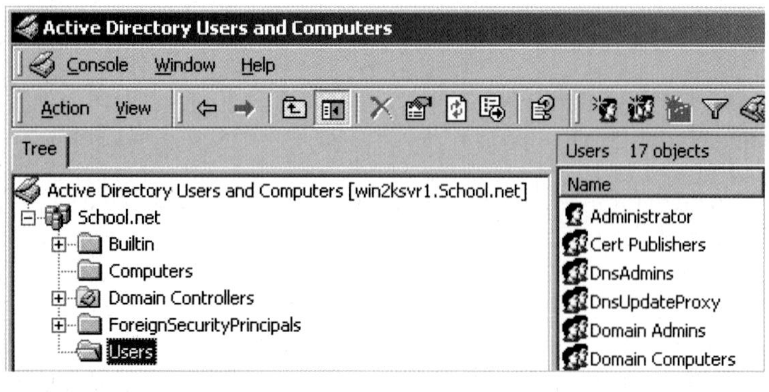

• The Active Directory Users and Computers window

File and Print Server

When you use a computer at school or work, do you save the word processing, spreadsheet, graphics, and other data files to a network server? A computer that allows you to connect to it to store files is a **file server**. Do you access a printer connected to the network? A server that gives you access to a network printer is a **print server**. These two roles are often combined and performed by the same server—a **file and print server**. In Microsoft networking, this combined service is called File and Printer Sharing for Microsoft Networks. The client side is called Client for Microsoft Networks. Most, if not all, NOSs have a file and print service as a base service that does not have to be added to the NOS.

Data is saved on file servers for a variety of reasons. The following is not a comprehensive list, but includes the most common reasons for saving data on a file server:

- It is easier to physically ensure the security of a server, which can be removed from direct access, while still available on the network to authorized users. This is in contrast to a desktop computer, which may be in a very public location.
- Data stored on a server can be made available to two or more users.
- Data stored on a server can be used in a collaborative effort by two or more users.
- Data stored on a server can be backed up more easily than data saved on many desktop computers.

Remember that the word *share* is both a verb and a noun. This has often been a source of confusion. Computers *share* (verb) resources. A *share* (noun) is the name for the point at which one computer can access the resources of another. Do not confuse these two uses of this word!

The most important word here is *share.* A user of a networked PC can share a file folder, printer, or other resource with other computers and access the resources of other network computers as well. When a PC's resources are shared, it is offering a service to other computers on the network. At that moment, it is a server. When a user at a PC accesses a share on another networked computer, that user's computer is a *client* of the service offered by the other computer. So a PC can be both server and client at the same time. Without a network, each PC is just an island, something that is not generally desirable in computing today.

While this service is available on Windows desktop operating systems, which can then act as network servers, a desktop operating system does not have some of the same capabilities and services as a server operating system, such as Windows Server 2003 or Novell NetWare. Server operating systems can handle many simultaneous connections and can take advantage of very high-end server computers with many processors,

Try This!

View the File and Printer Sharing Service

The Windows File and Printer Sharing Service is turned on by default. The instructions are for Windows XP, but these instructions are very similar to those you will use in Windows NT 4.0 or Windows 2000. Try this:

1. Log onto your lab computer as Administrator or a member of the Administrators group.
2. Select Start | Control Panel | Network Connections. Right-click the icon for a network connection and select Properties.
3. Locate the item named "File and Printer Sharing for Microsoft Networks." If this item is listed *and* the check box contains a check mark, it is turned on, and you may share files and printers from this computer. If the item is listed but does not have a check mark, it is turned off, and the computer may not act as a file and printer server.
4. Close all dialog boxes and open windows when you are finished.

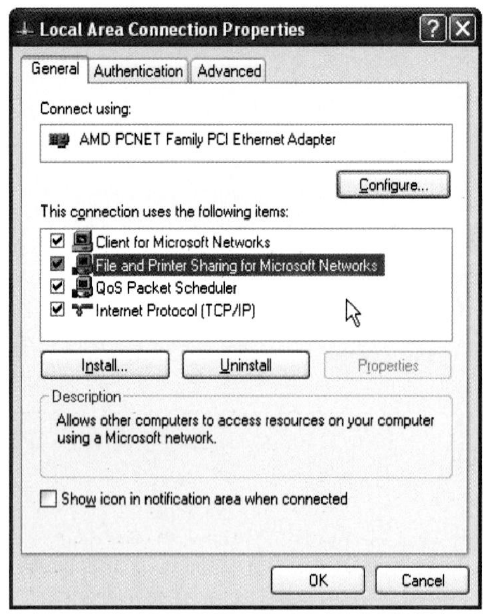

• File and Printer Sharing for Microsoft Networks

high-speed disk drives, and gigabytes of RAM memory. Such computers, attached to high-speed networks, provide file and print services on large enterprise networks.

E-Mail Server

In the early days of PC networks, the basic information sharing need was satisfied by file and printer sharing. The electronic delivery and management of messages within most large private and governmental organizations was already the turf of the mainframe systems. However, as LAN networks proliferated and became more reliable and more interconnected, communication of messages within organizations was gradually moved from the larger systems to servers on these networks. A server that transmits, receives, and stores e-mail is called a **mail server** or **e-mail server**. The messages transmitted electronically are called e-mail.

Today, in addition to the mail servers within organizations, there are many Internet-based mail servers. Most people can communicate via e-mail seamlessly both within organizations and over the Internet. In fact, for many individuals, e-mail is the most compelling reason to have Internet access from home. In the 1980s, we subscribed to an Internet messaging service (CompuServe), but found that we received only infrequent messages from a few other technical people. Today, we conduct most of our business by Internet e-mail and stay in touch with many family members connected to the Internet, in addition to our technical and business associates.

In a Microsoft network, the e-mail server is Exchange; in a NetWare environment, it is GroupWise. Both of these products do much more than simply manage e-mail.

Data Backup Servers

Centralized data backup has long been an important network service. For real data safety, the data is frequently put on removable media (tape, disk, and so on) and stored somewhere safely away from the computer. In the simplest scenario, users save all of their data to one or more network servers. Each server is then backed up nightly. This moves the backup task from the desktop to the server room. A small organization may have a tape backup system on each server, but things can become messy as the number of servers grows. Several vendors sell centralized backup systems that use a dedicated backup server, large tape archiving systems, and specialized client

Try This!

Find a Backup Service

You are looking for an Internet-based backup service to back up the 15 desktop computers in a small office. Connect to the Internet and find a service that will allow you to back up 5GB of data from each computer nightly.

1. Use your favorite search engine to find Internet-based backup services. Search for a product that will work for a small office.

   ____

2. Find the cost of subscribing for 15 computers. Do you consider the cost reasonable for this service? Why?

   ____

3. Look for a free trial version of the product you want to try.

   ____

software that runs on each computer that has its data backed up to the central backup server. Just a few of these vendors are Novastor, Syncsort, and Computer Associates. Most major vendors have backup services that run on Windows (various versions), Novell, and UNIX OSs.

Also, a large number of Internet-based backup services allow subscribers to back up data over the Internet to their servers. Some of the vendors who sell backup software have added Internet backup services to their list of products. Just a few of these vendors are CapSure, Connected, Xdrive, Clunk Click, and 1stForData.

Application Servers

An **application server** is a program that acts as an intermediary between users running client software and a large back-end business application or database. The client-side component may be a program running on a PC, or it may be a simple web browser on a minimally configured network computer called a **thin client** that may not even have a hard disk. This model is replacing the client/server application, in which a more robust, or "fat," client was required to connect to and interact with the server application. Another Internet-based service now is provided by application service providers (ASPs), which manage application servers for many customers from a central location.

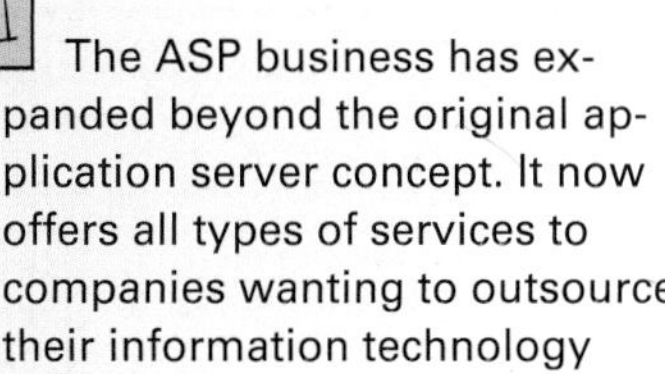

The ASP business has expanded beyond the original application server concept. It now offers all types of services to companies wanting to outsource their information technology needs in order to reduce costs.

Web Servers

Web servers are found on the Internet, hosting millions of web pages. They are also found on private networks, replacing file servers in some cases. Some content that was previously made available to employees and students on file servers, or even on physical bulletin boards and in-house publications, is now published on the company intranet. An intranet is a private internal network using Internet technologies such as web servers.

For many years, users connecting to the Internet could see only text content. There were no graphical pages such as we now see on the Web. The Internet existed, but not the Web. People often think that the Internet and the Web are simply different names for the same thing. They are not. The Web uses the Internet, but it uses a special set of protocols.

The Web came about thanks to the efforts of Tim Berners-Lee, a communications and text-handling expert who worked in the CERN physics laboratory in Geneva, Switzerland. He sought to help physicists from around the world as they collaborated on projects. He is credited with designing the hypertext markup language (HTML), the "killer technology" that made the World Wide Web possible. HTML is the language of the World Wide Web. The pages you view on the Web with your browser are written in

Cross Check

Server Roles

Like many aspects of networking, server roles continue to evolve. Consider what you have learned here, and perhaps some of your own experiences, and answer the following questions:

1. Has the file server role been made obsolete?

   ____

2. If you use a computer network at work or at school, identify the various server roles you access.

   ____

this language, which your browser transfers to your computer, which then uses the Hypertext Transfer Protocol (HTTP) to interpret the text commands on the page into the graphical elements you see on your screen. A uniform resource locator (URL) pointing to a web page starts with "http" to tell your browser software which protocol to use. In this book, we usually omit the protocol prefix, because your browser will attempt to use the HTTP protocol by default.

Microsoft and Novell both offer web server add-ons for their operating systems. Another product, Apache Server, developed by the Apache Software Foundation, comes in versions for several different NOSs and is reportedly used on as many as 60 percent of all web servers.

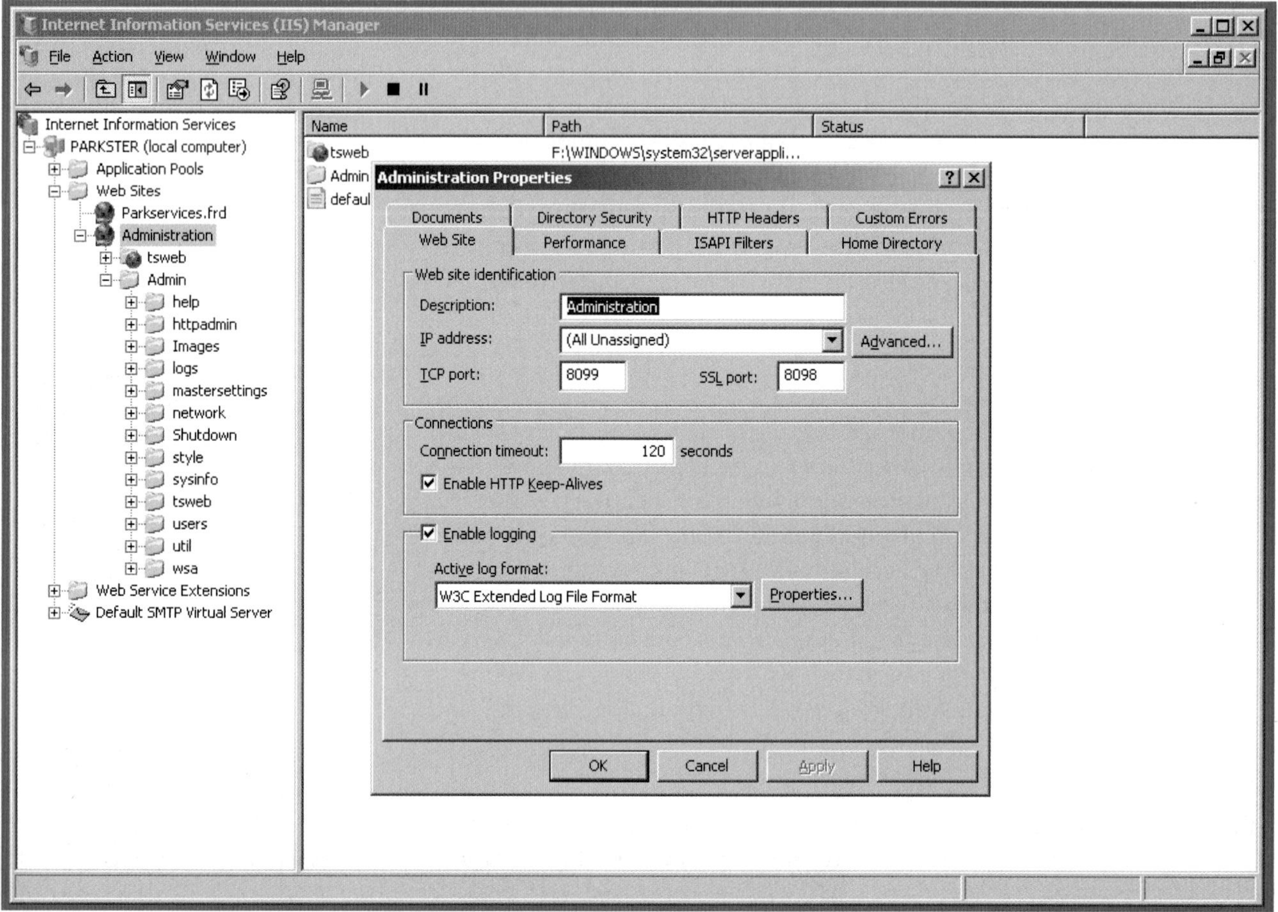

• An Administration console for Microsoft Web Server software IIS

Sharing and Protecting Resources

Effective sharing and protection of network resources is always carefully planned. In a medium- to large-sized organization, this plan is developed taking into consideration the work processes, company goals, user needs, and a host of other issues. The person who implements this plan is the administrator. In this section, we look at some of the tasks of the administrator who must implement the plan for sharing and protecting network resources. Our perspective is that of a Windows Active Directory domain administrator. The server-side tasks include adding a computer to a domain, creating user accounts and groups, and creating file and print shares. The client-side tasks include connecting to resources and testing the network security.

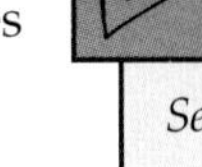

Inside Information

Get Server Software Free (Almost)

Server OSs are very expensive, but both Microsoft and Novell have in the past made evaluation copies of their OSs available. Evaluation copies stop working after a specified period. They are intended for people who want to learn about the software before buying it. Presently, Microsoft sells a 180-day evaluation version of Windows Server 2003 Edition (32-bit version) for $7.35. To get it, connect to `http://microsoft.order-2.com/trialstore/`. *Select Windows Server System and then scroll down on the following page until you find Windows Server 2003 Edition. Then check out, at which time you must fill out a form and provide a method of paying for the purchase. Do not be put off if the site states that it will take many weeks to deliver the CD. In our experience, CDs have been delivered from Microsoft in about half the time predicted.*

Adding Computers to a Microsoft Domain

A Windows Active Directory domain has several types of security accounts. A security account is one to which permissions and rights can be assigned. There are security accounts for computers, users, and groups. A computer account actually has a password it provides when it logs onto the domain (yes, computers log on, too) and when it connects to another computer.

Some Computers Can Join a Domain

An administrator has two tasks to perform before a computer can log onto a domain. First, the administrator must create an account for the computer in the domain, and then the administrator must have the computer join the domain. It takes a special right in the domain to create an account, and only someone with special rights to a computer can make it join a domain.

If you want to log onto a Windows domain from a Windows NT, Windows 2000, or Windows XP Professional computer, the computer must be a member of the domain. Once a computer joins a domain, it has a computer account in the domain. This is how even desktop computers become resources of a domain.

One of the differences between the Windows XP Home and Windows XP Professional products (other than the lower price of the former) is that a Windows XP Home computer cannot join a Windows NT or Active Directory domain.

Some Computers Cannot Join a Domain

Not all computers that can connect to Windows domain networks have security accounts. In particular, computers running Windows 9*x* or Windows XP Home cannot join a domain and have a security account in the domain. What they can do is enjoy some of the benefits of membership. The first one is that a user can log onto a domain from Windows 9*x* computers (but not a Windows XP Home computer) if it is configured for a user domain logon. Then, once logged onto the domain, a user can assign permissions to access local shares to users and groups in the domain. With Windows NT, Windows 2000, Windows XP Professional, and Windows Server 2003 computers, each computer must have an account in a domain and be logged onto a domain before a user sitting at that computer can log onto a domain.

Joining a computer to a domain is important even if you never intend to share a folder or printer on that computer, because there are other benefits of membership. These include centralized management of the desktop computer by administrators in the domain and your ability to log onto that computer using a domain user account. These things are possible because when the computer joins the domain, certain group accounts in the domain become members of local groups, which gives the domain administrators administrative rights on the local computer and allows domain users to log onto the local computer.

Inside Information

Computer and User Domains Can Differ

A computer's domain and that of the user logging on can be different if the two domains have a special relationship called a trust. A ***trust*** *relationship allows the accounts from one domain to use the resources of another domain. Therefore, if a computer is in a domain that trusts the user's domain, the user will be permitted to log onto the user domain from that computer. This is an advanced topic that server and network administrators must master.*

Step-by-Step 9.02

Adding a Computer to a Domain

In this exercise, you will add a Windows computer to a domain. To complete this exercise, you will need the following:

- A computer with Windows 2000 Professional or Windows XP Professional (Windows XP Home cannot join a domain) that is a member of a workgroup
- A user name and password of an account with local administrator rights
- A user name and password of a user account in the domain
- The name of a Windows domain on your network
- A user name and password of an account in the domain with permission to join a computer to the domain (you will need an Administrator account for a Windows NT domain, but an ordinary user account for an Active Directory domain)

Step 1

Log onto the local machine with an account that is a member of the Administrators group. Right-click on My Computer and then select Properties. In the System Properties dialog box, select Computer Name (Windows XP) or Network Identification (Windows 2000).

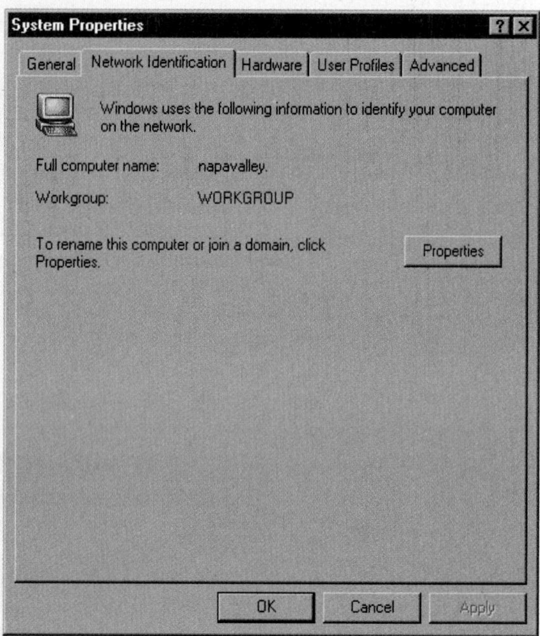

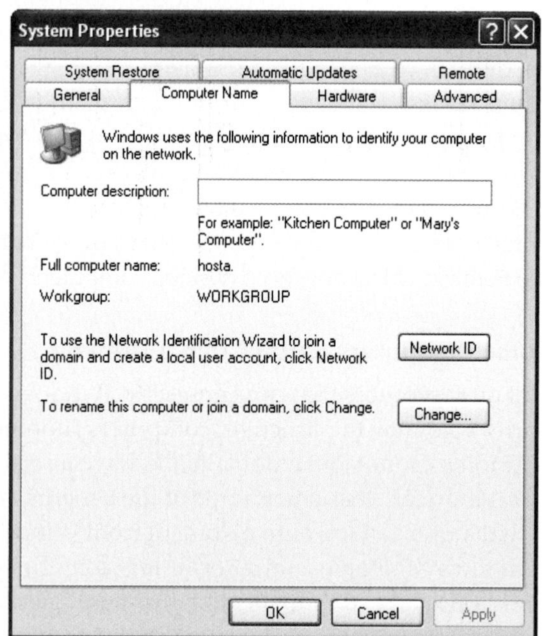

Step 2

In Windows XP, click Network ID to run the Network Identification wizard (for Windows 2000, skip to Step 4). Provide the answers for a computer on a business network with a domain. Be sure to enter the domain name in the Domain box on the User Account And Domain Information page, as well as the user name and password for an account in the domain. The Network Identification wizard will add this domain user to your local Users group, and it will create a local user profile for the domain user.

Step 3

Windows XP only: Now determine the level of access to grant to the user. Then, unless an administrator has already created a computer account in the domain, provide a user name and password for an account that can join a computer to a domain (a member of the Domain Administrators group works in both types of Microsoft domains). Click OK twice and then click Yes to reboot. Skip to Step 5.

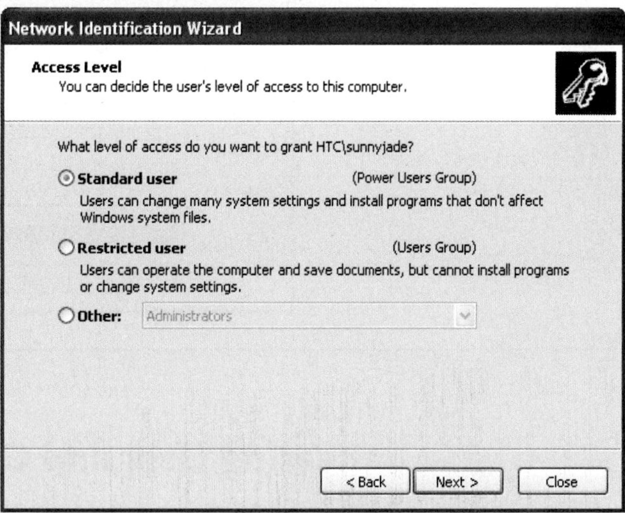

Step 4

In Windows 2000, click Properties and complete the Identification Changes dialog box, selecting Domain and entering the name of the domain you want to join. Click OK. Enter the name and password of a user with permission to join the domain, click OK twice, and then click Yes to reboot.

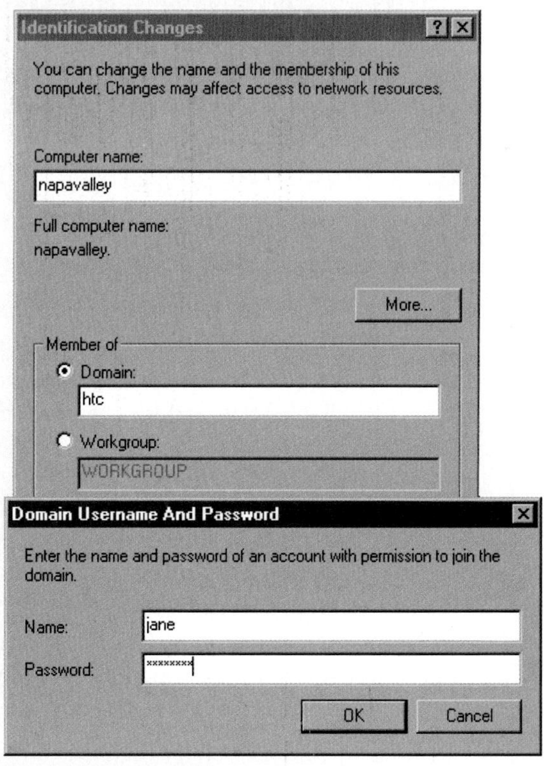

Step 5

After the reboot, log onto the domain using a domain user account. Be sure to select the domain by clicking Options to make the Log On To box visible.

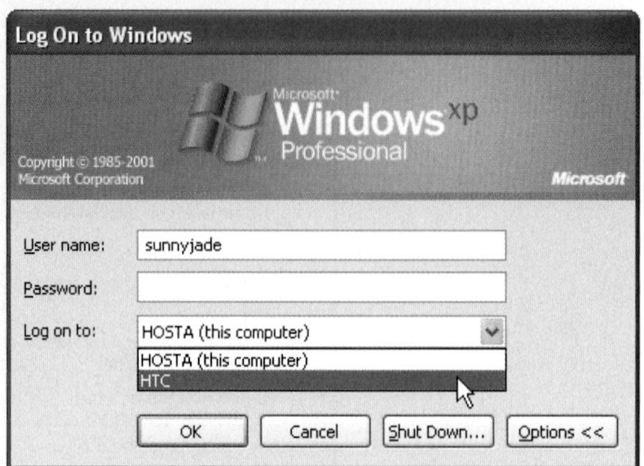

Creating User and Group Accounts

Using worksheets created from the network administration plan, an administrator creates the domain user and group accounts. Organizing users into groups that have common resource access needs allows an administrator to avoid the many steps involved in assigning unique permissions to each user in the organization. That would be too much like administering a workgroup! Now you will learn about the types of groups in a Windows domain, the account policies, and the permissions that can be assigned to users and groups.

Users and Group Membership

A Windows NT domain accepts passwords of up to 14 characters, and an Active Directory domain accepts passwords of up to 104 characters. In a mixed environment, to maintain compatibility across the board, keep password length to 14 or fewer characters.

In a Windows domain, the administrator can create several types of groups. These group types are similar, but they vary in scope and membership between Windows NT domains and Active Directory domains.

Domain Users Each user who logs onto a domain must have a domain user account. Domain user accounts contain identifying information about each user. At minimum, each user must have a user name and password to use to log on. This name can be up to 20 characters, and most organizations establish a standard for creating the user name from the user's full name.

Windows NT Domain Groups An NT domain (one in which all the domain controllers are Windows NT Server systems) has two types of groups: local and global. A local group is used to assign permissions to resources on those same domain controllers and can contain only user and group accounts from that domain. A global group is used to assign permissions to resources on other computers in the domain, and to resources in a domain that trusts the domain in which the global group resides. A global group can contain only users from the local domain.

Here is how an administrator works with these group types. Consider an NT domain named SchoolDom. The domain includes several shared folders and printers that should be accessed only by the managers and clerks in the school registration office. The group membership plan recognizes that the managers and clerks will have different access needs to various resources; therefore, they will be placed into two separate global groups, named Regmgrs and Regclerks. The registration printers should be available to all registration employees, but not to other employees; therefore, a local group, RegPrint, will be used for the registration printers.

Are you still with us? Good! Note that there are certain data files that only managers need to access, so another local group, RegData1, is created for giving access to these folders. Yet another set of data files must be available to all of the users in the Registration department; therefore, another local group is created, RegData2. Table 9-1 shows a sample group membership planning sheet for a Windows NT domain, with the user name shown in parentheses next to each user's full name. User names are created using the first initial and the last name. A naming policy should also define what is to be done to avoid duplicate names, such as for John Brown and James Brown. In that case, the policy may allow the use of the middle initial or a number in the name.

Recall that case is not significant in file and folder names in Windows OSs. Similarly, case is not significant in user and group names in Windows networks. RedData1 and regdata1 are treated the same. A mixture of upper- and lowercase is used in this chapter only for ease of reading.

Active Directory Domain Groups Active Directory domains are those with Windows 2000 or newer domain controllers. The group story here is much more complicated than that of Windows NT domains, and we will tell only a part of it here, because the finer details will help you only if you are close to becoming an Active Directory administrator.

An Active Directory domain also has local and global groups, but the local groups are called domain local groups, and although they work much like the local groups of Windows NT domains, they have greater scope. Whereas the local groups for a Windows NT domain can be used only to assign permissions to resources on the actual domain controllers, in a Windows Active Directory domain, the domain local groups can be used to assign permissions to resources on any computer with an account in the domain. Domain local groups can contain user accounts from the same domain, global groups from the same domain or a trusted domain, and other domain local groups. This last is a practice called nesting, and it should be used with caution, because it does add a level of real complexity to your administration.

Table 9-2 shows the scenario from Table 9-1 using Active Directory groups. There is also an additional global group for night clerks in the

Acquire Good Habits! In reality, if you are working with small groups of people, you will be tempted to use a shortcut instead of using local groups to set access to resources and global groups to hold user accounts. Go ahead; you can easily assign permissions directly to the global group, and not bother creating special local groups containing the global groups to assign permissions to resources. You can also assign permissions directly to individual user accounts. However, small networks have a way of becoming large networks, and proper practices applied early save work in the long run.

Table 9-1 Group Member Planning Sheet—Windows NT Domain

Group Name	Group Type	Group Membership
RegPrint	Local	Regmgrs Regclerks
RegData1	Local	Regmgrs
RegData2	Local	Regclerks
Regmgrs	Global	Mai Ling (mling) Juan Martinez (jmartinez)
Regclerks	Global	Sarah Webster (swebster) Allison Romain (sromain) Tom Harrah (tharrah) Walter Brown (wbrown)

Table 9-2 Group Members Planning Sheet—Active Directory Domain

Group Name	Group Type	Group Membership
RegPrint	Domain local	Regmgrs Regclerks Regprint2
RegData1	Domain local	Regmgrs
RegData2	Domain local	Regclerks
Regmgrs	Global	Mai Ling (mling) Juan Martinez (jmartinez)
Regclerks	Global	Sarah Webster (swebster) Allison Romain (aromain) Tom Harrah (tharrah) Walter Brown (wbrown)
Regnight	Global	Marisa Tortelli (mtortelli) Glen Olson (golson)
RegPrint2	Domain local	Regnight

registration office. They produce reports on a special printer for which a new domain local group has been created, Regprint2. They also must print to the same printers as the Regprint domain local group; therefore, these groups are nested. Now, if this all seems like too much trouble considering the number of users involved, you are correct. However, when there are dozens or hundreds of users in each global group, this scheme actually saves work.

Step-by-Step 9.03

Creating User Accounts

Use your local computer to practice working with domain groups. If your classroom lab has a Windows NT or Windows Active Directory domain, your instructor will have created the appropriate accounts from Table 9-1 or Table 9-2. In the lab, you will create the local group accounts on your computer so that each person in the classroom can work independently.

To complete this step-by-step exercise, you will need the following:

- A computer with Windows 2000 Professional or Windows XP Professional that is a member of a domain
- A domain account that is a member of your computer's Power Users or Administrators group
- The user accounts defined in Table 9-1 created in the computer

Step 1

Log onto the domain with an account that is a member of the local computer's Power Users or Administrators group. Right-click on My Computer and then select Manage. Expand Local Users and Groups, and then Local Users. Right-click on an empty area in the right window pane, and then select New User. Create new user accounts for the users listed under the Group Membership column in Table 9-1. You do not need to create a user account for the first four items in this list (those are groups); the users in this list begin with Mai Ling.

Step 2

In the Computer Management window, expand Local Users and Groups and then Groups. You will see the default groups created on your local computer. Right-click in an empty area in the right window pane and then select New Group.

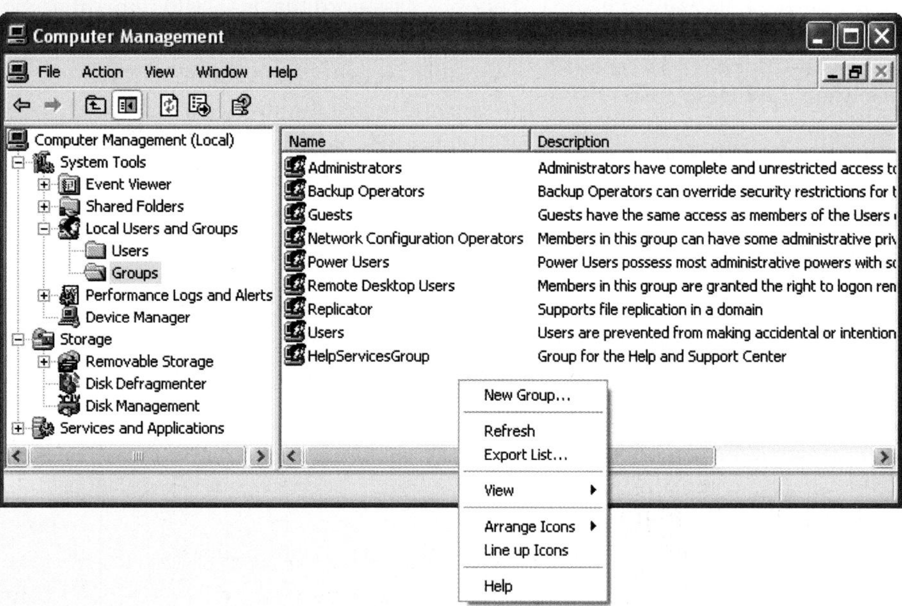

Step 3

Complete the New Group form for RegPrint by first entering the group name and then clicking the Add button. Then, in the Select Users dialog box, add the members from the domain, as shown in Table 9-1, that were added in Step 1. Remember that you need to add groups from the domain to this group. If you need help in completing the form, search the Help (or Help and Support) program.

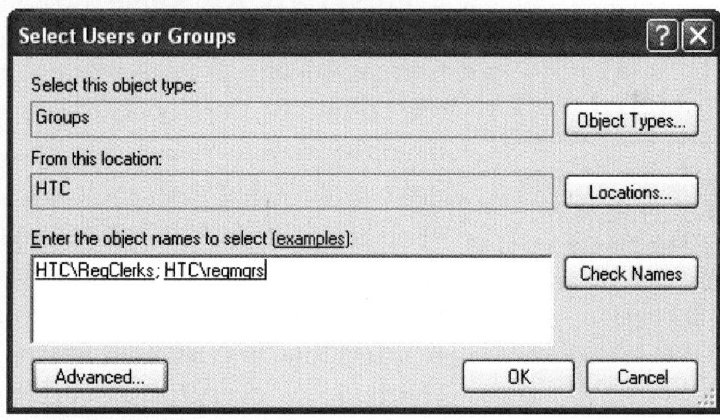

Step 4

Repeat Step 2, creating the local groups RegData1 and RegData2. You will use these groups in the next step-by-step exercise.

Passwords

Although Windows (all versions) allows you to use a blank password by default, you should always use a password on a computer that is on a network. This can be enforced by local password policies in Windows NT and the versions of Windows that have evolved from Windows NT. In fact, Windows Server 2003 is configured by default to require a complex password.

Domain-level password policies override local-level password policies when users are logging onto a domain.

Windows *is not* case sensitive in regard to user names, computer names, domains, workgroups, or file names (although it can remember file name case). But it *is* case sensitive when it comes to passwords, so be sure you carefully enter your password and remember the exact password, including uppercase and lowercase and special symbols.

A domain-level password policy affects all users who log onto the domain. Some administrative tasks are required to set either local or domain-level password policies.

In your class lab, you may not be concerned about security, and you may choose a password that is easy to remember. Your instructor will advise you on the password policies in the computer lab. Anytime you are concerned about computer security, we recommend that you use all security features available to you and create the strongest password possible. For instance, Windows NT, Windows XP, and Windows 2000 all allow you to have mixed case in a password, as well as a mix of alphabetic characters, numeric characters, and other symbols. We recommend that you create strong passwords that have more than eight characters and a mix of uppercase and lowercase characters, numeric characters, and symbols. Creating such a password is easy—the hard part is remembering the password after you create it. Do not use your name or any common words, because an intruder can discover such a password simply by knowing a little about you and guessing, or by using password-cracking software that simply uses a dictionary of common names and words. You should also change your password frequently. Oh yeah—do not write your password on your office calendar, on sticky notes, or on a whiteboard!

Cross Check

Account Policies

Flip back to Chapter 7, and review the information about account policies. Then answer the following questions:

1. What two groups of settings are included in account policies?

   ____

2. What is the relationship between these groups of settings?

   ____

Creating Shares

A new share starts with very lax permissions. Therefore, if NTFS file security is not set before a share is created, unauthorized users may be able to access the share before you can set restrictive permissions at the NTFS level!

Once users and groups are created, you can assign permissions to them for the resources they need to access. Creating shares after you know who needs to access a resource enables you to assign the appropriate permissions immediately, but you can create shares at any time. If the shares are to be on an NTFS volume, you need to perform a preparation step before actually creating shares: setting NTFS file and folder permissions. We highly recommend the use of NTFS on any Windows computer that supports NTFS and that has multiple users accessing the file system, either interactively at the computer or over the network. After you have set permissions, create the share and set share-level permissions.

Setting File-Level Permissions

The file permissions on an NTFS volume are the last defense against unauthorized users coming over the network. Set permissions at the most restrictive level that will allow the right users to accomplish their work. Table 9-3 shows our NTFS permissions worksheet.

Creating a Share and Setting Share-Level Permissions

Your local files and folders are not visible over the network until one or more shares are created. Remember: A file share is the point at which a user, using client software, can access your file system. This is called *file* sharing,

Table 9-3 NTFS Permissions Worksheet

Folder	Users/Groups	Permissions
Registration	RegData1	Everything but Full Control and Take Ownership
Registration	RegData2	Read, Write, and Execute
Registration	Administrators (local computer) SYSTEM CREATOR OWNER	Full Control
Registration\database	RegData1	Everything but Full Control and Take Ownership
	RegData2	Read, Write, and Execute
	Administrators (local computer) SYSTEM CREATOR OWNER	Full Control
Registration\forms	RegData1	Everything but Full Control and Take Ownership
	RegData2	Read, Write, and Execute
	Administrators (local computer) SYSTEM CREATOR OWNER	Full Control

but a share point must point to a *folder*. Once a share is created, permissions can be set. This is important because the default permissions on desktop Windows and some of the server versions give the group Everyone full control. Windows Server 2003 only grants the Read permission to this group by default. The Everyone group is every user connected to the network. This means that in those cases in which the Everyone group is given full control to a share at creation, anyone coming over the network can access these shares. That is, unless an administrator has the foresight to first set NTFS permissions (when available) on the folders and files under the share, and then to create the share.

> The share name is the name seen from over a network. When you create a share, you can use the name of the disk folder as the share name, or you can optionally give it another name. On *rare* occasions, it is necessary to create a short share name for DOS and Windows 3.1 network clients, because they cannot access shares with names longer than 11 characters.

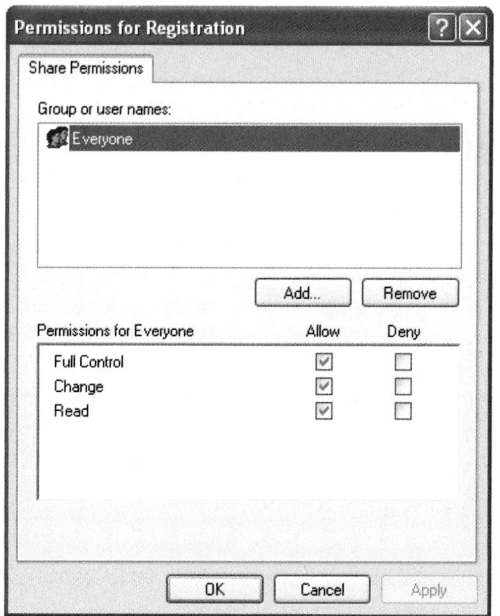

• Share Permissions page

At each door, the most permissive permission level applies, with the effective permissions determined by combining all permissions applied at that point to the user and to all groups to which the user belongs. However, when the user goes through more than one door, it is the least permissive of the effective permissions that applies.

The most important step is to remove the Everyone group from the share permissions. Beyond that, you must assign permissions that are not more restrictive than the NTFS permissions you have assigned to the underlying folders and files. Combining share permissions and NTFS permissions is like sending the network user through two doors. As the user approaches the share door, the user is carrying a backpack full of permissions that add up to full control. At the share door, the share permissions act as an electronic customs agent, confiscating the permissions not granted to this user's individual or group accounts. Now the user's backpack is lighter as the user approaches the NTFS door to the folder or file he or she is accessing. At that door, an agent again looks at the NTFS permissions for this user and for all of the groups the user belongs to, combines them, and declares that although the user is allowed Full Control permissions, since the user left some permissions at the share door, the user cannot be allowed to have full control.

Step-by-Step 9.04

Setting Permissions and Sharing Folders

In this step-by-step exercise, you will implement the folder-sharing plan for the registration office. Rather than do this on a server, you will perform these steps on your lab computer, using the local groups you created in Step-by-Step 9.03. You will first create the folder hierarchy and NTFS permissions required for the registration office employees, using the NTFS permission worksheet in Table 9-3. Then you will create the share. Finally, you will set permissions on the share. To complete this step-by-step exercise, you will need the following:

- A computer with Windows 2000 Professional or Windows XP Professional that is a member of a domain
- A domain account that is a member of your computer's Power Users or Administrators group

Step 1

Log onto the domain using an account that is a member of your computer's Power Users or Administrators group. Open Windows Explorer or My Computer and expand drive C:. Create the folders shown on the NTFS permission worksheet (Table 9-3).

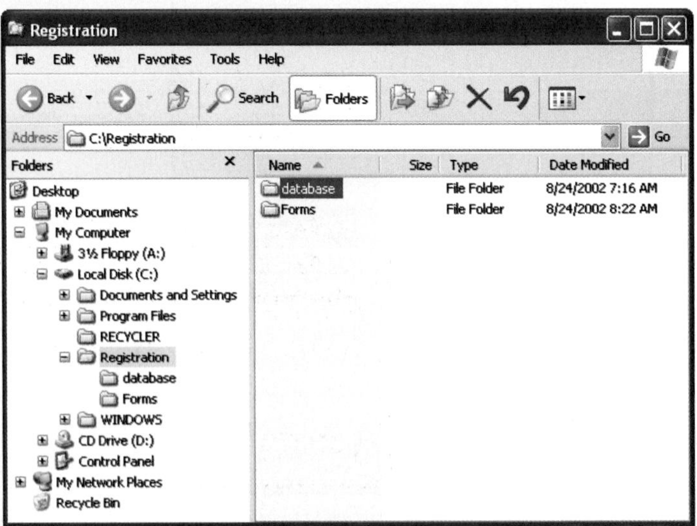

Step 2

After creating the folders, you need to block inheritance on the Registration folder so that it will not inherit the permissions of the parent folder. This will enable you to remove some of the permissions. To block inheritance, right-click the Registration folder and then select Properties | Security. On the Security tab, click Advanced. In the Advanced Security Settings dialog box, clear the Inherit From Parent The Permission Entries That Apply To Child Objects check box. In the Security box, select Copy.

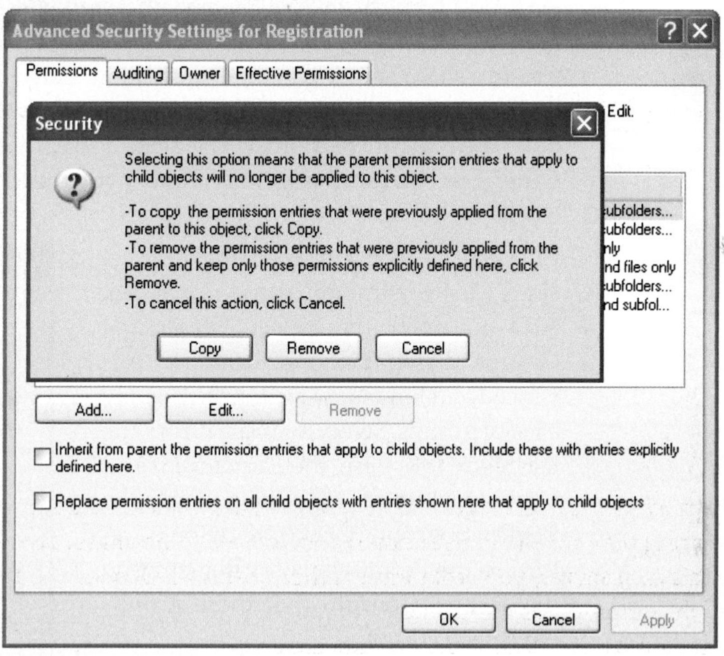

Step 3

On the Permissions page, remove permissions for users and groups that are not included on the NTFS permission worksheet. Add the permissions for the RegData1 and RegData2 groups. If you need help in assigning permissions, check out Help (Help and Support).

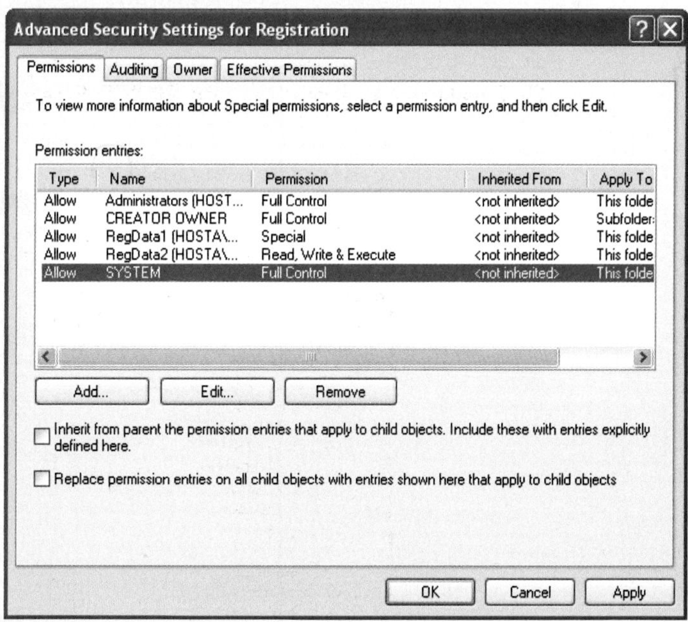

Step 4

In Step 2, you blocked inheritance of permissions from the parent of the Registration folder and copied the parent's permissions. Then in Step 3 you removed any accounts that were not in your planning sheet for the Registration folder. You do not need to block inheritance on the folders below Registration because the permissions you set for Registration are identical to what you need for the folders below, and these permissions will be inherited by those folders. You still need to remove any accounts not included on your NTFS permissions worksheet, as you did in Step 3. Do that now.

Step 5

Create a share pointing to the Registration folder, by right-clicking the Registration folder and selecting Sharing And Security. This opens the Sharing tab of the Properties dialog box. Select Share This Folder. The default share name is the same as that of the underlying folder, but you can change this name if you wish. Leave the share name as Registration.

Step 6

Click Permissions to open the Permissions for Registration dialog box. Click Add to open the Select Users and Groups dialog box and use the Advanced and Find Now buttons to display a list of groups. Select RegData1 from the list, click OK. Use the Advanced and Find Now buttons to locate and add the RegData2 group. Click OK twice to return to the Permissions for Registration dialog box. Confirm that these groups have been added.

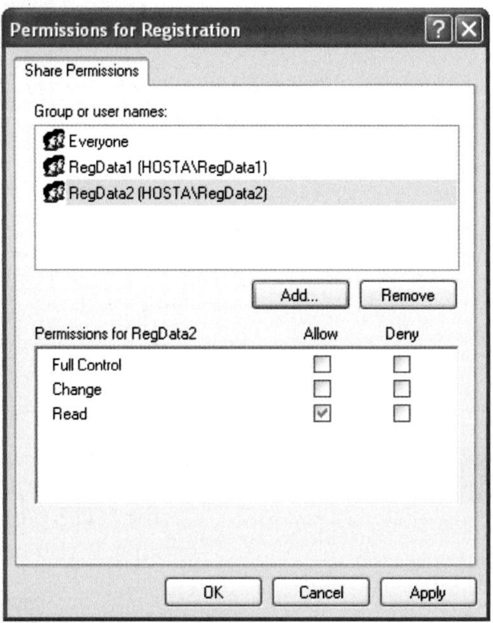

Step 7

Now that you have added groups, you can remove the Everyone group. Give the RegData1 and RegData2 group Full Control permissions. The registration share is now open for business!

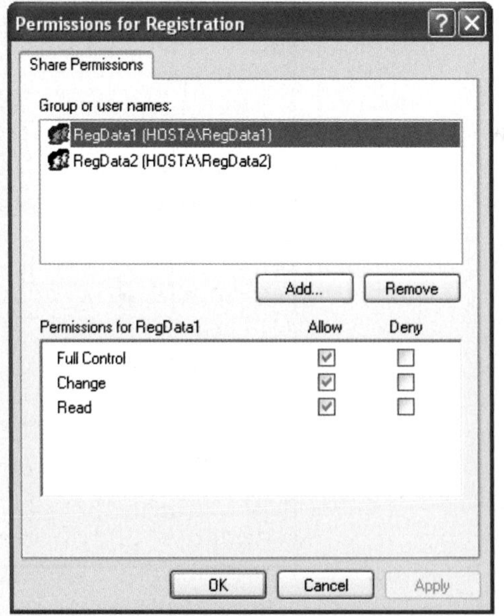

Chapter 9 Review

Chapter Summary

After reading this chapter and completing the Step-by-Step tutorials and Try This! exercises, you should understand the following facts about networking:

Basic of Networking

- PCs are networked for resource sharing, communicating, and network resource management.
- The single-server security model works when just one or a very few servers are required.
- The many-server security model centralizes security management for a large number of servers.
- A computer network consists of two or more computers connected by communications media in order to share resources, communicate, and centralize management of resources.
- A LAN is limited geographically to a room, a floor of a building, an entire building, or a campus that is all connected with a common network technology, usually at the fastest speeds (10 Mbps, 100 Mbps, 1 Gbps, or 10 Gbps).
- A MAN is a network that covers a metropolitan area, usually connected by a high-speed fiber-optic cable, and that runs at speeds measured in gigabits per second.
- A WAN is two or more networks connected over long distances using phone lines or satellite communications with speeds normally ranging from thousands of bits per second to millions of bits per second.
- A peer-to-peer network (a workgroup in Microsoft terminology) has no central authority responsible for security, and the management of resources becomes more difficult as the number of PCs increases.
- A server-based network provides a central place for keeping and controlling resources.
- A client is the software that requests services from server software.
- A Microsoft server-based network with central administration is called a domain.
- Network hardware components include network interface, media, hubs, switches, bridges, routers, and firewalls.
- Network software components include network operating systems, device drivers, services, and protocols.
- Network communication protocols suites include TCP/IP (by far the most common), NetBEUI (very rarely used today), Apple's AppleTalk (replaced by TCP/IP), and Novell's IPX/SPX (also being replace by TCP/IP).

Basic Server Concepts

- A server is a computer on a network that provides a service to other computers.
- A client is a computer on a network that accesses the service of the server.
- Microsoft's major server versions in use today include Windows NT 4.0, Windows 2000, and Windows Server 2003.
- Windows NT 4.0 is still running on many servers today. Its server products include the Server and Enterprise editions.
- Windows 2000 Server products include Windows 2000 Server, Windows 2000 Advanced Server, and Windows 2000 Datacenter Server.
- Windows Server 2003 products include Windows Server 2003 Standard Edition, Windows Server 2003 Enterprise Edition, Windows Server 2003 Web Edition, and Windows Server 2003 Datacenter Edition.
- UNIX runs on a variety of platforms and is offered by vendors such as IBM, Compaq, Caldera, Hewlett-Packard, and Sun. It has long been the server of choice for hosting network infrastructure services. It remains the top choice for servers that host large databases shared by hundreds or thousands of users, especially in industries such as insurance, medicine, banking, and manufacturing.
- The many versions of Linux, distributed by vendors such as Red Hat, Novell, Hewlett-Packard, the Gentoo Foundation, and MandrakeSoft SA, are growing in popularity within organizations, competing with all other server operating system in many arenas.

- Novell's NetWare server OS dominated the LAN server market in the 1980s, but declined in the 1990s, although Novell introduced Novell Directory Services (NDS) in 1994, years ahead of Microsoft's competing Active Directory.
- Currently, NetWare is just one server product line offered by Novell. They have added two Linux Server products: SuSE Enterprise, for a broad range of computers up to mainframes, and SuSE Standard, for basic small business or departmental servers.

Server Roles—Past and Present

- File and printer sharing was the earliest role for servers. It is still a huge function of servers.
- A server that transmits, receives, and stores e-mail is called a mail server.
- A server that maintains a directory service database is a directory service server. A Microsoft Active Directory server is called a domain controller.
- In a Microsoft network, the e-mail server is called Exchange. In a NetWare environment, the e-mail server is GroupWise. Both of these products do much more than simply manage e-mail.
- Centralized data backup has long been an important network service, and several vendors sell centralized backup systems that use a dedicated backup server, large tape archiving systems, and specialized client software.
- A large number of Internet-based backup services allow subscribers to back up data over the Internet to their servers.
- An application server is a program that acts as an intermediary between users running client software and a large back-end business application or database.
- Web servers are found on the Internet, hosting millions of web pages, and they are also found on private networks, replacing file servers in some cases.

Sharing and Protecting Resources

- Effective sharing and protection of network resources requires careful planning.
- The network administrator implements the plan for sharing and protecting network resources.
- An administrator's server-side tasks include adding a computer to a domain, creating user accounts and groups, and creating file and print shares.
- A Windows 9*x* or Windows XP Home computer cannot join a domain, but a user at a Windows 9*x* computer can log onto a domain, while one using Windows XP Home cannot.
- An administrator's client-side tasks include connecting to resources and testing network security.
- A Windows Active Directory domain has several types of security accounts.
- Administrators save time and effort by organizing users into groups that have common resource needs.
- Groups in Windows NT domains and Active Directory domains are similar but vary in scope and membership.
- Planning for effective use of user accounts and group accounts is complex but worthwhile.
- After users and groups have been created, create shares to give users access to the resources they need. If a share is on an NTFS volume, set NTFS permissions on the underlying files and folders before creating the share.
- When you create a new share, immediately set the permissions on the share. You should usually remove the Everyone group from the permissions list.
- Once shares have been created, network clients can connect to the shares from their computers.

Key Terms List

application server *(459)*
bridge *(447)*
client/server networking *(451)*
directory service *(442)*
domain controller *(451)*
domain name *(445)*
e-mail server *(458)*
enterprise network *(456)*
file and print server *(457)*
file server *(457)*
hub *(447)*
internetwork *(444)*
mail server *(458)*
media *(447)*
network resource *(440)*
node *(447)*
print server *(457)*
protocol *(449)*
router *(447)*
scalable *(452)*
share *(441)*
switch *(447)*
thin client *(459)*
trust *(461)*

■ Key Terms Quiz

1. A user may access network services using a minimally configured network computer called a/an thin client.
2. A/an domain controller is a server that maintains the directory service accounts database in a Microsoft network.
3. Bridges and routers(s) are network connection devices that carry traffic from network to network.
4. In networking an agreed-upon rule that is applied to hardware or software is called a protocol.
5. A/an directory service is a network service that can manage all types of network resources, based on certain international standards.
6. When a computer or other physical device is connected to a network, it is called a/an node.
7. A/an enterprise network contains all the connected networks of a single organization and all the resources on that network.
8. PCs on a network share much more than data; they share network resources(s).
9. Making a resource, such as a file or folder, available to other computers on a Microsoft network is called creating a/an share.
10. A NOS that is scalable is capable of easily adapting to increased demands.

■ Multiple-Choice Quiz

1. What are the fundamental reasons for connecting computers to a network?
   - **a.** To share resources, communicate, and manage network resources
   - **b.** To share money, communicate, and manage traffic
   - **c.** To play Internet games
   - **d.** To facilitate data cleansing
   - **e.** To facilitate inventory control
2. A specialty mail-order company has 25 computer users who need to access inventory and customer databases on a network server. Which administrative network structure would you expect to find in the company's office?
   - **a.** Peer-to-peer
   - **b.** Quality circle
   - **c.** Ethernet
   - **d.** Server-based
   - **e.** Dialog box
3. Which of the following is not a common network server role?
   - **a.** File and print
   - **b.** Mail
   - **c.** Defragmenter
   - **d.** Data backup
   - **e.** Application
4. Which web server software is on more web servers than any other similar product?
   - **a.** IIS
   - **b.** Exchange
   - **c.** GroupWise
   - **d.** Apache Server
   - **e.** Novell NetWare 6.5
5. The variety of hardware and software on a network can work together and communicate, thanks to sets of rules called ________________.
   - **a.** Laws of physics
   - **b.** Services
   - **c.** Security
   - **d.** NOSs
   - **e.** Protocols
6. Select an example of network media ________________.
   - **a.** CD-ROM
   - **b.** DVD
   - **c.** Walls
   - **d.** Keyboard
   - **e.** Wire

7. Why would an administrator want a trust relationship between two Windows domains?
   - a. To allow the resources of one domain to exist in another domain
   - b. To allow the accounts from one domain to use the resources of another
   - c. To create groups in two domains at a time
   - d. To create user accounts in two domains at a time
   - e. To allow users to access the Internet
8. Why can't Peggy Sue log onto the domain at work? She has a new Windows XP Professional computer at her desk that has a tested IP configuration. Previously, she could log onto the company domain, but now she can log onto only the computer itself. There is no choice for a domain in the Logon box.
   - a. She needs a new local user account.
   - b. Her computer needs to join the domain and have an account in the domain.
   - c. Her computer needs a service pack.
   - d. Her computer does not have all of its services turned on.
   - e. She must be an administrator to log onto the domain.
9. Why are users placed into group accounts?
   - a. To simplify administration.
   - b. To confuse you.
   - c. It is the only way to assign permissions to users.
   - d. To classify users by student or employee ID number.
   - e. To enable users to log on.
10. Why create a share?
    - a. To give users an e-mail account
    - b. To allow users to log onto a domain
    - c. To provide a point of access to a file system
    - d. To give users access to an entire domain
    - e. To keep unauthorized users out of your computer
11. Other than having their own backup services within their organization, what other choice is available to a company desiring regular backups of their networked data?
    - a. Sneaker net
    - b. Storing backup tapes in a vault
    - c. Internet-based backup services
    - d. Windows Backup
    - e. MS Backup

12. Which server role is included with most, if not all, NOSs?
    - a. Web
    - b. File and print
    - c. Database
    - d. E-mail
    - e. Backup
13. Which server role acts as an intermediary between users running client software and a large back-end business application or database?
    - a. Backup
    - b. File and print
    - c. Database
    - d. Application server
    - e. Directory services

14. Tim Berners-Lee, a communications and text-handling expert who worked in the CERN physics laboratory in Geneva, Switzerland, is credited with designing this core technology of the World Wide Web.
    - a. TCP/IP
    - b. URL
    - c. DNS
    - d. Sharing
    - e. Hypertext markup language (HTML)
15. In a Windows Active Directory domain, a domain local group can contain all of the following, with one exception. Find the exception.
    - a. User accounts from the same domain
    - b. Local shares
    - c. Global groups from the same domain
    - d. Global groups from a trusted domain
    - e. Other domain local groups from the same domain

■ Essay Quiz

1. Write a few sentences describing why managers should want backup systems on their networks. Feel free to draw on your own experience and to include your own assumptions and conclusions.
2. One network communication method that was discussed in this chapter may, by itself, be the most compelling reason for many people to be on a network or on the Internet. Come to your own conclusion about which method this is, and support your answer with an explanation. You can use your own experience and opinion, or do a little research to answer this question.
3. What is TCP/IP and why is it called a protocol suite?
4. Why is it important to set permissions at the NTFS level before creating a share?
5. Describe the differences between domain local groups in an Active Directory domain and the local groups in a Windows NT domain.

Lab Projects

• Lab Project 9.1

Conduct a survey. Gather information about the networks of six organizations (businesses or schools) in your area, and complete the following table. Try to vary the size of the organizations you approach for this information, so that you have a variety of results. You may find that some organizations have both peer-to-peer and dedicated servers on their networks. Use Table 9-4 to organize your information.

After gathering the information, attempt to determine whether these organizations match the model for keeping a strictly peer-to-peer network to less than ten users. If your results vary from this model, try to determine whether there was justification for going beyond ten users on a peer-to-peer network.

• Lab Project 9.2

You work for a company that provides desktop support services to small business clients. Today you have been asked to go to the site of a potential new client company and gather information about its computers and network. This is the information your company will use to determine the level of service the customer will require and the monthly fee scale for a one-year contract. You have decided that some of the information you need to gather is that which is included in the Network Survey Form in Table 9-4. Describe other information that you believe your boss needs to know.

Gather information about the current network computers, hardware, and software. Determine the

Table 9-4 Network Survey Form

Company Name	Number of Employees	Number of Employees Who Use Computers	Peer-to-Peer (Y/N) / Number of Computers	Number of Dedicated Servers / Number of Clients

information you will need, and create two or more forms that will help you gather the information. To give you a head start, you can use the form provided in Lab Project 9.1 as one form (or part of one form), but more information is required. Create at least one more form with additional information you will gather.

• Lab Project 9.3 (Optional)

In this project, we suggest that you build a network. That's right—build a network. Maybe you can do this at school through some special arrangement, or at home. Or maybe you work in a company that supports your effort to learn more. We encourage you to look for an opportunity to build even the simplest of networks. How extensive a network it is depends on what you can access and the cooperation of your instructor or a mentor. We simply feel that hands-on experience is always valuable.

Since this is just an overview chapter on networks, we have left out many details of building a network, but a basic network can begin rather simply. Consider the following suggested activities:

1. Use as few as two computers, each with a NIC, and each with an OS that includes networking components. Any of the OSs studied in this book will work.
2. Connect the computers. If you are connecting only two computers, assuming that the NICs are Ethernet (it is pretty darned hard to buy anything else), you could use a simple Ethernet cross-over cable to connect them directly. Otherwise, if you have an Ethernet hub or switch, you can connect each computer to that device using a standard Ethernet cable from each computer to the hub or switch.
3. To make things more interesting, install a server OS on one of the computers on your network. Recall that you can order Microsoft Windows Server 2003 Edition at `http://microsoft.order-2.com/trialstore/`. Move the folders you created on the local computers to the server, and create new user and group accounts on the server.

The Client Side of Networking

The new information technology, Internet and e-mail, have practically eliminated the physical costs of communications.

—Peter Drucker

In previous chapters, you worked with various versions of Windows and learned about server roles on networks. At work, at school, and at home, computer users depend on client software to participate on a network—whether they are doing research over the Internet, playing an Internet game, using e-mail, or transferring files from a server to the desktop computer.

In this chapter, you will study the client side of networking. Because a client cannot interact with network servers unless the OS is properly configured to communicate on a network, we will begin with an overview of the TCP/IP protocol suite and how to configure TCP/IP settings on a client computer. You will learn about the file and print clients used most often on private networks. Then you will move on to the Internet, first examining methods for connecting to the Internet, and then examining the most common Internet clients. Finally, you will practice methods for troubleshooting common connection problems.

In this chapter, you will learn how to:

- **Apply basic TCP/IP knowledge and skills**
- **Use a file and print client to connect to shares**
- **List methods for connecting to the Internet**
- **Identify and configure common Internet clients**
- **Troubleshoot common client connection problems**

Many students enjoy using TCP/IP tutorials available on the Internet. A search on "TCP/IP Tutorial" using any Internet search engine will give you links to many sites. Our favorite is at www.learntcpip.com. Another good one is at www.learntosubnet.com. Pick one and spend a rainy Saturday (or a sunny Sunday) learning more about TCP/IP and binary math!

Understanding the TCP/IP Protocol Suite

TCP/IP is a suite of protocols that work together to allow both similar and dissimilar computers to communicate. This protocol suite is needed to access the Internet and is the most common protocol suite used on private intranets. It gets its name from two of its many protocols: Transmission Control Protocol (TCP) and Internet Protocol (IP)—the core protocols of TCP/IP. If a network adapter is detected during Windows installation, a driver will be installed for that adapter card, and the TCP/IP protocol will automatically be installed.

TCP/IP is a subject of epic proportions! In the following sections, we offer only an introduction to TCP/IP in which we attempt to arm you with useful information but not to overwhelm you with detail. Our goal is to give you an overview of TCP/IP and to familiarize you with the settings that you may need to enter or modify for your Windows desktop computer.

Transmission Control Protocol (TCP)

Transmission Control Protocol (TCP) is the protocol responsible for the accurate delivery of messages, verifying and resending pieces that fail to make the trip from source to destination. Several other protocols act as sub-protocols, helping TCP accomplish this.

Internet Protocol (IP)

Internet Protocol (IP) is a protocol that packages your communications in chunks, called packets. This protocol allows your computer to be identified on an internetwork by a logical address called an IP address. Each packet is given a header that contains information including the source address (local host address) and the destination address. Special routing protocols can use a destination IP address to choose the best route for a packet to take through a very complex internetwork. IP also has sub-protocols that help it accomplish its work. We will not discuss the sub-protocols, but it is important for you to learn about IP addresses, because you cannot participate on a TCP/IP network without a valid IP address.

IP Addressing Fundamentals

In your first computer-related job, you might not have any responsibility for IP addressing on your network, so you might think that this section is not necessary or can be ignored. However, even as a junior networking associate or power user in a company (or at home as a customer of an Internet service provider), you might have to look up an IP address on your own workstation or the workstation of others. Why? Because a senior network administrator (or technical support person at the ISP) may need the information, and you may be physically at the computer while the senior network administrator may be elsewhere. Thus, the needed information must be obtained by you. What does this mean to you personally and professionally? It means that you should get used to identifying information sources of

IP addressing so that your encounters with senior networking staff are *less* stressful and more educational.

Let's now explore the basics of IP addressing. First of all, an IP address is not really assigned to a computer, but to each network adapter (Ethernet or wireless) or modem in that computer that connects it to a network. If more than one device is present, each connects your computer to a different network—the Ethernet or wireless adapter is a connection to a LAN or WLAN, and the modem is a dial-up WAN connection to a remote network. A desktop computer usually has only a single network device connecting it to a specific network, so that is the only address by which the computer is known on that network.

The Internet Protocol is a property of a network connection in Windows (Figure 10-1). The Connect Using box near the top of the Local Area Connection Properties dialog box shows the connecting device to which these settings apply.

An IP address has four parts, and you will usually see it in dotted decimal format, such as 192.168.100.48, the address shown in the Internet Protocol (TCP/IP) Properties dialog box in Figure 10-2. Between the dots you will see four sets of base-10 numbers (decimal—the numbering system we learned as children), and each number is from 0 to 255. Because this is a very simplified explanation, we will not go into the exact rules for these addresses, just an overview.

There are almost 4.3 billion possible IP addresses, but the way in which they have been allocated has reduced that number. Someday we will use a different addressing scheme that will provide many more addresses, but this new addressing scheme depends on a new version of the IP protocol. The current version is IP Protocol 4 (IPv4), so we will stick to the present addressing scheme in this explanation.

As you can see, there is more to an IP configuration than the address of the device itself, but before we discuss these other settings, we will first tell you more about IP addresses.

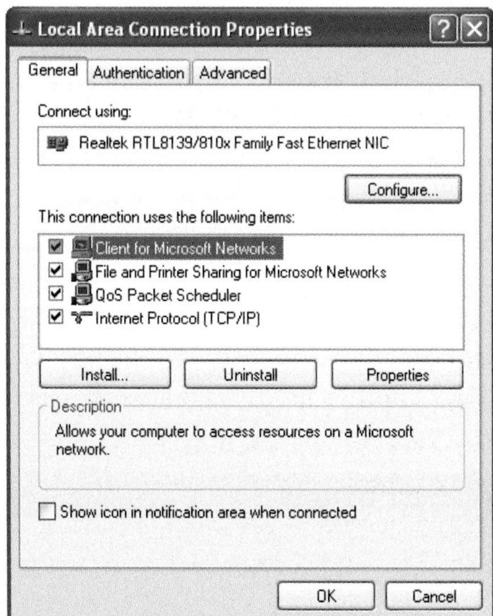

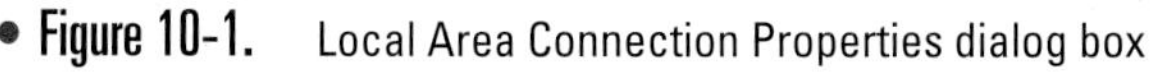

• **Figure 10-1.** Local Area Connection Properties dialog box

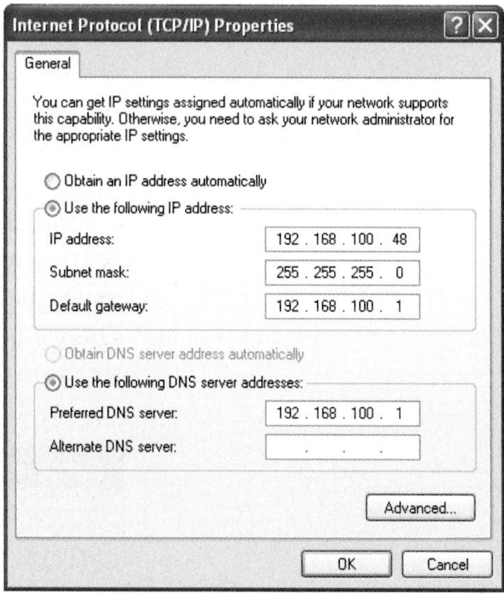

• **Figure 10-2.** Internet Protocol Properties dialog box

Which Addresses Can Be Used?

There are billions of addresses, so how do you pick an address to use? It all depends. Will the address be used on a public network (the Internet) or on a private network? A central organization decides how to allocate all these addresses for use on the public Internet. They also understand that many organizations need to use IP addresses within their private networks. Therefore, they have divided up the possible IP addresses into two broad categories: public addresses and private addresses.

Public Addresses **Public IP addresses** are used for hosts on the Internet. In IP terminology a host is any computer or device that has an IP address. To communicate over the Internet, your message must be sent from an IP address that is unique on the entire Internet, and your message must be directed to an IP address that is unique on the entire Internet. The centrally responsible organization for allocation of public IP addresses is the Internet Assigned Numbers Authority (IANA). They allocate numbers to various Regional Internet Registries (RIRs), which are organizations given the task of allocating IP addresses to Internet service providers (ISPs). The largest ISPs, in turn, allocate addresses to other ISPs. You, or your school or employer, receive addresses for each Internet connection from your ISP. The addresses they provide are from selected portions of those billions of possible addresses that are specifically used on the Internet.

Private Addresses A **private IP address** is an address from one of three ranges of IP addresses designated for use only on private networks. They are not to be used on the Internet. The address in our earlier example (192.168.100.48) is such an address. In fact, many organizations use these addresses on their private IP networks, and you do not need to get permission to do so. If a computer with a private address is connected directly to the Internet, the Internet routers (network devices that route packets based on their destination IP addresses) will not let packets with these addresses pass. Table 10-1 shows the three ranges used as private IP addresses. All other addresses either have specialized uses or are public addresses valid for computers and devices that are on the Internet.

If a computer user on a private network that uses private IP addresses wishes to connect to the Internet, each data packet from that computer must be intercepted, repackaged, and given a public IP address as its source address before being sent out onto the Internet. Then, if there is a response, each packet will be repackaged and returned to the private address.

If you are connecting to the Internet through an ISP from home, school, or work, there is probably a device between your computer and the Internet that replaces (or translates) your private IP address with a public IP address. There are a couple of methods for doing this. One involves a special network service called a proxy server, and another involves a special service called

Table 10-1 Private IP Address Ranges

Private IP Address Ranges
10.0.0.0 through 10.255.255.255
172.16.0.0 through 172.31.255.255
192.168.0.0 through 192.168.255.255

network address translation (NAT), which is provided by a NAT router. These are services that your ISP or network administrator manages for your school or organization. Such services are also packaged into the common devices, named Internet routers, now sold in consumer electronics stores, which allow home or small office computers to be connected to the Internet, usually through a cable or DSL connection.

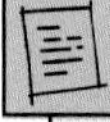

Cable/DSL routers make it easy for a novice to connect one or more computers to the Internet with default settings that will assign private addresses to any hosts on the local side. The only configuration required is to provide the settings needed for the Internet side of the router.

How Does a Host Get an IP Address?

A host gets an IP address in one of two ways. An address can be assigned as a static address, which means someone manually configures the computer or other network device requiring an IP address. Alternatively, an address can be assigned automatically, which means that it is given out over the network by a specialized service designed to give out IP addresses.

Static Address Assignment A **static IP address** is one that is manually configured for a host and can, therefore, be considered semipermanent—that is, it stays with the device until someone takes action to change it. Manually configuring an IP address involves manually entering the IP address and other necessary IP settings. In most organizations, static IP addressing is done only on servers, network printers, and network devices such as routers that are required to have permanent addresses.

Incorrect IP configuration settings can make your network connection useless. Modify IP configuration settings only if you are instructed to and if you have been provided with settings from a network administrator or from your ISP. Then take great care to be accurate!

Where will you find this information in the rare event that you are required to use a static address on your desktop or laptop computer? Actually, unless you are setting up your own TCP/IP network (a very advanced task!), you will be given the IP addressing information by a network administrator if you are connecting to a LAN, or by your Internet service provider if you are configuring an Internet connection. If you find yourself having to do this, be sure to carefully enter the numbers given to you, and double-check them! In Windows, you will enter these in the TCP/IP properties found in the properties dialog box for the network connection.

Internet routers use DHCP to give out IP addresses to hosts on the local network.

Automatic Address Assignment (DHCP and APIPA) After seeing all those IP settings, you will be relieved to learn that there is a method by which a computer can be assigned an IP address, and all the additional configuration settings, automatically. This method, **automatic IP addressing**, is used by most organizations for their desktop computers. It requires a special server or service on the network, called a **Dynamic Host Configuration Protocol (DHCP) server**, which issues IP addresses and settings to computers that are configured to obtain an IP address automatically, thus making them DHCP clients. The news gets even better, since the default configuration of TCP/IP on a Windows computer is to obtain an IP address automatically!

Do not confuse *automatic* with *automatic private*. Beginning with Windows 98, Microsoft added a new twist to the DHCP client—**Automatic Private IP Addressing (APIPA)**, whereby a DHCP client computer that fails to receive an address from a DHCP server will automatically give itself an address from a special range that has the value 169 (base-10) in the first octet (eight binary digits) of the IP address. If a computer uses this range of addresses, it will not be able to communicate with other devices on the network unless they also have addresses using the same network ID.

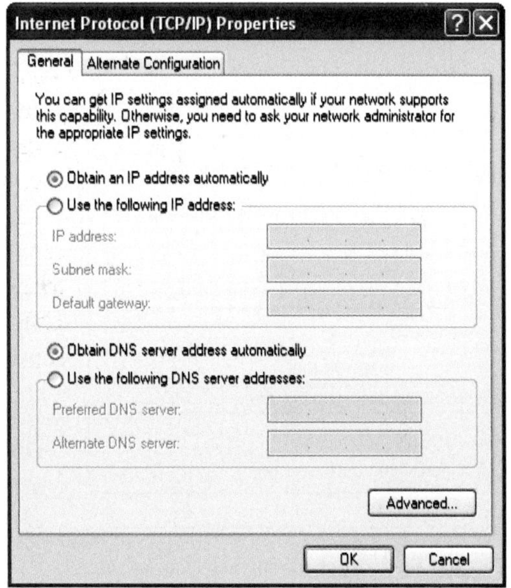

• Obtaining an IP address automatically

APIPA was designed to allow a novice to set up a small TCP/IP network and not have to bother learning about IP addressing. Each computer would use APIPA to assign itself an address, first testing that no other computer on the LAN is also using that same address. Theoretically, two or more computers on the same network using this method could do file and printer sharing.

IP Configuration Settings

If you must manually configure IP, you will need to understand the other settings that are entered in addition to the IP address.

Subnet Mask When a network device is given an IP address, it must also be given a subnet mask. The **subnet mask** is as critical as the address itself, because it takes what looks like a single address and divides it into two addresses by masking off part of the address. It is like your house address. The house number gives the address on the street, but you also need the street name. In our example, the address 192.168.100.48 has a mask of 255.255.255.0. The IP protocol now knows that this network device has the host address of 48 (its house number) on network 192.168.100 (its street name). The host portion is called the host ID, or host address, and the network portion is called the net ID, or network address.

Take a brief look at how masking works. Technically, it is done using binary math (base-2 math that uses only 0's and 1's), but you do not have to be a binary math whiz to understand the concept of masking; just look at the IP address and mask in their binary form. You can use the scientific setting of the Calculator program that comes with Windows to convert each octet (or group of eight binary digits) of an IP address from binary to decimal or vice versa. If you convert the IP address 192.168.100.2 to binary, it looks like this: 11000000.10101000.01100100.00000010. If you convert the mask we are using, 255.255.255.0, to binary, it looks like this: 11111111.11111111.11111111.00000000. If you lay the mask on top of the IP address, the 1's cover (mask) the first 24 bits (short for binary digits). What falls under the 1's of the mask is the network address, and what falls under the 0's of the mask is the host address. Figure 10-3 should make this concept clearer for you.

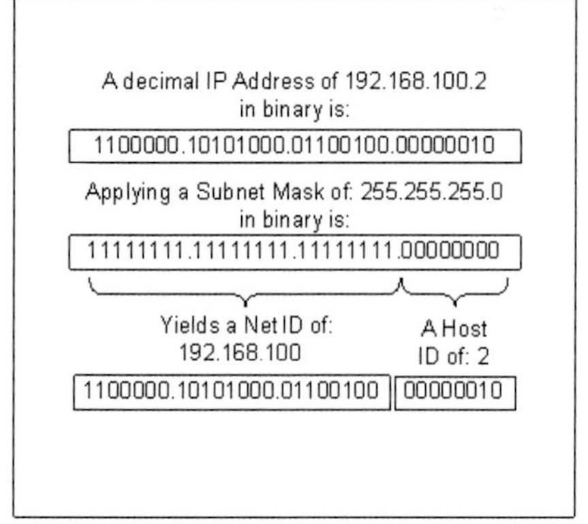

• **Figure 10-3.** A subnet mask "masks" or "covers" a portion of an IP address.

Default Gateway The next entry is the **default gateway**. This is the IP address of the router connected to your network. The net ID of the default gateway address should be identical to that of your NIC. A router is a network device that sits between networks, and directs traffic to destinations beyond the local network. Without this, you will not get beyond your network. In our example, the default gateway router connects network 192.168.100 to other networks. Anytime your computer has a packet destined for a network with an address other than 192.168.100, IP will send the packet to the gateway address.

DNS Servers The names used on the Internet, such as mcgraw-hill.com, are part of the **Domain Name System (DNS)**, a distributed online database of domain names mapped to IP addresses. Thousands of name servers maintain this distributed database; when you attempt to connect to a web site your computer's DNS client queries a DNS server to determine the IP address of the web site. For instance, a query of "mcgraw-hill.com" may return the address of 198.45.18.151. The last two settings in Windows' IP configuration are addresses of Domain Name System (DNS) servers. You may enter two addresses here—first, a primary DNS server, the one that should be contacted anytime you make a request to connect to a server using a domain name rather than an IP address. The DNS server looks up the name in its database (or asks other DNS servers to do so) and resolves the name to the IP address of the web server and sends this information back to your computer, so that it can communicate with the server. The second DNS server address is used by the client only if there is no response from the first DNS server, but it is not used when the first DNS server responds that it cannot resolve the name. This is when you see an error similar to: "DNS query for *www.somedomainname.com* failed: host not found."

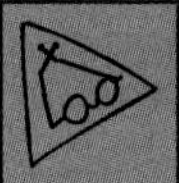

Inside Information

Naming Names...

The Internet Corporation for Assigned Names and Numbers (ICANN), a California nonprofit corporation, currently oversees the Domain Name System. It replaced an organization called InterNIC. ICANN is sanctioned by the U.S. government and reports to the U.S. Department of Commerce. Anyone wishing to acquire a domain name contacts one of the roughly 200 domain name registrars of top-level domains (.com, .org, .pro, .info, .biz, and so on) accredited by ICANN. Once registered with ICANN, each domain name and its IP address is listed on the Internet Domain Name Servers so that users can access Internet services offered under those domain names. You can go to `http://www.icann.org/` *for name registration information.*

Advanced TCP/IP Settings

On the Advanced menu in the IP Configuration Properties dialog box are several settings you will probably never touch, but there are two, DNS and WINS, that deserve mention here, because in some networks, these settings must be modified beyond the default settings. Such changes should only be done automatically (through a DHCP server) or manually by an experienced administrator or a user receiving expert advice.

DNS The advanced DNS settings can be found by clicking the Advanced button on the Internet Protocol (TCP/IP) Properties dialog box and then selecting the DNS tab in the resulting Advanced TCP/IP Settings dialog box. Figure 10-4 shows this page. The first setting allows you to add more than two DNS server addresses, and to change the order in which they are used. The remaining settings allow the Windows DNS client to request a name search for a domain name, even when an incomplete one is entered. For instance, say you are trying to point your browser to `www.microsoft.com`, but you enter

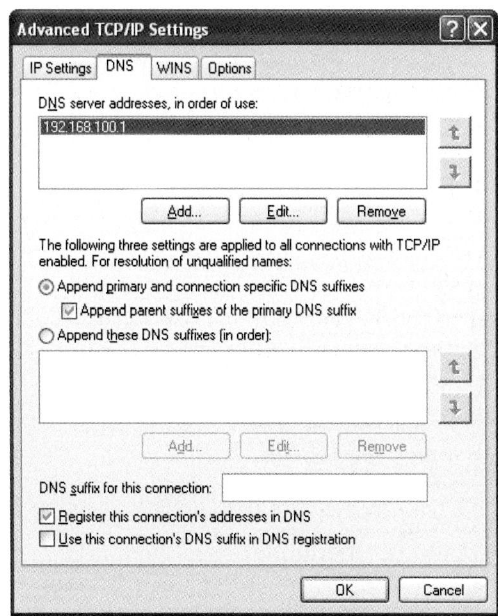

• **Figure 10-4.** The advanced DNS settings

Try This!

Examine TCP/IP Properties

Use this method to learn how your computer gets its IP address. Try this:

1. Locate My Network Places, right-click on it, and choose Properties.
2. In the Network Connections dialog box, right-click on Local Area Connection and choose Properties.
3. In the Local Area Connections Properties dialog box, click on Internet Protocol (TCP/IP) and click the Properties button.
4. Determine whether your computer has a static IP address or receives an address automatically, and then close all open dialog boxes *without* making any changes.

only `www.microsoft`. This is an unqualified domain name. What it lacks is the DNS suffix, which is another way of saying "top-level domain name." Suffixes include names like .com, .net, .gov, or .biz. An administrator can configure the DNS client to attempt additional searches by substituting (in turn) each suffix listed here.

WINS Servers Figure 10-5 shows the Advanced WINS settings. If your computer is in a Microsoft network, you may also need to include the IP address for one or more Windows Internet Naming Service (WINS) servers. A WINS server is similar to a DNS server in that it resolves names to IP addresses. These names are not the type of names you see on the Internet, but names that were used in Microsoft networks before Active Directory was developed. Active Directory uses Internet-style names. The naming system used by WINS is called NetBIOS and requires an additional software component that runs on top of the network protocols and is used for accessing computers with NetBIOS names. The NetBIOS component that Microsoft uses with the TCP/IP stack is called NetBIOS over TCP/IP (NBT) and is automatically installed with the TCP/IP stack. NetBIOS is still used in Microsoft workgroups, Microsoft NT domains, and in Active Directory domains that have a mixture of old and new Windows clients and domain servers or applications that require NetBIOS.

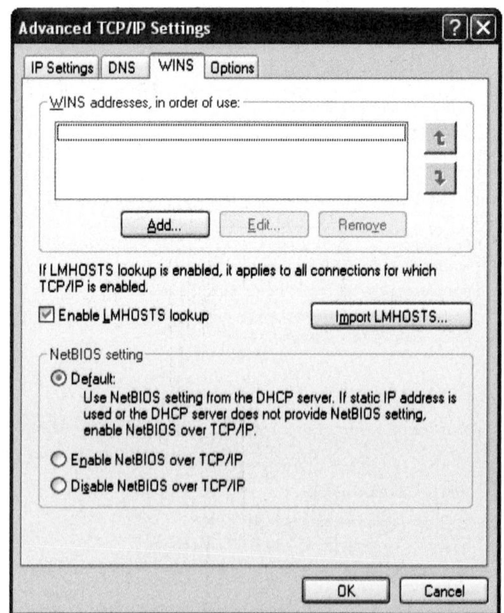

• **Figure 10-5.** The advanced WINS settings

Viewing an IP Configuration with IPCONFIG

IPCONFIG is a command-line command that displays the IP configuration of your computer's network interfaces. You may be thinking that you already know how to look at that—in Windows, you simply view the TCP/IP properties of a network connection. However, the Properties dialog box is not very helpful when your computer is a DHCP client, acquiring its address automatically from a DHCP server on the network. In that case, the Properties dialog box will show only that the interface is obtaining an address automatically, and not what the address or other configuration settings are.

The IPCONFIG command is not installed with TCP/IP in Windows 95, but it is in Windows NT 4.0 and all of the versions of Windows from Windows 98 on. The equivalent program in Windows 95 is WINIPCFG. Windows 98 has both programs.

Using the command without any command-line switches will have it display only the IP address, subnet mask, and default gateway for each network interface. Using the command with the `/all` switch will display all the IP configuration information for each network interface on a computer.

Try This!

View Your IP Configuration

Check out your current IP configuration using the IPCONFIG command. Try this:

1. Open a command prompt by selecting Start | Run, and in the Open dialog box, type **cmd** and press ENTER.
2. At the command prompt, type **ipconfig**.
3. After viewing the results of the command, type the command again with the `/all` switch: **ipconfig /all**.
4. Notice the additional information the `/all` switch provides.

Cross Check

Test Your IP IQ

Test what you have learned about IP addresses by answering the following questions:

1. What is the difference between a private IP address and a public IP address?

   ____

2. What is the difference between a static IP address and an automatic IP address?

   ____

3. Give a simple definition of a subnet mask.

   ____

File and Print Clients on Private Networks

Windows has included a file and print client since Windows for Workgroups, allowing users to access file shares and to print to printers shared by other computers on a network. A file and print client includes both the user interface and the underlying file sharing protocols to access a file sharing system on a network server. Examples of file sharing protocols are Microsoft's **Server Message Block (SMB)** protocol; Novell's venerable **NetWare Core Protocol (NCP)**; the newer **Common Internet File System (CIFS)**, a standard used by Microsoft, Novell, and many others; the network file system (NFS), used in Linux and most UNIX versions; and even the P2P file sharing protocol used to

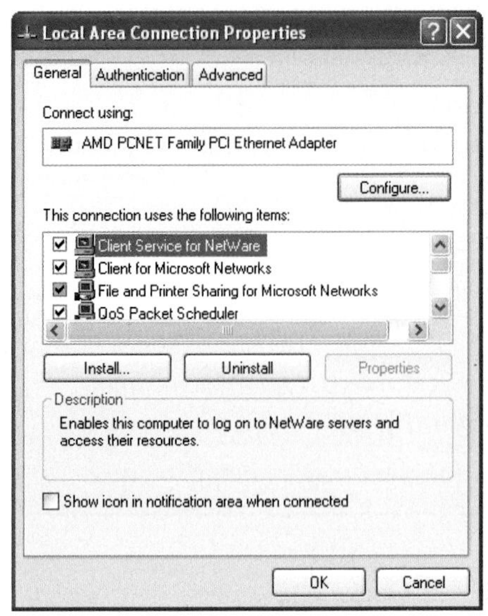

• **Figure 10-6.** Local Area Connection Properties dialog box

share files over the Internet. Most of these file sharing protocols include support for sharing a printer attached to the local server and are also contained in dedicated network devices for sharing a printer. Windows allows you to have more than one client installed, so your connection properties may look like Figure 10-6. When you install a new service or client, it is by default installed for all available connections. Once it is installed, you can turn it off or on for individual connections, but uninstalling a service or client uninstalls it for all connections. Now learn more about just a few of these file and print clients.

Client for Microsoft Networks

The Client for Microsoft Networks is automatically installed and enabled when a Windows operating system is installed. With the client installed, you are able to use the Windows GUI to see those Microsoft computers on the network that have file and printer sharing turned on, whether they are using the older SMB file sharing protocol or the newer CIFS protocol standard. You can see both dedicated Windows network servers and Windows desktops that have file and print sharing turned on. You will be able to see servers on your network in My Computer | My Network Places, but your ability to connect to any shares on those computers depends on the permissions applied to each share. You will also have mixed results viewing the properties of these objects in My Network Places. You may even be surprised at what you find. Figure 10-7 shows the properties of a print server, a dedicated device packaged in a small case that uses the Microsoft SMB protocol to allow users to print to one or more printers attached to it.

Try This!

Find Microsoft File and Print Servers

You can use My Network Places to look for the file and print servers on your network. Try this:

1. Open My Network Places. If this shortcut is not on your Start menu, open My Computer and select My Network Places.
2. Select View Workgroup Computers.
3. Right-click on one of the computer icons and select Properties. If it is a network server, you may see an error message if you do not have permissions to view its properties.

Novell Clients

A computer user requiring access to file and print services on a Novell server needs a Novell client. Both Microsoft and Novell offer Windows clients for Novell networks. Novell offers clients for almost any operating system, including several versions of UNIX and Linux, Macintosh, mainframe, and (at last count) eight versions of Windows.

Microsoft's Client Service for NetWare

While Microsoft's Novell client for Windows is not automatically installed on a Windows computer, one comes with each version of Windows and can be installed after the fact through the properties of a network connection. The computer will have to be restarted after installation.

After the restart, complete the Select NetWare Logon dialog box, in which you either select a NetWare server, or a NetWare Directory Services (NDS)

As a rule, a desktop computer should not have the File and Print Sharing service turned on, especially if the computer is a member of a domain and connects to dedicated servers for file and print services. The exception to this is when a desktop computer is participating in a workgroup rather than in a domain and must share local files or printers with other workgroup members.

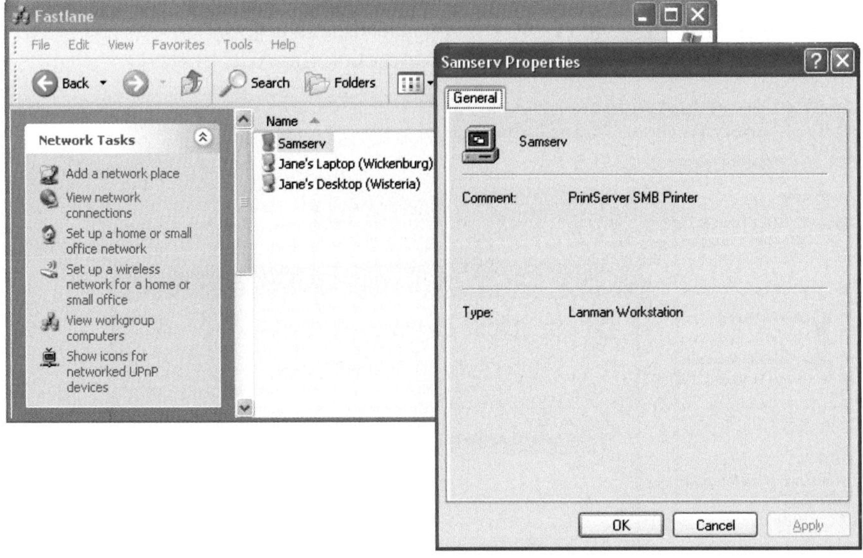

• **Figure 10-7.** Print Server properties

tree and context. If you select a server, you will need the name of a Novell NetWare server on the network that is either running an older version (previous to version 4) of NetWare, or is running a newer version but emulating the older version for logon purposes. Alternatively, selecting a tree and context allows you to log onto NDS, Novell's distributed directory service introduced in Novell NetWare 4.0.

The Microsoft client for Novell is generally considered less capable than the one provided by Novell, and network administrators may select this client for a network with just a few Novell file and print servers or for compatibility with certain software.

Do not be confused. Previous to Windows XP, the Client Service for NetWare was known as Novell Client by Microsoft for Windows. You will see this term used in certain articles and documentation.

Step-by-Step 10.01

Install the Client Service for NetWare

In this exercise, you will install a second file and print client in Windows. If you do not have a Novell server on your network, you may still complete it, but cancel out of the dialog box in Step 4. To complete this exercise, you will need the following:

- A computer with Windows 2000 Professional or Windows XP
- A CD containing the version of Windows installed on the computer you are using
- A user name and password of an account with local administrator rights
- A user name and password of a user account on a NetWare server or in an NDS tree and context
- The name of the tree and context if you will be logging onto a NDS directory

Step 1

Open Control Panel | Network Connections, right-click on a network connection (preferably your LAN connection), and select Properties.

Step 2

In the Connection Properties dialog box, click the Install button. The choices will normally be Client, Service, or Protocol. Select Client and click the Add button.

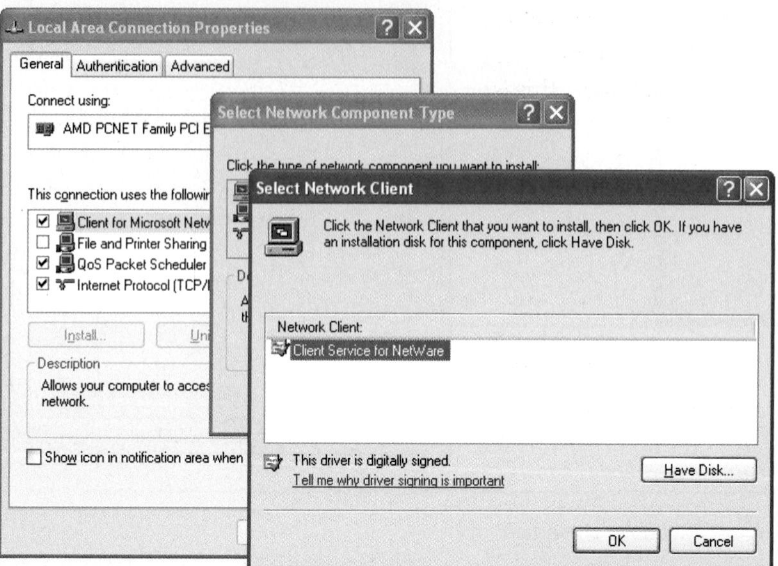

Step 3

In the Select Network Client dialog box, select Client Service For NetWare and click OK. If requested, provide the Windows CD. When prompted, select Yes to restart the computer.

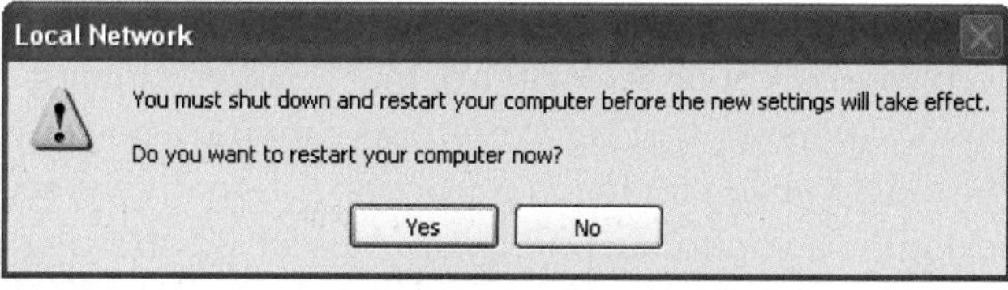

Step 4

After the restart, complete the Select NetWare Logon dialog box with the information you gathered at the beginning and then click OK. When prompted, supply the user name and password to log on. (If you were unable to complete the Select NetWare Logon dialog box, simply select Cancel.)

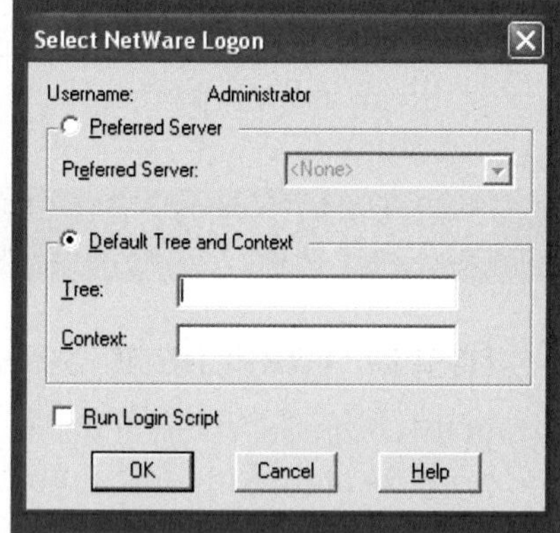

Step 5

Open Control Panel | Network Connections, and view the Properties dialog box of the network connection you used in Step 1. Verify that two clients are now installed. If this client is not needed, remove it at this time, by selecting it and clicking the Uninstall button. Click Yes when asked in the dialog box that informs you that this will uninstall it for all connections. Click Yes again to allow the computer to restart.

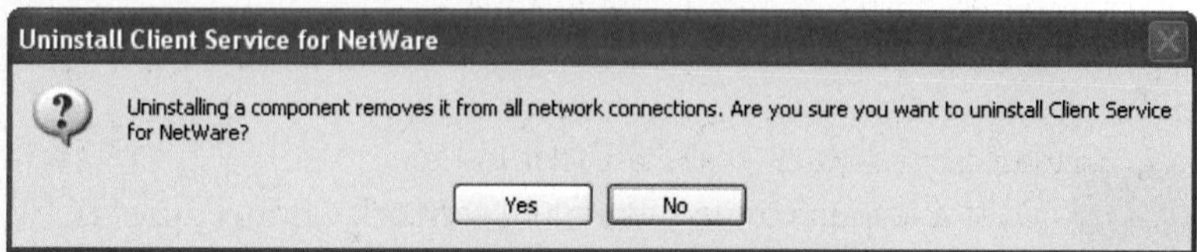

Novell Client by Novell for Windows

Novell also offers a client to allow Microsoft computers to connect to Novell services. If your network is primarily a Novell network, this is the preferred client for Novell, because it has better software tools for use by a Novell server administrator, who will normally administer the server or servers from a desktop computer. There are separate Novell clients for the various Windows versions and for other operating systems. The clients themselves are also issued in numbered versions.

The Novell clients can be downloaded for free from the Novell site (`www.novell.com`).

Try This!

Find the Novell Client for Windows

You will need a computer running Windows XP or Windows 2000 and an Internet connection. Try this:

1. Point your web browser to the Novell site at `www.novell.com`. Click the link to the Download page (at this time, the link is easy to miss—the word *download* is near the top of the home page in *very* small print).
2. On the download page, open the drop-down box labeled "Any Platform/OS" and notice the long list of clients available."
3. If you need one of these clients, download it now and follow the instructions to install it on your computer. When done, close all open windows.

Connecting Clients to Shares

Once shares have been created on servers or on peer computers, network clients can connect to the shares from their computers. In the past this has depended on the user knowing the name of the file server and the share, or browsing through each network server to locate a share. While this is still common practice, beginning with Windows 2000, a client for Microsoft networks has some additional features when working within an Active Directory domain. The client will allow you to search the Active Directory for file shares and shared printers without requiring that you memorize the name of the specific server hosting the share. Shares that can be found via this method are said to be published in the directory, something an AD administrator can do for shares that must be searchable to AD users.

Connecting to a File Share

You can locate a share to connect to by browsing to it in My Computer or Windows Explorer, entering a Universal Naming Convention (UNC) name in Internet Explorer or Windows Explorer, or by searching for it in an AD domain. A UNC name is used on Microsoft networks and has this syntax: *servername**sharename*. For instance, to connect to the folder shared as *data* on the computer named *Wickenburg*, type **\\wickenburg\ data**. For a frequently accessed share, select **Tools | Map Network Drive** to assign a drive letter to the share, and have it reconnect at logon. This is called **mapping** and it assigns one of your local, unused drive letters to a share out on the network. This provides a logical connection to the share from your computer.

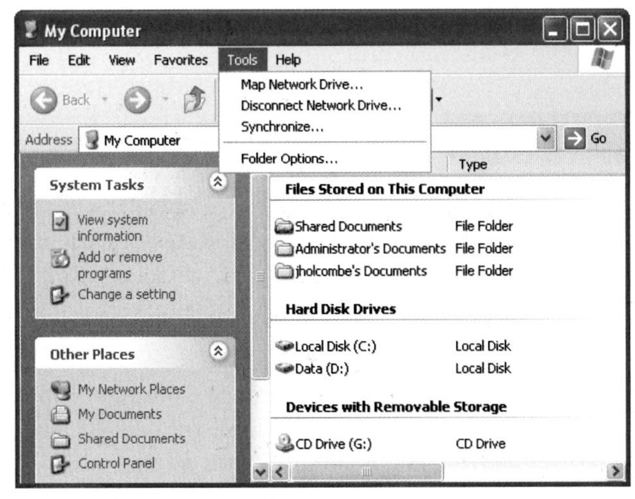

• Tools | Map Network Drive

Step-by-Step 10.02

Connecting to a Share

Administrators and users often need to connect from a desktop computer to one or more network shares. As is true for many operations, there are several ways to do this. Using the accounts and the shares you created in step-by-step exercises in Chapter 9, practice connecting to a share. To complete this step-by-step exercise, you will need the following:

- A computer with Windows 2000 Professional or Windows XP Professional that is a member of a domain as a result of Step-by-Step 9.02
- The domain user and group accounts from Table 9-1 (NT domain) or Table 9-2 (Active Directory domain) created by the instructor
- The name of another computer on the network that successfully completed the following Step-by-Steps: 9.02, 9.03, and 9.04

Step 1

If you are still logged on from the previous step-by-step exercise, log off and log back on to the domain as Sarah Webster (swebster). Right-click on My Computer, and then select Map Network Drive. In the Folder text box within the Map Network Drive dialog box, type ***computername*\registration**, where *computername* is the name of another lab computer on which Step-by-Step 9.04 was completed. You can select a different drive letter if you wish. Then confirm that the Reconnect At Logon check box is selected and click Finish.

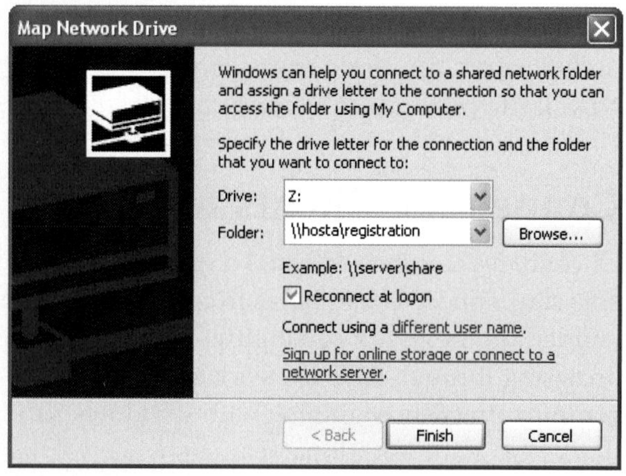

Step 2

Test the connection. Open My Computer and locate the new mapped drive. Notice that you can also see the folder below that drive. Open the database folder and create a text file and name it **SARAH.TXT**.

Step 3

Log off as Sarah Webster and log back on as Allison Romain (aromain). Open My Computer or Windows Explorer. Give Allison a connection that does not have a drive mapping. Choose Start | Run. In the Open text box, type ***computername*\registration**. Click OK.

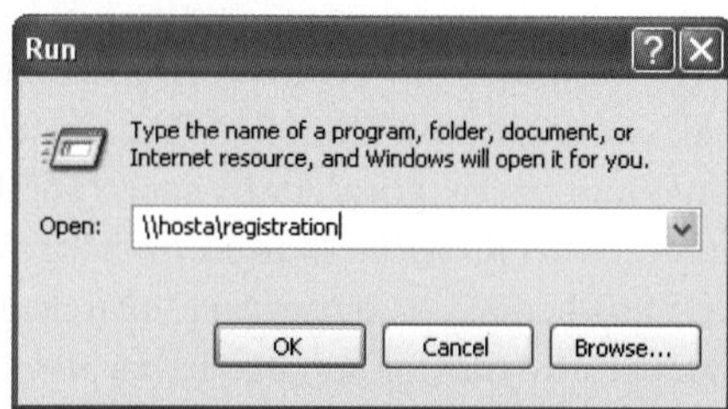

Step 4

Back in My Computer, open the database folder and attempt to delete the file SARAH.TXT. At first, it appears that you will be permitted to delete the file, but if the permissions are set correctly, you will not be able to delete it. Click OK to close the error message.

Step 5 Create a text file in the database folder and name it **ALLISON.TXT**. Log off as Allison.

Step 6 Log back on as Mai Ling (mling). Open My Computer and notice that Mai Ling does not have a drive mapping to the Registration share. Now use another method to connect to a drive. You will not need to provide a drive letter; this method maps the drive to the next highest unused drive letter on the local computer. Open a command prompt and type **net use * *computername*\registration**.

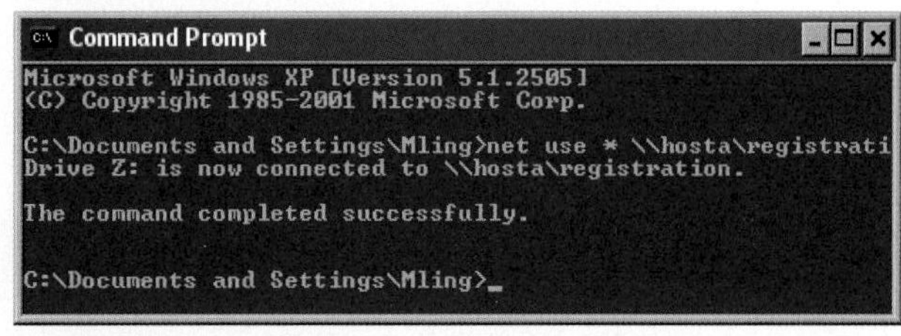

Step 7 Return to My Computer, open the new database folder, and delete the files SARAH.TXT and ALLISON.TXT.

Connecting Clients to Shared Printers

A file and print client also allows you to access a shared printer that is physically attached to another computer, as well as a printer connected directly to the network (Microsoft calls this a network printer).

Connecting to Printers Using UNC Names As with connecting to shared folders, the standard for connecting to shared printers on Microsoft networks has long included the use of UNC names. For instance, if you have a computer named Wickenburg with a print share named legal01, the UNC name is \\wickenburg\legal01. Enter this name in the Add Printer wizard when you first connect to a printer, or in Internet Explorer. In addition, the printers and faxes folder on each Windows XP computer that has file and print sharing turned on has the share name of *Printers and Faxes*. Therefore, you can view the list of shared printers on the computer named Wickenburg by entering the UNC name **\\wickenburg\printers and faxes** in the Address box of Internet Explorer.

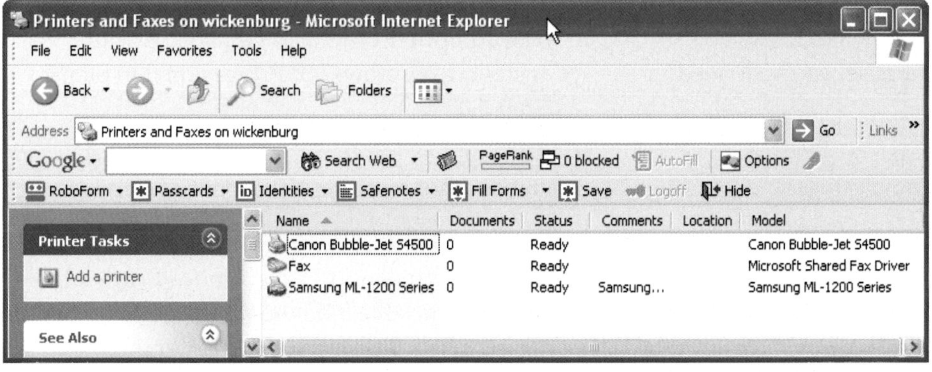

• The result of using the UNC \\wickenburg\printers and faxes

Connecting to Printers Using IPP Windows 2000 and greater clients also have a feature known as IPP, or Internet Protocol Printing. This feature allows you to use your browser to connect to a printer by using a URL. For instance, to see the list of printers on a server named `PrintServer01`, point your browser to `http://PrintServer01/printers`, which will display the list of shared printers on that server. Or, if you already know the name of the printer, enter the URL for the Printer. The URL `http://PrintServer01/Legal01` will enable you to connect to the printer named Legal01 on the printer server.

Adding a Standard TCP/IP Printer Port When connecting to a Network printer that is connected to a TCP/IP network, part of the configuration is to add a TCP/IP printer port, which will include providing the IP address of the network printer. This is quite common in many organizations today, including school computer labs. When you installed your new Windows OS in earlier chapters, your instructor may have helped you with this task, or your logon to the school's network may have included a script that ran automatically and set this up for you.

Try This!

Add a TCP/IP Printer Port

It is easy to add a standard TCP/IP port, thanks to the Add Printer and the Add Printer Port wizards. You will need to be logged on as an Administrator, you will need the IP address of the printer, and the printer will need to be turned on. Try this:

1. To do this, open Printers and Faxes, and select Add A Printer, which will open the Add Printer wizard. Click Next, select Local Printer Attached To This Computer, clear the check box by Automatically Detect And Install My Plug And Play Printer, and then click Next.
2. Select Create A New Port, use the drop-down list to select Standard TCP/IP Port, and then click Next.
3. In the Welcome page of the Add Standard TCP/IP Printer Port wizard, click Next. In the Add Port dialog box, enter the printer's IP address and a name for this port (the default name resembles IP_192.168.100.1), and then follow the instructions to complete the installation. Once the port is added, the Add Printer wizard will open. Follow the instructions to install the printer driver for the printer.

Step-by-Step 10.03

Connecting to a Shared Printer

Connect to a shared printer on the lab LAN. To complete this step-by-step exercise, you will need the following:

- The computer on which you successfully installed Windows XP Professional in Step-by-Step 5.02
- The name of another computer on the LAN and the name of a printer share on that computer

Step 1

Open the Printers folder by choosing Start | Printers and Faxes. Under Printer Tasks, select Add A Printer. In the Add Printer wizard, click Next on the Welcome page. On the Local Or Network Printer page, select A Network Printer, Or A Printer Attached To Another Computer. Click Next.

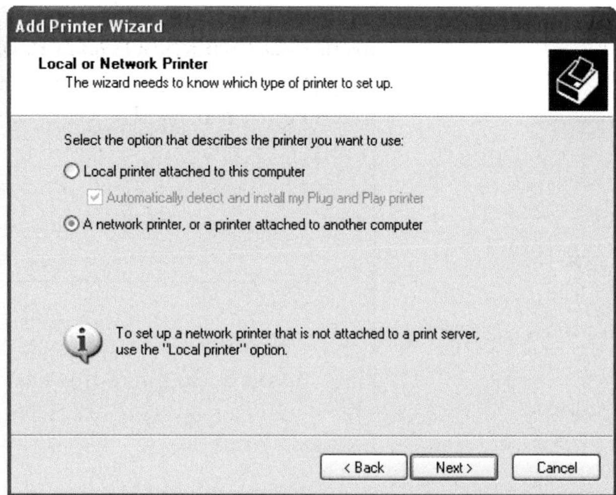

Step 2

On the Specify A Printer page, notice the options for locating a shared printer. Leave Browse For A Printer selected and click Next.

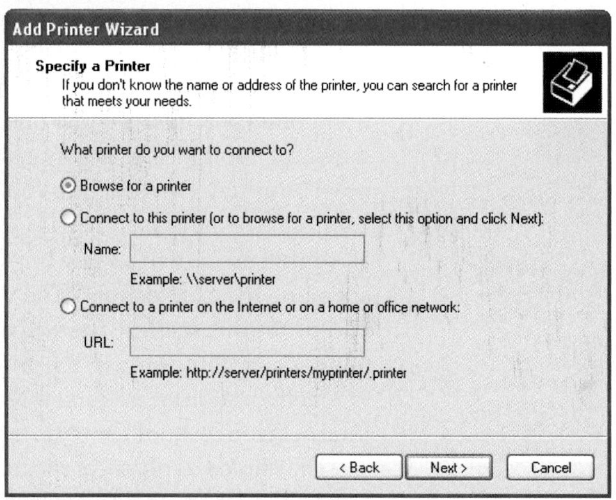

Step 3

There may be a brief delay before the list appears under Shared Printers in the Browse For Printer page. Once it does, select the printer you wish to connect to and click Next. Click Yes in the Connect To Printer dialog box.

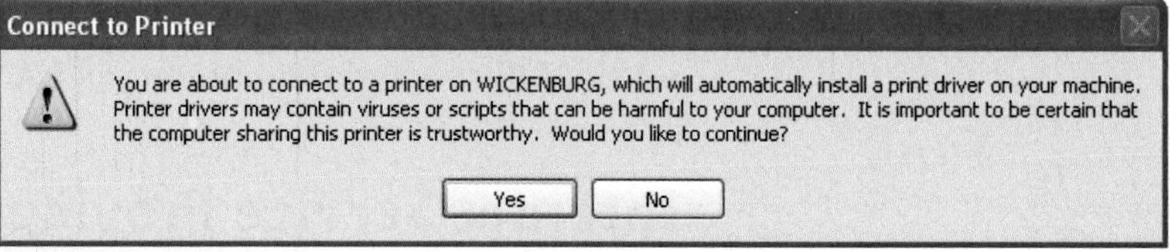

Step 4

There will be another brief delay while the driver is installed on your computer (unless the driver is already installed). Then (if this is not the first printer you have installed) you will see the Default Printer page. Select Yes or No, depending on whether or not you want this to be the default printer (the one used automatically when you print from most applications). Then click Next, and click Finish in the Completing The Add Printer Wizard page.

Step 5

Confirm the addition of the new printer by opening Printers and Faxes from the start menu and locating the new printer. When you are done, close all open windows.

Cross Check

Making the Connection with File and Print Clients

Test what you have learned about file and print clients by answering the following questions:

1. List three methods for locating shares on your network.

   ____

2. If you need to connect to the same share repeatedly, what can you do to make this easier?

   ____

Connecting to the Internet

How do you connect a computer to the Internet? You have so many choices—which one is right for you? You can choose from several WAN technologies for the connection point to the Internet, whether that connection point is created for just one computer or for several. Some of these are wired technologies, and some are wireless technologies. Some connections must be initiated every time you wish to connect to the Internet, while many connection methods remain available 24/7, in which case, Internet access is as simple as opening your browser or sending an e-mail. What about the speed of the connection? The choices you have include a wide range of speeds. In this section, we will compare the various means of connecting a network or computer to the Internet so that you can make a decision for yourself, or at least understand a little about how you are connected to the Internet from school or work.

The choice of physical means of connecting to the Internet is closely related to your choice of an organization that will give you access to the Internet. Such an organization is called an Internet service provider, and you will learn about these organizations first. Then you will consider the differences between a direct computer-to-Internet connection versus a computer-to-LAN-to-Internet connection. And finally, you will learn about the technologies used at the connection point to the Internet, regardless of whether it is a single computer or a LAN connection.

Internet Service Providers

An **Internet service provider (ISP)** is an organization that provides individuals or entire companies access to the Internet. For a fee, an ISP provides this connection service and may offer other Internet-related services such as web server hosting and e-mail. Many ISPs provide proprietary software for web browsing, e-mail management, and accessing other Internet services. Some ISPs specialize in certain connection types. For instance, Ground Control (`www.groundcontrol.com`) specializes in satellite Internet services and T-Mobile (`www.tmobile.com`) provides ISP services for their cellular customers. Your local telephone company may provide ISP services for dial-up and DSL customers, and Comcast (`www.comcast.com`) offers cable Internet access.

Computer-to-Internet vs. LAN-to-Internet

Try This!

Find Internet Service Providers

You can use the Internet itself to find ISPs you might want to use. Try this:

1. Use your web browser to connect to your favorite search engine, search on "Internet Service Provider," and brace yourself for a *long* list of ISPs and sites related to ISPs!
2. Look for an option to search within the results (in Google this is found at the bottom of the search results). To find ISPs that specialize in satellite connections, search within the previous search results for "satellite."
3. Further refine your search to just one country by entering a country name in the search by results box.

A computer might be connected to the Internet, but not to a LAN. A computer that is connected to a LAN may have access to the Internet through that LAN if the LAN itself, or another LAN to which it has a connection, is connected to the Internet (see Figure 10-8). A computer may be connected to a LAN, but not to the Internet, if the LAN has no Internet connection. A computer connected to a LAN may also have a separate connection to the Internet. So many choices! We will try to simplify this.

Wired Connectivity Technologies

Most, but not all, wired WAN technologies used for connecting to the Internet utilize the telecommunications infrastructure of the telephone system—either in its traditional state or with some upgrades and equipment added to that infrastructure. Another private network often used for wired Internet connections belongs to the cable TV companies, who in recent years have added Internet access for their customers.

Dial-Up Connections

A technology that clearly takes advantage of the traditional phone system is **dial-up**—an inexpensive WAN option available to anyone with a phone line

Inside Information

Internet Connection = WAN Connection

A connection to the Internet is a WAN connection, but even the fastest commonly available WAN connections are not as fast as the slowest LAN connections. For example, the slowest LAN speeds now are about 10 megabits per second (10 Mbps), while the fastest WAN speeds are about 8 megabits per second. Many LANs now operate at speeds of 100 Mbps or 1+ Gbps. It is easy to see that the connection to the Internet is a potential bottleneck if many users on a LAN are using the same WAN connection!

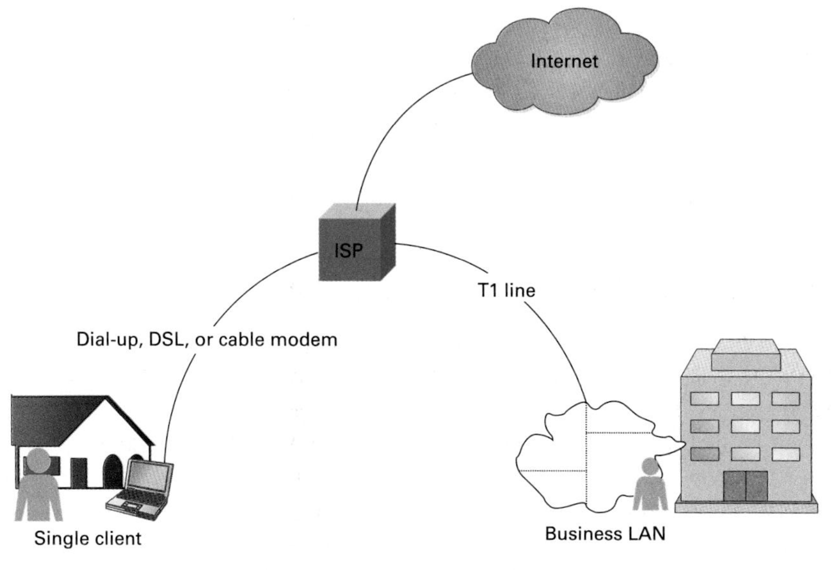

• **Figure 10-8.** Connecting to the Internet from a single computer or from a LAN

and a standard modem (the longtime standard runs at 56 Kbps). It is not quite that easy—you also need to subscribe to an Internet connection service from an Internet service provider (ISP).

The cost of the ISP subscription should be your only additional cost. There is usually no additional fee for using a modem on your voice line, but it is an either/or situation—you may either use the modem *or* use the phone *or* use a fax machine. You may not use the phone line for multiple purposes simultaneously when using dial-up technology.

In a dial-up connection to the Internet, your computer uses its modem to dial a telephone number provided by the ISP (hence the term *dial-up connection*). Your computer's call is answered by one of many modems maintained by the ISP at its facility, you are authenticated by a server maintained by the ISP for authenticating customers, and then the ISP routes traffic between your computer and the Internet for that session. Like a voice phone conversation, the connection is only temporary and ends when either your PC or the ISP's server ends the call. Most ISP servers disconnect a dial-up connection automatically after a certain period of inactivity.

Furthermore, a dial-up connection can also be used to connect a remote computer to a private network at school or work. In this case, the modem that "answers" the call and the server that authenticates the user are located on a private network and allow the users to work on the network as if they were physically at school or work, as shown in Figure 10-9. Note that the

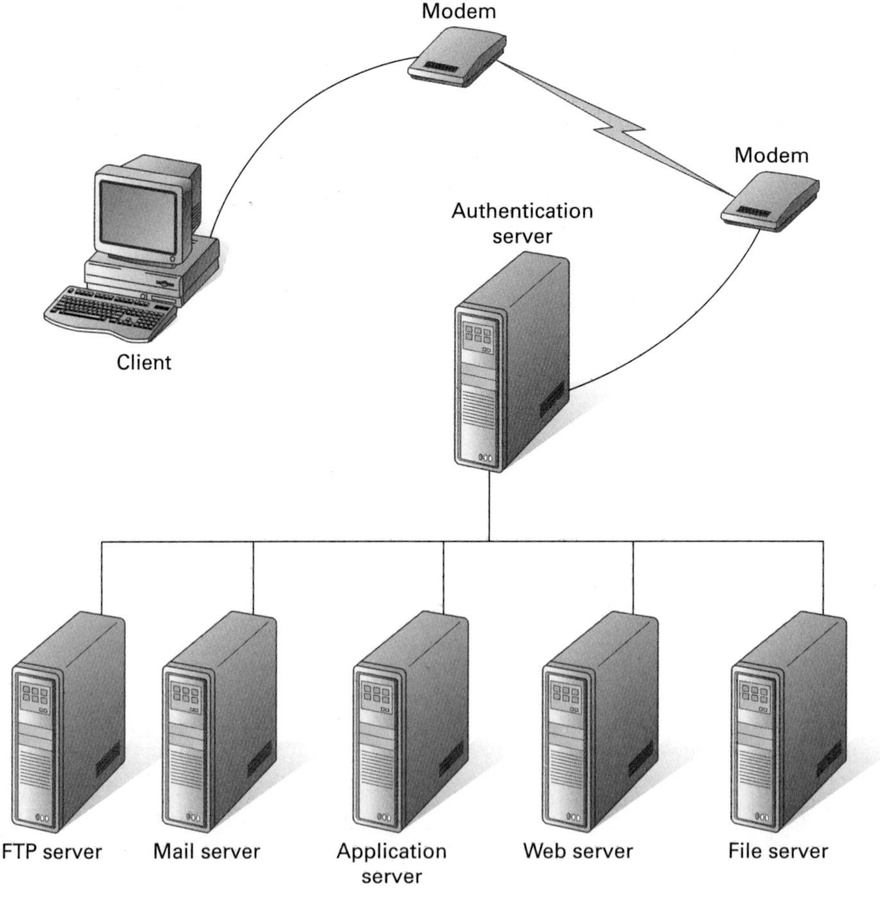

• **Figure 10-9.** A remote client dials in to the network.

• **Figure 10-10.** The Phone and Modem Options dialog box

dial-up connection at 56 Kbps will be very slow compared to a LAN running at 10 Mbps, 100 Mbps, or 1 Gbps.

Installing a Modem To prepare for a dial-up connection, first verify that you have a working modem. If the modem is an external modem, ensure that it is connected and powered on (an internal modem is by definition connected, and it is powered on with the computer). Then open the Phone and Modem Options applet in Control Panel, and click on the Modems tab. Figure 10-10 shows the Modems page with two modems—one using COM3, and a USB modem that was powered off and shown as "Not present." When the USB modem is powered up, that state is indicated by showing a communications port in the Attached To column.

Step-by-Step 10.04

Installing a Modem in Windows

In this step-by-step, you will manually install a modem driver. Because we assume lab computers will not have a physical modem connected to each computer and installed in Windows, you will create a fictitious modem to use for the next step-by-step. If you have a modem, this exercise is optional. This lab will fail in Step 4 on some computers (mostly laptops) that do not have unassigned serial ports. You will need

- A computer with Windows XP
- To be logged on with local administrator privileges

Step 1

Start the Phone and Modem Options applet from the Control Panel. If the Phone and Modem Options applet opens without opening any other window, proceed to Step 2. If this is the first modem to be installed on this computer, you will need to complete the Location Information page. Fill in the page and click OK. When the Phone and Modem Options applet is displayed, proceed to Step 2.

Step 2

Select the Modems page and click the Add button. The Install New Modem page of the Add Hardware wizard appears. Select Don't Detect My Modem; I Will Select It From A List, and then click Next.

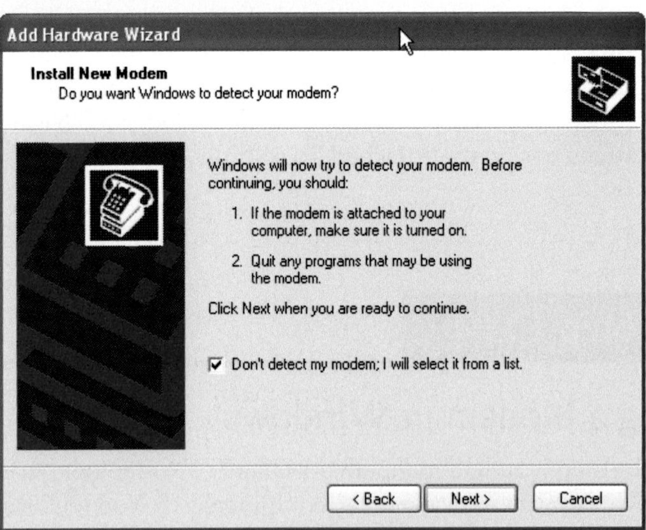

Step 3

Select [Standard Modem Types] in the list of manufacturers, select Standard 56000 bps Modem from the list of models, and click Next.

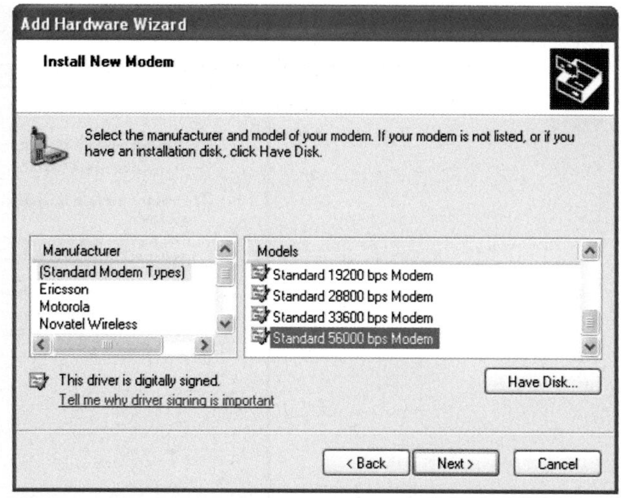

Step 4

Select a Port and click Next. Then click Finish. Verify that your new modem is installed in the Modems page, and then click OK to close the Phone And Modem Options dialog box. Your modem is installed and you are ready to configure a dial-up connection using this modem.

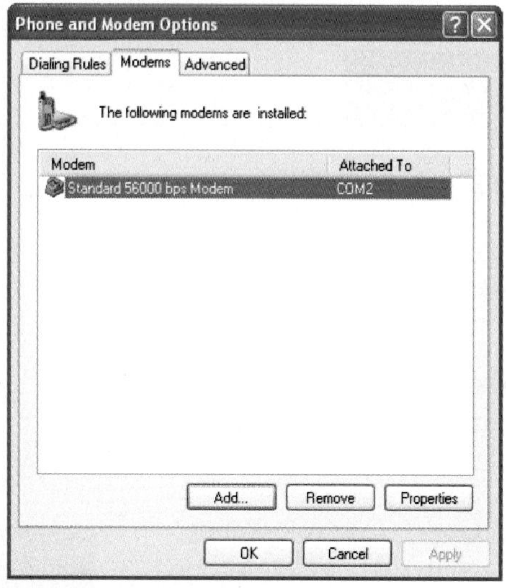

Creating a Dial-Up Connection With a modem installed, you can run the New Connection wizard in Windows XP to create and configure a connection and to provide all the required information for any type of Internet connection (see Figure 10-11). If you use an online service, such as AOL or CompuServe, you will usually not run the New Connection wizard, but will instead use the service's installation program that configures a connection and installs client software that dials the connection for you. This software may also include a specialized browser, e-mail client, and other features.

Once a connection is configured on your computer, you can initiate a dial-up session by using the connection applet for that specific connection. If you have accessed the Internet without using a "connection applet," it is because certain applications, such as a browser or e-mail client, will automatically open an Internet connection whenever the application is started.

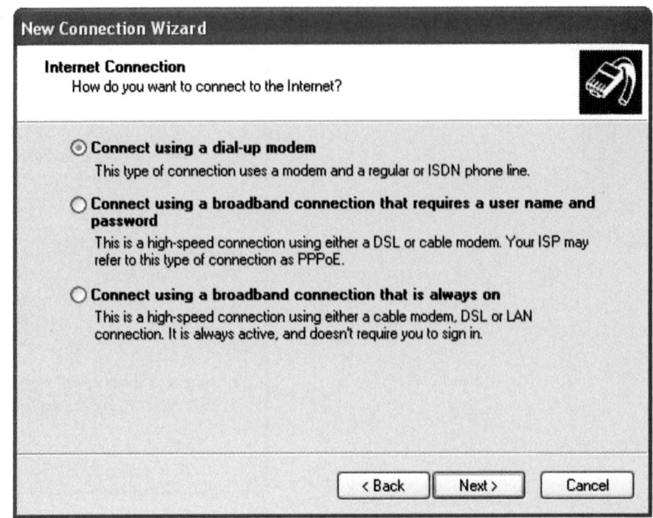

• **Figure 10-11.** The New Connection wizard in Windows XP will guide you through the process of configuring any type of network connection.

Step-by-Step 10.05

Configuring a Dial-Up Client

In this step-by-step, you will configure a dial-up client by creating a new dial-up connection. You will need

- A computer with Windows XP that has a modem installed (see previous step-by-step)
- To be logged on with local administrator privileges

Step 1

Open Control Panel | Network Connections, and select Create A New Connection, located in the Network Actions list on the left (if the list is not there, click the Folders button on the button bar). On the Welcome page of the New Connection wizard, click Next.

Step 2

On the Network Connection Type page, select Connect To The Internet and click Next. On the Getting Ready page, select Set Up My Connection Manually and click Next.

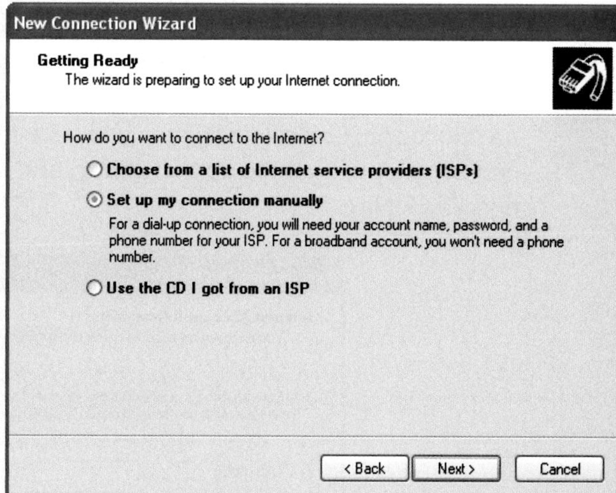

Step 3

On the Internet Connection page, select Connect Using A Dial-Up Modem and click Next. On the Connection Name page, enter the name of an ISP (use a fictitious ISP name for this lab) and click Next.

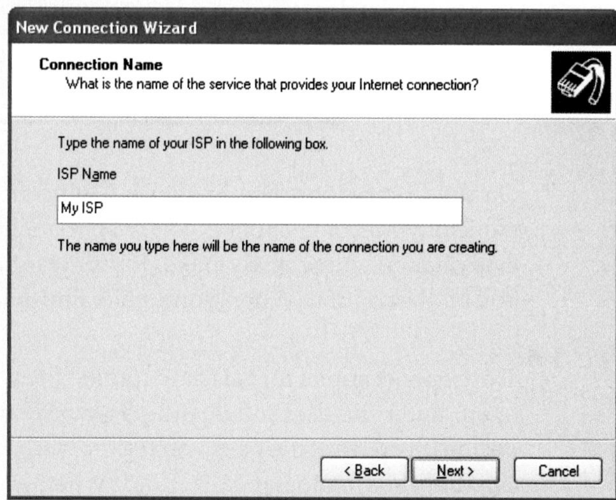

On the Phone Number To Dial page, enter a phone number and click Next.

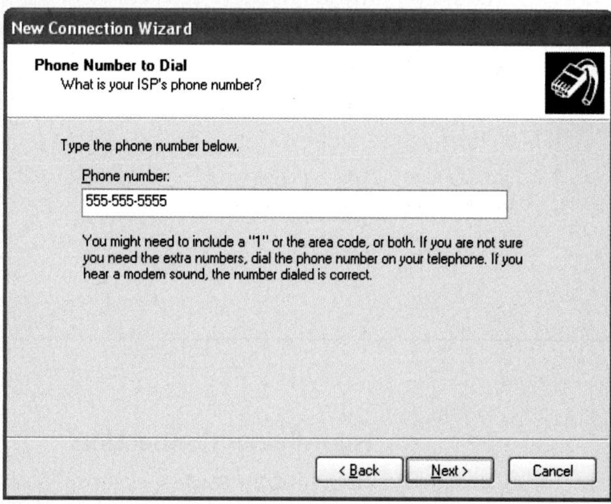

Step 4

On the Internet Account Information page, enter a user name and password and confirm the password. Notice the two settings below the Confirm Password box. The first setting will allow you to restrict the use of this connection to the current account (the one you used to log on) or to allow anyone who uses this computer to use the connection. The second setting makes it the default connection for all applications that can open a connection. Click Next.

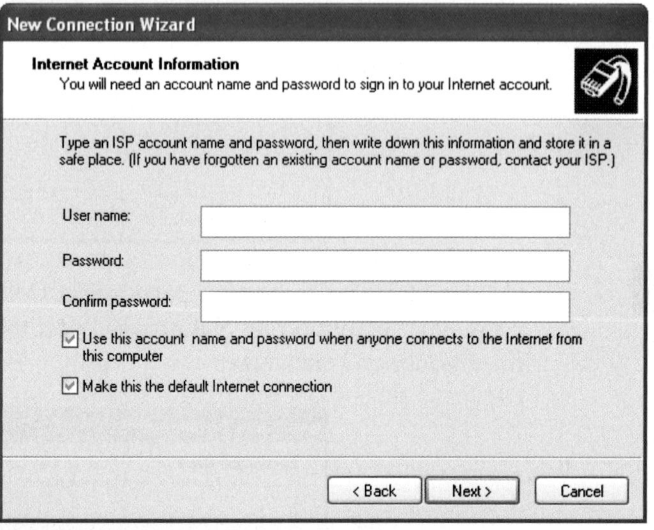

Step 5

On the Completing The Network Connection Wizard page, review the list under the name of your connection. If you wish to make any changes, select Back and make whatever change you wish to make. If you want a shortcut on the desktop, select the check box by that option. When done, click Finish.

Step 6

The Connect applet for this new connection will open. Enter the user name and password, and decide if you want the password saved so that it can be used automatically, and whether it should only be saved for you or for other users of the computer. If you followed the lab and created a fictitious modem and connection settings, cancel out of this dialog box. If the modem is real and the connections settings are valid, click Dial and test your new connection.

High-Speed Connection

Any type of Internet connection can be shared through a LAN, but if many users need to share an Internet connection, the connection between the network and the ISP must be adequate to carry the traffic. This means it must support the traffic created by all the users simultaneously at peak usage times.

Dedicated high-speed data circuits are available from telephone companies, cable network services, and other suppliers such as large networking companies and satellite service providers. These high-speed services are called broadband connections when they can handle multiple communications channels. Broadband connections communicate over media such as fiber optics, microwave, radio waves (wireless LANs), cable, and other technologies. In contrast, wired LAN technologies are usually baseband, with only a single communication channel.

The Yankee Group, a communications and networking research and consulting company, estimates that by 2008 the number of households in the USA using broadband Internet connections will reach 61.5 million.

Integrated Services Digital Network (ISDN) Integrated services digital network (ISDN) is a digital telephone service that simultaneously transmits voice, data, and control signaling over a single telephone line. ISDN service operates on standard telephone lines but requires a special modem and phone service, which adds to the cost. An ISDN data connection can transfer data at up to 128,000 bits per second (128 Kbps). Most telephone companies offer ISDN at a slightly higher cost than the modem dial-up service that it replaces. It is rarely used in homes in the United States. But in some areas, especially outside of the United States, it may be all that is available for a wired WAN connection.

The benefits of ISDN (beyond the faster speed compared to a dial-up connection) include being able to connect a PC, telephone, and fax machine to a single ISDN line and use them simultaneously. Many ISPs and local telephone companies that offer Internet access services support ISDN connections.

However, ISDN is dropping out of favor because of the increasing availability of higher-performance broadband options, such as cable and DSL, discussed next. In remote parts of the world, another optional broadband service, satellite communications, may be a more viable option than ISDN.

Digital Subscriber Line (DSL) **Digital subscriber line (DSL)** service is similar to ISDN in its use of the telephone network, but it uses more advanced digital signal processing to compress more signals through the telephone lines. DSL also requires changes in components on the telephone network before it can be offered in an area since it can only be used within a few miles of the central office. Like ISDN, DSL service can provide simultaneous data, voice, and fax transmissions on the same line. It gives you a dedicated circuit from your home or office to a central office, and they can usually guarantee consistent upload and download speeds.

- Several versions of DSL services are available for home and business use. Each version provides a different level of service, speed, and distance, and they normally provide full-time connections. The two most common are Asynchronous DSL (ADSL) and Synchronous DSL (SDSL). ADSL is the type of service normally available to home users. Others include High-bit-rate DSL (HDSL) and Very high bit-rate DSL (VDSL). The abbreviation often used to refer to DSL service in general begins with an *x* (*x*DSL), reflecting the variation of the first character in the DSL versions.

Across the DSL standards, data transmission speeds range from 128 Kbps for basic DSL service through 52 Mbps for high-end service.

When DSL speeds are described, they are usually the speed of traffic flowing "downstream"—that is, from the Internet to your computer. For instance, ADSL's downstream speed (commonly 256 Kbps, 512 Kbps, or 768 Kbps) is much faster than its upstream speed, which may be as low as 16 Kbps. While SDSL provides the same speed in each direction, it is much more expensive and not widely available. Most people only require the higher speeds for downloads (browsing the Internet, downloading multimedia files, and so on), so SDSL service is only recommended for customers who must upload a great deal of data.

T-Carrier System If you connect through a LAN at school or work, the LAN's connection to the Internet may be through the T-Carrier System offered by your telephone company. The T-Carrier System offers high-speed connections identified as a T-1, fractional T-1 or T-3. Even with hundreds of users on the network, large files and complex Web pages download quickly. T-1 consists of 24 individual channels that transmit 64Kbps each, and offer a combined throughput of 1.544Mbps. Fractional T-1 is one or more of the T-1 channels, leased as a cheaper alternative to T-1. The much more expensive T-3 service offers a connection with 672 channels, with a combined throughput of 44.736Mbps.

Cable Many cable television companies now use a portion of their network's bandwidth to offer Internet access through existing cable television connections. This Internet connection option is called cable modem service because of the need to use a special cable modem to connect.

Cable networks use coaxial cable, which can transmit data as much as 100 times faster than common telephone lines. Coaxial cable allows transmission over several channels simultaneously. Internet data can be transmitted on one channel, while audio, video, and control signals are transmitted separately. A user can access the Internet from his or her computer and watch cable television at the same time, over the same cable connection, and without the two data streams interfering with one another.

The biggest drawbacks to cable modem service involve the fact that the signal is shared between the subscribers in a defined area. As the number of users in an area increases, less bandwidth is available to each user. Therefore, while cable providers advertise higher speeds than DSL, they cannot guarantee consistent speeds.

Wireless Connectivity Technologies

Wireless communications over a very wide area is not a recent phenomenon. Radio technology has been around for over 100 years and was used to send information before wired telephone networks were common. The use of Morse code over wireless (radio) by ships at sea was just beginning to catch on when the *Titanic* sank in 1912. But as radio technology progressed, the use of radio transmissions for voice became dominant.

Like wired communications, wireless has moved from analog to digital over the years. Today, you can connect to the Internet through cellular networks, wireless wide area networks (WWANs), wireless LAN (WLAN) connections (if the WLAN ultimately connects to the Internet), and by satellite.

New wireless hand-held devices take advantage of WWAN technology, allowing users to surf the Internet from any location offering the required signal.

Enhanced personal digital assistants have cellular communications features and web browsing and e-mail client software, but they are being overshadowed by smart phones that have added many of the features of PDAs plus screens and software for working on the Internet.

Wireless WAN (WWAN) Connections

A wireless wide area network (WWAN) is a digital wireless network that extends over a large geographical area. A WWAN receives and transmits data using radio signals over cellular sites and satellites, which makes the network accessible to mobile computer systems. At the switching center, the WWAN splits off into segments and then connects to either a specialized public or private network via telephone or other high-speed communication links. The data traffic is then linked to an organization's existing LAN/WAN infrastructure (see Figure 10-12). The coverage area for a WWAN is normally measured in miles (or kilometers), and it is therefore more susceptible to environmental factors, like weather and terrain, than wired networks.

A WWAN is a fully bidirectional wireless network capable of data transfer at speeds in excess of 100 Mbps for a cost comparable with most DSL connections. Usually, basic WWAN services offer connection speeds between 1 and 10 Mbps. With dedicated equipment, the speeds can reach 100 Mbps. A WWAN system requires an antenna tuned to receive the proper radio frequency (RF).

A cellular Internet connection is an example of a WWAN. Many cellular services offer Internet access. That access may be directly from the cell phone, in which case, special software is included in the phone to provide a

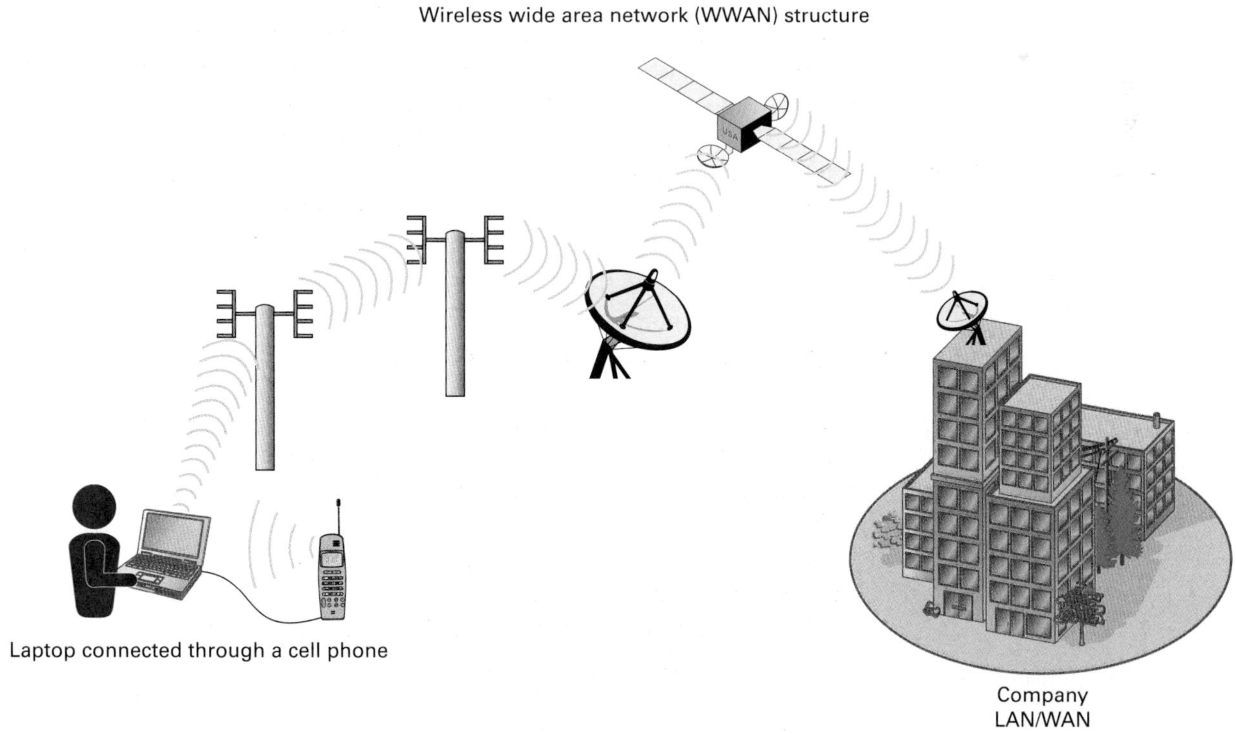

Wireless wide area network (WWAN) structure

Laptop connected through a cell phone

Company
LAN/WAN

• Figure 10-12. A WWAN includes devices that retransmit the wireless signal.

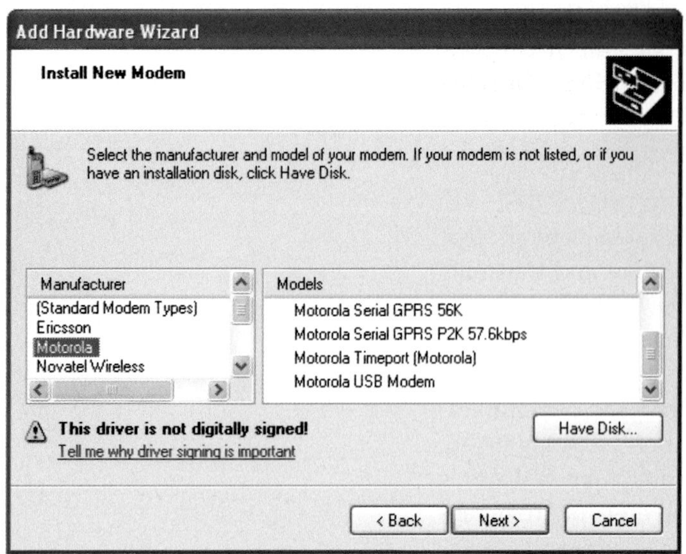

• Cellular modem drivers available with Windows XP

user interface. Some cellular providers also allow for cellular modems to be used with a desktop or laptop computer. Cellular customers may have a choice of buying a cellular modem card or of purchasing a special cable to connect their cell phone to a computer as a modem. One popular cellular data technology is Global Packet Radio Service (GPRS), and drivers to support several GPRS modems come with Windows XP. Install drivers for one of these modems, much as you would install a standard 56 Kbps modem. For over two years the authors have used a Motorola phone/modem as backup Internet access (via T-Mobile), and it has performed as well as a standard 56-Kbps modem.

Satellite

Many places in the world (even some in the United States) do not have a wired telephone network that can support broadband, nor do they have cellular coverage. For these locations, and for those who require Internet access while traveling, data satellites are the answer, and satellite connection services are becoming more affordable.

In fact, satellite communications are estimated to be used for a significant percentage of all worldwide ISP links to the Internet backbone and to customers. Further, it is estimated that 10 percent of the worldwide broadband traffic in 2003 involved satellite communications, and the trend is for more such use of satellite communications.

Satellite connections are suitable for large businesses and for small offices, cyber-cafes, and homes. They also are used for mobile communications by the armed forces, business, and individuals.

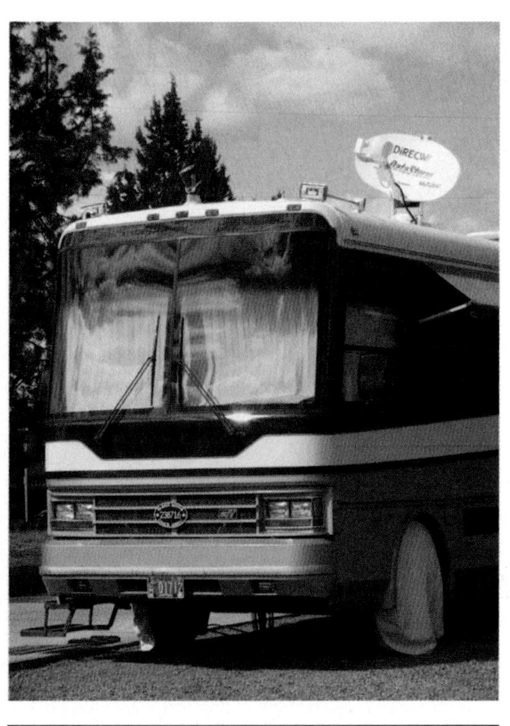

• A mobile satellite dish mounted on a motor home

Like ADSL, satellite data communication is usually faster downstream than upstream. The discrepancy can be huge, as we have found with our own mobile satellite system installed on our motor home. We often achieve download speeds of 400 Kbps to 800 Kbps (and occasionally more), but upload speeds are in the range of 25–45 Kbps. The system works well for us because, like most Internet users, our greatest need is for fast downloads as we browse the Internet or download files.

When an individual or organization contracts with an ISP for satellite service, an earth-based communications station is installed. It includes two parts: a transceiver, in the form of a satellite dish, and a modem-like device. The satellite dish is placed outdoors in direct line of sight of one of several special data satellites in geostationary orbit around the earth. The modem is connected to the dish and to the computer or LAN. A mobile installation (on a land- or water-based vehicle) is generally much more expensive than a stationery installation, because the mount must be designed to allow for moving the dish to align on the satellite, and therefore requires controlling circuitry and a costly motor-driven mount to achieve this with precision.

A satellite traveling in a geostationary orbit moves at the same speed as the earth's rotation and thus is always positioned over the same place on the earth—therefore the dish can be aligned precisely on the satellite. The satellite links the user's satellite dish to a land-based satellite operations center, through which the signal is routed to the Internet. (See Figure 10-13.)

WLAN Connections

A wireless LAN (WLAN) is a local area network, usually using one of the standards referred to as Wi-Fi (for wireless fidelity). The Wi-Fi standards of the Institute of Electrical and Electronics Engineers (IEEE) include 802.11a, 802.11b, and 802.11g. The distance covered by a WLAN is usually measured in feet (or meters) rather than miles. Therefore, this is not a technology that connects directly to an ISP (as a WWAN or satellite connection will) but can be used to connect to another LAN or device through which Internet access is achieved. This is the technology of Internet cafes and wireless notebooks. With enough wireless connect hubs, called access points, an entire community can gain wireless access to a shared Internet connection.

802.11g network adapters and access points are usually downward compatible with 802.11b devices. Therefore, you can take your new laptop with its built-in 802.11g wireless adapter to a public Wi-Fi venue and connect to either type of wireless network.

802.11a The IEEE 802.11a standard provides for speeds up to 54 Mbps. This may inspire you to run out and buy an 802.11a device for your computer, but the problem with this standard is compatibility. Most of the public access to WLANs is provided for by standards that use the 2.4-GHz band, but 802.11a uses the 5-GHz band. Therefore, an 802.11a device would be useless in most Internet cafes, public libraries, and other such sites.

802.11b The IEEE 802.11b standard is the one most often associated with the term Wi-Fi. This standard provides speeds up to 11 Mbps. While it is much slower than the 802.11a standard, it offers compatibility with most public WLAN access points.

802.11g The IEEE 802.11g standard offers speeds of up to 54 Mbps with a sustained throughput of 25 Mbps. Because it uses the 2.4-GHz band, a WLAN using 802.11g access points is usually accessible to users with either 802.11g or 802.11b network adapters.

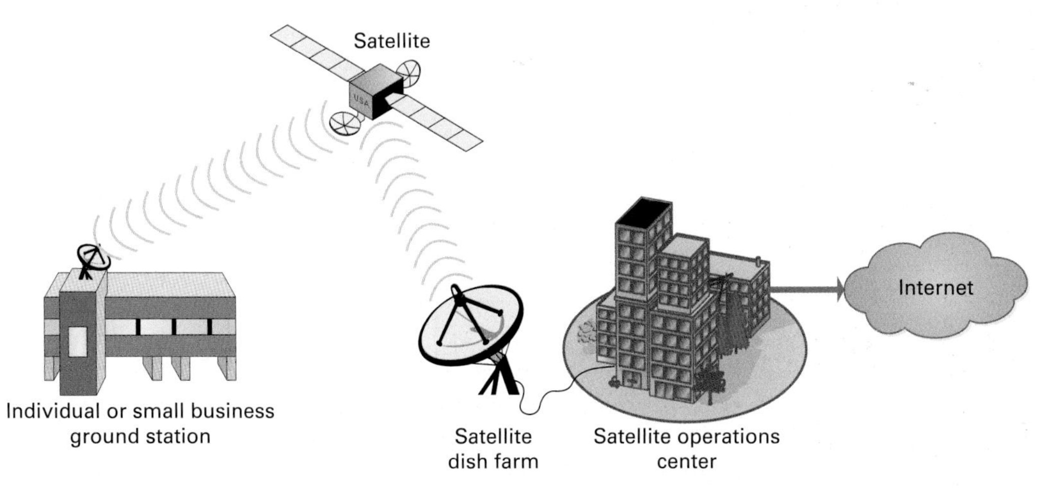

• **Figure 10-13.** Accessing the Internet through a satellite

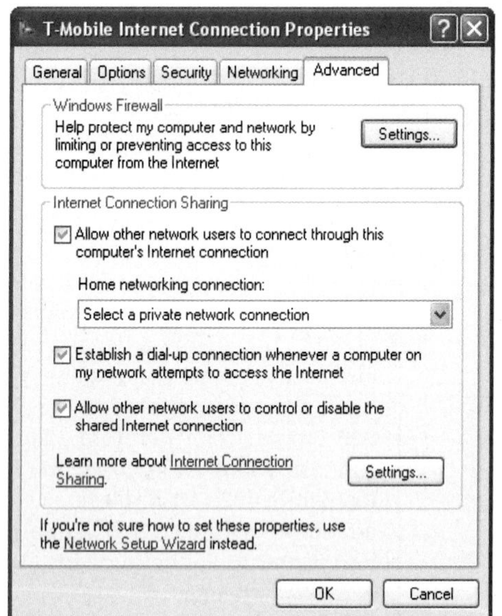

• **Figure 10-14.** Internet Connection Sharing settings for Windows XP

Sharing an Internet Connection

An Internet connection in a home or small office can be shared much like an Internet connection to a LAN is shared. They use similar technologies, although they generally offer fewer options and are simplified for home use.

Sharing a Dial-Up Connection

You can share a dial-up connection with other computers if those computers and the one that has the dial-up connection are on a network. This network may be a WLAN, as described on the previous page, or a more conventional Ethernet LAN. Windows 98 Second Edition (SE), Windows Me, Windows 2000, and XP all come with software that you enable and configure on the computer sharing the connection. See Figure 10-14.

Sharing a Broadband Connection

While you can share a dial-up connection, it is more practical to share one of the broadband technologies discussed next. A broadband connection to a single computer can be shared through ICS in the same way that you would share a dial-up connection, but a hardware solution usually works better for sharing a broadband connection. This kind of sharing just requires installation of a simple device called a broadband router, which is available in most computer stores. This device actually plays more roles than that of a router, but this is the term generally used. First, ensure that the broadband router includes enough Ethernet ports for the number of PCs you wish to have share the connection; otherwise, add an Ethernet hub or switch with enough ports, and connect the PCs as well as the broadband router to the hub or switch. Then connect the broadband modem to the broadband router—and do not worry about IP addresses for the private LAN. One of the many roles the device plays is that of a scaled-down DHCP server, so each computer receives a private address on the Internet LAN (yes, you now have a LAN), and some configuration will be required for the broadband interface. These devices are usually very easy to install.

Use this same technique to share an Internet connection with computers on a wireless LAN. Simply connect a wireless access point and broadband router via an Ethernet cable.

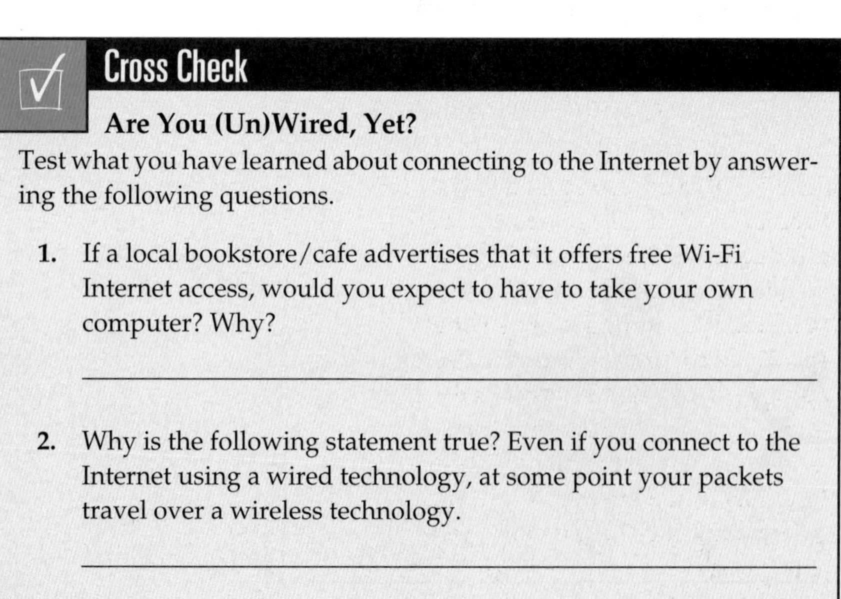

Cross Check

Are You (Un)Wired, Yet?

Test what you have learned about connecting to the Internet by answering the following questions.

1. If a local bookstore/cafe advertises that it offers free Wi-Fi Internet access, would you expect to have to take your own computer? Why?

2. Why is the following statement true? Even if you connect to the Internet using a wired technology, at some point your packets travel over a wireless technology.

Using a Virtual Private Network

Mobile users and remote offices often need to connect to a corporate intranet through the Internet by using any of the connection technologies discussed earlier. Such a connection can be made more secure by connecting through a virtual private network (VPN), which can be made over an existing network connection. For mobile users this will normally be made over a dial-up connection to the Internet and is called a remote access VPN (see Figure 10-15). When two networks are connected by a VPN, it is called a site-to-site VPN.

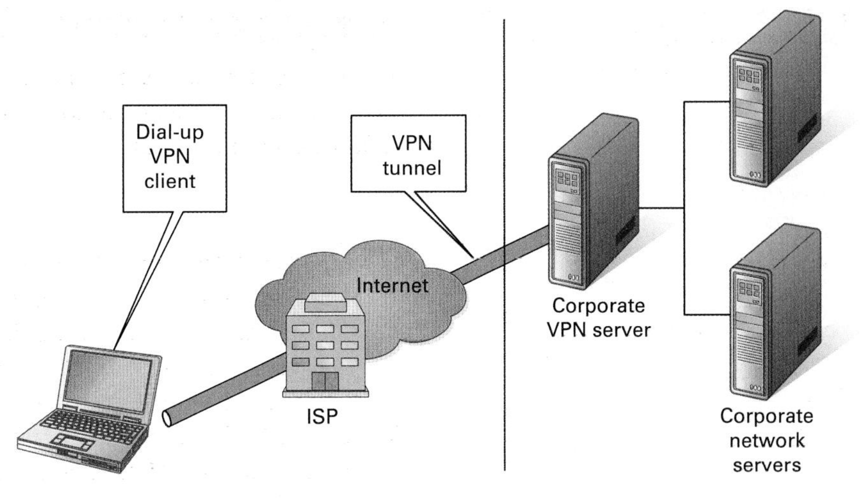

• **Figure 10-15.** A remote access VPN

Think of a virtual private network (VPN) as a simulated private network that runs inside a "tunnel" from endpoint to endpoint. One endpoint may be a user's computer using dial-up networking, while the other end will be a VPN Server in the private network. The tunnel effect is achieved by encapsulating each data packet sent from one end of the tunnel and removing it from the encapsulation at the receiving end. The encapsulation itself provides a very small amount of protection; other measures need to be applied to truly protect the data. Such measures include encrypting the data and requiring authentication of both endpoints of the tunnel.

Internet Clients

The growth of Internet services has increased the types of clients required to access those services. We will limit our discussion of Internet clients to web browsers, e-mail clients, and FTP clients. Many services are accessible through web browsers. E-mail may be the most important service on the Internet—many people who have no other use for the Internet use e-mail. And finally, the File Transfer Protocol (FTP) remains an important file transfer method on the Internet.

Web Browsers

While the World Wide Web (the Web) is just one of many services that exist on the Internet, it alone is responsible for most of the huge growth in Internet use that began after the Web's introduction in the 1990s. Web technologies changed the look of Internet content from all text to rich and colorful graphics, and made it simple to navigate the Web through the use of a special type of client called a web browser. The web browser's ease of use hides the complexity of the Internet, as protocols are used to transfer the content of a web page to the user's computer. There the web browser translates the plain text language into a rich, colorful document that may contain links to other pages—often at disparate locations on the Internet. You were introduced to servers in Chapter 9. Here we examine the common web browsers used on the Web.

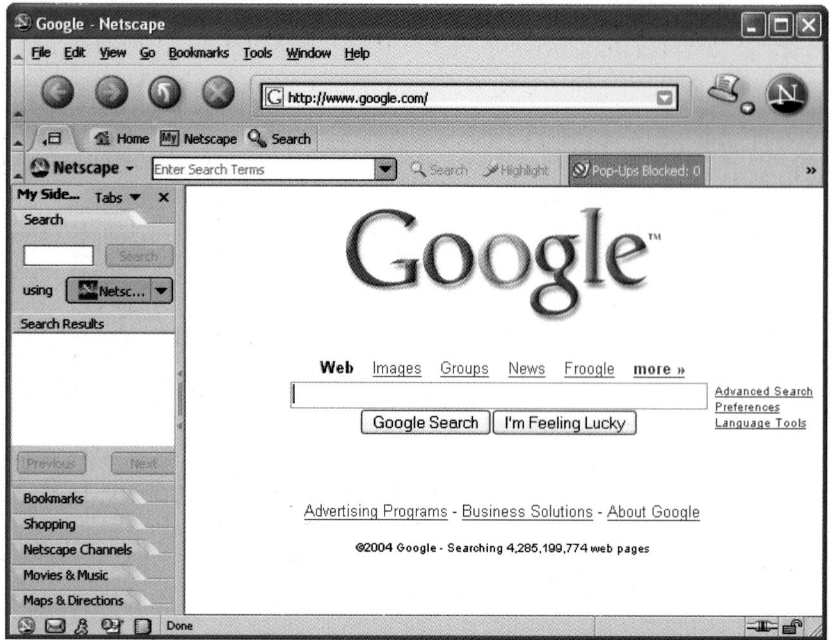

• **Figure 10-16.** Netscape Navigator

Netscape Navigator

In 1994, Mosaic Communications (later renamed Netscape Communications) was formed to develop a web browser called Netscape Navigator (Figure 10-16 shows a recent version of this browser). It was designed to compete directly with a web browser developed earlier at the National Center for Supercomputing Applications (NCSA). Mosaic's plan was to give the browser away and to sell web server software and other services. When they released Netscape Navigator, the company announced that they intended to develop it into a platform-independent GUI, obviously to compete head-to-head with Microsoft. Although Netscape was then far from achieving that goal, they succeeded in getting the attention of Microsoft, which eventually followed up with their own Internet browser, Internet Explorer. Netscape Communications, now owned by AOL, continues to update the Navigator and offers it for free—they also sell a variety of services and specialized server software. They maintain a membership-based free web portal called Netscape Network at `www.netscape.com`. A web portal is a web site that offers links to other sites as well as a variety of services.

In addition to the Navigator browser, Netscape now includes an e-mail client, newsgroup client, instant messaging, the Composer Web page editor, and an address book.

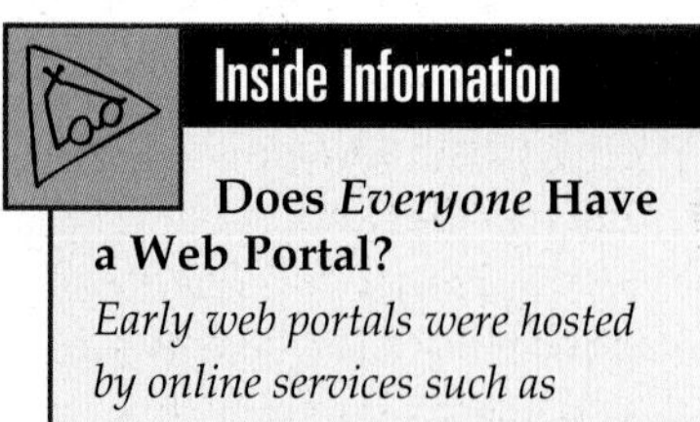

Inside Information

Does *Everyone* Have a Web Portal?

Early web portals were hosted by online services such as CompuServe and AOL. Many organizations now provide web portals, sometimes targeted to specific audiences. Even search engines, such as Google, AltaVista, and Lycos, have evolved into web portals.

Internet Explorer

In August 1995, in response to the introduction of the Netscape web browser, Microsoft introduced the Internet Explorer (IE) web browser along with the launch of the Windows 95 operating system. IE was included (or bundled) free with the operating system. IE is still bundled with Windows, and free updates to newer versions of IE for Windows and Mac OSs are available at the Microsoft web site. Figure 10-17 shows IE.

IE is primarily a web browser; the Mail and News options found on the Tools menu will actually call up your default e-mail program and Outlook News Reader. Similarly, selecting the Windows Messenger option will call up the Windows Messenger applet. IE on Windows XP with Service Pack 2 includes a pop-up blocker and an add-on manager.

Others

While Internet Explorer and Netscape are the two most widely used web browsers for Windows, there are alternatives. A recent addition is Firefox, free from Mozilla (`www.mozilla.org`). If you need a web browser that works on desktop computers, phones, and other mobile products, look into

Opera (www.opera.com). They offer versions of their browser for several platforms, including Windows, Mac, Linux, FreeBSD, Solaris, and more. Their Opera Mobile product runs on cell phones that use the Symbian OS and allows users to browse ordinary web pages as the software formats the pages to fit the small cell phone screen.

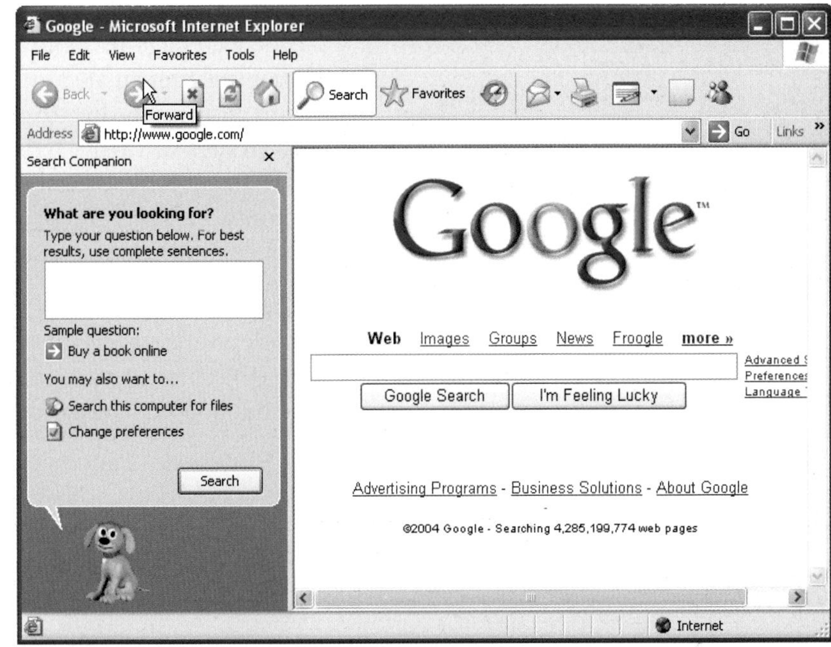

• **Figure 10-17.** Microsoft Internet Explorer

Browser Configuration Options

Browsers are now full-featured applications that go beyond simple web browsing and, as such, have a multitude of settings. Both Netscape Navigator and IE have a large number of configuration settings that range from GUI preferences to critical settings to protect your privacy and maintain security for your computer and personal data. To modify the settings in Netscape Navigator, use the menu option Edit | Preferences and select the Navigator node, which opens the preference settings, as shown in Figure 10-18. Similarly, Microsoft's Internet Explorer has no less than seven pages of settings in the Internet Options dialog box, shown in Figure 10-19. Open this dialog box from within IE by selecting Tools | Internet Options, and explore the settings as you read about them next.

An identical dialog box with a slightly different title (Internet Properties) can be opened from the Internet Options applet from within Control Panel.

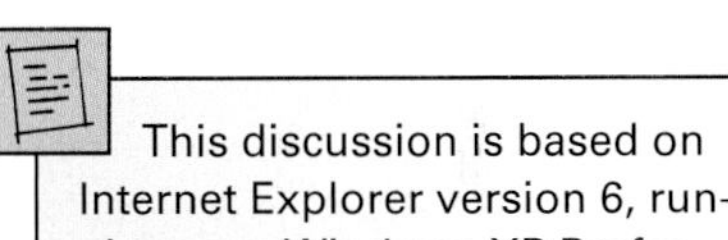

This discussion is based on Internet Explorer version 6, running on a Windows XP Professional computer with Service Pack 2 installed.

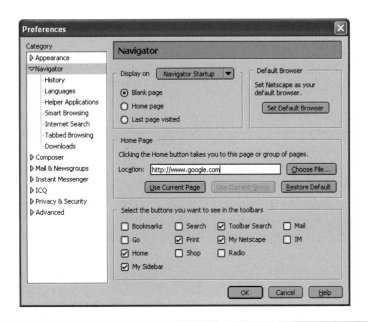

• **Figure 10-18.** Preference Settings for Netscape Navigator

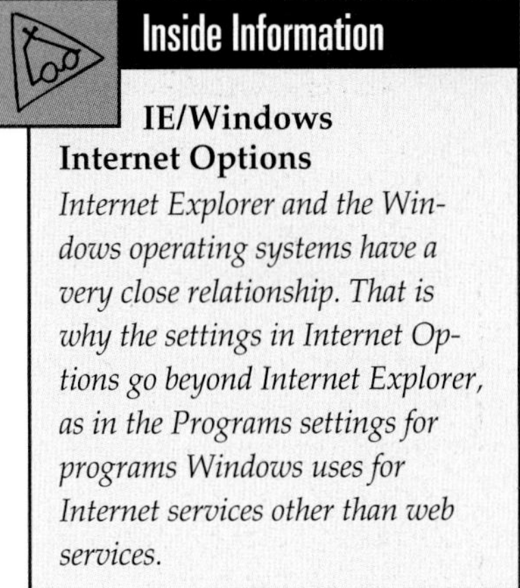

Inside Information

IE/Windows Internet Options

Internet Explorer and the Windows operating systems have a very close relationship. That is why the settings in Internet Options go beyond Internet Explorer, as in the Programs settings for programs Windows uses for Internet services other than web services.

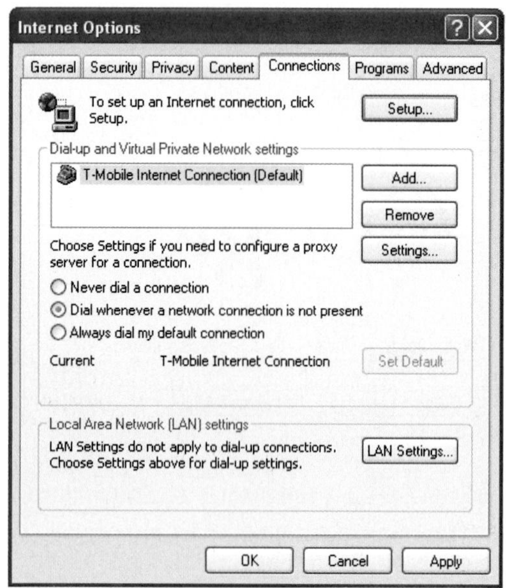

• **Figure 10-19.** Internet Options for Internet Explorer

General The General page contains settings for the Home page (the web page IE connects to when it starts), Temporary Internet files (the files created locally when you are browsing the Internet), and History (the length of time the history folder should save links to all sites you visit). In addition, a row of buttons on the bottom of this page lets you customize the Internet Explorer GUI to make it more accessible, and to make it more personal through changes to colors, fonts, and languages.

Security The Security page allows you to set security levels for various areas called zones. A **zone** contains one or more web sites to which you can assign restrictions. These security settings are all about how IE handles cookies. There are four predefined zones:

- **Internet** This zone contains any web site that has not been assigned to another zone, is not on your local computer, and is not on an intranet. The default setting for this zone is medium, which means that Internet Explorer will save cookies locally when instructed by code on web pages in this zone, and will allow each web site to read the cookies it previously created. You cannot add sites to this zone.
- **Local intranet** Any web site that can be reached without going through a proxy server is considered part of this zone. The default setting for this zone is medium, which means that Internet Explorer will save cookies locally when instructed by code on web pages in this zone, and will allow each web site to read the cookies it previously created.
- **Trusted sites** This zone does not contain any sites by default. You assign any sites to this zone that you trust completely, because the default setting for this zone is low, meaning that IE will allow all cookies from these web sites to be saved locally and will allow each web site to read the cookies it previously created.
- **Restricted sites** This zone does not contain any sites by default. You assign any sites to this zone that you trust completely, because the default setting for this zone is high, meaning that IE will block all cookies from these web sites.

Privacy Two groups of settings are on this page: Settings and Pop-up Blocker. Settings allow you to set the privacy settings for the Internet zone. The Sites button will allow you to create a list of managed sites. For each managed site, you can specify that IE always allow cookies or never allow cookies, regardless of the privacy setting for the Internet zone. The Pop-up Blocker settings let you turn this feature on or off. When blocking is turned on, you can designate sites for which IE will allow pop-ups. In addition, you can select notification and filter levels. Notification can be in the form of a sound played whenever IE blocks a pop-up and/or an information bar that appears under the IE toolbar after a pop-up has been blocked. This second option enables you to allow the individual pop-up or to ignore it. The filter levels are High (all pop-ups blocked), Medium (most automatic pop-ups blocked), and Low (allow pop-ups from secure sites).

Content The Content page has three groups of settings: Content Advisor, Certificates, and Personal Information.

- **Content Advisor** allows an administrator to block access from sites based on their ratings in a variety of categories. The rating systems used are provided as a service by various companies, and you can use the default rating system, or add a rating system to Content Advisor. The Content Advisor is turned off by default.
- **Certificates** settings control **Secure Sockets Layer (SSL)** certificate settings. SSL is a security protocol included in web browsers and web servers that uses a special encryption method involving a public key and a private key. In this context a **key** is a password or other code that is used to encrypt ("lock") or decrypt ("unlock") a message. A public key is used to encrypt a message, and a private key is used to decrypt a message. A certificate is actually a digital document issued by a certificate-issuing authority, such as VeriSign (`www.verisign.com`) and GeoTrust (`geocerts.com`). Certificates contain identifying information used for verifying the holder of the certificate and also contain the holder's public key. This can be used to encrypt a message for the user. Only the user holds the private key to decrypt the message.
- **Personal Information** settings include AutoComplete and personal information stored by Microsoft Profile Assistant. AutoComplete will save your previously entered web address to complete web addresses as you type them in, and save personal information for completing forms and entering user name and password. This last is the setting that allows IE to prompt you to decide to save passwords.

Connections Consider this page "Internet connections central" for your computer. Clicking the Setup button will launch the New Connections wizard. Once a connection is configured, use the appropriate groups of settings to modify each connection. Under Dial-Up and Virtual Private Network settings, add or remove dial-up or VPN connections, or change the settings for one of these connections. Use the LAN settings to configure how IE will use an Internet connection through your LAN. If your Internet connection depends on a proxy server, you will need to enter the address and port number of the proxy server for that connection for each protocol or service the proxy server supports. In Figure 10-20 the HTTP protocol and Secure (SSL) are supported by the proxy server.

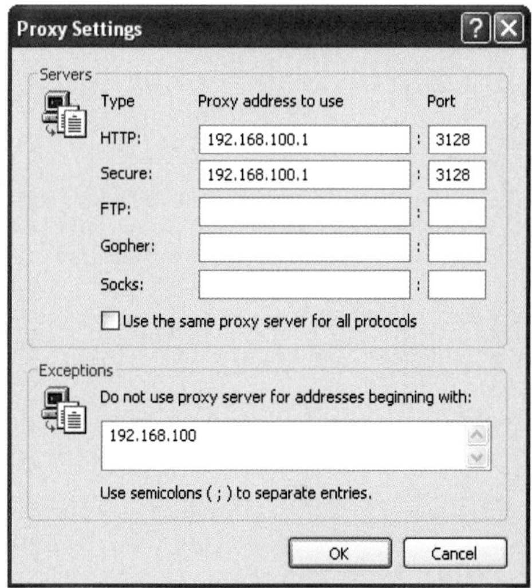

• **Figure 10-20.** Proxy Settings for one connection

Programs It is not uncommon to have more than one e-mail client or web browser, or to have other Internet clients or programs handy to use while on the Internet. The Programs page allows you to select just one program of each type to be the default. The list includes HTML editor, calendar, and contact list programs as well as the following clients: e-mail, newsgroup, and Internet call. This page also contains a button for resetting the default home and search pages and another button that brings up the Manage Add-Ons dialog box, where you can add the programs that have been added to IE to enhance it. This last is an excellent feature, since these add-ons seem to appear out of nowhere, and you may want to disable those that you do not want to use. Figure 10-21 shows the Manage Add-Ons dialog box.

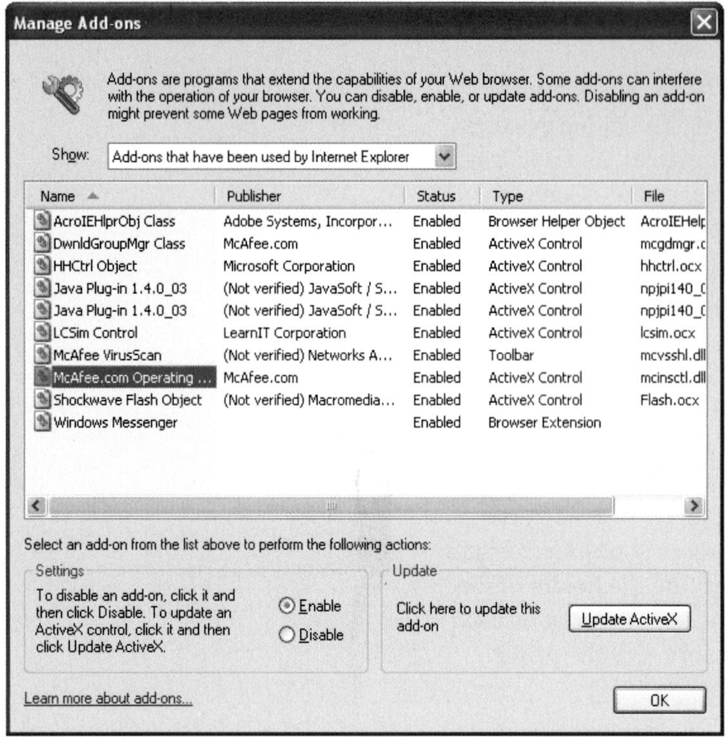

• **Figure 10-21.** Use the Manage Add-ons dialog box to disable add-ons you do not use.

Advanced This page contains a long list of settings in several categories: Accessibility, Browsing, HTTP 1.1 Settings, Java (Sun), Microsoft VM, Multimedia, Printing, Search From The Address Bar, and Security. If you have been advised to disable or enable script support for Java applets, look under Microsoft VM, and deselect or select the option titled "Java Console Enabled."

E-Mail Clients

The scope of Internet e-mail has made several major leaps in the last few decades—from being used mainly by academics and government workers, through the period when early PC users accessed services such as CompuServe, to today's casual PC users, numbered in the millions, who joined the Internet after the advent of the World Wide Web. Because of the past decade's explosion in the use of the Internet, e-mail has long been the most compelling reason to own a PC—but today you do not even need to use a PC to participate in personal e-mail. Now a plethora of hand-held devices, including cell phones and PDAs, allows users to send and receive e-mail over the Internet. Many of these do not allow attachments, but most messages do not include attachments. Further, you do not even need to own the device you use for Internet access! Today you can visit your local library or Internet cafe to keep up with the travels of Uncle Alonzo.

A mail client used in a school or corporate network may be specific to the mail servers the user connects to (Exchange, Notes, Domino, GroupWise), or the client may be one of several that can be used for different types of mail servers. Many users have access to e-mail client software such as Microsoft Outlook, Outlook Express, Eudora, or Pegasus. Users who subscribe to free e-mail services such as MSN or Yahoo! can use a web browser rather than special e-mail client software. Regardless of the type of client software, they all accomplish the task of sending and receiving the same way.

The client software will show a list of all of the messages in the mailbox by displaying information it reads from the message header. The message header is information added to the beginning of the message that contains details such as who sent it and the subject, and also may show the time and date of the message along with the message's size. Then the user may click on a message to open it and read the body of the e-mail. Users can then respond to the message, save the message, create a new message, add attachments, and/or send it to the intended recipient.

Outlook

Outlook is Microsoft's e-mail client that is sold both as a separate product and as part of the Microsoft Office suite. It can be used as a client to

Microsoft's Exchange Server e-mail service, as well as to any of several Internet e-mail services. It offers core e-mail features, such as an address book and folders for organizing mail, plus additional personal productivity features like an appointment calendar, a to-do list, and scheduling. It supports the use of more than one e-mail account.

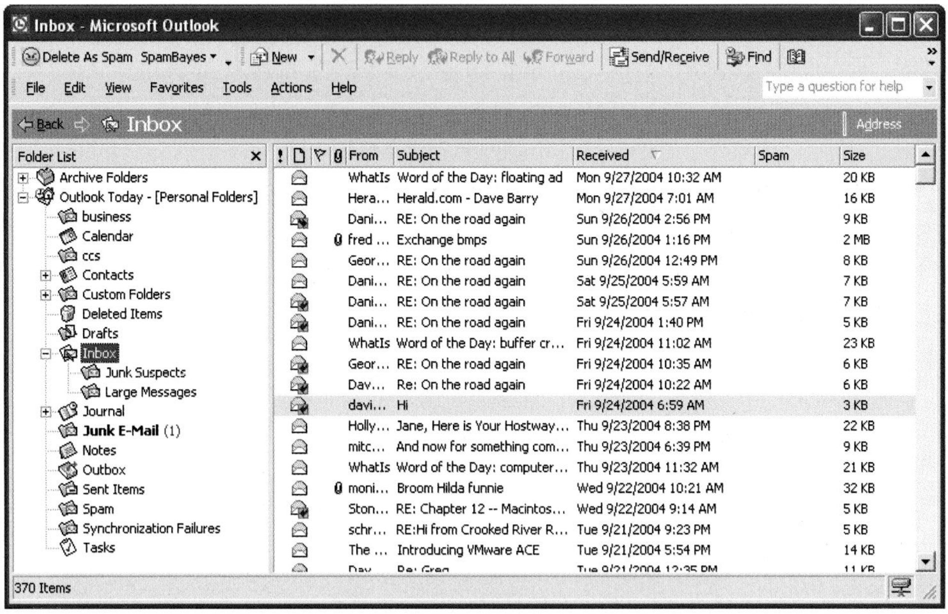

• Outlook e-mail client

Outlook Express

Outlook Express, an e-mail client and news reader, is bundled with Windows and installed during Windows installation. It does not have all the features of the commercial Outlook product. For instance, it can only be used for Internet e-mail accounts, but like Outlook, Outlook Express will manage multiple e-mail accounts.

Configuring and Using an E-Mail Client

Whether you use Outlook, Outlook Express, or one of many third-party e-mail clients, you will need to know the same set of information to configure your e-mail client. This includes

- The type of mail server you are accessing (POP3, IMAP, or HTTP)
- Your account name and password
- The DNS name of the incoming mail server
- The name of an outgoing mail server if you are preparing to connect to a POP3 or IMAP server

If you do not have this information, ask your ISP in the case of a private account, or network administrator if your mail server is a corporate mail server. ISPs often provide e-mail configuration information on their web sites. Check this out before configuring your e-mail client because it will help you avoid certain pitfalls. For instance, a client using a cell modem may have to be configured to authenticate to a certain mail server in their home service area.

Step-by-Step 10.06

Configure an E-MailClient

To complete this lab, you will need a PC with Windows 2000 or Windows XP with a previously configured Internet connection and the following information:

- The type of mail server
- Your account name and password
- The DNS name of the outgoing and incoming mail server
- Outlook Express installed into Windows
- An Internet e-mail address
- The DNS name or IP address of an incoming mail server for POP3, IMAP, or HTTP
- The DNS name or IP address of an outgoing mail server (SMTP)
- The HTTP mail service provider (if needed)

Step 1

Open Outlook Express by selecting Start | Programs | Outlook Express. The Internet Connection wizard will appear and be open to the Your Name page. Enter the name you would like to display when you respond to e-mail messages; then click Next.

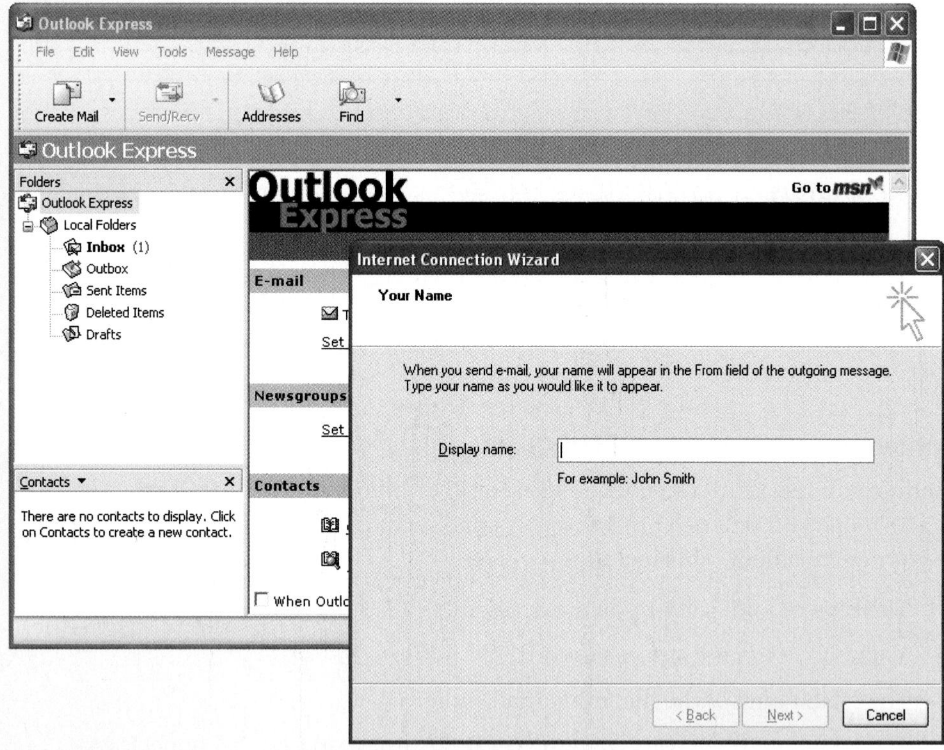

Step 2

On the Internet E-Mail Address page, enter your e-mail address, and then click Next.

Step 3

On the E-Mail Server Names page, select the protocol of your incoming mail server (POP3, IMAP, or HTTP). If you select POP3, IMAP, or HTTP, you will enter the DNS name of your incoming mail server on this page. With all but HTTP, you will also enter the DNS name of your outgoing mail server. The E-Mail Server Names page appears when you select POP3 or IMAP.

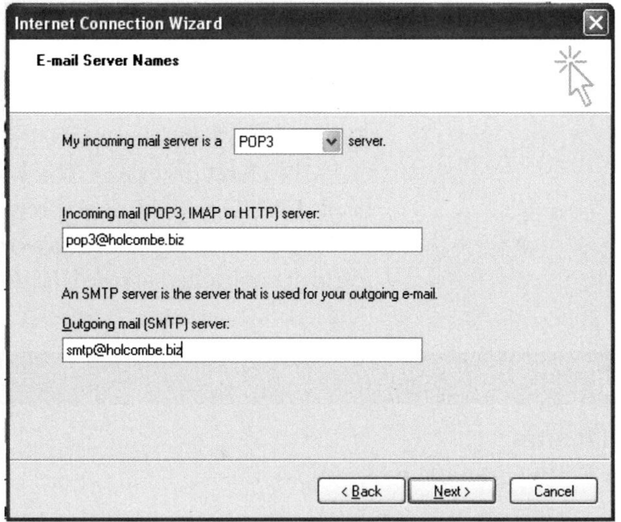

Step 4

If you select HTTP as the protocol for your incoming mail server, the E-Mail Server Names page displays an additional option: HTTP Mail Service Provider. Your choices are Hotmail or Other, and the outgoing SMTP server is no longer available and is grayed out.

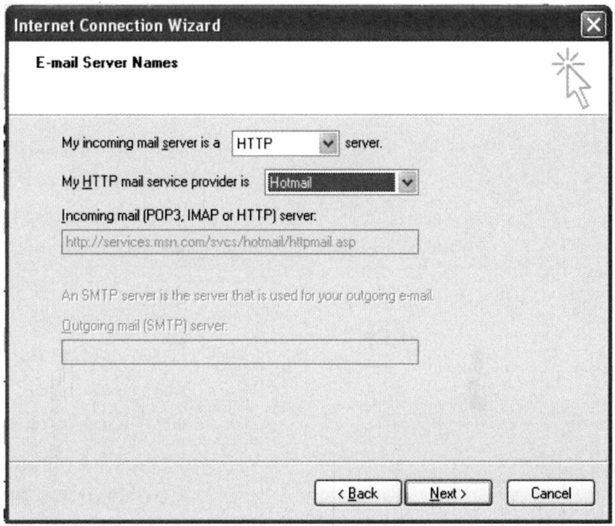

When you enter the incoming mail server for an HTTP mail server, be sure to include the complete URL for the mail server, including the prefix for the HTTP protocol (http) and a file name (select Hotmail and notice that it uses an ASP file). Click Next.

Step 5

On the Internet Mail Logon page, enter your account name and password, and leave the check box next to Log On Using Secure Password Authentication (SPA) blank unless you know that this is required. Choose Remember Password only if you are the only person who uses your user name to log onto your computer. Click Next.

Step 6

On the Congratulations page, click Finish, and close the Internet Accounts dialog box. To pick up your e-mail (optional), click the Inbox in Outlook Express. Then on the menu bar, click Tools | Send And Receive | Receive All.

FTP Clients

File Transfer Protocol (FTP) is a protocol used to transfer files between a computer running the FTP server service and an FTP client. It is a preferred method of transferring files over a TCP/IP network, especially the Internet, because it is simple and fast. Before the advent of the World Wide Web and the use of GUI tools for working on the Internet, people used character-mode FTP clients, because character mode was all there was. Because of the tremendous growth in the number of Internet and web users, you can use a variety of GUI FTP client programs. You can even use some of the popular web browsers as FTP clients, although programs designed specifically as FTP clients are usually easier to use and allow you to save the settings for connecting, including (but not limited to) the URL for the site, the user name, and the password.

Try This!

Find FTP Sites

Look for lists of FTP sites on the Internet. Try this:

1. Use your web browser to connect to your favorite search engine; search on "FTP sites."
2. Browse through the results. Notice that many of the results are links to compiled lists of sites, often organized by topic.

Anonymous FTP

If an FTP site does not require a user name and password, it is said to allow anonymous connection, which means that all users connecting are using the Anonymous account. As such, each user only has the permissions assigned to the Anonymous account, which may mean they can only read and copy the files from the FTP site, but cannot copy files to the site. An FTP site that allows anonymous connections is referred to as an **anonymous FTP site**. It is simple to connect to such a site using your browser by entering the URL, including the protocol suffix. For instance, to connect to the 3COM anonymous FTP site at `ftp.3com.com`, enter **ftp://ftp.3com.com** in the browser's address box. If you are using IE, it will open a new FTP window. Once connected, navigate through the list of folders and files, much as you do with your local folders and files. Then, to copy the item to your local hard drive, right-click on a file or folder, and select the Copy To Folder option.

Configuring an FTP Client

When connecting to a site that requires a user name and password, you can use a web browser. In IE 6, you will be prompted to log in, or, if you are already connected as Anonymous and want to log in with a different user account, select File | Login. IE is fine for connecting to an FTP site you will only visit once, but when you wish to save the settings for a site and manage settings for many FTP sites, you should find a free or commercial FTP client that suits your needs. A quick search of "FTP client" using an Internet search engine will yield a long list of clients. Our favorite is WS_FTP Professional, an inexpensive, full-featured client, which is also available in a freeware version (WS_FTP LE) for personal use. To configure an FTP client you will need

- The host name of the FTP server
- User ID and password (if applicable)
- Account (if applicable)

You may also need to know if the FTP server allows passive mode connections and/or Secure (SSL) connections. Figure 10-22 shows a list of sites saved in WS_FTP and the configuration options for one of the sites.

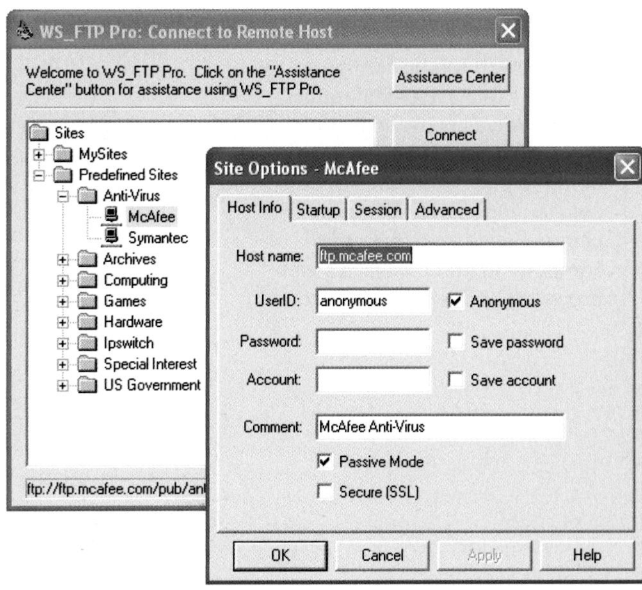

• **Figure 10-22.** An FTP client will save settings for each FTP site.

Troubleshooting Common Network Client Problems

If you are unable to access another computer on the network, several command-line utilities will help in pinpointing the source of a problem and arriving at a solution. In this section, you will learn to troubleshoot common client connection problems using each of these utilities, as required by the problem symptoms. Each utility provides different information and is most valuable when used appropriately. For instance, you should first view the IP configuration using the IPCONFIG utility and verify that it is correct for the network to which you are connected. If any obvious problems are discovered when you view the IP configuration, correct them before proceeding. Then test the ability to communicate using the PING command. Next you will practice this procedure and a few others.

Testing IP Configurations and Connectivity

When the TCP/IP suite is installed on a computer, it includes many protocols and many handy little programs that network professionals quickly learn to use. There are two that you should learn right away, for those times when you find yourself sitting at your computer and talking to a network professional while trying to resolve a network problem. These commands are IPCONFIG and PING. Learn about these commands next, and then do Step-by-Step 10.07, in which you will use both of these commands to test a network connection.

Verifying IP Configuration with IPCONFIG

Recall that the IPCONFIG command will display the IP configuration of all network interfaces, even those that receive their addresses and configuration through DHCP. Using this command shows whether the IP settings have been successfully bound to your network adapter. Bound means that there is a linking relationship, called a binding, between network components—in this case, between the network protocol and the adapter. A binding establishes the order in which each network component handles network communications. When troubleshooting network connectivity problems on an IP network, always use the IPCONFIG command to verify the IP configuration.

If you connect to the Internet from home, you can view your IP configuration. If you do not have a full-time connection, you must first connect to the Internet. Once connected, open a command prompt and enter the command **IPCONFIG /ALL**. If you are using Windows 95, use the command **WINIPCFG**.

A firewall can be configured to block specific types of traffic, so if a firewall is between your computer and the one you are trying to ping, you may not be able to ping it, even if you can communicate with that same computer in other ways like web browsing or downloading e-mail.

Troubleshooting Connection Errors with the PING Command

The **PING** command-line command is useful for testing the communications between two computers. The name of this command is actually an acronym for Packet Internet Groper, but we prefer to think (as many do) that it was named after the action of underwater sonar. Instead of bouncing sound waves off surfaces, the PING command uses data packets, and it sends them to specific IP addresses, requesting a response (hence the idea of pinging). This is a great test to see if you can access a certain computer. To run this command, you give it an address, it sends packets to the specified address, and then it "listens" for a reply. Pinging the IP address of the computer's own network interface and receiving a successful response indicates that the IP protocol and the local address are working. Ping another computer on the same network to test the ability to communicate between the two computers. Ping the gateway address to ensure that your computer can communicate with the router, and ping an address beyond your network, to test the router and the ability to communicate with a computer via the router.

Step-by-Step 10.07

Testing an IP Configuration

In this step-by-step exercise, you will look at the IP configuration settings to determine whether they are automatic or static, and then you will test the current configuration. The first test will let you confirm that you can communicate with a computer on your network, and the second test will confirm that you can communicate with a router on your network. The last test you will do will confirm that you can communicate with a computer beyond your network. To complete this step-by-step exercise, you will need the following:

- A computer with Windows 2000 Professional or Windows XP Professional
- A working connection to a TCP/IP network
- The IP address of another computer on your local network (use this when a step asks for *localIPaddress*)
- The IP address of a computer beyond your local network (use this when a step asks for *remoteIPaddress*)
- The user name and password of an account that is a member of your computer's Administrators account

Step 1

Log onto your computer with an account that is a member of the local Administrators group. If this is not possible, log on with whatever account you can, and just go through the steps. You will not be able to complete them all, but you will be able to see some of the settings.

Step 2

Check out your current IP configuration using the IPCONFIG command. To do that, first open a command prompt by selecting Start | Run, and in the Open text box, type **CMD** and press ENTER. Type **ipconfig /all** at the command prompt.

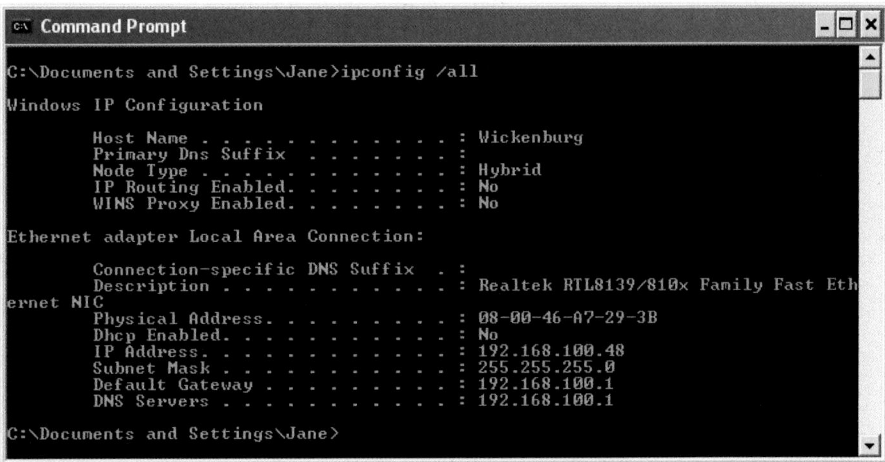
Command Prompt
C:\Documents and Settings\Jane>ipconfig /all
Windows IP Configuration
Host Name . . . . : Wickenburg
Primary Dns Suffix . . . . :
Node Type . . . . : Hybrid
IP Routing Enabled. . . . . : No
WINS Proxy Enabled. . . . . : No
Ethernet adapter Local Area Connection:
Connection-specific DNS Suffix . :
Description . . . . : Realtek RTL8139/810x Family Fast Ethernet NIC
Physical Address. . . . . : 08-00-46-A7-29-3B
Dhcp Enabled. . . . . : No
IP Address. . . . . : 192.168.100.48
Subnet Mask . . . . : 255.255.255.0
Default Gateway . . . . : 192.168.100.1
DNS Servers . . . . : 192.168.100.1
C:\Documents and Settings\Jane>

Step 3

If the current settings show an IP address other than 0.0.0.0, IP has successfully bound an IP address to the network adapter. If the current settings include DHCP enabled = Yes and also show an IP address for a DHCP server, then your network adapter is configured to receive an address automatically. If your DHCP Enabled setting equals No and your computer has a set of values for the IP address, then it has a static IP configuration that has a successful binding to the network adapter.

Step 4

Gather the information from the IPCONFIG command in the space provided next. You will need these addresses in the following steps.

IPaddress: ____________________________

Default Gateway: ______________________

DNS Server: __________________________

Step 5

At the command prompt, enter **ping *IPaddress***, where *IPaddress* is the address of your computer. You should receive four replies if your computer is properly configured. If you receive an error message or fewer than four replies, report this to your instructor.

Step 6

At the command prompt, enter **ping *localIPaddress***, where *localIPaddress* is the address of another computer on your same network. You should receive four replies if your computer is properly configured and if the other computer is also on the network and configured properly. If you receive an error message or fewer than four replies, report this to your instructor.

```
Command Prompt

C:\Documents and Settings\Jane>ping 192.168.100.48

Pinging 192.168.100.48 with 32 bytes of data:

Reply from 192.168.100.48: bytes=32 time<1ms TTL=128
Reply from 192.168.100.48: bytes=32 time<1ms TTL=128
Reply from 192.168.100.48: bytes=32 time<1ms TTL=128
Reply from 192.168.100.48: bytes=32 time<1ms TTL=128

Ping statistics for 192.168.100.48:
    Packets: Sent = 4, Received = 4, Lost = 0 (0% loss),
Approximate round trip times in milli-seconds:
    Minimum = 0ms, Maximum = 0ms, Average = 0ms

C:\Documents and Settings\Jane>_
```

Step 7

If the last test was successful, and if your computer has a gateway address, test this address now. Return to the command prompt and enter **ping *Default Gateway***, where *Default Gateway* equals the Default Gateway address recorded in Step 4. You should receive four replies if your computer is properly configured and if the default gateway is active on your network.

```
C:\WINDOWS\system32\CMD.exe

C:\Documents and Settings\Jane>ping 192.168.100.1

Pinging 192.168.100.1 with 32 bytes of data:

Reply from 192.168.100.1: bytes=32 time<1ms TTL=128
Reply from 192.168.100.1: bytes=32 time=1ms TTL=128
Reply from 192.168.100.1: bytes=32 time<1ms TTL=128
Reply from 192.168.100.1: bytes=32 time<1ms TTL=128

Ping statistics for 192.168.100.1:
    Packets: Sent = 4, Received = 4, Lost = 0 (0% loss),
Approximate round trip times in milli-seconds:
    Minimum = 0ms, Maximum = 1ms, Average = 0ms

C:\Documents and Settings\Jane>
```

Step 8

If your IP configuration includes the address of a DNS server, you should test connectivity to the DNS server now. Return to the command prompt and enter **ping *DNS Server***, where *DNS Server* equals the DNS Server address recorded in Step 4. You should receive four replies if your computer is properly configured and if the default gateway is active on your network.

Step 9

If you were given the address of a computer beyond your local network, test this address now by returning to the command prompt and entering **ping *remoteIPaddress***, where *remoteIPaddress* is the address of the remote computer.

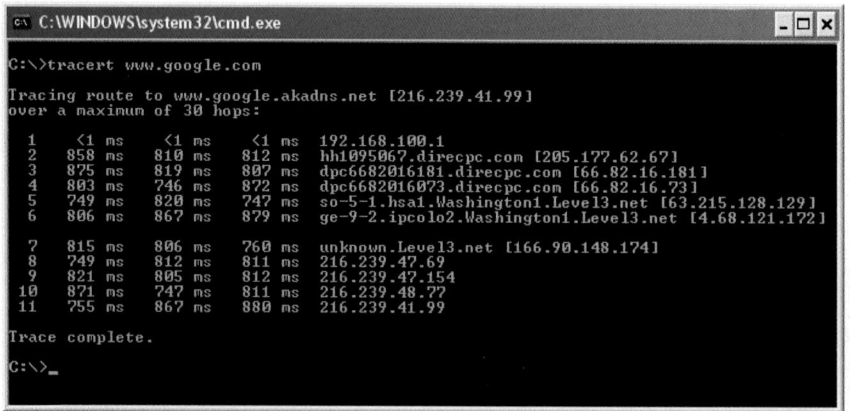
```
C:\WINDOWS\system32\cmd.exe

C:\>tracert www.google.com

Tracing route to www.google.akadns.net [216.239.41.99]
over a maximum of 30 hops:

  1    <1 ms    <1 ms    <1 ms  192.168.100.1
  2   858 ms   810 ms   812 ms  hh1095067.direcpc.com [205.177.62.67]
  3   875 ms   819 ms   807 ms  dpc6682016181.direcpc.com [66.82.16.181]
  4   803 ms   746 ms   872 ms  dpc6682016073.direcpc.com [66.82.16.73]
  5   749 ms   820 ms   747 ms  so-5-1.hsa1.Washington1.Level3.net [63.215.128.129]
  6   806 ms   867 ms   879 ms  ge-9-2.ipcolo2.Washington1.Level3.net [4.68.121.172]

  7   815 ms   806 ms   760 ms  unknown.Level3.net [166.90.148.174]
  8   749 ms   812 ms   811 ms  216.239.47.69
  9   821 ms   805 ms   812 ms  216.239.47.154
 10   871 ms   747 ms   811 ms  216.239.48.77
 11   755 ms   867 ms   880 ms  216.239.41.99

Trace complete.

C:\>_
```

Troubleshooting Connection Problems with TRACERT

You may have situations in which you can connect to a web site or other remote resource, but the connection is very slow. If this connection is critical to business, you will want to gather information so that a network administrator or ISP can troubleshoot the source of the bottleneck. You can use the TRACERT command to gather this information. **TRACERT** is a command-line utility that traces the route taken by packets to a destination. When you use TRACERT with the name or IP address of the target host, it will ping each of the intervening routers, from the nearest to the farthest. You see the delay at each router, and you will be able to determine the location of the bottleneck. You can then provide this information to the people who will troubleshoot it for you. Consider a scenario in which your connection to the Google web (`www.google.com`) is extremely slow. Use the following to run Tracert and save the result to a file: tracert www.google >trace01.txt.

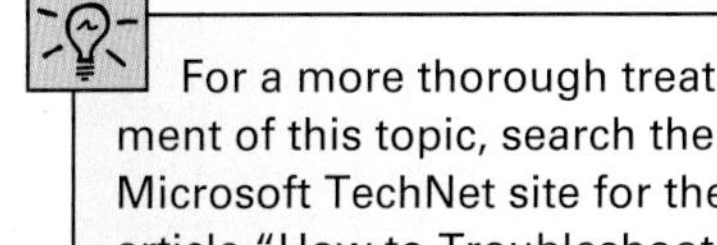

For a more thorough treatment of this topic, search the Microsoft TechNet site for the article "How to Troubleshoot Basic TCP/IP Problems."

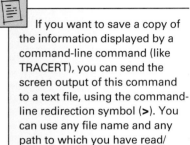

If you want to save a copy of the information displayed by a command-line command (like TRACERT), you can send the screen output of this command to a text file, using the command-line redirection symbol (**>**). You can use any file name and any path to which you have read/write access. No output will appear on the screen. Here is an example of a command with the output sent to a file in the current directory: `TRACERT www.google.com >tracegoogle.txt`

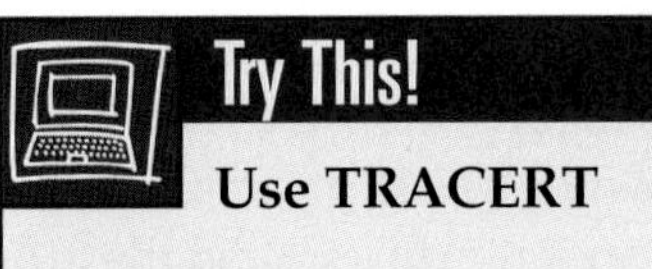

Try This!

Use TRACERT

1. Open a command prompt.
2. Type **tracert www.google.com**.
3. The numbered lines represent routers, and the highest delay, measured in milliseconds (MS), shows the slowest router.

Troubleshooting DNS Errors by Using PING, NETSTAT, and NSLOOKUP

Have you ever attempted to browse to a web page, only to have your browser display an error message such as "Cannot find server or DNS Error?" This may be a name resolution problem, since the fully qualified domain name (FQDN) portion of a URL, such as `www.google.com`, must be resolved to an IP address before a single packet will be sent to the web site.

One way to test if the problem is a connectivity problem or a DNS error is to first test for connectivity by either pinging (using the PING command) the IP address of the web site, or by using the IP address in place of the FQDN in the uniform resource locator (URL). If you cannot reach the web site by using its IP address, then it is a connectivity problem and should be resolved by contacting your network administrator or ISP.

If you can reach the web site by pinging the IP address, but cannot access it through your browser, then it is a name resolution problem, and a simple test of DNS name resolution is to ping the FQDN. Figure 10-23 shows the

```
C:\WINDOWS\system32\CMD.exe
C:\>ping www.google.com

Pinging www.google.akadns.net [216.239.41.104] with 32 bytes of data:

Reply from 216.239.41.104: bytes=32 time=923ms TTL=245
Reply from 216.239.41.104: bytes=32 time=856ms TTL=245
Reply from 216.239.41.104: bytes=32 time=855ms TTL=245
Reply from 216.239.41.104: bytes=32 time=858ms TTL=245

Ping statistics for 216.239.41.104:
    Packets: Sent = 4, Received = 4, Lost = 0 (0% loss),
Approximate round trip times in milli-seconds:
    Minimum = 855ms, Maximum = 923ms, Average = 873ms

C:\>
```

• **Figure 10-23.** Pinging the FQDN `www.google.com` reveals the IP address.

result of pinging the FQDN `www.google.com`. Notice that this displays the IP address of the web site, confirming the DNS name-to-IP address resolution is working.

When you are troubleshooting networking problems, it is very helpful to have a second computer that does not display the same problems. Then you can use the second computer to discover the IP address of a web site by using your browser to connect. Once connected, you can use the NETSTAT command to discover the IP address of the web site. NETSTAT displays network statistics, protocol statistics, and information about current TCP/IP connections. Figure 10-24 shows the result of running the NETSTAT command after connecting to a web site with a browser. The IP address for this web site, `www.google.com`, is shown under Foreign Address, and the protocol used to connect to the web site, http, is shown after the colon in the foreign address.

Finally, the classic command for troubleshooting DNS, used for many years on the Internet and other TCP/IP networks, is **NSLOOKUP**. The *NS* in this command name stands for "name server." This command allows you to send queries to a DNS name server directly and to see the results. It is a very powerful command, but you can use it to test your DNS setting without learning all of its subcommands. Running NSLOOKUP in a command prompt without any additional command-line parameters will cause it to attempt to connect to the name server address in your IP configuration. Then it displays the NSLOOKUP prompt, a greater-than sign (>). You may enter subcommands at this prompt. If it cannot connect to the DNS server, it will display an error, as shown in Figure 10-25. If you see this error, contact your network administrator or ISP. Type **Exit** at the NSLOOKUP prompt to exit from the command. Then type **Exit** again to exit from the command prompt.

To learn more about the NSLOOKUP command, search on "NSLOOKUP" in the Windows Help program.

Troubleshooting Logon Problems

By some estimates 60 to 80 percent of calls to help desks of private networks involve forgotten or incorrectly entered passwords. Help stamp out this

• **Figure 10-24.** NETSTAT displays the IP address and protocol information of current connections.

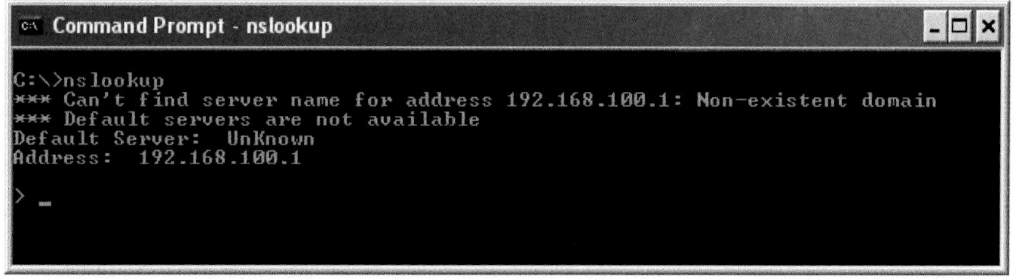

• **Figure 10-25.** NSLOOKUP reveals a DNS problem.

scourge of productivity by memorizing passwords, and anytime you cannot log onto the network, do the following steps before calling for help:

1. Ensure that Caps Lock is not on, and carefully reenter your user name and password.
2. If you are confident that you have entered the correct user name and password, treat it like a connectivity problem.
3. If you are confident that there is no connectivity problem, call your network administrator or ISP (as appropriate).

Chapter 10 Review

Chapter Summary

After reading this chapter and completing the Step-by-Step tutorials and Try This! exercises, you should understand the following facts about networking:

Understanding the TCP/IP Protocol Suite

- TCP/IP is a commonly used suite of protocols that allows dissimilar computers to communicate. It is the protocol suite needed to access the Internet.
- Transmission Control Protocol (TCP) and Internet Protocol (IP) are the core protocols of TCP/IP.
- TCP is responsible for the accurate delivery of messages, verifying and resending pieces that fail to make the trip.
- IP is a protocol that packages your communications in chunks, called packets. This protocol allows your computer to be identified on an internetwork by a logical address, called an IP address, and is responsible for the route that a packet takes through a very complex internetwork.
- An IP address is assigned to a network adapter (usually, but not always, Ethernet) or modem in a computer that connects it to a network.
- An IP address has four parts, and you will usually see it in dotted decimal format, such as 192.168.100.48. Each number must be within the range from 0 to 255, and rules define exactly which numbers can be used.
- Public IP addresses are used for hosts on the Internet, and each address must be unique on the entire Internet.
- The organization that is centrally responsible for allocation of public IP addresses is the Internet Assigned Numbers Authority (IANA). They allocate numbers to various Regional Internet Registries (RIRs), organizations given the task of allocating IP addresses to Internet service providers (ISPs).
- The largest ISPs allocate addresses to other ISPs, who in turn allocate addresses to individuals and businesses.
- A private IP address is one of three ranges of IP addresses designated for use only on private networks. They are not to be used on the Internet, and you do not need to obtain permission to use these addresses on a private network.
- Computers on a private network using private IP addresses get access to the Internet through a specialized device using one of several methods. One method involves a proxy server, and another method uses a network address translation (NAT) router.
- The devices commonly sold as "Internet routers" for use in homes and small offices allow one or more computers on a private network to communicate over the Internet by using one of several methods for temporarily providing a valid public IP address for the source address of each internal client that is using a private address.
- Each host on a TCP/IP network must have an IP address. There are two general methods by which a host receives an address: automatically as a DHCP client via a network DHCP server or a self-assigned APIPA address, or statically, which involves someone manually assigning an address to the host.
- In addition to the IP address, several IP configuration settings include subnet mask, default gateway, DNS server, advanced DNS settings, and WINS settings.

File and Print Clients on Private Networks

- A file and print client includes both the user interface and the underlying file sharing protocols to access a file sharing system on a network file and print server.
- File sharing protocols include Microsoft's Server Message Block (SMB) protocol; Novell's NetWare Core Protocol (NCP); the newer Common Internet File System (CIFS), a standard used by Microsoft, Novell, and many others; the network file system (NFS) used in Linux and most UNIX versions; and

the P2P file sharing protocol used to share files over the Internet.

- The client for Microsoft networks, installed when a Windows operating system is installed, allows users to use the Windows GUI to see those Microsoft computers on the network that have file and printer sharing turned on, whether they are using the older SMB file sharing protocol or the newer CIFS protocol standard.
- A computer user requiring access to file and print services on a Novell server needs a Novell client. Windows clients can choose from two: the client for Novell that comes with Windows or Novell's client software.
- You can connect to a share by browsing to it in My Computer (or Windows Explorer), by entering a Universal Naming Convention (UNC) name in a browser, or you may search for it in an Active Directory domain.
- For a frequently accessed share, map a drive letter to the share and select to have it reconnect at logon.
- Connecting to a shared printer is much like connecting to a file share. You can browse to a shared printer, use a UNC name to point to one, and you can even use a URL to connect to a printer.
- Active Directory clients may also search Active Directory for files or printers that have been published in the directory.
- A mail client used in a school or corporate network may be specific to the mail servers the user connects to (Exchange, Notes, Domino, GroupWise), or the client may be one of several that can be used for different types of mail servers.
- The client software will show a list of all of the messages in the mailbox by displaying information it read from the message header, which contains details such as who sent the mail and the subject of the mail, and also may show the time and date of the message along with the message's size.

Connecting to the Internet

- An Internet service provider (ISP) is an organization that provides individuals or entire companies access to the Internet.
- A computer might be connected to the Internet but not to a LAN. A computer that is connected to a LAN may have access to the Internet through that LAN if the LAN itself or another LAN to which it has a connection is connected to the Internet.
- Most, but not all, wired WAN technologies used for connecting to the Internet utilize the telecommunications infrastructure of the telephone system.
- Dial-up is an inexpensive choice available to anyone with a phone line and a standard modem (the longtime standard runs at 56 Kbps).
- Like a voice phone conversation, a dial-up connection is only temporary and ends when either your PC or the ISP's server ends the call.
- Use the Phone and Modem Options applet in Control Panel to verify that a modem is properly installed and configured, or to install a new modem.
- After a modem is installed and configured, use the New Connection wizard to configure the connection unless you have software from your ISP that will automatically configure the connection.
- Use the connection applet whenever you wish to open a dial-up connection.
- Of the wired high-speed connection options, ISDN is the oldest technology and generally slower than the other two: cable and digital subscriber line (DSL).
- ISDN is a digital telephone service that simultaneously transmits voice, data, and control signaling over a single telephone line and can transfer data at up to 128,000 bits per second (128 Kbps).
- Digital subscriber line (DSL) service is similar to ISDN in its use of the telephone network, but it uses more advanced digital signal processing to compress more signals through the telephone lines.
- Several versions of DSL services are available; each version provides a different level of service, speed, and distances; and they normally provide full-time connections. The two most common are Asynchronous DSL (ADSL) and Synchronous DSL (SDSL). Others include High-bit-rate DSL (HDSL) and Very high bit-rate DSL (VDSL).
- Across the standards, data transmission speeds range from 128 Kbps for basic DSL service through 8.448 Mbps for high-end service.

- ADSL's downstream speed is much faster than its upstream speed, while SDSL provides the same speed in each direction, but is usually much more expensive. Most people only require the higher speeds for downloads (browsing the Internet, downloading multimedia files, and so on).
- For organizations requiring high-speed Internet access for hundreds of users, the telephone company offers high-speed T-Carrier connections, including T1 at 1.544Mbps, fractional T1 using one or more of the 64Kbps T1 channels, or T3 with a maximum throughput of 44.736Mbps.
- Many cable television companies now offer Internet access through existing cable television connections using special cable modems that provide speeds of up to 5MB downstream and up to 768MB upstream.
- Wireless options for connecting to the Internet include cellular networks, wireless wide area networks (WWANs), wireless LAN (WLAN) connections (if the WLAN ultimately connects to the Internet), and by satellite.
- An Internet connection in a home or small office can be shared much like an Internet connection to a LAN is shared. They use similar technologies, although they generally offer fewer options and are simplified for home use.
- Mobile users and remote offices often need to connect to the corporate intranet through the Internet using any of the connection technologies discussed earlier, with the addition of a virtual private network (VPN) for security.

Internet Clients

- Web technologies changed the look of Internet content from all text to rich and colorful graphics and made it simple to navigate the Web through the use of a special type of client called a web browser.
- The Netscape Navigator and Microsoft Internet Explorer (IE) web browsers are available free for Windows and other operating systems.
- Both Netscape Navigator and IE have a large number of configuration settings that range from GUI preferences to settings critical to protecting your privacy and maintaining security for your computer and personal data.
- To modify the settings in Netscape Navigator, use the menu option Edit | Preferences and select the Navigator node, which opens the preference settings.
- Configuration settings for IE can be found at Tools | Internet Settings.
- While some e-mail services require dedicated clients, some e-mail clients can interact with a variety of e-mail server types. Microsoft Outlook can be used as a client to Microsoft's Exchange Server e-mail service, as well as to any of several Internet e-mail services. It supports the use of more than one e-mail account and also offers a variety of related productivity tools such as address book, folders for organizing mail, an appointment calendar, to-do list, and scheduling.
- Outlook Express is an e-mail client and news reader, bundled with Windows and installed during Windows installation. It can only be used for Internet e-mail accounts, but like Outlook, it will manage multiple e-mail accounts.
- To configure any e-mail client, you need a specific set of information:
  - The type of mail server you are accessing (POP3, IMAP, or HTTP)
  - Your account name and password
  - The DNS name of the incoming mail server
  - The name of an outgoing mail server if you are preparing to connect to a POP3 or IMAP server
- File Transfer Protocol (FTP) is a protocol used to transfer files between a computer running the FTP server service and an FTP client. It is a preferred method of transferring files over a TCP/IP network, because it is simple and fast.
- An FTP site that allows anonymous connections is referred to as an anonymous FTP site.
- If a site requires a user name and password, you will be prompted, whether you are using a web browser to connect or an FTP client.
- A web browser is fine for occasionally connecting to FTP sites, but use an FTP client to save settings for FTP sites you visit repeatedly.

- To configure an FTP client you will need
  - The host name of the FTP server.
  - User ID and password (if applicable).
  - Account (if applicable).
  - You may also need to know if the FTP server allows passive mode connections and/or secure (SSL) connections.

Troubleshooting Common Network Client Connection Problems

- Several command-line commands help in diagnosing and solving network client connection problems. These utilities include
  - IPCONFIG
  - PING
  - TRACERT
  - NETSTAT
  - NSLOOKUP
- Do not contribute to the 60 to 80 percent of help desk calls associated with forgotten or incorrectly entered passwords. Memorize your passwords and do the following steps before calling for help when you have difficulty logging onto the network:
  - Ensure that Caps Lock is not on, and carefully reenter your user name and password.
  - If you are confident that you have entered the correct user name and password, treat it like a connectivity problem.
  - If you are confident that there is no connectivity problem, call your network administrator or ISP (as appropriate).

Key Terms List

anonymous FTP site *(520)*
automatic IP addressing *(483)*
Automatic Private IP Addressing (APIPA) *(483)*
Common Internet File System (CIFS) *(487)*
default gateway *(484)*
dial-up *(497)*
digital subscriber line (DSL) *(505)*
Domain Name System (DNS) *(484)*
Dynamic Host Configuration Protocol (DHCP) server *(483)*
File Transfer Protocol (FTP) *(520)*
Internet Protocol (IP) *(480)*
Internet service provider (ISP) *(496)*
IPCONFIG *(487)*
key *(515)*
mapping *(491)*
NetWare Core Protocol (NCP) *(487)*
NSLOOKUP *(526)*
PING *(522)*
private IP address *(482)*
public IP addresses *(482)*
Secure Sockets Layer (SSL) *(515)*
Server Message Block (SMB) *(487)*
static IP address *(483)*
subnet mask *(484)*
TCP/IP *(480)*
TRACERT *(524)*
Transmission Control Protocol (TCP) *(480)*
zone *(514)*

Key Terms Quiz

1. ____________________ are used for hosts on the Internet.
2. In addition to the Server Message Block (SMB) file sharing protocol, Microsoft Windows uses ____________________.
3. A/an ____________________ is a portion of the Web or private intranet to which you can assign web sites for the purpose of setting or removing restrictions.
4. ____________________ is a security protocol included in web browsers and web servers that uses a special encryption method involving both a public key and a private key.
5. A/an ____________________ is not used for hosts on the Internet.
6. A/an ____________________ is an organization that provides individuals or entire companies with access to the Internet.
7. A/an ____________________ is a password or other code that is used to encrypt ("lock") or decrypt ("unlock") a message.

8. ________________ assigns one of your local, unused drive letters to a share out on the network(s).

9. ________________ service is a term for a group of wired broadband technologies offered through the phone company, and capable of higher speeds than Integrated Services Digital Network (ISDN).

10. Most organizations use ________________ to assign IP addresses to desktop computers.

■ Multiple-Choice Quiz

1. The IP address 192.168.30.24 is an example of one of these.
   - **a.** DNS server address
   - **b.** Public IP address
   - **c.** Private IP address
   - **d.** Automatic private IP address
   - **e.** WINS server address

2. A computer requiring access to file and print services on a network server running a Windows operating system must have a Microsoft file and print client installed. Where can you find this?
   - **a.** It is included with Windows and must be installed after setup.
   - **b.** It is included with Windows and installed during setup.
   - **c.** It is not included with Windows and must be downloaded from the Microsoft web site.
   - **d.** It can be downloaded from the Novell web site.
   - **e.** It must be installed and configured in the Connection properties dialog box.

3. In the chapter, which form of DSL is described as having the same speed upstream as downstream?
   - **a.** ADSL
   - **b.** *x*DSL
   - **c.** VDSL
   - **d.** HDSL
   - **e.** SDSL

4. Your neighbor tells you that he has to initiate a connection to the Internet and complains that the connection is much slower than the connection he enjoys at work—and he is disconnected if there is a period of inactivity. From his description, which type of connection do you believe he has?
   - **a.** ISDN
   - **b.** Dial-up
   - **c.** ADSL
   - **d.** SDSL
   - **e.** Cable

5. What appears in the Connect Using box in the Connection properties dialog box?
   - **a.** A connection device
   - **b.** An ISP name
   - **c.** A user name
   - **d.** A password
   - **e.** A phone number

6. Which of the following is obviously *not* a valid IP address?
   - **a.** 192.168.100.48
   - **b.** 10.0.33.50
   - **c.** 172.300.256.100
   - **d.** 30.88.29.1
   - **e.** 200.100.99.99

7. You have two e-mail clients installed on your computer. Where can you configure Windows to use one of them as your default e-mail client?
   - **a.** Control Panel | Internet Options | Programs
   - **b.** Control Panel | Network Connections
   - **c.** Start | Run | CMD
   - **d.** Control Panel | Internet Options | Advanced
   - **e.** Start | All Programs | Outlook Express

8. What command can you use to view the status of current connections, including the IP address and protocol used for each connection?
   - **a.** IPCONFIG
   - **b.** CMD
   - **c.** PING

d. NETSTAT

e. TRACERT

9. Which of the following is a relatively newer file and print sharing protocol standard, used by more than one vendor?

   a. Server Message Block (SMB)

   b. NetWare Core Protocol (NCP)

   c. Network file system (NFS)

   d. Common Internet File System (CIFS)

   e. File and print sharing

10. Which command would you use as a test to see if a DNS server will respond to a request to resolve a name?

    a. PING

    b. NSLOOKUP

    c. IPCONFIG

    d. NETSTAT

    e. TRACERT

11. What, according to some sources, is the reason for the majority of calls to computer help desks?

    a. Internet connection problems

    b. Forgotten or incorrectly entered passwords

    c. E-mail problems

    d. FTP problems

    e. Installation problems

12. The settings on the Security page of Internet Options are all about how Internet Explorer handles these.

    a. Web pages

    b. FTP sites

    c. E-mail messages

    d. Cookies

    e. Error messages

13. Your neighbor, a retiree on a fixed income, has asked your help in acquiring an Internet connection for his computer, a desktop computer running Windows 2000. His only interest in Internet access is to use e-mail to keep in touch with his children, who live in other states. He has a reliable phone connection. Based on this information, which service will you recommend?

    a. Cable

    b. ISDN

    c. Dial-up

    d. DSL

    e. Satellite

14. Which of the following is the printer that will be used automatically when you print from an application?

    a. HP LaserJet

    b. Network printer

    c. Local printer

    d. Shared network printer

    e. Default printer

15. What is the protocol responsible for the accurate delivery of messages, verifying and resending pieces that fail to make the trip from source to destination?

    a. Internet Protocol (IP)

    b. Transmit Control Protocol (TCP)

    c. Secure Sockets Layer (SSL)

    d. File Transfer Protocol (FTP)

    e. Transmission Control Protocol (TCP)

Essay Quiz

1. Your computer was recently connected via a network adapter to a LAN that includes a router through which traffic passes to the Internet. You know the adapter was configured to use TCP/IP, and you need to test its ability to communicate with computers on the LAN and on the Internet. In your own words, describe the steps you will take.

2. Your school uses an FTP site where each instructor posts documents, such as course assignments, white papers, and schedules for students to download. In addition, for each course, every student has a folder and is expected to upload class assignments to his or her folder. Each student has a user name and password to access the FTP site and must connect to a specific folder for each course. Would you use a web browser, or would you use an FTP client program? In your own words, explain your choice, including why it is the right choice for you.

3. A state agency that dispatches mobile units to disaster areas to monitor the disaster sites for hazardous chemical and biological contamination requires reliable Internet access for these units from any location in the state. They need to keep up-to-date with technical information via postings on federal web sites and to upload their data to state and federal FTP sites. Which Internet connection option is the best fit for their needs? Explain your answer.

4. You are the desktop support person for a law firm that has a Microsoft Active Directory domain in place, but one department requires a single Novell server to run a special application. All the desktops have Windows XP, and you are meeting with the network administrator to determine which Novell client should be used on the desktop computer requiring access to this server. Describe how you and the administrator should determine which client to use, and give your opinion (with the information provided) of which client should be used.

5. In your own words, explain subnet masking in simple terms, including why a subnet mask is required when an adapter is configured with an IP address.

Lab Projects

• Lab Project 10.1

Survey your classmates, coworkers, and other acquaintances to determine the following:

1. What percentage of them have Internet access from home?
2. Of those who have Internet access from home, what percentage have had it for ten years or more?
3. Of those who have Internet access from home, what percentage have had it for five years or more?
4. Of those who have Internet access from home, what percentage have had Internet access for less than one year?
5. Why is home Internet access important to those who have it?

What percentage change (plus or minus) did you discover between adoption of home Internet connections between the ten years and greater group and the five years and greater group? What percentage change (plus or minus) did you discover between each of the earlier groups and the group who have had Internet access from home for less than one year? What was the most common reason home Internet access was important?

Discuss the results with your classmates.

• Lab Project 10.2

This project requires the use of a Windows computer that has Internet access. Using methods you learned in this chapter, find the answers to the following questions:

1. Does the lab computer have its own connection to the Internet, or does it connect to the Internet through a LAN?
2. How is an IP address assigned to the lab computer?
3. Record the IP configuration settings for the lab computer:
   a. IP address
   b. Subnet mask
   c. Default gateway
   d. DNS server

• Lab Project 10.3

Interview the IT staff at your school, place of work, or another organization, and determine what clients are in use on their networks. Create a list of the clients.

Linux on the Desktop

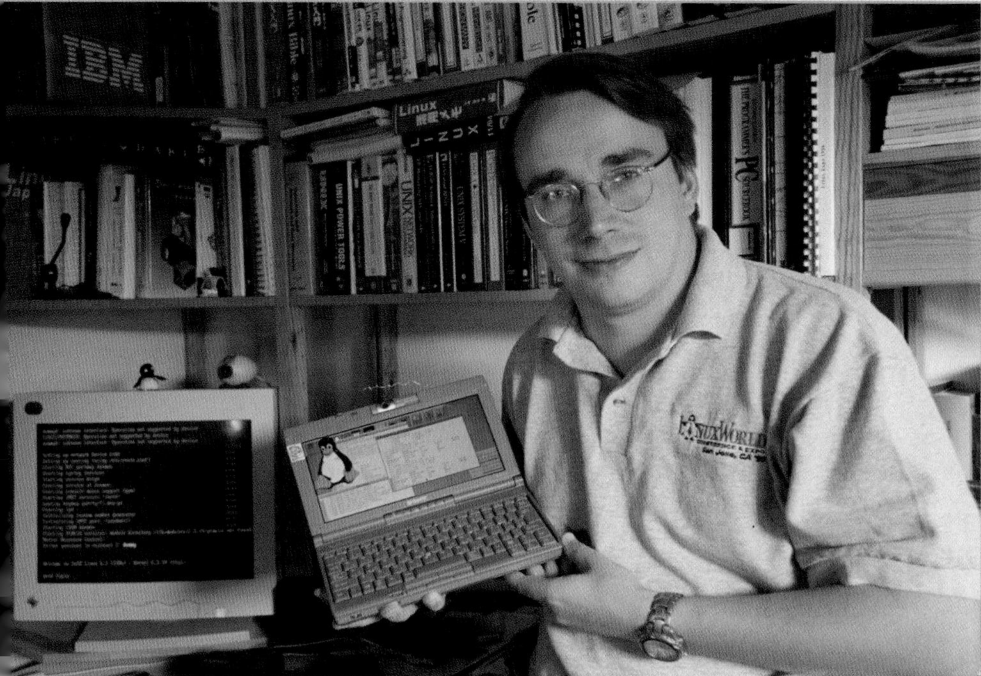

The Linux philosophy is "Laugh in the face of danger." Oops. Wrong one. "Do it yourself." Yes, that's it.

—LINUS TORVALDS

In the early 1970s, Ken Thompson, a developer working at Bell Labs, was criticized for playing a computer game on company equipment. Ken's response to the criticism was to find an unused computer and write an operating system that would run his game. This operating system was the foundation of UNIX, which has gone on to power the computers of most of the universities, corporations, and governments of the world. UNIX is known as a powerful, stable, and fast system.

In 1991, Linus Torvalds developed an open-source operating system based on UNIX called **Linux**. Today, Linux has many flavors and can be found on computers ranging from desktops to corporate servers. Linux is a very powerful and popular alternative to Microsoft operating systems for servers and desktops. In fact, in the server market, Linux has become a strong competitor to all major server OS products.

In this chapter, you will learn how to:

- **Describe Linux features, benefits, and limitations**
- **Install Linux**
- **Log in, log out, and use Linux commands**
- **Manage files and directories**
- **Use a GUI desktop in Linux**
- **Configure Linux for users**
- **Troubleshoot common Linux problems**

There are many distributions of Linux, which range from free barebones distributions to those sold with bundled drivers and utilities. An industry has grown up around products and services relating to Linux. A prime example of a participant in this industry is **Red Hat** (`www.redhat.com`), a company that was founded in 1993, and has grown into a premier distributor of Linux, sold as Red Hat Linux. They offer both products and services built around the open-source model. They also have a global training program and offer a Linux certification called RHCE (Red Hat Certified Engineer). In this chapter, we use examples from Red Hat Linux Desktop. Linux is far too broad a topic to explore in detail here, but you will learn why Linux is so popular and when Linux can be a viable choice for use in an organization. You will learn how to install and customize Linux, and to work in a Linux environment.

Linux Overview

Linux may be new to you, but it has been a hot topic in the computer industry since the mid-1990s. At that time, traditional SCO Group and Berkeley UNIX installations cost thousands of dollars, and services like programming languages or the TCP/IP protocol were an additional charge. Since TCP/IP is the protocol suite of the Internet and most UNIX networks, many people felt that charging more for this crucial service made UNIX too expensive.

Linux, a free operating system with many of the same qualities as UNIX, has the potential to save corporations millions of dollars. But corporate managers and accountants, while liking the premise of a free OS, didn't know anything about the software, so Linux experts were hired or trained to provide the answers that corporations needed.

To grasp how important a free operating system is, compare Linux to the engine in your car. An engine costs thousands of dollars, but if a company started making and distributing free engines, the cost of your new car would drop dramatically.

Why Learn Linux?

Learning Linux can be quite beneficial to your future career, regardless of your field of study, because of its growing importance on all types of computers. You will find Linux, like Windows, on both desktop and server computers. However, it is not as easy to use as Windows. If you implement Linux as your desktop OS, be prepared to spend a lot of time configuring Linux and training other users who might need to use your computer.

Qualifying for a Job

The first reason to learn Linux is to help you get a job. Linux and UNIX have long been regarded as the "difficult" operating systems. If you learn Linux and list this fact on your resume, you are advertising your intelligence, initiative, and computer ability. An organization reviewing your resume would see Linux as a big plus. Their reasoning is simple. If you can learn Linux, then you should learn their internal computer systems very quickly.

For instance, as an undergraduate majoring in mathematics, Cameron landed a job as a debt collector with a small law firm. The firm had problems in the past with employees being unable to work with its debtor system. The system was based on Linux and was not easy to work with. The company rightly figured that Cameron's experience with Linux would allow him to learn their system quickly.

Linux is used in several industries. Major banks, investment houses, retail establishments, and scientific organizations use Linux to run employee computers. If you want to work in these organizations, Linux knowledge is a must.

Freedom to Choose Your Operating System

A second reason to learn Linux is to give you the freedom and knowledge to choose your operating system. To date, you probably have had experience only with Windows and Apple products, and both make excellent operating systems. But if you know only Windows and Mac OSs, you are likely to choose only a Windows or Mac OS. Understanding Linux in addition to other operating systems allows you to choose the operating system that best fits your needs.

Improving Your Skills

A final reason to learn Linux is to improve your computer skills. Linux, unlike Windows and Mac OSs, is very unforgiving. It forces you to be precise when entering commands; acquiring the habit of being precise now will help you succeed in future computer work.

The Evolution of Linux

The **GNU** organization was created in 1984 for the purpose of developing a free version of a UNIX-like operating system. GNU, a recursive acronym for GNU's Not UNIX, has developed thousands of applications that run on UNIX and Linux platforms. Many are distributed with versions of Linux.

Learn more about GNU at `www.gnu.org`.

In 1988 a group of UNIX licensees formed the Open Systems Foundation (OSF) to lobby for an "open" UNIX after AT&T formed a partnership with Sun Microsystems to develop a single UNIX with the best features of many versions.

In response, AT&T and other licensees formed UNIX International in order to oppose the OSF. The trade press called the maneuverings of these two groups the "UNIX wars."

In spite of opposition to the notion of free and open software, with no one entity owning the source code, such software thrives today, and has the support of many organizations that previously opposed it. Linux is the best example of this phenomenon and its popularity is growing. Manufacturers such as IBM and Sun have added Linux to their server lines that previously featured mostly UNIX servers. These vendors offer inexpensive web servers running Apache Web Server on Linux. These products help make high-quality, inexpensive web hosting available to the public. Dell offers its customers the option of having Red Hat Linux installed on new server purchases, which reduces the cost of new server equipment by thousands of dollars. Red Hat offers a series of classes and certification exams, and

The kernel is the core of the operating system. It contains all of the programs needed to allow the user to interact with the computer. The Linux kernel's code is freely available to any who wish to download it. Along with a great deal of other information, you can find the latest version of the Linux kernel at www.kernel.org.

CompTIA offers a Linux+ certification. The independent research group International Data Corporation (IDC) has stated that Linux is the fastest growing operating system in the world.

In 1991, Linus Torvalds started a new hobby. Other people might try inline skating, but Linus wanted to write a better, open-source version of MINIX, a UNIX-like operating system. **Open-source software** is distributed with all of its source code, which allows developers to customize the software as necessary. In turn, the modified code must also be freely distributed.

Since the software was open source, many individuals and several companies modified the kernel. Two of the versions available in 1994 were the Slackware and Red Hat kernels. Both included the C++ language, TCP/IP functionality, and primitive web servers. Of course, the code for the kernels was available as well. To obtain a copy, you simply went to an Internet site and selected the products to download.

Today open source is a movement that has gained credibility since such vendors as Novell and IBM have integrated open-source software into their product mix. At this writing, the open-source debate continues between proponents and vendors such as Microsoft who, while trying to satisfy customer demand for open-source software, want to retain control of their products. For instance, Microsoft has proposed a system of "shared code" in which they make the source code of some of their products available to customers and partners, but still maintain intellectual property rights.

Try This!

Research the Open-Source Debate

View the current arguments in the open-source debate. Try this:

1. Use your favorite Internet search engine to find recent articles on "source debate."
2. Look at the arguments on the pro-open-source side and the anti-open-source side.
3. Who appear to be the major players on each side?

Benefits of Linux

Initially, Linux was popular with the "geek" crowd simply because it was new. It was a badge of honor to be able to run Linux on your home computer *and* be productive. But then the users soon found out that Linux was capable of being cool on its own. They demonstrated that there are several benefits to having Linux on your computer.

Linux Is Inexpensive

The first benefit of Linux is cost. Numerous versions of Linux may be freely downloaded from the Web. Many sites, such as www.linuxlookup.com, offer the Linux distributions in convenient ISO images. An **ISO image** is a copy of the entire contents of a CD that can be easily transferred to a writeable CD with ISO image copy software. If you don't want to download these distributions, prepackaged versions of Linux may be purchased online or in computer stores for modest cost. In addition, the software may be legally shared with your friends.

The savings for a company can be incredible. Imagine an IT manager who needs to roll out 1,000 desktop computers. Rolling out 1,000 Linux computers could cost the company nothing for the operating system software, but rolling out 1,000 Windows XP workstations, at $71 per station, could cost the company over $71,000. In addition, when the time comes to upgrade the operating system, the Linux upgrade would still be free, whereas there would be a significant upgrade cost for the Windows solution. All together, in upfront costs, the Windows solution would be more expensive than the Linux solution. Of course, upfront costs are only a small part of the picture. The long-term cost of using and supporting Linux on the desktop versus Windows is a hotly debated topic, with convincing arguments on both sides.

Linux Can Run on Old Equipment

In addition to being free or inexpensive (when bundled), Linux can run on old equipment. Slackware states that its products can run on i386-class machines, which were popular in the late 1980s. A nonprofit organization could provide computers for its employees with donated or very inexpensive equipment. And consider this: in countless situations, computers too underpowered to run even an outdated version of Windows continue to run reliably for years—as web servers!

Linux Is Fast

Linux runs respectably well on old computers, and it is even faster on newer, faster computers. This is because Linux programs are very efficient and lean. They use as few resources as possible, and unlike Windows, the use of graphics in Linux is optional, and many Linux applications use few, if any, graphics. Graphics can slow a system's response time, making it seem slower than it truly is. Linux may not be pretty, but it sure is fast.

Linux Is Stable

Linux code is well written. This both increases the speed at which Linux runs and improves the stability of the operating system. Linux is next to impossible to crash. If an application crashes, you can simply remove the program from memory and restart your computer. In older versions of Windows, a crashing program had the potential to take down the entire computer. This is one of the reasons why Linux is used on many web servers where stability is crucial. With Linux, web hosting providers can guarantee 99.9 percent (or better) uptime.

Linux Is Open Source

Finally, Linux is open-source software. This means that users can read the source code and modify it as needed. This probably means little to the average user of the final version of a Linux kernel. However, during development, "beta" releases of the kernel are available to developers who will download the code and test it thoroughly. When possible, they will find any problems and correct the code. This process helps to ensure that the final release of the kernel is as well written as possible.

Once the final version is released, developers can adjust the kernel as needed. We know a developer who modified his kernel to be more usable for vision-impaired users. He added better support for large print output and a command-line narrator that reads the information on the command line. Open source allowed the developer to modify his code to suit his needs.

Drawbacks of Linux

Even though Linux is widely used on corporate servers, web sites, and large-scale networking environments, you still won't find many people using it on their desktop computers or workstations at home. There are several reasons for this.

Lack of Centralized Support

No system is 100 percent secure; however, Microsoft products do have extensive documentation and support. Microsoft releases service packs and updates frequently to fix discovered vulnerabilities. Linux does not have this centralized support. Although Linux purchased from vendors is often supported by vendor-provided documentation and user groups, support and documentation for free Linux can be spotty. A user who downloads Linux from a server may receive only an electronic manual and access to online help pages. It is true that the Linux community is growing and there are many active user groups, but you must search them out and expend considerable effort and time to get answers to questions.

Limited Software Selection

Several browsers for Linux are available; however, if you want to see animation, find out if a browser supports JavaScript (which powers much of the animation on the Web) before installing it into Linux. Use your favorite search utility to find web sites that have more information on Linux browsers and other available software for Linux.

People purchase computers to run software. Users of Windows computers have many software titles to choose from, and some of these titles have become the "gold standard" to employers when describing skills they desire in new hire employees. For example, experience with the Microsoft Office Suite, especially Microsoft Word and Excel, is often listed in employment advertisements. Application software in every category is available for Linux, but you will not, as yet, find the Microsoft Office Suite running on Linux. As alternatives, StarOffice and OpenOffice have been bundled with different versions of Linux. Although both are very nice products, a proficient Microsoft Word user must learn some new skills to use either of them.

In other categories, old standbys are available for Linux. For example, consider Internet browsers. The two most popular browsers, Netscape Navigator and Microsoft Internet Explorer, are available for Linux. In addition, other browsers such as Opera and Mozilla can easily be found in versions for Linux.

Limited Hardware Support

If you cannot find a printer driver for a new printer, look for an older driver for another, similar printer by the same manufacturer. New printer features will not be available, but you will be able to print most documents successfully.

Just as not all popular software runs on Linux, not all hardware products work with Linux, but we see this improving. Red Hat and the other Linux vendors work hard to support the more common devices. They provide drivers for hardware devices. A driver is a small program that allows the operating system to communicate with the device. Having the correct driver is crucial. If you have a new or unusual device, you may need to search the Internet. Maybe the vendor has not created a Linux driver for your new device, but there is great support among Linux users who create drivers and make them available on the Internet.

Complexity

The last block in the wall between Linux and greater success is Linux's difficulty of use, meaning that only a limited subset of users cares to invest the time and effort to learn its intricacies. Linux, like UNIX, assumes that you know what you are doing, and it assumes that you know the consequences of every command you type. In contrast, Windows XP asks you to verify everything and then shows you a pretty animation to confirm the action.

For a beginning user, Linux can be intimidating to use; entering the wrong command can have serious consequences. It doesn't help that Linux is also case sensitive, so you must enter the commands in lowercase, and be careful to use the correct case for each subcommand you use with a command. Upper- and lowercase versions of the same word often denote different actions. Don't let this frighten you, however. By now, you have spent sufficient time working with operating systems so that you know the basic theory. You'll do fine in Linux.

Case sensitivity in a password is a security benefit. Case sensitivity in command syntax is an inconvenience that adds complexity and increases the level of difficulty in learning Linux.

When to Use Linux

While Linux does have drawbacks, it is useful in several situations. Cost, stability, and security are major factors when deciding to go with Linux. Here are a few examples of situations in which a Linux solution was a viable option.

Education: Small Budget Combined with Skilled Staff

Pittsburgh Computer School needed to teach its students UNIX. As a private school with limited funds, the administration opted to install Slackware Linux. Slackware does an excellent job of emulating UNIX at a fraction of the cost. The savings allowed the school to purchase other necessary equipment without increasing student tuition.

Inexpensive Web Servers

Martinez Lawn Service needed a web presence but did not want to pay a lot of money. The company found a hosting solution that uses Linux. The hosting company is able to charge a low fee in part because the OS fee was zero.

Web Development

Amanda is a freelance web developer. For testing purposes, she needs an environment that supports PHP, Perl, and XML, all programming languages for the Web. Amanda installed Red Hat Linux Server along with the Apache Web Server. Apache and other web servers deliver web pages to a person's computer. A web server powers every page you visit on the Web. Apache is one of the most popular servers due to its stability, security, and cost. By having Apache installed at home, Amanda can test her web pages in a realistic setting. If the page works on her computer, it will likely work on the Web. She writes the web pages on her Windows computer and uploads them to her Linux installation for testing.

Preparing for Your Future

John is applying to a bank for a position in the trust department. The software that controls the trust accounts is based on a UNIX database, and the employees are expected to know UNIX. John installed Linux on his computer to gain familiarity with UNIX commands.

Inside Information

What about FreeBSD?

In discussions of Linux distributions, people often mention FreeBSD, but we don't consider this a version of Linux. FreeBSD is an operating system based on the Berkeley UNIX distribution. As far as we can tell, FreeBSD is not derived from the code created by Linus Torvalds and the many contributors to Linux.

Installing Linux

When you encounter a new operating system, nothing makes you feel more in control than completing a successful installation. However, it is important to make certain decisions and preparations before beginning an installation. The most important decision (after the decision to go with Linux!) is which distribution to acquire. Once that decision is made, you need to prepare for the Linux installation.

Acquiring Linux

There are many sources of the Linux OS. Using an Internet search engine to search on "Linux download" (without the quotes) produced over 9 million results! Why are so many people offering free Linux software? You might need to know about old-fashioned razors and razor blades to truly understand that. King Gillette, the founder of Gillette Corporation, actually gave away the razor handles, and the company made their money selling the blades. Along those lines, many organizations that distribute Linux offer the OS code for free (like the old razors that were free or sold cheap) and then make their money on the many add-ons they offer. These add-ons include drivers, GUI interfaces, utilities, installation programs, and applications they bundle with the OS. All use the most recent Linux kernel in their products. Here are just a few of these vendors:

- Mandrake (`www.mandrake.com`)
- Red Hat (`www.RedHat.com`)
- Slackware (`www.slackware.com`)
- SuSE (`http://www.novell.com/linux/suse/`)

If you browse to any of these web sites, you will find that these vendors sell many products and services related to Linux. For instance, the Red Hat site shows a long list of products, but unfortunately Red Hat has discontinued the practice of providing free downloads and no longer sells individual licenses for Red Hat Linux Desktop. At this writing, the only free download of Linux Desktop available at the Red Hat site is a demo copy that expires in 30 days, and which is intended only for people evaluating the product to make a purchase of multiple licenses. The minimum sale point today is ten licenses for $2,500! However, we have chosen to use Red Hat in our examples for two reasons:

- If you encounter Linux in the workplace, the odds are pretty good that it will be Red Hat Linux rather than another version, due to their marketing efforts and the fact that they sell software bundles that appeal to businesses.
- The various versions of Linux have many things in common, so what you learn about one version will carry over to another version.

The Fedora Project

Separate from any of their commercial projects, Red Hat sponsors the Fedora Project, a merger of two separate Linux projects—the Red Hat Linux Project and the Fedora Linux Project, which is a separate entity from Red Hat. The new project organization involves members of the Linux community in developing and maintaining a separate distribution of Linux known as Fedora. At this writing, the merger is not quite complete; check out the status of this project at `fedora.redhat.com`.

Preparing for Linux Installation

Before installing Linux, review the installation documentation and decide how you wish to install. Do you plan to dedicate a computer to Linux?

Do you have a single Windows computer and wish to be able to boot between the two operating systems? In either case, you must ensure that you have enough free space to install Linux and any other applications you desire. In addition, you should plan to have extra free space for your data. Remember, you cannot have too much hard disk space!

Keep Your Linux Installation Simple

As is true when installing any operating system, keep it simple by accepting the detected devices to allow a basic installation, and wait to fine-tune the operating system to work with specific devices until after the installation.

Hardware Requirements, Compatibility, and Minimums

There are versions of Linux for several computer platforms, including those based on Intel, AMD, and Cyrix processors. In addition, there are distributions for Alpha, MIPs, PowerPC, SPARC, and Motorola processors.

Linux memory requirements are small compared to Windows operating systems. You can install most versions of Linux on a system with as little as 8MB of RAM, but a minimum of 16MB is recommended. You can never have too much memory.

If you wish to have a minimal installation, you can boot Linux from a floppy disk, but this is not practical for a working system. Distributions, such as Red Hat Linux, come with a large number of packages (programs), and selecting some of these packages will greatly increase your disk space needs, so you will want to install it on a hard disk. Check the documentation of the version of Linux you plan to install. Linux supports a number of hard disk controllers, but plan to read the documentation to verify that Linux will install on your computer before beginning an installation. Linux also supports CD and DVD drives.

Linux supports all the standard video graphics adapters and monitors, but generally supports the use of a mouse only in graphic interfaces. In addition, Linux supports many printers, modems, and network adapters.

Be Prepared to Work with the Root Account

Before you install Linux, you need to understand the root account, often simply called "**root**." It is the most powerful account on a Linux (or UNIX) computer, and, like the Administrator account on a Windows computer, it is capable of doing anything. It can access any file or program on a computer. It is also required to shut down Linux from the command prompt. Be very careful with your use of root. Log in as root only when you need to perform system maintenance tasks. Create a strong password for root, and take steps to remember and protect this password. If you forget this password, you will not be able to access administrative functions on your system, which will ultimately require entering the root password recovery process—something you will not enjoy!

In your encounters with Linux, you may see the term *superuser*. The superuser is not a comic book hero; **superuser** is simply another name for root. This name still appears in Linux or UNIX help pages and chat rooms, and if you're going to be surfing these Internet spots, you need to be savvy about the vocabulary. While you may refer to this account as superuser, remember that the login name is "root."

Inside Information

Munich, Germany

In addition to its ever-increasing presence on network and Internet servers, Linux is gaining popularity as a desktop operating system. In July of 2004, the city of Munich, Germany, began installing Linux and open-source word processing, spreadsheet, and web-browsing programs—in place of Microsoft Windows and Microsoft Office—on desktop PCs and laptops for 14,000 city workers. The software is to be provided by SuSE (Novell) and IBM, but at this writing, the project is being delayed by concern over patent issues.

Recall what you learned in Chapter 7 about creating and protecting strong passwords. Look for more helpful hints by using a search engine to find topics containing "creating passwords."

Standard Installation vs. Dual Booting

When you are installing Linux on a computer that already has another operating system, you have the option to create a dual-boot installation. When planning for a dual-boot configuration, plan for each operating system having its own hard disk partition. This is a very common installation for someone who is currently running Windows and wants to learn about Linux, but does not have a spare computer to devote to Linux. However, you will need unpartitioned disk space before you begin. The result will be a dual-boot installation that will allow you to select which operating system you boot into when you restart your computer.

The following lab is written for a clean installation, but if you wish to create a dual-boot configuration, depart from the instructions on the Installation Type page, and follow the instructions on the screen.

> **Inside Information**
>
> **Install Linux into a Virtual Machine!**
>
> *Another option for installing and testing Linux is to install it into a virtual machine on a Windows computer. This requires investment in one of the virtual machine products, such as VMWare Workstation (`www.vmware.com`) or Microsoft Virtual PC (`www.microsoft.com/windows/virtualpc/`). With this software, you can create separate virtual environments—each emulating an entire PC system (processor, memory, network adapter, harddrive, floppy drive, etc.), and install a different operating system into each. We have used VMWare Workstation during the writing of this and several earlier books. We also find it handy to test software updates in Windows installed in a virtual PC before installing them on our production PCs.*

Booting into the Linux Installation Program

If you have a Linux distribution on a bootable CD, you can boot into the Linux installation program. If you do not have a bootable CD, or if your computer will not boot from CD, you will need a bootable floppy disk that you can create with a utility, sometimes called **raw write**, that comes with most distributions of Linux. Using the version of this utility for Windows (RAWRITEWIN) requires a Windows computer from which you will run the program and create the raw write floppy disk. Using this utility, you place a boot image onto the floppy disk. A **boot image** is a special file that contains a boot sector and all the files required to boot up Linux. The image is in a format that can be placed on the floppy disk sector-by-sector. This boot image file (boot.img) is found in the images directory of the first CD. Then you take the floppy disk and the CDs, insert the floppy disk and CD #1 into the computer on which you wish to install Linux, and restart the computer to begin the installation.

The step-by-step that follows assumes that you have a computer that will boot from the Linux distribution CD.

Performing the Installation

Once the Linux installation program begins, you are guided through the process by successive pages providing choices. If you use Red Hat Linux, the installation program provides a great GUI with online help in a pane on the left side of the screen. The right side of the screen contains a larger pane containing the current page of the installation program.

A page you will see early in the installation process is the Installation Type page shown in Figure 11-1. You have two big choices here: Install On System versus Upgrade Existing System. Install On System is a full installation that is equivalent to a clean installation onto the targeted partition, which wipes out any previous OS or data on

> **Cross Check**
>
> **Compare Linux with Windows XP**
>
> After installing Linux in Step-by-Step 11.01, compare Windows XP to Linux.
>
> 1. During installation, both Windows XP and Linux discover hardware. What differences did you observe between the two installations in how this was accomplished in each?
>
> ______________________________
>
> 2. Which installation comes with more applications to install: Windows XP or Linux?
>
> ______________________________

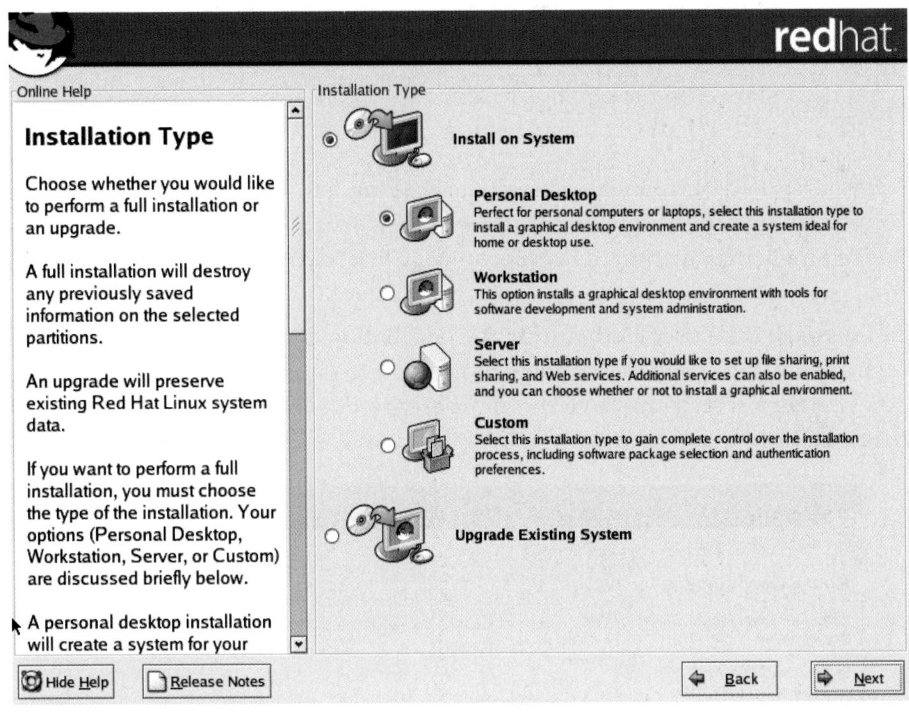
redhat
Online Help
Installation Type
Choose whether you would like to perform a full installation or an upgrade.
A full installation will destroy any previously saved information on the selected partitions.
An upgrade will preserve existing Red Hat Linux system data.
If you want to perform a full installation, you must choose the type of the installation. Your options (Personal Desktop, Workstation, Server, or Custom) are discussed briefly below.
A personal desktop installation will create a system for your
Installation Type
Install on System
Personal Desktop
Perfect for personal computers or laptops, select this installation type to install a graphical desktop environment and create a system ideal for home or desktop use.
Workstation
This option installs a graphical desktop environment with tools for software development and system administration.
Server
Select this installation type if you would like to set up file sharing, print sharing, and Web services. Additional services can also be enabled, and you can choose whether or not to install a graphical environment.
Custom
Select this installation type to gain complete control over the installation process, including software package selection and authentication preferences.
Upgrade Existing System
Hide Help
Release Notes
Back
Next

• **Figure 11-1.** The Installation Type page

that partition. The Upgrade Existing System choice will install into a previous Linux installation.

For any new installation, select Install On System, and then choose the type of new installation: Personal Desktop, Workstation, Server, or Custom. The step-by-step has you select Custom, but if you are new to Linux and wish to get up and running on a spare computer at once, consider the Personal Desktop option.

Step-by-Step 11.01

Installing Linux

This lab includes the steps for installing Linux as the only OS on a computer. We use Red Hat Linux as an example, but if you install any version of Linux with an automated installation, the steps will be similar. The steps describe many but not all pages that are displayed. We strongly suggest that you accept the defaults, and be sure that the GNOME desktop is selected when that page appears. To complete this step-by-step, you will need:

- A computer that meets or exceeds the minimum hardware requirements for the version of Linux you are using and that will boot up from the CD-ROM drive
- A bootable CD distribution of Linux with an installation program that guides you through the steps
- The TCP/IP configuration required for your lab computer (automatic addressing or IP address, mask, and so on)
- A hostname that you will enter in Step 7
- Account Configuration information to be entered in Step 10, including a password for the root account and a user name and password for your personal account.

Step 1

Insert the Red Hat CD # 1 into the CD-ROM drive, and start or restart your computer. When the first screen of the installation program appears, press ENTER to start the graphical mode installation.

Step 2

At the Welcome To Red Hat Linux screen, note that the left side of the screen can be scrolled to provide you with explanations of the steps that each screen provides. Remember to read these explanations as you proceed. Click Next to proceed.

Step 3

Choose the language to be used both during the installation and as the default language of the system. Click Next. The next screen allows you to choose the keyboard layout. Click Next. The next screen displays the mouse type detected. Accept the detected mouse and click Next.

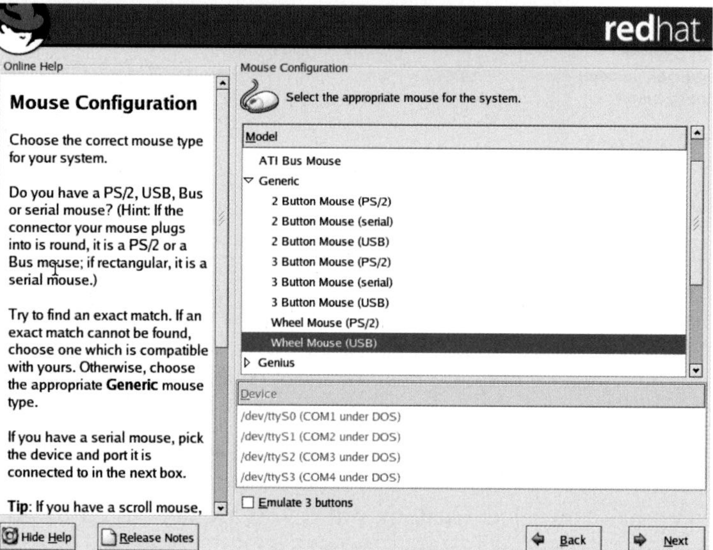

Step 4

On the Installation Type screen, select Custom and click Next. The following screen allows you to choose the disk partitioning method. Select Automatically Partition and then click Next.

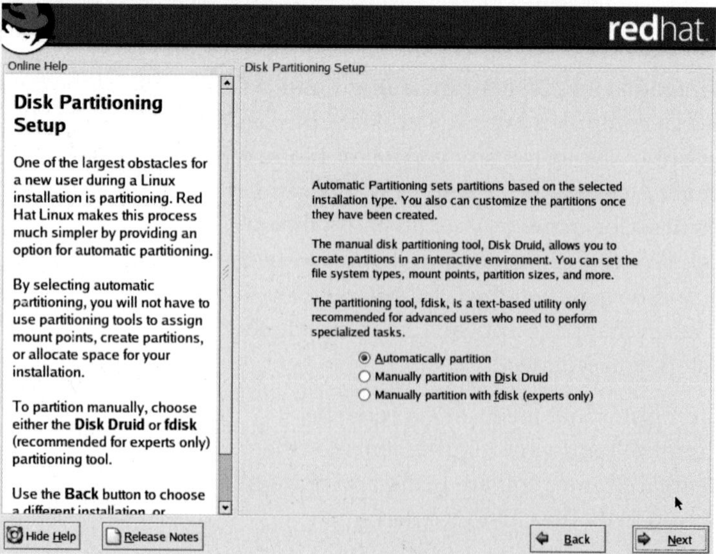

Step 5

On the following screen, you can define how automatic partitioning treats existing partitions. As this is to be a clean installation, choose the option to remove all Linux partitions. This will only remove previous Linux partitions, but should leave intact partitions devoted to other operating systems. Note that the Review And Modify If Needed option is set by default. Uncheck this option and then click Next.

Step 6

If a Warning dialog box displays at this point, click Yes. In the Boot Loader Configuration screen, use the default boot loader (GRUB, in the example shown). As this is not a dual installation, you will only see one OS listed. Clear the check box for Use A Boot Loader Password and then click Next.

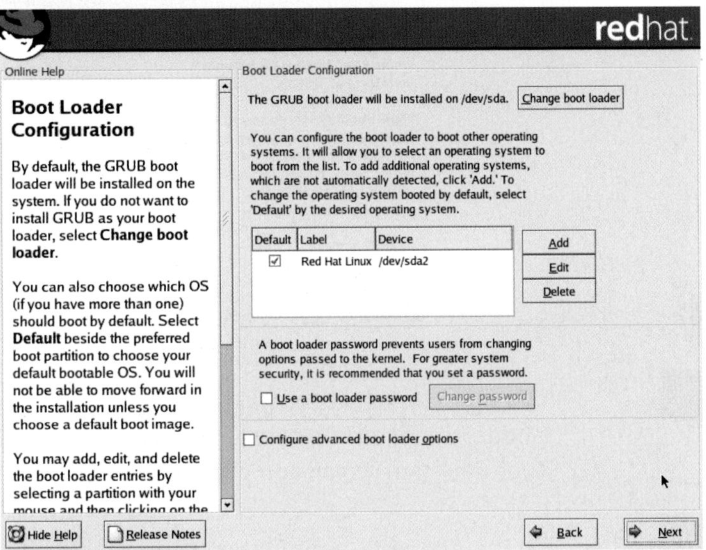

Step 7

If you are on a network, the Network Configuration screen will display. Your NIC should be listed under Device as eth0. Confirm that it is marked as Active On Boot. Modify the settings per the TCP/IP configuration requirements for your lab computer. In the Hostname area of the dialog box, click the button labeled "manually" and enter a name. If you do not provide a hostname, it will be given the default hostname of localhost. When you have completed this page, click Next.

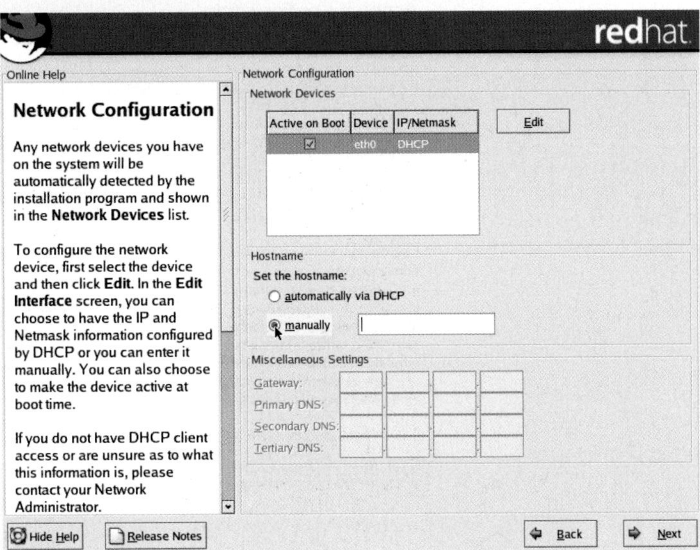

Step 8

In the Firewall Configuration screen, confirm that Medium security level is selected. If your computer is configured as a DHCP client, the installation program will configure the firewall to allow incoming DHCP traffic. Click Next.

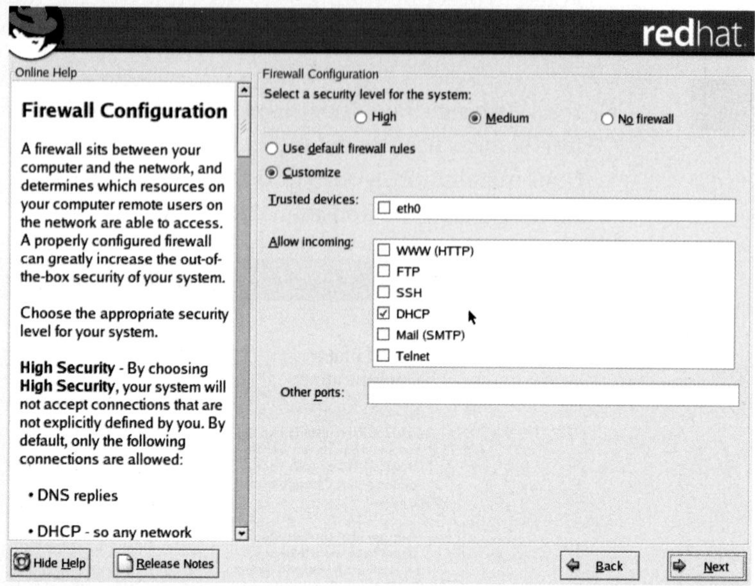

Step 9

You may choose additional language support, which allows you to change the default language after installation. Click Next. Select your time zone in the scroll box of the Time Zone Selection screen and click Next.

Step 10

On the Account Configuration page, assign a password for the root account. You must type this password twice in order to confirm your selection. Do *not* proceed until you also create a personal account that you will use as an ordinary user of the system. Click on the Add button and enter a user name, a password (twice), and a full name, and then click OK. Then click Next.

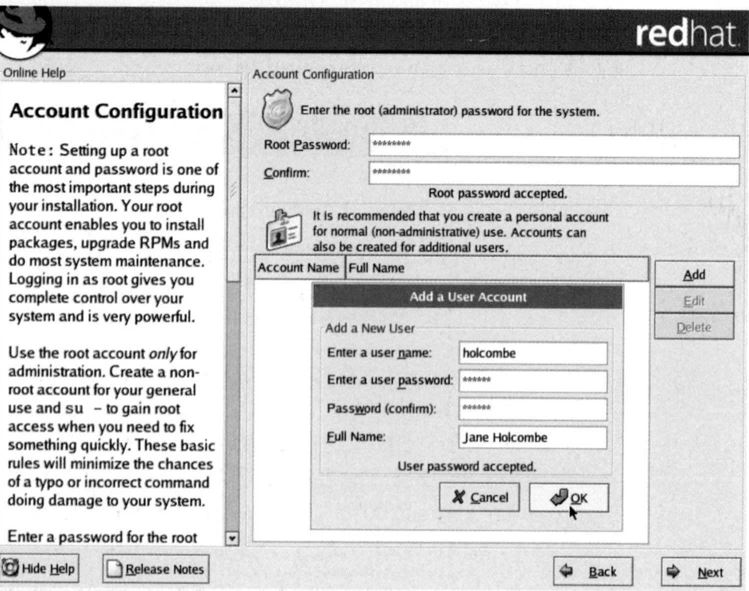

Step 11

On the Personal Desktop Defaults screen, select Customize The Packages To Be Installed and click Next. On the Package Group Selection screen, view the selection, and accept the default selections, unless told otherwise by your instructor. Ensure that GNOME is selected, because later exercises depend on it, and then click Next.

Step 12

The About To Install screen is next. It tells you how to confirm the installation options selected by reviewing log files after the install is completed. Click Next.

Step 13

The installation proceeds, copying files to the hard drive and prompting you to insert the CDs needed for the installation. This will take about an hour. If the screen goes blank, press the space bar to reactivate it. The next step is to create a boot disk. Place a blank floppy disk in the drive and click Next. Remove the floppy disk when prompted and click Next.

Step 14

The system may now ask you to confirm your video adapter for the X Window interface. The adapter for your system should have been detected properly. Click Next to proceed. On the Monitor Configuration screen, choose Unprobed Monitor, and do not enter horizontal and vertical sync ranges, to avoid damaging your monitor. Click Next.

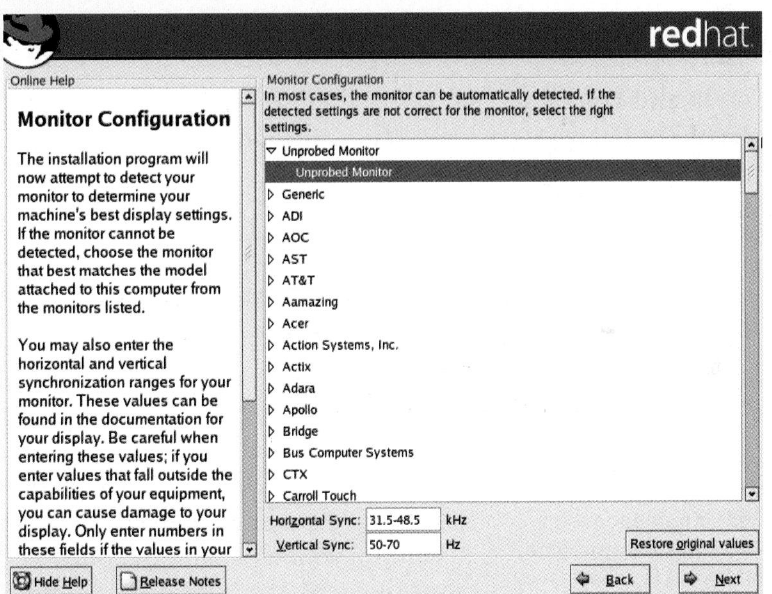

Step 15

On the Customize Graphics Configuration screen, change the login type from graphical to text. Select the desired color depth and screen resolution settings, and then click the Test Setting button. After a successful test of the configuration, click Next.

Step 16

The Congratulations screen should appear. Click Exit to reboot. If your installation is dual-boot, select Linux from the choice menu and boot into Linux. The Red Hat Setup Agent will display a Welcome screen. Follow the instructions to complete the basic configuration tasks, including testing a sound card (if detected), registering with Red Hat (if desired), and installing any additional Red Hat or other software. When finished, the computer will reboot. Wait to log back on until the following Try This.

Basic Linux Skills and Concepts

There are some basic Linux skills and concepts that everyone working with Linux should know. In this section, you will practice these skills, including logging in and out, working with Linux commands at the Linux prompt, and shutting down the computer.

Logging into Linux

Whether you are logging in from the command shell or a GUI, a Linux password never shows on the screen, and the cursor does not move while you type in the password.

Just as in other OSs, Linux requires authentication of each user with a valid user name and password from a user account. If your Linux computer is configured for a command-line login (per the instructions in the installation step-by-step), when you start a Linux computer, it will display the login prompt, which consists of the name of the computer, followed by a space and the word *login,* followed by a colon and a blinking cursor, as shown in Figure 11-2. Once you type in your user name at this prompt and press ENTER, it will prompt you for the password. Type your password (it will not be displayed, and the cursor will not move to indicate that you entered anything) and press ENTER.

Try This!

Log In and Log Out

Log in using the ordinary user account you created during the Linux installation. Try this:

1. Start Linux (if necessary). At the login prompt, type your user name and then press ENTER. You will be prompted for a password. Type your password and press ENTER. If all is correct, you will see the Linux prompt.
2. To log out, type **exit** at the $ prompt.

If the user name and password are correct, you will see information about the last time you logged in, followed by the standard command-line prompt. This prompt, shown in Figure 11-3, consists of your user name and the computer name (hostname) separated by an @ sign that is followed by your user name again. All this is contained within square brackets and followed by a $ sign, which is the traditional end of a Linux prompt for an ordinary user. This entire assemblage is often called the **$ prompt**. (When the root account logs in at the command shell, the prompt ends with a # sign.) The second instance of your user name indicates the current directory. When you create a user account, Linux creates a directory for that user and names it with the user name; that directory is made current every time that user logs in. Other users cannot easily access a user's directory.

The act of authentication in Windows is called logging on, while in Linux it is called logging in.

When you are through working in Linux, you will normally log out so that someone else can use the computer. Logging out allows you to leave Linux without shutting it down. Typing **exit** at the $ prompt, or pressing CTRL-D, logs you out of Linux, which is similar to the Log Off option in Windows.

```
classlab01 login: _
```

• **Figure 11-2.** The Login prompt

```
classlab01 login: jh
Password:
Last login: Mon Nov 29 22:37:46 on :0
[jh@classlab01 jh]$ _
```

• **Figure 11-3.** The $ prompt shows user name, computer name, and current directory.

Shutting Down Linux

Only root can shut down Linux from the command line. This is accomplished with the shutdown command, which has many switches. A switch is a subcommand that changes the outcome of a command. Entering **shutdown -h now** tells Linux to shut down immediately and then to halt (turn off the computer) after shutting down. The process will take a few minutes. The shutdown command has several other switches that can be used in place of the `-h` and `now` options. One option is the `-r` switch. This will reboot the system after the shutdown. For a complete list of switches, type **man shutdown** at a Linux prompt.

Try This!

Shutting Down a Linux Computer

If you want to turn off your computer, you should shut down Linux correctly. Try this:

1. To shut down a Linux computer when working at the command line when you are logged in as an ordinary user, log out, and then log in as root.
2. After logging in as root, issue the command **shutdown -h now**.

When working in a GUI in Linux, an ordinary user can shut down Linux from the main menu (for instance, the GNOME menu) by selecting the Log Out option and then selecting Shutdown. This option is often turned on by default in a GUI, but can be disabled by an administrator using the root account. However, if someone is using a GUI on his or her desktop computer, he or she should be able to shut down the system without logging in as root.

When working in Linux within a GUI such as GNOME, you can select a command to shut down Linux without logging in as root.

Working with Linux Commands

If you went through both the "Log In and Log Out" and "Shutting Down a Linux Computer" Try This! exercises, you can now log in, log out, and shut down Linux. You should feel pretty pleased, but you probably realize that you still have a lot to learn before you can be productive. Your experience with DOS, or the Windows command prompt, will be very helpful in your initial explorations of Linux because of the many similarities between them. So we will start with a comparison between the DOS or Windows command line and that of Linux.

Comparing DOS and Linux

There is a world of difference between DOS and Linux, not the least of which is that DOS is single user, single tasking, and Linux is multi-user, multitasking. However, a comparison of the command-line interfaces of these two OSs may help the new Linux user who has some command-line experience—either in DOS or in using the command-line in Windows. We will make comparisons of shells, case sensitivity, use of switches, use of spaces, paths, and command feedback.

The more generic term to use for the prompt in the BASH shell is shell prompt, which applies whether you are logged on as root or as an ordinary user.

The Shell The operating system component that provides the character-mode user interface is called a **shell**. This shell processes commands and issues error messages and other limited feedback, when appropriate. Commands used in the shell are referred to as **shell commands**. In DOS this shell is the

The developers of Linux were also users of DOS, and they included several DOS commands in Linux. In particular, the `dir` command works in Linux—that is, you can use `dir` instead of `ls`. However, `dir` in Linux supports the same switches as `ls` does, which has its roots in UNIX, rather than in the DOS switches you may be more familiar with.

COMMAND.COM program, while in Linux it is called **BASH**, an acronym for Bourne Again Shell. This is another example of Linux humor. The original Linux shell was the Bourne shell. The Bourne developers added several features to improve the shell. Thus, the Bourne shell was "born again." Don't worry if you're not laughing—it takes a true Linux aficionado to appreciate much of Linux humor.

Case Sensitivity An important difference for those of us transitioning from DOS or the Windows command line is case sensitivity. An operating system that is case sensitive treats *A* differently then *a*. DOS is case *in*sensitive. Thus, *DIR* is the same command as *dir*. Linux is case sensitive. The command *exit* is much different than *EXIT* (which is not a command).

Try This!

Test Case Sensitivity in Linux

If you have access to a computer with Linux, test its case sensitivity. Try this:

1. Log into Linux and enter **man ls**
2. Notice that you get an error message.
3. Now reenter the command in all lowercase.

Inside Information

***Flag* Those *switches* and *options* Just for the Sake of *argument*!**

Everything that you enter on a command line has a purpose. Each string of characters must be separated by a space. The first string of characters on a command line is the command itself. All that follows will either modify the behavior of the command and/or provide it with the name of a file or other object on which to perform its function. There are several commonly used terms for the string or strings that modify the behavior of a command. They include argument, switch, option, *and* flag *(just to name the most common). In addition, the string that provides the name of a file or other object (sometimes referred to as the data) that a command works on is sometimes called a* parameter. *When you view the documentation for a Linux command, be prepared to see any or all of these terms used. P.S. Did you notice the humor in the title?*

Designation of Switches Compare the use of switches in DOS and Linux. A switch changes the way that a command runs. For example, in DOS, `dir /w` displays the files in a directory in a column layout. The forward slash (/) indicates that the following character or characters are to be interpreted as a switch. Linux switches start with a hyphen (-) character. For example, the `shutdown -h now` command uses the `-h` switch. Some Windows shell commands also use hyphens; these are usually commands that originated on UNIX systems.

Use of Spaces Compare the use of spaces in shell commands. DOS allows you to forget a space before a switch. For example, `dir /ad` works with or without a space before the `/`. In Linux, each part of a command-line entry must be separated by a space. For example, neither of these commands will work in Linux:

shutdown-h now
shutdown -hnow

Figure 11-4 shows the error message the first example will generate.

```
[root@classlab01 root]# shutdown-h now
-bash: shutdown-h: command not found
[root@classlab01 root]# _
```

• **Figure 11-4.** Example of a BASH error

Paths There are differences in how paths are built. In DOS and Windows, a full path to a file or directory begins with the drive designator (letter plus colon) and is built using the backslash (\) character as separators between the drive and root directory (first backslash) and each of the subsequent directories in the path. Thus, a valid DOS or Windows path is C:\Winnt\System32. In Linux, you do not use a drive letter, and you use the forward slash (/) character to separate directories. A valid path is `/etc/gtk`. Also, each drive and other device is simply shown as a part of the file system and given a path that begins at the root of the file system (/). Drives and other devices are given names, such as `/dev/sda0` (the first hard drive on a SCSI interface) or `/dev/hda1` (the first hard drive on an IDE interface).

Linux Feedback DOS and Linux commands are actually similar in the area of feedback—they both provide cryptic feedback, communicating with you only if there is a problem. They will not report that they are successful, though you're warned if the command is incorrect. Figure 11-5 illustrates this trait of Linux. The first command successfully renames a file. Notice that no message is returned to the user. The second command returns an error message. This is helpful, although cryptic, information.

In addition to providing little feedback, Linux provides only the bare minimum output. For example, `ls` is the Linux equivalent of the DOS DIR command. Whereas `dir` returns considerable information about the files it finds, `ls` returns only the file names. If you want more information, you need to enter a switch. Figure 11-6 shows the results of two different `ls` options. The first command, `ls`, simply lists the files. The second command returns a long listing that includes the file attributes. You'll learn more about the `ls` command later.

The Command Syntax

When you're working at the command line, or shell, the Linux command syntax is pretty basic. All lines start with a Linux command (the first string of characters). Then, separated by spaces, come options specific to that command. Order is usually of little importance, but the space between the command and each option is crucial. Certain (but not all) options are referred to as switches. These are the options that are preceded by a hyphen (-). However, if you want to use multiple switches for a command, you can combine them into one long switch with a single hyphen at the beginning. Then there is the parameter, which is often a file name, directory, or device name. The parameter is usually placed at the end of the command line. In general, the command syntax in Linux follows this format:

command -switch parameter

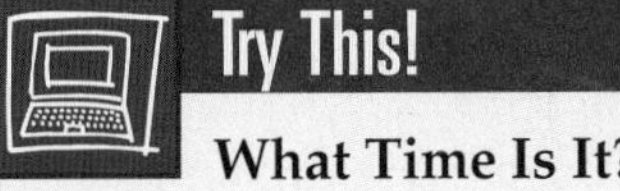

What Time Is It?

Practice entering the date and calendar commands. Try this:

1. Type the command **date** and press ENTER. This will display the date.
2. Now type the command **cal** and press ENTER. This will display the current month's calendar.

```
classlab01 login: jh
Password:
Last login: Tue Nov 30 09:53:52 on tty1
[jh@classlab01 jh]$ ls
EngLitJH01   TODO-List
[jh@classlab01 jh]$ mv TODO-List old-list
[jh@classlab01 jh]$ mv TODO-List new-list
mv: cannot stat `TODO-List': No such file or directory
[jh@classlab01 jh]$ _
```

• **Figure 11-5.** Linux messages

```
login: jh
Password:
Last login: Tue Nov 30 10:08:39 on tty1
[jh@classlab01 jh]$ ls
EngLitJH01  old-list
[jh@classlab01 jh]$ ls -l
total 4
-rw-r--r--    1 jh       jh              0 Nov 29 22:49 EngLitJH01
-rw-r--r--    1 jh       jh             20 Nov 29 22:26 old-list
[jh@classlab01 jh]$ _
```

• **Figure 11-6.** Output from the `ls` and `ls -l` commands

You may also combine switches and have more than one parameter, depending on the command. For example, consider the Linux command `ls`, which lists files in a directory. The `ls` command has several switches, two of which are `a` and `l`. To use `ls` with the `a` switch, enter **ls -a**. To use both switches, enter either **ls -al** or **ls -la**—either will work. If you want to use a switch and list the `/etc` directory, you can enter **ls -a /etc**. In all cases, spaces *separate the items on the command line.*

Try This!

Using the Linux Electronic Manual

Use the online manual to view the documentation for the `ls` command. Try this:

1. Log into Linux and enter **man ls**.
2. The `man` command displays the help screen for the `ls` command, a command analogous to the DIR command in DOS.
3. Scan through the options for the `ls` command displayed on your screen, and then press the space bar to move to the next page. Continue pressing the space bar until you reach the end. You will know you are at the end by what you see at the bottom left of your screen.
4. When you reach the end, press Q to exit the manual.

Command-Line History The shell commands you enter during a session are saved for the duration of the session, and you can scroll through these old commands while at the $ prompt. Simply use the UP ARROW and DOWN ARROW keys to move through the history. When you find a command you would like to use, you can edit the command by moving back and forth through it with the LEFT ARROW and RIGHT ARROW keys. When you are ready to use the command, simply press ENTER. These commands are saved in a file called bash_history, but you do not need to know about this file to take advantage of this feature.

Command Completion As you enter a command at the $ prompt, experiment with the command completion feature. Enter the command name and just a few more characters of the switches and options; then press TAB. BASH tries to guess what you wish to type and is especially clever at doing this when it looks like you are entering a directory name, indicated by the forward slash (/)—but you need to give it more information than just the forward slash. For instance, if you enter **cd /e** and then press TAB, it will guess that you intended to type `etc/` and will complete it.

View help files and the syntax of commands with the `man` command.

The Help Manual Help is always at hand in the form of the online manual, accessed with the `man` command. The simple syntax for the `man` command is `man` *command* where *command* is the shell command you wish to view.

You can even see the documentation for the `man` command itself by entering **man man** at the $ prompt. Figure 11-7 shows the results of doing this. There are many pages of documentation. The colon (:) positioned by itself at the bottom of the screen indicates that there are more pages to view. Whenever you see this symbol at the bottom of your screen in the shell, use PAGE DOWN and PAGE UP keys to scroll through the documentation one screen at a time, and use UP ARROW and DOWN ARROW to scroll through one line at a time. Even very simple commands have extensive help pages.

Cross Check

Test Your Knowledge of Linux Basics

Consider the basic skills and concepts you just learned and answer the following questions:

1. After you log in to Linux at the BASH shell, what information appears on the next two lines?

   ____

2. Briefly describe Linux's case sensitivity.

   ____

3. Give a simple description of the Linux command syntax.

   ____

Managing Files and Directories with Shell Commands

The terms *folder* and *directory* are synonymous in Linux, as they are in Windows. However, it is customary to use the term *folder* in a GUI and *directory* in a command-line interface. Suit yourself!

File management is one of the most important tasks to learn for any operating system. Learning how to create, manipulate, and use files is crucial to your development as a Linux user. This section begins with an overview of Linux shell commands used for file and directory management. You will practice using the `ls` command, with its most common options, and then you will create a file using the text editor pico and the commands to copy,

```
man(1)                                                              man(1)

NAME
       man - format and display the on-line manual pages
       manpath - determine user's search path for man pages

SYNOPSIS
       man  [-acdfFhkKtwW]  [--path]  [-m system] [-p string] [-C config_file]
       [-M pathlist] [-P pager] [-S section_list] [section] name ...

DESCRIPTION
       man formats and displays the on-line manual pages.  If you specify sec-
       tion,  man  only looks  in that section of the manual.  name is normally
       the name of the manual page, which is typically the name of a  command,
       function,  or  file.   However,  if  name contains a slash (/) then man
       interprets it as a file specification, so that you can do  man  ./foo.5
       or even man /cd/foo/bar.1.gz.

       See  below  for  a  description  of where man looks for the manual page
       files.

OPTIONS
       -C  config_file
              Specify  the  configuration  file  to  use;   the   default   is
:_
```

• **Figure 11-7.** Documentation for the `man` command

move, and delete this file. Finally, you will learn how to create a directory and protect the contents of that directory.

To learn the commands, you must enter them at a Linux prompt. Sit at a Linux computer while reading the following sections, which will examine various commands and give you frequent opportunities to try most of them. Feel free to also experiment on your own. Note that your screen may not look exactly like the ones shown in this book. This is okay.

Working with Directories in Linux

Linux relies heavily on a directory structure and in order to work with Linux, you must understand the Linux directory structore. The structure is similar to that used by Windows XP, which has several predefined directories that are needed by the system. Some hold important system files and others hold user data. Linux is very similar. It has several directories for system files and a home directory for each user.

The Linux directory structure can be categorized into two types. The first type consists of directories in which an ordinary user can make changes. These are called home directories. Every user has a **home directory**, which is created for the user, using the user's login name, and located under the /home directory. Your home directory is the one place in Linux where you have full control over files without being logged in as the root account. By default, the other category consists of directories that you cannot change. These are often system directories, such as /etc and /bin, or other user's home directories.

When you log into Linux, your home directory becomes your current (or working) directory. If you installed Linux with the defaults, your home directory path is /home/*username.* A shorthand for this path in a shell command is ~. The default installation includes several other directories. The bin directory within your home director contains many of the Linux commands. The /etc directory contains settings and configuration data for your Linux computer. Do not change anything in this directory unless you know what you are doing.

The /etc and /bin directories are not the only directories included with a Linux installation. After learning how to use the `ls` command in the next section, spend some time exploring your Linux computer to see others. Some have pretty strange names. Table 11-1 shows some of the default directories created during a Linux installation.

Now that you know something about the directory structure on your Linux computer, you will learn how to use shell commands to work with files and directories on your computer. Table 11-2 provides a list of basic file management commands for your reference.

Listing the Contents of a Directory

The `ls` command is the Linux equivalent of the DOS command DIR. The `ls` command lists the contents of a directory. By default, `ls` provides only the names of visible files in the current directory. Using switches changes the

Table 11-1 Linux Default Directories

Directory	Purpose/Contents
/	The top, or root directory
/bin	Linux commands
/boot	Files to be loaded during Linux bootup
/dev	Device files
/etc	Linux system configuration files
/home	The home directories for each user
/lib	Shared libraries for programs and commands to use
/mnt	Mount points for removable devices such as floppy disk drives, zip drives, and CD-ROMs
/opt	Optional (add-on) software packages
/sbin	System commands and binary files
/tmp	Temporary files
/usr	Secondary hierarchy
/var	Several directories containing variable data

way that the command runs. Table 11-3 lists the commonly used switches for `ls`. For a complete list of switches, enter the following: **man ls**.

Simple Directory Listings If you enter the command **ls**, you will get a list of all files in the current directory. Figure 11-8 shows the result of typing `ls /etc`. In this listing of the etc directory, different colors have different meanings. White files are simple files. Dark blue files are directories. Green files are either programs that you can run at the command prompt or binary files like JPEGs. Light blue files are like Windows shortcuts; they are links to files in a different directory.

Fancy Directory Listings You might notice that when you enter the `ls` command without any switches, details like date of creation and length were omitted from the output. You must tell `ls` that you want these details, which requires a switch. To view more detail of the /etc directory, enter the

Table 11-2 Basic Shell Commands for File Management

Command	Description
cd	Changes to another directory
chmod	Changes the mode or file permissions
cp	Copies a file
head	Displays the first ten lines of a file
ls	Lists contents of a directory
mkdir	Makes a directory
more	Displays a text file, one screenful at a time
pico, vi, or emacs	Creates or edits a text file
pwd	Prints the working directory
rm	Deletes a file

Table 11-3 Commonly Used Switches for the `ls` Command

ls Switch	Description
-a	Lists all files in the directory, including the hidden files. Files are hidden in Linux by making the first character a period, like this: .bash_profile.
-l	Displays a long listing of the directory contents. All file attributes and permissions are listed.
-F	Classifies the listed objects. In particular, directory names have a / character after the name.
-S	Sorts the output by size.
-t	Sorts the output by time.

Try This!

Finding Hidden Files

View the hidden files in the current directory. Try this:

1. Enter **ls -a** to see only the hidden files and directories in the current directory.
2. Practice using the `more` and `head` commands to display one of the files shown in white. Be sure to include the period in the file name. For instance, to display the file in which BASH saves a history of the commands you use in a session, type **more .bash_history**.

command **ls -l /etc**. The output will be similar to that shown in Figure 11-9. The first column lists the attributes on the file or folder, which you will examine a little later in this chapter. The next column indicates the type of file. The number 1 indicates a normal file, and 2 indicates a directory. Higher numbers indicate that the file is either a special system file or a link, which is like a shortcut in Windows—a file that points to another file. The next two columns list the owner (normally the user who created the file) and last modifier of the file, respectively. The next number indicates the size of the file. The date

```
gnome                  minicom.users     skel
gnome-vfs-2.0          modules.conf      slrn.rc
gnome-vfs-mime-magic   modules.conf~     smrsh
gpm-root.conf          motd              snmp
group                  mtab              sound
group-                 mtools.conf       ssh
grub.conf              Muttrc            sudoers
gshadow                nscd.conf         sysconfig
gshadow-               nsswitch.conf     sysctl.conf
gtk                    ntp               syslog.conf
gtk-2.0                ntp.conf          termcap
host.conf              oaf               updatedb.conf
hosts                  openldap          updfstab.conf
hosts.allow            openoffice        updfstab.conf.default
hosts.deny             opt               vfontcap
hotplug                pam.d             vfs
htdig.conf             pam_smb.conf      warnquota.conf
im_palette.pal         pango             wgetrc
im_palette-small.pal   paper.config      X11
im_palette-tiny.pal    passwd            xinetd.conf
imrc                   passwd-           xinetd.d
info-dir               passwd.OLD        xml
init.d                 pbm2ppa.conf      xpdfrc
initlog.conf           pcmcia            yp.conf
[jh@classlab01 jh]$ _
```

• **Figure 11-8.** File listing of the /etc directory

```
-rwxr-xr-x     1 root      root          22476 Jul  9  2002 slrn.rc
drwxr-xr-x     2 root      root           4096 Aug 29  2002 smrsh
drwxr-xr-x     2 root      root           4096 Oct  4 17:52 snmp
drwxr-xr-x     3 root      root           4096 Aug 27  2002 sound
drwxr-xr-x     2 root      root           4096 Oct  4 23:14 ssh
-r--r-----     1 root      root            580 Jun 27  2002 sudoers
drwxr-xr-x     7 root      root           4096 Oct  4 23:38 sysconfig
-rw-r--r--     1 root      root            526 Sep  4  2002 sysctl.conf
-rw-r--r--     1 root      root            693 Jun 23  2002 syslog.conf
-rw-r--r--     1 root      root         737535 Jun 23  2002 termcap
-rw-r--r--     1 root      root            140 Jun 23  2002 updatedb.conf
-rw-r--r--     1 root      root             35 Sep  3  2002 updfstab.conf
-rw-r--r--     1 root      root            772 Sep  3  2002 updfstab.conf.default
lrwxrwxrwx     1 root      root             34 Oct  4 17:54 vfontcap -> ../usr/share
/VFlib/2.25.6/vfontcap
drwxr-xr-x     3 root      root           4096 Oct  4 17:58 vfs
-rw-r--r--     1 root      root            864 Sep  6  2002 warnquota.conf
-rw-r--r--     1 root      root           4022 Jul 24  2002 wgetrc
drwxr-xr-x    17 root      root           4096 Nov 29 20:11 X11
-rw-r--r--     1 root      root            289 Aug 15  2002 xinetd.conf
drwxr-xr-x     2 root      root           4096 Oct  4 17:52 xinetd.d
drwxr-xr-x     2 root      root           4096 Oct  4 17:54 xml
-rw-r--r--     1 root      root           4941 Aug 26  2002 xpdfrc
-rw-r--r--     1 root      root            361 Oct  4 18:17 yp.conf
[jh@classlab01 jh]$ _
```

• **Figure 11-9.** File listing with more details

and time columns indicate when the file was created. Last, the name of the file is shown. If a file is a link (shown in light blue), the link location is listed; the file after the arrow is the original file, and the light blue file name in this directory is a shortcut to the original file.

Whenever you need to use a shell command to perform an operation on a hidden file or directory, be sure to include the period (.) that precedes the name.

Like all Microsoft OSs, Linux automatically hides certain files and directories. There are even files and directories hidden in your home directory. For instance, if you are logged in with the user name rex, then your home directory is named rex.

Using the `ls` command with the `-a` switch will reveal the entire contents of a directory, including hidden files, as shown in Figure 11-10. The period (.) preceding a file indicates that it is hidden. Notice that most of the hidden files in the listing are actually directories, which is evident by their blue color.

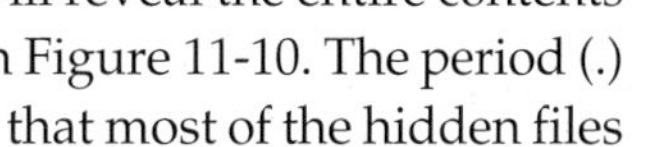

When using shell commands, you often need to use several switches. This is done by combining the switches. You simply type the hyphen just once, and type the appropriate set of characters after the hyphen. For instance, to tell the `ls` command to display a long listing, and to include all entries, the combined switches look like this: `-la`.

Try This!

Using Multiple Switches

Practice using the `ls`. Run the command with a single switch and then with multiple switches. Try this:

1. Enter the command **ls /etc**.
2. Notice that `ls` defaults to column output.
3. To get a long listing of this directory, enter **ls -l /etc**. This runs the `-l` switch on the /etc directory.
4. Now use multiple switches. Enter **ls -la /etc**. This provides a long listing for all files, including hidden files, in the /etc directory.

Changing the Current Directory

As in DOS, the command to change the current directory in Linux is `cd`. The `cd` command requires just one parameter to run: the directory to change to. If the

```
[jh@classlab01 jh]$ ls -a
.                        .file-roller          .gtkrc-1.2-gnome2    .openoffice
..                       .fonts.cache-1        .ICEauthority        .qt
.bash_history            .gconf                .kde                 .rhn-applet.conf
.bash_logout             .gconfd               letter               .sversionrc
.bash_profile            .gnome                .mailcap             .Trash
.bashrc                  .gnome2               .metacity            Untitled 1
.DCOPserver_classlab01__0  .gnome2_private     .mime.types          .user60.rdb
.DCOPserver_classlab01_:0  .gnome-desktop      .nautilus            .Xauthority
.emacs                   .gphoto               .netscape            .xsession-errors
EngLitJH01               .gqview               .netscape6
.esd_auth                .gtkrc                old-list
[jh@classlab01 jh]$ _
```

• **Figure 11-10.** A listing with all entries displayed

directory is a child of the current directory, then only the name is needed to change to this directory. For example, suppose that in your home directory you have a child directory called private. To change to this directory, you enter **cd private**. If the directory is not a child of the current directory, you will need to enter the path to the directory. Typically, the path will start with / (the root directory). Each directory in the path is listed after the / and separated by another /. For example, to change to the sbin directory under the / usr directory, you would enter **cd /usr/sbin**.

When you correctly use `cd` to change to a different directory, you are rewarded with a change in your prompt. In Figure 11-11, the user started in the jh directory and changed to the sbin directory. The prompt changed to reflect the new directory. You can quickly change back to your personal home directory by entering **cd** ~. Figure 11-12 shows the result of entering this command.

Unfortunately, the Linux prompt does not (by default) show the entire path to the current directory. If you are unsure what directory you are in, use the command `pwd`. The `pwd` command stands for *print working directory.* It does not send anything to your printer; rather it displays the path to the working (current) directory on your screen.

Relative Path

Linux allows you to use commands to navigate directories, using special symbols as shorthand for moving to directories that are relative to your current directory. For instance, the command **cd ..** will change the current directory to the next directory up in the hierarchy. If you are in your personal home directory, this command will move you to the home directory, one level up. You can also place the **..** characters between forward slashes (/) to move up additional levels. Also, you can throw in a specific directory that exists at that level. For example, the command `cd ../../etc` moves up two levels and then to the etc directory. Be sure you know where you want

```
[jh@classlab01 jh]$ cd /usr/sbin
[jh@classlab01 sbin]$ _
```

• **Figure 11-11.** Changing directories

```
[jh@classlab01 sbin]$ cd ~
[jh@classlab01 jh]$ _
```

• **Figure 11-12.** Changing back to a home directory using the tilde (~)

to go, and remember, using one of these characters is supposed to save you typing. Rather than use the command string `cd ../../etc`, it is shorter to type `cd /etc`. Another special symbol is the single dot (.), which refers to the current directory. While you are first learning Linux, any path that gets you to the right place is the right path!

Using Relative Path Statements

A little practice with relative paths is helpful. Try this:

1. Type the command **cd ..**
2. Return to your home directory by typing **cd ~**
3. Now move to the /etc directory using a relative path: **cd ../../etc**
4. Return to your home directory by typing **cd ~**

Wildcards

Linux supports the use of wildcards at the command prompt, which are symbols that replace any character or characters. For instance, the use of the asterisk in a file name or directory name replaces all the characters from the point at which the asterisk is placed to the end of the name. For example, `bi*` would include all files or directories that begin with "bi". Linux wildcard support is more flexible than that of DOS. You can enter a range of characters as a wildcard. For instance, if you enter **ls [c-d]***, the `ls` command will display all files in the current directory that begin with the letters *c* through *d*. The [ ] symbols are part of a Linux feature called regular expressions. Linux also allows you to use the dollar sign ($) to represent a single character within a file name. We considered ourselves very experienced DOS users (in its heyday), and we found that the $ sign was rarely worth bothering with.

Using Wildcards

1. Change to the /etc directory
2. Enter the command **ls e***. You'll see all files that begin with the letter *e*
3. Now enter the command **ls [c-d]***

```
[jh@classlab01 etc]$ ls e*
esd.conf   exports

ethereal:
diameter   manuf
[jh@classlab01 etc]$ ls [b-c]*
bashrc   cdrecord.conf   crontab   csh.cshrc   csh.login

bonobo-activation:
bonobo-activation-config.xml

cron.d:

cron.daily:
00-logwatch   0anacron   logrotate   makewhatis.cron   rpm   slocate.cron   tmpwatch

cron.hourly:

cron.monthly:
0anacron

cron.weekly:
0anacron   makewhatis.cron
[jh@classlab01 etc]$ _
```

• Using wildcards

Try This!

Create Directories

Create directories in your home folder. Try this:

1. Enter the command **mkdir data**.
2. Use the `ls` command to confirm that the data directory was created.
3. Make several directories by entering the `mkdir` command followed by several names for new directories.
4. Use the `ls` command to confirm that the new directories were created.

Creating Directories

Creating a directory in Linux is done with the `mkdir` command, which requires at least one parameter: the name of the directory to create. For example, to create a directory called junk within the current directory, enter the command **mkdir junk**. Because Linux gives you no feedback after you create a directory, use `ls` to verify that the directory was built.

If more than one parameter is listed, then a directory will be created for each. Therefore, to create several directories at once, enter the command **mkdir perl html bin data**. (See Figure 11-13.)

A file you may want to copy is your .bash_profile file. This file is run when you log into Linux. A mistake in this file can cause Linux to not work. By creating a copy of the file, you can recover if you make a mistake when changing this file.

Copying Files in Linux

Like DOS and Windows, Linux allows you to copy files. The command to copy files in Linux is `cp`. If you are wise, you will make a copy of a file before you change it. This allows you to go back and recover from any changes you make.

The `cp` command requires two parameters. The first is the source file, which can be a file in the current directory or a file in another directory. The second parameter is the target, which can be a target location to copy to and/or a name for the file. Like the DOS copy command, this makes more sense after you practice using the command.

As you can see in Figure 11-14, the file ntp.conf has been copied to the current directory. (The period at the end represents the current directory.) The file ntp.conf resides in the /etc directory. Notice that Linux does not report that it copied a file. The figure also shows that we used the `ls` command to verify that the file was successfully copied.

Creating and Editing Files in Linux

In any operating system, sometimes it is useful to create and edit files with a text editor. A text editor works with plain text—that is, it works with a

```
[jh@classlab01 jh]$ mkdir junk
[jh@classlab01 jh]$ ls
EngLitJH01  junk  letter  old-list  Untitled 1
[jh@classlab01 jh]$ mkdir perl html bin data
[jh@classlab01 jh]$ ls
bin  data  EngLitJH01  html  junk  letter  old-list  perl  Untitled 1
[jh@classlab01 jh]$ _
```

• **Figure 11-13.** Using `mkdir` to create directories and `ls` to show them

simple alphanumeric character set with just the minimal formatting codes reminiscent of old typewriters: carriage return (move to the beginning of the line) and line feed (move to the next line). There are also no special codes for formatting characters, as you find in word processing. Text editors are used for creating simple script files, programming code, and any other occasion when you do not want extraneous code in a file. There are many text editors available for Linux. A few that you may encounter are pico, vi, and emacs. Learn how to use a text editor if you ever plan to write a script or program in Linux.

```
[jh@classlab01 jh]$ cp /etc/ntp.conf .
[jh@classlab01 jh]$ ls
EngLitJH01  letter  ntp.conf  old-list  Untitled 1
[jh@classlab01 jh]$ _
```

• **Figure 11-14.** Copying the ntp.conf file

Using pico

Pico is perhaps the easiest text editor, because it has some features that make it attractive to a new user:

- It provides a series of commands at the bottom of the screen.
- It allows you to use the keyboards as expected—BACKSPACE and DELETE work as usual.
- Text will wrap to the next line after you enter 80 characters (a feature we take for granted in a word processor, but which is not always included in a text editor).

For anyone with even a little experience with a word processor, entering text into pico seems to work as you expect. If you need help with spelling, you are in luck because pico includes a spell checker, accessed by pressing CTRL-T, but you will quickly notice that the checker is not quite as nice as the spell checker in Microsoft Word.

Table 11-4 lists handy pico commands. Figure 11-15 shows pico with an open document. (Saying nice things to a teacher or instructor will rarely hurt your grade!)

Try This!

Create a File

Use a Linux text editor to create a file. Try this:

1. For instance, to use pico, create a file named "letter01", type the following at the $ prompt: **pico letter01**.
2. Type a letter. When you are done, use the command to save a file. In pico this command is CTRL-O.
3. Exit from the text editor. In pico the command to exit is CTRL-X.

Table 11-4 Common pico Commands

pico Command	Description
CTRL-O	Saves the current file. If it is unnamed, you will be prompted to name it.
CTRL-R	Opens another text file. You will need to enter the name of the file you want to open.
CTRL-T	Spell-checks the current document.
CTRL-X	Exits pico. If the current file is unsaved, you will be prompted to save the file.

```
UW PICO(tm) 4.2                    File: letter                    Modified

Dear Instructor,

Your class is the best class I have ever taken. This Linux is really neat.
I hope I get a job where I have to use Linux every day!

Yours truly,

Rex Holcombe_

^G Get Help   ^O WriteOut   ^R Read File ^Y Prev Pg    ^K Cut Text   ^C Cur Pos
^X Exit       ^J Justify    ^W Where is  ^V Next Pg    ^U UnCut Text ^T To Spell
```

• **Figure 11-15.** The pico editor with an open document

The vi Text Editor

One of the oldest editors around is vi, which is a line editor. You essentially edit one line at a time. The vi editor has three modes: text, colon, and graphical. To use vi, you must master all three modes.

The emacs Text Editor

Another popular Linux editor is emacs. Emacs is especially popular with developers because it has several programming features. One of these features is called the emacs dance. When you close a pair of quotation marks or parentheses, the cursor jumps back to the item that you are closing. This feature helps developers with complex code. A downside to emacs is that the BACKSPACE key does not always work as expected. In a default installation, the BACKSPACE key opens help after the third use. This behavior can be changed by root.

Only delete files that you created yourself and that you are certain are not needed by the operating system or other programs.

Deleting Files in Linux

When you find you no longer need a file, you should delete it to free up disk space. The command to delete a file is `rm`. The `rm` command requires at least one parameter: the name of the file to delete. If you include more than one file name, each file will be erased. Figure 11-16 shows a listing of the home directory for jh; then the `rm` command is run with the names of two files: letter and ntp.conf. Finally, a listing shows that those files no longer exist in the directory.

Try This!

Deleting Files

Practice deleting files. Try this:

1. To delete the file you copied earlier, enter this command: **rm ntp.conf**.
2. Enter **ls** to list your files to verify that the copy operation worked.

```
[jh@classlab01 jh]$ ls
EngLitJH01  letter  letter02  ntp.conf  old-list  Untitled 1
[jh@classlab01 jh]$ rm letter ntp.conf
[jh@classlab01 jh]$ ls
EngLitJH01  letter02  old-list  Untitled 1
[jh@classlab01 jh]$ _
```

• **Figure 11-16.** Using the `rm` command to delete a file

Renaming or Moving Files in Linux

The `cp` command allows you to have two versions of a file, which is a good thing to do before making changes to an important file. Also, sometimes you want to rename a file. The net result is one instance of the file, not two instances like you get with the copy command. Copying the file and then deleting the original file can accomplish this, but it is handy to be able to do this in just one operation, which you can do with the `mv` command. The `mv` command can rename a file in the current directory, or move the file from the current directory to a different directory.

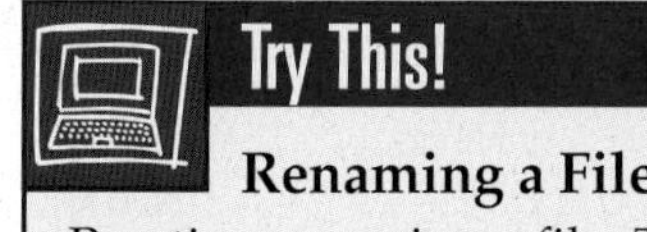

Renaming a File

Practice renaming a file. Try this:

1. Log in as a regular user, not root. Use `mv` to rename your file. Enter the command **mv letter01 instructor_letter**.
2. Use the `ls` command to verify the name change.

The `mv` command requires two parameters: the name of the original file and the new name or location of the file. If the original file does not exist, then you will get an error message. If you cannot delete or change the original file, then `mv` will generate an error message.

```
[jh@classlab01 jh]$ mv letter instructor_letter
[jh@classlab01 jh]$ ls
instructor_letter
[jh@classlab01 jh]$ _
```

• Renaming a file with the `mv` command

Viewing the Contents of a File

A typical Linux directory contains many files. You often need to know what is in the files. Several Linux commands let you view files. These include `more`, `head`, `less`, `tail`, and `cat`. These commands are viewers for text files. When you use one of these commands on a text file, you will see standard text characters. However, if you use one of these commands to view a program (binary) file, you will see mostly nonsense (techies call it garbage) on your screen.

more The `more` command displays the entire contents of a file page (or screenful) at a time. Press the space bar to view another page; press ENTER to see another line. The `more` command can be used on more than file contents. You can use the `more` command for those shell commands that put so much information on the screen that the beginning scrolls off before you can read it. In fact, experienced DOS users will recognize this use of the `more` command. When you get ready to enter a command that you believe will scroll off the screen, simply add | **more** to the end of the command line. For instance, the command `ls -a` will often produce more than a

```
[jh@classlab01 jh]$ ls -a | more
.
..
.bash_history
.bash_logout
.bash_proback
.bash_profile
.bashrc
.emacs
.esd_auth
.fonts.cache-1
.gconf
.gconfd
.gnome
.gnome2
.gnome2_private
.gnome-desktop
.gtkrc
.gtkrc-1.2-gnome2
.ICEauthority
instructor_letter
.kde
.metacity
.mozilla
--More--
```

• **Figure 11-17.** Using the `more` command

screenful of output, so add the `more` command: `ls -a | more`. The vertical bar is called a pipe symbol, and when it's used this way, you are "piping" the output of the first command to the `more` command, and it, in turn, displays the output from the first command, one page at a time. See Figure 11-17.

head The `head` command displays just the first ten lines of a file, which is helpful on occasions when you don't want to see the entire file, and the first few lines will suffice.

less The `less` command is nearly equivalent to the `more` command. The difference is that the `less` command allows you to move forward and backward in the file, whereas the `more` command allows you to move only forward. Thus, the `less` command has more features than the `more` command. (This is more Linux humor.)

tail The `tail` command displays the last ten lines of a file.

cat The `cat` command displays the entire contents of a file. Be careful with the `cat` command because "catting" a large file can take some time.

Step-by-Step 11.02

Displaying the Contents of Files

To complete this step-by-step, you need the following:

- A Linux computer
- A text file saved in your home directory (the file instructor_letter is used in the steps)

Step 1

Enter this command: **more instructor_letter**. The instructor_letter file that we used was very small, so the entire contents displayed on one screen.

```
[jh@classlab01 jh]$ more instructor_letter
Dear Instructor,

Your class is the best class I have ever taken. This Linux is really neat.
I hope I get a job where I have to use Linux every day!

Yours truly,

Rex Holcombe
[jh@classlab01 jh]$ _
```

Step 2

Now view a larger file. Type the following command: **more /etc/ntp.conf**. You will see a screen like the one shown here. To move through the file, use the space bar to jump one page (screen) at a time, or press ENTER to move just one line at a time. If you tire of viewing the file before you reach the end, simply press CTRL-C to exit the file.

```
[jh@classlab01 jh]$ more /etc/ntp.conf
# Prohibit general access to this service.
restrict default ignore

# Permit all access over the loopback interface.  This could
# be tightened as well, but to do so would effect some of
# the administrative functions.
restrict 127.0.0.1


# -- CLIENT NETWORK -------
# Permit systems on this network to synchronize with this
# time service.  Do not permit those systems to modify the
# configuration of this service.  Also, do not use those
# systems as peers for synchronization.
# restrict 192.168.1.0 mask 255.255.255.0 notrust nomodify notrap


# --- OUR TIMESERVERS -----
# or remove the default restrict line
# Permit time synchronization with our time source, but do not
# permit the source to query or modify the service on this system.

# restrict mytrustedtimeserverip mask 255.255.255.255 nomodify notrap noquery
--More--(29%)_
```

Step 3

Use the `more` command to display the output from another command. At the command line, type **ls –a | more**.

Step 4

Now use the `head` command to view just the first ten lines of a file. Type the following command: **head /etc/ntp.conf**. Notice that only the first ten lines are shown.

```
[jh@classlab01 jh]$ head /etc/ntp.conf
# Prohibit general access to this service.
restrict default ignore

# Permit all access over the loopback interface.  This could
# be tightened as well, but to do so would effect some of
# the administrative functions.
restrict 127.0.0.1


# -- CLIENT NETWORK -------
[jh@classlab01 jh]$ _
```

Step 5

Now use the command that will let you move forward and backward through a file. Type the following command: **less /etc/ntp.conf**. Use the DOWN ARROW and UP ARROW keys and the PAGE UP and PAGE DOWN keys to move through the document. When you reach the end, press Q to quit.

Step 6

View the last ten lines of a file. Type the command **tail /etc/ntp.conf**.

```
[jh@classlab01 jh]$ tail /etc/ntp.conf
# Keys file.  If you want to diddle your server at run time, make a
# keys file (mode 600 for sure) and define the key number to be
# used for making requests.
#
# PLEASE DO NOT USE THE DEFAULT VALUES HERE. Pick your own, or remote
# systems might be able to reset your clock at will. Note also that
# ntpd is started with a -A flag, disabling authentication, that
# will have to be removed as well.
#
keys            /etc/ntp/keys
[jh@classlab01 jh]$ _
```

File and Folder Permissions

One of the benefits of Linux is the security. However, unless you implement the security features, anyone can access anyone else's directories and files on the Linux computer. To secure your files, you need to decide which files you want to secure.

To implement security for a file or folder, you must first understand Linux file and folder attributes. When you use the `-l` switch with the `ls` command, you will see the attributes listed in a column of ten characters on the far left. Each character is significant in both its placement (first, second, and so on) and in what each single character represents. The first character at the far left indicates whether the entry is a file (-), directory (d), or link (l). The next nine characters show the permissions on the file or folder. Figure 11-18 shows a listing of a directory using both the `-a` and `-l` switches to show the attributes of all entries. To decode the permissions, which are the second through tenth characters, use the following list:

r = read

w = write

x = execute

- = disabled

Notice the set of permissions for the link named *awk*. They repeat *rwx* three times. Linux is not repeating itself; it is listing permissions for three different groups of people. The first three permissions apply to the user who owns the files (owner). The user account that creates a file or directory is the **owner**. The second set of permissions applies to the group the user belongs to. Groups are used to organize users, grouping together those with similar needs and access privileges. For example, a school may group

Inside Information

Web Pages and UNIX/Linux

In the early days of the Web, most webmasters had little knowledge of how UNIX worked. They simply knew that they could post their pages on a UNIX web server, and the world could read them. Unfortunately, many did not pay close attention to the modes of the files. Typically, the webmaster set the permissions as 777. This, of course, allowed anyone to change the files.

*Several famous web pages were hacked because of this lack of care. Two that stand out as gutsy moves on the part of the hacker were the FBI's web page and the Pentagon's page. Both were hacked in a very visible manner. If you start writing web pages on a Linux or UNIX computer, be sure to set permissions for your pages to **755**. This lets the world read and execute the page, but the world cannot change the files.*

all faculty members into a single group. This will allow instructors to create files that other instructors can read, but that students cannot read. The third set of permissions is applied to all others. So the read, write, and execute permissions on *awk* apply to the owner (root), the owner's groups, and all others. The permissions on the file *arch* are set so that the owner has read, write, and execute permissions, but the owner's group and all others have only read and execute permissions, meaning only the owner can change or delete the file.

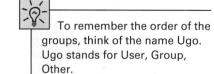

> To remember the order of the groups, think of the name Ugo. Ugo stands for User, Group, Other.

Permissions are also referred to as "modes," and the command to change a file's permissions is `chmod` (called "change mode"). The `chmod` command requires two parameters. The first parameter is the **access mode number**, a value calculated from values assigned to a permission. The second parameter is the file to change.

There is a small calculation to be performed to determine the access mode number. In Figure 11-18, the file *awk* has access mode number 777, and *arch* has access mode number 755. The number can be calculated using the values in Table 11-5. Determine the permission for each user or group by adding the values together.

Cross Check

Manage This!

Working with files and folders in any operating system involves certain common concepts, but each OS has its own implementation. Test your knowledge of Linux file management now.

1. What symbol represents the very top of the Linux file system?

 ____

2. What command will allow you to rename or move a file?

 ____

3. What is the exact command and syntax you would use to set the permissions on the file "calendar" to rw-r--r--?

 ____

```
[jh@classlab01 bin]$ ls -al |more
total 7040
drwxr-xr-x    2 root     root         4096 Dec  2 08:11 .
drwxr-xr-x   19 root     root         4096 Dec  3 06:37 ..
-rwxr-xr-x    1 root     root         4330 Aug 30  2002 arch
-rwxr-xr-x    1 root     root       110048 Jul 17  2002 ash
-rwxr-xr-x    1 root     root       505685 Jul 17  2002 ash.static
-rwxr-xr-x    1 root     root        10296 Aug  4  2002 aumix-minimal
lrwxrwxrwx    1 root     root            4 Dec  2 07:38 awk -> gawk
-rwxr-xr-x    1 root     root        10680 Aug 29  2002 basename
-rwxr-xr-x    1 root     root       626188 Aug 23  2002 bash
lrwxrwxrwx    1 root     root            4 Dec  2 07:38 bash2 -> bash
lrwxrwxrwx    1 root     root            3 Dec  2 07:40 bsh -> ash
-rwxr-xr-x    1 root     root        19154 Jul  1  2002 cat
-rwxr-xr-x    1 root     root        18136 Sep  2  2002 chgrp
-rwxr-xr-x    1 root     root        18072 Sep  2  2002 chmod
-rwxr-xr-x    1 root     root        20120 Sep  2  2002 chown
-rwxr-xr-x    1 root     root        49548 Sep  2  2002 cp
-rwxr-xr-x    1 root     root        64706 Jun 23  2002 cpio
lrwxrwxrwx    1 root     root            4 Dec  2 07:45 csh -> tcsh
-rwxr-xr-x    1 root     root        21854 Jul  1  2002 cut
-rwxr-xr-x    1 root     root        40600 Aug 29  2002 date
-rwxr-xr-x    1 root     root        32044 Sep  2  2002 dd
-rwxr-xr-x    1 root     root        28972 Sep  2  2002 df
--More--_
```

• **Figure 11-18.** A sample listing showing attributes

Always be sure the file owner has an access mode number of at least 6 for a file, which allows for read and write permissions. If the mode for the owner drops below 6 on some Linux installations, any future access to this file is blocked. You should rarely have a file with permissions of 777, because it means that anyone can change the file.

Table 11-5 Access Mode Numbers

Permission	Value
Read	4
Write	2
Execute	1

Thus, if the owner needs to read, write, and execute a file, the first number is 4 + 2 + 1 = 7. If the group is to also read, write, and execute the file, the second number is also 7. If a user has permission only to read and execute a file, the value is 4 + 1 = 5.

Step-by-Step 11.03

Working with Directories

Imagine that you have been hired by a marketing firm that uses Linux as its primary OS. You will work with a group of users. You will need to create a series of directories that the group can see, as well as a private directory that no one else but you can see. Be sure that you are logged in as a regular user. The following steps will allow you to create directories and set permissions on the directories. You will create these directories in your own home directory. You will need the following:

- A Linux computer
- An account on this computer
- Read access to the /etc directory

Step 1

First create the directories needed to work. Use `mkdir` to create two directories, called *wineProject* and *private,* entering this command: **mkdir wineProject private**.

Step 2

Use the command **ls -l** to verify that the directories were created and to view the permissions that were assigned to the directories by default.

```
[jh@classlab01 wineProject]$ ls -l
total 8
-rw-rw-r--    1 jh       jh          70 Dec  3 10:11 busplan2006
-rw-rw-r--    1 jh       jh         178 Dec  3 10:10 instructor_letter
[jh@classlab01 wineProject]$ cd ~
[jh@classlab01 jh]$ ls -l
total 216
-rw-rw-r--    1 jh       jh          70 Dec  3 08:14 busplan2006
-rw-rw-r--    1 jh       jh         178 Dec  2 19:51 instructor_letter
-rw-r--r--    1 jh       jh        9283 Dec  2 22:03 mailcap
-rw-r--r--    1 jh       jh         112 Dec  2 22:03 mail.rc
-rw-r--r--    1 jh       jh        4426 Dec  2 22:03 man.config
-rw-r--r--    1 jh       jh       36823 Dec  3 06:49 mime-magic
-rw-r--r--    1 jh       jh       99960 Dec  2 22:03 mime-magic.dat
-rw-r--r--    1 jh       jh       12786 Dec  2 22:03 mime.types
-rw-r--r--    1 jh       jh        1110 Dec  2 22:03 minicom.users
-rw-r--r--    1 jh       jh         311 Dec  2 22:03 modules.conf
-rw-r--r--    1 jh       jh         281 Dec  2 22:03 modules.conf~
-rw-r--r--    1 jh       jh           0 Dec  2 22:03 motd
-rw-r--r--    1 jh       jh         242 Dec  2 22:03 mtab
-rw-r--r--    1 jh       jh        1913 Dec  2 22:04 mtools.conf
drwxrwxr-x    2 jh       jh        4096 Dec  3 10:10 private
drwxrwxr-x    2 jh       jh        4096 Dec  3 10:11 wineProject
[jh@classlab01 jh]$ _
```

Step 3

You are now the owner of these directories. Set the permissions on the private directory so that it can be accessed only by you, and on the wineProject directory, give yourself read, write, and execute permissions, but only read and write permissions to users in your group, and set no permissions for others. To set the permissions appropriately, enter these two commands: **chmod 700 private** and **chmod 760 wineProject**.

Step 4

Confirm the new permissions using **ls -l**.

```
[jh@classlab01 jh]$ chmod 700 private
[jh@classlab01 jh]$ chmod 760 wineProject
[jh@classlab01 jh]$ ls -l
total 216
-rw-rw-r--    1 jh       jh            70 Dec  3 08:14 busplan2006
-rw-rw-r--    1 jh       jh           178 Dec  2 19:51 instructor_letter
-rw-r--r--    1 jh       jh          9283 Dec  2 22:03 mailcap
-rw-r--r--    1 jh       jh           112 Dec  2 22:03 mail.rc
-rw-r--r--    1 jh       jh          4426 Dec  2 22:03 man.config
-rw-r--r--    1 jh       jh         36823 Dec  3 06:49 mime-magic
-rw-r--r--    1 jh       jh         99960 Dec  2 22:03 mime-magic.dat
-rw-r--r--    1 jh       jh         12786 Dec  2 22:03 mime.types
-rw-r--r--    1 jh       jh          1110 Dec  2 22:03 minicom.users
-rw-r--r--    1 jh       jh           311 Dec  2 22:03 modules.conf
-rw-r--r--    1 jh       jh           281 Dec  2 22:03 modules.conf~
-rw-r--r--    1 jh       jh             0 Dec  2 22:03 motd
-rw-r--r--    1 jh       jh           242 Dec  2 22:03 mtab
-rw-r--r--    1 jh       jh          1913 Dec  2 22:04 mtools.conf
drwx------    2 jh       jh          4096 Dec  3 10:10 private
drwxrw----    2 jh       jh          4096 Dec  3 10:11 wineProject
[jh@classlab01 jh]$ _
```

Step 5

Populate the wineProject directory by copying two files into it from your home directory, using the cp command. For instance, to copy the file named *letter*, type **cp letter wineProject**.

Step 6

Change to the wineProject directory by entering the command **cd wineProject**. Confirm that the files are there, and view the permissions on the files. They do not inherit the permissions of the directory. You will need to modify the permissions on the files if you wish permissions more restrictive than those assigned to the directory. However, any restrictive directory permissions will keep users from accessing the contents of the directory.

```
[jh@classlab01 jh]$ cp instructor_letter wineProject
[jh@classlab01 jh]$ cp busplan2006 wineProject
[jh@classlab01 jh]$ cd wineProject
[jh@classlab01 wineProject]$ ls
busplan2006   instructor_letter
[jh@classlab01 wineProject]$ ls -l
total 8
-rw-rw-r--    1 jh       jh            70 Dec  3 10:11 busplan2006
-rw-rw-r--    1 jh       jh           178 Dec  3 10:10 instructor_letter
[jh@classlab01 wineProject]$ _
```

Using a GUI Desktop in Linux

You are showing Linux to your neighbor Laurie one day. Laurie is a proficient Microsoft Windows user, who does not want to type everything at a prompt. She complains that Linux should be as easy to use as Windows.

Inside Information

X Window System and NextStep

The X Window System has its proponents and detractors. One famous detractor is Steve Jobs. In the early 1990s, Jobs, after leaving Apple Computer, founded a new computer company called NeXT, intending to build high-powered graphic workstations. In his search for an operating system, Jobs tried the X Window System. He publicly declared it "brain dead." He decided to create a new operating system called NextStep. While NextStep was a good OS running on a wonderful computer, it failed, leaving the "brain dead" X Window system surviving.

Part of the problem with NextStep was it was way ahead of its time. The operating system was a dream to work with, and the hardware was exceptional. However, the newest and greatest is not necessarily the best choice for the job at hand. What is important is to pick technology that solves your problems now.

GNOME stands for GNU Network Object Model Environment.

Once you start GNOME, you will log out using the GNOME menu. Shutdown can be accomplished from here as well, without logging in as root.

Laurie is not alone. Most users are uncomfortable with the command prompt. Visual interfaces are much easier to use, but at a cost. It typically takes longer to perform a task in a graphical user interface (GUI) than it does to perform the same task at a command prompt. However, some actions are better performed in a GUI. During the installation step-by-step, you had the option to install one or more GUIs. Examples of Linux GUIs are GNOME and KDE. In this section, we'll examine the GNOME GUI.

The GNOME and many other Linux and UNIX GUI desktops are implementations of the **X Window System**, which was first developed in 1984 at MIT as Project Athena. The X Consortium was founded in 1986 to continue the development of the X Window System (alternatively called "X Windows" or even simply "X"). The Open Group continued the X Window System development in 1997. Today, the X Window System is the program code used as the basis for many GUIs for Linux or UNIX. Once installed into Linux, the `startx` command will load an X Window System GUI. This runs as a client, depending on a local X Window System server component called an X Server, which manages the GUI.

The GNOME Desktop

Recall that during the installation process, you selected the **GNOME** desktop. GNOME, an acronym for GNU network object model environment, is a UNIX GUI that uses the **X Window System**. You also had an option to choose between a text login or a GUI login. If you selected a text login, then you start at the command prompt and run a command to start a GUI. If you selected the GUI login, you log in via a GUI dialog box, and the GUI (GNOME or other) starts up automatically.

Starting a GUI after a Text Login

To start GNOME, type **startx** at the $ prompt. After a delay, you will see a screen like Figure 11-19. You use your mouse to navigate, and there are icons on the desktop, an object called a **panel** (resembling the Windows taskbar) residing at the bottom of the screen, and on the left of the panel is a Red Hat icon with a tiny triangle that can be used to open the GNOME menu. This last is reminiscent of the Start menu in Windows. In fact, these GUI interfaces have many similar GUI objects. Applications run in windows, which you can manipulate with your mouse exactly as you would in

Try This!

Start GNOME

It is easy to start your GUI environment from the Linux command prompt. Try this:

1. If necessary, log in with the user account (not root).
2. At the $ prompt, type **startx** and press ENTER. After a slight delay, the GNOME desktop should display. Leave GNOME open for the following step-by-step.

Microsoft Windows. You will also notice that directories are represented by folder icons, so while we are in GNOME, we will use the term "folder" rather than "directory."

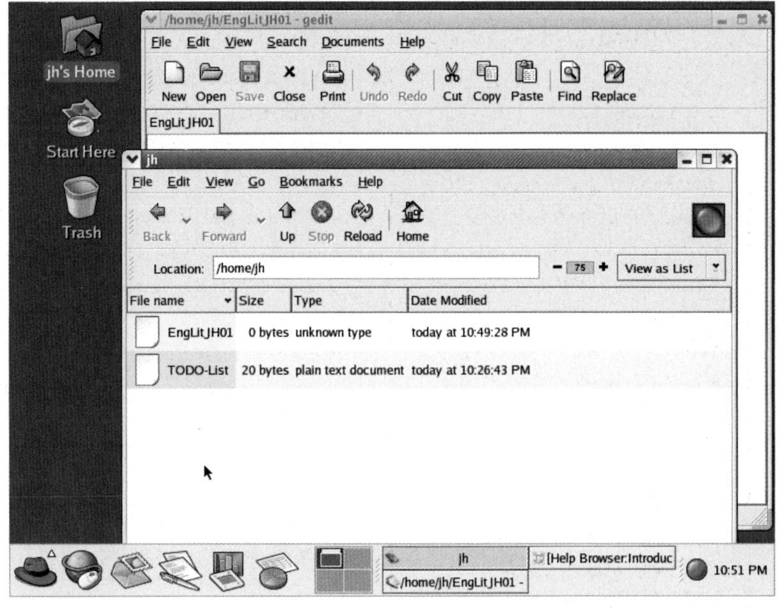

• **Figure 11-19.** The GNOME desktop with icons and open windows

The Workspace Switcher

If you have worked with computers, you may have noticed that you open applications in certain groupings. For example, when you write, you may have a word processor and a music program open. When you are preparing a report or class assignment, you may have an entirely different set of applications open, such as a database program, a spreadsheet program, and a web browser. In Windows, while you can certainly multitask, you can have only one set of applications open at a time. GNOME, through the GNOME Workspace Switcher, lets you have different sets of applications open and easily accessible, but not always visible. Each set of programs is in its own workspace (hence, the name). The Workspace Switcher is located in the middle of the taskbar, and it shows four squares, each of which represents a workspace. By default, the upper-left box is the first workspace, the upper-right is the second workspace, and the bottom-left and -right boxes are the third and fourth workspaces, respectively. You may switch between them by simply clicking on the square that represents the workspace you wish to open. Preferences changed in one workspace will carry over into all four workspaces. It is only the open applications that are unique, so you cannot count on keeping track of things based on the wallpaper or background color.

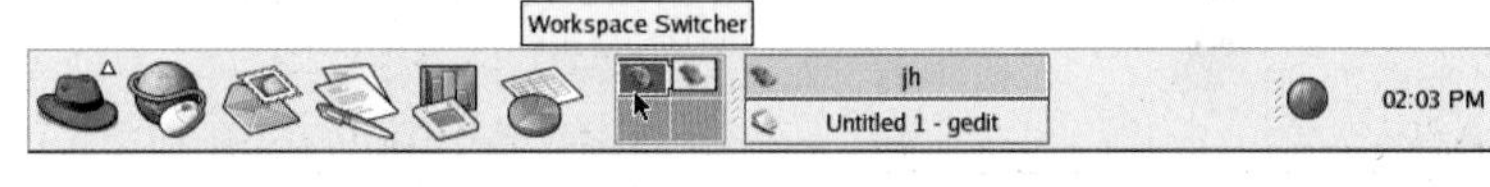

• The Workspace Switcher on the panel

Step-by-Step 11.04

Managing Workspaces in GNOME

The following step-by-step exercise will set up two different workspaces in GNOME. It will also give you a chance to explore and use a few of the GNOME menu options.

You will need the following:

- A computer with Linux installed
- GNOME installed

Step 1

If necessary, log in with your user (your not-root) account and start GNOME. On the GNOME desktop, double-click on your home folder. This open window will help you distinguish this first workspace from the new one you will create.

Step 2

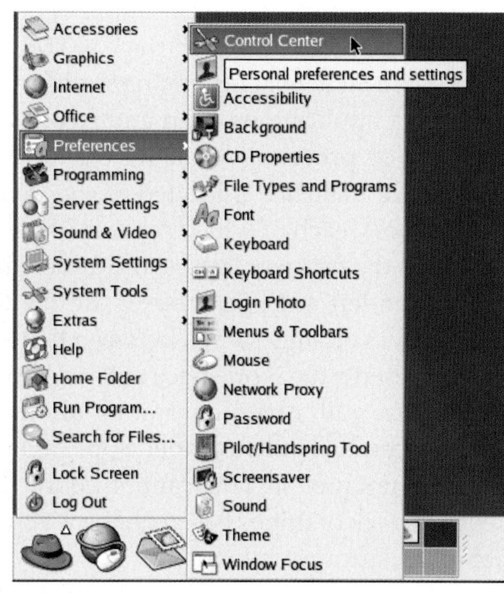

Click the square in the upper-right of the Workspace Switcher. In the new workspace, you will see basically the same screen you had, but without the open window. Now change the appearance of your desktop. Open GNOME menu (the red hat icon) on the panel and select Preferences. View the long list of user preferences you can use to personalize your GNOME workspaces. From the Preferences menu, select Control Center.

Step 3

Notice that the Workspace Switcher now shows an open window in each of two of the workspaces. In the Control Center, double-click the background icon to open the Background Preferences dialog box. Under Picture Options, click No Picture and then click Top Color, which will open the Pick A Color dialog box. Pause your mouse cursor over the color wheel for instructions on how to select a color using this really clever device. When you have selected a color, click OK in this dialog box, and then Close in Background Preferences.

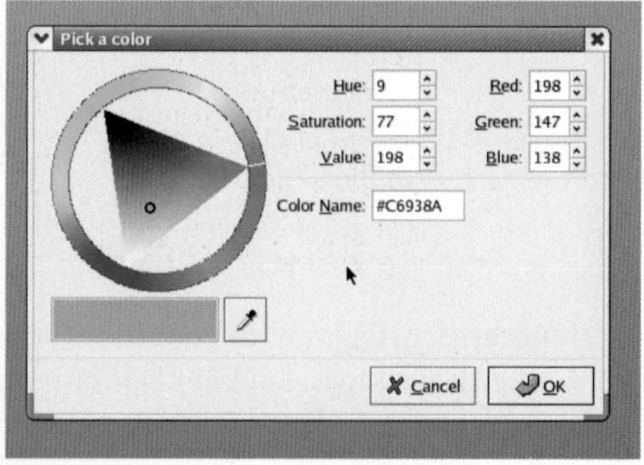

Step 4

Open two or three applications from the GNOME | Accessories menu.

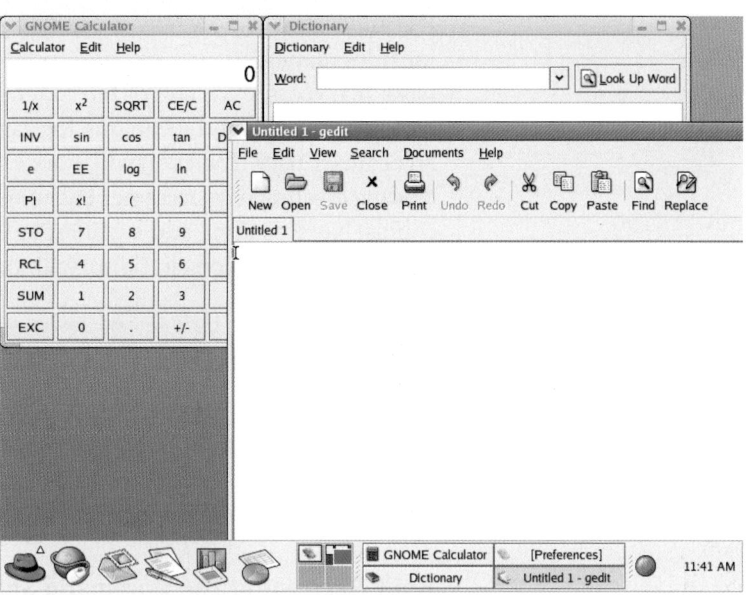

Step 5

Use the Workspace Switcher to move back and forth between the two workspaces. Notice the common preferences, but a different set of open applications, in each workspace.

Step 6

Select the Logout option from the GNOME menu. Click the check box by Save Current Setup to place a check. Now if you log out, shut down, or restart the computer, your workspace will be saved. The next time you start GNOME, these applications will open for you in their own workspace. Be sure you have selected the check box, and then select Restart.

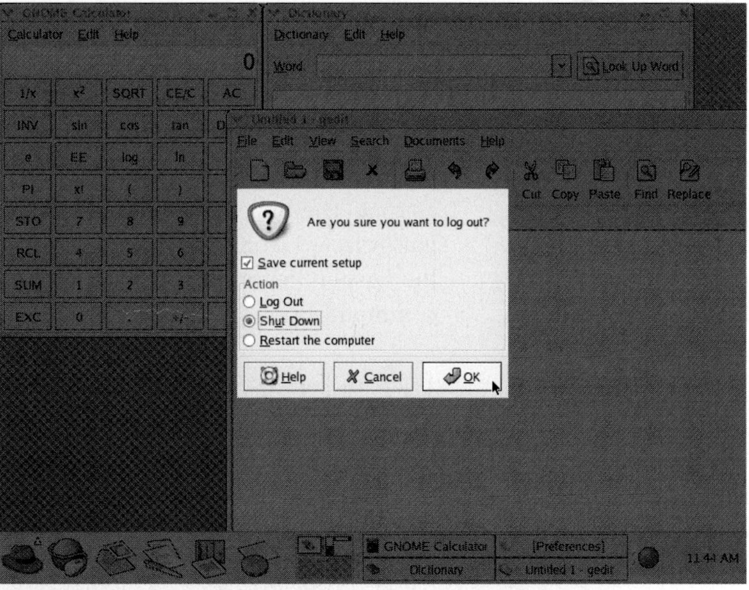

Step 7

After the restart, if necessary, log in at the command prompt and start GNOME with **startx**. When GNOME opens, your two workspaces should also open.

Configuring Linux for Users

It is important to know how to configure a computer for the needs of users. This includes managing user accounts, printers, and applications. These all involve tasks that require the use of the root account. In this section, you will learn a handy command and technique for using the root account while logged in as an ordinary user. Then you will work with user account management tasks, including creating new accounts, changing user passwords, and deleting user accounts. Next you will add a printer to Linux, and finally, you will learn about managing applications in Linux with the Red Hat Package Manager.

Using the Root Account

The root account must be used when creating and managing users, and when making system changes. While logged in as a regular user, you can log in as root without logging out. This is true both if you are working at the $ prompt and if you are working in a GUI.

Root Account at the Command Shell

Be careful when logged in as root. You have the ability to do anything you want to the system. Remember that Linux does not warn you when you are deleting files. This behavior is especially dangerous when you are logged in as root.

If you are logged in as an ordinary user and realize that you need to perform a task that requires superuser capabilities, enter the command **su root**, and then enter the root password. You will then have root permissions. The su command stands for substitute user, but if it helps you to remember the command, think of it as standing for "superuser," although it allows you to substitute the current user with any other user. If no user name is specified, then it is assumed that you are logging in as root. Figure 11-20 shows user jh logging in as root. The only clue you'll see that she is logged in as root is the # prompt that indicates the root account.

Using the Root Account in a GUI

When you are in the GNOME GUI in Linux, you can rely on it to give you the opportunity to log in as root any time you attempt to do a task that requires root privileges. For instance, if you attempt to run any of the programs on the GNOME System Setting menu, you will be prompted to log in as root. The dialog box in Figure 11-21 popped up when the Display item was selected from the System Settings menu. After entering the password, the Display Setting dialog box opened, and this is a lot friendlier than its command-line equivalent!

Managing Users

Linux allows several users to use one computer; but each user must have a unique account. As you learned earlier, at the time a user account is created,

```
[jh@classlab01 jh]$ su
Password:
[root@classlab01 jh]# _
```

• **Figure 11-20.** After logging in as root, the # prompt displays.

Linux also creates a home directory for the new user in which that user can save files, as well as create new subdirectories. Users can further protect files from other users by changing the permissions on files and folders in their home directories.

To manage users, you will need to learn how to create users, delete users, and change user passwords. For speed, we will create users at the command prompt. User accounts can be created from the command shell or from within a GUI, using a tool such as Red Hat User Manager, as shown in Figure 11-22.

We find it faster and more convenient to add and change users at the prompt than to do so using a GUI. Table 11-6 lists some useful commands for managing users.

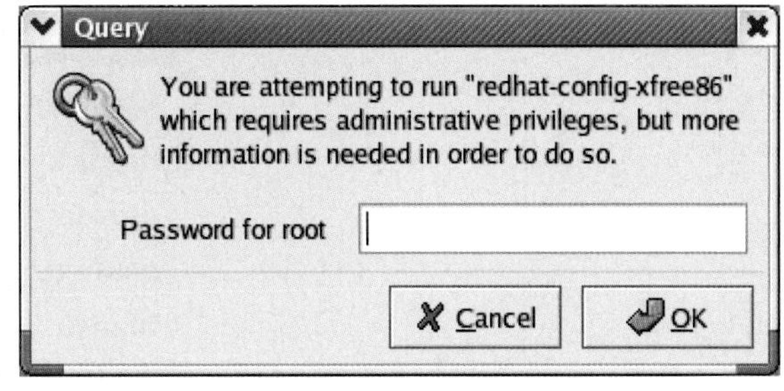

• **Figure 11-21.** GNOME dialog box warning requesting root password

Creating User Accounts

Before creating user accounts, you should determine at least an informal naming convention for creating user names—the names the users will use to log in. For ease of use, the user name should be short and, of course, it must be unique in the accounts database. A common rule is to use the first letter of the first name plus the last name, or a portion of the last name. From the command shell, use the `useradd` command to create a user. This command requires at least one parameter, the user name to be added. For instance, to create an account for Ashley Phoenix, using the user name of aphoenix, enter the command **useradd aphoenix**. To verify that the user account was created, use the `finger` command: **finger aphoenix**. See Figure 11-23.

Creating New Users

Practice creating user accounts for Ashley Phoenix, Jose Martinez, Kiesha Olson, and Beverly Chung. The naming convention method you will use for user name logins is a combination of the first letter of the first name with the last name, so the user names will be aphoenix, jmartinez, kolson, and bchung. Try this:

1. Log into the system as root. Start by creating one user, Ashley Phoenix.
2. Enter the command **useradd aphoenix**.
3. Confirm that the account was added by entering the command **finger aphoenix**.
4. Now add the remaining three names.

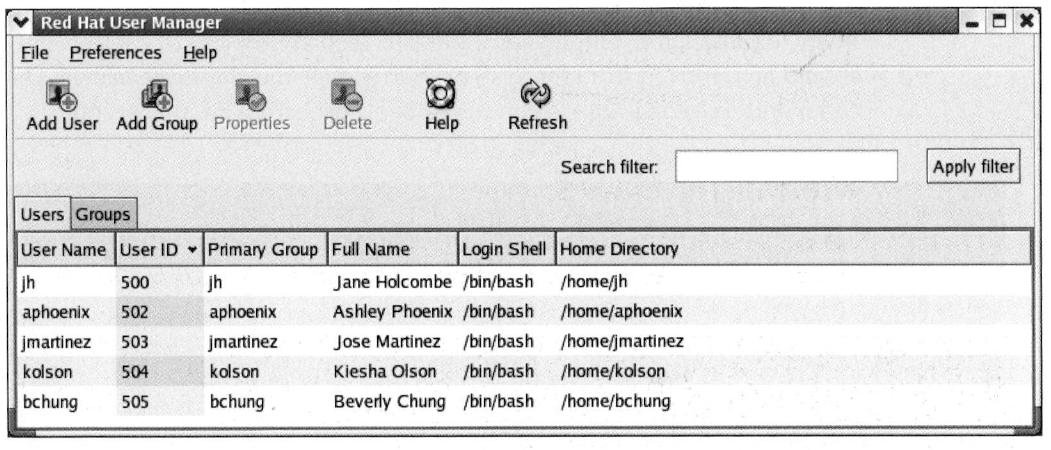

• **Figure 11-22.** A GUI tool for user management

Table 11-6	Shell Commands for User Management
Command	**Description**
useradd	Adds a user to the system
userdel	Removes a user from the system
passwd	Changes a user's password
finger	Finds a user name

Changing User Passwords

Setting up a user without a password is a bad idea. The password proves that it is truly user aphoenix who is logging in. Changing a user's password involves the command `passwd`. Entering **passwd** without any additional parameters will let you change your own password. Any user can change his or her password, but only root can change the password on other user accounts. For example, entering **passwd aphoenix** will enable the root account to change the password for the aphoenix account. The user logged in as root does not need to know the current password for the account before changing it to the new one, but can simply enter the new password twice. Figure 11-24 shows a successful password change. Note that, as always, Linux doesn't display passwords.

Try This!

Change a Password

Create passwords for the accounts you created. Try this:

1. Create passwords for Ashley Phoenix (aphoenix), Jose Martinez (jmartinez), Kiesha Olson (kolson) and Beverly Chung (bchung). Use the `passwd` command individually for each account.
2. Change the password for the root account. Enter the command **passwd** with no user name. Be sure to memorize this password!

Note that selecting passwords can be difficult. Linux will force the password to be complex. No password based on a word or popular character from fiction will work. We like to use the names of bands and albums. For example, Pink Floyd's *Dark Side of the Moon* is a nice basis for a password. Use the first letters of each word, and capitalize one word to get pfDsotm. This password is very hard to guess, and if you pick an album you like, you are unlikely to forget it.

Deleting Users

In any organization, employees leave. For security reasons, these accounts should be removed from the system shortly after the employee leaves. The command `userdel` allows you to remove a user from a Linux account.

```
[root@classlab01 root]# useradd aphoenix
[root@classlab01 root]# finger aphoenix
Login: aphoenix                                 Name: (null)
Directory: /home/aphoenix                       Shell: /bin/bash
Never logged in.
No mail.
No Plan.
[root@classlab01 root]# _
```

• **Figure 11-23.** Using the `useradd` command to create a user

```
[root@classlab01 root]# passwd aphoenix
Changing password for user aphoenix.
New password:
Retype new password:
passwd: all authentication tokens updated successfully.
[root@classlab01 root]# _
```

• **Figure 11-24.** Using root to change another account's password

The syntax for `userdel` is similar to that for `passwd` and `useradd`. You use this format: **userdel *username***

For example, you can remove the aphoenix account with the command **userdel aphoenix**.

Recall that every user gets a home directory in which to store his or her files. This directory is not removed when the user is deleted—you must remove these files manually. Linux does not provide a good command to handle this. You will need to delete the files contained in the home directory first and then delete the directory itself. However, if a directory has subdirectories, you first need to change into each subdirectory and delete all files in them as well. Once the files are deleted, you change directory to one level above and use the `rmdir` command. The syntax for `rmdir` is as follows: `rmdir` *`directoryname`*.

Step-by-Step 11.05

Deleting an Account

In this step-by-step, you will delete the account Ashley Phoenix.

To perform this exercise, you will need the following:

- An account on the system named aphoenix
- The root password

Step 1

Log into the Linux system as root. Delete the user by entering this command: **userdel aphoenix**. Wait for a moment while the command executes.

```
[root@classlab01 root]# userdel aphoenix
[root@classlab01 root]# _
```

Step 2

Change to aphoenix's home directory with the command **cd /home/aphoenix**. Enter **pwd** to verify that you have successfully changed to user aphoenix's directory.

Step 3

List all of user aphoenix's files. Be sure to include the hidden files. Enter the command **ls -a** to see all files.

```
[root@classlab01 root]# cd /home/aphoenix
[root@classlab01 aphoenix]# ls -a
.  ..  .bash_logout  .bash_profile  .bashrc  .emacs  .gtkrc  .kde
[root@classlab01 aphoenix]# _
```

Step 4

Delete all files in the aphoenix directory with the command **rm .***. Ignore the two lines that state "rm: cannot remove '.' or '..'." These are actually pointer files for the directory itself, and they will be removed later. Type **y** when prompted for each file name.

```
[root@classlab01 aphoenix]# rm .*
rm: cannot remove `.' or `..'
rm: cannot remove `.' or `..'
rm: remove regular file `.bash_logout'? y
rm: remove regular file `.bash_profile'? y
rm: remove regular file `.bashrc'? y
rm: remove regular file `.emacs'? y
rm: remove regular file `.gtkrc'? y
rm: remove directory `.kde'? y
rm: remove directory `.kde/Autostart'? y
rm: remove regular file `.kde/Autostart/Autorun.desktop'? y
rm: remove regular file `.kde/Autostart/.directory'? y
rm: remove directory `.kde/Autostart'? y
rm: remove directory `.kde'? y
[root@classlab01 aphoenix]# _
```

Step 5

Reenter **ls -a** to verify that all files are gone. The directory entries "**.**" and "**..**" should remain visible. If any files remain, use the `rm` command to delete them. If any directories remain, use the `cd` command to change into each directory and delete files.

Step 6

To remove a directory, use the `cd` command to move to the parent, and then use the `rmdir` command. For instance, if the aphoenix directory is totally empty (except for the "**.**" and "**..**", enter the command **cd /home**. To remove the aphoenix directory, enter the command **rmdir aphoenix**. Again list your files and verify that the aphoenix directory is gone.

```
[root@classlab01 aphoenix]# ls -a
.  ..
[root@classlab01 aphoenix]# cd /home
[root@classlab01 home]# rmdir aphoenix
[root@classlab01 home]# ls
bchung  brenda  jh  jmartinez  kolson
[root@classlab01 home]# _
```

Configuring a Printer

The users you added to the Linux computer will need some way to print. Linux supports many printers. Configuring printers requires the use of a program called Printtool. Like the Add Printer wizard in Windows, Printtool allows you to select the printer and the port to which the printer is attached. *Port* is a name for a connector on the back of a computer to which a peripheral device attaches. The port for most printers is LPT1 (the first parallel port), which in Linux is represented by `/dev/lp0`.

Notice the path reference for LPT1. Recall that in Linux, hardware devices are treated as files.

Printtool is best run in the GUI. Printtool is a command-line program that starts a GUI configuration program for your printer. Before you can run Printtool, you need to open a **terminal window** in GNOME. A terminal window is a window in a Linux GUI that provides a command line for entering

Linux shell commands. This will allow you to enter command-line Linux commands from within the GUI.

Printtool provides a wizard to help you create the printer. It asks you to describe how the printer is connected to the computer and to give the printer a name. Names are typically descriptive of the type of printer. For example, you might name your printer hp842c if you have a Hewlett-Packard 842c printer. You then pick the driver for the printer. Linux will suggest what it thinks will work. Unless you know differently, you should use the driver suggested by Linux. When the wizard finishes, you should print a test page. This verifies that your printer truly works.

Step-by-Step 11.06

Adding a Printer

In this step-by-step, you will add a printer driver and print queue to a Linux computer. The instructions show how to use the Printtool program for this purpose. Depending on the version of Linux you are using, the dialog boxes you see may vary from those shown.

To complete this exercise, you will need the following:

- A Linux computer
- The root password
- A printer attached to the computer

Step 1

Log in as root and start the GUI. After the desktop loads, open a terminal window. Right-click on the desktop and select New Terminal. At the prompt within the terminal window, enter the command **printtool**. After a short pause, the Printtool Printer Config window will open.

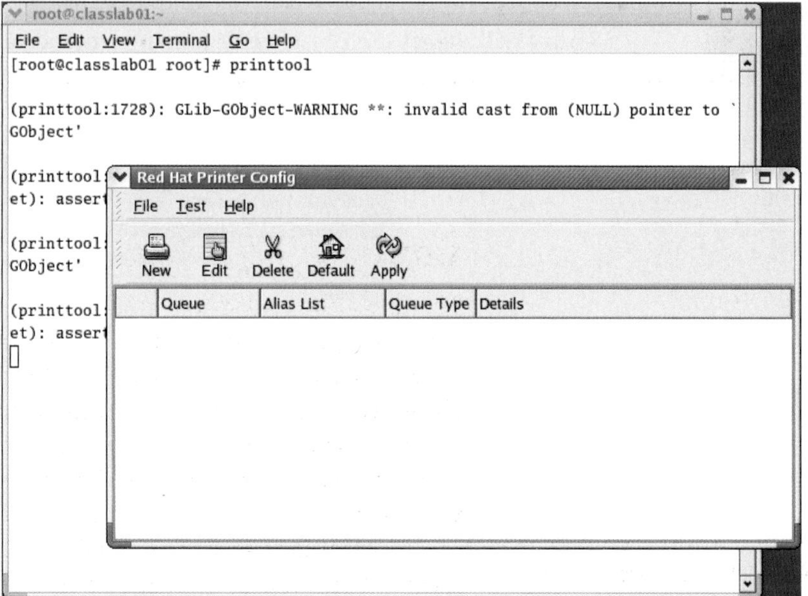

Step 2

Click the New button in the button bar of the Printer Config window. Click Next to start the configuration. In the Add A New Print Queue page, click Forward.

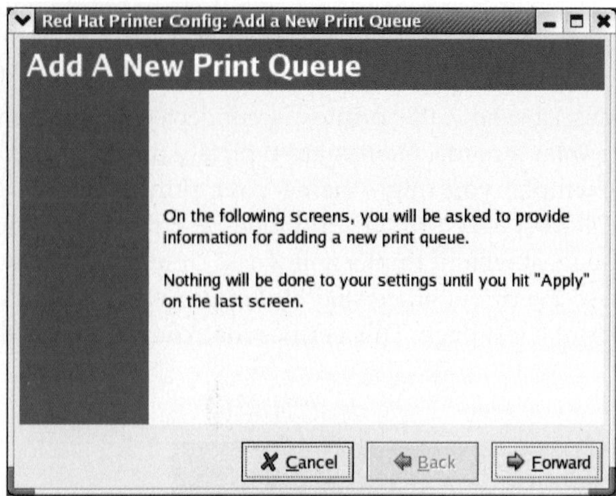

Step 3

Provide a name for the print queue, and select the queue type, which for this exercise should be Local Printer. When you have completed this page, click Forward.

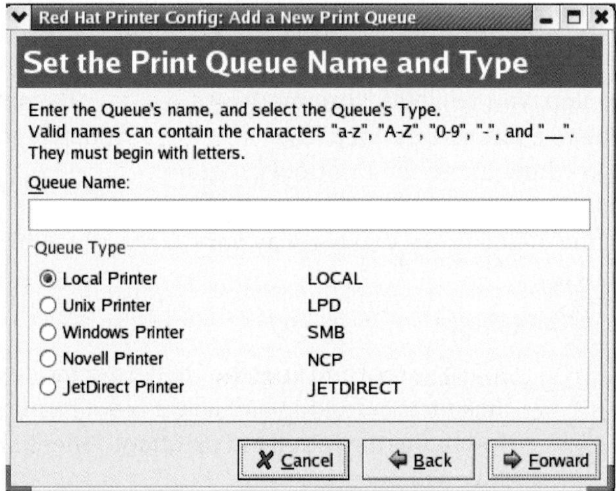

Step 4

Linux will detect the presence of a printer device and list it in the Configure A Local Printer page. Click Forward to the Select A Print Driver page, and scroll through the list to select a printer driver. Once you have selected a printer driver, click Forward.

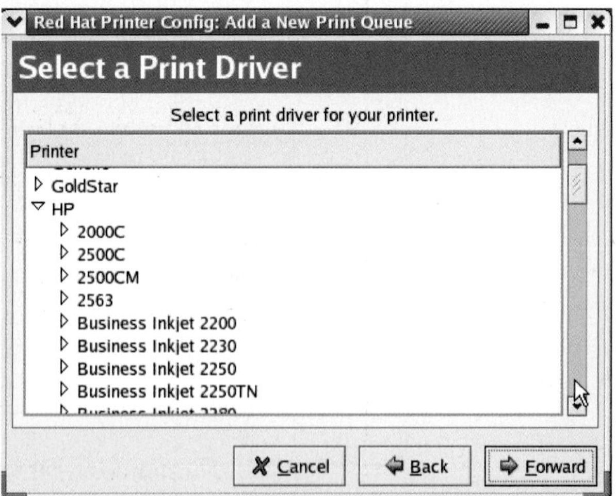

Step 5

In the Finish page, click Apply. The current window will close. Click the Red Hat Printer Config button on the panel to see the new printer listed. Close the open window when you are finished.

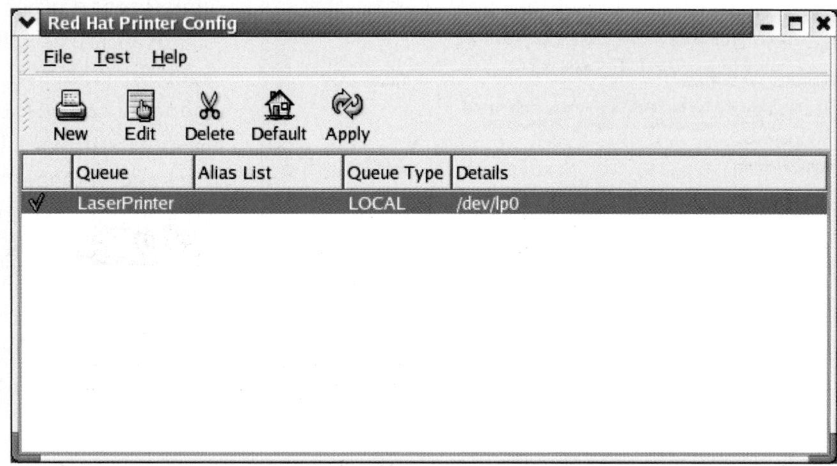

Installing Software

Only root can run the Package Manager and install software.

All this focus on learning Linux functions and commands should not lead you to believe that a Linux computer will meet all your needs without any additions. As with any operating system, you need to install the appropriate programs to accomplish work (or entertainment). When you install a bundled version of Linux, such as Red Hat or Mandrake, there are many, many programs to choose from during the installation. You can also go back to your distribution CDs and install more programs after installation.

Savvy Linux users know that many programs for Linux come in a special format referred to as an RPM package. RPM stands for **Red Hat Package Manager**, a system designed by Red Hat to standardize the processes of installing, uninstalling, and updating Linux software packages. Packages that can be used with RPM have all the program code and installation instructions compressed into a single file, and sometimes a package comes with additional update files. It is easy to identify an RPM package because it will have an RPM file extension. You will find

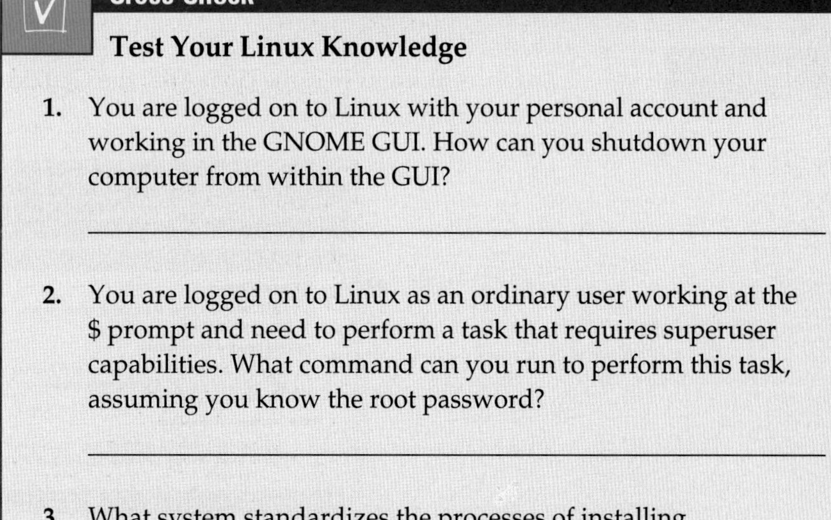

Cross Check

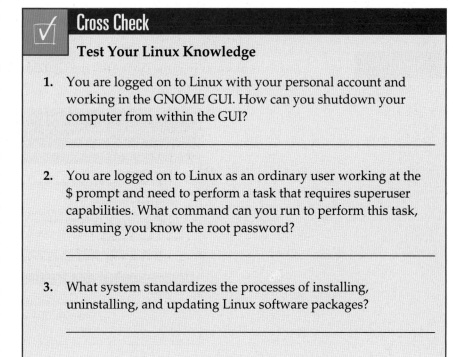

Test Your Linux Knowledge

1. You are logged on to Linux with your personal account and working in the GNOME GUI. How can you shutdown your computer from within the GUI?

   ____

2. You are logged on to Linux as an ordinary user working at the $ prompt and need to perform a task that requires superuser capabilities. What command can you run to perform this task, assuming you know the root password?

   ____

3. What system standardizes the processes of installing, uninstalling, and updating Linux software packages?

   ____

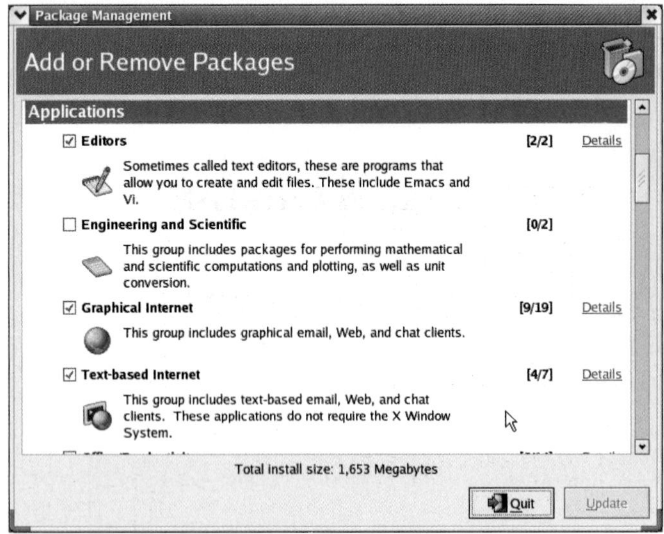

• **Figure 11-25.** Red Hat Package Manager

many such files on your Linux distribution CDs and at a large number of download sites on the Internet. Because Red Hat makes RPM available to other vendors, RPM packages are available for installation on other versions of Linux.

In a Linux GUI you should find a package manager. In GNOME in Red Hat Linux, the package manager can be found by selecting GNOME Menu | System Settings | Packages. Figure 11-25 shows the Package Management program. With this program, you do not have to search for the package file. You simply place a check mark next to the program or programs you wish to add to your computer. Further, Package Manager allows you to deselect programs you wish to uninstall. It works very much like Windows Add or Remove Programs.

Step-by-Step 11.07

Software Installation with RPM

In the following steps, you will install an application using Red Hat Package Manager. These steps describe the use of Red Hat Package Manager in Red Hat Linux using GNOME, but the steps will be similar in another GUI or another version of Linux.

To complete this exercise, you will need the following:

- A Linux computer with a GUI and RPM, or other package management program
- The Linux distribution CDs

Step 1

Log in as root and start the GUI. After the GUI desktop comes up, select GNOME Menu | System Settings | Packages.

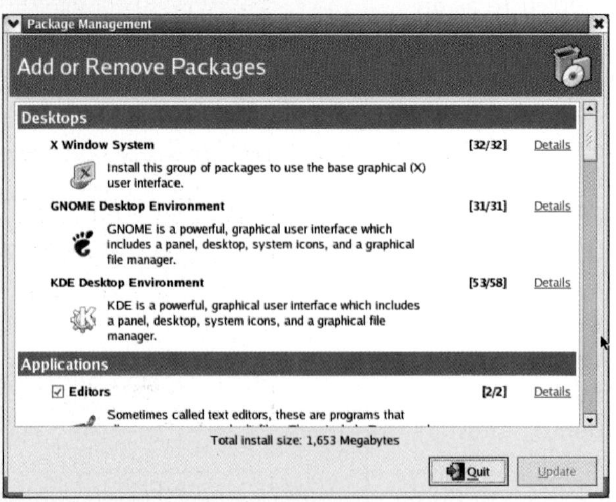

Step 2

Scroll through the Add Or Remove Packages page of Package Management, and locate an application group that has not been installed on your computer. Click a check box to place a check by the application group you wish to install. We selected Engineering And Scientific. Then click Update.

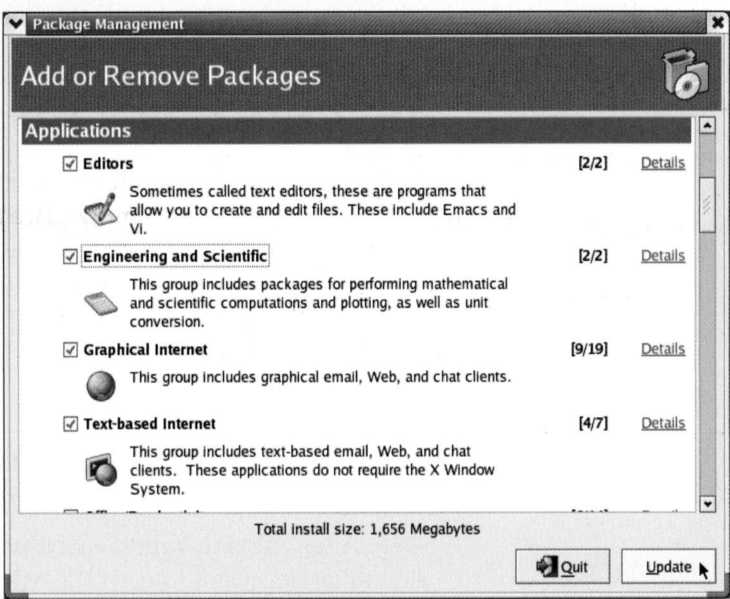

Step 3

After a brief delay during which a message window will open showing the progress, the system will be prepared for the installation, and the packages will be queued for installation. Click Continue.

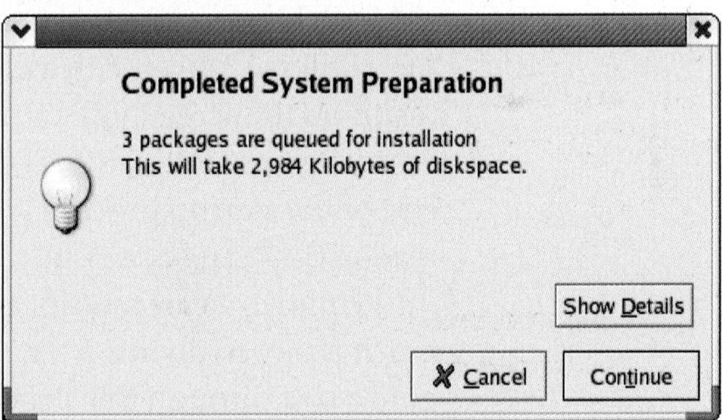

Step 4

When prompted, supply the appropriate distribution CD. If the CD requested is CD 1, be prepared to select No when asked if you wish to run autorun. The installation will proceed, and the Update Complete message box will be displayed. Click OK and remove the CD.

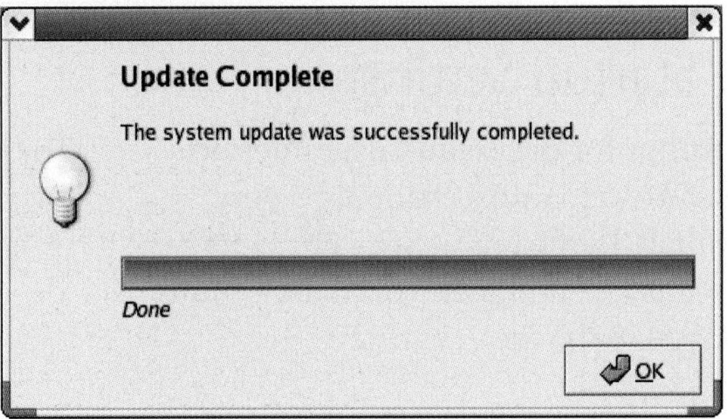

Troubleshooting Common Linux Problems

This section describes some typical problems you may encounter when using Linux, and some possible solutions.

The GNOME Will Not Start

Sometimes, the GNOME will not start. Typically, the problem is an improperly selected video card or monitor. It also may not start after a new video card or monitor is added. The solution is to run the Xconfigurator program in Red Hat distributions previous to version 8 or redhat-config-xfree86 in later versions. Both commands allow you to change the video and monitor drivers.

Make GNOME Start Automatically

When you installed Linux, you chose to have it start up to the command shell. After working with the GNOME desktop for some time, you've decided that you want to use GNOME instead of working at the command shell, and you would like it to start up automatically. To do so, you need to make a simple change to the /etc/inittab file.

Inittab is a text file that is read as a script by a Linux process at bootup. Included in the file are run levels that control how Linux behaves as it boots up. The two run levels we will look at here are 3 and 5. Runlevel 3 will result in Linux being started up in multi-user mode with networking. In the inittab file, runlevel 3 is set with a line that reads `id:3:initdefault:`. The visual result on the screen will be a command shell login. Runlevel 5 will result in Linux being started in a GUI, and it will display a GUI login prompt at the end of the startup process. In the inittab file, runlevel 5 is set with a line that reads `id:5:initdefault:`.

While you can modify this file using a command-line text editor, it is much easier to do this from within the GUI. The following step-by-step will guide you through this procedure.

Step-by-Step 11.08

Modify the Startup Settings

To change the settings for the default user interface that is chosen at startup requires changing a very important file, inittab. In the following steps, you will first back up this file, and then you will carefully make a small change in the file.

To complete this exercise, you will need the following:

- A Linux computer with a GUI

Step 1

Log in as root and start GNOME with the **startx** command. Double-click your home folder, and after the window opens, click the Up arrow in the button bar to move up to the root directory (/). From the root, navigate to the /etc folder.

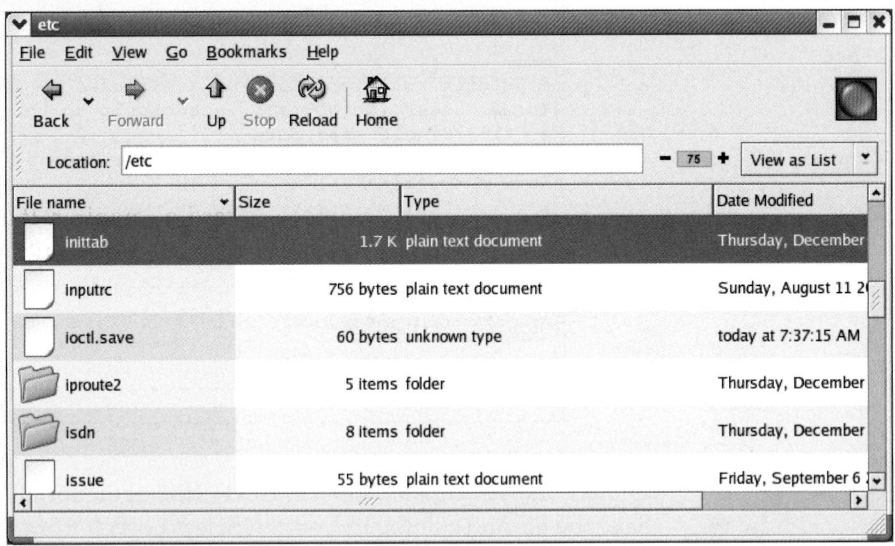

Step 2

Right-click on the inittab file and select Copy File. Right-click on an empty area of the desktop and select Paste Files.

Step 3

Return to the open window containing the etc folder, and right-click on the inittab file again. This time select Open With. On the Open With menu, select a text editor, such as gedit (our choice).

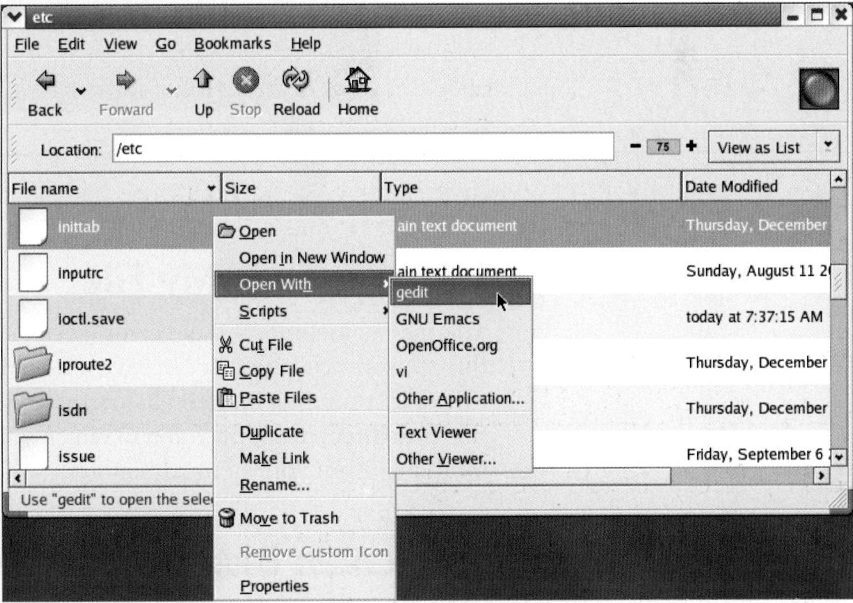

Step 4

In the text editor, scroll down until you find this line: `id:3:initdefault:`.

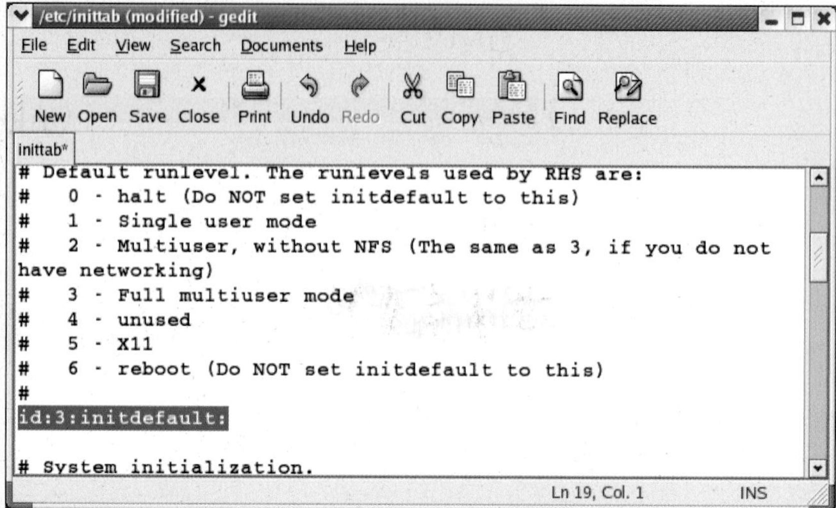

/etc/inittab (modified) - gedit
File Edit View Search Documents Help
New Open Save Close Print Undo Redo Cut Copy Paste Find Replace
inittab*
Default runlevel. The runlevels used by RHS are:
0 - halt (Do NOT set initdefault to this)
1 - Single user mode
2 - Multiuser, without NFS (The same as 3, if you do not have networking)
3 - Full multiuser mode
4 - unused
5 - X11
6 - reboot (Do NOT set initdefault to this)
#
id:3:initdefault:
System initialization.
Ln 19, Col. 1
INS

Step 5

Replace the 3 with a 5. This forces X11 (the name for all Linux GUIs) to run at bootup. Save the file and exit the text editor. Select Logout from the GNOME menu and then select Restart. After a delay while the system shuts down and reloads, you will see a GUI screen with a login dialog box.

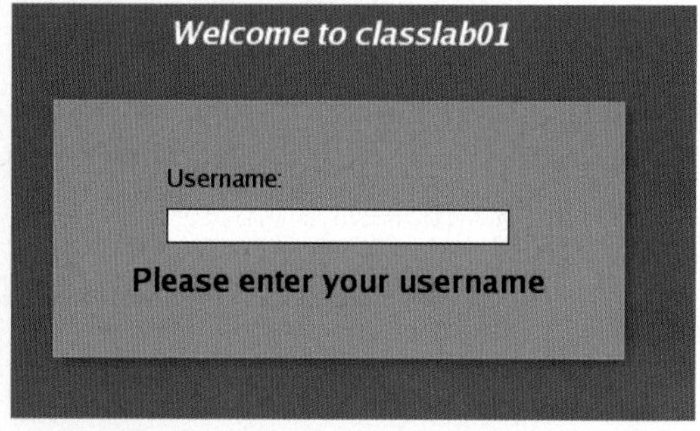

I Cannot Save My File

You may sometimes see the error screen shown in Figure 11-26. Typically, this appears when you try to save a file anywhere but in your home directory or in a subdirectory you have created in your home directory. The solution is to direct the application in which you are working to save the file in a location within your home directory.

A.out is written in machine language. This is actually binary code. The reason you see characters is that some of the binary instructions in the file happen to match ASCII values.

My Screen Displays Gibberish

Does your screen display gibberish? This error usually occurs when you use the `head` or `cat` command on a file that contains nontext data. Figure 11-27 shows the results of entering a `head` command for the file a.out.

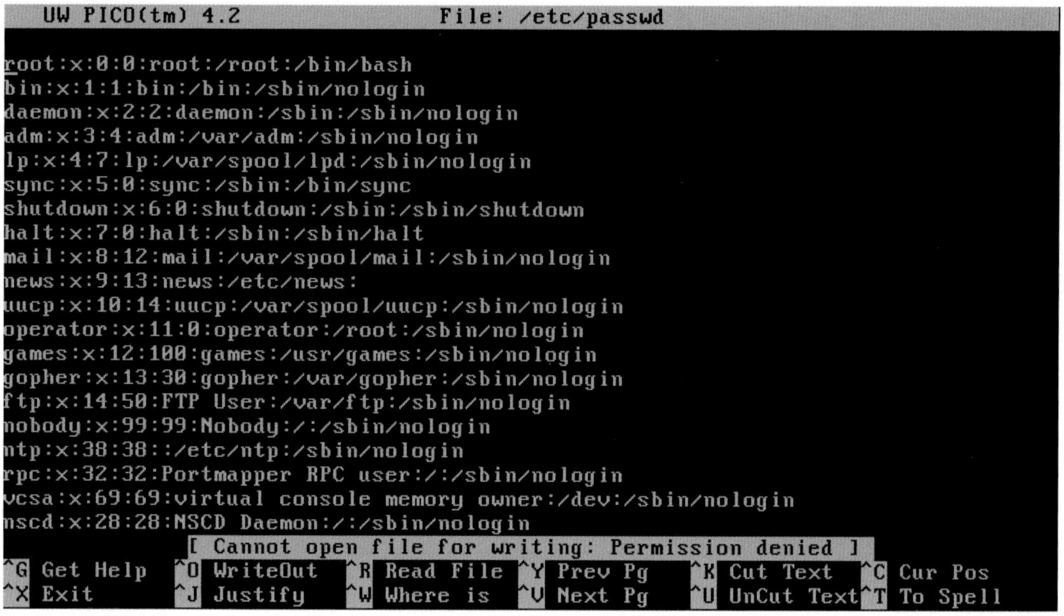

```
  UW PICO(tm) 4.2                    File: /etc/passwd

root:x:0:0:root:/root:/bin/bash
bin:x:1:1:bin:/bin:/sbin/nologin
daemon:x:2:2:daemon:/sbin:/sbin/nologin
adm:x:3:4:adm:/var/adm:/sbin/nologin
lp:x:4:7:lp:/var/spool/lpd:/sbin/nologin
sync:x:5:0:sync:/sbin:/bin/sync
shutdown:x:6:0:shutdown:/sbin:/sbin/shutdown
halt:x:7:0:halt:/sbin:/sbin/halt
mail:x:8:12:mail:/var/spool/mail:/sbin/nologin
news:x:9:13:news:/etc/news:
uucp:x:10:14:uucp:/var/spool/uucp:/sbin/nologin
operator:x:11:0:operator:/root:/sbin/nologin
games:x:12:100:games:/usr/games:/sbin/nologin
gopher:x:13:30:gopher:/var/gopher:/sbin/nologin
ftp:x:14:50:FTP User:/var/ftp:/sbin/nologin
nobody:x:99:99:Nobody:/:/sbin/nologin
ntp:x:38:38::/etc/ntp:/sbin/nologin
rpc:x:32:32:Portmapper RPC user:/:/sbin/nologin
vcsa:x:69:69:virtual console memory owner:/dev:/sbin/nologin
nscd:x:28:28:NSCD Daemon:/:/sbin/nologin
              [ Cannot open file for writing: Permission denied ]
^G Get Help  ^O WriteOut  ^R Read File ^Y Prev Pg   ^K Cut Text  ^C Cur Pos
^X Exit      ^J Justify   ^W Where is  ^V Next Pg   ^U UnCut Text^T To Spell
```

• **Figure 11-26.** Error screen in an application indicating trouble saving a file

This is not an error—it is simply the result of trying to view executable or binary code. The code is written in a language that your CPU can understand—but you can't.

Often, after a gibberish display, your prompt and input will be messed up. Linux is now confused and displays the wrong characters. The last line of Figure 11-27 is an attempt to type `ls` at the $ prompt. The easiest way to fix this problem is to log out and then in again.

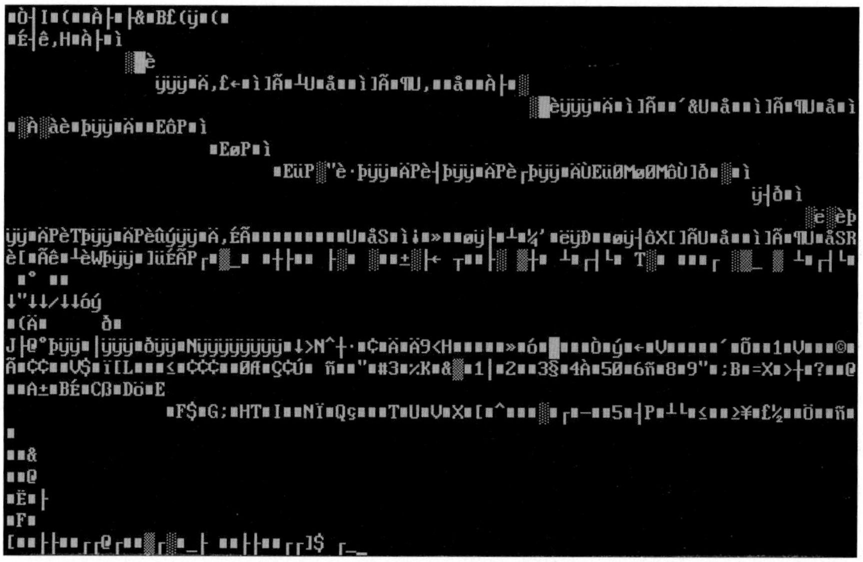

• **Figure 11-27.** Results of entering a `head` command for a.out

Command Not Found Error

When working at the command shell, you are almost guaranteed to see the error "Command not found." The number one cause of such an error is typos. Use the UP ARROW on the keyboard to move up through the command-line history and double-check the string you entered. Use the LEFT ARROW and RIGHT ARROW keys to move through the line and correct your error. Press ENTER when you are ready to test the corrected command.

Chapter 11 Review

■ Chapter Summary

After reading this chapter and completing the Step-by-Step tutorials and Try This! exercises, you should understand the following facts about Linux:

Linux Overview

- Linux, originally created by Linus Torvalds, is free, open-source software that is like UNIX in stability and function.
- Many versions of Linux exist for all types of computers, and Linux is often used on web servers.
- Linux benefits include cost (it is free or inexpensively bundled), the ability to run on old hardware, speed, and stability.
- Drawbacks of Linux include lack of centralized support, limited software selection, limited hardware support, and complexity.
- Use Linux when cost, stability, and security are major factors, such as in schools, or any time an inexpensive web server is required. It is also a great platform for web development.

Installing Linux

- Acquire Linux from many sources, including free downloads and inexpensive bundles from such vendors as Mandrake, Red Hat, Slackware, and SuSE (Novell).
- Decide how to install—clean installation, upgrade, or dual-boot.
- Keep the installation simple, and fine-tune it later, especially as far as undetected devices go.
- Linux memory requirements are small compared to Windows operating systems.
- While the OS itself has minimal hard disk space requirements, many distributions come with a large number of packages that will greatly increase hard disk space needs.
- Verify that the version of Linux you are installing is compatible with your hard disk controller.
- Linux supports all standard video graphics adapters and monitors, supports the use of a mouse, primarily in graphics interfaces, and supports many printers, modems, and network adapters.
- Be prepared to work with the root account (super user) before installing Linux; give this account a strong password, and only use it when you need to perform system maintenance tasks, such as changing the configuration or installing software packages.
- When planning for a dual-boot installation, plan to give each operating system a separate hard disk partition.
- You can boot into a Linux installation program from a bootable CD. If this is not possible, then create a bootable floppy disk to boot using the raw write program usually available with the installation files.
- The Red Hat installation program can be run in GUI mode, providing online help in a pane onscreen throughout the process.

Basic Linux Skills

- Linux requires authentication via a login—either in the command shell or in a GUI.
- Whether you are logging in from the command shell or a GUI, a Linux password never shows on the screen, and the cursor does not move while you type in the password.
- When an ordinary user logs into the command shell, the prompt consists of the user name and the computer name (hostname) separated by an @ sign, followed again by the user name. The second instance of your user name indicates the current directory. All this is contained within square brackets and followed by a $ sign. This is often called the $ (dollar) prompt.
- When the root account logs in at the command shell, the prompt is similar, but ends with a # sign.
- Log out of Linux by typing **exit** at the $ prompt, which allows you to leave Linux without shutting down.
- Only root can shut down Linux from the command line. This is accomplished with the `shutdown` command, which has many switches (that change the outcome of a command). Entering **shutdown -h now** tells Linux to shut down immediately and then to halt after shutting down.

Working with Linux Commands

- The Linux shell is called BASH, while the DOS shell is COMMAND.COM.
- Linux is case sensitive, while DOS is case *in*sensitive.
- A switch is a subcommand that changes the outcome of a command. Switches in DOS are preceded by a forward slash (/), while switches in Linux are preceded by a hyphen (-).
- DOS will allow you to forget a space before a switch, but Linux requires that each part of a command-line entry be separated by a space.
- In DOS a full path to a file or directory begins with a drive letter, but Linux does not use drive letters.
- Each device in Linux is also shown as part of the file system, as in /dev/sda0 (the first hard drive on a SCSI interface).
- Linux, like DOS, provides very little feedback at the command shell.
- The Linux command-line syntax is *command -switch parameter*. You may also combine switches and have more than one parameter, depending on the command.
- Linux saves command-line history during a command shell session, which allows you to use the UP ARROW and DOWN ARROW keys to retrieve and reuse commands you have used since you logged in.
- Linux also provides command completion that will complete part of the command line, particularly if it recognizes a portion of a directory path. Use the TAB key to retrieve the rest of a directory name.
- The `man` command gives you access to the Linux shell commands help manual.

Manage Files and Directories with Shell Commands

- File management is crucial, particularly since everything in Linux is a file.
- Linux has several directories for system files and a home directory for each user.
- Your home directory is the only place you can save files, and when you log in, this directory becomes your current (or working) directory.
- Your home directory path is /home/*username*. A shorthand for this path in a shell command is ~.
- The /bin directory within your home director contains many of the Linux commands.
- The /etc directory contains settings and configuration data for your Linux computer.
- There are many other directories created for the use of the system, and an ordinary user cannot access these directories.
- The `ls` command is the Linux equivalent of the DOS command DIR, because it lists the contents of a directory.
- The `cd` command allows you to change the current directory.
- The `more` command displays a file one screen at a time.
- You can use special symbols with the shell commands to navigate to directories that are relative to your current directory. The double dot (..) refers to one level up, the single dot (.) refers to the current directory, and the tilde (~) refers to the home directory.
- The asterisk (*) is used as a wildcard to replace all the characters from the point at which the asterisk is placed to the end of the name.
- Square brackets can be used with the asterisk to include a range of characters to precede the wildcard.
- Linux also allows you to use the dollar sign ($) to represent a single character within a file name.
- The `mkdir` command creates directories.
- The `cp` command copies files.
- A text editor works with plain text.
- Pico, vi, and emacs are text editors that come with some distributions of Linux.
- The `rm` command deletes a file. The `mv` command renames or moves files.
- The `more`, `head`, `less`, `tail`, and `cat` commands can be used to view files.
- Use permission attributes on files and folders to control access to them.
- The permissions include r (read), w (write), x (execute), and - (disabled).
- Use the `chmode` command to modify attributes, based on mode number.
- Permission attribute modes are 1 (execute), 2 (write), and 4 (read).

Use a GUI Desktop in Linux

- GNOME and KDE are Linux GUIs.
- Many Linux GUIs use the X Window System for their underlying program code.
- To run the GNOME from the command shell, enter the command **startx**.
- The GNOME GUI resembles Windows and Apple Mac OS interfaces with windows, icons, menus, folder icons, and other familiar GUI objects.
- The GNOME Workspace Switcher lets you switch between different sets of applications.

Configure Linux

- The root account must be used to create and manage users, and to make system changes.
- When logged in as an ordinary user, use the `su` command to log on as another user (most often root).
- When logged in as an ordinary user in a GUI, you will automatically be prompted to provide the root password anytime you attempt to perform a root-only function.
- The `useradd` command creates a user at the command prompt.
- The `finger` command displays information about a user.
- The `passwd` command changes user passwords.
- The `userdel` command deletes a user, but it does not delete the associated home directory. The home directories must be manually deleted by root.
- The LPT1 port is represented by the file /dev/lp0.
- The Printtool utility is used in either the command shell or in the GUI to install printers into Linux.
- Many programs for Linux come in a special format so that they can be installed and managed with the Red Hat Package Manager (RPM), a system designed by Red Hat.
- An RPM package has a file extension of RPM. These packages are available from many sources and will install in any version of Linux with Red Hat Package Manager or a similar system.
- When installing software in a Linux GUI, look for a package manager; it will work very much like Windows Add or Remove Programs.

Troubleshoot Common Linux Problems

- Video problems are solved using the XConfigurator.
- To change the behavior of Linux at startup, modify the inittab file and provide the correct run level.
- You must have permission to save a file in a directory.
- Displaying a binary file results in garbage on the screen.
- The "Command Not Found Error" usually results from a typo at the command prompt.

Key Terms

$ prompt *(550)*
access mode number *(569)*
BASH *(552)*
boot image *(544)*
GNOME *(572)*
GNU *(537)*
home directory *(556)*
ISO image *(538)*
Linux *(535)*
open-source software *(538)*
owner *(568)*
panel *(572)*
raw write *(544)*
Red Hat *(536)*
Red Hat Package Manager *(583)*
root *(543)*
shell *(551)*
shell command *(551)*
superuser *(543)*
terminal window *(580)*
X Window System *(572)*

■ Key Terms Quiz

Use the Key Terms list to complete the sentences that follow. Not all terms will be used.

1. To access the command line in GNOME, you start a ____________.
2. GNOME and KDE are Linux GUIs that use the ____________.
3. When you are logged in as an ordinary (non-root) user, you enter commands at the ____________.
4. When a user is created in Linux, the OS creates a ____________ on disk for that user.
5. If you cannot boot from CD to begin the Linux installation, use the raw write utility to place a ____________ onto a floppy disk.
6. The `startx` command will start the ____________ GUI, provided it is installed in Linux.
7. The ____________ organization was created for the purpose of developing a free UNIX-like operating system.
8. A ____________ is a command that must be entered at the command prompt.
9. ____________ is distributed with all of its source code, which allows the purchaser to customize the software as necessary.
10. The most powerful account in Linux has the login name of ____________.

■ Multiple-Choice Quiz

1. Linux is modeled on which operating system?
   - **a.** Windows
   - **b.** UNIX
   - **c.** NT
   - **d.** VMS
   - **e.** CP/M
2. If the access mode number for the owner drops below this on some Linux installations, any future access to this file is blocked.
   - **a.** 5
   - **b.** 8
   - **c.** 1
   - **d.** 7
   - **e.** 6
3. Who was the initial developer responsible for Linux?
   - **a.** Ken Thompson
   - **b.** Linus Torvalds
   - **c.** Steve Jobs
   - **d.** Dennis Ritchie
   - **e.** Fred Cohen
4. Which user has the most power and privileges in Linux?
   - **a.** Administrator
   - **b.** Admin
   - **c.** Absolute
   - **d.** Root
   - **e.** Linus
5. What is the command a user invokes to leave (log off) Linux from the command shell?
   - **a.** `exit`
   - **b.** `shutdown`
   - **c.** `bye`
   - **d.** `log off`
   - **e.** `quit`
6. What is the Linux command to copy a file?
   - **a.** `cpy`
   - **b.** `rm`
   - **c.** `mv`
   - **d.** `copy`
   - **e.** `cp`
7. What switch for the `ls` command lists all files in a directory, including the hidden files?
   - **a.** `-s`
   - **b.** `-f`
   - **c.** `-l`

d. `-a`

e. `-t`

8. What is the command to turn off Linux?

a. `down`

b. `shutdown`

c. `exit`

d. `off`

e. `power`

9. When you are using pico, what is the key combination to save a file?

a. CTRL-O

b. CTRL-S

c. CTRL-D

d. CTRL-W

e. CTRL-V

10. What command displays only the first ten lines of a file?

a. `more`

b. `begin`

c. `tail`

d. `top`

e. `head`

11. Which command displays a text file, one page at a time?

a. `mkdir`

b. `more`

c. `pwd`

d. `pico`

e. `rm`

12. Why is Linux fast?

a. It uses resources efficiently.

b. It only runs on Pentium III or newer.

c. Linux is graphics-intensive.

d. It has no security.

e. It only runs in real mode.

13. Which Linux command would you use to change file permissions?

a. `cd`

b. `ls`

c. `cp`

d. `chmod`

e. `head`

14. Why would you use the command line rather than the GNOME when you are creating and changing users?

a. The command line is more intuitive.

b. GNOME is too cryptic.

c. The command line is faster.

d. The command line is more secure.

e. You cannot create users from GNOME.

15. What tool is recommended for installing and configuring a printer in Linux?

a. Control Panel

b. Add Printer wizard

c. Port

d. LPT1

e. Printtool

■ Essay Quiz

1. List and explain the reasons that Linux has not yet taken over the desktop OS market.
2. Discuss how Linux could be used in your school or at work.
3. Discuss how open-source software can benefit an organization.
4. The Helping Hand, a charitable organization, has asked you to set up its computer systems. The organization has a very limited budget. Describe how Linux can allow users to be productive while costing very little.
5. You try to start the GNOME for the first time on your Linux computer, but it fails. Explain what you learned that may be the most likely problem, and how you will resolve it. Be sure to explain how the tool you use works.

Lab Projects

• Lab Project 11.1

Linux and Windows products can share disks. You would like to back up your files to a Windows computer. In particular, you wish to copy the .bash_profile file in your home directory to a Windows computer. Use `man` to learn the mtools suite. Copy the .bash_profile file to a floppy disk for use in a Windows computer.

• Lab Project 11.2

Use the network configuration tool in GNOME to set up a NIC for use on a LAN. You will need to create a hostname, IP address, net mask, and default gateway. Your instructor will supply you with the appropriate information for your lab. If no settings are available, use the following values for a statically set IP address:

Setting	Value
Hostname	Your name
Address	192.168.110.30
Net mask	255.255.255.0
Default gateway	192.168.110.1

The program is found by choosing Panel | Programs | System | Network Configuration. You will need to add an Ethernet connection.

Macintosh OS X

chapter 12

People tell you about their great vision. I honestly say that the only guy I've ever met—well, I've met two guys. Paul Allen has some vision and Steve Jobs has some vision.

—Bill Gates

We have been talking for 11 chapters now about operating systems in general, and we have specifically covered a number of Microsoft Windows OSs as well as Linux. Other companies make OSs as well, and now we will discuss the Macintosh OS by Apple Computer.

In this chapter, you will explore the Macintosh OS X operating system, beginning with a history of this OS. You will learn how to install it, and then get to know the features of the Mac OS workspace. You will practice managing drives, files, printers, and users, and then take a look at troubleshooting common Mac OS problems.

In this chapter, you will learn how to:

- **Describe the history of Apple and the Mac OS**
- **Install and configure Mac OS X**
- **Use the features of the Mac desktop**
- **Get to know the Mac OS X workspace**
- **Troubleshoot common Mac OS problems**

Introducing Apple and the Macintosh Operating System

Come explore the Mac OS, its history and place in the world of computing, and learn about the main features of Apple's OS X.

Courtesy Apple Computer

- Power Mac G5

A Colorful Contribution to the World of Computing

Apple Computer was founded on April 1, 1976, when high school friends Stephen Wozniak and Steven Jobs began marketing the Apple I computer from a garage in Los Altos, California. In those days, personal computing was a hobby industry, and the initial reception to the Apple I was lukewarm. The following year's version, the Apple II, was a different story. Debuting at a local trade show, it was the first personal computer to come in a plastic case and include color graphics, which is not to say that it had a graphical interface. In 1983, Apple launched the Lisa, the first production computer to use a graphical user interface (GUI). The following year Apple launched the Macintosh 128k with much fanfare—the first *affordable* personal computer with a GUI.

Courtesy Apple Computer

- Two versions of the iMac. Tasteful? Beauty is in the eye of the beholder.

From these earliest incarnations—credited with popularizing the personal computer beyond the world of techies—to the Smithsonian Institution's awarding of the National Design Award in 2000 to the admittedly not always tasteful but certainly colorful iMac, Apple computers have without question had a profound impact on the computer industry and have inspired a strong community of proponents.

Macintosh Characteristics

One of the quirks of Apple's history is that, barring one experiment lasting from 1993 to 1997, Apple has never licensed its OS to any other hardware manufacturer, thus irrevocably binding together the OS and the often interesting looking boxes it comes in. This has tended to make the Mac "the sum of more than its parts" in the minds of its dedicated users—and is also noted as one of the key contributing factors to Apple's small overall market share in total units sold.

Although Apple accounts for only a small percentage of the overall market, in the fields they specialize in, such as graphics, commercial publishing, multimedia software development, and the education sector, its market share is much more significant. Because of its fine hardware and hallmark easy-to-use OS, Apple has disproportionately penetrated niche markets.

With its latest operating system, OS X (referred to as either OS "ten" or OS "X" and initially launched in March 2001), Apple has further refined its user interface while placing it on top of a UNIX system, offering increased stability, networking potential, and security.

OS X was so revolutionary that it has been quickly adopted by those who can make the change. OS 9 remains the OS of choice for those with less capable hardware or who use OS 9–dependent applications that run too slowly in the Classic compatibility mode of OS X. In this chapter, we will focus on OS X. As with most other personal computers, Macintosh operating systems share common metaphors such as the desktop, files and folders, and the trash can. Similarly, hardware falls into certain types.

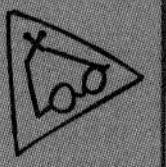

Inside Information

Why the Name "Mac"?

*The nickname for Apple's computers, "**Mac**," comes from its 1984 model: the Macintosh 128k. The Mac was the first computer in which Apple invested serious mainstream advertising dollars and was the first* affordable *computer boasting a GUI, originally selling for $2,495. Apple's seminal and infamous 1984-style, anti-IBM Super Bowl commercial for the Macintosh 128k was directed by Ridley Scott, well known at the time for cult films* Alien *(1979) and* Blade Runner *(1982). The commercial can be viewed by pointing your web browser to* `apple-history.com` *and selecting the link to the 1984 commercial found in the timeline.*

Built-in Multimedia Hardware and Software in the Mac OS

Apple's standard inclusion of what has historically been considered by other hardware manufacturers to be *optional* multimedia elements has tended to make Mac users low maintenance insofar as their technical needs are concerned, compared with users of other operating systems.

The authors of Mac's operating systems have typically had to consider only one or two hardware platforms, built with basically the same architecture, which makes problems such as component-software conflicts less likely to be issues than with PCs running Windows, which require that the operating systems be designed to work on hardware manufactured by a host of other companies.

Macs have contained sound cards, the hardware interface that allows your computer to accept and output high-fidelity audio, from surprisingly early in their history. In fact, if you mention the phrase "sound card" to Mac users, many will not understand what you're talking about; a sound card was never presented to them as an option when purchasing their computers, but was included as standard. This is a manifestation of a far harder-to-quantify aspect of the Mac OS: its ease of use.

The standard hardware and software configurations that Macs are distributed with are sufficient to organize a music or photo collection, edit home video, and burn CDs and DVDs. Apple raised the bar, and the personal computer industry followed suit, making multimedia features and support for writeable CDs and DVDs standard on most consumer Windows desktops. Ultimately, the computer you choose these days—Apple or PC—matters less and less, as companies rush to match and better their competitors, usually within a matter of months.

Inside Information

The Hills Are Alive with the Sound of...Data Backup?

Burning CD-Rs and DVD-Rs is not just a feature for users who want to work with music and home video! Both of these media offer a cheap storage solution for data backup. CD-Rs typically cost just pennies apiece when bought in bulk and hold up to 800MB of data. DVD-Rs are more expensive at present, but can hold a staggering 4.7GB of data.

Ease of Use of the Mac OS

Elijah, age six, is an experienced Mac user. He has used educational software on his mother's Mac since age three, when he apparently picked up the mouse skills just from observing his mother and did as well as his toddler eye-hand coordination would allow. The Mac OS interface is as simple as possible, involving users with as little of the back-end functionality as possible. In hardware terms, this has meant delivery of a minimum system configuration of computers that contains many extras as standard.

In software terms, the Mac OS has tended to minimize user intervention as much as possible. Elijah's mother knows when she buys new software that all she has to do is insert the disk, and the program will be installed automatically with very little intervention. During software installations, the user is typically asked the fewest questions needed to complete the task. If you compare Windows and Mac installation instructions in software booklets, you'll find that Mac instructions typically are shorter.

Macs—with their single-source hardware, operating system, and software—tend to break only when they're really broken, rather than because someone did something to something while adding a new component or installing some new software. This is an advantage of single-source hardware and software manufacturers.

Installing and Configuring Mac OS X

This section details the process of installing and configuring Mac OS X, including the minimum hardware and software requirements, installation process, and system configuration options following installation. If you purchase a new computer with Mac OS X preinstalled, the OS will be installed, but not configured. In that case, you begin with Step 6 in the following step-by-step.

Minimum Requirements

Anyone purchasing a new Apple Mac computer will have Mac OS X preinstalled, but many people with existing Macs will upgrade to this greatly improved OS. Therefore, we will begin by discussing the minimum OS required to upgrade to OS X. Then you will see in the following sections that the official Mac OS X minimum hardware requirements are higher than those typically published by Microsoft for its Windows OSs. This is mostly because of the Mac's more multimedia-focused basic hardware platform.

Try This!

Determine Which Version of the Mac OS Is Installed

It is simple to check out the version of Mac OS installed. Try this:

1. Log into a Macintosh computer, and click an empty area of the desktop.
2. Click the Apple menu in the top-left corner of your desktop, and select About This Computer or About This Mac. The screen that pops up shows which version of the Mac OS is installed.

Software Requirements When Upgrading

To use OS 9 applications from within OS X, you need at least OS 9.1 installed on your computer before installing OS X. If your OS is not up to this level, a message will appear at the beginning of the OS X installation process stating that you can upgrade after the installation of OS X. You can upgrade your computer from the Mac OS 9.1 CD included with OS X, or you can download the update from Apple's Software Update web site. For more information see `www.apple.com/macosx/upgrade/`.

To be prepared, verify the version of Mac OS before installing OS X. Simply open the Apple menu, and select either About This Computer or About This Mac (depending on the version), and the version information will display.

Before you start the installation of OS X, you may need to update your computer's firmware. Check whether a Firmware Updater is available for your computer on the OS X CD. If you find one, undertake the update process before you install Mac OS X. A good resource for firmware information is Apple's Support site (`www.apple.com/support/`).

• Mac OS version information from the Apple menu

Hardware Requirements

The minimum hardware requirements for installing Mac OS X are shown in Table 12-1. We view these requirements as realistic for most functions, but you will want to beef up the memory and hard disk space if you plan to regularly undertake image or video editing with your computer.

Table 12-1	Minimum Hardware Requirements for OS X
Computer	Power Macintosh G3; PowerBook G3 (except the original PowerBook G3, distinguished by the rainbow-colored Apple logo on its outside case—PowerBook G3s with a white logo are compatible but may require a firmware update); Power Mac G4; PowerBook G4; iMac G4; iBook; iMacG5; Power Mac G5; PowerBook G5.
Hard disk	1.5GB or more disk space available. Installation of Mac OS X on FireWire or USB disks is not fully supported by Apple. In the case of earlier PowerBooks, OS X needs to be installed on a partition that falls within the first 8MB of the hard disk.
RAM	128MB or more.
Video card	Internal monitor support or an Apple-supplied IXMicro, ATI, or NVidia video card.

Inside Information

Blast from the Past: System Requirements for OS 9

Compared to OS X, OS 9 has light dietary needs. If you find yourself with very old Macs and only the earliest versions of OS 9 available to install, this list details what you will need as a minimum.

- *Mac OS–based Apple computer with a PowerPC processor (PowerPC upgrade cards and 680X0 processors and OS X Server are* not *supported)*
- *150 to 250MB of free disk space for an easy installation (the universal installation can be as large as 400MB)*
- *40MB of RAM*

Step-by-Step 12.01

Installing Mac OS X

In this step-by-step exercise, you will install Mac OS X and create a configuration necessary for a typical user. To complete this exercise, you will need the following:

- A Mac computer with any version of OS 9 installed, 9.1 if you want to complete the installation without interruption to update to OS 9.1
- A user name and password that will allow you to log into your computer
- The OS X installation CD

Step 1

Insert the OS X CD and double-click the Install Mac OS X icon. When prompted to restart the computer, click the Restart button. If the Installer does not open, restart your computer while holding down the C key on your keyboard.

Step 2

The OS X installer loads. This may take several minutes, depending on your system. In the Select Language window that appears, click the radio button for the main language you want to use on your computer and then click Continue.

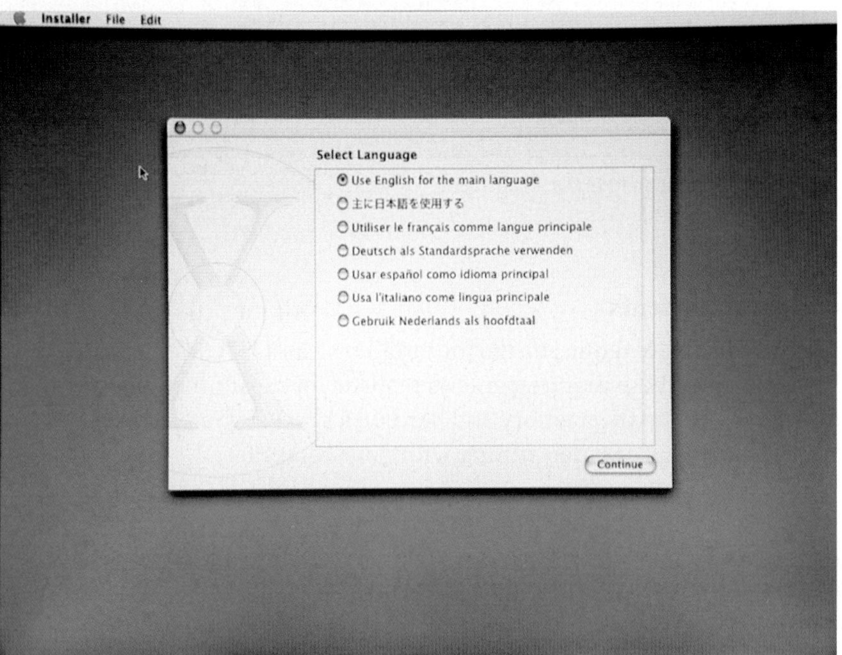

Step 3

In the Welcome To The Mac OS X Installer window, read Important Information About OS X and then click Continue. Read the information in the Software License Agreement window and then click Continue. A dialog box appears, asking if you agree to the terms. Click Agree.

Step 4

The Select A Destination window appears asking you to select a destination disk on which to install OS X. Select the disk on which you want to install the OS, making sure it has enough space for the installation. If the version of OS 9 you have is lower than what is required, this is the point where you will find out, because you will not be able to select a disk. The selected disk shows a green arrow. If you select the Erase Destination And

Format As option, all data on the destination disk will be overwritten and lost. Click Continue to proceed.

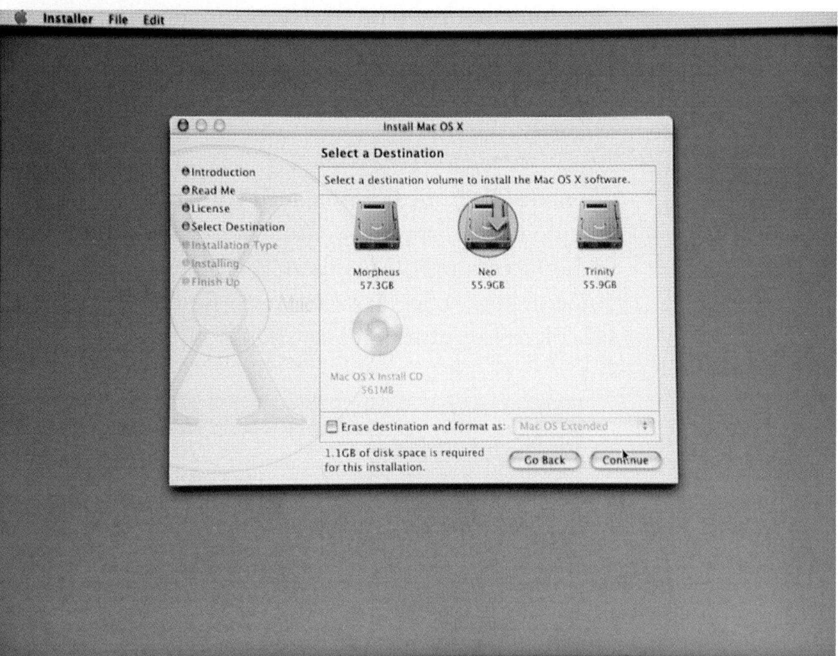

Step 5

In the Installation Type window, leave Easy Install as it is and click Install. Mac OS X installation begins. A status bar shows the progress and gives a rough idea of where you are in the process. When the OS is installed, the computer restarts and the Mac OS Setup Assistant opens. *If you purchased your computer with OS X installed, you will begin from this point.*

Step 6

The Mac OS Setup Assistant now asks you a series of questions beginning with the name of the country you are in. Select the answer and click Continue. The Personalize Your Settings window appears. Select a keyboard layout and click Continue.

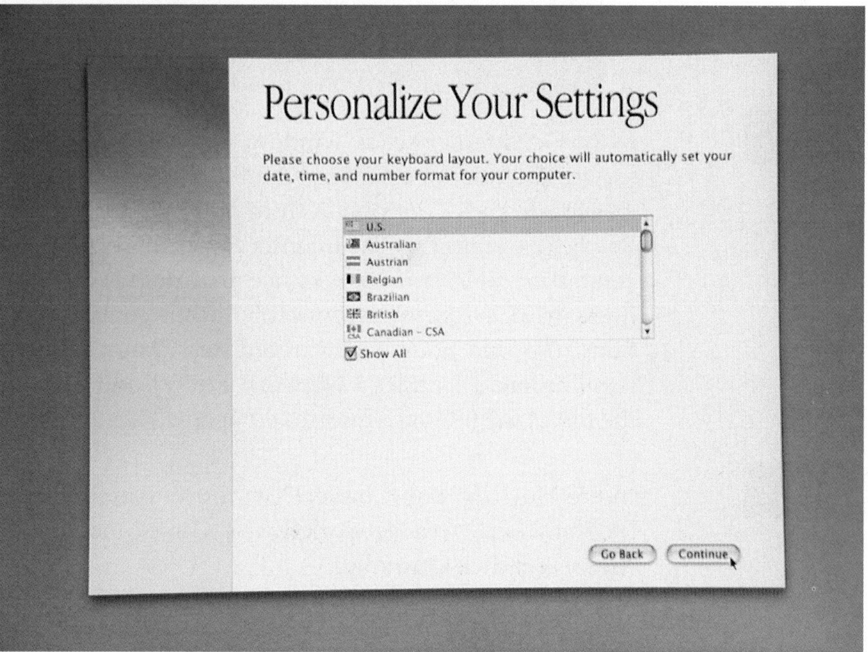

Step 7

You will be taken to the Registration Information window to fill out a form with your personal details. Fill these in and click Continue. You are now asked some marketing questions that have no practical function in the setup process, such as where you use the computer and what best describes your type of work. Fill these in and click Continue. This information will be sent to Apple after the Get Internet Ready step, coming right up.

Step 8

Click the Continue buttons until you arrive at the Create Your Account window. This is where you register and set up the administrator account for OS X, an account that has higher access privileges than other users. To administer your computer in the future, you will need to log in as this user. Remember to keep the user name and password in a safe place for future access. Click Continue.

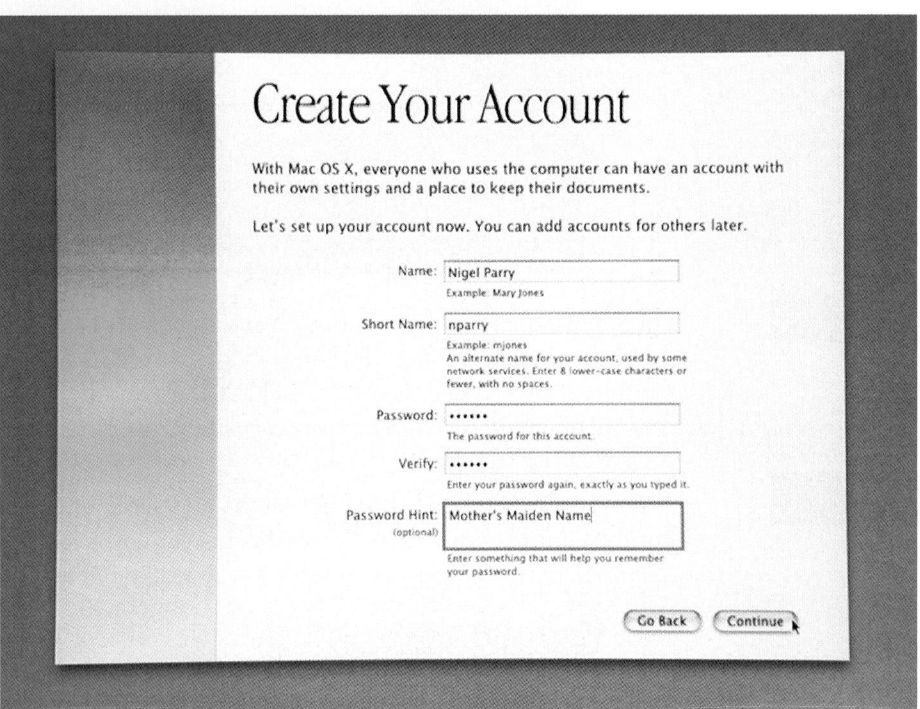

Step 9

In the Get Internet Ready window, you are asked to sign up with a third-party Internet service provider or to choose the I'll Use My Existing Internet Service option. Make a choice and click Continue. A third option in the Get Internet Ready window is I'm Not Ready To Connect To The Internet. Select this option if you prefer to set up your Internet connection later, or if your service provider requires you to provide your hardware address (MAC address) to connect, which is common for DSL and cable modem connections. (To find your hardware address, launch Network Utility [found in Finder | Applications | Utilities | Network Utility], and write down the address that appears at the top of the Interface Information panel.)

Step 10

In the How Do You Connect? window, you are asked to choose among Telephone Modem, Local Area Network (LAN), Cable Modem, DSL, and AirPort Wireless. Make a choice and click Continue.

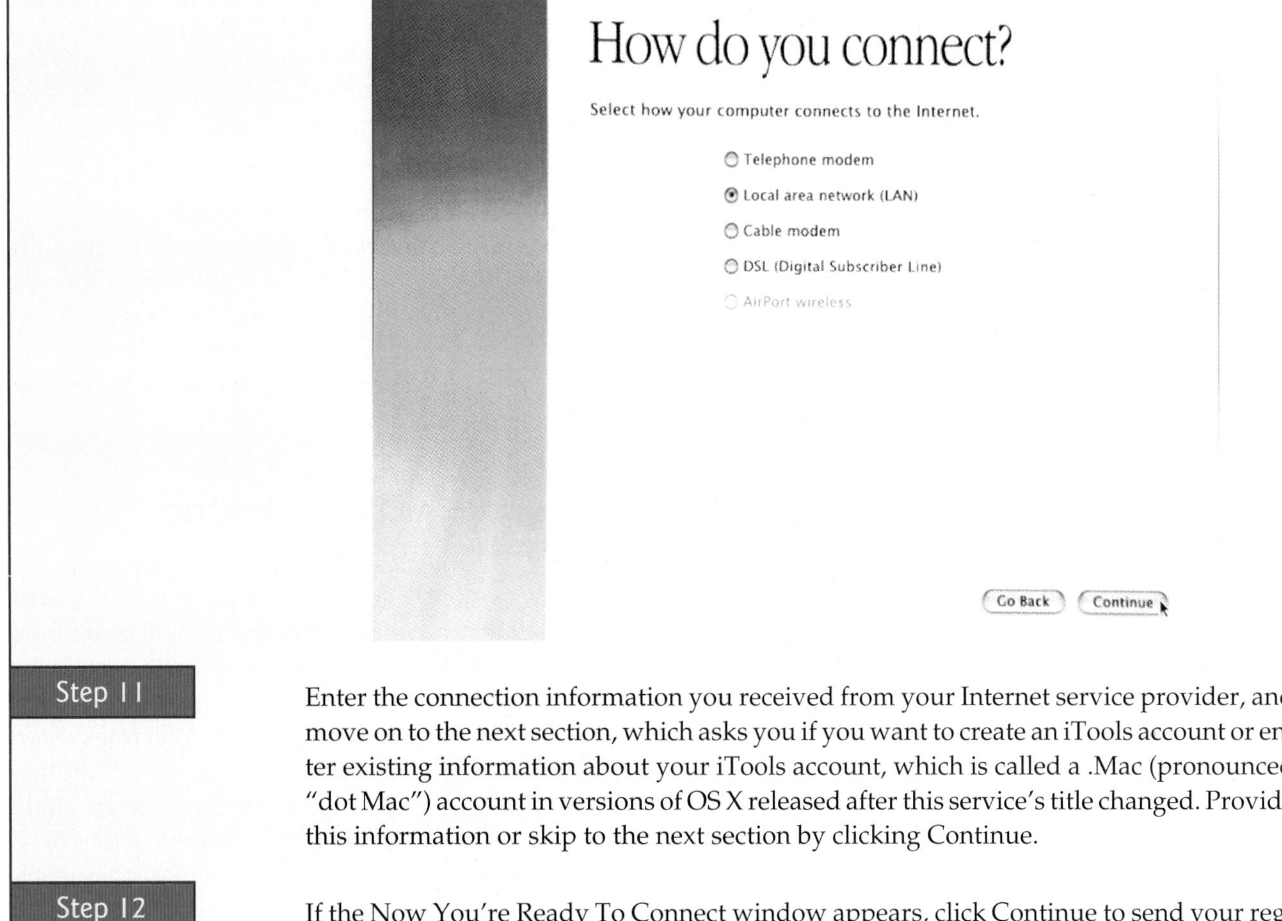

Step 11

Enter the connection information you received from your Internet service provider, and move on to the next section, which asks you if you want to create an iTools account or enter existing information about your iTools account, which is called a .Mac (pronounced "dot Mac") account in versions of OS X released after this service's title changed. Provide this information or skip to the next section by clicking Continue.

Step 12

If the Now You're Ready To Connect window appears, click Continue to send your registration to Apple via your Internet connection. If you provided marketing information earlier, it will also be sent at this point.

Step 13

The Select Time Zone window appears. Choose an option from the pop-up menu and click Continue. The Set Your Date And Time window appears. Enter the correct settings, click Save, and then click Continue. In the final window that appears, click Go.

Features of the Mac OS X Desktop

Let's take a tour of the Mac OS X desktop, beginning with the startup and login processes that quickly get you to the desktop, the overall appearance of the desktop, and the tools you will find there, including the Finder, Apple menu, and Dock.

Startup

From the first light of the screen, you'll notice that Macs don't expose users to system-level commands that most users are in no position to assess the importance of. Mac users aren't expected to know any of that "under the hood" stuff.

• OS X startup screen

Even as an administrator, your interaction with the computer is simplified, and your capacity to customize the machine is largely limited to system preferences and folder permissions.

Login

Mac OS X, like earlier versions, comes with multiple-user capability. If the computer you are using comes with this multiuser ability turned on, you will need to be assigned a login. When prompted, select your name from the list during the startup process and, as with logins everywhere, enter your password and then click OK. Passwords are encrypted and saved in a database known as the **system keychain**.

Try This!

Startup and Login

You can quickly start and log in and be ready to tour the desktop. If using Mac OS X setup for multiple users, you will need a user account and password. Try this:

1. Turn on the computer by pressing the power-on switch.
2. When (if) prompted for your user name, enter it or select it from the list.
3. Enter your password and click OK. You should now proceed to the desktop.

The Desktop

Once the desktop appears, new visitors familiar with Windows operating systems will be relieved to see the same basic metaphors visible: a trash can, a menu reminiscent of the Windows Start menu, and some sort of application launcher. Yes, there are slight differences between the OS X desktop and non-Mac systems, but this is not entirely unfamiliar territory.

The Finder

For the user, the **Finder** is the foundation of the Mac OS X desktop. At startup, the OS 9 Finder visibly loads system extensions, which add modular functionality to the operating system. In OS X, such extensions load invisibly, but the Finder still appears by default after startup; and is the default GUI/desktop view before any application software runs (see Figure 12-1). The Finder is equivalent to Windows Explorer, the Windows file management tool. Where previous versions of Mac OS used the Finder as a task switcher, this function has been delegated to the Dock in OS X.

The Finder menus in OS X—Finder, File, Edit, View, Go, Window, and Help—offer a variety of file management and power-on/-off tools. The Finder menu is new in OS X, containing the functions of the Special menu found in previous versions. A Window menu arranges window views, and a new Go menu offers shortcuts to folders used for storage both on the computer and on the Internet, as in the case of Apple's **.Mac** online file storage and file sharing service (previously known as **iTools**), found at `www.mac.com`. The .Mac service operates as a virtual hard drive for storing private files and as a web site where you can upload files such as photographs and movies for others to view.

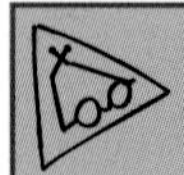

Inside Information

Where Did the Chooser Go?

Longtime Mac users seem perplexed when they first see the Mac OS X desktop because they miss the Chooser of OS 9. The Chooser is still here in spirit if not in graphical splendor. Its functions have been taken over by other tools such as the Finder and System Tools, which have also improved on them.

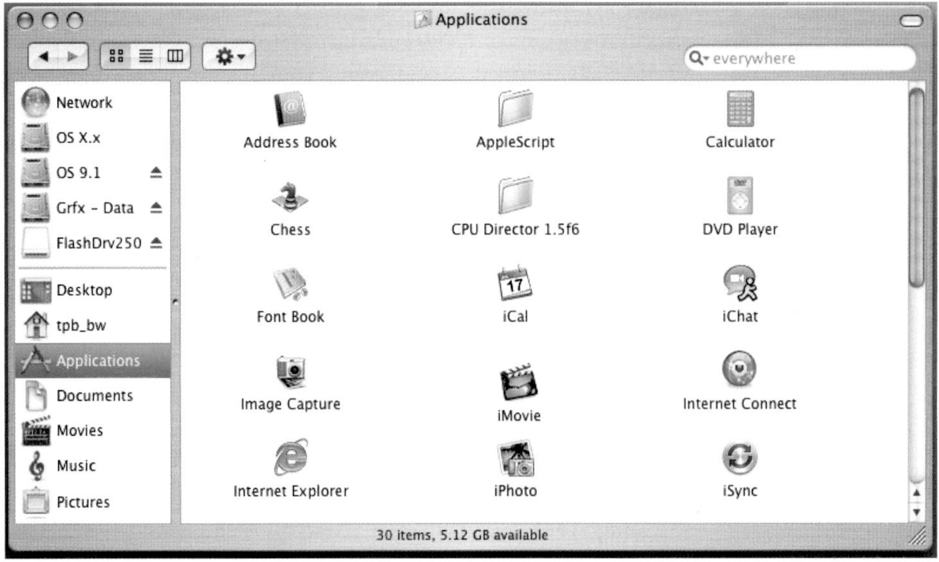

• Finder window with Applications folder open

The Apple Menu

Found on the top-left of the desktop, the **Apple menu** is a pop-up menu that opens when you click a tiny Apple logo. In OS X, the Apple menu is something of a disappointment after the long list of options available from this

• **Figure 12-1.** Key features of the Mac OS X desktop

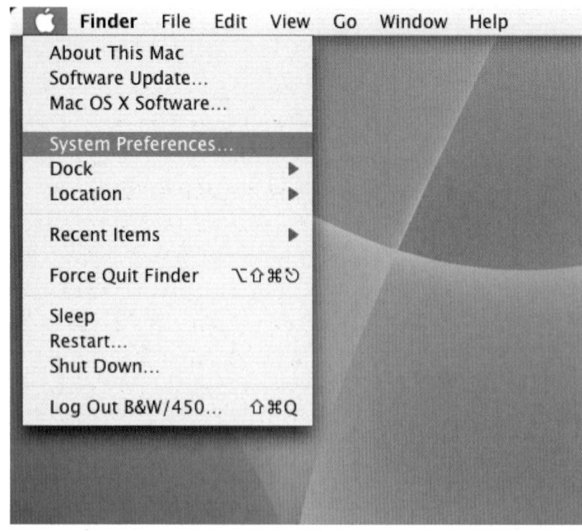

• The OS X Apple menu

• The OS X Dock

• The Dock with a new shortcut to a drive device (on the right)

menu in OS 9. It has been reduced to a startup and shutdown menu, with recent items and a shortcut to system preferences. It is not customizable. That functionality has been passed to the Dock.

However, all is not lost for diehard Apple menu buffs. The System/Disk Utilities section of Apple's OS X Downloads page (`apple.com/downloads/macosx/`) has several third-party utilities that will restore functionality to OS X's Apple menu, including the ability to browse the entire hard disk from this menu.

The Dock

New in OS X, the **Dock** is a floating bar on the desktop that replaces the OS 9 Control Strip. The Dock gives access to a variety of system preferences, including location, Internet dial-up, and screen resolution. It is an improvement over the Control Strip, which required modules to be specially programmed for it, and shortcuts to files and folders could not be added by the casual user. This has changed with the Dock. In OS X, the Dock's default installation state includes shortcuts to Mail (Apple's e-mail software), Internet Explorer, iTunes (or .Mac), iMovie, Sherlock, QuickTime, Apple's OS X, System Preferences, and Trash.

Want a file, folder, application, or Internet bookmark to be in the Dock? Drag it on. Want to remove something from the Dock? Drag it off the Dock and onto the desktop and let go. It will disappear in a puff of smoke, quite literally.

Preferences allow you to choose to have the Dock appear on the right, left, or bottom of the screen; to hide it so that it appears only when the mouse rolls over that area; to size it larger or smaller; and to turn its mouse-over magnification feature on and off. If you plan to have a lot of shortcuts on the Dock and have consequently set its size to be small to fit them all, the magnification feature is useful, allowing you to see the tiny icons as you roll the mouse over them.

Try This!

Adding a Shortcut to the Dock

Add a shortcut to the OS X Dock. Try this:

1. Look around the OS X desktop for something for which you want to create a shortcut on the Dock. This can be a hard disk, an application, a file or folder, or a CD. You can choose something from your hard disk if you like.
2. Click the item's icon and drag it onto the Dock. Before letting go of the mouse button, move the icon around over the Dock to position it between the existing Dock icons where you want it to appear. Application and file icons can be positioned anywhere to the left of the vertical divider, while icons representing devices, such as drives, can only be positioned to the right of the divider.
3. Release the mouse button. The icon will stay on the Dock and will now function as a shortcut to the item. Want to remove it? Click the item on the Dock, and drag it onto the desktop. No, that puff of smoke we were talking about wasn't a figure of speech!

Under-the-Hood Features of Mac OS X

In OS X, Apple has enhanced the best aspect of the earlier OS 9 and Macs in general—the GUI—and married it with a stable, tried-and-tested UNIX core. Apple has therefore finally responded to the main criticisms of Macs by system administrators who typically work with other platforms, by offering an OS that:

- Is based on a rock solid platform
- Complies with international networking standards
- Adopts tried-and-tested open standard security protocols
- Is better designed to multitask and fulfill a server role
- Allows familiar root-level access to developers and administrators

Whereas before, Apple seemed focused on appealing to creative professionals at the user end of the purchasing scale, OS X signals Apple's acknowledgment of the people who make up the majority of computer users and require mainstream productivity tools.

The OS X GUI—known as **Aqua** because of its blue, fluid appearance—ensures that OS X's interface will feel familiar, although its under-the-hood functionality is clearly aimed at advanced technical users.

While it's always painful to upgrade any computer system, the system performance and usability of OS X when compared to OS 9—to say nothing of the new, free multimedia software that comes bundled with it and which is not available for OS 9—makes upgrading worthwhile.

OS X seems to be a work in progress, as Apple creates new major releases—four within four years, beginning with 10.0. At the time of this writing, the most recent release of OS X is version 10.3, code-named **Panther**. The fourth release, 10.4, code-named **Tiger**, will be out by the time this book is in distribution. And between the major releases have been minor releases (10.0.1, 10.0.2, and so on). The release we used for most of the screen shots in this chapter is 10.3.5 (released August 2004). Each release has added a variety of improvements and new features, and, as you may notice while comparing the illustrations in this book to OS X on your lab computer, has made frequent changes to the look of existing GUI components.

At the time of this writing, the list price for OS X single-user version is around $129, although many online retailers are offering it for just over $100, after rebate, in the United States. A Family Pack with 5 licenses is only $199.

From the network-ready interface and multidevice connectivity present even in Apple's lower-end hardware to the compatibility and stability advantages brought by OS X's new UNIX core, Apple's latest computers are more functional in a multimedia and multi-operating system environment than ever before.

The notable characteristics of Apple computers and the Mac OS discussed in the following paragraphs are not exclusive, but represent discernable traits or major strengths in the OS and hardware that will be recognizable to regular users of the OS.

Table 12-2 Release Dates of Major OS X Versions

Major OS X Release	Release Date
10.0 (Initial release)	March 2001
10.2 Jaguar	August 2002
10.3 Panther	October 2003
10.4 Tiger	First half 2005

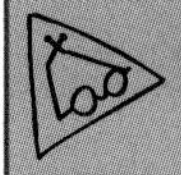

Inside Information

The Hierarchy of Mac Operating Systems

OS 9 made its precursor OS 8 obsolete by the addition of Internet tools that include a hard disk search utility integrated with Internet search engines, multiple-user capacity, Internet file sharing and remote administration, strong file encryption, and a network browser.

Until January 2003, new Mac computers were distributed with the ability to start up in either OS 9 or OS X. Since that date, new Macs offer only the **compatibility layer** *(also known as Classic) as an option for running OS 9 applications under OS X. This allows new users of OS X to run older software until newer versions are available that will run in OS X natively. They may then upgrade their older software at their own pace, or at the speed their budget allows.*

However, in the day-to-day reality of working with these two operating systems, anyone with OS X installed will soon find that the OS 9 compatibility layer is relegated from the background to obscurity. There is really no compelling reason, barring simple installation requirements, to continue using OS 9. As a result, in this chapter, OS 9 is referred to only where OS X users need to deal with it, and by way of comparison to introduce users familiar with OS 9 to OS X.

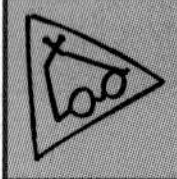

Inside Information

Prosumers—Valuable Customers

In the Internet age, when everyone has a previously unheard-of capacity to research products prior to purchase and where home computer advances have brought a hugely increased demand for connectivity with myriad digital devices, we have seen the emergence of a new type of consumer who expects consumer-level affordability combined with professional-level features.

***Prosumers**, as they are termed, increasingly drive the digital device and home computer market, especially in the case of Apple, which has historically prospered in the multimedia sector with features that are now becoming part of mainstream computer functionality.*

AirPort is Apple's term for the IEEE 802.11**b** wireless networking standard. AirPort Extreme is their term for the IEEE 802.11**g** wireless networking standard.

Built-in Networking Hardware and Software

These days, every Apple computer, from the consumer-level iBooks and iMacs to the prosumer-level and professional-level PowerBooks and G5 desktops, ships with Ethernet, FireWire (IEEE 1394), and USB ports and is AirPort or AirPort Extreme ready. This makes Apple computers more versatile in terms of the peripherals and networks they can connect with.

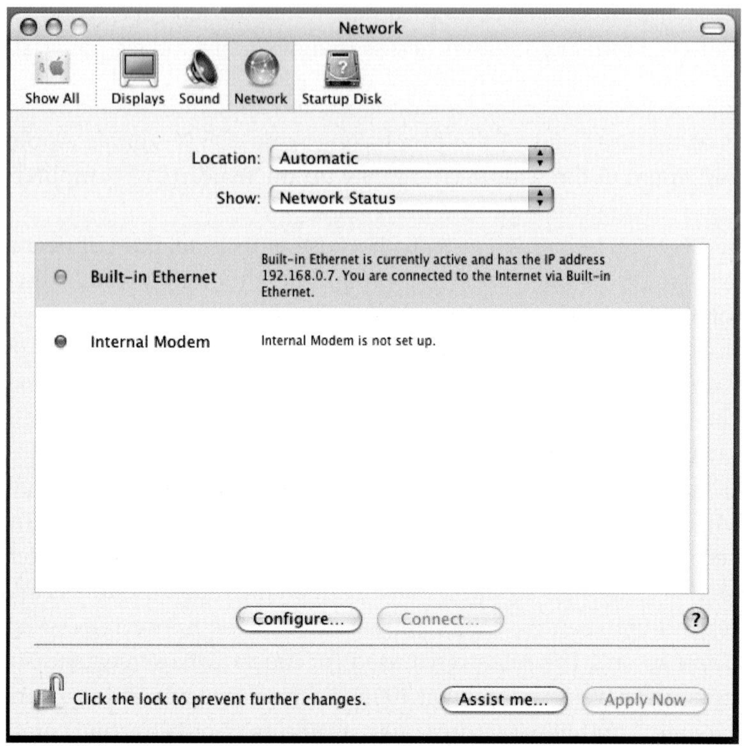

• View the Network settings at Apple | System Preferences | Network.

Earlier versions of the Mac OS required third-party software for network connectivity—that is, client software that allowed Macs running OS 8 and 9 to connect to Windows-based networks. OS X (beginning with **Jaguar** version 10.2) includes a PPTP-based virtual private network (VPN) client to connect to both Windows and other remote networks.

OS X's Personal File Services for Windows allows Windows users to connect to a Mac and share files without needing any additional software. OS X also allows users to log into a Microsoft Windows domain, which eases the task of network administrators who need to integrate Macs into Windows networks.

OS X Is Less Vulnerable to Crashes

Previous to OS X, the Mac OS was built on the same core OS that existed in 1984. OS X is a departure from that practice, and is built on a core operating system known as **Darwin** (`developer.apple.com/darwin/`). Its most noticeable feature, when compared to OS 9, is vastly improved system performance.

Darwin is a product of the open-source community. Open source, a development model that evolved naturally on the Internet, makes freely available the nuts and bolts of the code that powers software to encourage widespread debugging and modification for the betterment of the entire community. This model has provided the Internet community with an impressive list of software that includes BSD, Linux, Sendmail, Apache, and Perl.

Darwin integrates a number of technologies including a Mach 3.0 kernel, BSD UNIX operating system services, high-performance networking facilities, and support for multiple integrated file systems. This use of Darwin is of particular interest to developers, whose programming efforts on a Mac are now immeasurably more portable to other operating systems.

UNIX is an operating system that was designed to allow multiple users to carry out multiple processes on interconnected computers. As an open-source platform, it has weathered years of public testing on the Internet and has come to be respected as a reliable, efficient, and secure operating system particularly suited to multitasking processes.

Inside Information

FireWire: Apple's Peripheral Interface Technology

Connecting peripherals to computers at speeds of up to 400 Mbps, Apple's FireWire interface technology is comparable to the USB 2.0 standard, but 30 times faster than the USB 1.0 standard. Each computer can support up to 63 devices using cable lengths up to 14 feet long. Connections are ***hot swappable****, which means that peripherals and the computer do not need to be restarted while connecting or disconnecting. The Institute of Electrical and Electronics Engineers made FireWire, also known as iLink, a standard (IEEE 1394) now found in most new PCs. For more information about FireWire, see* `developer.apple.com/firewire`.

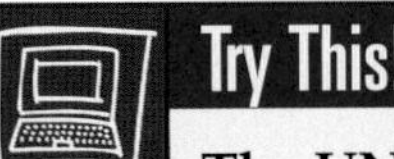

Try This!

The UNIX Core of OS X

Want to know more about UNIX in OS X? Try this:

1. Open your Internet browser.
2. Type **www.apple.com/macosx/features/unix/** in the location bar to go to the site.

Security

The exposure of the Internet and the open-source nature of the UNIX operating system have forced commercial UNIX vendors to be open about security issues with their systems. Security holes resulting from a user's turning on a feature that was switched off by default are not dismissed but rather are considered challenges to the UNIX community, whose users and programmers are so numerous that security fixes are provided swiftly and made readily available to alert users who check for such updates. Apple now can contribute to and benefit from this large communal effort. They make updates available on their web site and also provide a Software Update program in the Mac OS. You will learn more about this later.

For those interested in the development of the Mac's hardware architecture from the earliest days of the 1977 1-MHz CPU Apple 1 to the processors of today, `www.apple-history.com` is a professional and comprehensive information resource.

Advanced User System Access

Macs were long criticized for not paying attention to advanced users who have an interest in programming. OS X, unlike OS 9, now offers terminal access to its system. OS X includes the open-source GCC 3.1 compiler, which offers increased code compilation speeds. Standard UNIX math libraries have been optimized to work with Apple's Power PC G4 chip, giving programmers optimal performance without their needing to write Apple-specific code and increased portability to others' operating systems after development.

Apple's Terminal application (found by selecting Applications | Utilities | Terminal) supports vt100/vt220 emulation and—here's how you know that it's a piece of Apple software—it can actually be made translucent, so you can see other windows through it.

For detailed technical information, see the Mac OS X Developer Connection Documentation on the Apple web site (`developer.apple.com/documentation/`).

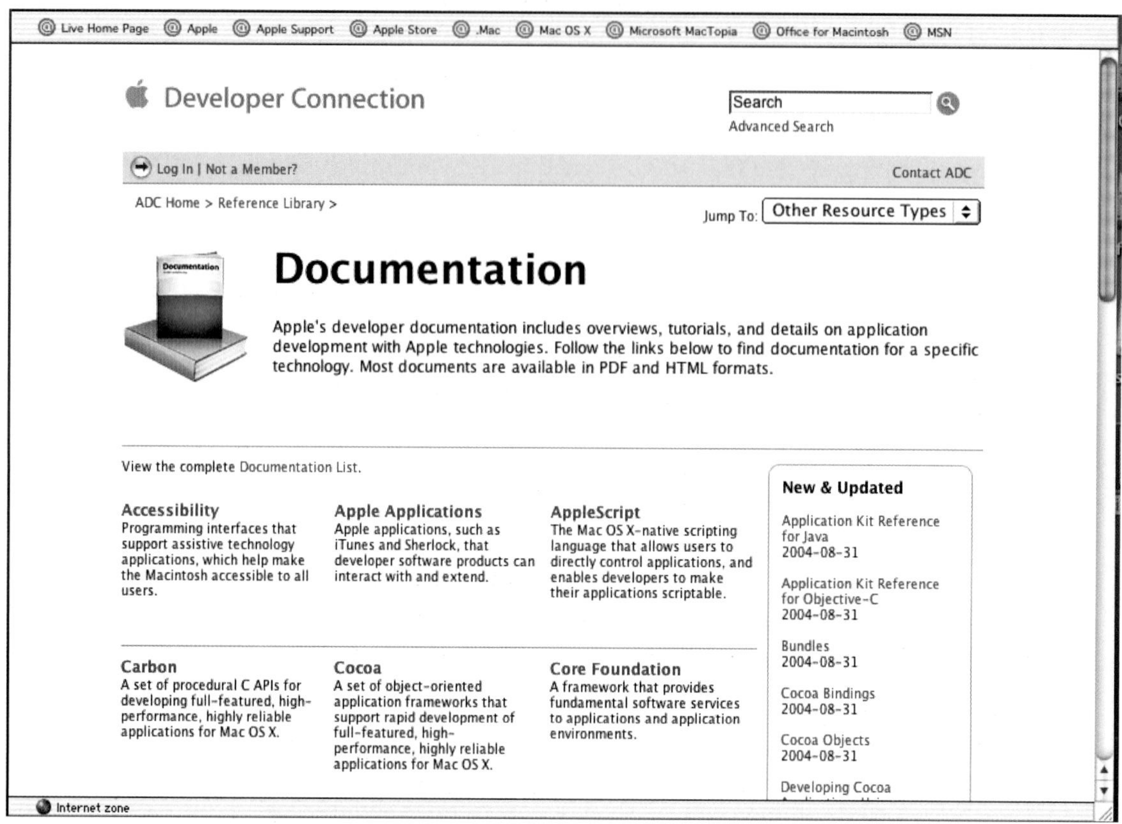

• Mac OS X developer's web site

Strong Multi-User Support

As OS X is a UNIX system, Apple computers now boast very powerful multiuser functionality, including not only customized, password-protected user home directories on the hard disk, but also the capacity for administrators to prevent access to core systems and key areas of the hard disk.

For example, when you begin the process of installing any new software in OS X, no matter how small, the system asks you for an administrator password. This is particularly appreciated in situations where the computer is exposed to many people with minimal supervision, as is the case in educational settings, Internet cafes, and households with children.

Choose the Hardware Type for the User Level

Greg owns a professional recording studio that currently offers 24-track analog recording onto 2-inch tape, but he wants to institute a solution whereby he can offer hard disk recording to smaller music groups that cannot afford his high-end analog service.

After some research, in which he learns that an iMac is appropriate for a SOHO (small office, home office) user but not for a Prosumer user, he decides on a Mac G5 desktop system with dual 64-bit 2.5-GHz G5 processors, an interface with eight inputs, and a copy of ProTools for mixing and mastering. He feels this is a good beginning for most recording situations that this digital studio will likely deal with. Because Greg travels a lot, he also bought a Titanium G5 PowerBook equipped with ProTools so he can take work with him on the road.

Greg is confident that his chosen solution is adequate, not least because the G5 desktop is expandable to 8GB of RAM and has slots for two additional hard disks.

At home, Greg's wife, Kammy, has her own dog-walking business and a new baby and, in addition to simple word processing, needs to run basic client-billing software. They decided a few years ago on an iMac—the Dalmatian model, of course—and upgraded to OS X to better control their teenage daughter's use of the computer; Kammy was worried about her business files being deleted by accident.

> **Cross Check**
>
> **Compare Windows and Mac OS Features**
>
> Compare what you know about Windows and Mac OS X features and answer the following questions:
>
> 1. Describe a feature of the Windows OSs you have studied in this course that is comparable to the Mac OS X compatibility layer.
>
> ______________________________
>
> ______________________________
>
> 2. Using your own observations, list five features of the Mac desktops that are similar to the Windows desktop and that make the transition between the two easy. These features can include actions required to do tasks.
>
> ______________________________
>
> ______________________________

Apple's hardware is aimed at a variety of user levels. For users wanting the potential to expand their computers to meet new challenges, the G5 desktop and PowerBook laptop allow expansion. For users wanting a robust home or school computer, the sturdily built iMac and iBook are suitable, allowing RAM upgrades but limited hardware expansion.

When Brian bought his 867-MHz G4 desktop, it came with 256MB of RAM and a 60GB hard disk, which was a welcome upgrade from his previous G3 233-MHz PowerBook with 160MB of RAM and a 20GB hard disk. A year later, Brian's web design business has increased his need for basic video editing for clients.

While the G4 system is powerful enough to deal with the processor-intensive rendering that video requires, the hard disk space was pushed to the limit, and multitasking with several different programs at once necessitated change. The latter issue was resolved with the addition of RAM to take the system up to just under 1GB. Brian purchased a second 120GB hard disk to handle the massive files that digital video capture produces. With an iMac, which was a tempting option at the time Brian was considering this purchase, this wouldn't have been possible, because the iMac allows RAM upgrades but little else.

Today, however, as users' needs grow, excellent FireWire and USB 2.0 external drives and peripherals expand a computer's capacity virtually infinitely.

True Plug and Play

Although there are, of course, exceptions to the rule, if you plug a peripheral such as a printer into a Mac, it will typically start working immediately.

This holds true for installed items even if you plug them in while the computer is already switched on.

Try This!

Mac Viruses

To find out more about the Mac and viruses, try this:

1. Go to `Google.com` or any other search engine. Search on "viruses and the Mac."
2. The resulting sites and pages will provide an interesting introduction to the issue of viruses and the Mac.
3. For more information about Mac viruses and viruses that affect other computer operating systems, use your search engine to locate the `alt.comp.virus` newsgroup.

Viruses

Because the Mac OS has been a minority operating system, Macs have tended not to be plagued by viruses, unlike Windows systems. OS X's insistence on an administrator password before new software is installed offers an additional barrier of protection. Commercially available virus programs such as Norton AntiVirus (`www.symantec.com/mac/`) are recommended nonetheless. As Mac sales expand, the likelihood of becoming more vulnerable to attacks will probably increase.

Getting to Know the Mac OS X Workspace

This section offers an introduction to basic functions and customization options within the Mac OS X workspace, with reference to Mac OS 9 where appropriate. You will learn how to set up system preferences, manage files, print, and create and manage user accounts.

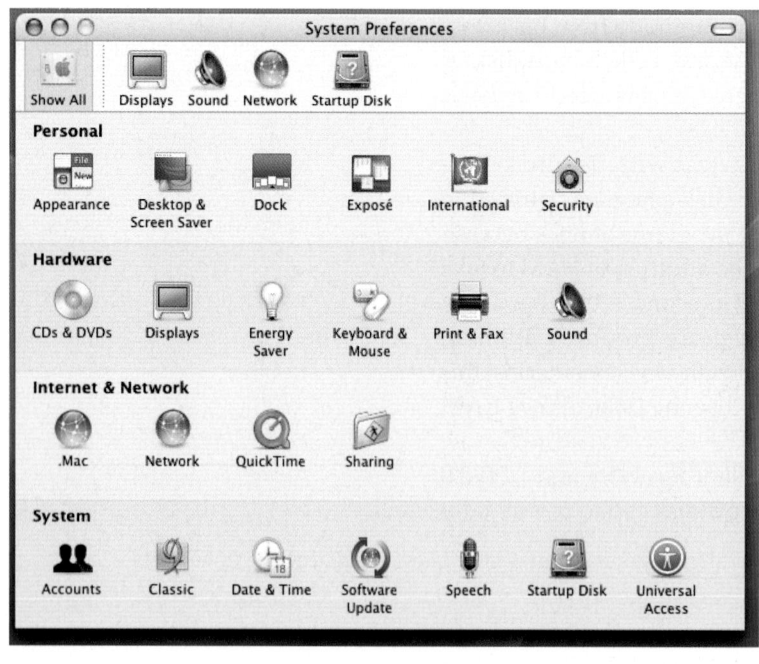

• The System Preferences window showing shortcuts to all system preferences

Changing System Preferences

In OS 9, system preferences were changed through the Control Panels folder, accessed through the Apple menu or by browsing the hard disk (/System Folder/Control Panels). In OS X, system preferences can be accessed from the Apple menu or Dock or by browsing the hard disk (Applications | System Preferences). While it is still possible to change preferences in OS 9 from within OS X, note that some control panels can no longer be run in Classic mode, the Control Strip being an example.

The following is a list of system preferences (each preference screen is known as a preference pane) found in OS X release 10.3.5. A few did not make an appearance until sub-versions (10.2, 10.3, and so on).

The preferences are explained next as they appear in the System Preferences window. They are arranged in rows, with the top row containing the Show All button that allows you to switch from each preference pane to the overview of all preference objects. In addition, this row contains shortcuts to several frequently used preference panes. Where there is an OS 9 equivalent—which conveniently covers the main functions—the corresponding name of the OS 9 control panel is given.

As of this writing, each new release of OS X includes many minor changes to the GUI, so any screenshot you see here may differ somewhat from the release of OS X you are using.

Personal Preferences

The preferences found in the row labeled "Personal" are settings that control visual and security preferences for the currently logged-on user.

Appearance The Appearance preference allows you to alter the color of buttons, menus, and windows; select a text and list highlight color; choose the location and behavior of scroll arrows and the scroll bar; and determine the number of applications and documents that appear in the Recent Items (both applications and documents) submenu of the Apple menu (choose from 5 to 50). These functions were previously available in the Appearance control panel in OS 9, with the exception of the number of recent items listed, which was customizable from the Apple menu's Options control panel in OS 9.

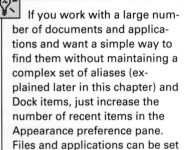

If you work with a large number of documents and applications and want a simple way to find them without maintaining a complex set of aliases (explained later in this chapter) and Dock items, just increase the number of recent items in the Appearance preference pane. Files and applications can be set separately with a maximum setting for each at 50. These are then accessible from Apple Menu | Recent Items.

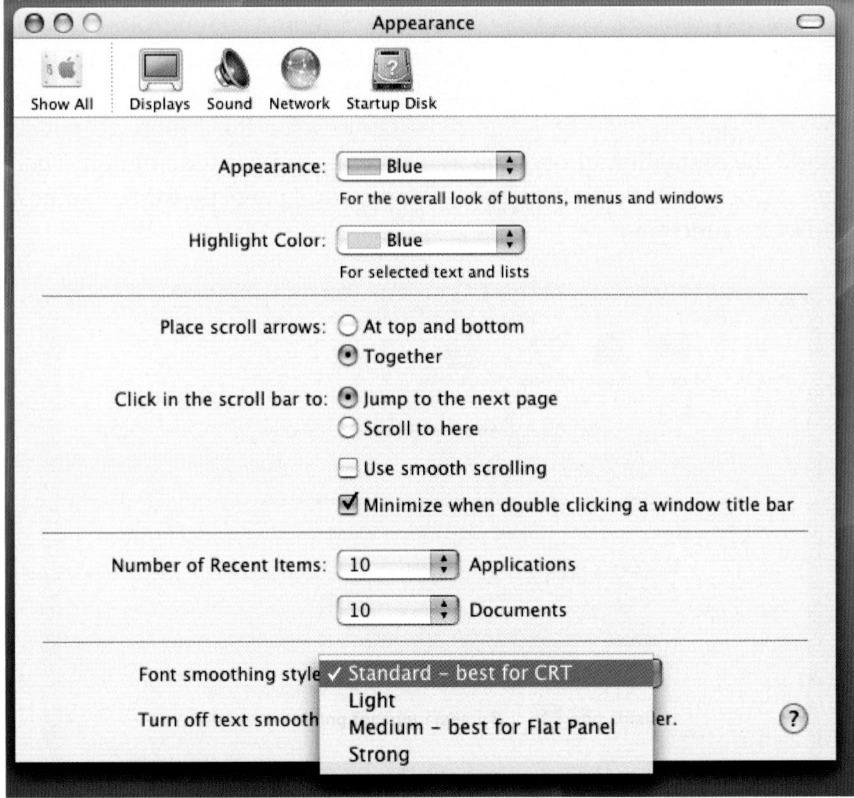

• Appearance preferences

Desktop & Screen Saver The Desktop & Screen Saver preference allows you to select a screen saver or background for your desktop. Click on Desktop to view the desktop settings, and click on Screen Saver to view the screen

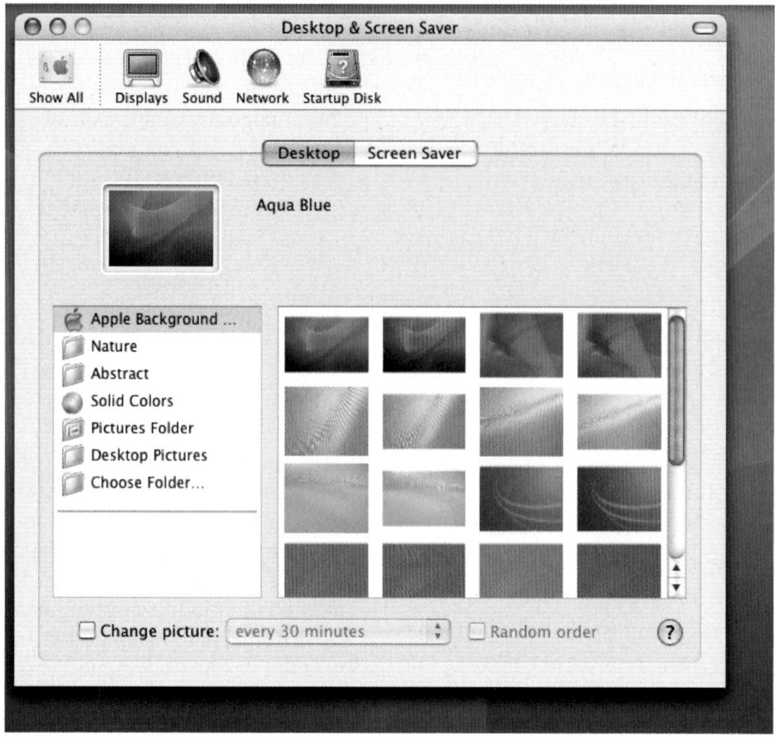

• The Desktop preferences

savers available on your Mac. In the Desktop settings, to select a different group of images, choose another option from the list on the left. Clicking on the Screen Saver button presents more preferences, including a selection of screen savers and settings for the selected screen saver. The Hot Corners button allows you to select one or more corners as Active Screen Corners and to choose an action (start screen saver or disable screen saver) that will occur when you move the mouse to the active screen corner. The Appearance control panel in OS 9 offered the Desktop function, and though there were third-party screen savers for OS 9, there was no dedicated control panel for them.

Dock The Dock preference allows you to control the size and position of your Dock. Slider controls allow you to control the Dock Size and Magnification. Radio buttons allow you to position the Dock on the Left, Bottom, or Right, while a box gives choices for the Minimize effects. Toggle the animation of opening applications and the hide option. There was no Dock in OS 9, but the Control Strip control panel performed some of the Dock's functions.

> Keep the Dock out of your way! Although the Dock is a useful utility, the magnification option can cause it to get in the way when positioned near application toolbars or open application windows. A simple solution in Dock preferences is to turn off magnification and reduce the size of the floating launch bar.

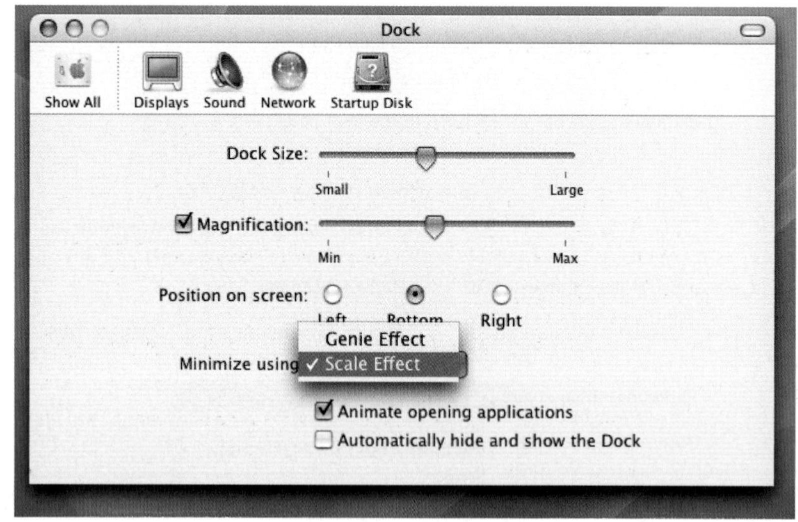

• The Dock preference

Exposé When you open Exposé, you are greeted by the Active Screen Corners settings that are also available through the Hot Corners button in Screen Savers. But Exposé is really about letting you assign actions to certain keys or mouse buttons that will expose all open windows at once, or switch between the open documents in a single application, or the desktop. This is very handy when you are working in one application with many documents open at once, and need to quickly find a particular document.

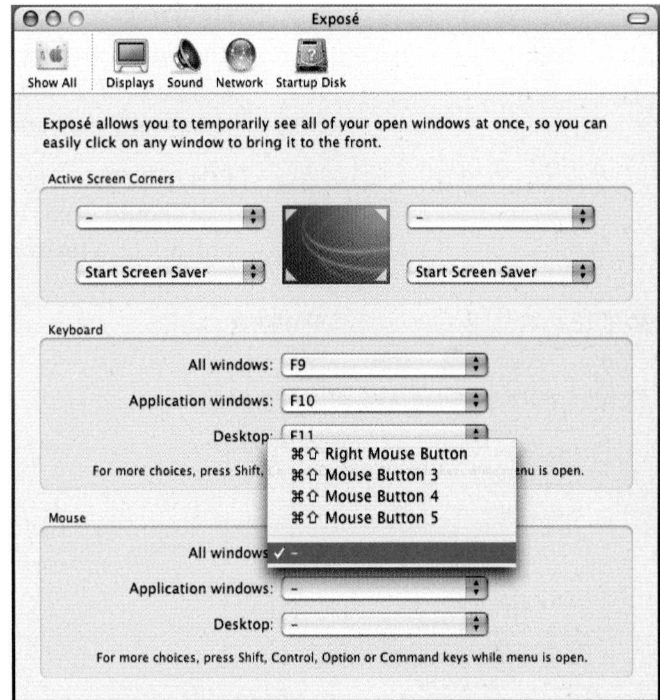

• Assign keys or mouse buttons to actions that will quickly reveal all open documents.

International The International preference allows you to choose the language that appears in application menus and dialog boxes and the text behaviors of languages; date, time, and numbering conventions; and the keyboard layout. In OS 9 these functions were offered in four different control panels: Text, Numbers, Date And Time, and Keyboard.

Security The Security preference includes, as you might suspect, security settings. This is where you can turn on and configure FileVault, the file encryption feature, and set a master password for encrypted files. You may also configure a password requirement for waking the computer from sleep or screen saver, and determine systemwide settings to enable or disable automatic login (only enable this in an extremely safe environment), require a password to unlock each secure system preference, and configure an automatic logout after a predetermined period of time.

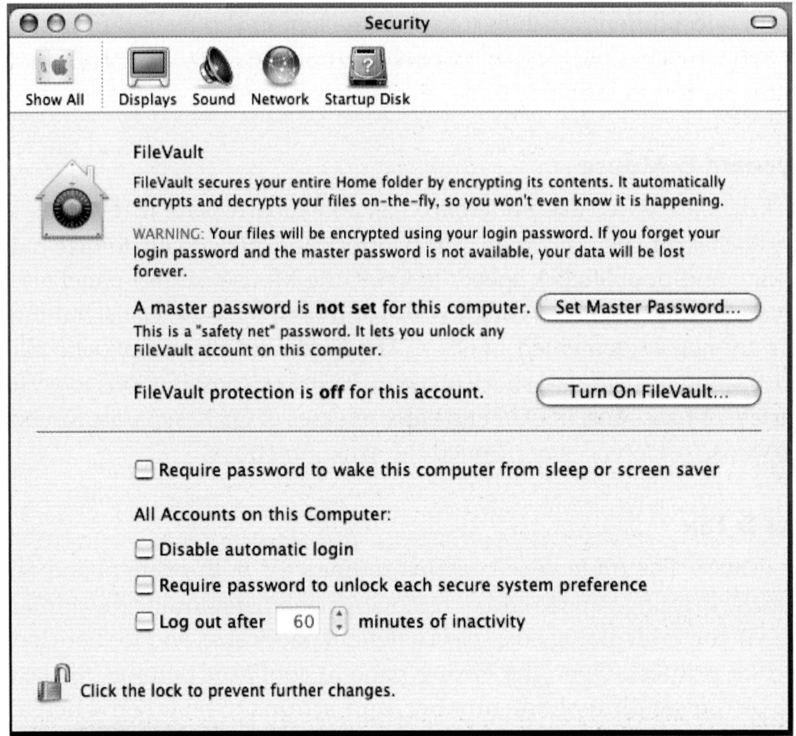

• Security preferences

Hardware

The Hardware row contains panes for setting preferences for such hardware areas as CDs and DVDs, displays, power management, keyboard and mouse, printers and faxes, and sound.

CDs & DVDs The CDs & DVDs preference allows you to select the action that should occur when you insert a blank CD or DVD (separate actions), a music CD, a picture CD, or a video DVD.

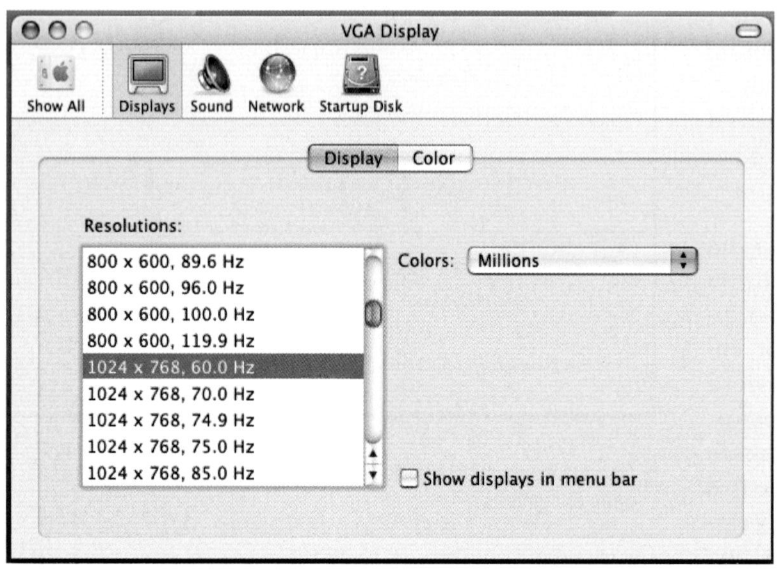

• Displays preference pane

Displays The Displays preference allows users to customize the resolution, number of colors, refresh rate, and display profiles for each supported monitor connected to the computer. You can also calibrate the monitor using the Color option within the Displays preference. The calibration includes a ColorSync component, which enables you to specify the ColorSync profile for displays and printers for better screen rendering and print output. In OS 9, the Monitors control panel managed these functions.

Energy Saver The Energy Saver preference offers options for putting your system, display, or hard disk to sleep after a defined period of inactivity and determines what situations will wake the sleeping computer. On laptops, it is possible to select different values for when the laptop is powered from its battery and when it is plugged into a power supply. In OS 9, the corresponding control panel had the same title.

Everyone types differently. Some people type faster and therefore require a higher key repeat rate than others, and some are frustrated when their slower keypresses result in too many of the same characters. On the Settings tab of the Keyboard preference, try adjusting the Key Repeat Rate and Delay Until Repeat slider bars until you are comfortable with the results.

Keyboard & Mouse

The Keyboard & Mouse preference has a keyboard pane that allows keyboard behavior customization. The Mouse pane lets you customize mouse tracking and double-click speed. In OS 9, the Mouse control panel also allowed users to customize cursor width and toggle mouse trails, but mouse trails are not implemented in OS X. The Keyboard Shortcuts pane allows modification of keyboard shortcuts, which are key combinations to perform a variety of functions. In OS 9 and early releases of OS X, separate Keyboard and Mouse preferences performed the same functions.

Print & Fax

The Print & Fax preference contains settings for both printers and faxes. Open the Printing pane to add or remove a printer, determine the printer selected in the Print dialog box, select a default paper size, and to share locally attached printers. Open the Faxing pane to configure settings for faxing, such as the sending phone number, and actions to be taken when a fax arrives.

Sound

The Sound preference permits users to select system alert sounds and the alert volume, main volume, and speaker balance, and to choose between connected devices for sound input and output. The Sound control panel in OS 9 was no different.

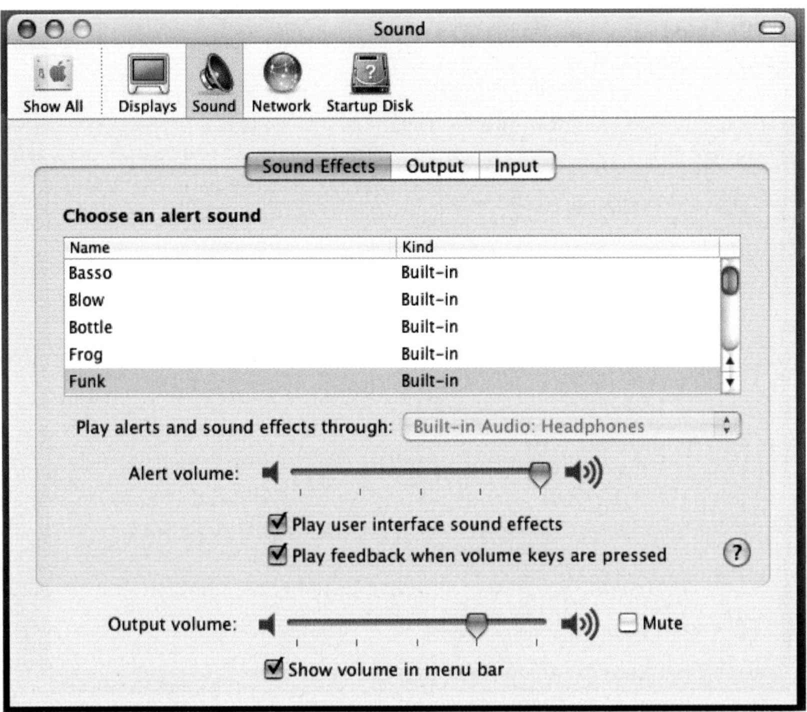

• Sound preference pane

Internet & Network

The Internet & Network row contains preferences that apply to networking.

.Mac The .Mac preference allows users to set up a .Mac (formerly Apple iTools) account, which allows online storage and multimedia file sharing with others.

Network The Network preference allows you to manage locations that have a bearing on your network connection (a function more appropriate

Try This!

Changing the Alert Sounds

Not every sound is pleasing to every ear. For those sounds that need changing, we recommend the following:

1. Go to the Sound preference pane in OS X.
2. On the Alert or Sound Effects tab, click the name of a new sound other than the one currently highlighted.
3. You will hear the sound. Repeat this process until you find a sound you like; then close the panel.

for laptops), and to configure TCP/IP, PPP, proxies, and modem settings. In OS 9, this role was handled by the TCP/IP, Modem, and Remote Access control panels.

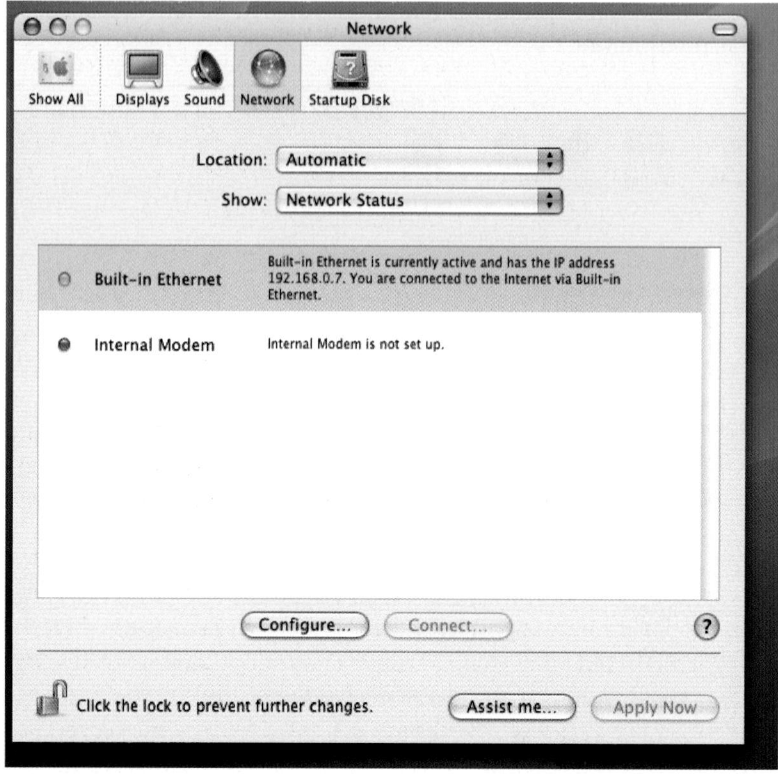

• Click the Configure button to change the configuration of the selected device.

It also allows users to specify the default e-mail and web browser software, home and search pages, newsreader and server preferences, and file download destination. Newer versions of Mac OS X reflect Apple's change in the name of this online service from iTools to .Mac.

QuickTime The QuickTime preference allows customization of QuickTime functionality. QuickTime is Apple's own multimedia software architecture that has become a multiplatform, industry standard for multimedia content delivery and is used by software developers and hardware manufacturers to offer integrated and coordinated graphics, sounds, video, text, music, virtual reality, and other 3-D media.

QuickTime works seamlessly at the system level with OS X as well as the earlier OS 9 (which had a corresponding control panel, called QuickTime Settings).

Sharing

The Sharing preference has three subpanes: Services, Firewall, and Internet. Services enables file sharing with other computers, Apple's Web Sharing, and remote login and management options. In OS 9, the File Sharing and Web Sharing control panels handled these functions. Firewall allows you to control the firewall and to select the types of incoming traffic (if any) to allow in for the purposes of sharing. Internet contains settings for allowing sharing of local resources to Internet users.

System

The preferences in the System row include non-hardware settings common to all users of the computer.

Users/Accounts The OS X Users preference pane allows you to add, delete, and edit users from your computer. You will learn about adding users later in this chapter. In OS 9, the corresponding control panel was Multiple Users. In addition, this pane allows for a variety of login options, including the password, a password hint, select a picture to be used when logging in, FileVault Settings (see Security preferences earlier), and startup items for each user.

Classic The Classic preference enables users to perform a variety of functions relating to the **OS 9 Classic environment**, the compatibility layer that allows users to run OS 9 software from within OS X. The Start/Stop tab of the pane allows you to stop, restart, or forcibly quit Classic mode. The Advanced tab allows you to restart Classic mode with several options and offers an optional Sleep When Inactive setting. Use the Memory/Versions tab when the Classic environment is running to view memory usage of each OS 9 application and its version information.

> Software updates have an order. Some software updates are visible only when previous updates have been installed. If you are installing a system from an older version of OS X, be sure to click the Update Now button in the Software Update preference pane after each new update has been installed to check for these stacked updates. Only when your Mac tells you that no further updates are available do you know that your work is truly complete!

Date & Time Although the Date & Time preference has seemingly limited functionality, it actually lets you perform a variety of functions. Obviously, it allows you to set the date and time, but the panel also enables you to control the appearance and specifics of the menu bar clock, specify your time zone, and synchronize with one of three global network time servers so that your computer clock is regularly adjusted to the global standard time. OS 9 contained a similar Date And Time control panel.

Software Update Software Update is a utility that automatically or manually checks for system security and other bug-fix upgrades and new versions of common software programs such as Internet Explorer, downloads them when you agree to installation, and keeps track of what you've downloaded and installed and what you haven't. Software Update existed for Mac OS 9 as well.

In OS X, the utility proves to be more useful as Apple releases bug fixes and does feature tweaking. We recommend that you set the update option in Software Update to Automatic rather than Manual so that it checks for and downloads updates regularly. After an update has been downloaded, it is displayed in a list from which you may choose it to install.

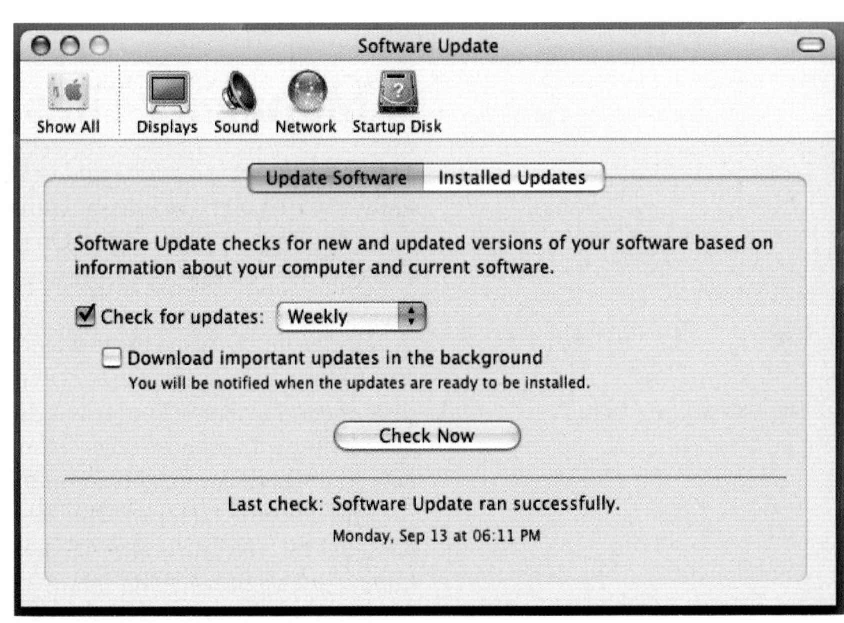

• Software Update application

Speech Speech is a system preference panel that can enable the use of spoken commands for your computer and offers a place where you can customize the voice with which your computer speaks back. This functionality obviously has great potential in environments where computers are being implemented for people with severe physical disabilities; it has been implemented in Macs for many years. OS 9 had a Speech control panel.

Startup Disk The Startup Disk preference allows you to select which operating system boots up the computer on restart. In OS X, this is typically split between OS 9 and OS X. One reason why you would want to boot from OS 9, for those of you who remember the discussion about the Classic environment, is that OS X offers limited functionality for some OS 9 applications it runs from within the compatibility layer. This is particularly true in the case of third-party peripherals such as scanners, which have either refused to work in OS X or have behaved so badly that booting into OS 9 is the only reasonable option. As more scanner drivers are written for OS X, this will become less of an issue.

Printers and digital camera card readers, on the other hand, when attached to OS X computers, seem to work fine.

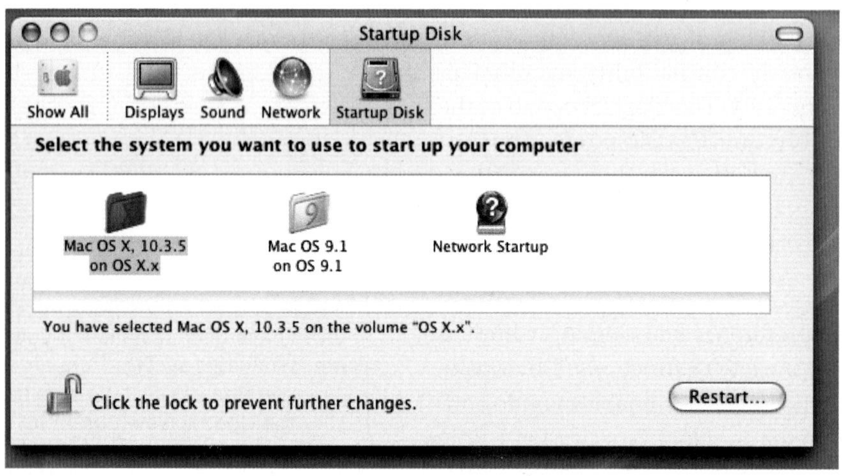

• Startup Disk preference pane

Universal Access The Universal Access preference enables custom keyboard and mouse responsiveness for computer users who require such customization. In OS 9, this functionality required an optional installation from the OS 9 disk.

Managing Files in OS X

The OS X Finder is all you need to know about for file system navigation for daily use of your Macintosh. Unlike Windows, there is no separate Windows Explorer–type interface. On the Mac, the default desktop state *is* "Mac Explorer," if you like. Click the icon for your hard disk, and you've begun to explore.

Finder in OS X has three ways of displaying objects: through icon, list, and column views. The Finder saves the preferred view of the first folder or disk opened in a new Finder window. OS 9 offered two of these three ways of viewing folders and files—icon and list—making the transition to the new Mac OS easier for those comfortable with OS 9.

The unifying factor in all three viewing modes in OS X is the ability to navigate the file and folder structure of your disks and to open files and folders by double-clicking them.

Different Ways of Viewing Files and Folders

Here you will be introduced to the different options you will need to know when viewing files and folders. First, you need to know how these different views are selected.

Open your hard disk structure or any folder by double-clicking it. In Mac OS 9 and OS X, you can set view options from the View menu of the Finder. In OS X, you can also set view options from the toolbar of any open folder or disk.

Mimic OS X! In OS 9, if you hold down the OPTION key while double-clicking a folder, when the new folder opens, the old folder closes!

Icon View

Icon view is the original Mac approach to viewing folders and files, first implemented in 1984. Not that much has changed. You still select items by clicking them once, and you open them by double-clicking them to open them in a new window.

The new twist that OS X has brought to this viewing option is that you can set an option so that a folder opens in the same window when you double-click. In OS 9, this action opened the subfolder in a new window. In OS X, this behavior takes place in all three of the view modes. You can turn this option on and off in the Finder preferences (Finder | Preferences).

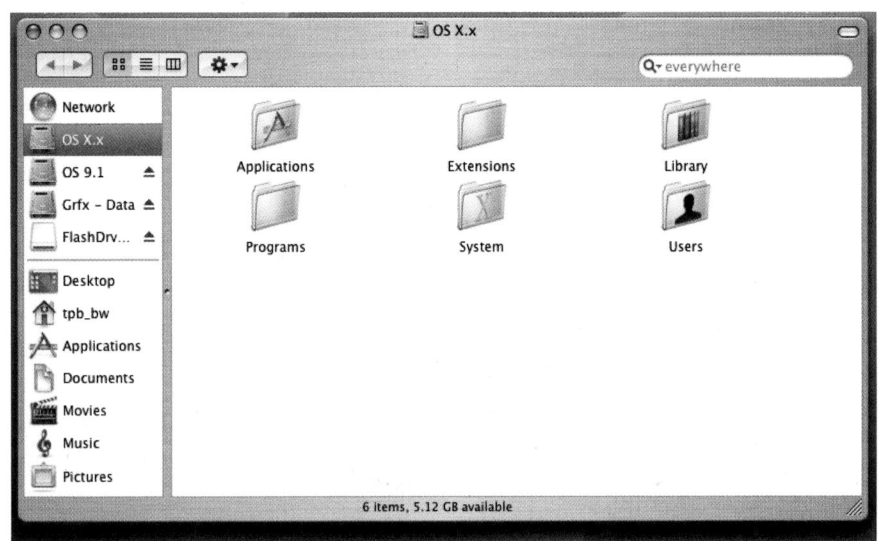

• Finder window in Icon view

List View

Just as in OS 9, List view displays content in an indented outline format that allows you to see the contents of enclosed folders. This is a powerful means of viewing and organizing your folders and files without having to open new windows for each subfolder, a process that can make your virtual desktop as messy as a real one!

To open a folder, click the triangular icon to the left of the folder icon. To close the folder, simply click the icon again to hide the contents of that folder.

The List view offers a wealth of information about folders and

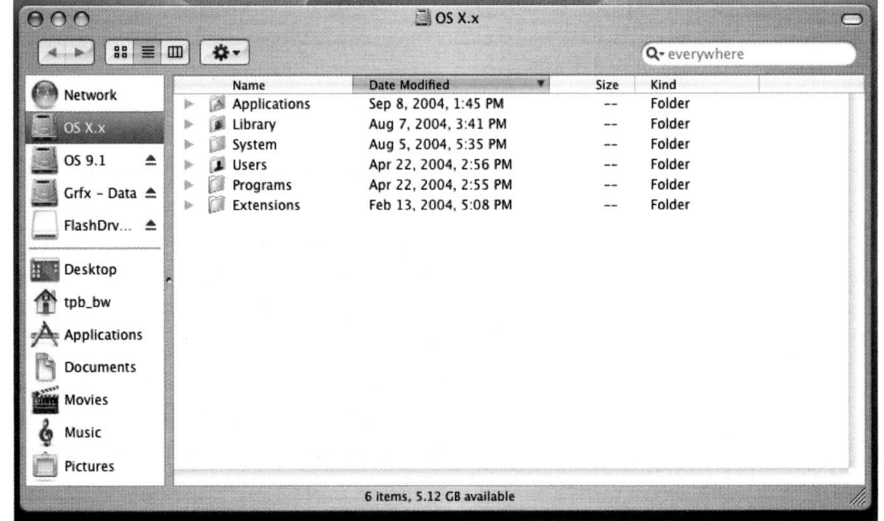

• Finder window in List view

Try This!

Sorting Files in List View

In List view, four columns offer information about your files: Name, Date Modified, Size, and Kind. The default view is an alphabetical sort by name. You can change that order of things. Try this:

1. Double-click a folder or hard disk.
2. Click the title of any of these columns, and you will see your files sorted by that attribute. Sorting based on the Kind column is useful when you want to recover hard disk space. Look for big, obsolete files this way.
3. Click the same title again to see the files sorted by that attribute in reverse order. This technique is most often used with the Date column when you want to search for recently changed or out-of-date files.

files, such as date modified, size, and kind (for example, application or file). If you double-click a folder, that folder opens inside itself, as in the other two view options.

Column View

The Column view is new to the Mac OS, appearing in OS X, although its roots originate in the shareware utility Greg's Browser, released in 1989. In Column view, when you select a file by clicking it once, the file's icon or a preview of its contents, either text or graphics, is displayed to the right of the selected item.

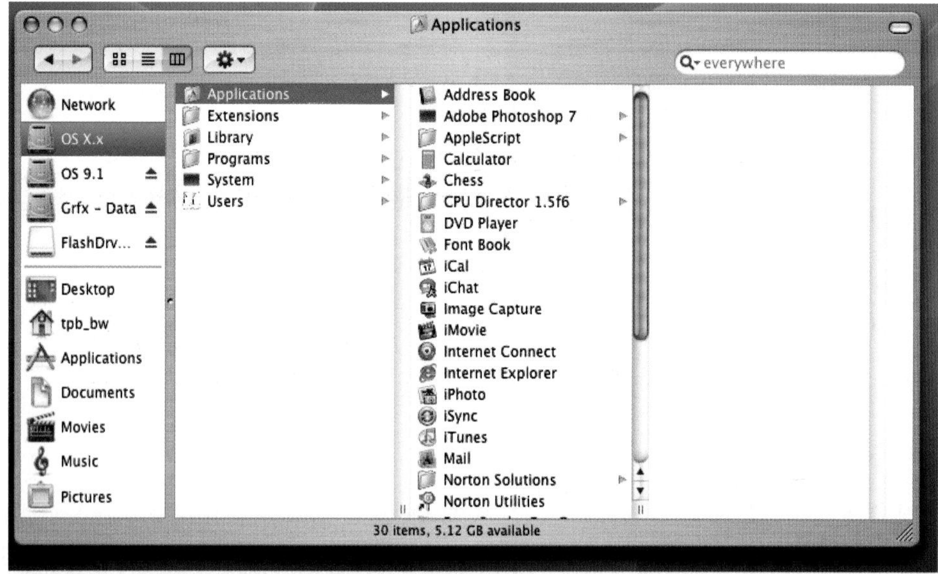

• Finder window in Column view

When you open a file from within an application, Column view is the default browsing behavior. UNIX users and webmasters will appreciate the following shortcut: If you type a forward slash (/) in the Go To box and press RETURN, you will find yourself browsing at the root of your current hard disk. If you're lost, this is your down-and-dirty compass to get to the root of the matter.

This view can be very confusing when you first start using it because it resembles an Open dialog box in OS 9 or Windows, but it behaves differently. It is easy to get confused when clicking a folder and having it leap to the left and open something on the right rather than up and down. A sideways scroll bar at the bottom of the dialog box helps you keep track of where you are.

When a window is in Column view, you can change the size of columns by dragging the bottom of the column divider.

The Toolbar

In OS X, you use the toolbar to select which one of the three view types you want, and the toolbar also offers plenty of space in which to place often-used folder, file, and application aliases. To add items to the toolbar, all you need to do is drag the original item into the bar and release, similar to the action of the Dock. This makes an alias of the item (which is essentially a shortcut to the item) that can be accessed from any open window. You can toggle the visibility of the toolbar by clicking the thin lozenge-shaped button located in the upper-right corner or the top of the open window.

Introduction to Searching with Sherlock

Sherlock is Apple's combination hard disk and Internet search utility. You can use Sherlock to find files on your hard disk or a variety of information on the Internet. Sherlock can perform as complicated or as simple a search as you like through application of a series of attribute filters to narrow down the search criteria. Although OS X Sherlock has a new look, it performs most of the same functions as the OS 9 version, Sherlock 2.

There are two quick ways to open Sherlock.

From an Alias

You can access Sherlock from the Applications folder, or put an alias of Sherlock in any Finder toolbar (which would be available anytime you open a new window) or on the desktop or in the Dock.

To create an alias—which you can do for any type of application, file, or folder—just select the item and select Make Alias from the File menu, and then drag the alias to wherever you'd like it.

If you'll be dragging the alias to the Dock or a window toolbar, you don't even have to create the alias; just select the item and drag it into either location, and an alias will automatically be created.

Finder Shortcuts

When you're working in the Finder, you open a small Find window by choosing File and then selecting Find or by using a simple keyboard shortcut: COMMAND-F.

Detailed Searching with Sherlock

The Sherlock window, looking from the top to the bottom, has four basic areas: Channels, Criteria, Sources/Results, and Details.

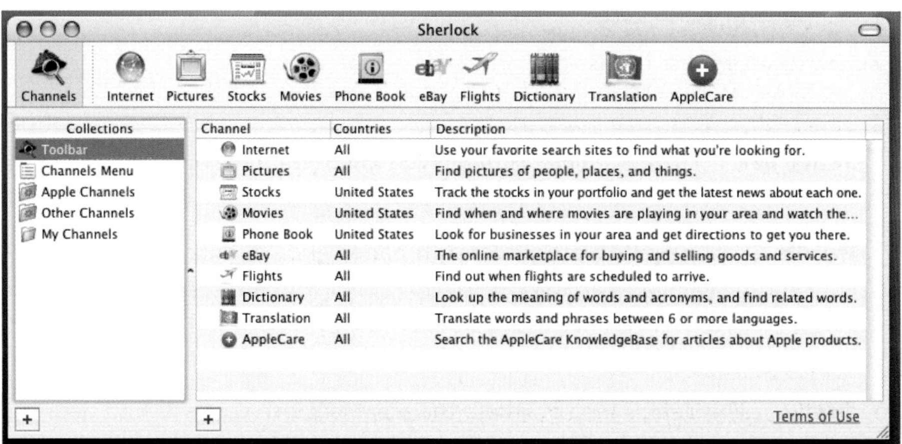

• Sherlock window with channels listed

Channels At the top of the Sherlock window is a button bar containing shortcuts to various search locations, called channels. The buttons that appear here are associated with one of the collections of channels in the Collections pane on the left. Clicking one of the collection icons in the left pane displays the buttons at the top and shows them as a list in the right pane.

Each icon represents a different group of search locations, including a general Internet search and a variety of searches that also involve the Internet, but are targeted to areas such as pictures, stocks, movies, and so on. In reality, most give you access to groups of Internet sites and expose you to advertisements, more than being a useful function. When you click on the button for a channel, it will perform its default search, but each of the channels can be configured. For instance, the default search performed by the Stocks channel displays the latest information on Apple Computer stock, but this channel can be configured to open with the latest information on your favorite stocks.

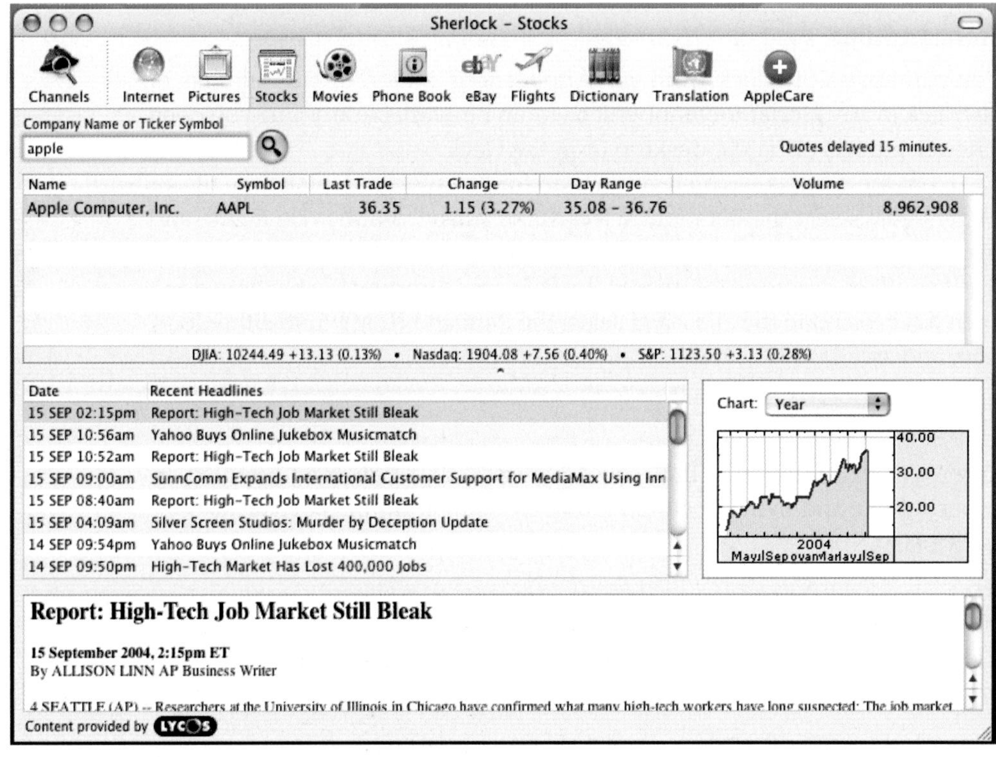

• Sherlock window showing search results

Search Box The search box is displayed after you have opened a channel, allowing you to enter an appropriate search string for the channel.

Results The results window is multi-paned and contains appropriate results for the channel you have searched. To view details of a file or Internet search, click one of the results. The information will be displayed in the details window below.

Details The details area is where the meat is. Here you will find detailed information about the selected search results, and with a simple double-click, you will be taken to its location, be it a web page, file, or folder.

Creating Folders in the Finder

With folders, you can organize your documents and applications in the contents pane. Create a new folder by choosing File | New Folder in the Finder or by right-clicking an area of the contents pane and selecting New Folder.

Copying, Pasting, and Deleting Files and Folders

You can copy and paste files and folders into the same or a different document or folder.

- To copy, select the item and choose Copy from the Edit menu (or press COMMAND-C).
- To cut, select the item and choose Cut from the Edit menu (or press COMMAND-X).
- To paste, first either copy or cut a file or folder. Then open the destination folder and select Paste from the Edit menu (or press COMMAND-V).
- To delete, choose Delete from the Edit menu (or press COMMAND-DELETE). This moves the file or folder into the Trash. To empty the Trash, select Empty Trash from the Finder menu of the Finder (or press COMMAND-SHIFT-DELETE).

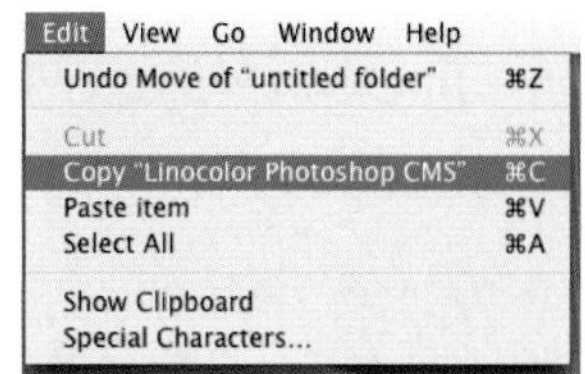

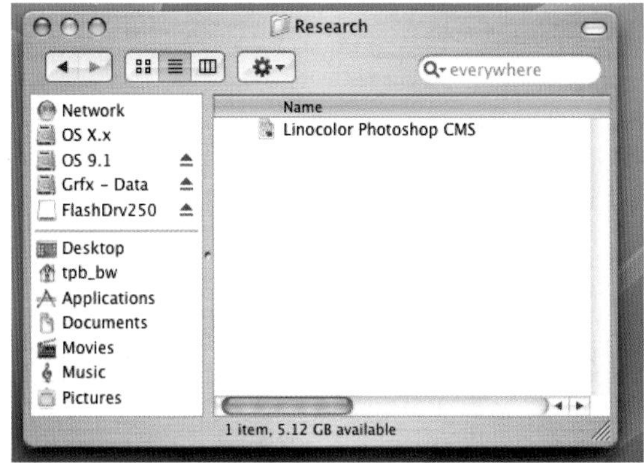

• Copying a folder

Moving and Renaming Files

Moving files and folders is as simple as selecting the item with your mouse, dragging it into the new location, and letting go. You may also select an item and use the cut and paste option described in the preceding section. To copy a file, hold down the OPTION key as you let go of the file or folder.

There are two ways to rename a file:

- Find the desired item to rename and click twice—*but* with a short pause between the two clicks. The name of the item will be highlighted, and you will be able to edit the file name. Click off the item or press RETURN to save the new name.
- Select the item, and in the Finder choose File and then Get Info (formerly File Info) or press COMMAND-I. This will bring up the information window. In the pop-up menu that displays General Information by default, select Name and Extension. In the box, replace the name and extension with whatever new name you want and then close the window.

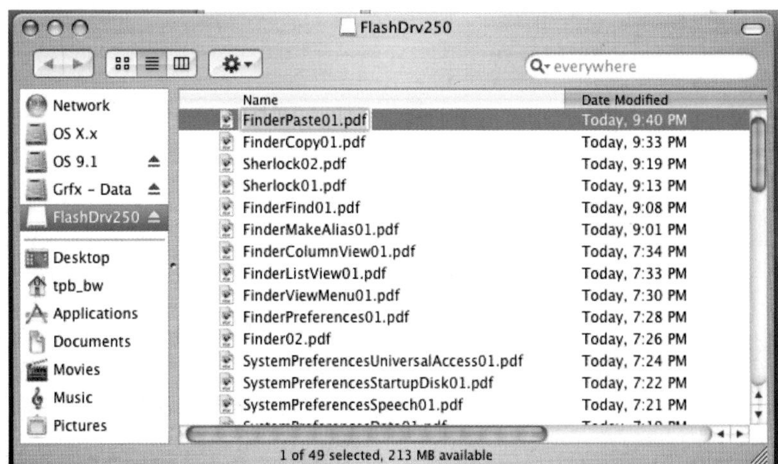

• Info window

Step-By-Step 12.02

Creating a New Folder to Organize Files

In this exercise, you will create a folder within an existing folder, rename it, and move some files into it. To complete this exercise, you will need the following:

- A Mac computer with Mac OS X installed
- A user name and password that will allow you to log onto your computer
- Files in at least one of the folders of your home directory

Step 1 Open your hard drive by double-clicking its icon. In the Finder window that opens, you will see a list of folders. Double-click on a folder that contains some files.

Step 2 Create a new folder. Press COMMAND-SHIFT-N or select New Folder from the Finder's File menu. A new folder, called "untitled folder," will appear in the list of files and folders.

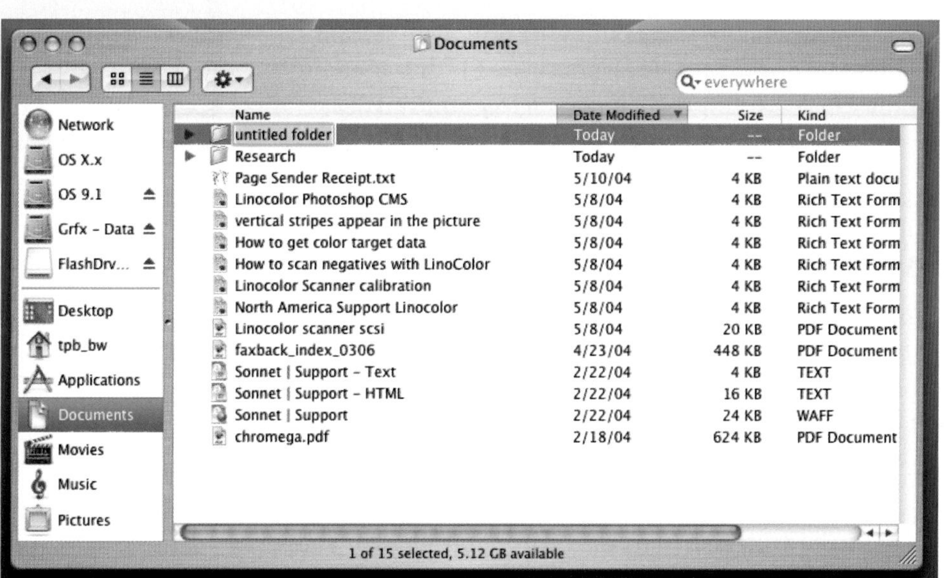

Step 3 Begin typing a new name for the folder; or click the folder once, pause, and then click it a second time to highlight its name, and then type a new name.

Step 4 Select a file or folder that you want to place into this folder by clicking it once. If you want to select multiple files or folders to drag into the folder, hold down the SHIFT key while clicking them.

Step 5 When you are finished selecting items you want to put into the new folder you have created, select one of the highlighted items, drag it over the new folder you created until the folder is highlighted, and then let go. The files will be moved into the new folder. Double-click this folder to check that everything moved as you wanted.

Printing in Mac OS X

No matter what type of printer you have, almost every OS X application manages the printing process in the same way, including giving you the ability to create an Adobe PDF document from any Print menu.

Installing a Printer

The Print command, accessed from the File menu of OS X applications, is your one-stop shop for all printing needs. As in OS 9, printer names appear when printer drivers have been installed. These print drivers prepare page descriptions for printing and also talk with the printer. OS X comes with a large set of common USB printer drivers from Epson, Canon, and Hewlett-Packard, as well as several for Ethernet-connected printers.

If you have one of the included USB printers, OS X will automatically set that printer as the default printer when it is plugged in. If your printer happens to not use one of the many common printer drivers supplied, you can add drivers to Library | Printers and activate them through the Print menu, which we will discuss later.

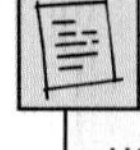

Library is a folder in each user's Home directory (with the user login name).

In OS 9, you would choose your printer through the Chooser, but in OS X, the Chooser represents a now-obsolete step; therefore, most of your printer interaction takes place within the Print dialog box within applications. During printing, the Print Center icon appears in the Dock, allowing you to view, hold, or delete jobs.

Step-by-Step 12.03

Adding a Printer

This step-by-step exercise will take you through the process of installing a new printer. To complete this step-by-step exercise, you will need the following:

- A Mac computer with any version of X installed
- A user name and password that will allow you to log onto your computer
- A printer to connect to the computer or a connection to a network printer

Step 1

If you are not going to connect to a printer via a network and have a local printer to connect, connect the printer cable to your computer, and make sure that the printer is turned on.

Step 2

Select Apple Menu | System Preferences | Print & Fax. On the Printing tab of the Print & Fax pane, click Set Up Printers. This brings up the Printer List window of the Printer Setup Utility.

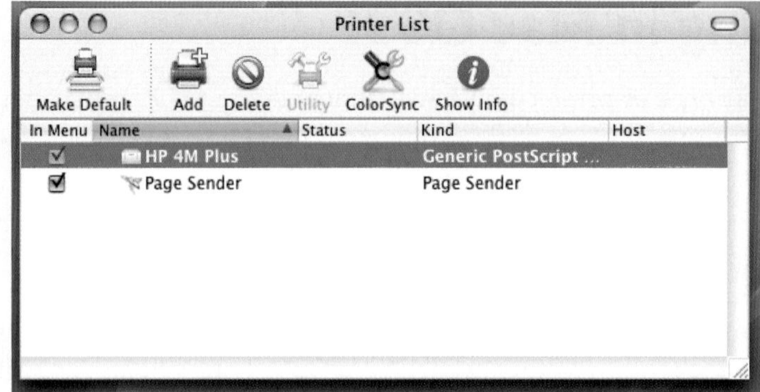

Step 3

Click the Add button to display a drop-down form in which you select and configure the printer. Select the appropriate connection type/protocol from the drop-down menu: AppleTalk, Bluetooth, IP Printing, Open Directory, Rendezvous, USB, Windows Printing, and so on.

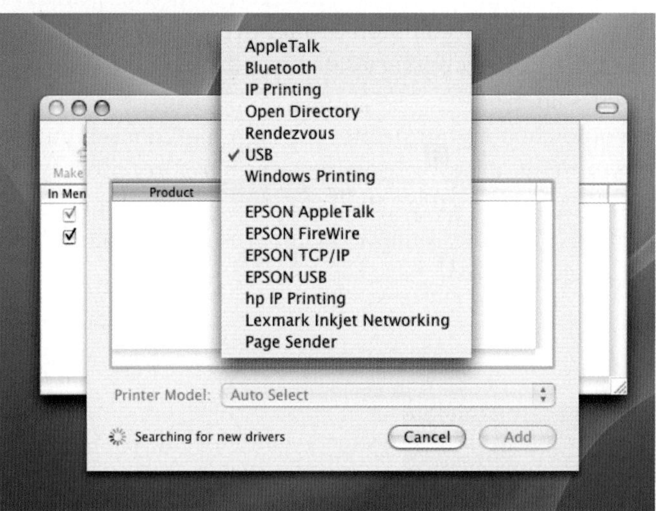

Step 4

When you have selected the connection type/protocol, a form opens in which you can provide more information about the printer. In the example, we show the configuration for a network printer on a TCP/IP network (IP Printing). Select the correct address and Printer Model (Manufacturer), and a list of Models will be displayed.

Step 5

Select the Model Name that matches your printer, and then click Add. The Printer List will appear with the new printer included.

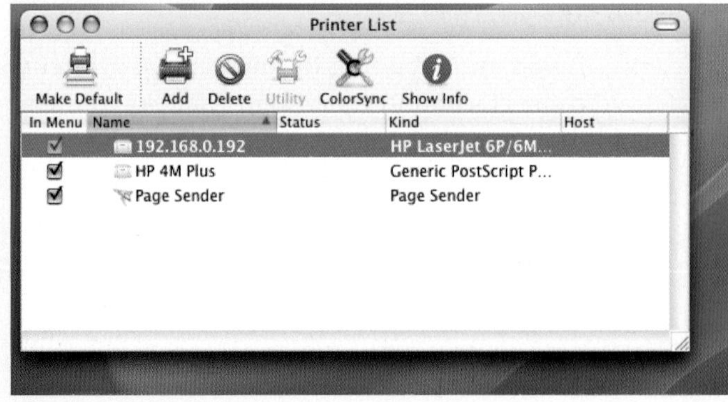

Setting Printing Options

Most printers have a variety of configurable options, which you may modify from the Print menu in an application's File menu. In the Print dialog box, you will have access to a variety of configurable options from a pop-up menu. These options are specific to the printer model, and you will see a variety of options depending on the printer you have selected. You should explore these options for your own printer so that you can take advantage of them.

> **Inside Information**
>
> **ColorSync and Publishing**
>
> *ColorSync is actually an important feature to be aware of if the computers you are using are to be used for print or multimedia design. ColorSync is an industry-standard color management technology that tries to ensure consistent color throughout an entire production cycle. By correctly configuring ColorSync throughout your workflow, you can minimize the chance of unhappy surprises in the often turbulent world of prepress and publishing. Apple's web site has some introductory information at* `http://www.apple.com/colorsync/`.

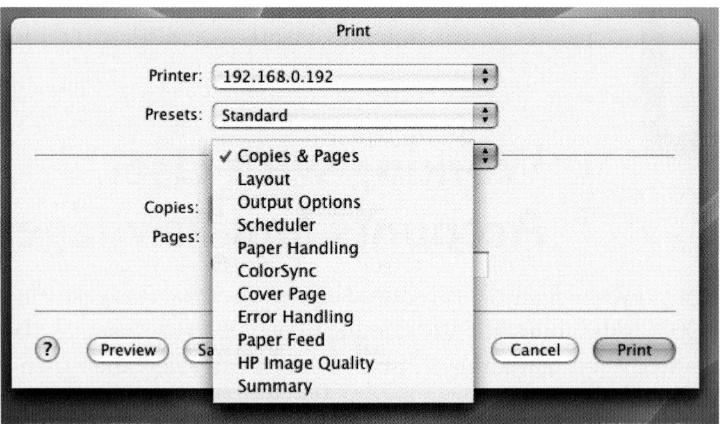

• A set of print options for one model of HP printer

ColorSync, an option on many printers, enables users to specify the ColorSync profile for displays and printers, for better screen rendering and print output. OS 9 had a ColorSync control panel. The first few revisions of OS X had ColorSync in the System Preferences.

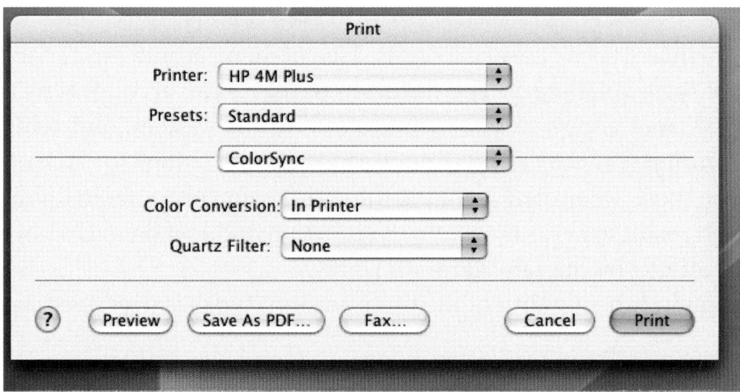

• ColorSync control panel

Where to Find the Print Queue

You can find the print queue for an individual printer by calling up the Printer Setup Utility. One way to do this outside an application is to open the Apple menu and select System Preferences | Print & Fax | Set Up Printers. This will display the Printer List. Double-click on any printer to view its print queue. When you print, the Printer Setup Utility icon can be seen on the Dock, and if you're fast, you can open it in time to see the print

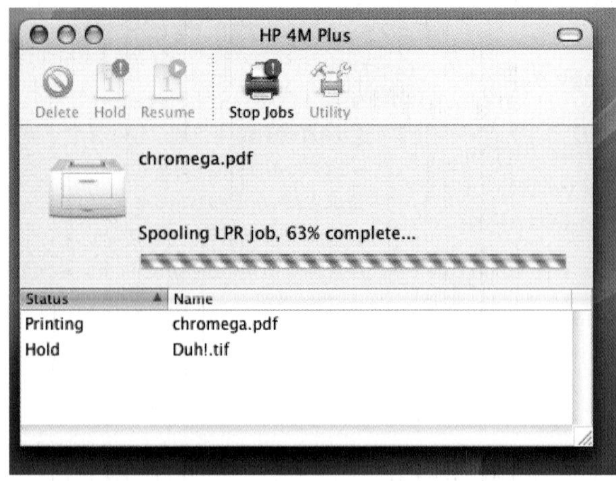

• The Printer Setup Utility with the print queue visible

queue, which closes when the print job is finished. In OS 9, printers are saved on the desktop, where you can double-click them to access the print queue.

Where to Find Page Setup

As in other operating systems, Page Setup is found on the File menu of most applications. Here, you will find options for paper size, orientation, and scaling. Depending on your printer driver, you may be offered additional options.

Working with User Accounts and Privileges

One of the powerful features introduced in Mac OS 9 that was vastly improved in Mac OS X is the ability for any number of people to use a single Mac. Once granted a login account, individual users can select their own custom settings, such as desktop views and bookmarks, and access their own private storage space: the Home folder, located in the Users folder in the hard disk root directory.

For example, one user might choose a right vertical Dock, but this will not affect the next logged-in user's settings, which may be completely different. Other users may have limited access to your Home folder and vice versa; however, all users have access to a shared folder.

> The first-created user account on your computer is automatically designated an administrator. If you happen to forget or lose the administrator password, you can reset it by using the OS X installation CD. To do this, insert the CD and choose Reset Password from the Installer menu. You should keep the CD in a safe place, because anyone with the OS X CD can gain complete access to your system.

> Don't forget that the basis of OS X is UNIX, so references in the text to UNIX are not mistakes!

Types of Users and Privileges

There are three types of user accounts. Two of them, administrator and standard, are self-explanatory. The third, super user, is an account type that offers UNIX root access to your computer and file system, and which you should implement only if you understand the restrictions (or lack of them) placed on these accounts. Changing things on your computer in this account mode can result in serious system dysfunction and lost data. Do not implement it unless you are familiar with UNIX.

The main functionality of the three account types is described here.

Administrator Account

This account type is for advanced users or for the person who will administer this computer, add more users, install software, and the like. This level allows you to:

- Change all system preference settings and install software in the main application and library folders
- Create, modify, and delete user accounts

Standard Account

This account type is for ordinary users, those whom you typically need to save from themselves on a regular basis. This account level will minimize those desperate tech support calls! This level has the following restrictions:

- File access is limited to only the user's Home folder and the shared folder (/Users/Shared/).
- Access is denied to higher-level system preferences, such as network settings, sharing, software update settings, user setup, and date and time settings.

Super User Account

This account type is only for people familiar with the inner workings of UNIX. It is not for normal software installation or use. This level of account:

- Gives you complete control over all folders and files on the Mac
- Is seldom needed for normal use

You will seldom need the amount of control over OS X system files that the super user account allows. OS X is specifically organized to limit the need to change the system files and folders. The files that most users will want to change are located in the main Library folder (administrator access required) or in the user's private Library folder (/Users/*YourUsername*/ Library/), where the Ordinary user has access.

Advanced users may enable this option via the NetInfo Manager (Applications | Utilities | NetInfo Manager).

Creating User Accounts

The first user account is set up when you first install OS X. This account is automatically set up with administrator access. After the installation process is complete, you can create additional user accounts.

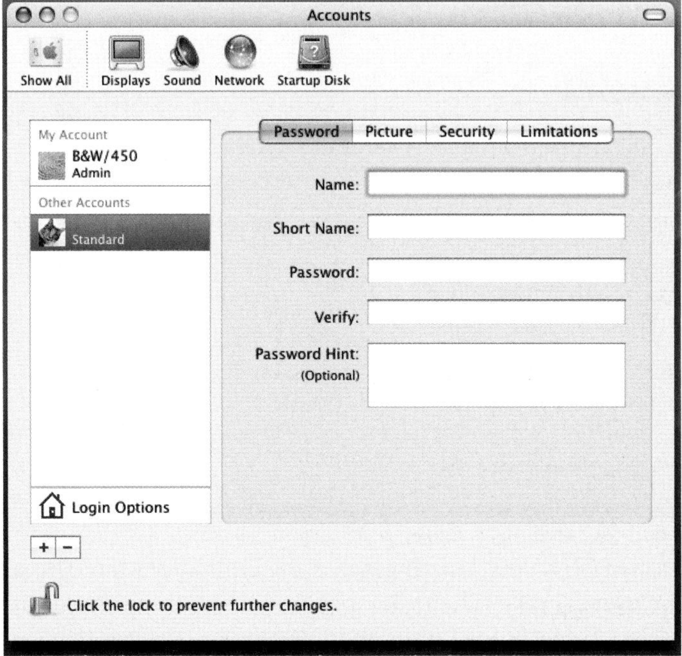

• Adding a user account

Step-by-Step 12.04

Adding a New User

In this exercise, you will add a new user to your computer. To complete this exercise, you will need the following:

- A Mac computer with OS X installed
- An administrator account and password that will allow you to log onto your computer

Step 1

Begin the process of creating a new user by choosing System Preferences from the Apple menu, clicking the Accounts (or Users) preference pane, and clicking the button with the Plus sign (or the New User button).

Step 2

Type a long and a short name in the corresponding boxes. Both are case sensitive, and the short name is limited to a maximum of eight characters with no spaces. OS X uses the short name for the user's home folder as well as to recognize the user during login processes. The full name and password can be changed later, but the short name is permanent. The user can log in as either.

Step 3

Assign the user password. A password can be anything, even blank for any user not needing administrator access. For highest security, the password should contain, at minimum, one number or symbol: for example, 5$muffins. In some early releases of OS X, this page included a check box labeled "Allow User to Administer This Computer," which you would only check if applicable.

Step 4

If available in the release of OS X you are using, select the Limitations tab. This allows an administrator to set the user's limits. When you open it, it shows three levels without detail if No Limits is selected. Select Some Limits and view the restrictions that can be configured. Then select Simple Finder to see a very restricted user.

Step 5

In some versions of OS X, you must click OK at this point to create the new user, but in 10.3.5, the account is created as soon as you provided the Name, Short Name, and password. If you are using an older release of OS X, click OK now to create the user account or Cancel to start over.

Step 6

Automatic login bypasses the login window during startup and logs into the designated user account when the computer is powered on. With Automatic Login turned off, users are prompted to choose their individual accounts and passwords when the computer boots up. Depending on the version of OS X you are using, you will configure automatic login on the Login panel of System Preferences (old releases), or by using the Login Options in the Accounts preference.

Troubleshooting Common Mac OS Problems

In this section, you learn where to find basic help and a guide to the system utilities and keyboard shortcuts that can help you get out of trouble. You'll also learn how to handle the larger files that you'll encounter in today's computing environment.

Where to Find Help

Where do you go to find general help in Mac OS 9 and OS X or from within an application?

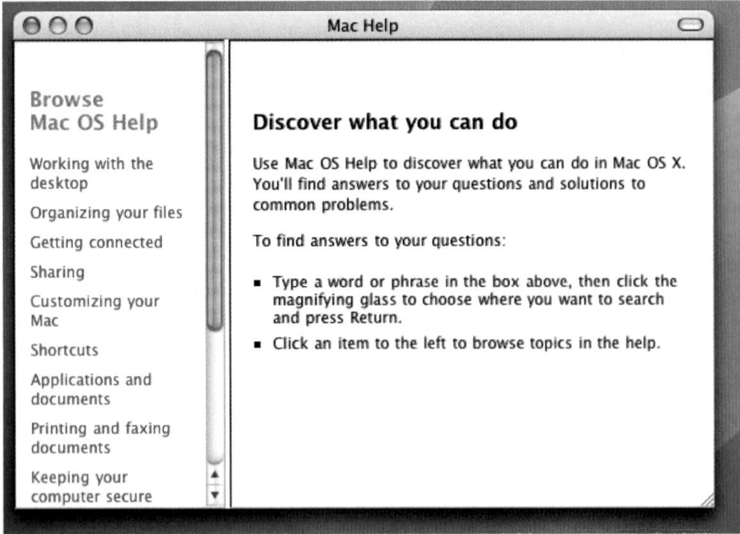

• OS X Mac Help window

Help with the OS

If you have questions about how the Mac OS works, the first port of call is the help facility built into the Mac OS. From the Finder, go to the Help menu and select Mac Help. If the system help does not answer your questions and solve your problem, connect to the Internet and visit Apple's support center at `http://www.apple.com/support/`. Information there is well organized, and Apple's Knowledge Base, manuals, and related discussion groups are all fully searchable.

Help Within Applications

If you are having difficulties with specific software you are using, click the Help menu at the top of the application window, and select the option you need. In many cases, there will be a local help file and an option to find online help for the application.

Inside Information

Alternative Support Options

If self-help fails and your computer is still under warranty, you might want to dial Apple at 1-800-MY-APPLE for help.

Technical support is expensive if your computer is outside its warranty period. Novice users who use their computers enough to increase the likelihood of multiple requests for support should consider signing up for an AppleCare service and support package to keep technical support costs down. More information can be found at `www.apple.com/support/products/`.

Alternatively, you can contact a network of Apple user groups around the world to get support from other users and to learn more about your computer. Apple user groups are a useful and affordable way to increase your knowledge of your system and the software you choose and use. For more information, see `www.apple.com/usergroups/`.

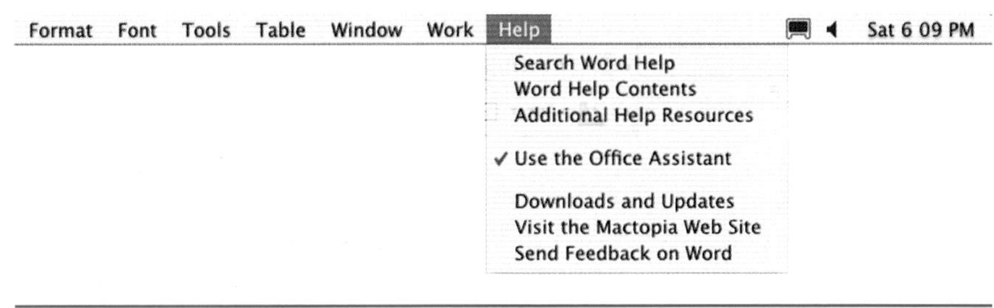

• Help menu in MS Word

Useful System Utilities

The utilities described here for OS X are useful for basic troubleshooting. As with any situation, if you find yourself in deep water, seek expert advice. OS X system utilities offer the same basic functionality as their OS 9 predecessors. A main difference is that some OS X utilities combine some of the disparate functions of several OS 9 utilities into a single application. Here is a quick guide to OS X's hard disk and network software utilities.

Disk Utility

Found in the OS X Utilities folder (Applications/Utilities/Disk Utility), Disk Utility offers a summary and usage statistics for all volumes attached to the computer. The utility also includes Disk First Aid, which enables you to verify or repair Mac OS Standard, Mac OS Extended, and UFS formatted disks, including hard disks and CD-ROMs. The software also works as a one-stop shop for erasing and partitioning volumes.

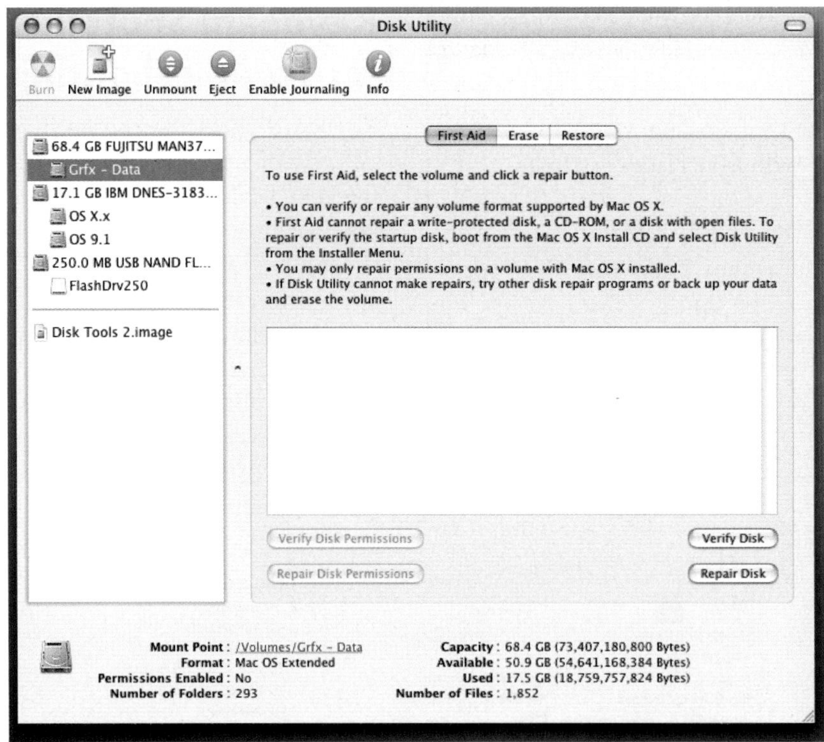

• Disk Utility window

If your system is crashing a lot, one of the reasons may be damage to the hard disk. Running a diagnostic test with Disk Utility can help you find out if there is damage.

Network Utility

Also found in the OS X Utilities folder (Applications/Utilities/Network Utility), Network Utility identifies your hardware and IP address, gives you transfer and other network statistics, and performs a variety of other network and Internet scans, lookups, and directory searches, including ping, lookup, traceroute, whois, finger, and port scan.

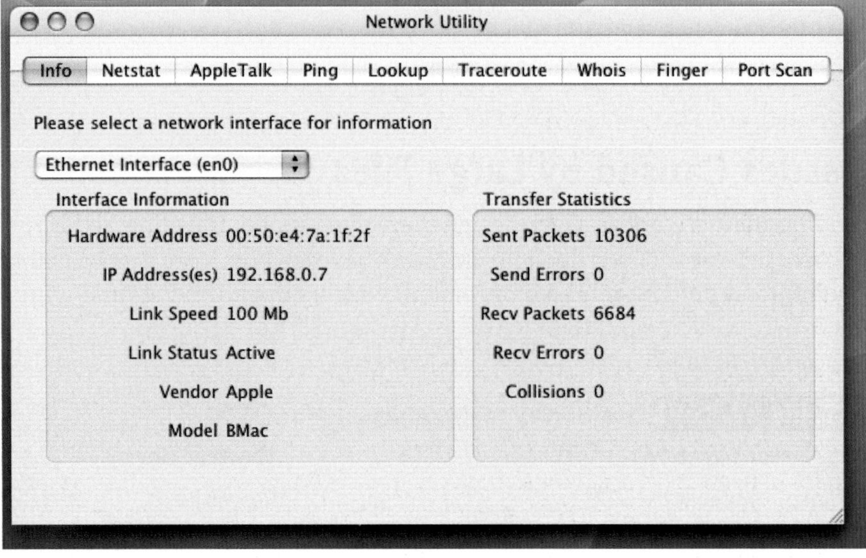

• Network Utility window

Try This!

Mac Help to the Rescue!

If you're in OS X and can't remember the keyboard shortcuts for escaping a program freeze, jog your memory with Mac Help. Try this:

1. Click the desktop to make sure you're in the Finder.
2. Move the mouse to the Finder's Help menu and select Mac Help or press COMMAND-SHIFT-?.
3. Type **Freeze** in the search field.
4. Click the Ask button.
5. Choose Shortcuts For Freezes.

Keyboard Shortcuts for Troubleshooting

Keyboard shortcuts can help you get out of application or system freezes. Table 12-3 lists common keyboard shortcuts for OS X.

In OS 9, sometimes forcing an application to quit also forced the user to restart the computer, because the freeze would transfer to the Finder. In OS X, forced quits of applications rarely affect the performance of the rest of the computer's functions.

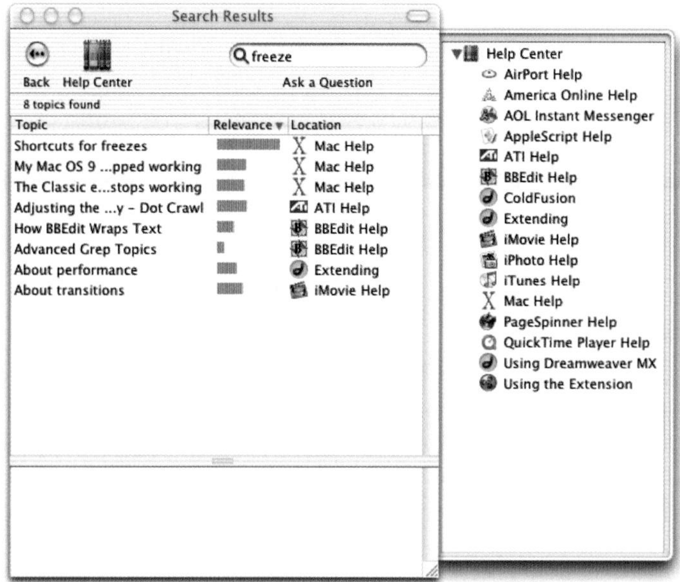

• Freeze recovery information in OS X Mac Help

Issues Caused by Large Files

In 1998, John's work as a web designer involved a lot of traveling, so he purchased an Apple PowerBook. As he didn't have a whole lot of money at that point, John bought a 233-MHz version, which shipped at the time with a 6GB hard disk and 32MB of RAM.

Table 12-3 Useful Keyboard Shortcuts for OS X

Shortcut Function	Shortcut Keys
Turn computer ON/OFF	Power key
Stop a process/cancel an operation in progress	COMMAND -. (period)
Force an application to quit	COMMAND-OPTION-ESC
Start computer from CD	Press C during startup

Because the graphic design aspect of web design is aimed at a screen destination rather than print, most of the Photoshop work John did involved small files with a screen resolution of 72 dpi (dots per inch), and therefore 32MB of RAM felt sufficient. While it's nice to have extra RAM on your computer to enable optimum software speed, the system operated at an acceptable level for the workload John had.

As time went on and the number of files John created in the course of his work steadily increased, John became aware that he needed to institute some backup for the data. Literally the week before he purchased an external CD-RW drive to accomplish this, disaster struck. Before John's PowerBook reached its first birthday, his computer's hard disk crashed and refused to reboot. Third-party utilities that he rushed to get hold of couldn't help.

John took the computer to an authorized Apple repair shop that specialized in data recovery. After $800 in data rescue fees, he had an answer as to why his system had crashed. Although Photoshop and the other graphic and multimedia software John used were functioning fine for his purposes, something else was going on behind the scenes.

The temporary files that Photoshop creates for its processor-intensive graphical functions are large. When a computer doesn't have much RAM, these files are not held in RAM but are written and rewritten to the hard disk's free space over and over and over. In the case of John's system, this caused massive fragmentation of the hard disk, to the point where the huge database that keeps track of such things became corrupted beyond the system's capacity to recover it.

These days—especially with Apple's promotion of the Mac as "the hub of your digital lifestyle" and its inclusion of music burning, movie editing, photo processing, and DVD creation software on its consumer-level computers—normal users who don't necessarily use their computer as much as John does are increasingly dealing with massive files on a regular basis.

Users who fit the pattern described here should take the following steps to ensure that they don't fall into the same costly trap that John did:

- Get enough RAM. Remember: There's no such thing as too much RAM—get as much as you can afford for your system. Applications will run faster and more smoothly, and your hard disk is less likely to misbehave.
- Purchase some form of backup solution. CD-RW drives offer an affordable means, and each CD-R has a capacity of 750 to 800MB.
- Make regular backups of all your data. It is up to you to determine which data you have is most valuable. This data should be backed up regularly. Some software can automate this process: for example, Retrospect Express Backup software by Dantz (distributed as part of Norton's SystemWorks for Macintosh) copies files to a huge variety of removable disks or cartridges, including CD-R, CD-R/RW, Zip, Jaz, SuperDisk, magneto-optical, and DVD devices.
- Once every six months or so, either run third-party optimization software such as Norton Speed Disk (part of the SystemWorks package), which defragments and organizes files on your hard disk, or reformat your computer's hard disk from scratch and reinstall everything. This will ensure that your hard disk is not fragmented, even in the case of excessive use.

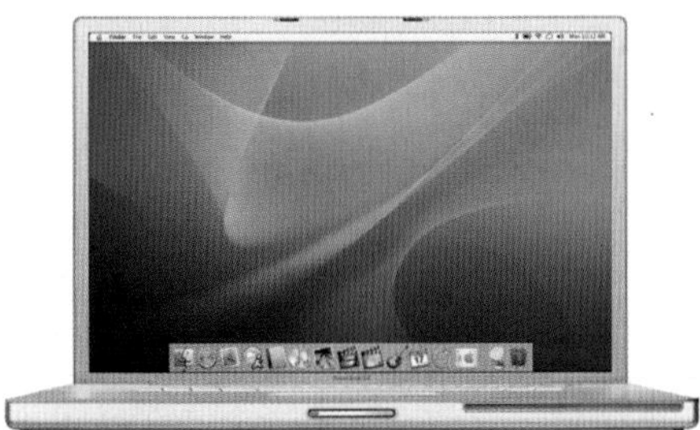

Courtesy Apple Computer

• PowerBook

Other Backup Options

Other backup options include the following:

- If you have an Apple computer with a SuperDrive that burns DVDs, each DVD-R can be used to hold 4.7GB of data. Data backup onto DVD-R is available only for OS X.
- Purchase an external FireWire drive or a second internal hard disk (for desktop systems only).
- Back up your files to a workplace LAN (speak to your system administrator).
- If you don't have access to a LAN, you can make use of various online storage solutions such as Apple's iDisk (`www.mac.com/`). These typically are limited to a few hundred megabytes of storage.

Useful System Diagnostic/Repair and Backup Utilities

The following sites offer access to useful software utilities for system diagnosis and repair (SystemWorks, Drive 10, TechTool Pro, and Hard Disk Toolkit) and data backup (Synchronize! Pro X and Backup Toolkit):

- SystemWorks (`www.norton.com/`)
- Drive 10 and TechTool Pro (`www.micromat.com/`)
- Synchronize! Pro X (`www.Qdea.com/`)
- Hard Disk Toolkit and Backup Toolkit (`www.fwb.com/`)

Chapter Summary

After reading this chapter and completing the Step-by-Step tutorials and Try This! exercises, you should understand the following facts about Apple computers and the Mac OS:

Introducing Apple and the Macintosh Operating System

- Apple sold the first affordable personal computer with a graphical user interface.
- Apple has never licensed its operating system (except briefly and experimentally) to any other company, meaning that the hardware and software of the Mac are a proprietary combination.
- Apple accounts for only a small percentage of personal computer sales in the United States.
- Macs have traditionally been popular with creative professionals, particularly those needing strong graphical and multimedia performance, and the publishing industry.
- Apple computers are well known for ease of use and an attractive graphical user interface.
- There are two distinct Mac operating systems in wide use: Mac OS 9 and Mac OS X. The GUIs are basically comparable and will not be entirely unfamiliar to Windows users.
- Loaded Apple computers these days ship with the software and hardware that allow you to perform a variety of multimedia tasks, including video editing and CD and DVD burning.
- OS 9 software can run on OS X from within a compatibility layer known as Classic.
- OS X is based on a UNIX core and so enjoys greater stability, complies with networking and security standards, and appeals more to system administrators and developers.
- OS X's graphical user interface is known as Aqua.
- All Macs these days ship with Ethernet, FireWire, and USB ports and are AirPort or AirPort Extreme ready.
- Jaguar, the code name for OS X's 10.2 build, has vastly improved connectivity support for Windows and other non-Apple servers.
- Panther, the code name for OS X's 10.3 build was released in October 2003.
- Tiger is the code name for OS X's 10.4 build, which should be released by the time you read this book.
- Apple's UNIX core is known as Darwin and is a product of the open-source development community, with all the advantages that brings.
- OS X offers strong multi-user support.
- OS X comes ready for many common peripherals such as Canon, Epson, and Hewlett-Packard printers.
- Macs tend to be less likely to be affected by computer viruses than Windows computers.

Installing and Configuring Mac OS X

- You will need to determine which version of the Mac OS is currently installed. OS 9.1 is the minimum required for an installation of OS X. You may need to upgrade your software.
- Even though Apple's software runs on Apple's proprietary hardware, some hardware configurations will not be sufficient to run OS 9 or OS X. Check to see that your hardware meets the minimum requirements. You may need to upgrade your firmware.
- Have your Internet configuration ready before setup. If your Internet connection is a DSL connection, you will need to get your hardware address registered with your Internet service provider. Do this before installation to avoid an interruption in the process.

Features of the Mac OS Desktop

- The Mac typically hides back-end operations that its users do not need to know.
- The Finder is the default state and file management interface of the Mac OS.
- The Dock is a key component of OS X.
- Sherlock is the native local file and Internet content search utility of the Mac.
- The Print menus of applications in OS X contain most printing functionality, and the print queue opens automatically during printing as a page of the Printer Setup Utility.

Getting to Know the Mac OS X Workspace

- Many OS X system preferences correspond to the earlier OS 9 control panels. Some OS X system preferences incorporate functionality previously found in more than one control panel.
- The Software Update preference is very important because it notifies you when Apple has released important security and functionality updates to your operating system.

Managing Files in OS X

- Files and folders may be viewed in three different modes in OS X: Icon view, List view, and Column view. OS 9 has the Icon and List views, does not have Column view, but offers an additional Button view.
- The Sherlock search utility can search local hard disks, the Internet, and even content channels such as news or shopping.

Printing in Mac OS X

- Adding printers is typically a simple process in the Mac OS.
- Multiple user accounts for Apple computers are a strong feature of OS X and are simple to manage.
- ColorSync is an important printer setting to configure for those in the design and publishing industries, as it manages color consistently throughout a multifunction workflow process.

Working with User Accounts and Privileges

- Mac OS X allows an administrator to configure a Mac so that any number of people may have individual user accounts and private storage space in personal home folders. Each user will also have his or her preferences.
- The first user account in the Mac OS X is automatically designated an administrator. If you forget the user name or password for this account, you can use the OS X installation CD to reset the password.
- The types of user accounts in OS X are administrator, standard account, and super user.
- The administrator account type can change all system preference settings and install software in the main application and library folders.
- The standard user account type can only access files in the user's home folder and in the shared folder (/users/shared/). The super user account type has complete control over all folders and files on the Mac and is seldom needed. Create and manage user accounts through System Preferences | Accounts (or Users).

Troubleshooting Common Mac OS Problems

- Pressing COMMAND-OPTION-ESC forces an application to quit in both versions of the Mac OS. OS X handles this extreme measure very well.
- Use of software that creates large temporary and other files on a computer with limited RAM causes excessive fragmentation of the hard disk. Solutions are to increase RAM and optimize your hard drive a couple of times a year.

Key Terms

Apple menu *(607)*
Aqua *(609)*
compatibility layer *(609)*
Darwin *(610)*
Dock *(608)*
Finder *(606)*
hot swappable *(611)*
iTools *(606)*
Jaguar *(610)*
.Mac *(606)*
Mac *(599)*
OS 9 Classic environment *(621)*
Panther *(609)*
prosumer *(610)*
Sherlock *(625)*
system keychain *(606)*
Tiger *(609)*

Key Terms Quiz

Use the Key Terms List to complete the sentences that follow. Not all terms will be used.

1. Apple is the company, and ____________ is the nickname for the computer.
2. To search for files, the utility you need is called ____________.
3. User's login passwords are saved in a database called the ____________.
4. At the core of OS X is a powerful UNIX system called ____________.
5. The 10.4 version of OS X is nicknamed ____________.
6. ____________ is the name of the OS X GUI.
7. A new type of consumer who expects consumer-level affordability combined with professional-level features is called a/an ____________.
8. Where previous versions of Mac OS used the Finder as a task switcher, this task has been delegated to the ____________ in OS X.
9. As the foundation of the Mac OS X desktop, the ____________ is the Apple equivalent to Windows Explorer.
10. The ____________, which is accessed through a small icon at the extreme top-left of the Mac OS X screen, sounds like something you might be given as you are seated in a vegetarian restaurant.

Multiple-Choice Quiz

1. Which of the following is the name of Apple's OS X compatibility layer in which older programs can be run?
   - **a.** Jaguar
   - **b.** Sherlock
   - **c.** Finder
   - **d.** Classic
   - **e.** Darwin
2. What is the minimum version of OS 9 that is needed to run older programs from within OS X?
   - **a.** 8.0
   - **b.** 9.0
   - **c.** 9.3
   - **d.** 9.2
   - **e.** 9.1
3. Which of the following is *not* a requirement for installing OS X on a Mac?
   - **a.** 128MB of RAM
   - **b.** A video card or Apple internal monitor support
   - **c.** A DOS partition
   - **d.** The installation disk
   - **e.** An Apple Mac computer
4. Complete this sentence: In OS X, forced quits of applications…
   - **a.** Often cause other applications to fail
   - **b.** Always require a restart of the OS
   - **c.** Have the same effect on the OS as in OS 9
   - **d.** Usually cause a system crash
   - **e.** Rarely affect the performance of the rest of the computer's functions
5. The ___ key is a handy shortcut when browsing in an Open menu to return to the root of the hard disk you currently are working in.
   - **a.** *
   - **b.** $
   - **c.** #
   - **d.** /
   - **e.** DELETE
6. Which of the following is one of the three file and folder views available when browsing Finder windows?
   - **a.** Date
   - **b.** Icon
   - **c.** Reverse
   - **d.** Finder
   - **e.** Aqua

7. Apple's consumer-level laptop is known as the:
   a. iMac
   b. iTop
   c. iLap
   d. iBook
   e. iCarry
8. OS X's Date and Time system preference can be configured to keep the correct time by regularly comparing your system time with:
   a. GMT
   b. The BBC
   c. A network time server
   d. Your watch
   e. The DOS clock
9. Which type of account must be used to make changes to system files in Mac OS X?
   a. Standard
   b. Group
   c. Administrator
   d. Super user
   e. Global
10. The following is a list of advantages typical of open-source software development. Which item does *not* belong in this list?
   a. Widely available pool of programmers
   b. Fast bug fixing
   c. Free software
   d. Wide distribution
   e. Faster Internet speeds
11. Find the odd one out. Apple's search utility Sherlock can be used to search by all but one of the following:
   a. File name
   b. Contents
   c. File size
   d. Modification date
   e. Usage
12. What keyboard shortcut can be used to force an application to quit?
   a. COMMAND-power key
   b. SHIFT-ESC
   c. SHIFT-RETURN
   d. COMMAND-OPTION-ESC
   e. Pressing C during startup
13. Which of the following is the name of the command-line interface in OS X that allows you to access core systems from a command prompt?
   a. DOS Editor
   b. ResEdit
   c. Terminal
   d. End User
   e. iMonkey
14. Which of the following is not customizable in the OS X Dock?
   a. Size
   b. Position on the screen
   c. Magnification turned on or off
   d. Color
   e. Icons that appear on the Dock
15. Which of the following preference panes allows you to change the time zone?
   a. Time Zone
   b. Date and Time
   c. World Time
   d. Latitude
   e. Longitude

Essay Quiz

1. Write a few sentences explaining why OS X is a superior operating system to OS 9.
2. You are the network administrator at a school. You need to purchase at least five computers for a new classroom extension that has been added. These computers will need to offer basic multimedia services and support multiple users. Your purchase order allows you to buy either the latest G-model Apple desktop computers or iMacs, which cost half the price. Which do you buy and why?

3. Your copy of Microsoft Word suddenly freezes in mid-sentence. Describe the best way to regain control of your Mac.
4. When you brought your new iMac home and completed the information in the Mac OS Setup Assistant, you did not have Internet access. You have signed up for Internet access, and the setup instructions from your ISP request the (MAC address) of your network card. Explain where you will find this information within the Mac OS X GUI.
5. Describe the purpose of the Dock.

Lab Projects

• Lab Project 12.1

One of the users of your network, Helen Bandora, married a longtime friend, Jon Moz, and changed her name to Helen Moz.

While it is simple enough to log into OS X as an administrator and alter her long user name to reflect her name change, changing her short name is not possible in OS X because it was used to create the Home directory *hbandora.* Her Home directory is not particularly full, with some Microsoft Word files in the Documents folder and some MP3s in her Music folder.

You decide that it would be only polite to change both login names. What do you do to get her set up with a correctly named account?

You will need a computer with OS X installed on which you have administrator rights.

You will need to do the following:

1. Determine the solution for setting up Helen Moz with a correctly named account.
2. Find Helen's Home directory on the hard drive.
3. Implement your solution on the lab computer.

• Lab Project 12.2

The manager of your department has asked you to set up a Mac with two USB printers attached and to teach a user how to print something on each of the two printers.

You will need a computer with OS X installed on which you have administrator rights, plus two USB printers. To make this lab true-to-life, it would be useful if one printer were a black-and-white laser printer and the other a color inkjet, so there's a good reason someone might switch between the two.

You will need to do the following:

1. Install and check that both printers are working on your lab computer.
2. Find a willing volunteer.
3. Show the volunteer how to use the Print menu from any application to switch between printers.

• Lab Project 12.3

If you ever find yourself the administrator of a large network, you would want to minimize your network's electricity consumption by instituting good energy practices.

You will need a computer with OS X installed.

You will need to do the following:

1. Go into the Energy Saver control panel, and assess the various options you have for controlling the display and hard disk sleep features. Your goal is to reduce the display and hard disk sleep times to the minimum possible without causing the display to dim or the hard disk to spin down intrusively for users.

2. This is a chance to be creative and aware of the types of users of your network and how they interact with the lab environment. Are computers used constantly, requiring a generous display or hard disk sleep time? Is the amount of RAM sufficient for working with files in memory, or does the hard disk need to be accessed constantly? What kinds of software do your users use: processor- and hard drive–intensive programs such as image manipulation and multimedia programs, or e-mail and word processing software?

About A+ Certification

This book is designed to introduce you to microcomputer operating systems and to help you build the skills you'll need to enjoy a successful career in the field of information technology. As you gain valuable experience and load up on a treasure trove of skills, you'll find that many doors will open to you. But when you're starting out on your new career, one way that you can show potential employers you have the skills to do the job is to earn an industry certification.

What's Certification?

A certification is a license that documents a certain level of skill and knowledge in a particular area of expertise. To attain a certification, you usually have to pass one or more exams. A lot of professions use certifications as a way to demonstrate skills and show potential employers or clients they are qualified to do the job. For example, if you want a job in accounting, you need to get a *Certified Public Accountant* (CPA) certification. If you want to be an auto mechanic, you should get an *Automotive Service Excellence* (ASE) certification. These certifications are recognized by everyone in the industry as proof of a certain level of competence and ability.

Certifications in the field of computer technology are particularly important because changes in technology happen so quickly. Even after you graduate from school, you'll need to keep up with changes in technology in order to advance your career. This doesn't mean you need to keep going back to school every few months, but it does mean you should keep up with the latest changes. Certifications are one way you can show that you are up to date on the latest technologies that matter to your profession.

You can study for a certification in a lot of ways. You can buy a self-study guide at a bookstore, take a course at your local college or university, or find information online. Various vendor certifications will verify that you have the skills and knowledge in a particular company's product. You can find information about vendor-specific certifications at the company's web site. For example, Microsoft (`www.microsoft.com`) offers several different certifications for its software. The *Microsoft Certified Systems Administrator* (MCSA) and *Microsoft Certified Systems Engineer* (MCSE) are two popular certifications that experienced network administrators use to demonstrate their ability to use and manage Microsoft Windows networking technologies.

A+ Certification

The place most PC technicians and other computer specialists start is the A+ Certification, which is an industry-supported, vendor-neutral certification designed to demonstrate basic knowledge and skills in supporting microcomputers. A+ Certification is composed of two exams: hardware technologies and operating system technologies. By passing both these exams, you demonstrate the skills of a PC technician with at least six months experience.

A+ Certification is part of a program developed by the *Computing Technology Industry Association* (CompTIA), which is a nonprofit trade organization with a membership of over 8,000 computer resellers, distributors, manufacturers, and training companies. In addition to A+ Certification, CompTIA offers additional certifications that cover other areas of the computer industry.

Preparing for the A+ Operating System Technologies Exam

The *Survey of Operating Systems, Second Edition* has been expanded to include the objectives for the CompTIA A+ Operating System Technologies exam. Tables listing the exam objectives and the chapters in which the objectives are taught follow.

Domain 1 Operating System Fundamentals

Objectives	Chapters
1.1 Identify the major desktop components and interfaces, and their functions. Differentiate the characteristics of Windows 9*x*/Me, Windows NT 4.0 Workstation, Windows 2000 Professional, and Windows XP.	1, 2, 3, 4, 5, 6, 8, 13 (Windows 98 Bonus Chapter)
1.2 Identify the names, locations, purposes, and contents of major system files.	2, 3, 4, 5, 6, 8, 13
1.3 Demonstrate the ability to use command-line functions and utilities to manage the operating system, including the proper syntax and switches.	2, 3, 4, 5, 6, 8,
1.4 Identify basic concepts and procedures for creating, viewing, and managing disks, directories, and files. This includes procedures for changing file attributes and the ramifications of those changes (for example, security issues).	2, 3, 4, 5, 6, 7, 8, 13
1.5 Identify the major operating system utilities, their purpose, location, and available switches.	2, 3, 4, 5, 6, 7, 8, 13

Domain 2 Installation, Configuration, and Upgrading

Objectives	Chapters
2.1 Identify the procedures for installing Windows 9*x*/Me, Windows NT 4.0 Workstation, Windows 2000 Professional, and Windows XP, and bringing the operating system to a basic operational level.	2, 3, 4, 5, 8, 13
2.2 Identify steps to perform an operating system upgrade from Windows 9*x*/Me, Windows NT 4.0 Workstation, Windows 2000 Professional, and Windows XP. Given an upgrade scenario, choose the appropriate next steps.	2, 3, 4, 5, 13
2.3 Identify the basic system boot sequences and boot methods, including the steps to create an emergency boot disk with utilities installed for Windows 9*x*/Me, Windows NT 4.0 Workstation, Windows 2000 Professional, and Windows XP.	2, 8, 13
2.4 Identify procedures for installing/adding a device, including loading, adding, and configuring device drivers, and required software.	2, 3, 4, 5, 8, 13
2.5 Identify procedures necessary to optimize the operating system and major operating system subsystems.	2, 8, 13

Domain 3 Diagnosing and Troubleshooting

Objectives	Chapters
3.1 Recognize and interpret the meaning of common error codes and startup messages from the boot sequence, and identify steps to correct the problems.	2, 3, 4, 5, 8, 13
3.2 Recognize when to use common diagnostic utilities and tools. Given a diagnostic scenario involving one of these utilities or tools, select the appropriate steps needed to resolve the problem.	2, 3, 4, 5, 7, 8, 13
3.3 Recognize common operational and usability problems and determine how to resolve them.	2, 3, 4, 5, 6, 7, 8, 13

Domain 4 Networks

Objectives	Chapters
4.1 Identify the networking capabilities of Windows. Given configuration parameters, configure the operating system to connect to a network.	9, 10, 13
4.2 Identify the basic Internet protocols and terminologies. Identify procedures for establishing Internet connectivity. In a given scenario, configure the operating system to connect to and use Internet resources.	9, 10, 13

The number at the end of the entry refers to the chapter where the term is introduced. Chapter 13 can be found on the book's web site.

.Mac (Pronounced "dot Mac.") The online file storage and file sharing service provided by Apple. It operates as a virtual hard drive for storing private files and as a web site where you can upload files such as photographs and movies for others to view. (12)

$ prompt (Pronounced "dollar prompt.") The Linux command prompt that is displayed in the BASH shell when you are logged on as an ordinary (nonroot) user. (11)

286 protected mode An operating mode of the Intel processors that first appeared in the 80286 (286) processor. In this mode, only 16MB of RAM is available, and there is no support for virtual DOS machines. (1)

386 protected mode An operating mode of the Intel processors that first appeared in the 80386 (386) processor. In this mode 4GB of RAM can be used by the operating system and programs, and there is support for 32-bit code, virtual machines, and virtual memory. (1)

8.3 alias In Windows versions beginning with Windows NT, an 8.3 file system–compliant name given to a file with a long file name (LFN) in addition to the LFN. (3)

access mode number A value assigned to a file permission in Linux. The user (owner), group, and others each have a different access mode number that is calculated using the following values: read = 4, write = 2, and execute = 1. (11)

account lockout policy An account policy that includes three important settings: (1) the number of tries a user has when entering a password before being locked out, (2) the length of time that an account will be locked out of the system, and (3) when the counter for the number of attempts is reset to zero. (7)

account policies Settings stored on a computer that control how user accounts can interact with the computer. Account policies exist in Windows NT 4.0 Workstation, Windows 2000 Professional, and Windows XP Professional. (7)

activation A method of combating software piracy, intended to ensure that each license for Windows XP is used solely on a single computer. Many vendors now use activation. Microsoft's implementation of activation is Microsoft Product Activation (MPA). (5)

Active Channel web site A web site that delivers updated information to a subscriber's computer on a regular schedule. (13)

Active Desktop A feature introduced in Windows 98 that lets you put web content directly on your Windows desktop. In web view, objects on the desktop behave like links in a web page that you can open with a single click. (6)

Active Directory domain A Microsoft administrative unit organized around a distributed directory services database. Some or all of the network servers maintaining a replica of the directory services database are running Windows 2000 Server or a newer version of Windows Server OSs. (4)

Add Printer wizard A series of onscreen instructions that guide you through the installation of a printer's driver and utilities. (5)

address A pointer to a specific location in memory. (1)

allocation unit See *cluster*. (1)

anonymous FTP site An FTP site that does not require a user name and password, but allows anonymous connection, which means that all users connecting are using the Anonymous account. As such, a user only has the permissions assigned to the Anonymous account. (10)

anti-pop-up A program that blocks pop-ups. (7)

antivirus program A program that examines the contents of a disk or RAM for hidden viruses and files that may act as hosts for virus code. Effective antivirus products not only detect and remove viruses, but also help you recover data that has been lost because of a virus. (7)

Apple menu A pop-up menu opened by clicking on the Apple icon in the upper left of the Mac OS desktop. (12)

applet A mini-application, such as those in the Windows Control Panel, that allows an administrator to configure software or hardware. (6)

application Software that allows a computer user to perform useful functions such as writing a report or calculating a budget. (2)

application server A program that acts as an intermediary between users running client software and a large back-end business application or database. (9)

Aqua The code name for the Apple X OS GUI when it was in development—so named for its blue, fluid appearance. (12)

authentication Validation of a user account and password that occurs before the security components of an OS give a user access to the computer or network. (7)

authorization The process of both authenticating a user and determining the permissions that the user has for a resource. (7)

automated installation An installation of an OS that uses scripts prepared ahead of time. An automated install can run either independently, or with very little input from a user, because the scripts provide some or all responses to queries posed during installation. (3)

automatic IP addressing A method by which a host can be assigned an IP address and all the additional configuration settings automatically. (10)

Automatic Private IP Addressing (APIPA) A method by which a DHCP client computer that fails to receive an address from a DHCP server will automatically give itself an address from a special range that has the value 169 (base-10) in the first octet (eight binary digits) of the IP address. (10)

Automated System Recovery (ASR) New in Windows XP, this replaces the Emergency Repair process of Windows NT and Windows 2000. ASR is available from the Windows Backup program (NTBACKUP.EXE). (5)

Automatic Update A Windows utility that can be configured to automatically connect to the Microsoft site and download updates. (5)

autorun A feature that enables Windows to automatically find and run a program on a CD when it is placed in a drive. (4)

back door A way to bypass security and gain access to a computer. (7)

Backup Utility A utility that can be used to back up system data files. Beginning with Windows XP, the Windows Backup Utility (NTBACKUP.EXE) can also be used to create a set of disks for Automated System Recovery. (5)

BASH An acronym for Bourne Again Shell. The component (shell) that provides the character-mode user interface for entering and processing commands, issuing error messages and other limited feedback. (11)

basic disk Beginning with Windows 2000, a disk type that can have up to four partitions and is compatible with older operating systems. The partition types are primary and extended, of which there can be a maximum of four primary partitions or three primaries and one extended partition. Each primary partition may have only one drive letter assigned to it, while an extended partition must have one or more logical drives (each with a drive letter). (4)

binary digit The smallest unit of storage on disk or in memory. (Also called "bit.") A single bit is like a light switch: either on or off. The "on" state represents 1, and the "off" state represents 0. (1)

binary file A file that contains program code, as opposed to a file containing data. (8)

binding A linking relationship between network components—such as between the network protocol and the adapter. A binding establishes the order in which each network component handles network communications. (10)

bit See *binary digit.* (1)

Blue Screen of Death (BSOD) A widely used term for the blue character-mode screen that displays a Stop or Fatal Error message, indicating that Windows has become unstable and has stopped. (3)

boot disk A floppy disk containing the programs that are used to start an OS. In the case of DOS, the whole computer OS can fit on a single floppy disk. Windows NT, Windows 2000, and Windows XP are all too big to fit on a diskette, and normally these OSs must boot from a hard disk. It is possible to create a limited boot floppy disk for one of these bigger operating systems, but it can only contain the initial boot files from the root directory of the system partition. (2)

boot files In Windows, operating system files that reside in the root of drive C: and are required during the bootup of the operating system. (8)

boot image A special file that contains a boot sector and all the files required to boot up an operating system. A boot image is in a format that can be placed on the disk sector-by-sector. (11)

boot partition In Windows NT/2000/XP/2003, Microsoft's term for the partition containing the system files. (8)

bootstrap loader A small ROM-BIOS program that searches for a boot sector on disk. Once it finds one, it loads it into memory. The boot sector program then looks on the disk from which it was loaded for operating system files, which it will load into memory. (2)

bot Short for robot, a program that runs automatically. (7)

bridge A network connection device that carries traffic from network to network. (9)

built-in security principals Special built-in groups that cannot be modified. Their membership is predefined, and some of them are available to you only when you assign permissions or rights. In Windows NT and Windows 2000, these groups are called special groups; in Windows XP, these are referred to as built-in security principals. (7)

byte A group of eight bits. A single byte can represent a character, like the letter *A*, or represent a very simple command, like "move down one line." (1)

central processing unit (CPU) An integrated circuit (chip) that performs the calculations, or processing, for a computer. See also *microprocessor*. (1)

certificate A digital document issued by a certificate-issuing authority, such as VeriSign (`www.verisign.com`) and GeoTrust (`geocerts.com`). Certificates contain identifying information used for verifying the holder of the certificate and also contain the holder's public key. This can be used to encrypt a message for the user. Only the user holds the private key to decrypt the message. (10)

clean installation An installation of an OS onto a completely empty new hard disk or one from which all data has been removed. (3)

client A software component on a computer that accesses services from a network server. (1)

client/server networking A network dynamic in which client software sends requests to a server asking for information or action, and the server responds. (9)

cluster The minimum space that a file system can give to a file. This is also known as an allocation unit. (2)

code signing A practice introduced in Windows 2000 in which all of the operating system code is digitally signed to show that it has not been tampered with. See also *driver signing*. (4)

cold boot A method of starting up a computer by turning on the power switch. (2)

command prompt In a simple character-mode interface, a place in which commands can be entered. Windows offers a character-mode command prompt for entering commands. Some commands, such as IPCONFIG, can only be entered at the command prompt. (6)

Common Internet File System (CIFS) A file sharing protocol standard used by Microsoft, Novell, and many others. (10)

compatibility layer Apple's term for the environment in which an older operating system (OS 9) runs in OS X. This allows new users of OS X to run older software until newer versions are available that will run natively in OS X. (12)

Computer Administrator account In Windows XP, a type of account that is a member of the local Administrators group. (7)

content filter In an Internet browser, software that blocks content. (7)

Control Panel A Windows folder that contains numerous applets that you can use to adjust the configuration of many different aspects of the OS. (4)

conventional memory In real mode, the first 640KB of RAM that can be used as the workspace for the operating system, application programs, and data. (2)

cookies Very small text files an Internet browser saves on the local hard drive at the request of a web site. Cookies may contain user preferences for a specific site, information entered into a form at a web site (including personal information), browsing activity, and shopping selections made at a web site. (7)

copy An operation in which a file remains in the source location while a duplicate of the file is placed in a target location. (6)

critical update Program code offered by a vendor to modify or update their software in order to solve security problems or problems that can potentially cause major failures. (3)

cursor A graphical pointer that can be moved around a GUI by manipulating a mouse or other pointing device. (1)

Darwin The name of the core operating system on which Mac OS X is based. A product of the open-source community, it allows OS X to provide vastly improved system performance over OS 9. (12)

data type A special data format in the Windows registry. There are several registry data types, such as REG_BINARY, REG_DWORD, and so forth. (8)

default gateway The IP address of the router connected to your network. The net ID of the default gateway address should be identical to that of your NIC. The router is a network device that sits between networks and directs traffic to destinations beyond the local network. (10)

defragmentation The process of rearranging the data stored on disk so that all portions of each file are stored contiguously. (3)

device driver Software that is added to an OS to control a physical component (device). A component-specific device driver is needed for each unique hardware device connected to a computer. (1)

device management An OS function that controls hardware devices through the use of device drivers. (1)

dial-up An inexpensive WAN option available to anyone with a phone line and a standard modem (the longtime standard runs at 56 Kbps). (10)

dialog box A computerized form that you fill in much like a paper form, using the keyboard and mouse rather than a pen or pencil. You encounter many dialog boxes in Windows. (6)

digital certificate A special file stored on a computer that may hold a secret key for decrypting data. (7)

digital signature In Windows, encrypted data that can be unencrypted by Windows in a process called file signature verification. (8)

digital subscriber line (DSL) A WAN service similar to ISDN in its use of the telephone network, but using more advanced digital signal processing to compress more signals through the telephone lines. (10)

directory A special file that can contain files as well as other directories. This term is most often used with non-GUI operating systems, while *folder* is most often used when describing a directory in a GUI. (1)

directory service A network service that can manage all types of network resources, based on certain international standards. (9)

Disk Administrator The Windows NT administrative tool for managing hard disk partitions and logical drive letters. (3)

disk drive A data and program storage device that works by encoding data onto the surface of platters called disks. A disk drive may use magnetic or optical methods, although a platter in an optical drive is one of several types of special removable optical platters, often referred to as a *disc*. (1)

Disk Management Introduced in Windows 2000, this console is the Windows administrative tool for creating and deleting hard disk partitions, formatting volumes, assigning drive letters, and changing the disk type from basic to dynamic. (4)

display screen An output device that shows the visible output from a computer. A traditional display screen is built around a cathode-ray tube (CRT). CRT display screens are fast being replaced by flat-panel displays. (1)

DNS Suffix A top-level Internet domain name such as .com, .net, .gov, or .biz. An administrator can configure a Windows DNS client to attempt additional searches by substituting (in turn) each suffix listed in the Advanced DNS setting. (10)

Dock A floating bar on the Mac OS X desktop that replaces the OS 9 Control Strip. The Dock gives access to a variety of system preferences, including location, Internet dial-up, and screen resolution. (12)

domain In a Microsoft Windows network, an administrative organization with a centralized security accounts database maintained on one or more special servers called domain controllers. This centralized database contains accounts for users, groups, and computers participating in the domain and can be used to authenticate a user for access to any resource of the domain. (6)

domain controller A server that maintains the directory service accounts database in a Microsoft network. (9)

domain name A special label for an administrative unit called a domain. (9)

Domain Name System (DNS) A distributed online database containing registered domain names mapped to IP addresses. Thousands of name servers on the Internet maintain this distributed database. When you attempt to connect to a web site, your computer's DNS client queries a DNS server to determine the IP address of the web site. (10)

DOS prompt The user interface of DOS, also called the command prompt. It includes, at minimum, the current drive letter followed by a blinking cursor, indicating that the command interpreter is ready for input. (2)

drive-by download A program downloaded to a user's computer without consent. Often the simple act of browsing to a web site or opening an HTML e-mail message may result in such a surreptitious download. A drive-by download may also occur when installing another application. (7)

drive path The path from a mount point to a partition or volume. (4)

driver See *device driver.* (2)

driver signing Code signing of device drivers that indicates two things: the integrity of the file or files, and that the device driver has passed Microsoft's tests for compatibility. (4, 8)

dump file In Windows, a file to which memory contents are copied (dumped) when a stop error occurs. The information in a dump file can be used when debugging stop errors. This file can be sent to Microsoft for evaluation of a problem. (5)

dynamic disk A new disk type, introduced in Windows 2000 as a way to allocate disk space and manage hard disks. In dynamic disk types, Microsoft most often describes the space allocated in volumes, not partitions. There is no limit to the number of volumes on a dynamic disk. A dynamic disk volume can be extended to include available space on any hard disk in the computer. The configuration information for a dynamic disk is saved on the disk (outside the dynamic disk volumes), rather than in the registry. (4)

Dynamic Host Configuration Protocol (DHCP) server A server that issues IP addresses and settings to computers that are configured to obtain an IP address automatically, thus making them DHCP clients. (10)

e-mail server A server that transmits, receives, and stores e-mail. (9)

emergency repair disk (ERD) An ERD for Windows NT 4.0 and Windows 2000 contains a backup of the REPAIR directory, found under the WINNT directory. A repair disk can be created during installation of these versions of Windows or by using RDISK in Windows NT 4.0 or NTBACKUP in Windows 2000. It is important to create and keep an ERD up-to-date, because it is needed to recover from damage to the operating system files through the emergency repair process. (3)

Encrypting File System (EFS) An NTFS file encryption feature introduced with Windows 2000 and NTFS5. (7)

encryption The transformation of data into a code that can only be decrypted through the use of a secret key or password. (7)

enterprise network All the connected networks of an organization and all the resources on that network. (9)

extended partition A partition type that can contain one or more logical drives, each of which can use a portion of the partition. FDISK can create only two partitions on a physical drive; only one can be primary, and one can be extended. MS-DOS will boot from a primary partition, but not from an extended partition. (2)

external command A command program stored on disk, rather than within the operating system code that remains in memory. MS-DOS looks for an external command program on disk if it cannot find it in memory. (2)

FAT16 file system A version of the FAT file system used on hard disks by DOS and other operating systems. (2)

FAT32 file system The FAT file system available with Windows since Windows 95 OSR2 (OEM Service Release 2) in the fall of 1996. (2)

file allocation table (FAT) The component of the FAT file system that an OS uses to track where files reside on disk as it allocates space to the files. (2)

file and print server A network server that gives client computers access to files and printers. (9)

file attribute A component of file or directory entries that determines how an operating system handles the file or directory. In the FAT file system, the attributes are read-only, archive, system, hidden, volume label, and directory. (2)

file management An operating system function that allows the operating system to read, write, and modify data and programs organized into files. (1)

file server A network server that gives client computers access to files. (9)

file signature verification The process by which Windows unencrypts a digital signature and verifies that the file has not been tampered with in any way. (8)

File Transfer Protocol (FTP) A protocol used to transfer files between a computer running the FTP server service and an FTP client. It is a preferred method of transferring files over a TCP/IP network, especially the Internet, because it is simple and fast. (10)

Finder The foundation of the Mac OS desktop, the Finder appears by default after startup and is the default GUI/desktop view before any application software runs. It is equivalent to Windows Explorer, the Windows file management tool. (12)

firmware The software contents of ROM. (12)

folder A special file that can contain files as well as other directories. This term is most often used with GUI operating systems, while *directory* is most often used when describing a directory in a non-GUI. (1)

fully qualified domain name (FQDN) The human-readable TCP/IP name corresponding to the TCP/IP address of a host, as found on a computer, router, or other networked device. It includes both its hostname and its domain name. (10)

gigabyte (GB) 1,073,741,824 bytes, or 2^{30} bytes. The prefix "giga" means a billion. (1)

GNOME An acronym for GNU network object model environment, a UNIX GUI that uses the X Windows system. (11)

GNU An organization created in 1984 for the purpose of developing a free version of a UNIX-like operating system. GNU, a recursive acronym for GNU's Not UNIX, has developed thousands of applications that run on UNIX and Linux platforms. Many are distributed with versions of Linux. (11)

graphical user interface (GUI) A user interface that takes advantage of a computer's graphics capabilities to make it easier to use with graphical elements that can be manipulated to perform tasks such as system and file management and running applications. (1)

group account A security account that may contain one or more individual accounts. In some security accounts databases, it may contain other groups. (7)

group policy A grouping of policies (rules) for controlling not only the many security settings, but also configuration settings for the OS. This is done to give administrators the ability to centrally manage many hundreds of settings by using a single administrative tool. (4)

guest A special account used when someone connects to a computer over a network but is not a member of a security account recognized on that computer. That person connects as a guest (if the guest account is enabled) and will only have the permissions assigned to the guest account. (7)

hardware compatibility list (HCL) A list of hardware supported by the OS. Some versions of Windows come with an HCL. (4)

hardware profile In Windows a hardware profile consists of registry keys that contain the following: settings defining the devices that must be started during Windows startup, the list of files associated with each device, and configuration settings for each device. (8)

Help and Support Center The improved Help utility found in Windows XP. (5)

hive The portion of the Windows registry represented in one registry file. (8)

home directory A directory created for a user, using the user's login name, and located under the /home directory. This is the one place in Linux where an ordinary user account has full control over files without being logged in as the root account. (11)

host ID The portion of an IP address that identifies the host on a network, as determined using the subnet mask. (10)

hot swappable A feature of certain hardware that eliminates the need to power off a computer before connecting or disconnecting peripherals. (12)

hub A network device that the media from each node connects to. (9)

hyperlink A link to a different location or document. That location can be elsewhere in the same document, or in another document, or it can be a uniform resource locator (URL) that points to a web page, FTP site, or other resource on a network. (13)

hypertext markup language (HTML) The language of the World Wide Web. The pages you view on the Web with your browser are written in this language, which your browser interprets in order to display the pages on the screen. (9)

icon A tiny graphic representing an object such as a file, folder, disk, menu item, or program. (6)

identity theft This occurs when someone collects personal information belonging to another person and uses that information to fraudulently make purchases, open new credit accounts, or even obtain new driver's licenses and other forms of identification in the victim's name. (7)

image An exact duplicate of the entire hard drive contents, including the OS and all installed software, that is used to install copies of an OS and associated applications on multiple computers. (3)

imaged installation An installation that uses an image of a hard disk. (13)

Indexing Service A service, introduced in Windows 2000, which maintains indexes of the files (both properties and contents) on your hard drive. This service watches for changes on the drive and updates the indexes every time changes occur. These indexes speed up searches by any program (such as the Search program) that knows how to use them. (4)

input To send something into a computer. Keyboard entry is input, as is having your word processing program read a file from disk. (1)

input/output (I/O) Anything sent into a computer (input); anything coming out of a computer (output). Every keystroke you enter, all files read in, and even voice commands, are input. Output can include a printed page, what you see on the screen, and even sounds. (1)

InstallShield A special installation program developed by InstallShield Software Corporation (now owned by Macrovision Corporation) that runs as a wizard and guides the user through the installation of software. (5)

integrated services digital network (ISDN) A digital telephone service that simultaneously transmits voice, data, and control signaling over a single telephone line. ISDN service operates on standard telephone lines, but requires a special modem and phone service, which adds to the cost. An ISDN data connection can transfer data at up to 128,000 bits per second (128 Kbps). (10)

internal command A command program within the operating system code that remains in memory. MS-DOS internal commands are stored within COMMAND .COM. (2)

Internet Assigned Numbers Authority (IANA) The central organization responsible for allocation of public IP addresses. They allocate numbers to various Regional Internet Registries (RIRs), which are organizations given the task of allocating IP addresses to Internet service providers (ISPs). (10)

Internet Protocol (IP) A core TCP/IP protocol that packages your communications in chunks, called packets. This protocol allows your computer to be identified on an internetwork by a logical address called an IP address. Special routing protocols can use a destination IP address to choose the best route for a packet to take through a very complex internetwork. IP also has subprotocols that help it accomplish its work. (10)

Internet service provider (ISP) An organization that provides individuals or entire organizations access to the Internet. For a fee, an ISP provides you with this connection service and may offer other Internet-related services such as web server hosting and e-mail. (10)

internetwork Two or more interconnected networks. (9)

IPCONFIG A command-line command that displays the IP configuration of a computer's network interfaces. (10)

ISO image A copy of the entire contents of a CD that can be easily transferred to a writeable CD with ISO image copy software. (11)

iTools The former name of the .Mac online file storage and file sharing service provided by Apple. It operates as a virtual hard drive for storing private files and as a web site where you can upload files such as photographs and movies for others to view. (12)

Jaguar The code name for version 10.2 of Mac OS X. (12)

job management An operating system function that controls the order and time in which programs are run. For example, an operating system's print program can manage and prioritize multiple print jobs. (1)

kernel The main component of an operating system that always remains in memory while a computer is running. (1)

key In the Windows registry, a folder object that may contain one or more sets of settings as well as other keys. (8)

key A password or other code that is used to encrypt ("lock") or decrypt ("unlock") a message. A public key is used to encrypt a message, and a private key is used to decrypt a message. (10)

Knowledge Base A database of articles on problems and solutions created by Microsoft Support Services for Microsoft products, and by other vendors for their own products. (13)

launch by association The ability to start up an application by double-clicking a data file that is associated with the application. The application starts, and the data file is opened with the application. (6)

limited account An account type in Windows XP that is a simplistic reference to an account that only belongs to the Local Users group. (7)

Linux An open-source operating system based on UNIX that was developed by Linus Torvalds and others beginning in 1991. (11)

local group A security account that contains one or more local user accounts and, when a computer is a member of a Windows domain, may also contain domain user or group accounts. (7)

logical drive A portion of a physical hard drive that is treated as a separate drive with a drive letter assigned to it. (2)

long file name (LFN) A file name that breaks the 8.3 file naming rules by allowing up to 255 characters (including spaces). LFNs are supported by the VFAT driver on all implementations of FAT in 32-bit Windows. (3)

Mac The nickname for Apple's computers. (12)

mail server A server that transmits, receives, and stores e-mail. (9)

manual installation A method of installing an OS or application that requires interaction between the user and the installation program throughout the entire process. The user must provide information and respond to messages. (3)

mapping The act of assigning a drive letter to a network share. (10)

media In a network, that which carries the signals between devices on the network. (9)

megabyte (MB) 1,048,576 bytes, or 2^{20} bytes. The prefix "mega" means million. (1)

memory The physical chips that store programs and data. There are two basic types: random-access memory (RAM) and read-only memory (ROM). (1)

memory management An operating system function that manages and tracks the placement of programs and data in memory. Advanced operating systems, such as Windows, Linux, and Mac OS X, use memory management to make optimal use of memory. (1)

menu A list of choices that launch applications, start utilities, or open dialog boxes. Menus are available in both GUI and non-GUI interfaces. (6)

message header Information added to the beginning of an e-mail message that contains details such as who sent it and the subject; it also may show the time and date of the message along with the message's size. (10)

microcomputer A computer built around a microprocessor. (1)

microprocessor An integrated circuit (chip) which performs the calculations, or processing, for a computer.

Also called a processor or central processing unit (CPU). (1)

Microsoft Product Activation (MPA) See *activation*. (5)

mirrored volume A dynamic disk volume available only in the Windows 2000 Server and Windows Server 2003 products. A mirrored volume includes two identical copies of a simple volume, on separate physical disks, created nearly simultaneously. Therefore, if one disk in a mirrored volume fails, Windows 2000 will "fail-over" to the still-working member of the mirrored volume, drop the failed member, and use only the surviving member. (4)

motherboard The central circuit board of a computer to which all other devices connect. (1)

mount point Beginning with Windows 2000, a new feature is available on both basic and dynamic disks. Using a mount point (an empty directory on an NTFS volume), a partition (basic disk) or volume (dynamic disk) need not have a drive letter assigned at all, but can be "connected" to an empty folder on another volume. The path to the partition or volume is called a drive path. A partition or volume can have both a drive letter and one or more drive paths. (4)

mouse An input device. Movement of a mouse over a surface is translated into movement of the cursor on the display screen. (1)

move An operation in which a file is copied to a target location and deleted from the source location. (6)

MS-DOS compatibility mode A mode that allows Windows 9*x* to use MS-DOS device drivers for older devices. Running in MS-DOS compatibility mode enables use of both 16-bit and 32-bit device drivers, but such use slows down the OS and makes it more prone to failure. (13)

MS-DOS mode A special mode for DOS applications that do not run well in a DOS virtual machine under Windows 9*x*. Once this mode is configured from the properties of the DOS application or its shortcut, whenever the application is run, Windows 9*x* removes much of its own program code from memory and loads a real-mode copy of MS-DOS. It may even reboot into MS-DOS mode to load special drivers or other programs required by the DOS application. When the application is closed, the system boots back into Windows 9*x*. (13)

multitasking Two or more programs (tasks) running simultaneously on a computer. (1)

net ID The network portion of an IP address, as determined through the subnet mask. (10)

NETSTAT A command that displays network statistics, protocol statistics, and information about current TCP/IP connections. (10)

NetWare Core Protocol (NCP) Novell's file sharing protocol, used in their server products for many years. (10)

network operating system (NOS) Software that enhances a basic OS by adding networking features. (1)

network resource Anything that can be shared over a network. (9)

node A computer, when connected to a network. (9)

NSLOOKUP The classic command-line command for troubleshooting DNS, used for many years on the Internet and other TCP/IP networks. (10)

NTFS Short for NT file system. NTFS has features to improve reliability over the FAT file system, such as transaction logs to help recover from disk failures. It also allows controlled file access via permissions for directories and/or individual files. (3)

NT file system version 4 (NTFS4) The version of NTFS introduced with Windows 2000. (3)

octet A group of eight binary digits. (10)

open source A certification standard issued by the Open Source Initiative (OSI) that requires that the source code of a computer program be made available free of charge to the general public. (1)

open-source software Software distributed with all its source code, allowing developers to customize it as necessary. (11)

operating system (OS) A collection of programming code that provides a computer with critical functionality, such as a user interface, management of hardware and software, and ways of creating, managing, and using files. (1)

OS 9 Classic environment The compatibility layer that allows Mac users to run OS 9 software from within OS X. (12)

output That which comes out of a computer, such as text or graphics on a screen display or printed page. Output also includes sounds that come from the computer speaker. (1)

owner In Linux, the user account that creates a file or directory. (11)

packet A piece of a message packaged by the Internet Protocol. In addition to the portion of a message, each packet is given a header that contains information including the source address (local host address) and the destination address. (10)

panel An object in the GNOME GUI (for Linux) resembling the Windows taskbar and residing at the bottom of the screen. On the left of the panel is a Red Hat icon with a tiny triangle that can be used to open the GNOME menu, which is similar to the Windows Start menu. (11)

Panther The code name for version 10.3 of Mac OS X. (12)

parse Used in the context of an operating system's treatment of a command entered at the command line, *parse* means to divide the command into its components. DOS's command interpreter parses an entry based on special delimiter characters, such as the space character. (2)

partition (n.) An area of a physical hard disk that defines space that will be used for logical drives. (v.) To define the space to be used for logical drives using a program such as the MS-DOS FDISK program. (2)

pass-through authentication The act of passing a user's authentication information to a domain controller for authentication. (4)

password A confidential string of characters that a user enters (along with a user name) in order to be authenticated. (7)

password policy A group of settings for passwords, such as the requirement for password length, and the length of time before a password must be changed. (7)

password reset disk A disk that can be used to log on in the case of a forgotten password. This is very important to have, because if you forget your password, and an administrator resets the password using User Accounts or Local Users and Groups, then when you log on using the new password, you will find that you will lose access to some items, including files that you encrypted when logged on with the forgotten password. When you reset a password with a password reset disk, you can log on using the new password, and still have access to previously encrypted files. (7)

patches Software fixes to correct problems with an operating system or application. (3)

peer-to-peer networking A type of networking in which desktop computers act as file and print servers to their peers on the network. (1)

peripheral device A very broad term most often used to refer to nonessential add-on computer devices, such as digital cameras, printers, scanners, pointing devices, and external modems and disk drives. (1)

permission A level of access to an object, such as a file or folder, that is granted to a user account or group account. (4)

personal computer (PC) A microcomputer that complies with the Microsoft/Intel standards. (1)

personal folders A set of special folders saved on disk for each user who logs on. (6)

PING A command-line command that is useful for testing the communications between two computers. The name is an acronym for Packet Internet Groper. It behaves in a manner similar to underwater sonar, but instead of bouncing sound waves off surfaces, the PING command sends data packets to specific IP addresses, requesting a response. (10).

plug and play The ability of a computer to automatically detect and configure a hardware device. To work, the computer, the device, and the OS must all comply with the same plug-and-play standard. (1)

pointing device An input device that is used to move a cursor around on a graphical user interface (GUI). The most common pointing device is a mouse, but others include track balls, joysticks, and light pens. (1)

pop-ups An ad that runs in a separate browser window that you must close before you can continue with your present task. (7)

pop-up download A program that is downloaded to a user's computer through the use of a pop-up page that appears while surfing the Web. (7)

prefetching A technique Microsoft uses to decrease the boot time in Windows XP, in which the OS learns what is needed at bootup and creates a list of code or data that it can bring into memory and have ready in advance. (5)

primary directory entry On a FAT file system, the directory entry Windows uses to store the standard directory information, including an 8.3 file name. In the case of a long file name, additional (secondary) directory entries are needed to store the long file name itself. (13)

primary partition A partition type that can only have one logical drive, which is assigned to the entire space defined by the partition. MS-DOS and Windows 9*x* can only have a single primary partition, while Windows NT/2000/XP can have up to four primary partitions. (2)

print server A network server that gives client computers access to printers. (9)

private IP address An address from one of three ranges of IP addresses designated for use only on private networks and not to be used on the Internet. The private IP address ranges are 10.0.0.0 through 10.255.255.255, 172.16.0.0 through 172.31.255.255, and 192.168.0.0 through 192.168.255.255. (10)

private key A password or other confidential code used to decrypt a message. (10)

processor See *microprocessor*. (1)

Program Compatibility wizard A Windows XP wizard that enables you to set compatibility options for an older application that will "trick" the older program into thinking that the OS is actually the earlier version of Windows required by the application (such as Windows 95). You can also set these options manually from the properties of the application's shortcut or program file. (5)

prosumer A new type of consumer who expects consumer-level affordability combined with professional-level features. (12)

protected memory space The method employed by Windows NT/2000/XP to isolate running applications. Thanks to the use of protected memory space, when a program crashes, other running applications or the OS itself will not be affected. (4)

protocol A set of agreed-upon rules or standards. (9)

public IP addresses IP addresses assigned to hosts on the Internet. (10)

public key A password or other code used to encrypt a message. (10)

Quick Launch toolbar An area of the taskbar where you can place icons for programs you wish to activate with a single click. (6)

RAID-5 volume A type of dynamic volume that provides fault tolerance. A RAID-5 volume is a type of striped volume with added information that enables it to recover from a failure of one of the physical disks in the volume. It requires at least three physical disks in a computer running a Windows 2000 Server OS or greater. (4)

RAM See *random-access memory*. (1)

random-access memory (RAM) Volatile memory that stores active programs and data while the computer is operating. (1)

raw write A utility that comes with most distributions of Linux and is used to create a bootable floppy disk. (11)

read-only memory (ROM) Nonvolatile memory that is used to store programs permanently. When the computer is turned off, the contents of ROM remain intact. (1)

read-only memory basic input/output system (ROM BIOS) A set of program instructions for starting the computer, as well as for controlling communications between the processor and other components (input and output). (1)

real mode The mode in which an Intel processor starts when the computer is first turned on. It is very limited, offers the operating system just a small amount of memory to work with, and does not allow for multitasking, protection of the hardware from other software, or support for virtual machines. (1)

real-time application An application that responds to certain inputs extremely quickly—thousandths or millionths of a second (milliseconds or microseconds, respectively). Real-time applications are needed to run medical diagnostics equipment, life-support systems, machinery, scientific instruments, and industrial systems. (1)

Red Hat A company that was founded in 1993 and has grown into a premier distributor of Linux, sold as Red Hat Linux. (11)

Red Hat Package Manager (RPM) A system designed by Red Hat to standardize the processes of installing, uninstalling, and updating Linux software packages. (11)

refresh rate A measurement of how often a computer display is refreshed (or redrawn) to keep the image flicker free. This setting must be above 60 Hertz to reduce eyestrain. (4)

Regional Internet Registries (RIRs) Organizations given the task of allocating IP addresses to Internet service providers (ISPs). (10)

registry A database of all configuration settings in Windows. (8)

restore point A snapshot of Windows, its configuration, and all installed programs. If your computer has nonfatal problems after you have made a change, you can use System Restore to roll it back to a restore point. (5)

ROM BIOS See *read-only memory basic input/output system.* (1)

root The most powerful account on a Linux (or UNIX) computer, and, like the Administrator account on a Windows computer, an account that is capable of doing anything. It can access any file or program on a computer and is also required to shut down Linux from the command prompt. (11)

root directory In a FAT file system, a directory with special characteristics: it is at the top level of the directory hierarchy, and it is the only directory created automatically when a logical drive is formatted. (2)

root key The top five folders are root keys, often called subtrees in Microsoft documentation. Each of these subtrees is the top of a hierarchical structure containing folders called keys. (8)

router A network device that sits between networks and directs (routes) traffic to destinations beyond the local network. (9)

Safe Mode A startup mode in which Windows 9*x*, Windows 2000, and Windows XP start without using all of the drivers and components that would normally be loaded. Use Safe Mode when your Windows computer will not start normally. (8)

scalable Capable of easily adapting to increased demands. (9)

secondary directory entry A directory entry used on a FAT volume in a Windows OS to store a long file name. (13)

secret key A special code that can be used to decrypt encrypted data. (7)

Secure Sockets Layer (SSL) A security protocol included in web browsers and web servers that uses a special encryption method involving a public key and a private key. A public key is used to encrypt a message, and a private key is used to decrypt a message. (10)

security An operating system function that provides password-protected authentication of the user before allowing access to the local computer. Security features may restrict what a user can do on a computer. (1)

security account In a security accounts database, a security account is a listing of information about a user, group, or computer. A user or computer account is used for authentication; both user and group accounts are used for authorization with assigned permissions. (7)

security ID (SID) A unique string of numbers preceded by *S-1-5* that identifies a security principal in a Windows security accounts database. (8)

server A computer that plays one or more of several important roles on a network. In all of these roles, the server provides services to other computers (clients). (1)

Server Message Block (SMB) A file and print sharing protocol used on Microsoft networks that is being replaced by a newer protocol, Common Internet File System (CIFS). (10)

service pack A bundle of patches or software updates released periodically by a software publisher. (3)

share (n.) A resource, such as a file folder or printer, that is made available to clients on a network. (v.) To make a resource available on a network. (9)

shell The operating system component that provides the character-mode user interface—processing commands and issuing error messages and other limited feedback. (11)

shell commands Commands used in the shell. (11)

Sherlock Apple's combination hard disk and Internet search utility. (12)

shortcut An icon that represents a link to any object that can be represented by an icon. Activating a shortcut (by clicking on it) is a quick way to access an object or to start up a program from any location without having to find the actual location of the object on your computer. (6)

Show Desktop button A button that is included by default on the Quick Launch toolbar in Windows beginning with Windows 98. When you click this button, all open windows are minimized so that you can see the desktop. (4)

simple volume A dynamic disk volume type that includes disk space on a single hard disk. When you convert a basic disk to a dynamic disk, each existing volume becomes a simple volume. A simple volume can be created in Windows 2000 Professional and Windows 2000 Server products, as well as Windows XP and Windows Server 2003. (4)

single-tasking The ability of an operating system to run just one task at a time. (2)

small office, home office (SOHO) A business with one or very few employees based in a very small office or private home. (12)

spam Unsolicited e-mail. This includes e-mail from a legitimate source selling a real service or product, but if you did not give them permission to send such information to you, it is considered spam. (7)

spam filter Software designed to combat spam. (7)

spanned volume A dynamic disk volume type that combines space on two or more physical disks. The operating system writes data into the first disk; and when the first disk runs out of space in the portion allocated to the spanned volume, the operating system moves on to the second disk in the spanned volume, writing to it until it is full, and then moving on to the next disk that has space allocated to the spanned volume. (4)

special folder Certain disk folders including Start Menu, My Documents, Favorites, Desktop, and many others. (6)

special group A special built-in group that cannot be created or modified. Its membership is predefined, and it is available to you only when you assign permissions or rights. In Windows NT and Windows 2000, these groups are called special groups; in Windows XP, these are referred to as built-in security principals. A few important special groups are Creator Owner (the user who created the file or folder), System (the operating system), and the Everyone group, which includes all users on a network, even those who haven't been authenticated. (7)

spim An acronym for "Spam over Instant Messaging"; the perpetrators are called spimmers. (7)

spyware A category of software that runs surreptitiously on a user's computer, gathers information without permission from the user, and then sends that information to the people or organizations that requested the information. (7)

startup disk See *boot disk.* (2)

static IP address An IP address that is manually configured for a host and can, therefore, be considered semipermanent—that is, it stays with the device until someone takes action to change it. (10)

striped volume A dynamic disk volume type that combines space on two or more disks into a single volume. Data on a striped volume is written in 64KB blocks across all the physical disks in the volume in turn, using up to 32 disks, and using an equal amount of disk space on each disk. (4)

strong password A password that meets certain criteria, which change over time as hackers create more techniques and tools for discovering passwords. Microsoft defines a strong password as one that contains at least eight characters, includes a combination of letters, numbers, and other symbols (+, -, $, and so on), and is easy for you to remember but difficult for others to guess. (7)

subkey In the Windows registry, a key that exists within another key. (8)

subnet mask An important IP configuration parameter as critical as the address itself, because it takes what looks like a single address and divides it into two addresses by masking off part of the address. (10)

subtree In the Windows registry, a folder object at the top of a hierarchical structure containing folders called keys. A subtree is also called a root key. (8)

superuser Another name for the root account in Linux, although the login name is "root." (11)

swap file The file an operating system creates and uses as virtual memory, moving portions of programs and data to and from this disk space when space in RAM memory is low. (3)

switch A network device that the media from each node connects to. (9)

switch A subcommand that changes the outcome of a command. (11)

syntax A set of rules for correctly entering a specific command at the command line. The rules include the placement of the command name and the parameters that can be used to modify the behavior of the command. (2 & 11)

system file A file that is a critical component of an operating system. (8)

system keychain A database in which OS X saved encrypted passwords. (12)

system partition In Microsoft terminology, the partition containing the boot files. (8)

System Restore A recovery tool introduced in Windows Me and upgraded in Windows XP. System Restore creates restore points, which are snapshots of Windows, its configuration, and all installed programs. If your computer has nonfatal problems after you have made a change, you can use System Restore to roll it back to a restore point. (5)

taskbar A GUI object in the shape of a long slender bar that usually is at the bottom of a Windows desktop, with some variations in the default buttons on the bar. (6)

task management An operating system function in multitasking OSs that controls the focus. The user can switch between tasks by bringing an application to the foreground, which gives the focus to that application. (1)

TCP/IP A suite of protocols that work together to allow both similar and dissimilar computers to communicate. This protocol suite is needed to access the Internet and is the most common protocol suite used on private intranets. It gets its name from two of its many protocols: Transmission Control Protocol (TCP) and Internet Protocol (IP)—the core protocols of TCP/IP. (10)

terabyte (TB) 1,099,511,627,776 bytes, or 2^{40} bytes. The prefix "tera" means trillion. (1)

terminal client Software on a computer that establishes a connection to a terminal server. (1)

terminal server A single network server with a multi-user/multitasking operating system that allows multiple users to run programs simultaneously in separate sessions on the server. (1)

terminal window A window in a Linux GUI that provides a command line for entering Linux shell commands. (11)

terminate and stay resident (TSR) The characteristic of some small DOS programs that stay loaded in memory when inactive but can be quickly activated when needed. (2)

thin client A minimally configured network computer. (9)

Tiger The code name for version 10.4 of Mac OS X. (12)

token A physical device that can be used in authentication, either alone or together with a user name and password. (7)

TRACERT A command-line utility that traces the route taken by packets to a destination. When you use TRACERT with the name or IP address of the target host, it will ping each of the intervening routers, from the nearest to the farthest. You see the delay at each router, and you will be able to determine the location of the bottleneck. (10)

Transmission Control Protocol (TCP) The protocol responsible for the accurate delivery of messages, verifying and resending pieces that fail to make the trip from source to destination. Several other protocols act as sub-protocols, helping TCP accomplish this. (10)

Trojan horse A program that is installed and activated on a computer by appearing to be something harmless, which the user innocently installs. This is a common way that a virus or a worm can infect a computer. (7)

trust In a Microsoft domain network, a relationship that allows the accounts from one domain to use the resources of another domain. (9)

Universal Naming Convention (UNC) name A path used on Microsoft networks with this syntax: *servername**sharename*. For instance, to refer to the folder shared as *data* on the computer named Wickenburg, type **\\wickenburg\data**. (10)

Upgrade Advisor A compatibility checker that can be run from the Windows XP CD by selecting Check System Compatibility on the Welcome To Microsoft Windows XP screen that runs automatically (autorun) or after invoking the Setup program. (5)

upgrade installation An installation in which a new OS is installed into the same directory as the previous OS. An update can only be done with a successor OS to the currently installed OS, and the new OS must be capable of taking on the settings of the previous OS. Upgrades are possible between most adjacent versions of Windows and between Mac OS versions, but never from Windows to Mac OS or vice versa. (3)

user account A record in an accounts database that represents a single person and that is used for authentication. (6)

user interface The software layer, sometimes called the shell, through which the user communicates with the OS, which, in turn, controls the computer. (1)

user profile In Windows, a set of folders and desktop settings that are unique for each user. (13)

user right In Windows, the privilege to perform a systemwide function, such as access the computer from the network, log on locally, log onto a computer from the network, back up files, change the system time, or load and unload device drivers. (7)

utility A program that allows a user to perform useful tasks, such as computer management or diagnostics. A utility is distinguished from an application program, which is usually used for office productivity, or other non–computer management tasks. (2)

value entries The settings within a Windows registry key. (8)

VFAT See *virtual file allocation table.* (3)

VFAT file system driver A driver that Windows OSs use as the interface between applications and the file systems. (13)

virtual device driver (VXD) A device driver that allows more than one program to use a device. (4)

virtual file allocation table (VFAT) Introduced in Windows 95, an implementation of FAT that supports long file names. (3)

virtual machine A software simulation of a computer. In Windows, when a DOS application is launched, the OS creates a DOS virtual machine that simulates both the hardware of a PC and the DOS operating system. When a 16-bit (Windows 3.*x*) Windows application is launched, Windows creates a virtual machine that includes the Windows 3.*x* OS. (6)

virtual memory A system of memory management in which the OS moves programs and data in and out of memory as needed. (1 & 8)

virtual memory manager An operating system component that moves code and data, as necessary, to the virtual memory file (swap file) on disk. (1)

virtual private network (VPN) A virtual tunnel created between two endpoints over a real network or internetwork. This is done by encapsulating the packets. Other security methods are also usually applied, such as encryption of the data and encrypted authentication. When set up in combination with properly configured firewalls, a VPN is the safest way to connect two private networks over the Internet. (7)

virus A program that is installed and activated on a computer without the knowledge or permission of the user. At the least the intent is mischief, but most often it is intended to be genuinely damaging in one way or another. (7)

Visual Effects A group of settings that includes treatments of the GUI that make Windows more visually interesting and even fun to use. (8)

volume On a hard disk, each area that is defined as a drive. A primary partition has a single volume, and an extended partition can contain one or more volumes. (3)

war driving The act of moving through a neighborhood in a vehicle or on foot, using either a laptop equipped with Wi-Fi wireless network capability or a simple Wi-Fi sensor available for a few dollars from many sources. War drivers seek to exploit open hotspots, areas where a Wi-Fi network is connected to the Internet without the use of security to keep out intruders. (7)

warm boot Restarting a computer without a power-down and power-up cycle, by using a key combination (for example, CTRL-ALT-DELETE) or a hardware reset button. (2)

web browser A special type of client software used to navigate the Web. Examples include Netscape

Navigator, Microsoft Internet Explorer, and Mozilla's Firefox. (10)

window A bordered area of the desktop used by a single program. (6)

Windows NT domain A Microsoft administrative unit organized around one distributed directory services database and in which all servers maintaining the domain database are running a Windows NT Server OS. (4)

Windows Update A Windows program that allows you to interactively connect to the Windows Update web page. (5)

WINVER A program that displays the Windows version information. (3)

wireless LAN (WLAN) A local area network using one of the standards referred to as Wi-Fi (for wireless fidelity). The Wi-Fi standards of the Institute of Electrical and Electronics Engineers (IEEE) include 802.11a, 802.11b, and 802.11g. The distance covered by a WLAN is usually measured in feet (or meters) rather than miles. (10)

wireless wide area network (WWAN) A digital wireless network that extends over a large geographical area. A WWAN receives and transmits data using radio signals over cellular sites and satellites, which makes the network accessible to mobile computer systems. At the switching center, the WWAN splits off into segments and then connects to either a specialized public or private network via telephone or other high-speed communication links. The data then is linked to an organization's existing LAN/WAN infrastructure. (10)

workgroup A grouping of computers on a network for the sake of sharing printers and folders with other users in the group. Generically, this is called a peer-to-peer network. (6)

worm A replicating computer virus. (7)

X Windows system The program code used as the basis for many GUIs for Linux or UNIX. (11)

zone An area that contains one or more web sites to which you can assign restrictions that control how Internet Explorer handles cookies. (10)

INDEX

B

C

D

E

F

G

H

I

J

K

L

M

N

O

P

T

U

V

W

X

Z